Parvaneh Pourshariati is Associate Professor of History at New York City College of Technology (CUNY).

'A very important and original book, which makes a significant contribution to many aspects of late antique and early Islamic Iran. Scholars will spend many years digesting it, no doubt disagreeing with certain aspects of it, but it will surely remain a vital point of reference.'
Speculum

'This is a monumental work of first-class scholarship. Its publication represents a landmark, and it immediately becomes the point of departure for further work on the many subjects it deals with. I can think of few other books I have read over the years that can match this work's astounding combination of originality, bold vision, clarity of presentation, meticulous examination of the sources, and practical puzzle-solving. I learned immensely from reading it. Dr. Pourshariati's book is in my view one of the most important individual contributions to our understanding of the history of Iran since Christensen's *L'Iran sous les Sassanides*, published seventy years ago. Especially remarkable is the breadth of the author's agenda, and the way in which she has convincingly woven together different strands. These include: the political rivalry of the great families, the Sasanians' collapse before Byzantine and Muslim attacks, the religious diversity of medieval Iran, questions of historiography, the substance of the Iranian popular epic, and the important details to be gleaned from seals and other documents. Any one of these would be (and for many scholars has been) a subject for full immersion for many years, but Pourshariati has integrated each into a complex and meaningful whole, even as she has made signal contributions to the more detailed study of each one.'
Fred M. Donner, Professor of Near Eastern History, University of Chicago

'A fundamental reappraisal of a major issue in Near Eastern history, and a book that will be referred to whenever the subject is discussed, *Decline and Fall of the Sasanian Empire* is the most important re-examination of late Sasanian and early Islamic history since the work of Christensen in the 1940s.'
Hugh N. Kennedy, Professor of Arabic, SOAS, University of London

'Dr. Pourshariati's book proposes a reinterpretation of the structure of the Sasanian Empire and of the power struggle that followed the end of the Byzantine–Persian War of 602–628. The author argues that throughout most of its history the Sasanian state was a confederative structure, in which the north and east (the old Parthian territories of Media and Khurasan) were highly autonomous both politically and culturally. It was Khusraw II's (590–628) disastrous effort to centralize the state that led to its collapse and to the Arab Conquests. Dr. Pourshariati also argues for a significant redating of critical moments in the Arab conquests in Iraq. Taken as a whole, *Decline and Fall of the Sasanian Empire* is original, innovative, bold, and generally persuasive.'
Stephen Humphreys, Professor of Islamic and Middle Eastern History, University of California, Santa Barbara

'Both impressive and intellectually exciting, *Decline and Fall of the Sasanian Empire* is a major, even pathbreaking, work in the field—a field which this book should revolutionize.'
Stephen Dale, Professor of History, Ohio State University

Decline and Fall of the Sasanian Empire

The Sasanian–Parthian Confederacy and the Arab Conquest of Iran

Parvaneh Pourshariati

I.B. TAURIS
LONDON · NEW YORK

Paperback edition published in 2017 by
I.B.Tauris & Co. Ltd
London • New York
Reprinted 2018
www.ibtauris.com

Hardback edition first published in 2008 by
I.B.Tauris & Co. Ltd

In association with the Iran Heritage Foundation

Layout: Hans Schoutens

ISBN: 978 1 78453 747 0
eISBN: 978 1 78672 981 1
ePDF: 978 0 85771 199 1

A full CIP record for this book is available from the British Library
A full CIP record is available from the Library of Congress

Library of Congress Catalog Card Number: available

Printed and bound by CPI Group (UK) Ltd, Croydon, CR0 4YY
From camera-ready copy edited and supplied by the author

MIX
Paper from responsible sources
FSC® C013604
FSC www.fsc.org

In loving memory
of my father:
Houshang Pourshariati
(1934–2004)

روانش خرد بود و تن جان پاك
تو گفتی که بهره ندارد ز خاك

فردوسی

Contents

Note on transliteration and citation xi
Acknowledgments xiii

Introduction **1**
The problem 6
Sources and methodology 10

1 Preliminaries **19**
1.1 The Arsacids 19
1.2 Agnatic families 27

I Political History **31**

2 Sasanian polity revisited: the Sasanian–Parthian confederacy **33**
2.1 Sasanians / Arsacids 37
2.1.1 Christensen's thesis 47
2.1.2 Dynasticism 53
2.1.3 Early Sasanian period 56
2.2 Yazdgird I, Bahrām V Gūr, and Yazdgird II / the Sūrens 59
2.2.1 Mihr Narseh Sūren 60
2.2.2 Yazdgird I 65
2.2.3 Bahrām V Gūr 67
2.2.4 Yazdgird II 70
2.3 Pīrūz / the Mihrāns 70
2.3.1 Īzad Gushnasp Mihrān 71
2.3.2 Shāpūr Mihrān 74
2.4 Bilāsh and Qubād / the Kārins 75
2.4.1 Bilāsh 75
2.4.2 Sukhrā Kārin 76
2.4.3 Qubād 78

2.4.4 Shāpūr Rāzī Mihrān 80
2.4.5 Mazdakite uprising 82
2.5 Khusrow I Nowshīrvān / the Mihrāns, the Ispahbudhān, and the Kārins 83
2.5.1 Khusrow I's reforms 83
2.5.2 Interlude: *Letter of Tansar* 85
2.5.3 The four generals 94
2.5.4 The Mihrāns 101
2.5.5 The Ispahbudhān 104
2.5.6 The Kārins 112
2.6 Hormozd IV / the Mihrāns 118
2.6.1 Bahrām-i Māh Ādhar 119
2.6.2 Sīmāh-i Burzīn Kārin 120
2.6.3 Bahrām-i Chūbīn Mihrān 122
2.7 Khusrow II Parvīz / the Ispahbudhān 130
2.7.1 Vistāhm Ispahbudhān 131
2.7.2 Smbat Bagratuni 136
2.7.3 The last great war of antiquity 140
2.7.4 Shahrvarāz Mihrān 142
2.7.5 Farrukh Hormozd Ispahbudhān 146
2.7.6 Khusrow II's deposition 153

3 The Arab conquest of Iran **161**
3.1 Question of sources: the futūḥ and X^{w}adāy-Nāmag traditions . 161
3.1.1 Futūḥ 164
3.1.2 Revisiting Sayf's dating 166
3.2 Shīrūyih Qubād and Ardashīr III: the three armies 173
3.2.1 Shīrūyih Qubād 173
3.2.2 Ardashīr III 178
3.2.3 Shahrvarāz's insurgency 179
3.3 Būrāndukht and Azarmīdukht: the Pārsīg–Pahlav rivalry . . . 183
3.3.1 The Ispahbudhān 186
3.3.2 Analepsis: Arab conquest of Iraq 190
3.3.3 Azarmīdukht and the Pārsīg 204
3.3.4 Būrāndukht and the Pahlav 207
3.3.5 The battle of Bridge 214
3.4 Yazdgird III: Arab conquest of Iran 219
3.4.1 The conquest of Ctesiphon 224
3.4.2 The conquest of Khuzistān 236
3.4.3 The conquest of Media 240
3.4.4 The conquest of Rayy 249
3.4.5 The conquest of Gurgān and Ṭabaristān 253

3.4.6 The mutiny of Farrukhzād 260
3.4.7 The conquest of Khurāsān and the mutiny of the Kanārangīyān 265
3.4.8 The conquest of Azarbāyjān 278
3.5 Epilogue: repercussions for early Islamic history 281

4 Dynastic polities of Ṭabaristān 287

4.1 The Āl-i Bāvand 288
4.1.1 Kayūs 288
4.1.2 Bāv 289
4.2 The Kārins in Ṭabaristān 294
4.3 The Āl-i Jāmāsp 298
4.3.1 Jāmāsp 298
4.3.2 Pīrūz 301
4.3.3 Jīl-i Jīlānshāh 302
4.4 The Arab conquest of Ṭabaristān 303
4.4.1 Peace treaty with Farrukhzād and Jīl-i Jīlānshāh 304
4.4.2 Farrukhān-i Bozorg Dhu 'l-Manāqib 308
4.4.3 Yazīd b. Muhallab's unsuccessful conquest of 716–718 . 310
4.5 Khurshīd Shāh 314
4.5.1 The spāhbed Kārin 314
4.5.2 Sunbād's murder 315
4.5.3 Khurshīd's death and the final conquest of Ṭabaristān . 316

II Religious Currents 319

5 Sasanian religious landscape 321

5.1 Post-Avestan period 321
5.2 Orthodoxy – Heterodoxy 324
5.2.1 Two pillars: the monarchy and the clergy? 324
5.2.2 Kirdīr 327
5.2.3 Āturpāt 334
5.2.4 Zurvanism 339
5.2.5 Zandīks 341
5.2.6 Circle of Justice 342
5.2.7 Mazdakite heresy 344
5.2.8 Jewish and Christian communities 347
5.3 Mihr worship 350
5.3.1 Mithra 351
5.3.2 Mihr worship in the Achaemenid and the Arsacid periods 358
5.3.3 The Pārsīg–Pahlav religious dichotomy 360

5.4 Mihr worship in the quarters of the north and east 368
5.4.1 Mihr worship in Ṭabaristān 369
5.4.2 Mihr worship among the Mihrān 378
5.4.3 Mihr worship among the Kārin 379
5.4.4 Mihr worship in Armenia 386
5.5 Conclusion 392

6 Revolts of late antiquity in Khurāsān and Ṭabaristān 397
6.1 Bahrām-i Chūbīn 397
6.1.1 Mithraic purview of Bahrām-i Chūbīn's rebellion . . . 398
6.1.2 Bahrām-i Chūbīn and the apocalypse 404
6.2 The ʿAbbāsid revolution 414
6.2.1 Inner–Outer Khurāsān 417
6.2.2 Post-conquest Iran and contemporary scholarship . . . 420
6.3 Bihāfarīd 426
6.3.1 Interlude: *Ardā Wīrāz Nāma* 431
6.3.2 Mithraic purview of Bihāfarīd's rebellion 432
6.4 Sunbād the Sun Worshipper 437
6.4.1 Sunbād and Bahrām-i Chūbīn: recurrent narrative motifs 441
6.4.2 Mithraic purview of Sunbād's rebellion 442
6.4.3 Sunbād and the apocalypse 445
6.4.4 Gentilitial background of Sunbād 447
6.5 Conclusion 451

Conclusion 453

Tables, figures and map 467
Key 467
Conquest of Iraq 468
Conquest of Iran 469
Seals 470
Genealogical tree 471
Map of the Sasanian empire 472

Bibliography 473

Glossary 499

Index 509

Note on transliteration and citation

As this book deals with sources from many languages, it has been virtually impossible to be consistent in nomenclature. In general, we adopted the following ranking of languages in descending order of priority in our transliteration of foreign words: English, New Persian, Middle Persian, Arabic, Armenian, Greek, Avestan. A name or a term is then rendered in the first of these languages in which it is well attested. For instance, the third Achaemenid king in these languages is respectively *Darius*, *Dāryūsh*, *Dārā*, *Dārāb*, *Dara*, *Dareios*, *Dāraiiauuaš*. Since the first, English, form is already in common use, we render his name as *Darius*. Likewise, although Middle Persian *spāhbed* can be translated in English as *general*, or rendered in New Persian as *ispahbud*, we have opted to keep its Middle Persian rendition in order to remain as true to its intended meaning as possible. Similarly, we will use New Persian *Nīshāpūr*, rather than *Nishapur* (English), *Nēw-Shābuhr* (Middle Persian), or *Nīsābūr* (Arabic). These examples also underline another issue: names of places or offices may have changed over time, and so we will use the name that was prevalent at the period in question. Hence in the case of *Nīshāpūr*, the older name *Abarshahr* is not used when discussing events in later Sasanian times. Similarly, instead of modern *Istanbul*, Roman *Byzantium*, or late Roman *Augusta Antonina*, we will refer to the capital of the Byzantine empire during the Sasanian period by its official East-Roman name, *Constantinople*.

The context and/or the intended meaning will also determine our adoption of a particular transliteration. We shall, therefore, use Armenian *Mirranes* instead of New Persian *Mihrān*, for the commander of Petra under Khusrow I; and we shall use Middle Persian *kūst-i ādurbādagān*, rather than its New Persian form *kūst-i Azarbāyjān*, for the quarter of the north. Likewise, to refer to the deity that plays a germane role in this work, the New Persian form *Mihr*, or on occasion the older form *Mithra*, derived from Avestan *Miθra*, is used in the Iranian context, whereas the English form *Mithras* is reserved for the Roman context (Roman Mithraism). In the index and the glossary, an attempt is made to provide cross-references to the most commonly attested forms.

In working with many different sources, the language as well as the script can cause problems. For scripts other than Arabic (like Aramaic, Pahlavi,

Armenian, Avestan, or Greek), we have followed the conventions of the translated source. To transliterate Arabic into Latin script, we have more or less followed the transliteration scheme used by the *Encyclopaedia of Islam*. As we had to deal with both Persian and Arabic sources, we felt that following the *Encyclopaedia of Islam* rather than the *Encyclopaedia Iranica* would yield a more consistent scheme. We have, however, simplified this system for the four letters خ, ژ, چ, and ش, which we transliterate *kh*, *zh*, *ch*, and *sh* instead of the respective underlined forms *kh*, *zh*, *ch*, and *sh*. Thus we write *Kheshm* instead of *Kheshm* or *Xešm*. An additional complication of transliterating Arabic script is vowelization.[1] This is reflected, for instance, in the name of the Iranian general *Hurmuzān*. As his name is only attested in Arabic sources, we have maintained the Arabic transliteration, although its Persian form would have been *Hormozān*, derived from Persian *Hormozd*. We also opted to render Persian *iḍāfih* as *-i*, and New Persian final ه as *ih* instead of *e* or *eh*.

Works are cited following the Harvard style (author plus year of publication),[2] except for the first citation, which is given in full.[3] Articles in the *Encyclopaedia Iranica* and the *Encyclopaedia of Islam* are now readily available online. As we have availed ourselves of the online versions, our references to these may no longer have page numbers. We have dated each online article without a page reference to the present, that is to say, to 2007.[4] For the benefit of the non-Arabic speaking reader, we have cited Ṭabarī's history, which is used extensively in this study, both in English (published in the series *The History of Ṭabarī*) and in Arabic (de Goeje's edition). For example, the citation Ṭabarī 1999, p. 295, de Goeje, 988, means: page 295 in *The Sāsānids, the Byzantines, the Lakhmids, and Yemen*, and page 988 in de Goeje's edition. Furthermore, for the benefit of the Persian speaking reader, many citations of non-English sources are followed by a citation to its Persian translation, whenever such a translation is available. As Khaleghi Motlagh's last volume of his critical edition of the *Shāhnāma* has not yet been published, we had, unfortunately, only recourse to less critical editions. We ultimately opted for two, the Nafisi and Moscow editions, and where possible, we have cited both.

[1]This mainly applies to the short vowels *a, e, i, o, u*, but even و when denoting a vowel, can be rendered as *ō* or *ū* depending on the word. The vocalization *ē* is only used in Middle Persian or other older languages and never represents ی.

[2]In case there is no author, an alternative key is provided. All dates are converted to the CE calendar.

[3]E.g., the first citation would be: Ṭabarī, *The Sāsānids, the Byzantines, the Lakhmids, and Yemen*, vol. V of *The History of Ṭabarī*, Albany, 1999, translated and annotated by C.E. Bosworth (Ṭabarī 1999); with any subsequent citation to this work given by the form between parenthesis.

[4]The same rule applies to papers that have not yet been published.

Acknowledgments

The acknowledgments of any book are my personal favorite. For they bear testimony not only to what sustains the solitary works of scholarship, but also to the debt that such endeavors carry. In lieu of acknowledgments, one could very well write a contextual social and psychoanalytic analysis of the stimuli that have sustained any piece of scholarship. And so it is with much regret that the author is following the trends in the field and is giving a short synopsis. This work would not have been possible without the support that the author has received through the years leading to the present study: Iraj Afshar, Peter Awn, Michael L. Bates, Kathryn Babayan, Elton L. Daniel, Fred M. Donner, Touraj Daryaee, Dick Davis, Rika Gyselen, Stephen Humphreys, Manuchehr Kasheff, Hugh N. Kennedy, Christian Maetzener, Jalal Matini, Robert D. McChesney, Sam A. Meier, Julie S. Meisami, Charles Melville, Margaret Mills, Michael G. Morony, James Russell, Pari Shirazi, Zeev Rubin, Sabra Webber, and Ehsan Yarshater, each bear a sustaining responsibility for a juncture of this journey. To Richard W. Bulliet, my promoter in the course of my graduate studies, I owe my initial training in historical enquiry. For this, I shall remain indebted to him. I would also like to extend my gratitude to my colleagues in the Department of Near Eastern Languages and Cultures at the Ohio State University, to the AAUW, SSRC, and the Department of Women's Studies at OSU for their support, giving a special thanks to my colleague Joseph Zeidan for lending me his support when I was in dire need of it. To our chief librarians, Dona Straley and Patrick Visel, I owe a debt of gratitude for always coming to my rescue with charm and caring. I would also like to acknowledge the kindness and support of the staff at the Āstān-i Quds-i Raḍavī and the Bibliothèque Nationale for accommodating me during my research visits to those libraries.

There are a few friends and colleagues who travel with you throughout the unsettling world that has become the academe, especially if you are a female of the species. My dear friends Sussan Babaie, Ariana Barkeshli, Habib and Maryam Borjian, Marina Gaillard, Jane Hathaway, Tameron Keyes, Larry Potter, Nader Sohrabi, Rosemary Stanfield-Johnston, Shahrbanou Tadjbakhsh, and Faramarz Vaziri are among these. I remain indebted to Jane Hathaway for volunteering the truly Rustamian job of editing a first draft of this manuscript, and to Rosemary Stanfield-Johnston, who read and edited a second version of two chapters of this work. My dear colleague, Stephen Dale, was one of the first not only to read the initial draft of a manuscript that had been submitted to him in trepidation, but also to support it subsequently. I am extremely grateful to him. The support of Fred M. Donner and Hugh Kennedy, who have also read a first draft of the present book, has been invaluable. For any infelicity, the author bears the sole responsibility. One of my greatest fans throughout this journey has been my very good friend and colleague, Asef Kholdani. Through many years of uncertainty in the course of this study, his support has been unrelenting. Hours of stimulating telephone conversations with Asef filled my void in the twilight zone of late antique Iranian studies.

A handful of momentous influences affect the lives of each of us. Had it not been for my cherished friend Mamad Shirazi, I would probably not have considered an academic career when the Iranian revolution metamorphosed the lives of many. His friendship through the past three decades has been the hallmark of my intellectual and emotional life. There are those who catapult you in life and those who sustain you through it. This work would, literally, have not been in front of you had it not been for the loving support of my husband, partner, and soul mate Hans Schoutens, my pillar in all of this. It is he who bears responsibility, among other things, for the meticulous index, glossary, and charts, and the whole layout and format of this manuscript. I would not have been here without him.

To I.B.Tauris, Iradj Bagherzade, and Alex Wright, I extend my sincere gratitude for seeing a work of this magnitude, quantitatively, through production, in a publishing atmosphere where pre-modern Iranian studies is not given the attention it deserves and needs. Besides my husband, a secondary dedication of this work is to Farhad, Shapoor, Shirin, Mallika, Kate, Taji, Soheila, Bahar, and Minou Pourshariati, Shahriyar Zargham, and the rest of my family. My adoptive family, the Schoutens, but most of all my adoptive mother and father, the late Josephine Van Passel-Schoutens, and Louis Schoutens, know full well the contribution that they have made to this study.

My primary debt, however, is reflected in the dedicatory page of the present study. Had it not been for the inspiration of my father, Houshang Pourshariati, the ideals that he cherished, the life he led, and the mark that he left on me, I would not have embarked on a journey that has now been more than four decades in the making. It is on account of the turn of the wheels that he is not here to see this. He is sorely missed. Above all, none of this would have been possible had it not been for my mother, Iran Pourshariati, whose nurturing sustained all else in order to make this contribution what it is.

Introduction

The history of Iran in the late antique, early medieval period (circa 500–750 CE) remains one of the least investigated fields of enquiry in recent scholarship. This, in spite of the fact that some of the most crucial social and political processes transpiring during this period in what Hodgson has termed the *Nile to Oxus* cultural zone, directly implicate Iranian history. The "last great war of antiquity" of 603–628 CE, between the two great empires of the Near East, the Byzantines (330?–1453 CE)[5] and the Sasanians (224–651 CE), was on the verge of drastically redrawing the map of the world of late antiquity. For almost two decades during this period, the Sasanian empire was successful in re-establishing the boundaries of the Achaemenid (559–330 BCE) empire at the height of its successful campaigns against the Byzantines. As Sebeos' account bears witness, when in 615 the Persians reached Chalcedon,[6] the Byzantine emperor Heraclius (610–641) was about ready to become a client of the Sasanian emperor Khusrow II (591–628).[7] When, in 622, a small, obscure, religio-political community in Mecca is said to have embarked on an emigration (*hijra*) to Medina—an emigration that in subsequent decades came to be perceived as the watershed for the birth of a new community, the Muslim *ʾumma*—the Sasanians were poised for world dominion.

Unexpectedly, however, the tides turned. For in the wake of what has been termed "one of the most astonishing reversals of fortune in the annals of war,"[8] and after the ultimate defeat of the Sasanians in the last crucial years of the war (621–628 CE)—itself a tremendously perplexing question—a sociopolitical upheaval unprecedented in the world of late antiquity began: the Arab conquest of the Near East. While the event truncated Byzantium beyond recognition by the 640s, its consequences were even more dire for the Sasanians. For with the

[5]There is no consensus among scholars as to when, precisely, one must date the end of the Roman and the beginning of the Byzantine empire. Dates varying from the early fourth to the early seventh century have been proposed.

[6]A district near present-day Istanbul (the former Byzantine capital, Constantinople), called Kadiköy, Chalcedon was an ancient maritime town in the Roman province of Bithynia.

[7]Sebeos, *The Armenian History Attributed to Sebeos*, Liverpool University Press, 1999, translated with notes by Robert Thomson, Historical Commentary by James Howard-Johnston with assistance from Tim Greenwood (Sebeos 1999), part I, pp. 78–79 and part II, p. 212.

[8]Sebeos 1999, p. xxiv.

death of the last Sasanian king, Yazdgird III (632–651), in the aftermath of the Arab conquest of Iran, came the end of more than a millennium of Iranian rule in substantial sections of the Near East. The Sasanian empire was toppled and swallowed up by the Arab armies. What had happened? Why was an empire that was poised for the dominion of the Near East in 620, when successfully engaging the powerful Byzantines, utterly defeated by 650 by the forces of a people hitherto under its suzerainty, the Arab armies? This work is an attempt to make sense of this crucial juncture of Iranian and Middle Eastern history. It will seek to explain the success of the Arab conquest of Iran in the early seventh century, as well as the prior defeat of the Sasanians by the Byzantines, with reference to the *internal dynamics* of late Sasanian history. Our very conceptualization of the internal dynamics of Sasanian history, however, will involve a heretical assessment of this history, for it will take serious issue with the Christensenian view of the Sasanians as an *étatiste/centralized* polity, a perspective that ever since the 1930s, when Christensen published *L'Iran sous les Sassanides*, has become paradigmatic in scholarship.[9] The overarching thesis of the present work is that, episodic and unsuccessful attempts of the Sasanians at centralization notwithstanding, the Sasanian monarchs ruled their realm through a decentralized dynastic system, the backbone of which was the *Sasanian–Parthian confederacy*.[10]

The theses proposed in this work have been formed after an exhaustive investigation and at times reevaluation of a host of external and internal sources pertaining to this period of Iranian history. Armenian, Greek, Syriac, and classical Islamic histories, especially the *futūḥ* (or conquest) narratives, have been utilized in a source-critical juxtaposition with literary and primary sources of Sasanian history, the *X^w adāy-Nāmag* (Khudāynāmag or the *Book of Kings*)[11] tradition(s) as they appear in classical Arabic histories but especially in the *Shāhnāma* of Ferdowsī; Middle Persian literature produced in the late antique period of Iranian history; local Iranian histories; and, above all, the numismatic and sigillographic evidence of late Sasanian history. The present work, therefore, engages in a continuous and pervasive critical dialogue between the ways in which the Sasanians *were perceived* by their foreign, generally hostile, contemporary or near contemporaries, the ways in which they *wished to be perceived* from an imperial, central perspective, and the ways in which they *were actually perceived* by the powerful polities within their own periphery—polities which in fact forcefully articulated their own perception of the Sasanians. The end result, as we shall see, is that the historiographical strengths evinced by each of

[9]Christensen, Arthur, *L'Iran sous les Sassanides*, Copenhagen, 1944 (Christensen 1944). See also page 7 and §2.1.1 below.

[10]Throughout this study, the term *Parthian*, referring to various powerful Parthian families, is used in contradistinction to the term *Arsacid*. As we shall see in greater detail in §1.1, the Arsacids were the particular dynastic branch of the Parthians who ruled Iran from about 250 BCE to about 226 CE. For a definition of dynasticism as used in this study, see §2.1.2.

[11]Shahbazi, Shapur, 'On the Xwadāy-Nāmag', *Acta Iranica: Papers in Honor of Professor Ehsan Yarshater* VXI, (1990), pp. 218–223 (Shahbazi 1990); see also page 171ff.

these depictions of the Sasanians come to form a critical commentary on the shortcomings inherent in the others. The final picture that is formed is explicitly and irrefutably confirmed by the one corpus of data that suffers the least harm in a people's historiographical production of their history: the primary sources of Sasanian history, the numismatic and sigillographic evidence. For the recently discovered seals pertaining to late Sasanian history remarkably confirm one of the main theses of this study, namely, that throughout the Sasanian history there was a dichotomy between the *Pārsīg* (Sasanians) and the *Pahlav*,[12] which forced the Sasanians into a confederate arrangement with the powerful Parthian dynastic families living in their domains.[13] As late as the seventh century, some of the dynastic bearers of the seals insist on identifying themselves as either a *Pahlav* or a *Pārsīg*.

As already mentioned, one of the central themes of this study is that the Sasanians ruled their realm by what we have termed the Sasanian–Parthian confederacy. This was a predominantly *decentralized*,[14] and—borrowing a term from Cyril Toumanoff[15]—*dynastic* system of government where, save for brief and unsuccessful attempts at centralization by the Sasanians in the third and the sixth centuries, the powerful dynastic Parthian families of the Kārins, the Mihrāns, the Ispahbudhān, the Sūrens,[16] and the Kanārangīyān were, for all practical purposes, co-partners in rule with the Sasanians. In Chapter 2, we shall abandon the centrist/monarchical image of the Sasanians currently in vogue in scholarship, and, revisiting the Sasanians from the perspective of the Parthian dynastic families, we shall trace the ebb and flow of the Sasanian–Parthian confederacy and the tensions inherent in it. This Sasanian–Parthian confederacy ultimately collapsed, however. The inception of its debacle occurred in the midst of the "astonishing reversal of fortune in the annals of war," when the tide turned and the Sasanians suffered their inexplicable defeats of 624–628 at the hands of the Byzantines. As we shall see, had it not been for the Parthian withdrawal from the Sasanian–Parthian confederacy toward the end of the rule of Khusrow II Parvīz (591–628), the Byzantines might very well have become a client state of the Sasanians, and Heraclius a son instead of a "brother of Khusrow II."[17] The debacle of the Sasanian–Parthian confederacy during the last years of the Sasanian–Byzantine wars, however, had a far greater consequence for late antique Iranian history: the ultimate defeat of the Sasanians by the Arab armies and the eradication of their empire by the middle of the seventh century.

[12]The Middle Persian term for *Parthian*.

[13]For the geographical extent of these domains, see footnote 145.

[14]Our conceptualization of any given system of government as a centralized or decentralized polity, needless to say, ought not entail any value judgments as to the successful functioning of that polity.

[15]Toumanoff, C., *Studies in Christian Caucasian History*, Georgetown University Press, 1963 (Toumanoff 1963); see §2.1.2 below.

[16]While a detailed analysis of the Sūrens will not be undertaken in this study, they were in fact an integral part of this confederacy.

[17]Sebeos 1999, part II, p. 212.

It was in the *immediate* aftermath of the final collapse of the Sasanian–Parthian confederacy, in the wake of Khusrow II's deposition and murder in 628 CE, that the unprecedented chain of events that ultimately led to the total annihilation of the Sasanian monarchy after four centuries of rule commenced: the early Arab conquest of Sasanian territories. A second central theme of the present study—arrived at through a critical examination of the *futūḥ* narratives in *juxtaposition* with the Sasanian *Xʷadāy-Nāmag* historiography[18]—therefore, is that the early Arab conquest of Iraq took place, *not*, as has been conventionally believed, in the years 632–634, after the accession of the last Sasanian king Yazdgird III (632–651) to power, but in the period from 628 to 632.[19] The conquest of Iraq occurred precisely during the period of internecine warfare between the Pahlav and the Pārsig. The two factions, engrossed in their strife in promoting their own candidates to the throne, were incapable of putting up a united defense against the encroaching Arab armies. The subsequent conquest of the Iranian plateau, moreover, was ultimately successful because powerful Parthian dynastic families of the *kūst-i khwarāsān* (quarter of the east) and *kūst-i ādurbādagān* (quarter of the north) abandoned the last Sasanian king, Yazdgird III, withdrew their support from Sasanian kingship, and made peace with the Arab armies. In exchange, most of these retained *de facto* power over their territories.

The recalculation of the chronology of the early conquest of Iraq to the period between 628–632, in turn, has crucial implications, not only for the chronology of the conquest of Syria and the famous desert march of Khālid b. Walīd, but also for a host of other significant events in early Islamic history. If, as we claim, the conquest of Iraq took place in 628–632, how then are we to perceive the role and whereabouts of the Prophet Muḥammad[20] at the onset of the conquests of Iraq according to this alternative chronology? The conquest of Iraq is traditionally believed to have occurred *after* the death of the Prophet in 632 and, *after* the *ridda*[21] wars (or wars of apostasy). If Prophet Muḥammad was alive according to this newly offered scheme, how then will this affect our traditional understanding of early Islamic history? What of our conventional view of the roles of Abū Bakr and ʿUmar as *caliphs* in this period of Islamic history? If Muḥammad was alive, what of apostasy?

Our chronological reconstruction of the conquest of Iraq could potentially have revolutionary implications for our understanding of early Islamic history. We shall offer one possible, conjectural answer to these crucial questions here,[22] for by the time we have expounded our thesis, it will become clear

[18]For an elaboration of this, see page 15ff below.

[19]As we shall see, the implications of what might initially seem to be a minor chronological recalculation, are in fact far-reaching.

[20]According to the generally accepted chronology, the Prophet Muḥammad was born sometime in 570 CE and died in 632 CE.

[21]See footnote 900.

[22]See §3.5.

that its implications will require a thorough reevaluation of a number of crucial episodes of early Islamic history, a task beyond the confines of the present study. One thing will remain a constant in the midst of all of this: understanding the nature of the Sasanian–Parthian confederacy and disentangling its gradual and final collapse will lead to a better understanding of the nature and rise of the Arabo-Islamic polity. So much for the implications of our thesis vis-à-vis early Islamic history. How are we to view the effects of the Arab conquest in the context of the post-conquest Iranian history?

The Arab conquest of Iran has long been viewed by some as a watershed in Iranian history. Through it, the *pre-Islamic* history of Iran is presumed to have led to its *Islamic* history. Examining the histories of Ṭabaristān, Gīlān, and partially Khurāsān, from the late Sasanian period through the conquest and up to the middle of the eighth century, we shall highlight the fallacies of this perspective. We shall argue that the Arab conquest of Iran ought not be viewed as a total overhaul of the political structures of Iran in late antiquity. For while the kingship of the house of Sāsān was destroyed as a result of the onslaught of the Arab armies, the Pahlav domains and the Parthian power over these territories remained predominantly intact throughout the Umayyad period. Here then we shall follow our methodology of investigating the history of Iran not through the center—this time of the Caliphate—but through the periphery. This then becomes a testimony to the strength of the Parthian legacy: as the Parthians had not disappeared with the advent of the Sasanians in the third century, neither did they leave the scene after the Arab conquest of Iran in the middle of the seventh century, their polities and cultural traditions long outliving the demise of the Sasanian dynasty.

This thesis is, in turn, closely connected to our assessment of the aims of the Arab armies in their conquest of Iranian territories. The course of the Arab conquest, the subsequent pattern of Arab settlement, and the topography of the ʿAbbāsid revolution,[23] all give evidence of one significant fact: the overthrow of the Sasanian dynasty was not an intended aim of the Arab armies, but only an incidental by-product of it, precipitated by the prior debacle of the Sasanian–Parthian confederacy. For the primary objective of the Arab conquerors was not the actual conquest and colonization of Iranian territories, but to bypass these, in order to gain access to the trade entrepôts in Transoxiana. Recognizing this, chief Pahlav families reached a *modus vivendi* with the Arab armies.

In part two of the present study we shall turn our attention to the spiritual landscape of Iran during the Sasanian period. Providing a synopsis of the state of research on this theme during the past two decades, we shall then put forth the fourth major thesis of this study: the Sasanian/Parthian political dichotomy was replicated in the realms of spirituality, where the Pahlav predominantly adhered to Mihr worship, a Mithraic spiritual universe that was distinct from the Zoroastrian orthodoxy—whatever the nature of this—that the Sasanians

[23] These latter two themes will be addressed in detail in a sequel to this study.

ostensibly tried to impose on the populace living in their territories. As the concentration of Pahlav power had always been in their traditional homelands, Parthava[24] and Media[25]—what the Sasanians later termed the *kūst-i khwarāsān* and *kūst-i ādurbādagān*, the quarters of the east and north—so too was the preponderance of Mihr worship in these territories. Our evidence for the prevalence of Mihr worship in the northern, northeastern, and northwestern parts of the Sasanian domains will hopefully also become relevant, not only for further deciphering the religious proclivity of the Arsacids, but also for engaging the ongoing debate between Iranists and classicists about the provenance of Mihr worship in Roman Mithraism—a debate that has been resumed during the past three decades within the scholarly community.

Finally, we shall conclude our study with an analysis of the Mithraic features of the revolt of the Mihrānid Bahrām-i Chūbīn at the end of the sixth century, and the continuity of these Mithraic themes in the revolts of Bihāfarīd and Sunbād in the middle of the eighth century. The upshot of our contention here is that, far from betraying a presumed synthesis of Iranian and Islamic themes, the aforementioned revolts evince startling evidence for the continuity of Mihr worship in Pahlav territories. In a sequel to this study, we shall trace the continuity of this Parthian heritage to the revolts of the Kārinid Māzīyār in Ṭabaristān and Bābak-i Khurramdīn in Azarbāyjān, assessing the connections of these to the cultural heritage that we perceive to have affected the ʿAbbāsid revolutionaries. A word needs to be said about the issues that instigated this study, and further remarks about the author's methodology, before we proceed.

The problem

In 1992, Walter Kaegi wrote his magisterial work *Byzantium and the Early Islamic Conquests.* Here he provided an explanatory exposé of the rationale behind his opus. "For some scholars of Islamic history," he wrote, "this subject may appear to be ill-conceived, because for them there is no reason why the Muslims should not have defeated and supplanted Byzantium. No adequate Byzantine historical research exists on these problems, certainly none that includes the use of untranslated Arabic sources."[26] In 1981, Fred M. Donner had already written *The Early Islamic Conquests*, a work that in the tradition of nearly a century of highly erudite scholarship sought not only to "provide a new interpretation of the Islamic conquest movement, ... [but also to argue that] Muḥammad's career and the doctrines of Islam revolutionized both the ideological bases and the political structures of Arabian society, to the extent

[24]See footnote 77.

[25]For the historical boundaries of Media, see Dandamayev, M. and Medvedskaya, I., 'Media', in Ehsan Yarshater (ed.), *Encyclopaedia Iranica*, New York, 2007 (Dandamayev and Medvedskaya 2007).

[26]Kaegi, Walter, *Byzantium and the Early Islamic Conquests*, Cambridge University Press, 1992 (Kaegi 1992), pp. 1–2.

that they transformed ... the face of ... a large part of the globe."[27] Kaegi and Donner's works are symptomatic of the state of the field in late antique studies. For, at the very least during the past half century, the late antique and early medieval history of Iran has found itself in a paradigmatic quagmire of research, where the parameters of the field have been set by Byzantinists and Arabists.[28] While a host of erudite scholars continue to exert their efforts in disentangling the perplexing questions surrounding the nature and rise of the Arabo-Islamic polity and its dizzying successes, and while a number of erudite works have addressed aspects of Sasanian history, except for general observations and artificial asides, no one has bothered to address the Arab conquest of Iran and its aftermath *from a Sasanian perspective*.

The last *magnum opus* on Sasanian history was Christensen's *L'Iran sous les Sassanides*, published in 1936.[29] The path for all subsequent research on the Sasanians, including that of Christensen, however, had already been paved by the masterpiece of the nineteenth-century semitist, philologist, and classicist, Theodore Nöldeke, *Geschichte der Perser und Araber zur Zeit der Sasaniden*, which appeared in 1879.[30] If Nöldeke had been the father of Sasanian studies, however, it was the Christensenian thesis that had set the subsequent paradigm for Sasanian historiography. Building on Nöldeke's work, and using the then available primary sources of Sasanian history—sources which belong predominantly to the third and partly to the sixth centuries only—and relying more or less credulously on the *X^w adāy-Nāmag* tradition of Sasanian historiography and other secondary accounts of this history, Christensen argued that the rise of Sasanians, after their defeat of the Arsacids in the third century, heralded a new epoch in Iranian history. From this period onward, and through most of their subsequent history, some lapses notwithstanding, argued Christensen, the Sasanians were able to establish a highly efficient and *centralized* system of

[27] Donner, Fred M., *The Early Islamic Conquests*, Princeton University Press, 1981 (Donner 1981), p. ix and p. 8, respectively.

[28] To give the reader a sense of this, one needs only mention the impressive series launched by Irfan Shahîd, *Byzantium and the Arabs*, in which, in multi-volume format, the author has thus far treated the fifth and sixth centuries of this relationship. Shahîd, Irfan, *Byzantium and the Arabs in the Sixth Century, Volume 1, Part 1: Political and Military History*, Dumbarton Oaks Research Library and Collection, Washington, 1995 (Shahîd 1995). Equally remarkable for the depth of its scholarship, is the series edited by Averil Cameron on *The Byzantine and Early Islamic Near East*. In this series see, for example, Cameron, Averil and Conrad, Lawrence I. (eds.), *The Byzantine and Early Islamic Near East, III: States, Resources and Armies*, Princeton, 1995, papers of the Third Workshop on Late Antiquity and Early Islam (Cameron and Conrad 1995). An article by Zeev Rubin on the reforms of Khusrow I is included in the volume mentioned here. It must be said that the proclivity of the majority of Iranists, who in the wake of the Iranian revolution of 1978–79 have been obsessed with the modern and contemporary history of Iran, has also exacerbated this void in the field. Those who, like the present author, adhere to a *long durée* conceptualization of pre-modern history, will reckon that on some fundamental level, the implications of the present work also engage contemporary Iranian history.

[29] We will use here the second edition, Christensen 1944.

[30] Nöldeke, Theodore, *Geschichte der Perser und Araber zur Zeit der Sasaniden*, Leiden, 1879 (Nöldeke 1879).

government in which the monarchs functioned as the supreme rulers of the land.[31] The lapses, Christensen argued, were significant and occasioned by *decentralizing* forces exerted on the monarchy by the various strata of the nobility of the empire, some of whom were of Parthian origin. In spite of these recurrent lapses, one of which incidentally, as he himself admitted, continued through most of the fourth century, Christensen insisted that the Sasanians were always able to reassert their control and rule their empire as a centralized monarchical system. The height of this monarchical power came with Khusrow I Nowshīrvān (531–579), who implemented a series of important reforms in the wake of another surge of the nobility's power and the revolutionary Mazdakite uprisings. Through these reforms Khusrow I was able to inaugurate one of the most splendid phases of Sasanian history. In the tradition of Ardashīr I (224–241) and Shāpūr I (241–271), this exemplary king restored the normative dimensions of Sasanian kingship: a powerful, centralized monarchy capable of mustering its resources in order to ameliorate and stabilize the internal conditions of the realm, maintain its boundaries, and, when appropriate, launch expansionist policies. What had happened to the centrifugal forces of prior centuries, most importantly, to those of the powerful Parthian nobility? Allegedly, in the process of his reforms, Khusrow I had metamorphosed these into a "nobility of the robe," bereft of any substantive authority. Meanwhile, in the late sixth century, for some inexplicable reason, two major rebellions sapped the power of the centralizing Sasanian monarchs, the rebellions of Bahrām-i Chūbīn (590–591) and Vistāhm (595–600). Curiously, both rebellions were launched by Parthian dynastic families. Unexpectedly, the Parthians had come to question the very legitimacy of the Sasanian kings. For a while they even usurped Sasanian kingship. The Mihrānid Bahrām-i Chūbīn forced the Sasanian king Khusrow II Parvīz to take refuge in the bosoms of their ancient enemies, the Byzantines. The Ispahbudhān Vistāhm carved, for all practical purposes, an independent realm in an extensive stretch of territory that ran from Khurāsān to Azarbāyjān. Even more Parthian insurgencies followed in the wake of these. Such outright rebellion against the legitimacy of the kingship of the house of Sāsān was unprecedented in the annals of Sasanian history. What is more, it was in the wake of the presumably successful and forceful centralizing reforms of Khusrow I that this trend was established. What had happened? Had Khusrow I not sapped the authority of the powerful Parthian families? Why had they come to question the very legitimacy of Sasanian kingship, unleashing havoc at the height of Sasanian supremacy? The Christensenian thesis could not address this. Neither could it address the reasons why the last Sasanian monarch of substantial power, Khusrow II Parvīz (591–628), the same monarch during whose rule the Sasanian empire was poised for world dominion, was suddenly to lose not only the war, but his very head by 628 CE. Christensen, likewise, did not address the subsequent turbulent history of the Sasanians in

[31] A more in depth analysis of his thesis will be given in §2.1.1.

any great detail. For him, as for all subsequent scholars of Sasanian history, the period from 628 to the last feeble Sasanian king, Yazdgird III (632–651), was simply too chaotic to be amenable to any systematic research. Christensen's magnificent opus, therefore, stopped with the ascension of Yazdgird III, which was presumably when the Arab conquests had begun according to him and subsequent scholars of Sasanian history. And so the Christensenian reconstruction of Sasanian history came to an abrupt, perplexing end, leaving the student of Sasanian history baffled by the inexplicable spiraling demise of the dynasty.

One of the primary sources which Christensen had used in order to arrive at this thesis was an official historiography, patronized by the Sasanians and known as the *X^{w}adāy-Nāmag*, or the *Book of Kings*. The Sasanians, in fact, were the first to promote a literary account of Iranian history.[32] Through this official historiography, the Iranian national history was traced from the first mythic Iranian monarch, Kayūmarth,[33] to the last Sasanian king, Yazdgird III. While patronizing this national history, however, the Sasanians also undertook another feat: they deleted most of the annals of their defeated foes, the Arsacids (250 BCE–224 CE), from the pages of history, cutting in half the duration of their rule. In *Das iranische Nationalepos*, Nöldeke had already argued that in spite of this Sasanian censorial effort at deleting Arsacid history, the accounts of particular, powerful, Parthian families do appear in the pages of the Iranian national history. Thus, while there is next to nothing left of the history of the Arsacids in the *X^{w}adāy-Nāmag* tradition, several Parthian families did superimpose their histories during the Arsacid period onto the heroic sections of the Iranian national history.[34] While Nöldeke and others underlined the continued cultural and political legacy of the Parthians to Sasanian history, and while some, including Christensen, even highlighted the continued presence of particular Parthian families in the course of Sasanian history, the Christensenian paradigm of Sasanian history continued to hold sway: with the defeat of the Arsacids and the murder of Ardavān in 224 CE, the Sasanians inaugurated a new era in Iranian history, establishing a centralized, *étatiste*, imperial power which, in collaboration with the clergy, imposed an orthodox creed on the flock living in its territories. But this was precisely the image that the Sasanians wanted to present of themselves. It might have been constructed under the influence of the model of *caesaropapism* effected in Byzantium from the fourth century. This étatiste model can certainly not be substantiated with reference to the primary sources of Sasanian history, for these, belonging primarily to the third

[32]Yarshater, Ehsan, 'Iranian National History', in Ehsan Yarshater (ed.), *Cambridge History of Iran: The Seleucid, Parthian, and Sasanian Periods*, vol. 3(1), pp. 359–477, Cambridge University Press, 1983b (Yarshater 1983b).

[33]In the Iranian religious tradition, Kayūmarth or Gayōmart, literally meaning the *mortal man*, was the protoplast of man. See Shaki, Mansour, 'Gayōmart', in Ehsan Yarshater (ed.), *Encyclopaedia Iranica*, New York, 2007a (Shaki 2007a).

[34]Shahbazi refers to this as the *Ctesian* method of historical writing, that is, the superimposition of contemporary histories onto remote antiquity.

and the sixth centuries, are far too disjointed to give us a picture of the nature of Sasanian administrative polity throughout its history.

Yet the *X^w adāy-Nāmag* image of the Sasanians was uncritically accepted by Christensen and adopted by those who followed him. So convinced were they by the Sasanian censorial effort in deleting Arsacid history, and so accepting were they of the Sasanians' view of themselves as a benevolent and centralized monarchy, that none paid any heed to the implications of Nöldeke's observation. When and how, then, had the Parthians engaged in their own historiographical endeavors in the official histories patronized by the Sasanians? One must certainly reckon with the oral dimension of Parthian historiography during the Arsacid period, as the late matriarch of Zoroastrian studies, Mary Boyce, underlined in her study of the Parthian *Gōsāns*.[35] Yet this does not explain everything. For if the accounts of Arsacid history were deleted from the pages of the Sasanian *X^w adāy-Nāmag* histories and if the few Parthian families that existed under the Sasanians were ultimately under the *étatiste* pressure of the Sasanian polity, how then, as we shall see, were the sagas of various Parthian families so *intimately, systematically, and integrally intertwined* with the stories of successive Sasanian kings and queens in these histories? In fact, as soon as the historical, Sasanian, section of the *X^w adāy-Nāmag* tradition begins to acquire flesh, whether in the classical Arabic histories or in the *Shāhnāma* of Ferdowsī, the Parthian dynastic families appear side-by-side of the Sasanian kings. Some of these towering Parthian figures of Sasanian history are, moreover, depicted very positively in the histories of the Sasanians. A corollary of the present thesis, therefore, is that while the Sasanians were successful in deleting Arsacid history, they seriously failed in obliterating the history of the Parthian families from the pages of history. The Sasanians were unsuccessful in this attempt, because the Parthians co-authored substantial sections of the *X^w adāy-Nāmag* traditions, and they did so during the Sasanian period and most probably afterwards as well.[36] This is patently clear from an examination of the *X^w adāy-Nāmag* tradition, which observation necessitates a word about the sources for Sasanian history and our methodology.

Sources and methodology

To reconstruct Sasanian history one relies on the *X^w adāy-Nāmag* tradition as contained, for example, in classical Arabic historiography; on Middle Persian sources written in the late Sasanian or early caliphal period; on Armenian, Greek, and Syriac sources dealing with Sasanian history; and finally on coins, seals, inscriptions, and other products of material cultural. The order of priority has been reckoned to be the reverse of what we have enumerated. These

[35] Boyce, Mary, 'The Parthian Gōsān and Iranian Minstrel Tradition', *Journal of the Royal Asiatic Society* 1, (1957a), pp. 10–45 (Boyce 1957a).

[36] Nöldeke had already postulated this, but he had not examined it in any detail in his pioneering work on the Iranian national epic.

have been respectively termed the tertiary, secondary, and primary sources for Sasanian history.[37]

Numismatists and scholars of material culture have long reprimanded historians for their inordinate emphasis and reliance on literary history, both foreign and native, at the expense of the material sources for Sasanian history. It is not for nothing that these latter have been considered *primary* for reconstructing Sasanian history. Seals, coins, and inscriptions speak clearly, succinctly, and usually far more reliably and explicitly than the corpora of literary narratives, foreign or native, that suffer from layers of ideological underpinning, editorial rewriting, and hazards of transmission over centuries. They are, therefore, crucial for reconstructing Sasanian history and can serve as a gauge of the reliability of the information that we cull from literary sources. This study makes ample use of coins and seals. Among the latter is Rika Gyselen's recently discovered collection of seals pertaining to the late Sasanian period. These seals put to rest, once and for all, the debate about the veracity of the military and administrative(?) quadripartition of the Sasanian realm following the much-discussed reforms of Khusrow I in the sixth century.[38] They are by all accounts the greatest discovery of the past half century of primary sources for late Sasanian history; as such they are unprecedented in terms of their implications for this history. Remarkably, they corroborate, explicitly and concretely, our conclusions regarding the Pārsīg/Pahlav dichotomy prevalent throughout Sasanian history, for they give clear testimony to the continued significance of this dichotomous imperial identity late in Sasanian history.[39] Recent scholarship in numismatics has likewise contributed substantially to disentangling crucial episodes of late Sasanian history. Recent works of Malik and Curtis, and Tyler-Smith on Sasanian numismatics, in particular, have added to our understanding of the chronologies of, respectively, the reign of the Sasanian queen Būrāndukht, and the crucial battle of Qādisiya between the Arab and Iranian armies. It is only within the context of the narrative histories at our disposal, however, that the full ramifications of these significant recent strides in Sasanian numismatic history can be established.

While crucial, the primary sources for Sasanian history suffer from a clear limitation: they belong predominantly to the third and sixth century, leaving a substantial lacuna for the centuries in between. This in itself might be a telling indicator of the course of Sasanian history and the *étatiste* junctures of this history. Even numismatists acknowledge that our primary sources for Sasanian

[37]Gignoux, Philippe, 'Problèmes de distinction et de priorité des sources', in J. Harmatta (ed.), *Prolegomena to the Sources on the History of Pre-Islamic Central Asia*, pp. 137–141, Budapest, 1979 (Gignoux 1979). It is not clear where exactly in Gignoux's scheme we should put the *X^w adāy-Nāmag*.

[38]Gyselen, Rika, *The Four Generals of the Sasanian Empire: Some Sigillographic Evidence*, vol. 14 of *Conferenze*, Rome, 2001a (Gyselen 2001a). For an enumeration of these seals, see notes 473 and 477, as well as Table 6.3 on page 470.

[39]Significantly, the author became apprised of these seals *after* she had already formed the theses of this study based on literary narratives.

history are remarkably disjointed and comparatively limited to begin with.[40] Besides, seals, coins, and reliefs, while clarifying crucial dimensions of Sasanian history, do not always give us a narrative. Coins and seals are not storytellers. As such they do not provide a context within which we can evaluate the sagas of significant personae and social collectivities powering Sasanian history. For this we have to resort to what Gignoux has termed the secondary and tertiary sources, the native and foreign sources for reconstructing Sasanian history.

Throughout this study we attempt to integrate—to the extent possible, but at times in detail—the strong and pervasive interdependencies of Iranian and Armenian sociopolitical, religious, and cultural history. Here, we shall underline the crucial significance of the rule of the Arsacids (53–428 CE)[41] in Armenia into the fifth, and its legacies in the subsequent two centuries, in the context of the Sasanian–Parthian confederacy.[42] To this end we make ample use of Armenian histories in our study.[43] Explicit confirmation of the significant and central contribution of the Parthian dynastic families to Sasanian history abounds in the pages of Armenian histories.

Armenian historical writing was born under the aegis of the Christian Armenian Church in the fifth century.[44] The birth of the Armenian alphabet, in fact, was integrally connected to the production of Christian Armenian histories. This overwhelmingly Christian dimension to Armenian historical literature, coupled with the increasing Byzantine pull on Armenia, ultimately led to a worldview in which Armenian chroniclers systematically downplayed the Iranian dimension of the kingdom's political and cultural history.[45] Yet, as we shall see, precisely because the heritage of Arsacid rule was a recent and vivid memory in Armenian historical memory, the Parthian dimension of Sasanian history was systematically highlighted and underlined in early Christian Armenian historiography. As Lang, Garsoian, and Russell have been at pains to point out, furthermore, in spite of the ideological proclivities of Armenian

---

[40] Gyselen, Rika, 'Nouveaux matériaux', *Studia Iranica* 24, (2002), pp. 61–69 (Gyselen 2002), here p. 180.

[41] For a synopsis of the history of the Arsacids in Armenia and sources for further study, see Chaumont, M.L., 'Armenia and Iran: The pre-Islamic Period', in Ehsan Yarshater (ed.), *Encyclopaedia Iranica*, pp. 417–438, New York, 1991 (Chaumont 1991). Also see page 43 and footnotes 82 and 192.

[42] The author has merely been able to peck at this important fount of information for Sasanian history and the Sasanian–Parthian confederacy. It is hoped that future studies will further integrate this crucial Armenian dimension of Sasanian history into the late antique history of Iran.

[43] Thanks to the tireless efforts of scholars of Armenian history who have admirably edited and translated a substantial collection of the primary sources of this history, students of the late antique history of Iran who have no knowledge of Armenian, such as the author, can now overcome this linguistic barrier and access this important historical corpus. These sources will be listed in the course of this study.

[44] See, among others, the introduction by Robert W. Thompson to Ełishē, *History of Vardan and the Armenian War*, Harvard University Press, 1982, translated and commentary by R. Thomson (Ełishē 1982), pp. 1–3.

[45] Garsoian, Nina G., *Armenia between Byzantium and the Sasanians*, London, 1985b (Garsoian 1985b).

historians, it is still possible to disentangle the pervasive Iranian undercurrents of Armenian history.[46] Pending further research, one might even postulate that the commentaries that Christian Armenian chroniclers made on the religious landscape of the Sasanian realm were informed more by the recent pagan heritage of Armenia itself than by the religious inclinations of particular Sasanian kings, and, therefore, constituted a Christian commentary on the legacies of the Armenian past.

Alternatively, the picture that Armenian histories painted of the religious panorama of the Sasanian domains might have been a depiction of the religious predilections of the Iranian Parthian dynastic families, who struck deep roots in Armenia. In this context, we underline not only the significance of Arsacid rule in Armenia to the Sasanian–Parthian confederacy, but also the clear evidence of Mihr worship in Armenia,[47] and the connection of this to the evident prevalence of Mihr worship in the Pahlav territories in Iran. Besides Armenian histories, selective use has also been made of other foreign sources, especially Greek and Syriac sources relevant to the history of the Sasanians in late .

The *X^w adāy-Nāmag* traditions, the *futūḥ* narratives, and other accounts of Iranian national history, as they appear in classical Arabic histories,[48] are central to the present study. It has long been recognized that the *X^w adāy-Nāmag* traditions were incorporated into the classical Arabic histories which were composed in the ninth and tenth centuries. Some of these, such as Ṭabarī's (839–923) *Taʾrīkh al-Rusul wa 'l-Mulūk (Annales)*,[49] Balʿamī's (d. between 992 and 997) *Tārīkh*,[50] Thaʿālibī's (961–1038) *Ghurar Akhbār Mulūk al-Furs wa Sīyarihim*,[51] Dīnawarī's (d. between 894 and 903) *Akhbār al-Ṭiwāl*,[52] Ibn Balkhī's *Fārsnāma* (written sometime between 1105 and 1116),[53] and, finally, Yaʿqūbī's (d. early tenth century) *Taʾrīkh*,[54] incorporate the *X^w adāy-Nāmag* traditions systematically. We regularly resort to these in order to reconstruct Sasanian history. The most important of these works are those of Ṭabarī and Thaʿālibī.[55]

[46]Lang, David M., 'Iran, Armenia, and Georgia', in Ehsan Yarshater (ed.), *Cambridge History of Iran: The Seleucid, Parthian, and Sasanian Periods*, vol. 3(1), pp. 505–537, Cambridge University Press, 1983 (Lang 1983); Garsoian 1985b; Russell, James R., 'Armenia and Iran: III Armenian Religion', in Ehsan Yarshater (ed.), *Encyclopaedia Iranica*, pp. 438–444, New York, 1991 (Russell 1991).

[47]Russell, James R., 'On the Armeno-Iranian Roots of Mithraism', in John R. Hinnells (ed.), *Studies in Mithraism*, pp. 553–565, Rome, 1990b (Russell 1990b). See §5.4.4.

[48]Yarshater 1983b, pp. 360–363.

[49]Ṭabarī, Muḥammad b. Jarīr, *Taʾrīkh al-Rusul wa 'l-Mulūk (Annales)*, Leiden, 1879–1901, edited by M.J. de Goeje (Ṭabarī 1879–1901).

[50]Balʿamī, *Tarjumih-i Tārīkh-i Ṭabarī*, Tehran, 1959, edited by M.J. Mashkur (Balʿamī 1959).

[51]Thaʿālibī, Abū Manṣūr, *Ghurar Akhbār Mulūk al-Furs wa Sīyarihim*, Paris, 1900, edited by H. Zotenberg (Thaʿālibī 1900).

[52]Dīnawarī, Abū Ḥanīfa Aḥmad, *Akhbār al-Ṭiwāl*, Cairo, 1960, edited by Abd al-Mun'im 'Amir Jamal al-Din al-Shayyal (Dīnawarī 1960).

[53]Ibn Balkhī, *Fārsnāma*, Shiraz, 1995, edited by Mansur Rastgar Fasai (Ibn Balkhī 1995).

[54]Yaʿqūbi, Aḥmad b. Abī Yaʿqūb, *Ibn Wādhih qui Dicitur al-Yaʿqūbī, Historiae*, Leiden, 1969, edited by M.T. Houtsma (Yaʿqūbi 1969).

[55]For other chronicles, such as Bīrūnī, Muḥammad b. Aḥmad, *Āthār al-Bāqiya*, Tehran, 1984, translated by Akbar Danasirisht (Bīrūnī 1984), Bīrūnī, Muḥammad b. Aḥmad, *The Chronology*

Among the most important sources containing the *X^w adāy-Nāmag* (or *Book of Kings*) tradition, however, is the *Shāhnāma* of Ferdowsī (940–1019 or 1025).[56] The *Shāhnāma*, the poetic epic of the scholar/poet Ferdowsī, was itself based on a prose account compiled at the orders of a compatriot of the poet, Abū Manṣūr ʿAbdalrazzāq-i Ṭūsī (d. 962).[57] One of the primary sources of the *Shāhnāma-i Abū Manṣūrī*, was, in turn, the *X^w adāy-Nāmag*(s). Scholars of Iran have long admired the *Shāhnāma* as one of the greatest poetic opera of Iranian national tradition, or of any ethnic community, for that matter. For an inordinate span of time, however, they have also dismissed the *Shāhnāma* as a source for reconstructing Iranian history. Not only Iranists, but also solitary classicists who touch on Sasanian history, have generally regarded the *Shāhnāma* as merely a literary epic, worthless for reconstructing Sasanian history. The reason: more than three fourths of this approximately 50,000-couplet epic poem details mythic and legendary accounts of Iranian history. And if one were to reckon the latter of no academic merit, one might just as well abandon the entire *Shāhnāma* of Ferdowsī.[58] One fourth of the book, however, presumes to detail Sasanian history. What do we do with this? Until quite recently, when Zeev Rubin reprimanded the field, Iranists threw the ill-fated baby out with the bathwater. And why did they do this? Because its medium was *poetic* and as such it was presumed to take *poetic license* and hence more liberties than, say, the works of Ibn Farazdaq, Ibn Isḥāq, or Ṭabarī, the last of which, incorporating the *X^w adāy-Nāmag* tradition,[59] we, incidentally, do use regularly for reconstructing Sasanian history.

The present work uses the Sasanian sections of the *Shāhnāma* of Ferdowsī systematically. And it will show that the *Shāhnāma* is not merely one of the sources, but often the *only* source that provides us with details corroborating the information contained in some of the primary sources for Sasanian history, such as the crucially significant sigillographic evidence, or in some of the secondary sources for Sasanian history, such as the history of the Armenian Bishop Sebeos.[60] This is so because, as Omidsalar, Khaleqi Motlaq, and others

of Ancient Nations, London, 1879, translation by C.E. Sachau (Bīrūnī 1879); or Masʿūdī, ʿAlī b. Ḥusayn, *Murūj al-Dhahab wa Maʿādin al-Jawhar*, Paris, 1869, edited by Barbier de Meynard (Masʿūdī 1869), which provide other significant information pertaining to Sasanian history, see Yarshater 1983b, pp. 360–363.

[56]Shahbazi, Shapur, *Ferdowsī: A Critical Bibliography*, Center for Middle Eastern Studies, Harvard University Press, 1991d (Shahbazi 1991d).

[57]For Abū Manṣūr, see, among others, Motlagh, Djalal Khaleghi, 'Yikī Mihtarī Būd Gardan-farāz', *Majallih-i Dānishkadih-i Adabīyāt o ʿUlūm-i Insānī-i Dānishgāh-i Ferdowsī* 13, (1977), pp. 197–215 (Motlagh 1977); and Pourshariati, Parvaneh, *Iranian Tradition in Ṭūs and the Arab Presence in Khurāsān*, Ph.D. thesis, Columbia University, 1995 (Pourshariati 1995), Ch. II.

[58]Naturally, students and scholars of Iranian myths, legends and pre-history may be justifiably appalled by this. For they regularly appeal to the *Shāhnāma* for assessing this dimension of Iranian history and identity. Besides, through the Ctesian method we will see examples of pertinent information on Sasanian history hidden even within these legendary tales.

[59]Nöldeke 1879, pp. xxi–xxii apud Yarshater 1983b, p. 360.

[60]Sebeos 1999.

have warned us, Ferdowsī in fact slavishly followed the sources which had been entrusted to him in order to compile his opus on Iranian national history.[61]

As we shall be investigating the Arab conquest of Iranian territories, the *futūḥ* narratives of classical Islamic historiography become essential to our study. As Albrecht Noth notes, an overwhelming majority of histories that deal with the period of the first four caliphs, also deal with the theme of the Arab conquest of territories outside Arabia.[62] These are designated under the rubric of *futūḥ* narratives.[63] Examining the *futūḥ* narratives in the context of the *X*ʷ*adāy-Nāmag* historiography, we shall establish that Noth's contention that Iran is a *primary* theme in classical Arab historiography is unmistakably valid. We shall also underline the ways in which the introduction of the *hijra*, *annalistic*, and *caliphal* structures of historical writing, as they appear in the works of Ṭabarī and those who followed him, have seriously undermined the chronology of the early Arab conquest of Sasanian territories as well as that of early Islamic history. Nevertheless, here we highlight the substantial reliability and the tremendous value of Sayf b. ʿUmar's account, upon which Ṭabarī and later authors predominantly based themselves, in his *retention of the primary theme of Iran* in his narrative of the early conquest of Iraq. We shall demonstrate that a critical juxtaposition of the *X*ʷ*adāy-Nāmag* traditions with the *futūḥ* narratives not only disentangles the complex web of the Sasanian–Parthian confederacy, but does so for a crucial juncture in Sasanian history: the early Arab conquest of the Sasanian territories in Iraq. This is one of the numerous instances where we resort to Armenian histories in order to gauge the reliability of the conclusions that we have reached.

For a variety of reasons having to do with the nature of classical Islamic historiography, Crone once remarked that the "obvious way to tackle early Islamic history is ... prosopographical," and proceeded to do this in her *Slaves on Horses: The Evolution of Islamic Polity*.[64] A year after these words appeared in print, so did Donner's work, *The Early Islamic Conquests*, where he likewise engaged in a prosopographical study of important Arab figures of early Islamic history, specifically those who had participated in the conquest of the Fertile Crescent. In contrast, in the translated volume of Ṭabarī's work dealing with the early Arab conquest of Iraq, a majority of the important Iranian figures

[61] Omidsalar, Mahmoud, 'The Text of Ferdowsi's Shâhnâma and the Burden of the Past', *Journal of the American Oriental Society* 118, (1998), pp. 63–68, review of Olga M. Davidson's *Poet and Hero in the Persian Book of Kings* (Omidsalar 1998); Omidsalar, Mahmoud, 'Unburdening Ferdowsi', *Journal of the American Oriental Society* 116, (1996), pp. 235–242 (Omidsalar 1996); Omidsalar, Mahmoud, 'Could al-Thaʿālibī Have Used the *Shāhnāma* as a Source?', in *Jostārhāy-i Shāhnāma-shināsī*, pp. 113–126, Tehran, 2002 (Omidsalar 2002); Motlagh, Djalal Khaleghi, 'Badīhih Sarāyī-i Shafāhī va *Shāhnāma*', in *Jostārhāy-i Shāhnāma-shināsī*, pp. 153–167, Tehran, 2002 (Motlagh 2002).

[62] Noth, Albrecht, *The Early Arabic Historical Tradition: A Source Critical Study*, Princeton, 1994, second edition in collaboration with Lawrence I. Conrad, translated by Michael Bonner (Noth 1994), p. 31.

[63] For a more detailed discussion, see §3.1.1 below.

[64] Crone, Patricia, *Slaves on Horses: The Evolution of Islamic Polity*, Cambridge University Press, 1980 (Crone 1980), here, p. 16.

appearing in Sayf b. ʿUmar's narrative have been reckoned to be creations of Sayf's fertile imagination.[65] Sayf, it appears, comfortably and systematically concocted *Iranian* names and genealogies. The resultant prosopographical map that we have been left with is one in which the Arabs fight a host of ghosts in Iranian territories. And as ghosts cannot be active participants in any history, it is not clear whom precisely the Arabs fought in their wars of conquest in the Sasanian territories. The present work indulges in a heavy dose of prosopographical research in order to bring back to life the ghosts of the Iranian protagonists in late antique Iranian history, specifically those of Parthian ancestry. The reader must bear with us as we attempt to reconstruct these in the course of our narrative.

Prosopographical research on the late antique history of Iran, however, especially when we are dealing with the Iranian side of things, is complicated by the nature of the sources with which we have to deal. Except in minor, but crucial, instances, our primary sources are of comparatively much less use than our foreign and native literary sources. These latter, in turn, have their own shortcomings, for whether we cull our data from the Armenian, Greek, Syriac, or classical Arabic sources, including the *futūḥ* narratives, or even from the *Xʷadāy-Nāmag* traditions, the fact remains that they have been handed down to us through centuries of transmission and after undergoing transformations at the hands of authors not at home in Middle Persian naming practice. Consequently, depending on the source, the names of important Iranian historical figures have been metamorphosed through the languages in which they have been carried. As we shall see, the *Shāhnāma* of Ferdowsī—apart from some mild use of poetic license—comes closest to the original Pahlavi rendition of these names. The inflation of titles in Sasanian political and administrative culture exacerbates this problem. Particularly in Greek and Arabic sources, the titles of significant personae of Sasanian history are at times confused with their personal names. To complicate matters, in Arabic texts the names of important figures are often Arabicized. What aids us *significantly* in disentangling this confusing web in which Middle Persian names have been bastardized, and in identifying figures appearing in different sources under various names, titles, or epithets, however, is the crucial importance of genealogical heritage in Sasanian history. If tribal traditions ensured the retention of identities in early Arabic histories—albeit we know too well of forged genealogies—so too the *agnatic* social structure of Iran in late antiquity, and the crucial significance of belonging to an agnatic family, guaranteed the preservation of ancestral lines in Sasanian history.[66] Genealogies were not simply the obsession of Arab genealogists. The upper crust of the hierarchical Iranian society, especially the Parthian dynastic families, were also adept at it. As this work deals with the saga of these families, it also serves as a prosopographical investigation into the fortunes of

[65] Ṭabarī, *The Challenge to the Empires*, vol. XI of *The History of Ṭabarī*, Albany, 1993, translated and annotated by Khalid Yahya Blankinship (Ṭabarī 1993).

[66] See §1.2.

important Parthian dynastic families in Sasanian history. In the course of the many identifications that are made, there will doubtless be some inaccuracies and inconsistencies. These will not detract, however, from the greater scheme that the author is proposing, namely, the Sasanian–Parthian confederacy.

A word remains to be said about what this work does not purport to be. This is not a work on Sasanian administrative history, nor the much neglected domain of Sasanian economic history. For the former, the standard works remain those of Christensen, Rika Gyselen, and a host of other scholars of Sasanian history. The economic history of the Sasanian empire continues to remain a barren field and, unfortunately, we shall not rectify this.[67] While the Sasanian–Parthian confederacy and the general contours of the dynastic sociopolitical arrangement in Sasanian history will be investigated through the course of the present study, the precise administrative mechanisms through which this Sasanian–Parthian confederacy came to be implemented lie beyond its scope. This study is likewise not a detailed investigation of Sasanian religious life. While we stand by our postulate regarding the Mithraic dimensions of Parthian religiosity in the Sasanian period, and while we hope to offer significant insights into the religious inclinations of some of the Parthian families, this is a study neither of Mihr worship, nor of the precise nature of the Mihr worship prevailing among various Parthian families. All that we are proposing is that there is substantial evidence for the popularity of Mihr worship in the *kūst-i khwarāsān* and *kūst-i ādurbādagān* of the Sasanian domains and among particular Parthian families, and that this Pahlav version of Mihr worship was distinct from the place of Mihr not only in the orthodox Mazdean creed, but also in that which was current among the Sasanians (Pārsīg). And even here one must probably reckon with the religious inclinations of particular Sasanian kings. In bringing to bear the results of the recent fascinating research on the Sasanian religious landscape, and while discussing evidence of Mihr worship among the Pahlav, it is hoped that subsequent scholarship on the post-conquest[68] religious history of Iran will reckon with the multifarious religious landscape of the Sasanian empire.[69] For at some point we need to abandon the notion, still prevalent

[67]Except sporadically and in passing, moreover, scholarship has yet to engage the dialectic of the natural environment and human agency in Sasanian history. Michael Morony and Fred M. Donner's works, as well as Christensen, Peter, *The Decline of Iranshahr: Irrigation and Environments in the History of the Middle East 500 B.C. to 1500 A.D.*, Copenhagen, 1993b (Christensen 1993b), are valuable exceptions to this.

[68]I owe this terminology to my good friend and colleague Dr. Asef Kholdani. As the process of conversion in Iran took many centuries to complete, the dichotomous conceptualization of history of Iran into *pre-Islamic* and *Islamic* periods seems unwarranted and superficial for the purposes of this study. As this study hopes to establish, the political and cultural currents of Iranian history in the period under study fall more properly into late antique history of Iran, the Islamic periodization marking an artificial watershed imposed on this history.

[69]The multifarious character of Islamic sectarian movements in early medieval Iran is itself a testimony to the source which fed it. Madelung, Wilferd, *Religious Trends in Early Islamic Iran*, Albany, 1988 (Madelung 1988); Madelung, Wilferd, *Religious and Ethnic Movements in Medieval Islam*, Brookfield, 1992 (Madelung 1992); Madelung, Wilferd, *Religious Schools and Sects in Medieval*

in some corners, that the strict hold of an orthodox Zoroastrian religious culture on its flock eased the way for the conversion of Iranians into a coherently formed and egalitarian Muslim creed. A systematic methodology for investigating the course of conversion in Iran,[70] and detailed studies of a host of other issues in late antique history of Iran are yet to be devised and undertaken. While this remains to be the case, we need only to acknowledge, as does the present author, that our investigations of late antique history of Iran are preliminary.

Offering a number of dissenting perspectives, this study picks many fights. But it does so in the habit of a rebellious disciple indulging in a *zandīk* reading of the orthodox creed. For in the final analysis, it has been the nurturing of the latter that has paved the way for the present analysis. This debt will become apparent in the course of this study.

Islam, London, 1985 (Madelung 1985).

[70]The only viable study on this crucial topic thus far remains Bulliet, Richard W., *Conversion to Islam in the Medieval Period: An Essay in Quantitative History*, Harvard University Press, 1979 (Bulliet 1979). See our discussion in §6.2; also see Choksy, Jamsheed K., *Conflict and Cooperation: Zoroastrian Subalterns and Muslim Elites in Medieval Iranian Society*, Columbia University Press, 1997 (Choksy 1997).

CHAPTER 1

Preliminaries

1.1 The Arsacids

Sometime before the middle of the third century BCE, an Iranian people known as the Dahae[71] appear in our records on the southeastern borders of the Caspian Sea.[72] To this region they ultimately gave their name, the land of the Dahae, or Dihistān. Shortly thereafter, a group of these, known as the Parni, entered the Iranian plateau through the corridor established by the Atrak[73] valley in the mountainous regions of northeastern Iran. Somewhere here, in the ancient city of Asaak,[74] they established their capital. In Asaak, around 247 BCE, they crowned their king, Arsaces (Ashk) I.

What had facilitated these momentous events was the turmoil that had engulfed the comparatively short-lived, post-Alexandrian, Seleucid kingdom of Iran,[75] and the rebellions that had erupted against the Seleucids—preoccupied

[71]For the Dahae, see de Blois, F. and Vogelsang, W., 'Dahae', in Ehsan Yarshater (ed.), *Encyclopaedia Iranica*, pp. 581–582, New York, 1991 (de Blois and Vogelsang 1991).

[72]Which territories comprised the original homeland of the Dahae and their settlements have been the subject of intense debate in recent scholarship. See footnote 94 below.

[73]The Atrak is a river in northeastern Iran, in the region of Khurāsān. Following a northwest and subsequently a southwest course, the Atrak river flows into the Caspian Sea. See Bosworth, C.E., 'Atrak', in Ehsan Yarshater (ed.), *Encyclopaedia Iranica*, New York, 2007a (Bosworth 2007a).

[74]The precise location of Asaak is open to dispute. It has been postulated, however, that it was somewhere near the modern city of Qūchān in the Atrak valley.

[75]After defeating the Achaemenid Darius III in 331 BCE, Alexander conquered Iran and the regions to the east. Upon his return from India, he died in Mesopotamia in 323 BCE. After Alexander's death, the eastern parts of the conquered regions, including Iran, fell into the hands of one of his generals, Seleucus, who subsequently established the Seleucid empire. The Seleucids, however, became a western-oriented empire from early on. As Bickerman remarks, Seleucus' transfer of his headquarters to the newly established city of Antioch in Syria in 300 BCE, was a momentous decision that "changed the course of Iranian history." Bickerman, E., 'The Seleucid Period', in Ehsan Yarshater (ed.), *Cambridge History of Iran: The Seleucid, Parthian, and Sasanian Periods*, vol. 3(1), Cambridge University Press, 1983 (Bickerman 1983), p. 4. Thereafter, the Seleucids lost their Iranian possessions "within a period of roughly fifteen years from 250 to 235 BCE." See Shahbazi, Shapur, Schipmman, K., Alram, M., Boyce, Mary, and Toumanoff, C., 'Arsacids', in Ehsan Yarshater (ed.), *Encyclopaedia Iranica*, pp. 525–546, New York, 1991 (Shahbazi et al. 1991), here p. 525.

in Egypt and Syria—in Bactria (Balkh) and Khurāsān.[76] Taking advantage of the unsettled situation in the east, the Parni moved on to take over the province (*satrapy*) that—at least since the Achaemenid period—had come to be known as Parthava.[77] This was around 238 BCE. Shortly afterwards, they also conquered Hyrcania. Hyrcania, an extensive territory to the east of the Caspian Sea, included the regions later known as Gurgān (the land of the wolves) as well as Ṭabaristān.[78] Thenceforth, together with Parthava, the province of Hyrcania/Gurgān became one of the most important centers of the Dahae (Parni).

After their king, the dynasty that this group of the Parni established came to be known as the Arsacids (Persian Ashkānīyān). After the new region which they occupied as their homeland, they came to be known as the Parthians, that is, the people of Parthava. The Parthians, then, were the collectivity—composed of many large agnatic families[79]—of the Iranian people that entered the plateau in the middle of the third century BCE. The term Parthian, in other words, is an Iranian *ethnicon* that has been coined after a territory, Parthava. The Arsacids, on the other hand, were the particular branch of the Parthians that came to rule Iran. Arsacid, therefore, is a dynastic name.

By 170 BCE, the Arsacids had consolidated their rule in the southern regions of the Caspian Sea.[80] The rule of one of their greatest kings, Mithradates (Mihrdād) I (171–138 BCE), saw further expansions to the west against the Seleucids, and later against Rome. By 148 BCE, they had conquered the important and ancient region of Media in western Iran. And by 141 BCE, Mithradates I's power was recognized as far as the ancient city of Uruk in Mesopotamia.[81] Around this time, Mithradates I also conquered the important Seleucid city Seleucia, where he crowned himself king. By this time, Arsacid power in Mesopotamia was beyond doubt. In the process the Arsacids had made another crucial conquest: the conquest of Armenia.

Ultimately, Arsacid rule (247 BCE–224 CE) over Iran and Mesopotamia lasted for more than four and a half centuries—more than their predecessors, the Achaemenids (559–330 BCE), or their successors, the Sasanians (224–651 CE). As we shall see in the course of this study, their control of Armenia

[76]Besides the rebellion in Bactria, the most important uprising was that of the Seleucid *satrap* (governor) of Parthava and Hyrcania, Andragoras, who rebelled against his Seleucid overlord, Antiochus II, around 245 BCE. It has been suggested, though not without controversy, that Andragoras himself was probably a Persian, his original old Persian name being Narisanka. For Andragoras, see Frye, Richard N., 'Andragoras', in Ehsan Yarshater (ed.), *Encyclopaedia Iranica*, p. 26, New York, 1991 (Frye 1991), p. 26.

[77]The boundaries of the province of Parthava were subject to change depending on the political situation in which the region found itself. As a general rule of thumb, it might be said to have included the provinces of Khurāsān and Hyrcania.

[78]Bivar, A.D.H., 'Gorgān', in Ehsan Yarshater (ed.), *Encyclopaedia Iranica*, New York, 2007a (Bivar 2007a).

[79]For the agnatic social structure of Iranian society, see §1.2 below.

[80]Shahbazi et al. 1991.

[81]Shahbazi et al. 1991.

also lasted for close to four centuries.[82] The Parthians remained the greatest unconquered foes of the imperialistic Romans through most of their rule. Any impartial observer of antiquity ought to have reckoned them as the equals of the Romans during this period. Early in the twentieth century some began to recognize this. Debevoise remarked in 1931, for example, that "the most cursory examination of the [classical] literature ... [underlined the fact] that Parthia was no second-rate power in the minds of the ancients ... Poet and historian, dramatist and technician, all speak of the military and political strength of the Arsacidae. Collections of Latin inscriptions teem with references to Parthia. It was frankly admitted that there were but two great powers in the world: Rome and Parthia."[83]

Debevoise's sentiments, however, reflected a very new trend in scholarship. For prior to this, the Parthians were the subjects of some of the most partial scholarly accounts. They were thus considered the barbarian hordes of antiquity.[84] As late as 1977 they were still characterized as the political "clowns of

[82] After the conquest of Armenia by the Arsacids, the Arsacid king Vologeses (Valakhsh I, 51–78), appointed his younger brother, Tiridates, to the Armenian throne in 62 CE. This junior branch of the Arsacids remained in power in Armenia until the Sasanians conquered the region under Shāpūr I (241–272). The Sasanian king then appointed his brother Hormozd-Ardashīr as governor of Armenia. While Armenia remained a bone of contention between the Romans and the Parthians and, subsequently, the Byzantines and the Sasanians throughout its history, after a short hiatus, Arsacid rule was restored in Armenia under Bahrām II (276–293) in 286–87. The Arsacids continued to rule Armenia until 428 when their kingdom was officially abolished (see footnote 192). As Garsoian underlines, therefore, there is no question that the "Armenian Arsacids were a junior branch of the Parthian royal house." Garsoian, Nina G., 'Prolegomena to a Study of the Iranian Aspect of Arsacid Armenia', in *Armenia between Byzantium and the Sasanians*, pp. 1–46, London, 1985e (Garsoian 1985e), p. 3.

[83] Debevoise, Neilson C., 'Parthian Problems', *The American Journal of Semitic Languages and Literature* 47, (1931), pp. 73–82 (Debevoise 1931), here, p. 74. Debevoise also gives a good summary of the extant, and unfortunately lost, classical literature dealing with the Parthians.

[84] After the publication of Rawlison, George, *The Sixth Oriental Monarchy, or The Geography, History, and Antiquities of Parthia, Collected and Illustrated from Ancient and Modern Sources*, New York, 1837 (Rawlison 1837), the first serious attempt at critically examining Parthian history was undertaken by Neilson Debevoise. In 1931, in an article entitled 'Parthian Problems', Debevoise first articulated the results of his research, and the problems confronting scholars interested in Parthian history; this was followed seven years later by Debevoise, Neilson C., *A Political History of Parthia*, Chicago University Press, 1938 (Debevoise 1938). In the early 1960s, there also appeared Lozinski, Philip, *The Original Homeland of the Parthians*, 's-Gravenhage, 1959 (Lozinski 1959); Ghirshman, Roman, *Persian Art, Parthian and Sassanian Dynasties 249 B.C.–651 A.D.*, New York, 1962, translated by Stuart Gilbert and James Emmons (Ghirshman 1962); and Neusner, J., 'Parthian Political Ideology', *Iranica Antiqua* 3, (1963), pp. 40–59 (Neusner 1963). Debevoise's work, however, remained the standard on the topic. In 1967, Colledge published Colledge, Malcolm A.R., *The Parthians*, New York, 1967 (Colledge 1967), and two decades later Colledge, Malcolm A.R., *The Parthian Period*, Leiden, 1986 (Colledge 1986). Most recently, other works have appeared: Schippmann, Klaus, *Grundzüge der parthischen Geschichte*, Darmstadt, 1980 (Schippmann 1980); translated into Persian as Schippmann, Klaus, *Mabānī-i Tārīkh-i Pārtīyān*, Tehran, 2005, translation of Schippmann 1980 by Houshang Sadighi (Schippmann 2005); Wiesehöfer, Josef, *Das Partherreich und seine Zeugnisse: The Arsacid Empire: Sources and Documentation*, Stuttgart, 1998 (Wiesehöfer 1998); Brunner, Christopher, 'Geographical and Administrative Divisions: Settlements and Economy', in Ehsan Yarshater (ed.), *Cambridge History of Iran: The Seleucid, Parthian, and Sasanian Periods*, vol. 3(2),

the millennium."[85] And until recently, when Soviet archaeological investigations in Dihistān, Transoxiana, and the surrounding regions led to the discoveries of ancient, settled civilizations and communities,[86] the nomadic background of the Parthians was established wisdom, as was their want of any notable cultural and political legacy to posterity.

The Arsacids, we are told, never really committed their history to writing.[87] The skewed image through which they had been presented, therefore, was partly a legacy of Rome, of the ambivalence with which the classical authors had represented their enemies. Another group of foes, however, were equally and centrally involved in drawing this dismal image of Parthians and their history. These were an Iranian people, the Persīs, the early migrants to the Iranian plateau who had settled in the region of Fārs (Pārs) in southwestern Iran, from much prior to the arrival of the Parni—at least a millennium before the common era.[88] Many centuries later, it was from this same region of Fārs, with its tradition of hostility toward Parthava, that the Sasanians hailed. And, thus, having defeated the Parthians in the early third century, the Sasanians also inherited the added antagonism of the Persīs toward their conquered foes, the Arsacids.[89] While the Arsacids had presumably left us few written records of their history,[90] under the patronage of the Sasanians the first history of Iran, including what little they had left of Arsacid history, was committed to writing: in the *X^{w}adāy-Nāmag* or *Book of Kings*.[91]

Literary sources for Parthian history, therefore, are predominantly based on these two sets of hostile historical sources with all the problems contained in them.[92] In the combined hands of modern classicists, who had based themselves

pp. 747–778, Cambridge University Press, 1983 (Brunner 1983); Bivar, A.D.H., 'The Political History of Iran under the Arsacids', in Ehsan Yarshater (ed.), *Cambridge History of Iran: The Seleucid, Parthian, and Sasanian Periods*, vol. 3(1), Cambridge University Press, 1983 (Bivar 1983); Wolski, Józef, *L'empire des Arsacides*, Leuven, 1993 (Wolski 1993); and Wissemann, Michael, *Die Parther in der augusteischen Dichtung*, Frankfurt, 1982 (Wissemann 1982).

[85] Keall, E.J., 'Political, Economic, and Social Factors on the Parthian Landscape of Mesapotamia and Western Iran', *Bibliotheca Mesopotamica* 7 (Keall 1977), p. 81, cited in Wenke, Robert J., 'Elymeans, Parthians, and the Evolution of Empires in Southwestern Iran', *Journal of the American Oriental Society* 101, (1981), pp. 303–315 (Wenke 1981), here p. 303, n. 5.

[86] Schippmann 1980; see footnote 94.

[87] See in this context our discussion of sources on pages 10 and 459, as well as Boyce 1957a.

[88] The Achaemenids, for instance, were Persīs.

[89] See also our discussion at the beginning of §5.1.

[90] The many epic traditions and romances which have a clear Parthian provenance, such as *Vīs o Rāmīn*, *Samak-i ʿAyyār*, and others, should warn us against taking this too literally.

[91] See also page 171ff below.

[92] The wealth of the sources pertaining to Parthian history is in material culture, specifically numismatic evidence. Besides recent archaeological investigations, through which, for instance, the *ostraca* of Nisā (near modern Ashkābād), have been found, there are *papyri* from the western regions of Iran and Dura Europos (see footnote 2250) as well as Chinese sources. It should be mentioned, however, that archaeological investigations of Parthian homelands, Khurāsān and Ṭabaristān, have been practically nonexistent. Besides the sources listed above, also see Lukonin, V.G., 'Political, Social and Administrative Institutions: Taxes and Trade', in Ehsan Yarshater (ed.), *Cambridge History of Iran: The Seleucid, Parthian, and Sasanian Periods*, vol. 3(2), pp. 119–120, Cambridge University

on classical authors, and modern Iranists, some of whom uncritically accepted the *X^w adāy-Nāmag* versions of Iranian history, the Parthians thus suffered, at best, from collective historical amnesia and, at worst, from bouts of hostile historiography.

A revival of Parthian studies in recent decades, however, has partially corrected this hostile representation of the Parthians and their contributions to the history of antiquity. Although we remain many decades behind a substantive knowledge of Parthian and Arsacid rule, our previous blind spots are being increasingly fixed.[93] Recent archaeological discoveries, for example, have established that we can no longer date the beginnings of urbanization in Dihistān, Kopet Dāgh and the Murghāb regions—regions in which the nuclei of the Arsacid state were originally formed—to the Achaemenid or the Hellenistic periods, but to a much earlier period: the end of the third millennium BCE. By the beginnings of the first millennium BCE, the Iron Age, the pace of urbanization in these areas became even more rapid. The question that has now risen, therefore, is the extent to which the Dahae partook in the advanced settled cultures of these territories. What is clear, according to Schippmann and others, is that we can no longer simply speak of the *nomadic* Dahae/Parni.[94] Critically reexamining our historical givens, the Parthian contribution to the contemporary and subsequent cultures of the area have been increasingly recognized. At its simplest, we now recognize, for example, that had it not been for the Parthian

Press, 1983 (Lukonin 1983); Widengren, Geo, 'Sources of Parthian and Sasanian History', in Ehsan Yarshater (ed.), *Cambridge History of Iran: The Seleucid, Parthian, and Sasanian Periods*, vol. 3(2), pp. 1261–1284, Cambridge University Press, 1983 (Widengren 1983).

[93]Schippmann's work gives a very good synopsis of the state of the field in Parthian studies. Schippmann 1980; Schippmann 2005. Disregarding conventional practice, mention also should be made of an electronic resource, parthia.com, whose authors have done an admirable job of presenting a bibliographic survey of works on Parthian history.

[94]Archaeological investigations have unearthed three major cultures, belonging to the late Bronze Age (circa 3500–1450 BCE), in southern Turkmenistan: 1) The *Dihistān culture* in western Turkmenistan, belonging to 1200–650 BCE, takes its name from the Dahae, who at some point lived in the region. Settlements ranging from one to fifty acres and extensive irrigation networks testify to a centralized rule. The question of whether or not this culture belonged to the Dahae, however, has polarized scholarship. Wolski, basing himself on classical sources, argues that the Dahae only migrated to this region in the third century BCE. In opposition to him, I. N. Chlopin has argued that the Dahae had always lived in the eastern regions of the Caspian Sea, in ancient Hyrcania, and that archaeological investigations in this area do not give any evidence of an aggressive inroad of nomadic populations in the third century BCE. This culture, argues Chlopin, does in fact belong to the Dahae; 2) The second culture, sometimes called the *Namazga VI* culture, was found at the base of the Kopet Dāgh mountains. Extensive settlements, some as large as 70 acres, have been found here as well. The chronology of this culture has been traced to the third and second millennium BCE. It has been argued that, with intermittent periods of decline, this culture reached its height in the seventh to the fourth centuries BCE; 3) Finally, there was the *culture of the Murghāb*, belonging to 1500–1200 BCE. Over all, according to Schippman, we can now propose that prior to the first millennium BCE, and in the case of Dihistān even prior to this, large political confederations did exist in Dihistān and neighboring territories. Extensive irrigation networks, enclosed fortresses and settlements, as well as the emergence of iron, all testify to the fact that these three cultures developed on a comparable basis, although the details of their connection to one another is not yet clear. Schippmann 1980, pp. 78–81, Schippmann 2005, pp. 98–100.

protection of the frontier territories in Central Asia and Caucasia, even Rome would have suffered under the pressure of nomadic populations in these sensitive corridors of the East. In art, architecture,[95] and even traditions of rule, the Parthian contributions to subsequent Iranian culture and to the cultural traditions of the region as a whole are being gradually and increasingly established—albeit at a snail's pace—by scholarship. There is much that remains unclear about this era of Iranian history.[96] One of the least investigated dimensions of the Parthian cultural contribution to posterity, for example, is the impact they made on the religions of the Near East and the Mediterranean world.[97] A discussion of the state-of-the-field in Parthian studies is beyond the scopes of the present study and the reader is urged to look elsewhere for this.[98] By way of background, however, some preliminary notes about the political and social structure of Parthian rule and their role in preserving and disseminating Iranian national history must be given.

Political organization of the Parthian empire

As mentioned, the Arsacids were only one of the families of the collectivity that we have come to know as Parthians, namely, the ruling family that had assumed power with the coronation of Arsaces I. There were besides these other, important, Parthian (Pahlav) families, who exerted tremendous power throughout the Arsacid period. Traditionally, it is said that there were seven of these, although this is most likely legendary. As it stands, besides significant, yet disjointed, sets of information, the details of the histories of these other Parthian families during the Arsacid period escape our knowledge. In fact, a substantial part of the information that we do have on these families pertains not to their histories during the Arsacid period, but to their saga among the Sasanians. This book is partly an account of this latter history.

What little we do know about these Parthian families during the Arsacid period relates to the later period of Arsacid history. Based on these, some have argued that the Parthian families' participation in Arsacid history had rendered the sociopolitical and economic structures of the Arsacids feudal. As Schippmann, Neusner, and others have observed, however, the matter is not so simple.[99] The problem, once again, pertains to the question of sources for Arsacid history. The dearth of sources for the early Arsacid period has been debilitating

[95]See, among others, Curtis, Vesta Sarkhosh, Hillenbrand, Robert, and Rogers, J.M., *The Art and Archaeology of Ancient Persia: New Light on the Parthian and Sasanian Empires*, British Institute of Persian Studies, London, 1998 (Curtis et al. 1998).

[96]Fortunately during the past decade a thorough investigation of the Parthian numismatic and political history has been undertaken by Farhad Assar. The scholarly community eagerly awaits the publication of his results, as well as the volume covering the Parthian period of the *History of Zoroastrianism* by Frantz Grenet and the late Mary Boyce.

[97]The growth and spread of Mithraism in the Roman empire took place, after all, during the Parthian period. In a subsequent study, the author hopes to contribute to this topic.

[98]For a summary bibliography, see footnote 84.

[99]Schippmann 1980, pp. 81–89, especially p. 88–89, Schippmann 2005, pp. 100–107; Neusner 1963.

for scholarship. Here we are in the realm of conjectural history. Schippman provides one scenario for this: after his coronation, Arsaces I, as the commander of a small army, at once found himself sovereign not only over the Parni, but also over the population living in the conquered territories. Arsaces had to exert, therefore, all his efforts during this period toward strengthening his rule. His coronation in Asaak, the establishment of this as the beginning of the Arsacid calendar, and the minting of coinage bearing Arsaces' effigy, are all evidence of measures taken by the king toward solidifying his rule in these territories. Already during this early period, however, we hear of a small number of powerful vassals, vassals who controlled extensive tracts of land and ruled over provinces next to the king. The lands under the control of these families were hereditary. From the rule of Mithradates I (171–138 BCE) onward, especially during the reign of Mithradates II (123–88 BCE), and in the wake of the extensive Parthian conquests in the west and the incorporation of the western city-states into their domains, we witness an imperial structure of rule developing within Parthian territories. The power and strength of the nobility, however, continued and, in fact, seems to have increased from then on. From the first century BCE onward, therefore, there seems to be clear evidence that the power of these families vis-à-vis the king was growing.[100]

The nature of the political and economic structure of the Parthian state has thus raised two central questions in Parthian studies: 1) whether the selection of the king was effected through a council of nobility, a *senatus* or *mahistān*, or was based on the concept of hereditary kingship; and related to this, 2) the extent to which we can speak of a feudal structure when studying Parthian history. To begin with the first, we have evidence for the existence of such an executive body for some periods of Arsacid history, and we therefore presume its continued existence throughout. Our evidence also suggests that during the early period, that is, prior to the first century BCE, the power of the Arsacid king far outweighed the power of the nobility.[101] The increasing power of the Parthian families in the late Arsacid period seems to be reflected in Arsacid political ideology, as we can reconstruct these from sources.

Basing himself on the accounts given by Strabo (64/63 BCE–21 CE) and Justinus' epitome of Pompeius Trogus' *Historiae Philippicae*, which was probably written in the third century, Jacob Neusner argues that the conditions of a conquering people who established hegemony by force of arms[102] is reflected in the realities of the early Arsacid state, which "was governed by a king and a council, and was apparently centralized to some degree." This state of affairs reflects conditions up to the first century BCE.[103] This then was a "feudal, but still centralized state, in which authority rested in the hands of a king, the royal family, priesthood, and a council of powerful nobles." As the earliest coins

[100] Schippmann 1980, pp. 81–88; Schippmann 2005, pp. 100–107.
[101] Schippmann 1980, pp. 100–106; Schippmann 2005.
[102] Neusner seems to accept the nomadic background of the Dahae.
[103] Neusner 1963, p. 43.

of the Arsacids, which mostly lack any honorifics, bear witness, such a state "would have considered itself legitimate by force of arms, requiring no further political authority to explain its authority."[104] Once we turn to the accounts of Flavius Arrianus of the second century CE, and consider the numismatic evidence of later Arsacid history, however, we realize that the political ideology of the Arsacids had undergone a transformation, incorporating in the process an important dimension into their claim for legitimacy: the Arsacids now claimed an Achaemenid genealogy. This claim, Neusner argues, was not advanced by the Arsacids before the end of the second century BCE. From then on, however, Arsacid co-option of Achaemenid heritage is evidenced not only in their coins, which bear the title *King of Kings* (*shāhānshāh*), but also by their use in writing of Pahlavi side-by-side of Greek as well as other symbolic associations that they sought to make with ancient Iranian rule and the Achaemenids.[105] Neusner believes that this change in Arsacid political ideology was a reflection of the changing fortunes of the dynasty. Initially instigated by the victories of the Parthians in the course of the first century, victories which recalled "the glories of Achaemenid Persia," the change in Arsacid political ideology was thereafter sustained when, by the end of the first century BCE, "the powerful [Parthian] armies and government ... fell apart ... and the fundamental weakness of Arsacid rule became evident."[106] From then on the power of the nobility increased, while the strength of the state in the face of external enemies decreased. In view of this, there was a greater need for the state to continue to emphasize its legitimacy by resorting to extra-Parthian, ancient Iranian traditions of rule and hegemony.[107] At this point, according to Neusner, a "feudal theory was required, which unlike an étatiste one, made a great matter out of original legitimacy, pure lineage, and proper succession of the monarch."[108]

Who were the Parthian feudal families exerting such power throughout Arsacid history? An impressionistic and romanticized account of the provenance of the Parthian families, an origins myth, is preserved for us in the accounts of the Armenian historian Moses Khorenats'i.[109] The Arsacid king, Phraat IV (circa 38–2 BCE), relates Khorenats'i, had three sons and a daughter: Artashēs (Artaxerxes), Kārin, Sūren, and Koshm, respectively. The first son became the successor to his father and ruled as Phraat V (circa 2 BCE–4 CE).[110] The other two sons became the progenitors of the houses bearing their name, namely, the Kārins and the Sūrens. Koshm married a "general of all Iranians" after whom

[104]Neusner 1963, p. 44.

[105]Neusner 1963, pp. 45–47.

[106]Neusner 1963, p. 51.

[107]Neusner 1963, p. 57.

[108]Neusner 1963, pp. 50–58.

[109]For a critical account of Khorenats'i and his work, which Thomson dates to the "first decades of Abbasid control over Armenia," see the introduction by Thomson, pp. 1–63, here p. 60, in Khorenats'i, Moses, *Moses Khorenats'i: History of the Armenians*, Harvard University Press, 1978, translated by Robert W. Thomson (Khorenats'i 1978).

[110]Also known as Phraataces.

his progeny "bore the title of Aspahpet Pahlav,"[111] the family who later came to be known as the Ispahbudhān family. This account is, doubtless, mythic. For, as Christensen argues, the existence of these families as great feudal nobility is established long prior to the periodization provided by Khorenats'i.[112] Unfortunately, we have little more than myths to go by for reconstructing the details of the histories of these families during the Parthian period itself.[113]

It is suggested that these Parthian families considered the Arsacids only as *primus inter pares*, first among equals.[114] As a collectivity, these families had agreed to Arsacid rule for a substantial period of their history. Evidence seems to suggest, moreover, that this was increasingly not the case in the last century of Arsacid history, during which period internal struggles beset the dynasty. It was at the end of this period of inter-Parthian rivalry, during the early third century, that from Persīs, the land of the Pārsīg, the forebears of the Sasanians rose. Our study traces the relationship of the various Parthian families, the Pahlav, with the Sasanians, the Pārsīg. Before we embark, a final word needs to be said about the nature of the Iranian family structure.

1.2 Agnatic families

From well before the Arsacid times, the family had been the primary unit of Iranian society.[115] A host of social constructs and restrictions bound the Iranian family together. Besides a strict system of rights and obligations, the family was also cemented together by important social customs and economic systems. The family shared worship that was structured around the "domestic altar and the cult of the souls of ancestors on the father's side," as well as specific religious rites. The family owned property as a collectivity. And, finally, the family engaged in common activities in production and consumption of resources. The life of the individual within the family, in other words, was bound to the latter by a network that reinforced itself on multiple levels, continuously.

Both the small and extended families, designated respectively by the terms *dūtak* (literally smoke) and *katak* (house), consisted of "a group of agnates limited to three or four generations counting in descending order from the head of the family." The crucial concept, however, is the *agnatic* group. For, whether small or extended, the family itself was only a nucleus that functioned within a larger network of a community of kinsmen, the "agnatic group." As Perikhanian observes, the agnatic group, referred to in the Parthian and Sasanian society

[111]Khorenatsʿi 1978, p. 166.

[112]Christensen 1944, p. 104, n. 1.

[113]Hopefully, the work of Assar will shed light on this.

[114]Although recently this too seems to have been the subject of some debate.

[115]Unless otherwise noted, the following discussion is indebted to Perikhanian, A., 'Iranian Society and Law', in Ehsan Yarshater (ed.), *Cambridge History of Iran: The Seleucid, Parthian, and Sasanian Periods*, vol. 3(2), pp. 627–681, Cambridge University Press, 1983 (Perikhanian 1983).

as *nāf* (family), *tōkhm* (seed), and *gōhar* (substance, essence, lineage),[116] the two latter terms, incidentally, permeating the *Shāhnāma* of Ferdowsī, "was the most important structure within the civic community, replacing the earlier clan and tribal systems."[117] In its simplest form the agnatic group included several dozen extended families who defined themselves based on their lineage from a common ancestor from the father's side three or four generations down the line.

In terms of the social and organizational patterns, perhaps the most important consideration to keep in mind is the impact of the agnatic group on Iranian society. According to Perikhanian, the agnatic group entailed a "(1) community of economic life, (2) solidarity in obligations, (3) community of political life, (4) territorial community."[118] While with the growth of the family as a social unit, property rights eventually came to accrue to the individual families, furthermore, "the agnatic group continued to retain latent rights over the possession of all families forming part of the group."[119] The characteristics of the agnatic social structure of the society under investigation here will be of crucial importance to the crux of the present investigation. When discussing the power of the dynastic[120] families over the population living in their domains during the Sasanian period, it will be important to bear in mind, for example, that "the larger group also retained collective ownership of the common pastures, mills, irrigation works, farm buildings and so on."[121] Community of worship was also closely controlled by one's agnatic group. The rites of passage of a youth into adulthood were celebrated by solemn ceremonies in the presence of the agnates. Other important ceremonies, such as marriages and juridical acts, equally required the presence of adult members of the agnatic group.[122] By far, one of the most crucial characteristics of the agnatic group for our purposes, however, is the fact that each agnatic group constituted a territorial unit. Members of an agnatic group, in other words, lived in the confines of one and the same territory. Modern ethnographic studies of Iran, where whole villages are sometimes made up of kinsmen, corroborate the tremendous continuity of this aspect of the agnatic group in Iranian society.

The specific features of the agnatic group in Iran had important socio-cultural and political ramifications. Insofar as the religious panorama of Iran was concerned, for example, and in light of the diversity of the religious landscape in the region,[123] community of worship would have probably meant that religious diversity in Iran had a local dimension to it. As we shall see, semi-regional or

[116]MacKenzie, D.N., *A Concise Pahlavi Dictionary*, Oxford University Press, 1971 (MacKenzie 1971).

[117]Perikhanian 1983, p. 642.

[118]Perikhanian 1983, p. 643.

[119]"In a large family, the undivided brothers had only theoretical shares ... and were from the legal standpoint partners." Perikhanian 1983, p. 642

[120]For a discussion of the notion of *dynasticism*, see §2.1.2 below.

[121]Perikhanian 1983, p. 643.

[122]Perikhanian 1983, p. 644.

[123]See Chapter 5, especially §5.4.

regional communities had access not only to local religious traditions and lore, but also to their local forms of worship.[124]

As Perikhanian observes, it was membership in an agnatic group that determined not only one's legal capacity as a citizen, which in the Pahlavi legal terminology was rendered by the term *āzāt*,[125] but also one's membership in one of the *estates* of the nobility. Among these latter were the agnatic or dynastic families, who held the most prestigious places in the hierarchical Sasanian societal structure. Their local power bases set aside, we know that to the dynastic families, by virtue of their birth, also accrued privileges in the empire's administration. With proper agnatic ties, in other words, came political power. Membership in a noble agnatic group, therefore, gave "one access to appointment to any state or court office of importance." In the administrative public law documents, the word *āzāt* is, in fact, "used in the sense of member of an agnatic group of nobility, representative of the noble estate, noblemen."[126] Perhaps even more important for our purposes is Perikhanian's observation that certain "offices even became, with the passing of time, hereditary in a particular group, and that branch of the clan which had acquired preferential right to hold a given office could take the title of this office as the basis of its gentilitial name." The classic articulation of this, depicting the Parthian agnatic families, is found in Simocatta's narrative which, while formulaic and articulating an idealized rendition of Sasanian sociopolitical structure, nevertheless, encapsulates the realities of the Sasanian–Parthian confederacy. Simocatta here quotes a "certain Babylonian, a sacred official who had gained very great experience in the composition of royal epistles," as maintaining the following: "For seven peoples among the Medes, allocated by ancient law, perform the sagacious and most honoured of their actions; and he [i.e., the sacred official] stated that the procedures could not be otherwise; and they say that the people entitled Arsacid hold the kingship and these place the diadem on the king, another is in charge of the military disposition, another is invested with the cares of state, another resolves the differences of those who have some dispute and need an arbitrator, the fifth commands the cavalry, the next levies taxes on subjects and is overseer of the royal treasuries, the seventh is appointed custodian of arms and military uniforms." This Simocatta claims, had been established since the time of "Darius [III (380–330 BCE)] the son of Hydaspes."[127]

[124]The growth of regional traditions which, according to Boyce, sought to co-opt the homeland of Zoroaster into their own cultural milieu was only one of the consequences of this; see page 321ff.

[125]Zakeri, Mohsen, *Sasanid Soldiers in Early Muslim Society: the Origins of ʿAyyārān and Futuwwa*, Wiesbaden, 1995 (Zakeri 1995), *passim*.

[126]Perikhanian 1983, p. 645. It is to be noted incidentally that this terminology is also replete in the *Shāhnāma*, especially when referring to the court nobility.

[127]Simocatta, *The History of Theophylact Simocatta*, Oxford, 1986, English translation with introduction and notes by Michael and Mary Whitby (Simocatta 1986), p. 101. As we shall see, the fact that Simocatta diverges into this exposition when discussing the genealogy of Bahrām-i Chūbīn is particularly significant in the context of our study (see §6.1).

The Byzantine historian Theophylact Simocatta wrote in the early seventh century, during the reign of Heraclius (610–641).[128] His *History*, which covers the reign of the Emperor Maurice (582–602), is therefore not an eyewitness account. According to Simocatta's editors, when giving the above passage, the "rare mention by Theophylact of an oral source may refer to a Persian ambassador to Constantinople during Heraclius' reign."[129] If this is the case, then the germ of the tradition that he gives concerning the Parthian dynastic power in late Sasanian history must nevertheless be very valid. It is the dynamic of this Sasanian–Parthian relationship that we shall seek to disentangle as we proceed.

[128]For a discussion of the life of Simocatta and the sources on which he based his history, see Simocatta 1986, pp. xiii–xxviii.

[129]Simocatta 1986, p. 101, n. 87.

Part I

Political History

CHAPTER 2

Sasanian polity revisited: the Sasanian–Parthian confederacy

Gradually and in the course of their long history, the Sasanians learned to be incredibly able propagandists. They attempted to obliterate the history of their defeated foes, the Arsacids (247 BCE–224 CE), through, among other exertions, a recalculation of the Parthian rule to half of its actual duration.[130] They endeavored to connect their rather humble origins to remote antiquity.[131] They envisioned and tried to implement the clerical-monarchical cooperation as the pillar of their polity, and to fuse the national and religious traditions in the service of a political agenda.[132] And they attempted to subsume—and at

[130]Based on astrological calculations in vogue, and in order to make their rise coincide with the dawn of a new millennium, the Sasanians recalculated Arsacid rule from 474 to 266 (or 260) years. For a detailed investigation of this see, Shahbazi 1990.

[131]Broadly speaking, the Iranian national tradition divides the history of the Iranians into four periods: (1) the Pīshdādīs, "the early kings who ruled over the world and contributed to the progress of civilization by their teachings and institution;" (2) the Kayānids (Kayānīyān), "who were the kings of Iran proper and who were in continual conflict with their neighbors, the Tūrānians" (see also page 385ff); (3) the Ashkānīs (Arsacids), "who headed a feudal system and allegedly presided over the dark ages of Iranian history" (see also §1.1); and (4) the Sāsānīs (Sasanians). Yarshater 1983b, p. 366. As we shall see on page 385ff, the Sasanians eventually connected their ancestry to the Kayānids. For an extensive assessment of Iranian national history also see Nöldeke, Theodore, *The Iranian National Epic*, Philadelphia, 1979, translated by L. Bogdanov (Nöldeke 1979); Yarshater 1983b, especially pp. 386–87; Gnoli, Gherarldo, *The Idea of Iran*, Rome, 1989 (Gnoli 1989), *passim*, especially pp. 122–123; Yarshater, Ehsan, 'Were the Sasanians Heirs to the Achaemenids?', in *La Persia Nel Medioevo*, pp. 517–531, Rome, 1971 (Yarshater 1971); and Daryaee, Touraj, 'National History or Kayanid History?: The Nature of Sasanid Zoroastrian Historiography', *Iranian Studies* 28, (1995), pp. 129–141 (Daryaee 1995).

[132]The very "concept of Ērānshahr ... was an integral part of the politico-religious propaganda of the early Sasanians ... which linked the destiny of the Iranian nation to that of the Mazdean religion of the *mobeds*." Gnoli has, systematically and convincingly, traced the origins of the fusion of the national tradition with the religious tradition to the pre-Avestan period. The coalescence of the national and religious traditions of Iran, therefore, has an ancient history that harks back to remote antiquity, and was not an innovation of the Sasanians. As we shall see below, however, and as Gnoli himself argues, the systematic formulation of a worldview which depicted the state and the church as the two pillars of government, and the use of this for political propaganda and as an ideology, was a legacy of the Sasanians (see §5.2.1). The development of Mazdaism into a state church through "successive redaction of the sacred texts by means of selection and censorship," the establishment of a doctrinal and liturgic orthodoxy, the development of an official chronology, and the definite

times aspired to subordinate—a multifarious Iranian religious landscape under the aegis of an orthodox Zoroastrian system of belief and a controlled and hierarchical religious structure. In retrospect, the propagandistic efforts of the Sasanians were incredibly successful. Their crowning achievement in this direction was surely their patronage and promulgation of an official historiography, a feat hitherto unprecedented in the annals of pre-Islamic Iran, although perhaps in tune with historical processes current in the Mediterranean world by the third century. Setting aside for the moment other instruments pertaining to material culture for effecting political propaganda, such as inscriptions and coinage, the Sasanians were unique in that the first official history of Iran was written under their auspices. The importance of the above observation cannot be taken lightly. Most of the other efforts of the dynasty in promulgating and sustaining a political ideology, enumerated above, were subsumed under, written into, and articulated through this same official history. And so the Sasanians were successful in leaving to posterity an image of their fascinating story in the corpus that has come to be known as the *X*ʷ*adāy-Nāmag*, or the Book of Kings.[133]

But it is surely not incidental that the most concerted efforts of the dynasty in the writing and rewriting of its history took place at junctures when it experienced acute crises in its history, as in the revolt of Bahrām-i Chūbīn (590–591), when the last effective Sasanian king, Khusrow II Parvīz (591–628), inherited a fragmented realm as his legacy.[134] Already by the time of Bahrām V Gūr (420–438), we have evidence of the *Book of Kings*, and by the time of Khusrow I (531–579), "the history of ancient Iran was definitely compiled." It was under Khusrow II, however, when "much new material was added to the *X*ʷ*adāy-Nāmag*, and this then became the source of all early Islamic histories on ancient Iran." According to Jāḥiz, when Khusrow II asked his paladin whether he knew of anyone more heroic than himself, the latter replied with a narrative of Bahrām-i Chūbīn. Furious, the king made sure that the tale did not appear in the *Book of Kings*. In the context of the late Shahbazi's disagreement with Nöldeke concerning the date of the compilation of this national history,[135] we should note that the historical information about the Sasanians begins to take flesh by the mid-fifth century, during the reigns of Yazdgird II (438–457) and Pīrūz (459–484). As we shall see,[136] these were also junctures in which the

"demonization of the figure of Alexander … [as part] of the political and religious propaganda of the new dynasty," all of these processes are thought to have begun in the third century. Gnoli 1989, pp. 152, 140, 151. For the history of the demonization of the figure of Alexander in Iran, one of the first articulations of which can be found in Book IV of *The Sibylline Oracles*, where the author prophesies the death of Alexander "at the hands of coming Oriental successors of the Achaemenids on account of his injustice and cruelty," see Eddy, Samuel K., *The King is Dead: Studies in the Near Eastern Resistance to Hellenism 334–31 B.C.*, University of Nebraska Press, 1961 (Eddy 1961). Eddy dates *The Sibylline Oracles* to 325 BCE, Eddy 1961, pp. 10–14.

133 Shahbazi 1990. For a further discussion of the *X*ʷ*adāy-Nāmag*, see page 171ff.

134 For Bahrām-i Chūbīn's revolt, see §2.6.3 below.

135 Shahbazi 1990, pp. 213–215 and p. 226, n. 52; Nöldeke 1979, p. 9.

136 See §2.2.4, §2.3, and page 380 below.

Sasanians experienced acute crises. This then remains an important caveat to the Sasanian efforts at writing their history: they seem to have embarked upon it in an hour of need and at a time when their desire to create a hegemonic polity was forcefully questioned by forces that, as we shall see shortly, had agreed upon a partnership with the Sasanian, namely the Parthian dynastic[137] families. The belated effort of the Sasanians at representing their realm and their history proved successful. It remains one of our most basic founts for reconstructing the Sasanian history of Iran with any degree of certainty. It portrays the Sasanians from a legitimist, monarchical perspective. It sanctifies, naturally, the Sasanians' view of themselves as a centralized and benevolent hegemonic polity. And, in view of what seems to have been the wholesale destruction of this corpus in its original Pahlavi renditions, and through the process of translation, this history was adopted *in toto* by classical Islamic history, a historiography through which, besides the Persian *Shāhnāma*-genre, including the *magnum opus* of Ferdowsī,[138] we have reconstructed the dynasty's history. Ironically, the legitimistic bent of Sasanian historiography suited the purposes of a nascent Islamic caliphate admirably. Islamic historiography not only faithfully retained the legitimist monarchical tradition of Sasanian history in its transmission of this history, but highlighted this very dimension of it.[139] As Gutas has brilliantly argued, the ʿAbbāsids considered their polity direct heir to that of the Sasanians. The Sasanian imperial ideology, with its emphasis on a centralized, semi-theocratic polity, furnished the nascent ʿAbbāsid regime with a normative model based on which it would depict the nature of its own polity.[140]

One of the crucial dimensions of the Sasanian patronage of the *X^w adāy-Nāmag* tradition, in turn, was that it had come to subsume an east-Iranian tradition.[141] Whether this process had already been effected during the Arsacid

[137]For the term dynasticism, see §2.1.2.

[138]Safa, D., *Ḥamāsih Sarāyī dar Irān*, Tehran, 1945 (Safa 1945), p. 93; Qazvini, Muhammad, '*Muqaddamih-i Qadīm-i Shāhnāma*', in Abbas Iqbal and Ustad Purdavud (eds.), *Bīst Maqalih-i Qazvīnī*, 1984 (Qazvini 1984), p. 16; Yarshater 1983b, pp. 359–363.

[139]This historiography was produced during the ʿAbbāsid period and the nature of the ʿAbbāsid political ideology was very different from that of the Umayyads. The ʿAbbāsids became the direct heirs to the Sasanian political ideology with its emphasis on the twin pillar aspect of government. Gutas, Dimitri, *Greek Thought, Arabic Culture: The Graeco-Arabic Translation Movement in Baghdad and Early Abbasid Society (2nd–4th/8th–10th Centuries)*, London, 1998 (Gutas 1998). But see also Crone, Patricia, *God's Caliph: Religious Authority in the First Centuries of Islam*, Cambridge University Press, 1986 (Crone 1986), and Goldziher, 'Islam et Parsism', in *Religion of the Iranian Peoples*, Bombay, 1912, translated by Nariman (Goldziher 1912), quoted in Sadighi, Ghulam Husayn, *Les mouvements réligieux Iraniens au IIe et au IIIe siècle de l'hégire*, Paris, 1938 (Sadighi 1938), p. 118.

[140]In the *Annals* of Ṭabarī, the legitimistic and centrist portrayal of the Sasanian kings and their polity can be fruitfully compared with the representation of the ʿAbbāsids and their conception of the caliphate. The sort of detailed narratives, moreover, that we get in the Islamic historical tradition on the fall of Ctesiphon, the emphasis of this tradition on the battle of Qādisiya and the battle of Nihāvand, and the rendition of Khusrow I Nowshīrvān as the typologically ideal monarch, all bespeak the preoccupation of the Islamic historiographical tradition with the Sasanian imperial tradition, co-opting an imperial tradition, which, providentially, had ceased to exist.

[141]Eddy 1961, pp. 3–80, here p. 80.

period, or whether it was under the patronage of the Sasanians that it took shape,[142] it is certain that the Sasanians became heir to the traditions of Persīs, the region from which they themselves had risen and which had been the cradle of the Achaemenids. Ever since the rise of the Arsacids,[143] however, the Persīs (Pārsīg), as we shall see below,[144] had not only clearly distinguished themselves from the Parthians (Pahlav), but had adopted a very hostile attitude to the newly rising power of Parthava in the east. This trend was continued in the political ideology of the Sasanians. During the Sasanian period, the geographical term Pahlav (Parthia, Parthava) referred to an extensive territory that was bounded in the east by Gurgān, in the north by the Caspian Sea, and in the southwest by the region between Khuzistān and Media.[145] Masᶜūdī, quoting the Nabateans, claims that the Pārsīg were in "Fārs … [whereas] Māhāt[146] and other regions were Pahlav territories."[147]

So while the patronage of the national Iranian historiography during the Sasanian period had the unprecedented effect of concocting a linear history with a remarkable degree of continuity—a history that ran from the first human-king, Kayūmarth, to the last Sasanian king, Yazdgird III (632–651), through the paradigmatic model of kingship—the tensions inherent in this juxtaposition of the traditions of Persīs with those of Parthava continued to inform the national Iranian tradition that was promulgated by the Sasanians. This conflictual relationship can best be seen in the uneasy correspondence that exists between the kingly and heroic traditions contained within the national Iranian tradition.[148] The present study, however, is not a literary investigation of the Iranian national tradition. Nor shall we attempt to give a theoretical assessment of this relationship. For it has long been recognized that a substantial portion of the Iranian national tradition, above all the heroic elements of this tradition, were

[142]For the debate over whether this eastern Iranian tradition was spread to the west by the Parthians, as argued by Yarshater, or whether it remained confined to the east and was incorporated into the *Xʷadāy-Nāmag* tradition through the auspices of the Sasanians, see Yarshater 1983b, pp. 388–391; Christensen, Arthur, *The Kayanians*, Bombay, 1993a, translated by F. N. Tumboowalla (Christensen 1993a), pp. 39–41.

[143]See §1.1.

[144]See §5.3.3.

[145]Gyselen, Rika, *La géographie administrative de l'empire Sassanide: Les témoignages sigillographiques*, vol. I of *Res Orientales*, Paris, 1989 (Gyselen 1989), p. 73. Also see Bivar 1983, pp. 24–27.

[146]Māhāt (Māhān, Māhayn) were the names given by the Arabs to the two districts of Nihāvand and Dīnawar in Media. Although some Arab sources claim that *Māh* is the Middle Persian term for city, it more likely stands for Media (Mād). According to the Islamic tradition, Nihāvand was conquered by the forces of Baṣrah and Dīnawar by those of Kūfa. Thereafter the regions came to be called Māh al-Baṣrah and Māh al-Kūfa, respectively.

[147]Masᶜūdī, ᶜAlī b. Ḥusayn, *al-Tanbīh wa 'l-Ashrāf*, Beirut, 1965, edited by V.R. Baron Rosen (Masᶜūdī 1965), p. 37:

ان الفرس كانت بفارس و الماهات و غيرها من بلاد الفهلويّون.

[148]One of the best efforts at disentangling this relationship is that of Davis, Dick, *Epic and Sedition: The Case of Ferdowsi's Shāhnāmeh*, University of Arkansas Press, 1992 (Davis 1992).

in fact sustained, elaborated, and promoted under the patronage of the Parthian families, not only during the Parthian period but, more importantly, during the Sasanian period.[149] Try as they may, therefore, to obliterate the annals of the Arsacids from the pages of their history, the Sasanians were never successful in obliterating the traditions which they inherited from the Parthians, neither in their historical writing nor in the historical reality of their four centuries long rule in Iranian history. A vivid, constant reminder of the Parthian heritage infused, perforce, the very polity that the Sasanians had constructed. For as we shall argue in this chapter, in spite of the sporadic attempts of the Sasanians to leash the centrifugal forces of the Parthian dynastic families who continued to hold tremendous power in their domains, they were never successful in ridding themselves of their influence. In fact, had it not been for the cooperation, what in this study we have termed the *Sasanian–Parthian confederacy*, that the Sasanians established with the Parthian dynastic families of their domain, they could never have sustained their rule for as long as they did.

2.1 Sasanians / Arsacids

The Sasanian tradition of rule owed a great deal to the Parthians. It is generally recognized that through a substantial part of their history the Arsacids ruled through a decentralized system of government the backbone of which was the feudal[150] nobility. Heir to the heritage of the Achaemenids and the Seleucids, the administrative and social structure of the Arsacid empire was a heterogeneous medley: there was first the predominantly Semitic, and substantially urbanized Mesopotamia; independent states in Mesopotamia and other Iranian frontiers; and finally *the social and political conditions existing in the heartland of Parthia*, the east and northeast of Iran.[151] In the middle of the first century CE, even the Romans recognized the decentralized nature of the Arsacid administration, Pliny counting as eighteen the number of kingdoms that comprised the Parthian polity.[152]

While a centrist perspective continues to inform our view of the Sasanian polity, a very cursory examination of the Sasanian social and economic infrastructure suggests that the above picture was not substantially changed under the Sasanians. The centrist depiction of Sasanian polity highlights the Sasanian efforts in assuming direct control of the provinces through the creation of

[149]Christensen 1993a, pp. 127–129; Nöldeke 1979, pp. 12–14.

[150]The term feudal and its attendant economic and political structures in the Iranian context have been the subject of much debate. It is used in this study for lack of a better term. The present author follows the analysis of the term by Toumanoff discussed in §2.1.2, although she disagrees with his conclusions regarding Sasanian Iran; see page 55. Also see Frye, Richard N., 'Feudalism in Iran', *Jerulasem Studies in Arabic Islam* 9, (1987), pp. 13–18 (Frye 1987); Widengren, Geo, *Der Feudalismus im alten Iran*, Cologne, 1969 (Widengren 1969).

[151]Lukonin 1983, p. 714.

[152]Lukonin 1983, p. 728. For a more detailed discussion, see page 24ff.

kingly cities beginning in the third century CE[153] One theory explains the background to this process:[154] Ancient cities in the east had for a long time operated on the basis of slavery and were run by temple priests and city councils that had substantial land under their control. During the Hellenistic period these cities were granted self-rule as a *polis*. The Hellenistic kingdoms relied on these semi-independent cities in order to run their realms. These kinds of cities were the instrument for implementing the policies of Hellenistic dynasties and were required to give part of the income from their vast lands to the central treasury. Besides these, the Hellenistic kingdoms also created new cities, *poleis*, in the east.

In the third century, as a result of broader economic transformations, the slave basis of the economy of these cities was disrupted and the influence of kings increased. The Sasanians, who took over Mesopotamia, had as one of their aims the incorporation of this region into their *dastgirds* as kingly cities.[155] When a city was turned into a kingly city, its affairs were put under the king's representative (*shahrab*, governor),[156] the city itself thus becoming a pillar of kingly authority.[157] So, as Lukonin notes, while Ardashīr I (224–241) was only able to create two such cities, Veh Ardashīr and Ardashīr Khurrah, with two *shahrabs* included in the list of his court nobility, by Shāpūr I's (241–272) rule there were fifteen such *shahrabs* mentioned in the inscriptions of the *Ka'ba-i Zartusht*.[158]

What needs to be highlighted when considering the centralizing efforts of the early Sasanian kings, however, is that by far the most systematic focus of their efforts in this direction was in the west and southwestern parts of their domains, especially in the core regions of Sasanian power in Fārs and Mesopotamia. Compared to the rigor of their urban construction activity in the west during their long reign, very few cities were constructed by the Sasanians in the non-western parts of their domains. Pigulevskaja's study[159] confirms that the Sasanians' efforts at urbanization and urban construction were

[153] Lukonin, V.G., *Tamaddun-i Īrān-i Sāsānī: Īrān dar Sadih-hā-i Sivvum tā Panjum-i Milādī*, Tehran, 1986, translation of Lukonin 1969 by Inayat Allah Riza (Lukonin 1986), p. 101.

[154] Pigulevskaja, Nina, *Les villes de l'état Iranien aux époques Parthe et Sassanide*, Paris, 1963 (Pigulevskaja 1963), *passim*.

[155] *Dastgird*, from Avestan *dasta-kṛta*, "made by hand, handiwork, a term originally designating a royal or seigneurial estate." Gignoux, Philippe, 'Dastgerd', in Ehsan Yarshater (ed.), *Encyclopaedia Iranica*, New York, 2007b (Gignoux 2007b).

[156] See glossary.

[157] Lukonin 1986, p. 101–102.

[158] The *Ka'ba-i Zartusht* is an Achaemenid structure at Naqsh-i Rustam in Fārs, on which a series of trilingual inscriptions were later carved by the Sasanian king Shāpūr I; usually cited as *ŠKZ*. Gignoux, Philippe, 'Middle Persian Inscriptions', in Ehsan Yarshater (ed.), *Cambridge History of Iran: The Seleucid, Parthian, and Sasanian Periods*, vol. 3(2), pp. 1205–1216, Cambridge University Press, 1983 (Gignoux 1983), pp. 1207–1208; Huyse, Philip, 'Die dreisprachige Inschrift Shâbuhrs I an der Ka'ba-i Zardusht', in *Pahlavi Inscriptions*, vol. 3 of *Corpus Inscriptionum Iranicarum*, 1999a (Huyse 1999a); Lukonin 1986, pp. 102–103.

[159] Pigulevskaja 1963.

concentrated in Fārs and Mesopotamia, the latter of which had a long history of urbanization harking back to the ancient period. While Pigulevskaja conclusions were reached based on evidence provided for the western regions of Iran, therefore, they do in fact reflect the reality of urban construction, and by extension Sasanian efforts at centralization, throughout their realm. The most forceful evidence for Sasanian lack of interest in urban construction, or perhaps their economic and sociopolitical inability to undertake such construction, in non-western parts of their domain, can be found in the Middle Persian text *Shahrestānīha-ī Ērānshahr* (or, *Provincial Capitals of Ērānshahr*).[160] Composed under the patronage of the Sasanians themselves, the text describes the foundation histories of various cities in Iran.

While the final redaction of the *Shahrestānīha-ī Ērānshahr* dates back to the ʿAbbāsid period (late eighth century), it was probably originally composed in the sixth century, sometime during the reigns of Qubād (488–531),[161] Khusrow I (531–579), or Khusrow II (590–628),[162] a period when the Sasanians had finally exhausted most of their construction activities. Even a cursory examination of the list of cities in the *Shahrestānīha-ī Ērānshahr* and the foundation myths and histories attributed to them reveals a striking fact: of the twenty-three cities listed in the territories comprising the quarters (*kūsts*)[163] of the east (*kūst-i khwarāsān*), north (*kūst-i ādurbādagān*[164]), and south (*kūst-i nēmrōz*)—that is the regions of Khurāsān, Sīstān, Azarbāyjān, and Ṭabaristān—only five are credited to the Sasanians. Of the rest, one is attributed to the mythic period of Iranian history, ten others to the semi-historical and legendary Kayānid history,[165] two to Alexander, and three to the Parthian period.[166] Of the remaining cities in these three quarters, the construction of one dates partly to the Parthian and partly to the Sasanian period,[167] that of another to mythic

[160]Shahrestan 2002, *Šahrestānīha-ī Ērānšahr: A Middle Persian Text on Late Antique Geography, Epic and History*, Costa Mesa, 2002, translated by Touraj Daryaee (Shahrestan 2002); Marquart, J., *A Catalogue of the Provincial Capitals of Ērānshahr*, Rome, 1931, edited by G. Messina (Marquart 1931).

[161]For Qubād's reign, which was interrupted for about two years around 497, see §2.4.3 below.

[162]Shahrestan 2002, p. 7. The reigns of the two Khusrows will be discussed extensively below.

[163]A *kūst* was an administrative and military division of the Sasanian realm introduced under Khusrow I. For a comparative enumeration of these quarters, as they appear in various sources, see Brunner 1983, pp. 750–771, especially p. 750. For the meaning of the term *kūst*, see Marquart 1931, p. 25, No. 2, and Gyselen 2001a, pp. 13–14 and the references cited therein.

[164]Instead "of the word *abākhtar*, north, the geographical name Adurbāygān was also used for the region in general, to avoid naming north, the region in which, according to the Zoroastrian belief, the gate of hell is situated." Tafazzoli, Ahmad, *Sasanian Society*, Winona Lake, 2000 (Tafazzoli 2000), pp. 8–9.

[165]As Yarshater observes, whereas "earlier kings are often of a mythical nature ... the Kayanian kings from Kai Kavād to Kai Khusrau form a coherent group which exhibits dynastic features." Yarshater 1983b, p. 436.

[166]These include the cities of Khwārazm, Marv al-Rūd, Pūshang, Nīshāpūr, and Kirmān. Shahrestan 2002, pp. 18, 20. For further notes on these see, ibid., pp. 37 and 49.

[167]Qūmis. Shahrestan 2002, pp. 18, 39–40.

times, though the Sasanians are credited with finishing it,[168] in yet another site the Sasanians are said to have constructed only a fortress,[169] and a last city is thought to have been built by Mazdak![170] The construction of twenty-one other cities in Padhashkhwārgar, which, in the *Letter of Tansar*,[171] includes the territories of Ṭabaristān, Barshawādgān, Gīlān, Deylamān, Rūyān, and Damāvand (Dumbāvand), are traced to the mythic period.[172]

By contrast, of the twenty-four cities named in the quarter of the west (*kūst-i khwarbarān*), the construction of sixteen is credited to the Sasanians.[173] Naturally, this brief analysis is not meant to be an exhaustive history of urban construction activity of the Sasanians, nor of the history of urbanization in Iran. Other studies, including that of Pigulevskaya, have investigated aspects of the process of urbanization during the Sasanian period in general, and have implicitly highlighted the concentration of this development in the western parts of the Sasanian kingdom.[174] Neither have we attempted to investigate the administrative infrastructure of the Sasanian domains, through which they exerted their putative central control.[175] Significantly, as Gyselen has observed, our knowledge about the administrative infrastructure of the Sasanians is seriously hampered by the fact that the primary sources[176] at our disposal for reconstructing this history suffer from a serious gap of about three centuries.[177] As has been observed in this connection, a "more carefully nuanced picture of the rate and effectiveness with which royal control was extended is obviously desirable, but large gaps in the evidence make it difficult to trace developments with precision." It has been appropriately remarked, therefore, that as "most information for Sasanian administrative history pertains to the reign of Khusro I in the sixth century, when a centralised bureaucracy of some complexity functioned in the

[168]Zarang. Shahrestan 2002, pp. 19, 49.

[169]In Media. Shahrestan 2002, pp. 19, 43.

[170]Āmul. Shahrestan 2002, pp. 21, 57.

[171]For the *Letter of Tansar*, see §2.5.2 below.

[172]Following the orders of Armāyīl—one of the two righteous men who decided to pose as cooks in order to save some of the children whose brains were being fed daily to the evil Ḍaḥḥāk (see footnote 2115)—these were built by seven families of mountaineers, some of whom are postulated to be historical. Shahrestan 2002, pp. 19, 44–45.

[173]This enumeration does not include cities in Arabia, Syria, Africa, and Yemen, which also figure in the *Shahrestānīha-ī Ērānshahr*. For the imperial outlook that the inclusion of these regions in the conception of Ērānshahr reflects, and the deduction that the incorporation of these territories is a reflection of the territorial expansions during the combined reigns of Qubād to Khusrow II, see Shahrestan 2002, pp. 1–7; also see Daryaee, Touraj, 'The Changing 'Image of the World': Geography and Imperial Propaganda in Ancient Persia', *Electrum: Studies in Ancient History* 6, (2002), pp. 99–109 (Daryaee 2002).

[174]Marquart 1931, p. 121, Shahbazi, Shapur, 'Capital Cities', in Ehsan Yarshater (ed.), *Encyclopaedia Iranica*, pp. 768–770, New York, 1991c (Shahbazi 1991c), p. 768. See also Christensen 1993b, and Pigulevskaja 1963.

[175]For this the most admirable study remains that of Christensen 1944, and Gyselen 1989.

[176]For a categorization of sources available for Sasanian history as primary, secondary, and tertiary, see our discussion on page 10.

[177]Gyselen 1989.

capital Ctesiphon, ... *it is clearly illegitimate to assume that such a level of organisation was characteristic of earlier centuries of Sasanian rule.*"[178]

Our superficial enumeration of Sasanian urban construction activity, therefore, is meant to bring to the fore one important fact: for all their preoccupation with the eastern parts of their domains, the Sasanians were, due to the balance of power in the region and logistic and sociopolitical considerations, a western-oriented empire, within which context we must gauge the equation of urbanization with centralization and the conclusions that we derive from this. This observation, likewise, is no epiphany. It is one, however, that seems to be constantly ignored in the investigation of Sasanian sociopolitical history. In their western gaze, and even in their initial administrative structures, the Sasanians were no different from the Parthians before them.[179] The difference was the degree of control that they sought to exert on the heterogeneous population of their western and southwestern regions. Our ensuing discussion on the continued participation of the Parthian dynasts in Sasanian polity, therefore, needs to be put in the context of the predominantly agrarian economy of the non-western parts of the Sasanian domains, and the social relations that proceeded from this.[180]

Altheim's assessment of the economic landscape of the Sasanian state becomes pertinent here, although the conclusions that he reaches are not corroborated by the evidence. According to Altheim, "the Sasanian economic landscape divide[d] itself into two parts: on the one side [stood] the domain directly under royal rule, and on the other the domain of the landowning nobility in which central power operated only indirectly. It was in the interest of powerful, far-reaching royal control to increase the number of royal cities, and their attendant districts ... [This] had the effect of converting indirectly ruled into directly ruled districts, and only partly taxed districts into fully-covered ones. *The history of the royal founding of cities thus also concerns the struggle between royal power and that of nobility.*"[181] If this was indeed the case, and if, as we have seen, the Sasanians could boast of the construction of very few cities in the eastern, northeastern, northern, and even northwestern parts of their domains,

---

[178] Lee, A.D., *Information and Frontiers: Roman Foreign Relations in Late Antiquity*, Cambridge University Press, 1993 (Lee 1993), p. 16. Emphasis mine.

[179] As Lee observes, the overall picture of the third century "is one of initial continuity with the predominantly feudal arrangements of the Parthians." Lee 1993, p. 17. See also Lukonin 1983, p. 730.

[180] It is evidently understood that even while heavily urbanized, the western regions of the Sasanian domains were likewise dominated by a predominantly agricultural infrastructure, as their extensive construction of irrigation networks in Mesopotamia attests; see footnote 181.

[181] Altheim, Franz and Stiehl, Ruth, *Ein asiatischer Staat: Feudalismus unter den Sasaniden und ihren Nachbarn*, Wiesbaden, 1954 (Altheim and Stiehl 1954), as quoted in Lee 1993, p. 17. Emphasis added. Lee also notes "that the most powerful testimony to the actual growth of centralizing control [during the Sasanian period] is the vast network of systematically laid-out irrigation canals and accompanying engineering projects which *archeologists have found in southern Iran and Iraq.*" Ibid., p. 16. Emphasis mine. Needless to say these indicate only direct Sasanian control over the aforementioned regions.

it follows that for a variety of reasons, not yet fully understood, "the struggle between royal power and ... [the] nobility," as evidenced through the construction of royal cities, did not play itself out in extensive territories of the Sasanian realm. One of the primary reasons for this situation, it will be argued in this study, was the predominant power of the Parthian dynastic families in the quarters of the east and the north, *kūst-i khwarāsān* and *kūst-i ādurbādagān*, a power that continued to exert itself over these territories, in spite of the sporadic efforts of the Sasanians toward centralization.

One of the paramount legacies of the Arsacid dynasty to the Sasanian polity was the forceful continuity of the power of the Parthian dynastic families in these domains. As we shall be arguing in this study, Parthian dynasts, who were the co-partners in rule for the Arsacid dynasty,[182] came to form a confederacy with the Sasanians as well. The names of some of these families appear in the origins myth of the Armenian historian Moses Khorenats'i discussed above: the Kārins, the Sūrens, and the Ispahbudhān.[183] Two others, the Mihrān and the Kanārangīyān, must be added to these. Khorenats'i also narrates, with much passion, a fascinating tale that details the part played by the Parthian dynastic families in the rise of the upstart Sasanian Ardashīr I to power: "After Artashir, son of Sasan, had killed Artavan [the last Arsacid king] and gained the throne, two branches of the Pahlav family called Aspahapet [i.e., Ispahbudhān] and Surēn Pahlav were jealous at the rule of the branch of their own kin, that is Artashēs, [—who ruled over Parthava—] and willingly accepted the rule of Artashir, son of Sasan. But the house of Karēn Pahlav, remaining friendly toward their brother and kin, opposed in war Artashir, son of Sasan."[184] Khorenats'i then proceeds to narrate the actions taken by the Arsacid Armenian king Khusrov on behalf of the Arsacid dynasty of Iran in the wake of the turmoil that ensued after the murder of Ardavān. Khusrov's call to arms and his promise that upon victory he would bestow the crown of Iran on one of the Iranian Parthian families, went unheeded by the Sūren and the Ispahbudhān families. The news also reached Khusrov that in the process of their struggle against Ardashīr I, the Kārins had been decimated, save for one child, Perozamat, who became "the ancestor of our great family of Kamsarakan."[185] Khorenats'i's account surely combines fact with fiction. It does, however, highlight one important fact: as the Sasanian primary sources for the third century testify,[186] the end of the Arsacid dynasty did not mean the end of the Parthian dynastic families in Iran. As late as Ardashīr II's (379–383) reign, the Sasanians still recalled the services rendered to them by Parthian dynastic families in the third century. According

[182]See page 24ff.

[183]Khorenats'i 1978, p. 166. See page 26.

[184]Khorenats'i 1978, p. 218. Also see Lukonin 1986, p. 58.

[185]Khorenats'i 1978, p. 218–219. As we shall see, traditions that underline the total decimation of a particular Parthian dynastic family are replete in our sources and are nothing but *topoi* meant to highlight the defeat of these families at various junctures. For again and again these families appear on the scene after having been allegedly executed to the last man.

[186]For further discussion of these third century primary sources, see page 48 below.

to Khorenats'i, the Sasanian king recalled for Vṙamshapuh, the Arsacid king of Armenia (392–414),[187] that he "remembered the services of his [i.e., Bishop Sahak, who was of Parthian ancestry] ancestors, the Princes of the line of Surēn Pahlav, who willingly accepted the sovereignty of my ancestor and homonym Artashir."[188] As we shall see, there is reason to suspect that the Sūren continued their loyal service to the Sasanians to the very end of the dynasty.

Armenian Arsacids

Even if we were to start with the fallacy that the ascendancy of the Sasanians ushered in a new age that obliterated the Parthian legacy and their traditions of rule, as the canonical Sasanian history would have us believe, we cannot afford to lose sight of a crucial dimension of Sasanian history, namely, its intimate and involved relationship with its northwestern neighbor Armenia, where an Arsacid dynasty continued to rule up until 428 CE. It has been poignantly argued, in fact, that the "political history of Iran during [both] the Parthian and Sasanian periods ... is scarcely intelligible without reference to Armenia and Georgia."[189] The connection of Iran to Armenia harks back to remote antiquity and the Urartan period. When in 66 CE, emperor Nero (54–68) officially crowned the Arsacid Prince Tiridates I (53–75) king of Armenia, however, a new chapter was opened in the Armenian–Iranian relationship. The defeat of the Arsacids in Iran in the early third century, therefore, did not mean the disappearance of the Parthians from the scene. Far from it. For, in fact, when "the Parthians were overthrown by the Sasanians in 226 CE, the old Armenian royal house became redoubtable foes of the new Great Kings of Iran."[190] As Garsoian argues this theme of "Arsacid blood vengeance is ubiquitous in early Armenian literature ... [and] is repeated from generation to generation ... in Armenian literature. It [even] appears in as late a work as that of Moses Chorenatsi."[191] Not until 428, when the Armenian Arsacid dynasty was abolished, was this situation changed.[192] As David Lang argues, the continued rule of the Arsacids in Armenia "helps to explain the singular bitterness of the relations

[187]Vṙamshapuh was the father of Artashēs, last king of Armenia. Ełishē 1982, p. 60, n. 5.

[188]Khorenats'i 1978, p. 317. Parpeci 1991, *History of Łazar P'arpec'i*, vol. 4 of *Columbia University Program in Armenian Studies*, Atlanta, 1991, edited by R.W. Thomson (Parpeci 1991), p. 53.

[189]Lang 1983, p. 517.

[190]Lang 1983, p. 518.

[191]Garsoian 1985e, pp. 2–3, n. 5. Moses Khorenats'i devotes a whole section at the end of his work to the "*lament over the removal of the Armenian throne from the Arsacid family and of the archbishopry from the family of Saint Gregory.*" Khorenats'i 1978, pp. 350–354.

[192]In 416, the Sasanian Shāpūr, son of Yazdgird I, had been appointed king of Armenia after the deaths of the Armenian Arsacid kings Vṙamshapuh and Khosrov III. When Shāpūr died in 420 in an attempt to gain the Sasanian throne after the death of his father (see §2.2.3 below), Artashēs, the son of Vṙamshapuh, assumed the Armenian throne in 423. As a result of the dynastic struggles in Armenia, the latter was deposed in 428 by Bahrām V Gūr (420–438) upon the request of the *naxarars* of the country. Thus ended the line of the Arsacids in Armenia. Thereafter, "the government of Armenia was conducted by *marzbāns*, who were sometimes picked from the Armenian nobility." Chaumont 1991, p. 429.

between Arsacid Armenia and Sasanian Iran, extending right up to and even after the abolition of the Armenian Arsacid dynasty in 428."[193] Armenian Arsacids continued to claim to be the champions of Iranian legitimacy.[194] Until the Armenian Arsacids made Christianity the state religion of Armenia in 301 under Tiridates III (283–330), moreover, and probably for a substantial period after that,[195] the Sasanians were forced to reckon with an Armenia that was not only Arsacid but also most probably predominantly Mithraist. This aspect of Armenian tradition and its connection to the religious panorama of the Sasanians also has important ramifications, which we will discuss below.[196] What is more, not only the royal house but also a good number of Armenian noble houses, as well as one of the most illustrious Christian dynastic lines of Armenia, that of the Armenian patron saint, St. Gregory the Illuminator, claimed descent from the Arsacids, in the latter case from the Sūrens, St. Gregory being remembered by the Armenian church "to this day by the surname Partev, the Parthian."[197]

Not only in Armenia but in Georgia as well, the Parthian legacy continued well into the Sasanian period. After the kingdom of Amazaspes of the Third Parnabazid dynasty in Iberia was replaced, sometime in the 180s CE, with that of Rev, the son of the sister of Amazaspes, there was for over a century "an Arsacid or Parthian dynasty in eastern Georgia, allied by blood to the Armenian Arsacids."[198] Upon the extinction of this Arsacid line in eastern Georgia in the fourth century, when the kingdom passed to king Mirian III, the latter established a dynasty called the Chosroids. These Chosroids "were [also] a branch of the Iranian [Parthian] Mihranids [i.e., Mihrāns]."[199] As late as the reign of Khusrow I (531–579), when the Armenians were hard-pressed by the Byzantines, and a group of them went to the Sasanian king in order to solicit his aid, they continued to recall their Arsacid ancestry. Procopius preserves a narrative that underscores this Arsacid consciousness among the Armenians: "Many of us, O Master, are Arsacidae, descendants of that Arsaces who was not unrelated to the Parthian kings when the Persian realm lay under the hand of the

[193] Lang 1983, p. 518.

[194] Lang 1983, p. 518.

[195] As Thomson remarks, "Koriun's biography of Mashtots' makes it clear that even in the early fifth century there were many in Armenia still unconverted." Ełishē 1982, p. 12. See also footnote 2232 below.

[196] See §5.4.4.

[197] Lang 1983, p. 518. Moses Khorenats'i emphasizes St. Gregory's descent from the line of the Parthian Sūren Pahlav. Khorenats'i 1978, pp. 166, 250.

[198] Lang 1983, p. 520.

[199] Beginning with Mirian III, the Chosroid dynasty also turned Christian. As Lang observes, the "political systems of Armenia and Georgia had much in common with the great monarchies of Iran. Considering that the Arsacids of Armenia were Parthian princes, and the Mihranids, Chosroids and Guaramids of Iberia all closely connected with one or other of the Seven Great Houses of Iran, this was only to be expected ... It is [also] necessary to stress the many close links between Iran, Armenian and Georgia in religion, architecture and the arts, which continued even after the latter two countries had officially adopted Christianity." Lang 1983, pp. 520, 527–528, 531, respectively.

Parthians, and who proved himself an illustrious king, inferior to none of his time. Now we have come to thee, and all of us have become slaves and fugitives, not, however, of our own will, but under most hard constraint ... of the Roman power."[200] The close connection of Iran to Armenia will become apparent in the pages that follow.[201] Suffice it to say here that the *de facto* termination of Arsacid rule in Iran—even while ignoring the history of the Sasanian–Parthian confederacy with which we shall be dealing in the pages that follow—did not mean the destruction of the Parthian legacy among the Sasanians. For up to the first quarter of the fifth century, at the very least, the Sasanians were forced to reckon with an Armenia that was not only Arsacid but also conscious of the defeat of their brethren, the Iranian Arsacids, by the Sasanians.[202] The Sasanians, for their part, could not have afforded to ignore this persistent legacy.

The continued relevance of the Parthian legacy to Sasanian history, and in fact their centrality in the affairs of the Sasanian dynasty, at its inception and throughout their history, was so overwhelming that popular traditions connected the lineage of the first Sasanian rulers to the last defeated Arsacid king.[203] There are numerous versions of this tradition, all bearing the same theme. According to these narratives, when Ardashīr I killed the last Arsacid king, Ardavān, and "vow[ed] not to leave a single soul from Ardavān's house alive," he inadvertently married a member of the Arsacid royal family.[204] According to Ṭabarī, the bride was none other than Ardavān's daughter.[205] The *Nihāyat*[206]

[200] Procopius, *The History of the Wars*, London, 1914, translated by H.B. Dewing (Procopius 1914), here p. 279.

[201] Although, naturally, a detailed investigation of this is beyond the confines of our study. The work of Toumanoff remains to date the *magnum opus* on the history Caucasia, Toumanoff 1963. For a series of fascinating studies on the Irano-Armenian cultural relationship, with aspects of which we shall be dealing further in this study, also see Garsoian 1985b; Russell 1991; Russell, James R. (ed.), *Armenian and Iranian Studies*, vol. 9 of *Harvard Armenian Texts and Studies*, Cambridge, Mass., 2004 (Russell 2004).

[202] The intimate affinity of Armenia with Iran was not confined to this. For as Garsoian observes, the very "fabric of Armenian life, its social, legal and administrative institutions as well as its tastes and mores, reveals a far greater coincidence with the Iranian tradition." Garsoian 1985e, p. 6.

[203] A line of debate in the Sasanian creation of an image of itself revolves around how the dynasty conceived of its relationship to the Achaemenids. For these see Yarshater 1971; also see Daryaee 1995 and the sources cited therein.

[204] Yarshater 1983b, p. 380.

[205] Ṭabarī, *The Sāsānids, the Byzantines, the Lakhmids, and Yemen*, vol. V of *The History of Ṭabarī*, Albany, 1999, translated and annotated by C.E. Bosworth (Ṭabarī 1999), p. 25, and n. 86, de Goeje, 824. Bosworth, in the prior note, as well as Nöldeke 1879, pp. 26–28 and p. 28, n. 1, Nöldeke, Theodore, *Tārīkh-i Īrāniyān va ʿArab-hā dar zamān-i Sāsāniyān*, Tehran, 1979, translation of Nöldeke 1879 by Abbas Zaryab (Nöldeke 1979), pp. 76–78 and p. 89, n. 7; and Lukonin 1986, p. 49, question the veracity of this genealogy, an issue not relevant to the arguments presented here. It is interesting to note, however, that this genealogical tradition is not found in Thaʿālibī, for instance. Thaʿālibī 1900, pp. 473–486.

[206] Another important source for Sasanian history is the anonymous Nihayat 1996, *Nihāyat al-ʾIrab fī Akhbār al-Furis wa ʾl-ʿArab*, vol. 162, Tehran, 1996, translated by M.T. Danish-Pazhuh (Nihayat 1996). For some crucial junctures of the Sasanian history, it adds important details not found in other recensions of the *X^w adāy-Nāmag* tradition. For the value of the *Nihāyat* as a source, see Rubin,

maintains that she was a cousin of the Arsacid king,[207] and Dīnawarī claims her to be the daughter of another Arsacid prince.[208]

In the *Kārnāmag-i Ardashīr-i Pāpagān*, written apparently toward the end of the Sasanian period and containing a popular and romanticized version of the life of Ardashīr I, this Parthian connection is pervasive. In one version of this matrimony given by the *Kārnāmag-i Ardashīr-i Pāpagān*, after defeating Ardavān,[209] Ardashīr I marries the unnamed daughter of the last Parthian king.[210] The brothers of Ardavān, having found sanctuary with Kābulshāh, later wrote to their sister and, chastising her for being oblivious to familial bonds, urged her to poison Ardashīr I. Providentially, the poisoned cup that Ardashīr I was about to drink was spilt and the king realized his wife's mutiny. When the *mōbadhān mōbad* informed the king that the punishment for such acts against the king was death, and subsequently was ordered by Ardashīr I to carry out the sentence against the Parthian princess, the latter informed the *mōbad* that she was seven months pregnant with the child of the Sasanian king. Realizing the king's fleeting anger and anticipating his future regret, the *mōbad* forewent killing the princess and hid her from Ardashīr I. The son that was subsequently born was the future king, Shāpūr I.[211] It is significant that this same story is also contained in the *Shāhnāma* of Ferdowsī.[212] The narrative of Shāpūr I's matrimony to a daughter of Mihrak-i Nūshzādān, resulting in the birth of Hormozd I, is equally revealing. For while the precise Parthian ancestry of Mihrak cannot be established, the theophoric Mithraic name of Mihrak, the continued profusion of Mithraic terminology in his narrative, and the intense enmity existing between him and Ardashīr I underline Mihrak's exalted and perhaps Parthian genealogy. So important Mihrak's ancestry seems to have been, in fact, that the Indian astrologers are said to have prognosticated that the kingship of Iran could be obtained only by him who was an offspring from the seed of Mihrak-i Nūshzādān and Ardashīr I.[213] In spite of Ardashīr I's insistence on the impossibility

Zeev, 'The Reforms of Khusrow Anūshirwān', in Averil Cameron and Lawrence I. Conrad (eds.), *The Byzantine and Early Islamic Near East, III: States, Resources and Armies*, pp. 227–297, Princeton, 1995 (Rubin 1995), here pp. 237–239, and the sources cited therein, providing a history of the source from E. G. Browne to M. Grignaschi.

[207]Nihayat 1996, pp. 181, 183–185.

[208]Dīnawarī, Abū Ḥanīfa Aḥmad, *Akhbār al-Ṭiwāl*, Tehran, 1967, translated by Sadiq Nash'at (Dīnawarī 1967), pp. 46–47. All quoted as well in Yarshater 1983b, p. 380.

[209]At the inception of this story, with Ardavān's favorite slave girl in his company, Ardashīr I flees from the last Arsacid king. As we shall see on page 366, the imagery surrounding this flight is full of portent Mithraic symbolism, that is, symbolism borrowed from the predominant religious predilections of the Parthian families. Ardashir 1963, *Kārnāmag-i Ardashīr-i Pāpagān*, Tehran, 1963, translated by Sadegh Hedayat (Ardashir 1963), p. 182. For Mithraism among the Parthians, see Chapter 5, especially §5.4.

[210]Ardashir 1963, p. 184.

[211]Ardashir 1963, pp. 195–202.

[212]Ferdowsī, *Shāhnāma*, Moscow, 1971 (Ferdowsī 1971), vol. VII, pp. 156–164.

[213]Ardashir 1963, p. 203.

of this mixture,[214] from the union of the daughter of Mihrak with Shāpūr I, Hormozd I was born.[215] What is significant about these genealogical traditions is not their possible historical veracity, but the fact that in some quarters at least, the early Sasanians could gain legitimacy only by genealogical connections to the Arsacids. This belief, moreover, circulated even in late Sasanian period. For the purposes of the later Sasanian history examined in this study, moreover, it is important to keep in mind that the strongholds of Ardavān throughout his struggle against Ardashīr I were the regions of Rayy, Damāvand, Deylam, and Padhashkhwārgar (Ṭabaristān), the traditional homelands of the Arsacid dynasty.[216]

2.1.1 Christensen's thesis

The continued power of the Parthian families is acknowledged—in some corners more than others—by current scholarship on the Sasanians. The details of Sasanian administrative structure, based predominantly on the primary evidence of the third and the sixth centuries, and the secondary and tertiary literary sources, was long ago investigated in Christensen's magnum opus, *L'Iran sous les Sassanides*, a highly erudite work which continues to be the reference point of all current scholarship on the Sasanians. The paradigmatic narrative constructed by Christensen runs something like this:[217] In its broad outlines, the social and administrative structure of Sasanian society harked back to antiquity. Its hierarchy was articulated in the Younger Avestā[218] as the class of the priests, *āϑravan*; the warriors, *raϑaēštar*; and finally the agriculturalists, *vāstryōfšuyant*. In one instance, a fourth class of artisans or *hūiti* is also mentioned.[219] Superimposed on the politically and socially more complex Sasanian society was a similar division: the clerical class, *asravān*; the class of the warriors, *artēshtārān*; the bureaucrats, *dibhērān*; and finally the people. Included among the last were the farmers, *vāstryōshān*, and the artisans, *hutukhshān*. Each class was itself stratified into various categories. The head of the priestly class was the *mōbadhān mōbadh*; that of the warriors, *ērān-spāhbadh*; the bureaucrats, *ērān-dibhērbadh*; and finally the people were headed by the *vāstryōshān sālār*.

[214] Ardashir 1963, p. 204:

ان روز مباد که از تخم مهرك و اردوان کسی به ایرانشهر کامکار شود.

[215] Ardashir 1963, pp. 203–209; Ferdowsī 1971, vol. VII, pp. 164–172.

[216] Ardashir 1963, p. 184. Yarshater 1983b, p. 365.

[217] The discussion of the Sasanian social and administrative structure is based on Christensen 1944, pp. 96–137. Also see Tafazzoli 2000.

[218] For the periodization of the various parts of the Avestā, see Kellens, J., 'Avesta', in Ehsan Yarshater (ed.), *Encyclopaedia Iranica*, pp. 35–44, New York, 1991 (Kellens 1991).

[219] Zamyad Yasht 1883, *Zamyād Yasht*, vol. 23 of *Sacred Books of the East*, Oxford University Press, 1883, translated by James Darmesteter (Zamyad Yasht 1883), §17, as cited in Christensen 1944, p. 98.

Third-century inscriptions

A second and for our purposes more important social division of the Sasanians, however, according to this narrative, was inherited from more recent times, the period of the Arsacid dynasty (247 BCE–224 CE). In the bilingual inscription of Shāpūr I at Ḥājī Abād (ŠH) in the province of Fārs,[220] these are listed as the Princes of the Empire, or *shahrdārān*; the high-ranking elite or *vāspuhrān*; the grandees, or *wuzurgān*, and finally the freemen or *azādhān*.[221] Divine Glory (or *farr*) was a quality possessed by the King of Kings. "Originally meaning life force, activity, or splendor, it [gradually] came to mean victory, fortune, and especially royal fortune."[222] But the King of Kings was not the only dignitary in possession of *farr*. The *shahrdārān* of the realm could also boast the attribute of Divine Glory. The highest members of the *vāspuhrān* came from the seven great feudal families of the realm. In fact, the Sasanians were themselves only the first of these. As Christensen observes, "the members of these seven great families had the right to carry a crown, being in their origin the equals of the kings of Iran. Only the size of their crown was smaller than that of the Sasanian kings."[223] The *shahrdārān* were subordinate to the King of Kings, *Shāhanshāh*. These subordinate kings also included the large fief holders, as well as the vassal kings of other regions under the protection of the Sasanian king. Also included among those carrying the title of king and the splendor that accompanied it were a number of *marzbāns* (wardens of marches) "whose territories were particularly susceptible to enemy attacks and who were entitled to a reward in return for their defense of the realm."[224]

[220]Lukonin 1983, p. 682; Boyce, Mary, 'Parthian Writings and Literature', in Ehsan Yarshater (ed.), *Cambridge History of Iran: The Seleucid, Parthian, and Sasanian Periods*, vol. 3(2), pp. 1151–1166, Cambridge University Press, 1983b (Boyce 1983b), p. 1165, and the sources cited therein.

[221]See also footnote 126.

[222]Meaning glory, derived etymologically from the Iranian word *xu̯ar/n* for sun, and attested in various forms in other Iranian languages (Median and Old Persian *farnah*, Soghdian *farn*), the concept traversed into other cultural zones (in Buddhist Soghdian signifying the position of Buddha, and in Armenian signifying glory, honor, for example). It is "at the root of ideas that were widespread in the Hellenistic and Roman period ... such as *tyche basileus*, *fortuna regia*," and in Islamic Iran, it was translated into the concept of *farr-i ilāhī*. *Farr* was a royal and divine attribute. Besides meaning "glory, splendor, luminosity and shine, [and besides being] connected with sun and fire ... [its] secondary meaning ... related to prosperity, (good) fortune, and (kingly) majesty." It was associated with the stars and the great luminaries, various divinities, most importantly, as we shall see, with Mithra, as well as with waters and mountains. Its iconographical representations ranged from winged sun disks to rings in investiture scenes, figural images connected with light and fire, and finally to birds and rams, although there continues to be controversies surrounding some of these representations. See Gnoli, Gherardo, 'Farr(ah)', in Ehsan Yarshater (ed.), *Encyclopaedia Iranica*, New York, 2007 (Gnoli 2007); Frye, Richard N., *The Golden Age of Persia: The Arabs in the East*, London, 1975a (Frye 1975a), p. 8. See the religion chapter for further discussion of this important Iranian concept, especially page 354ff.

[223]Christensen 1944, p. 103.

[224]Christensen, Arthur, *Vaz‘-i Milat va Dowlat va Darbār dar Dowrih-i Shāhanshāhī-i Sāsāniyān*, Tehran, 1935, translated and annotated by Mujtaba Minovi (Christensen 1935), p. 28. In the acts of the Syrian martyrs we find, among others, Mihrānid *marzbāns* from Bet-Darāyē and from Georgia, called respectively Shahrēn and Pīrān Gushnasp. Hoffmann, G., *Auszüge aus syrischen Akten per-*

The seven great feudal families of the Sasanian period traced their descent to the Parthians. In fact only three, Christensen argues, seem to have held the same elevated position in the Arsacid feudal structure inherited by the Sasanians. These were the families of the Kārins, the Sūrens, and the Ispahbudhān. These all carried the title of Pahlav, or Parthian. The three other families were the Spandīyādhs (or Isfandīyār), the Mihrān,[225] and "possibly the Zīks."[226] Together they formed a sort of feudal nobility. Their power primarily accrued to them from their large fiefs. A number of these families in time came to be associated with certain provinces in the empire. The family of Kārins, therefore, are known to have resided in the Nihāvand area (in Media), the Sūrens in Sīstān, and the Ispahbudhān in Dihistān in Gurgān.[227] The centrifugal powers of this Parthian feudal nobility in Sasanian society has been acknowledged. Long ago Lukonin argued, for example, that "political centralization *appears* to have been achieved in Iran only at the end of the Sasanian epoch, when the reform[s of Khusrow I were] ... completed."[228] Pioneering scholars have even attempted to trace the bare outlines of the history of some of these great Parthian feudal families in early Sasanian history.[229] Patkanian, for example, highlighted that the Sasanians devoted a substantial part of their early history to combating the traditions of Parthava, traditions which still forcefully presented themselves against that of the Persīs.[230] It has been further observed that the high place that these dignitaries continued to hold in the court of the first Sasanian kings is a reflection of the fact that they formed a confederacy without the aid of which Ardashīr I could not have assumed power to begin with. The list of the nobility in the inscriptions of the first Sasanian kings in the *Kaʿba-i Zartusht* (ŠKZ), for example, argued Lukonin, makes it amply clear that it was as a result

sischer Märtyrer, vol. 7 of *Abhandlungen für die Kunde des Morgenlandes*, Leipzig, 1980 (Hoffmann 1980), pp. 64, 68 apud Khurshudian, Eduard, *Die Partischen und Sasanidischen Verwaltungsinstitutionen nach den literarischen und epigraphischen Quellen*, Yerevan, 1998 (Khurshudian 1998), p. 71.

[225]Patkanian claims that indirect allusions in the works of Armenian historians seem to indicate that the Mihrāns were in fact a branch of the Ispahbudhān family. But he does not elaborate on this. Patkanian, M.K., 'D'une histoire de la dynastie des Sassanides', *Journal Asiatique* pp. 101–238, translated by M. Evariste Prud'homme (Patkanian 1866), p. 129. Nöldeke questions whether the Mihrāns were the same house as the Isfandīyār family for the base of both seems to have been in Rayy. I do not know based on what he conjectures the identity of the Isfandīyārs and the Mihrāns.

[226]Christensen 1944, p. 103.

[227]When describing the celebration of Isfandārmadh (Spandarmad), the Amahraspand of earth, called *mard-qīrān*, Bīrūnī maintains that this celebration was prevalent in the *Parthian domains, in which he includes Isfahān and Rayy*. Bīrūnī 1984, p. 355. As we shall see, contrary to Christensen's claims, there is little doubt that the concentration of the power of the Parthians families of the Kārin, the Mihrān, the Ispahbudhān, and the Kanārangīyān during the Sasanian period remained in the lands of Pahlav and Media, the isolated names of villages and rivers outside of these territories notwithstanding. Christensen 1944, pp. 105–106.

[228]Through these reforms, argues Lukonin, "the system of *shahrs* was changed to a system of four large divisions of the state [*kūst*], headed by vice-regents appointed by the central government and each wielding both military and civil power in his vice-regency—a kind of revival of the institution of the *shahrab*." Lukonin 1983, p. 731. Emphasis mine. Nöldeke 1979, p. 88, n. 1.

[229]Patkanian 1866.

[230]Patkanian 1866, pp. 119–120 and 126–128.

of the cooperation of the kings of Andīgān, Kirmān, Aprenak, Sakistān, and Marv, *as well as the cooperation of the Parthian feudal families* of the Razz, the Sūrens, the Kārins, and not to mention the cooperation of the minor kings of Mesopotamia, that Ardashīr I was able to assume power.[231] Lukonin further argued that it is rather certain that in the court of Ardashīr I, "the Sūrens, Kārens, Varāzes and the kings of Andīgān held positions of great honor, *ousting the representatives of the noble clan of Persis*. In this instance there is a complete analogy with the appearance, at the court of the King of Kings of Iran of the new dynasty, of the kings of Marv, Abarshahr, Carmenia, Sakastān, Iberia and Adiabene." After all, argued Lukonin, "*the extensive domains of the Sūrens, Kārens and Varāzes must also have originally become part of the Sasanian state as semi-independent states*,"[232] and the king most probably could not interfere much in the regions under their control.[233] In spite of the ostensible decimation of the Kārins at the hands of the Sasanians, therefore, even these continue to appear in the court of the Ardashīr I as high dignitaries.[234] There are also indications that the scribal personnel of early Sasanian society, a group that belonged to the third estate, were inherited from the Parthian scribal personnel. Thus, among the retinue of Shāpūr I (241–272) at the *Ka'ba-i Zartusht* (ŠKZ), there is mention of one Aštād, "the (letter) scribe [*pad frawardag dibīr* in Parthian] from Rayy, *from the Mihrān family*."[235] As far as the rule of the early Sasanians are concerned, therefore, the continuity of the political power of the Parthians in their polity is acknowledged by most scholars of Sasanian history. In spite of these reservations about the power of the Sasanians at the inception of their rule and during subsequent centuries, however, it was the Christensenian paradigm that came to dominate the field.

While acknowledging decentralizing forces operating at the inception of Sasanian history, Christensen argued that during the third century the monarchy obtained great powers. During this period the Sasanians attempted to assert their control over newly acquired territories formerly under the control of the Parthian dynasts and various other petty kings and leashed the decentralizing forces of their realm. During this century, argued Christensen, the Sasanians attempted to rid themselves of the legacy of the Parthians. "In few years, and with a heavy hand, he [Ardashīr] welded together the rarely cohesive parts of the Parthian kingdom into a firm and solid unity ... and *created a political*

[231]Lukonin 1986, p. 57.

[232]Lukonin 1983, p. 705. Emphasis mine. In the depictions of Shāpūr I at Naqsh-i Rajab likewise, after the king, the princes of the realm and the queen, and the commander of king's guard, come representatives of the families of Varāz (Ardashīr Varāz), Sūren (Ardashīr Sūren), and Kārin. Lukonin 1986, p. 108–109.

[233]Besides the Parthian dynasts, we also know that the kings of Abarshahr, Marv, Kirmān, and Sakastān continued to rule their own territories during Ardashīr I's reign. Lukonin 1986, p. 21.

[234]Frye, Richard N., 'The Political History of Iran Under the Sasanians', in Ehsan Yarshater (ed.), *Cambridge History of Iran: The Seleucid, Parthian, and Sasanian Periods*, vol. 3(1), pp. 119–120, Cambridge University Press, 1983 (Frye 1983). See also note 185.

[235]Tafazzoli 2000, p. 21.

and religious organism that lasted for more than four centuries[!]"[236] Thus, Christensen argued, the advent of the Sasanians was not simply a political event: it marked the appearance of a "novel spirit in the Iranian empire ... The two characteristic traits of the system of the Sasanian state ... [were] *heavy centralization and the creation of a state church*."[237]

What then of the power of the Parthian feudal families, those who were thought to be on a par with Sasanian kings, and those without whose aid Ardashīr I could not have assumed kingship? Christensen argued that as the territories of these Parthian nobles came to be dispersed in the different parts of the kingdom—it is not clear how—this undermined their continued control over vast estates. The fragmentation of the territorial possessions of the Parthian feudal families was perhaps one of the causes, according to Christensen, through which, in time, these became more and more a "nobility of the robe and of the court," losing the characteristics of real feudal nobility. In comparison to the area under the direct control of the state and administered by the royal governors, the territories under the control of the feudal nobility were never extensive.[238] While this remained the case, we do not know the nature of the king's jurisdiction over the territories under the control of the Parthian feudal nobility, and whether these had total or partial immunity. It is true that certain offices in the Sasanian realm belonged to these families on a hereditary basis and through ancient custom, Christensen admitted.[239] Quoting the narrative of Simocatta about the hereditary positions of the nobility in Sasanian administration,[240] he proceeded to argue that "[i]t is difficult to assess to which family each of the aforementioned posts belonged." As the families of Sūren and Mihrān are generally mentioned among the generals of the army, one might conclude that each of these families controlled one of the military posts, Christensen conceded. As for the distribution of the civilian posts among these families, "we know absolutely nothing about this."[241] Finally, "all considered ..., while it is true that the hereditary posts were very important positions, they were not the most important ... In fact it is not likely that the primary posts of the empire, that of the prime minister, the commander in chief of all the armies of the king etc., should have been transmitted on a hereditary basis, and that the king would not have had the choice of his counselors ... *This kind of institution would have been incompatible with the absolutist government that was in effect the base of the Sasanian state, and it would have, in a short time, brought about the ruin of the empire*."[242] The hereditary posts in the Sasanian empire, therefore, "were *positions of honor* that marked the privileged status of the seven Parthian

[236] Christensen 1944, p. 96. Emphasis mine.
[237] Christensen 1944, p. 97. Emphasis mine.
[238] Christensen 1944, p. 106.
[239] Christensen 1944, pp. 106–107.
[240] See page 29.
[241] Christensen 1944, p. 109.
[242] Christensen 1944, p. 108–109. Emphasis added.

families. The power of these, especially in the period anterior to Qubād and Khusrow I, rested equally in the *revenues of their fiefs, and on the force of feudal ties between these Parthian families and their subjects*."[243] What then did these Parthian families do with the wealth and manpower under their control? They used this as a "prerogative in the nomination of the highest posts in the empire," according to Christensen. As we shall see, however, this included the appointment of the Sasanian kings themselves! While acknowledging long stretches of Sasanian history wherein the feudal nobility held sway, Christensen nevertheless carried his thesis of an absolutist, centralized monarchy to the end of the Sasanian period, making Khusrow I the quintessential absolute monarch, and devoting to him a substantial part of his opus. The Christensenian thesis carried the field. Accordingly, it was subsequently argued, for example, that while "the nobility from time to time during the Sasanian empire showed its power, on the whole the importance of the ruler and the centralization of authority continued ... *The reign of Shāpūr II (309–379) can be considered the culmination of the process of centralization under the early Sasanian kings*."[244]

As we shall see, however, the centrist monarchical perspective promoted by this thesis falls seriously short of explaining the ongoing tension between the Sasanian monarchy and the decentralizing forces operating within its polity. Specifically, and most importantly, it fails to properly appreciate the tremendous and continuous power of the Parthian feudal nobility, the Pahlav, within the Sasanian realm. It cannot explain why episodic surges of the Sasanians' attempt at centralization were thoroughly overshadowed by substantial periods when there was almost a total collapse of the power of the monarchy, and a resurgence of the power of the Parthian feudal families. If the Sasanians were so successful in creating an absolutist and powerful centralized polity, then we are at a loss to account for the stories of a multitude of Sasanian kings who were enthroned and deposed, sometimes in their infancy, at the whim of this same Parthian feudal nobility. If the height of Sasanian centralization was achieved in the sixth century, why was it that even after the reforms of the archetypal centrist Sasanian monarch, Khusrow I, Sasanian control was on the verge of collapse through the rebellions of Bahrām-i Chūbīn and Vistāhm, both belonging to the Parthian families?[245]

A *longue durée* investigation of Sasanian sociopolitical history, one which does not read the evidence for the third and sixth centuries into the rest of Sasanian history, reveals that, except for short periods in their history, the Sasanians were rarely able to centralize their rule and leash the power of the Parthian feudal nobility. In fact, if we were to read the history of the Sasanians not from the monarchical perspective or from the point of view of the Sasanian court in western Iran and Mesopotamia, the result would be a thoroughly different history, dominated by the tremendous power of the Pahlav families. The power

[243] Christensen 1944, p. 110.
[244] Frye 1983, p. 133. Emphasis added.
[245] See §2.6.3 and §2.7.1.

of the Sasanian monarchy at the center, it will be argued in this study, was always contingent on the cooperation of the Pahlav families with the Sasanians, the inheritors of the traditions of Persīs. The Sasanians realized this early in their reign and recognized that the only viable and enduring polity that they could ever hope to establish was one in which the long-established power of the Pahlav families was acknowledged and rendered continuous. Thus, in direct continuity with the history of the Arsacids, the Sasanians knew they had to establish a confederacy with the Pahlav families. This policy was made viable by the fact that, throughout their long history, the Pahlav families had never been a homogeneous group to begin with. The divisions and rivalries long established among them made the Sasanians' task easy, and the Sasanian–Parthian confederacy worked admirably, albeit with the ebb and flow inherent in any such political arrangement, throughout most of Sasanian history. In fact, the dissolution of the Sasanian polity was caused primarily by Sasanian efforts, late in their history, to do away with this confederacy. Part of the problem in appreciating the dynamics of the relationship between the Sasanian monarchy and the Parthian families is the conceptual framework that scholarship has adopted in order to investigate Sasanian sociopolitical and administrative history, a conceptual framework which, sustained by Christensen's thesis, nevertheless fails to account for the realities of Sasanian history. Toumanoff's study[246] of Caucasia offers an alternative conceptual framework that is much more applicable to Sasanian society, through which we can appreciate the nature of the Pārsīg–Pahlav relationship throughout Sasanian history.

2.1.2 Dynasticism

In a detailed study of the history of Caucasia through the centuries, Toumanoff argues that the "social history of Caucasia is marked by an extraordinary *permanence of form*, which offers a sharp contrast to the vicissitudes of its political history ... The perdurable form in question is one of a strongly aristocratic society which combined in an unusual way the features of a *feudal regime* with those of a *dynastic regime* evolved from earlier tribal conditions."[247] Citing recent studies of feudalism, Toumanoff notes that unfortunately in these studies "no notice was taken of Caucasian society, or that other component which may, in *contradistinction to feudalism*, be termed *dynasticism*."[248] Toumanoff then proceeds to conceptualize what he understands to be the nature of the two regimes of feudalism and dynasticism. *Feudalism*, Toumanoff argues, is born "of the revolutionary encounter of two more or less moribund elements." One of these elements is the "state: a civilized, bureaucratic and centralized, cosmocratic, yet disintegrating polity—or, at least, an abortive attempt at one."[249] The other element "is the tribe in what has been called its Heroic Age, when,

[246] Toumanoff 1963.
[247] Toumanoff 1963, p. 34.
[248] Toumanoff 1963, p. 34, nn. 1–2. Emphasis added.
[249] Toumanoff 1963, p. 35.

instead of a gradual evolution into a polity, it suffers, under the impact of a too-pronounced outside influence of a State, the disruption of the ties of mystic kingship that have held it together and which are now replaced by personal and contractual bonds of lord–vassal relationship."[250] The feudal society that results from the meeting of these two elements at a particular juncture of a society can thus be described as "a system of government, a polity, which is marked by the diffusion of sovereign power."[251] In spite of the horizontal and vertical ways in which sovereignty is pulverized in such a society, Toumanoff argues, "there is nevertheless unity in this society, besides diversity; it derives from *the tradition of a centralized state, and, once enforced by the ruler–subject bonds, is now affected by the lord–vassal relations of the pyramidal group.*" Relations, in such a system, "converge in the person of supreme overlord, or king, who is the theoretical source of sovereignty and of landownership in the polity."[252]

Opposed to this system, according to Toumanoff, stands that of *dynasticism*. In a dynastic system, the "same elements as with feudalism" are at work, only "here the tribe is basic and the State secondary." Dynasticism is the "result not of the disruption of a tribal society and of the meeting of Heroic-Age warriors with a decaying cosmocracy, *but of a gradual evolution of tribes into a polity.*"[253] The evolution of a society into a dynastic form of sovereignty "is brought about by the coalescence [presumably over an extended period] of clans and tribes dwelling in close vicinity, within a geographically and—though not necessarily—ethnically unified area; by the acquisition of the prerequisites of statehood: sovereignty, independence or at least autonomy, and of course, territory; and by the achieving of a higher degree of civilization, manifested, for instance, in written records."[254] What prompts this evolution, besides outside forces, according to Toumanoff, is the development "of a new social force inside: the rising class of the dynasts." The monarchical regimes that thus rise in a dynastic system "display a greater degree of interpenetration of religion and polity ... for they inherit more fully the theophonism of the tribe and in fact develop it further."[255] The unity of such a system "rests on geographical, cultural and ethnic, rather than political foundations." In such a society when "a number of small States coexist in a circumscribed area, the group of kingly dynasties ruling in them, though each unique in its own polity, come to form together, in the multiplicity of States, as it were one class."[256] This class cuts across political boundaries and comes to constitute "the highest stratum of the society of the entire area." According to Toumanoff, this class might be called a dynastic aristocracy. Political unification in such a society involves not the "complete

[250] Toumanoff 1963, p. 35.
[251] Toumanoff 1963, p. 35.
[252] Toumanoff 1963, p. 36. Emphasis added.
[253] Toumanoff 1963, p. 36. Emphasis added.
[254] Toumanoff 1963, p. 36.
[255] Toumanoff 1963, p. 37.
[256] Toumanoff 1963, p. 37.

reduction of the fellow dynasts by the super dynasts, as in a centralized state ... [but] *the imposition upon them of only his political hegemony*." In such a system, a "hierarchy of political, but also economic, or at least fiscal, and social, relationships is established which holds together the super-dynast or High King, the other dynasts ... in the common governance of the nation."[257] The sovereign power, here, is polygenetic. In contradistinction to this, a *feudal* regime "presupposes the fragmentation of the theoretically monogenetic sovereign power ... to an essentially non-sovereign, noble group." There is however, a greater difference between the two regimes that transcends political differences, and that is the condition of land tenure. While in dynastic regimes land ownership is "*absolute and inalienable*, feudal land tenure is conditional, contractual, and limited."[258] As with the polygenetic nature of the political regimes that are thus established, land tenure in a dynastic society is also polygenetic, *dominium directum*, "as opposed to the unitary, monogenetic one, which reduces the land tenure of all save the supreme lord to a mere *dominium utile*." A feudal society, on the other hand, is one in which there is a complete "political, social, and economic *dependence* of vassal on suzerain."[259] Finally, a feudal state is something of "a middle way between dynasticism, on the one hand, and an anti-nobiliary and bureaucratic, total *étatisme*, such as characterized by the Roman Empire, on the other."[260] Toumanoff then proceeds to argue that Caucasian societies were indeed dynastic. In Iran and western Europe, however, it was a feudal system that supplanted dynasticism.

Like scholars before and after him, however, Toumanoff based his study of Sasanian Iran on Christensen's thesis, and not on an independent investigation of the Sasanian sociopolitical regime.[261] While he maintained that in Iran "the super-dynastic Crown early became powerful and, moreover, imperial, and evinced *étatiste* tendencies", he also stated that the "*only* dynastic group in Iran was, to give it its Sassanian name, that of *shahrdārān* or vassal kings." Comparing the "seven great houses of the *vāspuhrān*," sociologically and juridically, to the "Caucasian lesser, non-dynastic, nobility," moreover, Toumanoff significantly maintained that the "political and social importance of ... [these Parthian families] *was commensurable with that of the greatest* of the Caucasian [dynastic] Princes."[262] It will be proposed in this study that a non-centrist investigation of Sasanian sociopolitical history highlights the fact that in spite of sporadic efforts of the Sasanians to create a feudal and, at times, an *étatiste* sociopolitical regime, the monarchy can in fact best be viewed as a dynastic regime. This dimension of Sasanian sociopolitical history can be corroborated with

[257] Toumanoff 1963, p. 38. Emphasis added.

[258] Toumanoff 1963, p. 39.

[259] Toumanoff 1963, p. 39. Emphasis added.

[260] Toumanoff 1963, p. 39.

[261] The first reference that he makes once he assesses the Sasanian political structure is to Christensen's work, Christensen 1944. Toumanoff 1963, p. 40, n. 14. Emphasis added.

[262] Toumanoff 1963, p. 40, n. 14.

reference to the agnatic sociopolitical and cultural infrastructure that characterized Iranian society throughout the Sasanian period.[263] There is little doubt that the seven great Pahlav families were in fact dynastic sociopolitical regimes, over whom, ideally, the Sasanians would have liked to establish an étatiste or a feudal regime, but with whom the Sasanians were forced to enter into a dynastic confederacy, a confederacy in which, by agreement, the Sasanians functioned as the Kings of Kings (*Shāhanshāh*).

2.1.3 Early Sasanian period

Even without our knowledge of the Pahlav dynastic families' substantial power in the court of Ardashīr I, where they ousted the representatives of the noble clan of Persīs, and even without all the other evidence adduced here to substantiate the continued forceful legacy of the Pahlav families and the western-focused nature of Sasanian attempts at centralization and urbanization during the third and subsequent centuries, the well-established fourth-century history of the Sasanians should have led to the realization that something is terribly skewed in this disproportionate emphasis on the centralizing measures undertaken by the Sasanians during the reigns of Ardashīr I and Shāpūr I (241–272). For while the third century has been characterized as the century of the monarchy, it has also been almost unanimously acknowledged that in "the fourth [century,] until Shāpūr II [(309–379)] reached manhood, the nobility and the priesthood held sway."[264] Once Shāpūr II comes of age, his reign is said to have witnessed the height of centralization in Iran. What is not highlighted in this appreciation of Shāpūr II's regime, however, is that he himself owed his very kingship to the designs of the nobility. The father of Shāpūr II, Hormozd II (302–309), had left many sons behind. At the death of Hormozd II, as Ṭabarī narrates, the "*great men of the state and the Zoroastrian priesthood* saw their chance of securing a dominant influence in affairs, hence killed the natural successor to power, Hormozd II's eldest son Ādhar Narseh, blinded another, and forced a third to flee to Roman territory, and then raised to nominal headship of the realm the *infant* Shābūr II, *born forty days after his father's death*."[265] Of the first thirty years of Shāpūr II's reign, that is until the 330s, we seem to know next to nothing. But the king's belated renewed warfare against the Byzantines, led even Christensen to suspect that once of age, Shāpūr II must have had "difficulties to surmount in the interior of his realm."[266] Whether or not these had to do with leashing the nobility who had put him on the throne as an infant can only be surmised. As we shall see later on in this study, a major factor behind the power of the Parthian dynasts, and the Sasanian king's reliance on them, was the military prowess of the Parthians and the manpower that they contributed to the Sasanian army. It is therefore indicative of their

[263]See §1.2.

[264]Frye 1983, p. 136. Emphasis added.

[265]Ṭabarī 1999, p. 50, and n. 146, de Goeje, 836.

[266]Christensen 1944, p. 238.

continued strength at the height of Shāpūr II's reign that some of his major campaigns during this period were headed by the Parthian dynastic families. In the wars that Shāpūr II undertook against emperor Julian (361–363)—who boasted of having among his own ranks the Arsacid king of Armenia, Arshak III—a general from the dynastic Pahlav family of the Mihrans led the Sasanian forces, gaining for the Iranians a victory that was crowned with the murder of Julian in 363 CE.[267] In his war against the Byzantines over Armenia and against the Armenian Arsacids, likewise, Shāpūr II was ultimately forced to send yet another Parthian dynastic family, the Sūren. Even Christensen admitted that during the fourth century, the "traditions of the Arsacid period continued to be strong in the blood of the great nobility, and the moment when a less energetic king unleashed the bridle of their ambitions, the danger of preponderance of the nobility and feudal anarchy" presented itself.[268]

Given the current paradigms in scholarship on the Sasanians, it is curious that this same scholarship acknowledges that after Shāpūr II's rule the monarchy became a pawn in the hands of the nobility. In fact, the course of Sasanian history during the fourth century must force us to reconsider the rule of Shāpūr II and his ostensible success in centralizing the Sasanian polity. For the reign of Shāpūr II's successor, Ardashīr II (379–383), betrays the continued hold of the Parthian dynasts over the Sasanians. Ardashīr II's assumption of the throne seems to have been approved by the *great men of the state*. Once secured in power, however, Ardashīr II "turned his attention to the great men and holders of authority, and killed a great number of them."[269] Naturally, this proved to be Ardashīr II's undoing. For "*the people* then deposed him of power," after a reign of only four years.[270] It is indicative of our mainstream monarchist perspective on Sasanian history that the above episode has been interpreted in the following terms: "Ṭabarī's information that Ardashīr II slaughtered many nobility points to his being a personality who continued Shābūr's policy of firm rule." This may very well have been true. What seems to be forgotten in this picture, however, is that Ardashīr II lost his very head as a result of this undertaking after only four years of rule! The next monarch, Shāpūr III (383–388), did not fare much better than Ardashīr II. In his accession speech Shāpūr III declared to the nobility that henceforth deceit, tale-bearing, greed, and self-righteousness would have no place in his court and his polity.[271] This,

[267] Christensen 1944, p. 238.

[268] Christensen 1944, p. 235. It has been argued that the "belief that the *farr* or mythical majesty of kingship had descended on a Prince would cause nobles to rally to one member of the royal family rather than another." Frye 1983, p. 134. In all objectivity, however, this perspective does not give due credence to sociopolitical and economic expediencies that must have informed the relationship of the Sasanians with their Parthian constituents.

[269] Ṭabarī 1999, pp. 67–68, de Goeje, 846.

[270] Ṭabarī 1999, p. 68, n. 183. Emphasis added.

[271] Ferdowsī 1971, vol. VII, pp. 259–260:

بدانید که انکس که گوید دروغ — از ان پس نگیرد بر ما فروغ ...
کسی را کجا مغز باشد بسی — گواژه نباید زدن بر کسی ...

however, was too much to ask of the nobility. For the anecdotal narratives that briefly trace the short rule of this Sasanian monarch also apprise us that after a rule of five years, the great men of state (*al-ʿuẓamāʾ*) and the members of noble houses (*ahl al-buyūtāt*) finally proceeded to kill the king by cutting "the ropes of a large tent Shābūr had had erected in one of his palace courts, [so that] the tent fell down on top of him." As a result of the antagonism that his policies created among the great men of state and the members of noble houses, therefore, Shāpūr III also ruled for only five years.[272] The successor to the throne, Bahrām IV (388–399), seems to have been dethroned under unclear circumstances. He is said to have enjoined his army commanders to obedience,[273] and to have been a self-involved king who never held *maẓālim* court.[274] He too suffered a violent death.

Even Christensen admitted, therefore, that Ardashīr II, Shāpūr III, and Bahrām IV "were weak kings under whose reigns the grand nobility easily *reconquered the grounds that they had lost under the great Shāpūr II*,"[275] and that these were "times of trouble for the Sasanian state, with enfeeblement of the crown and aggrandizement of the nobility."[276] The successors of Shāpūr II, wrote Christensen, "were for the most part figures of little significance, and so the death of Shāpūr II marks *the beginning of a period of close to 125 years[!] in which the king and the grandees of the empire vied for power.* The great nobility, who had found an ally in the clergy,[277] became, once again, a danger for the power of the royalty."[278] The end point of this rivalry, which apparently reached its height in the initial phases of Qubād's reign (488–531), is presumed to have been the reign of the quintessential Sasanian monarch, Khusrow I Nowshīrvān (531–579), to be discussed shortly.

As we have seen thus far, while the continued forceful participation of the nobility in Sasanian history is not disputed, the problem remains, nevertheless, that due to the nature of the sources at our disposal up to the rule of Yazdgird I (399–420), the actual noble families who came to wield such direct influence on the crown remain, for the most part, anonymous. Except for significant yet solitary figures in the monarchically patronized accounts of the *X^wadāy-Nāmag* tradition as reflected in the *Shāhnāma* or the classical Arabic histories, we are forced to deal up to this point with anonymous collectivities that are

---

دل مرد طامع بود پر ز درد　　بگرد طمع تا توانی مگرد …
چهارم نراند سخن از گزاف　　ز بی دانشی نام جوید ز لاف

[272]Ṭabarī 1999, p. 68, de Goeje, 846. Thaʿālibī 1900, pp. 534–535, Thaʿālibī, Abū Manṣūr, *Tārīkh-i Thaʿālibī*, 1989, translation of Thaʿālibī 1900 by Muhammad Fada'ili (Thaʿālibī 1989), p. 345; Ibn Balkhī 1995, p. 148; Dīnawarī 1967, p. 54.

[273]Ṭabarī 1999, p. 69, de Goeje, 847.

[274]Ibn Balkhī 1995, p. 198.

[275]Christensen 1944, p. 253. Italics mine.

[276]Paraphrased by Bosworth in Ṭabarī 1999, pp. 68–69, n. 184. Emphasis added.

[277]For a discussion of the presumed power of the clergy, see Chapter 5.

[278]Christensen 1944, p. 260. Emphasis added.

referred to by such generic terms as *ahl al-buyūtāt*, *al-ʿuzamā*, *bozorgān*, and so forth.[279] From the rule of Yazdgird I, however, the nature of the information at our disposal begins to change. Henceforth, sporadically, yet meaningfully, the dynastic forces assume identity. From this point onward it is possible to identify the major noble families whose power and rivalries directed the affairs of the country in crucial ways. As we shall see, predominant among these noble families were the Parthian dynastic families. The information on these dynastic families becomes more and more substantial as we proceed further into Sasanian history—although the infrastructural base of the power of these families is not always explicit in our sources. Ironically, the emergence of the Pahlav families into the full light of history from Yazdgird I's reign onward is most probably connected not only to the initial efforts of the Sasanians at creating a historiography, but, as Nöldeke acknowledged close to a century ago, also to the contribution of these same Parthian families to the creation of the Iranian national history and the *Xʷadāy-Nāmag* tradition during the Sasanian period itself. For invariably, as we shall see, the Pahlav families are depicted in a very positive light in the *Xʷadāy-Nāmag* tradition.

2.2 Yazdgird I, Bahrām V Gūr, and Yazdgird II / the Sūrens

We shall commence our story, therefore, with the rule of Yazdgird I the Sinner (399–420), an epithet bestowed upon him precisely by those who defeated him.[280] Yazdgird I is said to have commenced his rule on a platform of justice. Now, bereft of its religio-ethical connotations,[281] the platform of justice attributed to specific Sasanian kings must be understood in terms of their intention in agreeing to a dynastic/confederate arrangement. In contradistinction, the Sasanian kings who are accused of injustice, such as Khusrow II, are precisely those who did not abide by the natural order of things, that is, the explicit understanding that the Sasanian polity was a confederacy wherein the independent power of the Parthian dynastic families was left undisturbed.[282] Thus, in the case of Yazdgird I the Sinner, in an inaugural speech to the elite of his realm, the king warned the families that he would restrain their unbridled powers. He warned those who had power in his realm, and through this power inflicted injustice upon the needy, that he would deal with them harshly and that they ought to be wary of his wrath.[283] In elaborating on Yazdgird I's

[279]It might still be possible to give some flesh to these through the use of other sources, such as the Armenian. This examination has not been undertaken in the present study.

[280]Christensen 1944, p. 269.

[281]For an exposition of this, see §5.2.6.

[282]That this should be couched in terms of *justice* fits very well the Mithraic proclivity of most of the Pahlav families. See Chapter 5, especially pages 351 and 354.

[283]Ibn Balkhī 1995, pp. 200–203; Thaʿālibī 1900, pp. 537–539; Ferdowsī 1971, vol. VII, pp. 264–265:

کسی را کجا پر ز اهو بود   روانش ز بیشی بنیرو بود
به بیچارگان بر ستم سازد اوی   گر از چیز درویش بفرازد اوی

relations with the elite of his realm, Ṭabarī in fact maintains that Yazdgird I "had begun his reign over them with lenience and equity; but then they, or at least some of them, had rejected that policy and not shown themselves submissive, as servants and slaves should in fact show themselves toward kings. This had impelled him into harsh policies: he had *beaten people and shed blood*."[284]

2.2.1 Mihr Narseh Sūren

Now during the rule of Yazdgird I begins the career of one of the most preeminent men of his kingdom, whom the king chose as his vizier, Mihr Narseh.[285] Narseh, son of Burāzih (Gurāzih), went by the name of Mihr Narseh and the title of *hazārbandih*, which is most probably a corruption of the title *hazārbed* (*hazarpat*), the Chief of the Thousands.[286] As Khorenats'i and Łazar P'arpec'i inform us, Mihr Narseh belonged to the Sūren Pahlav family.[287] Mihr Narseh is

---

بکوشیم و نیروش بیرون کنیم   به درویش ما نازش افزون کنیم
کسی کو نپرهیزد از خشم ما   همی بگذرد تیز بر چشم ما

[284] Ṭabarī 1999, p. 98, de Goeje, 865. Emphasis added.

[285] Based on Mihr Narseh's long career, and the fact that forty years later he appears as the general of the army, Nöldeke has argued that it seems improbable that Mihr Narseh was appointed as the minister immediately after Yazdgird I's accession to power as maintained by Ṭabarī. Nöldeke 1879, p. 76, n. 1, Nöldeke 1979, p. 177, n. 8. Based partially on Nöldeke's statement, and the fact that there seems to have been a change of policy for the worse toward the Christians of the realm in the latter parts of Yazdgird I's reign, Christensen implicitly argues that Mihr Narseh might have been appointed toward the end of the reign of Yazdgird I. Christensen 1944, p. 273. From this Zaehner concludes that it was toward the end of Yazdgird I's reign that Mihr Narseh was appointed. But Nöldeke never specified a date for Mihr Narseh's appointment, and Christensen only postulated a late appointment based on Nöldeke. In any event the whole reasoning seems unsound as Mihr Narseh could have been appointed in his mid-twenties for all we know. And in any event the whole discussion is not crucial to the gist of the arguments that follow. It must be noted that the story of Mihr Narseh and his family is not found in Thaʿālibī 1900, pp. 537–539.

[286] Nöldeke 1879, p. 76, n. 2, Nöldeke 1979, p. 177, n. 9; Ṭabarī 1999, p. 72, de Goeje, 849; Gyselen 2001a, pp. 20–22.

[287] As we shall see shortly, the Sūren continued to hold the most important offices in the Sasanian domains during the reign of Yazdgird I (399–420), Bahrām V Gūr (420–438) and Yazdgird II (438–457). According to Khorenats'i, during the reign of Bahrām V Gūr (Vram), the minister of the Aryans, the *hazarpat*, "was of the Surenean Pahlav" family. Khorenatsʿi 1978, p. 340. In fact, Bahrām V Gūr, under whose rule the Sūren continued in power, had the Sūrenid minister persuade Sahak the Great of Armenia, also of the Sūren family, to willingly abdicate his position, underlining their common descent in order to convince Sahak. The Surenean Pahlav *hazarpat* told Sahak that since "you are my blood and kin, I speak out of consideration for your own good." Khorenatsʿi 1978, p. 340. The kinship of Sahak to the Surenean Pahlav *hazarpat* is reiterated in other places. Ibid., p. 344. Łazar P'arpec'i mentions the *hazarpat* of Yazdgird as the infamous Mihr Narseh. He also calls him, like Moses, the *hazarpat* of the Aryans. Parpeci 1991, p. 75. In the court of Bahrām V Gūr (Vram), Łazar P'arpec'i calls him the Surēn Pahlav, the *hazarpat* of the royal court. Ibid., p. 58. Based on a genealogy that Ṭabarī provides for this family, which is found only in the Sprenger manuscript, however, Christensen and Nöldeke suspected that Mihr Narseh belonged to the Isfandīyār family. Nöldeke 1879, pp. 76–77, 139–140, n. 2, Nöldeke 1979, pp. 170–171, 241, n. 81; Christensen 1944, p. 104, n. 1. Nöldeke, however, as he himself admits, was only guessing this genealogical connection.

said to have come from the town (*qarya*) of Abruwān in the district of Dasht-i Bārīn in the southwestern province of Fārs, in Ardashīr Khurrah.

The extensive powers of the Sūren family during the combined reigns of Yazdgird I (399–420), Bahrām V Gūr (420–438), and Yazdgird II (438–457) are reflected in all of our sources. Ṭabarī devotes an extensive section to this Pahlav family, without identifying them as Sūrens,[288] and praises them highly. Of Mihr Narseh's several sons he singles out three as having reached an outstanding position. According to Ṭabarī, one of the sons of Mihr Narseh was called Zurvāndād and was chosen to pursue a career in religious law. So strong was the continuity of the power base of the Sūren family that under the rule of Bahrām V Gūr, Zurvāndād was appointed the Chief *herbad* of the realm, a position second only to that of the Chief *mōbad*.[289] A second son of Mihr Narseh, Mājusnas, or Māhgushnasp, with the rank of *vāstryōshān sālār*, Chief Agriculturalist,[290] was in control of the financially crucial department of the land tax all through the reign of Bahrām V Gūr.

Yet the powers of the Sūrens through the first half of the fifth century were not limited to influential standing within the clergy and extensive control over the agricultural wealth of the empire. A third important office was also filled by a third son of Mihr Narseh, *Kārdār*,[291] who was supreme commander of the army, and held the title *rathashtārān sālār*,[292] a rank, according to Ṭabarī, higher than that of *spāhbed* and near to that of *arjbadh* (*hargbed*). Lofty constructions in the region are attributed to him.[293] Not only did the Sūrens exert a tremendous influence over the administrative, financial, and military affairs of the Sasanian state during this period. In their cooperation and connection to the religious hierarchy, they also exerted a moral hold on their contemporary society. At Jirih in Fārs, Mihr Narseh established a fire temple, called Mihr Narsīyān, which, according to Ṭabarī, was "still in existence today, with its fire burning to this present moment."[294] As if this were not enough, in the process of founding four other villages in the environs of Abruwān, Mihr Narseh established four more fire temples—one for each village, naming these after himself and his sons: Faraz-marā-āwar-khudāyā, Zurvāndādhān, Kārdādhān, and Mājusnasān. The three gardens that Mihr Narseh constructed in this area are said to have contained 12,000 date palms, 12,000 olive trees, and 12,000

[288]Nöldeke 1879, pp. 110–113, Nöldeke 1979, pp. 169–173; Ṭabarī 1999, pp. 103–105, de Goeje, 868–870.

[289]Nöldeke 1879, p. 110, Nöldeke 1979, p. 172. For a detailed discussion of the different classes of the Zoroastrian clergy, among which were included the high priests, the *herbads* and the *mōbads*, see Kreyenbroek, Philip G., 'The Zoroastrian Priesthood after the Fall of the Sasanian Empire', in *Transition Periods in Iranian History*, Societas Iranologica Europaea, pp. 151–166, Fribourg-en-Brisgau, 1987 (Kreyenbroek 1987), p. 151.

[290]Nöldeke 1879, pp. 110–111, Nöldeke 1979, pp. 172, 197, n. 100.

[291]*Kārdār* is most probably the title and not the name of this figure. See also Khurshudian 1998, p. 280.

[292]Tafazzoli 2000, p. 9.

[293]Nöldeke 1879, p. 111, Nöldeke 1979, p. 172.

[294]Nöldeke 1879, p. 111, Nöldeke 1979, pp. 172–173.

cypress trees.[295] Ṭabarī maintains that these "villages, with the gardens and the fire temples, have remained continuously in the hands of his descendants, who are well known till today, and it has been mentioned that all these remain in the best possible condition at the present time."[296] Mihr Narseh's religious zeal was evident in his constructions of numerous fire temples. This zeal seems to have been intensified by his implacable hatred of Christians. It is a function of the hold of this Pahlav family over the monarchy that the persecution of Christians under Bahrām V Gūr (420–438) and the flight of Christian refugees to Byzantine territory are said to have been largely the result of the influence of Mihr Narseh—who instigated as well the Perso-Byzantine war of 421–422—over the Sasanians during this period. Mihr Narseh himself led the Sasanian armies against Byzantium, in which he "played a notable role ... and returned home having achieved all that Bahrām V Gūr had desired, and the latter heaped honors unceasingly on Mihr Narsī."[297] Mihr Narseh continued to hold the office of prime minister, *hazārbed*,[298] throughout the reign of Yazdgird II (438–457). It is indicative of the independent historiographical contributions of these Parthian dynastic families to the formation of the *X^w adāy-Nāmag* tradition that, according to Nöldeke, in a number of places in the Sprenger manuscript, Ṭabarī mentions a certain *mōbad* called Abū Jaʿfar Zarātusht, the son of Aḥrāʾ, who lived at the time of the ʿAbbāsid caliph al-Muʿtaṣim (833–842) "as the narrator of the last wars of Mihr Narsī with the Byzantines ... and probably [for the name here has been changed] as the narrator for the events surrounding the family of Mihr Narseh."[299]

Here, then, we have evidence of a tremendously powerful Parthian dynastic family, the house of Sūren, who were basically the confederates in rule of Yazdgird I (399–420), Bahrām V Gūr (420–438), and Yazdgird II (438–457) for a period of close to half a century. Even if the Sūren family rose to prominence only at the end of Yazdgird I's reign, they were literally at the center of power for a substantial period of time. While we do not know to which period Ṭabarī's observation of the continued social power of the family refers, it is significant that there was a tremendous continuity of the land holdings of the family in subsequent centuries, most likely into the post-conquest period, for it was only at this point that historians began using such phrases as "to this day". We are fortunate in having this sort of detailed information about the infrastructural power of the Pahlav. The nature of our information and the positive light that it sheds on this Pahlav family most probably hint at the direct hand that the family had in writing this segment of the national history. They are portrayed

[295]Twelve thousand, of course, is one of the eschatological numbers in the Zoroastrian tradition.

[296]Ṭabarī 1999, p. 72, n. 192, de Goeje, 849.

[297]Ṭabarī 1999, p. 103, de Goeje, 868.

[298]During Bahrām V Gūr's reign, Mihr Narseh held the office of *Buzurjfarmadhār*, that is, *wuzurg framādār* (prime minister). Ṭabarī 1999, pp. 99, 105, de Goeje, 866, 870. For the office of *wuzurg framādār* and its relation to *hazārbed*, see Khurshudian 1998, pp. 76–90.

[299]Nöldeke 1879, p. xxiii, n. 1, Nöldeke 1979, p. 37, n. 23.

in extremely positive terms in almost all our histories. While the rivalries of the dynastic families vis-à-vis the crown and among themselves assume a greater and greater focus through the rest of the Sasanian history, the sort of detailed information that we get about the actual basis of the Sūrens' power is lacking for other Pahlav dynasties in subsequent Sasanian history. Notwithstanding, the information on the Sūrens in the first half of the fifth century can be considered indicative of the power that accrued to other Parthian dynastic families in later Sasanian history.

But it is appropriate to pause and consider the precise nature of the Sūren's power during their almost half a century of rule. Here we have a family that basically shared the government with the Sasanian monarchy. The Sūren were the *hazārbeds*, or prime ministers, of the realm. Isolated examples, pertaining to different junctures of Sasanian history, testify to the tremendous power of the *hazārbeds* in the Sasanian polity. As Gyselen points out, a royal inscription of the late third, early fourth century, "names the *hazārbed* among those who *upheld [the Sasanian] Narseh in his reconquest of the throne.*"[300] As we shall see, a *hazārbed* of Hormozd IV's (579–590) reign, one Wahrām Ādurmāh,[301] who held this office during Khusrow I's reign as well, was among the dynastic leaders murdered by Hormozd IV in the course of his efforts at restraining the powers of the nobility in his realm. A third, tremendously powerful *hazārbed* of late Sasanian history, Wistaxm[302] (the infamous Vistāhm of Hormozd IV's and Khusrow II's reigns, from the Parthian Ispahbudhān family), was, as we shall see,[303] not only responsible for bringing Khusrow II to power, but led a rebellion that crippled the Sasanians late in their reign. There is every indication, moreover, that as the examples of the Sūrens and the Ispahbudhān indicate, the tremendously powerful figure of *hazārbed* was generally chosen from the Parthian dynastic families. From the Pahlav Sūrens of the first half of the fifth century, however, were not only the *hazārbeds* of the realm chosen, but also the *vāstryōshān sālār* (Chief Agriculturalist) and the *rathāshtārān sālār* (Commander of the Army). The Sūrens, in other words, had a central hold over the administration, military, and treasury of the realm, not to mention the leadership of the clergy in Fārs. All this they managed to achieve at the very center of the empire. They had extensive, productive lands in their domains and exerted a direct influence over the spiritual direction of the regions under their control. Naturally, with all of this came the manpower that sustained their authority, hence their leadership in the wars that the Sasanians waged during this period. As we shall see, moreover, the military power of these Pahlav families was itself predicated upon the fact that they not only provided the backbone of the Sasanian army with their cavalry, but, through their peasant population, their slave contingents, and possibly mercenaries, also with their infantry. Slave ownership

[300] Gyselen 2001a, p. 21, and note 45.

[301] Gyselen 2001a. See also §2.6.1.

[302] Gyselen 2001a, p. 42–43, seals 3a, 3b.

[303] See page 107ff and §2.7.1.

was in fact a key source of wealth for the dynastic families. We have evidence of slave ownership among the Sūren family as far back as the Arsacid period, when Plutarch informs us that the Parthian general Surena had many slaves in his army.[304] After the siege of Āmid, in southeastern Anatolia,[305] during Qubād's reign (488–531), certain "senior commanders in the Persian army asked Kawad [Qubād] to hand over one-tenth of the captives to them, arguing that the deaths of so many of their relatives during the siege had to be requited."[306] At any rate, Ełishē summed up the powers of Mihr Narseh best: "He was the Prince and the commander (*hramanatar*) of the whole Persian Empire ... There was no one at all who could escape his clutches. Not only the greatest and the least, *but even the king himself obeyed his command.*"[307]

What seems to have been specific to the Sūrens, however, is that their intimate collaboration with the Sasanians ran throughout the course of Sasanian history. In this sense they can be said to have maintained—as Khorenats'i's folkloric tradition and the list of the nobility in the inscriptions of the first Sasanian kings in the inscriptions of *Ka'ba-i Zartusht* (ŠKZ) confirm—the alliance that they had initially made with the early Sasanians at the inception of Ardashīr I's rise to power, so much so that they might even have come to adopt the title of *Pārsīg* itself.[308] The original base of the Sūrens was the region of Sīstān in southeastern Iran, a region incorporated into the quarter of the south after Khusrow I's reforms. The proximity of the traditional territory of the Sūrens to the Sasanians' home territory in Fārs, in other words, might explain the strong hold that this Pahlav dynastic family exerted over the Sasanians at the very center of their power. What powers could have accrued to the rest of the seven great dynastic powers of the realm in their own territories, and away from the reaches of the central authorities during the first half of the fifth century, we can only imagine. Whether or not the Sūrens adopted the epithet Pārsīg, there is no doubt that they were a Parthian family. The reliance of Yazdgird I, Bahrām V Gūr, and Yazdgird II on this great dynastic Parthian family for the very administration and control of their realm is symptomatic of a general

---

[304]Perikhanian 1983, p. 635. The title of Mihr Narseh, *hazārbandak*, has also been interpreted to mean the "owner of a thousand slaves." Ibid., pp. 627–681 and 635.

[305]A strategically important city on the west bank of the Tigris, and the intersection of the north-south and east-west trade routes, the city of Āmid (Amida, modern day Dīyārbakr), was a bone of contention between the Byzantines and the Sasanians, from the early fourth century onward. Sellwood, David, 'Amida', in Ehsan Yarshater (ed.), *Encyclopaedia Iranica*, p. 938, New York, 1991 (Sellwood 1991), p. 998.

[306]The Persians then "murdered the captives with a variety of techniques that none of our sources had the stomach to report." Joshua the Stylite, *The Chronicle of Pseudo-Joshua the Stylite*, Liverpool University Press, 2000, translated with notes and introduction by Frank R. Trombley and John W. Watt (Joshua the Stylite 2000), pp. 62–63.

[307]Ełishē 1982, p. 140. Emphasis mine. For Ełishē, see footnote 309.

[308]Garsoian, in league with Justi and Christensen, suspects that the Sūren Pārsīg are actually a branch of the Sūrens. Buzandaran 1989, *The Epic Histories: Buzandaran Patmut'iwnk'*, Harvard University Press, 1989, translation and commentary by Nina Garsoian (Buzandaran 1989), p. 410, and the sources cited therein.

trend in Sasanian history from the reign of the Sasanian king Pīrūz (459–484) onward: the monarchical institution itself was sustained, and in fact could not have functioned without the help of at least one of the powerful Parthian dynastic families of the realm.

2.2.2 Yazdgird I

The power of Mihr Narseh, as well as the dynastic structure of the Sasanian army during this period, is clearly borne out by the account of Ełishē.[309] According to Ełishē, in Yazdgird I's wars against the Armenians, postulated by some to have been instigated by Mihr Narseh himself, the Sūrenid *hazarpat* gathered the armies of nobility in order to fight against the Armenian rebels. Mihr Narseh then "addressed the greatest nobles at the king's behest, saying: 'Each of you remember the command of the great king and set as your goal the fame of bravery. Choose death over a cowardly life. Do not forget the oil, the crown, the laurels, and the liberal gifts which will be granted you from the royal treasury. *You are lords each of your own province, and you possess great power.* You yourselves know the bravery of the Armenians and the heroic valor of each one of them. *If perchance you are defeated, though alive you will be deprived of the great property you now have. Remember your wives and children, remember your dear friends.*' Likewise he reminded them of their many companions who had fled; although they survived the battle, they had received the penalty of death by the sword. Their sons and daughters and their entire families had been banished, and all their ancestral lands taken from them."[310] In other words, Mihr Narseh organized an army from various regions. Among the contingents that were thus gathered, Ełishē mentions "the contingents of the Aparhatsik‘, the Katishk‘, the Huns and the Gel̃k, and all the rest of the army's elite ... [which were] assembled in one place."[311] The Aparhatsik‘ were the people of *Apar*, that is, Abarshahr, the region of Nīshāpūr of medieval Muslim geographers; the Katishk‘, a population from Herāt; and the Gel̃k, the people of Gīlān.[312] The *hazarpat* Mihr Narseh, then, had not only the power to dictate foreign policy, but to gather the regional armies under his command. While the identities of the commanders of these armies are unfortunately not given, there is little doubt that the armies thus gathered were those of the dynastic families of the realm, who "*are lords each of [their] own province, and ... possess great power.*"

[309] Ełishē was an Armenian priest and historian, who wrote an account of the Armenian uprising of 451 against the Sasanians. While he claims to have been an eye-witness to these events, it is now generally agreed that he probably lived toward the end of the sixth century. It is also agreed, however, that this does not detract from the authenticity of his writing. Ełishē 1982.

[310] Ełishē 1982, p. 167. Emphasis added.

[311] Ełishē 1982, pp. 167–168.

[312] He then set these in order and "extended his battle line ... he disposed the three thousand armed men to the right and left of each elephant, and surrounded himself with the elite of his warriors. In this fashion he strengthened the center [of the army] like a powerful tower or an impregnable castle. He distributed banners, unfurled flags and ordered them to be ready at the sound of the great trumpet." Ełishē 1982, p. 168, nos. 10, 11, and 12 respectively.

For the purposes of later Sasanian history, it is important to keep in mind, therefore, that Mihr Narseh's armies were regional armies of the realm.

Ełishē's account also betrays the circumstances through which Yazdgird I came to be given the epithet the Sinner. Having had the thorough cooperation of one dynastic family, the Pahlav Sūrens, Yazdgird I attempted to impose a feudal arrangement on them by usurping their land. It is rather certain that the policies pursued by Yazdgird I did not sit well with the grandees of the empire—who, except for the Sūren, remain anonymous in our sources—and that these were meant to undermine their wealth and power. According to Thaʿālibī, the elite became base during Yazdgird I's reign, and "the leaders of the Pārsīs were destroyed."[313] It is said that he was "ill thinking, ill-natured, and bloodthirsty." He would use any excuse in order to usurp a grandee's wealth. In this way he "ran the great families into desperation."[314] The *Shāhnāma* devotes an extensive section to Yazdgird I: When he took control of affairs his grandeur increased, but his kindness diminished. The wise became base next to him and he forgot the kingly ways. The nobility lost all their repute with him. His nature turned toward tyranny.[315] The *mōbads* were, likewise, unsettled by his policies.[316] In fact the autocratic rule that Yazdgird I sought to impose, with the very help of the Sūren dynastic family, was most probably of the sort that the other nobility of the realm could not stomach. And hence the fate of the unfortunate king Yazdgird I the Sinner: he is said to have been kicked to death by a white horse that miraculously appeared from the Chishmih-i Sū or Chishmih-i Sabz (the green spring) next to the ancient city of Ṭūs, in northeastern Iran,[317] and

[313]Thaʿālibī 1900, p. 538:

و نکس رؤوس الفرس.

Thaʿālibī 1989, pp. 347–348:

سران پارسیان را سر بکوفت.

[314]Ibn Balkhī 1995, p. 200:

خاندانهاء بزرگ را استیصال کردی.

[315]Ferdowsī 1971, vol. VII, p. 265:

چو شد بر جهان پاد شاهیش راست   بزرگی فزون گشت و مهرش بکاست
خردمند نزدیك او خوار گشت   همه رسم شاهیش بیکار گشت
کنارنگ با پهلوان و ردان   همان دانش و پر هنر بخردان
یکی گشت با باد نزدیك اوی   جفا پیشه شد جان تاریك اوی

Significantly, Ferdowsī's section on Yazdgird I is more elaborate than that of Ṭabarī. Ferdowsī 1971, vol. VII, pp. 264–303; Ṭabarī 1999, pp. 70–74, de Goeje, 847–850. By contrast, Thaʿālibī devotes barely a page and a half to him. Thaʿālibī 1989, pp. 347–348, Thaʿālibī 1900, pp. 537–538. Ibn Balkhī's rendition is likewise short. Ibn Balkhī 1995, pp. 200–203.

[316]See page 335 below.

[317]Monchi-Zadeh, Davoud, *Topographisch-Historische Studien zum Iranischen Nationalepos*, Wiesbaden, 1975 (Monchi-Zadeh 1975), pp. 201–202, and the notes cited therein. The color green and the messianic symbolism of a white horse appearing from a body of water in order to kill an unjust king are all symbolic representations of the God Mihr, in whose safekeeping not only the custody of the *farr* (xwarra or Divine Glory) rests, but who also bestows this *farr* on a suitable royal candidate;

inexplicably disappeared after trampling the king to death. This narrative is sure to have been inserted in the account of the king's death by the Parthian dynasts who cherished the traditions of Parthava at the expense of Persīs, for it puts Yazdgird I in the company of other illustrious figures who met their deaths in one of the capitals of Parthava.[318] Nöldeke realized this: "I think that this narrative was constructed with a purpose in mind . . . They had killed the king, who was despised by the nobility, secretly and in distant Hyrcania (Gurgān), and later spread this story."[319] Nöldeke also suspected that Ferdowsī had fecklessly grafted this tradition onto traditions of his hometown, Ṭūs. This tradition, however, certainly belongs to a far earlier period than that of Ferdowsī. Whether Hyrcania or Ṭūs, the place remains squarely within the traditional homeland of the Parthians and within the realm of at least three powerful Parthian dynastic families. In fact, among the dynastic families whose power had been undermined by Yazdgird I, the one Ferdowsī does list is the Kanārangīyān family. The Kanārangīyān, as we shall see, was a Pahlav family who had their traditional fiefdom in Ṭūs.[320]

2.2.3 Bahrām V Gūr

The power vacuum left at the death of Yazdgird I set the stage for the intrigues of the dynastic families. As Ṭabarī notes, having done away with Yazdgird I, the elite decided not to support any of his offspring as the successor to the crown, and settled instead on a prince from "a collateral line of descent from the first Sasanian king" called Khusrow.[321] We have a number of lists of these nobles who conspired against Yazdgird I's offspring. While two of these lists are anachronistic superimpositions of powerful Parthian figures of the sixth century onto a mid-fifth century account, the list is nonetheless significant for the dynastic leaders it mentions.[322] Among the nobility listed in Bahrām V

see §5.3.1, especially page 354ff.

[318]Ibn Balkhī in fact gives a folkloric rendition of this that is quite significant: "They say that [the horse] was an angel that god . . . made into the guise of a horse and [given the task] of ridding the world of his oppression." Ibn Balkhī 1995, p. 203:

و گفتند این فرشته بود که خدای عزّ و جلّ به صورت اسپی گماشت که ظلم او را از سر جهانیان برداشت.

In *Nuzhat al-Qulūb*, Ḥamdallāh Mustawfī also mentions that the pious, who hold vigil by night near the spring, "behold on the borders of the spring, the forms of water-camels, and water-cows, and water-men [!] . . . seen to graze all around it." Ḥamdallāh Mustawfī, *Nuzhat al-Qulūb*, Leiden, 1919 (Ḥamdallāh Mustawfī 1919), p. 18f, cited in Monchi-Zadeh 1975, p. 201. Ṭūs, the fiefdom of the Kanārangīyān, has a long history of having dignitaries been brought to their death. For this see Pourshariati, Parvaneh, 'Khurāsān and the Crisis of Legitimacy: A Comparative Historiographical Approach', in Neguin Yavari, Lawrence G. Potter, and Jean-Marc Ran Oppenheim (eds.), *Views From the Edge: Essays in Honor of Richard W. Bulliet*, pp. 208–229, Columbia University Press, 2004 (Pourshariati 2004).

[319]Nöldeke 1979, p. 178, n. 10.

[320]See page 266ff.

[321]Ṭabarī 1999, p. 87, de Goeje, 858.

[322]Ferdowsī 1971, vol. VII, p. 387. Besides Ferdowsī's list, we also have one in Dīnawarī 1960, p. 55, Dīnawarī 1967, p. 59. See page 109ff for further discussion.

Gūr's realm, Ferdowsī includes members of the Parthian dynastic families of the Kārin, the Mihrān and the Kanārangīyān: Gostaham, or Vistāhm, who was the minister (*dastūr*); Kharrād-i Mihr Pīrūz, Farhād-i Mihr Burzīn, Bahrām and Pīrūz-i Bahrāmīyān, and Rahām.[323]

After the news of his father's death in 420 reached him, the Prince Shāpūr—who had been appointed king of Armenia by Yazdgird I in 416 CE[324]—hastened to Ctesiphon to take over the throne of his father. But it was not to be. At the capital he was killed by the nobles and the clergy of the realm.[325] At this juncture Bahrām V Gūr (420–438) enters the story. The romanticized story of Bahrām V Gūr's heroic assumption of the throne, in which the prince is forced to snatch the regalia from the midst of two lions, among other things, need not detain us here.[326] According to Ferdowsī, when, after seven years of rule, Yazdgird I fathered Bahrām V Gūr and the astrologers predicted that the child would become a great king, the *mōbads*, the king's minister, and the elite gathered and, anxious that the crown prince would have the same nature as the king, proposed to the king that he should send the prince abroad for his

[323]Rahām is certainly a Mihrān, as we shall see in §2.3 below. In Chapter 5, we will show that the theophoric dimensions of most of these names, incorporating the name of the Mithraic Burzīn Mihr fire of Khurāsān, or simply the god Mihr, also points to the Pahlav affiliation of these figures. There is a strong possibility that the Bahrāmīyān mentioned also belong to the Mihrān family. Other nobles mentioned are Gīlān Shāh, the king of Rayy—Rayy, as we shall see, was an ancient center of the Mihrān; Dād Burzīn, who was in control of Zābulistān, Kārin-i Borzmihr (Burzīn-Mihr), and finally Rādburzīn. Ferdowsī, *Shāhnāma*, Tehran, 1935, edited by S. Nafisi (Ferdowsī 1935), p. 2196. Neither Ferdowsī's nor Dīnawarī's list should be trusted, however, for, as we will argue on page 109ff below, they are in fact anachronistic lists that belong to the period of Khusrow II and his struggle against Bahrām-i Chūbīn, which has been superimposed onto the struggle of Bahrām V Gūr with the nobility. It is most probably as a result of this that Christensen, who took the list at face value, observed that it is remarkable that within the list of names provided by Dīnawarī we do not see the name of the Sūrenid Mihr Narseh, the powerful minister of Yazdgird I and later of Bahrām V Gūr. Christensen 1944, p. 275. This also explains why the wars that Bahrām V Gūr is supposed to have undertaken in the east sound so anachronistic given the historical conditions. See Nöldeke 1879, p. 99, n. 1, p. 103, n. 1, Nöldeke 1979, p. 189, n. 72, and p. 192, n. 80.

[324]Khorenatsʿi 1978, p. 323. Shāpūr had ruled over Armenia for four years at this point. Ibid., p. 326. See also Chaumont 1991, as well as footnote 192.

[325]Khorenatsʿi 1978, p. 326; also see Ṭabarī 1999, p. 87, n. 229. Ferdowsī names these in the following account:

چو در دخمه شد شهریار جهان ز ایران برفتند گریان مهان
کنارنگ با موبد و پهلوان هشیوار دستور روشن روان
همه پاك در پارس گرد امدند بر دخمه یزدگرد امدند
چو گستهم کوپیل کستی بر اسپ دگر قارن گرد پور گشسپ
چو میلاد و چون پارس مرزبان چو پیروز اسپ افگن از گرزبان
دگر هر که بودند ز ایران مهان بزرگان و کنداوران جهان
کجا خوارشان داشتی یزدگرد همه امدند اندر ان شهر گرد

It is important to note that, while this list appears in the *Shāhnāma*, it is not given by Thaʿālibī. Moreover, in Ṭabarī's account, of all the nobility, besides Mihr Narseh and his family, only the name of Vistāhm is given. Nöldeke 1879, p. 96, Nöldeke 1979, p. 162.

[326]Ṭabarī 1999, pp. 91–92, de Goeje, 861–862. Ibn Balkhī 1995, p. 210.

upbringing.[327] The stage was thus set for the exile of Bahrām V Gūr to Mundhir, the king of Ḥīra.[328] Upon Yazdgird I's death Bahrām V Gūr claimed the throne but was faced with the stern opposition of the elite of the realm.[329] Bahrām V Gūr tried to appease them by acknowledging all "[of which] they have accused Yazdgird I of responsibility." In assurance, Bahrām V Gūr promised the nobility of the realm that if God would bestow upon him the royal power, he would "put right all that he [i.e., Yazdgird I] has done wrong and repair what he has split asunder." Bahrām V Gūr allegedly even asked for a year of probationary rule in order to fulfill his promise.[330] Nöldeke remarks that the Sprenger manuscript details these promises as the lowering of taxes, an increase in the army's pay, and the promise of even greater offices to the nobility.[331] As there does not seem to have been a standing army at the disposal of the Sasanians prior to the reforms of Khusrow I, the first two conditions presented to Bahrām V Gūr by the dynastic families in lieu of their agreement to his kingship must have involved one and the same thing. For prior to Khusrow I's reforms,[332] the money the dynasts calculated for the upkeep of each cavalry that they provided was deducted from the amount that they were required to direct to the central treasury. One of Bahrām V Gūr's first acts, therefore, was to resume payment of the army in a timely fashion.[333] He then proceeded to make amends with the nobility who had initially opposed him. He gathered all those whom Yazdgird I had dispersed, and allocated, or, most probably, restored to them various regions (*kishvar*) and their revenues (*badr*).[334] Bahrām V Gūr also maintained

---

[327]Ferdowsī 1935, pp. 2078–2079, Ferdowsī 1971, vol. VII, pp. 266–267.

[328]Ferdowsī 1935, pp. 2080–2085, Ferdowsī 1971, vol. VII, pp. 266–273. Ṭabarī 1999, p. 86, n. 227, de Goeje, 857–858. The city of al-Ḥīra was the capital of the Sasanian vassal kingdom of the Arab Lakhmids, situated on the "fringes of the Iraqi alluvium." See Beeston, A.F.L. and Shahîd, Irfan, 'Ḥīra', in P. Bearman, Th. Bianquis, C.E. Bosworth, E. van Donzel, and W.P. Heinrichs (eds.), *Encyclopaedia of Islam*, Leiden, 2007 (Beeston and Shahîd 2007); Donner 1981, pp. 45–47.

[329]According to Thaʿālibī at least three groups were by now vying to put their own candidate in power: those who were inclined to Bahrām V Gūr, those who favored Khusrow, and others with their own candidate for the Sasanian kingship. At any rate, it is clear that the dynastic forces that conspired in the murder of Yazdgird I and against the succession of his offspring were those whose authority had been directly undermined by Yazdgird I. This is articulated in no uncertain terms by Ferdowsī. Ferdowsī 1935, pp. 2097–2098, Ferdowsī 1971, vol. VII, pp. 285–286. Thaʿālibī 1900, p. 550, Thaʿālibī 1989, p. 355.

[330]Ṭabarī 1999, p. 90, de Goeje, 860.

[331]Nöldeke 1879, p. 187, n. 62, Nöldeke 1979, p. 94, n. 2.

[332]See §2.5.1.

[333]Ferdowsī 1971, vol. VII, p. 309, Ferdowsī 1935, p. 2110.

[334]Ferdowsī 1935, p. 2120:

کسی را کجا رانده بد یزدگرد — بجست و به یك شهرشان کرد گرد
بدان تا شود نامه شهریار — که ازادگان را کند خواستار
فرستاد خلعت به هر مهتری — ببخشید با بدرشان کشوری

with the following variant in Ferdowsī 1971, vol. VII, p. 309:

فرستاد خلعت به هر مهتری — ببخشید باندازه شان کشوری

the Sūrenid Mihr Narseh in the office of prime minister.[335]

2.2.4 Yazdgird II

Of the rather long career of Yazdgird II (438–457) our sources have very little to offer. Invariably their treatment is short.[336] Invariably as well, they give a very positive representation of the king, applauding his justice, although a tradition preserved in Thaᶜālibī highlights the continuing strife between the king and the dynastic families. According to Thaᶜālibī, Yazdgird II followed for a while his father's policies, presumably vis-à-vis the elite. But after a while, he turned away from these. When the elite informed him that his new policies had offended the populace, he objected that "it is not correct for you to presume that the ways in which my father behaved towards you, maintaining you close to him, and bestowing upon you all that bounty, are *incumbent upon all the kings that come after him … each age has its own customs*."[337] Yazdgird II did not name either of his two sons, Hormozd and Pīrūz, as his successor, delegating the matter of succession "to the elite of the realm and the major *marzbāns*."[338] What is certain about Yazdgird II's reign, however, besides his many wars, is that Mihr Narseh continued as his vizier. While ultimately defeated, the Sūrenid Pahlav dynasty led the campaigns of Yazdgird II in the east as well as the west, and is accused by Ełishē of being "guilty of treachery on many counts … [and bearing] responsibility for the ruin of Armenia."[339] On account of these defeats, Mihr Narseh "was [finally] dismissed to his home in great dishonor."[340] The total silence of the sources on Yazdgird II's twenty years of rule is, nevertheless, hard to explain. Which dynastic families, besides that of the Sūrens, played precisely what roles during Bahrām V Gūr and Yazdgird II's reigns unfortunately cannot be ascertained given the sources at our disposal.

2.3 Pīrūz / the Mihrāns

As much as the Sūrens were intimately and powerfully enmeshed in Sasanian rule, the very rise to power of Pīrūz (459–484), the son of Yazdgird II, was brought about through the efforts of a member of another dynastic family:

[335]Ṭabarī 1999, pp. 99, 105, de Goeje, 866, 870. Ṭabarī adds that Bahrām V Gūr "gave them hopes of future beneficence." Ibid., p. 93, de Goeje, 863.

[336]Ṭabarī 1999, pp. 106–109, de Goeje, 871–872; Ferdowsī 1935, p. 2263–2264, Ferdowsī 1971, vol. VIII, pp. 6–7; Thaᶜālibī 1900, pp. 569–573, Thaᶜālibī 1989, pp. 365–368; Dīnawarī 1960, p. 58, Dīnawarī 1967, p. 62, a total of two lines; and Ibn Balkhī 1995, p. 216, a total of four and a half lines.

[337]Thaᶜālibī 1900, pp. 571–572, Thaᶜālibī 1989, p. 367.

[338]Thaᶜālibī 1900, p. 573, Thaᶜālibī 1989, p. 368.

[339]Ełishē attributes these defeats to the "disunity of his army," and maintains that after the defeat Mihr Narseh was "much afraid, for he himself was the cause of all the disasters that had occurred." Ełishē 1982, p. 193. In the aftermath of his defeat and, in order to redirect the king's wrath, Mihr Narseh is also accused by Ełishē of instigating the king's slaughter of the Armenian captives in Nīshāpūr. Ibid., p. 194.

[340]Ełishē 1982, p. 238.

Rahām from the Parthian Mihrāns. Eḷishē specifically informs us that Pīrūz was a protégé of the Mihrānid Rahām. Upon the death of Yazdgird II, when the army of Aryans had become divided in two, according to Eḷishē, the Parthian Mihrānid Rahām was in command of one of the armies of the realm. Rahām defeated and massacred the army of the "king's elder son [Hormozd III] ... and capturing the king's son ordered him to be put to death on the spot ... The surviving troops he brought into submission, unifying the whole army of the Aryans." Rahām then "crowned his own protégé Peroz."[341]

2.3.1 Īzad Gushnasp Mihrān

The significant part played by the house of Mihrān during Pīrūz's reign is corroborated by Armenian historians. In fact, Pīrūz seems to have established what the Armenian historians term foster relationships with the house of Mihrān. According to Łazar P'arpec'i, at the inception of Pīrūz's reign his foster brother (*dayeakordi*, son of one's tutor) was a certain Yĕzatvšnasp (Īzad Gushnasp) "whom he loved very dearly."[342] This Īzad Gushnasp was the son of Aštat (Ashtāt) from the Mihrān family. Father and son played a prominent part in the significant revolt of the Armenians in 451–452, and, together with other, seemingly more significant members of the Mihrān family, also in the course of Pīrūz's reign. Łazar P'arpec'i[343] relates the role played by father and son in the release of the Armenian nobility who had participated in the Armenian revolt[344] and who, together with their priest, had been captured and, by Yazdgird II's order, imprisoned in the vicinity of "Niwšapuh [Nīshāpūr], the capital of the land of Apar," near the village of Rewan.[345] At the inception of Pīrūz's reign, the king ordered his foster-brother Īzad Gushnasp (Yĕzatvšnasp) "to take the Armenian nobility, together with their families and their cavalry, to his father Aštat [i.e., Ashtāt], to the city of Hrev [i.e., Herāt], in order to settle these there and use them as cavalry in Aštat's army."[346]

Łazar P'arpec'i's account gives us significant insight into this branch of the Mihrān family. Īzad Gushnasp was the commander of the fortress of Bolberd, northeast of the Armenian city of Karin. Bolberd, also known as Bolum, was the site of the gold mines run by the Sasanians. Its control was a matter of

[341] Eḷishē 1982, p. 242. Also see Nöldeke 1979, p. 222, n. 6; Ṭabarī 1999, p. 109, de Goeje, 872.

[342] Parpeci 1991, p. 159.

[343] For a critical assessment of Łazar P'arpec'i, who was writing on behalf of the Armenian dynastic house of Vahan Mamikonian, and his work, *History of Łazar P'arpec'i*, see the introduction provided by Robert Thomson, in Parpeci 1991, pp. 1–31.

[344] The Armenian revolt of 451–452 is said to have been precipitated by the efforts of Yazdgird II to impose Mazdaism on the Armenian population. Most likely, these measures were instigated in part by Mihr Narseh. For accounts of the revolt see Eḷishē 1982; Parpeci 1991; Chaumont 1991, pp. 428–429.

[345] Parpeci 1991, p. 133.

[346] "Let them stay there," he said, "with their cavalry, and carry out whatever task Aštat, father of Yĕzatvšnasp, may set them to do." Parpeci 1991, p. 159. We should note the discrepancy between the accounts of Eḷishē and Łazar P'arpec'i regarding the treatment of the Armenian captives in Nīshāpūr. See footnote 339.

great dispute between the Sasanians and the Byzantines.[347] The wealth obtained from the gold mines in Armenia must have been great, for one of the charges brought against the leader of the later Armenian rebellion in 482–484, Vahan Mamikonean,[348] was that he did not allow Persian officials to attend to their duties in the mines. He intended instead to offer the gold to the Byzantine emperor or to the Huns in return for support for his rebellion. In fact, in what Łazar P'arpec'i implies was a ruse, Vahan came to Pīrūz's court with great quantities of gold and argued in the king's presence that this voluntary offering ought to be enough to assure the king of his loyalty to the Sasanian crown.[349] Łazar P'arpec'i informs us as well that the slanderers of this same Vahan reminded Pīrūz "of his [i.e. Vahan's] ancestors one by one: 'Which of them had not disturbed the land of Aryans and had not caused tremendous damage and many deaths'." This, without doubt, is a recollection of the hostility of this branch of the Armenian Arsacids toward the Sasanians.[350] The position of the commander of this valuable fortress was, therefore, a very sensitive post, which was bequeathed to Īzad Gushnasp, described by Łazar P'arpec'i as the confidant of Pīrūz.[351] The father of Īzad Gushnasp, Ashtāt, was the general of the army. The participation of the Mihrāns in the military organization of Pīrūz's realm, however, was not confined to this.

The author of the fascinating *Tārīkh-i Ṭabaristān*, Ibn Isfandīyār, gives us further information on Īzad Gushnasp (rendered by the author as Yazdān) and Ashtāt, whom he considers to be brothers. According to him, they were from the mountainous region of Deylam, southwest of the Caspian Sea, but as a result of antagonism between them and a member of another noble house, "one of the grandees and prominent men of Deylam,"[352] they left Deylam and settled in Ṭabaristān.[353] We cannot ascertain to what particular history Ibn Isfandīyār is referring for his account of the brothers' migration. What is interesting, however, is that the familial relationship of this branch of Mihrāns with Pīrūz is included in the guise of a romantic narrative in the history of Ibn Isfandīyār.[354] In this narrative, Pīrūz dreams of a beauty with whom he falls helplessly in love. To find her, he sends yet another of his relatives from the Mihrān family, one Mihrfīrūz. According to Ibn Isfandīyār, this Mihrānid Mihrfīrūz was also very close to the king, residing with him at the royal court, which Ibn Isfandīyār

---

[347]Procopius 1914, n. 15:18, 32, 33, 22:3, 18. Cited also by Parpeci 1991, p. 205, n. 5.

[348]For Vahan Mamikonean, see Buzandaran 1989, pp. 419–420 and the sources cited therein.

[349]Parpeci 1991, p. 170.

[350]Parpeci 1991, p. 168.

[351]Parpeci 1991, p. 166.

[352]Ibn Isfandīyār, Muḥammad b. Ḥasan, *Tārīkh-i Ṭabaristān*, Tehran, 1941, edited by 'Abbas Iqbal (Ibn Isfandīyār 1941), p. 69:

شخصی را از کبّار دیالم و معروفان ان ناهیت.

[353]Ṭabaristān is an extensive territory south/southeast of the Caspian Sea, originally known by the name Māzandarān. We will discuss its history in more detail in Chapter 4.

[354]Ibn Isfandīyār 1941, pp. 62–71.

locates in Balkh.[355] The beloved turns out to be none other than the daughter of Ashtāt. The king marries this Mihrānid princess and at her behest builds the city of Āmul in Ṭabaristān.[356] What exact status Īzad Gushnasp, Ashtāt, and Ibn Isfandīyār's Mihrfīrūz had at the court of Pīrūz we cannot ascertain. There were other, more significant members of the house of Mihrān, however, about whose status and activities during the reign of Pīrūz we have more information.

Almost contemporaneous with the Armenian revolt of 482, the Sasanians experienced troubles in Georgia.[357] They seem to have feared the cooperation of the two rebellious regions, and the possibility of the Georgians enlisting the aid of the Huns. While Zarmihr of the house of Kārin[358] was sent against the rebellious forces of Vahan Mamikonean and other insurgent Armenian nobles,[359] a certain Mihrān was sent to the Georgian front.[360] As events unfolded, Mihrān engaged his forces also against the Armenians.[361] In his wars against the Armenians, Mihrān is reported to have been surrounded by a numerous army and powerful warriors. His role, not only as one of Pīrūz's foremost generals but as his confidant, is underlined in Łazar P'arpec'i's narrative.[362] Mihrān advised Vahan Mamikonean to submit to Pīrūz, assuring Vahan that he would intercede on his behalf to the Sasanian king. The king, he told Vahan, "loves me and listens to my words ... I shall beseech the king and reconcile him with you. And whatever it is right for you to be given, I shall try to see that he

[355]Ibn Isfandīyār 1941, p. 66:

مهرفیروز نام خویشی داشت به قربت او قرابت مخصوص.

[356]Ibn Isfandīyār 1941, p. 72. The Mihrāns are the third Parthian dynastic family who are given credit for the construction of the city of Āmul in Ibn Isfandīyār's account. This, doubtless, is a reflection of the different Parthian traditions on urban construction in Ṭabaristān circulating in the region. For the etymology of the city's name, see Marquart 1931, p. 110.

[357]For the intimate connection of Iran to Georgia, analogous in cultural terms to that which existed between Iran and Armenia, see Lang 1983.

[358]As we shall see shortly, another important Kārinid leader is Sukhrā. Our sources sometimes confuse Zarmihr with Sukhrā. Moreover, toward the end of Qubād's reign, a son of Sukhrā with the name Zarmihr also appears. It is rather unlikely that this is the same Zarmihr mentioned here. Christensen suggested that Sukhrā seems to have been the family name of the dynastic family of the Kārins to which Zarmihr belonged. Christensen 1944, p. 294, n. 5. Equally plausible is that Zarmihr was the name of both Sukhrā's father and son.

[359]The commander-in-chief of the operations in Armenia during this violent phase of the Armenian–Sasanian relationship was Zarmihr Hazarwuxt (*hazārbed*), who prior to the outbreak of the revolt was commander-in-chief of the forces fighting the rebellion of the Georgian king Vaxt'ang (Vakhtang I Gorgasali, 452–502), in Albania (Arrān). Under his command Zarmihr (see previous note) had contingents of Armenians. Parpeci 1991, pp. 166, 184. For a fascinating article on Caucasia and its topography, and the role of the Parthians, specifically the Mihrāns, in Arrān, see Minorsky, V., 'Caucasia IV', *Bulletin of the School of Oriental and African Studies* 15, (1953), pp. 504–529 (Minorsky 1953). An assessment of the connection of this history to the rebellion of Bābak Khurramdīn in Azarbāyjān in the early ninth century will be made in the author's forthcoming work.

[360]Parpeci 1991, pp. 172–189.

[361]Parpeci 1991, pp. 192–193.

[362]Parpeci 1991, p. 193.

gives."[363] It is to Mihrān that Vahan Mamikonean likewise argued his case for his loyal behavior toward the Sasanian kings and the unfair recompense that he and Armenia had received through the Sasanians' destructive policies in the region.[364] Mihrān urged the insurgent rebels to convert and "take refuge in fire and worship the sun." In the midst of his negotiations with the Armenians, Mihrān was suddenly summoned back to the court by Pīrūz.[365]

2.3.2 Shāpūr Mihrān

During the next campaign season in the spring of 484, it was the turn of the Kārinid Zarmihr to be sent to Armenia with a large force. After a while, however, Zarmihr was also recalled by Pīrūz, who informed him of his attack on the Hephthalites.[366] The king then advised Zarmihr first to go to Georgia and either to kill or expel the Georgian king. At this point in his narrative Łazar P'arpec'i introduces a certain Šapuh (Shāpūr) of the house of Mihrān. Pīrūz had advised Zarmihr to install this Shāpūr Mihrān as the *marzpan* of Georgia with a detachment of troops. Whatever the case, Shāpūr Mihrān takes to Bolberd some of the Armenians earlier captured by Zarmihr, specifically the wives of the Kamsarakan noble house, and entrusts them to the care of Īzad Gushnasp, the Mihrānid commander of the fortress in control of the gold mines.[367] Shāpūr Mihrān seems to have been from the same branch of the Mihrāns as Īzad Gushnasp, for as the latter is described as a foster brother of Pīrūz, the former also partook in the *dayeak* system of foster family. He too is described as having known the devotion of the Kamsarakan family to Christianity because he had been raised among the Armenians.[368] Like Īzad Gushnasp, Shāpūr Mihrān had the power of intercession with the Sasanian king. He advised the Kamsarakan family: "fear not, and do not abandon the service of the king of kings ... [for] through my mediation, I shall have the king of kings forgive your guilt. Whatever is right I shall have granted to you ... And because I love you like sons, I am advising you like children as to the way you can live and survive." That the Mihrāns at this point no longer enjoyed the same power as the Kārins is borne

[363]It is significant, as we will discuss on page 392ff below, that the term used by Łazar P'arpec'i for mediation is *mijnord*. Parpeci 1991, p. 193 and n. 1.

[364]Parpeci 1991, pp. 193–196.

[365]Parpeci 1991, p. 199 and 196.

[366]Parpeci 1991, p. 202. The identity of the Hephthalites/White Huns (or Hayāṭila), a steppe people from Mongolia, is unknown. The Armenian sources call them, anachronistically, "Kushāns or Huns who were Kushāns." They were apparently just beginning to arrive in Transoxiana, Bactria, and the northern fringes of Khurāsān at this time. They are mentioned in the Chinese sources as having their original home in Central Asia. It was in the fifth century that they moved to Bactria. Once there, they adopted the local written language, Bactrian, which was written in modified Greek. For the Hephthalites, see Bivar, A.D.H., 'Hayāṭila', in P. Bearman, Th. Bianquis, C.E. Bosworth, E. van Donzel, and W.P. Heinrichs (eds.), *Encyclopaedia of Islam*, Leiden, 2007b (Bivar 2007b); Frye, Frye 1983, p. 146.

[367]Parpeci 1991, p. 205. See §2.3.1.

[368]See Parpeci 1991, p. 206, and n. 1, where Thomson remarks that this is a reference to the system of *san* and *dayeak*.

out by the fact that they were put under the command of the Kārinid Zarmihr in Armenia. In the midst of his wars against the Armenians, Shāpūr Mihrān received a grievous and distressing letter from the "Persian nobles and ... other relatives and friends who had escaped the crushing defeat by the Hephthalites," informing him of the death of Pīrūz in battle.[369] It is noteworthy that according to Łazar P'arpec'i, Shāpūr had other relatives who had participated in Pīrūz's campaigns against the Hephthalites. It is also significant that in line with the traditions contained in the *X^w adāy-Nāmag*, the messenger who brought the news of the disaster to Shāpūr blamed the whole affair on the folly of Pīrūz.[370]

Now it is almost certain that in the figure of Shāpūr Mihrān we are actually dealing with the son of the great Mihrān, the general who was sent against the Armenian rebel Vahan Mamikonean in 481–482. This was, in other words, yet another father and son couple from the house of Mihrān with whom Pīrūz was on intimate terms, as he was with Īzad Gushnasp and Ashtāt from the same family. Shāpūr and his father, however, are also closely connected with Pīrūz's administration and described by the Armenian sources as the king's closest confidants. They had the authority not only to cajole the king but, together with the Kārins, to function as king-makers by bringing Bilāsh (484–488) to power on Pīrūz's death. It is quite possible that the elder Mihrān was recalled by Pīrūz to participate in the Hephthalite campaign, leaving the son to deal with the Armenian situation alone. This would explain Shāpūr Mihrān's own recall after the news of Pīrūz's disastrous defeat, the murder of the king, and the loss of the greater part of his army. It was at this point, then, that Shāpūr Mihrān hastened to the capital to take part in the selection of the new king, Bilāsh, an appointment in which the Mihrāns must have followed the lead of the Kārinid Sukhrā, to be discussed below. At any rate one thing is clear: the prominent role of the Mihrāns both in the Armenian campaign and at the court of Pīrūz, and his successor, Bilāsh, is amply demonstrated through the narratives of Łazar P'arpec'i of the events of 482–484.

2.4 Bilāsh and Qubād / the Kārins

2.4.1 Bilāsh

Bilāsh's accession (484–488), however, marks the start of an all-out dynastic rivalry between the Mihrān and the Kārin families.[371] Just as the career of the

[369]Parpeci 1991, p. 214.

[370]"The cause was no one else save the king." Parpeci 1991, p. 214. The theme of the covenant that Pīrūz had made with the Hephthalite king and then broken, as well as the notion of an unjust war, also looms large in Łazar P'arpec'i's narrative. Ibid., pp. 214–215. For the significance of this, see Chapter 5, especially page 380ff.

[371]After Pīrūz's death yet another civil war engulfed Iran. According to Ṭabarī, when Bilāsh assumed the throne, he had to contend for power with one of his nephews, Qubād, who was twice forced to flee to the east. But sources based on Ibn Muqaffaʿ claim that Qubād fled only once, from his brother Jāmāsp—whose saga we will follow in §4.3.1—when he was forced to stay with the Hephthalites for two years as a hostage. Bilāsh nonetheless was forced to fight his other brother

Sūrens and the Mihrāns enmeshed the Sasanian monarchs during the first half of the fifth century, the tremendous power of another Parthian dynastic family, the Kārins, overshadowed the very rule of Sasanian monarchs for more than half a century subsequent to this.[372] The career of Sukhrā of the Kārin therefore takes the center stage during the latter part of the reign of Pīrūz (459–484), the entire reign of Bilāsh (484–488), and the first part of the reign of Qubād (488–531). In fact, from the end of Pīrūz's reign to the Mazdakite uprising,[373] the fortunes of the Sasanian kings can best be understood through the saga of the Parthian house of the Kārin.

2.4.2 Sukhrā Kārin

In Ṭabarī's narrative,[374] transmitted through Ibn Muqaffaʿ, Sukhrā appears as the avenger of Pīrūz's second, humiliating, and foolhardy defeat at the hands of his enemies in the east,[375] a defeat the "like[s] of which ... [the Persian army] had never before experienced," when Pīrūz's "womenfolk, his wealth, and his administrative bureaus" had fallen into enemy hands. Sukhrā is here identified as coming from the district of Ardashīr Khurrah.[376] In a heroic feat, Sukhrā defeated the enemy, rescued the captives, and secured all the wealth that had fallen into enemy hands. According to Ṭabarī, when Sukhrā returned victorious to Iran, the Persians "received him with great honor, extolled his feats, and *raised him to a lofty status such as none but kings were able to attain after*

Zarih (or Zarīr) for the throne. Nöldeke 1879, p. 133, n. 6, Nöldeke 1979, p. 236, n. 61. Ṭabarī 1999, p. 126, n. 324.

[372]As the career of Surena of the house of Sūren found its way into the national historical tradition in the saga of the mythical hero Rustam, so too the Kārins are almost certain to have left their mark on the national historiography. Nöldeke compares the part played by Sukhrā in avenging Pīrūz's humiliating defeat to that of Kārin in the legendary sections of the national history. Nöldeke, Theodore, 'Das iranische Nationalepos', *Grundriss der iranischen Philologie* II, (1896), pp. 130–211 (Nöldeke 1896), p. 9; Ṭabarī 1999, pp. 120–121, and n. 308, de Goeje, 880.

[373]For a discussion of the controversy surrounding the chronology of the Mazdakite uprising, see §2.4.5 below.

[374]Ṭabarī gives three narratives on the rule of Pīrūz. The first one is apparently taken from Ibn Hishām. The second, much longer and more detailed, was, according to Nöldeke, transmitted through Ibn Muqaffaʿ. And a third, given without attribution, is also found in Ferdowsī's *Shāhnāma*. Nöldeke 1879, p. 119, n. 1, p. 121, n. 1, and p. 128, n. 3, Nöldeke 1979, pp. 200–201, p. 227, n. 19, p. 229, n. 21, p. 233, n. 43. Cited also in Ṭabarī 1999, p. 111, n. 287.

[375]Bosworth notes that Pīrūz actually undertook three wars against the peoples of the east. "At the time of his first war with the powers of the eastern lands, Fīrūz's enemies there were probably still the Kidarites, who controlled Balkh, as they were the Persian ruler's foes in his second war of 467 ... It would thus have been natural for Fīrūz to have sought aid from the Kidarites' enemies, soon to replace them as the dominant power in Transoxiana and Bactria, the Hephthalites, and equally natural that he should fall out with his erstwhile allies once the formidable power of the Hephthalites was firmly established just across his eastern frontiers." Ṭabarī 1999, p. 110, n. 284, de Goeje, 873. For the wars of Pīrūz against the Hephthalites in the east and the Caucasus also see Joshua the Stylite 2000, pp. 10–21.

[376]In Ṭabarī's first narrative, Sukhrā appeared as the avenger of the death of Pīrūz and is identified as a man from Fārs.

him."[377] Here, Ṭabarī gives the exalted genealogy of the Kārins, who traced their descent, as it had become fashionable, even among the Sasanians, from Pīrūz's reign onward,[378] to the Kayānid king Manūchihr.[379]

According to Ferdowsī, before leaving for his last war in the east Pīrūz left his brother Bilāsh, presumably as vice-regent, in the capital. He installed Sukhrā, whose name is rendered first as Surkhāb and later as Sūfrāy in Ferdowsī, as minister to Bilāsh. Upon hearing of Pīrūz's defeat, Sukhrā set out to avenge the king. He defeated Khushnavāz, the Hephthalite king, negotiated a truce, and returned to Iran in the company of Qubād,[380] who had been taken captive by Khushnavāz.[381]

Łazar P'arpec'i emphasized the dominant role in Bilāsh's accession played by the Kārins, although he calls their main leader Zarmihr rather than Sukhrā.[382] After detailing the mindless follies of Pīrūz, the Kārinid Zarmihr instructed the incumbent king Bilāsh: "[You are] to reduce by soft words and friendship the nations who have rebelled; to acknowledge each person among the Aryans and non-Aryans according to his individual worth, to recognize and distinguish the excellent and the worthless, to consult with the wise; to love well-wishers, but to scorn and destroy the envious and slanderous."[383] Even Christensen admits that the Kārinid Zarmihr (Sukhrā?) was the real ruler of Iran during Bilāsh's short reign.[384] In Ferdowsī's narrative, after avenging the death of Pīrūz and returning to the capital in the company of Qubād, the Kārinid Sukhrā became the true ruler of the Sasanian realm. Sukhrā gets the lion's share of Ferdowsī's attention in this account. He was the hero responsible for restoring kingship. All the other grandees of the empire were at his command, all the affairs of the country under his control.[385]

---

377 Ṭabarī 1999, p. 117, de Goeje, 877. Emphasis mine.

378 See page 385.

379 Ṭabarī 1999, p. 117, de Goeje, 878. In a third narrative—this version is also very much in agreement with that given by Ibn Isfandīyār—Ṭabarī maintains that Sukhrā was in fact put as deputy of the king over the cities of Ctesiphon and Bahurasīr (Veh Ardashīr)—the two royal residences. In this narrative, Sukhrā is made the governor of Sīstān and the two cities. Ibid., p. 118. Other sources claim Sukhrā to be the governor (*marzbān*) of Sīstān and Zābulistān. Thaʿālibī 1900, p. 582, Thaʿālibī 1989, p. 374. His name is given as Shūkhar in Dīnawarī 1960, p. 60, Dīnawarī 1967, p. 63. In the Iranian national history, the Kayānid king Manūchihr avenges the murder of Fereydūn's son, Iraj, by his brothers. During his reign the incessant feud between Iran and Tūrān begins, to which the Sīstāni cycle of the Iranian national history is added. For the primacy of Manūchihr, see page 375ff in Chapter 5.

380 According to Christensen (via Nöldeke and Ṭabarī) it is a daughter of Pīrūz, the future mother-in-law of Qubād, who is brought back, not Qubād himself; and even that he thinks is fiction. Christensen 1944, p. 296.

381 Ferdowsī 1935, p. 2286–2287, Ferdowsī 1971, vol. VIII, pp. 26–27.

382 See footnote 358.

383 Parpeci 1991, p. 218.

384 Christensen 1944, p. 295.

385 Ferdowsī 1935, p. 2286–2287, Ferdowsī 1971, vol. VIII, pp. 27–28:

مهان را همه چشم بر سوفرای — از او گشته شاد و بدو داده رای ...
بید سوفرای از جهان بی همال — همی رفت زین گونه تا چار سال

2.4.3 Qubād

Finally Sukhrā set out to depose Bilāsh and crown Qubād (488–531) king. He reproached Bilāsh that he did not know the way of kingship, making a mockery of it, and that Qubād was more fit for this.[386] So after four years of Bilāsh's rule, Sukhrā deposed him from the throne and installed Qubād in his stead.

The Kārin/Mihrān rivalry reached its heights during Qubād's reign. It was one of the most important instigators of Qubād's Mazdakite phase, and it most certainly precipitated Qubād's and Khusrow I's (531–579) reforms,[387] the most important dimension of which was concentrating the power of the Sasanians in the monarch's hand and undermining the centrifugal tendencies of the dynastic houses of the empire. What, then, was the nature of this rivalry? With a juvenile king at the throne, according to the chroniclers, Sukhrā ruled the country. It was as if Qubād was not king, for Sukhrā controlled all the affairs of the empire. None had access to the king except Sukhrā, and even the clergy were not under Qubād's authority.[388] Ṭabarī's narrative corroborates that of Ferdowsī. He portrays Sukhrā's power in an account detailing Qubād's supposed flight to the Khāqān of the Turks during Bilāsh's reign.[389] When Qubād finally came back to Madā'in (Ctesiphon), "he sought out Sūkhrā ... [and] delegated to him all his executive powers."[390] Sukhrā "was in charge of government of the kingdom and the management of affairs ... [T]he people came to Sūkhrā and undertook all their dealings with him, treating Qubād as a person of no importance and regarding his commands with contempt."[391] Ferdowsī provides

---

نبودی جز انچیز کو خواستی   جهان را به رای خود اراستی

[386]Ferdowsī 1971, vol. VIII, pp. 26–27, Ferdowsī 1935, p. 2286–2287:

چو فرمان او در جهان گشت فاش   به چربی بپرداخت گاه از بلاش
بدو گفت شاهی ندانی همی   بدانرا ز نیکان ندانی همی
همی پادشاهی به بازی کنی   ز کژی و از بی نیازی کنی
قباد از تو در کار دانا تر است   بدین پادشاهی توانا تر است
به ایوان خویش اندر امد بلاش   نیارست گفتن که ایدر مباش

Dīnawarī confirms that Qubād was put on the throne by Sukhrā. Dīnawarī 1960, pp. 59–60, Dīnawarī 1967, p. 64.

[387]See §2.5.1 below.

[388]Ferdowsī 1971, vol. VIII, pp. 30–31, Ferdowsī 1935, p. 2289:

جوان بود، سالش سه پنج و یکی   ز شاهی ورا بهره بد اندکی
همی راند کار جهان سوفرای   قباد اندر ایران نبد کدخدای
همه کار او پهلوان راندی   کسی را بر شاه ننشاندی
نه موبد بد او را نه فرمان نه رای   جهان پر ز دستوری سوفرای
چنین بود تا بیست و یك ساله گشت   بجام اندرون باده چون لاله گشت
بیامد بر تاجور سوفرای   بدستوری بازگشتن بجای
سپهبد خود و لشکرش ساز کرد   بزد کوس و اهنگ شیراز کرد

[389]According to Bosworth the historicity of this flight is difficult to accept, "Ṭabarī having confused, probably, Qubād's one or two stays with the Hephthalites." Ṭabarī 1999, p. 128, n. 330.

[390]Ṭabarī 1999, p. 130, de Goeje, 884–885.

[391]Ṭabarī 1999, p. 131, de Goeje, 885.

even more details on the extent of Sukhrā's power. After five years in which Sukhrā was for all practical purposes ruling, his power went beyond what the king could tolerate, and Qubād began to assert his control.[392] One of his first acts was to send Sukhra into exile, away from Ctesiphon, to his native Shīrāz in southwestern Iran. Once back in his native land, according to Ferdowsī, Sukhrā controlled all except the kingly crown. He boasted of putting the king on the throne. It was to him that various regions and the other members of the elite paid their tribute. Rumor had it that the king ruled only in name, for neither the treasury nor the army were under his control. No one heeded his orders. Those privy to Qubād enquired into the reasons behind his complacency. In search of a remedy, Qubād decided against sending an army to attack Sukhrā, lest he rebel. In any case, Qubād had no army to speak of, as the military was under Sukhrā's control.[393]

Two points stand out in Ferdowsī's depiction of Sukhrā's power. One is the wealth at the disposal of the chief of the Kārins. Great wealth is in fact the one common denominator of all the Pahlav dynasts covered in this study. Ferdowsī highlights a number of times how the Parthian Kārinid Sukhrā—like the Sūren in the first half of the fifth century—was in control of the treasury of the realm to which all the tributes of the various provinces came. All regions under the presumed authority of the Sasanian king Qubād, as well as all the elite of his realm, paid their taxes (*bāj*) to Sukhrā. In fact Sukhrā actively solicited these.[394]

[392]According to Ferdowsī, Qubād was sixteen years old when Sukhrā promoted him as the Sasanian king; see footnote 388.

[393]Ferdowsī 1971, vol. VIII, pp. 30-31, Ferdowsī 1935, pp. 2290–2291:

همی رفت شادان سوی شهر خویش   ز هر کام برداشته بهر خویش
همه پارس او را شده چون رهی   همه بود جز تاج شاهنشی
بران بد که من شاه بنشاندم   به شاهی برو افرین خواندم ...
همی باژ جستی ز هر کشوری   ز هر نامداری و هر مهتری
چو اگاهی امد سوی کیقباد   ز شیراز و از کار بیداد و داد
همی گفت هر کس که جز نام شاه   ندارد از ایران نه گنج و سپاه
نه فرمانش باشد به چیزی نه رای   جهان شد همه بنده سوخرای
هر انکس که بود رازدار قباد   برو این سخنها همی کرد یاد
که از پادشاهی به نامی بسند   چرا کردی ای شهریار بلند
ز گنج تو اگنده تر گنج او   بباید گسست از جهان رنج او
همه پارس چون بنده او شدند   بزرگان پرستنده او شدند
ز گفتار بد شد دل کیقباد   ز رنجش بدل بر نکرد ایچ یاد

[394]Ferdowsī 1971, vol. VIII, p. 31, Ferdowsī 1935, p. 2290:

همی باج جستی ز هر کشوری   ز هر نامداری و هر مهتری

Or again, Ferdowsī 1971, vol. VIII, p. 31, Ferdowsī 1935, p. 2290:

ز گنج تو اگنده تر گنج او   بباید گسست از جهان رنج او

Or again when Shāpūr Rāzī, on whom see §2.4.4 below, advises Qubād to write a letter to Sukhrā maintaining among other things, that from kingship all that has remained at his disposal is the title and an empty treasury. Ferdowsī 1971, vol. VIII, p. 33, Ferdowsī 1935, p. 2291:

بگویی که از تاج شاهنشهی   مرا بهره رنجست و گنج تهی

A second characteristic of the Pahlav dynasts is their control of independent sources of manpower. The Sasanians came to rely on them militarily. Ferdowsī makes this abundantly clear in his narrative, never more so than when he describes Qubād's lack of manpower with which to confront Sukhrā. In fact, Qubād shirked the possibility of sending troops against Sukhrā, had he been able to, for this would have made Sukhrā an even more formidable enemy and led him to rebellion.[395] The manpower at the disposal of the Parthian dynastic families is a theme reiterated again and again in the chronicles. Detailing the crises incapacitating the monarchy in the wake of the rebellions of Bahrām-i Chūbīn and Vistāhm in the late sixth, early seventh centuries below,[396] we still observe this continued reliance of the Sasanians on the military force provided by the Parthian dynasts even after Khusrow I's ostensible military reforms and the creation of a standing army.

2.4.4 Shāpūr Rāzī Mihrān

It is indicative of the nature of the power of the dynastic families during this period that in order to rescue his kingship from the stranglehold of the Kārins, Qubād was forced to turn to another Parthian dynastic family, the Mihrāns. When Qubād complained that he did not have an army, or a commander in chief (*razmkhāh*), for that matter, with which to confront Sukhrā, he was reminded that he did still possess loyal subjects who were powerful. Our sources are unanimous in calling the Mihrānid protagonist at whose hands and power Sukhrā and the Kārins lost their hegemony as one Shāpūr Rāzī, that is, Shāpūr of Rayy, a clear reference to the Mihrānid power base in Ṭabaristān, of which Rayy was the chief city. Significantly, Dīnawarī clearly identifies him as Shāpūr Rāzī, "one of the sons of the great Mihrān, and his [i.e., Qubād's] governor over Khuṭrāniya and Babylonia."[397] Ṭabarī identifies him as the supreme commander of the land (*iṣbahbadh al-bilād*) and remarks, as does Ferdowsī in his long narrative, that Shāpūr Rāzī was asked to come to the king with the troops under his command.[398] Ferdowsī leaves us no doubt that in his recall of Shāpūr Rāzī,

---

تويي با جناه و منم با گناه نخواهم که خوانی مرا نیز شاه

395Dīnawarī 1960, p. 65, Dīnawarī 1967, p. 69; Ferdowsī 1971, vol. VIII, pp. 31–32, Ferdowsī 1935, pp. 2290–2291:

همی گفت اگر من فرستم سپاه سر او بگردد، شود رزمخواه
چنو دشمنی کرده باشم به گنج ازو دید باید بسی درد و رنج
ندارم در ایران همی رزمخواه کز ایدر شود پیش او با سپاه
بدو گفت فرزانه مندیش از این که او شهریاری شود بافرین؟
ترا بندگانند و سالار هست که سایند با چرخ گردنده دست
چو شاپور رازی بیاید ز جای بدرد دل بد کنش سفرای

396See §2.6.3 and §2.7.1 respectively.

397Khuṭrāniya and Bābil were districts in southern Iraq, irrigated by the Ṣūrā canal. Donner 1981, p. 163; Dīnawarī 1960, p. 65, Dīnawarī 1967, p. 69.

398Ṭabarī 1999, pp. 130–131, de Goeje, 885.

Qubād was relying on one of the staunchest enemies of Sukhrā.[399] It was he who could destroy the Kārinid Sukhrā. The aftermath of Qubād's beckoning of Shāpūr Rāzī was a war that took place not between Qubād and Sukhrā, but between the agnates of two dynastic families: the Mihrānid Shāpūr Rāzī and the Kārinid Sukhrā. Together with his army, Shāpūr Rāzī collected that of other discontented nobles and set out against Sukhrā to Shīrāz. Sukhrā was defeated, captured, and brought back to Ctesiphon together with his treasury. Even in captivity in Ctesiphon, however, he was deemed to be too powerful. And so Sukhrā was put to death.[400]

The rivalry of the houses of Kārin and Mihrān, and the ephemeral positions of one or the other vis-à-vis the monarchy is said to have become proverbial in their contemporary society. The expression that "Sukhrā's wind has died away, and a wind belonging to Mihrān has now started to blow," circulated among the people.[401] Still, as we shall see, it was with the aid of Zarmihr, the son of Sukhrā, that Qubād regained his throne after being deposed by the nobility and the clergy on account of his adoption of the Mazdakite creed.[402]

The rivalry between the Parthian Mihrāns and the Kārins during this period also highlights a crucial factor in the dynamic between the monarchy and the nobility that is symptomatic of the sociopolitical history examined here: in spite of their corporate interests, the various Parthian dynastic families did not always function in a unitary fashion. The maneuverability of the monarchy, and the ability of the Sasanians to sustain themselves in the face of Parthians' hold on the monarchy was, therefore, to a great degree contingent on the divisions and rivalries among the Pahlav dynasts. Division within one and the same family—or even patricide and fratricide, a common enough means of succession at the disposal of the Sasanian monarchy—were certainly nothing unprecedented, as the careers of Bahrām-i Chūbīn[403] and his brother Gorduyih,[404] and that of Sukhrā and his son Zarmihr, amply demonstrate.

---

399 "Nowhere in the world was there a greater enemy of Sukhrā than he." Ferdowsī 1971, vol. VIII, p. 32, Ferdowsī 1935, p. 2291:

که بر سوفرا دشمن اندر جهان — نبودی جز او اشکار و نهان

400 Ferdowsī 1971, vol. VIII, p. 35, Ferdowsī 1935, p. 2293:

چنین گفت پس شاه را رهنمون — که یارند با او همه تیسفون

همان لشکر و زیردستان ما — ز دهقان و از دور پرستان ما

گر او اندر ایران بماند درست — ز شاهی بباید ترا دست شست

401 Ṭabarī 1999, p. 132, de Goeje, 885.

402 Dīnawarī 1960, p. 65, Dīnawarī 1967, p. 69. For a discussion of the Mazdakite rebellion, see §2.4.5 and §5.2.7.

403 For the rebellion of Bahrām-i Chūbīn, see §2.6.3 below.

404 Ṭabarī 1999, p. 308, de Goeje, 997.

2.4.5 Mazdakite uprising

Much has been said about the hold of the so-called nobility over Qubād in his initial stages of his kingship, and the fact that this situation precipitated his ultimate resort to the Mazdakite creed in order to stamp out their power.[405] The history of the Sasanians at this crucial juncture will lack any substance, however, if we fail to identify the Parthian dynasts involved and ignore their far reaching rivalries. The conventional narrative of this episode of Sasanian history runs something like this: So strong was the hold of the nobility over the monarchy that at some point during his long career, presumably during his second term in office, Qubād rebelled against them. A felicitous opportunity presented itself to the king in the form of the Mazdakite doctrine, in whose adherents Qubād is said to have found the perfect constituency with which to combat the powers of the nobility.[406] And so, presumably, during his reign and with his tacit support, was unleashed one of the most remarkable upheavals in Sasanian history: the Mazdakite uprising. The effects of this rebellion on the nobility are thought to have been nothing short of devastating. The financial and social infrastructures that sustained the nobility are thought to have been attacked systematically by a mass popular movement. Whole families among the nobility are presumed to have lost their power in an apparently extended revolutionary phase, although the chronology again is utterly confusing. As a result of the Mazdakite predilection for *ibāha 'l-nisā* (communal sharing of women), by the time Khusrow I took power, multitudes of children are said to have been conceived out of wedlock by noble women! It has even been argued that the Mazdakite uprising was orchestrated from above in order to achieve Qubād's aim after his epiphany that the noble houses had become overbearing.[407] It was presumably also to undermine the dependency of the monarchy on the manpower of the nobility that Qubād began a cadastral survey as a preliminary step toward a taxation reform. As his son's later reforms, this was meant to bring enough resources to the central treasury to establish a standing army, a new nobility that would ensure the strength of the Sasanian monarch in the face of centrifugal powers within his realm. In short, as Zeev Rubin observes, while there has been much controversy about the nature and chronology of the Mazdakite uprising, there has been little disagreement about its outcome: "The old Iranian aristocracy was its main victim, and once its power was swept away the road to change was opened."[408]

[405] We will discuss the popular and possibly communist nature of the Mazdakite rebellion below in §5.2.7.

[406] See §5.2.7.

[407] Gaube, H., 'Mazdak: Historical Reality or Invention?', *Studia Iranica* 11, (1982), pp. 111–122 (Gaube 1982). Also see Shaki, Mansour, 'The Cosmogonical and Cosmological Teachings of Mazdak', in *Papers in Honour of Professor Mary Boyce*, vol. 24 of *Acta Iranica*, pp. 527–543, Leiden, 1985 (Shaki 1985).

[408] Rubin 1995, p. 229.

An incapacitated nobility opened the way, therefore, it has been argued, for the unprecedented reforms of Qubād's son and successor, Khusrow I. Rubin again recapitulates the near consensus of the field: "Something drastic must have happened to enable a king to override the powerful nobility of the country which so far [had] ... successfully managed to block any initiative for change. The explanation is supplied by the Mazdakite revolt under Khusrow I's father and predecessor Kavād I."[409] And so enters one of the most paradigmatic figures in Sasanian history, Khusrow I Nowshīrvān, of Immortal Soul, whose auspicious reign epitomizes what the Sasanians had always aspired to be and nearly achieved, a centralized, powerful oriental polity. What, however, was the fate of the Mihrāns and other great feudal families in the wake of the Mazdakite uprising?

However one answers the question of periodization, and whatever the nature of Khusrow I's fiscal and military reforms, there is no doubt about this, as we shall see: the pattern of a confederacy between the Sasanian monarchy and the Parthian dynastic families did not change. Neither did the history of the ebb and flow of the fortunes of the dynasts vis-à-vis each other and the monarchy. Players on the scene might have changed, but the paradigm of Sasanian history remained unscathed. For one of the astounding facts of the post-Mazdakite and post-reform narrative of Sasanian history is that with the Kārins conveniently out of the way, thanks to the resources and manpower of the Mihrāns, the stage was now set for the ascendancy, once more, of the Mihrān during Khusrow I's rule. Another great feudal family, however, the Ispahbudhān, likewise assumed center stage in subsequent Sasanian history.

2.5 Khusrow I Nowshīrvān / the Mihrāns, the Ispahbudhān, and the Kārins

2.5.1 Khusrow I's reforms

The kernel of the image of Khusrow I Nowshīrvān is that of a powerful king who, through his reforms, inaugurated one of the most splendid phases of Sasanian history, restoring, in the tradition of Ardashīr I, Shāpūr I, and Shāpūr II, the normative dimensions of Sasanian kingship: a powerful centralized monarchy capable of mustering the empire's resources to stabilize the realm internally while solidifying its external boundaries and even engaging in expansionist policies. As mentioned previously, the chief architect of this image is doubtless Arthur Christensen,[410] who, in his seminal work draws its contours, systematically and persistently. Commencing his chapter on Khusrow I with the letter, preserved in Ṭabarī, which the king is said to have written to his *pādhūspān*[411]

[409] Rubin 1995, p. 229.

[410] He in fact devotes almost one sixth of his œuvre to an assessment of Khusrow I's reign. Christensen 1944.

[411] For the office of *pāygōspān* (*pādhūspān*, protector of the land), see, for instance, Khurshudian 1998, §1.2.

of the north,[412] Christensen observes that we have in the fragments of the letter a "king who has clearly reemerged as the center of all authority. He rules *in an absolute manner over the nobility as well as the commoners, even the clergy are under his sway*."[413] The glory of the Sasanian kings reached its apogee during his reign and Iran entered one of the most brilliant phases of its history. In his systematic construction activity, among which was the building of the Ṭāq-i Kisrā, the most illustrious example of the Sasanian monarchy's celebration of itself, Ctesiphon witnessed its greatest expansion during his reign. Together with his rigorous and systematic patronage of the arts and sciences, Khusrow I inaugurated "one of the most brilliant epochs of Sasanian history,"[414] achieving a grandeur surpassing even "the periods of the great Shāhpūrs."[415] Minor reservations notwithstanding, Khusrow I remains the epitome of Sasanian kingly glory.

There is indeed much to commend in Christensen's portrayal of Khusrow I and his times, an image the deconstruction of the exaggerated aspects of which has begun elsewhere and is not within the purview of the present study.[416] Even so, the image has in the meantime acquired paradigmatic dimensions. It is not a question of whether or not the Sasanians during this period, or indeed throughout their history, were one of the two major powers on the international scene of late antiquity, a role that the Byzantines, their only other peer in late antiquity, recognized "after a delay for mental adjustment."[417] Likewise, there is no denying the cultural achievements of the Sasanians throughout their history. A bare knowledge of antiquity bears witness to this. It is not even a matter of questioning the notion that "the apparatus of government, administrative, fiscal, and military, both at the center and in the province, reached a relatively advanced stage of development early in the Sasanian era of Iranian history,"[418] although this latter notion is itself based more on deductions than on any detailed investigation of a wealth of information contained in the literary or extant primary sources that at times defy any attempt at chronological reconstruction. Here a question of methodology comes in, which we will discuss shortly. Suffice it to underline here that one of the foremost authorities investigating the administrative geography of the Sasanian history warns against the disequilibrium of the information contained even in the primary sources at our disposal—inscriptions, coinage and seals—for reconstructing a detailed

[412]Christensen 1944, p. 363.

[413]Christensen 1944, p. 364. Emphasis mine.

[414]Christensen 1944, pp. 363–442.

[415]Christensen 1944, p. 438.

[416]See most importantly Rubin 1995, and Rubin, Zeev, 'The Financial Affairs of the Sasanian Empire under Khusrow II Parvez', 2006, MESA talk (Rubin 2006). I would like to thank professor Zeev Rubin for providing me with a draft version of his fascinating article.

[417]Howard-Johnston, James, 'The Two Great Powers in Late Antiquity: A Comparison', in Averil Cameron and Lawrence I. Conrad (eds.), *The Byzantine and Early Islamic Near East, III: States, Resources and Armies*, pp. 157–227, 1995 (Howard-Johnston 1995), p. 165.

[418]Howard-Johnston 1995, p. 169.

administrative geography of the span of Sasanian history. For even from the purely chronological point of view, our current data belong to two distinct periods of Sasanian history. On the one hand, there are the monumental inscriptions belonging to the third century, and on the other, the administrative seals that belong to the sixth and seventh centuries.[419]

The question, rather, is the following: How does one reconcile the ostensible success of Khusrow I's centralizing reforms with the understanding that, as we shall see, it was ultimately centrifugal forces that brought about the demise of the Sasanian dynasty? This is not the place to engage in a detailed study of Khusrow I's reforms. A recent study by Zeev Rubin has done this admirably.[420] In brief, Khusrow I's reform is said to have attempted a modernization of the Sasanian fiscal system, involving, above all, a rationalization of the empire's taxation system in order to ensure a stable source of income for the central treasury.[421] Having established a financially sound fiscal system under the strict supervision of the central administration, Khusrow I is said to have used his newly acquired resource for the ultimate purpose that the fiscal restructuring had been conceived to begin with: the creation of a standing army that would replace the problematic and unreliable "army of retainers, brought to the field by powerful feudal lords over whom the king had little effective control."[422]

This too is thought to have been achieved. It is here that the social crisis in the wake of the Mazdakite uprising is said to have come in handy. With the great noble families presumably out of the way as a result of the Mazdakite uprising, the king reportedly set out to turn his new military recruits into a new nobility. As Rubin remarks, there is a crack here in the consensus of the field: while some have suggested that "they were recruited from among the gentry of the *dehkān*s, … the more common view is that they belonged to a higher social rank."[423] The scholarly consensus of Khusrow I's rule then builds upon the image constructed by Christensen of a powerful centralizing monarch who, through a keen sense of expediency and farsighted measures, managed to achieve what had hitherto remained unrealizable: a sound fiscal system as well as a standing army. As Rubin's fascinating study points out, however, there are a number of problems with this scenario. Before proceeding with Rubin's analysis, however, we should highlight a number of points about the forces that might have instigated Khusrow I's reforms.

2.5.2 Interlude: *Letter of Tansar*

In order to do so we may start with a document authored during the Sasanian period, the *Letter of Tansar*. The greater part of the *Letter of Tansar* presumes to be the response of Tansar (or Tosar), the chief *herbad* of Ardashīr I, to the

419 For this and other problematics inherent in our primary sources, see Gyselen 2002, p. 180.
420 Rubin 1995.
421 Christensen 1944, p. 367.
422 Rubin 1995, p. 228.
423 Rubin 1995, p. 228, and the references given in n. 5.

charges that the ruler of Ṭabaristān, Gushnāsp, is supposed to have made against the first Sasanian king, Ardashīr I, when the *herbad* had asked Gushnāsp to submit to Ardashīr I. Now the precise date of the *Letter of Tansar* has been the subject of debate. While the letter presents itself as being written during the reign of Ardashīr I at the inception of Sasanian rule, and while there is some agreement that parts of the *Letter of Tansar* might in fact pertain to this period, the evidence for a sixth-century authorship is too overwhelming to be simply brushed aside as instances of interpolations.[424] One of the primary criteria for attributing a sixth-century date to the letter, in fact, is its informational content: it refers to the post-reform period of Khusrow I's administration.[425] The letter appears to transpose the events that transpired during Khusrow I's reign onto the conditions that are presumed to have existed during the reign of Ardashīr I.

To begin with, there can be no doubt that the *Letter of Tansar* contains a veiled description of the Mazdakite rebellion. Among the first few charges against Ardashīr I, the *Letter* articulates Gushnāsp's accusation that "the King of Kings demands of men *earnings and work* (*makāsib o m-r-d-h*)."[426] Tansar then proceeds to give a classic articulation of the desirability of maintaining the *four estates* of the kingdom, enumerating these as the clergy, military, scribes, and artisans and tillers of land at the head of which stands the king, arguing that it "is through these four estates that humanity will prosper as long as it endures," and reminding Gushnāsp that assuredly there ought not be any "passing from one to another" estate except under exceptional circumstances.[427] He then describes for Gushnāsp the ways in which this four-fold division of society had been threatened with destruction—the point of reference always being presumably the Arsacid period—when "men fell upon evil days" and "fixed their desires upon what was not justly theirs." When this transpired, argues Tansar, "violence became open and men assailed one another *over variance of rank and*

[424]Among these one can list the usage of the old Kayānid names, which became prevalent only after Pīrūz's reign (see our discussion on page 385ff); the mention of the "Lords of Marches, of Alan and the western region, of Khwārezm and Kābul," who can be called kings—a situation which only transpired during Khusrow I's reign; the reference to the Turks who appear in the northeastern parts of Iran only in the sixth century; the borders given of the Sasanian empire; and finally the references to the treatment inflicted on the heretics and the emphasis on the ranked order of the social structure, which betray a Mazdakite context (see our discussion below). In her assessment of the authorship of the *Letter of Tansar*, Boyce admits that "the evidence for a 6th century date for the *Letter* is ... considerable." She also acknowledges the fact that the "consensus of scholarly opinion has come to be that the treatise is in fact a literary forgery perpetrated for political purposes, the prestige of the founder of the dynasty and his great herbad, Tansar, being drawn on to help Xusrau to re-establish the authority of both state and church." Tansar 1968, *Letter of Tansar*, vol. XXXVIII of *Istituto Italiano Per Il Medio Ed Estremo Oriente*, Rome, 1968, translated by Mary Boyce (Tansar 1968), p. 16.

[425]For further evidence, see Tansar 1968, and the references cited therein.

[426]Tansar 1968, p. 37. Ibn Isfandīyār 1941, p. 19. Boyce notes significantly that the "reading of the word *m-r-d-h* translated as work is doubtful." Tansar 1968, p. 37, n. 5, where she refers to Minovi's Tehran edition, p. 12, n. 5 of the *Letter*. I am following Iqbal's edition of *Tārīkh-i Ṭabaristān* in which the *Letter* is contained. Can an emended reading of *m-r-d-h* be *mard*, meaning men, here?

[427]Tansar 1968, p. 38, Ibn Isfandīyār 1941, pp. 19–20.

opinion." It is to be noted that what Tansar is describing here is an antagonism among the people of *rank*, a horizontal war as a result of *variance of rank and opinion*, and not a vertical antagonism between the four estates. Immediately afterwards this is made amply clear. For it was at this point, Tansar reminds Gushnāsp, that the "veil of modesty and decency was lifted, and a people appeared *not enhanced by nobleness or skill or achievement nor possessed of ancestral lands; indifferent to personal worth and lineage . . . ignorant of any trade, fit only to play the part of informers and evil-doers.*" Through their exertions in this direction, Tansar continues, these people "*gained a livelihood and reached the pinnacle of prosperity and amassed fortunes.*" What we are dealing with here, in other words, is analogous to the creation of a bourgeoisie, for lack of a better term, a class amassing fortune through means other than land ownership. The significance of this will become clear as we proceed. Thus far we do not have a description of the Mazdakite uprising, for among all our accounts of the latter it is the theme of the destruction of property that is highlighted, and while passing reference is also made to the low-born acquiring wealth, no account maintains that as a result of the uprising the Mazdakites reached the "pinnacle of prosperity and amassed fortunes." Tansar then continues to describe this same state of affairs while replying to another, related aspect of Gushnāsp's accusation, the fact that Ardashīr I had committed excessive bloodshed. There used to be no reason to impose unduly harsh punishments on the population, because "people were not given to disobedience and the *breach of good order.*" "Were you not aware," Tansar rhetorically asks Gushnāsp, "that chastity and modesty and contentment, the observance of friendship, true judgment and *maintenance of blood ties*, all depend upon *freedom from greed*?"[428]

Tansar then begins to describe the consequences of this state of affairs, a mass popular uprising. It is here therefore that Tansar's description of the Mazdakite uprising starts. When "*greed* became manifest and corruption became rife and men ceased to submit to religion, reason, and the state," then the "populace [*ʿāmma*], like demons, set at large, abandoned their tasks, and were scattered through the cities in theft and riot, roguery and evil pursuits, *until it came to this, that slaves (bandigān) ruffled it over their masters (khudāvandigān) and wives laid commands upon their husbands.*" Here, then, is a replica of all the other accounts contained in various versions of the *X*^{w}*adāy-Nāmag* tradition describing the Mazdakite uprising.[429] At this point, Tansar explains, Ardashīr I was compelled to use excessive force. In all probability, then, this account is not a description of the events during late Arsacid period, but of those prevailing during Qubād's and Khusrow I's reign. Tansar then describes the measures

[428]Tansar 1968, p. 38, Ibn Isfandīyār 1941, pp. 19–20.

[429]It is to be noted that the actual term used by the *Letter of Tansar*, and rendered as roguery in the translation, is *ʿayyāri*. This is one of the many pieces of evidence at our disposal connecting the Mazdakite social movement with the phenomenon of *ʿayyāri*. This latter, in turn, as we have noted elsewhere, clearly replicated the ethos of Mihr worship. The author hopes to address this in her upcoming work on *ʿayyāri* and Mihr worship.

taken by the king in order to rectify the turbulent conditions of the realm.[430] But before proceeding with this, it is necessary to describe the following section where the theme of *greed* and *blood-line* is taken up once again.

Tansar here addresses Gushnāsp's concerns about the affairs of the great families (*ahl al-buyūtāt*), and his complaint that "the king of kings has established new customs and new ways." To this charge Tansar replies that "the decay of family and rank is two-fold in nature. In the one case men pull down the family and allow rank to be unjustly lowered [that is presumably by the king or other families]." The other case, however, and that which forms the greater cause for concern, is when "time itself ... deprives them of honour and worth ... Degenerate heirs appear, who adopt boorish ways and forsake noble manners ... *They busy themselves like tradesmen with the earning of money and neglect to garner fair fame. They marry among the vulgar and those who are not their peers, and from that birth and begetting men of lower rank appear.*"[431] Here we have likewise a description of the conditions that existed *prior to the Mazdakite uprising*, when greed and corruption were the order of the day and cause for neglecting the "maintenance of blood ties," and when people busied themselves "like tradesmen with the earning of money."

The king, Tansar now explains, "set a chief (*ra'īs*) over each and after the chief an intendant (*'ārid*) *to number them, and after him a trusty inspector (mufattish) to investigate their revenues.*" A teacher was likewise appointed to each man from childhood to instruct him in his trade and calling. The king also appointed judges and priests who busied themselves with preaching and teaching. Another crucial dimension of the measures that the king undertook, however, was that he "ordered the instructor of the chivalry [Middle Persian *andarzbad ī aspwāragan*, Arabic *mu'addib al-asāwira*] to keep the fighting-men in town and countryside practiced in the use of arms and all kindred arts that all the people of the realm may set about their own tasks."[432]

Of two facts there can be no doubt: First, these passages deal with the corruption that had supposedly engulfed the affairs of the great families (*ahl al-buyūtāt*), that is, the Parthian dynastic families, in the period immediately preceding Khusrow I's reign—a period that, as all agree, engendered the Mazdakite uprising. And second, after detailing the Mazdakite uprising, the section describes the measures undertaken by Khusrow I in remedying the greed and corruption of the great families. The *Letter of Tansar* is thus describing the reforms that Khusrow I undertook in order to bridle the Parthian dynastic families, the *ahl al-buyūtāt*. Among the sources of their power, the letter informs us, was the

[430] Tansar 1968, p. 40; Ibn Isfandīyār 1941, pp. 20–21.

[431] Tansar 1968, pp. 43–44, Ibn Isfandīyār 1941, p. 23. The emphasis of the *Letter of Tansar* on the newly fashionable trading interest of the great families is in fact quite interesting for as we know both the nobility as well as the Zoroastrian orthodoxy "relegated trading to the lowest rung of their ethic, the *Dinkard* considering trade as the lowest and least of activities." Gnoli 1989, pp. 160–161, n. 37.

[432] Tansar 1968, p. 41, Ibn Isfandīyār 1941, p. 21.

fact that they busied themselves like tradesmen with the earning of money. The fame that they achieved in this manner was not fair fame. Khusrow I's measures consisted in the appointment of a chief and an intendant (*ʿāriẓ*) over these dynastic families in their provinces. The function of this *ʿāriẓ* is, in fact, extremely significant. His responsibility was "to number them", that is to say, to take a census. This census, however, was not only of the tillers of the land under the dynasts' control, but also of the fighting men whom the Parthian dynasts contributed to the kings' army. The responsibility of the inspector (*mufattish*), in turn, was an investigation of the revenues produced by the tillers.

Part of Balʿamī's account on Khusrow I's reforms seems to be, in fact, an abridgment of the *Letter of Tansar*.[433] Here Balʿamī informs us that after Khusrow I Nowshīrvān implemented the taxation reforms, he used these revenues to re-arrange the army, "so that, *as we know whence this wealth comes, so we would know where it is going.*"[434] The information that Balʿamī subsequently provides is of significant value for assessing not only the maladies affecting the Sasanian army prior to Khusrow I Nowshīrvān's reign, but also the part played by the Parthian dynastic families, who provided the backbone of this very army. Khusrow I appointed a certain Bābak-i Behruwān[435] to pinpoint the precise problems affecting the army. He complained to Bābak-i Behruwān that the criteria through which they distributed remuneration to the army lacked any justice and logic whatsoever. He then instructed Bābak-i Behruwān to implement measures to rectify the situation, allocating to the grandees (*mahābudhān*) what they deserved. A long list of problems are then enumerated by the king. "There are those, whose worth is 1000 *dirham* who receive only 100. There are those who do not have a mount, but who receive the pay of the cavalry. There are those who have a mount, but who do not know how to ride. There exist those who are not archers, but receive the salary of an archer, and the same with swords and lances."[436] Bābak-i Behruwān was then instructed to restructure the army[437] and allocate to each member of the cavalry and the infantry a fixed pay,

[433] The reforms of Khusrow I in one of the recensions of Balʿamī's work appear under the headings "taxation measures" and "reform of the army." Balʿamī 1959, pp. 169–171 and 171–175 respectively. For an erudite exposition of the variant recensions of this work, see Daniel, Elton L., 'Manuscripts and Editions of Bal'ami's *Tarjamah-yi Tarikh-i Tabari*', *Journal of the American Oriental Society* pp. 282–321 (Daniel 1990).

[434] Balʿamī 1959, p. 172:

تا چنان که میدانم که این خواسته از کجا میاید، نیز دانم که کجا میرود.

[435] For the reading of the name see Tafazzoli 2000, p. 23, n. 25, and p. 15, n. 86.

[436] Balʿamī 1959, p. 172.

[437] A similarly detailed list of the precise measures to be implemented is also given. Each cavalry is then required to wear complete armor, their mail, with complete upper part, together with a stirrup. On their heads must be a helmet, and they should carry chains and foreleg covers (*bar sar khud va silsila o sāghayn*). On their arms must be iron forearms (*va andar dast sāʿidayn-i āhanīn*). On their mounts there must be a mail (*bargustvān bar asp*). They should have a spear, a sword, and a shield, and they should be wearing a belt, have a feed bag, and an ironed mace. On the saddle bow (*bih yik sūy-i kūhih*) there must be a battle ax and on the back of the saddle a bow-holder (*kamāndān*)

the latter not receiving less than a 100 *dirhams*. In the symbolic narrative that follows, however, the jackals appearing in the lands of the Arabs heralded the injustices precipitated by the reforms undertaken by Khusrow I Nowshīrvān. Characteristically, the *mōbadhān mōbadh* articulated this: the *kārdārān* (tax collectors) in charge of collecting the taxes (*harag, kharāj*) after the reforms, had been oppressing the peasantry. They were collecting more than the regulated taxes and were inflicting injustice. Khusrow I Nowshīrvān then appointed *mōbads* over the *kārdārs*, hence the profusion of seals belonging to *mōbads* (*maguh*) in precisely the regions belonging to the Parthian families.[438]

The dynamics of the relationship of the Parthian dynasts with the central administration prior to the reforms is thus fully exposed in Balʿamī's narratives. Prior to the reforms, the dynasts were responsible for forwarding to the central treasury the revenue that they had procured from their domains. In the assessment of their revenue, and the part that they were expected to forward to the central administration, however, they entered calculations that did not reflect the actual amount of wealth that they had collected or needed to spend. Taxation from trade through their territories, as the *Letter of Tansar* informs us, most probably greatly augmented this wealth. A cadastral survey and the imposition of a fixed rate of taxation, which, once decided upon, was no longer left to the self-serving calculations of the dynasts but was to be forwarded directly to the central administration, was meant to fund the central treasury with the actual wealth of the empire.

But, as Balʿamī's narrative significantly underlines, there was a second, very important mechanism through which the central treasury lost a substantial amount of wealth: the Parthian dynasts deducted exaggerated expenses for the armies that they provided. They counted as cavalry those who were only infantry and without any mounts. They deducted inflated expenses for providing their armies with costly armor and war gear, which they then did not provide. As the organization of their army was at their own discretion, they might have used untrained peasants or slaves, or mercenaries whom they probably paid less, as cavalry, the reduced expenses of which they nevertheless calculated as cavalry pay. They might have refused to pay a cavalry member his proper dues as a member, hence the king's complaint that there were mounts without riders. In short, they greatly overestimated their expenses and thereafter deducted these when they provided the Sasanians with armed contingents. Add to this the proceeds from trade, and one could very well imagine the substantial amount of wealth that never actually left Parthian domains in order to make its way to the central Sasanian treasury. No wonder the *Letter of Tansar* complains that the *ahl al-buyūtāt* had acquired tremendous wealth. Part of this wealth, as the *Letter of Tansar* maintains, came from trade, when degenerate heirs adopted boorish

with two bows. Balʿamī 1959, p. 172.

438 Balʿamī 1959, p. 172. For the seals, the majority of which belong to the Pahlav lands of Āmul, Damāvand, Hamadān, Gurgān, Rayy, Ṭūs, and Qūmis; see Gyselen 2002, pp. 61–69.

ways and, forsaking noble manners, busied "themselves like tradesmen with the earning of money and neglect[ed] to garner fair fame." As Balʿamī's narrative makes clear, however, a substantial part of this wealth was gained as a result of the direct control that these dynasts had on the collection of revenue from their domains and the liberty that they had in dispensing this wealth. The Sasanians had very little control over all of this, and hence the dire need for a reform of the system. A strict echelon of control, of checks and balances and counter-checks, had to be imposed in order to even begin to address the problem. As Gushnāsp put it, "the King of Kings demands of men *earnings and work*."[439] As Zeev Rubin's admirable studies have shown, however, the system introduced was itself very soon beset with problems and, as Balʿamī's narrative highlights, susceptible to perennial abuse, over-collection, and under-accountability of the wealth produced by the empire. Such extensive and potentially meticulous degrees of control over Parthian domains and interference in their affairs were probably unprecedented in Sasanian history; hence the rebellion of one Parthian dynast after another during and after the reign of Khusrow I's son, Hormozd IV, and the downward spiral of the Sasanian state when the measures imposed sapped the decentralized system that had hitherto functioned with comparatively much greater success.

Rubin argues that Khusrow I does not seem to have been as vigorous a personality as conventional sources make him to be. Newly tapped sources for Khusrow I's reform present him as "a vacillating and temperamental ruler who bows to pressure and contents himself at the very end of the day with the introduction of half measures."[440] The fiscal reform that he is said to have successfully implemented, moreover, took a long time to implement, and was susceptible to tremendous abuse. The built-in control mechanism imposed by Khusrow I implied an intense involvement of the *mōbads*, as they were supposed to ensure the just implementation of the reforms.[441] But this control mechanism, supervised by "the *quḍāt al-kuwar*, none other than provincial *mūbads*, under the authority of the great *mūbads*, proved to be as susceptible to corruption as the system that had to be controlled."[442] To be sure, for "a time the new system *appeared* to be functioning in perfect order. [And] [r]oyal revenues from the land and poll taxes were doubled."[443] But there were other, perhaps even more powerful forces at work that seem to have helped Khusrow I to achieve this.

There is first the issue of other, substantial sources of income that aided Khusrow I through his first four decades of rule. One of the most important of these was the customs on the silk trade that ran through the Iranian territories,

[439]Tansar 1968, p. 37. Ibn Isfandīyār 1941, p. 19.

[440]Rubin 1995, p. 251.

[441]Rubin 1995, p. 256. The remarkable involvement of *mōbads* in implementing Khusrow I's reforms is corroborated by the primary sources recently unearthed (see footnote 438), a discovery that proves the substantial soundness of not only Rubin's conclusions, but also his methodology.

[442]Rubin 1995, p. 293.

[443]Rubin 1995, p. 292. Emphasis mine

specifically the Parthian regions, one might add. This wealth seems to have augmented the income of the central treasury of Khusrow I. As the *Letter of Tansar* implies, Khusrow I was envious of the wealth from the silk trade revenues monopolized by the Parthian dynasts. Neither were the subsidies paid by the Byzantines, amounting to 11,000 pounds of gold, an unwelcome windfall for Khusrow I at the conclusion of their peace treaty.[444] The circulation of currency in the market seems to have been also plentiful, and this not on account of the "economic soundness of the system as whole," but due to the fact that the volume of silver currency was on the rise ever since Shāpūr II's reign, becoming especially noticeable during the rule of Pīrūz. Other economic indices, such as agricultural productivity, seem also to have been on the rise, offsetting inflationary tendencies inherent in the increased flow of currency.[445] The successes of Khusrow I both internally and in his external relations seem, therefore, to have been affected by other factors besides the putative success of his fiscal reforms. As for the question of the manpower necessary to sustain a standing army, Rubin's study shows clearly that the dearth of manpower contemporaneous even with the reforms of Khusrow I seems to have led to, as Rubin put it, a "barbarization of the Sasanian army."[446] Rubin's evidence pertaining to the end of Khusrow I's reign, "when enough time had passed for his fiscal reforms to have an impact on the organization of the army,"[447] contains the startling feature that even after the reforms, Khusrow I was forced to continue enlisting nomadic groups as a source of manpower for the army, a practice without which Qubād himself could not have regained his kingdom. What is more, this evidence suggests that the standing army created by Khusrow I was "significantly ineffective in warfare against the Turks [the Sasanian enemies in the East], prone to alarm and demoralization."[448] In short, as Rubin observes, the picture that may be drawn from this evidence "is a far cry from that of an army whose backbone is provided by a restored class of rural landlords, the *dehkāns*."[449] In fact, the continuing use of dynastic armies during Khusrow I's reign is clearly reflected in Simocatta's narrative: As the Byzantine campaigns "ravaged through Azerbaijan as far as the Caspian (Hyrcanian) Sea in 577, ... unlike the Romans going on campaign, Persians do not receive payment from the treasury, not even when they are assembled in their villages and fields; but the customary distributions from the king constitute a law of self-sufficiency for them, they administer these provisions to obtain a subsistence and hence *are forced to support themselves together with their animals until such time as they*

[444] Rubin 1995, pp. 262–263, nn. 86–90.

[445] For this and the complicated issues of Sasanian monetary system, see Rubin 1995, pp. 262–263, and the sources cited there.

[446] Rubin 1995, p. 285.

[447] Rubin 1995, p. 280.

[448] Simocatta also observes that in Hormozd IV's war against the Byzantines in 582–586, the Parthian general Kardārīgan "was marching against the Romans. Having enrolled *throngs, who were not soldiers but men inexperienced in martial clamour.*" Simocatta 1986, p. 52.

[449] Rubin 1995, p. 283.

invade a land."[450] That there were recruits from the nobility is acknowledged by Rubin. These, however, must have been drawn from the ranks of those nobility whose parentage was not clear. Why would Khusrow I recruit from among the ranks of these? The answer brings us full circle to the Mazdakite social uprising.[451] For the problem created by the Mazdakite movement, with its supposed indulgence in the practice of *ibāha 'l-nisā*, "was not that there [were] no young men of aristocratic origin [as the noble families will have been blessed as a rule with many children] but rather that there were too many youngsters of unrecognized parenthood at the fringes of the aristocracy, which Khusrow I was striving to restore."[452] Why would Khusrow I—whose quintessential aim in the reforms is said to have been the sapping of the powers of the nobility—want to restore this same nobility? Contemporary scholarship has yet to answer this. For the contention that these were a nobility of the robe and therefore directly answerable to Khusrow I, not only disregards the subsequent course of Sasanian history, but neither can it accommodate the new evidence brought forth in the present study. What is clear is that the effects of Khusrow I's reforms are wrought with so many complications and uncertainties that the Christensenian thesis of a strong centralizing monarch in the person of Khusrow I falls seriously short. The whole issue, however, takes us back to the Mazdakite social uprising.

As far as the Mazdakite rebellion(s)[?] is concerned, what must be borne in mind is that in spite of the tremendous social and doctrinal influence of the Mazdakites—and in spite of the legacy that they left well into the Islamic centuries—their revolutionary dictum of overhauling the rigid class-based order of society was evidently never achieved. The social, political, and economic ramifications of the Mazdakite doctrine, even if we were to uncritically follow the sources, were simply too threatening to the status quo. There is no denying the fact that as an ideology the Mazdakite heresy had a long-lasting effect. As an ideology it had successfully exploited, as we shall see,[453] the Mithraic ethos of the Circle of Justice,[454] and there are a number of indications that, as an ideology, Mazdakism had permeated Iranian society for an extended period prior to its eruption as a mass popular uprising.[455] This does not seem to have been the case as far as the social consequences of the Mazdakite uprising are concerned, however. Much has been said of these destructive effects of the Mazdakite uprising on the class structure of Iranian society. There is probably some truth to this, as these effects are the focus of many of the sources dealing with it. As far as

[450] "In this instance, [i.e., toward the end of Khusrow I's reign,] the king of the Persians, *fearing mutinies in his army*, resolved to participate in discussions about peace with Tiberius [II] the Caesar [(574, 578–582)]." Simocatta 1986, iii. 15.4, 5, p. 95, n. 66 and p. 96. Emphasis added.

[451] Rubin 1995, p. 291.

[452] Rubin 1995, p. 291.

[453] See §5.2.7.

[454] See page 354.

[455] Crone, Patricia, 'Kavād's Heresy and Mazdak's Revolt', *Iran: Journal of Persian Studies* XXIX, (1991b), pp. 21–42 (Crone 1991b).

overhauling, or even seriously threatening, the rigid class structure of Sasanian society is concerned, however, the testimony of the sources—which, after all, bear witness to the normative, strictly class-based, dimensions of Iranian society and which were reworked by the Sasanians after the eruption of the revolts—needs to be dealt with cautiously. This is especially the case where the effects of the movement on the upper echelons of Iranian society, like the Parthian dynastic families, are concerned. The crucial problem here is that the testimony of these sources needs to be weighed against the agnatic character of Iranian society.[456] The economic, politico-religious, and finally territorial dimensions of the agnatic structure of Iranian society, and the strong cohesive bonds that these established, rendered the fabric of Iranian society far too interconnected for it to be overhauled easily. This agnatic structure especially applied to the Parthian dynastic families. The disruptions ostensibly caused by the Mazdakite uprising in the fabric of dynastic communities, therefore, have to be gauged against the formation of these latter as agnatic groups.

In view of this, the contention that the Mazdakite social uprising—even if we were to believe its destructive force as our sources would have us believe—severely disrupted the power bases of the great dynastic families needs to be reassessed. An extensive destruction of property in times of revolutionary fervor is one thing, but to romanticize the effects of the Mazdakite social uprising and argue that it decimated substantial agnatic groups of dynastic families implies a revolutionary upheaval of such intensity that, considering the coercive powers at the disposal of these same dynastic families, is hard to imagine. Members of a particular branch of agnatically based dynastic families might have been particularly hard hit, but there were, as Rubin notes, certainly enough of them to go around. In keeping with the Sasanian legal system, another branch of the same family could very well have claimed and inherited the powers of the family as a whole subsequently. That neither the Mazdakite uprising, nor the reforms of Khusrow I were able to undermine—or, in the case of the latter, were even meant to undermine—the power of these families is, in fact, borne out clearly by the course of Sasanian history from the reign of Khusrow I onward. In order to assess this, we shall have to abandon temporarily our chronological narrative for the reigns of Khusrow I, Hormozd IV, and Khusrow II.

2.5.3 The four generals

One of the many points of controversy over Khusrow I's reforms has had to do with whether or not, in the course of his military and administrative reforms, the king replaced—as our literary sources inform us—the office of *ērān-spāhbed* (*iṣpahbadh al-bilād* or *supreme commander* of the land) with that of four *spāhbeds* assigned to the four cardinal points of the Sasanian empire. The thesis that such a reorganization was undertaken by Khusrow I was first promulgated

[456] As Perikhanian observes the agnatic structure was a quality intrinsic to "the [social] structures ... [and] organization of the whole civic population of Iran." Perikhanian 1983, pp. 641–642; see also our discussion in §1.2.

most forcefully by Christensen. In recent decades, however, this measure of Khusrow I's reforms has come under intense scrutiny. In 1984, for example, Gignoux questioned the historicity of the alleged quadripartition of the empire under Khusrow I. Arguing on the basis of the dearth of primary inscriptions, stamps, seals, coins, and so on—as opposed to literary sources—that testify to such a reorganization, Gignoux contended that the notion of an administrative quadripartition of the empire was most probably largely symbolic with no correspondence to any historical reality.[457] Following Gignoux, others accepted his conclusion that the administrative quadripartition was probably no more than a literary *topos*, but argued that the military quadripartition of the empire was probably "not totally devoid of historical value."[458] While questions surrounding the precise boundaries of the four *kūsts* are still outstanding,[459] and while the longevity of this quadripartition after Khusrow I is still open to dispute,[460] its implementation under Khusrow I is now established beyond doubt by Gyselen's sigillographic discovery.[461]

Quadripartition of the empire

One paramount feature of Khusrow I's reform was the military and possibly administrative quadripartition of the empire, where the king divided his realm into four quarters or *kūsts*.[462] Over each of these he appointed a supreme commander, a *spāhbed*. Khusrow I Nowshīrvān undertook these measures, it was argued, in order to further centralize his rule. This was yet another attempt at undercutting the powers of the nobility, in other words. The king was successful in achieving this and through his reign there were no major uprisings. These *spāhbeds*, it was argued, like the new army that Khusrow I created, did not belong to the ranks of the nobility and most certainly did not come from the Parthian dynastic families. During the rule of Hormozd IV, however, something unprecedented happened: For some inexplicable reason, a Parthian dynast, Bahrām-i Chūbīn of the house of Mihrān, launched a major uprising that engulfed the quarters of the north (*kūst-i ādurbādagān*) and

[457] Gignoux, Philippe, 'Les quatres régions administratives de l'Iran Sassanide et la symbolique des nombres trois et quatre', *Annali dell'Istituto Universitario Orientale* 44, (1984), pp. 555-572 (Gignoux 1984), pp. 555–572.

[458] Gnoli, Gherarldo, 'The Quadripartition of the Sassanian Empire', *East and West* 35, (1985), pp. 265–270 (Gnoli 1985), p. 266.

[459] Gyselen 2001a, pp. 15–16, and the references cited therein.

[460] Gnoli 1985, pp. 268–269. We will argue below that it was even in place as late as Khusrow II's reign.

[461] A seal fragment of a *nēmrōz spāhbed* (supreme commander of the south/Nīmrūz), discovered in 1991, was already acknowledged by Gignoux as sufficient evidence to this effect. Gignoux, Philippe, 'A propos de quelque inscriptions et bulles Sassanides', in *Histoires et Cultes de l'Asie Centrale préislamique: Sources écrites et documents archéologique*, pp. 65–69, 1991b (Gignoux 1991b).

[462] The paradigmatic articulation of this, as other aspects of Khusrow I's reforms, seems to have been made in Christensen 1944, pp. 364-373. For some of the subsequent scholarship on this see Gignoux 1984; Gnoli 1985; and most recently, Rubin 1995, and the sources cited therein.

east (*kūst-i khwarāsān*).[463] Bahrām-i Chūbīn's rebellion was unprecedented in a number of ways. To begin with, it marked the first time in Sasanian history when a Parthian dynast questioned the very legitimacy of the Sasanians and rebelled against the Pārsīg. Significantly, as Boyce underlines, the rebellion also showed "how sturdy a resistance Iran had put up to Persian propaganda about the illegitimacy of the Arsacids."[464] Bahrām-i Chūbīn's rebellion was ultimately put down and the rebel killed. In order to do this, however, as we shall see, the Sasanians were forced to muster all of their resources, including, significantly, the aid of other Parthian dynastic families. What is more, the Parthian Bahrām-i Chūbīn and his powerful constituency had in a sense achieved part of their intended aim before their defeat: they had deposed and murdered the ruling king, Hormozd IV, and had raised to the throne another, Khusrow II Parvīz. In fact, Bahrām-i Chūbīn's rebellion was only put down at the inception of Khusrow II's reign. Even considering what little we have enumerated so far about the saga of Bahrām-i Chūbīn, historical hindsight should have already alerted us to the problems in Christensen's thesis and led us to suspect the continued and forceful power of this Parthian dynastic family in the post-reform period of Sasanian history.

We recall that it was the Mihrāns who had helped secure Qubād's power against the stranglehold of the Kārins. As far as Khusrow I's quadripartition of his realm—intended to further undermine the power base of the nobility—is concerned, therefore, the questions before us are as follows: what happened to the Mihrāns after Khusrow I's reforms? And if in fact they had been decimated in the course of these reforms, as we are led to believe, why did they so forcefully appear again during the reign of Hormozd IV? The problem, furthermore, is that the Mihrāns were not the only Parthian dynastic family who reappeared, almost volcanically, in subsequent Sasanian history. Shortly after Khusrow II's accession to power, yet another powerful Pārthian dynast, Vistāhm of the Ispahbudhān family, launched a second major rebellion.[465] This time, Vistāhm did not limit himself to merely disrupting the kingdom and engaging in rhetoric over the legitimacy of the Sasanians. He in fact carved for himself an independent kingdom covering most of the quarters of the north (*kūst-i ādurbādagān*) and east (*kūst-i khwarāsān*). Neither would this be the last time the Pahlav rebelled against the Pārsīg and assumed the crown. To the details of each of these episodes in Sasanian history, we shall get shortly. For now it is worth highlighting again the inadequacies of the conventional portrayal of the rule of Khusrow I Nowshīrvān as a centralizing monarch and his presumed success in establishing an absolutist polity. Why did Parthian dynasts rise one after another if Khusrow I was in fact so successful in his reformist

[463] For our discussion of the political and religious aspects of this rebellion, see §2.6.3 and §6.1 respectively.

[464] Boyce, Mary, *Zoroastrians: Their Religious Beliefs and Practices*, London, 1979 (Boyce 1979), p. 142.

[465] See §2.7.1 below.

policies? What then of the destructive effects of the Mazdakite rebellion on the elitist fabric of Sasanian society? The paradigmatic Christensenian thesis once again falls short, because it uncritically accepts the Sasanians' portrayal of themselves. Khusrow I's quadripartition of his empire in fact engaged the same long-established pattern of Sasanian polity: the Sasanian–Parthian confederacy, through which it continued to function. There was no discontinuity in the power of Parthian dynastic families, and no overhaul of the power of these, during his reign. To the contrary, major Pahlav families continued to be as much involved in the power structure of Khusrow I's administration as previously. To be sure, there continued to be the ebb and flow of the fortunes of particular dynastic families. But even in this the power structure of Sasanian polity had remained unscathed. What is our evidence for this?

All our literary sources, Armenian, Greek, and Arabic, as well as the *Shāhnāma*, attest that the paradigmatic image of Khusrow I as an all-powerful monarch who through his reforms undermined the power of the great nobility needs to be substantially revised. The pattern of the Sasanian–Parthian confederacy lasted through the reforms of Khusrow I Nowshīrvān and into the reigns of Hormozd IV (579–590) and Khusrow II Parvīz (591–628). Already by Hormozd IV's time, however, and partly as result of the reforms of Khusrow I, the mechanisms that had ensured the collaboration of the Pahlav with the Pārsīg began to crumble, however. The end result of this was that the Sasanians lost their legitimacy, a legitimacy that they had in fact sustained through this confederacy. The collaboration between the Pahlav and the Pārsīg was predicated upon a broad understanding through which the Pahlav agreed to Sasanian kingship in return for maintaining a substantial degree of independence in their respective Pahlav territories. These were concentrated in the quarters of the east and the north, including the Partho-Median territory, the control of which remained, in the words of Toumanoff, allodial, that is, absolute and inalienable, to the Pahlav dynastic families.[466] Within the heavily agricultural territories of the north, east, and south—the last of which will not be the focus of our studies—the agnatic dynasts maintained their hegemony, while upholding the Sasanians by contributing military manpower and agricultural revenues to the central treasury.

In the process of dividing his realm into four quarters, however, Khusrow I introduced, as we shall see, one other novelty: he uprooted some of the chief agnates of key dynastic families from their traditional territories and relocated these to other parts of the realm, putting them in charge of the home territories of other agnatic families. By this means he seems to have intended to undermine the agnatic bonds of these families with their constituency. This measure of reform, like the others, not only did not have its anticipated results, but even further antagonized the dynastic families. Khusrow I had attempted to break the tradition of non-interference in the affairs of the Parthian dynastic families.

[466] Toumanoff 1963, p. 39.

Recently discovered spāhbed seals

The remarkable fact about the continued dependence of the Sasanians on the Parthian dynasts is that the recent sigillographic evidence corroborates the literary evidence. What then is the nature of the sigillographic evidence? In 2001, Rika Gyselen published the results of an incredible discovery that she had recently made in London.[467] These were a set of seal impressions or bullae. Upon closer examination, she ascertained these to belong to the period of the quadripartition of the empire, and to the various *spāhbeds* assigned to the four quarters of the Sasanian empire. One of the greatest finds of the past century, as far as the primary sources for Sasanian history are concerned, this set of sigillographic evidence contains a wealth of information as to the identity of the four generals, *spāhbeds*, who, in the wake of Khusrow I's reforms, were appointed to the four quarters of the realm. To begin with, the seals provide us with the names and the titles of these *spāhbeds*. Literary evidence can be particularly notorious if used for identification of paramount figures of Sasanian history. Where available, names are subject to scribal errors, linguistic transformations from one language to another, and limitations of the literary sources in general. In terms of our ability to identify these figures, therefore, the seals are, in and of themselves, highly significant. For, as we shall presently see, where identification is possible we can now investigate the tremendous part played by the Parthian dynastic families in late Sasanian history by comparing the names of these generals, as they appear on the seals, to those given in our secondary and tertiary sources, and where possible to follow their sagas in late Sasanian history.

At times, however, the seals also provide us with crucial information on the gentilitial background of these figures, thereby clarifying the dynastic family to which they belong. For among the seals recently discovered, there are those that insist on distinguishing the holder of the office as a *Parthian aspbed*, *aspbed i pahlaw*,[468] or, alternatively, as a *Persian aspbed*, *aspbed i pārsig*,[469] confirming in fact one of the theses proposed in this study. As the seals bear witness, the incredible dichotomy of the Parthian (Pahlav) versus Persīs (Pārsīg) affiliation

[467] I was not aware of Gyselen's work on the *Four Generals* until I had finished investigating the literary evidence for the Parthian participation in Sasanian history. The fact that the sigillographic evidence in fact corroborates the hypotheses that I had reached prior to having access to these becomes therefore all the more significant and testifies to the value inherent in literary sources for reconstructing Sasanian history. The present discussion is based on Gyselen 2001a; Gyselen 2002; Gyselen, Rika, 'Lorsque l'archéologie rencontre la tradition littéraire: les titres des chefs d'armée de l'Iran Sassanide', *Comptes Rendus de l'Académie des Inscriptions et Belles Lettres* Jan, (2001b), pp. 447–459 (Gyselen 2001b); Gyselen, Rika, 'La notion Sassanide du Kust î Âdurbâdagân: les premières attestations sigillographiques', *Bulletin de la Société Française de Numismatique* 55, (2000), pp. 213–220 (Gyselen 2000). I am indebted to Rika Gyselen for kindly providing me with copies of her valuable works. For a complete list of the seals, see notes 473 and 477, as well as Table 6.3 on page 470.

[468] Gyselen 2001a, seal 1b of a figure called Dād-Burz-Mihr, p. 36, and the personal seal of this same figure, seal A, p. 46.

[469] Gyselen 2001a, seal 2c, p. 39, and the personal seal of this same figure, seal B, p. 46.

of members of high nobility and the clear importance of such affiliations, persisted through the reforms of Khusrow I and in fact to the end of the Sasanian period. Taken together with the names, this information on the gentilitial background of the four generals, the territorial domains under their control, as well as the kings under whom they served,[470] enables us finally not only to prove the continued participation of the Parthian dynastic families in the sociopolitical structure of late Sasanian history, but, through our literary sources, also to investigate the nature of this participation at this crucial juncture of Iranian history. Significantly, the seals underline one crucial fact: the Sasanians were unable to destroy either the Parthian dynastic families or their consciousness of their Pahlav ancestry. The Pārsīg–Pahlav dichotomy which had begun, as Eddy underlines, with the very rise of the Parthians in the third century BCE,[471] therefore, continued to inform Iranian history through the end of the Sasanian period. Finally, as we shall see in our examination of the religious panorama of the Sasanians, the seals also shed light on the religious affiliations of the four generals,[472] information which becomes tremendously significant in the context of the debates surrounding the religious trends existing within the Sasanian empire. Specifically, as we shall see, this information highlights the fact that the Pārsīg–Pahlav consciousness of their heritage percolated, as a general rule, into the religious traditions that the members of each group embraced.

There are two crucial issues, moreover, that this evidence establishes beyond any doubt. First and foremost, not only did the power of major Parthian dynastic families already on the rise not abate in the post-Mazdakite and post-reform period of Sasanian history, but, in fact, Khusrow I continued to avail himself of the powers of at least three of these families, the Mihrāns, the Kārins, and the Ispahbudhān—whose saga we shall shortly discuss. Second, the sigillographic evidence corroborates the literary evidence and above all the information contained in the *Shāhnāma*. It is time, therefore, to search these literary traditions, including the *Shāhnāma*, which are predominantly based on the *X^{w}adāy-Nāmag* tradition, for further evidence. For these in fact do allow us to reconstruct the Sasanian history not only from the center, the cradle of Pārsīg domination, but also from the edge, the domains of the Parthian dynastic families.

The collection unearthed by Gyselen contains eleven seals belonging to eight different *spāhbeds*, of all four quarters of the Sasanian realm, from the reign of Khusrow I onward.[473] Two *spāhbeds* have seals showing their appointment

[470]The monarchs named on the seals are Khusrow and Hormozd. As we shall argue shortly, these pertain to the rules of Khusrow I, Hormozd IV, and Khusrow II.

[471]See our discussion in §5.3.3.

[472]Gyselen, Rika, 'Les grands feux de l'empire Sassanide: quelques témoignages sigillographiques', in *Religious themes and texts of pre-Islamic Iran and Central Asia: Studies in honour of Professor Gherardo Gnoli*, Wiesbaden, 2003 (Gyselen 2003), especially pp. 134–135. See Chapter 5, especially page 364.

[473]Seal 1a, "Čihr-Burzēn ... *ērān-spāhbed* of the side of the east (*kūst-i khwarāsān*)," belonging to Khusrow's reign; seal 1b, "Dād-Burz-Mihr, Parthian *aspbed* ... *ērān-spāhbed* of the side of the east (*kūst-i khwarāsān*)," belonging to Hormozd IV's reign; seal 2a, "Wahrām ... Ādurmāh ... *ērān-spāh-*

under two separate kings, one of the two Khusrows[474] and Hormozd IV;[475] one *spāhbed* has two seals which are identical except for the addition "[of the] Mihrān [family]" on the second;[476] and the remaining five seals pertain each to a *spāhbed* under a single king. Apart from these eleven *spāhbed* seals, the collection also contains two personal seals, each belonging to one of the individuals already named on the *spāhbed* seals.[477] Hence in total, the collection consists of thirteen seals. Significantly, of these thirteen seals, two that belong to the same individual identify the bearer as a Parthian *aspbed*,[478] and two, also belonging to one individual, identify the bearer as a Persian *aspbed*.[479] Three seals, belonging to three separate figures, moreover identify the bearer as belonging to the Mihrān family.[480] Because the Mihrāns also claimed a Parthian ancestry, together with the two Parthian *aspbed* seals, according to the given information of the seals alone, five[481] out of the thirteen seals unearthed by Gyselen already belong to Parthian dynastic families.

But the seals can further corroborate the continued participation of the Parthian dynastic families in the post-reform period and in fact through the rest of Sasanian history. For with the aid of narrative histories, central among which

bed of the side of the south (*kūst-i nēmrōz*)," belonging to Khusrow's reign; seal 2b, "Wahrām ... Ādurmāh ... *ērān-spāhbed* of the side of the south (*kūst-i nēmrōz*)," belonging to Hormozd IV's reign; seal 2c, "Wēh-Šābuhr, Persian *aspbed*, ... *ērān-spāhbed* of the side of the south (*kūst-i nēmrōz*)," belonging to Khusrow's reign; seal 2d/1, "Pīrag-i Šahrwarāz ... *ērān-spāhbed* of the side of the south (*kūst-i nēmrōz*)," belonging to Khusrow's reign; seal 2d/2, "Pīrag-i Šahrwarāz ... *ērān-spāhbed* of the side of the south (*kūst-i nēmrōz*), [of the] Mihrān [family]," belonging to Khusrow's reign; seal 3a, "Wistaxm, *hazārbed* ... *ērān-spāhbed* of the side of the west (*kūst-i khwarārān* [sic])," belonging to Khusrow's reign; seal 3b, "Wistaxm, *hazārbed* ... *ērān-spāhbed* of the side of the west (*kūst-i khwarbarān*)," belonging to Hormozd IV's reign; seal 4a, "Gōr-gōn [of the] Mihrān [family] ... *ērān-spāhbed* of the side of the north (*kūst-i ādurbādagān*)," belonging to Khusrow's reign; seal 4b, "Sēd-hōš [of the] Mihrān [family] ... *ērān-spāhbed* of the side of the north (*kūst-i ādurbādagān*)," belonging to Khusrow's reign. Gyselen 2001a, pp. 35-45 consecutively.

[474]The name of the king only appears as Khusrow on the seals, making an identification of which Khusrow extremely difficult. Rika Gyselen has argued that all of these seals must belong to the period of Khusrow I and Hormozd IV. Gyselen 2001a, pp. 18–20. As we shall see, the present study will argue that while some of the attributions of the seals to Khusrow I remain valid, others must be dated to Khusrow II.

[475]Seals of Wahrām Ādurmāh, seals 2a and 2b; and Wistakhm, seals 3a and 3b. Gyselen 2001a, pp. 37–38, 40–41 and 42–43 respectively.

[476]Pīrag-i Shahrwarāz, seals 2d/1 and 2d/2 respectively. Gyselen 2001a, p. 43.

[477]Seal A, "Dād-Burz-Mihr, Parthian *aspbed*, refuge into Burzēn-Mihr"; seal B, "Wēh-Šābuhr, Persian *aspbed*," who are identical with those mentioned in seals 1b and 2c respectively. Gyselen 2001a, pp. 36 and 39. For a table with all these seals, see page 470.

[478]Dād-Burz-Mihr, seal 1b and seal A. Gyselen 2001a, pp. 36 and 46 respectively. It is extremely interesting to note that on the personal seal, Seal A, "on trouve le motif, plutôt rare, de deux chevaux ailès, choix qui peut être mis en relation avec le titre *aspbed*, litteralement maître du cheval." This also applies, however, to Seal B, p. 46, which has the same motif of two horses facing each other, but with the addition of a tree between them. See also footnote 602.

[479]Wēh-Shābuhr, seal 2c and seal B. Gyselen 2001a, pp. 39 and 46 respectively.

[480]Those of Pīrag-i Shahrwarāz, seal 2d/2, of Gōr-gōn, seal 4a, and of Sēd-hōsh. Gyselen 2001a, pp. 41, 42 and 43 respectively. As already noted, Pīrag-i Shahrwarāz has a second seal, seal 2d/1, without his family name Mihrān, but otherwise identical to seal 2d/2; see also footnote 768.

[481]In fact, six, when we also count seal 2d/1, of the same person as seal 2d/2.

is the *Shāhnāma* of Ferdowsī, we will establish that, except for the two seals of the Persian *aspbed*,[482] and two seals of a figure whose gentilitial background remains unclear,[483] in fact nine seals belonged to Parthian dynastic families.[484] What is more, we can now confirm that together with the Mihrāns already mentioned in the seals, we have also *spāhbeds* among the Parthian Kārin and Ispahbudhān families. Moreover, some of the seals that have been identified by Gyselen as belonging to the reign of Khusrow I Nowshīrvān actually belong to that of Khusrow II Parvīz. The ramifications of this novel piece of information for understanding the course of Sasanian history are tremendous. The seals confirm not only the continued participation of Parthian dynasts after the Mazdakite uprising through the reigns of Khusrow I, Hormozd IV, and Khusrow II, but also prove that neither Qubād nor Khusrow I were able to significantly change the fundamental dynamics of the Sasanian–Parthian confederacy.

In order to establish our claims we should return to our narrative. We recall that faced with the overwhelming military and financial powers of the Kārinid Sukhrā, Qubād had been forced to appeal to the Mihrānid Shāpūr Rāzī, his supreme commander of the land (*iṣpahbadh al-bilād*), thus setting off a war between the two dynastic families. This dynastic struggle among the Parthians led to the victory of the Mihrāns, and the temporary fall from power of the Kārins. What then was the fate of the Mihrāns and other dynastic families in the wake of the Mazdakite uprising, Khusrow I's assumption of power, and the military reforms that he inaugurated? We should reiterate that, according to conventional wisdom, both the Mazdakite uprising and Khusrow I's reforms are thought to have seriously undermined the power of the hitherto independent Parthian dynastic families.

2.5.4 The Mihrāns

Significantly, the seals already give substantial evidence of the paramount role of the Mihrāns in Khusrow I's military administration. On Gyselen's seals, three out of the eight *spāhbeds* who assumed office during and subsequent to the rule of Khusrow I belong to the Mihrān family. Of these, two[485] were *spāhbeds* of the north (*kūst-i ādurbādagān*), and one, belonging to a certain Pīrag-i Shahrwarāz of the Mihrān family, was a *spāhbed* of the south.[486] All of these seals have been attributed by Gyselen to Khusrow I's administration.[487]

---

[482] Wēh-Shābuhr, seal 2c and seal B. Gyselen 2001a, pp. 39 and 46 respectively. See, however, footnote 840, postulating its Sūrenid affiliation.

[483] Wahrām Ādurmāh, seals 2a and 2b. Although we will further identify this figure in §2.6.1 below as Bahrām-i Māh Ādhar, I have not been able to determine the dynastic family to which he belongs.

[484] For a summary, see Table 6.3 on page 470.

[485] These are the seals of Gōrgōn and Sēd-hōsh, seals 4a and 4b. Gyselen 2001a, pp. 44–45.

[486] Gyselen 2001a, pp. 41, seal 2d/2. The other seal of Pīrag-i Shahrvarāz, seal 2d/1, is almost identical with the aforementioned seal and only lacks the gentilitial patronymic Mihrān, and therefore most certainly belongs to the same Pīrag just mentioned. Ibid., p. 40.

[487] Gyselen 2001a, pp. 18–20.

However, the attribution of the seals of Pīrag-i Shahrvarāz to the period of Khusrow I is problematic. We claim that this Pīrag-i Shahrvarāz is none other than the famous general Shahrvaraz of Khusrow II Parvīz, who was one of the most powerful commanders of Khusrow II's army in his wars against the Byzantines. In fact, Shahrvarāz's subsequent mutiny—aided, as we shall see, by another dynastic leader[488]—would lead to the very collapse of the Sasanian military efforts against the Byzantines, and bring him to briefly usurp kingship during the dynastic havoc of 628–632.[489] Of even greater significance for our purposes, however, is that we can now assert that the towering figure of Shahrvarāz belonged to the Mihrān family.[490] This leaves us with the seals of the Mihrānids Gōrgōn and Sēd-hōsh, both of whom were appointed as the *spāhbeds* of the quarters of the north (*kūst-i ādurbādagān*). Significantly, therefore, the Mihrāns continued to hold the *spāhbedī* of the quarter of the north, their traditional homeland, after Khusrow I Nowshīrvān divided his realm into four quarters and appointed a *spāhbed* over each.

Literary evidence substantiates the tremendous role of the Mihrāns in Khusrow I's administration. Their presence in Khusrow I's military and civil administration is in fact overwhelming. One of Khusrow I's viziers, the Mihrānid Īzadgushasp,[491] whose fate under Hormozd IV's reign we shall see shortly,[492] is mentioned by Ferdowsī as one of the highest dignitaries of Khusrow I's administration. He is identical to Procopius' Isdigousnas whom, together with his brother Phabrizus (Farīburz), the Greek historian describes as "both holding most important offices … and at the same time reckoned to be the basest of all Persians, having a great reputation for their cleverness and evil ways."[493] They aided Khusrow I in his plans to capture Dara in Upper Mesopotamia,[494] and Lazica (Lazistān) in western Georgia.[495] In the annals of the Sasanian–Byzantine negotiations, the favorable reception of Īzadgushasp by the emperor Justinian (527–565) on this occasion is said to have been unprecedented, Izadgushasp returning to Khusrow I with more than "ten centenaria of gold" as gifts presented by the Byzantine emperor.[496] Īzadgushasp's brother Farīburz was also involved in Khusrow I's wars in the west. Having been sent against the Lazi (circa 549–555), but forced to retreat, he left a certain Mirranes, yet another Mihrānid,

[488]See page 143ff below.

[489]See §2.7.4 and §3.2.3 below.

[490]We will substantiate this identification further on page 110 below.

[491]Ferdowsī 1971, vol. VIII, p. 319, Ferdowsī 1935, p. 2570. Justi, Ferdinand, *Iranisches Namenbuch*, Marburg, 1895 (Justi 1895), p. 149.

[492]See page 119.

[493]Procopius 1914, p. 519.

[494]The Byzantine fortified city and trading center of Dara, built in 507 CE, was of tremendous strategic importance, both to the Byzantines and the Sasanians, and especially significant in the war between Khusrow I and the Byzantines. See Weiskopf, Michael, 'Dara', in Ehsan Yarshater (ed.), *Encyclopaedia Iranica*, pp. 671–672, New York, 1991 (Weiskopf 1991).

[495]Sebeos 1999, pp. 7, 163.

[496]Procopius 1914, p. 527. Also see Justi 1895.

to protect the garrison in the city of Petra in Lazica.[497] Khusrow I also resorted to Mermeroes (i.e., Shāpūr Rāzī)[498] when Farīburz's attempt resulted in a stalemate in the war against the Lazis.[499]

Seal of Gołon Mihrān

According to Sebeos, another Mihrānid, a certain Mihrān Mihrewandak, also called Gołon Mihrān, was sent to the Armenian theater of war in 573–575, where he advanced into Iberia in the Caucasus but was defeated. He then led an expedition into southern Armenia, where he seized Angł in Bagrewand, probably in 575 CE[500] Now as we have seen, among the seals unearthed by Gyselen, one belongs to a certain Gōrgōn from the Mihrān family, the *spāhbed* of the quarter of the north during one of the Khusrows. There is a strong possibility that this Gōrgōn of the seals is in fact the Gołon Mihrān of Sebeos.[501] In her remarks on the names of these figures, Gyselen notes that the name Gōrgōn might actually be Gōrgēn.[502] If this figure is in fact Gōrgēn, and if he is identical with the Gołon Mihrān of Sebeos, then quite likely this *spāhbed* of the north was the grandfather of Bahrām-i Chūbīn. What makes this identification more probable, besides the association of all Mihrāns with the quarter of the north and with Armenia and Azarbāyjān, is that Gołon Mihrān is the only other figure, besides Bahrām-i Chūbīn, who bears the epithet Mihrewandak in Sebeos' narrative.[503] Bahrām-i Chūbīn, also called Mihrewandak, in fact claimed to be the great-grandson of Gorgēn Mīlād. While Gorgēn Mīlād, ancestor of the Mihrāns is a legendary, Kayānid figure to whom the Mihrāns traced their genealogy,[504] in the person of Gōrgōn or Gōrgēn of the seals we are most probably dealing in fact with a historical figure, the grandfather of Bahrām-i Chūbīn. At any rate, with such direct involvement of the Mihrāns in the Armenian theater of war in the late sixth century, it is not surprising that Bahrām-i Chūbīn is also said to have been stationed as a *marzbān* of Armenia by some of our sources, as we shall see.

Mihrānsitād Mihrān

The continued reliance of Khusrow I's administration upon the Mihrāns went beyond this. During one of Khusrow I's eastern wars, when the Khāqān of the Turks sued for peace and offered, as a gesture of friendship, his daughter to the Sasanian king, it was a Mihrān, identified by Ferdowsī as Mihrānsitād,[505] whom

[497]Procopius 1914, pp. 529–531, 543.

[498]See §2.4.4.

[499]Procopius 1914, pp. 531–551.

[500]Sebeos 1999, pp. 7, 10, 163.

[501]A *spāhbed* Glon is listed as having taken part in the siege in 502 of Āmid during Qubād's reign. Joshua the Stylite 2000, p. 62, n. 297, and p. 68, n. 324.

[502]"[P]rovided that it is a case of the -*ē*- being badly written." Gyselen 2001a, p. 32, n. 85.

[503]See §2.6.3 and §6.1; for a discussion of the epithet, see page 399.

[504]For a more detailed discussion, see page 116ff below.

[505]Ferdowsī 1971, vol. VIII, p. 178.

Khusrow I sent to appraise the Khāqān's daughter for the king. This daughter became the future queen of Iran, and from her union with Khusrow I, Hormozd IV was born. Mihrānsitād later boasted to Hormozd IV of his significant role in this union.[506] Mihrānsitād's son, Nastūh, was also centrally incorporated in the military and administrative state of Khusrow I and took part in the wars in the east.[507]

The predominant role of the Mihrāns in Khusrow I's administration, therefore, is beyond any doubt. We know now of at least two Mihrāns, Gōrgōn and Sēd-hōsh, who assumed the post of *spāhbed* of the north. Whether or not our identification of Gōrgōn Mihrān with Gołon Mihrān of Sebeos holds, it is extremely probable that Gōrgōn Mihrān was the grandfather of Bahrām-i Chūbīn. Where exactly in the dynastic line of the Mihrāns Sēd-hōsh should be placed, and what the family tree of the Mihrāns at this juncture of history would actually look like, requires further research, as does the sequence in which Gōrgōn and Sēd-hōsh were appointed to the *spāhbedī* of the quarter of the north.[508] If we follow, however, the military career of the Mihrāns from Shāpūr Rāzī Mihrān—on whose manpower and military prowess Qubād relied in his struggle against the Kārinid Sukhrā[509]—to Bahrām-i Chūbīn, we see that the Mihrāns continued to muster substantial forces from the reign of Qubād to that of Hormozd IV and Khusrow II at the very least. Bahrām-i Chūbīn was also able to gather together a huge army from within his traditional homeland with which he debilitated the forces of Khusrow II Parvīz.[510] Considering that the Mihrāns continued to be appointed *spāhbeds* of the north even after Khusrow I's reforms, and keeping in mind that the careers of Shāpūr Rāzī Mihrān and Bahrām-i Chūbīn were at their height precisely before and after the presumed reforms of Khusrow I Nowshīrvān, it stands to reason that the Mihrāns never lost either their control over their traditional homeland or the military force which they could muster from these lands. As we shall see, they continued to function as king makers in subsequent Sasanian history. The Mihrāns, however, were not the only Parthian family upon whom Khusrow I depended during his reign. Once again, we begin our account with the sigillographic evidence that has recently come to light.

2.5.5 The Ispahbudhān

Among the seals discovered by Gyselen, two others deserve attention. Both belong to a certain Wistaxm and identify him as "Wistakhm, *hazārbed … ērān-spāhbed* of the side of the west" and "Wistakhm, *hazārbed … ērān-spāhbed* of the side of the west, blessed."[511] One of these seals, seal 3a, identifies Wistaxm

506 Ferdowsī 1971, vol. VIII, pp. 177–179, Ferdowsī 1935, pp. 2586–2587. See page 124 below.
507 See page 124.
508 For an identification of Sēd-hōsh with a legendary Kayānid general, see page 116ff below.
509 See §2.4.4.
510 See §2.6.3 below.
511 Gyselen 2001a, p. 42–43, seals 3a, 3b.

as the *ērān-spāhbed* of Khusrow; it is not clear which Khusrow, although the seal has been attributed to Khusrow I.[512] The other, seal 3b, has Hormozd IV as king. While both seals are thought to identify Wistaxm as the *ērān-spāhbed* of the west, however, the reading of one of these seals, seal 3a, as belonging to the quarter of the west (namely, *kūst-i khwarārān*) is conjectural.[513] Who was this Wistaxm? To answer this, we must look at another of the Parthian houses.[514]

Asparapet, the great Parthian and Pahlav aspet

In his accounts of Khusrow I's reign (531–579), Sebeos writes extensively of the part taken by a figure he calls *the great Parthian and Pahlaw aspet*, one of "the generals of the Persian king who came one after another to this land of Armenia."[515] The one crucial thing that we have to keep in mind about the gentilitial background of this *aspet* of Sebeos, therefore, is that he was a Parthian and a Pahlav. At times Sebeos calls this same figure Asparapet, or *sparapet*,[516] and deals extensively with the fate of his offspring. In Sebeos' narrative, therefore, we are dealing with a figure who holds two separate offices:[517] the general of the cavalry (*aspet*) and the general of the army (*asparapet*) or *spāhbed*—the titles of which are given in their Armenian rendition.[518] Following Sebeos' chronology, Thomson assigns the duration of the tenure of this *Parthian and Pahlaw aspet*, Asparapet (*sparapet* or *spāhbed*) in Armenia as taking place between 580 and 586, that is during the reign of Hormozd IV.[519] In the accounts of Sebeos, therefore, we are given the identity of a Parthian *spāhbed* who ruled precisely during the reign of Hormozd IV and who was intimately connected—like all the other

[512] Gyselen 2001a, pp. 18–20.

[513] Gyselen 2001a, pp. 14–15.

[514] See also Pourshariati, Parvaneh, 'Recently Discovered Seals of Wistaxm, Uncle of Khusrow II?', *Studia Iranica* 35, (2006), pp. 163–180 (Pourshariati 2006).

[515] Sebeos lists a total of ten figures here. "[T]he *great* Parthian and Pahlaw *aspet*" appears fifth in the list. Sebeos 1999, pp. 11, 14, 166 (v).

[516] In one instance he refers to him as "the great Asparapet, the Parthian and Pahlaw," giving us a combination of the terms of identification for this personage. Sebeos 1999, p. 14.

[517] In Sebeos' narrative the office of *sparapet* is linked to the Mamikonean house on a hereditary basis. Unlike his usage of the term *aspet*, however, of the total of four occasions that Sebeos uses the term *asparapet*, or *sparapet*, three have a Persian context, and refer to the aforementioned figure. Sebeos 1999, p. 14, 17, 318. See Pourshariati 2006.

[518] As Philip Huyse has noted, the title *aspabédes* "is not to be confused with [the title] *aspipīdes*." The latter term comes from Mp. *'sppt/aspbed* (general of the cavalry) < OIr. **aspa-pati*, and is rendered in Armenian as *aspet*. The former term, *aspabédes*, "goes back to Mp. *sp'hpt/spāhbed* (general of the army) < OIr. **spāda-pati*, cf., Arm. *aspahapet* and *(a)sparapet*: the latter word was borrowed twice into Armenian, once in Parthian times from Parth. *sp'dpty/sp̄bed* > Arm. *(a)sparapet* and again in Sasanian times from Mp. *sp'hpt/spāhbed* > Arm. *aspahapet*." See Huyse, Philip, 'Sprachkontakte und Entlehnungen zwischen dem Griechisch / Lateinischen und dem Mitteliranischen', in A. Luther, U. Hartmann, and M. Schuol (eds.), *Grenzüberschreitungen: Formen des Kontakts und Wege des Kulturtransfers zwischen Orient und Okzident im Altertum*, vol. 3 of *Oriens et Occidens*, pp. 197–234, Stuttgart, 2002 (Huyse 2002). For the Armenian office of *sparapet*, see footnote 684 below. I am extremely grateful to Professor Huyse for providing me with this important observation in a personal correspondence. See Pourshariati 2006.

[519] See §2.6 for a more detailed account.

Parthian dynasts so far examined—with the events in Armenia and the west, and was in fact the Asparapet over Armenia, among other regions. All the literary and contextual evidence suggest that Sebeos' Asparapet, the *Parthian and Pahlaw aspet*, is in fact the *spāhbed* of the west, in this case during Hormozd IV's reign (under whose control came the troops of Iraq up to the frontier of the Byzantine empire[520]) Sebeos confusing here the title of the figure with his personal name.[521]

Now according to Sebeos, this Asparapet was the father of Vindūyih and Vistāhm.[522] The daughter of Asparapet had married Hormozd IV, and it was from this union that Khusrow II was born.[523] The *Parthian and Pahlaw* Asparapet, therefore, was the father-in-law of Hormozd IV, and the grandfather, on the mother's side, of Khusrow II, making Vindūyih and Vistāhm the maternal uncles of Khusrow II. Now Vindūyih and Vistāhm, as has been long established, came from the Parthian Ispahbudhān family.[524] There is very little doubt, therefore, that Sebeos' Asparapet, the *Parthian and Pahlaw aspet*, was the patronymic member of the Ispahbudhān family and the figure who in all probability held the office of the *spāhbed* of the quarter of the west during Hormozd IV's rule. Now, as Perikhanian observes, and as Khorenats'i's tradition confirms, the Ispahbudhān were probably the original holders of the office of *spāhbed*, and as a result came to use the title of the office as their gentilitial name.[525] Based on literary evidence, Patkanian, Justi, and Christensen, among others, consider the gentilitial name of Ispahbudhān a given, Justi even reconstructing a family tree for them.[526] According to Sebeos, in an episode corroborated by classical Islamic histories, Hormozd IV recalled and killed this senior member of the Ispahbudhān family, Asparapet, his father-in-law and the Parthian *spāhbed* of the west, in 586, about six years into his reign.[527]

What we cannot ascertain at the moment is the name of this *spāhbed* of the west. Dīnawarī maintains that his name was Shāpūr and that he was the

[520] Christensen 1944, p. 370.

[521] The confusion of the title with the personal name seems to be a common practice in Greek sources as well. Theophylact Simocatta calls this same figure Aspebedes. Simocatta 1986, iv. 3.5. Once again I owe this observation to a personal correspondence from Philip Huyse. See Huyse 2002. Another Aspebedes appears in Procopius' narrative as an important general during Qubād's reign, who is probably the father of Sebeos' Asparapet, and whose saga we will discuss on page 110ff below. Procopius 1914, pp. 83–84.

[522] Sebeos 1999, p. 14. For a detailed assessment of the tremendous role of these figures in late Sasanian history, see page 127ff.

[523] Sebeos 1999, p. 17. See also the genealogical tree on page 471.

[524] Shahbazi, Shapur, 'Besṭām o Bendōy', in Ehsan Yarshater (ed.), *Encyclopaedia Iranica*, pp. 181–182, New York, 1991b (Shahbazi 1991b).

[525] Perikhanian 1983, p. 645.

[526] As we shall see at the conclusion of this study, we can now add to the family tree that Justi had reconstructed; see page 471. For the Ispahbudhān family see, among others, Patkanian 1866, pp. 128–129; Justi 1895, p. 429; Christensen 1944, p. 104. Lukonin 1983, p. 704, disagrees with this identification.

[527] "He [i.e., Hormozd IV] killed the great Asparapet, Parthian and Pahlaw, who was descended from the criminal Anak's offsprings." Sebeos 1999, p. 14.

son of Khurbundād.[528] The *Nihāyat* omits Shāpūr and calls him Khurbundādhūyih, which is probably a combination of the name Khurbundād and the title *jādhūyih*.[529] Finally, the *Shāhnāma* gives his name as Kharrād, which is a diminutive of Khurradād.[530] According to Joshua the Stylite, in 503 CE, during Qubād's war against the Byzantines, the Persian *astabid*[531] (the Syriac rendition of Iranian title *spāhbed*) was called Bawi.[532] The order of the genealogical tree of the Parthian Ispahbudhān family, therefore, might be Bawi (Boe, Procopius' Aspebedes); Shāpūr (Sebeos' Asparapet); Vistāhm and Vindūyih. The names given by other sources as Khurbundād, Khurbundādūyih, and Kharrād in lieu of Shāpūr are merely a combination of the titles *khurra*, *farrokh*,[533] *dād*,[534] and *jādhūyih*.[535] Significantly, the title *farrokh* is also carried by Wistaxm on one of his seals.[536] This genealogy then is the pedigree of the Ispahbudhān family, who acquired their name by virtue of the fact that traditionally the office had remained in their family. It is a genealogy that is extremely significant for later Sasanian history, as well as the history of Ṭabaristān.[537]

Seal of Vistāhm Ispahbudhān

As a general rule, even after Khusrow I's reforms, the offices of the *spāhbed* remained hereditary, certainly within the same Parthian dynastic families.[538] This claim is now corroborated above all—and besides other evidence thus far presented—by the seals of Gōrgōn (of the) Mihrān (family) and Sēd-hōsh (of the) Mihrān (family), both of whom were *spāhbeds* of the side of the north during Khusrow I's rule. What is of crucial importance is that this general rule also applied to the Parthian Ispahbudhān family, a family that after the Sasanians was probably the second most important family in Sasanian history. As Sebeos maintains, the *spāhbed* in Armenia from 580–586 was the father of

528Dīnawarī 1960, p. 102, Dīnawarī 1967, p. 111.

529Nihayat 1996, p. 361:

بندویه و بسطام ابنی خربنداضویه

and p. 391:

بسطام بن شهربنداد

The office of *jādhūyih* was probably a judiciary office with possible religious overtones. For further elaboration, see page 197.

530Ferdowsī 1971, vol. IX, p. 42. All also cited in Shahbazi 1991b, p. 180.

531Procopius calls him Aspebedes. Procopius 1914, pp. 83–84.

532Joshua the Stylite 2000, p. 76.

533From *farr*, for which see footnote 222.

534From the Avestan word *dātā*, meaning law, right, rule, regulation, the term *dād* "is the most general word for the concept of law in the Iranian religious tradition." It stands in contrast to *dādestān*, meaning "civil law, justice, judicial decision." Shaki, Mansour, 'Dād', in Ehsan Yarshater (ed.), *Encyclopaedia Iranica*, pp. 544–545, New York, 1991 (Shaki 1991).

535See page 197.

536As we shall see below, some of the names of other important members of this family are also composed with *-farrokh-*; see §3.3.1 and the family's genealogical tree on page 471.

537For the connection with the Āl-i Bāvand of Ṭabaristān, see §4.1.2.

538We shall see further examples of this.

Vistāhm and Vindūyih, the Parthian figure who was also the *spāhbed* of the west, and was recalled and killed by Hormozd IV. The secondary and tertiary sources provide plenty of evidence about the paramount figure of Vistāhm, the uncle of Khusrow II, a figure who became intimately involved in the Parthian dynastic struggles that, as we shall see, engulfed the Sasanian dynasty precisely during the reigns of Hormozd IV and Khusrow II. Finally we should keep in mind that, as Gyselen remarks, the name Vistāhm is a "less common name."[539] Considering all this, and considering the subsequent course of Sasanian history, there is very little doubt that the figure whom the seals identify as Wistaxm, the *spāhbed* of ***kūst-i khwarbarān*** (the quarter of the west) of Hormozd IV,[540] is the extremely powerful Parthian dynast Vistāhm of the Ispahbudhān family, whom Hormozd IV appointed *spāhbed* of the west after murdering his father Asparapet. The other seal of Vistāhm, seal 3a, as we have argued elsewhere,[541] most probably belongs to the rule of Khusrow II, not Khusrow I, and to the period when Vistāhm was appointed *spāhbed* of the east by Khusrow II, as a reward for the central role that he played, together with his brother, Vindūyih, in bringing Khusrow II Parvīz to power.[542] Shortly after this, Vistāhm led a rebellion in Khurāsān.[543] It is important to observe that according to Sebeos, the original land of the family of Asparapet, the *Parthian and Pahlaw aspet*, was the "region of the Parthians," which clearly refers, in the context of Sebeos' narrative, to Khurāsān. In the midst of his rebellion, Sebeos informs us, Vistāhm, the son of Asparapet, moved from the region of Gīlān to "the region of the Parthians, to the original land of his own principality."[544] When Vistāhm was appointed *spāhbed* of the east, therefore, he had finally assumed power over the original land of his own principality, the land of Parthava.[545]

Gyselen, who argues that seal 3a of Wistaxm belongs to the *spāhbed* of the west as opposed to the east—an identification with which, as noted, we disagree—bases part of her reasoning "on the identity of the person who is *spāhbed* of the western side. A person named Wistaxm appears in the literary tradition as a *spāhbed* of the Sawād, a region which was definitely on the western side of the Sasanian empire."[546] The literary tradition to which Gyselen refers, unique in its identification of Wistaxm as the "*spāhbed* of the Sawād who

---

[539]Gyselen 2001a, p. 32.

[540]Gyselen 2001a, p. 43.

[541]Pourshariati 2006.

[542]Ferdowsī 1935, p. 2798, Ferdowsī 1971, vol. IX, p. 136:

بدان کار بندوی بد کدخدای — جهان دیده و راد و فرخنده رای
خراسان سراسر به گستهم داد — بفرمود تا نو کند رسم و داد

We will discuss this episode in more detail in §2.7.1 below.

[543]See page 132ff.

[544]Sebeos 1999, p. 42.

[545]Sebeos 1999, p. 42.

[546]Gyselen 2001a, p. 15.

had the position of *hazāraft*," is the *Akhbār al-Ṭiwāl* of Dīnawarī.[547] Dīnawarī, therefore, confirms that a *spāhbed* of the west was called Wistaxm. The next question, therefore, is under which king did this Wistaxm serve?

Dīnawarī's anachronistic account

Now Dīnawarī's citation appears in the course of his narrative on the end of Yazdgird I's reign (399–420), and the accession of his son, Bahrām V Gūr (420–438). As in other sources that we examined above, Dīnawarī points out that after the death of Yazdgird I, the nobility of Iran decided that, on account of the injustices committed by this king, none of his offspring should succeed him.[548] Among the nobility, Dīnawarī mentions Wistaxm, the *spāhbed* of Sawād who held the position of *hazāraft*.[549] Gyselen aptly remarks that "unless we have here two homonyms, the Wistaxm whose *spāhbed* seal we possess could well be the same as the one mentioned by Dīnawarī." As for the fact that the Wistaxm of Dīnawarī belongs to the fifth century, while the seals of Wistaxm "would rather appear to be from the second half of the 6th century," Gyselen observes correctly that "here we have one of those chronological confusions very common in the historiographical tradition concerning the Sasanian Empire."[550] As she remarks, we are in fact dealing here with a chronological confusion, but, as we shall argue, a confusion that has been caused by Dīnawarī's transference of events pertaining to *Khusrow II's reign* to those occurring in the aftermath of Yazdgird I. The confusion, in other words, does not pertain to the reign of Khusrow I.

Dīnawarī notes that after the death of Yazdgird I, the elite of Iran decided that on account of the deceased king's injustices, none of his offspring ought to be considered fit for rule and therefore opted for a certain Khusrow, "from a side line," to succeed to the throne. Upon hearing the news, one of Yazdgird I's sons, Bahrām V Gūr, who was exiled to Ḥīra,[551] considering himself the natural heir to the throne, rebelled against the nobility and their puppet king Khusrow and seized the throne. Now, among Khusrow's supporters, Dīnawarī mentions Wistaxm, the *spāhbed* of Sawād.[552] The two protagonists of the dynastic struggle in Dīnawarī's account of the aftermath of Yazdgird I's death were, therefore, Khusrow, from a side line, and Bahrām, the pretender to the throne—the namesakes of the figures of the dynastic struggle between Khusrow II and Bahrām-i Chūbīn.[553] Dīnawarī has confused, in other words, the story of the struggle between Khusrow II and Bahrām-i Chūbīn with the accounts of the struggle between Khusrow and Bahrām V Gūr. Given that other historical narratives,

[547] Dīnawarī 1960, p. 55, Dīnawarī 1967, p. 59.
[548] Dīnawarī 1960, p. 55, Dīnawarī 1967, p. 59. See §2.2.3.
[549] Dīnawarī 1960, p. 55, Dīnawarī 1967, p. 59.
[550] Gyselen 2001a, p. 22.
[551] See page 69.
[552] See footnote 549.
[553] For Bahrām-i Chūbīn's rebellion, see §2.6.3 and §6.1 below.

including Dīnawarī's, speak extensively of a Vistāhm who actively participated in Sasanian politics during the second half of the sixth century—namely, the uncle of Khusrow II, the Parthian dynast of the Ispahbudhān family—little doubt ought to remain as to the transposition of Dīnawarī's narrative from the time of Khusrow II to that of Yazdgird I.

What strongly corroborates this hypothesis are the seals of Pīrag-i Shahrvarāz of the Mihrān family. Among Bisṭām's (Vistāhm's) fellow notables, Dīnawarī mentions a "Fīrak, entitled Mihrān." We claim that this Fīrak is none other than "Pīrag-i Shahrvarāz ... *spāhbed* of the side of the south, [of the] Mihrān [family]."[554] As Gyselen observes, the literary sources always identify Shahrvarāz in the same context:[555] as a powerful figure who played a dominant role in Khusrow II's long drawn out wars with the Byzantines (603–630) and who finally mutinied against him.[556] Like Wistaxm, therefore, the Parthian Mihrānid Pīrag-i Shahrvarāz is a powerful general of Khusrow II Parvīz. Dīnawarī thus identifies in his anachronistic account four figures from the second half of the sixth century: the king Khusrow II Parvīz, the rebel Bahrām-i Chūbīn, and the two Parthian generals Wistaxm and Shahrvarāz.

The Ispahbudhān and the Sasanians

Before we proceed with the identification of other seals, which further substantiate the confederacy of other Parthian dynastic families besides the Mihrāns and the Ispahbudhān with the Sasanian monarchy after Khusrow I's reforms, a few words must be said about the tremendous power of the Ispahbudhān family. The Parthian Ispahbudhān family was traditionally closely related to the Sasanian kings. At least since the time of Qubād—but most probably from early on in Sasanian history[557]—there seems to have been a tradition according to which one of the daughters and/or sisters of the senior branch of the Ispahbudhān family would marry the incumbent Sasanian Prince. Procopius informs us of Qubād's marriage into the Ispahbudhān family. In his desire to have Khusrow I Nowshīrvān, rather than any other of his offspring,[558] succeed him, Qubād schemed to have Khusrow I "be made the adopted son of the emperor Justinus,"

[554]Seals 2d/1 and 2d/2. Contra Gyselen, who, in line with her previous argument, has identified the seals of Pīrag, as belonging to the reign of Khusrow I. Gyselen 2001a, pp. 40–41.

[555]Gyselen 2001a, pp. 22–23.

[556]See respectively §2.7.4 and §2.7.6 below.

[557]As we have seen on page 26, in the tradition given by Moses Khorenats'i, Koshm, the daughter of the Arsacid king Phraat IV, "married the general of all the Aryans who had been appointed by her father ... [with the result that her progenies' name became] Aspahapet Pahlav, taking this name from the principality of her husband." Khorenats'i 1978, p. 166. That the Sasanians could have been following the practice of the Achaemenids and taking wives either among their own family or from those of the six other great noble houses is accepted by Christensen, who cites, besides the mother of Khusrow II (for which see page 132), a son of a sister of Khusrow II, "who carries the name Mihran" as evidence of this practice (see footnote 1137). For this and for further references to the Ispahbudhān family see Christensen 1944, pp. 109–110, n. 2 and p. 104, respectively. See also our discussion in §3.3.1.

[558]These were Zames (i.e., Jāmāsp) (497–499) and Caoses (i.e., Kayūs), for whom see §4.1.1.

thereby enlisting the support of the Byzantines if necessary.[559] For Qubād, Procopius maintains, "loved Khusrow I, who was born to him by the sister of Aspebedes, exceedingly."[560] Both of the Khusrows, therefore, had direct Ispahbudhān lineage, their fathers Qubād and Hormozd IV having married into the family. No wonder Dīnawarī calls the Ispahbudhān family the "brothers of the Sasanians and their partners [in rule]."[561]

Throughout Qubād's reign, the Parthian dynast Aspebedes of the Ispahbudhān family was one of the paramount figures of the king's court. He arranged the peace treaty of 506 with the Byzantines.[562] And together with Mermeroes (Shāpūr Rāzī)[563] and Chanaranges (Ādhargulbād) of the Kanārangīyān family,[564] he played a central role in the siege of the important city of Amida, contested between the Byzantines and the Sasanians in late antiquity.[565] Like their relationship with other Parthian dynastic families, however, the connection of the Sasanians with the Ispahbudhān was also marked by periods of tremendous belligerency.

The nobility's plot against Khusrow I

Early in Khusrow I's reign, Aspebedes joined a group of other discontented dynasts plotting to bring Qubād, a child of Khusrow I's brother Jāmāsp (Procopius' Zames) to power. Having discovered the plot, Khusrow I killed Jāmāsp, together with the rest of his brothers and their offspring as well as "all the *Persian notables* who had either begun or taken part in any way in the plot against him. Among these was Aspebedes, the brother of Khusrow I's mother."[566] In fact, the plot that Procopius mentions seems to have been nothing short of yet another Parthian dynastic struggle for the control of the throne of the Sasanians, for it was in vexation over Khusrow I's "unruly turn of mind" and his strange "fond[ness] of innovation" that Aspebedes had joined other discontented dynasts and strove for dethroning Khusrow I from Sasanian kingship.[567] In this plot, Aspebedes was joined by yet another extremely powerful Parthian dynast, the Chanaranges, the Kanārangīyān Ādhargulbād, who had secretly raised Jāmāsp's son Qubād at his court in Khurāsān.[568] As a result of this plot, therefore, Khusrow I killed Aspebedes.

559 According to Procopius, Qubād was certain that "*the Persians [would]... make some attempt to overthrow his house as soon as he [had] ended his life,... [He] was [also] certain that he would not pass on the kingdom to any one of his sons without opposition.*" Procopius 1914, pp. 83–84. Emphasis mine.

560 Procopius 1914, pp. 83–84. This Aspebedes is presumably the father (or grandfather) of Sebeos' Asparapet, where again the title is substituted in the sources for his actual name.

561 Dīnawarī 1967, p. 111, Dīnawarī 1960, p. 102.

562 Procopius 1914, p. 77.

563 See §2.4.4.

564 For the Kanārangīyān family, see page 266ff. For the name, see footnote 1545.

565 Procopius 1914, p. 195. Joshua the Stylite 2000, pp. 60–61, n. 292 especially. For Amida, see footnote 305.

566 Procopius 1914, p. 211. Emphasis added.

567 Procopius 1914, pp. xxiii, 4–10, 211.

568 Procopius 1914, p. 211. For a more detailed account, see page 266ff below.

Khusrow I was not the only Sasanian king to kill a close relative from the powerful Ispahbudhān family. As we have mentioned and will further discuss, Hormozd IV also killed his father-in-law, the great Asparapet, in the course of his purge of Parthian magnates. Likewise, as we shall see shortly,[569] Khusrow II killed his uncles Vindūyih and Vistāhm of the Ispahbudhān family—the sons of the great Asparapet—to whom he owned his very kingship. The rivalry between the Sasanians and the Ispahbudhān family was perhaps the most contentious of all the relationships of the Sasanians with the Parthian dynastic families, and we shall have occasion to see the tremendous implications of this. Having highlighted the role of the Mihrān and the Ispahbudhān families in the military and civil administration of Khusrow I, we can now turn to the saga of the Kārins.

2.5.6 The Kārins

According to Dīnawarī and the *Nihāyat*, in the final stages of the Mihrānid Bahrām-i Chūbīn's rebellion against Hormozd IV and Khusrow II,[570] when he was finally forced to flee east to Khurāsān, Bahrām-i Chūbīn and his forces were intercepted by their age old enemies, the Kārins.[571] According to both narratives, in Qūmis,[572] Bahrām-i Chūbīn was prevented from proceeding further east by one Kārin, the governor of Khurāsān,[573] who according to both accounts, was over hundred years old, and therefore sent his son to confront Bahrām-i Chūbīn.[574] In Khurāsān, according to Dīnawarī, the Kārins were in charge of "war and peace, collecting taxation and the administration" of the region. Qūmis and Gurgān were also part of the Kārins' governorship.[575] Both sources assert that the Kārins were appointed the governorship, *spāhbedī*, of the region by Khusrow I Nowshīrvān,[576] and continued to hold this position during the reign of

---

[569] See page 132 below.

[570] For Bahrām-i Chūbīn's rebellion during this period see §2.6.3 and §6.1 below.

[571] Dīnawarī 1960, pp. 94–95, Dīnawarī 1967, pp. 102–103. Nihayat 1996, p. 380.

[572] The province of Qūmis was located to the south of the Caspian Sea, with Rayy and Khurāsān forming its western and eastern boundaries respectively. Its main city, also called Qūmis, and known as Hecatompylos (the city of hundred gates) by the classical authors, was one of the ancient capitals of the Arsacids. One of its eastern-most cities was called Bisṭām, a name which might hark back to its association with the Ispahbudhān Vistāhm. Also see Bosworth, C.E., 'Kūmis', in P. Bearman, Th. Bianquis, C.E. Bosworth, E. van Donzel, and W.P. Heinrichs (eds.), *Encyclopaedia of Islam*, Leiden, 2007b (Bosworth 2007b).

[573] *Nihāyat* obviously exaggerates by maintaining that Kārin was the governor of Khurāsān up to the borders of Byzantium. Nihayat 1996, p. 380.

[574] In this crucial episode, Kārin's son was killed, his army scattered, and Kārin himself retreated eventually to Qūmis. Nihayat 1996, p. 380, Dīnawarī 1960, p. 94, Dīnawarī 1967, p. 103.

[575] Dīnawarī 1967, pp. 102–103, Dīnawarī 1960, p. 94:

و كان بقومس قارن الجبلى و كان عاملا على خراسان الى بلاد روم [!] و كان مستوطنه بقومس و كان شيخا كبيرا قد اناف على المائة من السنين و كان عامل كسرى انوشروان. ثم اقرّه هرمزد على عمله فلما تولى الامر بهرام اقرّه ايضا على عمله.

[576] Dīnawarī 1960, p. 94, Dīnawarī 1967, p. 103. Nihayat 1996, p. 380.

Hormozd IV.[577] In his short term of usurping kingship, even Bahrām-i Chūbīn (590–591) had confirmed their rule over the region.[578]

We recall that during Qubād's rule the power of the Kārinid Sukhrā had reached such heights that the king was forced to solicit the help of the Mihrāns to undermine and defeat him.[579] What happened to the Kārins after this can be reconstructed with the aid of Ibn Isfandīyār's *Tārīkh-i Ṭabaristān* and the seals. Although the Kārins appear in Ibn Isfandīyār's narrative in the garb of an anecdotal story[580] that betrays the circulation of popular traditions surrounding them, it is quite remarkable, in fact, that the historicity of the germ of this story can now be substantiated in reference to our sigillographic evidence.

According to the *Tārīkh-i Ṭabaristān*, after his fall from absolutist power, Sukhrā fled to Ṭabaristān with his nine sons.[581] We recall that according to Ferdowsī, Sukhrā was killed.[582] His reappearance in Ṭabaristān in the *Tārīkh-i Ṭabaristān*, therefore, must be excused on account of the anecdotal story in which it is garbed and which is meant to underline the Kārins' appointment over Ṭabaristān by Khusrow I. When Qubād died, however, Khusrow I (531–579) regretted his father's treatment of the Kārins and sought to reincorporate them into his administration.[583] According to Ibn Isfandīyār's narrative, the Kārins heard about Khusrow I's intentions and came with their army *clad in green*,[584] and aided the king in his war against the Khāqān of the Turks.[585] In return for their aid, Khusrow I took measures the effects of which clarify part of the subsequent history of Ṭabaristān[586] and Khurāsān. According to Ibn Isfandīyār, Khusrow I gave control of Zābulistān[587] to Zarmihr, the eldest son of the late Sukhrā.[588] One Kārin, apparently a younger son, received parts of

---

[577] Dīnawarī 1960, p. 94, Dīnawarī 1967, p. 103. Nihayat 1996, p. 380.

[578] Dīnawarī 1960, p. 94, Dīnawarī 1967, p. 103. Nihayat 1996, p. 380.

[579] See §2.4.2 and §2.4.3.

[580] See also page 380.

[581] Ibn Isfandīyār 1941, p. 151. Marʿashī, Mīr Seyyed Ẓahīr al-Dīn, *Tārīkh-i Ṭabaristān o Rūyān o Māzandarān*, 1966, edited by M. Tasbih with an introduction by Muhammad Javad Mashkur (Marʿashī 1966), p. 6.

[582] See footnote 400.

[583] Ibn Isfandīyār 1941, p. 152. Marʿashī 1966, pp. 6–7.

[584] For the significance of the color green and for the details of this episode, see page 380 below.

[585] Ibn Isfandīyār 1941, p. 151 and 150. Marʿashī 1966, p. 7.

[586] See §4.2 below.

[587] For Zābulistān, in present day eastern Afghanistan, see Bosworth, C.E., 'Zābul, Zābulistān', in P. Bearman, Th. Bianquis, C.E. Bosworth, E. van Donzel, and W.P. Heinrichs (eds.), *Encyclopaedia of Islam*, Leiden, 2007c (Bosworth 2007c).

[588] Note that the control of Zarmihr over Zābulistān might explain the revolt of the Kārins in the Qūhistān and Nīshāpūr regions in 654, shortly after the Arab conquest of Khurāsān, for which see page 277 below. Ferdowsī mentions a Dādburzīn, who was another son of Sukhrā, as being in control of Zābulistān during Bahrām V Gūr's reign. The list of nobles that Ferdowsī provides, here, however, is most probably affected by the *Ctesian* method (see footnote 609 below). Ferdowsī 1935, p. 2196. Besides a Burzmihr, Thaʿālibī also mentions a Bahrām Adharmahān as one of the grandees of Khusrow I's administration (for more on this figure, see §2.6.1). Thaʿālibī 1900, p. 638, Thaʿālibī 1989, p. 411.

Ṭabaristān. For our future purposes, it is important to note that included in this region were Vand Omīd Kūh, Āmul, Lafūr, and Farīm, the latter of which was called Kūh-i Kārin.[589] Khusrow I followed this Kārin to Ṭabaristān, sojourned for a while in Tammīsha, and gave parts of other territories to other rulers.[590] Kārin was called the *isfahbudh*[591] or *spāhbed* of Ṭabaristān.[592]

Seal of Dādmihr Kārin

The sigillographic evidence corroborates the narratives of Dīnawarī and the *Nihāyat*: the Kārins had indeed been installed as the *spāhbeds* of the east, which included not only Khurāsān but also parts of Ṭabaristān, during the reign of Khusrow I Nowshīrvān. In his reconstructed family tree of the families ruling in Gīlān and Ṭabaristān, which we will discuss in Chapter 4, the late Ferdinand Justi includes a genealogical table for the Kārins.[593] Here he gives Sukhrā's sons as Zarmihr, whom he dates to 537–558, and Kārin. Of Zarmihr's five sons, one is given as Dādmihr, obviously a shortened version of Dādburzmihr.[594] Justi's reconstruction of Dādmihr's identity, whom he dates to 558–575 CE,[595] is corroborated by other literary sources besides the one he cites. Among the three figures whom Ferdowsī lists as having high positions in Khusrow I's administration, figures who were later murdered by Hormozd IV as a result of this,[596] there was one Burzmihr. This Burzmihr is already listed among the sons of Sukhrā during Qubād's reign. According to Thaʿālibī, when Qubād returned from the campaigns against the Hephthalites with a large army, the elite, the *mōbads*, as well as Jāmāsp[597] decided to avert another civil war and accept Qubād as king on condition that he would not harm either Jāmāsp or any of the elite. Qubād accepted and appointed Burzmihr, whom Thaʿālibī identifies as the son of Sukhrā, as his minister and remunerated him for his services. The Parthian dynast Burzmihr encouraged Qubād to avert taxation on fruits and grain from the peasantry.[598] Motlagh, following Justi, identifies this figure with the legendary wise vizier Bozorg-Mehr of Khusrow I.[599] We can now add that this illustrious figure of Islamic wisdom literature was in fact a Kārin; this is affirmed explicitly by Ferdowsī.[600] Sigillographic evidence further confirms the information provided by Dīnawarī, *Nihāyat*, Ferdowsī, and Justi. We now

[589]Ibn Isfandīyār 1941, p. 152. Marʿashī 1966, p. 7.
[590]Ibn Isfandīyār 1941, p. 152.
[591]*Isfahbudh* is the Arabicized version of the Middle Persian term *spāhbed* or *ispahbud*.
[592]Ibn Isfandīyār 1941, p. 151.
[593]Justi 1895, p. 430.
[594]Justi 1895, p. 75. See also §2.6.2.
[595]Justi 1895, p. 75.
[596]See the beginning of §2.6.
[597]See §4.3.1 below.
[598]After a while, however, "Ahrīman began to influence Qubād and afflicted him with Mazdak." Thaʿālibī 1900, pp. 596–603, Thaʿālibī 1989, p. 384–388.
[599]Motlagh, Djalal Khaleghi, 'Bozorgmehr-i Bokhtagān', in Ehsan Yarshater (ed.), *Encyclopaedia Iranica*, New York, 2007a (Motlagh 2007a).
[600]Ferdowsī 1971, vol. VII, p. 387.

possess seals from the Kārinid Dādmihr (Dādburzmihr, Burzmihr) as the *spāhbed* of Khurāsān during the rule of Khusrow I. Two seals in fact are in Gyselen's collection, one maintaining Dādburzmihr as the *ērān-spāhbed* of the side of the east,[601] and another personal seal of the same figure.[602] There is no doubt that the Dādburzmihr of the seals is the same figure as the Dādmihr of Justi and the Burzmihr of Ferdowsī, the two latter names being the shortened versions of the name as it appears on the seals. In both seals, moreover, Dādburzmihr insists on his Parthian genealogy by claiming to be a Parthian *aspbed*. Both seals, furthermore, have the added theophoric dimension of claiming the holder as taking refuge in the Burzīn Mihr fire of Khurāsān, thus once again confirming the local dimensions of the agnatic spiritual beliefs.[603] There is, therefore, no doubt: the Kārins were appointed as *spāhbeds* of the side of Khurāsān (*kūst-i khwarāsān*) by Khusrow I Nowshīrvān in the course of the administrative/military reforms that he implemented when dividing his realm into four quarters. The novelty in Khusrow I's reforms, was that, in order to establish control over the Parthian dynastic families in their extensive traditional homelands, he apparently assigned some of them to territories outside their ancestral domains, thus engendering further antagonism among the Parthian dynastic families and increasing the maneuverability of the monarchy vis-à-vis these.[604] For Khurāsān, we recall, was the traditional homeland of the Ispahbudhān family[605] and not that of the Kārins, whose ancestral land seems to have been Nihāvand.[606] This then also explains Ibn Isfandīyār's contention that in the course of his reforms Khusrow I partitioned the territories,[607] for he must have done this to further divide the Parthian dynastic families. This certainly was the case with the Ispahbudhān and the Kārin families. The unfortunate results of this will become apparent in one of the most crucial junctures of Sasanian history, the Arab conquest of Khurāsān in the mid-seventh century.[608]

We can now sum up the identifications proposed thus far as follows. In the course of the reforms that Khusrow I implemented, the Parthian families continued their cooperation with the Sasanian king. The Kārins were assigned as the *spāhbeds* of the east (*kūst-i khwarāsān*), the Ispahbudhān as the *spāhbeds* of the west (*kūst-i khwarbarān*), and the Mihrāns as the *spāhbeds* of the quarter

[601] Gyselen 2001a, seal 1b, p. 36.

[602] Gyselen 2001a, seal A, p. 36. In the Hermitage Museum in St. Petersburg, there is also a silver bowl with the inscription "Dādburzmihr, son of Farrokhān from the Gīlsarān(?) family, *spāhbed* of the east;" see Khurshudian 1998, p. 153. How this can be reconciled with our gentilitial analysis requires further study. Another seal that most likely belongs to the same figure is the seal of a *driyōšān jādaggōw ud dādvar* (*jādhūyih*, see page 197) with the inscription "Dādburzmihr, aspbed-i pahlav, [seeking] protection in the Exalted", depicting two facing winged horses as on the personal seal of Dādburzmihr. Gyselen 1989, p. 159.

[603] Gyselen 2001a, seals, 1b and A, pp. 36 and 46. For the Burzīn Mihr fire, see page 364 below.

[604] We will elaborate on this point as we proceed.

[605] Sebeos 1999, p. 42.

[606] See for instance our discussion on page 243ff below.

[607] See also page 295 below.

[608] See §3.4.7 below, especially page 271ff.

of the north (*kūst-i ādurbādagān*). Therefore, not much seems to have changed in the dynamics between the Sasanians and the Parthian dynastic families even after the presumed Mazdakite uprising and Khusrow I Nowshīrvān's reform. By now, we must have also partially explicated the falsity of the scenarios about the presumed consequences of the Mazdakite uprising: even if there was any such mass uprising, it barely affected the fortunes of the Parthian dynastic families, or, as we shall shortly see, the dynamics of their relationship with the Sasanian monarchy.

Kai Khusrow's army

This is corroborated by Ferdowsī's description of Kai Khusrow's battle against Afrāsīyāb, a classic example of the anachronistic editing that took place during the reign of the Sasanians, in all likelihood by the Parthian dynastic families. The late Shahbazi labeled this use of anachronism as the *Ctesian method*.[609] According to Shahbazi, in this battle that is said to have taken place around Fārāb near Dihistān in the east, Ferdowsī gives a detailed description of the battle formation of Kai Khusrow's army together with a list of names, most of which "are unfamiliar in Firdausī's narrative of Kai Xusrau's reign."[610] Included in the army, are, moreover, foreign contingents such as the Yemenite, Roman, Moorish, and Caucasian units whose incorporation in the ranks of the army of the mythic king Kai Khusrow is bewildering. Shahbazi concludes, therefore, that the mention of these units as well as the detailed and careful description of the battle proves not only that Ferdowsī resorted to a "written record which, necessarily, related to the Sasanian army," but also that the document must have been describing the battle of Khusrow I Nowshīrvān against the Hephthalites.[611]

What Shahbazi did not highlight,[612] however, is that the ranks of Kai Khusrow's army were populated with the Parthian dynasts thus far discussed. To start with, one Shēdōsh was fighting together with the men of Bardaʿa in Arrān[613] and of Ardabīl in Azarbāyjān. The whole contingent was put under the command of one Gūdarz the Kārin, who led Kai Khusrow's left flank. It is almost certain that this Shēdōsh was none other than Sēd-hōsh of the Mihrān family, the *ērān-spāhbed* of the side of the north form the seals.[614] The Mihrāns,

[609]The *Ctesian method* is what we have already alluded to: an anachronistic editing of the text, in this case the *X*^{w}*adāy-Nāmag* tradition. According to Shahbazi, "Iranian compilers of a national history sometimes used what we may term the *Ctesian method* of anachronism whereby old history was enriched and its lacunae filled in by the projection of recent events or their reflections into remoter times." Shahbazi 1990, p. 211.

[610]Shahbazi 1990, p. 213.

[611]Shahbazi 1990, p. 213.

[612]See also the diagram that he provides.

[613]Bardaʿa, modern-day Barda, the former capital of Arrān (Albania), was called Pērōzāpāt in Persian and, significantly, Partav in Armenian, being its etymology. Dunlop, D.M., 'Barḍaʿa', in P. Bearman, Th. Bianquis, C.E. Bosworth, E. van Donzel, and W.P. Heinrichs (eds.), *Encyclopaedia of Islam*, Leiden, 2007 (Dunlop 2007).

[614]It must be noted significantly that, as Gyselen remarks, the name Sēd-hōsh is not a common name but is extremely rare. Gyselen 2001a, seal 4b, p. 45. As she maintains, "although proper

with their home base in the quarter of the north, a quarter which included parts of Azarbāyjān, and having a long connection with Armenia, were therefore naturally in charge of the contingent of Bardaʿa and Ardabīl. Included in the left flank was yet another familiar figure of Khusrow I's establishment, one Farēburz. In all probability, Farēburz was none other than the Mihrānid Phabrizus of Procopius, who, together with his brother Īzadgushasp (Procopius' Isdigousnas) was directly involved in Khusrow I's wars against the Byzantines.[615] One Nastūh, the son of the Mihrānid Mihrānsitād of Khusrow I's administration,[616] also participated in this same left flank. Participating in the rear lines was also a certain Gorgēn Mīlād who appeared together "with men of Rey."[617] As we already mentioned, this Gorgēn Mīlād was probably the same Gōrgōn of the seals, called Gołon Mihrān in Sebeos.[618] In other words, in the figures of Gorgēn Mīlād and Shēdōsh we have most probably confirmed the identities of the two *spāhbeds* of the northern quarter during the reign of Khusrow I Nowshīrvān, Gōrgōn and Sēd-hōsh.[619] Besides being the *ērān-spāhbed* of the side of the north, Sēd-hōsh is called on his seals the *aspbed* (leader of the cavalry) of the empire. Appropriately, therefore, in the army formation of Kai Khusrow, Shēdōsh appeared in the left wing, under the command of Gūdarz the Kārin.

We cannot ascertain why the name of this Kārin is given as Gūdarz. There are two possibilities. This Gūdarz may be one of the nine sons of Sukhrā, some of whose names have been lost in our historical records, or Ferdowsī can be simply following through his Ctesian method, where the real name of the historical Kārinid figure, the one who was appointed as the *spāhbed* of the east, is supplemented by the name of a mythic ancestor of the house. In the course of restructuring his realm, Khusrow I, we further recall, had given Ṭabaristān and Zābulistān to the sons of the Kārinid Sukhrā. An army of Zābulistān in fact did appear in Kai Khusrow's battle formation under the command of one Rustam, who is put in charge of the right wing. In this same right wing were also the "Caucasian mercenaries under Gēv the Kāren."[620] Two other Kārins, Bīzhan and Rahām, also participated in the rear lines.[621] There is every reason to suppose that Ṭūs, the commander of the right flank, who carried the Imperial banner, is a representation of the Asparapet of Sebeos, the *spāhbed* of the western quarter, the father of Vistāhm and Vindūyih. His authority over the armies of Khuzistān and Yemen makes sense, as he was the *spāhbed* of the

names with *sēd* are known, *hōš* is not attested." Gyselen 2001a, p. 32 and n. 87 and 88. Indeed the one example that Justi provides, Sēd-hōsh, son of Gūdarz, belongs to the legendary period. Justi 1895, p. 294.

[615]See page 102.

[616]See page 103.

[617]Shahbazi 1990, p. 213.

[618]Gyselen 2001a, p. 44, seal 4a. See our discussion on page 103.

[619]Gyselen 2001a, pp. 44–45, seals 4a and 4b respectively.

[620]Shahbazi 1990, p. 213.

[621]Shahbazi 1990, p. 213.

west.[622] Finally, it is rather certain that in Rustam, who was put in command of the right wing, we are actually dealing with an agnate of the Sūren family, whose exploits replicate those of the mythic character Rustam.

The identity of so many of these figures with those contained in our Armenian, Greek, and Persian accounts supports Shahbazi's assertion as to the use of *Ctesian method* and the substitution of figures from the reign of Khusrow I to that of the semi-legendary king Kai Khusrow. Moreover, it not only substantiates the reliability of Ferdowsī but also the contention of the present study. For, even if none of the postulates as to the identity of these figures with actual historical figures of Khusrow I's reign were to be admitted—quite unlikely in view of the overwhelming nature of the evidence—the list of the Mihrāns, the Kārins, and possibly the Ispahbudhān and the Sūrens in Kai Khusrow's army proves that the superimposition in question in fact replicates not only the rule of Khusrow I Nowshīrvān but also that of all the dynastic figures participating in the defense and administration of his realm. Returning to our narrative, however, enables us to identify even more of the figures appearing on the seals as members of these same Parthian dynastic families.

2.6 Hormozd IV / the Mihrāns

For all the fanfare surrounding Khusrow I's reforms, the one Sasanian monarch who actually attempted to do away with major Parthian dynastic families in a systematic manner, as we have already briefly mentioned, was Hormozd IV (579–590). His actions, as we shall see, had dire results: they led to the unprecedented rebellions of two Parthian dynasts, the Mihrānid Bahrām-i Chūbīn and the Ispahbudhān Vistāhm. According to Ṭabarī, Hormozd IV had "benevolence toward the weak and destitute, but he attacked the power of the *nobles*, so that they showed themselves hostile and hated him, exactly as he in turn hated them."[623] Both Ṭabarī and Ibn Balkhī relate that Hormozd IV removed the nobles from his court and killed "13,600 [!] men from the religious classes and from those of good family and noble birth."[624] It is Ferdowsī, however, who actually provides us with substantive information on some of the leading members of the nobility decimated by Hormozd IV. At the beginning of this narrative, Ferdowsī specifically informs us that Hormozd IV wanted to do away with the elite that had obtained privileged positions in the court of his father Khusrow I Nowshīrvān and had become immune from harm therein.[625]

---

[622]See page 105ff. In this contingent, Ferdowsī also mentions one Tukhār, which is a title rather than a name; see footnote 825.

[623]Ṭabarī 1999, p. 295, de Goeje, 988. Emphasis added.

[624]Ṭabarī 1999, p. 297, de Goeje, 990. Ibn Balkhī 1995, p. 242; Dīnawarī 1960, p. 84, Dīnawarī 1967, p. 90.

[625]Ferdowsī 1971, vol. VIII, p. 319:

هر انکس که نزد پدرش ارجمند بدی شاد و ایمن ز بیم و گزند
یکایك تباه کردشان بی گناه بدین گونه بد راه و آیین شاه

Hormozd IV is portrayed as being preoccupied with the welfare of the poor and the peasantry. Significantly, he warned those with kingly pretensions (*shāhvash*) and those in search of treasuries, that they would find their demise if they were to pursue accumulation of wealth.[626] Immediately afterwards Ferdowsī provides us with concrete information, singling out three dynasts whom Hormozd IV murdered. The identity of these can be compared against our recent sigillographic evidence.

The three magnates against whom Hormozd IV's wrath was especially directed were Īzadgushasp, Sīmāh-i Burzīn, and Bahrām-i Māh Ādhar.[627] One by one, these high dignitaries of Khusrow I's administration were done away with by Hormozd IV. We have already become quite familiar with the Mihrānid Īzadgushasp.[628] He is identified by Ferdowsī as a vizier[629] and *dabīr* to Khusrow I. One of the first casualties of Hormozd IV's wrath was this Īzadgushasp, who, according to a detailed narrative in the *Shāhnāma*, was first imprisoned and then killed by Hormozd IV.[630]

2.6.1 Bahrām-i Māh Ādhar

The fate of two other leading feudal figures under Hormozd IV's administration is even more revealing, for here we can actually match the identity of those singled out by Ferdowsī with the figures mentioned on the recently discovered seals. This identification is beyond any doubt at least for one of these figures,

[626]Ferdowsī 1971, vol. VIII, p. 318, Ferdowsī 1935, p. 2569:

همه کار درویش دارد دلم   نخواهم که اندیشه زو بگسلم
همی خواهم از پاك پروردگار   که چندان مرا بردهد روزگار
که درویش را شاد دارم به گنج   نیارم دل پارسا را به رنج
هر انکس که شد در جهان شاهوش   سرش گردد از گنج دینار کش
سرش را بپیچم ز کنداوری   نخواهم که جوید کسی مهتری ...
چو بشنید گفتار او انجمن   پر اندیشه گشتند از ان تن به تن
سر گنجداران پر از بیم گشت   ستمگاره را دل بدو نیم گشت
خردمند و درویش زان هر که بود   بدلش اندرون شادمانی فزود

[627]Ferdowsī 1971, vol. VIII, p. 319:

بر تخت نوشیروان این سه پیر   چو دستور بودند و همچون وزیر
چو ایزد گشسپ و دگر برزمهر   دبیر خردمند با فرّ و چهر
سه دیگر که ماه اذرش بود نام   خردمند و روشن دل و شاد کام

Ferdowsī 1935, p. 2574–2575:

همی خواست هرمز کزین هر سه مرد   بر ارد یکایك ز ناگاه گرد

[628]See page 102.

[629]Also Dīnawarī 1960, p. 84, Dīnawarī 1967, p. 89.

[630]Bosworth maintains that this Īzadgushasp is the same figure who later appears among the supporters of Bahrām-i Chūbīn. If Ferdowsī's detailed narrative about the murder of Īzadgushasp is to be trusted—there is no reason why it should not be—and considering that Ferdowsī, in fact, counts a certain Īzadgushasp among the supporters of Bahrām-i Chūbīn—around the role of whom in Bahrām-i Chūbīn's army there is likewise a detailed narrative—Bosworth's identification of the two figures is not warranted. Ṭabarī 1999, p. 299, n. 703. Justi, in fact, appropriately separates the two figures in this instance. Justi 1895, p. 149, under Yazdwšnasp, numbers 4 and 5, and p. 429.

Bahrām-i Māh Ādhar. For among Gyselen's collection, there are two seals that identify the bearer as Wahrām, son of Ādurmāh, seals 2a and 2b. According to Gyselen, one belongs to the reign of Khusrow I and the other to that of Hormozd IV.[631] Both of these identifications of Gyselen are correct. There is no doubt that Ferdowsī's figure Bahrām-i Māh Ādhar[632] is the same personage whose seals have been recently discovered. This Bahrām, who is identified in both of the seals as the *spāhbed* of the south (*kūst-i nēmrōz*) is further identified with a number of epithets. For the reign of Khusrow I, he bears the title "chief of ... and eunuch."[633] For that of Hormozd IV, his epithet is "chief of ... and eunuch, hazāruft of the empire."[634] Following Ferdowsī's narrative, it may therefore be supposed that at the inception of Hormozd IV's reign, Bahrām-i Māh Ādhar was in fact maintained and promoted in his administration. Shortly thereafter, under unclear circumstances that seemed to have led to a change of policy under Hormozd IV, this leading figure of Khusrow I's administration was done away with.[635] The problem with Bahrām-i Māh Ādhar's identity, however, is that in our present state of knowledge, and unlike the Mihrānid Īzadgushasp, we cannot clearly establish his gentilitial background. If there is any validity to Justi's claim about the possible Sasanian lineage of this figure,[636] and considering the fact that there might have been a greater participation of the nobility of Persīs in the quarter of the south, then Bahrām-i Māh Ādhar was probably a Pārsīg. This leaves us with the third figure listed by Ferdowsī, that of Sīmāh-i Burzīn.

2.6.2 Sīmāh-i Burzīn Kārin

As we have seen, there are two seals which belong to the *spāhbeds* of the east. We have already become familiar with one, that of Dād-Burz-Mihr, the Parthian *aspbed* of the Kārin. He was one of the sons of the Kārinid Sukhrā whom Khusrow I had appointed *spāhbed* of the east (*kūst-i khwarāsān*) and whom Hormozd IV retained for a while in this capacity.[637] The other seal identifies yet another

[631] Gyselen 2001a, pp. 37–38, seals 2a, 2b.

[632] Ferdowsī 1971, vol. VIII, pp. 324–328, Ferdowsī 1935, pp. 2574–2578. In Thaʿālibī's narrative, he is called Bahrām-i Ādharmahān and identified as one of the grandees of Khusrow I's reign. Thaʿālibī 1900, p. 638, Thaʿālibī 1989, p. 411. A great *marzbān* (*marzbānā rabbā*), Ādurmāhān, is also mentioned by Johannes from Ephesus as a general of Khusrow I. Khurshudian 1998, p. 71.

[633] Gyselen 2001a, p. 37, seal 2a.

[634] Gyselen 2001a, p. 38, seal 2b.

[635] Justi cites him as being mentioned also by Theophanes. Justi identifies this figure as the *mōbad* of Hormozd IV's reign. Under this same entry, however, he cites a seal of this Bahrām in which he is identified as "Bahrām, son of Āturmāh, descended from gods." Here, Justi questions, in brackets, whether this is meant to signify that he is a Sasanian. Justi 1895, p. 362, numbers 21 and 22, respectively. Ferdowsī 1935, p. 2578, Ferdowsī 1971, vol. VIII, pp. 319–320. Clearly, as the evidence of the seals makes it apparent, Justi's identification of this figure as a *mōbad* is not warranted. That a seal from him already exists in which he claims descent from gods, however, is revealing, and might indeed point to a close relation between this figure and the Sasanians.

[636] See previous footnote.

[637] See page 114ff.

spāhbed assigned to the east for the reign of Hormozd IV, one Chihr Burzīn.[638] This latter figure might be identical with a personage called Sīmāh-i Burzīn in the *Shāhnāma*. Chihr Burzīn, the literal translation of which is "having the face of Burzīn [fire]," is the exact equivalent of Sīmāh-i Burzīn, where *chihr* and *sīmāh* are identical in meaning. Using poetic license, one may postulate, therefore, that Ferdowsī substituted the name of Chihr Burzīn with that of Sīmāh-i Burzīn for the purposes of rhyme and rhythm, a practice in which the poet regularly indulges.[639] In Ferdowsī's narrative, Sīmāh-i Burzīn is depicted as one of the high elite of the reign of Khusrow I Nowshirvān, who together with Bahrām-i Māh Ādhar and Īzadgushasp were among the nobility that were consulted by Khusrow I for choosing a successor. As Ferdowsī and Thaʿālibī's accounts inform us, Hormozd IV began his onslaught on the Parthian dynastic nobility, partly through the age old mechanism available to the Sasanians: the instigation of one dynastic family against another.[640] Ferdowsī informs us that in order to undermine the power of the dynastic factions of his realm, Hormozd IV instigated Bahrām-i Māh Ādhar, the *spāhbed* of the quarter of the south (*kūst-i nēmrōz*) during Khusrow I (seal 2a), as well as his own reign (seal 2b), against Sīmāh-i Burzīn, that is, if our identification is correct, against Khusrow I's *spāhbed* Chihr Burzīn (seal 1a). In a private correspondence between the two powerful figures of Hormozd IV's realm, and in response to Sīmāh-i Burzīn's astonishment at the sudden change of demeanor of Bahrām-i Māh Ādhar against him, the latter explained that Sīmāh-i Burzīn himself was to be held responsible for the turn of events, for he belonged to the faction that had voted for Hormozd IV's kingship to begin with.[641]

The dynastic background of Sīmāh-i Burzīn can only be conjectured. If even after Khusrow I's reforms important offices of the realm, in this case the office of *spāhbed*, remained hereditary, and if Dād-Burz-Mihr, the Parthian *aspbed* (*aspbed ī pahlaw*) and *spāhbed* of the east during Hormozd IV's reign (seal 1b) is none other than the Kārinid Dādmihr,[642] then it might be conjectured that Sīmāh-i Burzīn or Chihr Burzīn, the *spāhbed* of the east during Khusrow I's reign, also belonged to the Kārin family. In fact, the Kārins continued to maintain the *spāhbedī* of the east until after Bahrām-i Chūbīn's rebellion.[643] As we have argued, the tradition of giving the *spāhbedī* of the east to the Kārins in fact began with the rule of Khusrow I. When Hormozd IV instigated Bahrām-i Māh Ādhar, the *spāhbed* of the quarter of the south (*kūst-i nēmrōz*) during his father's reign, against Sīmāh-i Burzīn, or Chihr Burzīn, the *spāhbed* of the east during Khusrow I's reign, therefore, he was instigating one leading dynastic agnate, Bahrām-i Māh Ādhar, whose agnatic affiliation is not clear, against

[638] Gyselen 2001a, pp. 37–38, seals 1a, 1b.

[639] See also our discussion of Bahrām-i Chūbīn's epithet on page 399.

[640] Thaʿālibī 1900, pp. 638–639, Thaʿālibī 1989, p. 411.

[641] Ferdowsī 1935, p. 2575–2576, Ferdowsī 1971, vol. VIII, pp. 323–325.

[642] Gyselen 2001a, seal 1b, p. 36 and seal A, p. 46. See our argument on page 114ff.

[643] For the details of this see the narrative of Bahrām-i Chūbīn in §2.6.3 below.

another leading dynastic figure, who belonged to the house of the Kārins, Sīmāh-i Burzīn. Having done so, however, Hormozd IV could not take away the *spāhbedī* of the east from the Kārin family. For, as we have seen, the *spāhbed* that he ended up assigning in the quarter of the east, Dād-Burz-Mihr (Dādmihr), the Parthian *aspbed* of seal 1b, was still a Kārinid.

At any rate, what is significant for the purposes of the present discussion is that ultimately both Bahrām-i Māh Ādhar as well as the Kārinid Sīmāh-i Burzīn were killed by Hormozd IV,[644] and joined the fate of the Mihrānid Īzadgushasp as the leading dynastic figures of Khusrow I's reign who were murdered by Hormozd IV.[645] But that is not all. All our sources, including Sebeos,[646] maintain that the father of Vindūyih and Vistāhm, Asparapet, the *Parthian aspet* of the Ispahbudhān family, of whom we have heard in detail,[647] the father-in-law of Hormozd IV and the grandfather of Khusrow II, was also murdered during Hormozd IV's purge of magnates. Such slaughter of leading agnates of Parthian families belonging to different dynastic houses was probably unprecedented in Sasanian history. That this decimation could not have been total and the king nevertheless was forced to continue to rely on the powers of the nobility is evidenced not only by Hormozd IV's retention of the Ispahbudhān Vindūyih and Vistāhm in his administration and the tremendous power base of these, as we shall see, but also by the continued reliance of the king on the power of the Mihrāns and the Kārins. The ultimate treatment of these in the hands of Hormozd IV and his son, Khusrow II, however, commenced the unprecedented upheavals that led the Parthian dynastic families to question the very legitimacy of the Sasanians for kingship. We are referring here to the revolts of Bahrām-i Chūbīn of the Mihrān family and that of Vistāhm of the Ispahbudhān family. The Parthian confederacy with the Sasanians was for the first time violently disrupted through the rebellion of Bahrām-i Chūbīn.

2.6.3 Bahrām-i Chūbīn Mihrān

Bahrām-i Chūbīn's rebellion was unlike any other in Sasanian history. Except perhaps in Armenia, and not since the last Parthian king, Ardavān, was any Parthian dynast audacious enough to question the very legitimacy of Sasanian kingship. The monarchy might be dominated, directed, abused, and possibly mocked by the Parthian dynastic families. But the tradition had been established: even an infant Sasanian was deemed to be more legitimate for kingship—or so at least the *X^{w}adāy-Nāmag* tradition would have us believe—than any member of the Parthian nobility, at least formally. As far as the Parthian dynastic families were concerned, the name of the game was confederacy. Bahrām-i Chūbīn's rebellion changed most of this. As with the rise of the Parthians from the perspective of the Sasanians, Bahrām-i Chūbīn's rebellion was also

[644] Thaʿālibī 1900, pp. 638–639, Thaʿālibī 1989, pp. 411–413.
[645] Ferdowsī 1935, p. 2570; see also footnote 627.
[646] Sebeos 1999, p. 14.
[647] See §2.5.5.

attended by a religious dichotomy,[648] that of Parthava versus Persīs, and a powerful messianic fervor. All the narratives of the rebellion in the literary sources are infused with millennial motifs. We shall deal with the religious dimensions of Bahrām-i Chūbīn's rebellion below. For now, however, we concern ourselves only with the sociopolitical dimensions of his rebellion.[649]

Prognostication of Hormozd IV's demise

According to the narratives at our disposal, some years into his reign, previously prognosticated to be, significantly, the messianic number twelve, Hormozd IV found his realm attacked by the Turks from the east, the Byzantines from the west, the Khazars from the northwestern Caspian region, and the Arabs from the west.[650] Significantly, it was Bahrām-i Ādhar-māhān (Bahrām-i Māh Ādhar) who had informed Hormozd IV that the apocalypse would soon arrive and that Hormozd IV was to be blamed for it on account of his injustice.[651] Hormozd IV had become unjust because of the crimes that he had committed against the grandees of his realm, turning against custom and tradition (*āʾīn o kīsh*).[652] For the first time in Sasanian history, Hormozd IV had unleashed an all-out attack against almost every single leading agnate of the Parthian and other dynastic families. Among the measures taken by Hormozd IV was a further reduction of the size of their cavalry, and a decrease in the army's pay.[653] Although Hormozd IV's policies were in a sense the continuation of reforms inaugurated by Khusrow I, especially his taxation policies, his systematic onslaught on the Parthian dynastic families was of such intensity that in Bahrām-i Chūbīn's rebellion, the theme of Parthian claim to rule was voiced for the first time in Sasanian history. While there continued to be dissension in their ranks, and while they finally lost as a result of it, at the inception of Bahrām-i Chūbīn's rebellion, a powerful Parthian alliance was formed. It is for this reason that the theme of Sasanian–Parthian rivalry infuses not only the Persian and Arabic accounts of Bahrām-i Chūbīn, but also that of the western sources that were witness to its actual unfolding.

As already mentioned, the first episode of millennial prognostication is communicated to Hormozd IV by his and his father's *spāhbed* of the south, Bahrām-i Ādhar Mahān (Bahrām-i Māh Ādhar), or, as he appears on the seals,

[648]See §6.1 for the religious connotations of this rebellion, and §5.3.3 for the dichotomy.

[649]For a synopsis of the state of the field on Bahrām-i Chūbīn's rebellion, see Shahbazi, Shapur, 'Bahrām VI Čōbīn', in Ehsan Yarshater (ed.), *Encyclopaedia Iranica*, New York, 2007a (Shahbazi 2007a).

[650]Ṭabarī 1999, pp. 298–301, de Goeje, 991; Ferdowsī 1971, vol. VIII, pp. 331–332, Ferdowsī 1935, p. 2582–2583. For a synopsis of these histories, see Ṭabarī 1999, nn. 701, 703–705, and the citations given therein.

[651]Ferdowsī 1971, vol. VIII, p. 327, Ferdowsī 1935, p. 2578.

[652]Ferdowsī 1971, vol. VIII, p. 319, Ferdowsī 1935, pp. 2582–2583:

همه موبدان و دبیران خویش بکشتی و گشتی زائین و کیش

[653]Shahbazi 2007a, p. 519.

Wahrām, son of Ādurmāh, the *hazāruft*.[654] Recognizing his imminent doom, Bahrām-i Māh Ādhar decided to make life unbearable thenceforth for the Sasanian king, and forecasted the demise of the king in twelve years.[655] But the prognostication did not stop here. It was reiterated once more, this time, significantly, from the mouth of the Parthian Mihrāns. When the enemy attacked from all sides, the Mihrānid Nastūh, the son of Mihrānsitād,[656] informed the king that his father's knowledge would be of use to the king.[657] Hormozd IV then sent for Mihrānsitād, who had taken up seclusion in Rayy, the traditional home-base of the Mihrāns, occupying himself, significantly, with Zand and the Avestā.[658] When Mihrānsitād was summoned to the king's court, he first narrated for Hormozd IV, presumably out of fear, his own central role in choosing the king's mother, the daughter of the Turkish Khāqān, and then informed Hormozd IV that the astrologers who had read the stars for the Khaqān had also forecasted that when the Turks attacked Iran, the savior of Hormozd IV's throne would be a certain Bahrām-i Chūbīn of Pahlav ancestry. Mihrānsitād then advised Hormozd IV to search and summon Bahrām-i Chūbīn to his court. According to Ferdowsī, having given this prognostication and introduced Bahrām-i Chūbīn's narrative, the aged Mihrānsitād died instantly.[659] As Ferdowsī's poetic rendition informs us, this prompted Hormozd IV to avail himself of the services of the Parthian Mihrānid dynast Bahrām-i Chūbīn, who in the course of his military campaigns in the west and the east in fact did help Hormozd IV sustain his kingship.[660]

---

[654] Gyselen 2001a, pp. 37–38, seals 2a and 2b, respectively.

[655] While in prison Bahrām-i Māh Ādhar sent a message to Hormozd IV that he should avail himself of a black box, left for posterity by Khusrow I Nowshīrvān, and that he should read the message contained therein, written on a white silk cloth. The message predicted the onslaught of enemies from the four corners of Iran, the blinding of the king, and his demise in the twelfth year of his kingship. Ferdowsī 1971, vol. VIII, p. 327, Ferdowsī 1935, pp. 2582–2583. Thaʿālibī 1900, pp. 637–642, Thaʿālibī 1989, pp. 411–413.

[656] See page 103.

[657] Ferdowsī 1971, vol. VIII, p. 335, Ferdowsī 1935, pp. 2586–2587.

[658] Ferdowsī 1971, vol. VIII, p. 335, Ferdowsī 1935, pp. 2586–2587. For the significance of reading the Zand, that is, the interpretation of the Avestā, see §5.2.5.

[659] Ferdowsī 1971, vol. VIII, pp. 336–337, Ferdowsī 1935, p. 2587–2588:

به پرسش گرفت اختر دخترش　　که تا چون بود گردش اخترش
ستاره شمر گفت جز نیکویی　　نبینی و جز راست نشنوی
از این دخت و از شاه ایرانیان　　یکی پور زاید چو شیر ژیان
به بالا بلند و به بازو ستبر　　به مردی چو شیر و به بخشش چو ابر …
فراوان ز گنج پدر بر خورد　　بسی روزگاران به بد نسپرد
وزان پس یکی شاه خیزد سترگ　　ز ترکان سپاهی بیارد بزرگ …
یکی کهتری باشدش دوردست　　سواری سرافراز مهترپرست …
جهانجوی چوبینه دارد لقب　　هم از پهلوانانش باشد نسب

[660] Sebeos 1999, p. 15; Czegledy, K., 'Bahrām Chubīn and the Persian Apocalyptic Literature', *Acta Orientalia Hungarica* 8, (1958), pp. 21–43 (Czegledy 1958); Shahbazi 2007a.

Bahrām-i Chūbīn's western campaigns

Already in 572, at the end of the rule of Khusrow I, Bahrām-i Chūbīn had participated in the king's campaigns against the Byzantines and in the Caucasus, and had been in charge of the cavalry that captured the Byzantine city of Dara.[661] According to some of our sources, Bahrām-i Chūbīn, son of Bahrām Gushnāsp, started as a margrave of Rayy.[662] This piece of information fits quite well with the fact that the *spāhbeds* of the north during Khusrow I's reign were in fact from the Mihrān family. If our theory as to the familial relationship of Bahrām-i Chūbīn with Gōrgōn[663] is correct, then the appointment of Bahrām-i Chūbīn after his grandfather as *spāhbed* of the north further confirms our contention that the *spāhbedī* of particular quarters was maintained within the same dynastic family. At any rate, Dīnawarī calls Bahrām-i Chūbīn the *marzbān* of Armenia and Azarbāyjān,[664] a military and administrative jurisdiction that in fact corresponds to the *spāhbedī* of the *kūst-i ādurbādagān*.

The Parthian genealogical claims of Bahrām-i Chūbīn, as well as his provenance from the Mihrānid capital Rayy, are highlighted by most of our narratives.[665] In the *Shāhnāma*, Rayy, as the capital of the Mihrāns, is clearly pitted against Persīs. Jumping ahead for a moment in our narrative, in the mutual diatribe of the antagonists, Bahrām-i Chūbīn and Khusrow II Parvīz, when they are confronted in the battle scene near Lake Urumiya in Azarbāyjān, the Sasanian Khusrow II accused the Parthians of Rayy of complicity with Alexander and then of assuming kingship.[666] The regional dimension of the rivalry between the house of Sāsān and the descendants of Ardavān is underlined with Bahrām-i Chūbīn's threat to relocate majesty from Fārs to Rayy.[667] The theme of restoring Arsacid glory is in fact central to Bahrām-i Chūbīn's platform for rebellion.[668] In yet another exchange, Bahrām-i Chūbīn reminded Khusrow II

[661]Simocatta 1986, 3.18.10f., pp. 101–102. For Bahrām-i Chūbīn western campaigns, also see Shahbazi 2007a, p. 519.

[662]Ferdowsī 1935, p. 2662, Ferdowsī 1971, vol. IX, p. 32; Mas'ūdī 1869, p. 215, Mas'ūdī, 'Alī b. Ḥusayn, *Murūj al-Dhahab*, Tehran, 1968, translation of Mas'ūdī 1869 by Abolqasim Payandih (Mas'ūdī 1968); Ṭabarī 1999, p. 301, n. 706, de Goeje, 992; Simocatta 1986, iii. 18.6, p. 101.

[663]Gyselen 2001a, seal, 4a, p. 44. See page 103 above.

[664]Dīnawarī 1960, p. 79, Dīnawarī 1967, p. 84.

[665]Czegledy 1958; Shahbazi 2007a.

[666]Ferdowsī 1971, vol. IX, p. 30, Ferdowsī 1935, p. 2696:

همان از ری امد سپاه اندکی که شد با سپاه سکندر یکی
میانها ببستند با رومیان گرفتند ناگاه تخت کیان

[667]Ferdowsī 1971, vol. IX, p. 32, Ferdowsī 1935, p. 2697:

بزرگی من از پارس ارم به ری نمانم کزین پس بود نام کی

[668]Ferdowsī 1971, vol. IX, p. 30:

بیازم بدین کار ساسانیان چو اشفته شیری که گردد ژیان
ز دفتر همه نامشان بسترم سر تخت ساسانیان بسپرم
بزرگی مر اشکانیان را سزاست اگر بشنود مرد داننده راست

that his Sasanian ancestors had in fact usurped kingship from the Arsacids. After five hundred years, however, Bahrām-i Chūbīn claimed, the demise of the Sasanians was imminent, and kingship must revert to the Arsacids.[669] He would not rest, Bahrām-i Chūbīn claimed, until he destroyed Kayānid kingship—a clear reference to the Sasanians' forged claim of being the progenies of the Kayānids.[670]

Bahrām-i Chūbīn's eastern campaigns

The substantial power of Bahrām-i Chūbīn at Hormozd IV's court is established beyond doubt. Simocatta maintains that once Bahrām-i Chūbīn's military successes increased, for example, he became the *darigbedum* (*darīgbed*) of the royal hearth of Hormozd IV.[671] While the precise powers of the *darīgbed* are not clear, it is clear that this must have been an extremely important office of late the Sasanian period.[672] One of the few figures who carried this title in late Sasanian history, was the towering figure of Farrukhzād,[673] whose story we examine in depth in Chapter 3. In 588, in the aftermath of the Hephthalites' attack against Iran, Bahrām-i Chūbīn was appointed as the commander-in-chief of the Sasanian forces and sent against the invading army. This is where our apocalyptic as well as historical narratives begin. Leading a messianic number of 12,000 cavalry to the east,[674] Bahrām-i Chūbīn conquered Balkh and the Hephthalite territories in what is now Afghanistan, crossed the Oxus, and killed the Khāqān of the Turks.[675] He finally advanced to a place called the Copper Fortress, Rūyīn Dizh, near Bukhārā.[676]

[669]Ferdowsī 1971, vol. IX, p. 29, Ferdowsī 1935, p. 2695:

بدو گفت بهرام کی مرد گرد   سزا ان بود کز تو شاهی ببرد
چو از دخت بابك بزاد اردشیر   نه اشکانیان را بد ان دار و گیر؟
نه چون اردشیر اردوان را بکشت   به نیرو شد و تختش اندر به مشت؟
کنون سال چون پانصد اندر گذشت   سر و تاج ساسانیان سرد گشت
کنون تخت و دیهیم را روز ماست   سر و کار با بخت پیروز ماست ...
بزرگی مر اشکانیان را سزاست   اگر بشنوی مرد داننده راست

For the millennial calculations involved in this reckoning, see Shahbazi et al. 1991, p. vi.

[670]See page 385ff for an elaboration of this.

[671]Simocatta 1986, iii.18.12, p. 102. For the office of *darīgbed*, see Gyselen 2002, pp. 113–114; Khurshudian 1998, pp. 109–113.

[672]Gyselen 2002, pp. 113–114. Khurshudian argues for a parallel with the Byzantine *cura palatii*, and the substantial growth of importance of this office at both courts. Khurshudian 1998, pp. 112–113.

[673]Gyselen 2002, pp. 113–114. Khusrow I's vizier Bozorg-Mehr (Dādmihr; see page 114) is also called a *darīgbed* in Bozorgmehr 1971, *Andarz-nāma-i Bozorgmehr-i Ḥakīm*, Isfahan, 1971, translated by F. Abadani (Bozorgmehr 1971); Gyselen 2002, pp. 113–114, citing Shaked, Shaul, 'Some Legal and Administrative Terms of the Sasanian Period', in *Momentum H. S. Nyberg*, vol. 5, pp. 213–225, 1975 (Shaked 1975), here pp. 223–225.

[674]Czegledy 1958; see also §6.1.2.

[675]This latter figure is mistakenly rendered as Shāwa, Sāva, Sāba. Shahbazi 2007a, p. 520.

[676]Shahbazi 2007a, p. 520. For Rūyīn Dizh, see page 406ff.

Our sources claim that Bahrām-i Chūbīn's successes in his western[677] and eastern campaigns prompted the jealousy of the king, and instigated Hormozd IV to undermine him. In the face of Hormozd IV's harassment, and prompted by other leading magnates who had gathered against Hormozd IV's anti-elite policies, therefore, Bahrām-i Chūbīn rebelled in the east in 590 CE, collecting around him a substantial force from the quarters of the east and the north.[678]

Hormozd IV and the Ispahbudhān

The Parthian rebel then set out for the capital of the ungrateful and foolhardy Sasanian king, Hormozd IV. Meanwhile, in the face of the tremendous support gained by the Mihrānid Bahrām-i Chūbīn, another significant coup was launched. Partly in revenge for Hormozd IV's murder of their father, Asparapet, in 586, the Ispahbudhān brothers Vistāhm and Vindūyih, now spearheaded a palace coup. The Sasanians proved once again to be at the mercy of the Parthians: two Parthian dynastic families came to steer the very fate of the Sasanian kinship. The Ispahbudhān brothers reenacted a recurrent chronicle of the house of Sāsān: they blinded, imprisoned, and finally murdered Hormozd IV, and attempted to enthrone his feeble son Khusrow II Parvīz.[679] So powerless were Khusrow II Parvīz and his forces against Bahrām-i Chūbīn's insurrection, that under the watchful guard of Vindūyih and Vistāhm, he was forced to flee to the bosom of the Sasanian's age-old enemy, the Byzantines, until such time that they could muster an army.[680] According to some accounts, one of the options discussed by the Parthian Ispahbudhān brothers and Khusrow II was to take refuge with the Arabs and seek their aid.[681] With the Persian crown now vacant, Bahrām-i Chūbīn seized it when he entered Ctesiphon in 590 CE. A Parthian dynast had finally nullified the contract of the Sasanian–Parthian confederacy by declaring himself king.

Even among the Parthians, however, this was hard to concede, especially by the Ispahbudhān brothers, who considered themselves "brothers [to] the Sasanians and their partners [in rule]."[682] Moreover, with the support of the Byzantine emperor Maurice and the army that had finally gathered around the Ispahbudhān brothers, Bahrām-i Chūbīn's chances and rhetoric had lost their appeal. A substantial sector of Bahrām-i Chūbīn's constituency therefore deserted him. Under the command of Maurice's brother, Khusrow II advanced toward Azarbāyjān to rendezvous with the 12,000-strong cavalry of Armenian forces under Mušeł Mamikonean, and the 8,000-strong cavalry organized by

---

677 See page 125.

678 On his way Bahrām-i Chūbīn passed via the Mihrānid capital Rayy and was joined by many veterans from the western front. Shahbazi 2007a, p. 521.

679 The young age of Khusrow II and his lack of manpower is highlighted in Sebeos' narrative among others: "For he [i.e., Khusrow II Parvīz] was a youth and the strength of his army was weak and modest." Sebeos 1999, p. 26.

680 Shahbazi 2007a, p. 521, and the sources cited therein.

681 Sebeos 1999, p. 18, but also Nihayat 1996, p. 366.

682 Dīnawarī 1960, p. 102, Dīnawarī 1967, p. 111. See our discussion on page 110.

Vindūyih and Vistāhm. Sebeos confirms that the Ispahbudhān's base of operation was now Azarbāyjān, where they rallied "support ... under the watchful eye of John Mystacon, *Magister Militum per Armeniam*, who was mobilizing troops throughout Armenia."[683] For our future purposes it is important to note that at this point the *army of Nīmrūz*, the army of the south, also set out to aid Khusrow II Parvīz.

Bahrām-i Chūbīn's defeat

This predicament of the Sasanian king Khusrow II Parvīz must be kept in mind in any assessment of the military reforms undertaken by his grandfather, Khusrow I Nowshīrvān: Two generations after the latter was presumed to have established his absolutist kingship, overshadowing even the powers of Shāpūr II, the Sasanian crown could only be salvaged with the aid of the Byzantines, the Armenians, and, most importantly, their closest of kin, the Parthian Ispahbudhān family. It was with the combined power of these armed forces—itself a reflection of the continued dependency of the Sasanians on the military prowess of the Parthian dynastic families—that Khusrow II was finally able to defeat the by now depleted forces of Bahrām-i Chūbīn. It is symptomatic of Sasanian history and the traditional part played by Armenia in this history, that, as Sebeos informs us, at this point Bahrām-i Chūbīn even wrote letters to the Armenian *sparapet* Mušeł Mamikonean.[684] Now, by hereditary right, the Mamikoneans held the office of *spāhbed* (*sparapet*) throughout the fourth century and even after. They claimed, moreover, Arsacid ancestry.[685] It is certain, therefore, that the Parthian Bahrām-i Chūbīn had his common ancestry with the Mamikonean house, as well as their shared heritage vis-à-vis the Sasanians, in mind when in his letter to Mušeł, he wrote: "As for you Armenians

[683]Sebeos puts the number of Byzantine forces at 3,000 cavalry and that of the Armenian as 15,000, presumably in both cavalry and infantry. Sebeos 1999, pp. 19–20, 172; Ferdowsī 1971, vol. IX, pp. 98–105, Ferdowsī 1935, p. 2676–2677.

[684]The office of *sparapet*, i.e., Middle Persian *spāhbed*, in Armenia, like most Armenian institutions replicated the office in Sasanian Iran before the reforms of Khusrow I. As Garsoian informs us, the "office of *sparapet* was clearly the most important one after that of the king. [Throughout the fourth century it] was hereditary in the Mamikonean house, which held it by nature, fundamentally, originally ... *Like the other contemporary offices of this type it belonged to the family as a whole and did not pass in direct line from father to son* ... [T]he hereditary character of the office was such that it was not affected by the inability of the holder of the title to perform the duties of his office because of his extreme youth ... The royal [Armenian Arsacid] attempt to interfere in the normal succession and to bestow this office on a member of another family was viewed as flagrant abuse naturally ending in tragedy. The evidence ... makes it amply clear that the power of the Mamikonean *sparapets* did not depend on the favor of the [Armenian Arsacid] kings whom they outlived." Buzandaran 1989, pp. 560–561.

[685]As Garsoian maintains, "rightly or wrongly the Mamikonean were traditionally considered to have been of royal [i.e., Arsacid] ancestry ... The family may also have had Persian kinsmen." After the second Armenian revolt against Iran in 572 CE, the "family's fortunes began a slow decline, leading to the disappearance of its senior branch in the ninth century." A "cadet branch [also] survived in Tarōn, while other members of the family played important roles at the Byzantine court." Buzandaran 1989, pp. 385–386.

who demonstrate an unseasonable loyalty, did not the house of Sasan destroy your land and sovereignty? Why otherwise did your fathers rebel and extricate themselves from their service, fighting up until today for your country?"[686] As Howard–Johnston remarks, the extensive territorial and political concessions that Bahrām-i Chūbīn promised to the Arsacid Mamikonean house in this letter were tantamount to offering the Armenians a "junior partnership in the Sasanian empire (the kingdom of the Aryans)," a Sasanian empire ruled by a Parthian dynastic family, that is.[687] Bahrām-i Chūbīn's offer, however, was rejected by the Mamikoneans. It is indicative of the support for Bahrām-i Chūbīn that it took the combined forces of the Byzantines, the Armenians, and the Parthian Ispahbudhān family to defeat him. The Sasanian crown was thus saved, thanks to the sagacity of another Parthian dynastic family, the Ispahbudhān. For as all our sources agree: as the Ispahbudhān brothers later reminded the ungrateful Khusrow II Parvīz, had it not been for their protection of his kingship and for the forces that they were able to muster in Azarbāyjān—where the family had come to run deep roots, as we shall see also below[688]—Bahrām-i Chūbīn's rebellion could very well have marked the end of the Sasanian dynasty.

When, in the wake of his defeat, Bahrām-i Chūbīn was forced to flee east, he ran into yet another Parthian dynastic family, the Kārins. Even in flight, Bahrām-i Chūbīn was able to defeat the Kārins, after which he proceeded to take refuge with the Khāqān of the Turks.[689] As his continued existence was a humiliating affront to the Sasanians, however, Bahrām-i Chūbīn was finally murdered. Two variant narratives trace the semi-folkloric take on his murder, one of which claims that he was assassinated, through a ruse, by an agent of the Sasanians.[690] Here ends, temporarily,[691] our account of Bahrām-i Chūbīn's saga.

The rebellion of the Mihrāns against Hormozd IV and subsequently his son Khusrow II Parvīz galvanized the northern and northeastern territories of Iran, the former of which were the traditional homelands of the dynasty. Much of Khurāsān seemed to have supported the aspirations of the Mihrānid rebel, although, as the example of the Kārins bears witness, not all Parthians lent him their support. We recall from the seals that the Mihrāns were the *spāhbeds* of the north (*kūst-i ādurbādagān*[692]) throughout the rule of Khusrow I and presumably all of that of Hormozd IV. The *kūst-i ādurbādagān* included not only parts of Gīlān and Ṭabaristān, but also Azarbāyjān.[693] The incorporation of

[686]Sebeos 1999, p. 20.

[687]Sebeos 1999, p. 173.

[688]See, for instance, footnote 806.

[689]For Bahrām-i Chūbīn's flight to the east, see Ṭabarī 1999, pp. 314–316, nn. 736 and 740, and the sources cited therein, and Nihayat 1996, p. 380.

[690]Shahbazi 2007a, p. 521 and the sources cited there.

[691]For its powerful effects on the post-conquest history of Iran, see §6.1 below.

[692]See footnote 164.

[693]The exact boundaries between the quarter of the north and that of the east are not clear. At

parts of Azarbāyjān in the quarter of the north explains the confusion in the sources for referring to Bahrām-i Chūbīn as respectively the *marzbān* of Bardaʿa and Ardabīl,[694] or Azarbāyjān.[695] The support that Bahrām-i Chūbīn received in the east is also significant. According to the *Shāhnāma*, when gauging the endorsement of other dynasts prior to his rebellion, a certain Khizravān Khusrow encouraged Bahrām-i Chūbīn to forego rebellion and settle instead in Khurāsān. In Khurāsān, he told Bahrām-i Chūbīn, he would be able to rule in an independent manner.[696]

What is of course significant in all of this is the fact that the regions in which the Mihrāns and, as we shall see, the Ispahbudhān found their staunchest support were precisely those regions designated by the term Parthava and Media in the classical sources. Included in this was also Ṭabaristān. The age-old antagonism of Parthava against Persis was in full swing in the course of Bahrām-i Chūbīn's rebellion, and it was perhaps this, more than any other single element in Sasanian history, that brought about the demise of the Sasanians in the wake of the Arab conquest.[697] As always, the problem, of course, was that the Parthian nobility was never a unified collectivity. There were not only divisions within the Mihrāns, but also between them and the other major Parthian family at this point in Sasanian history, the Ispahbudhān. In Khurāsān, the Mihrāns also came into conflict with their age old enemies, the Kārins. Added to this was, as we shall see in Chapter 4, the history of Ṭabaristān as a refuge for rebellious factions within the house of Sāsān. What is significant for our purposes, therefore, is that all these divisions not only played into the hands of the Sasanians—for a while—but also played themselves out in the northern, northeastern, and northwestern territories of the Sasanian realm, Gīlān and Ṭabaristān, Khurāsān, and Azarbāyjān, respectively. They engulfed, in other words, the quarters of the north and east.[698]

2.7 Khusrow II Parvīz / the Ispahbudhān

The Parthian Ispahbudhān family remained the staunchest supporters of the Sasanians during Bahrām-i Chūbīn's rebellion. Of this, our sources leave us no doubt. It was not so much that the Ispahbudhān were in favor of the legitimist claims of the Sasanians, having, as we have seen, their own volatile relation

any given time after the reforms, however, it seems that the *kūst-i ādurbādagān* started somewhere in the environs of Rayy and included parts of Azarbāyjān.

[694]Ferdowsī 1971, vol. VIII, p. 338, Ferdowsī 1935, p. 2708.

[695]Thaʿālibī 1900, p. 643, Thaʿālibī 1989, p. 414; Dīnawarī 1960, pp. 78–79, Dīnawarī 1967, p. 84.

[696]Ferdowsī 1935, p. 2724:

و گر بیم داری ز خسرو بدل   ی از پارس وز تیسپون بر گسل
به شهر خراسان تن اسان بزی   که اسانی و مهتری را سزی

[697]We do not mean to downplay a host of other internal and external forces that affected the demise of the dynasty, only to highlight a crucial pattern in their history.

[698]In addition, Sīstān also had a long tradition of independence.

with them. At issue, rather, seems to have been the newly found absolutist claims of the Sasanians under Hormozd IV—and not Khusrow I. The fact that it was a rather junior branch of the Parthians, the Mihrāns, that was now claiming sovereignty was probably also hard to swallow for the Ispahbudhān family. For the antiquity of their claim to Parthian nobility seems to have been much greater than that of the Mihrāns, not to mention their close familial relationship with the Sasanians.[699] And thus is connected the saga of the Mihrāns to that of the Ispahbudhān family.

2.7.1 Vistāhm Ispahbudhān

Shortly after having saved his crown and secured the throne, Khusrow II turned in fact against his maternal uncles, Vindūyih and Vistāhm. The upshot of what transpired was the rebellion of the venerable Vistāhm of the Ispahbudhān family. What, however, instigated Khusrow II's turn of heart? We recall that Vistāhm was appointed the *spāhbed* of Sawād (that is to say, the *kūst-i khwarbarān*) after his father's murder in 586 by Hormozd IV.[700] Sebeos, however, provides us with an invaluable piece of information: the traditional homeland of the Ispahbudhān family was not in the west but in the east, that is to say, in the Pahlav dominions. Twice in the course of his narrative Sebeos informs us that the "regions of the Parthians ... [were] the original homeland of his [i.e., Vistāhm's] own principality ... under ... [whose] *control [lay] the troops of that region*."[701] This post, Sebeos maintains, had been given to Vistāhm's family in the third century when the Persian king restored to the ancestor of the Ispahbudhān family "his original Parthian and Pahlaw [lands], crowned him and honoured him, and made him second in the kingdom."[702] With such heritage and power at their disposal, it was only natural that the Ispahbudhān would not have acquiesced to being partisan to the schemes of Bahrām-i Chūbīn.

Hormozd IV and Khusrow II were cognizant of their dependence on the Ispahbudhān. Prior to Khusrow II's flight to the Byzantines, when Bahrām-i Chūbīn was approaching to overtake the capital, Hormozd IV prompted Khusrow II to destroy Vistāhm and Vindūyih. Khusrow II refused his father's advise, arguing that, faced with the forces gathered around Bahrām-i Chūbīn, any

[699]See page 110ff.

[700]See page 107ff.

[701]Here Sebeos is talking about the inception of Vistāhm's rebellion and his attempt to bring the troops of Khurāsān under his own control. It is clear, however, that as the land was his original homeland, he was not going to achieve this through force, but through gathering support in the region. Sebeos 1999, p. 42. Emphasis mine.

[702]Sebeos 1999, p. 14. Sebeos claims that the ancestor of the Ispahbudhān family was the Parthian "criminal Anak's offspring." Other Armenian sources inform us that Anak was also the father of St. Gregory, the Illuminator. According to Armenian sources, however, Anak was from the Sūren family. In no other source, however, do we come across the information that the Ispahbudhān were from the Sūren family. Chaumont observes, on the other hand, that there is a greater probability that St. Gregory was from Greek descent rather than from the Sūren family as the Armenian sources would have us believe. Chaumont 1991, p. 426. For the Anak family, see Buzandaran 1989, pp. 346–347.

assault on the Ispahbudhān family would be tantamount to the end of Sasanian hegemony (*sipāhast bā ū fuzūn az shomār*).[703] Bahrām-i Chūbīn, meanwhile, devised a brilliant plan: he minted coins in the name of Khusrow II Parvīz. Becoming suspicious that Khusrow II was in consort with the rebels, Hormozd IV contemplated his son's murder.[704] It was in fear for his life, therefore, that the young king Khusrow II fled to Azarbāyjān and thence to the Byzantines. And it was under these circumstances that the palace mutiny took place. In some traditions the whereabouts of Vistāhm at this time are not clear. Significantly, according to Sebeos, Vistāhm had already "stirred up no few wars in those days on his own account."[705] According to Sebeos, when Hormozd IV had Vindūyih imprisoned, Vistāhm had already fled from the king.[706] In any event it is clear from the sources that the Ispahbudhān either directly led the palace mutiny against Hormozd IV, or were chosen as the leaders of the uprising. Sebeos underlines the Ispahbudhān's claim for leadership of the group: "[b]ecause the queen, mother of the royal Prince and daughter of the *Asparapet* who was a noble of the house of the Parthians who had died, [was] sister of Vndoy and of Vstam, and Vndoy himself was a wise and prudent man valiant of heart, they [the nobility at Hormozd IV's court] planned to release him [i.e., Vindūyih] and make him their leader and head of their undertaking."[707] By now we know the rest of the story: Hormozd IV was murdered in the palace coup, Bahrām-i Chūbīn was defeated at the combined hands of the Ispahbudhān, the Armenians, and the Byzantines, and Khusrow II Parvīz was crowned as new king.

Vistāhm's rebellion

After taking power, presumably in 590, Khusrow II began rewarding his supporters.[708] Above all he remunerated his uncles, the chief architects of his victory: he made Vindūyih his first minister and Vistāhm his *spāhbed* of the east,[709] in the traditional homeland of the family. Yet in a matter of months, Khusrow II is said to have changed course; his excuse: avenging his father's murder. According to our sources, shortly after assuming the throne, he murdered Vindūyih. When news reached Vistāhm, he rebelled in the east. All territories

[703]Ferdowsī 1935, p. 2676–2677:

ولیکن نگاه کن به روشن روان — که بهرام چوبینه شد پهلوان
سپاهست با او فزون از شمار — سواران و گردان خنجر گزار
اگر ما به گستهم یازیم دست — به گیتی نیابیم جای نشست

Significantly, here, once again, the theme of lack of manpower of the Sasanians against the Parthians is reiterated in the narrative.

[704]Nihayat 1996, p. 360.

[705]Sebeos 1999, p. 15.

[706]Sebeos 1999, pp. 39–40; Nihayat 1996, p. 361.

[707]Sebeos 1999, p. 17.

[708]Shahbazi 1991b, pp. 180–182; Ferdowsī 1971, vol. IX, p. 136, Ferdowsī 1935, p. 2798.

[709]Mas'ūdī 1869, p. 223, Mas'ūdī 1968, p. 270. See also our discussion of his seals on page 107.

previously galvanized in Bahrām-i Chūbīn's rebellion were now overtaken by this prominent Parthian dynast. Much of Bahrām-i Chūbīn's army joined him. A substantial group of the Parthians, therefore, had left, once again, the confederacy. This time, their success was half complete: Under the leadership of Vistāhm, for seven years at least, the *kūst-i ādurbādagān* and the *kūst-i khwarāsān* ceded from Sasanian territories. The Parthian Vistāhm began minting coins in the territories under his control. We possess coins belonging to the second to seventh years of his reign and minted, significantly, at Rayy, on which the Ispahbudhān rebel is called Pīrūz Vistāhm, victorious Vistāhm. As traditionally coinage reflected the regnal years of the king, however, a problem remains with the exact chronology of Vistāhm's kingship in the Pahlav domains. A consensus, nevertheless, reckons this to be circa 590–96 CE.

Vahewuni incident

The traditional chronology fails to explain, however, how a young and inexperienced Sasanian king, brought to power by the collective forces of the Ispahbudhān family, the Armenians, and the Byzantines, could in a single year become so powerful as to move against the powerful Parthian Ispahbudhān family. Howard–Johnston's alternative chronology, supported by other sources at our disposal, addresses this. According to him, shortly after defeating Bahrām-i Chūbīn, Khusrow II was faced with the Vahewuni rebellion of 594–595 in Armenia.[710] Vistāhm's rebellion took place shortly after this. Howard–Johnston, therefore, dates Vistāhm's rebellion from 594 to 599–600.[711] Indeed, if the Vahewuni incident is to be solidly dated to 594–595, then we must envision a situation in which the still feeble Khusrow II Parvīz was forced to deal with two major upheavals that engulfed all of his northern territories simultaneously. There is nothing unprecedented in this, as having to face wars on two fronts was a familiar paradigm in both Sasanian and Byzantine history. And indeed this might explain Khusrow II Parvīz's diplomacy: collaborating with the Byzantines in undermining the Vahewuni insurrection. The idea that Khusrow II was forced to deal with the Vahewuni incident at precisely a time when almost half of his realm had ceded seems, nevertheless, quite unlikely. As Howard–Johnston maintains, it is more likely that Khusrow II dealt with the initial stages of Vistāhm's rebellion almost toward the end of the Vahewuni incident, where either through force or cajoling, he was able to bring a group of Armenian nobles in consort with him.[712] This included settling these in Iṣfahān. According to Howard–Johnston, "incidental remarks [in Sebeos] reveal

[710]For the Vahewuni incident, when a group of Armenian noblemen rebelled against their overlords, the Byzantines and the Sasanians, see Howard–Johnston's historical commentary in Sebeos 1999, pp. 175–179. See also page 301 below.

[711]Sebeos 1999, pp. 179–180.

[712]Among those who joined the Persian side, after the combined Sasanian and Byzantine forces had pursued the rebels to the Araxes valley area, were Mamak Mamikonean, Kotit, lord of Amatunik', Step'anos Siwni, and other unnamed. See Howard–Johnston's historical commentary in Sebeos 1999, p. 177.

that the troops mobilized in Persarmenia in Spring of 595 and their noble leaders accompanied Khosrov on his campaign against the rebels ... The campaign should therefore be dated to 595. This points to 594 as the year in which Vstam rebelled and gathered support."[713] Both the *Nihāyat* and Dīnawarī confirm this dating of Vistāhm's rebellion, for both put it ten years into Khusrow II's reign, in 599/600.[714]

Citing the Khuzistan Chronicle, Howard-Johnston argues justifiably that there was also more than simple vengeance to Khusrow II's onslaught on his uncles. The *Nihāyat* confirms this. The combined accounts also aid us in settling the question of chronology. According to Howard-Johnston, after consolidating his rule, Khusrow II faced too much criticism by Vindūyih—who was now his prime minister—of his policies.[715] This, and not simple vengeance, was in fact the true cause of Khusrow II's belated epiphany about the culprits of his father's murder. According to the *Nihāyat*, after the revolt of Bahrām-i Chūbīn, when Khusrow II had established his affairs (*lammā istadaffa 'l-amr li kisrā*) and his power increased (*'aẓuma sulṭānuhu*), the king pondered what his uncles had done to his father. "Bindūyah was *in control of his affairs and he had [all the] influence in his kingdom*,"[716] while Vistāhm was in control of Khurāsān up to the borders of Rayy. Khusrow II "watched Bindūyah with a great fury, but he did not divulge any of it to him."[717] Until ten years passed, according to the *Nihāyat*, under this state of affairs, Khusrow II found an auspicious opportunity.[718] The anecdotal story in which the *Nihāyat* subsequently garbs Vindūyih's power itself bespeaks the ease with which the Parthian dynast opined on state matters and Khusrow II's policies. For an incident in which Khusrow II exhibited his lavish spending provided the opportunity for the supreme minister to proclaim to the king that the "public treasury cannot withstand this kind of squandering."[719] As *Nihāyat*'s account makes clear, therefore, the saga of Khusrow II Parvīz vis-à-vis his powerful uncles was no different than the

[713] Sebeos 1999, pp. 179–180.

[714] Nihayat 1996, p. 390; Dīnawarī 1967, p. 110, Dīnawarī 1960, p. 101:

فمكث كسرى و يكاثرهما عشر سنين.

[715] Sebeos 1999, p. 180.

[716] Nihayat 1996, p. 390:

و قد كان اسند اموره الى بندى و كان نافذ الامر فى مملكته.

[717] Nihayat 1996, p. 390:

و كان ينظر الى بندويه بالحنق الشديد، و لا يظهر له شيئا من ذلك

[718] Nihayat 1996, p. 390:

حتّى مضت عشر سنين.

[719] Nihayat 1996, p. 390:

ان بيوت الاموال لا تقوم بهذا التبذير.

saga of Qubād under the Kārins or that of other Sasanian kings against their respective Parthian dynastic family: the Sasanians were at the mercy of their power.

According to Sebeos, when Vistāhm first rebelled and stationed himself in Rayy, Khusrow II set out to fight him. The *Nihāyat*, which is the only Arabic source other than Dīnawarī providing us with a detailed narrative of Vistāhm's rebellion—for in fact the rebellion and secession against Khusrow II Parvīz are *absent from all our other Arabic sources as well as the Shāhnāma*[720]—incorporates a series of correspondences between Khusrow II and Vistāhm. In these, Vistāhm detailed the debt that Khusrow II had incurred toward his family. "Woe onto you, the companion of the devil (*ansāka 'l-shayṭān*), didn't my brother free you … and did he not give his life for you … when the heavens and the earth had dejected you. Did he not kill your father in order to consolidate your kingdom for you and set up your kingship?"[721] According to Sebeos, contemporaneous with Vistāhm's rebellion, the lands "called Amal [i.e., Āmul in Ṭabaristān], Ṙoyean, [i.e., Rūyān to the west of Ṭabaristān and] Zrēchan and Taparistan [i.e., Ṭabaristān] also rebelled against the Persian king."[722] Vistāhm's supporters incited him to rebellion using, as did the supporters of Bahrām-i Chūbīn, his claim to Parthian ancestry, and his privileged position in Sasanian history: "You are the son of Khurrbundād,[723] with an ancestry that goes back to Bahman the son of Isfandīyār. You have been the *confederates and brothers* of the Sasanians. Why should Khusrow II have precedence over you in kingship?"[724] Convinced by their arguments, and with a great army behind him, Vistāhm thus followed in the footsteps of the pioneering Mihrānid rebel Bahrām-i Chūbīn. He derided the Sasanian genealogy and boasted about his own, more exalted, pedigree: "Your ancestors," Vistāhm told Khusrow II Parvīz, were after all no more than shepherds who usurped kingship from us.[725]

[720]The *X^w adāy-Nāmag* tradition remains silent on Vistāhm's rebellion: neither Ṭabarī, the *Shāhnāma*, Thaʿālibī, nor Ibn Balkhī have anything to say about it. This leaves room for thought. The *X^w adāy-Nāmag*'s rendition of Bahrām-i Chūbīn's rebellion might still be used in articulating the legitimist claims of the Sasanians against a rebel of the Mihrān family. But how was this tradition to portray one of the most embarrassing episodes of Sasanian history: the secession for at least seven years of the northern regions of the realm, where a Parthian family set up a separate kingdom in what was ostensibly Sasanian domains?

[721]Nihayat 1996, p. 293.

[722]Howard-Johnston appropriately notes that these rebellions were "surely not spontaneous but engineered by Vstam." Ibid., p. 181.

[723]This is a variant of the name of Vistāhm's father, as we have seen on page 106.

[724]Dīnawarī 1967, p. 111, Dīnawarī 1960, p. 102:

و انكم لاخوة بنى ساسان و شركاؤهم

[725]Dīnawarī 1967, p. 112, Dīnawarī 1960, p. 102:

و اعلم انك لست بأحق بهذا الامر منى بل انا احق به منك … غير انكم يا بنى ساسان غلبتمونا على حقنا و ظلمتونا و انما كان ابوكم ساسان راعى غنم

It is symptomatic of the Sasanian predicament at this and future junctures of their history that in order to combat the Parthian Vistāhm, an Armenian contingent came to hold a central place in what subsequently transpired.[726] The initial battle of Khusrow II against Vistāhm came to no fruitful conclusion, Vistāhm and his army having taken refuge in Gīlān from whence Vistāhm "journeyed to the regions of the Parthians, to the original land of his own principality."[727] Meanwhile the Armenian forces who had been settled in Iṣfahān[728] by Khusrow II also rebelled and set out for Gīlān, where they came across the Sasanian cadet Pīrūz,[729] while others finally reached Vistāhm in Khurāsān. With an insurgence in most of the northern parts of his territory, the quarters of the north and the east, the regions predominantly under Parthian rule, the Sasanian monarch's vulnerability was now complete. Khusrow II Parviz was forced to turn to the great Armenian dynastic family and its leader Smbat Bagratuni.[730] Khusrow II gave Smbat the *marzpanate* of Vrkan, that is Gurgān, and dispatched him against his powerful enemy, the Parthian dynast Vistāhm of the Ispahbudhān family.[731] Smbat was said to have achieved success and much else.[732]

2.7.2 Smbat Bagratuni

Smbat's governorship of Gurgān

Thomson argues that Sebeos puts Smbat's term of office in Gurgān from 596–602 CE,[733] a date that fits well with the traditional rendering of Vistāhm's rebellion as taking place between 590 and 596, since Smbat was instrumental in ending Vistāhm's rebellion. He maintains, however, that this date seems to be too early because, after having successfully completed his assignments in the east, Smbat was called to the court by Khusrow II in the eighteenth year of the latter's reign, which brings us to 606–607.[734] This, Thomson argues, is another indication that Vistāhm's rebellion must be dated to somewhere around 594/599–600 CE.[735] For by this time, Vistāhm was preparing a second major expedition against Khusrow II with the help of the Kūshāns, and it is fairly

[726]The *Nihāyat* calls the leader of the Armenian contingent by that of his office, al-Nakhārjān, i.e., *naxarar*. Nihayat 1996, p. 393.

[727]Sebeos 1999, p. 42.

[728]See page 133.

[729]See §4.3.2.

[730]Sebeos 1999, p. 42. For the Bagratuni family, see Buzandaran 1989, pp. 362–363 and the references cited therein.

[731]Sebeos 1999, pp. 43–44.

[732]According to Sebeos, Smbat also quelled the rebellions in Āmul, Rūyān, Zrēchan, and Ṭabaristān "and brought them into subjection to the Persian king. He established prosperity over all the area of his *marzpanate*, because that land had been ravaged." Sebeos 1999, p. 44.

[733]Sebeos 1999, p. 44, n. 271.

[734]Howard-Johnston has no qualms about the matter: "His [i.e., Smbat's] appointment as the governor (*marzbān*) of Vrkan (Gurgān) . . . , can precisely be dated to 599/600, since his retirement after eight years on the post is dated to Khusrov's 18th regnal year (606/607)." Sebeos 1999, p. 181.

[735]Sebeos 1999, p. 48, n. 297.

certain that he was killed in 600, at the hands of one of his Kūshān allies.[736] Gurgān, Howard-Johnston correctly observes, "was of crucial strategic importance since it was wedged between the Elburz range and Khurasan (the region of the east), which was now actively supporting Vstam."[737]

Besides the evidence provided by the *Nihāyat* and the arguments presented by Howard-Johnston, there is a curious numismatic peculiarity that corroborates the dating proposed by him, that is, the end of Vistāhm's rebellion after ten years of Khusrow II's rule. For, according to Gobl "[a]fter the 11th year of the reign of Khusrow II, and only in this particular year, we find the word *'pd* (praise) in the second quadrant of the border of the obverse of the coins issued by the king, although this terminology does not appear on every mint of Khusrow II Parvīz during this year." While the precise significance of this inscription is not clear, according to Gobl,[738] such novel innovation in precisely the eleventh year of Khusrow II's reign, cannot be devoid of meaning: the appearance of this terminology on Khusrow II's coinage during his eleventh regnal year supports Dīnawarī's and *Nihāyat*'s dating of (the end of) Vistāhm's rebellion to the tenth year of the king's reign.

Whatever the chronology of Vistāhm's rebellion, Sebeos' narrative leaves no doubt that Smbat was instrumental in putting an end to it. The joint forces of Vistāhm, his supporters from Gīlān and Ṭabaristān, and the Armenian nobility that had joined the Ispahbudhān's camp engaged the combined large forces of Smbat and a figure that Sebeos calls Shahr Vahrich[739] in a village called Khekewand in the Komsh (Qūmis) area.[740] Although the Parthian secessionist Vistāhm was killed, his murder did not mark the end of the rebellion of the regions where he found his support, according to Howard-Johnston. For after the murder of Vistāhm, Smbat himself was defeated in Qūmis by the supporters of Vistāhm in Gīlān, who could bring to the field their own Armenian allies.[741] It was only in 601, according to Howard-Johnston, in Smbat's second expedition against the rebels that he was finally successful.[742] When this news reached

[736]Howard-Johnston uses Dīnawarī to further corroborate his chronology. "For if his [i.e., Dīnawarī's] chronology of Khosrov's reign lags one year behind the true reckoning, as does Tabari's, the only date which he gives in his full account of Vstam's rebellion—Khusrov's tenth regnal year (598/599+1)—would correspond exactly to the first year of Smbat's governorship (599/600)." It should be noted though that Dīnawarī attaches this date to the start rather than the end of the rebellion (see footnote 714). Sebeos 1999, p. 181.

[737]Sebeos 1999, p. 181.

[738]Göbl, Robert, 'Sasanian Coins', in Ehsan Yarshater (ed.), *Cambridge History of Iran: The Seleucid, Parthian, and Sasanian Periods*, vol. 3(1), pp. 322–343, Cambridge University Press, 1983 (Göbl 1983), pp. 330–331.

[739]It is not clear whether this figure can be identified with the Mihrānid Shahrvarāz, who in the next decade also rebelled against the Sasanian king.

[740]Sebeos 1999, pp. 44–45.

[741]Most likely, the ruler of Gīlān at that time was the Āl-i Jāmāsp Pīrūz, whom we shall discuss briefly at the beginning of §4.3.3.

[742]According to Howard-Johnston "Sebeos' account of Vstam's rebellion is superior to those of the other sources. Whereas the others compress a complex series of events apparently into a single

Khusrow II, Smbat was greatly exalted in the king's eyes.

Smbat's governorship of Khurāsān

It is indicative of the Sasanian monarch's policies during this period that in the face of the power vacuum in Khurāsān in particular, Khusrow II not only appointed Smbat as the governor of the region,[743] but also greatly honored and promoted "him above all the *marzbāns of his kingdom*."[744] It is significant that immediately after Bahrām-i Chūbīn's rebellion (590–591), and Vistāhm's *spāhbedī* of Khurāsān (590–593?) and his rebellion (594–600), Khusrow II was forced to resort to an Armenian dynast, Smbat, in order to calm the revolutionary fervor in the northern and the northeastern parts of his realm. The precise nature of Smbat's activities in the region during this period is hard to follow. Whatever their course, it is clear that Smbat and his army were in control. In 606/607, however, Smbat asked Khusrow II for a leave in order to go to Armenia.[745] Howard-Johnston's chronology of the rest of Smbat's career in Khusrow II's administration appears quite sound. After his stay in Armenia, Smbat was once again recalled by Khusrow II. Smbat's date of recall from Armenia and his second dispatch to Khurāsān, can be "inferred from the date later given for his death, the twenty-eighth year of Khosrov's reign (616–617)."

Khusrow II's remuneration of this Armenian nobleman upon his arrival at the court is symptomatic for the Sasanians' posture vis-à-vis their native Pahlav dynasts. Howard-Johnston summarizes this: "Extraordinary powers were granted to him [i.e., Smbat]: together with the supreme command in the East, he was given *delegated authority to appoint marzbāns* ... and was granted simultaneously a probably lucrative civilian office in charge of a central financial ministry."[746] From 599/600 to 606/607, on one occasion, and 614–616/617 on another, for a total period of almost a decade, therefore, a substantial part of Khurāsān was put under the command of the Armenian dynastic figure Smbat Bagratuni. Extensive powers were also granted to him in the capital of the Sasanian empire by the king. This then is indicative of the predicament in which the Sasanian monarchy had found itself after it was confronted with the rebellions of one Parthian dynastic family after another in the northern and eastern parts of its realm: for a not insignificant period, under what seems to have been

year (the deaths of Vstam and Vndoy are reported side by side in *Khuzistan Chronicle*), focusing either on the 595 campaign (*Chronique de Seert* and Dīnawarī), or 600 (Khuzistan Chronicle), Sebeos provides the crucial dating indications and distinguishes several phases in the rebellion." Sebeos 1999, p. 182.

[743]Once from about 600–607, and the second time from 614–616/617. Sebeos 1999, pp. 183–184.

[744]Sebeos 1999, pp. 47–48. This might actually mean that Smbat was appointed the *spāhbed* of the east, replacing Vistāhm (see page 107).

[745]There seems to be very little information about Smbat's stay in Armenia, for unlike other detailed accounts provided by Sebeos about this Bagratuni dynast, part of Sebeos' text seems to be missing here. According to Howard-Johnston, Sebeos seems to have availed himself of a lost encomiastic biography of Bagratuni, from which information about Smbat's stay in Armenia was perhaps lost in the excerption process. Sebeos 1999, pp. 178–79 and 184, respectively.

[746]Sebeos 1999, pp. 44–45, 181. Emphasis added.

extraordinary circumstances, the Sasanian king was forced to exert his power in Khurāsān through the agency of neighboring Armenian nobility!

The only information we have on Smbat Bagratuni's governorship in Khurāsān during the second half of his tenure in the east in 614–616/617, are the detailed accounts given by Sebeos of two military expeditions that he undertook in Khurāsān. According to Howard-Johnston, the first of these took place when a Kūshān army invaded the region.[747] In Qūmis,[748] Smbat summoned about 2,000 Armenian cavalry from Gurgān,[749] which he had stationed there during his first stay in the region in 606/607. At this initial encounter, Smbat's forces defeated the Kūshāns, withdrew "and camped at Apr Shahr [i.e., Nīshāpūr], *in the province of Tus*; and with 300 men took up quarters in the walled village called Khrokht." At this point the Kūshāns asked for Turkish aid, and a great force of 300,000 [!] answered the call and crossed the Oxus (Vehṙot). A raiding party besieged the walled village, "for the village had a strong wall encircling it." Smbat managed to flee from the debacle with three of his followers, leaving the village to be defended by the commander (*hrmanatar*) "of their force[750] [who] was a certain Persian Prince named Datoyean, [appointed] by royal command." Needless to say, Smbat and Datoyean's forces were defeated by the Turks. The Turkish army then moved westwards and got "as far as the borders of Reyy and of the province of Ispahan," and after plundering the region, returned to its camp.[751] An inspector from the court, a certain Shahrapan Bandakan, was then sent to Smbat and Datoyean. It is, once again, indicative of Khusrow II's policies that Smbat was exonerated, but Shahrapan Bandakan was taken to court and executed.[752] In Khusrow II's second campaign, which, according to Howard-Johnston, took place a year later,[753] Smbat reorganized his army and attacked "the nation of Kushans and the Hephthalite king."[754] Smbat's forces defeated the enemy and followed them on their heels to their capital Balkh. Herāt, all of Tukharistan, and Ṭāliqān were plundered before Smbat returned and, with much booty, settled in Marv.[755] At the news of Smbat's victory "king Khosrov was happy and greatly rejoiced. Once again the king summoned the Armenian nobleman *of Parthian descent* ... to the court. He ordered his son to be promoted and be called Javitean Khosrov. Smbat himself

[747]Sebeos 1999, p. 50.

[748]It is significant in this context to recall that one of the residences of the Arsacids was in Qūmis. Marquart 1931, p. 12, no. 18.

[749]Sebeos 1999, p. 50.

[750]According to Thomson this figure was the commander of the relief force, not the commander of the 300. Sebeos 1999, p. 51, n. 320.

[751]Sebeos 1999, p. 51.

[752]Sebeos 1999, p. 51–52.

[753]For the reasons why the Sasanians were able to engage the enemy on two fronts at this point, being heavily engaged in the west (see §2.7.3 below) conquering, for example, Jerusalem in 614, while Smbat was dealing with the Turks in the east, as well as for an explanation of the appearance of the Kūshāns in the east, see Sebeos 1999, pp. 184–188.

[754]Sebeos 1999, p. 52.

[755]Sebeos 1999, p. 53.

got two honorific titles of Armenian *tanutēr*, and Persian *Khusrov-Shum* [i.e., Khusrow Shenūm], and the investiture and insignia of five sorts."[756] Treasures were distributed to his followers. Smbat then became "the third nobleman in the palace of king Khusrov and after remaining [there] a short time ... die[d] in the 28th year of his [i.e., Khusrow II's] reign," in 616/7 CE.[757] Clearly, Smbat's services to Khusrow II Parvīz were thought to have been so tremendous by the Sasanian king that he deemed it justifiable to shower him with honors hitherto bestowed only on the Iranian Parthian dynastic families. This then brings to an end the second most important episode of the breakdown of the Sasanian–Parthian confederacy.

2.7.3 The last great war of antiquity

From 603–630, Khusrow II Parvīz engulfed Iran in one of the most devastating and long periods of warfare against its traditional enemy, the Byzantine Empire. In human and material terms, the costs of the war, which perhaps precipitated the onslaught of the horrific bubonic plague in the course of it, was staggering for the world of late antiquity. While Khusrow II was filling the coffers of his treasury with fantastic treasures all the while, and while in terms of territorial gains, at the height of Khusrow II's victories, the monarch could boast of extending his boundaries to that which existed at the height of the Achaemenid empire, the Sasanian empire was engaged in an ultimately disastrous feat. It arguably suffered the most. That Khusrow II lost his crown in 628 through the familiar and paradigmatic mechanism of the joint forces of Parthian dynastic families unleashing their power against an exhausted monarchy paled in comparison to what was to come. The causes, courses, and effects of the last war of antiquity between a Sasanian monarchy that was soon no longer to be and a Byzantine empire that was soon to be truncated beyond recognition have been discussed in great detail in a corpus of erudite literature and are beyond the scope of the present study. What happened in the course of the war in terms of the balance of power within the Sasanian Empire between the monarchy and the Parthian dynastic families, however, is of central concern to us. We shall therefore turn our attention to the final chapter of this conflictual relationship.

First phase (603–610)

In order to provide a context for the issues under consideration, a very brief outline of the course of the last great war of antiquity between the Byzantines and the Sasanians is in order. Three clear phases of the wars of 603–628 can be discerned.[758] The theaters of war in its first phase from 603 to 610 were Mesopotamia and the Caucasus. The fall of the strategically important city of

[756] Sebeos 1999, p. 183. Emphasis added.

[757] Sebeos 1999, p. 54.

[758] The following outline is based on James Howard-Johnston's account in Sebeos 1999, pp. xxii–xxv, 197–221, who reconstructs a detailed course of events as a commentary to Sebeos' text in Part I, pp. 54–84.

Dara in 604 to the Sasanians and the opening of Armenia as a diversionary front of the war were probably two of the most important aspects of this phase, besides the fact that Khusrow II seems to have taken, initially at least, personal charge of directing the Mesopotamian war front. An important Sasanian general, Shāhīn—whom Nöldeke believes to have belonged to one of the seven great Parthian dynastic families, but whose pedigree we cannot establish with any degree of certainty[759]—appeared on the western Armenian front, "before making a forward thrust into Cappadocia" and capturing Caesaria at the beginning of the second phase of the war, 610–621.

Second phase (610–621)

In this phase, the Persians overran northern Syria, thrust deep into Anatolia (611), reached the Bosphurus (615), pushed through southern Syria, and finally conquered Egypt (619–621). The conquests of Damascus (613), Jerusalem (614), and Egypt were, for both sides, the emotive hallmarks of this second phase. The direction of the wars in this phase were under the command of two of the foremost generals of the Sasanian armies, the aforementioned general Shāhīn and the towering figure of Shahrvarāz. Important aspects of their role in these wars remain unclear, however. Whether or not it was Shahrvarāz or Shāhīn who should be credited with the conquest of Egypt, for example, is one of these. The Sasanians were so successful during these first two phases that by 615 they had reached Chalcedon,[760] across the Sea of Marmara from Constantinople. It was at this point that, according to Sebeos, the emperor Heraclius had agreed to stand down, allow the Roman empire to become a Persian client state, and even allow Khusrow II to choose the emperor. Heraclius would become a "son rather than a brother of the Sasanian king."[761] But in the late 620s, the Sasanians suffered "*one of the most astonishing reversals of fortune in the annals of war.*"[762]

As Kaegi and Cobb have argued, a catalyst in this last phase of the war was the mutiny of the general Shahrvarāz. The aggregate of evidence here seems to corroborate Kaegi and Cobb's argument that the relationship of Khusrow II and his foremost general turned sour "probably late in the year 626 or early in 627."[763] But who was this Shahrvarāz whose role in the last eventful years of Sasanian history was so paramount? Besides the name through which he has come to be known to posterity, Shahrvarāz is said to have carried at least two other names, a situation which has created substantial confusion in the study of the course of the Persian war efforts in Byzantine territory and the internal

[759] Nöldeke 1879, p. 291, n. 2, p. 439, n. 3, Nöldeke 1979, p. 483, n. 44, p. 661 and p. 681, n. 12.

[760] See footnote 6.

[761] Sebeos 1999, p. 211.

[762] Sebeos 1999, p. xxiv. Emphasis added.

[763] Cobb, Paul M. and Kaegi, Walter E., 'Heraclius, Shahrbarāz and Ṭabarī', in Hugh Kennedy (ed.), *Al-Ṭabarī: A Medieval Muslim Historian and His Work*, pp. 121–143, Princeton, 2002 (Cobb and Kaegi 2002).

conditions that led to Khusrow II's deposition.[764] To this confusion, we will get shortly,[765] but for now, we recall that throughout this period, when he was preoccupied with the events in the west, Khusrow II had put the east under the command of Smbat Bagratuni.

2.7.4 Shahrvarāz Mihrān

In the accounts of the eventful years that led to the Byzantine victory over Khusrow II, the role of one of the foremost generals of Khusrow II, a certain Shahrvarāz, looms large. What is clear from the complicated course of events is that Shahrvarāz rebelled and mutinied, probably late in 626 or early in 627, and formed an alliance with the Byzantine emperor Heraclius. As Kaegi and Cobb observe, Shahrvarāz's mutiny is "*critical for understanding Heraclius' victory over Chosroes II, the disintegration of Persian authority in the region, as well as the historical background to the Persian evacuation of Byzantine territory, and, in general, conditions on the eve of the Islamic conquest.*"[766] What is of crucial concern for us here is the identity of this famous general of the Sasanian realm and the context of his mutiny. The timing of the outbreak of hostilities between Shahrvarāz and Khusrow II Parvīz is also of crucial importance. The issue is not a moot one. For if, as Kaegi and Paul have argued, the mutiny of Khusrow II's armed forces under Shahrvarāz was crucial in undermining the Sasanian power and the Byzantine victory over them, then, at the very least, it highlights the continued dependency of Khusrow II's military power, in whatever reformed form, on the generals that steered his war effort. The gentilitial background of Shahrvarāz can now be reconstructed through sigillographic evidence, which in turn has tremendous ramifications for understanding the last crucial years of Khusrow II Parvīz's reign. As we have seen,[767] the seals establish that the enigmatic figure of Shahrvarāz was (1) the *spāhbed* of the south, and (2) a Mihrānid.[768] This brings us to a second important concern, closely tied in with the first: Shahrvarāz was most probably not alone in reaching an agreement with

[764] Kaegi and Cobb's investigation does not aim at deciphering the problem that we will be investigating. It should be pointed out, however, that one of their important conclusions, namely the fact that it was Shahrvarāz who should be credited with the conquest of Egypt, is corroborated by the *Fārsnāma*: "Shahrvarāz went to Jerusalem and then to Egypt and Alexandria and conquered these." Ibn Balkhī 1995, p. 253–254.

[765] See page 143ff below.

[766] For the latest investigation into this, see the important article Cobb and Kaegi 2002, p. 123. Emphasis added. I would like to thank Professors Walter Kaegi and Paul Cobb for providing me with a copy of their forthcoming work. I would especially like to thank Paul Cobb for sending the article to me.

[767] See §2.5.4.

[768] Gyselen 2001a, seal 2d/2, p. 41. It is remarkable that according to Gyselen, the gentilitial name of Mihrān is clearly added to the seal at a later date for we do possess one bulla (impression) "which was made by the seal under its first form (seal 2d/1) and *several* made by the same seal under its second form (seal 2d/2), where the word -mtr'n- (Mihrān) has been added to the end of the inscription on a third line, just below the word *spāhbed*, which addition might in fact be a sign of the growing independence of Shahrvarāz." Gyselen 2001a, p. 11. Emphasis mine.

the Byzantines. The activities of another important dynastic power in Iran was also crucial in explaining the turn of events. Before we proceed, we ought to recall that in Dīnawarī's anachronistic account,[769] Shahrvarāz is listed together with Vistāhm from the Ispahbudhān family.

Two figures in one: Shahrvarāz and Farrukhān

Shahrvarāz's name has been rendered in a number of forms in our sources.[770] This, however, is not so much of a problem as the epithets through which the general has come to be known. For an outline of these it is best to follow the accounts of Ṭabarī and compare these with other narratives at our disposal. According to Ṭabarī, at the inception of the mutiny that led to the deposition and murder of the Byzantine emperor Maurice (582–602) and the accession of Phocas (602–610), Khusrow II decided to wage war against the Byzantines on behalf of Maurice's son, who had taken refugee with him. To this effect he set out three armies under the command of three separate figures. One of these commanders of Khusrow II, Ṭabarī informs us, was called Rumiyūzān, and was sent to Syria and Palestine; a second general, our aforementioned Shāhīn, who according to Ṭabarī "was the *fādhūsbān* (*pādhūspān*) of the west," proceeded to capture "Egypt and Alexandria and the land of Nubia." The third general appointed to the war front was a certain Farruhān, or Farrukhān. Here starts the confusion. For according to Ṭabarī and some other sources, this Farruhān "had the rank of Shahrbarāz" and carried the expedition against Constantinople.[771] Of the three commanders named by Ṭabarī the identity of one, Shāhīn, does not seem to be in dispute.[772] The precise identities of the other two, however, remain unclear, so much so that it is not certain whether or not we are in fact dealing with two figures here. In part, the remark that Nöldeke made more than a century ago about the confusion surrounding these names still stands in the scholarship on the subject.[773] It has been maintained, for example, that the figure of Rumiyūzān might in fact be identical with that of Shahrvarāz, for there is little doubt that it was the latter who captured Jerusalem in 614 CE.[774]

[769]See page 109ff.

[770]For a list of these, see Justi 1895, pp. 277–278.

[771]Ṭabarī 1999, pp. 318–319, de Goeje, 1002.

[772]As some sources, including Ṭabarī, called Shāhīn one of the *pādhūspāns* of Khusrow II, Nöldeke argued that Shāhīn, therefore, was one of the four *satraps*, that is to say, *spāhbeds*, of Khusrow II Parvīz. Now the *Chronicon Paschale* calls Shāhīn the "famous Babaman Zādigān." This Babaman Zādigān, argues Nöldeke, is presumably nothing but a scribal error for Vahūman Zādag, that is a descendent of Bahman. This figure, therefore, argues Nöldeke, is from the progeny of Bahman, the son of Isfandīyār. Nöldeke 1879, p. 291, n. 2, p. 439, n. 3, Nöldeke 1979, p. 483, n. 44, p. 661 and p. 681, n. 12.

[773]"In general one cannot decipher the truth, through the names that the Greeks, the Armenians, the Syrians, and the Arabs have given to the[se] Iranian generals, unless an expert Armenionologist corrects these names on the basis of the Armenian sources." Nöldeke 1879, pp. 290–291, n. 3, Nöldeke 1979, p. 482, n. 42.

[774]Bosworth seems to maintain the identity of Rumiyūzān with Shahrbarāz and Farrukhān. Ṭabarī 1999, pp. 318–319, nn. 745 and 749, de Goeje, 1002.

Nöldeke's suspicions about the identity of Shahrvarāz and Farrukhān, as we shall presently see, are in fact valid, although he himself did not offer an explanation for it.[775] Thus far, to the author's knowledge, no detailed investigation of the topic seems to have been made.

In the identification of Shahrvarāz with Farrukhān, two powerful figures have been in fact superimposed onto each other. It is apt to begin with a narrative that highlights this superimposition. In the course of their investigation of the circumstances that led to Shahrvarāz's rapprochement with Heraclius and his eventual mutiny against Khusrow II, Kaegi and Cobb highlight the importance of the narrative contained in Zuhrī's *Kitāb Futūḥ Miṣr wa Akhbārihā*,[776] which, in conjunction with Ṭabarī's narrative, can be used for reconstructing the course of events. Here Zuhrī gives us a narrative "concerning the cause of the Persian withdrawal from [Byzantium]." When Shahrvarāz's stay in Syria was prolonged, Khusrow II reprimanded him. Frustrated with Shahrvarāz's actions, Khusrow II then wrote letters to "the greatest of the Persian lords," ordering him to kill Shahrvarāz, take charge of the Persian armies, and return to the capital. This Persian lord, who is not named in Zuhrī's narrative, tried to persuade Khusrow II, in a series of three correspondences, against his decision, at which point Khusrow II became so aggravated that he now wrote a letter to Shahrvarāz ordering him to kill the Persian lord. When Shahrvarāz, reluctantly, set about executing Khusrow II's command by informing the "greatest of the Persian lords" of the king's orders, the lord produced the letters that Khusrow II had initially sent to him. At his submission of the first letter to Shahrvarāz, the latter proclaimed to the Persian lord: "You are better than I." When the lord produced the second letter, Shahrvarāz "descended from his throne and" asked the Persian lord to "[b]e seated upon it." Refusing the offer, the Persian lord then produced the third letter, at which point Shahrvarāz declared: "I swear by God to do evil to Chosroes! And he made up his mind to betray Chosroes."[777]

While the use of letters as a *topos* in Islamic historiography must be acknowledged and while the anecdotal nature of the letters under consideration speaks for itself, not every letter in the tradition can be dismissed as mere *topos*. There is no reason to doubt the fact that throughout the war preparations, Khusrow II must have kept in touch with his generals in the field. In fact, it is unrealistic to presume that some form of correspondence did not take place between the center, which had precipitated the war, and the armies in charge of directing the war efforts. In Ṭabarī's rendition of the same account, for example, Khusrow II

[775] Nöldeke seems to have remained undecided: once he argued that the identity of Rumiyūzān with Khurrahān, or Farrukhān, "which is the name of Shahrbarāz," is probably correct, and once that "it seems inconceivable to suppose that Shahrvarāz's name was Farrukhān or Khurrahān." Nöldeke 1879, pp. 290–291, n. 3, p. 292, n. 2, Nöldeke 1979, p. 482, n. 42, and p. 484, n. 46.

[776] Zuhrī, b. ʿAbd al-Ḥakam, *Kitāb Futūḥ Miṣr wa Akhbārihā*, New Haven, 1922, edited by C. Torrey (Zuhrī 1922), pp. 35–37, cited in Cobb and Kaegi 2002, pp. 138–141.

[777] Zuhrī 1922, as cited in Cobb and Kaegi 2002, p. 139.

availed himself of the services of the *barīd* (courier service), an institution the crucial function of which was probably all the more obvious during times of crisis.[778] While the precise content of the letters as produced by Zuhrī is not altogether trustworthy, there is every reason to assume that their general tenor is valid.

For one thing, Zuhrī's narrative highlights the close connection, or even the participation of a second figure, the Persian lord, in Shahrvarāz's campaigns. The existence of this second figure in close association with Shahrvarāz is confirmed through other sources. Whereas in Zuhrī's narrative the identity of this greatest of Persian lords remains unknown, in Ṭabarī's accounts of this same episode his name is disclosed, while the actions of the two figures are now transposed. We recall that at the inception of his narrative Ṭabarī had maintained that "Farruhān [i.e., Farrukhān], … had the rank of Shahrbarāz." However, this is only one of the two traditions concerning this episode in Ṭabarī, given in fact without any *isnād*. The second tradition, narrated through Abū ʾIkramah, separates the two personalities. In this narrative, Farrukhān and Shahrvarāz are depicted as brothers.[779] The following story is then given: "When the Persians were victorious over the Byzantines, Farrukhān was once sitting and drinking, and said to his companions, '*I had a dream, and it was as if I saw myself on Kisrā's throne*'."[780] When the news of Farrukhān's design for the throne reached Khusrow II, the latter wrote a letter to Shahrvarāz ordering him to send him Farrukhān's head. Shahrvarāz entreated Khusrow II to change his mind, arguing that he would "never find anyone like Farrukhān *who had inflicted so much damage on the enemy or had such a formidable reputation among them.*" Abū ʾIkramah's narrative, like that of Zuhrī, underlines not only Farrukhān's participation in Khusrow II's campaigns in the west, but also his power and centrality in these war efforts. Confronted with the obstinacy of Shahrvarāz, Khusrow II, furious, had a radical change of heart and declared to the people of Persia: "I hereby remove Shahrbarāz from power over you and appoint Farrukhān over you in his stead." He then sent a letter containing the transfer of power from one to the other as well as the order of the execution of Shahrvarāz by Farrukhān. In ʾIkramah's narrative, it was when Farrukhān proceeded to implement the king's order that Shahrvarāz produced for him the letters that Khusrow II had initially sent him ordering the execution of Farrukhān. At this point Farrukhān relinquished power back to Shahrvarāz. This then instigated Shahrvarāz's rebellion and mutiny and his cooperation with Heraclius.

In his commentary on this section of Ṭabarī, Bosworth, doubting the identity of Shahrvarāz and Farrukhān as two separate figures, notes that here "the separation of Shahrbarāz-Farrukhān into two different persons" continues in

[778] Ṭabarī 1999, p. 328 and n. 774, also n. 147, de Goeje, 1008.

[779] Ṭabarī 1999, p. 328, de Goeje, 1008. The information that the two figures were brothers is, as we shall see, apocryphal.

[780] Ṭabarī 1999, pp. 327–328, de Goeje, 1008. See also footnote 1141, putting this story in a different light.

Ṭabarī's narrative and remarks that "the second commander involved in the story is presumably in reality the Shāhīn mentioned" by Ṭabarī prior to this.[781] In fact, however, we are dealing not with one, but with two distinct figures, neither of whom is Shāhīn, whose sagas during this period are closely connected.

Some of the other eastern Christian sources (in Greek, Syriac, and Arabic) that have been investigated by Kaegi and Cobb give variant names for this second commander involved. Michael the Syrian's account, for example, gives the name of the second commander as Kardārīgan. Now according to Simocatta, Kardārīgan is a Parthian title, the Persians being fond of being "called by their titles."[782] Agapius of Manjib renders the name Mardif and Chronique de Seert gives Farinjān. Again Shāhīn is nowhere to be found.[783] Foreign names, of course, are rendered differently and sometimes mutilated beyond recognition in the process of transcultural transmission. Farrukhān, the name given by the early Arabic sources—themselves based on the *X^w adāy-Nāmag* tradition—is in fact closest to what was probably the actual name or possibly the title of the figure concerned. For deciphering this and for our argument that we are in fact dealing with two separate figures and not one, we fortunately possess a source that in this, as in many other cases, contains valuable information, and here must be deemed the most reliable, namely the *Shāhnāma* of Ferdowsī.

2.7.5 Farrukh Hormozd Ispahbudhān

Ferdowsī begins his narrative on the "injustices of Khusrow II and the ingratitude of the army" by naming three figures who were deeply involved at this juncture. The first of these is a figure called Gorāz, the second Ẕād Farrukh, and a third Farrukhzād Ādharmagān. The last figure, Farrukhzād Ādharmagān, was a despised tax collector.[784] What, however, of the other two? According to Ferdowsī, Gorāz, about whom the author has not a few unkind words to say, was always in charge of protecting the Byzantine frontier, and was the first to become rebellious when the just king commenced his injustices. There is no doubt that Ferdowsī's Gorāz is the same figure as Shahrvarāz, *gorāz*, *borāz*, or *varāz*, that is boar, being the suffix to *shahr*, that is, region or empire, whence *boar of the empire*, Shahrvarāz.[785] For our future purposes it is also important to note that the wild boar has a significant religious symbolism, being

[781]Ṭabarī 1999, n. 775, pp. 328–329, de Goeje, 1008.

[782]In Hormozd IV's wars against the Byzantines in 582–586, a Kardārīgan, the *satrap*, is centrally involved. It is possible that Kardārīgan's name is derived from the title *kārdār*, tax collector, in which case Michael the Syrian might have confused this commander with Farrukhzād Ādharmagān; see footnote 784 below.

[783]Michael the Syrian, *Chronique de Michel le Syrien*, Paris, 1899, edited and translated by J.-B. Chabot (Michael the Syrian 1899), IV. 408–409 and II. 408–409. Agapius of Manjib, *Kitāb al-ʿUnvān*, vol. 8 of *Patrologia Orientalis*, 1911, edited and translated by A. Vasiliev (Agapius of Manjib 1911); Seert 1918, *Chronique de Seert*, vol. 13 of *Patrologia Orientalis*, 1918, translated by R. Griveau and A. Scher (Seert 1918). All cited in Cobb and Kaegi 2002, pp. 124–125, 126 and 127 respectively.

[784]See Nöldeke 1979, pp. 563–564, n. 68.

[785]Justi 1895, pp. 277–278.

a representation of the God Mihr.[786] Ferdowsī's account, therefore, confirms the identity of Shahrvaraz as a leading figure of the Sasanian-Byzantine wars. In the second figure, Zād Farrukh, however, as we shall see, we are most probably dealing with the son of the Farrukhān of Ṭabarī. So what is Ferdowsī's narrative, and who are Zād Farrukh and Farrukhān?

According to Ferdowsī, once Shahrvarāz/Gorāz became rebellious, Zād Farrukh—who was "so close to Khusrow II that none dared to approach him without his permission"[787]—also rebelled and joined forces with Shahrvarāz. Ferdowsī hints at the correspondence between Zād Farrukh and Shahrvarāz, at the end of which Shahrvarāz commenced his own correspondence with the Byzantine emperor, Heraclius, encouraging him to attack Iran.[788] After it became clear that Shahrvarāz had mutinied against him, Khusrow II wrote a letter which he anticipated to be intercepted by Heraclius' men. Khusrow II, in other words, used a ruse. In it, he encouraged Shahrvarāz to prepare for a coordinated attack against Heraclius, whereby the army of Shahrvarāz and that of Khusrow II himself would clamp that of Heraclius from two sides. Ferdowsī's narrative makes it clear that Heraclius was either very close to or already within the Iranian territory. As intended, the message was intercepted by Heraclius and achieved its purpose of arousing his suspicions of Shahrvarāz's peaceful intentions.[789]

Meanwhile Khusrow II sent another message to Shahrvarāz, instructing him to send the mutinous members of his army to him. Shahrvarāz then instructed 12,000[790] of his army to move toward Iran, set up camp at Ardashīr Khurrah, not to cross the water, and remain united.[791] Khusrow II, who "was not pleased with [the army's] arrival," sent Zād Farrukh to reprimand them for letting Heraclius invade Iran. Zād Farrukh delivered Khusrow II's message. But in the guise of a messenger he, too, mutinied: he entered into secret negotiations with the mutinous army. As he was sympathetic toward the cause of Shahrvarāz

---

[786]The wild boar is singled out twice in *Mihr Yasht* as the fifth incarnation of Mithra. Mihr Yasht 1883, *Mihr Yasht*, vol. 23 of *Sacred Books of the East*, Oxford University Press, 1883, translated by James Darmesteter (Mihr Yasht 1883), §§70, 127, cited in Garsoian, Nina G., 'The Iranian Substratum of Agatʿangelos Cycle', in *Armenia between Byzantium and the Sasanians*, pp. 151–189, London, 1985a, reprinted from Nina G. Garsoian, *East of Byzantium: Syria and Armenia in the Formative Period*, Washington, 1982 (Garsoian 1985a), p. 160. See also footnote 2257 below.

[787]Ferdowsī 1971, vol. IX, p. 238, Ferdowsī 1935, p. 2894:

یکی بی هنر بود نامش گراز   کزو یافتی نام و ارام و ناز
که بودی همیشه نگهبان روم   یکی دیو سر بود بیداد و شوم
چو شد شاه با داد بیدادگر   از ایران نخست او بپیچید سر
دگر زاد فرّخ که نامی بدی   بنزدیك خسرو گرامی بدی
نیارست کس رفت نزدیك شاه   مگر زاد فرّخ بدی بارخواه

[788]Ferdowsī 1971, vol. IX, pp. 243–244, Ferdowsī 1935, pp. 2899–2900.

[789]Ferdowsī 1971, vol. IX, pp. 243–244, Ferdowsī 1935, pp. 2895–2897.

[790]Note, again, the messianic number.

[791]For a detailed exposition of the course of this last phase of the Sasanian-Byzantine war see Sebeos 1999, pp. 214–220.

(*payāmbar yekī bod bih dil bā Gorāz*), he instructed Shahrvarāz's army to remain united and not to divulge the name of the mutinous members among them. Through a second set of correspondences with the army, Zād Farrukh reiterated his support and encouraged them not to fear the wrath of Khusrow II, arguing that it was he who had scattered the army to the corners of the world, and assured them that there were no longer any grandees at Khusrow II's court who would lend him their support. Meanwhile, he retained his posture of loyalty vis-à-vis Khusrow II. The king, however, suspected Zād Farrukh's mutinous intentions but did not divulge it. Here, Ferdowsī provides us with an extremely crucial piece of information: Khusrow II kept his knowledge of Zād Farrukh's intent to himself because he was afraid of his brother, Rustam, who, with 10,000 men under his command, had already rebelled in his region.[792] Zād Farrukh meanwhile gathered support for his mutiny. It was decided that Khusrow II's time had come and that a new king must assume the throne. The above narrative is presented in a somewhat similar fashion in Ibn Balkhī's account. According to him, it was to Zād Farrukh, rendered as Zādān Farrukh, the commander of Khusrow II's army, that the order of murdering 36,000 men from the "famous and elite and Princes and soldiers and Arabs" was given. When the latter refused to carry out the king's orders and news reached the army, tumult spread among them, and the commanders of the regions, fearing their lot, each started strengthening the realm under their control. These finally conspired, in secret (*dar sirr*), with the elite of Fārs and the king's ministers and deposed the king.[793] They cast lots for Shīrūyih Qubād, Khusrow II's son, who had been imprisoned by his father.[794]

Ferdowsī's account, therefore, leaves no doubt about two facts: first, the Parthian Shahrvarāz did indeed mutiny, and second, in his rebellion he was not

---

[792]Ferdowsī 1971, vol. IX, pp. 243–244, Ferdowsī 1935, pp. 2899–2900:

سبك زاد فرّخ زبان بر گشاد	همی کرد گفتار ناخوب یاد
کزین سان سپاهی دلیر و جوان	نبینم کس اندر میان ناتوان
شما را چرا ترس باید ز شاه	به گیتی پراگنده از در سپاه
بزرگی نبینم به درگاه او	که روشن کند اختر و ماه او
به دشنام لبها گشایید باز	چه بر من چه بر شاه گردنفراز ...
همه یکسر از جای برخواستند	به دشنام لبها بیاراستند
بشد زاد فرّخ به خسرو بگفت	که لشکر همه یار گشتند و جفت
مرا بیم جانست اگر نیز شاه	فرستد به پیغام نزد سپاه
بدانست خسرو که ان کژّی گوی	همان اب و خون ارد به جوی
ز بیم برادرش چیزی نگفت	همی داشت این راستی در نهفت
که پیچیده بد رستم از شهریار	به جای خود تیغزن ده هزار
دل زاد فرّخ نگه داشت نیز	سپه را همی روی برگاشت نیز

For a discussion of the regions under the control of the Ispahbudhān family, see page 188ff.

[793]Ibn Balkhī 1995, p. 257.

[794]Howard-Johnston maintains that at this point Shīrūyih Qubād "made contact with a leading disaffected magnate, the former supreme commander of Sasanian forces. The latter gathered support for a coup at the court and in the higher echelons of the army, sent a deputation to inform Heraclius of the conspirators' plans, and put them into action on the night of 23–24 February 628." Sebeos does not give the name of this leading disaffected magnate. Sebeos 1999, p. 221.

alone and, in fact, had the collaboration of another force, stationed at the capital, and identified by Ferdowsī as the powerful Zād Farrukh.[795] The figure of Zād Farrukh, and his conspiracy and correspondence with the army of Shahrvarāz, was crucial to the mutiny that subsequently took place against Khusrow II Parvīz. But Ferdowsī also furnishes us with another significant piece of information: with 10,000 troops at his disposal, Zād Farrukh's brother, Rustam, had already staged a rebellion of his own during this period. This piece of information is of significant value in determining the period during the latter parts of Khusrow II's reign in which these events took place.

Third phase (621–628)

We know that in the third phase of the Sasanian–Byzantine wars, in 624, there was a dramatic reversal of the course of the war in which, under the banner of holy war, Heraclius effected the conquest of Transcaucasia and, taking the northern route through Armenia, captured Dvin. Afterwards, the northwestern parts of Sasanian realms were at Heraclius' mercy. Under the personal command of the emperor, the Byzantine army invaded Azarbāyjān and Media. In the same year, Gandzak was sacked by Heraclius' army.[796] The initial conquest of Azarbāyjān then, was the first important phase of the reversal of the course of the war. It was at this point that Khusrow II Parvīz recalled the Mihrānid Shahrvarāz.[797] Azarbāyjān, however, was invaded by the Byzantines on two separate occasions, not only in 624–626, but also in 627–628.[798] The combination of the information at our disposal therefore informs us that by 624 Heraclius' army was in Azarbāyjān. By 626–627, Shahrvarāz had mutinied and Zād Farrukh had become a coconspirator of the Mihrānid in his mutiny against Khusrow II. Prior to the mutiny of Zād Farrukh and Shahrvarāz, the brother of Zād Farrukh, Rustam had already rebelled. All these crucial rebellions, therefore, took place in the period between 624–627, the period in which Heraclius invaded Azarbāyjān. Who, however, were the brothers Rustam and Zād Farrukh who held such tremendous power in Khusrow II's realm? Who was the Persian lord conspiring with Shahrvarāz? And how was all this connected with Heraclius' invasion of Azarbāyjān?

[795]Theophanes, who calls the other general Kardarigas, specifically highlights his complicity with Heraclius. When Heraclius intercepts the letter that Khusrow II had sent to Kardarigas in which the Sasanian king had ordered the latter to murder Shahrvarāz, he showed the letter to Shahrvarāz. Shahrvarāz in turn asked Kardarigas whether he was resolved to do this. Theophanes then maintains, the "commanders were filled with anger and renounced Chosroes, and *they made a peaceful settlement with the emperor*." Theophanes, *The Chronicle of Theophanes Confessor: Byzantyine and Near Eastern History AD 284–813*, Oxford, 1997, translated with introduction and commentary by Cyril Mango and Roger Scott (Theophanes 1997), pp. 452–453. Emphasis mine.

[796]Sebeos 1999, p. 214.

[797]Sebeos 1999, p. 215.

[798]Minorsky, V., 'Roman and Byzantine Campaigns in Atropatene', *Bulletin of the School of Oriental and African Studies* 11, (1944), pp. 243–265 (Minorsky 1944), p. 248. For a campaign said to have been undertaken in 621/2 in southern Azarbāyjān, "we have no authentic report." Ibid.

Prince of the Medes

On a number of occasions Sebeos mentions a figure whom he calls the Prince of the Medes,[799] Khoṙokh Ormizd (Farrukh Hormozd).[800] The Prince of the Medes, Sebeos informs us, "was the Prince of the region of Atrpatakan [Azarbāyjān]."[801] As Sebeos, Ferdowsī, and some of our Arabic sources clearly inform us, moreover, Rustam and Zād Farrukh, or Farrukhzād—Zād Farrukh being simply an inverted rendition of the name—were the *sons* of Farrukh Hormozd (Khoṙokh Ormizd), Sebeos' Prince of the Medes and Prince of Azarbāyjān.[802] Sebeos further provides us with a fascinating and crucial piece of information: On the eve of Shahrvarāz's rebellion, the army of the Persian empire had divided into three main parts. "One force was in Persia and the East; one force was Khoṙeam's [i.e., Shahrvarāz's] in the area of Asorestan; and one force in Atrpatakan."[803] By the end of the Sasanian–Byzantine wars, therefore, the Iranian army had divided into three. As we shall see in Chapter 3, this division of the Iranian armed forces into three camps did not only precipitate the deposition and murder of Khusrow II Parvīz, but it also led to four subsequent years of tumultuous crisis. For it is as a result of this factionalism that during the period 628–632 one Sasanian king and queen succeeded the other. We have, however, jumped ahead of our narrative. Which are the three armed factions enumerated by Sebeos? We will discuss the army of Persia and the East below.[804] The army under Khoṙeam, it is clear, was none other than the conquest army under the Parthian dynast, the Mihrānid Shahrvarāz in Āsōristān.[805]

It is the leadership and constituency of the third army, however, that once and for all clarifies the identity of the Persian lord. For there is no doubt that the army of Atrpatakan mentioned by Sebeos was the force under the command of Khoṙokh Ormizd (Farrukh Hormozd), the Prince of the Medes, and his sons Farrukhzād (Ferdowsī's Zād Farrukh) and Rustam. As we have seen, Sebeos specifically maintains that Khoṙokh Ormizd was the "Prince of the region of

[799] Sebeos 1999, pp. 107, 243–246, 253, and n. 661.

[800] Sebeos 1999, p. 107.

[801] Sebeos 1999, p. 89.

[802] Sebeos 1999, p. 92. As we shall see in the next chapter, many layers of confusion have been imposed on the traditions of this important Parthian dynastic family. On the most trivial level this has led to an obvious yet crucial mistake in the simple genealogy of this family where, even in some of our contemporary secondary accounts, Rustam is considered the son, as opposed to the brother of Farrukhzād! For a detailed discussion of this family, see §3.3.1 below, but see also the genealogical tree on page 471.

[803] Sebeos 1999, p. 89.

[804] See page 155.

[805] As we shall see in Chapter 3, the precise constituency of the force under Shahrvarāz's control cannot be deciphered. This was a force that had probably seen years of exile during the Persian–Byzantine conflict. The force under his command included most likely a good number number of his Mihrānid constituency, but we should also recall that Pīrag-i Shahrvarāz had been assigned as *spāhbed* of the quarter of the south (*kūst-i nēmrōz*) by Khusrow II. This might explain Shahrvarāz's complicity with the native Sīstāni contingents in deposing Ardashīr III, as we shall see in §3.2.3.

Atrpatakan."[806] At some point shortly before the deposition of Khusrow II in 628, when Zād Farrukh, the son of the Prince of Atrpatakan, was secretly in correspondence with the forces of Shahrvarāz, and most probably contemporaneous with, or shortly after, Heraclius' invasion of Azarbāyjān in 624, Rustam, the son of Farrukh Hormozd, had also rebelled, most probably in the same region over which his father ruled, Azarbāyjān.

In Ferdowsī's narrative the name of the dynastic leader of the family, Farrukh Hormozd, is missing or is mistakingly replaced by that of his son, Zād Farrukh (Farrukhzād). Indeed, virtually the same actions performed by the father Farrukh Hormozd, who is called Farrukhān in Ṭabarī, are attributed by Ferdowsī to Zād Farrukh (Farrukhzād).[807] This is yet another example of the confusion in the sources about a father–son pair, to which we have already hinted,[808] and which in any case is quite understandable in view of the agnatic power structure within a dynastic family, where a son could very well be acting on behalf of his father.[809] That Farrukh Hormozd, however, was the prime instigator of the family's policies and that therefore in the person of Farrukhān of Ṭabarī we are in all likelihood dealing with this same figure, is most clearly reflected in the subsequent history of the Sasanians. The army under the leadership of Farrukh Hormozd (Farrukhān or Khurrukhān) was, next to those of Shahrvarāz and of Shāhīn, most likely the third army division involved in the Sasanian–Byzantine wars, reflecting the accuracy of all the narratives at our disposal.

Shahrvarāz presented the case for his defection as well as that of his putative brother Farrukhān (Farrukh Hormozd) to Heraclius: "The ones who laid waste to your towns were my brother and my self, with our stratagems and our valor. But now Kisrā has come to envy us and wants to kill my brother. When I refused to do so, he ordered my brother to kill me. Hence *both of us have thrown off allegiance to him, and are ready to fight at your side.*"[810] A presumed brother and accomplice of Shahrvarāz is in this case apocryphal.[811] The coconspirators of the Parthian Mihrānid dynast, therefore, were the family of the Prince of the Medes. As Ferdowsī's narrative's inform us, the two factions collaborated

[806] Sebeos 1999, p. 89. This might be an indication that Farrukh Hormozd was appointed as the *spāhbed* of the *kūst-i ādurbādagān*. We must assume that the Ispahbudhān, to which family Farrukh Hormozd belonged as we shall argue shortly, had lost their *spāhbedī* over the *kūst-i khwarāsān* in the aftermath of Vistāhm's rebellion and the appointment of Smbat Bagratuni over the region (see note 744).

[807] This confusion between Farrukh Hormozd and his son Farrukhzād, with slightly different renderings of their names, persists in the narratives about the deposition of Ardashīr III and the ascension of Būrāndukht, as we shall see on pages 184 and 187.

[808] See for instance the confusion between the Kārinid Sukhrā and his son Zarmihr discussed in §2.4.3.

[809] See §1.2.

[810] Ṭabarī 1999, p. 330, de Goeje, 1008.

[811] So far as I can establish, there was no familial relationship between Farrukh Hormozd and Shahrvarāz, and in fact, we will shortly argue that Farrukh Hormozd belonged to the Ispahbudhān family.

secretly. Although Khusrow II was aware of their conspiracy and he did order the leadership of one faction—Farrukhān in Ṭabarī, Zād Farrukh in Ferdowsī—to kill the other, Shahrvarāz, he had to keep at least a semblance of cordiality toward the former family, that of the Prince of the Medes, Farrukh Hormozd.

And so all the motifs of the anecdotal series of letters between Khusrow II and his powerful generals, Shahrvarāz and the Persian lord Farrukhān (Farrukh Hormozd), are in fact historically valid. There is no need to conflate the identity of personalities that are clearly portrayed as two separate figures in most of our narratives.[812] In the last decisive months of the Sasanian–Byzantine wars, not only Shahrvarāz mutinied, but also Farrukh Hormozd, the Prince of the Medes, withdrew his army of Azarbāyjān, and indirectly, at least, cooperated with Heraclius. Moreover, the family of Farrukh Hormozd pursued a collective policy. It was perhaps this significant rebellion of the Prince of the Medes, or rather, as Sebeos and Ferdowsī maintain, of his son Rustam, in Azarbāyjān, that allowed Heraclius to invade Azarbāyjān in 624. An alternative scenario is equally plausible: the success of Heraclius in the eastern wars, together with the collective policies of Khusrow II, led the Prince of the Medes to withdraw his support from Khusrow II, thus allowing Heraclius to invade through Azarbāyjān, the territory under his control.

The precise turn of events as a result of the policies pursued by the Parthian leaders of the two great armies of Iran at this point, Shahrvarāz and Farrukh Hormozd, and their postures vis-à-vis Heraclius and Khusrow II Parvīz, need to be placed in the context of the theater of war in Azarbāyjān.[813] Those who maintain an earlier date for the agreement of Heraclius with Shahrvarāz and the figure that we have now identified as Farrukh Hormozd, namely 624–626/627 CE,[814] provide a more convincing version of events.[815] As Ṭabarī's account highlights, Heraclius, Shahrvarāz, and Farrukh Hormozd must have reached some sort of understanding either prior to or in the midst of Heraclius' invasion of Azarbāyjān. A thorough reexamination of the course of the war of 624–626 must account for the active participation of the army of Azarbāyjān, under the leadership of the dynastic family of Farrukh Hormozd, whose territory was invaded when the course of the war was reversed. In this campaign, Heraclius invaded Azarbāyjān, sacked Gandzak, Ormi, Hamadān, and Media. The fire of

[812]Incidentally, the confusion in the sources between these two figures might also be explained by the fact that Shahrvarāz's full name, as it appears on the seals, was Pīrag-i Shahrvarāz, the first part of which would be rendered in Arabic as *Fīrak* and therefore could very well have been confused with *Farrukh*.

[813]For the third phase of the war, see also page 149ff above.

[814]Minorsky 1944, p. 248.

[815]Howard-Johnston claims that there "is no hint ... [in Sebeos] of any earlier political understanding, such as that alleged to have been reached by Heraclius and Shahrvaraz in 626 by *Chronique de Seert*, Tabari and Dionysius. The allegation should probably be rejected as a piece of deliberate disinformation, circulated to further Roman interests as the war reached a climax in 627–628." Sebeos 1999, p. 223. In the face of the overwhelming evidence presented by the sources, however, to which we can now add Ferdowsī, Howard-Johnston's claim is not tenable here. Also see Cobb and Kaegi 2002, *passim*.

Ādhar Gushnasp was ransacked and extinguished.[816] Most significantly, when Khusrow II was deposed in February 628 CE,[817] and his son, Shīrūyih Qubād enthroned in April 628, suing for peace, the new king's envoy was dispatched to Gandzak in Azarbāyjān, the territory of Farrukh Hormozd, where Heraclius' army had encamped.[818]

What led to "one of the most astonishing reversals of fortune in the annals of war,"[819] and the final victory of the Byzantines over the Sasanians in one of the great wars of late antiquity, therefore, was the desertion and mutiny of the leaders of two of the major armies that had steered the course of the war prior to this in favor of Khusrow II Parvīz. One mutinous party was Pīrag-i Shahrvarāz, the *ērān-spāhbed* of the *kūst-i nēmrōz* of the Mihrān family, the Parthian general of Khusrow II. The other was the dynastic family of the Prince of the Medes, Farrukh Hormozd, and his sons Farrukhzād and Rustam. While Shahrvarāz was from the Parthian Mihrānid family, moreover, it will be argued below that the family of Farrukh Hormozd was most probably none other than the Ispahbudhān family,[820] whose power extended not only over Azarbāyjān but also, as we shall establish,[821] over Khurāsān. It was as a result of the mutiny of these two towering *Parthian* dynastic families that the last powerful Sasanian king, Khusrow II Parvīz lost one of the greatest wars of late antiquity, and eventually his very crown. Who, however, were the other factions involved in the mutiny?

2.7.6 Khusrow II's deposition

In the aftermath of his conspiracy with Shahrvarāz, Farrukhzād, the son of the Prince of the Medes, set upon toppling Khusrow II Parvīz and bringing another Sasanian king to power.[822] According to Ferdowsī, Farrukhzād gathered a numerous army and met with the Armenian *spāhbed* Tukhār, another leading conspirator against Khusrow II. This Tukhār was none other than Varaztirots', the son of Khusrow II's previous rescuer in the east, Smbat Bagratuni. Varaztirots' had been educated at the Sasanian court and was later appointed *marzbān* of Armenia, acquiring the title of Javitean Khusrow.[823] For reasons that require further research, however, his relationship with Khusrow II Parvīz soured. The

[816]Sebeos 1999, pp. 214–215. For the Ādhar Gushnasp fire, see page 362 below.

[817]Nöldeke 1879, p. 382, n. 2, Nöldeke 1979, p. 580, n. 135.

[818]Sebeos 1999, p. 222.

[819]Sebeos 1999, p. xxiv.

[820]This is an important claim of this study, a detailed investigation of which has to be postponed to a more relevant section, §3.3.1. For now we mention that in some of our sources Farrukh Hormozd is clearly maintained to be the son of the Ispahbudhān Vindūyih; see page 187.

[821]See page 188ff.

[822]Ṭabarī 1999, p. 379, 381, de Goeje, 1043, 1045; Ferdowsī 1971, vol. IX, p. 244, Ferdowsī 1935, p. 2900:

همی راند با هر کسی داستان — شدند اندر ان کار همداستان
که شاهی دگر بر نشاند به تخت — کزین دور شد فرّ و ایین و بخت

[823]Chaumont 1991, p. 432. See page 139.

term *tukhār* in Ferdowsī's narrative refers to the office of *tanutēr*, which was first given to Smbat Bagratuni.[824] The *tanutēr* was the "senior member of a *naxarar* family," in this case the Bagratuni house.[825]

As we have seen, the Bagratuni house had become centrally involved in the military and administrative organization of the Sasanian realm during Khusrow II's tenure, with Smbat being largely responsible for putting down Vistāhm's rebellion.[826] Varaztirots', however, joined the ranks of the rebellious factions who, according to Ferdowsī, were being led by Farrukhzād in the capital. That Varaztirots' played a central role in the rebellion that toppled Khusrow II and led to Shīrūyih Qubād's succession is corroborated by the fact that upon assuming the throne, Shīrūyih Qubād "summoned Varaztirots', son of Smbat Bagratuni called Jāvītān, and gave him the office of *tanutēr*."[827] An Armenian faction, therefore, was also involved in the deposition of Khusrow II.

A third important faction involved in Khusrow II's deposition was that of another Parthian dynastic family, the Kanārangīyān, whom we shall examine in detail later.[828] For when Farrukhzād informed Tukhār (Varaztirots') of the factions' choice for the Iranian throne, the Armenian *naxarar* responded that "the choice would be pleasing to the *kanārang* as well."[829] Farrukhzād's coup was successful and, according to Thaʿālibī, Shīrūyih Qubād was taken to the house of Farrukhzād, whom the author depicts as the *ḥājib* of the king, where he was declared king the next morning.[830] But with a young king on the throne, and in what is typical of the course of Sasanian history, Farrukhzād seemed to be actually running affairs.[831]

There is a lengthy set of correspondences of Shīrūyih Qubād who, at the instigation of the dynastic factions, enumerated those aspects of Khusrow II's policies that had wreaked havoc on Iran. A key issue, as Shahbazi puts it, thirty years after the fact,[832] was Khusrow II's treatment of the Ispahbudhān brothers

---

[824]Sebeos 1999, p. 86, n. 534 and p. 49, n. 307. See also §2.7.2.

[825]Buzandaran 1989, p. 563. *Tukhār* is the Persian rendition of the Armenian title *tanutēr* of a *naxarar* family (from Parthian *naxvadar*), "the general term designating the first Aršakuni society superior to the *azat* and referring to the nobility rather than a particular rank or office." Buzandaran 1989, p. 549. In the revolt of Bahrām-i Chūbīn the two houses that had aided Khusrow II in regaining his throne were the houses of Mušeł Mamikonean and Smbat Bagratuni. In 602, when the Byzantine emperor Maurice ordered the deportation and resettlement of a substantial section of the Armenian population, the Armenian nobility split. Mušeł wavered between Khusrow II and Maurice, while Smbat's house always took the side of Khusrow II. Chaumont 1991, p. 432.

[826]See §2.7.2.

[827]Sebeos 1999, p. 86.

[828]See page 266ff.

[829]Ferdowsī 1971, vol. IX, p. 245, Ferdowsī 1935, p. 2901:

گرامی بد این شهریار جوان   به نزد کنارنگ و هم پهلوان

For the connection of the Kanārangīyān to the Ispahbudhān, see page 266.

[830]Thaʿālibī 1900, p. 714, Thaʿālibī 1989, pp. 455–457.

[831]Ferdowsī 1971, vol. IX, pp. 250–253, Ferdowsī 1935, pp. 2905–2908.

[832]Shahbazi 1991b, p. 182.

Vindūyih and Vistāhm. In the *Shāhnāma*, after being accused of the regicide against his father Hormozd IV, Khusrow II is called upon to explain his treatment of the Ispahbudhān brothers. "They were my uncles," Khusrow II Parvīz retorted, "without equals in all the regions. They had put their lives on the line for me. They were kind and of my blood. Yet, when they committed regicide and killed my father [Hormozd IV], I had no choice but to kill them."[833] In Ferdowsī's rendition of the events it was Farrukhzād who finally sent an assassin to murder Khusrow II Parvīz. This, as we shall see later, also corroborates our contention that the Prince of the Medes was from the Ispahbudhān family.[834]

Nīmrūzī army

Apart from Shahrvarāz and Farrukh Hormozd's forces, an Armenian faction and the Kanārangīyān were also among the central players involved in the deposition of the last powerful Sasanian king. What, however, does Sebeos mean by the army of Persia and the East? While there is a probability that he is here referring to the forces of the Kanārangīyān family, the army of Persia and the East most probably refers to the army of Nīmrūz, that is Sīstān.[835] While the *Shāhnāma* highlights the role of Zād Farrukh (Farrukhzād) from the Ispahbudhān family in the deposition of Khusrow II, Ṭabarī's account, together with a group of other narratives, highlights the part played by the *spāhbed* of Nīmrūz and his son,[836] making its identification with Sebeos' army of Persia and the East all the more likely.

From the end of Khusrow II's rule onward, the army of Nīmrūz is one of three main factions that struggle for the control of the Sasanian throne, the others being those of Shahrvarāz and of Farrukh Hormozd. Unfortunately, the dynastic affiliation of the Nīmrūzī faction requires further research, and we can only conjecture that it was controlled by the Sūren dynastic family, as Sīstān

[833]Ferdowsī 1971, vol. IX, pp. 254–276, here, pp. 262–263, Ferdowsī 1935, pp. 2912–2923, here p. 2917:

چو بندوی و گستهم خالان بدند — بهر کشوری بی همالان بدند
چو خون پدر بود و درد جگر — نکردیم سستی بخون پدر
بریدیم بندوی را دست و پای — کجا کرد بر شاه تاریك جای
چو گستهم شد در جهان ناپدید — ز گیتی یکی گوشه ای برگزید
بفرمان ما ناگهان کشته شد — سرو رای خون خوارگان گشته شد

Significantly, once again, Ferdowsī disguises here the protracted rebellion of Vistāhm.

[834]See §3.3.1. It is also reflective of the nature of the opposition against Khusrow II Parvīz's rule that one of the issues raised by the factions was the charge that the Sasanian king had positioned armies in distant regions. Ferdowsī 1971, vol. IX, pp. 269–270, Ferdowsī 1935, pp. 2922–2923; Thaʿālibī 1900, p. 722, Thaʿālibī 1989, p. 458.

[835]A third, less likely alternative is that the army of Persia and the East refers to a force that had gathered in the Outer Khurāsān regions (see §6.2.1), an army that ultimately tried to set up the child Khusrow III as king. What could have been the make-up of this force, if in fact this alternative is valid, I have not been able to ascertain.

[836]Ṭabarī 1999, p. 396, de Goeje, 1059.

was the original fiefdom of the Sūrens.[837] We propose that the Sūrenid dynastic family of Sīstān in southeastern Iran had become so enmeshed with the house of Persīs, on account of the greater coincidence of their sociopolitical interest with the Sasanians, that at least a group of them adopted the dynastic epithet *Pārsīg*, and functioned under the umbrella faction of the Pārsīg. What lends credence to this hypothesis is that we in fact have evidence of Sūrens who carried the epithet *Pārsīg*. Remarkably, as Christensen has already pointed out a long time ago, in the narratives of Faustus of Byzance we find two Sūrens who carry the Pārsīg epithet in addition to their dynastic family name.[838] Among the *spāhbed* seals unearthed by Gyselen, furthermore, those of Wēh-Shābuhr, the *ērān-spāhbed* of the *kūst-i nēmrōz*, bear the epithet *aspbed i pārsīg*, Persian aspbed.[839] It is, furthermore, extremely probable that he had a Sūren agnatic affiliation. Citing the evidence pointed out by Christensen, Gyselen herself conjectures as much, although, again, all the evidence at our disposal remains inconclusive.[840]

Several accounts underline the preponderant role of the Nīmrūzī faction in the dynastic struggles that ensued, reaching their height at precisely the time when the Arab onslaught on Sasanian territories began. In these narratives, the Nīmrūzī faction's involvement began with the deposition and murder of Khusrow II and the accession of Shīrūyih Qubād in 628. We have evidence of an army of Nīmrūz, however, at other crucial junctures of Sasanian history. We recall, for example, that when the Byzantines, the Armenians, and the Ispahbudhān brothers coalesced around Khusrow II against Bahrām-i Chūbīn, the army of Nīmrūz also set out to aid the feeble Sasanian king.[841] As we shall see later on, at another highly critical juncture, when the Arab onslaught threatened the Sasanian monarchy, Rustam asked his brother Farrukhzād to solicit the cooperation of the army of Sīstān. The army of Sīstān, periodically mentioned at crucial junctures of Sasanian history, is therefore, in all likelihood, the force that Sebeos calls the army of Persia and the East.

According to Ṭabarī, when the Parthian led conspiracy of the house of the Prince of the Medes and the army of Shahrvarāz had brought Shīrūyih Qubād to power, Khusrow II was put in prison. The great men of the state then told Shīrūyih Qubād: "It is not fitting that we should have two kings: either you kill Kisrā, and we will be your faithful and obedient servants, or we shall depose you and give our obedience to him [i.e., Khusrow II Parvīz] *just as we always did before you secured the royal power*."[842] Struck with fear and crushed,[843] Shīrūyih Qubād then sent an envoy, one Asfādjushnas,[844] to

[837] Sīstān was one of the main regions of the *kūst-i nēmrōz*.

[838] Christensen 1944, p. 105, n. 2, as cited in Gyselen 2001a, p. 23, n. 56. See also note 308.

[839] Gyselen 2001a, seals 2c and B, p. 46.

[840] "One cannot rule out that the title of *aspbed i pārsīg* might have been reserved for the Sūrēn family. But this is clearly only purely speculation." Gyselen 2001a, p. 23, n. 56.

[841] Ferdowsī 1971, vol. IX, p. 105, Ferdowsī 1935, pp. 2676–2677. See page 128.

[842] Ṭabarī 1999, pp. 381–382, de Goeje, 1046. Emphasis added.

[843] Ṭabarī 1999, p. 382, de Goeje, 1046.

[844] There is confusion surrounding the position of this figure. Based on Dīnawarī, who claims that

Khusrow II Parvīz. Asfādjushnas was charged with communicating to the deposed king all his evil actions, and the reasons for his deposition and final murder.[845] Asfādjushnas then met with Jīlinūs or Jālīnūs, a figure whom Ṭabarī identifies as the commander of the guard in charge of keeping ward over Khusrow II. It is possible that Jālīnūs was in fact one of the Armenian dynasts ensnared in Sasanian history at this important juncture.[846] If this was the case, then Ṭabarī's folkloric rendition is meant to highlight the complicity of the Armenian faction in the deposition of Khusrow II. At any rate, Ṭabarī reiterates an elaborate exchange of grievances against Khusrow II and the latter's reply to these.[847] Being hard-pressed, Shīrūyih Qubād then ordered the execution of his father.[848] From among "several men who had *duties incumbent upon them of vengeance against* Khusrow II Parvīz," no one dared to undertake the task of regicide, however. Finally a "youth named Mihr Hurmuz [i.e., Mihr Hormozd], son of Mardānshāh,"[849] volunteered his services.

Mardānshāh Sūren

According to one version of Ṭabarī's narrative, Mardānshāh was Khusrow II's *pādhūspān* over the province of Nīmrūz.[850] It is to be noted that the cooperation of Mardānshāh, the *pādhūspān* of Nīmrūz, with Shahrvarāz, the (former) *spāhbed* of the *kūst-i nēmrōz*, makes perfect sense, for the office of *pādhūspān* was subordinate to that of the *spāhbed* of any given *kūst*. While Ṭabarī's narrative only implicitly connects the Mihrānid Shahrvarāz with the Sīstānī faction, other sources make their conspiracy explicit. Ṭabarī, however, provides us with a piece of information that is possibly quite significant for Sīstān's history of affiliation with the house of Sāsān in the late Sasanian period. Mardānshāh, Ṭabarī maintains, was one of Khusrow II's most obedient and trusty retainers.

he was "the head of the secretaries responsible for official correspondence (*ra'īs kuttāb al-rasā'il*)," Bosworth has emended Ṭabarī's *ra'īs al-katībah* (head of the cavalry) with that in Dīnawarī, making Asfādjushnas the "head of the [royal] secretaries." Ṭabarī 1999, p. 382 and n. 948, de Goeje, 1046. It is more than likely, however, that Ṭabarī's original title for this figure is valid.

[845]Ṭabarī 1999, p. 382, de Goeje, 1046.

[846]In an attempt to identify this figure, Bosworth notes that his name "looks Greek rather than Persian; possibly he was a Christian and had adopted a Christian name in addition to an unknown, purely Persian one." Ṭabarī 1999, p. 384 and n. 953, de Goeje, 1047. Citing other sources Bosworth further identifies him as someone who became a "leading general of the Persian troops combating the Arab invaders of Iraq and fell in the battle of Qādisiya." Ṭabarī 1999, p. 384, n. 953; see §3.4.1. This Jālīnūs took part in the initial wars of the Sasanian against the Arabs. His name, therefore, might be the Arabic rendition, probably the title, of one of the Armenian dynasts that were at this point intimately involved in Sasanian affairs. As a son of Dawit', Mušeł Mamikonean, and Gregory of Siwnik' both fought under Rustam in the battle of Qādisiya and were killed in 636, Jālīnūs might well refer to one of these figures. Sebeos 1999, p. 98.

[847]Ṭabarī 1999, pp. 385–394, de Goeje, 1048–1057.

[848]Ṭabarī 1999, p. 395, de Goeje, 1058.

[849]Ṭabarī 1999, p. 395, de Goeje, 1058.

[850]Ṭabarī 1999, p. 395, de Goeje, 1058. Justi calls Mardānshāh a brother of the Mihrānid Bahrām-i Chūbīn. Justi 1895, p. 196. As we shall presently see, we are more inclined, in view of his Sīstānī provenance, to assign him to the Sūren family, who did call themselves at times Pārsīgs; see notes 308 and 838.

Some "two years before his deposition, astrologers and diviners ... had told him [i.e., Khusrow II] that his fated death would come from the direction of Nīmrūz."[851] Khusrow II had therefore grown suspicious of Mardānshāh and become "fearful of his proximity, *on account of Mardānshāh's great prestige and because there was no one in that region [i.e., Sīstān] who could equal him in strength and power.*"[852]

Cognizant of Mardānshāh's "faithful obedience to him, his good counsel to him, and his eagerness to please the king," Khusrow II, however, spared Mardānshāh's life but cut off his right hand, rendering him incapable of holding office.[853] Having his hand cut off in "the open space before the royal palace," Mardānshāh was so grief-stricken that when the news of this reached Khusrow II Parvīz, the latter, in remorse, promised the *pādhūspān* of Nīmrūz that he would grant him anything he wished. The *pādhūspān* chose death over living mutilated and dishonored. Reluctantly and with a heavy dose of guilt, Khusrow II granted his wish. "[T]he heart of all the *ʿajam* was distressed by this," Ṭabarī's narrative maintains.

At the prospects of murdering Khusrow II Parvīz, therefore, it was Mihr Hormozd, the son of Mardānshāh, who volunteered for the regicide. Khusrow II Parvīz was "only too happy to have his life cut short by the son of a dignitary whom he had previously unjustly recompensed for his faithful service."[854] In Balʿamī's account, the Sīstānī faction spearheaded the revolt that toppled Khusrow II Parvīz and appointed Shīrūyih Qubād as king. They were the ones who solicited the cooperation of the son of Vindūyih—unnamed in Balʿamī's account—in the deposition of Khusrow II.[855] It is interesting to note that in Balʿamī's account, the list of grievances against Khusrow II included the murder of Mardānshāh rather than that of Vindūyih and Vistāhm: Mardānshāh's murder was listed as one of the king's gravest sins.[856]

An important note on the provenance of the sources must be added. Khusrow II's murder in vengeance has either been attributed to Farrukhzād or to Mihr Hormozd in our sources. Each of these figures actually represents a

[851]Ṭabarī 1999, pp. 395–396, de Goeje, 1058–1059.

[852]Ṭabarī 1999, pp. 395–396, de Goeje, 1058–1059. Emphasis mine.

[853]Ṭabarī 1999, pp. 396–397, and n. 974, de Goeje, 1059. The same story is given in Balʿamī's *Tarjumih-i Tārīkh-i Ṭabarī*, where he is also called Mardānshāh. His title, however, is given as the *amīr* (governor) of Bābil and Nīmrūz. Balʿamī 1959, p. 241.

[854]Ṭabarī 1999, p. 397, de Goeje, 1060.

[855]In Balʿamī's version, after Khusrow II killed Mardānshāh, he decided to appoint the latter's son, Hormozd, in the position of his father. Hormozd, later called Mihr Hormozd (p. 253), however, refused, and gave up his position (*az lashkarī towbih kard*). In this account, Jālīnūs was the general, *sarhang*, who was put in charge of keeping guard over Khusrow II. The house in which Khusrow II was kept as a prisoner belonged to a personage called Māh Isfand, whose title is again *sarhang*. Finally, the person who was in charge of taking the list of the grievances against Khusrow II is called Asʿād Ḥusayn or Asʿād Ḥasīs(?), the figure whom Ṭabarī calls Asfādjushnas. Balʿamī 1959, pp. 242–244.

[856]This, together with the general Sīstānī emphasis of Balʿamī's account, highlights the Sūren provenance of Balʿamī's sources.

faction: Farrukhzād that of the Prince of the Medes (the Ispahbudhān[857]), with control over the army of Azarbāyjān, and Mihr Hormozd that of Nīmrūz, that is to say, Sebeos' army of Persia and the East. If our identifications thus far are valid, therefore, what triggered "one of the most astonishing reversals of fortune in the annals of war" and the ultimate demise of the last effective Sasanian king, Khusrow II Parvīz in 628—commencing the downfall of the Sasanian dynasty—was the refusal of the powerful Parthian dynastic agnates to continue their confederacy with the Sasanian dynasty. The division of the Sasanian army during the last years of Khusrow II Parvīz into three separate entities, Shahrvarāz's conquest army, Farrukh Hormozd's army of Azarbāyjān, and the army of Persia and the East (the Nīmrūzī forces[858]), had devastating consequences for the Sasanians. Sebeos' work is unique among all sources at our disposal in explicitly highlighting this debilitating aspect of the Sasanian state's defensive and offensive posture at this crucial juncture.[859] The Sasanians finally came to lose the greatest war of antiquity substantially because the two Parthian dynasts, Shahrvarāz of the Mihrān family and Farrukh Hormozd of the Ispahbudhān family,[860] mutinied against Khusrow II Parvīz. In insisting on taking credit for the murder of one of the most maligned Sasanian kings, furthermore, the narrative sources betray two separate traditions, emanating from the Ispahbudhān faction on the one hand and the Sīstānī (Nīmrūzī) faction on the other. The discrepancies in these narratives therefore also betray the ways in which the Parthian dynastic families edited the *X^w adāy-Nāmag* tradition.[861]

There is a reason, however, why of all possible dynasts involved at this crucial juncture of Sasanian history, our narratives underline the role of the Ispahbudhān and the Nīmrūzī factions in the deposition of Khusrow II Parvīz. For overshadowing the tripartite division of the Sasanian forces was the Sasanian–Parthian confederacy. It was under the respective Ispahbudhān and Nīmrūzī factions, established shortly after the deposition of Khusrow II, that the Iranians finally divided into two camps: the Pārsīg versus the Pahlav.[862] The Sasanian–Parthian confederacy ultimately collapsed, and this at a highly critical moment in Sasanian history, when "from the Arab [regions] strong winds were blowing."[863] It is our goal to disentangle this ultimately disastrous episode for the Sasanians in the continuation of our story. A number of important

857 See page 187ff

858 See page 155.

859 The recent analysis of Howard-Johnston sheds much light on our understanding of this important phase of Sasanian history. Unfortunately, Howard-Johnston totally overlooks the significant role of the army of Atrapatkan (Azarbāyjān) under the Prince of the Medes, and therefore fails to assess the true nature of this division and its ramifications.

860 As mentioned earlier, this identification will be substantiated in the next chapter; see page 187ff.

861 For an elaboration of this point, see also Chapter 6.5, especially page 462ff.

862 See page 214ff below.

863 Thaʿālibī 1989, p. 465, Thaʿālibī 1900, p. 731:

و تحرّكت الاعد آء و هبّت ريح العرب.

historiographical observations must be addressed in detail, however, before we can again pick up our narrative and discuss the effects of the Pārsīg–Pahlav debacle on the Arab conquest of Iranian territories.

CHAPTER 3

The Arab conquest of Iran

On the face of it, the saga of the Sasanians in the last decades of their rule seems to defy any understanding. From the deposition of the powerful Khusrow II in 628 CE to the accession of the last Sasanian king Yazdgird III in 632 CE, no less than half a dozen monarchs are officially counted in the roster of Sasanian kings in a period of about four years.[864] Ṭabarī lists eight kings and two queens.[865] It has been suggested that some of these ruled simultaneously.[866] Exasperation has been voiced over how little we know of these rulers.[867] There is a similar unsubstantiated consensus that these ephemeral monarchs were put on the throne by various *factions* of the nobility, a nobility that was created in the wake of Khusrow I's reforms.[868] Which were the factions who spearheaded the candidacy of these monarchs, however? To date, no systematic effort in elucidating the tangled web of Sasanian history at this crucial juncture has been undertaken. The picture has been deemed too chaotic to be amenable to any logical disentanglement.

3.1 Question of sources: the futūḥ and X^{w}adāy-Nāmag traditions

There is a bewildering array of Iranian names and personalities involved in this crucial period of Sasanian history. Through the process of transmission in the course of centuries, some of these names have all but metamorphosed into illegibility. Scholarly attitudes in dealing with this quagmire have been flippant. In certain respects Noth's analysis is representative of the consensus. In investigating the personal names of some of the commanders in the wars of

[864]Five monarchs, inclusive of Yazdgird III, are listed in the chapter dealing with Sasanian history in the *Cambridge History of Iran*. Frye 1983, p. 178.

[865]Ṭabarī 1999, pp. 381–409, de Goeje, 1045–1067.

[866]Nöldeke 1879, pp. 397–398, n. 5, Nöldeke 1979, pp. 594–595, n. 183. Analyzing Sebeos' data, Howard-Johnston also comes to this conclusion, although, as we shall see, in line with the scholarship's current consensus, the dates that he postulates for the Persian succession crisis are flawed. Sebeos 1999, p. 225.

[867]Frye 1983, p. 171.

[868]Christensen 1944, p. 497 and especially pp. 500–501.

conquest—names that are given in the *futūḥ*[869] narratives—for example, Noth lumps together the order of the battles listed for the Arabs as well as those of the Iranians as mere *topoi* and argues that "it is impossible to say anything precise about the relation of these *topoi* to actual historical circumstances."[870] Noth then proceeds to examine the names of the *Arab* generals involved in these battles[871] and concludes that "it is not clear if any or all of the formations and units which appear in a number of these traditions were already in existence in the early period."[872] Given the fact that Noth considers the theme of Iran as a primary theme[873] in the early Arabic historical tradition, and given our knowledge of the nature of the *futūḥ* narratives,[874] one would have expected Noth to have proposed caveats to this aspect of his thesis. This, unfortunately, is not the case. With very little investigation, Noth proceeds to argue that in "the description of the opposing side, especially the Persian side, we have to do with pure fiction."[875]

The present study will take serious issue with this aspect of Noth's thesis. We cannot afford to continue to reckon with this period of Iranian history in a vacuum that has been occasioned by our own lack of research. And where, as Noth himself admits, we are given detailed and unique information, it behooves us to investigate such information in depth before dismissing it as fiction or the result of a fertile imagination of, for instance, Sayf b. ʿUmar,[876] through whom posterity has received some of these traditions.[877]

To begin with, while we might not have enough information about Arab

[869] As Noth observes, the "great majority of the traditions which deal with the time of the first four caliphs is concerned with the first large-scale conquests of the Muslims outside the Arabian peninsula ... These are designated over all as *futūḥ*. *Futūḥ* thus constituted a—if not the—principal historical rubric under which the early traditionalists considered the first decades of history after the death of Muḥammad." Noth 1994, p. 31. For an assessment of the *futūḥ* narratives, see ibid., pp. 28–31; or our discussion in §3.1.1 below, as well as footnote 934. For some of the latest works on this theme, besides Noth's, see, among others, Donner, Fred M., *Narratives of Islamic Origin: The Beginnings of Islamic Historical Writing*, vol. 14 of *Studies in Late Antiquity and Early Islam*, Princeton, 1998 (Donner 1998); Robinson, Chase F., *Islamic Historiography: Themes in Islamic History*, Cambridge University Press, 2003 (Robinson 2003).

[870] Noth 1994, p. 114.

[871] Noth 1994, p. 114, n. 34 where he gives references to pp. 97–98, 100–101.

[872] Noth 1994, p. 114.

[873] Noth defines a primary theme as a "subject area which, so far as the extant evidence allows us to judge, represents a genuine topic of interest, as opposed to an offshoot derived from—and therefore secondary to—one or several such early topics." Noth 1994, p. 27 and p. 39. For our subsequent purposes we should point out that besides Iran, Noth considers the themes of *ridda* and *futūḥ* as primary themes as well. Ibid., pp. 28–30, 31–33, respectively.

[874] For a comprehensive survey of Islamic historiography in the classical period, see Humphreys, R. Stephen, *Islamic History: A Framework for Inquiry*, vol. 9, Minneapolis, 1991 (Humphreys 1991), especially pp. 4–127.

[875] Noth 1994, p. 114.

[876] See footnote 894 below.

[877] Ṭabarī diligently starts each of his narratives by giving its chain of transmission (*isnād*), so that we almost always know when a tradition is due to Sayf.

warfare and battle formation in pre-Islamic Arabia,[878] we do possess enough information about the logistics of war, war strategies, and battle formations of the Sasanian army.[879] Battle formations in right and left flanks, main body, complemented with cavalry, infantry, rearguard and vanguard, and so forth—all aspects of Sasanian battle strategy that Noth was examining—have had a long history in Iranian warfare.[880] One needs only to browse the *Shāhnāma* of Ferdowsī in order to come across battle formations throughout the text, an observation that cannot be dismissed on account of Ferdowsī's poetic imagination. In fact, as opposed to considering the explicit information given on Sasanian battle formations in the conquest accounts as a mere *topos*, we should reckon it an extremely valuable tool for deciphering the identities of the leaders of the factions involved in the Sasanian war efforts at this crucial juncture of their history.[881] The Sasanians kept records of their campaigns.[882] To argue that the "credibility of these statements [—in which the names of the commanders, and their battle formations have been given in specific battles—] is ... weakened by the occurrence of *rhyming* names such as Bandaway/Tīraway,"[883] is only to betray unfamiliarity, replete in studies of the late antique period, with the Iranian side of events. Bandaway, whose name is in fact misspelled to utter illegibility—easily rectified with reference to Justi's *Iranisches Namenbuch*[884]—was in fact Vindūyih. Tīraway, that is Tīrūyih, is a theophoric name after one of the *Yazatas* of the Iranian religious pantheon, Tīr. And the suffix *-ūyih* contained in the aforementioned names, as well as in others such as Shīrūyih and Gurdūyih, is regularly used in Iranian names. Ironically, *both* Vindūyih and Tīrūyih were *historical* figures and none other than the sons of the Parthian dynast Vistāhm of the Ispahbudhān family.[885] They participated, quite logically and appropriately, therefore, in the forces that were brought to the war front against the Arab armies by the Parthian Ispahbudhān dynastic family of Rustam.[886] The fact that Bandaway was named after his murdered uncle, Vindūyih, in commemoration

[878] See the important article of Landua-Tasseron, Ella, 'Features of the pre-Conquest Muslim Armies in the Time of Muḥammad', in *The Byzantine and Early Islamic Near East III: States, Resources and Armies*, pp. 299–337, Princeton, 1995 (Landua-Tasseron 1995).

[879] Shahbazi, Shapur, 'Army: I. pre-Islamic', in Ehsan Yarshater (ed.), *Encyclopaedia Iranica*, pp. 489–499, New York, 1991a (Shahbazi 1991a), pp. 489–499. Tafazzoli 2000, pp. 12–18, especially p. 15, where it is argued that the later structure of the Muslim armies were based on the military organizations of the Sasanians.

[880] Shahbazi 1991a, pp. 494–499.

[881] In fact, as it has been justifiably observed, one of the chief problems of the Sasanian army was that "the Persians placed too great a reliance on the presence of their leader: the moment the commander fell or fled, his men gave way regardless of the course of action." As we shall see, there were good reasons for this. Shahbazi 1991a, p. 498.

[882] Shahbazi 1991a, pp. 498–499.

[883] Noth 1994, p. 112.

[884] Justi 1895.

[885] Ibn al-Athīr, ʿIzz al-Dīn, *Al-Kāmil fi 'l-Taʾrīkh*, Beirut, 1862, edited by C.J. Tornberg (Ibn al-Athīr 1862), vol. 2, p. 436. See also page 187ff, as well as the genealogical tree of the Ispahbudhān family on page 471.

[886] As we will argue below on page 187, Rustam was a grandson of Vistāhm's brother Vindūyih.

of this illustrious member of the family, makes perfect sense, and is not a figment of the imagination of the authors or the collectors of these traditions. The names of these figures rhyme because they use suffixes prevalent in Iranian naming practice.

3.1.1 Futūḥ

The superficial incomprehensibility of this period of Sasanian history, 628–632 CE, is further confounded by the fact that a whole new genre of *Islamic* historiography professes to give historical accounts of events that presumably transpired shortly after this period, namely the *futūḥ* narratives.[887] The Arab bias inherent in this genre of Islamic histories, one of the avowed purposes of which was to highlight the meritocracy of the Arab generals and tribes who undertook the *Islamic* conquests and established the Muslim polity, dominated the historiography of the early Islamic period and possibly even constructed the Arabist bias that dominates contemporary scholarship. As a result, while modern scholarship has been busy researching which Arab tribe at which juncture and for what purpose chose to participate—or did not actually participate—in which battles under the command of which Arab general,[888] it has practically all but written off any effort in reconstructing some of the same, potentially analogous, variables for this period of Sasanian history from an *Iranian* perspective.[889] In some very crucial sense the victors have managed to write the Iranian history of late antiquity.[890] Our efforts in rectifying the skewed reconstruction of this period of Iranian history, however, will prove rewarding, for they will explicate not only the ultimate success of the Arab conquests of Sasanian territories and the dissolution of the Sasanian polity from the perspective

[887]See footnote 869.

[888]If one is predominantly interested in constructing the political dimensions of early Arabo-Islamic history and polity, prosopography might very well be the only viable methodology at our disposal, as Crone has argued, and as both she and Donner—both also addressing the religious dimensions of the emerging polity—have successfully undertaken for early Islamic history. As one of Donner's latest works on the subject emphasizes, the two approaches have more in common than meets the eye at first sight. See Donner, Fred M., 'Centralized Authority and Military Autonomy in the Early Islamic Conquest', in Averil Cameron and Lawrence I. Conrad (eds.), *The Byzantine and Early Islamic Near East, III: States, Resources and Armies*, pp. 337-361, Princeton, 1995 (Donner 1995), p. 341 and n. 3; Crone 1980, especially p. 15; and Donner 1981, especially the appendices, pp. 357–438; Leder, Stefen, 'The Literary Use of the Khabar', in Averil Cameron and Lawrence I. Conrad (eds.), *The Byzantine and Early Islamic Near East, I: Problems in Literary Source Material*, pp. 277–317, Princeton, 1992 (Leder 1992), pp. 309–310.

[889]In *The Challenge to the Empires*, admittedly, two diagrams seek to reconstruct the family tree of one of the Parthian dynastic families, the Ispahbudhān family, which we shall further study. However, the commentaries provided for these family trees are so dismissive that they make these very charts superfluous. Ṭabarī 1993, pp. xxxi–xxxii.

[890]Our point of reference here is the interregnum period 628–632 and the conquest of Iran up until the 650s. Nöldeke's investigation for the interregnum remains the last serious effort in this direction. Numerous other works that have dealt with this period from a general perspective will be cited as we proceed.

of Iranian history,[891] but also important aspects of the sociopolitical history of the northern and eastern quarters of Iran during the first two post-conquest centuries.[892]

In assessing the reliability of the information provided by our sources about the events in Iran, however, an examination of the material at our disposal obliges us to unequivocally side with Noth's assertion that the topic of Iran was one of the primary themes of early Arabic historical tradition. Noth argues justifiably that the information on Iran has been for the most part "connected with the theme of *futūḥ* in such a manner as to explain Muslim successes through Sasanian precedents, while at the same time identifying *the futūḥ of Islam as the cause of certain developments in Iranian history.*"[893] The *futūḥ* narratives, primarily those of Ṭabarī, are based substantially on the traditions of Sayf b. ʿUmar.[894] All of the *futūḥ* accounts of this period of Iranian history contain a serious

[891]The wealth of literature that has addressed this specific issue thus far has fallen short of arriving at a satisfactory answer. The contention that the Arab conquests can be explained in terms of the "fortuitous weakness of the Byzantines and Sasanians just when the Muslims began their expansion … [raise the question of] whether the mighty empires were not weaker in the eyes of the scholars baffled by the astounding success of the conquests than they were in actual fact," gives very little credit to what has been termed one of the greatest wars of late antiquity, that between the Byzantines and the Sasanians from 603–628 or the internal dynamics of either of these two empires during the previous centuries. Donner 1981, pp. 8–9. Kaegi 1992, *passim*.

[892]We will provide in this study only a detailed political investigation of these two centuries for the Ṭabaristān region; see Chapter 4.

[893]Noth 1994, p. 39. Emphasis mine.

[894]We know next to nothing of the life of Sayf b. ʿUmar, the compiler of early Islamic history, "except that he lived in Kufa …, probably belonged to the Usayyid clan," of the Tamīm tribe, and possibly died during the reign of Hārūn al-Rashīd (170–193 AH/786–809 CE). We also know that medieval *ḥadīth* specialists denigrated him, considered his material as untrustworthy, and accused him of being a *zandīk* (see §5.2.5). Sayf in fact did not belong to their circle. Indeed most of the authorities to whom Sayf credits the source of his information are unknown figures of early Islamic history. Yet, as Blankenship argues, Sayf's traditions "made an enormous impact on the Islamic historical tradition, especially because Ṭabarī chose to rely mainly on them for the events of 11 [*sic*]-36 (632 [*sic*]-56), a period that spanned the reigns of the first three caliphs and included all the conquests of Iraq, Syria, Egypt and Iran … The overwhelming bulk of [Ṭabarī's] material for this period is from Sayf." In spite of his importance, and solitary efforts to the contrary notwithstanding, however, Sayf's material remains one of the most maligned corpora of early Arabic histories. Blankenship, summing up the consensus of the medieval and modern *muḥaddithūn*, proclaims in his introduction to the volume on the conquest of Iraq and Syria, for example, that Sayf's materials "belong more to the realm of historical romance than to that of history." One internet blogger even maintained recently that if Sayf were to be resurrected, he would kill him! See Blankenship's preface to Ṭabarī 1993, pp. xiii–xxx. Important exceptions to the negative scholarly assessments of Sayf include Landua-Tasseron, Ella, 'Sayf b. ʿUmar in Medieval and Modern Scholarship', *Der Islam* 67, (1990), pp. 1–26 (Landua-Tasseron 1990); Donner 1981, pp. 143–144, p. 303, n. 36, p. 306, n. 94, p. 317, n. 212, p. 319, n. 247, p. 333, n. 118, and p. 338, n. 179; Crone 1980, pp. 9–10, and p. 206, n. 51. Also see Donner, Fred M., 'Sayf b. ʿUmar', in P. Bearman, Th. Bianquis, C.E. Bosworth, E. van Donzel, and W.P. Heinrichs (eds.), *Encyclopaedia of Islam*, Leiden, 2007b (Donner 2007b) and Robinson, Chase, 'The Conquest of Khuzistān: a Historiographical Reassessment', *Bulletin of the School of Oriental and African Studies* 68, (2004), pp. 14–39 (Robinson 2004), p. 38. As Donner maintains, "a definitive study of the historiographical complexities of all Sayf's traditions remains an important desideratum." The assessment of the present author of Sayf's material will become amply clear at the conclusion of this chapter.

problematic, however: their chronology. While Sayf, and the sources that follow him, provide significant information about this period of Iranian history, 628–632 CE, they give these while detailing the initial conquest of Iraq, dated to the years 12–13 AH/633–634 CE, under the presumed command of Khālid b. Walīd and Muthannā b. Ḥāritha. While current scholarship acknowledges the problematic nature of this chronology and, while all admit that the course and details of this initial stage of the conquest of Iran are hard to reconstruct, the basic chronology of this phase of the Arab conquest of Mesopotamia has been accepted as 12–13 AH/633–634 CE.[895] The present study will offer a revised chronology for this crucial juncture of Middle Eastern history, the early Arab conquest of Iraq.[896] While doing so, we shall not provide an exhaustive and critical survey of these conquests.[897] In fact, we shall neither be dealing with a detailed itinerary of the conquests, nor the topography or sociopolitical context of the Mesopotamian society on the eve of the Arab conquest. Neither will we be concerned with the logistic of wars on either side. These have been addressed admirably by other scholars.[898] As we shall see, however, if the postulates that we are offering are valid, they will have important implications for a number of crucial issues in those debates that address early Islamic history, especially those that concern chronology, but also those that address the causes of the conquests.[899] With these debates, we shall not engage in the course of the pages that will follow, for all deserve independent studies on their own. Having provided this disclaimer, a number of general observations must, nevertheless, frame our subsequent analysis.

3.1.2 Revisiting Sayf's dating

Three primary themes have been confounded in the histories of the early conquest of Iraq: the overriding themes of 1) the *ridda* (or wars of apostasy),[900] 2) the *futūḥ*,[901] and 3) Iran.[902] Sayf seems to have been the first to have combined these three themes. What complicates matters, however, is that secondary themes have been superimposed on these primary themes. The conquest narratives are arranged, especially in the works of Ṭabarī and other classical authors,

[895]Donner 1981, p. 173; Morony, Michael G., 'Arab: II. Arab Conquest of Iran', in Ehsan Yarshater (ed.), *Encyclopaedia Iranica*, pp. 203–210, New York, 1991 (Morony 1991), pp. 203–210.

[896]See §3.3.2.

[897]Nonetheless, for a tentative timeline, see Tables 6.1 and 6.2 on pages 468–469.

[898]See most importantly Donner 1981, pp. 157–217, especially pp. 157–173; Morony, Michael G., *Iraq After the Muslim Conquest*, Princeton University Press, 1984 (Morony 1984), especially pp. 169–431.

[899]For a succinct overview of the state of the field, see Donner 1981, pp. 3–9. For a brief discussion of these ramifications, see §3.5.

[900]According to Islamic tradition, shortly after the Prophet's death, presumably in 11/632, a number of nomadic and sedentary tribes left the fold of the recently established *umma* and apostatized. The term *ridda* refers to the series of battles undertaken in order to bring these back. For an alternative perspective, see our discussion on page 284.

[901]Noth 1994, p. 29.

[902]Noth 1994, pp. 28–33 and 39.

which, in turn, are based predominantly on the traditions of Sayf and analogous sources, in *both* an annalistic fashion as well as according to the rule of particular caliphs, in this case Abū Bakr and ʿUmar.[903] Now, as Noth notes, the "original arrangement of the great majority of traditions collected" in the works of such authors as Ṭabarī, could not have been the annalistic structure we currently possess. "The formula *and in this year (wa fī hādhihi l-sanna / wa fīhā)* does not belong to the [originally transmitted] text."[904] Collections of material arranged according to the rule of caliphs, also typical of the work of Ṭabarī and others, moreover, appeared even later than the annalistic style in Islamic historiography,[905] long after the conquest narratives were first formulated. These annalistic and caliphal arrangements, as Noth observes, were secondary themes in this literature.[906]

Hijra calendar

The problem of reconciling Sayf's account of Iran for this period with his accounts of the early conquest of Iraq is further confounded by the fact that the annalistic style adopted in these reports is based on the *hijra* calendar.[907] Now, as we know, a uniform chronology that was established with reference to the migration (*hijra*) of Prophet Muḥammad from Mecca to Medina (conventionally dated to 622 CE) "was first introduced under ʿUmar in 16 AH/637 CE (the years 17 and 18 are also named)."[908] As Noth observes, even several decades after ʿUmar introduced this dating the "confusion that prevailed ... and the arbitrary manner in which *hijra* dates were imposed in later times, is clear ... [S]harp and irresolvable contradiction[s] ... prevail ... on not only dating, but even the order, of even the most central events in this history of the expansion of Islam."[909] This of course is a perfectly understandable situation given the limitations affecting the dissemination of information in the post-conquest

[903] Noth perceptively maintained that both of these themes, the annalistic style and the caliphal arrangement, were secondary themes of the early Arabic historical tradition. Secondary themes, according to Noth, were all those themes that can be considered as offshoots of primary themes. These themes "are of no fundamental use in reconstructing what actually happened, however plausible and logical they may appear." Noth 1994, pp. 39–48. As we shall see shortly, another important secondary theme is the *hijra* calendar.

[904] Noth 1994, p. 43.

[905] Noth 1994, p. 45.

[906] Noth 1994, pp. 42–48.

[907] As the *hijra* calendar is a lunar calendar without intercalary months, it is about 11 days shorter than a solar year as used in the Sasanian and Gregorian calendars. Since therefore 100 *hijra* years correspond roughly to 97 solar years, and since 1 AH corresponds to 622 CE, an approximate conversion between the two calendars is given by the formula $CE = 621 + .97 * AH$ (this formula is only correct for the first few centuries AH, and even then only of course when ignoring the particular month of the year).

[908] Noth 1994, p. 40 and n. 2. For the chronological uncertainties affecting crucial events in early Islamic history, also see Cook, Michael and Crone, Patricia, *Hagarism: The Making of the Islamic World*, Cambridge University Press, 1977 (Cook and Crone 1977), pp. 4, 24, 157, n. 39; and Crone 1980, pp. 15, 212 and nn. 92, 93, 95 and 96.

[909] Noth 1994, p. 41 and n. 7, and the references cited therein.

centuries and given that "the Arabs in earliest Islamic times were for the most part unfamiliar with any formal chronological system."[910] How then is Sayf's report on the early conquest of Iraq arranged? And what kind of relationship does this arrangement have with his account on the conditions prevailing in Iran *in the period between 628–632* CE?

In Sayf's narratives, the early conquests of Iranian territories in Iraq are arranged according to both *hijra* dates and reigns of particular Sasanian kings or queens. Sayf's account puts these during the caliphates of Abū Bakr (632–634) and ʿUmar (634–644), specifically during the years 12–13 AH/633–634 CE, that is, *after the death of the Prophet in 632* CE. As Blankenship observes, Ṭabarī devotes a major section of his work to only these two years of the conquest of the Fertile Crescent.[911] What is more, the space devoted to the conquest of Iraq in this section of Ṭabarī is double that devoted to the conquest of Syria.[912]

While major debates have surrounded crucial aspects of these conquests,[913] and while substantive issues have been raised, thus far the investigations of this initial phase of the conquest of Iraq have adopted this *hijra* dating wholesale. Following Ṭabarī's arrangement, this is how the translated volume of this section of Ṭabarī is organized, for example. For the most part, the chronology of the accounts of these conquests—which include the battle of Madhār,[914] the battle of Walajah,[915] the battle of ʿAyn Tamr,[916] the battle of Firāḍ,[917] the battle of Namāriq,[918] and finally the battle of Bridge[919] (the former four dated by Sayf to 12 AH/633 CE, and the latter two to 13 AH/634 CE)—as told by Ṭabarī, through Sayf and other sources, have been followed in most of the secondary literature, their major flaws being noted intermittently.[920]

The *hijra* chronology provided in the accounts of the *futūḥ*, however, occur side-by-side with a different set of chronological indicators, those of the rules of

[910]Noth 1994, p. 41.

[911]This comprises the whole of the translated volume, *The Challenge to the Empires* (Ṭabarī 1993, de Goeje, 2016–2212).

[912]Ṭabarī 1993, p. xiii.

[913]In this context we have to reckon, for example, with the fact that the traditions detailing Khālid b. Walīd's participation in the conquest of Iraq might be spurious. Crone, Patricia, 'Khālid b. Walīd', in Ehsan Yarshater (ed.), *Encyclopaedia Iranica*, p. 928a, New York, 1991a (Crone 1991a); Ṭabarī 1993, p. 1., n. 2.

[914]Both Morony and Donner have argued for example that this battle seems to have taken place later. Based on this, Blankenship maintains that Madhār was "actually … conquered by ʿUtbah b. Ghazwān later, so that *Sayf's report here is chronologically improbable*." Morony 1984, pp. 127 and 160; Donner 1981, p. 329, n. 66; Ṭabarī 1993, p. 15, n. 97. See also page 193ff below.

[915]See page 195ff.

[916]See page 201ff.

[917]See page 201ff.

[918]See page 211ff.

[919]See §3.3.5.

[920]Zarrinkub, Abd al-Husayn, 'Arab Conquest of Iran and its Aftermath', in Ehsan Yarshater (ed.), *Cambridge History of Iran: The Seleucid, Parthian, and Sasanian Periods*, vol. 4, pp. 1–57, Cambridge University Press, 1975 (Zarrinkub 1975), pp. 1–57; Morony 1991, pp. 203–210; Donner 1981, pp. 157–217, especially p. 173.

various Sasanian kings and queens given in the course of recounting these same conquest narratives. The acute problem confronting us a result of this juxtaposition is that the two sets of chronologies *do not* correspond to each other.[921] Almost every war that Sayf attributes to the years 12 to 13 AH (633–634 CE), is *systematically attached to the particular reign of a Sasanian king or queen*, Shīrūyih Qubād (628), Ardashīr III (628–630), Shahrvarāz (630), Būrāndukht (630–632),[922] Azarmīdukht (630–631), and Farrukh Hormozd (631), ending with the inception of the rule of Yazdgird III in 632, corresponding, therefore, to the years 8–11 *hijra*.[923] That is, based on this alternative chronology, the striking fact is that these wars fall, *not* as it has been conventionally believed, following the *hijra* calendar, in the years 633–634 CE, but between 628 and 632 CE, when the Sasanian monarchy was engulfed in a factional strife spearheaded by its nobility. As we shall see, there is such a cogent *internal logic* between the conquest accounts of particular important battles and the events that transpired under the rule of specific Sasanian kings or queens associated with each of them, that these two traditions could never have been haphazardly juxtaposed next to each other by the original narrators of these events or the subsequent collectors of the traditions. Unlike the characteristic *static* dimensions of individual *khabars* (reports),[924] furthermore, Sayf's narrative provides us with temporal, and at times, spatial movement.

Following this alternative, Sasanian-based chronology, then, these wars or raids would have taken place almost *immediately* after the Byzantine–Sasanian warfare, and during the period when the two empires were in the process of negotiating their peace treaty and attempting to implement the terms of it. This, for example,[925] might explain the cooperation of the Byzantines and the Persians in the war that Sayf reports as Firāḍ—attached by him to the year 12 AH (633 CE)—when the Byzantines as well as the Persians became "hot and angry … and sought reinforcements from the Taghlib, Iyād and Namir," and encouraged each other to keep "[their] sovereignty in [their] own hands."[926] If we follow the Sasanian chronological indicators, therefore, this war took place *not* as reported by Sayf and traditionally accepted in 12 AH/633 CE,[927] but after Ardashīr III's deposition and around the time when the Byzantines were inciting Shahrvarāz to assume power, that is around 9 AH/630 CE, a period in which

[921] While Greek, Syriac, Armenian, and Coptic sources have been used, unsuccessfully, in order to comparatively resolve these chronological inconsistencies, no examination of the Sasanian chronological indicators have thus far been undertaken. Noth 1994, p. 42.

[922] For our revised chronology for this queen, see §3.3.4 below.

[923] To avoid confusion, we will provide henceforth only a *hijra* date when it is pertinent to our discussion.

[924] See footnote 934.

[925] The following examples are only given as illustration, and will be discussed in more detail in their appropriate context below.

[926] Ṭabarī 1993, p. 67, de Goeje, 2074.

[927] Ṭabarī 1993, p. 47, de Goeje, 2056.

Byzantine–Sasanian cooperation in fact would make perfect sense.[928]

Similarly, Ḥamza Iṣfahānī maintains, for example, that "the arrival of Khālid b. Walīd in Ḥīra coincided with the regency of Būrāndukht and *12 years* after the *hijra* ... for Būrāndukht's regency took place toward the end of the caliphate of Abū Bakr ... [She ruled] three months in the period of Abū Bakr and four months in the period of ʿUmar."[929] Now, the chronological indicator of Būrāndukht's regency would put the arrival of Khālid b. Walīd sometime in the years 629–631 CE, or possibly in 632 CE,[930] during which period the cooperation of the Byzantines, the Arabs and the Iranians would still make sense. The chronological indicator equating the regency of Būrāndukht with *12 years after the hijra ... toward the end of the caliphate of Abū Bakr [in 634* CE*]*, however, would throw the whole thing off, for clearly it was not Būrāndukht who ruled in 634 CE, but Yazdgird III. How then can we possibly circumvent this and attempt to reconcile the two accounts, when faced with such blatant chronological confusion?

An objective methodology warrants that the Sasanian chronological indicators given by Sayf be taken *more* seriously than his *hijra* dating. There are no legitimate reasons for ignoring these Sasanian chronological indicators.[931] After all, the chronology of the rule of important Sasanian kings and queens during this period—for whom we even have numismatic evidence—although still problematic, is nevertheless *comparatively* far better established than the uncertain early *hijra* calendar superimposed *post facto* onto these narratives. Here, therefore, we have an *independent* chronological scheme *against* which we can gauge our *hijra* dating. There should be no reason, therefore, to dismiss Sayf's often maintained, alternative chronological indicators which place these wars in the period between 628–632 CE. The inertia in tackling this question of chronology has been conditioned by an uncritical acceptance of what the *futūḥ* narratives promote as the ideological locomotive of these wars, namely, that these wars were driven by the presumed policies of the first two Muslim caliphs *after the death of the Prophet*.

The methodology we propose for tackling the chronological confusion that permeates the *futūḥ* narratives comprises a threefold scheme. First, in §3.2 and

---

[928] See §3.2.3. Sayf's contention that the Byzantines, Persians, and Arab tribes cooperated together in this war, and were defeated by Khālid b. Walīd, has therefore led Fück to argue that this is a dubious piece of information. Fück, J.W., 'Iyād', in P. Bearman, Th. Bianquis, C.E. Bosworth, E. van Donzel, and W.P. Heinrichs (eds.), *Encyclopaedia of Islam*, Leiden, 2007 (Fück 2007) apud Ṭabarī 1993, p. 67, n. 383. According to our proposed revised chronology, however, Fück's argument becomes moot, as we shall see.

[929] Ḥamza Iṣfahānī, *Taʾrīkh Sinnī Mulūk al-Arḍ wa ʾl-Anbiyāʾ*, Beirut, 1961, edited by Yusuf Ya'qub Maskuni (Ḥamza Iṣfahānī 1961), p. 97, Ḥamza Iṣfahānī, *Taʾrīkh Sinnī Mulūk al-Arḍ wa ʾl-Anbiyāʾ*, Tehran, 1988, translation of Ḥamza Iṣfahānī 1961 by Jaʿfar Shiʿar (Ḥamza Iṣfahānī 1988), p. 115.

[930] For Būrāndukht's double regency, see §3.3, especially page 203ff, and §3.3.4, especially 210ff; for her dates based on a reassessment of the new and old numismatic evidence, see page 208ff.

[931] At the very least, one ought to satisfactorily answer why some of these wars are so systematically and seemingly anachronistically attached to the rule of ephemeral Sasanian kings and queens of this period.

the first part of §3.3, we will collect the information on the conditions prevailing in Iran during the reign of the Sasanian kings and queens who ruled from the deposition of Khusrow II in 628 to the accession of Yazdgird III in 632 CE, from sources that have their purview *outside* the provenance of the early Arabic historical tradition and the *futūḥ* narratives.[932] Then, starting in §3.3.2, we shall turn to Sayf's account of the conquest. Here, we shall temporarily ignore the *hijra* dates provided by Sayf and other *futūḥ* literature on the early conquest of Iraq and Iran, as well as any information pertaining to Arab generals, and concentrate instead on the data given for the conditions prevailing in Iran in these same accounts. Here, in other words, we shall proceed from the assumption that the information provided by the *futūḥ* literature on Iran on this juncture of Sasanian history ought to be collected and examined as if it originated from a separate, independent corpus.[933]

Finally, we shall investigate how the information provided by Sayf *in the course of his narrative on the early conquest of Iraq* correlates with the Sasanian data of the same period that we had initially collected, in order to determine the *internal* logic of the information provided by Sayf. Based on this methodology, we shall conclude that, because Sayf's information about internal Sasanian affairs in the context of his account of the early conquest of Iraq proves to be solid, these two sets of data, so *systematically connected to each other*, must, therefore, be interrelated. So much so that at some crucial junctures one set of events in fact explains the other. In the historical memory of the participants and early narrators of these events, these early conquests were so forcefully related to the conditions prevailing in Iran and to the reigns of specific Sasanian kings and queens of this period, that they *inevitably* maintained these connections.[934] We shall conclude, therefore, that the events which Sayf systematically attaches to the rule of a particular Sasanian monarch did in fact transpire in that period and *not at the hijra dates proposed by him*.

Xʷadāy-Nāmag tradition

In assessing the reliability of the information provided *on Iran* by Sayf for these crucial four years, 628–632, we are fortunate in that we are not simply confined to the accounts of the conquest. Besides these we can resort to Persian and Arabic sources that have their provenance in the *Xʷadāy-Nāmag*tradition,[935] foreign sources such as Sebeos—which probably are themselves based on Persian sources—and numismatic and sigillographic evidence. The fount of all of these sources, needless to say, is completely outside that of the *futūḥ* literature. A separate section of Ṭabarī details the accounts of the Sasanian dynasty including

[932] We will discuss the nature of these sources shortly.

[933] Albeit this will only be a working hypothesis, for as we shall see, we do not believe this to be the case.

[934] We are well aware that the information contained in the *futūḥ* narratives was originally collected as individual short *khabars* on the conquest of particular districts, cities, or regions. Noth 1994, p. 32. Also see Leder 1992.

[935] See also our discussion on page 13.

those monarchs ruling during the period of our concern. As has been established during the past century, this section of Ṭabarī as well as all most other sources dealing with this period of Iranian history, were most probably based on the various renditions of the *X^w adāy-Nāmag* tradition, and hence *completely independent from the futūḥ literature*.[936] The *X^w adāy-Nāmag* tradition has its own problems, especially during these tumultuous years. Nevertheless, as we hope to show, the greater scheme of the events transpiring in Iran can be reconstructed with reference to these sources. The material provided by Sayf not only corroborates these outside sources, but also adds significantly to the information contained in them. What we shall be attempting to do, in other words, is to ignore the artificial rupture that is contained within our sources, where the *futūḥ* literature is thought to have begun when the *X^w adāy-Nāmag* tradition is reaching its end with the inception of Yazdgird III's rule. The net effect of this rupture in our sources has created a situation in which it has been difficult to understand the progression of the conquests in the context of the events that are transpiring in Iran itself during this period. Specifically, it has been hard to examine the successes and the failures of the Sasanian army against the Arabs during this period in the context of the *alliances* and *rivalries* unfolding within Iran.[937]

Once we have disentangled and streamlined the confusing narratives of the last quarter of a century of Sasanian history beginning with the murder of Khusrow II Parvīz in 628, a major theme emerges. Although the bewildering array of personalities and groups do not seem to lend themselves at first to any logical or systematic understanding, they actually partake in a quite comprehensible dynamic that bespeaks the course of Sasanian history: the struggle of the Pārsīg against the Pahlav. As we shall see, the Sasanian–Parthian confederacy finally exhausted itself in the last decades of Sasanian history. In this final period of Sasanian history, a regional dynamic superimposed itself on all other contextual historical givens. The quarters of the north and the east, where the regional power of all the dynastic Parthian families thus far examined was concentrated,

[936] Most of the narratives contained in this part of Ṭabarī's opus do not contain a *sanad*, and the three or so that do are attributed to ʾIkramah, Ibn Isḥāq, or Hishām b. Muḥammad. See respectively, Ṭabarī 1999, pp. 324–327, de Goeje, 1005–1007; Ṭabarī 1999, p. 335, de Goeje, 1013; and Ṭabarī 1999, p. 379, de Goeje, 1044.

[937] Walter Kaegi reflects on a similar problem when dealing with the Arab conquests of Byzantine territories. Investigating the chronological or regional structures of the Arabic sources on the conquest of Byzantine territories, Kaegi observes that these "structures of organization have their value and of course without specific chronological references the task of the historian would be even more formidable." He notes, however, that what "has been lost in all these narratives, irrespective of the reliability of the traditions that they report, *is any understanding of the interrelationship and potential coherence of those events*." Kaegi further argues justifiably that "there is always the danger that coherence can be overemphasized ... But the disconnected and fragmentary historical approach has tended, unconsciously, *to obscure the inter-connections between the warfare and diplomacy in Syria and that of Egypt and Byzantine Mesopotamia*." Kaegi 1992, p. 13. The nature of the predicament of the Iranist investigating this juncture of Sasanian history is, therefore, quite analogous to that of the Byzantinist.

ultimately ceded from those of the south and the west with the end result that the house of Sāsān, which so successfully had managed to link these regions together through the course of four centuries, was finally destroyed. There was order within the chaos of latter day Sasanian history. And while we do not claim to be able to explain this process in all of its sociopolitical complexities, and while we are cognizant of other crucial factors that affected this period of Sasanian history—of which the Sasanian wars against the Byzantines during Khusrow II's reign surely take the lion's share of the responsibility for explaining the economic and political exhaustion of the empire—it is the contours of the Sasanian–Parthian confederacy and its final collapse, that we shall attempt to elucidate. What then were the conditions prevailing in Iran at the outset of Khusrow II's murder that moved the Parthian dynastic families to the final dissolution of their confederacy with the Sasanian polity?

3.2 Shīrūyih Qubād and Ardashīr III: the three armies

As explained previously, we shall begin our reconstruction of the interregnum period 628–632 using sources outside the *futūḥ* literature. The reader should anticipate that as a result of the particular methodology adopted, layers of information will become available on a piece-meal basis, the complete picture emerging only at the end of this chapter.

3.2.1 Shīrūyih Qubād

We recall that the deposition of Khusrow II and the appointment of his son Shīrūyih Qubād (628) to power was brought about by the collective conspiracy of a number of very powerful dynastic factions. It is important to recall that except for the Nīmrūzī faction led by Mihr Hormozd, who, probably belonging to a branch of the Sūren family,[938] had adopted the title of Pārsīg,[939] most other factions involved in overthrowing Khusrow II hailed from Parthian families: the Ispahbudhān, represented by the powerful scions of the dynasty, Farrukh Hormozd, Farrukhzād and Rustam; a branch of the Mihrāns, under the leadership of Khusrow II's *ērān-spāhbed* of the *kūst-i nēmrōz*, Shahrvarāz; the Armenian faction, represented by the son of Smbat Bagratuni, Varaztirots' (Javitean Khosrov);[940] and finally the Kanārangīyān.[941] The Iranian forces had at this point also broken up, we recollect, in three distinct armies: the army of Azarbāyjān under the leadership of Farrukh Hormozd; the occupation army of Shahrvarāz; and the army of Nīmrūz, what Sebeos calls the army of Persia and the East, under the leadership of Mihr Hormozd.

Before we proceed with the story of the Sasanians during this turbulent period, a word of caution is in order. In line with their monarchical bias, the

---

[938] See footnote 850.

[939] See footnotes 308 and 838.

[940] Sebeos 1999, p. 53. For Smbat Bagratuni, see §2.7.2.

[941] For the Kanārangīyān family's agnatic background, see page 266ff.

sources at our disposal attribute substantial powers to the short-lived monarchs who ruled Iran from the deposition of Khusrow II onward. As the pendulum of Sasanian history had now swung in favor of the dynastic families, however, this was rarely the case, and certainly not for Khusrow II's successor, Shīrūyih Qubād. Sebeos and some of the accounts based on the *X^w adāy-Nāmag* tradition make it appear as though Shīrūyih Qubād held a great deal of power. The peace treaty with Heraclius and the termination of the hostilities with Byzantium are both attributed to his actions.[942] The appointment of Varaztirots', the son of Smbat Bagratuni, as the *tanutēr* of Iranian-controlled Armenia, where he enlisted the support of some of the other Armenian factions, is also attributed to Shīrūyih Qubād.[943] Some Arabic sources based on the *X^w adāy-Nāmag* tradition even depict Shīrūyih Qubād as a despot and, tangentially, as a womanizer.[944] In order to drive home the latter aspect of the king's personality, Ferdowsī includes an account of how Shīrūyih Qubād attempted to woo Shīrīn, the favorite wife of his father, Khusrow II Parvīz, into marrying him.[945]

Shīrūyih Qubād might very well have been a womanizer. It is doubtful, however, that a king who was brought to power by the collective conspiracy of the dynastic families, had any substantial power at his disposal. The peace treaty with Heraclius was, as we have seen, instigated by Shahrvarāz and the Prince of the Medes, Farrukh Hormozd.[946] Shīrūyih Qubād, in fact, was born to Khusrow II through Maryam, the Byzantine emperor's daughter.[947] It might very well have been the case, therefore, that in their selection of Shīrūyih Qubād as king, the factions also considered the young king's Byzantine connection. The support of the Armenian Varaztirots', moreover, was also most certainly made with the understanding that Varaztirots' would continue to function as the *tanutēr* of Armenia under the new king. Shīrūyih Qubād's acquiescence to this expectation was most probably already written into his promotion to the throne.

Shīrūyih Qubād's minister Fīrūzān

Ferdowsī, in fact, graphically portrays the powerlessness of the youthful Shīrūyih Qubād in the hands of the nobility. He depicts him as being frightened and inexperienced (*tarsandih o khām*). When the dynastic factions had pressured Shīrūyih Qubād into killing his father, Khusrow II, the king was acting "like a

[942] Sebeos 1999, pp. 84–85.

[943] According to Sebeos the "king Kawat [i.e., Shīrūyih Qubād] summoned Varaztirots', son of Smbat Bagratuni, called Khosrov Shum, and gave him the office of *tanutēr*. He made him *marzpan* [*marzbān*], and sent him to Armenia with [authority over] all his ancestral possessions in order to keep in prosperity." Sebeos 1999, pp. 86–87. Sebeos in fact equates the office of *tanutēr* with the title Khosrov-Shum (Khusrow Shenūm). Ibid., p. 49.

[944] Thaʿālibī 1900, p. 728, Thaʿālibī 1989, p. 463.

[945] This queen Shīrīn, probably of Armenian descent, is also the main character in the medieval romance of *Shīrīn and Farhād*, where this time her suitor, *Farhād*, was an architect at Khusrow II Parvīz's court. Nīzāmī, Ganjavī, *Khusrow o Shīrīn*, London, 1844, edited N. Bland (Nīzāmī 1844).

[946] See page 149ff.

[947] Ferdowsī 1971, vol. IX, pp. 197–198, Ferdowsī 1935, p. 2857.

slave in their pawns," fearful of disobeying their collective order.[948] Whereas, as we have seen, one set of traditions, including Ferdowsī's, depicts the Pahlav dynast Zād Farrukh (Farrukhzād) as the primary instigator of both Khusrow II's deposition and Shīrūyih Qubād's promotion, and hence as the one in control of the young king,[949] other sources emphasize the role of a Fayrūz, Fīrūzān, or Pīrūz, as he is variously called. Shīrūyih Qubād's murder of seventeen of his brothers, for example, is said to have been instigated by this same Fīrūzān, called the minister of Shīrūyih Qubād by Ṭabarī.[950] The *Nihāyat* also belongs to the set of traditions which maintain that Fīrūz ran state affairs under Shīrūyih Qubād.[951] In the *Shāhnāma*, he is called Pīrūz Khusrow, and is depicted as the commander of the army.[952] The identity of this Fīrūzān is crucial for understanding the subsequent events. For now it is sufficient to note that this Fīrūzān, belonging to the same camp as the Nīmrūzīs, as we shall see, ultimately assumed leadership of the Pārsīg.[953] The factions responsible for bringing down Khusrow II Parvīz, therefore, continued to take charge of affairs during the rule of Shīrūyih Qubād.

---

948 Ferdowsī 1971, vol. IX, p. 280, Ferdowsī 1935, p. 2933:

بترسید شیرویه و ترسنده بود   که در چنگ ایشان یکی بنده بود

949 See §2.7.6.

950 Nöldeke 1879, pp. 381–382, Nöldeke 1979, p. 542. This Fīrūzān collaborated with a certain Shamṭā, one of the sons of Yazdīn, "the official in charge of [the collection of the] land tax ... from the entire lands." Ṭabarī 1999, p. 398, de Goeje, 1061. Bosworth notes that Nöldeke had identified Yazdīn from the Syriac sources as Khusrow II's treasurer Yazdīn. Thomas of Margā-described Shamṭā as the "real driving force behind the conspiracy to dethrone the Khusrow II." As we have seen thus far, however, the conspiracy that led to the overthrow of Khusrow II Parvīz involved far too many factions and was far too long in the making to have been instigated by a single individual. Nevertheless a question posed by Bosworth is worth pursuing, namely whether this Yazdīn is the same figure mentioned by Sebeos as the governor of Armenia under Khusrow II Parvīz. Considering the Armenian faction's direct involvement in the overthrow of Khusrow II, this is by no means unlikely. Ṭabarī 1999, p. 398, n. 980, de Goeje, 1061.

951 He is referred to as Barmak b. Fīrūz in the *Nihāyat*. Nihayat 1996, p. 438:

و جعل رئیس مرازبته و وزرائه برمك بن فیروز، و هو الذی کان جد البرامکة، و فوض الیه جمیع اموره.

In Bal'amī's account, Shīrūyih Qubād's minister is called Fīrūz (Fīrūzān) and considered the ancestor of the Barmakids. This tradition is most probably spurious for the ancestors of the Barmakids were likely either Zoroastrian high priests, or Buddhist chiefs of the *Nowbahār* temple in Balkh. The tradition, however, even if forged, and especially if forged, is nevertheless extremely significant, for it testifies to the continued currents of consciousness of Pārsīg identity through the eighth century and thereafter. The Barmakids also held the governorship of Fārs, and it might have been in this region that this ancestral pedigree was attached to them. Bal'amī 1959, p. 253. For the Barmakids, see Abbas, I., 'Barmakids', in Ehsan Yarshater (ed.), *Encyclopaedia Iranica*, pp. 806–809, New York, 1991 (Abbas 1991).

952 According to Ferdowsī, Būrāndukht killed a Pīrūz Khusrow, which therefore this time cannot be Fīrūzān, as he only died around 642 at the battle of Nihāvand (see page 241ff). Ferdowsī 1971, pp. 305–306.

953 For more details on Fīrūzān, see page 196 below.

The Byzantine-Sasanian peace treaty

Shīrūyih Qubād's powerlessness is also apparent in the decision-making process that led to the Byzantine-Sasanian peace treaty, bringing thirty years of warfare to an end.[954] As we have seen and shall further elaborate upon, our evidence suggests that the peace treaty between the Persians and the Byzantines was concluded not only as the result of an understanding reached by Shahrvarāz and Heraclius, but also with the cooperation of Farrukh Hormozd and his sons Rustam and Farrukhzād, who, at this juncture of Sasanian history, probably represented all the factions, including the Nīmrūzī faction.[955] As in later periods,[956] all the contextual evidence at our disposal highlights the fact that the Prince of the Medes was involved in the negotiations that resulted in the peace proposals of 629. We should recall that during the third phase of the Byzantine-Sasanian war,[957] Heraclius' army had overrun the territories of the Prince of the Medes (Farrukh Hormozd) in 624. When in 8 April 628, the Sasanian king Shīrūyih Qubād is said to have dispatched a letter proposing peace to the Byzantine emperor Heraclius, the latter *was encamped in Gandzak*, the territory of the Prince of the Medes in Azarbāyjān.[958] A peace treaty with the Byzantines now in partial control of his territories suited therefore the purposes of Farrukh Hormozd admirably.

It took a while, however, to effect Shahrvarāz's agreement to the peace treaty. For as Sebeos informs us, when Shahrvarāz was "ordered [ostensibly by Shīrūyih Qubād to] collect his troops, come back to Persia, and abandon Greek territory ... [the latter] *did not wish to obey that order*."[959] According to Kaegi, it was in all probability only after Heraclius met with Shahrvarāz in July 629, that the latter agreed to withdraw his forces.[960] Shahrvarāz's initial

[954]Sebeos' account hints as much. For, prior to making peace, the king took "council with the nobles of his kingdom." Sebeos 1999, p. 85.

[955]Sebeos 1999, p. 107. Howard-Johnston takes Sebeos' account at face value. Ibid., pp. 222-223.

[956]The intimate relations between the Prince of the Medes and the Byzantines is, in fact, specifically highlighted for later periods. In describing the coalition that was being formed in 642-643 between the Byzantines, the Armenians, and the Ispahbudhān, Sebeos informs us that in his capacity as the successor to his father the Prince of the Medes (Farrukh Hormozd), Farrukhzād had already made a pact with the Byzantine emperor Constans II (Constantine, 641-668), the grandson of Heraclius, who had become the new emperor of Byzantium. The newly appointed governor of Armenia, Tu'mas "did not wish to break the pact between the emperor and the [son of the] Prince of the Medes. He brought all the princes [of Armenia] into agreement with himself, went to the [son of the] Prince of the Medes and made peace proposals to him. He received from him many gifts, and promised him with an oath that he would have T'ēodoros brought in bonds to the palace, because he was the prince of Armenia." Sebeos 1999, p. 107. We should add here that the epithet *Prince of the Medes* is applied by Sebeos also to other members of the family, as it is here to Farrukhzād (Khoṙokhzat).

[957]See page 149ff.

[958]Sebeos 1999, p. 222.

[959]Sebeos 1999, p. 86.

[960]The True Cross, the relic believed to be the cross upon which Jesus was crucified, was taken as a trophy to Khusrow II in 614. Its return to Jerusalem on 21 March 630, after the peace agreement with Shahrvarāz, therefore, only took place toward the end of the reign of Ardashīr III. Kaegi 1992,

refusal to abide by this peace treaty indicates that, while his army was still in the western war-ridden territories, the affairs of the kingdom were conducted not only by Fīrūzān and the army of Nīmrūz, but also by the Ispahbudhān Farrukh Hormozd and the army of Azarbāyjān. Being absent from the center, it was this collaboration that must have been worrisome to Shahrvarāz.

Heraclius, cognizant of the rivalries among the dynastic families, took full advantage of the situation, for he played the two important factions, the Mihrānid Shahrvarāz and the Ispahbudhān Farrukh Hormozd, against one another. Upon the death of Shīrūyih Qubād in 628, Heraclius wrote to Shahrvarāz, whose armies were still in control of substantial sections of Byzantine territory: Now that the Iranian king is dead, "the throne and the kingdom has come to you. I bestow it on you, and on your offspring after you. If an army is necessary,[961] I shall send to your assistance as many [troops] as you may need."[962] This gesture persuaded Shahrvarāz. For in the face of Farrukh Hormozd and the Sīstānī contingent's alliance, a collaboration between the Byzantine emperor and Shahrvarāz was a necessity. Howard–Johnston, while dismissing any prior understanding between Heraclius and Shahrvarāz in 626 as political propaganda articulated by the Byzantines,[963] maintains that that was *no longer* the case in the events that transpired at the end of Shīrūyih Qubād's reign, for by "629 ... both Heraclius and Sharvaraz had compelling reasons for reaching an accommodation."[964] What were these compelling reasons for both sides? Heraclius' predicament was clear enough. Shahrvarāz was the commander-in-chief of the actual occupation forces in control of substantial sections of the Byzantine territory.[965]

Shahrvarāz, on the other hand, was very well aware that his faction was only one of the factions side-by-side of the Ispahbudhān, the Nīmrūzī, the Armenians, and the Kanārangīyān that had participated in deposing Khusrow II Parvīz. As the two traditions discussed above bear witness, moreover, during Shīrūyih Qubād's rule, the Ispahbudhān with their army of Atrapatkan

pp. 66 and 67 respectively.

961 Heraclius probably realized that Shahrvarāz's army on its own could not reckon with the combined forces of the army of Azarbāyjān and the army of Nīmrūz.

962 Sebeos 1999, p. 88.

963 The "allegation [contained in *Chronique de Seert*, Ṭabarī and Dionysius] should probably be rejected as a piece of deliberate disinformation, circulated to further *Roman interests* as the war reached a climax in 627–628 CE." Sebeos 1999, p. 223.

964 Sebeos 1999, p. 223.

965 As the peace treaty between the Byzantine emperor and the Mihrānid dynast makes clear, these included the territories of Jerusalem, Caesaria in Palestine, all the regions of Antioch, Tarsus in Cilicia, and the greater part of Armenia. Sebeos 1999, p. 224. It is extremely noteworthy that in the stipulations of the terms of this treaty Shahrvarāz was not willing to abandon all the advantages that the Sasanian forces of Khusrow II had gained in the course of the war. According to Howard–Johnston, "*Chronique de Seert* 724 states unequivocally that the Euphrates was recognized as the frontier between them, implying thereby that Shahrvaraz had insisted on retaining some of the territory beyond the traditional post-387 frontier which he and his troops had conquered, that is, the Roman provinces of Mesopotamia and Osrhoene which lay east of the Euphrates (with their principal cities, Amida and Edessa)." Sebeos 1999, p. 224.

(Azarbāyjān) and the Nīmrūzī faction of Fīrūzān had forged an alliance under the leadership of the powerful and towering figure of the Prince of the Medes, Farrukh Hormozd. Hence, as Howard–Johnston explains, "Sharvaraz needed to strengthen his position now that *he was at odds with the government in Ctesiphon.*"[966] Shīrūyih Qubād managed to stay in power for six to seven months only. Ṭabarī does not give an account of how he met his demise.[967] In anticipation of our examination of the *futūḥ* narratives, and jumping ahead of our story for a moment, we should underline at this point that the *X^w adāy-Nāmag* tradition provides a crucial piece of information about the aftermath of Shīrūyih Qubād's death. According to Thaʿālibī, when the puppet king died, "enemies were on the march, and *from the Arab [regions] strong winds were blowing* ... Shahrvarāz also started rebelling and conquered some of the cities in Byzantium and his affairs grew strong."[968] According to Thaʿālibī, therefore, at the death of Shīrūyih Qubād in 628, when the child king Ardashīr III (628–630) was elevated to kingship, *the Arabs, too, were on the move* against the Sāsanian empire. Dīnawarī also furnishes us with a chronology that closely corresponds to Thaʿālibī's. For according to Dīnawarī, when Būrāndukht assumed power, to be discussed shortly, and the news reached the Arabs that there were no kings left to the Persians, who therefore had resorted to a woman, Muthannā b. Ḥāritha from Ḥīra and Muqarrin from Ubullah, together with their tribe Bakr b. Wāʾil, began attacking the Persian realm.[969] The promotion of Būrāndukht to regency, as we shall see further, however, actually started in 630 CE.[970]

3.2.2 Ardashīr III

The next Sasanian king, Ardashīr III (628–630), son of Shīrūyih Qubād, was only a child, by some accounts seven years of age, when he was placed upon the Sasanian throne. On his coinage he is distinctly portrayed as a child.[971] Considering his youth, it is clear that his appointment was a symbolic act meant only to ensure the presence of a Sasanian figure on the throne of the kingdom. It goes without saying that the child king's actual power during this period must have inhered in one or another of the factions. Our evidence indicates that the same factions which had brought Shīrūyih Qubād to power, especially those

[966] Sebeos 1999, p. 231. Emphasis added.

[967] Bosworth notes that according to Ibn Qutaybah and Ibn al-Athīr, the king ultimately died from a plague that had spread through the war-ridden territories of Iraq at this juncture (for which see §3.3.2 below), while Theophanes claims that the king was poisoned. Ṭabarī 1999, p. 399. n. 984.

[968] Thaʿālibī 1989, p. 465.

[969] Dīnawarī 1960, p. 111, Dīnawarī 1967, p. 121. According to Dīnawarī, throughout the caliphate of Abū Bakr (633–634), Muthannā b. Ḥāritha attacked the Sawād from various corners. Dīnawarī 1960, p. 112, Dīnawarī 1967, p. 123.

[970] See §3.3.4.

[971] Nöldeke 1879, p. 386, n. 1, Nöldeke 1979, p. 584, n. 145; Thaʿālibī 1900, p. 731:

لمّا توفّى شيرويه ملك ابنه اردشير على شكّ فى بلوغه الحلم.

For further references for his coinage, see Ṭabarī 1999, p. 401, n. 990.

of the Prince of the Medes, Farrukh Hormozd, and of the Pārsīg, promoted and—for a while at least—sustained Ardashīr III's regency.[972]

Ardashīr III's minister Māhādharjushnas

One set of narratives maintains, that the minister "in charge of the child's upbringing and carrying the administration of the kingdom" during Ardashīr III's reign was one Mih Ādhar Jushnas or Māhādharjushnas,[973] who apparently was also a cousin of Khusrow II.[974] According to Ṭabarī, Māhādharjushnas "carried on the administration of the kingdom in [such] an excellent fashion, [and with such] ... firm conduct ... [that] no one would have been aware of Ardashīr III's youthfulness."[975] Other sources such as the *Shāhnāma*, however, single out a figure called Pīrūz Khusrow. It was to Pīrūz Khusrow that the child king supposedly relegated the control of his army.[976] Thaʿālibī identifies this figure as Khusrow Fīrūz and maintains that he was in charge of all of the king's affairs.[977] There is very little doubt that Pīrūz Khusrow of Ferdowsī and Khusrow Fīrūz of Thaʿālibī are none other than Ṭabarī's Fayrūzān (Fīrūzān), Shīrūyih Qubād's minister responsible for instigating the king's fratricide.[978] The two sets of narratives, therefore, betray, yet again, two separate founts of historical provenance: a Pārsīg and a Pahlav, for we will presently see that Fīrūzān and Māhādharjushnas, respectively, each belong to one of these factions continuing to sustain Ardashīr III's kingship.

3.2.3 Shahrvarāz's insurgency

A while into Ardashīr III's reign, Shahrvarāz rebelled against the child-king under the pretext that "the great men of the state had not consulted him about

[972] Agreeing with Flusin's dating of the event, Johnston maintains that "Shahrvarāz must have exercised power initially as regent for the young Artashir, since his execution of the boy and his own ascent onto the throne took place on 27 April 630, after Artashir had reigned one year and six months." Sebeos 1999, p. 224. None of our Arabic or Persian sources contain any reference to this.

[973] Justi 1895, p. 354.

[974] According to Ṭabarī this figure "held the office of high steward of the table (*riʾāsat aṣḥāb al-māʾidah*)." Ṭabarī 1999, p. 400, de Goeje, 1061. Ibn al-Athīr calls him Māhādharjushnas (appearing in the text mistakenly as Bahādur Jusnas). Ibn al-Athīr 1862, vol. 1, p. 498. Yaʿqūbi 1969, vol. 1, p. 196, Yaʿqūbi, Aḥmad b. Abī Yaʿqūb, *Taʾrīkh*, Shirkat-i intishārāt-i ʿIlmī va Farhangī, 1983, translation of Yaʿqūbi 1969 (Yaʿqūbi 1983), pp. 213–214. The *Fārsnāma* also calls him Māhādharjushnas and gives him the title *atābak*. Ibn Balkhī 1995, p. 261. Balʿamī calls him Mihr Ḥasīs, clearly a typographical error, and maintains that he was killed by Shahrvarāz. Balʿamī 1959, p. 256.

[975] Ṭabarī 1999, p. 400, de Goeje, 1061.

[976] Ferdowsī 1971, vol. IX, p. 294:

بپروز خسرو سپردم سپاه   که از داد شادست و شادان ز شاه
به ایران چو باشد چنو پهلوان   بمانید شادان و روشن روان

[977] Thaʿālibī 1989, p. 464, Thaʿālibī 1900, p. 732:

خسرو فیروز المتولی لامور اردشیر

[978] See page 174.

raising Ardashīr III to the throne."[979] According to Ibn Balkhī, Shahrvarāz reprimanded Māhādharjushnas for not consulting him.[980] Alone, however, his army could not have withstood the combined forces of the Nīmrūzī and the Pahlav.[981] He needed therefore to break the bonds of the recently established alliance. And so, he approached the leaders of the Pārsīg and forged an alliance with the Nīmrūzīs.[982] Along with 6,000 men from among the Persian army on the Byzantine frontier, Shahrvarāz set out for the capital of the Sasanian king.[983] Together with Nöldeke, Bosworth notes that "it was indicative of the chaos and weakness into which the Persian state had fallen that such a modest force was able to take over the capital and secure power for Shahrbarāz himself."[984] The point, however, is that the army of the Persian state had already divided into three factions in the midst of the events that led to Khusrow II's deposition.

We recall that the Byzantine emperor had in fact encouraged Shahrvarāz to mutiny and had promised him backup forces if he needed them.[985] Māhādharjushnas, confronted by the eminent arrival of Shahrvarāz and his army, took charge of protecting the king and the Sasanian capital. The conspiratorial atmosphere is reflected in an anecdote relayed by Ṭabarī. When Shahrvarāz's army besieged the capital, it was unable to gain entry. In need of help, the aspiring Mihrānid made recourse to a ruse. "He kept inciting a man named Nēw Khusrow, who was the commander of Ardashīr III's guard, and Nāmdār Jushnas,[986] the *iṣbabadh* (*ispahbud*, *spāhbed*) of Nīmrūz, to treachery, until the *two of them opened the gates of the city to Shahrbarāz*."[987] Surely, Nāmdār Jushnas, the *spāhbed* of Nīmrūz, and Nēw Khusrow, the commander of Ardashīr III's guard, had more important affairs on their hands than to open single-handedly the gate of the city for a besieging army. Potentially, Nēw Khusrow (the heroic Khusrow) is most probably a substitute for Pīrūz Khusrow (the victorious Khusrow), and hence was none other than Fīrūzān, the leader of the Pārsīg. Ferdowsī clearly portrays his power, when he writes of Pīrūz Khusrow (Fīrūzān): "whether young warriors or old warrior paladins, all were the cohorts of him."[988] In

[979] Ṭabarī 1999, p. 400, de Goeje, 1062. Ferdowsī 1971, vol. IX, p. 295, Ferdowsī 1935, p. 2946.

[980] Ibn Balkhī 1995, p. 261.

[981] Realizing this, Shahrvarāz exclaimed, according to Ferdowsī, that "the king may have many designs, but his affairs are in control of another army." Ferdowsī 1971, vol. IX, p. 295, n. 11, Ferdowsī 1935, p. 2227:

اگر چند بی شاه شد روزگار نخواهم که باشد چنو شهریار
که اورا بسی داوری در سر است همان رای با لشکر دیگر است

[982] Ṭabarī 1999, pp. 400–401, de Goeje, 1062. Ferdowsī 1935, p. 2946.

[983] Ṭabarī 1999, p. 401, de Goeje, 1062.

[984] Ṭabarī 1999, p. 400, n. 989.

[985] See footnote 961.

[986] Most certainly a different personage than Māhādharjushnas, as will become apparent in the remainder of the story.

[987] Ṭabarī 1999, p. 401, de Goeje, 1062. Emphasis added.

[988] Ferdowsī 1971, vol. IX, p. 298, Ferdowsī 1935, p. 2948:

همه یار پیروز خسرو بدند اگر نو جهانجوی اگر گو بدند

any case, the figures of Nēw Khusrow and Nāmdār Jushnas are meant only to represent collectively the armies at their disposal, made up of the Nīmrūzī and Pārsīg factions, what Sebeos had called the "army of Persia and the East."[989]

Incidentally, Ṭabarī's narratives on the depositions of Khusrow II Parvīz and Ardashīr III compliment one another. Mardānshāh,[990] mentioned in the conspiracy against Khusrow II, was a *pādhūspān*[991] of Nīmrūz, while in the mutiny against Ardashīr III, Nāmdār Jushnas appears as the *spāhbed* of the region. There remains a discrepancy, however, insofar as Shahrvarāz's seals also identify him as the *spāhbed* of the *kūst-i nēmrōz* under Khusrow II.[992] This anomaly can be easily explained, however, if we consider that Shahrvarāz had already mutinied against Khusrow II toward the end of his reign,[993] leaving the latter ample time to dispossess his general from his post. Besides, the unsettled conditions after Khusrow II was deposed were perfectly amenable to a Nīmrūzī faction assuming the title of *spāhbed*, if the title in fact meant anything during this tumultuous period of Sasanian history. As the previous *ērān-spāhbed* of the quarter of the south (*kūst-i nēmrōz*), moreover, Shahrvarāz had presumably come to collaborate intimately with the Pārsīg during his tenure.

So, once again, the Pahlav were divided in their promotion of a Sasanian king. Moreover, the fate of the Sasanian monarch Ardashīr III was decided by the complicity of at least two of the three armies of the realm: the army of Persia and the East under the control of the *spāhbed* Nāmdār Jushnas of Nīmrūz in collaboration with the Pārsīg leader Fīrūzān; and Shahrvarāz's army. Having seized the capital of the Sasanians, Shahrvarāz seized a number of leading men and, appropriating their wealth, put them to death, along with the seven year old king. Among these was Māhādharjushnas, the minister who had assumed the responsibility of raising and protecting the young king. Thus, in 630, the Nīmrūzī faction collaborated with Shahrvarāz to topple the child Ardashīr III.

There then transpired an event that had only two other precedents in the four hundred years of Sasanian history, the accession of a non-Sasanian to the throne. Having deposed Ardashīr III, with the complicity of the army of Persia and the East, the Parthian Mihrānid Shahrvarāz crowned himself king on 27 April 630. What is perhaps the most significant aspect of Shahrvarāz's coronation, however, is that together with the Mihrānid Bahrām-i Chūbīn and the Ispahbudhān Vistāhm, he became the third *Parthian* dynast to claim Sasanian kingship. The *X^wadāy-Nāmag* narrative in Ṭabarī cloaks the Sasanian legitimist perspective on the sacrilege of having a non-Sasanian on the throne in the garb of an anecdote that highlights the usurper's illegitimacy. As Shahrvarāz was not from the "royal house of the kingdom ... when he sat down on the royal

[989]See page 155ff.
[990]See page 157ff.
[991]See footnote 411.
[992]See §2.5.4.
[993]See page 149ff.

throne, his belly began to gripe, and this affected him so violently that he had no time to get to a latrine, hence he [swiftly] called for a bowl ... had it set down before the throne, and relieved himself in it."[994] Bosworth notes that this story "is meant to heighten the enormity of Shahrbarāz's temerity and his sacrilege by sitting down on the royal throne *when he was not from the royal houses of the Arsacids or the Sasanians.*"[995]

In fact, prior to the discovery of the seal of Pīrag-i Shahrvarāz, on which he *insisted* on his dynastic affiliation as a Mihrānid, and prior to our identification of this seal as belonging to the towering figure of Shahrvarāz,[996] while his non-Sasanian descent was acknowledged, his gentilitial background remained unclear. Now however, we have a better understanding of Sasanian history from the late sixth century onward: a number of processes, including the reforms of Khusrow I Nowshīrvān and the policies of his son Hormozd IV, violently disrupted the confederacy of the Parthians with the Sasanians with the effect that, in the span of only four decades, from the 590s to 630, three Parthian dynasts had claimed the Sasanian throne: Bahrām-i Chūbīn from the Mihrān,[997] Vistahm from the Ispahbudhān,[998] and Shahrvarāz from the Mihrān. This, however, is not the end of the Parthian aspiration to Sasanian kingship, as we shall see shortly.[999]

To belong to the Parthian dynastic families, to have a substantial and loyal army, and to uphold Sasanian kingship through their confederation with the house of Sāsān was one thing. To usurp the title *Shāhanshāh*, King of Kings, however, was, yet again, an altogether different story. The predicament of the Parthians throughout Sasanian history, after all, had always been their agreement to Sasanian kingship. To add insult to injury, upon usurping the throne, Shahrvarāz murdered many of the elite, among them Māhādharjushnas.[1000] The resulting opposition meant that Shahrvarāz's rule would also be short-lived, lasting a total of only forty days, from 27 April to his murder on 9 June 630.[1001] Who then was responsible for the murder of the Parthian Shahrvarāz?

In Ṭabarī's account the actual murder of Shahrvarāz is attributed to one Fus Farrukh, the son of Māh Khurshīdān.[1002] In Balʿamī's account this figure is called Saqrūkh, which is clearly a scribal error for Fus Farrukh.[1003] In Thaʿālibī's narrative the name of this figure is given as Hormozd-i Iṣ.takhrī; together

[994] Ṭabarī 1999, p. 402, de Goeje, 1063.
[995] Ṭabarī 1999, p. 402, n. 991.
[996] See §2.5.4.
[997] See §2.6.3.
[998] See §2.7.1.
[999] See page 205ff below.
[1000] Rendered in Balʿamī as Mihr Ḥasīs, as we have seen. Balʿamī 1959, p. 256.
[1001] Nöldeke 1879, p. 433, Nöldeke 1979, p. 641.
[1002] Ṭabarī 1999, p. 402, and n. 992, de Goeje, 1063.
[1003] Balʿamī 1959, p. 258. The first letter *fih* in Fus Farrukh is dropped whereas a dot is added to the second *fih* of the name, turning it into the letter *ghāf*.

with his army, he besieged Shahrvarāz, defeated and killed him.[1004] Ibn Balkhī calls him Pusfarrukh and maintains, significantly, that he was put in charge of killing Shahrvarāz by Būrāndukht.[1005] According to Ṭabarī, "two of his brothers were roused to great anger at Shahrbarāz's killing of Ardashīr III and his seizure of royal power."[1006] Fus Farrukh and his brothers were joined by a figure called Zādhān Farrukh-i Shahrdārān, as well as "a man called Māhyāy (?), who was the instructor of the cavalrymen (*mu'addib al-asāwira*). These were accompanied by a large number of the great men of state and members of the leading families."[1007] The group aided Fus Farrukh and his brothers "in killing various men who had assassinated Ardashīr III ... [and] various members of the class of the great men of state." Having done away with the Mihrānid usurper, the group "then raised to the throne Būrān, daughter of Kisra."[1008] In this version of Ṭabarī's account, therefore, two main personalities are depicted as serving a central role in the opposition to Shahrvarāz and are ultimately held responsible for the murder of this powerful Parthian dynastic leader: Fus Farrukh-i Māh Khurshīdān and Zādhān Farrukh-i Shahrdārān. Now we recall that the deposition and murder of the child-king Ardashīr III was effected through the collaboration of Shahrvarāz and the Nīmrūzī faction under the leadership of the Pārsīg Fīrūzān. It follows therefore that Fus Farrukh-i Māh Khurshīdān and his brothers, together with Zādhān Farrukh-i Shahrdārān, must have risen against these Pārsīg and Nīmrūzī factions gathered around Fīrūzān.

3.3 Būrāndukht and Azarmīdukht: the Pārsīg–Pahlav rivalry

According to Ṭabarī, upon the murder of Shahrvarāz, when Fus Farrukh and Zādhān Farrukh promoted Būrāndukht to Sasanian regency, the latter "entrusted Shahrvarāz's office to Fus Farrukh, and invested him with the office of her chief minister."[1009] This is reiterated also in Bal'amī's account: Būrāndukht, rendered here as Tūrān Dukht, gave her ministership to Fus Farrukh. Bal'amī adds one other significant piece of information: this Fus Farrukh was from Khurāsān.[1010] Fus Farrukh thus became the minister of Būrāndukht. Who then was Fus Farrukh? In order to attempt an answer we should begin by an observation regarding his name: Fus Farrukh (*fus* from Middle Persian *pus*, son) is the literal equivalent of Zādhān Farrukh (*zād*, child of), both meaning the son of Farrukh. Hence these names could simply be a substitute for the name Farrukhzād. And in fact, Fus Farrukh and Zādhān Farrukh are one and the same

[1004] Tha'ālibī 1900, pp. 733–735, Tha'ālibī 1989, pp. 467–468.
[1005] Ibn Balkhī 1995, p. 262.
[1006] Ṭabarī 1999, p. 402, de Goeje, 1063.
[1007] Ṭabarī 1999, p. 403, de Goeje, 1063.
[1008] Ṭabarī 1999, p. 403, de Goeje, 1064.
[1009] Ṭabarī 1999, p. 404, de Goeje, 1064.
[1010] Bal'amī 1959, p. 258.

figure, but not, as one would expect from the name, representing Farrukhzād, the son of Farrukh Hormozd, but in fact, as we shall see shortly, representing Farrukh Hormozd himself. Besides the literal identity of the name of Farrukhzād with both Zādhān Farrukh and Fus Farrukh, do we have any grounds for considering him, or his father, to be the prime minister of Būrāndukht and the figure—representative of a faction—responsible for toppling Shahrvarāz?

Before we proceed, two more observations are in order. Ṭabarī's epithet *shahrdārān* for Zādhān Farrukh clearly reflects his office, namely the governorship (*shahrdārī*) of a region (*shahr*).[1011] As for the epithet Māh Khurshīdān, considering the rarity of this name,[1012] one must forego Justi's explanation of Māh Khurshīdān as a patronym, namely, son of Māh Khurshīd, and simply opt for its meaning, someone who has "the spirit of the moon and the sun (as his protector)."[1013] Fus Farrukh thus becomes a dynastic figure who "seeks the protection of the sun and the moon," not a far fetched assumption considering the religious currents prevalent in the Sasanian realm by any means.[1014]

We can now state our main claim concerning Zādhān Farrukh-i Shahrdārān and Fus Farrukh-i Māh Khurshīdān: they are in fact none other than the famous Prince of the Medes, Farrukh Hormozd, the commander of the army of Azarbāyjān, under the leadership of whose family most other nobility were gathered to oppose Shahrvarāz and the army of Nīmrūz. A major problem, endemic to the Arabic as well as the Persian histories of the period, is the confusion of the name of this dynastic scion, Farrukh Hormozd, with that of his son, Farrukhzād.[1015] As we shall see, layers of confusion in our accounts have jumbled not only the identity of the members of this important Parthian dynastic family and their ancestry, but also their central and crucial involvement in the history of the Sasanians. Before we identify these layers of confusion, it is best to investigate the accounts that unmistakably identify this important minister of Būrāndukht's reign. We shall start with the account of the Armenian historian Sebeos.

According to Sebeos, shortly after Shahrvarāz attacked Ctesiphon and declared himself king, the elite rebelled, killed the mutinous general Shahrvarāz, and put Queen Bor (Būrāndukht), the daughter of Khusrow II, on the throne. After the enthronement "they appointed as chief minister at court Khoṙokh Ormizd, who was the prince of the region of Atrpatakan."[1016] This Khoṙokh Hormozd, of course, is none other than the Prince of the Medes, the Farrukh Hormozd of the Arabic sources.[1017] All other narratives at our disposal corroborate Sebeos' account on this point. However, Sebeos' narrative hereafter parts

[1011]Gyselen 1989, pp. 28–29.
[1012]Justi only cites this same figure. Justi 1895, p. 187
[1013]Justi 1895, p. 187. Ṭabarī 1999, p. 402, and n. 992.
[1014]See Chapter 5, especially page 357ff.
[1015]See also our discussions on pages 151 and 187.
[1016]Sebeos 1999, p. 89.
[1017]See page 150.

company with the Arabic and Persian sources. After narrating that queen Bor appointed Khoṙokh Hormozd as the chief minister of the court, Sebeos informs us that "this Khoṙokh sent a message to the queen [Bor]: 'Become my wife'." The queen consented to this matrimony.[1018] But as Sebeos informs us, this was nothing but a ruse, for under the pretense of marriage, Būrāndukht actually murdered Khoṙokh Hormozd (Farrukh Hormozd). Queen Bor (Būrāndukht) was in power for two years, according to Sebeos, before she died.

Our other sources also identify the minister of queen Būrāndukht as Farrukh Hormozd. About this, therefore, there is no doubt: it was the Prince of the Medes, the leader of the Pahlav, who promoted Būrāndukht to the throne and fought against Shahrvarāz's usurpation of the throne. The narrative of Farrukh Hormozd's request of matrimony from a Sasanian queen is also provided by other Arabic sources. Here, however, *all of our other sources deviate from Sebeos' account*: the queen in question is not Būrāndukht, but her sister, Azarmīdukht.[1019] The region under Farrukh Hormozd's jurisdiction, moreover, is at times said to be Azarbāyjān, but at other times Khurāsān. Furthermore, in all other narratives it was Azarmīdukht and not Būrāndukht who ultimately killed the Parthian dynast Farrukh Hormozd.

According to Yaʿqūbī, for example, when Azarmīdukht ascended the throne Farrukh Hormozd, the *ispahbud of Khurāsān*, approached her and declared: "Today I am the leader of the people and the pillar of the country of Iran." Farrukh Hormozd then asked the hand of Azarmīdukht in marriage. The story of the ruse of the queen and her murder of Farrukh Hormozd, attributed to Būrāndukht by Sebeos, is then also narrated by Yaʿqūbī, except that the queen in question is Azarmīdukht. Furthermore, after Azarmīdukht killed Farrukh Hormozd, "his son [i.e., the son of Farrukh Hormozd], Rustam, who was *in Khurāsān*, and who [later] fought Saʿd b. Abī Waqqāṣ in Qādisiya, came and killed Azarmīdukht."[1020]

Why does Yaʿqūbī maintain that Farrukh Hormozd was the *spāhbed* of Khurāsān, while Sebeos calls him the Prince of the Medes and Atrapatkan? Was Farrukh Hormozd in power over Azarbāyjān or over Khurāsān? Most Arabic sources confirm that Farrukh Hormozd was the *spāhbed* of Khurāsān. Ṭabarī, for example, maintains that during Azarmīdukht's reign "the outstanding great man of Persia was ... Farrukh Hurmuz, *iṣbahbadh* of Khurāsān."[1021] Ṭabarī also underlines for us the fact that during Azarmīdukht's reign "Rustam, son of Farrukh Hurmuz, the man whom Yazdjird (III) was later to send to combat the Arabs, was acting as his father's deputy in Khurāsān."[1022] The *Fārsnāma* identifies Farrukh Hormozd as the governor of Khurāsān and maintains that "there

[1018] Sebeos 1999, p. 89.

[1019] Yaʿqūbi 1969, vol. 1, pp. 197–198, Yaʿqūbi 1983, pp. 214–215, Ibn Balkhī 1995, p. 269.

[1020] Yaʿqūbi 1969, vol. 1, pp. 197–198, Yaʿqūbi 1983, pp. 214–215.

[1021] Ṭabarī 1999, pp. 406–407, de Goeje, 1065.

[1022] Ṭabarī 1999, pp. 406–407, de Goeje, 1065.

was none greater than him among the Persians."[1023] Balʿamī adds the significant piece of information that at the time of the murder of his father, the "great *spāhbed* of Khurāsān, Rustam, was himself in Khurāsān."[1024] It is Masʿūdī, however, who finally clarifies the confusion. According to him, when Khurra Hormozd (Farrukh Hormozd) was murdered by Azarmīdukht, his son Rustam, the future general at the battle of Qādisiya, and the figure who "*according to some was the successor of his father in Khurāsān and according to others in Azarbāyjān and Armenia*," came to queen Azarmīdukht and killed her.[1025] It is significant to note here tangentially that according to Masʿūdī, Rustam's murder of Azarmīdukht took place in 10 AH/631 CE.[1026] Rustam is called *Rostam-i Ādharī* (i.e., from Azarbāyjān) by Masʿūdī.[1027] This, for good reason, for initially Rustam was assigned the post of *darīgbed* of Azarbāyjān.[1028]

In short, while the confusion over the territorial domains of the family of the Prince of the Medes remains, all Arabic sources, unlike Sebeos, maintain that Farrukh Hormozd, the "leader of the people and the pillar of the country of Iran," and the figure besides whom "there was none greater ... among the Persians," asked the hand of Azarmīdukht and not Būrāndukht in matrimony. All maintain, moreover, that it was Azarmīdukht who was responsible for Farrukh Hormozd's murder in 631 and who lost her own life as a result at the hands of Rustam. Moreover, Rustam, sometimes called Āzarī, is most often identified as the *spāhbed* of Khurāsān, functioning in lieu of his father.

3.3.1 The Ispahbudhān

Our narratives, therefore, identify Farrukh Hormozd as one of the most important figures of the reigns of the two queens Būrāndukht and Azarmīdukht. Some sources call this figure either Fus Farrukh or Zādhān Farrukh, that is, Farrukhzād, the other son of Farrukh Hormozd. Hence, already we can detect three layers of confusion here. Firstly, the actual name of this towering figure is variously given as Fus Farrukh, Zādhān Farrukh or, alternatively, as Farrukh Hormozd. A simple confusion is at work here: the name of the father, Farrukh Hormozd, and the son, Farrukhzād, have been confused. A second layer of confusion surrounds the jurisdiction and power of this figure. Farrukh Hormozd is sometimes called the prince of Atrapatkan (Azarbāyjān) and at times the governor of Khurāsān. It is therefore not clear precisely over which of these

[1023] Ibn Balkhī 1995, p. 269.

[1024] Prior to this, Khusrow II Parvīz had given the governorship (*imārat*) of Khurāsān to Farrukh Hormozd. According to Balʿamī, while Farrukh Hormozd was in the capital serving Khusrow II, his son, Rustam, was serving as the representative (*khalīfa*) of his father in Khurāsān. Balʿamī also includes the story of Farrukh Hormozd's request of marriage from Azarmīdukht and the queen's refusal and ultimate murder of Farrukh Hormozd. Balʿamī 1959, p. 259.

[1025] Masʿūdī 1965 also contains Farrukh Hormozd's request of marriage from Azarmīdukht.

[1026] Masʿūdī 1965, p. 103.

[1027] Likewise, his father, Farrukh Hormozd, is said to be from Azarbāyjān. Masʿūdī 1965, p. 103.

[1028] For the office of *darīgbed*, see Gyselen 2002, pp. 113–114; Khurshudian 1998, pp. 109–113; see also our brief discussion on page 126.

two regions our figure(s) held control. Thirdly, with the exception of Sebeos, the *ministership* of Farrukh Hormozd is always attached to queen Būrāndukht, and never to Azarmīdukht, but it was from Azarmīdukht that Farrukh Hormozd requested matrimony, and at her hands that he lost his life. Rustam, the son of Farrukh Hormozd and his deputy in Khurāsān, then killed Azarmīdukht in revenge for his father's murder.

Farrukh Hormozd, son of Vindūyih

Now the confusion over the actual name of Farrukh Hormozd and the substitution of the name of the father for his son, Farrukhzād, is a common occurrence in our sources.[1029] This confusion has led to substantial misunderstandings, so much so that in some secondary literature to this day, Rustam, the other son of Farrukh Hormozd and the brother of Farrukhzād, has been rendered as Rustam-i Farrukhzād,[1030] that is, Rustam the son of Farrukhzād. This misunderstanding we must clear once and for all: Rustam was the *son* of Farrukh Hormozd and the *brother* of Farrukhzād.[1031]

The confusion of Farrukh Hormozd with his son Farrukhzād was pointed out long ago by Justi. Mīrkhwānd, for example, maintains that Farrukhzād was the *father* of Rustam.[1032] Ṭabarī also commits the same mistake switching, many times over, the name of Farrukh Hormozd with that of the latter's son Farrukhzād. Nöldeke noticed this confusion in Ṭabarī,[1033] but did not recognize the full ramifications of it. This confusion is clearly illustrated in Balʿamī's account. For while in one passage, Balʿamī correctly identifies Farrukh Hormozd as Rustam's father, later in this same narrative he contradicts himself by saying that "the name of the father of Rustam, the governor of Khurāsān, was Farrukhzād."

This confusion, in fact, had left a number of episodes of late Sasanian history inexplicable. Most significantly, it has in all probability thoroughly obscured the ancestry of the family of Farrukh Hormozd, the Prince of the Medes. With a high degree of confidence, we can now postulate that the family of Farrukh Hormozd is none other than the Ispahbudhān family. Farrukh Hormozd himself was the son of Vindūyih, the uncle and first minister of Khusrow II and the brother of the towering figure of Vistāhm, who both had helped Khusrow II to power, but later were killed by him.[1034] This crucial piece of information,

[1029]See for instance Gardīzī, Abū Saʿīd ʿAbd al-Ḥayy, *Taʾrīkh-i Gardīzī*, Tehran, 1984, edited by 'Abd al-Hayy Habibi (Gardīzī 1984), p. 103. See also our discussions on pages 151 and 184.

[1030]Zarrinkub 1975, p. 10. In the translated volume of Ṭabarī, he is even called Rustam b. Farrukhzād al-Armanī, Ṭabarī, *The Battle of al-Qādisiyyah and the Conquest of Syria and Palestine*, vol. XII of *The History of Ṭabarī*, Albany, 1992, translated and annotated by Yohanan Friedmann (Ṭabarī 1992), p. 232.

[1031]Sebeos 1999; Ḥamza Iṣfahānī 1988.

[1032]Justi 1895, p. 96. According to Justi, in his *Histoire des Rois de Perse*, Nikbī ben Massoud not only transposes the figure of Farrukh Hormozd on to, this time, his son Rustam, but calls him Farrukhzād.

[1033]Nöldeke 1879, pp. 393–394, and p. 344, n. 1, Nöldeke 1979, p. 591, n. 171.

[1034]See §2.7.1. For a reconstructed genealogical tree of the Ispahbudhān, see page 471.

however, has been lost as a result of the substantial confusion between the names of the father and son in our sources. For instance, as Balʿamī's editor observes,[1035] the name is given in Ṭabarī as Farrukhzād-i Binduwān, that is, Farrukhzād, *son of Bindū*.[1036] Ibn al-Athīr, too, succumbs to this confusion when he maintains that after the death of Ardashīr III, when the Sasanian crown had remained vacant, "the women of the Sasanian household spoke and instructed *Farrukhzād, ibn al-Bindhuwān* to choose a Sasanian king from wherever possible."[1037] Now, Bindū is the shortened, Arabicized version of Vindūyih. Moreover, in almost all of the cases where Farrukhzād is rendered as Farrukhzād-i Binduwān, the context makes it amply clear that the person talked about is in fact Farrukh Hormozd. We must therefore amend these sources appropriately: Farrukhzād and Rustam were the sons of Farrukh Hormozd, who in turn was the son of Vindūyih; Vindūyih of the Ispahbudhān family, the brother of Vistāhm and the son of the famous Asparapet whose exact name remains confused in our sources.

Territorial domains of the Ispahbudhān

What strengthens this identification is our awareness of the formidable power of the two families, the Ispahbudhān and the family of the Prince of the Medes, as well as our knowledge of the overlap of their territorial domains. As established in the previous chapter, Asparapet and his sons Vistāhm and Vindūyih held power, not only in the *kūst-i khwarbaran* (west), but also in the *kūst-i khwarāsān* (east),[1038] where their original homeland was located, and where Vistāhm eventually carved out an independent kingdom for almost seven years.[1039] Moreover, Sebeos makes it clear that in his fight against Bahrām-i Chūbīn, Vistāhm's power base was located in Azarbāyjān,[1040] although he does not comment on the extent of the Ispahbudhān's power in the latter region.[1041] Now, these same territories were also under the control of the family of the Prince of the Medes. The agnatic structure of the dynastic families made this continuity inevitable even after the reforms of Khusrow I: dynastic domains ultimately remained within the families of a particular dynast even if that dynast, Vistāhm in this case, *had lost his exalted position in the eyes of the Sasanians*. It is impossible to consider the incredibly powerful families of the Ispahbudhān and the Prince

[1035]Balʿamī 1959, p. 283 and n. 6.
[1036]The Persian possessive in names is often rendered by the suffix *-ān*, so that Farrukhzād-i Binduwān in this case means Farrukhzād of Bindū.
[1037]Ibn al-Athīr 1862, vol. 2, p. 393:

تكّم نساء آل كسرى فولّى الفرخزاد بن البنذوان الى ان يجتمع آل كسرى على من يملكونه إن وجدوه.

[1038]For the sigillographic evidence, see page 107ff.
[1039]See §2.7.1.
[1040]See page 128.
[1041]In the apocalyptic account that Sebeos provides from the prophecy of Daniel, he clearly connects the territory of the Medes and the Parthians: the "Sasanian kingdom ... [has] three ribs in its mouth, the kingdom of the Persians, Medes and Parthians." Sebeos 1999, p. 105.

of the Medes as two distinct families, if we take into consideration the genealogical tree that we have constructed and the agnatic infrastructure that regulated them together with the overlapping of the territorial domains of these families. The accounts of the *Xʷadāy-Nāmag* tradition highlight the familial relation of the Ispahbudhān with the family of the Prince of the Medes. In all the accounts that detail Khusrow II's deposition, the family of the Prince of the Medes is shown to have played a leading role. And in the list of grievances that was submitted to Khusrow II by Farrukhzād in a group of our narratives, as we have seen,[1042] the murders of Vistāhm and Vindūyih took a primary place.

What further corroborates this genealogical reconstruction is that in the wars that subsequently took place against the Arabs, Rustam of the family of the Prince of the Medes brought to the front what was tantamount to a dynastic army, in which the sons of Vistāhm, Vindūyih and Tīrūyih, together with other members of the Ispahbudhān family, fought side by side with Rustam, the grandson of Vindūyih, and other members of the family of the Prince of the Medes.[1043] Moreover, following the age-old tradition of rivalry among the Parthian dynastic families, the dynastic struggles in which the family of the Prince of the Medes became involved—in direct continuity of the rivalries that had engulfed the Ispahbudhān family—were against none other than the Mihrān family.[1044] In the unlikely event that the identification of Farrukh Hormozd's ancestry with that of the Ispahbudhān family does not hold under closer scrutiny, the postulate does not distract from the tenor of the rest of our argument, that is, from the period of Khusrow II onward, the Parthian family of Farrukh Hormozd, Farrukhzād, and Rustam was one of the most powerful dynastic families to hold power over both Azarbāyjān and Khurāsān, the latter being the traditional fiefdom of the Parthian families. Furthermore, Farrukh Hormozd's family was one of the primary factions that supported not only Shīrūyih Qubād's and Ardashīr III's kingship, but also Būrāndukht's regency, bringing her to power in 630 CE. What then explains the tenor of the narratives that claim that Farrukh Hormozd asked for the hand of Azarmīdukht in marriage? Here we shall have to stop our primary reliance on the *Xʷadāy-Nāmag* tradition. Our search for an answer must now involve a critical examination and juxtaposition of the *futūḥ* narratives—specifically the traditions handed down by Sayf b. ʿUmar and those following him—with those of the *Xʷadāy-Nāmag* tradition. Numismatic evidence will prove to be our corroborating gauge. Significantly, it is only in the course of examining some of the important battles in the early Arab conquest of Iraq that we can further reconstruct the nature of the over-arching rivalry between the Pahlav and the Pārsīg, the effect of this rivalry on the defensive war efforts of the Iranians against the encroaching Arab armies, and what we believe to be the chronology of this first phase of the Arab

[1042] See page 154.

[1043] See page 212 below.

[1044] This struggle culminated in the sacking of the Mihrāns' capital Rayy with the complicity of the Ispahbudhān; see §3.4.4, page 250ff, and page 264ff.

conquest of Iraq. The value of Sayf's *futūḥ* narratives, the precise relationship of Farrukh Hormozd to Azarmīdukht and Būrāndukht, as well as a host of other crucial dimensions of this juncture of Sasanian history, will only become fully explicated once we have undertaken this investigation. The reader must bear with us, however, for all of this will require that we go back to an earlier point, namely, the events that transpired during the reign of Shīrūyih Qubād, for it is at this juncture that the the narratives in the *futūḥ* literature begin.

3.3.2 Analepsis: Arab conquest of Iraq

Sayf's account of the initial phase of the conquest of Iraq begins with a very significant chronological and symbolic indicator: when "Khālid b. Walīd *was done with the business of Yamāmah*", Abū Bakr (632–634) wrote to him: "Go onward toward Iraq until you enter it. Begin with the gateway to India, which is Ubullah [i.e., Baṣrah, the port city near the Persian Gulf]. Render the people of Persia (Fārs) and those nations under their rule peaceable." Now Yamāmah was where Khālid had defeated the pseudo-prophet Musaylimah.[1045] The signifier, at the very inception of Sayf's account, therefore, is the *ridda*[1046] wars conducted under the direction of Abū Bakr.[1047] The accepted *hijra* chronology provided by Sayf, moreover, puts the start of these wars in 12 AH, conventionally dated to 633 CE.

The battle of Ubullah

The battle of Ubullah, one of the first wars reported during this phase of the conquest under Khālid b. Walīd's command has raised questions. Donner, for example, has maintained that the conquest of Ubullah was probably undertaken *somewhat later than 634* under the command of ʿUtbah b. Ghazwān.[1048] Blankinship, on the other hand, notes that Khalīfat b. Khayyāṭ records Khālid's campaigns in the vicinity of Baṣrah during this period, while Balādhurī also notes Khālid's presence around Baṣrah. All this suggests, Blankinship argues, that "Khālid at least may have led a raid there although ʿUtbah actually reduced the area."[1049] Controversy surrounds, therefore, the chronology of the inception of these wars. Who were the Persian commanders participating in the battle of Ubullah, however? And what are the *Sasanian* chronological indicators for this battle?

The Persian commanders mentioned in the course of this campaign are Jābān (Arabicized form of Middle Persian *gāwān*), the governor of Ullays;[1050] Āzādbih, the governor (*marzbān*) of Ḥīra and the commander of the Sasanian

[1045] Ṭabarī 1993, p. 1, n. 3, p. 2, n. 9.
[1046] See footnote 900.
[1047] This theme is reiterated a number of times in Sayf's account. See, for example, Ṭabarī 1993, pp. 4, 7 and 8, among others, de Goeje, 2018, 2020.
[1048] Donner 1981, p. 329, n. 66.
[1049] Ṭabarī 1993, p. 2, n. 9.
[1050] Ṭabarī 1993, p. 5, de Goeje, 2018.

cavalry;[1051] and the general Hurmuz (Hormozd), who might have been the commander of the Gateway to India, although it has been suggested that the appearance of this individual was Sayf's fabrication.[1052] During the course of this war, Khālid wrote to Hormozd and urged him to become a Muslim or opt to pay the *jizya*. Now these raids, as they are called, are described under the year 12 of *hijra* (633 CE) and are said to have been directed by Abū Bakr after the defeat of Musaylamah.

For our purposes, however, another significant chronological indicator is given here by Sayf. At the receipt of Khālid's letter, Hormozd *sent the news to Shīrūyih Qubād and to Ardashīr III*, after which he mobilized his forces.[1053] Unlike Sayf's account, where there is a confusion as to whether this war took place during Shīrūyih Qubād's reign (628) or during Ardashīr III's reign (628–630), however, Ibn al-Athīr maintains that the battle of Ubullah took place during the reign of Ardashīr III.[1054] The anachronism in Sayf's mention of these Sasanian kings was caught by Blankinship,[1055] who noted that, while Shīrūyih Qubād and Ardashīr III ruled in 7–9 AH/628–630 CE, these wars reportedly took place in 12 AH/633 CE, a year after the death of the Prophet and the inception of the rule of the Sasanian king Yazdgird III.[1056] If we continue to uphold the accepted *hijra* dating of these events, this objection would be valid. What would happen, however, if, as we suggested at the beginning of this chapter, we choose to ignore the *hijra* date altogether, and—even if we admit the participation of Khālid b. Walīd in these raids—presume that these raids in fact did take place around the time when Shīrūyih Qubād died and the seven-year old child Ardashīr III was enthroned? After all, why would the early traditionalist have connected this war to the rule of Ardashīr III when Yazdgird III was ruling? Would this alternative chronological scheme make sense if we compare it to the information that we have now garnered about Ardashīr III's reign from the *X^wadāy-Nāmag* tradition and other sources?

It can be readily observed that Sayf's information about the paramount Sasanian figures involved in the battle of Ubullah betrays a highly reasonable *internal logic when considered in isolation* from the remaining information on Arab generals and figures and when we disregard the *hijra* dating. According to Sayf, when Hormozd organized his army, he gave the command of the two wings to two brothers called Qubād and Anushjan. Qubād and Anūshjān were of Sasanian descent through the Sasanian kings Shīrūyih Qubād and Ardashīr III.[1057]

[1051] Ṭabarī 1993, p. 5, de Goeje, 2019.
[1052] Ṭabarī 1993, p. 9, n. 62.
[1053] Ṭabarī 1993, pp. 11, 16, de Goeje, 2023, 2027.
[1054] Ibn al-Athīr 1862, vol. 2, p. 141.
[1055] Blankinship's assessment, needless to say, is here given only as an example of the paradigmatic methodology relied upon in the field, which ultimately disregards the Sasanian chronological indicators in favor of the accepted *hijra* dating.
[1056] Ṭabarī 1993, p. 11, n. 73 and 74.
[1057] Ṭabarī 1993, p. 12, de Goeje, 2023.

Anūshjān is further identified as the son of Jushnasmāh.[1058] Who are these figures? Can we in fact establish any connection between these and the rule of Shīrūyih Qubād or Ardashīr III? We must start with an onomastic observation: the name *Jushnasmāh* is an abbreviated form of *Jushnas Māh Ādhar*, where the final suffix *ādhar* (fire) has been dropped,[1059] and hence in its inverted form, the name becomes *Māhādharjushnas*. As we recall, Māhādharjushnas (Jushnasmāh) was the minister of the child Ardashīr III "in charge of his upbringing and carrying the administration of the kingdom."[1060] He undertook to protect the child Ardashīr III and his capital, when the Nīmrūzī faction together with Shahrvarāz were conspiring to topple the king. And so we can expect the minister's sons Anūshjān and Qubād to have taken part in the battle of Ubullah. The executive powers under the command of Anūshjān were in fact so great that he undersigned a peace treaty with the Arabs after the battle.[1061] Now, Ardashīr III ruled for about one year and seven months, until Shahrvarāz usurped the Sasanian throne on 27 April 630. Based on our alternative chronology, therefore, the battle of Ubullah would have taken place anytime between September 628 CE and April 630 CE, that is 7–9 AH. However, since some of the accounts still mention Shīrūyih Qubād, we should conclude that this battle probably took place sometime in 7 AH/628 CE.

The battle of Dhāt al-Salāsil

A series of other battles, also placed by Sayf in the year 12 of *hijra*, follow this same internal logic. The battle that subsequently took place between Khālid and Hormozd is called the battle of Dhāt al-Salāsil. Significantly, Blankinship notes that this battle, which is reported only by Sayf, "*has the same name as the expedition of ʿAmr b. al-ʿĀṣ in the year 8/629, where it refers to a place.*" This war

[1058]Balādhurī, Aḥmad b. Yaḥyā, *Futūḥ al-Buldān*, Leiden, 1968, edited by M.J. de Goeje (Balādhurī 1968), p. 340; Ṭabarī 1993, p. 12, n. 78. The name of Anūshjān, therefore, might in fact be the abbreviated form of Anūsh Jushnasp, just as the name of his brother would be Qubād Jushnasp.

[1059]This name is formed on the same scheme as, for instance, a name attested on the seals: Bahrām-i Māh Ādhar; see §2.6.1.

[1060]Ṭabarī 1999, p. 400, de Goeje, 1061. See page 179ff.

[1061]His name is here given as Nūshjān b. Jusnāsmā. This information is provided by Balādhurī in the following context, although, naturally, he also puts these events in the year 12 of *hijra*: "They say that Suwayd b. Quṭbah, or according to some Quṭbat b. Qatādah, was constantly looting the ʿajam in the vicinity of Khuraybah in Baṣrah, as Muthannā ... was looting the environs of ... Ḥīra ... In the year 12 of *hijra*, when Khālid b. Walīd came to Baṣrah, and set out for Kūfa, he helped Suwayd [b. Muqarrin] in the battle of Ubullah. Others maintain that Khālid did not leave Baṣrah until he conquered Khuraybah. The arms depot (*zīnistān*) of the Persians was there ... They also say that he went to Nahr al-Marʾāt and conquered the palace there through a peace treaty with Nūshjān b. Jusnāsmā." The owner of the palace in Nahr al-Marʾāt, Kāmindār, the daughter of Nersī (Narsī), was the paternal cousin of Nūshjān. Balādhurī 1968, p. 340. Also see Khayyāṭ, Khalīfat b., *Taʾrīkh*, Beirut, 1977 (Khayyāṭ 1977), pp. 117–118. This Anūshjān is probably related to Anūshnād b. Ḥash-n-sh-bandih, whose name is a clear corruption of Anūsh Jushnasp, mentioned by Ḥamza Iṣfahānī among the Iranians who held the governorship over various Arab territories during the reign of Khusrow I and part of that of Hormozd IV. Ḥamza Iṣfahānī 1961, p. 116, Ḥamza Iṣfahānī 1988, pp. 141–142.

has also been reported by Ibn Hishām, Wāqidī, and Ibn Sa'd in the *Sīrah*, *Kitāb al-Maghāzī*, and *Ṭabaqāt al-Kabīr* respectively, as having taken place during the year 8 of *hijra*, that is, 629 CE.[1062] In other words, if we follow the Sasanian chronology, and compare it to the events described for the year 8 of *hijra* in other Arabic sources, then this war took place probably in 629. Hormozd, who was from "the highest nobility among the Persians ... [and] from [one of] the *seven houses*,"[1063] was killed in the battle of Dhāt al-Salāsil, whereas Anūshjān and Qubād escaped.[1064] Toward the end of this narrative, furthermore, Ṭabarī takes "the rare and unusual step of denouncing Sayf's story," observing that the narrative as we have it is "different from what the *true traditions have brought us.* For the battle of Ubullah was only in the days of 'Umar, when it was accomplished at the hands of 'Utbah in the year 14 of the *hijra* [i.e., 635–636 CE]."[1065] Blankinship takes issue with Ṭabarī's observation and notes that "*some of the points of* Sayf's story are related by Ibn Khayyāṭ ... with *isnāds* from others than Sayf."[1066]

The battle of Madhār

Sayf then narrates the battle of Madhār and claims that it, too, took place in 12 AH/633 CE.[1067] What, however, are the Sasanian chronological indicators provided by Sayf? According to Sayf, when Khālid b. Walīd had written to Hormozd urging him to become a Muslim or pay the *jizya*, Hormozd had in turn written to Shīrūyih Qubād and Ardashīr III and informed them of the content of the letter and the fact that Khālid "had *set out from al-Yamāmah against him.*"[1068] The child Ardashīr III allegedly responded to Hormozd's warning of impending warfare by sending one Qārīn to his aid. While the exact genealogy of this Qārīn cannot be reconstructed with the information at our disposal,[1069] there is no doubt that he belonged to the Parthian dynastic family of the Kārins. Qārīn put Qubād and Anūshjān, the sons of Jushnasmāh (Māhādharjushnas), the prime minister of Ardashīr III, once more in charge of the two wings of his

[1062] Ibn Hishām, b. Muḥammad, *Sīrah*, Cairo, 1956 (Ibn Hishām 1956), pp. 623–624; Wāqidī, Muḥammad b. 'Umar, *Kitāb al-Maghāzī*, London, 1966, edited by M. Jones (Wāqidī 1966), pp. 769–774; Ibn Sa'd, *Ṭabaqāt al-Kabīr*, Leiden, 1940, edited by E. Sachau (Ibn Sa'd 1940), p. 131; Ṭabarī 1993, p. 13, n. 86.

[1063] Ṭabarī 1993, p. 14, and n. 87, de Goeje, 2025.

[1064] Ṭabarī 1993, p. 13, de Goeje, 2025.

[1065] Ṭabarī 1993, p. 14, de Goeje, 2026.

[1066] Among the raids that Muḥammad ordered in 7 AH/628 CE, Khayyāṭ lists that of 'Amr b. al-'Āṣ and Zayd b. Hārithah to Dhāt al-Salāsil, in the direction of the regions in Iraq. Khayyāṭ 1977, p. 85; Ṭabarī 1993, p. 14, de Goeje, 2025. For the year 6 AH/627 CE, he mentions the message of Muḥammad to Khusrow II, the king's murder by Shīrūyih Qubād, and the death of the latter through pestilence. Khayyāṭ 1977, p. 79.

[1067] Blankinship again notes that this battle was actually fought by 'Utbah b. Ghazwān later, "so that Sayf's report here is chronologically improbable." Blankinship gives reference to Morony 1984, pp. 127 (map), 160, and Donner 1981, p. 329, n. 66.

[1068] Ṭabarī 1993, p. 16, de Goeje, 2027. Note the *ridda* indicator again.

[1069] The actual name of this Qārīn, according to Sayf, is Qārīn b. Qaryānis. Blankinship notes that the vocalization that he has given is conjectural. Ṭabarī 1993, p. 16, n. 104.

army. In other words, a predominantly Pahlav army was sent to Hormozd's aid. The *internal evidence* provided by Sayf on both of the major figures involved in the battle of Madhār, and his contention that these were active during the regency of Ardashīr III (628–630), continues to tally with the course of events transpiring in Iran as we have reconstructed these based on the *X^w adāy-Nāmag* tradition.

Presumably before reaching Hormozd, however, Qārīn and his forces hear of his defeat and death. Since Hormozd had been killed in the battle of Dhāt al-Salāsil, which took place prior to the battle of Madhār, the army commanded by Hormozd needed indeed a new commander, hence the dispatch of the Parthian general Qārīn. Qārīn arrived at the scene only to intercept the remnants of the fleeing army of Hormozd. Faced with the withdrawal of Sasanian forces they "encouraged each other [to return to the] fight once more." Who were these people encouraging each other? Sayf provides crucial evidence: The "remnants *[of the forces of] al-Ahwāz and Fārs* [said] ... *to the remnants of al-Sawād and al-Jabal*, 'If you split up, you will never join together afterward. Therefore join together to go back [to fight once more]'."[1070] Two groups of people are here distinguished: 1) the forces of Ahvāz and Fārs, and 2) the forces of Sawād and Jibāl. As the regional power of the Pahlav was partly in the north, here identified with Sawād and Jibāl, under the leadership of Māhādharjushnas and Qārīn, it follows that the forces of Hormozd must have hailed from Ahvāz and Fārs, that is, from the Pārsīg domains. Hence, we are dealing here with a regional distinction, north versus south, on to which a different sort of division is superimposed, the Pahlav versus the Pārsīg.[1071] For the moment we can summarize our narrative. We are still dealing with the reign of the child king Ardashīr III (628–630). A certain Hormozd was in command of the forces that were brought to the war against the Arabs. Two of the important commanders who were dispatched to serve under Hormozd, Qubād and Anūshjān, were the sons of the minister who was in charge of affairs during Ardashīr III's regency, Māhādharjushnas (Jushnasmāh). Hormozd, however, was defeated and killed in the battle of Dhāt al-Salāsil, which according to some sources took place during the year 8 of *hijra* (629 CE), precisely during the rule of Ardashīr III. When Hormozd died and his army was on the verge of withdrawing, however, the regional armies warned each other that to disperse would mean disaster. The command of the forces was then taken over by the Parthian general Qārīn. In the subsequent battle of Madhār, Qārīn, Qubād, and Anūshjān were all killed.[1072] For our purposes we should note here another piece of information provided by Sayf: "Qārīn's nobility had lapsed. After him the Muslims did not fight anyone whose nobility had lapsed among the Persians."[1073]

[1070]Ṭabarī 1993, p. 16, de Goeje, 2027.

[1071]We should recall here that according to Mas'ūdī, Fārs was the domain of the Pārsīg, while "Māhāt [Media] and other regions" belonged to the Pahlav. See footnote 145.

[1072]Ṭabarī 1993, p. 17, de Goeje, 2027.

[1073]Ṭabarī 1993, p. 17, de Goeje, 2028.

The battle of Walajah

In the battle of Walajah, described next, and placed among the wars taking place in 12 AH/633 CE, the news of the defeat and murder of Qārīn reached Ardashīr III. The child Ardashīr III reportedly sent a figure called Andarzghar, who "was a *Persian* from among the *mixed-bloods* of al-Sawād and one of its inhabitants, to the war front." Prior to this, he had been "in charge of the frontier of Khurāsān."[1074] This Andarzghar, however, Sayf informs us, "*was not among those who had been born at al-Madā'in, nor had he grown up there.* So Ardashīr III ... sent Bahman Jādhūyih after him with an army."[1075] There was, in other words, something wrong with Andarzghar, namely that he was of mixed blood and not from Ctesiphon. Andarzghar, it must be noted, is a title, not a name, made up of *andarz* (council) and *gar*, the Persian suffix denoting one who has a profession, in this case, a councillor.[1076] We can now recapitulate: Once Hormozd and Qārīn were dead, Ardashīr III—or rather, the factions in control of the child Ardashīr III—sent a figure called Andarzghar to the war front. The command of Andarzghar, however, was not accepted and Bahman Jādhūyih was sent in his stead. People then joined Andarzghar and Bahman Jādhūyih to engage the Arabs at the battle of Walajah.[1077] As we recall from the *X*ʷ*adāy-Nāmag* tradition, however, Ardashīr III's reign was thoroughly tumultuous.[1078] The Persians were, therefore, yet again defeated at the battle of Walajah.[1079]

The battle of Ullays

With the narrative of the war of the battle of Ullays, which is still taking place in the year 12 of *hijra* according to Sayf, we are given further significant *internal* Sasanian chronological indicators. Sayf's narrative connects in a continuous fashion to that given for the battle of Walajah. Bahman Jādhūyih, Sayf informs us, "was the spokesman of Persia on one day out of their month. They divided their months so that each month consisted of thirty days. On each day the Persians had a [different] spokesman, who was appointed to speak for them before the king. Their spokesman was Bahman Jādhūyih on the second day of the month."[1080] The child Ardashīr III supposedly wrote to this spokesman for the Persians and ordered him to go forth in order to engage the Arabs. Bahman Jādhūyih, however, *disobeyed* Ardashīr III's orders and sent Jābān in his stead,

[1074] Ṭabarī 1993, p. 19, de Goeje, 2030.
[1075] Ṭabarī 1993, p. 19, de Goeje, 2029.
[1076] According to Khurshudian, the title *andarzgar* was carried as a name by some Mazdakites, suggesting perhaps that this general Andarzghar was one of the allegedly illegitimate offspring from the noble houses during the Mazdakite uprising (§2.4.5). Khurshudian 1998, p. 92.
[1077] Ṭabarī 1993, p. 19, de Goeje, 2030.
[1078] See §3.2.2.
[1079] It must be noted that in this war there were still Arabs who aided the Persians. Ṭabarī 1993, p. 21, de Goeje, 2031.
[1080] Ṭabarī 1993, p. 22, de Goeje, 2032. Emphasis added. See footnote 1092 for a conjecture about the *jādhūyih* office which explains the peculiarities of this passage.

ordering him to not engage the enemy until he returned.[1081] This, according to Sayf, he did because he wanted to go to Ardashīr III "*to see him in person and consult with him about what he wanted to command.*" Bahman Jādhūyih, we are led to believe, wanted to seek the advice of a child king in power. The real reason why Bahman Jādhūyih was forced to leave the war front and go back to the capital, however, is subsequently given by Sayf. When Bahman Jādhūyih left the war zone to go to the capital, in Ctesiphon he found Ardashīr III sick![1082] We recall now the turmoil which had engulfed Iran when the Mihrānid Shahrvarāz under Heraclius' instigation moved toward the capital in order to topple Ardashīr III from power and declare himself king.[1083] The coconspirators of Shahrvarāz, moreover, were the army of Persia and the East, the Nīmrūzī faction, under the command of the *spāhbed* of Nīmrūz, Nāmdār Jushnas. Bahman Jādhūyih, in other words, was forced to leave the war arena because Ardashīr III was in the midst of being deposed through the collaboration of the army of Shahrvarāz and the army of Persia and the East. While Bahman Jādhūyih returned to the capital to take part in the strife that was unfolding, Jābān was forced to man the war front alone.

In the battle of Ullays, meanwhile, Sayf informs us, "the polytheists [i.e., the Iranians] were increased in rabidity and ferocity because they expected" Bahman Jādhūyih to return.[1084] With the forces of Jābān manning the war front on their own, with the chaos that must have been ongoing with the movement of Shahrvarāz's army toward the capital, and with the turmoil in Ctesiphon, the Arabs were once again victorious in their skirmishes in the battle of Ullays.[1085] We must now turn our attention to this Bahman Jādhūyih, who after the defeat and murder of Hormozd and Qārin took up the command of the army. Yet another brief onomastic diversion is necessary here before we can proceed with the rest of our examination.

Pārsīg leaders: Bahman Jādhūyih, Dhu 'l-Ḥājib, Mardānshāh, and Fīrūzān

The figure of Bahman Jādhūyih also bears the epithet Dhu 'l-Ḥājib. There is no doubt that *Dhu 'l-Ḥājib* is really an epithet, and not a name, some traditions giving what seems to be a popular etymology for it.[1086] The precise identity of this figure, however, remains unsettled. For at different historical junctures, at least three other names or epithets appear in the sources referring to a Pārsīg leader:

[1081] Ṭabarī 1993, p. 22, de Goeje, 2032. For Jābān, see footnote 1050.

[1082] Ṭabarī 1993, p. 22, de Goeje, 2032.

[1083] See §3.2.3.

[1084] Ṭabarī 1993, p. 23, de Goeje, 2034.

[1085] Ṭabarī 1993, pp. 24–25, de Goeje, 2034–2036.

[1086] See, for example, Balādhurī 1968, p. 251, where the epithet is given to Mardānshāh, whom we shall discuss shortly. Dhu 'l-Ḥājib is here described to mean the *eye-browed*, for his eye-brows were so long that he was forced to "lift them above his eyes."

Fīrūzān,[1087] Hormozd Jādhūyih, and Mardānshāh,[1088] with various traditions having substituted one name for the other. It should be remarked at the outset that whatever the confusion surrounding these figures, it is clear that they all belonged to the Pārsīg faction and functioned as the leader (or leaders) of this faction at different junctures.

The epithet *jādhūyih* is given not only to Bahman but also to Hormozd Jādhūyih.[1089] This epithet too can be explained. As sigillographic evidence bears witness, one of the important administrative offices of the Sasanian empire, possibly in the post-reform period (550–650), was the office of the *driyōšān jādaggōw ud dādvar*, the *defender of the poor and judge*. This seems to have been a judiciary office possibly with religious overtones.[1090] The title *jādhūyih*, then, is most probably the Arabicized and abbreviated version of the term *jādaggōw* given to the holder of the office of *driyōšān jādaggōw ud dādvar*,[1091] in this case, the important Pārsīg leader, Bahman Jādhūyih.[1092]

There remains, however, the issue that some traditions maintain Bahman Jādhūyih to have been one of the leading figures of the Sasanian war efforts, whereas, other traditions maintain this to have been Fīrūzān or Mardānshāh. For example, while some sources call the leader of the Pārsīg in the battle of

[1087] Justi 1895, pp. 250, 374.

[1088] Clearly, Mardānshāh cannot be the same person as Mardānshāh, the *pādhūspān* of Nīmrūz, discussed on page 157, as the latter was killed by Khusrow II.

[1089] See page 202ff. At least two other figures at this juncture of Sasanian history bore this epithet: Shahrvarāz Jādhūyih and Ābān Jādhūyih, see respectively page 247 and footnotes 1490 and 1528 below.

[1090] Gyselen 1989, pp. 6 and 31–33 and the sources cited therein; see also Daryaee, Touraj, 'The Judge and Protector of the Needy during the Sasanian Period', in A.A. Sadeghi (ed.), *Tafazzol Memorial*, pp. 179–187, Tehran, 2001 (Daryaee 2001).

[1091] Justi 1895, p. 107.

[1092] I am indebted to my husband Hans Schoutens for the following conjectural observation about the title *jādhūyih*. We recall that according to Sayf, the Persians had spokesmen who were appointed to speak on their behalf before the king, one for each day of the month. Bahman Jādhūyih was their spokesman on the second day of the month. Ṭabarī 1993, p. 22, de Goeje, 2032. Now, *jādhūyih*, from Persian *jādaggōw*, means *advocate, intercessor*, whence spokesman; see MacKenzie 1971, p. 46. Moreover, in the Zoroastrian calendar, the second day of the month is called Vohuman (Bahman). Bahman Jādhūyih therefore is the advocate (*jādhūyih*) on the second day of the month (Bahman). Similarly, Hormozd Jādhūyih must have been the *jādhūyih* on the first day of the month (Hormozd) and Ābān Jādhūyih on the tenth day (Ābān). We may even go further and suggest that the name of the general Shahrvarāz Jādhūyih—who participated in the battle of Iṣfahān (see page 247) and is not to be confused with the towering Mihrānid general Shahrvarāz under Khusrow II—is a corrupted version of Shahrīvar *jādhūyih*, that is, the *jādhūyih* on the fourth day (Shahrewar). Balʿamī, in fact, renders the name of this general as Shahrīyār. Balʿamī 1959, p. 328, n. 3. In particular, when dealing with a name composed with *jādhūyih*, the first part should be considered as the name of a day, like *Bahman* in Bahman Jādhūyih. As we shall argue shortly, Bahman Jādhūyih's actual name was most likely Mardānshāh. A Rustam Jādhūyih, who fell at the battle of Qādisiya, is mentioned in Yaqūt al-Hamawī, *Kitab Muʿjam al-Buldān*, Leipzig, 1866, edited by F. Wüstenfeld as *Jacut's Geographisches Wörterbuch* (Yaqūt al-Hamawī 1866) apud Justi 1895, p. 263. As there is no day named Rustam in the Zoroastrian calendar, this time Rustam must be the actual name of this *jādhūyih*, namely, the Ispahbudhān supreme commander Rustam, on whom see §3.4.1.

Bridge, Fīrūzān,[1093] others refer to him as Mardānshāh Dhu 'l-Ḥājib.[1094] In all probability, the substitution of Mardānshāh for Fīrūzān here is a simple case of scribal error, the orthography of both names being very close.[1095] On the other hand, some traditions substitute the figure of Mardānshāh for Bahman Jādhūyih, calling both Dhu 'l-Ḥājib, such as Balādhurī's contention that Mardānshāh Dhu 'l-Ḥājib, whom he lists as one of the main commanders of the battle of Bridge, also had the epithet Bahman.[1096] However, whereas Bahman Jādhūyih, Mardānshāh, and Dhu 'l-Ḥājib all seem to refer to the same person in the sources, their identity with Fīrūzān is more problematic: in the midst of the battle of Bridge, as we shall see, queen Būrāndukht recalled Bahman Jādhūyih and appointed in his stead Fīrūzān, but asked the latter to cooperate with the former;[1097] and after Fīrūzān died at the battle of Nihāvand, Bahman Jādhūyih was appointed in his stead.[1098] Based on this analysis, we therefore will proceed from the assumptions that Bahman Jādhūyih, Dhu 'l-Ḥājib, and Mardānshāh all refer to one and the same figure, distinct, however, from Fīrūzān. These Pārsīg dynastic leaders, nonetheless, either had a close familial relationship, or most certainly, closely collaborated with each other.

Returning to our narrative, we recall that Ardashīr III's deposition was effected by the cooperative efforts of the armies of Shahrvarāz and Nīmrūz.[1099] When Bahman Jādhūyih Dhu 'l-Ḥājib hurried back to the capital because the news had reached him that Ardashīr III was sick, therefore, as one of the leaders of the Pārsīg, he was in fact returning to the capital to aid Shahrvarāz and the Nīmrūzī faction in toppling the child king. Hence, based on the Sasānian chronological indicators, the battle of Ullays took place at the time when Shahrvarāz had mutinied and was about to take over Ctesiphon in his bid for power, that is around April 630.

The battle of Maqr

In the battle of Maqr, or the Day of al-Maqr, which according to Sayf took place subsequent to the battle of Ullays, Āzādbih, the *marzbān* of Ḥīra, who also fought at the battle of Ubullah,[1100] set out to dam the Euphrates.[1101] Āzādbih,

[1093] Ṭabarī, *The Conquest of Iraq, Southwestern Persia, and Egypt*, vol. XIII of *The History of Ṭabarī*, Albany, 1989a, translated and annotated by Gautier H.A. Juynboll (Ṭabarī 1989a), p. 193, de Goeje, 2608; Ibn al-Athīr 1862, vol. 2, pp. 434–435; Justi 1895, p. 250. For the battle of Bridge, see §3.3.5.

[1094] Balādhurī 1968, p. 251.

[1095] فيرزان *Fīruzān*, becoming فرزان *Firuzān* whence مردان *mardān*.

[1096] From Avestan Vohu Manah, Bahman means *Good Thought*. It was one of the divine *Amahraspands* in the post-Gathic Avestā. Narten, J., 'Bahman', in Ehsan Yarshater (ed.), *Encyclopaedia Iranica*, New York, 2007 (Narten 2007). See also footnote 1092.

[1097] Balʿamī 1959, pp. 290–291. For more details, see page 218.

[1098] *Bahman Jādhūyih alladhī jaʿala makān-i dhu-l-ḥājib*. Ṭabarī 1989a, p. 203, de Goeje, 2618; Balʿamī 1959, p. 317, n. 4.

[1099] See §3.2.3.

[1100] See page 190.

[1101] According to Sayf, "*they* used not to support each other except by permission of the king." Blankinship comments that *they* apparently meant the governors. Ṭabarī 1993, pp. 26–27 and

however, "was [also] *impelled to flee by the news that reached him about the death of Ardashīr III*, as well as the defeat of his own son." The mutiny of Shahrvarāz with the collaboration of the Pārsīg against Ardashīr III in 630 CE, therefore, seriously interrupted the Iranian defense against the encroaching Arabs. The series of defenses put up by Bahman Jādhūyih, Jabān, and Āzādbih were disrupted by the factionalism engulfing the Sasanian domains, pre-occupying the three armies of the realm: the army of Atrapatkan (Azarbāyjān), of Shahrvarāz, and of Nīmrūz. This allowed the Arabs to take the region of Ḥīra through skirmishes and negotiations.[1102] As the piecemeal affairs against Ḥīra were taking place, and Khālid had conquered one side of the Sawād, Sayf informs us, he sent a "letter to the Persians, who were then at al-Madā᾿in [Ctesiphon] *disputing and supporting [different parties] because of the death of Ardashīr III*."[1103]

The battle of Veh Ardashīr

While pre-occupied with their disputes in the capital, the Persians, nevertheless, "did send Bahman Jādhūyih to Bahurasīr (Veh Ardashīr)," accompanied by the forces of Āzādbih.[1104] It is the Pārsīg leader Bahman Jādhūyih, therefore, who nevertheless returned to the war front to engage the Arabs. Significantly, in the letter that Khālid sent to the *kings* of Persia he urged these to "enter [his] faith." If they would accept this, then the Arabs would *leave them as well as their land alone* and *pass beyond* them "*to others different from [theirs]*." If the kings of Persia did not accept the Arabs' conditions, then "they must engage the Arabs . . . , even though [they] loath [it]."[1105]

The chronology of the internal events as they transpired in the Sasanian domains is once again followed by Sayf. What is more, this chronology continues to corroborate the procession of events in Iran as reconstructed through other sources. The Persians, Sayf continues, "were left split after the death of Ardashīr III regarding the kingship but in agreement on fighting Khālid and supporting each other."[1106] This state of affairs continued "for a year, while the Muslims were penetrating up to the Tigris. The Persians held nothing between al-Ḥīra and the Tigris."[1107] If indeed the Persians were pre-occupied with this state of affairs for a year, this then takes us to the time that Būrāndukht became queen. Sayf confirms this: after a year of warfare, Khālid left Iraq and went to Syria at around the same time that Būrāndukht had come to power. As we saw earlier,[1108] this was sometime in July 630/early 9 AH. According to the *hijra* dating provided by Sayf, however, Khālid would have departed on 13 January 634

n. 161, de Goeje, 2037. As we shall see, however, *they* in fact is a reference to factions.

1102 Ṭabarī 1993, pp. 30–31, de Goeje, 2040–2041.

1103 Ṭabarī 1993, p. 43, de Goeje, 2053.

1104 Ṭabarī 1993, pp. 43–44, de Goeje, 2053.

1105 Ṭabarī 1993, p. 44, de Goeje, 2053.

1106 Ṭabarī 1993, p. 45, de Goeje, 2054.

1107 Ṭabarī 1993, p. 45, de Goeje, 2054.

1108 See the beginning of §3.3.

CE/4 Dhuʾl-Qaʿdah 12 AH.[1109] Let us point out once more the discrepancy of more than three years that is at work here, if we would trust Sayf's *hijra* dating.

What, however, was happening during this year according to Sayf? While "Khalid stayed in office for a year ... before his departure for Syria, ... [the] Persians were overthrowing kings and enthroning others, there being no defensive effort except at Bahurasīr [Veh Ardashīr]."[1110] And how did this state of affairs come about? "That was because Shīrūyih Qubād had slain all his [male] relatives descended" from Khusrow II, and "the people of Persia had risen after Shīrūyih Qubād and after Ardashīr III."[1111] Khālid, therefore, had remained in command for a year before his departure for Syria. During this period he had written a letter to the kings of Persia. However, because there were no Sasanian kings during this period with any real power, there is no doubt that the *kings* referred to here were, in fact, the dynastic leaders in charge of the regional armies vying for power. What then happened to Khālid's correspondence with the kings of Persia? When his dispatch "fell into the hands of the people of al-Madāʾin, *the women* of Kisrā's family spoke up." They put none other than "al-Farrukhzādh b. al-Bindawān ... in charge until such time as Kisrā's family agreed on a man [to make king], if they could find him."[1112] Here then we have finally come to the appointment of the Prince of the Medes, Farrukh Hormozd, as the prime minister of Būrāndukht, the Sasanian queen. This, however, is one of those instances where the name of Farrukh Hormozd is mistakenly rendered as al-Farrukhzādh.[1113]

We should recapitulate. Through the reign of the child king Ardashīr III, the Persians tried to put up a defense against the Arab armies. The last commander sent to the war front was the Pārsīg leader Bahman Jādhūyih. For a whole year after the deposition of Ardashīr III, the Iranian realm was then in turmoil. For at least three months during this period, the Parthian Shahrvarāz in fact usurped the Sasanian throne.[1114] Sayf subsequently follows the course of the events, filling in the lacunae for this one year, for not only was Khālid still in charge on the Arab side, and hence had not yet left for Syria, but also on the Persian side the participants remained the same.

The battle of Anbār

During this period, when the Persians were occupied with their internal concerns, a certain Shīrzād was unsuccessfully expending his efforts at defending Anbār. The lack of manpower at his disposal is highlighted when Sayf maintains that the people of Anbār had fortified themselves, and Khālid observed that he saw "groups of people ... *who had no knowledge of warfare*," fighting for

[1109] Ṭabarī 1993, p. 68, de Goeje, 2075.
[1110] Ṭabarī 1993, p. 47, de Goeje, 2056.
[1111] Ṭabarī 1993, p. 47, de Goeje, 2056.
[1112] Ṭabarī 1993, pp. 47–48, de Goeje, 2056–2057.
[1113] See our discussion on page 187.
[1114] See §3.2.3.

the Persians.[1115] The commander, Shīrzād, sued for peace and even requested to be allowed to retreat. Khālid granted his request. As Sayf's prior report had insisted, during this time Bahman Jādhūyih continued to lead the isolated war efforts of the Sasanians against the Arabs. It is to this chief commander, Bahman Jādhūyih therefore, that Shīrzād returned only to be reprimanded by him for his cowardice.[1116]

The battle of ʿAyn Tamr

The context of the subsequent battle of ʿAyn Tamr tallies best with the short period during which Shahrvarāz was in power (Muharram–Safar 9 AH/April–June 630).[1117] After the battle of Anbār, Khālid proceeded to ʿAyn Tamr, which was defended by a Parthian Mihrānid, called Mihrān b. Bahrām Jūbīn, clearly a descendent of Bahrām-i Chūbīn. Blankinship notes that this "would be a son of Bahrām-i Chūbīn," but objects that "in view of the fact the rebellion was put down and its adherents executed, *it is unlikely that anyone from this family would reemerge as a commander of a frontier garrison at this late date*[!]" He therefore dismisses this as "*another case of Sayf's adorning his reports with invented personages of illustrious ancestry*."[1118] Enough has been said here about the agnatic structure of the dynastic families to put Blankinship's remark in its proper context: Mihrān-i Bahrām-i Chūbīn was in all probability a direct descendent of the Parthian dynastic rebel Bahrām-i Chūbīn. The Arab tribes of Namir, the Christian Taghlib, and the Iyād reportedly encouraged Mihrān to leave this war to them,[1119] to which he agreed. But Mihrān together with his Arab allies were defeated at the battle of ʿAyn Tamr. Since Mihrāns were now commanding the war front, it is very likely that it was, in fact, Shahrvarāz who had sent them.[1120]

The battle of Firāḍ

The next significant Sasanian chronological indicator comes in the account of the battle of Firāḍ, where the Persian, Byzantines, and some Arab tribes joined

[1115] Ṭabarī 1993, p. 50, de Goeje, 2060.

[1116] Ṭabarī 1993, pp. 50–51, de Goeje, 2060. Ibn al-Athīr, however, lists Shīrzād's activities under the battle of Kaskar (see page 212 below). Ibn al-Athīr 1862, p. 206.

[1117] As we have seen, Heraclius and Shahrvarāz met in July 629, but Shahrvarāz's forces had already began evacuation of the occupied territories in June 629. Sebeos 1999, p. 223. The Byzantines defeated the Muslims in September 629 CE, at the battle of Mutʿah in Syria. Kaegi 1992, p. 67. How this fits into the schema of affairs remains to be assessed.

[1118] Ṭabarī 1993, p. 53, n. 289.

[1119] Ṭabarī 1993, p. 53, nn. 291–292, de Goeje, 2062. See also footnote 928.

[1120] Not much more can be said about the wars that are said to have taken place next, for very few Sasanian indicators are given. Although further research into the agnatic background of individuals appearing in these wars will probably clarify much. At the battle of Dūmat al-Jandal, the Persian commanders Rūzbih and Zarmihr were again joined by Arab tribes, while another Persian commander, Mahbūdhān, took part in the battle of Ḥuṣayd. In this latter war, both Zarmihr and Rūzbih were reportedly killed. Ṭabarī 1993, pp. 57–62, de Goeje, 2065–2069.

forces.[1121] Although traditionally believed to have been in 12 AH/633 CE, based on Sayf's *hijra* dating, we propose that it actually took place during Shahrvarāz's short reign. An attempted cooperation between the Byzantines and the Persians at this juncture of history is quite plausible,[1122] for Heraclius, we recall, had instigated the Mihrānid Shahrvaraz to usurp the throne, and had promised him manpower as well.[1123]

Sayf then recounts the battle of Yarmūk (in Syria) against the Byzantines, which he is said to have pushed two years earlier [!] to the year 13 of *hijra* (634). We shall not be concerned with the ways in which our newly constructed chronology of events affect our knowledge of the conquest of Syria. We turn, instead, to the continuation of Sayf's account on the early conquest of Iraq. The Sasanian chronological indicators in Sayf's narrative continue to fill in the gaps of the accounts that he has recently given: "The Persians ... found order, one year after Khālid had come to al-Ḥīra, a little after Khālid's departure, under the rule of Shahrvarāz b. Ardashīr b. Shahrīyār, one of the relatives of Kisrā, and then under Sābūr."[1124] Here, Sayf is actually referring to events during Shahrvarāz's reign, except that we are thrown off by the *hijra* dating interjection that Khālid had departed in 12 AH/634 CE. Significantly, when Sayf picks up his narrative here, the Arab commander in charge is not Khālid b. Walīd, but Muthannā b. Ḥāritha. Ibn al-Athīr notes that Muthannā came to Ḥīra after Khālid had left for Iraq.[1125]

Now Shahrvarāz sent a huge army against Muthannā, this time commanded by Hormozd Jādhūyih.[1126] The character of Hormozd Jādhūyih's army is quite significant: it was made up of mere "keepers of chickens and swine." The names of the putative commanders given are al-*Kawkabadh* and al-*Khūkbadh*, which are emended to al-Karukbadh and al-Kharukbadh by Ṭabarī's editor.[1127] The whole point of the story, however, is that Shahrvarāz's army was made up of mostly plebeian soldiers, as Muthannā observes, the rabble, who were "nothing but keepers of chickens and swine." *Kawkab* and *khuk* are in fact the Persian terms for chicken and swine respectively, and the suffix *badh* means a guardian

[1121] Among the tribes joining the Persian–Byzantine coalition, Ṭabarī mentions the Taghlib, the Iyād, and the Namir. Ṭabarī 1993, pp. 57–62, de Goeje, 2065–2068.

[1122] Because of the sorry state of the Byzantine armed forces at this juncture, it is likely that their aid could not have amounted to much, see Kaegi 1992, *passim*.

[1123] See footnote 961.

[1124] Ṭabarī 1993, p. 117, de Goeje, 2116. This Sābūr was most likely Shāpūr-i Shahrvarāz, the son of Shahrvarāz, whom we will discuss on page 204 below.

[1125] Ibn al-Athīr 1862, vol. 2, p. 415.

[1126] Ṭabarī 1993, p. 118, de Goeje, 2116. Ibn al-Athīr notes that the Iranian forces totaled 10,000 men. Ibn al-Athīr 1862, vol. 2, p. 415. It is possible that this Hormozd Jādhūyih is the father of Bahman Jādhūyih: according to Khayyāṭ, Bahman Jādhūyih was the son of Khorhormuzmān Dhu 'l-Ḥājib, and according to Dīnawarī, Mardānshāh was the son of Hormoz. Khayyāṭ 1977, p. 124. Fred M. Donner in fact suggested in a private correspondence that the substitution of Bahman Jādhūyih for Hormozd Jādhūyih could also involve a scribal error, the orthography of the names being very close in Arabic script. For an alternative conjecture, see footnote 1092.

[1127] Ṭabarī 1993, p. 118, nn. 637–638, de Goeje, 2117.

or a keeper. No need to emend here! Some knowledge of Persian, however, would have helped in distinguishing names of genuine historical figures from fictional or symbolic names, as is the case here.[1128] Now the meaning of this passage in the context of the factional rivalries becomes clear. Once he assumed power, ***and especially since he usurped power***, Shahrvarāz was left with very little support, as is evidenced by his short rule of three months. Apparently he was not able to bring to the war front enough manpower to put up a defense against the Arab armies; hence his use of the rabble and "groups of people ... *who [had] no knowledge of warfare.*"

Muthannā b. Ḥāritha and Shahrvarāz reportedly exchanged letters at this juncture. Shahrvarāz boasted to Muthannā: "I have sent against you an army consisting of the rabble of the Persians who are nothing but keepers of chickens and swine. I am not going to fight you except with them."[1129] Sayf then provides us with further significant internal indicators of factionalism. The Persians admonished Shahrvarāz: "You have encouraged our enemy against us by what you wrote to them. *When you write to anyone, consult [us first].*"[1130] Sayf informs us that Shahrvarāz was killed around the same time that Hormozd Jādhūyih was defeated,[1131] in June 630. Sayf's subsequent remark that after Shahrvarāz had died, "the Persians quarreled amongst themselves. The lands of the Sawād between the Tigris and Burs remained in the hand of the Muslims," indicates that he is here filling in the lacuna left in his previous accounts.[1132]

Būrāndukht's first regency

Then, Sayf maintains, after Shahrvarāz, "the Persians agreed ... on Dukht-i Zabān, the daughter of Kisrā, *but no order of hers was carried out.*"[1133] This Dukht-i Zabān is of course Būrāndukht, the first queen of the Persians. Two aspects of the Sasanian queens' regency will occupy us next, before we will return to the conquests: First we need to establish the sequence of the rules of Būrāndukht and Azarmīdukht, and next, we need to investigate what precisely transpired between the Pārsīg and the Pahlav factions. As we shall see, these two queries are related. Moreover, we need to assess the manner in which these *internal* processes affected the war efforts against the Arabs. Does Sayf's narrative on the processes unfolding in the Sasanian domains continue to betray an internal logic? Why would the Persians choose Būrāndukht but then refuse to obey her orders?

[1128]Ṭabarī 1993, p. 118, nn. 637–638.

[1129]Ṭabarī 1993, p. 118, de Goeje, 2117.

[1130]Ṭabarī 1993, p. 118, de Goeje, 2117.

[1131]Ṭabarī 1993, p. 120, de Goeje, 2119. According to Ibn al-Athīr, Hormozd Jādhūyih left the war front when Shahrvarāz was killed. Ibn al-Athīr 1862, vol. 2, p. 415.

[1132]According to Khalīfat b. Khayyāṭ, after the battle of Ullays, Khālid conquered Hurmuzjird and Bārusmā, after which he sent Muthannā toward the market of Baghdād [probably Anbār] in the year 10 AH. It is at this point that Khālid was sent to Syria where he attacked (*aghāra*) the Ghassanids in Marj al-Rāhiṭ. Khayyāṭ 1977, p. 119.

[1133]Ṭabarī 1993, p. 120, de Goeje, 2119.

Shāpūr-i Shahrvarāz

The continuation of Sayf's narrative provides crucial information that clarifies the situation: When Būrāndukht's orders were rejected, she was "*deposed*, and Sābūr b. Shahrbarāz was made king."[1134] Even more significant information is provided next. When Shāpūr-i Shahrvarāz became king, "al-Farrukhzādh b. al-Bindawān took charge of the affairs." It was from this Shāpūr-i Shahrvarāz that al-Farrukhzādh b. al-Bindawān asked for the hand of Azarmīdukht. Without doubt, al-Farrukhzādh b. al-Bindawān is actually Farrukh Hormozd, this being another one of the many instances that his name is confused with his son Farrukhzād's.[1135] We recall that all of our accounts agree that Farrukh Hormozd was the *minister* of Būrāndukht. He was the same figure who claimed to be the "leader of the people and the pillar of the country of Iran," and the same figure about whom our sources claim that "there was none greater ... [than him] among the Persians." As Būrāndukht held very little power, it is certain that she was promoted to the throne by Farrukh Hormozd and his faction, the Pahlav faction. While we do not have any coinage for Shāpūr-i Shahrvarāz, who vied for kingship after Būrāndukht's deposition, we can confirm nevertheless that he was a historical figure. Nonetheless, the Pārsīg, while willing to collaborate with the Mihrāns, had no intention of promoting once again one of them to Sasanian kingship, as is clear from Shahrvarāz's fate after usurping the throne. Therefore, if Shāpūr-i Shahrvarāz aspired to Sasanian kingship, he must have done so with very little support.

3.3.3 Azarmīdukht and the Pārsīg

Shāpūr-i Shahrvarāz's aspirations, however, were cut short and Azarmīdukht was raised to the throne with the aid of the Pārsīg faction. Numismatic evidence confirms her reign, sometime in 630–631 CE. According to Ṭabarī, Farrukh Hormozd then asked Shāpūr-i Shahrvarāz "to marry him to Azarmīdukht." Shāpūr-i Shahrvarāz obliged, but Azarmīdukht became angry, saying: "O cousin, would you marry me to my slave?" Whether the complicity of Shāpūr-i Shahrvarāz in Farrukh Hormozd's attempt at marrying Azarmīdukht is a spurious tradition or not, in folkloric garb Ṭabarī's narrative highlights a significant dimension of the dynastic struggles that were transpiring at this juncture: the dynastic faction of the late Shahrvarāz and his former army lent their support to Azarmīdukht,[1136] against the army of Azarbāyjān and its leaders, Farrukh Hormozd and his sons, who had supported Būrāndukht.

We must yet again recapitulate: after Shahrvarāz, Būrāndukht was promoted to the throne in 630 CE. Because her promotion was not agreed upon by all factions, however, she was *deposed*. The Mihrānid Shāpūr-i Shahrvarāz,

[1134] Ṭabarī 1993, p. 120, de Goeje, 2119.

[1135] However, the gentilitial connection to the Ispahbudhān Vindūyih is legitimate, as we have argued on page 187.

[1136] Thomson is therefore absolutely on the target when he makes this very assertion. Sebeos 1999, p. 225.

with or without the help of the Pārsīg, then attempted to fill in the vacant slot after Būrāndukht's deposition. But the Pahlav faction did not agree to this. So Azarmīdukht was made queen, sometime later in 630 CE. Then comes a crucial aspect of the regency of the Sasanian queens, Būrāndukht and Azarmīdukht. Here we finally realize why all our traditions, except for that of Sebeos, who is clearly in the wrong here, maintain that Farrukh Hormozd asked the hand of Azarmīdukht in marriage. Because Azarmīdukht was a Pārsīg candidate, the Pahlav leader Farrukh Hormozd, in asking for her hand, was trying to effect a *modus vivendi* with the Pārsīg faction. By marrying Azarmīdukht, he would have brought the two factions together. Our anecdotal tradition of Sayf also maintains that he sought to effect this union through the intermediary of the Mihrānid Shāpūr-i Shahrvarāz. Azarmīdukht, however, declined.

That Shāpūr-i Shahrvarāz was the cousin of Azarmīdukht is borne out by our evidence, underscoring the fact that, as the Ispahbudhān family had long-established familial ties with the Sasanians, so too did the Mihrāns, following an age-old tradition of marrying into the ruling Sasanian dynasty. A sister of Khusrow II carried the name Mihrān[1137] because she married into the Parthian Mihrān dynasty.[1138] The name of her husband is not given in the sources. However, if Shāpūr-i Shahrvarāz was the offspring of this marriage, thus making Azarmīdukht and Shāpūr-i Shahrvarāz cousins, then this sister of Khusrow II had actually married the powerful Parthian Mihrānid dynastic leader Shahrvarāz. In establishing Shahrvarāz as the *ērān-spāhbed* of Nīmrūz, therefore, Khusrow II had promoted his son-in-law to this important post.[1139]

Farrukh Hormozd as Hormozd V

After Azarmīdukht's refusal to marry Farrukh Hormozd, the latter no longer shied away from the throne itself. "Today I am the leader of the people and the pillar of the country of Iran," he claimed.[1140] And so, while Shāpūr-i Shahrvarāz's assumption of Sasanian kingship is subject to doubt, that of the Prince of the Medes, Farrukh Hormozd, is certain. All the evidence corroborates that the coinage of Hormozd V, minted in Stakhr in Fārs and Nihāvand in Media, belongs to Farrukh Hormozd, the Prince of the Medes.[1141] Furthermore, Farrukh Hormozd's attempt to co-opt Azarmīdukht in order to enhance his own

[1137] Christensen 1944, p. 109–110, n. 2 and p. 104 respectively. She is denoted by δ in the genealogical tree on page 471.

[1138] Justi 1895, p. 420.

[1139] Sebeos maintains that Queen Bor (Būrāndukht), that is to say, Khusrow II's daughter, rather than his sister, was Khoṙeam's (Shahrvarāz's) wife. Sebeos 1999, p. 89. Since our Arabic or Persian sources do not confirm this and, considering Sebeos' general confusion about the identities of the Sasanian queens, this account may be merely an echo of the marital relationships between the Sasanians and the Mihrāns.

[1140] Yaʿqūbi 1969, vol. 1, p. 197, Yaʿqūbi 1983, pp. 214–215.

[1141] Göbl, Robert, *Sasanian Numismatics*, New York, 1971 (Göbl 1971), p. 81. Incidentally, recall (see page 145) that Farrukhān, that is, Farrukh Hormozd himself, allegedly prognosticated this very feat: "I had a dream, and it was as if I saw myself on Kisrā's throne." Ṭabarī 1999, Ṭabarī 1999, pp. 327–328, de Goeje, 1008.

power—following the long established tradition of marriage alliance between the Ispahbudhān family and the Sasanians[1142]—is also reflected in numismatic evidence. For, among the coins of Azarmīdukht, who, according to various sources, ruled for a period ranging from four to six to sixteen months in 630–631, there is one, struck in the first regnal year, bearing the effigy of a man. Moshiri, who discovered and studied the coin, argued that the effigy belongs to Farrukh Hormozd, who came to power bearing the name Hormozd V and ruled *simultaneously* with Azarmīdukht for more than a year.[1143] All of our contextual evidence emphasizes that this was, indeed, the case. To the illustrious list of the Parthian dynasts who ascended the Sasanian throne, all during the last half century of Sasanian rule, therefore, the name of Farrukh Hormozd must be added. Like his predecessors, however, Farrukh Hormozd's attempt at usurping the Sasanian throne proved fatal, as is clear from Sayf's subsequent narrative.

This narrative bears out the complicity of another branch of the Mihrāns with the Pārsīg candidate, Azarmīdukht, against the Pahlav leader Farrukh Hormozd. Faced with the obduracy of the Prince of the Medes, Azarmīdukht allegedly solicited the aid of Sīyāvakhsh-i Rāzī from the house of Mihrān. The dynamic, needless to say, was probably the reverse of what is portrayed in our accounts. More likely it was Azarmīdukht who was under the control of the Mihrāns. According to Ṭabarī, this Sīyāvakhsh-i Rāzī, "who was one of the treacherous killers among the Persians," was the grandson of our famous Mihrānid rebel Bahrām-i Chūbīn.[1144] With the aid of Sīyāvakhsh-i Rāzī, Azarmīdukht subsequently killed Farrukh Hormozd.[1145] In search of a crown, therefore, the leader of the Pahlav lost his head, and thus ended the long career of the towering Parthian figure of Farrukh Hormozd, the Prince of the Medes, at the hand of the Mihrāns, who had joined the Pārsīg faction.

[1142] See page 110.

[1143] Moshiri, M.I., *Étude[s] de numismatique Iranienne sous les Sassanides*, vol. I, Tehran, 1972 (Moshiri 1972), pp. 11–16; Moshiri, M.I., *Étude[s] de numismatique Iranienne sous les Sassanides*, vol. II, Tehran, 1997 (Moshiri 1997), pp. 209–212, cited in Gignoux, Philippe, 'Āzarmīgduxt', in Ehsan Yarshater (ed.), *Encyclopaedia Iranica*, New York, 2007a (Gignoux 2007a), p. 190.

[1144] According to Blankinship, Sīyāvakhsh was "allegedly the grandson of the usurper Bahrām VI (590–591 CE) [i.e., Bahrām-i Chūbīn]. He *probably is yet another imaginary scion of a pre-Islamic house said to have been conquered by the Muslims in the early campaigns. Sayf improbably claims that he was the king of al-Rayy in 22/643 … His alleged father is mentioned above.*" Ṭabarī 1993, p. 120, n. 652. Emphasis added. We saw that his father, Mihrān-i Bahrām-i Chūbīn, was the Iranian commander during the battle of ʿAyn Tamr; see page 201. Below, during the conquest of Rayy in 651, we will encounter another progeny of Bahrām-i Chūbīn, called Sīyāvakhsh-i Mihrān-i Chūbīn, who was the ruler of Rayy; see §3.4.4. Sayf seems to imply that this is the same person as Sīyāvakhsh-i Rāzī (literally, Sīyāvakhsh from Rayy), but he then apparently contradicts himself by saying that the latter was killed by Rustam in 631. Justi also views these two figures as one and the same. Justi 1895, p. 300, n. 12.

[1145] Ṭabarī 1993, p. 120, de Goeje, 2119. This episode is also reported almost verbatim by Ibn al-Athīr 1862, vol. 2, pp. 415–416. Balʿamī calls Sīyāvakhsh-i Rāzī the commander of the army (*amīr-i ḥaras*). Balʿamī 1959, p. 259.

3.3.4 Būrāndukht and the Pahlav

The order of regency of the Sasanian queens that we have thus far established follows our conventional understanding of their chronology: after the murder of Shahrvarāz, Būrāndukht was placed on the throne, and once she was deposed and succeeded by the ephemeral interlude of Shāpūr-i Shahrvarāz, Azarmīdukht assumed power. In the process, Azarmīdukht's faction killed Farrukh Hormozd, the Pahlav leader. This is all fine and well. Except that this is not the end of the story of neither Azarmīdukht nor Būrāndukht, nor, for that matter, of the Ispahbudhān family of Farrukh Hormozd. For one thing, as was the case with other Parthian dynastic families, the murder of the scion of the Ispahbudhān house did not denote this Parthian dynastic family's loss of power. When the Pārsīg faction killed Farrukh Hormozd, his son Rustam in retribution killed the queen Azarmīdukht. Būrāndukht, meanwhile, *reappeared on the scene*. Indeed, all of our sources, except Sebeos, systematically connect the regency of Būrāndukht both to Farrukh Hormozd, whom she made her *minister*, and to his son, Rustam. We should recall, moreover, that while all of our sources emphasize the *deposition* of Būrāndukht and the *murder* of Azarmīdukht, none of them informs us of the fate of Būrāndukht after her initial deposition. In search of an answer, we continue our investigation of Sayf.

Sayf interrupts his account on the early conquest of Iraq, narrating the last days of the caliphate of Abū Bakr (634), the death of the latter, and other events pertaining to the first caliph, once more throwing us off with his Islamic chronological indicators.[1146] After a report on Muthannā b. Ḥāritha and Abū ʿUbayd,[1147] Sayf finally continues his narrative on the conquest of the Sawād with the battle of Namāriq under Muthannā,[1148] interposing almost forty-four pages,[1149] before the Persian narrative is picked up again.

Sayf's accounts of the wars in Ḥīra and the battle of Namāriq, as reported both in Ṭabarī and Ibn al-Athīr, coincide with the death of Abū Bakr and fall two years after the inception of Yazdgird III's rule, that is to say, in the year 13 AH/634 CE.[1150] Sayf, however, is reverting back to internal conditions in the Sasanian realm, which must be discussed before we deal with his conquest narrative.[1151] We stress, however, that the Sasanian chronological indicators are not referring to 13 AH/634 CE and the reign of Yazdgird III, but to the events after

[1146] Ṭabarī 1993, pp. 129–132, de Goeje, 2127–2129. Among the topics covered here we get, the ceremonies for Abū Bakr's burial, Ṭabarī 1993, pp. 133–138, de Goeje, 2129–2132; his appearances, Ṭabarī 1993, pp. 138–139, de Goeje, 2132–2133; his genealogy, Ṭabarī 1993, pp. 139–140, de Goeje, 2133–2134; his wives, Ṭabarī 1993, pp. 140–141, de Goeje, 2134–2135; his appointment of ʿUmar as successor, Ṭabarī 1993, pp. 145–153, de Goeje, 2137–2144; the caliphate of the latter, Ṭabarī 1993, pp. 157–158, de Goeje, 2144–2145; the expedition of Fiḥl, and finally, the conquest of Damascus and other regions, Ṭabarī 1993, pp. 159–173, de Goeje, 2145–2159.

[1147] Ṭabarī 1993, pp. 173–176, de Goeje, 2159–2162.

[1148] Ṭabarī 1993, p. 176, de Goeje, 2163.

[1149] In the translated version, and thirty-four in the de Goeje's edition.

[1150] Ṭabarī 1993, p. 177, de Goeje, 2163.

[1151] We will pick up the narrative with the battle of Namāriq on page 211 below.

Azarmīdukht's murder at the hand of Rustam in 631: "As often as the *people* would quarrel among themselves, *Būrān bt. Kisrā would act as an honest* arbiter *until they composed their differences.*"[1152] The context of this sudden reappearance of Būrāndukht is further elaborated: When "*Farrukhzād b. al-Binduwān [i.e., Farrukh Hormozd] was slain, and Rustam came forward to kill Azarmīdukht, … [Būrāndukht] acted as an arbiter until she brought forth Yazdgird III.*"[1153] The significant information that Sayf provides for us here, therefore, is that Būrāndukht was *still alive after Azarmīdukht was killed by Rustam* and that she acted as an *arbiter* among the quarreling parties. In other words, Būrāndukht, who had been put forward by the Pahlav faction under the leadership of the Ispahbudhān, eventually retrieved her status after overcoming the momentary ascension of her sister Azarmīdukht, who was supported by the Pārsīg faction. We therefore propose the following succession of the two queens: Būrāndukht—Azarmīdukht—Būrāndukht.[1154]

Būrāndukht's coinage during her first regency

A recent reassessment of the numismatic evidence for Būrāndukht's rule confirms our analysis.[1155] Malek and Curtis have argued that while "various traditions differ as to the length of her [i.e., Būrāndukht's] reign, ranging from six months to two years, … it is likely that she reigned for a little more than a year and perhaps the 1 year and 4 months referred to in a number of texts." This, they argue, "is consistent with numismatic evidence."[1156] To support their argument, Malek and Curtis analyze the coinage of Būrāndukht struck for years 1 to 3 of her rule. The Sasanians "dated their coins in accordance with regnal and not calendar years. Regnal years were [, in turn,] based on the New Year, … [since] the New Year in AD 629 fell on 17 June 629 this is likely to have been before Bōrān came to the throne. Her coins *from regnal year 1 would [therefore] cover the period up to 16 June 630* and those of regnal year 2 would cover 17 June 630 to 16 June 631. Regnal year 3 would have started on 17 June 631."[1157] Significantly, they conclude that while the "numismatic evidence cannot definitively assist in considering the precise dates of Bōrān's reign, … it points to her reign as having started in the year 17 June 629 to 16 June 630 … [Būrāndukht's reign] in all probability … *spanned 629 and 630*

[1152] Ṭabarī 1993, p. 176, de Goeje, 2163.

[1153] Ṭabarī 1993, p. 176, de Goeje, 2163.

[1154] It is also possible that for some period the two sisters ruled simultaneously, rather than sequentially.

[1155] Curtis, Vesta Sarkhosh and Malek, H.M., 'History of the Sasanian Queen Boran (AD 629–631)', *Numismatic Chronicle* 158, (1998), pp. 113–129 (Curtis and Malek 1998), pp. 113–129. We should also recall that at some point during the reign of Azarmīdukht, Farrukh Hormozd imprinted his own effigy on Azarmīdukht's coins. Also see Daryaee, Touraj, 'The Coinage of Queen Bōrān and its Significance for Late Sasanian Imperial Ideology', *Bulletin of the Asia Institute* 13, (1999), pp. 1–6 (Daryaee 1999).

[1156] Curtis and Malek 1998, pp. 115–116.

[1157] Curtis and Malek 1998, pp. 123.

and it is conceivable that it went into 631."[1158] Contrary to the assumption of the late Nöldeke, during whose time most of these coins had not yet been discovered,[1159] this recent numismatic evidence indicates that Būrāndukht started minting coins sometime between June 629 and June 630. However, we need to amend Malek and Curtis's argument here slightly. We recall that Ardashīr III was killed on 17 April 630 and Shahrvarāz on 6 June 630, and so Būrāndukht's regency was only accepted by all parties in late June 630. Hence the coins she had been minting in the year 1 were already in opposition to Ardashīr III, before she was officially ruling. This is confirmed by Sayf's remark that Būrāndukht "*was an opponent of Shīrā [i.e., Ardashīr III*[1160]*] for a year*."[1161] Her opposition to Ardashīr III also makes sense in view of the factional struggle during this period, when the Nīmrūzī faction had abandoned the Pārsīg–Pahlav alliance that had brought Ardashīr III to power and conspired with Shahrvarāz to topple the child king.[1162] In response, the Pahlav must have started promoting her regency already during that period. This is remarkably confirmed by her coinage, as almost all of the identifiable mints belong to Pahlav regions: six from Āmul (AM), one from Nīshāpūr (APL), two from Gurgān or Qum (GW), and two from Rayy (LD).[1163] As we will establish below,[1164] Būrāndukht's second regency, after the murder of Azarmīdukht by Rustam, lasted until Yazdgird III came to the throne in June 632. This, too, is in perfect accord with the findings of Malek and Curtis: Būrāndukht's regnal year 3 was from June 631 to June 632.[1165]

[1158] Curtis and Malek 1998, p. 123.

[1159] Nöldeke 1879, p. 433, Nöldeke 1979, p. 641.

[1160] Ardashīr III was also known as Ardashīr-i Shīrūyih Qubād, whence Sayf's mention of his name as simply Shīrā. It is unlikely that he actually meant Shīrūyih Qubād here, for the latter died sometime in 628.

[1161] Ṭabarī 1993, p. 177, de Goeje, 2163.

[1162] See §3.2.3.

[1163] We also have 18 coins of a mint called WYHC. As Malek and Curtis have argued, the WYHC mint "represents a major mint in the late Sasanian period, but its attribution is still to be conclusively established." Numismatists have proposed various places: Veh-az-Amid-Kavād (Arrajān, in Fārs); Veh Ardashīr (Southern Iraq); Visp-shad-Husrav (Media); Nishābuhr (Nīshāpūr, in Khurāsān). "The importance of this mint" under Būrāndukht, Malek and Curtis argue, "is reinforced by the number of drachms of regnal year 1 and the fact that the only bronze coins of Bōrān are from this mint." Curtis and Malek 1998, pp. 119–125. In view of what has been argued in this work, the location of this mint would most likely be found in the Pahlav territories, and so we suggest reading WYHC as Visp-shad-Husrav in Media. I cannot explain the existence of the two mints from Kirmān (KL). The two from Herāt (HL), however, might be explained by the fact that the Kārins seem to have had a base there (recall that the Kārinid Zarmihr was given control over Zābulistān by Khusrow I as reward for the Kārin's aid in the war against the Khāqān of the Turks; see page 113). At any rate, these anomalies could also be explained by the existence of petty factions that had joined the ranks of the Pahlav in their support of Būrāndukht.

[1164] See pages 210ff and 218ff.

[1165] For the continuation of our discussion of Būrāndukht's coinage, see page 217ff below.

Azarmīdukht's deposition and murder

Sayf maintains that after Azarmīdukht had become queen and after Sīyāvakhsh-i Rāzī had killed Farrukh Hormozd, "the Persians disputed amongst themselves and were diverted from the Muslims, *during the whole absence of Muthannā b. Ḥāritha*, until he came back from Medina." The deposed queen Būrāndukht then reappears in Sayf's account: when Muthannā returned from Medina, Būrāndukht sent "the news to Rustam and urged him to set out."[1166] At this point, Rustam "was in charge of the Khurāsān frontier and advanced until he stopped at al-Madā'in." On his way back from Khurāsān, Rustam "defeated every army of Azarmīdukht that he met." He then besieged Ctesiphon, where he defeated and killed Sīyāvakhsh. After capturing the capital, he blinded Azarmīdukht and established Būrāndukht in her stead.[1167]

Būrāndukht's second regency

Rustam's rise to power occurred during the rule of Būrāndukht, *after the murder of Azarmīdukht.* He took the place of his father, Farrukh Hormozd, and became the most important figure in Būrāndukht's realm—more important even than the queen herself, who is referred to as a mere *arbiter*. According to Sayf, Būrāndukht invited Rustam "to manage the affairs of the Persians, *whose weakness and decline she complained about to him*."[1168] Befitting the pretensions of his father, Rustam set up conditions for his family's continued collaboration with the Sasanian queen Būrāndukht: the queen should "entrust him [i.e., Rustam] with the rule for ten years," at which point sovereignty would return "to the family of Kisrā if they found any of their male offspring, and if not, then to their women." Būrāndukht accepted these conditions. She summoned the governors (*marāzibah*), that is, the other factions involved, the most important of which was the Pārsīg umbrella faction, and declared that Rustam would be "in charge of the armed forces of Persia ... There [would be] *no one above you save God ... Your judgment is applicable to them [i.e., the marāzibah] as long as it leads to the protection of their land and their being united rather than divided.*" Persia, therefore, Sayf concludes, submitted to Rustam after the coming of Abū ʿUbayd.[1169] Finally, under the sovereignty of Rustam, after he had killed Azarmīdukht, with Būrāndukht as the arbiter, the Pahlav and all the other factions agreed to cooperate. That the Pārsīg comprised the most important other faction is corroborated by other sources. Yaʿqūbī specifically confirms this: when

[1166] Ṭabarī 1993, p. 177, de Goeje, 2163.

[1167] Ṭabarī 1993, p. 177, de Goeje, 2163. Balʿamī 1959, p. 261. Some traditions maintain that the queen was poisoned. Ṭabarī 1999, pp. 406–407, de Goeje, 1065.

[1168] Ṭabarī 1993, p. 177, de Goeje, 2163–2164.

[1169] Ṭabarī 1993, p. 177, de Goeje, 2164. Ṭabarī also contains a variant narrative about Azarmīdukht, Shāpūr-i Shahrvarāz, Farrukhzād, and Rustam: after Shahrvarāz, Būrāndukht, rendered as Shah-i Zanān in the text, "held sovereign power until they agreed on Shāpūr-i Shahrvarāz." Azarmīdukht then rose in opposition to the Mihrānid contender Shāpūr-i Shahrvarāz, and killed him as well as Farrukh Hormozd. The news of this was given to Rustam, who was in charge of the Khurāsān frontier, by Būrāndukht. Ṭabarī 1993, p. 178, de Goeje, 2165.

"ʿUmar—naturally we shall ignore the Islamic signifier here—sent Abū ʿUbayd ..., together with an army to the aid of Muthannā b. Ḥāritha, ... Būrāndukht had assumed kingship and had installed Rustam *and Fīrūzān* ... in charge of the affairs of the kingdom."[1170] Fīrūzān, we recall, was one of the leaders of the Pārsīg faction.[1171] The agreement of the Pārsīg to collaborate with the Pahlav, moreover, was precipitated not only by the fact that, in Būrāndukht's words, Persia was in a state of weakness and decline,[1172] when already during the rule of Shahrvarāz "*from the Arab [regions] strong winds were blowing*,"[1173] but also as a result of the fact that, temporarily at least, their Mihrānid accomplices had been defeated by Rustam. As Sayf's account underscores and as the subsequent course of the war efforts of the Sasanians betrays, however, this collaboration of the Pārsīg with the Pahlav was effected under unequal conditions, because Rustam had assumed a substantial share of power in the Sasanian–Parthian confederacy under the arbitership of Būrāndukht.

We have therefore answered our initial questions regarding the two Sasanian queens. The order of rule of these queens was: Būrāndukht, Azarmīdukht, Būrāndukht—and for part of their candidacy they might have ruled in fact contemporaneously. Each was promoted by a different faction: Būrāndukht by the Pahlav, and Azarmīdukht by the Pārsīg. During the second term of Būrāndukht's regency, the Pahlav and the Pārsīg, under the respective leadership of Rustam and Fīrūzān, began to cooperate. It is time, therefore, to turn our attention again to the war front.

The battle of Namāriq

The immediate subsequent accounts given by Sayf have some points of interest for us, even though they are provided in a disjointed fashion. We will not be concerned with establishing a detailed sequence of these events.[1174] According to Sayf, when Muthannā b. Ḥāritha arrived in al-Ḥīra, he stayed there for fifteen nights. Rustam, meanwhile, summoned the *dihqāns* of al-Sawād. Most of the Iranian commanders appearing in the battle of Namāriq and the subsequent battle of Kaskar, however, belong to the Pahlav faction. Rustam sent Jābān[1175] and Narsī[1176] to the region. Jābān's two wings were under the command of

---

[1170] Yaʿqūbi 1983, p. 25, Yaʿqūbi 1969, vol. 2, p. 161:

و كان عمر قد بعث ابا عبيد بن مسعود الثقفى فى جيش مع المثنى بن حارثه الشيبانى الى العراق و كان كسرى قد توفى و قامت بوران ابنته بالملك و صيرت رستم و الفيروزان القيمين بامر الملك.

[1171] See pages 174ff and 196ff.

[1172] Ṭabarī 1993, p. 177, de Goeje, 2164.

[1173] Thaʿālibī 1900, p. 731, Thaʿālibī 1989, p. 465.

[1174] As Donner notes the "exact sequence of these raids cannot ... be reconstructed with any precision." Donner 1981, p. 192. But see nevertheless our provisional reconstructed chronological table on page 468.

[1175] The general who also fought at battle of Ullays and the battle of Maqr; see pages 195ff and 198ff.

[1176] The brother of the Ardashīr III's minister Māhādharjushnas; see footnotes 1061 and 1183.

Jushnasmāh,[1177] and Mardānshāh.[1178] In the battle of Namāriq, Jushnasmāh is killed and Jābān defeated. Ibn al-Athīr maintains that Mardānshāh also fell at this battle.[1179]

The battle of Kaskar

In the battle of Kaskar, which is reported next, the defeated Persians took refuge with Narsī. At the news of the defeat at the battle of Namāriq, Rustam and Būrāndukht ordered Narsī: "[go] off to your estate and protect it from your enemy and our enemy. Be a man."[1180] In the battle of Kaskar, Narsī's two flanks were "commanded by the two sons of his maternal uncle, who were the two sons of the uncle of Kisrā, Bindūyah [i.e., Vindūyih] and Tīrūyah [i.e., Tīrūyih], the two sons of Bisṭām [i.e., Vistāhm]."[1181] This, therefore, was an Ispahbudhān dynastic army, which was, quite appropriately, brought into the field by the Parthian Rustam.[1182] Moreover, Narsī, as Sayf informs us, "was the son of Kisrā's maternal aunt and Kaskar was [in fact] an estate of his."[1183] The powers of Narsī are described next. Narsī would protect his estates, "neither did humanity eat [of] it, *nor did anyone plant it besides them or the king of Persia ...* for this property was a protected reserve (*ḥimā*)."[1184] The generals leading Narsī's two flanks, Vistāhm's sons Vindūyih and Tīrūyih, were the two "sons of his [Narsī's] maternal uncle, who were [in turn] the two sons of the uncle of Kisrā [i.e., Khusrow II]."[1185] Māhādharjushnas, Ardashīr III's minister, furthermore, was a brother of Narsī, and was already killed by Shahrvarāz in 630.[1186] The close association that the names of the members of a dynastic family must have had, explains probably his posthumous presence on the battlefield in Sayf's narrative.[1187] Although Blankinship recognized these familial connections, he

[1177]See page 212 below, explaining this posthumous appearance of Jushnasmāh, i.e., Māhādharjushnas.

[1178]It is quite unlikely that this Mardānshāh is the Pārsīg leader Bahman Jādhūyih; see page 213 below. Also see Blankinship's notes on these, Ṭabarī 1993, nn. 903–904.

[1179]Ibn al-Athīr 1862, vol. 2, p. 435.

[1180]Ṭabarī 1993, p. 182, de Goeje, 2168.

[1181]Ṭabarī 1993, p. 183, n. 923, de Goeje, 2169.

[1182]See §3.3.1 for the Ispahbudhān, and page 471 for a genealogical tree of this family.

[1183]This maternal aunt is a sister of Vistāhm and Vindūyih, marked γ in our reconstructed genealogical tree on page 471.

[1184]In an interesting side note in Balʿamī's narrative, the author informs us that it was Khusrow II Parvīz who had given the villages of Kaskar to Narsī as a fief (*iqṭāʾ*), and that Narsī had been ruling these for 10 years. Balʿamī 1959, p. 286. Because these wars were being fought during the second term of Būrāndukht, probably in 631, Khusrow II's grant of Kaskar to Narsī must have been around 621 at the height of Khusrow II's victory against the Byzantines. Morony, however, dates this to 624 CE. Morony 1984, p. 186.

[1185]See footnote 1183 above.

[1186]See page 181.

[1187]Morony notes that the Parthian dynastic family under Narsī also had royal lineage. Morony 1984, pp. 185–186, n. 27. In any case, the familial ties of the Ispahbudhān to the Sasanians had a long history. Recall to this effect for instance Qubād's marriage with Aspebedes' sister discussed on page 110. For a reconstruction of Narsī's family, see also the family tree on page 471.

objected: "As this Bisṭām [Vistāhm] fought against Khusrow II for ten years (circa 591–601 CE) in a devastating civil war for the Persian crown, [however,] *it is not likely that any of Bisṭām's relatives would enjoy later prominence, least of all his sons, especially as there is no mention of this family after 601* CE, *except in the reports of Sayf b. ʿUmar*[1188] *... this is another instance of Sayf adorning his reports with claimed descendants of defunct pre-Islamic noble houses.*"[1189]

In line with their earlier cooperation with the Pahlav and the Pārsīg in toppling Khusrow II, an Armenian contingent also joined Rustam's war efforts. For, as Sayf maintains, when the news of Jaban and Narsī's imminent defeat was brought to Rustam and Būrandukht, they sent Jālīnūs to their aid.[1190] Jālīnūs "was commanded to begin by Narsī [, i.e., presumably aiding Narsī] and then to fight Abū ʿUbayd." Narsī and his followers hoped that Jālīnūs would "get to them before the battle."[1191] But Abū ʿUbayd "hastened against him [i.e., Narsī], leading his army off before al-Jālīnūs had drawn near ... [and so] God defeated the Persians [and] Narsī fled."[1192] In the engagement that followed, the Muslims defeated Jālīnūs as well, and the latter fled.[1193] How wholeheartedly Jālīnūs sought to engage the Arabs is not clear, but Sayf's subsequent remarks indicate that Jālīnūs's efforts were reserved. The numbers under his command might have also been exaggerated. What finally led to the defeat of the Pahlav forces that Rustam had sent to the war front, therefore, cannot be ascertained with any degree of certainty. Perhaps, as Donner puts it, the fact that the Arab forces had fanned out in the agricultural heartland of central Iraq had something to do with this.[1194] It is equally important to note, however, that, except for the Armenian contingent of Jālīnūs, who arrived too late, at any rate, the forces that were brought to bear in these wars comprised only the Pahlav faction. Without a doubt, the general Mardānshāh in Narsī's army was not the Pārsīg leader Bahman Jādhūyih Dhu 'l-Ḥājib,[1195] for it was only after Jālīnūs, too, was defeated, that Rustam brought in the Pārsīg faction, and cemented his collaboration with the Pārsīg forces under the leadership of Bahman Jādhūyih and Fīrūzān, leading to one of the only Persian victories against the Arabs: the battle of Bridge.

[1188]For a rebuttal of this particular objection of Blankinship, see page 462 below.

[1189]Ṭabarī 1993, p. 183, n. 923.

[1190]For Jālīnūs' possible identity, see footnote 846.

[1191]Ṭabarī 1993, p. 183, de Goeje, 2169. Jālīnūs is said to have brought to the front 20,000 men. Ibid., p. 183, n. 923; Balʿamī 1959, p. 287 and pp. 185–186.

[1192]Ṭabarī 1993, p. 183, de Goeje, 2169.

[1193]Ṭabarī 1993, p. 186, de Goeje, 2172.

[1194]Donner 1981, p. 192.

[1195]See page 196ff. Recall that according to Sayf, this general Mardānshāh died at the battle of Namāriq, whereas Bahman Jādhūyih only died in 642, at the battle of Iṣfahān; see page 247ff.

3.3.5 The battle of Bridge

The battle of Bridge[1196] may serve as the quintessential episode of Sasanian history illustrating both the strengths and weaknesses of the dynasty's four centuries of rule. While the failure of the Iranian war efforts thus far can be attributed to many factors, one of the most important of which was the Pārsīg-Pahlav debacle, there is no doubt that a paramount cause of the Iranian victory over the Arabs in the battle of Bridge—a victory that was never again repeated—was the unprecedented agreement between the Pārsīg and the Pahlav to forge an alliance under queen Būrāndukht, the arbiter.

The Pārsīg and the Pahlav

The unique articulation of this paradigmatic dimension of Sasanian history, that is, the crucial centrality of the Pahlav and Pārsīg terms of identity, is only explicitly stated by Sayf and, based on Sayf, by Ibn al-Athīr. Recounting the conquest of the Sawād, Ibn al-Athīr pauses to inform the reader about the internal turmoil that had swallowed up Iran during this period. "At this time, the people [of Iran] had divided into two groups: The *fahlawaj* [Pahlav] were supporting Rustam, while the inhabitants of Fārs (*ahl-i fārs*) were backing Fīruzān."[1197] What we have here, therefore, is a direct confirmation of one of the central theses of this study: the over-arching Pārsīg–Pahlav dimension of the Sasanian polity throughout their reign, and especially during the period examined in the course of this investigation. Sayf and Ibn al-Athīr, however, continue to maintain the untenable *hijra*–Sasanian chronological indicators, claiming that the battle of Bridge took place during Būrāndukht's regency (630–632), but maintaining at the same time that this was the year 13 of *hijra* (634). The chronology of the battle of Bridge, therefore, is one of the many examples of the chronological discrepancies which we have mentioned before, and all, including Blankinship, have remarked on.

We also find the above account in Ṭabarī's description of the battle of Bridge.[1198] Based on a faulty reading, however, this incredible piece of information on late Sasanian history is rendered meaningless in the recent translation of Ṭabarī's opus. To begin with, in two different translations, the term *fahlawaj*, the obvious Arabicized version of the Middle Persian term *Pahlav*, has been rendered as *al-Fahlūj*. Under the account of the battle of Bridge, therefore, we get the following translation, which curiously and, as we shall see, justifiably,

---

[1196] Also called the battle of Quss, al-Qarqus, Quss al-Nāṭif, or al-Mawaḥah.

[1197] Ibn al-Athīr 1862, vol. 2, p. 440:

و اراد بهمن جاذويه العبور خلف المسلمين فأتاه الخبر با اختلاف الفرس و انهم قد ثاروا برستم و نقضوا الذى بينهم و بينه و صاروا فرقتين: الفهلوج على رستم و اهل فارس على الفيروزان

[1198] Ṭabarī 1993, p. 188, de Goeje, 2174–2176:

و بينا اهل فارس يحاولون العبور أتاهم الخبر ان الناس با لمدائن قد ثاروا برستم و نقضوا الذى بينهم و بينه فصاروا فرقتين الفهلوج على رستم و اهل فارس على فيروزان·

includes a twist that appears in Sayf's narrative, but not in Ibn al-Athīr's version: "When the Persians were trying to cross [the Euphrates during the battle of Bridge], the news came to them that the people of Madā'in had revolted *against* Rustam, breaking that which was between them and him. *They became two parties*, al-Fahlūj [sic] *against Rustam* and the Persians *against al-Fayrūzān*." In Sayf's narrative, therefore, we also get the dichotomous division of the people of Madā'in into two parties, the *fahlawaj* and the Persians. Why, however, does Sayf here maintain that the Pahlav had revolted *against* Rustam, their leader, and that the *ahl-i fārs* had gathered in *opposition* to Fīrūzān? We shall attempt an answer to this later in this section. For now we should note the following: In the index to the translation of Ṭabarī the term *al-Fahlūj* (i.e., *fahlawaj*) is described as a party or ethnic group. A note explains that the term is "[d]efined in Ṭabarī, I, 2608,[1199] as the people from between al-Bāb [Darband] and Ḥulwān in the region of al-Jibāl in western Iran." As we know by now, of course, the term Pahlav denotes a considerably larger territory than that delimited here by Ṭabarī. The only reason Ṭabarī restricts his definition to the inhabitants of the Jibāl in the aforementioned section is that, in this case, he is relating the account of the future battle of Nihāvand[1200] squarely within the Jibāl region.[1201] The correct reading of this term, once again, is *not Fahlūj* but *fahlawaj* (Pahlav).[1202] Blankinship, however, is correct in considering the term as a party or ethnic group. For in fact Pahlav, as we have argued extensively through the course of this study, refers to the ethnicon of the Parthians who, through the course of the Sasanian history, consciously maintained their identity.

There is very little doubt, although the precise details await further research, that the Persīs–Parthian (*ahl-i fārs–fahlawaj*) division, unique to Sayf's accounts as reconstructed both in Ṭabarī and Ibn al-Athīr, comprised, *on a very broad level*, a regional division as well: the quarters of the south and west versus the quarters of the north and east. This regional division comes across quite clearly in Ṭabarī's account on the battle of Nihāvand, to be discussed in more detail shortly. When the Sasanian monarch, here correctly maintained to be Yazdgird III, is said to have issued a call for making a stance vis-à-vis the Arab armies in Nihāvand, Ṭabarī maintains that thus, "one after the other, there arrived those living in the territory between Khurāsān and Ḥulwān, those living in the territory between al-Bāb [i.e., Darband] and Ḥulwān, and those living in the territory between Sijistān [i.e., Sīstān] and Ḥulwān." Ṭabarī's account goes on to summarize these groupings: "The cavalry of *Fārs and of the Fahlūj [sic], the inhabitants of al-Jibāl joined forces*."[1203] In a second configuration, immediately

[1199] de Goeje, 2608.

[1200] See page 241ff.

[1201] Ṭabarī 1993, p. 189, n. 945, de Goeje, 2176.

[1202] Ṭabarī 1989a, p. 193, de Goeje, 2608. Under the *fahlawaj*, Juynboll notes that "he has not found another reference to" these. He gives however, a reference to Schwartz, Paul, *Iran im Mittelalter nach den arabischen Geographen*, Leipzig, 1896 (Schwartz 1896), p. 829. Ṭabarī 1989a, p. 193, n. 657.

[1203] Ṭabarī 1989a, p. 193, de Goeje, 2608.

following this, Ṭabarī makes this dichotomous territorial division even more lucid: "Those hailing from [1a] the *territory between Bāb (al-Abwāb) and Ḥulwān* numbered thirty thousand troops, those hailing from [1b] the *territory between Khurāsān and Ḥulwān* numbered sixty thousand, and those hailing from [2a] the *territory between Sijistān and Fārs* and [2b] *Ḥulwān*, numbered sixty thousand."[1204] If one were to conceptualize this division schematically, one would see that it roughly corresponds to the quadripartition into *kūsts* implemented during the rule of Khusrow I Nowshīrvān. A corrective to the four-fold territorial division given here by Ṭabarī is that the first area [1a], between Darband (Bāb) and Ḥulwān, naturally included Armenia with a number of its dynastic factions which were fighting the Arabs alongside the Iranians. Furthermore, because this is a description of the battle of Nihāvand, it naturally excludes the Sawād and Mesopotamian territories of the Sasanian empire, which had already been conquered by the Arabs in the battle of Qādisiya.[1205] As we shall see later on as well—and we are jumping ahead of our narrative here[1206]—by the time the battle of Nihāvand took place the Parthian general Rustam had already died at the battle of Qādisiya. Thus the army command at this point was taken over by the Pārsīg leader, Fīrūzān: "[and] they all set out to him [Fīrūzān], one after the other."[1207]

It is a testimony to the reliability of the secondary and tertiary sources for Sasanian studies, that this incredible, crucial, piece of information provided by Sayf, that is, the existence of a split between the Pahlav and the Pārsīg factions, is corroborated by our primary sources, namely by the recently discovered seals examined in this study, where, as we have seen, some of the *ērān-spāhbeds* on these seals insist on their affiliation as a Parthian *aspbed*, *aspbed-i pahlaw*,[1208] while others identify themselves as *aspbed-i Pārsīg*,[1209] that is, Persian *aspbed*. The terminology that they adopt for rendering this ethnic division, furthermore, is Pahlav, *fahlaw* or *fahlawaj*, and *Pārsīg*, what in Sayf's narrative has been rendered as *ahl-i fārs* (the people of Fārs).

The battle of Bridge

Let us return to our narrative on the battle of Bridge. Rustam's recognition of the Pārsīg's prowess is reflected in Sayf's subsequent narrative. After Jālīnūs was defeated at the battle of Kaskar and had returned to Rustam, the latter

[1204]With the numbers given here we are naturally not concerned, although as a ratio of the forces brought to the field by the two factions, these too might be revealing. Ṭabarī 1989a, p. 193, de Goeje, 2608.

[1205]So with these amendments, the above regional division roughly corresponds to the Pahlav regions [1a] of the *kūst-i ādurbādagān* and [1b] of the *kūst-i khwarāsān*, and the Pārsīg regions [2a] of the *kūst-i nēmrōz* and [2b] of the *kūst-i khwarbarān*.

[1206]See §3.4.3.

[1207]Ṭabarī 1989a, p. 193, de Goeje, 2608.

[1208]Gyselen 2001a, seal 1b of a figure called Dād-Burz-Mihr, p. 36, and the personal seal of this same figure, seal A, p. 46. See also the table on page 470.

[1209]Gyselen 2001a, seal 2c, p. 39, and the personal seal of this same figure, seal B, p. 46.

asked: "which of the Persians is the strongest in fighting the Arabs in your opinion?" He was directed to the Pārsīg leader Bahman Jādhūyih,[1210] whom he then put in charge of the Armenian faction. The chain of command that he established, moreover, reveals the friction between him and the Armenian dynasts. For Rustam ordered Bahman Jādhūyih thusly: if Jālīnūs "*returns to the like of his defeat*, then cut off his head."[1211] Befitting his status, Bahman Jādhūyih was given the Great Standard (*derafsh-i Kāvīyān*).[1212] In giving us a folkloric etymology for this general's epithet Dhu 'l-Ḥājib, Ibn al-Athīr highlights the seniority of Bahman Jādhūyih, maintaining that he was such an old man that he was forced to keep his eyebrows somehow maintained upwards in order to see in front of his own steps.[1213]

Thus, the Pārsīg leader Bahman Jādhūyih, under the tacitly acknowledged leadership of the Pahlav leader Rustam, commanded 30,000 of the grandees of the *ʿajam* at the battle of Bridge,[1214] defeating the Arab armies in battle. Although Ṭabarī dates this event to 13 AH/634CE, in a flagrant chronological invention, there is little doubt that the battle of Bridge was, in fact, fought *during the second term of Būrāndukht's regency*,[1215] after the murder of Azarmīdukht, when the Pahlav and the Pārsīg factions finally joined forces under the supreme command of Rustam sometime in 630–631, and not, as hitherto believed, in 634–635 CE.

Būrāndukht's coinage during her second regency

Significantly, Būrāndukht's coinage of the second and third year of her reign, and not of the first year, when most of the mints are from Pahlav lands,[1216] reflects the Pārsīg acceptance of her regency. For it is only for the second and third year that we have found numerous coins minted in Sīstān, Khuzistān, and Fārs,[1217] regions under the control of the Pārsīg. The number of coins found for Būrāndukht minted in Sīstān (SK) during these two years is amazing: 44 for her second regnal year and 59 for her third.[1218] There is no doubt, therefore, that once Būrāndukht assumed power after the murder of Azarmīdukht, the Pārsīg of the quarters of the south recognized her authority and joined forces with the Pahlav, the original faction to promote the queen, at the battle of Bridge, an engagement that could have potentially saved the Sasanian empire

[1210] As argued on page 196ff, he is also referred to as Mardānshāh or Dhu 'l-Ḥājib.

[1211] Ṭabarī 1993, p. 188, de Goeje, 2174.

[1212] Ṭabarī 1993, p. 188, de Goeje, 2174–2175.

[1213] Balādhurī 1968, p. 251; Ibn al-Athīr 1862, vol. 2, p. 437.

[1214] Balʿamī 1959, p. 287. Ṭabarī 1993, p. 190, de Goeje, 2176–2177.

[1215] As Būrāndukht was only the candidate of the Pahlav faction during her first regnal year, it is improbable that such a united opposition could have happened during her first regency.

[1216] See page 208.

[1217] Curtis and Malek 1998, pp. 124–128.

[1218] Others include one coin from Ardashīr Khurrah (ART) in Fārs, five from Hormozd Ardashīr (AW) in Khuzistān and five from Stakhr (ST) in Fārs. The latter, as well as Kirmān, for which we have one coin from the second year, also minted coins in her first year. Curtis and Malek 1998, pp. 124–128.

and averted the subsequent disaster. For the cooperation of the Pārsīg with the Pahlav finally payed off: they "inflicted a disastrous defeat on the Muslim forces."[1219]

A victory interrupted

In the midst of their victory at the battle of Bridge, however, something went terribly amiss. And as Morony maintains, that something was the resurgence of the factional strife in the Sasanian capital Ctesiphon.[1220] The Pahlav and the Pārsīg had, once again, broken ranks. For, "as the Persians were trying to cross [the bridge], the news came to them that the people of al-Madā'in [Ctesiphon] had revolted *against* Rustam."[1221] Ibn al-Athīr's narrative informs us, significantly, that, at this time, "*the people had* divided into two camps: The *fahlawaj* were supporting Rustam and the *parsīg* were supporting Fīrūzān."[1222] Bal'amī's narrative, furthermore, lends tremendous support to our contention that something in the successful cooperation of the Pahlav with the Pārsīg had gone awry in the midst of the battle of Bridge. In the midst of the Iranian triumph, while Bahman Jādhūyih was about to cross the bridge in pursuit of the fleeing Arab army, "news reached Muthannā that the army of the *'ajam* has risen against Tūrān [i.e., Būrāndukht] and they do not accept her in power and they have become fed up (*bīzār*) with the rule (*sipahsālārī*) of Rustam."[1223] There was, in other words, once again a revolt against Rustam's leadership. There is no doubt that the Pārsīg led the rebellion in the capital. For, as Sayf informs us, the insurgents were asking for Bahman Jādhūyih, who had been recalled by Būrāndukht.[1224] Moreover, after the uprising, the Sasanian queen Būrāndukht was killed, presumably strangled by the Pārsīg leader Fīrūzān.[1225]

The battle of Buwayb

The battle of Buwayb (near Kūfa),[1226] reported next and depicted as leading to a major victory for the forces of Muthannā b. Ḥāritha, is most probably part of a Muthannā lore, added to the accounts of the battle of Bridge and intended to "enhance the reputation of al-Muthannā and of his tribe ... [in order] to counter the disgrace of his humiliating defeat at the battle of Bridge."[1227] And

[1219]Morony 1991, p. 205.

[1220]Morony 1991, p. 205.

[1221]The story is reported through three different *isnād*: al-Sari b. Yaḥyā — Shu'ayb — Sayf — Muḥammad; Ṭalḥa; and al-Ziyād. Ṭabarī 1993, p. 188, de Goeje, 2174.

[1222]Ṭabarī 1993, p. 189, and n. 945 and 946, de Goeje, 2176. Ibn al-Athīr 1862, pp. 156–158 and p. 160.

[1223]Bal'amī 1959, pp. 290–291.

[1224]Bal'amī 1959, pp. 290–291.

[1225]Seert 1918.

[1226]Ṭabarī 1993, p. 197, de Goeje, 2184.

[1227]Donner 1981, pp. 198–200, here p. 199. According to Ya'qūbī, the battle of Madhār took place in 14 AH/635 CE, although he continues to put this in the context of Būrāndukht's rule, providing even the significant information that after this battle and the battle of Buwayb, which presumably takes place next, and as a result of their defeats, the Persians revolted against Rustam and Fīrū-

indeed the Sasanian account looses its internal cohesion here. For, while toward the end of the battle of Bridge it is made clear that the Pārsīg–Pahlav alliance had failed, in the accounts of the battle of Buwayb, and without further explanation, Fīrūzān and Rustam are depicted as working side by side again.[1228] So, if at all historic, we must date this battle as having taken place earlier than the battle of Bridge.[1229] The subsequent thick-headed refusal of the Pārsīg and the Pahlav to continue to cooperate is highlighted by the queen's presumed protest to Rustam and Fīrūzān: "Why will the Persians not go forth against the Arabs as they used to go forth before today." The Persians responded to her that fear "was with our enemy at that time but is among us today."[1230]

3.4 Yazdgird III: Arab conquest of Iran

Sayf then starts narrating "what stirred up the matter of al-Qādisiyyah."[1231] The Persians reprimanded Rustam and Fīrūzān:[1232] "To where are you being carried? Dispute has not left you alone, so that you have weakened the Persians and made their enemies greedy." The imminent mutiny of the whole constituency of the two factions against their respective leaders is further highlighted in Sayf's subsequent account: The "two of you have not reached such a rank that Persia will concur with you in this opinion and that you expose it to perdition. After Baghdād, Sābāṭ, and Tikrīt, there is only Madā'in. By God, *either the two of you unite, or else we will indeed begin with you.*"[1233] Threatened by rebellion against them, Fīrūzān and Rustam agreed to cooperate yet again.[1234]

zān and finally brought Yazdgird III to power. The Sasanian chronological indicator provided by Ya'qūbī in other words remains those provided by Sayf. Ya'qūbi 1983, pp. 24–25.

[1228]When the news reached Rustam and Fīrūzān that Muthannā was calling for reinforcement, "the two of them agreed to send forth Mihrān-i Hamadānī." Blankinship notes that the father of Mihrān-i Hamadānī was one "Mihrbundādh or Bādhān. He is mentioned twice in poetry quoted by Abū Mikhnaf." Ibn al-Āzādbih, who led the two flanks of Mihrān-i Hamadānī's army was evidently the son of the governor of Ḥīra, Āzādbih. Mardānshāh, the other commander, was most likely none other than Bahman Jādhūyih. A Shahrvarāz also appears in these wars. If the historicity of the battle of Buwayb is to be valid, this Shahrvarāz was in all probability a descendent of the infamous Mihrānid Shahrvarāz. Mihrān-i Hamadānī, was killed in this war, and so was Shahrvarāz, the commander of Mihrān-i Hamadānī's light cavalry. Ṭabarī 1993, pp. 205–206 and p. 208, de Goeje, 2192, 2194. Ibn al-Athīr 1862, p. 161. Once Mihrān-i Hamadānī was killed, the army of the Persians fled and the leadership of the army was taken up by Fīrūzān. Ibn al-Athīr 1862, pp. 163–164.

[1229]See Table 6.1 on page 468.

[1230]Ṭabarī 1993, p. 204, de Goeje, 2189.

[1231]Ṭabarī 1993, p. 221, de Goeje, 2209.

[1232]Presumably after the unsuccessful completion of their victory at the battle of Bridge, when the Persians were "held . . . back from [dealing with] their enemy." Ṭabarī 1993, p. 222, de Goeje, 2209; see also page 218.

[1233]Ṭabarī 1993, p. 222, de Goeje, 2209.

[1234]Ṭabarī 1993, p. 222, de Goeje, 2209. This threat against the leadership of Rustam and Fīrūzān is given in two different versions carrying two different chains of transmission through Sayf. Ṭabarī 1993, pp. 221–222, de Goeje, 2209.

So, right after their victory at the battle of Bridge and after Būrāndukht was deposed and finally killed, the debilitating rivalry of the interregnum 628–632 between the Pahlav and the Pārsīg over the control of the Sasanian monarchy ended. Under the respective leadership of Rustam and Fīrūzān, the Pahlav and the Pārsīg agreed to support Yazdgird III's ascendancy. Some time after his accession occurred the putative watershed of the Sasanian demise: the battle of Qādisiya. When Muthannā b. Ḥāritha sent the news of Yazdgird III's election to kingship to ʿUmar, Sayf continues, the "letter did not reach ʿUmar before the people of al-Sawād had rebelled (*kafara*), both those who had an agreement [with the Muslims] and those who had no agreement."[1235] Muthannā led his own garrison until they stopped at Dhū Qār. Here ʿUmar's response came to the Arabs: "regroup and become earnest, as the Persians have now become earnest."[1236] This, Sayf maintains, "was in Dhū 'l-Qaʿdah of the year 13 (early 635)."[1237]

This chronology provided by Sayf is the most plausible among all the dates provided by our sources for the battle of Qādisiya. As we shall see, not only did the Pahlav take their time before coming to terms with the Pārsīg's slaying of their candidate, Būrāndukht, and subsequently accepting the kingship of the Pārsīg nominee, Yazdgird III, but throughout this time their leader, Rustam, was also averse to engaging the Arab armies. Rustam, the immortal hero of Qādisiya, was, in fact, reluctant to fight. He followed a policy of procrastination through diplomatic correspondences with the Arabs before he was actually forced into battle. All of this took time. Numismatic evidence confirms the date of the battle of Qādisiya as 634–635 CE or, perhaps, a year afterwards. Were it not for this evidence and in view of the all too blatant problems with the *hijra* chronology for the previous battles, we would have continued to have difficulties in determining an exact date for the battle of Qādisiya. Unlike the data at our disposal for the previous period, the Sasanian chronological indicators from here on can no longer aid us in our analysis: all the subsequent engagements of the Arabs against the Iranians took place during the reign of the last Sasanian monarch Yazdgird III (632–651), so that we can no longer rely on the accession and deposition of various monarchs in order to trace the chronology of the Sasanian efforts against the Arab armies. Nevertheless, until the murder of the last Sasanian king Yazdgird III sometime in 651, we can still continue to trace the general contours of the Pārsīg–Pahlav dynamic and its effects on the Arab conquest of Iran.

Yazdgird III's coinage

Before we proceed, however, a word needs to be said about the numismatic evidence pertaining to the initial years of the kingship of Yazdgird III. For this evidence helps not only to delimit the chronology of the battle of Qādisiya,

[1235] Ṭabarī 1993, p. 223, de Goeje, 2210.
[1236] Ṭabarī 1993, p. 223, de Goeje, 2210.
[1237] Ṭabarī 1993, p. 224, de Goeje, 2211.

but also, and perhaps more significantly, to disentangle the sequence in which Yazdgird III's rule was eventually accepted by the Pahlav and the Pārsīg. To begin with the latter first.

The Pahlav did not wholeheartedly accept Yazdgird III's kingship. As Tyler-Smith observed, only seventeen mints are known "to have minted in the name of Yazdgird III, a *small number for a Sasanian king reigning 20 years.*"[1238] While the characteristics of this coinage present various problems limiting somewhat our interpretation of them, they do provide us with crucial information pertaining to Yazdgird III's rule. As Tyler-Smith remarks, if "one wishes to use the coins to help elucidate the literary sources and vice versa, the first essential step is to decide whether all coins struck in Yazdgird III's name, but without an Arabic inscription, were minted in towns he controlled at the material time."[1239] Significantly for our purposes, and as far as the number of mints are concerned, Tyler-Smith notes that of the sixteen mints other than Sakastān (Sīstān), one "would expect *his early years to be represented by the most mints*, the number diminishing as he was driven east, and by the year 20, a period of only 3 months, very few would be minting in his name." This, however, did not happen. For, while in year 1 (632–633 CE) only seven mints are recorded and in the middle years anywhere between "none to six in any given year," for the year 20 (651–652 CE) there are not only "a comparatively large number of mints, ... [but also a] large number of specimens/dies."[1240]

According to Tyler-Smith, Yazdgird III's coinage can be divided into "four major groups of closely allied coins with a fifth group of more diverse coins." The first group, dating to the years 1–3 of his reign (632–634), came from eight different mints. What is significant for our purposes is that most of the identifiable mints are located in the southwest of Iran, in Fārs or Khuzistān, that is to say, in Pārsīg domains. The principal exception is Sīstān, known for years 1 and 3. Sīstān, however, as we have noted, while under Sūren control, closely collaborated with the Pārsīg factions.[1241] According to Tyler-Smith, the fact that these early mints "were so restricted is curious, one possible explanation being that Yazdgird III did not in fact fully control the whole of Iran."[1242] In other words, all the coins from the first three years of Yazdgird III's rule are minted in Pārsīg territories: Sīstān, Fārs, and Khuzistān, roughly corresponding to the quarters

[1238]Tyler-Smith, Susan, 'Coinage in the Name of Yazdgerd III (AD 632–651) and the Arab Conquest of Iran', *Numismatic Chronicle* 160, (2000), pp. 135–170 (Tyler-Smith 2000), p. 138. Emphasis added. The Sīstān mint takes an exceptional place in Yazdgird III's coinage, as we shall see shortly. Of the remaining sixteen mints, only 194 specimens have thus far been identified. Tyler-Smith 2000, p. 137.

[1239]Tyler-Smith 2000, p. 137. For references to works on the Arab–Sasanian coins, see ibid., nn. 6, 7 and 8. For Sīstān's drachm coinage during the late Sasanian period, testifying to the predominant independence of this Sūrenid territory, also see Sears, Stuart D., 'The Sasanian Style Drachms of Sistan', *Yarmouk Numismatics* 11, (1999), pp. 18–28 (Sears 1999), here pp. 18–19.

[1240]Tyler-Smith 2000, pp. 138–139. All emphasis mine.

[1241]See for instance our discussion on page 155ff.

[1242]Tyler-Smith 2000, pp. 138–140.

of the south and west. Significantly, the important mint of WYHC of Būrāndukht's reign—the most favorable reading of which must be the one proposing Visp-shad-Husrav in Media[1243]—appears only in the second group of Yazdgird III's coins, those for the years 6 and 7 (637–639),[1244] and in the fifth category of mints, those belonging to the year 20 (651–652) of Yazdgird III's reign. What is even more remarkable is that unlike Būrāndukht's coins, no other coins of Yazdgird III have been found belonging to the Pahlav territories, the quarters of the north and the east. The one significant conclusion that this numismatic data afford us, therefore, is that while the Pahlav eventually did fight on behalf of Yazdgird III, throughout his rule, they *did not mint any coins on his behalf in their territories*, except for the rare issues of the WYHC mints.[1245] This observation becomes even more significant considering the following.

The mints of the first group, in Fārs and Khuzistān, stop striking coins from year 4 onward (636–637). This date tallies quite well with the chronology that we will establish for the conquest of Khuzistān in 636–637.[1246] In fact, the great majority of issues belong only to year 1 (632–633) of Yazdgird III's kingship, while from the year 10 through year 20 (642–652), there is an almost continuous production in the mints of Kirmān and, presumably, of Sīstān.[1247] One last remark is crucial in this connection. As Tyler-Smith observes, "*no coins appear to have been struck between* YE [i.e., Yazdgird Era] 3 (AD 634–635) and YE 10 (AD 641–642)."[1248] The absence of any coins from this period underscores a crucial observation: "a major shock [seems to have affected] ... the administration of the Sasanian empire in *year 3 or 4*." If so, and if "the absence of coins does really indicate the collapse of central administration it would strongly suggest that *an early date [i.e., 635–636] for the battle of Qādisiya is correct*."[1249] The numismatic evidence therefore corroborates the chronology that we have favored in this study: those traditions that put the date of the battle of Qādisiya between the years 13–15 AH/634–636 CE, that is during the first three years of Yazdgird III's reign, are the most reliable. Two more remarks are warranted here. Firstly, the absence of any coins from the mint of WYHC, from the year 7 (638–639), soon after this mint had begun to struck coins in the name of Yazdgird III, until the year 20 (651–652), can very well be explained as the consequence of a major thrust of Arab armies into Media proper following the battle of Nihāvand, the battle of Jalūlā᾽, and the conquest of Rayy, after

[1243]See footnote 1163.

[1244]Tyler-Smith 2000, p. 140.

[1245]Nöldeke already realized this, and referring to Sebeos, argued that the east, as well as Azarbāyjān, initially refused to accept Yazdgird III's regency. In spite of this observation, he continued to maintain that Rustam and Farrukhzād, immediately or almost immediately lent their support to Yazdgird III. Nöldeke 1879, pp. 307–308, n. 5, Nöldeke 1979, p. 594, n. 183.

[1246]See §3.4.2.

[1247]As we shall discuss below on page 244ff, Yazdgird III probably stayed in Kirmān and Sīstān from 642–648.

[1248]Tyler-Smith 2000, p. 140.

[1249]Tyler-Smith 2000, pp. 146–147.

which the Arabs had penetrated these Pahlav territories.[1250] Furthermore, the provinces of Iraq, Khuzistān, and Fārs had to be subdued before the Arab armies could head east, and, while the province of Kirmān may have been raided in 643–645,[1251] Kirmān was "protected for most of Yazdgerd's reign by the western provinces." Secondly, while "we do not know why the three Kirmān mints were not in use at the beginning of Yazdgerd's reign ... [p]resumably the Arab invasions *changed circumstances dramatically enough to make it worth while for the three towns [of Kirmān] to start minting*, though output, ... appears always to have been low." Thanks to Tyler-Smith's study, we will also be able now to realize Gobl's hope, expressed decades ago, that an investigation of Yazdgird III's mints "will one day put us in a position to trace the withdrawal route of the dynasty's last monarch."[1252]

We cannot reconstruct Yazdgird III's narrative, however, without addressing the controversy surrounding the age that he assumed the throne, for naturally, the younger the age of the king, the less validity to the presumption that he played a consequential role in the exigent course of affairs. Although the reverse does not necessarily follow, that is, even if not a child, Yazdgird III was certainly quite young when he was promoted to the Sasanian throne and was almost thoroughly controlled by the factions supporting him. According to Saʿīd b. Baṭrīq and Ibn Qutaybah, Yazdgird III was fifteen years old when he was placed on the throne,[1253] while according to Dīnawarī, he was sixteen.[1254] Ṭabarī noted, however, that Yazdgird III (632–651) lived for a total of twenty-eight years.[1255] If this latter tradition is correct, Yazdgird III must in fact have been only eight years old when he assumed kingship. Nöldeke already pointed out that the coinage for the tenth year of Yazdgird III's rule still portrays the king without a beard.[1256] Nöldeke therefore opted for a very young monarch, an eight-year old child. Whatever his age, however, it was not Yazdgird III who steered affairs, but the two most important factions, the Pahlav and the Pārsīg, under the respective leadership of Rustam and Fīrūzān. What then is our narrative?

[1250]For these three conquests, see respectively page 241, page 234, and §3.4.4 below. The usage of the WYHC mint in the year 20 remains, however, a mystery.

[1251]Ṭabarī, *The Conquest of Iran*, vol. XIV of *The History of Ṭabarī*, Albany, 1994, translated and annotated by G. Rex Smith (Ṭabarī 1994), p. 71, de Goeje, 2704. Also see Daryaee, Touraj, *Soghoot-i Sāsānīyān (The Fall of the Sasanians)*, Tehran, 1994 (Daryaee 1994), and Daryaee, Touraj, 'The Effect of the Arab Muslim Conquest on the Administrative Division of Sasanian Persis/Fars', *Iran: Journal of the British Institute of Persian Studies* 41, (2003), pp. 1–12 (Daryaee 2003).

[1252]Göbl 1971, p. 54. Yazdgird III's flight will be discussed on pages 244ff and 257ff below.

[1253]Nöldeke 1879, p. 397, n. 4, Nöldeke 1979, p. 593, n. 182.

[1254]Dīnawarī 1960, p. 119, Dīnawarī 1967, p. 130.

[1255]Nöldeke 1879, p. 399, Nöldeke 1979, p. 551.

[1256]Nöldeke 1879, p. 397, n. 4, Nöldeke 1979, p. 593, n. 182; Ṭabarī 1999, p. 409, n. 1014.

3.4.1 The conquest of Ctesiphon

The people of Sawād informed Yazdgird III that the Arabs had encamped at Qādisiya and "in a warlike manner … ruined everything between them and the Euphrates." Encamped in their forts, they warned Yazdgird III that "should help be slow in coming, we shall surrender." Yazdgird III then sent for Rustam in order to entrust the mission of subduing the Arabs to the son of the Prince of the Medes. At his inauguration, he addressed Rustam: "*Today you are the [most prominent] man among the Persians.* You see that the people of Persia have not faced a situation like this since the family of Ardashīr I assumed power."[1257] Incidentally, it is significant that the situation on the eve of the Arab conquest and at the time of the imminent demise of the Sasanians should be compared to what had transpired at the inception of the Sasanian rise to power. As with the rise of the Sasanians, so too on the eve of their destruction, the cooperation of the two polities, the houses of Ardavān and Ardashīr I, the Pahlav and the Pārsīg, was required.

From the onset of events that led to the battle of Qādisiya, all of our traditions depict what seems to have been a major disagreement between Rustam and Yazdgird III. Because, as we have argued above, Yazdgird III was too young to steer policy, any decisive action projected onto him in our narratives must be attributed to the faction that originally promoted him: the Pārsīg faction. It is with this caveat in mind, therefore, that we shall proceed. In anticipation of the battle, Yazdgird III and Rustam engaged in a discussion. Ṭabarī highlights this in the form of a parable that betrays the nature of the disagreement. When Yazdgird III put Rustam in command of the forces, he presumably also asked his commander to describe to him "the Arabs and their exploits since they have camped at Qādisiyyah and … what the Persians have suffered at their hands." Rustam replied that he believed the Arabs to be "a pack of wolves, falling upon unsuspecting shepherds and annihilating them."[1258] Significantly, however, Yazdgird III objected: "It is *not* like that … I put the question to you in the expectation that you would *describe them clearly* and that then I would be able to reinforce you so that you might act according to the [real situation]. But you did not say the right thing."[1259] The nature of the disagreement is not yet disclosed in Sayf's narrative, but from what follows, it is amply clear that at least some form of discord had come to exist between a king who owed his very crown to the agreement of the major factions and a dynastic commander who was in charge of one of the most powerful armies of the realm.

Yazdgird III then proceeded to give his own assessment of the situation. He compared the Arabs to an eagle who "looked upon a mountain where birds take shelter at night and stay in their nests at the foot of it." In the morning the birds recognized that the eagle is preying upon them. Whenever "a bird

[1257]Ṭabarī 1992, p. 43, de Goeje, 2247.
[1258]Ṭabarī 1992, p. 43, de Goeje, 2248.
[1259]Ṭabarī 1992, p. 43, de Goeje, 2248.

became separated from the rest, the eagle snatched him. When the birds saw him [doing this], they did not take off out of fear ... *If they had taken off all at once, they would have repelled him. The worst thing that could happen to them would be that all would escape save one. But if each group acted in turn and took off separately, they all perished.* This was the similarity between them and the Persians. Act according to this."[1260] What Yazdgird III was describing for Rustam in this parable was in fact the plight of the Persian armies: division and lack of collaboration among the factions. Clearly, Yazdgird III was urging Rustam into collective action. Rustam, however, was in favor of a different course of action. "O king, let me [act in my own way]. The Arabs still dread the Persians *as long as you do not arouse them against me.* It is to be hoped that my good fortune will last and that God will save us the trouble."[1261] Sayf then provides a crucial piece of information. Rustam allegedly believed that the king was inciting the Arabs against him. Clearly, this could not be the real reason for his fear. Instead, he must have been afraid of the harm that the Pārsīg faction might place in his way through their actions. Ṭabarī's subsequent account makes it clear that there was a substantial dispute between the Pahlav and the Pārsīg over the best strategy for engaging the Arabs encamped at Qādisiya.

Rustam favored patience and protracted warfare: We should "employ the right ruse," he insisted. "In war, patience is superior to haste, and the order of the day is now patience. *To fight one army after another is better than a single [and total] defeat and is also harder on our enemy.*" Yazdgird III, however, was obdurate.[1262] What is being exchanged here is of course not a correspondence between a puppet child king and his powerful commander, but a dialogue between the Parthians (*fahlawaj*) and the Pārsīg (*ahl-i Fārs*). Rustam pushed for isolated warfare, for biding their time to ascertain the true nature of the Arabs' intentions. But the situation had become desperate for the people of Sawād. Yazdgird III, that is, the Pārsīg, lost patience and pushed Rustam to engage the enemy. Rustam, however, refused to succumb to pressure, suggesting to send the Armenian Jālīnūs or another commander instead. Once these had "made them [i.e., the Arabs] weak and tired," Rustam argued, he could then proceed himself.[1263] No agreement, however, was reached, and Rustam was forced to prepare for battle.

Just prior to the battle, Rustam became again heavy-hearted, presumably on account of a dream. Now, it is true that apocalyptic dreams, like that of Rustam, are a later concoction, inserted in Ferdowsī's opus. As such they constitute nothing but a literary *topos*. For our purposes, however, they do contain significant information. Once again Rustam asked Yazdgird III (read, the Pārsīg)

[1260] Ṭabarī 1992, pp. 43–44, de Goeje, 2248.
[1261] Ṭabarī 1992, p. 44, de Goeje, 2248. Emphasis added.
[1262] Ṭabarī 1992, pp. 44, 52, de Goeje, 2248, 2257. Balʿamī also highlights this. Balʿamī 1959, p. 296. The theme of Rustam's initial disagreement with Yazdgird III is also reiterated in Yaʿqūbi 1969, vol. 2, pp. 160–162, Yaʿqūbi 1983, p. 27.
[1263] Ṭabarī 1992, pp. 44–45, de Goeje, 2249.

for permission to send Jālīnūs first. "The ability of Jālnūs is similar to mine, though they [i.e., the Arabs] dread my name more than his. [If Jālīnūs fails,] I shall send someone like him, and we shall ward these people off for some time. *The People of Persia still look up to me. As long as I am not defeated, they will act eagerly.* I am also at this time dreaded by the Arabs; they dread to move forward as long as I do not confront them. But once I do confront them, they will, at last, take heart, and the people of Persia will, in the end be defeated."[1264]

Arab trade interests

What has never been underlined apropos the battle of Qādisiya is that the Parthian general Rustam not only argued for procrastination and isolated warfare, being intent on deploying other commanders into action, but that he maintained this position while corresponding and negotiating with the Arabs. In the many pages of Ṭabarī that follow this is made clear. In the months that ultimately lead to the battle, Rustam sent a message to Zuhrah b. Ḥawiyah,[1265] with the intention of making peace. Rustam "wanted to make peace with Muslims and give Zuhrah a stipend on condition that they should depart."[1266] Rustam and Zuhrah then engaged in correspondence. Besides the heavy dose of rhetoric that infuses the narrative, significant information is interpolated into the text. Rustam reminded Zuhrah of the history of Persian behavior toward the Arabs, of the protection that they had given the latter, of how they gave them access to pasture land, and provided them with supplies, and finally of how they allowed the Arabs to trade in any part of the land. Zuhrah, acknowledging the veracity of Rustam's contentions, retorted that after the appearance of the Prophet and his religion of the truth, the Arabs were no longer seeking worldly gains. As we shall shortly see, this denunciation ought to be considered Muslim rhetoric, interpolated in the account by later traditionalists. Rustam now asked Zuhrah about their new religion. Zuhrah then enumerated the essential pillars of his newly found religion.[1267] Rustam then responded: "How excellent is this! ... *[And if] I agree to this matter and respond to you, together with my people, what will you do*? Will you return [to your country]?" In Zuhrah's final response, however, we are provided with a fascinating piece of information: "By God, if the Persians were to agree to all of these declarations, the Muslims would indeed never draw near ... [to their] land *except for [purposes] of trade* or some

[1264] Ṭabarī 1992, pp. 45–46, de Goeje, 2250.

[1265] One of the commanders of Saʿd b. Abī Waqqāṣ's army, who in the pre-Islamic period allegedly was made a tribal chieftain by the king of Hajar (in Bahrayn) and sent to the Prophet. Ṭabarī 1992, p. 17, and n. 65, de Goeje, 2224.

[1266] Ṭabarī 1992, p. 63, de Goeje, 2267.

[1267] There "is no god except Allāh and ... Muḥammad is His messenger." "Excellent," Rustam responded, and "what else?" "To extricate people from servitude to [other] people and to make them servants of God," Zuhrah replied. "Good," Rustam retorted, "and what else?" "Men are sons of Adam and Eve, brothers born of the same father and mother," Zuhrah continued. Ṭabarī 1992, p. 64, de Goeje, 2268.

necessity."[1268] The Arab intent therefore was not conquest for the sake of assuming power, but *trade*. The pre-occupation of the Arab conquerors with trade is also highlighted in a narrative of Balādhurī, where ʿAbbās b. ʿAbdalmuṭṭalib warned ʿUmar that if the latter established a *dīwān* (army registry), the Arabs would "be content with the *dīwān* [i.e., army stipend] and stop trading."[1269] Returning to our account, after some further discussions, Rustam went away, summoned the Persians, and communicated the Arabs' message to them. Here, we are finally appraised of the true identity of the party against whom Rustam maintained his position: once Rustam communicated the Arabs' message to the *Persians*, "they went into a rage and scornfully rejected [Zuhrah's proposals]." Rustam then cursed the *Persians*.[1270] A second tradition, also reported by Sayf, but through a different chain, has a certain Ribʿī b. ʿAmir as a messenger to Rustam. This narrative insists that it was Rustam who wished to engage in a dialogue with the Arabs. As in the previous narrative, again the classic three choices—tribute, conversion, or war—were offered. Rustam demanded time for consultation, a "delay [of] this matter until both parties consider it[s]" implications. Ribʿī offered one or two days. Rustam, however, asked for a longer delay: "*until we could exchange letters with our men of judgment and with the leaders of our people.*"[1271]

Ṭabarī's accounts make it amply clear that negotiations were contingent on the collective agreement of the factions who had by now implicitly agreed to Rustam's command.[1272] The collectivity, however, did not agree with Rustam's course of action. In the second narrative, after hearing Ribʿī's offer of the classic three, Rustam went "into private consultation with the Persian chieftains," and argued for the lucidity and honorable nature of their offer. Ṭabarī's sources for this narrative even imply that Rustam was prepared to convert. The Persian

[1268] Ṭabarī 1992, p. 64, de Goeje, 2269. Emphasis mine.

[1269] ʿUmar replied, "there is no option but this. The booty of the Muslims has become substantial indeed." Balādhurī 1968, p. 211. A tradition contained in Dīnawarī also highlights this crucial aspect of the agenda of the Arab conquerors. For according to Dīnawarī, when Mihrān-i Hamadānī and other grandees of Iran were defeated (see page 218) and the control of various regions of Sawād became feasible for the Arabs, the population of Ḥīra informed Muthannā that in their vicinity there was a village (*qariyā*) with a grand *bazār* in it. "Once every month, people from Fārs and Ahvāz and various other cities of Iran came there in order to trade in goods." The wealth attained by the Arabs after the conquest of Anbār is then highlighted by Dīnawarī. Concerning the conquest of Ubullah a similar observation is made. After the battle of Ubullah (see page 190), ʿUtbah b. Ghazwān wrote to ʿUmar: "Thank God that we have conquered Ubullah [Baṣrah] for this is the port city of the ships that come hither from ʿUmān, Bahrayn, Fārs and Hind o Chīn." Dīnawarī 1960, p. 117, Dīnawarī 1967, p. 127. Note, once more, the anachronism of the mention of ʿUmar, presumably as caliph.

[1270] Ṭabarī 1992, p. 65, de Goeje, 2269.

[1271] Ṭabarī 1992, pp. 68–69, de Goeje, 2272–2273. Emphasis added.

[1272] Noth studied the theme of negotiation in the *futūḥ* literature, and remarked on the many *topoi* that can be found in them. Noth, Albrecht, 'Iṣfahān-Nihāwand. Eine quellenkritische Studie zur frühislamischen Historiographie', *Zeitschrift der Deutschen Morgenländischen Gesellschaft* 118, (1968), pp. 274–296 (Noth 1968), p. 284. The information provided here about Iranian factionalism, however, should not be considered a *topos*.

chiefs warned Rustam: "May God save you from inclining toward ... abandoning your religion to this dog."[1273] This rhetorical exchange we can confidently disregard, for an agreement to conversion would have been all but impossible, given the context, for the son of the Prince of the Medes. The round of negotiations between Rustam and other factions "continued until *Rustam and his companions enraged each other.*"[1274] Rustam then asked for another messenger, and Mughīrah b. Shuʿbah was sent.[1275] Here, finally, Rustam's negotiations with the Arabs reached a dead-end. Rustam declared to Mughīrah: "We are firmly established in the land, victorious over our enemies, and noble among nations. None of the kings has our power, honor, dominion."[1276] Mughīrah interjected: "if you need our protection, then be our slave, and pay the poll tax out of hand while being humiliated; otherwise it is the sword." At this Rustam "flew into a rage, and *swore by the sun: 'Dawn will not break upon you tomorrow before I kill you all'.*"

Much has been said of the paramount role of Rustam in what is portrayed as one of the grand finales of Sasanian history, the battle of Qadisiya. It is to this foremost general of the Sasanian realm that the defense of Sasanian rule in Iran was entrusted, allegedly by a young puppet king, who himself owed his throne to the scheming of the factions to begin with. It is probably no exaggeration to argue that the death of no other figure in the long course of Sasanian history has acquired such poignant symbolism. Rustam's death at the battle of Qādisiya signals the end of Sasanian history. The *Shāhnāma*, together with the Iranian national historical memory, mourns the defeat and murder of this heroic figure. An apocryphal letter at the end of Ferdowsī's opus even prognosticates the end of Iranian national sovereignty through the mouth of Rustam, here depicted as having the Mithraic epithets of *Justice and Mihr* (*sitārih shomar būd bā dād o mihr*), before his fateful confrontation with the Arabs.[1277]

With all the fanfare around the heroic posture and tragic death of Rustam, however, little attention has been paid to the fact that, in defending the Sasanians at this important juncture of Iranian history, Rustam, like his brother, Farrukhzād and their father, Farrukh Hormozd, was not merely pitching his last efforts on behalf of the Sasanians—whose legitimacy his ancestral family, the Ispahbudhān, had questioned again and again in late Sasanian period, after

---

[1273]Ṭabarī 1992, p. 68–69, de Goeje, 2272.

[1274]Ṭabarī 1992, p. 70, de Goeje, 2274. Emphasis mine.

[1275]The continuation of this narrative is reported on the authority of Sayf with only one other transmitter listed after him. In this version, Mughīrah does not reiterate the classic three terms of surrender. In fact, it is only Rustam who speaks here.

[1276]Ṭabarī 1992, p. 73, de Goeje, 2277.

[1277]In a letter to his brother Farrukhzād, he predicted this end resorting to astrological signs. Ferdowsī 1935, p. 2965, Ferdowsī 1971, vol. IX, p. 314:

ز بهرام و زهره است ما را گزند — نشاید گذشتن ز چرخ بلند
همان تیر و کیوان برابر شدست — عطارد به برج دو پیکر شدست

We will discuss Mithraic symbolism below in §5.3.

all—but, more importantly, was defending the rights of his family and their fiefdoms in the east and west of the Sasanian territory. Even less is known about the likelihood that the family was probably the most significant player in accommodating the conquering army and betraying the Sasanians.

According to the *Shāhnāma*, in the process of preparing an army to face the Arabs, Rustam wrote a letter to his brother, Farrukhzād, instructing him to gather the army of Iran and Zābulistān, as well as anyone coming to him in refuge (*zīnhār khāh*), and to go to Azarbāyjān. Rustam encouraged Farrukhzād as well as all those who were from their agnatic group (*dūdih-i mā*), young or old,[1278] to pray for what was about to transpire, and he reminded them all that Yazdgird III was the only legacy left from the Sasanians.

The continuation of the letter as it appears in the *Shāhnāma* corroborates Sayf's account that the Arabs' aim in invading Iran was gaining direct access to trade entrepôts. Rustam informed Farrukhzād that the Arabs had assured him that the aim of their aggression was not the destruction of the monarchy and the assumption of power, but rather trade. They promised that they would leave the Iranians in control over the regions stretching from Qādisiya to Rūdbār. Now, while many rivers, villages, and districts in Iran are called Rūdbār, the context as well as topographical logic makes it amply clear that this Rūdbār is without doubt the Persian nomenclature for the Oxus.[1279] In other words, the Arabs pledged to go beyond the Oxus (*vazān sū*) *to the cities where there is trade*.[1280] The Arabs' sole purpose, in other words, was trade and nothing else. They even agreed to pay heavy tariffs and taxation and to respect the Sasanian king and the "crowns of the warriors", and even to provide hostages as insurance against their good conduct. Rustam, however, warned his brother: all this seemed to be their *rhetoric* and not their *intent*.[1281]

[1278]Ferdowsī 1971, vol. IX, pp. 313–316, Ferdowsī 1935, p. 2965:

تو با هر که از دوده ما بود   اگر پیر، اگر مرد برنا بود

[1279]Dihkhuda, *Lughat Nāma*, Tehran University Publications, 1998, edited by Muhammad Mo'in and Ja'far Shahidi (Dihkhuda 1998), pp. 12331–12333.

[1280]It is extremely important to note that Ṭabarī also highlights the role of trade. de Goeje, 1049; Nöldeke 1979, p. 529. This, however, is differently rendered both in Nöldeke's and in the English translation of Ṭabarī. In the English version, in the course of a prognostication that Khusrow II uttered when the famous list of grievances is given to him, the king informed the messenger that all "this happening indicates a bad omen, that the glory of the monarchs has passed into the hands of the *common masses*, that we have been deprived of royal power, and that it will not remain long in the hands of our successors before it passes to persons who are not of royal stock (*min ahl al-mamlakah*)." Ṭabarī 1999, p. 386. The actual phrase for the "glory of the monarchs has passed into the hands of the *common masses*" in Arabic, however, reads:

ان مجد الملوك قد صار عند السوق.

that is to say, "... has passed to the bazar [i.e., the *traders*]." de Goeje, 1049. For some reason, Nöldeke, too, has rendered this phrase as "dass die Herrlichkeit der Könige an *den Pöbel* gekommen ist." Nöldeke 1879, p. 368.

[1281]Ferdowsī 1935, p. 2966:

از ایشان فرستاده امد به من   سخن رفت هر گونه بر انجمن

It is important to underline the tremendous value of this piece of information provided by Ferdowsī. No other source, not even Sayf, gives this unique exchange of Rustam with the Arabs. To be sure, a substantial part of Ṭabarī's account details the futile negotiations that ultimately led to the battle of Qādisiya. And, as we have seen, the theme of trade is hinted at even in these narratives. In keeping with the classical Arab histories' Islamic rhetoric, however, Ṭabarī's accounts, while significant, highlight—probably *post facto*—the religious locomotive of the wars of conquest. Nowhere in the many pages of Ṭabarī,[1282] is the theme of trade so explicitly and in detail highlighted as in the poetic couplets of Ferdowsī.

Ferdowsī's narrative also underlines the forced final agreement of the Pahlav leader, Rustam, into the strategic policies and concerns of the Pārsīg and other factions. In the letter to his brother Farrukhzād, Rustam emphasized that it was they who had finally coerced him into engaging the enemy. The forces of Ṭabaristān, under the leadership of Mīrūy, those of Armenia and those under the control of the Sūrenid Kalbūy (Kalbūy-i Sūrī) were all unanimous in one opinion and one course of action, according to Rustam: "The Arabs are not to be trusted ... They are not even worthy of consideration. Why have they come to Iran and Māzandarān? *If they want access*, they have to obtain it through war."[1283]

Ṭabarī also mentions Rustam's letter to Farrukhzād. Here, we also are told

---

که از قادسی تا لب رودبار   زمین را ببخشیم به شهریار
وزان سو یکی بر گشایند راه   به شهری کجا هست بازارگاه
بدان تا خریم و فروشیم چیز   از ان پس فزونی نجوییم نیز
پذیریم ما ساو و باژ گران   نجوییم دیهیم کنداوران
شهنشاه را نیز فرمان بریم   گر از ما بخواهد گروگان بریم
چنینست گفتار، کردار نیست   جز از گردش کژ پرگار نیست

"A messenger came to me from them. Many subjects were discussed in the course of this assembly. [They promised] that from Qādisiya to Rūdbār, we shall leave the land to the king. Beyond that [i.e., Rūdbār, they promised] we will go to the cities where there are trade entrepôts [*bāzārgāh*], so that we could buy and sell. Besides this [they claimed] we pursue nothing. We shall even accept heavy tariffs. *We do not seek the crowns of the elite.* We shall also obey the king. If he desires, we shall even furnish him with hostages."

[1282] As Friedmann observes, many themes are highlighted in this section of Ṭabarī's narrative. These include the contemptuous treatment of the Arabs by the Persians, underlining their poverty and primitive way of life, and deriding their military prowess. These themes might very well reflect "anachronistic echoes of Shuʿūbī" controversy. The Persians' "repeated attempts to dissuade the Muslims from embarking on war by promises of material gain," however, fall short of the insights given by Ferdowsī. Ṭabarī 1992, p. xv.

[1283] Ferdowsī 1971, vol. IX, pp. 314–315, Ferdowsī 1935, p. 2966:

بزرگان که با من به جنگ اندرند   بگفتار ایشان همی ننگرند
چو میروی طبری و چون ارمنی   به جنگ اند با کیش اهریمنی
چو کلبوی سوری این مهتران   که گوپال دارند و گرز گران
همی سرفرازند، ایشان که اند   به ایران و مازندران بر چه اند
اگر مرز و راهست اگر نیك و بد   بگرز و بشمشیر باید ستد
بکوشیم و مردی بکار اوریم   بریشان جهان تنگ و تار اوریم

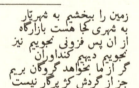

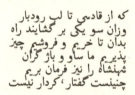

of the reasons why this other important scion of the Pahlav did not take part in the battle of Qādisiya. Rustam's letter was addressed to al-Binduwān and those who followed him. Al-Binduwān of course refers to Farrukhzād, who was indeed the grandson of Vindūyih,[1284] and is called here the "arrow of the people of Persia ... equal to every event, ... [through him] God will break every powerful army and conquer every impregnable fortress." Rustam warned his brother to strengthen himself "as if the Arabs have already arrived in *your country* to fight for *your land* and for your sons." He told Farrukhzād that he had "suggested [to the king] that we should ward them off and thus gain time until their auspicious stars become unlucky." The king, however, had refused this.[1285] As Ṭabarī informs us, Farrukhzād was the *marzbān* of al-Bāb, on the western coasts of the Caspian Sea,[1286] and he continued to be engaged in the Caucasus.

As both Ṭabarī's and Ferdowsī's narrative underline, therefore, the hero of the battle of Qādisiya participated in the fateful battle quite reluctantly and in spite of his preferred stratagems. In fact, according to Ṭabarī, between "the departure of Rustam from al-Madā'in, his camping at Sābāṭ, his departure from there, and his confrontation with Sa'd b. Abī Waqqāṣ's army, four months elapsed. During this time he did not move forward and did not fight."[1287] Rustam is portrayed as "hoping that the Arabs would become disgusted with the place, [and] would become exhausted, and ... leave."[1288] So long-lasting Rustam's procrastination is said to have been that the Arabs, realizing his strategy, followed suit and "made up their minds to be patient and to temporize with the Persians indefinitely, in order to throw them off balance," raiding meanwhile the Sawād and plundering "the area around them."[1289] Once the Persians realized "that the Arabs were not going to desist," however, they are said to have commenced their war efforts.

In all our narratives the theme of Rustam's procrastination, his insistence on having an isolated warfare strategy, and his initial refusal to start the war efforts, reflects his stance, not vis-à-vis the child king Yazdgird III, but vis-à-vis the other factions, most importantly the Pārsīg. The correspondence of Rustam with his brother Farrukhzād bears witness to this. The exhaustion of the Sasanian empire in the wake of the thirty-year Byzantine–Sasanian wars, which

[1284] See page 187 and the Ispahbudhān family tree on page 471. Ibn al-Athīr maintains that at the battle of Qādisiya, when Qa'qā supposedly slew Fīrūzān, Ḥārith also killed al-Binduwān. This, however, is most probably one of those forged traditions attributed to Qa'qā (see page 233 below). Ibn al-Athīr 1862, vol. 2, p. 474.

[1285] Ṭabarī 1992, pp. 46–47, de Goeje, 2251. Emphasis added.

[1286] Al-Bāb is the older name for the city of Darband, where successive Sasanian kings, most of all Khusrow I, are credited with constructing heavy fortifications against nomadic invasions. Ṭabarī 1992, p. 46, n. 183 and the sources cited therein, de Goeje, 2251. As we shall see on page 279ff, in the future course of the conquest, the Arabs encountered in precisely this same region a Mihrānid by the name of Shahrvarāz, leading the homeless soldiers under his command against the Khazars.

[1287] Ṭabarī 1992, p. 52, de Goeje, 2257.

[1288] Ṭabarī 1992, p. 52, de Goeje, 2257.

[1289] Ṭabarī 1992, pp. 52–53, de Goeje, 2257.

had only recently been brought to an end, perhaps helps explain Rustam's inclination toward placating the Arab armies. The Arab insistence on trade interests, was probably also responsible for the creation of those narratives that depict Rustam arguing for the lucidity and honorable nature of the Arab stance. All the traditions concerning Rustam's correspondence with the Arab armies, with his brother Farrukhzād, and with other factions bear witness, however, that the Pārsīg were bent on all-out war. Perhaps their promotion of this strategy was itself predicated upon their knowledge that, indeed, the latter did dread Rustam and his power more than they did that of the Pārsīg.

The battle of Qādisiya

Whatever the case, the list of commanders engaged in the battle of Qādisiya reflects the final participation of all parties who had gathered under the command of Rustam. Sebeos gives us the significant information that the "army of the land of the Medes gathered under the command of their general Rostom," numbering 80,000 armed men.[1290] Sebeos then provides a breakdown of this number in order to underline the Armenian participation in the battle of Qādisiya: from among the forces that had gathered under Rustam, 3,000 fully armed men participated in the battle under the command of the the Armenian general, Mušeł Mamikonean, son of Dawit'. Prince Grigor, lord of Siwnik', came with a force of 1,000.[1291] Sayf's account adds other contingents. Mušeł Mamikonean, possibly the figure rendered as Jālīnūs in our Arabic sources,[1292] was put in charge of the vanguard. He was ordered not to "rush [into battle]" without Rustam's permission. One Hurmuzān was put in charge of the right wing of the army.[1293] Mihrān-i Bahrām-i Rāzī, a Pahlav of the famous Mihrān family, took charge of the left wing, and finally Fīrūzān, the Pārsīg leader, commanded the rear guard.[1294] Significantly, a figure named Kanāra was commanding the light cavalry.[1295] This Kanāra, whose son Shahrīyār b. Kanārā also participated in the battle,[1296] was most probably the same Kanārang who played a major role in the deposition of Khusrow II,[1297] and who went on to play an even more significant role in the conquest of Khurāsān.[1298] Besides the contingents listed, and in true dynastic fashion, moreover, Rustam's next of kin were also heavily involved in all this. His cousins, Vindūyih and Tīrūyih, the sons of Vistāhm,[1299] were charged with commanding contingents from the Sawād.

[1290] Sebeos 1999, p. 98.

[1291] Sebeos 1999, p. 98.

[1292] See footnote 846.

[1293] As we shall see shortly on page 236 below, Hurmuzān belonged to the Pārsīg faction.

[1294] Ṭabarī 1992, p. 45, de Goeje, 2249.

[1295] Ṭabarī 1992, p. 53, de Goeje, 2258.

[1296] Ṭabarī 1992, p. 131, de Goeje, 2346.

[1297] See page 154ff.

[1298] See §3.4.7.

[1299] See the genealogical tree on page 471.

Perhaps one of the single most important causes of the Sasanian defeat at the battle of Qādisiya, besides the general exhaustion of the populace and the armies after years of warfare with Byzantium, the plague that had decimated the realm, and the atmosphere of distrust and factionalism that prevailed among the dynastic factions, was the fact that during the war *"[a]ll the leading nobles were killed, and the general Rostom was also killed."*[1300] Having long recognized the debilitating factionalism engulfing the Sasanian polity—where armies had gathered around their respective leaders—the Arabs also had realized that the best possible strategy was targeting these very leaders. For without these, the coalition of the Persians would crumble and their armies scatter. This strategy, perhaps, also explains the detailed narratives of the battle of Qādisiya which dramatize the capture, defeat, and murder of these leaders. Although these embellished accounts doubtless have little concrete historical value, recalling more the *ayyām* narratives,[1301] and *qiṣaṣ*, rather than accurate renditions of events, they portray emotionally the various climaxes of the battle. They also elucidate the controversy over whether ᶜUmar should participate in the wars of conquest in person, the fear being that in his capacity as the leader of the Arabs, the Iranians would likewise target him.[1302] In any event, whether targeting dynastic leaders was the strategic intention of Arabs or not, these were either first to fall in the course of the battle or first to flee. And a good number of dynastic leaders fell at Qādisiya: Mušeł Mamikonean, and two of his nephews, together with Grigor and his sons were among the casualties.[1303] Shahrīyār b. Kanārā, a member of the important Kanārangīyān family, "courageously courted death."[1304] Hurmuzān and Fīrūzān were among the first to flee the scene.[1305] A Sayf tradition maintains that Qaᶜqā killed the Pārsīg leader Fīrūzān (al-Bayrūzān).[1306] This, without a doubt, is one of those traditions that Sayf is regularly accused of fabricating, this time with justification. For as Blankinship maintains, the role of this Qaᶜqā—an alleged Companion of the Prophet, and a member of Sayf's own Usayyid tribe—in the accounts of the *futūḥ* of Sayf is "one of the most outstanding [examples]

1300 Sebeos 1999, p. 98.

1301 Naturally the reference here is to the battle scenes in this literature, not to their value as genre for historical study. See Mittwoch, E., 'Ayyām al-ᶜArab', in Ehsan Yarshater (ed.), *Encyclopaedia Iranica*, New York, 2007 (Mittwoch 2007).

1302 "All of them [i.e., the congregation that ᶜUmar had called in order to decide the matter] ... unanimously decided that he should stay, send out a man from the companions of the Prophet, and provide him with troops." In a different version, ᶜUmar is told to "stay and send an army ... If your army is defeated, it is not the same as if you [yourself] were defeated. *If you are killed or defeated at the outset, I am afraid that no Muslim will remain in existence,*" one of the Companions is said to have maintained. Friedman notes that the text actually reads: "I am afraid that Muslims will not say 'God is the greatest' and 'There is no god except Allāh'." He further notes that Masᶜūdī's *Murūj al-Dhahab* has the following: "If you are defeated or killed, the Muslims will *apostatize and will never attest that there is no god except Allāh.*" Ṭabarī 1992, pp. 4–6, de Goeje, 2213–2214.

1303 Sebeos 1999, p. 98–99.

1304 Ṭabarī 1992, p. 131, de Goeje, 2346.

1305 Fīrūzān is rendered here by Sayf as al-Bayrūzān. Ṭabarī 1992, p. 123, de Goeje, 2336.

1306 Ṭabarī 1992, p. 100, de Goeje, 2309.

of ... fabrications" of this traditionalist.[1307] In fact, Qaʿqā is said to have killed Fīrūzān not once, but twice: at the battle of Qādisiya as well as at the battle of Nihāvand.[1308] The dramatic and fabricated accounts of the murder of these dynastic leaders at the hands of particular Arabs, nonetheless, prove our point. The demise of important Pārsīg and Pahlav leaders was of such urgency and significance for the armies of conquest, that traditions portraying their actual demise might have been invented. Luckily for the Pārsīg, Fīrūzān was in fact able to flee.[1309] The most important Pahlav leader, Rustam, the one whom the Arabs were said to have feared the most, was not so lucky. The downfall of this towering dynast, together with the demise and flight of the other leaders, disheartened the various armies that had gathered around them, leading these, in turn, to flee from the battle scene.

As fortune would have it, however, the brother of Rustam, Farrukhzād, absent from the battle due to his engagement in the Caucasus, came to take over the leadership of the Pahlav, playing, as we shall see shortly, a crucial role in the subsequent fateful course of events. Initially, however, the dissolution of the armies that had gathered under the command of Rustam created a substantial power vacuum in Iran. The Arab recognition of this fact is reflected in most of our narratives. In Balʿamī's account, after the battle of Qādisiya, ʿUmar told Saʿd that if the Persians remained inactive, he should proceed. Saʿd realized in turn that after the death of Rustam "no-one ha[d] remained who would be capable of leading the Persians (*sipahsālārī rā shāyad*)."[1310] In fact, upon the death of Rustam, the two factions seemed for a while not to have been able to agree on a candidate for the supreme command of the army.[1311]

The battle of Qādisiya, and the heroic but fatal fight of Rustam at the scene, have at times been portrayed as a watershed of Iranian defeat at the hands of the Arab armies. This, however, was far from the case, for the battle of Qādisiya in fact functioned as a wake-up call for the Iranian armies, creating an awareness that continued factionalism could mean imminent destruction. With the defeat at the battle of Qādisiya, nonetheless, the way to the capital of the Sasanians was opened and Ctesiphon was taken by the armies of the Arab conquerors.

The battle of Jalūlāʾ

After the capture of Madāʾin (Ctesiphon), according to Ṭabarī, when "the people ... were about to go their separate ways, they started to incite one another:

[1307]This, therefore, is one of those instances where Sayf either invented, or glorified the deeds of certain Arabs precisely "in order to glorify further the exploits of the Arab conquerors." Ṭabarī 1993, p. xxiii.

[1308]Ṭabarī 1989a, p. 209, de Goeje, 2626.

[1309]As we shall see, with Rustam out of the picture, Fīrūzān not only participated in the next important battle, the battle of Jalūlāʾ, but later also came to lead the Persian armies in the next most important battle that took place after battle of Qādisiya, the battle of Nihāvand. See respectively pages 234ff and 241ff below.

[1310]Balʿamī 1959, p. 303.

[1311]Balʿamī 1959, p. 303.

'If you disperse now, you will never get together again; this is a spot that sends us in different directions'."[1312] A new army was eventually formed. Gathering in Atrpatakan (Azarbāyjān), they installed Khoṙokhazat (Farrukhzād) as their general.[1313] All the major groups that had participated in the battle of Qādisiya came together, once again, in the next important battle, the battle of Jalūlāʾ. Some of the *futūḥ* accounts date this important battle to the year 16 AH/637 CE. The date of the battle of Jalūlāʾ, however, is likewise debated in the tradition. While Ṭabarī lists this war among the wars that took place in the year 16 of *hijra* (637), he points out that according to a number of traditionalists, including Wāqidī, the conquest of Jalūlāʾ occurred in the year 19 AH/640 CE.[1314] If the battle of Qādisiya is to be put around 635 CE, however, the earlier date 637 for Jalūlāʾ seems to be the most accurate.[1315] Whatever the exact chronology of the battle, the Parthian Mihrān-i Bahrām-i Rāzī was in command.[1316] With the death of his brother Rustam, the Parthian dynast Farrukhzād, whose name has now been rendered correctly in Ṭabarī as Khurrazādh b. Khurrahurmuz, that is, Farrukhzād, son of Farrukh Hormozd, assumed the leadership of the Pahlav in the battle. The most important section of the Sasanian forces, the cavalry, was under his command.[1317] The Pārsīg leader Fīrūzān also participated in the battle, as did the Armenian contingents, under their new leader Khusrow Shenūm (Khusrov-Shum), that is to say, Varaztirots' Bagratuni.[1318] A host of factors, including low morale and exhaustion, basically incapacitated the Persians, however. The Persian forces were yet again defeated by the Arab armies under command of Hāshim b. ʿUtbah. Mihrān-i Bahrām-i Rāzī was killed and Fīrūzān fled, although Qaʿqā is said to have initially caught up with this commander whom he previously is said to have slain.[1319] The Armenian Khusrow Shenūm put up a resistance at Ḥulwān for a while, but was likewise forced to flee.[1320] As for the battle of Qādisiya, the logistics of a war where, in spite of the cooperation of the Pahlav and the Pārsīg, the Iranians were defeated, need to be reassessed.[1321] Exhaustion after at least four decades of warfare, low morale, and the sense of desperation after the murder of many dynastic leaders, surely were among the primary causes of the Iranian defeat. After the battle of Jalūlāʾ, Yazdgird III is said to have first gone from Ḥulwān in the direction of Jibāl,[1322]

1312 Ṭabarī 1989a, p. 37, de Goeje, 2457.

1313 Sebeos 1999, p. 99.

1314 Ṭabarī 1989a, pp. 160–161, de Goeje, 2579.

1315 Under this hypothesis, the conquest of Khuzistān, which we will discuss on page 236ff below, might actually have taken place prior to or at the same time as the battle of Jalūlāʾ.

1316 Ṭabarī 1989a, p. 37, de Goeje, 2457.

1317 Ṭabarī 1989a, p. 41, de Goeje, 2461.

1318 See footnote 943.

1319 Ṭabarī 1989a, p. 43, de Goeje, 2463. See page 233.

1320 Ṭabarī 1989a, p. 53, de Goeje, 2473.

1321 In fact, to the author's knowledge, very little attention has been payed to logistic considerations of warfare after the battle of Qādisiya, and given the limits imposed on this study, we can not take it much further either.

1322 Ṭabarī 1989a, p. 42, de Goeje, 2463.

and subsequently, and probably incorrectly here, in the direction of Rayy. The itinerary of Yazdgird III's flight, as we shall see, is very significant because it underscores the likelihood that the Pārsīg and the Pahlav took turns in protecting, for a while at least, the Sasanian king Yazdgird III.

3.4.2 The conquest of Khuzistān

In his accounts of the conquest of Iran, the next important battles that Sayf covers after the battle of Jalūlā' are the battle of Ahvāz,[1323] the raid into Fārs,[1324] and the conquest of Rām Hurmurz, al-Sūs and Tustar.[1325] All these he dates to 17 AH/638 CE.[1326]

Hurmuzān the Mede

The central commander in defense of Khuzistān was Hurmuzān, who fled to his own territory after the battle of Qādisiya.[1327] From his home territories, probably in Ahvāz,[1328] this important dynastic leader conducted raids against the people, that is, the Arabs, of Maysān and Dastimaysān.[1329] While we cannot identify unfortunately the gentilitial background of Hurmuzān, he belonged to one of the seven noble families.[1330] The *Khuzistan Chronicle* refers to him, significantly, as a Mede.[1331] That his fiefdom covered the districts of Ahvāz and Mihrijān Qadhaq, however, makes it probable that Hurmuzān belonged to the Pārsīg faction.[1332] At any rate, according to Sayf, Hurmuzān's family was "higher in rank than anybody in Fārs."[1333]

The absence of Hurmuzān at the battle of Jalūlā', and what must have been a substantial force under his command, is surely significant, and indicates several possibilities: a lack of coordinated action, a continuous disagreement among the factions on proper strategy, or the likelihood that Hurmuzān's armies were elsewhere engaging the Arabs. It is remarkable, therefore, that in the defense

[1323] Ṭabarī 1989a, pp. 114–123, de Goeje, 2534–2542.

[1324] Ṭabarī 1989a, pp. 126–132, de Goeje, 2545–2551. Hinds, Martin, 'The First Arab Conquests in Fārs', in *Studies in Early Islamic History*, pp. 199–232, Princeton, 1996 (Hinds 1996).

[1325] Ṭabarī 1989a, pp. 132–148, de Goeje, 2551–2567.

[1326] Although he acknowledges that some traditions put these wars in 16 AH/637 CE. Ṭabarī 1989a, p. 114, de Goeje, 2534.

[1327] Ṭabarī 1989a, p. 115, de Goeje, 2534.

[1328] Ahvāz is the name given by the Arab conquerors to Hormozd-Ardashīr, the Sasanian capital of Khuzistān (Susiana). Lockhart, L., 'al-Ahwāz', in P. Bearman, Th. Bianquis, C.E. Bosworth, E. van Donzel, and W.P. Heinrichs (eds.), *Encyclopaedia of Islam*, Leiden, 2007 (Lockhart 2007).

[1329] "These are districts north of al-Baṣrah and west of al-Ahwāz." Ṭabarī 1989a, p. 115, n. 395.

[1330] Ṭabarī 1989a, p. 140, de Goeje, 2560.

[1331] Khuzistan 1903, *Chronicon*, Chronica Minora, Paris, 1903, translated by I. Guidi (Khuzistan 1903), 35:20 / 29:30 apud Robinson 2004, p. 17.

[1332] Although we cannot be unequivocal in this claim, for there is also the possibility that he was a Pahlav with long roots in important Pārsīg territories. Ṭabarī 1989a, p. 114–115, de Goeje, 2534. According to Dīnawarī, he was the maternal uncle of Shīrūyih Qubād. Dīnawarī 1967, p. 141. This would make him the brother of Shīrūyih Qubād's mother, who, according to Ferdowsī, was the Byzantine emperor's daughter Maryam, which is quite unlikely. Ferdowsī 1935, p. 2857.

[1333] Ṭabarī 1989a, p. 115, de Goeje, 2534.

of Ahvāz, Hurmuzān's forces engaged the Arabs without the participation of the Pahlav forces. One might conjecture, based on his absence at the battle of Jalūlāʾ, that the first phase of the invasion of Khuzistān was simultaneous with, or even prior to, the battle of Jalūlāʾ, sometime during 636–637, thereby also explaining in turn the absence of the Pahlav at the defense of Khuzistān.[1334] How the first, presumably unauthorized, forays into the islands off the coast of southern Iran and subsequently into Fārs under al-ʿAlāʾ b. Ḥaḍramī and ʿArfajah b. Harthamah, conventionally dated to the years 13–14 AH/634–635 CE, relate to the Arab expeditions in Jalūlāʾ and Khuzistān, might also need reconsideration.[1335]

Hurmuzān's isolated warfare against the Arabs forced ʿUtbah b. Ghazwān to ask Saʿd b. Abī Waqqāṣ for reinforcements. Hurmuzān initially put up a stiff resistance against the Arabs. After a number of defeats, however, he sued for peace, in exchange for maintaining control of a truncated part of his territory.[1336] Meanwhile, the settlements in Baṣrah were proceeding apace.[1337] In the course of this, a conflict over territorial boundaries developed between Hurmuzān and the Arabs. Hurmuzān, therefore, stopped paying the agreed tribute to the Arab conquerors.[1338] It is symptomatic of the absence of the Pahlav faction in these conquests that, in anticipation of a second engagement with the Arabs, Hurmuzān was forced to ask for the aid of the Kurds, "whereupon his army grew in strength."[1339] War broke out and Hurmuzān was, once again, defeated, and fled to Rām Hurmurz.[1340] As Ahvāz had already been overtaken and "had become crammed full of Muslims settling in it," Hurmuzān sued for peace, once again. ʿUmar agreed to this and advised ʿUtbah to follow suit. This time the Muslims asked for control over territories not yet conquered, to wit, Rām Hurmurz, Tustar, Susa, Jundaysābūr, Bunyān and Mihrijān Qadhaq.[1341] Hurmuzān was left in charge of collecting the taxation, while the Muslims agreed to defend

[1334]Robinson also proposes the "terminus ante quem of late August of 636/Rajab of AH 15 for the end of ʾAshʿarī's campaigns [in Khuzistān]. That this dating is at *severe* variance with the consensus of Islamic sources [on the founding of Baṣrah] ... [and might] force a redating of the founding of Baṣrah." Robinson 2004, pp. 19–20. Emphasis mine. This of course tallies perfectly with the chronological scheme we have presented.

[1335]The claims that al-ʿAlāʾ b. Ḥaḍramī had to "respond to *ridda*" in Bahrayn in the years 11–12 AH/632–633, and that ʿArfajah b. Harthamah was to reinforce ʿUtbah b. Ghazwān at the battle of Ubullah, traditionally put in 12 AH/633 CE, but in our new dating scheme in 628 (see page 190), for example, will certainly be affected by this reconsideration. For the chronological scheme of the conquests of Khuzistān and Fārs, see, respectively, Robinson 2004; and Hinds 1996, p. 202.

[1336]This included "all of al-Ahwāz and Mihrijān Qadhaq with the exception of Nahr Tīrā and Manāḏhir and that area of Sūq al-Ahwāz that the Muslims had already conquered." Ṭabarī 1989a, p. 119, de Goeje, 2538.

[1337]The conventional date for the construction of Baṣrah is 17 AH/638 CE. Donner, Fred M., 'Baṣra', in Ehsan Yarshater (ed.), *Encyclopaedia Iranica*, New York, 2007a (Donner 2007a). See, however, also footnote 1334.

[1338]Ṭabarī 1989a, p. 120–121, de Goeje, 2540–2541.

[1339]Ṭabarī 1989a, p. 121, de Goeje, 2540.

[1340]Ṭabarī 1989a, p. 123, de Goeje, 2542.

[1341]Ṭabarī 1989a, p. 124, de Goeje, 2543.

him "in case the Kurds of Fārs were to make raids on him."[1342] The ambivalent part played by the Kurds in Hurmuzān's affairs is made clear here. Meanwhile, al-ʿAlāʾ b. Ḥaḍramī conducted an unauthorized raid from Bahrayn into Fārs. The resistance of the Persian Shahrak[1343] in the battle of Ṭāwūs came to nothing and the Persians were yet again defeated.[1344]

While there is a hint in our accounts that, at one point at least, part of the Pahlav joined forces with the Pārsīg,[1345] yet again apparent is the lack of military coordination between the Pahlav and the Pārsīg. The Pārsīg were forced to coordinate their efforts among themselves. For, in the course of these engagements, we are informed that the people of Fārs and those of Ahvāz entered into correspondence. Yazdgird III presumably encouraged these alliances through his correspondence *from Marv*.[1346] Hurmuzān, therefore, once again, prepared to engage the Arabs.[1347] In Tustar, Hurmuzān put up a stiff resistance.[1348] Yet again, however, he was forced, and this time for what was to be the last, to sue for peace with the Muslims.[1349] Captured, with all his royal paraphernalia and the crown of his kingdom on his head, the Muslims finally took this important Pārsīg leader to the Muslim caliph ʿUmar in Baṣrah.[1350] A long anecdotal narrative highlights Hurmuzān's ruse in saving his life when confronted with the prospects of being executed by ʿUmar.[1351] Once he realized that "he had to choose between death and Islam," however, the Pārsīg leader converted.[1352] With the ultimate defeat of the great dynastic figure of Hurmuzān, part of the power of the Pārsīg was also lost.

Sīyāh's conversion

While southwestern Iran was engulfed in turmoil, and while the conquest of Susa (Sūs) was taking place, as the tradition has it in 17 AH/638 CE, but in our revised scheme more likely around 637, Yazdgird III, from Iṣfahān on his way

[1342] Ṭabarī 1989a, p. 124, de Goeje, 2543.

[1343] *Shahrak* is, without a doubt, the Arabicized version of the Sasanian administrative title *shahrīg*, or possibly *shahrab* (see glossary).

[1344] Ṭabarī 1989a, pp. 128–130, de Goeje, 2547–2549.

[1345] Further research is required to determine in which phase of the conquest of Khuzistān the forces of Fārs, Ahvāz, *and* Jibāl could have joined Hurmuzān, if indeed they did, as maintained by Sayf. Ṭabarī 1989a, p. 134, de Goeje, 2553; Robinson 2004.

[1346] The whereabouts of Yazdgird III through all of this will occupy us shortly; see pages 244ff and 257ff. It is, however, quite unlikely that he had at this time already reached Marv; see our discussion on page 257 below.

[1347] Ṭabarī 1989a, p. 133, de Goeje, 2552.

[1348] Ṭabarī 1989a, pp. 134–135, de Goeje, 2553–2554.

[1349] Ṭabarī 1989a, p. 136, de Goeje, 2556.

[1350] While it is possible that depictions of the wealth of Iranians as opposed to that of the Arabs are *topoi*, as Noth observes, it is unwarranted to dismiss these wholesale. For in the general scheme of things, access to wealth was in fact an important motivation for conquest. Ṭabarī 1989a, p. 137, de Goeje, 2557. There is no doubt that as a dynastic leader, a Mede, Hurmuzān's grandeur and wealth must have appeared astounding to his conquerors.

[1351] Ṭabarī 1989a, pp. 138–139, de Goeje, 2558–2559.

[1352] Ṭabarī 1989a, p. 140, de Goeje, 2560.

to Iṣṭakhr, sent a certain Sīyāh,[1353] along with three hundred men, including seventy Persian aristocrats, against the Arabs. The numerical strength of what was meant to be a relief or possibly a reconnaissance force is worth notice. And here the tradition must be accepted for, if anything, our sources are prone to significant numerical exaggeration, as Juynboll argues, perhaps at times by a coefficient of a hundred.[1354] Much has been made of the story of the conversion of Sīyāh and the total of three hundred men who followed suit and submitted to the Arabs.[1355] In the narrative of their defection, however, a number of important points have rarely been highlighted. We must briefly occupy ourselves with these points, for they are relevant to our concerns.

To begin with, none of the Sasanian kings after Khusrow II ever elicited a strong sense of loyalty from the cavalry (*asāwira*) in charge of their protection, because of the political turmoil in the land. We must also keep in mind that we are not dealing here with a vast army but a mere figure of three hundred. These characterizations, however, do not even begin to describe the nature of Sīyāh and his followers' defection. The prelude to their defection is noteworthy. Before going over to the Arabs, Sīyāh reminded his comrades that these "invaders ... [have brought] misery and suffering ... [to] our kingdom ... [that their] animals [have] shat all over the courtyards of Iṣṭakhr." Most importantly, however, Sīyāh reminded his comrades that the Arabs "have subjugated our territory."[1356] Sīyāh and his collaborators, in other words, had become homeless, and hence the agreement into which they were forced to enter. The conditions that Sīyāh and his men set for the Arabs before their defection and supposed conversion are also significant.

According to Ṭabarī, they agreed to *become Muslims with the understanding that* they would fight the Persians, but not the Arabs, that they would settle wherever they pleased, and that they would be given maximum stipends. The Arabs agreed to these conditions. So Sīyāh and his cohorts *converted*. But in the siege of Tustar under ʾAshʿarī, they exhibited "*no application or military efforts*." When admonished and asked for an explanation, the leader of this group of *asāwira* retorted: "[w]e are not as attached to your religion as you are ... we lack the enthusiasm that you have and, living among you, we have no wives to protect, while you have not assigned the most generous stipend to us [i.e., as we stipulated]. And whereas we have weapons and animals, you face the enemy not even wearing helmets!"[1357] Having been informed of Sīyāh's sentiments, ʿUmar

[1353] Ṭabarī 1989a, pp. 142–144, de Goeje, 2562–2564. For Yazdgird III's whereabouts, see page 244 below.

[1354] Ṭabarī 1989a, pp. xiii–xv. Also see Kennedy, Hugh, *The Armies of the Caliphs: Military and Society in the Early Islamic State*, London, 2001 (Kennedy 2001), pp. 1–18.

[1355] Crone is one of the few scholars who actually argues against mass conversion of Iranian elite and their clientage. "Had the Iranian aristocracy converted in large numbers, the Marwanid evolution would certainly have taken a very different course. But the nature of the Arab conquest was such that aristocratic renegades were few and far between." Crone 1980, p. 50.

[1356] Ṭabarī 1989a, p. 143, de Goeje, 2562.

[1357] Ṭabarī 1989a, pp. 143–144, de Goeje, 2563.

then ordered that "the highest possible stipends [be allocated to them] according to their military record, in fact the largest amount [paid to] any Arab tribesman [was] paid [to them:] ... one hundred of the *asāwira* were to receive stipends of two thousand [*dirhams*], while six of them were even given two thousand five hundred."[1358] It is rather certain that Sīyāh and his comrades were originally fighting alongside the Pārsīg faction.[1359] Crone notes that while the "sources are unanimous that the [*asāwira*] converted in joining the Arabs, when they appear in the second civil war almost fifty years later, their leader is called Māh Afrīdhan [a Persian name indicating he had not yet converted] ... while another member of their ranks, Yazīd b. Sīyāh al-Uswārī clearly represents the first generation of Muslims."[1360] It is therefore certain that the conversion stories regarding the *asāwira* and other Iranian elite during the conquest period are *topoic* narration devices inserted post facto into the accounts.[1361]

3.4.3 The conquest of Media

Once the conquest of southwestern Iran was over, news reached ʿUmar that the Persians were assembling at Nihāvand. Aḥnaf advised ʿUmar that as long as "the king of the Persians is still alive among them, ... they will not seize to contend with us for the control of the region."[1362] ʿUmar was also informed "that the people of Mihrijan Qadhaq, [i.e., the home region of Hurmuzān] and those of the districts of al-Ahwāz *gravitated toward the point of view and the erstwhile ambitions of al-Hurmuzān.*" According to Sayf, these were the reasons that "*prompted ʿUmar to give the Muslims permission to venture out into Persian territory,*"[1363] but Hurmuzān's defeat must also have encouraged them.[1364] Whatever the cause, having conquered most of Iraq, the capital of the Sasanians and, finally, southwestern Iran, and having recognized that the only integrative force, however nominal, among the Persians was a Sasanian monarch on the throne, the Arabs set out on the trail of the last Sasanian king, Yazdgird III. If the ultimate goal of the Arabs was to reach the source of trade beyond the Oxus in order to do away with their hitherto middleman position in the east–west trade, there was certainly good logic in this decision.

[1358] Ṭabarī 1989a, p. 143, de Goeje, 2563.

[1359] According to Aʿtham al-Kūfī and the *Khuzistan Chronicle*, the *asāwira* were actually aiding Hurmuzān at Tustar. Robinson 2004, p. 27.

[1360] Crone 1980, n. 362.

[1361] As Robinson has put it in a slightly different manner, for "the early Muslim traditionalists it was probably not so much conversion that was at issue as the stipends that they were awarded." Robinson 2004.

[1362] Ṭabarī 1989a, p. 141, de Goeje, 2561.

[1363] Ṭabarī 1989a, p. 141, de Goeje, 2561. Emphasis added.

[1364] According to Robinson, "al-Hurmuzān, sent by Yazdgird III, played a crucial role in Sasanian defense." Robinson 2004, p. 21.

The battle of Nihāvand

While significant, the defeat of Hurmuzān did not bring about the total collapse of the Pārsīg or the Pahlav faction. The next major encounter with the Arabs under the command of Muqarrin took place in the battle of Nihāvand, which according to Ṭabarī was in 21 AH/641–642 CE. One of the most important features of the decisive battle of Nihāvand was, without a doubt, the fact that, although located in Media, in Parthian territory, the Pārsīg, and not the Pahlav, were leading the battle. For it was Fīrūzān, our famous Pārsīg dynast, who commanded the army that ultimately regrouped in Nihāvand in Median territory.[1365] Balʿamī implies the absence of the Pahlav leaders when he maintains that at the battle of Nihāvand, except for Fīrūzān, no one fit for assuming the command had remained.[1366] Why the Pārsīg rather than the Pahlav led this battle we shall shortly ascertain. For now it should be remarked that the absence of the leader of the Pahlav, Farrukhzād, from this important battle, with the substantial forces under his command, can be explained by determining the whereabouts at that point in time of the Sasanian king Yazdgird III.[1367]

The head and the wings of the bird

The interesting dialogue between ʿUmar and Hurmuzān regarding the choice of the battlefield, instead of being dismissed as a mere *topos*, should be read for the role of the Pahlav and the Pārsīg factional armies in their defense of the realm.[1368] In the course of this dialogue, ʿUmar asked Hurmuzān's advice as to where he should strike first. Hurmuzān answered with another question: "Where is the head?" ʿUmar replied that the head was Nihāvand under the "command of Bundār, [who] had the royal brigade of *asāwira* and troops from Iṣbahān [along] with him." De Goeje proposed that Bundār was a corruption of Mardānshāh Dhū 'l-Ḥājibayn,[1369] that is to say, the Pārsīg leader Mardānshāh Dhu 'l-Ḥājib (Bahman Jādhūyih).[1370] Nihāvand was chosen as head, not only on account of its important strategic and political location in Median territory, but also because the Iranian army had now gathered there. In this tradition provided by Ṭabarī the transmitter is said to have forgotten the regional identifications of the wings, but other traditions identify the wings with Fārs and Azarbāyjān.[1371] In an attempt to presumably misdirect ʿUmar,

[1365]Ṭabarī 1989a, p. 193, de Goeje, 2608.

[1366]Balʿamī 1959, p. 317, n. 4.

[1367]See page 244ff below.

[1368]It should be remarked at the outset that Noth's argument regarding the existence of *topoi* which appear in the accounts of both the battle of Nihāvand and the battle of Iṣfahān, confirms our earlier assessment of his analysis. For in fact all of the *topoi* which he enumerates are *Islamic* or *Arab topoi* and do not affect the information that Sayf provides regarding the Iranian side. An exception is this dialogue between ʿUmar and Hurmuzān, which appears to contain an echo of Sebeos' three armies. Noth 1968; see also footnote 1414.

[1369]Ṭabarī 1989a, p. 184, n. 629, de Goeje, DCXXII.

[1370]See our discussion of these epithets on page 196ff.

[1371]Another variant has the Persian king (Kisrā) as the head, and Fārs and Byzantium forming its wings. Noth 1968, pp. 283–284.

Hurmuzān nevertheless pressed on the caliph to "cut off the wings" of the empire. ʿUmar, however, realizing Hurmuzān's duplicity and ill-placed intentions retorted: "you speak lies ... I shall go for the head first."[1372] The repetition of this theme in the conquest accounts of both Nihāvand and Iṣfahān might give the appearance of a concocted literary device, but should not, however, detract from the *germ* of the narrative. Otherwise, the same narrative could very well have appeared in the accounts of the battle of Qādisiya or the battle of Jalūlāʾ, for example.

At any rate, Sayf reiterates the regrouping of the Persians after the defeat of Hurmuzān and the conquest of Khuzistān: "What precipitated the fighting at Nihāwand was that, after the fighters from al-Baṣrah had overpowered al-Hurmuzān and had forestalled the people of Fārs by preventing them from annihilating the army force of al-Alāʿ, ... the people of Fārs wrote to their king ... [and he rallied] the inhabitants of al-Jibāl, namely those of al-Bāb, al-Sind,[1373] Khurāsān, and Ḥulwān who were duly roused."[1374] The Armenian faction was also represented, under their leader Khusrow Shenūm (Varaztirotsʿ). After Hurmuzān's defeat, in other words, Yazdgird III is said to have appealed to the forces of the Pahlav. Continued discord emerges clearly in this narrative: "They agreed that they would show up at Nihāwand and *sort out their matters there*."[1375] Here then we are given the aforementioned south–north, Pārsīg–Pahlav territorial division.[1376] Thus, "one after the other, there arrived those living in the territory between Khurāsān and Ḥulwān, those living in the territory between al-Bāb and Ḥulwān, and those living in the territory between Sijistān and Ḥulwān ... The cavalry of Fārs and of the Fahlūj [*sic*, i.e., *fahlawaj*] ... joined forces ... [and they] assembled *under the command of al-Fayrūzān*, and they all set out to him, one after the other."[1377] Whereas sometime during the rule of Būrāndukht the Pahlav and the Pārsīg had joined forces only to divide again, in the battle of Nihāvand during the reign of Yazdgird III, they yet again joined forces. This is the second time, therefore, that Sayf has informed us of the over-arching Pahlav and Pārsīg factions coming under the command of Fīrūzān.[1378] And it is curious that while Yazdgird III sent a general appeal to all forces, Farrukhzād's were nevertheless missing from action in Nihāvand.

In spite of their coalition, the Persians were once again defeated at the battle of Nihāvand. The Pārsīg leader Fīrūzān was finally, and this time for real, killed.[1379] After Fīrūzān's death, Bahman Jādhūyih was appointed in

[1372] Ṭabarī 1989a, p. 184–185, de Goeje, 2601.

[1373] Who these might have been I have no idea.

[1374] Ṭabarī 1989a, pp. 189–190, de Goeje, 2605.

[1375] Ṭabarī 1989a, p. 190, de Goeje, 2605. Emphasis mine.

[1376] See our discussion on page 214ff.

[1377] Ṭabarī 1989a, p. 193, de Goeje, 2608. In our revised chronology, there will be a five year hiatus between the battle of Jalūlāʾ (637–638) and the regrouping of the forces at Nihāvand, if the conventional dating of the latter in 641–642 is assumed.

[1378] See our discussion on page 214ff.

[1379] Ṭabarī 1989a, p. 209, de Goeje, 2626.

his stead.[1380] Presumably, however, his appointment came too late to effect a change in the direction of the war, and part of the Persian army fled to Hamadān.[1381] Under the command of the Armenian Khusrow Shenūm (Varaztirots'), the Persians "sought immunity from the Muslims ... [and accepted to] surrender Hamadān and Dastabā [to the conquerors]."[1382] With Fīrūzān dead and Farrukhzād nowhere to be found, the Bagratuni dynast Varaztirots' sued for peace. The whereabouts of the treasury maintained by Varaztirots' was allegedly disclosed by a treacherous *herbad*, a tradition that might indicate signs of religious animosity between the two.[1383]

Dīnār's expropriation of Kārinid domains

In the wake of the defeat at the battle of Nihāvand and Varaztirots''s peace agreement with the Arabs, through which he relinquished the important Pahlav stronghold Hamadān to the conquering forces, the people in charge of the territories that eventually came to be called the Māh of Baṣrah and the Māh of Kūfa[1384] "followed Khusrawshunūm's [i.e., Khusrow Shenūm, Varaztirots'] example and corresponded with Ḥudhayfah." But in the course of these negotiations an unprecedented transformation took place. The Kārins, whose original homeland seems to have been the region of Nihāvand,[1385] were disenfranchised from the lands that had still remained in their possession. As our account puts it, "the people in charge of these territories ... were deceived by one of them, a man called Dīnār."[1386] This Dīnār, we are told, "was a king [in his own right] but of *lesser nobility* than the others, all of them being more exalted than he, with Qārin the noblest of them all."[1387] Significantly, Qārin (Kārin) was from "the ruling family in those days."[1388] The end result of Dīnār's ruse,[1389] advising the other noble families that it would not be prudent to approach the Arabs with their full regalia,[1390] was that the "Muslims concluded a treaty with him while disregarding his [fellow aristocrats, the outcome of this being that] ...

[1380]Bal'amī 1959, p. 317, n. 4; Ṭabarī 1989a, p. 203, de Goeje, 2618:

بهمن جاذويه الذى جعل مكان ذوالحاجب

[1381]Ṭabarī 1989a, p. 210, de Goeje, 2626.

[1382]Ṭabarī 1989a, p. 210, de Goeje, 2626.

[1383]Ṭabarī 1989a, p. 210, de Goeje, 2627. Varaztirots' (Khusrow Shenūm) is here identified as Nakhīrjān, the Arabicized form of Armenian *naxarar*; see also footnote 943.

[1384]See footnote 146.

[1385]That is, prior to their relocation to Khurāsān during Khusrow I's reign; see page 114. The nature and extent of the Kārins' identification with Nihāvand must be subjected to future research, for in the course of this study we have not been able to establish the *original* homeland of the Kārins with any certainty.

[1386]Ṭabarī 1989a, p. 211, de Goeje, 2628.

[1387]Ṭabarī 1989a, p. 211, de Goeje, 2628.

[1388]Ṭabarī 1989a, p. 215, de Goeje, 2631.

[1389]The theme of *traitor* in the accounts of conquest is also considered a *topos* by Noth. As we shall see, this observation cannot be applied as a general rule; see footnote 1447.

[1390]Ṭabarī 1989a, p. 211, de Goeje, 2628.

the latter saw no other way than to yield to Dīnār and to accept his authority." That is why, Ṭabarī explains, Nihāvand "came to be called Māh [i.e., Media] Dīnār."[1391] We have not been able to ascertain the true identity of Dīnār,[1392] who allegedly duped the rest of the nobility, including the Kārins. Clearly, in the wake of the defeat at the battle of Nihāvand, and analogous to the events that will transpire in Rayy,[1393] the Arabs were able to take advantage of factionalism in the Iranian ranks.

As we already pointed out, perhaps the most curious feature of the battle of Nihāvand was the conspicuous absence of Farrukhzād, the leader of the Pahlav, and his army. We recall that after his correspondence with Rustam prior to the battle of Qādisiya, the next and last thing that we hear about Farrukhzād is that he participated in the battle of Jalūlā'. As we have seen, the presence of almost all of the important dynastic leaders has been meticulously followed in our sources. But, from the subsequent engagements between the Arabs and the Persians after the battle of Jalūlā', Farrukhzād was patently missing. What happened then to this towering scion of the family of the Prince of the Medes? The answers to this crucial question must engage us in a discussion of the whereabouts of the Sasanian king, Yazdgird III, after the battle of Qādisiya. So, yet again, we briefly pause our war narratives to discuss the king's flight southwards.

Yazdgird III's flight southwards

The itinerary of the flight of Yazdgird III after the battle of Qādisiya has been the source of confusion.[1394] Sebeos' account aids us in reconstructing it. According to Sebeos, after the defeat of the Persians at the battle of Qādisiya and following the death of Rustam, when the "survivors of the Persian army reached Atrpatakan [Azarbāyjān], they gathered together in one place and installed Khoṙokhazat, [Farrukhzād] as their general."[1395] With the two important scions of the Ispahbudhān house of the Prince of the Medes, Farrukh Hormozd and Rustam, dead, Farrukhzād was appointed as the leader of the Pahlav faction. Instead of participating in the subsequent crucial battles, however, Farrukhzād took up an even more momentous responsibility: the safety of the last Sasanian king Yazdgird III. According to Sebeos, from Azarbāyjān, Farrukhzād "hastened to Ctesiphon, took all the treasures of the kingdom, the inhabitants of the cities, and *their king*, and made haste to bring them to

[1391] Ṭabarī 1989a, p. 212, de Goeje, 2628. For the use of *Māh*, see footnote 146.

[1392] Incidentally, Dīnār cannot have been the original Persian name of this dynast.

[1393] See §3.4.4.

[1394] Ya'qūbī maintains that Yazdgird III first went to Iṣfahān before going to some other region where he met the ruler of Ṭabaristān, who informed him of the sturdiness of his cities. Ya'qūbi 1983, p. 38. Bal'amī mistakenly maintains that Yazdgird III set out from Rayy to Khurāsān. Bal'amī 1959, p. 325.

[1395] Sebeos 1999, p. 99. Thomson notes that in Marquart 1931, the above passage is rendered as "when the survivors of the Persian troops from Atrpatakan gathered." Thomson argues, however, that "the text is clear as it stands." Ibid., p. 99, n. 611.

Atrpatakan."[1396] The flight of Farrukhzād and the king, together with the treasures of the kingdom, toward Azarbāyjān, however, was intercepted by the Arabs, called here *Ismaelites* by Sebeos. As Sebeos puts it, "after they had set out and had gone some distance, unexpectedly the Ismaelite army attacked them."[1397] The interception, or imminent interception of the Arab army, led Farrukhzād to "abandon ... the treasures and the inhabitants of the city."[1398] This unexpected arrival of the Arab army most probably refers to the battle of Jalūlāʾ (around 637). Farrukhzād's concern with the safety of Yazdgird III and the Sasanian treasury probably also explains the fact that the Pahlav leader was able to take charge only of the cavalry, and not of the entire army, in this battle. For in the battle of Jalūlāʾ, we recall, Mihrān-i Bahrām-i Rāzī was in command.[1399]

Upon this terrifying turn of events, Yazdgird III "fled and took refuge with the army of the south." The Arabs reportedly took all the treasures,[1400] returned to Ctesiphon, and "ravaged the whole land."[1401] Sometime after the sacking of Ctesiphon (around 635), therefore, Yazdgird III set out toward the south. Considering his absence, it is quite probable that Farrukhzād continued to follow the king, at least for a while, even when the latter took refuge with the army of the south (Nīmrūz). The flight of the king to the south is corroborated by our Arabic sources. According to Ṭabarī, sometime after the battle of Jalūlāʾ, Yazdgird III, who was then in Ḥulwān, was advised to go to Iṣṭakhr, "for that is the center of the kingdom."[1402] While he was further advised to "send ... [his] soldiers away" and keep his treasures, however, it is almost certain that the latter could not have been accomplished without the former. The treasury of the king must have required a strong force to safeguard, for it was to cause tremendous contention between the king and his protector Farrukhzād in the near future.[1403] It was at this point, when Yazdgird III began his arduous flight, from Ḥulwān via Iṣfahān to Iṣṭakhr, that he sent Sīyāh to lead the way. Sīyāh arrived at Iṣṭakhr at the same time that Abū Mūsā al-ʾAshʿarī was laying siege to Sūs (Susa). After he was sent to Susa, Sīyāh then mutinied.[1404] At this point Hurmuzān was in Tustar, and the people of Sūs, having heard about the news of Jalūlāʾ and the flight of their king to Iṣṭakhr, sued for peace with the Arabs.[1405]

Yazdgird III's flight took him first to the protective custody of the Pārsīg

---

1396 Sebeos 1999, p. 99.

1397 Sebeos 1999, p. 99.

1398 Sebeos 1999, p. 99.

1399 See page 234ff.

1400 That this could not actually have been the entire royal treasury will become clear later in the narrative; see for instance, page 258.

1401 Sebeos 1999, p. 99.

1402 Ṭabarī 1989a, p. 142, de Goeje, 2561.

1403 See page 258.

1404 See page 238ff. Note that we have dated his capture and conversion also at around 637.

1405 Ṭabarī 1989a, p. 142, de Goeje, 2562.

in the south. Ḥamza Iṣfahānī corroborates that Farrukhzād[1406] accompanied Yazdgird III in his flight south, then southeast and finally northeast, "to Iṣfahān ... Kirmān and finally to Marv."[1407] Other sources confirm this as well. An authority in Ṭabarī has it, for example, that Yazdgird III went first to Fārs, and thence to Kirmān and Sīstān, where he remained for five years. From Sīstān, Yazdgird III then went to Khurāsān, and finally to Marv. It seems likely that on his way to the northeast, Yazdgird III was also confronted with the unsettled situation in Ṭabaristān.[1408] Those traditions that claim that Yazdgird III went from Rayy to Khurāsān, therefore, might have a germ of truth in them.[1409] At any rate, Ṭabarī informs us that Farrukhzād was Yazdgird III's escort all the way to Khurāsān.[1410] That the Arab armies intended to follow Yazdgird III's trail is corroborated by the identical itinerary that they took northeast. Leading the way for the pursuing the Arabs, Yazdgird III went from Kirmān, via Ṭabasayn and Qūhistān, to Khurāsān.[1411]

Numismatic evidence confirms that Yazdgird III stayed for a somewhat extended period of time in the vicinity of Kirmān and Sīstān before heading northeast, sometime in the late 640s.[1412] In Kirmān and Sīstān, he was for a long while protected by the regions to the west. The authority in Ṭabarī who holds that Yazdgird III stayed for about five years in that region, provides the most trustworthy tradition. If our chronology for the battle of Nihāvand in or about 642 is correct, and if we accept the fact that Yazdgird III remained in the Kirmān and Sīstān regions for about five years, we can conjecture that Yazdgird III stayed in said regions from about 642 until around 648, after which he went northeast. It is not clear whether Farrukhzād remained with Yazdgird III throughout his stay in the southeast. What is clear is that after a long interlude, it was in the company of Farrukhzād and a substantial army under his command, that the last Sasanian king arrived in Khurāsān in search of protection. In Khurāsān the king's stay was very eventful, and we shall follow this saga in its appropriate place.[1413] For now, we proceed with the events after the battle of Nihāvand.

[1406]His name is correctly rendered here as Khurzād b. Khur Hurmuz, the brother of Rustam.

[1407]Ḥamza Iṣfahānī 1961, p. 55, Ḥamza Iṣfahānī 1988, p. 59.

[1408]For the political situation in Ṭabaristān around this time, see Chapter 4, especially page 302ff.

[1409]See footnotes 1394 and 1528.

[1410]Ṭabarī, *The Crisis of the Early Caliphate*, vol. 15 of *The History of Ṭabarī*, NY, 1990, translated and annotated by R. Stephen Humphreys (Ṭabarī 1990), p. 82, de Goeje, 2876.

[1411]Ṭabarī 1990, p. 87, de Goeje, 2881. Hence the tradition in the *Taʾrīkh-i Bayhaq* that Yazdgird III stayed for a while in Bayhaq. See Bayhaqī, Ibrāhīm b. Muḥammad, *Taʾrīkh-i Bayhaq*, Tehran, 1938, edited by Ahmad Bahmanyar (Bayhaqī 1938), p. 26; Pourshariati, Parvaneh, 'Local Historiography in Early Medieval Iran and the Taʾrīkh-i Bayhaq', *Journal of Iranian Studies* 33, (2000), pp. 133–164 (Pourshariati 2000).

[1412]See page 220.

[1413]For the continuation of Yazdgird III's flight to the east, see page 257ff.

The battle of Iṣfahān

After the battle of Nihāvand the Persians made a stand at the battle of Iṣfahān (641–642).[1414] The commander of the army at the battle of Iṣfahān was a certain Shahrvarāz Jādhūyih,[1415] "an important leader at the head of a large force."[1416] His name seems to suggest that this general was a member of Shahrvarāz's family, in other words, a Mihrān.[1417] A second figure introduced in the account of Iṣfahān is a certain al-Fādhūsfān, who was the ruler of the region. *Fādhūsfān*, that is, *pādhūspān*,[1418] clearly refers to an administrative title and not to the name of this figure. In Ṭabarī's account, the title of this general who commanded a grand army is given as *ustāndār* (*ōstāndār* or governor).[1419] The command structure of the Sasanian army in the battle of Iṣfahān, therefore, was quite distinct from that in the battle of Nihāvand, which had been under the command of Fīrūzān, containing not only Pārsīg, but also Pahlav and Armenian contingents.[1420] The congregation of the Pārsīg in Iṣfahān after the defeat at the battle of Nihāvand is clear in Sayf's account. According to Balʿamī, when the *pādhūspān* heard about the defeat at Nihāvand, he came to Iṣfahān, together with Shahrvarāz Jādhūyih, to confront the Arabs. Shahrvarāz Jādhūyih, however, was defeated and killed in this battle. Another Pārsīg leader who participated in the battle of Iṣfahān was Mardānshāh (Bahman Jādhūyih?).[1421] Mardānshāh and Shahrvarāz Jādhūyih are said to have alternated command. This confusion probably reflects isolated *khabars* concerning different episodes of the war. Whatever the case, it is quite clear that the commanders participating in the battle of Iṣfahān were predominantly of the Pārsīg faction, who had to confront the enemy without the participation of the Pahlav. After the defeat and death of Shahrvarāz Jādhūyih, the (unnamed) *pādhūspān* made peace in lieu of paying the *jizya*, on the condition that the Arabs let whosoever wanted to

[1414]According to Noth, there are grounds to argue that the account of the battle of Iṣfahān replicates some of the motifs of the battle of Nihāvand. Noth 1968. For instance, we find the same exchange between ʿUmar and Hurmuzān about the head and the wings of the bird. Ṭabarī 1994, p. 10, de Goeje, 2642; for the parable of the bird, see page 241. Interestingly enough, this account does not belong to Sayf. Another common motif between the two accounts is the meeting of Mughīrah with Dhu 'l-Ḥājib. Ṭabarī 1994, p. 11, de Goeje, 2642–2643. As already mentioned, since almost all of the *topoi* investigated by Noth are Islamic and most probably inserted in the traditions of the two battles in later periods, his analysis does not detract from the conclusions that we shall arrive at: The internal Sasanian indicators clearly testify to the retention of two separate episodes of conquest in the historical memory of its respective transmitters.

[1415]Balʿamī 1959, p. 328.

[1416]Ṭabarī 1994, p. 7, de Goeje, 2638.

[1417]Balʿamī calls him Shahrīyār, which could be a scribal error for Shahrvarāz. Balʿamī 1959, p. 328, n. 3. However, in footnote 1092 we offer an alternative reading, which no longer implies that he had to be a Mihrān.

[1418]See footnote 411.

[1419]Ṭabarī 1994, p. 7, de Goeje, 2638.

[1420]See page 241ff.

[1421]See page 196ff.

leave Iṣfahān free to depart.[1422] ʿAbdallāh b. ʿAbdallāh b. ʿItbān, who had been joined by Abū Mūsā ʾAshʿarī, accepted. Some traditions maintain that many people left the city upon the conclusion of the peace agreements.[1423] Others depict this migration as a minority who "opposed their people."[1424] Dhu 'l-Ḥājib (Mardānshāh, Bahman Jādhūyih) was also killed in this battle.

The battle of Wāj Rūdh

The sequence of conquests that follows in the accounts of Sayf is: Hamadān, Rayy, Gurgān, Ṭabaristān, and finally Azarbāyjān, all of which he puts in the year 18 of *hijra* (638), while most others put these conquests in the years 22 AH/642 CE, or 23 AH/643 CE. According to Sayf, after the battle of Nihāvand, Nuʿaym b. Muqarrin and Qaʿqā b. ʿAmr set out for Hamadān. In charge of Hamadān was the Armenian Bagratunid dynast Khusrow Shenūm (Varaztirotsʿ).[1425] Significantly, we are informed here that Varaztirotsʿ had broken the peace treaty that he had previously signed with Ḥudhayfah, and had gathered an enormous army around himself.[1426] In anticipation of Nuʿaym's arrival, Varaztirotsʿ requested the aid of the army of Azarbāyjān. Once a substantial enough force had gathered around him,[1427] he engaged the Arabs in one of the villages of Hamadān called Wāj Rūdh.[1428] As the accounts of this battle make clear, after the battle of Nihāvand, the battle of Wāj Rūdh became one of the most important battles in the north. The army of Daylam, under the command of one Mūtā, came to the aid of the Armenian dynast Varaztirotsʿ. Significantly, a member of the family of the Prince of the Medes, Isfandīyār, "did the same at the head of the Azerbaijan army."[1429]

Most of the commanders participating in the battle of Wāj Rūdh belong this time to the Pahlav faction, in collaboration with the Armenian contingent under the command of Varaztirotsʿ. The dynastic Pahlav leader, Farrukhzād, however, is still nowhere to be found! A new figure of substantial importance, however, is introduced. Bearing the enigmatic name al-Zīnabī Abū 'l-Farrukhān, he arrived "at the head of the Rayy army." That he too belonged to the

[1422] Balʿamī 1959, pp. 328–329. In Ṭabarī's version, the treaty that the *pādhūspān* made with the Arabs is also reproduced, but its contents are of no consequence to our concerns. Ṭabarī 1994, pp. 8–9, de Goeje, 2640–2641.

[1423] Balʿamī 1959, p. 329.

[1424] Ṭabarī claims these to be thirty in number. Ṭabarī 1994, p. 8, de Goeje, 2640.

[1425] Ṭabarī 1994, p. 19, de Goeje, 2648.

[1426] Ṭabarī 1994, p. 19, de Goeje, 2649. For the circumstances under which the previous peace treaty was effected, see page 243.

[1427] Balʿamī 1959, p. 331.

[1428] Ṭabarī 1994, p. 21, de Goeje, 2650.

[1429] Ṭabarī 1994, p. 21, de Goeje, 2650. Ṭabarī calls him mistakenly a *brother of Rustam*, but as will become clear later (see §3.4.8), he was a son of Farrukhzād. The editor, referring us to Zarrinkub 1975, observes that Isfandīyādh "was the brother of *Rustam b. Farrukhzād*, the Persian general defeated at Qādisiya." Ibid., n. 115. This, needless to reiterate, is yet another example of the scholarly confusion surrounding the genealogy of the Ispahbudhān. We should also recall that already during the Byzantine wars the army of Azarbāyjān was under the command of the Ispahbudhān family; see §2.7.5.

Pahlav faction will become amply clear once we have revealed his true identity.[1430] Considering the number of high-caliber dignitaries present in this battle, it is no wonder that Sayf claims the battle of Wāj Rūdh to be "a great battle like Nihāvand, not at all inferior, … [where] great, incalculable numbers were killed."[1431] The Persians lost, yet again, and the great Bagratunid dynast Khusrow Shenūm (Varaztirots') was killed.[1432] It is important to reiterate once again that the Iranian names contained in the *futūḥ* were not callously and haphazardly invented by the tradition. For, once identified, the names of these commanders become an important index for determining the chronology of events. In this case, for example, we can now ascertain that the battle of Wāj Rūdh took place *prior* to the conquest of Azarbāyjān, for it was only during the latter episode that the Ispahbudhān Isfandīyār made peace with the Arabs.[1433]

3.4.4 The conquest of Rayy

After the battle of Wāj Rūdh, when ʿUmar was finally informed of the Arab victory at the battle of Wāj Rūdh and the conquest of Hamadān,[1434] he was also told that yet again a great army had gathered, this time in Rayy, under the command of the grandson of Bahrām-i Chūbīn.[1435] The conquest of Rayy and Ṭabaristān and, as we shall see, Khurāsān and Azarbāyjān, connect together in a highly intricate fashion, in such a manner that, once the nuances in the narratives are deciphered and once the nature of the dynastic dynamics operating within these regions are disentangled, they clarify the histories of the *kūst-i ādurbādagān* and *kūst-i khwarāsān* in the two centuries following the conquest. For as we shall attempt to show in the pages that follow, the conquests of the quarters of the north and east of the Sasanian domains, which formed the hereditary territory of the Parthian dynastic families, actually led to the final collapse of the Sasanian–Parthian confederacy, to the demise of the house of the Sāsān, and most importantly, to the continued independence of these regions under the *de facto* rule of Parthian dynasts and under the *nominal* suzerainty of the caliphate. In the process, some Parthian dynasts did lose their long-held dominion of these territories, while others continued to rule with little change.[1436]

Sīyāvakhsh Mihrān

According to Ṭabarī, the ruler in Rayy at this juncture was one Sīyāvakhsh b. Mihrān b. Shūbīn.[1437] Now by way of context we should recall that Rayy and its vicinity had for a long time been the stronghold of the Parthian dynastic

[1430] However, a long tale still needs to be told before on page 264 we can finally identify this figure. See also page 250ff.
[1431] Ṭabarī 1994, p. 22, de Goeje, 2651.
[1432] Balʿamī 1959, p. 332.
[1433] See §3.4.8.
[1434] Balʿamī here notes that the news was delayed as the distance was great. Balʿamī 1959, p. 331.
[1435] Balʿamī 1959, p. 331.
[1436] We will elaborate this point further in Chapters 4 and 6.
[1437] Ṭabarī 1994, p. 24, de Goeje, 2653.

family of the Mihrāns. The Mihrāns, we recall, held the important office of the *ērān-spāhbedī* of the quarter of the north from at least Khusrow I's rule onward.[1438] The exception to this rule was the period of the rebellion and independence of Vistāhm[1439] in the quarters of the north and the east, when the office of the *ērān-spāhbed* was most likely meaningless in these regions. The rebellion of the Mihrānid Bahrām-i Chūbīn[1440] had set the precedent, even prior to Vistāhm's rebellion, for galvanizing these quarters against Hormozd IV and Khusrow II. There is, therefore, absolutely no reason to question the historicity of the figure of Sīyāvakhsh, the grandson of Bahrām-i Chūbīn, at this period.[1441]

By way of context we should also recall that while these regions had led uprisings against the Sasanians, and while the Parthian dynasts had at times come to collaborate against the latter, there had also long existed a strong antipathy between the Mihrāns and the Ispahbudhān, an antipathy that had reached its apex in the course of Bahrām-i Chūbīn's rebellion. During the latter episode, we remember, the Ispahbudhān family had ensured the destruction of the Mihrānid rebel.[1442] In the context of inter-Parthian dynastic struggles, in other words, the Mihrāns and the Ispahbudhāns were age-old rivals.

When Sīyāvakhsh heard that Nuʿaym b. Muqarrin was heading toward Rayy from Wāj Rūdh, he sent a messenger to the *ʿajam* (i.e., the Persians) and all the armies who were in the vicinity of Rayy and made an appeal to them: "The Arab army has set out toward Rayy, and the Arabs have spread elsewhere. None can stand up to them. And Yazdgird III is far from us." Sīyāvakhsh then proceeded to warn them of their imminent destruction, were they not to take action: "When the Arabs finally arrive at Rayy, you cannot remain where you are. *If you come to my aid, we can put up a fight against them. If you don't aid me, you will all be destroyed.*" All, Balʿamī maintains, answered Sīyāvakhsh's call for aid.[1443] According to Ṭabarī, Sīyāvakhsh had "asked the people of Dunbāwand, Ṭabaristān, Qūmis, and Jurjān for their help."[1444]

Zīnabī Abū 'l-Farrukhān

The Mihrānid Sīyāvakhsh, however, faced a serious rival. Balʿamī discloses the identity of this rival in a semi-folkloric account. In Rayy, there was in Sīyāvakhsh's army one of the "elite of the *ʿajam*, from among the *dihqāns* of Rayy," whose name was Rāmī. The father of this Rāmī, Balʿamī further maintains, "*was the grandee of Ray.* And between him and Sīyāvakhsh there had [always] been a struggle over the territories of Rayy." Now Balʿamī's editor justifiably notes that in other recensions, the name of this figure is given either as Vabī,

[1438]See §2.5.4, especially page 103ff, as well as the table on page 470.
[1439]See §2.7.1.
[1440]See §2.6.3.
[1441]For the likelihood of his identification with Sīyāvakhsh-i Rāzī, see footnote 1144.
[1442]See page 128ff.
[1443]Balʿamī 1959, pp. 331–332.
[1444]Ṭabarī 1994, p. 25, de Goeje, 2654.

the son of Farrukhān, or alternatively, as Zīnabī Abū 'l-Farrukhān.[1445] Who was this figure Rāmī, Vabī the son of Farrukhān, or Zīnabī Abū 'l-Farrukhān, and what was his role in the conquest of Rayy? According to Ṭabarī, when Sīyāvakhsh made an appeal for aid, in defiance of him, al-Zīnabī Abū 'l-Farrukhān, who "*had seen what the Muslims were like, [comparing their attitude] with the envy of Sīyāvakhsh and his family,*" came and met Nuʿaym in a place near Qazvīn called Qiha and made peace with him.[1446] Zīnabī proposed to Nuʿaym that the "enemy is numerous, whereas you are at the head of a small army. Send some cavalry with me. I shall take them into their town, [Rayy,] by a way that [even] (the locals) do not know."[1447] According to Ṭabarī, Zīnabī then collaborated with the Arabs and they engaged the army that had gathered around Sīyāvakhsh. With the aid of Zīnabī, Nuʿaym's army was victorious. After their victory, those who were among the original inhabitants of Rayy took refuge in Qūmis and Dāmghān. The Arab army then entered Rayy, looted the city and gained substantial booty. According to Sayf, "God gave the Muslims at al-Rayy about the same amount of spoils as those at Madāʾin."[1448] The wealth of the capital of the Mihrāns is thus compared to the wealth of the capital of the Sasanians themselves. Once again, there is no reason to consider the extent of this wealth as a *topos* created by the tradition.

In the account that follows we are apprised of one of the most important transformations that took place in the political structure of this important region of the Sasanian domains in the wake of the Arab conquest. The Arabs, we are informed, then gave Zīnabī and his followers promise of safety (*zinhār*), made Zīnabī the *marzbān* of Rayy, and made peace with him.[1449] As a result, Zīnabī gained a substantial treasury as well. With the conquest of Rayy, therefore, the Arab conquerors toppled one of the most powerful and ancient Parthian dynastic families of the region, the Mihrans, from its seat of power in Rayy. In this, however, they had the aid of one very able collaborator, our enigmatic figure Zīnabī Abū 'l-Farrukhān, who thenceforth assumed power, and as we shall see, not only in Rayy but also elsewhere.[1450] According to Sayf, thereafter the "honor of al-Rayy continued to be greatest among the family of al-Zīnabī, including Shahrām and Farrukhān. *The family of Bahrām [Chūbīn] fell from grace*, and Nuʿaym destroyed their town, which was called al-ʿAtīqah (the Old Town) . . . Al-Zīnabī [,however,] *gave orders for the building of the new town*

[1445] Balʿamī 1959, p. 332, and n. 2.

[1446] Ṭabarī 1994, p. 24, de Goeje, 2654. Ṭabarī maintains that Shahrām and Farrukhān were the sons of Zīnabī. This is a new piece of information, with which we should reckon in our analysis of Zīnabī's identity on page 264ff. Ṭabarī 1994, p. 25, de Goeje, 2655. Justi repeats this information. Justi 1895, p. 276.

[1447] Ṭabarī 1994, p. 25, de Goeje, 2654. Here then is an example of the ruse of a traitor, which although couched in a folkloric tale, is thoroughly historical, as we shall presently argue.

[1448] Ṭabarī 1994, p. 25, de Goeje, 2654.

[1449] Balʿamī 1959, p. 332; Ṭabarī 1994, p. 25, de Goeje, 2654–2655.

[1450] In Balʿamī's account we also get the curious passage that Zīnabī and his family had "*the same religion as the ʿajam* (*va īshān ham bar dīn-i ʿajam mībūdand*)." Balʿamī 1959, p. 333.

of al-Rayy."[1451] Nuʿaym's peace agreement was addressed to *al-Zīnabī b. Qūlah* and others with him.[1452] Zīnabī's *nisba* of Qūlah, or Kūlā, is important for our future purposes and we shall deal with it later.[1453] This then became a truly substantive transformation, somewhat analogous to the change in power in Khurāsān effected by Khusrow I's appointment of the Kārins as the new *spāhbeds* of the region.[1454] In keeping with the tradition of political rule in this important domain of the northern quarter, the region of Rayy, the Mihrāns were officially toppled and another family, the family of Zīnabī, was installed in their stead. What this might have meant in terms of the actual domains that had once been the property of the Mihrāns and how their tremendous social power was affected by this transformation, considering the nature of agnatic land-ownership and religious practices, must be left open for future research.[1455] What is clear, however, is that the *de facto* and age-old tradition of Mihrānid rule in Rayy came to an end in the wake of the conquests with, significantly, the aid of a faction that was likely an age-old rival, the family of Abū 'l-Farrukhān. This transformation in Rayy was altogether not dissimilar to what had transpired after the battle of Nihāvand, when Dīnār, who was of low nobility, allegedly duped the Arabs into accepting him as the ruler of the region, at the expense of the Kārins' status.[1456] For the transfer of power from one important dynastic family to another, as we witness here in Rayy, or the loss of status of an important dynastic family, as in Nihāvand, was of such a momentous nature that the details were highlighted in the traditions. By the same token we ought to have been given more information about the party to whom the power of the Mihrāns in Rayy was transferred. This, however, was not the case and the figure of Zīnabī, in spite of his importance, remains quite obscure.[1457]

Once the Mihrāns were defeated by the Arabs with Abū 'l-Farrukhān's collaboration, the petty rulers of the regions who had come to Siyavakhsh's aid also made peace with the Arabs. So, we are told, that after the conquest of

[1451] Ṭabarī 1994, p. 25, de Goeje, 2655.

[1452] Ṭabarī 1994, p. 26, de Goeje, 2655.

[1453] See pages 293 and 308.

[1454] See §2.5.6.

[1455] As with all other significant upheavals in the histories of the dynastic families, however, it is reasonable to assume that these transformations could not have totally destroyed the actual land-ownership, wealth, and power of the Mihrān family. Pending further research on precisely how land ownership from those who controlled these lands during the Sasanian period transferred to those who came to control the land under Muslim rule, this assertion remains a conjecture. The histories of Ṭabaristān and Qum suggest two ways in which such a transfer might have been effected. In the case of Ṭabaristān, by the late eight century when the caliphate finally conquered parts of the land, at least for some period, people began to convert in order to maintain their wealth and power. In the case of Qum, where Arab settlement actually took place, there was a gradual forced take-over of the land by the Arabs. For Qum, see Pourshariati, Parvaneh, 'Local Histories of Khurāsān and the Pattern of Arab Settlement', *Studia Iranica* 27, (1998), pp. 41–81 (Pourshariati 1998). We hope to deal with the case of Ṭabaristān in our forthcoming work.

[1456] See page 243.

[1457] Once more we must entreat upon the reader's patience until we can establish the identity of this figure and his family on page 264 below.

Rayy, Mardānshāh, the ruler of Dunbāwand (Damāvand), Khuwār, Lāriz, and Shirriz, whose title was *Maṣmughān*,[1458] sued for peace with the Arabs, and promised to "refrain [from hostile acts against them] ... [and] restrain the people of ... [his] territory." In return for an annual payment, Nuʿaym promised Mardānshāh that he "will not be attacked, nor ... approached save by permission."[1459] Suwayd b. Muqarrin subsequently conquered Qūmis, whose inhabitants had also come to the aid of the Mihrāns of Rayy, without any resistance on the part of its population.[1460] It is significant for our purposes to take note, moreover, that while the conquest of Rayy is narrated under the year 22 of *hijra* (643 CE), the actual account of the conquest gives no precise date.[1461]

3.4.5 The conquest of Gurgān and Ṭabaristān

The subsequent conquests of Gurgān and Ṭabaristān are extremely important, for it is through these, as well as through the conquest of Khurāsān, that the contours of the political conditions in northern and northeastern Iran in the next two centuries become clear. Moreover, these conquests, together with the conquest of Rayy, with its unprecedented transfer of power from the house of Mihrān to that of our enigmatic figure, Zīnabī Abū 'l-Farrukhān,[1462] must naturally be considered in the context of the history of Ṭabaristān[1463] and Khurāsān in the late Sasanian period, as well as in the context of the political events taking place once Yazdgird III reached Khurāsān during his flight from the encroaching Arab armies.[1464]

The Turkic leader Ṣūl

After he had conquered Rayy and concluded treaties with the ruler of Damāvand and the people of Qūmis, Suwayd b. Muqarrin moved east. Encamping in Bisṭām, he wrote to the "ruler of Jurjān [i.e., Gurgān], a figure called Rūzbān Ṣūl,"[1465] who hastened to make peace with him "[with the provision] that he [i.e., Ṣūl] should pay tribute and that he would *save [Suwayd] the trouble of making war on Jurjān*. If [he] were being defeated," Ṣūl promised Suwayd that he "would give him assistance." Suwayd then went to Gurgān, and stayed there until the taxes had been collected, and until he "had [specified] the various

[1458]Ṭabarī 1994, pp. 26–27, de Goeje, 2656. This Mardānshāh cannot be the Pārsīg leader Mardānshāh Dhu 'l-Ḥājib, as he had died already around 642 at the battle of Iṣfahān, see page 247ff. It is more likely that, being called a *Maṣmughān* (chief Magian?), he was a Kārinid; see footnote 1750.

[1459]Ṭabarī 1994, p. 27, de Goeje, 2656.

[1460]Significantly, the treaty with Qūmis was made with the people of Qūmis. Ṭabarī 1994, pp. 27–28, de Goeje, 2657.

[1461]Once we have identified our mysterious figure Zīnabī, we will be able to infer that the conquest of Rayy (and Gurgān, see below on page 255) must actually have taken place sometime in 650–652; see Table 6.2 on page 469.

[1462]See §3.4.4, especially page 250ff.

[1463]For a detailed account of this, see Chapter 4.

[1464]See page 257ff.

[1465]Ṭabarī 1994, pp. 28–29, de Goeje, 2658.

frontier regions of Jurjān by name."[1466] Suwayd then "allocated the Turks of Dihistān [to look after] them, removing the tribute from those who remained to defend them and taking taxes from the remainder of the people of Jurjān."[1467] Who this Ṣūl was, and what precisely was being negotiated, is clarified by the terms of the treaty that was subsequently drawn up between the two parties. In the treaty itself Ṣūl is no longer recognized as the ruler of Gurgān. Rather the treaty is addressed to "Rūzbān Ṣūl b. Rūzbān and the people of Dihistān and all of those of Jurjān." This Ṣūl was one of the Turkic leaders who in the post-Bagratuni period of Khurāsān had managed to carve for himself a domain, from where he imposed his rule on Gurgān and adjacent territories, such as Dihistān. Tangentially, we should mention a significant chronological issue before we proceed. While Sayf's narrative maintains that the conquest of Gurgān took place in 18 AH/639 CE,[1468] Ṭabarī also informs us that, according to al-Madāʾinī, the conquest of Gurgān took place in 30 AH/650–651 CE, more than a decade later. There is absolutely no indication, however, that the Arabs could have reached Gurgān at this early stage in 639 CE. To this important chronological dispute we will get shortly.

The treaty between Suwayd and Ṣūl stipulated that the tribute imposed on Ṣūl and his followers would not be in the form of monetary arrangements but "in the form of assistance."[1469] These treaty terms were analogous, as we shall see, to those the Arabs made with the Mihrānid Shahrvarāz in the Caucasus, where the tribute due from the conquered population was calculated in terms of the military assistance rendered.[1470] In Balʿamī's account, however, the terms of the agreement between Ṣūl and Suwayd were even more advantageous for Ṣūl: he entered into an agreement with Suwayd on the condition that the Arabs agreed to pay him a portion of the *kharāj* of Gurgān, as well as a portion of the dues given by "those who refuse to accept Islam."[1471] Another significant chronological indicator is provided by Balʿamī: Ṣūl persuaded Suwayd that this arrangement would also benefit the Arabs, for "once the *ispahbudān* [i.e., the plural of *spāhbed*] of Ṭabaristān realize that he, [i.e., Ṣūl,] has made peace, *they* will not engage in war with the Arabs." If they did nevertheless elect war, Ṣūl promised that he would come forth with the army of Gurgān, and wage war until Ṭabaristān was likewise conquered.[1472]

The ispahbud Farrukhān

Balʿamī then adds, significantly, that when the *ispahbudhān* (pl.), that is to say, the *collectivity of the ispahbuds* of Ṭabaristān, heard that Ṣūl had made peace

[1466]Ṭabarī 1994, p. 29, de Goeje, 2658.
[1467]Ṭabarī 1994, p. 29, de Goeje, 2658.
[1468]Ṭabarī 1994, p. 30, de Goeje, 2659.
[1469]Ṭabarī 1994, p. 29, de Goeje, 2658.
[1470]See page 279.
[1471]Balʿamī 1959, p. 334.
[1472]Balʿamī 1959, p. 334.

with Suwayd b. Muqarrin, they gathered around their ruler. This ruler's name was Farrukhān, "and he was the *ispahbud* of all of the *ispahbudhān*. And they [i.e., the other *ispahbuds*] were all under his rule. And *the ispahbud* was the commander of his army ... [Farrukhān] was [also] called the *Gīl of all of Gīlān* (Jīl-i Jīlān). And when he wrote letters, he would [address himself as the] '*ispahbud of all Ispahbudhān*'. And *today*, [i.e., presumably in Balʿamī's time,] they write the [name of the] *ispahbudhān* of Khurāsān in this manner [as well]."[1473] Once they realized that Ṣūl had made peace with Suwayd b. Muqarrin, Balʿamī proceeds, "*all of the ispahbudhān* gathered around Farrukhān and asked: 'what solution do you propose for us?'" Farrukhān, the Gīl-i Gīlān,[1474] Balʿamī continues, replied to the other *ispahbudān* that *peace seems to be the only option* (*ṣalāḥ ān ast kih ṣulḥ kunīm*). For the affairs of the *ʿajam* were in disarray (*kār-i ʿajam tār o pār shud*) and "the religion of Muḥammad was a new religion," so that it was prudent to make peace and pay the *jizya*.[1475] Farrukhān then wrote to Suwayd and asked for peace terms, and agreed to pay 500,000 *dirhams* per year for all of Ṭabaristān, and consented that in case the Muslims would engage in war, and asked for aid from Ṭabaristān, this would be rendered. Suwayd, who was in Gurgān, then informed ʿUmar that he had conquered *Qūmis, Gurgān, and Ṭabaristān*.[1476] Significantly, therefore, Farrukhān, too, made peace on behalf of Gurgān. What of Ṣūl, however? Here comes a further significant piece of chronological information. While according to Ṭabarī the conquest of Gurgān through Ṣūl was accomplished in 18 AH/639 CE by one account,[1477] Balʿamī maintains that Suwayd's peace with Farrukhān for Qūmis, Gurgān, and Ṭabaristān took place in 22 AH/643 CE.

Several chronologies for the conquests involving Gurgān therefore are provided. In the first, the treaty was allegedly put into effect through Ṣūl and deals only with the conquest of Gurgān. One tradition gives this conquest the improbable date of 18 AH/639 CE—when most of the battles discussed above still had to be fought in regions far to the west of Gurgān—while another tradition puts that conquest in the year 30 AH/650–651 CE.[1478] A second chronology given by Balʿamī for the year 22 AH/642–643 CE, claims that the peace treaty went into effect through Farrukhān and Gīl-i Gīlān, and involved Gurgān plus all of Ṭabaristān and Qūmis. There is another tradition which mentions no names or the extent of the territories involved, and which is dated to 30 AH/650–651 CE. Among the proposed dates, the latter is in all probability the correct one. However, our argument for this depends on our identification

1473 Balʿamī 1959, p. 334.

1474 The reader should be warned that the identification of Farrukhān with Gīl-i Gīlān (Jīl-i Jīlānshāh) will prove to be unwarranted, as we will argue shortly on page 256 below, and in more detail in §4.4.1.

1475 Balʿamī 1959, p. 334.

1476 Balʿamī 1959, p. 335.

1477 Ṭabarī 1994, p. 30, de Goeje, 2659.

1478 See next note.

of Farrukhān, and ultimately of Zīnabī Abū 'l-Farrukhān, which we will give below.[1479]

Now, in Balʿamī's account of the conquest of Gurgān and Ṭabaristān—reportedly in 22 AH/642–643 CE, but in our reconstructed chronology actually around 650–651[1480]—there occur so many *ispahbudhān* that, on the face of it, it would appear impossible to disentangle them. What is clear from the account is that the most powerful of the lot, the *ispahbud-i ispahbudhān*, was called Farrukhān, or Jīl-i Jīlān, and that he held authority over all the *ispahbuds*. To figure out Farrukhān's jurisdiction, we must turn to Ṭabarī's account of the conquest of Ṭabaristān. According to Ṭabarī, the ruler of Ṭabaristān, Farrukhān, wrote to Suwayd and sued for peace. The treaty as a whole, however, was addressed to Farrukhān, *the ruler of Khurāsān*, in authority over Ṭabaristān, and to the ruler Jīl-i Jīlānshāh, *our previous enemy*. Farrukhān therefore was the *ruler of Khurāsān*, but he also had authority over Ṭabaristān. As the syntax of Ṭabarī's passage indicates, moreover, and contrary to Balʿamī's narrative, Farrukhān and Jīl-i Jīlānshāh were not one and the same figure.[1481]

The combined powers of Farrukhān and Jīl-i Jīlānshāh vis-à-vis the Arabs was reflected in the peace treaty. Farrukhān, who was the first addressee of the treaty, promised not to harbor or aid any potential resistance coalition. Whereas Balʿamī maintains that Farrukhān agreed to aid the Arabs in case of military need, moreover, Ṭabarī maintains that one of the conditions that the rulers of Khurāsān and Ṭabaristān, Farrukhān and Jīl-i Jīlānshāh, stipulated in their peace agreement was that they would not be "obliged to render help or assistance against anyone."[1482] In other words, in exchange for peace, Farrukhān and Jīl-i Jīlānshāh demanded to be left alone. In return, the Arabs requested them to restrain their robbers, and the people on their borders: "You will harbor nobody or nothing we are seeking and you will ensure yourself [against military action against you] by [paying] anyone governing your border territory 500,000 dirhams." In conclusion, Farrukhān, the *ispahbud-i ispahbudhān*, the ruler of Khurāsān, in authority over Ṭabaristān, under whose rule all the other *spāhbeds* had now gathered, and Jīl-i Jīlānshāh, were required to ensure the calm around their borders by buying the cooperation of potentially insurgent governors of these territories. The Arabs agreed that they would not have a right to attack Farrukhān or invade the domains under his control, "or even to approach [him] without [his] permission."[1483] In order to further clarify the nature of the events that took place in Rayy, Ṭabaristān, and Khurāsān, we

[1479]See page 264ff, as well as page 291ff and §4.4.1 in the next chapter.

[1480]See §4.4.1.

[1481]For further background on Jīl-i Jīlānshāh, see §4.3.3 below.

[1482]Ṭabarī 1994, p. 30, de Goeje, 2659. As we have seen thus far, and shall continue to see, the practice of seeking the support and aid of one dynastic faction, or a branch of a dynastic faction, against another, was, in fact, one of the crucial ways in which the Arabs were able to effect the conquests and gradually move east. So, the Iranians' request to be left out these dynastic bargains fits in quite well with the scheme of things.

[1483]Ṭabarī 1994, p. 30–31, de Goeje, 2659.

must turn our attention once more to the fateful saga of the last Sasanian king, Yazdgird III, as he turned to Khurāsān. For, it was only after the destruction of the leadership of the Pārsīg faction, with Fīrūzān dead and Hurmuzān in captivity, that Yazdgird III came to lose the most important source of support left to him, that of the Pahlav faction under Farrukhzād's leadership.[1484]

Yazdgird III's flight eastwards

We recall that after the battle of Qādisiya and the battle of Jalūlā', Yazdgird III's flight first carried him south, then southeast, where he probably stayed in Sīstān, possibly for five years.[1485] We can now follow his trail as he turned finally to Khurāsān around 650. Some of our sources maintain that during his flight, Yazdgird III either went to the proximity of Ṭabaristān, or was at least invited to take refuge there. In any case, perhaps on his way to Khurāsān, Yazdgird III learned about the events in Ṭabaristān and Gurgān[1486] before he finally proceeded to Khurāsān, to Marv. We recall that most of our sources emphasize that the protection of the Sasanian king during his flight was undertaken by the most important scion of the Ispahbudhān family, Farrukhzād, the brother of Rustam, and the son of the Prince of the Medes, Farrukh Hormozd.

Whereas none of the anecdotal narratives that describe Yazdgird III's fate in Khurāsān and his presumed murder at the hands of a miller, rings of historical veracity, we do have substantive information that helps us clarify the course of events. The initial conquest of Khuzistān and Fārs by 'Ash'arī, we recall, took place sometime around 636–637 CE, according to our dating scheme,[1487] although some traditions maintain that this was shortly before Abū Bakr died, in 634 CE. The "real conquest of Fārs and the remainder of the Sasanian empire to the east," however, was undertaken by 'Abdallāh b. 'Āmir, the governor of Baṣrah, under 'Uthmān (23–35 AH/644–656 CE),[1488] when the latter sent Aḥnaf at the vanguard of an army to conquer Khurāsān from Ṭabasayn. According to Morony, it was after the second conquest of Fārs that Yazdgird III moved to Kirmān and thence, just ahead of the Arab forces, to Sīstān and Khurāsān.[1489] Yazdgird III, therefore, arrived in Khurāsān sometime in 650–651 CE. If Yazdgird III was eight years old when he ascended the throne in 632, moreover, by the time of his arrival in Khurāsān in 650–651, he was about twenty-six years old. From here on, the sources that depict the youthful Sasanian king as stubborn and thick-headed may carry some truth.

[1484] The conquest of Khurāsān will be discussed in §3.4.7 below, and the Arab peace treaty with Farrukhān and Jīl-i Jīlānshāh, in §4.4.1.

[1485] See page 244ff. A tentative chronology for his whereabouts is given in Table 6.2 on page 469.

[1486] See §3.4.5.

[1487] See §3.4.2 and Table 6.2.

[1488] Morony 1991, p. 207.

[1489] Morony 1991, p. 207. However, as we established on page 244ff, his stay in Kirmān and Sīstān was more likely during the years 642–648.

According to Ṭabarī, "historians are in disagreement" over Yazdgird III's journey to Khurāsān, and "how the whole affair happened."[1490] According to one tradition, once he arrived in Khurāsān, Yazdgird III "intended to join the ruler of the Turks, and *the Persians* asked him what he intended to do."[1491] Yazdgird III replied that "he wanted to join the ruler of the Turks and remain with him or [go] to China." Who were these Persians quarreling with the king? In this version of Ṭabarī's narrative the name of the figure(s) (or parties) is not disclosed. What is disclosed, however, is that a violent disagreement took place between the king and a faction whom Ṭabarī's source calls the *Khurāsānīs*. When Yazdgird III articulated his intentions, according to Ṭabarī, "they told him to tread warily, for this was a bad idea, going to a people in their own country, *while abandoning his own land and people*."[1492] They argued that he must go back to Iran and *make peace with the Arabs*, for having an "enemy ruling over Persians in their own land ... was a better political arrangement than an enemy ruling over them in his own land."[1493] Yazdgird III, however, refused to accept their arguments. The Khurāsānīs, likewise, "refused to give in to him."

The substantial treasury of the king and the issue of its ownership also complicated matters. The Khurāsānīs "told [Yazdgird III] to leave *their treasures alone*, ... [for they would] return them to their own territory and to its ruler."[1494] This seemed logical enough. But the young king refused to yield to pressure once again. Ṭabarī's narrative still does not disclose the precise identity of this collective *Persians*, except that they were *Khurāsānīs*. The dispute, however, got out of hand. For once Yazdgird III refused to relinquish the treasury, the Khurāsānīs "*told him that they would not let him go ... [they then] drew on one side and left him alone with his followers.*" Finally the Khurāsānīs took over "*the treasures and assuming complete control over them, abandon[ed] him completely.*"[1495]

According to this version of Ṭabarī's narrative, the Khurāsānī "polytheists [then] wrote to al-Aḥnaf", while driving Yazdgird III to Farghānah.[1496] Having made peace with Aḥnaf and "exchanging agreements with him," they handed over Yazdgird III's treasury to the Arabs and "gradually returned to their lands and wealth in *as good a state as they had been at the time of the Sasanian emperors. It was as if they were [still] under their rule except for the fact that the Muslims*

[1490] Ṭabarī 1994, p. 51, de Goeje, 2680. Here Sayf mentions Yazdgird III's flight to Rayy and his dispute with a figure called Ābān Jādhūyih, which quarrel led him to leave Rayy for Iṣfahān. Ṭabarī 1994, p. 52, de Goeje, 2681. For the office of *jādhūyih*, see page 197 and footnote 1092. For a conjectural identification of Ābān Jādhūyih, see footnote 1528.

[1491] Ṭabarī 1994, p. 59, de Goeje, 2688.

[1492] Ṭabarī 1994, p. 59, de Goeje, 2688–2689.

[1493] Ṭabarī 1994, p. 59, de Goeje, 2689.

[1494] Ṭabarī 1994, p. 59, de Goeje, 2689.

[1495] Ṭabarī 1994, p. 59, de Goeje, 2689.

[1496] Ṭabarī 1994, p. 59, de Goeje, 2689.

were more worthy of their confidence and acted justly toward them."[1497] While the tradition that the advent of the Arab army was the cause of Yazdgird III's withdrawal to Farghānah might or might not be valid, all evidence corroborates the rest of Ṭabarī's narrative, from which we receive yet another significant piece of information. Throughout the rule of ʿUmar (634–644), we are told, Yazdgird III maintained some form of correspondence with *at least some* of the Persians. "*So the people of Khurāsān rebelled*", it is interjected, "during the time of ʿUthmān ['s caliphate (644–656).]"[1498] It was at this point then that "the Khurāsānīs threw off their allegiance."[1499] Other sources clarify just who exactly these Khurāsānīs were.

According to Madāʾinī, when Yazdgird III arrived in Khurāsān, he was accompanied by "Khurrazādh Mihr, the brother of Rustam."[1500] There is, therefore, no doubt about what our sources had originally informed us: Yazdgird III was still in the company of Farrukhzād, the Ispahbudhān scion with claims to the *spāhbedī* of both Khurāsān and Azarbāyjān. In Marv, Farrukhzād reportedly reminded Māhūy, the *marzbān* of Marv,[1501] that he was entrusting the king to his protection and then "[he] left for Iraq." The tradition highlighting Yazdgird III's attempt at deposing Māhūy and the well-circulated traditions that the king was murdered at the hands of the latter or at his instigation, all betray the turmoil that engulfed the region as a result of the divergent policies of the young king and the supporters left to him, the *marzbān* of Marv and the Turks, in the face of the imminent arrival of the Arabs. Ibn al-Kalbī's tradition found in Ṭabarī adds a further point: after fleeing to Iṣfahān and then to Rayy, Yazdgird III entered into correspondence with the *overlord* (*ṣaḥib*) of Ṭabaristān. This overlord, who remains unidentified in Ibn al-Kalbī's transmission, then "described his lands for [Yazdgird III] and informed him of their impregnability," and asked the king to take refuge in his land. The overlord also cautioned the king that promptness was required in the king's decision, for otherwise he would not "receive ... [him] or give ... [him] refuge." Yazdgird III refused to take refuge in Ṭabaristān, but, as a gesture of appreciation, appointed the overlord (*ṣaḥib*) as the *spāhbed* of Ṭabaristān, where the latter "*had previously held a humbler rank.*"[1502] Following this narrative on the situation in Ṭabaristān, we receive another account where, once again, we are informed that the escort of Yazdgird III in his flight to Khurāsān was the Parthian dynast, Farrukhzād.[1503] The substantial power of Farrukhzād and the almost total dependency of Yazdgird

---

[1497] Ṭabarī 1994, p. 59, de Goeje, 2689.

[1498] Ṭabarī 1994, p. 59, de Goeje, 2689.

[1499] Ṭabarī 1994, p. 60, de Goeje, 2690.

[1500] Ṭabarī 1990, p. 79, de Goeje, 2873.

[1501] According to Thaʿālibī, the regions under the control of Māhūy included Marv, Marv al-Rūd, Ṭāliqān, Jūzjānān, and others. Thaʿālibī 1900, p. 744.

[1502] Ṭabarī 1990, p. 82, de Goeje, 2875. To properly identify this overlord and *spāhbed* of Ṭabaristān, we need to analyze the political situation in Ṭabaristān in more detail, which we postpone to the next chapter; see page 302ff.

[1503] Ṭabarī 1990, p. 82, de Goeje, 2876.

III on his protection comes across clearly in a subsequent account transmitted through an unidentified source in Ṭabarī.

3.4.6 The mutiny of Farrukhzād

According to Ṭabarī, Yazdgird III "had appointed Farrukhzād as governor of Marv and ordered Barāz, [the son of Māhūy] to turn the citadel and the city over to him." Māhūy, however, had opposed this. Farrukhzād knelt down before Yazdgird III, and proclaimed: "Marw has proved an intractable problem for you, and these Arabs have caught up with you." He advised Yazdgird III to go to the country of the Turks in refuge. Yazdgird III, however, "opposed [Farrukhzād] and did not accept his advice."[1504] The details of the discord that had been caused in Marv by Yazdgird III's arrival need not concern us here. The upshot of it was that Māhūy decided to mutiny. What becomes clear through the rest of the narrative, however, is that the army under the command of Farrukhzād was a central player in the dispute. According to this narrative, Māhūy wrote to the Turkic leader Nīzak Tarkhān, encouraging him to use a ruse and write to Yazdgird III "*in order to separate him from the main body of his soldiers, thereby leaving him with a weak and powerless segment of his army and personal retinue.*"[1505] Specifically, Māhūy prompted Nīzak to tell Yazdgird III "that … [he] will not come to meet him *until Farrukhzād parts from him.*"[1506] Nīzak followed Māhūy's instructions. When the letter reached Yazdgird III and he sought advice, no consensus was reached on the course to follow. One faction argued that it was not "*wise to dismiss your army and Farrukhzād for any reason.*" The other faction enjoined him to relieve himself of the Parthian dynast and his army. Yazdgird III accepted the latter's advice and "order[ed] … Farrukhzād to go to the reed beds of Sarakhs." Farrukhzād allegedly was heart-wrenched. He "crie[d] … out and rent the neck hole [of his garment]." Yet he did not leave until Yazdgird III had written the following letter to him: "This is a letter to Farrukhzād. Verily you have turned Yazdagird, his household and his children, his retinue, and his possessions over safe and secure to Māhawayh [Māhūy], the *dihqān* of Marw. And I hereby bear witness to this."[1507] In view of what will transpire, there is little doubt that this version was a history patronized by the Parthian Ispahbudhān family.[1508]

The *X*^{w}*adāy-Nāmag* tradition corroborates important details of various traditions provided by Ṭabarī, while adding other significant information. According to the *Shāhnāma*, it was Farrukhzād who urged Yazdgird III to go north to Ṭabaristān in the midst of his flight east, arguing that the population in

[1504]Ṭabarī 1990, p. 83, de Goeje, 2877. While Yazdgird III's disagreement with Farrukhzād is here correctly underlined, the stances of the two parties have been reversed. That is, it was actually Yazdgird III's idea to take refuge with the Turks and not Farrukhzād's.

[1505]Ṭabarī 1990, p. 84, de Goeje, 2878.

[1506]Ṭabarī 1990, p. 84, de Goeje, 2878.

[1507]Ṭabarī 1990, p. 85, de Goeje, 2879.

[1508]The narrative concerning Yazdgird III's appointment of the ruler of Ṭabaristān to the rank of *spāhbed*, however, is in all likelihood a Kārinid tradition; see page 302 below.

Ṭabaristān, Āmul, and Sārī were the king's supporters.[1509] Yazdgird III, however, rejected Farrukhzād's advice, and opted for Khurāsān instead. In Khurāsān, Yazdgird III argued, he was assured of the protection of the *marzbāns* of the region, who had a reputation for bravery and warring, as well as the aid of the Turks and the Khaqan of China. Chief among these *marzbāns*, Yazdgird III told Farrukhzād, was Māhūy, the *kanārang* of Marv.

According to the *Shāhnāma*, while Farrukhzād disagreed sternly with Yazdgird III's decision to go to Khurāsān and take refuge with Māhūy and the Turks, he did not abandon the king just yet. Leading the way with his substantial army, the Pahlav dynast proceeded toward Gurgān and thence to Būst (Bisṭām).[1510] Somewhere between Ṭūs and Marv, Māhūy came to greet the last Sasanian king. It was here, Ferdowsī informs us, that Farrukhzād left the king in Māhūy's custody and returned. And now, we are given a significant piece of information by Ferdowsī. After leaving the king, Farrukhzād set out for Rayy. In the meantime he adopted a new posture vis-à-vis Yazdgird III: he had a change of heart (*jodā shod zi maghz-ī bad andīsh mihr*) and the "*shepherd* came to covet the throne (*shabān rā hamī kard takht ārzūy*)." Pretending to be ill, Farrukhzād renounced his allegiance to Yazdgird III.[1511] And so the last Sasanian king lost his last and most formidable source of support: the Pahlav Farrukhzād mutinied. While leaving the king to the care of Māhūy, Farrukhzād revealed his intent: "I have to leave for Rayy, for *I do not know any longer whom I shall*

[1509] Ferdowsī 1971, vol. IX, pp. 333–334, Ferdowsī 1935, pp. 2980–2981:

چه بینید گفت اندر این داستان
چه دارید یاد از گه باستان
فرخزاد گوید که با انجمن
گذر کن بر بیشه نارون
به امل پرستندگان تواند
به ساری همه بندگان تواند
چو لشکر فراوان بود بازگرد
به مردم توان کرد جنگ و نبرد
شما را پسند اید این گفت اوی
باواز گفتند کینست روی
شهنشاه گفت این نه اندر خورست
مرا در دل اندیشه دیگر است ...
همان به که سوی خراسان شویم
ز پیکار دشمن تن اسان شویم
کز ان سو فراوان مرا لشکر است
همه پهلوانان کنداورست
بزرگان ترکان و خاقان چین
بیایند و بر ما کنند افرین
بران دوستی نیز پیشی کنم
ابا دخت فغفور خویشی کنم
بیاری بیاید سپاه گران
بزرگان توران و جنگ اوران

[1510] Ferdowsī 1971, vol. IX, p. 337, Ferdowsī 1935, p. 2983:

فرّخزاد هرمزد لشکر براند
از ایران جهاندیدگان را بخواند
چنین رفت با ناله و درد شاه
سپهبد به پیش اندرون با سپاه
چو منزل به منزل بیامد به ریّ
بر اسود یك چند با رود و می
ز ریّ سوی گرگان بر امد چو باد
همی بود یك چند ناشاد شاد
ز گرگان بیامد سوی راه بست
پر اژنگ رخسار دل نادرست

[1511] Ferdowsī 1971, vol. IX, pp. 347–348, Ferdowsī 1935, p. 2991:

فرّخزاد هرمزد از ان جایگاه
سوی ریّ بیامد به فرمان شاه
بدین نیز بگذشت چندی سپهر
جدا شد ز مغز بد اندیش مهر
شبان را همی کرد تخت ارزوی
دگرگونه شد به ایین و خوی
تن خویش یك چند بیمار کرد
پرستیدن پادشاه خوار کرد

consider the king" of this realm.[1512] Here, therefore, another part of the puzzle is finally solved. The Khurāsānīs of Ṭabarī were none other than Farrukhzād and his contingent. We recall, after all, that the family was not only dubbed the *princes of Azarbāyjān*, but also the *spāhbeds of Khurāsān*.[1513]

Sebeos corroborates the information on the Pahlav leader's mutiny provided by the Arabic sources and the *X^w^adāy-Nāmag* tradition, although his source might, in fact, have also been Persian. According to Sebeos, in the twentieth year of the reign of Yazdgird III, that is 651/652, the Arab armies that were "in the land of Persia [Fārs] and of Khuzhastan [Khuzistan] marched eastwards to the regions of the land called Pahlaw, which is the land of the Parthians, against Yaztkert king of Persia."[1514] Yazdgird III had already fled before them. After going east, however, the "Prince of the Medes [i.e., Farrukhzād]—*of whom I said above that he had gone to the east to their king and, having rebelled had fortified himself in some place—sought an oath from the Ismaelites [i.e., Arabs] and went into the desert in submission to the Ismaelites.*"[1515] As Howard-Johnston, Sebeos' editor, remarks, nowhere in his account does Sebeos mention the rebellion of the Prince of the Medes and his fortification somewhere. He suggests, therefore, that "either a passage has dropped out of Sebeos' text in its long transmission and the cross-reference is his, or, possibly the cross-reference was lifted together with the notice in which it was embedded, from Sebeos' source, probably the Persian Source."[1516] In all probability it is Howard-Johnston's second conjecture that is valid. For, as we shall see, not only are the details of Farrukhzād's rebellion against the Sasanian king generally hidden or implicit in our sources but, in almost all of them, this important Pahlav leader also disappeared from the scene altogether once he had left Yazdgird III behind. This, we shall propose, is one of the many instances of the editorial force that the Ispahbudhān exerted on the *X^w^adāy-Nāmag* tradition and, by extension, on other sources supplied by this tradition.[1517]

[1512]Ferdowsī 1971, vol. IX, p. 347:

مرا رفت باید سوی مرز ری   ندانم که کی دانم این تاج کی

In Thaʿālibī's version, it was Yazdgird III who ordered Farrukhzād to go to Iraq and make peace with the Arabs. Farrukhzād accepted the king's orders, warned him of Māhūy's malicious intentions, and left in distress. Thaʿālibī 1900, p. 744, Thaʿālibī 1989, p. 475. According to Ḥamza Iṣfahānī, the letter that Farrukhzād obtained from the king was not one that confirmed the safe transfer of the king to Māhūy's hand, but a contract through which the last Sasanian undertook to *relinquish his kingship* to the Parthian dynast Farrukhzād of the Ispahbudhān family. Ḥamza Iṣfahānī 1961, p. 55, Ḥamza Iṣfahānī 1988, pp. 59–60.

[1513]We should also reiterate that the Ispahbudhān were the *spāhbeds* of the *kūst-i khwarāsān* for an extended period; see pages 107ff and 188ff.

[1514]Sebeos 1999, p. 135.

[1515]Sebeos 1999, p. 135.

[1516]Sebeos 1999, pp. 135, 265.

[1517]For a more detailed discussion of their redactional efforts, see page 462ff below. For another example, see the two versions about Khusrow II's murder on page 158.

What is of crucial importance in the narratives just discussed is that until the end of Yazdgird III's flight to Khurāsān, it was the Pahlav leader, Farrukhzād, who continued to protect the king. Moreover, the aforementioned Khurāsānī rebellion[1518] was in fact a substantive disagreement over strategy and policy between Farrukhzād and Yazdgird, leading ultimately to Farrukhzād's mutiny. In line with the policies promoted by his brother Rustam,[1519] Farrukhzād even proposed to the king that making peace with the Arabs was a more prudent option, while Yazdgird III, in all likelihood fearful of Farrukhzād's power, opted for taking refuge with someone over whom he believed to have power, namely, Māhūy, the *marzbān* of Marv.[1520] It is important to note that in the last crucial months of Yazdgird III's life, when the Arabs had already reached the environs of Khurāsān, Farrukhzād still commanded a substantial army, whose withdrawal from Yazdgird III would expedite the king's demise.

With the quarters of the north and east in disarray at this juncture, Farrukhzād, *with a substantial army under his command*, headed west with the intention of making peace with the Arabs. Significantly, as Ferdowsī informs us, Farrukhzād set out for Rayy. The mutiny of Farrukhzād was momentous for the fate of the Sasanian empire. It conveniently explains the course of events in the *kūst-i khwarāsān* and the *kūst-i ādurbādagān*, the land of the Pahlav. It is to be noted that the *Xʷadāy-Nāmag* tradition does not follow what transpired in the wake of Farrukhzād's mutiny and his westbound departure in the direction of Rayy. This omission is partly due to the fact that this tradition ends with the death of Yazdgird III. On the face of it then, we are left in the dark about Farrukhzād's negotiations with the Arabs. The leader of the Pahlav, the progeny of the Ispahbudhān, the *spāhbed* of Khurāsān and Azarbāyjān, Farrukhzād, son of Farrukh Hormozd, seemingly vanishes from the accounts of our sources. That is, if we choose to neglect Sayf's traditions and the narratives of the conquests.

It is now time to recall[1521] that in the conquest of Rayy, the one who is said to have "seen what the Muslims were like, [comparing their attitude] with the envy of Sīyāvakhsh and his family," was a figure bearing the curious name Zīnabī Abū 'l-Farrukhān.[1522] We have, therefore, come full circle to our original question. Who was this Zīnabī Abū 'l-Farrukhān who on account of his age-old enmity with the Parthian Mihrāns, aided the Arabs in toppling this important family from their seat of power, and took over the control of their realm? It is here that the histories of Ṭabaristān and Gīlān tie in with the account of Yazdgird III's flight to Khurāsān, to provide a more coherent picture than had hitherto been possible.

[1518] See page 258ff.

[1519] See §3.4.1.

[1520] According to Yazdgird III, the Māhūy owed his position to the Sasanian monarchy and not, like the *Kanārang* (on whom below), to gentilitial claims. See our discussion at the beginning of §3.4.7.

[1521] See page 250ff.

[1522] Ṭabarī 1994, p. 25, de Goeje, 2654.

A hero unveiled: Zīnabī

We should start with an onomastic question: what is the meaning of the name Zīnabī? For on the face of it, the term seems neither to be Arabic nor Persian. Zīnabī, occurring in other sources as Zīnaband,[1523] is, in fact, the Arabicized, contracted form of the Persian term *zīnāvand*, meaning one who is wellarmed. The *Zand-i Vahuman Yasn*, for example, speaks of a large, well-armed (*zīnāvand*) army that is responsible for bestowing kingship to the Kayānids.[1524] The *Fārsnāma* also uses the term in this same sense.[1525] Zīnabī then is an epithet, not a name. It is an adjective describing the holder of the epithet as one who is wellarmed, in this case Abū 'l-Farrukhān. Balādhurī specifically maintains that Zīnabī was the nomenclature given by the Arabs to this figure.[1526]

The abrupt disappearance of the powerful figure of the Ispahbudhān Farrukhzād from our accounts, and the sudden appearance of the mysterious but equally powerful Zīnabī Abū 'l-Farrukhān at the exact juncture in our narratives is hardly coincidental. A closer examination of the latter's name leaves therefore very little doubt that Zīnabī Abū 'l-Farrukhān is none other than the Ispahbudhān Farrukhzād: Zīnabī Abū 'l-Farrukhān,[1527] the *wellarmed*, who with his large army mysteriously materialized to assist the Arabs in the conquest of Rayy and, as a result, gained supremacy over this important Mihrānid domain. Zīnabī, moreover, we notice, arrived on the scene at the precise moment when Farrukhzād had abandoned Yazdgird III in Khurāsān and, with his large army, was on his way to Rayy, the ancestral domain of his family's nemeses, the Mihrāns.[1528] Furthermore, in anticipation of our detailed study of the

[1523] Balādhurī 1968, p. 317.

[1524] Vahuman 1883, *Zand-i Vahuman Yasn*, Tehran, 1963, translated by Sadegh Hedayat (Vahuman 1883), p. 58, n. 9:

گند بیشمار زیناوند با درفش افراشته بیایند و پادشاهی به کی رسد·

[1525] Ibn Balkhī 1995, p. 95. Significantly, this army appears after the account of Bahrām-i Chūbīn and might in fact be a description of Bahrām-i Chūbīn's own army. See page 406ff. *Zīnāvand* was also the epithet of Ṭahmūrath. Ibn Balkhī maintains that he "was called Ṭahmūrath-i *zīnāvand* and *zīnāvand* was his epithet and [it] means well-armed." Ibn Balkhī 1995, p. 95 and n. 1. Bundahishn 1990, *Bundahish*, Tehran, 1990, translated by Mihrdad Bahar (Bundahishn 1990), n. 58.

[1526] Balādhurī 1968, p. 318.

[1527] In this respect, we should also recall the confusion in some of our sources between Farrukhzād and his father Farrukh Hormozd, who at times is called Farrukhān; see page 143ff. The Arabic *kunya*-prefix *Abū* (*father of*) when used in Iranian names is also notoriously unreliable, to the extent that it could even mean *son of*, so that we may interpret Abū 'l-Farrukhān here as the son of Farrukhān, that is to say, of Farrukh Hormozd (see §2.7.5). Indeed, some of our sources, we recall, refer to Zīnabī as the son of Farrukhān (i.e., Farrukh Hormozd); see footnote 1445.

[1528] We can now also shed some light on an enigmatic passage in Ṭabarī about the altercation between Yazdgird III and a certain Ābān Jādhūyih. When Yazdgird III on his flight eastwards arrived in Rayy, he was imprisoned by its ruler, called Ābān Jādhūyih. The king accused him of mutiny, to which Ābān Jādhūyih replied: "No, rather you have abandoned your empire, and it has fallen into the hands of someone else. I [only] want to record everything that is mine and nothing else". Ṭabarī 1994, p. 52, de Goeje, 2681. In other words, the dispute was over Rayy's treasury. Once the king agreed to grant Ābān Jādhūyih his properties, he left Rayy. His subsequent itinerary

political situation in Ṭabaristān,[1529] we shall further see that Farrukhzād was also the same figure who appeared in our accounts of the conquest of Ṭabaristān as Farrukhān, the *ispahbud-i ispahbudhān*, with authority over Ṭabaristān, and who signed, in collaboration with Jīl-i Jīlānshāh, a peace treaty with the Arabs.[1530] Who, however, are the other players on the scene? What else is transpiring in the Parthian domains at this juncture? We have left out thus far one last, crucial figure in the final saga of the Sasanian king: the Kanārang of Ṭūs.

3.4.7   The conquest of Khurāsān and the mutiny of the Kanārangīyān

According to Ferdowsī, during his eastward flight, Yazdgird III wrote two letters to the *kanārangs* of his choice in the east, Māhūy and the Kanārang-i Ṭūs. Faced with Farrukhzād's insistence that he should take refuge in Ṭabaristān, the king argued that he preferred to go under the protection of Māhūy, because of the latter's reputation as a warmonger and a slanderer. Yazdgird III further argued that since Māhūy owed his title (*nām*), land (*ard*), frontier (*marz*), and the rest of his possessions to the king, his loyalty to the Sasanians was guaranteed. That he was lowborn, was all the more to the king's advantage, since raising the ignoble to nobility would insure loyalty to the Sasanians. In Ferdowsī's rendition, there follows a didactic passage in which the king set forth the mutual benefits of forming a patron–client relationship, while the Parthian dynast Farrukhzād enumerated the evils of relying on non-nobility. Given the status of our current knowledge, we cannot ascertain the precise identity of this Māhūy-i Sūrī.[1531] As Ferdowsī's narrative unfolds, however, it becomes quite clear that the author's slander of Māhūy[1532] is meant to be juxtaposed with his praise for another *marzbān* of Khurāsān, the *Kanārang of Ṭūs*. The Kanārang's title, according to Ferdowsī, was deservedly bestowed, and he bore it in a normative fashion. These normative dimensions are enumerated in detail in the letter of Yazdgird III to the Kanārang of Ṭūs.[1533] The finale of this correspondence—

---

was Iṣfahān, Kirmān, and finally Khurāsān. Now, as Rayy was the capital of the Mihrāns, our first guess would be that its ruler Ābān Jādhūyih was a Mihrān, possibly Sīyāvakhsh. Ṭabarī 1994, p. 24, de Goeje, 2653. However, as we can readily see, this narrative is reminiscent of the treasury dispute between the king and Farrukhzād (see §3.4.6). As Farrukhzād, under the alias Zīnabī Abū 'l-Farrukhān, did become the ruler of Rayy with the aid of the Arabs (see §3.4.4, pages 250 and 254), we may conjecture that Ābān Jādhūyih is really Farrukhzād. We can link this conjectural identification also to our previous conjecture about the office of *jādhūyih*, in which Ābān, rather than being a proper name, stands for the tenth day of the month (see footnote 1092).

[1529] See §4.4.1.

[1530] See page 254. The reader should be forewarned that yet another enigmatic figure will appear in these accounts, which yet again turns out to be our notorious Farrukhzād; see page 291ff.

[1531] As this names suggests, it is possible that he actually belonged to the Sūren family.

[1532] Ferdowsī's narrative discredits Māhūy explicitly, questioning his loyalty and stressing his humble origins. Ferdowsī's debasing of the *kanārang* of Marv might of course have been formed by the poet's post-facto knowledge of Māhūy's complicity in the death of the king. According to Ḥamza Iṣfahānī, "down to his day in Marv and its vicinity people called the descendants of Mahoe ... king killers (*khudā-kushān*)." Ḥamza Iṣfahānī 1988, p. 43, as quoted in Yarshater, Yarshater 1983b, p. 404.

[1533] The first letter, as we have seen, was addressed to Māhūy-i Sūrī, the *kanārang* of Marv. All that the poet informs us of here is that the king described his plight, requested Māhūy to prepare

articulated, significantly, not in the *Shāhnāma*, but in the *Ghurar* of Thaʿālibī—reveals that Farrukhzād was not alone in his mutiny against Yazdgird III. As opposed to the curt letter written to Māhūy, Ferdowsī furnishes us with a lengthy—eighty three couplets in total—version of the contents of the second letter, written to the Kanārang of Ṭūs from the Kanārangīyān family.

The Kanārangīyān

The Kanārangīyān were in possession of "Kingly Glory," *farr*, land (*arḍ*), justice (*dād*) and law (*rāh*) in Ferdowsī's rendition. Their high lineage was well established and acknowledged. Ferdowsī then provides us with detailed information on the regional extent of the Kanārangīyān's power. Toward the end of Sasanian rule—and, yet again, the post-Bagratuni situation in Khurāsān needs to be kept in mind—the Kanārangīyān ruled over an extensive territory that included Shemīrān, Rūyīn Dizh, Rādih Kūh, and Kalāt.[1534] Now Shemīrān is most likely the fortress of Shamīlān in Ṭūs mentioned by Yāqūt,[1535] and not the famous village and fortress of Shemīrān located in Herāt, nor the fortress of the same name located in Balkh. For the topography of the region[1536] as well as the political situation of the realm on the eve of the conquests, would have precluded the Kanārangīyān's power over such a dispersed region.[1537] Rādih Kūh is part of a series of mountains located in the region of Ṭūs, Rādihkān being the name of a district in the environs of Ṭūs. Kalāt evidently refers to what in the later period came to be identified with the Kalāt-i Nāderī, one of the natural wonders and fortresses of Khurāsān, on the road to Nisā. The Islamic narratives, betraying a separate source, confirm Ferdowsī's delimitation of the territorial control of the Kanārangīyān.[1538] Who, however, were the Kanārangīyān, and what was their position in Sasanian history? We recall that in a number of significant episodes which we have recounted, they took their place among the important policy makers and military commanders of the realm. It is appropriate, therefore, to suspend temporarily the chronological order of our narrative for an examination of the Kanārangīyān's history during the Sasanian period.

We have information on the Kanārangīyān family as the rulers in the east going as far back as Yazdgird I's reign (399–420). As we shall see, the Kanārangīyān were a dynastic family, and there is little doubt that they were from Parthian ancestry. According to the *Shāhnāma*, the Kanārang was one of the central

his army for combat, and informed him that he himself would be following on the tail of the courier. The letter, as reproduced by Ferdowsī, is extremely short—nine couplets in total—and has a very general tone. Being the king's correspondence with the *kanārang* of his choice, its brevity as opposed to the subsequent letter to the Kanārang of Ṭūs is all the more puzzling. Ferdowsī 1971, vol. IX, pp. 339–340, Ferdowsī 1935, p. 458.

1534 Ferdowsī 1971, vol. IX, p. 339.

1535 Yaqūt al-Hamawī 1866.

1536 A detailed investigation of the topographical characteristics of Greater Khurāsān was undertaken in Pourshariati 1995, pp. 110–155. See also our brief discussion of Inner Khurāsān and Outer Khurāsān in §6.2.1 below.

1537 Dihkhuda 1998, p. 14505.

1538 See our discussion on page 276 below.

figures to conspire against the tyrannical rule of Yazdgird I the Sinner and to bring about the murder of the king.[1539] We recall, that Yazdgird I is said to have been kicked to death by a horse, specifically in Ṭūs.[1540] Two aspects of the Kanārangīyān's power are clearly established from the fourth century onward. Firstly, their office[1541] was of such great importance and its occupant so high in the ranks of the Parthian dynastic families, that they were directly involved in the dynastic struggles against the Sasanians from the late fourth century onward. Secondly and related to the first, the office was of such importance that it remained hereditary. Of both of these facts, Procopius informs us directly. After the nobility had put Bilāsh (484–488) in power,[1542] and "after the expression of many opinions … there came forward a certain man of repute among the Persians, whose name was Gousanastades (Gushnāspdād),[1543] and whose office was that of *chanaranges* … His official province lay on the very frontier of the Persian territory, in a district which adjoins the land of the Hephthalites." The *chanaranges* was one of the main parties advocating the murder of Qubād, Bilāsh's (484–488) rival. Holding up his knife, the *chanaranges* Gushnāspdād declared to the other factions: "You see this knife, how extremely small it is; nevertheless it is able at present time to accomplish a deed which, be assured, my dear Persians, a little later two myriads of mail clad men could not bring to pass." However, Gushnāspdād's opinion was overridden and Qubād was instead imprisoned.[1544] Under unclear circumstances, however, the king was able to escape from prison, flee, and take refuge with the Hephthalites. He was then able to return and assume power. On his way back west from the Hephthalites, Qubād had to cross the territory of the *chanaranges*, Gushnāspdād, in Khurāsān. Here Procopius furnishes us with further significant information about the office of *kanārang*. Qubād informed his supporters "that he would appoint as *chanaranges* the first man of the Persians who should on that day come to his presence." No sooner had he declared his intention, however, Qubād realized the impossibility of bringing it to fruition. For "even as he said this, he repented his speech, for there came to his mind a *law of the Persians which ordain[ed] that offices among the Persians shall not be conferred upon others than those to whom each particular honour belongs by right of birth*." Qubād's apprehension was subsequently articulated in no uncertain terms by Procopius. For, the king feared lest "someone should come to him first *who was not a kinsman of the present chanaranges, and that he would be compelled to set aside the law in order to keep his word*." As luck would have it, the first man to approach the Sasanian king was none other than Adergoudounbades (Ādhargulbād),[1545] "a young man

[1539]Ferdowsī 1971, vol. IX, pp. 285–287, Ferdowsī 1935, pp. 2097–2098. See §2.2.2.

[1540]Ibn Balkhī 1995, p. 203; Ferdowsī 1971, vol. IX, p. 284, Ferdowsī 1935, pp. 2097–2098. For the symbolism of the horse, see page 388.

[1541]For the office of *kanārang*, see for instance Khurshudian 1998, §1.4.

[1542]See §2.4.1.

[1543]For the name, see Khurshudian 1998, p. 74.

[1544]Procopius 1914, v. 1–7, p. 33.

[1545]We are trusting Khurshudian's reconstruction of Procopius' Adergoudounbades as the equiv-

who was a *relative* of Gousanastades [Gushnāspdād] and an especially capable warrior."[1546] Qubād was thus presented with an opportunity, so that after returning to the capital and assuming the throne, Gushnāspdād was put to death and "Adergoudounbades [Ādhargulbād] was established in his place in the office of *chanaranges*."[1547]

Throughout the reign of Qubād (488–531), the Kanārangīyān continued to hold substantial powers. In Qubād's last war against Byzantium, *chanaranges*, that is, Ādhargulbād, was one of the three commanders that led the Persian army into Mesopotamia, the others being, Mermeroes, our famous Mihrānid Shāpūr Rāzī,[1548] the supreme commander of the land (*iṣbahbadh al-bilād*), and Aspebedes from the Ispahbudhān family.[1549] In the early years of Khusrow I's reign, the Kanārangīyān partook in a mutiny mentioned by Procopius but rarely in other sources.[1550] "In vexation over Khusrow I's unruly turn of mind and strange fond[ness] of innovation," the Persians decided to bring Qubād, a child of Khusrow I's brother Jāmāsp, to power. Discovering the conspiracy, Khusrow I had the parties involved executed, including his uncle Aspebedes. Here comes the most interesting information, for as Procopius informs us, Khusrow I was "unable to kill [the child Qubād] for he was still being reared under the *chanaranges*, Adergoudounbades [Ādhargulbād]." By virtue of their power, therefore, the Kanārangīyān were directly tied to the Sasanian court, in this case by raising a potential rival to the throne. Their agnatic descent must have been of such high pedigree that they could engage in a practice similar to *dayeakordi*, or foster brother-ship. So Khusrow I sent a "message to the *chanaranges*, Adergoudounbades [Ādhargulbād], bidding him to kill the boy himself; *for he neither thought it well to show mistrust, nor yet had the power to compel him [i.e., Ādhargulbād]*."[1551] In consultation with his wife, however, Ādhargulbād decided to forego the kings orders, and hid the child "in the most secure concealment." He subsequently informed Khusrow I that they had in fact obeyed his orders and murdered the child. The whole affair was kept in such secrecy that no one came to suspect it except Ādhargulbād's own son Varrames (Bahrām), one of the Sasanians' trustworthy servants. As the child Qubād became of age, however, Ādhargulbād bid him to flee and save himself lest his identity become known to Khusrow I.[1552] This state of affairs remained hidden from Khusrow I until later when he was invading the land of the Colchis and Bahrām was accompanying him. On this occasion, Bahrām betrayed his father and,

---

alent of the Persian name Ādhargulbād, and henceforth will use the latter. Khurshudian 1998, p. 74.

[1546]Procopius 1914, vi. 9–17, p. 47.

[1547]Procopius 1914, vi. 17–vii., p. 49.

[1548]See §2.4.4.

[1549]Procopius 1914, xx. 12–xxi, p. 195. For Aspebedes, the grandfather of Vistāhm and Vindūyih, see page 110ff.

[1550]See page 111ff.

[1551]Procopius 1914, xxiii. 4–10, p. 211.

[1552]Procopius 1914, xxiii. 10–15, p. 213.

through an elaborate scheme, forced upon the king by his inability to directly harm the Kanārangīyān, Khusrow I finally had Ādhargulbād killed.[1553] According to Procopius, Adhargulbād was "a man who was in fact as well as in name an invincible general among the Persians, who had marched against twelve nations of barbarians and subjected them all to King Cabades. After Adergoudounbades had been removed from the world, *Varrames [Bahrām], his son, received the office of chanaranges.*"[1554] Procopius' fascinating narrative underscores three important issues. One is the fact that the Kanārangīyān held their exalted position in the east, in Parthava, a region that was the traditional homeland of the Ispahbudhān family, as Sebeos had previously informed us. Secondly, the office of the *kanārang* was an extremely important office in the Sasanian realm, an office that by law and tradition remained hereditary in the Kanārangīyān family. Finally, while their agnatic family is not specified in Procopius' nor in any other narrative, the Kanārangīyān are invariably associated with the Parthian Ispahbudhān family. Thus we might conjecture that the Kanārangīyān family was a branch of the Ispahbudhān family.[1555] Even Christensen admits that the Kanārangīyān must have belonged to one of the seven great feudal families of the realm.[1556] The Kanārangīyān continued to be centrally involved in Sasanian affairs in subsequent decades. In the coalition that had formed to depose Khusrow II,[1557] when Farrukhzād informed the Armenian dynast Varaztirots' that they had decided on Shīrūyih Qubād's kingship, the latter replied that the choice was acceptable not only to his party, but also to the Kanārangīyān family.[1558] At the battle of Qādisiya, we recall that a Kanāra commanded the light cavalry of Rustam's army,[1559] together with his son Shahrīyār b. Kanārā who fell at that battle.[1560]

It is in light of what we know of the exalted position of the Kanārangīyān family in Sasanian history, then, that we should consider Ferdowsī's narrative of Yazdgird III's correspondence with the Kanārang of Ṭūs on the eve of the Arab conquest. While the *Shāhnāma* informs us of Yazdgird III's correspondence with the Kanārang on his eastward flight, it remains, however, silent on the family's response to the last Sasanian king. There is no doubt that we are dealing

[1553] The king informed Ādhargulbād that he had decided to invade the Byzantine territory on two fronts and that he was giving the *kanārang* the honor of accompanying him on one of these fronts. Ādhargulbād obliged. It was in the course of this affair that the *kanārang* was put to death by Khusrow I. Procopius 1914, xxiii. 15–21, p. 215.

[1554] Procopius 1914, xxiii. 21–28, p. 217. We also recall that together with the Mihrānid Shāpūr Rāzī, the *chanaranges* Ādhargulbād occupied a central role in Qubād's campaigns against the Byzantines and the siege of Āmid. Ibid., p. 195. Joshua the Stylite 2000, pp. 60–61, especially n. 292.

[1555] For an elaboration on this postulate, see page 276ff below.

[1556] Christensen 1944, pp. 107–108, n. 3 and p. 351, n. 2.

[1557] See §2.7.6.

[1558] Ferdowsī 1971, vol. IX, p. 245, Ferdowsī 1935, p. 2901:

گرامی بد این شهریار جوان   به نزد کنارنگ و هم پهلوان

[1559] Ṭabarī 1992, p. 53, de Goeje, 2258.

[1560] Ṭabarī 1992, p. 131, de Goeje, 2346. See page 232.

here, yet again, with a case of Parthian editorial rewriting of the *Xʷadāy-Nāmag* tradition. For as the secessionist movement of Vistāhm and the mutiny of Farrukhzād were deleted from some recensions of this tradition, so too was the Kanārang's response to Yazdgird III deleted from the pages of the *Shāhnāma*, for reasons that will become clear shortly. For the Kanārangīyān's reply to Yazdgird III, therefore, we are forced to turn to the accounts of Thaʿālibī, a near contemporary of Ferdowsī, whose report at times, as in this instance, differs from that of the *Shāhnāma*. According to Thaʿālibī, when Yazdgird III reached the environ of Nīshāpūr "he was, on the one hand, fearful of the Arabs, and on the other, apprehensive of the Turks. He did not trust the walls (*ḥiṣār*) of Nīshāpūr and its fortification (*dizh*)."[1561] In search of a strategically sound refuge, Yazdgird III, who had heard the description of the strength and sturdiness of the fortifications of Ṭūs, "sent someone to acquaint himself with the situation there." The important information that Thaʿālibī's account provides is that the Kanārang of Ṭūs rejected Yazdgird III's request for protection: not pleased with the possibility of the king's arrival, the Kanārang "gave directions to a remote fortress and, together with presents, sent the envoy back." He asked the messenger to inform Yazdgird III that Ṭūs had "a small fortress that did not meet the needs of [the king] and his entourage."[1562] In this hour of need, therefore, the Kanārang, like Farrukhzād and his army, abandoned and betrayed Yazdgird III.

The contours of the events in Khurāsān have now been clarified. Upon the arrival of Yazdgird III in Khurāsān, there ensued a crisis: possibly in opposition to Yazdgird III's policies, the people of Khurāsān rebelled and Farrukhzād mutinied. Certainly simultaneously, the Kanārangīyān also refused to lend support to Yazdgird III. Yet there is more to what was transpiring in Khurāsān on the eve of the conquest of the region. While extremely partial to Arab affairs—and precisely because of this—the *futūḥ* narratives follow the course of events in the region just before the conquest. They invariably begin with the conquest of Ṭūs and Nīshāpūr and highlight the crucial role played by the Kanārangīyān. Interestingly enough, while the *Xʷadāy-Nāmag* tradition highlights the

[1561] As we have argued elsewhere, Yazdgird III's strategic considerations were in fact quite sound. Nīshāpūr was sheltered to its north by a chain of mountains that ran on a northwest–southeasterly axis. To its immediate south and southwest, however, the city opened up to the plateau. While the mountains could have provided protection from the Turks, the plain could not offer any protection from the Arabs on his trail. Such was not the case with Ṭūs. Ṭūs was situated in the midst of two mountain chains. It was, so to speak, clasped between them. In the turmoil that had engulfed the Sasanian realm, therefore, and in his flight east, the last Sasanian king Yazdgird III could have had protection from both enemies on either flank were he to position himself in the sturdy fortresses under the control of the Kanārangīyān in Ṭūs. Ferdowsī is explicit about this: "Verily in those high mountains and soaring peaks, from the Turk and Arab there shan't be injury." Ferdowsī 1971, vol. IX, p. 345:

همان بر ان راغ و کوه بلند   ز ترک و ز تازی نیاید گزند

For the strategic location of Ṭūs, see Pourshariati 1995, Chapter III.

[1562] Thaʿālibī 1900, p. 743.

correspondence of Yazdgird III with the Kanārang, the *futūḥ* narratives underline the complicity of the Kanārangīyān with the Arabs. Almost all of the narratives at our disposal inform us of what is purported to be some form of correspondence between the Kanārang and the Arab conquerors. In the Islamic sources, the Kanārang, as we shall call him henceforth, is variously identified as *kanārang*,[1563] *kanār*,[1564] Kanādbak, the ruler (*amīr*) of Ṭūs,[1565] Kanārī b. ʿĀmir,[1566] *marzbān*,[1567] king (*malik*) of Ṭūs,[1568] or the governor of Khurāsān.[1569] His letter, in which he invited the Arabs to conquer the region, according to some was addressed to ʿUthmān, the third Muslim caliph, or, according to others, to ʿAbdallāh b. ʿĀmir, the Arab general who initially overcame the region.

Dynastic struggles in Nīshāpūr

The *futūḥ* narratives on the conquest of Khurāsān make it unclear whether the conquest of Nīshāpūr took place peacefully (*ṣulḥan*) or through war (*anwatan*). The theme of *ṣulḥan/anwatan* is often, but not always, a reflection of legal discussions in later centuries.[1570] In this case, however, the controversy over the nature of the conquest of Khurāsān actually betrays a historical reality: dynastic factionalism on the eve of the Arab conquest of the region. One of the paramount reasons behind the confusion has to do with the fact that not all of the dynastic families with a stake in the region chose to cooperate with the Arabs. Specifically, the control over Nīshāpūr was in dispute at this juncture. Maʿmarī's narrative underscores this situation. According to the *Shāhnāma-i Abū Manṣūrī*, when "ʿUmar ... sent ʿAbdallāh b. ʿĀmir to call people to the religion of Muḥammad (Peace be upon Him and his Family), the Kanārang sent his son to Nīshāpūr to welcome him; [but] *people [who] were in the old fortress did not obey.* He [ʿAbdallāh b. ʿĀmir] asked his [i.e., the Kanārang's son's] help. He helped so affairs were set in order." According to the *Shāhnāma-i Abū Manṣūrī*, in exchange for their aid against the "people in the old fortress," ʿAbdallāh b. ʿĀmir added the governorship over *all of Nīshāpūr* to the jurisdiction of the Kanārangīyān.[1571]

1563 Nīshāpūrī, Abū ʿAbdallāh Ḥākim, *The Histories of Nishapur*, the Hague, 1965, edited by Richard Frye (Nīshāpūrī 1965), folio 61.

1564 Nöldeke 1979, pp. 2156–2157, de Goeje, 2886. See footnote 1596.

1565 Kufī, Abū Muḥammad Aḥmad b. Aʿtham, *Futūḥ*, Tehran, 1921, translation of Kufī 1986 by A.M. Mustowfi al-Hirawi (Kufī 1921), p. 115. See footnote 1578.

1566 Khayyāṭ 1977, pp. 164–165.

1567 Hamadānī, Ibn al-Faqīh, *al-Buldān*, Leiden, 1885, edited by M.J. de Goeje (Hamadānī 1885), p. 307.

1568 Balādhurī 1968, p. 405.

1569 Nīshāpūrī 1965, folio 60–61.

1570 See Robinson 2003 and the sources cited therein.

1571 "Then he [ʿAbdallāh b. ʿĀmir?] asked for a loan of a thousand dirhams. Then he [ʿAbdallāh b. ʿĀmir] asked for hostages (*girowgān*); [Kanārang] said that he didn't have any. So he [ʿAbdallāh b. ʿĀmir] asked for Nīshāpūr. He [Kanārang] gave him Nīshāpūr. When he [ʿAbdallāh b. ʿĀmir] took the money, he [ʿAbdallāh b. ʿĀmir] gave it [Nīshāpūr] back. ʿAbdallāh b. ʿĀmir gave him the war (*ān ḥarb ū rā dād*) and Kanārang fought him(?). And the story remains that Ṭūs belongs to

Initially, the Kanārang's control over Nīshāpūr was disputed. At least one segment of Nīshāpūr's population was fighting against the Arabs and the Kanārangīyān's complicity with the latter. They, therefore, rebelled. Most sources at our disposal highlight the problematic nature of the Kanārang's control over Nīshāpūr, for, according to some of these, he promised to aid the Arabs in exchange for being appointed governor of Khurāsān,[1572] whereas according to others, it was the governorship of Nīshāpūr that was at stake. According to Yaʿqūbī, for example, in his letter to ʿAbdallāh b. ʿĀmir, the Kanārang proposed: "I will [help] make you the first to reach Khurāsān if you promise the governorship of Nīshāpūr to me." Having fulfilled his promise, ʿAbdallāh gave the king of Ṭūs a letter which "to this day is with his offspring."[1573] Now Yaʿqūbī, who wrote in the last decades of the ninth century, was working at the Ṭāhirid court in Khurāsān, and probably in Nīshāpūr. He was, in other words, in a position to be well acquainted with the family in the nearby city of Ṭūs who claimed lineage, two and a half centuries back, to the ruler of Ṭūs from the Kanārangīyān family. The implications of this extremely significant piece of information, will be discussed elsewhere. For now it should be noted that the rendition of those accounts that refer to the Kanārang as the governor of Khurāsān,[1574] should be juxtaposed with those that refer to Farrukhzād as the *spāhbed* of Khurāsān.[1575]

That on the eve of the conquest, the Kanārang was no longer in complete control of Nīshāpūr is also borne out by a number of other sources, all of which seem to have a native Khurāsānī purview. The *Taʾrīkh-i Nīshāpūr*, for example,

so-and-so who holds Nīshāpūr as a hostage." In light of other sources at our disposal (see below), I offered here an alternative reading of the above passage than Minorsky, V., 'The Older Preface to the *Shāhnāma*', in *Studi orientalistici in onore de Giorgio Levi Della Vida*, pp. 260–273, Rome, 1964 (Minorsky 1964), p. 273. It should be noted that Qazvini's commentary on this passage agrees with my reading of the text: "[It was] ʿAbdallāh b. ʿĀmir who asked *kanārang* or his son for a thousand dirhams, and gave Nīshāpūr, which ʿAbdallāh had apparently conquered before, … as a hostage to the *kanārang*, and not the other way around." See Qazvini 1984, p. 89, n. 5.

[1572] According to Balādhurī, for example, in his letters to both ʿAbdallāh b. ʿĀmir and Saʿd b. ʿĀṣ b. Umaya, the governor (*wālī*) of Kūfa, the Kanārang invited them to conquer Khurāsān provided that whomever succeeded "would give him the governorship of Khurāsān." Balādhurī 1968, p. 334:

يدعوهما الى خراسان على ان يملكه عليها ايهما غلب و ظفر.

Also see Hamadānī 1885, p. 307.

[1573] Yaʿqūbi, Aḥmad b. Abī Yaʿqūb, *al-Buldān*, Tehran, 1977, translation of Yaʿqūbi 1967 by M.I. Ayati (Yaʿqūbi 1977), p. 114, Yaʿqūbi, Aḥmad b. Abī Yaʿqūb, *Kitâb al-Boldân*, Leiden, 1967, edited by M.J. de Goeje (Yaʿqūbi 1967), p. 296:

فكتب له كتابا هو عند ولده الى هاذه الغاية

[1574] "Imām Ḥākim … said … that at the time of the rule of ʿAbdallāh b. ʿĀmir … in Baṣrah and Saʿd b. ʿĀṣ in Kūfa … the *kanārang*, who was the governor of Khurāsān and a Magian, wrote a letter to them. He invited them to Khurāsān and [illegible] promised [illegible] and said that the ruthless Yazdgird III has been killed in Marv." Nīshāpūrī 1965, folio 60–61.

[1575] We shall discuss the exact nature of the Kanārang's relationship with Farrukhzād further on page 276.

corroborates this information provided by Maʿmarī. When ʿAbdallāh b. ʿĀmir and his army reached Nīshāpūr, they "came to the middle of the two gates of Jurjān and Fārs. The *fractious* people of Nīshāpūr ... [however] protested at the environs of the fortress and the ramparts [of the city]." The rebellion led to a stalemate that apparently lasted for nine months, after which peace ensued.[1576] This local history provides further, extremely significant, information about the identity of the leader of the rebellion in Nīshāpūr. When ʿAbdallāh b. ʿĀmir reached the environs of Nīshāpūr, "Barzān Jāh, the rebellious insurgent, who was ... the *governor of the territory*," put up a staunch resistance. Trying to secure himself against the offensive of the Arabs, Barzān Jāh set out for his "base [illegible] to the rampart and the *quhandiz*" with a group of other people. War ensued, and it was at this point and against Barzān Jāh, that the Kanārang aided the Arab army. Once the insurgents were defeated, the Kanārang came to ʿAbdallāh b. ʿĀmir and accepted the *kharāj* (tax) of Abarshahr, that is of Nīshāpūr and Ṭūs.[1577] We shall postulate here that the name Barzān is in all likelihood a scribal error for Burzīn, the famous Mithraic fire in the vicinity of Ṭūs and Nīshāpūr. The term Jāh is less clear. If we may hazard a guess, it could be a corruption of *shāh*, king, and hence this figure's name should be reconstructed as Burzīn Shāh. According to the local history of Nīshāpūr, therefore, Burzīn Shāh was a *governor* of this territory. By juxtaposing the facts that the Kanārang coveted the governorship of Khurāsān and that Burzīn Shāh claimed to be the governor of the territory, we can conclude that on the eve of the Arab conquest of the territory, a dynastic struggle was taking place in Khurāsān over the control of the region.

The *futūḥ* narratives corroborate the information provided by the native Khurāsānī tradition, adding other significant data. According to Aʿtham al-Kūfī, the name of the leader of the opposition faction in Nīshāpūr was Aswār and it was against Aswār's stalwartness that the Kanārang came to ʿAbdallāh b. ʿĀmir's aid.[1578] Information on the urban topography of Nīshāpūr will clarify

[1576] Nīshāpūrī 1965, folio 60–61.

[1577] This was "for 700,000 *dirhams*, which amount[ed] to 500,000 *mithqāls* of silver, together with other things." Nīshāpūrī 1965, folio 61.

[1578] "[After conquering Fārs] ʿAbdallāh [b. ʿĀmir] set out for Khurāsān. When ... he reached Nīshāpūr, there was a ruler (*malik*) there called Aswār [sic]. ʿAbdallāh pillaged the village ... and started a war with the people of the city. He killed whomever he found. His affair with the people of Nīshāpūr took up a long time. Meanwhile Kanādbak [i.e., the Kanārang], who was the ruler (*amīr*) of Ṭūs, wrote a letter to ʿAbdallāh and asked for safe-conduct from him, provided that if he granted him amnesty he would come to his service and aid him in conquering Nīshāpūr. ʿAbdallāh agreed and gave him safe conduct. Kanādbak came to ʿAbdallāh with a well-equipped army. ʿAbdallāh treated him kindly and gave him and the elite of his army robes of honor. He [then] set out for war with Nīshāpūr and fought valiantly. The two sides fought heavily. ʿAbdallāh promised that he would not leave Nīshāpūr until he had either conquered the city or had died in the process. When Aswār heard of ʿAbdallāh's pledge, he sent an envoy to the latter and asked for safe conduct, provided that if ʿAbdallāh granted him amnesty, he would open all the gates of the city for ... [the Arab army to enter]. He [ʿAbdallāh] agreed and pardoned him [Aswār]. The two sides then made up the stipulations of the agreement. The next day at sun-rise Aswār opened the gate of the city

the identity of these rebellious leaders, Burzīn Shāh and Aswār, who on the eve of the conquest of Khurāsān contested the governorship of Khurāsān with the Kanārangīyān family.

We recall that according to Nīshāpūrī, the armies of ʿAbdallāh b. ʿĀmir encountered the "fractious people of Nīshāpūr" near the two gates of Gurgān and Fārs.[1579] Now, Maqdisī, enumerating the gates of Nīshāpūr, mentions the gate of Aswār Kārīn next to the gate of Fārs.[1580] He also mentions, enumerating this time the *qanāts* (underground channels) of Khurāsān, a certain Sawār Kārīz.[1581] Instead of the reading *kārīz*, translated as *qanāt*, de Goeje proposes the reading *kārin*.[1582] There existed in Maqdisī's time, in other words, a gate, and possibly a *qanāt*, called *Sawār* or *Aswār*. Now *aswār* could be in fact an Arabic plural for the Persian word *sawār* (cavalry). The more common Arabic plural, however, is *asāwira*.[1583] The gate or *qanāt* of *Aswār* or *Sawār*, therefore, was in all probability simply the gate or *qanāt* next to which a section of the army was settled in Nīshāpūr. There is, however, an added significance to this information. For the gate of *Aswār* was not simply named after *any* member of the *asāwira*, but after a Kārin. We also recall that a second reading by de Goeje gives the name of a *qanāt* as Sawār Kārin. We have by now become quite familiar with the Parthian dynastic families of Khurāsān and Ṭabaristān, among whom the Kārin.[1584] Barzān Jāh (Burzīn Shāh) of our previous narrative, therefore, was in all probability a descendant of the Kārinid Sukhrā. It is apt to briefly recapitulate the history of the Kārins in Khurāsān, for it becomes extremely pertinent to what was transpiring in this region on the eve of the conquest.

We recall that Khusrow I had regretted his father's treatment of the Kārins and installed them as *spāhbeds* over Khurāsān and Ṭabaristān (*kūst-i khwarāsān*), the domains traditionally belonging to the Ispahbudhān family.[1585] The Kārins, who retained their *spāhbedī* of Khurāsān during Hormozd IV's reign, were demoted after Bahrām-i Chūbīn's rebellion by Khusrow II, who appointed in

and ʿAbdallāh entered [the city] with the Muslim army ... and started pillaging and looting the city. That day they were killing and looting until night time. Kanādbak, the ruler of Ṭūs, came to ʿAbdallāh and said: 'O amīr, once you have been victorious and triumphant forgiveness is a higher [virtue] than revenge and retribution.' ʿAbdallāh accepted the intercession of the Kanādbak and gave amnesty to the people of the city and ordered the army to stop pillaging. He [ʿAbdallāh, then] made Kanādbak the governor (*amīr*) of Nīshāpūr." Kufī, Abū Muḥammad Aḥmad b. Aʿtham, *al-Futūḥ*, Beirut, 1986 (Kufī 1986), vol I, pp. 338–339, Kufī 1921, pp. 115–116.

1579 Nīshāpūrī 1965, folio 60–61.

1580 Maqdisī, Shams al-Dīn, *Aḥsan al-Taqāsīm fī Maʿrifat al-ʾAqālīm*, Leiden, 1877, edited by M.J. de Goeje (Maqdisī 1877), p. 316.

1581 Maqdisī 1877, p. 329.

1582 Maqdisī 1877, p. 329.

1583 *Asāwira* is "the plural of the Pahlavi [word] *asvārān* or *asvāraghān*." Christensen 1944, p. 265. *Asāwira* also denotes one of the titles of the officers of the army. In hierarchical order Yaʿqūbī cites: *spāhbed* (the governor), *fādūsbān* (*pādhūspān*), *marzbān*, *shahrīj* (*shahrig*, *shahrab*, ruler of a canton), and finally the *asāwira*. Yaʿqūbi 1969, vol. 1, p. 203, Yaʿqūbi 1983, pp. 202–203. For the *asāwira*, see also Zakeri 1995.

1584 See §2.5.6. For Ṭabaristān, this will be discussed in more detail in Chapter 4, especially §4.2.

1585 See §2.5.6.

their stead the Ispahbudhān Vistāhm as the *spāhbed* of the *kūst-i khwarāsān*.[1586] As we shall see the, *Tārīkh-i Ṭabaristān* confirms the decline of the Kārin's power in Khurāsān and Ṭabaristān during this period.[1587] This was followed by the revolt of Vistāhm through which the Ispahbudhān family was able to reestablish their authority not only over their traditional homelands, the land of Parthava, but also over Ṭabaristān—their domains probably covering at this point not only the said regions, but also Azarbāyjān—for a period of close to a decade.[1588] The secessionist movement of the Ispahbudhān, however, was ended by the Armenian dynast, Smbat Bagratuni, who was delegated with this task by Khusrow II.[1589] After Smbat's tenure in Khurāsān,[1590] the situation in the region became, once again, very unsettled. In this post-Bagratuni situation, Farrukh Hormozd and his sons, Rustam and Farrukhzād, were able to reestablish their control in their dynastic homeland of Khurāsān, while maintaining control over Azarbāyjān, which situation explains the confusion of the sources in referring alternatively to Farrukhzād and Rustam as the *spāhbeds* of Azarbāyjān or Khurāsān.[1591] The Kārins, meanwhile, must have taken advantage of this post-Bagratuni situation to reclaim some territory and authority in Khurāsān. This, then, was the Kārin's position on the eve of the Arab conquest of Khurāsān. They were bent on preserving their authority in Khurāsān, and Ṭabaristān, even more so since, through the machinations of Dīnār in the wake of the defeat at the battle of Nihāvand, they had lost their control over Nihāvand.[1592]

In view of Farrukhzād's mutiny, the complicity of the Ispahbudhān and Kanārangīyān with the Arabs, and their own defeat at the battle of Nihāvand, the Kārins' antagonism toward the foreign invaders must have been great. In fact, during the conquest period and for centuries afterwards, the Kārins maintained a strong anti-Arab stance.[1593] What transpired in Khurāsān on the eve of the conquests, in other words, was analogous to what transpired in Rayy and its adjacent territories, and somewhat similar to what transpired in Azarbāyjān, as we shall see: one Parthian dynastic family threw in its lot with the conquering Arab armies, in opposition to an age-old Parthian rival in the region.[1594] With the Sasanians out of the picture, there remained the inter-Parthian rivalry. Like the Sasanians before them, the Arabs were quick to turn this situation to their own advantage. It is in this context, therefore, that the complicity of the Kanārang with the Arabs against the Kārins in Khurāsān, and that of Farrukhzād against the Mihrāns of Rayy and Ṭabaristān, makes sense. Without a doubt,

[1586] See page 107ff.
[1587] See §4.2.
[1588] See §2.7.1.
[1589] See §2.7.2.
[1590] See page 138ff.
[1591] See our discussion on page 188ff.
[1592] See page 241ff.
[1593] One example is the revolt of the Kārinid Sunbād during the early ʿAbbāsid period, which we will discuss in §6.4 below.
[1594] See §3.4.8 below.

the *fractious people of Nīshāpūr* under the leadership of Burzīn Shāh or Aswār were none other than the Kārins taking a vigorous stand against the incoming foreign power in order to protect their interests in the region.[1595] The *spāhbed* seals which we have now discovered testify to the Kārins' substantial control and presence in the region. How extensive, however, was the control of the Kanārangīyān over Khurāsān at this tumultuous juncture of the region's history? Or, turning the question around, how much territory were the Kārins and the Kanārangīyān competing for?

Most of our sources agree that the Kanārang was in control of Ṭūs and parts of Nīshāpūr, but that his dominion stopped somewhere to the east of Nīshāpūr. In none of the sources is there any suggestion of the involvement of the Kanārangīyān in the occupation of other major cities in Khurāsān. Whether conquered by peace (*ṣulḥan*), or through war (*anwatan*), every other city to the west of the Oxus, came to terms with the Arabs independently. Only Ṭūs and the rest of Abarshahr remained under the control of the Kanārang. This information is confirmed by Ṭabarī, who gives us the precise delimitation of the territory under the control of the Kanārangīyān. "[When ᶜAbdallāh b. ᶜĀmir] ... reached in front of the city [Nīshāpūr] ... he conquered half of it with war. The other half was under the control of a *kanār*, together with one half of Nisā and Ṭūs."[1596] These then were the limits of the jurisdiction of the Kanārangīyān family over Khurāsān on the eve of the conquest. What of the relationship between the Kanārangīyān and Farrukh Hormozd and his sons, Rustam and Farrukhzād, however? Isfazārī provides us with an answer.

The Ispahbudhān and the Kanārangīyān

According to Isfazārī, when the Kanārang made peace for Ṭūs and Nīshāpūr with ᶜAbdallāh b. ᶜĀmir, he informed the latter that among "all of the Pārsīs, after the house of Kisrā and Yazdgird III, there was no one [with the same status] as me (*dar jumlih-i Pārsīyān baᶜd az ahl-i bayt-i Kisrā va Yazdjird mānand-i man hīch kas nīst*)." The veracity of his claim, as well as the affinity of his house and his policies with the family of Farrukhzād, comes across in the rest of the narrative. While the Parthian Kanārang was highlighting his illustrious pedigree for ᶜAbdallāh b. ᶜĀmir, "Farrukhzād, who *was the minister of Yazdgird III* ... reached there. Kanāz went to welcome Farrukhzād. When he saw Farrukhzād, he threw himself unto the ground from his horse and proceeded in front of the [latter's] stirrup until [the reached] ᶜAbdallāh b. ᶜĀmir." Witnessing the Kanārang's expressions of reverence in front of Farrukhzād, ᶜAbdallāh was

[1595] Although Barzān Jāh (Burzīn Shāh) and Aswār were probably both Kārin dynasts, we can at present not ascertain whether they are in fact one and the same person.

[1596] Ṭabarī's narrative, incidentally, confirms our reading of Maᶜmarī's text (see footnote 1571). For according to Ṭabarī, when ᶜAbdallāh b. ᶜĀmir "made peace with the kanār ... [the latter] gave him his son, Abū Silt b. Kanārī, and the son of his brother Salim as hostages ... Ibn ᶜĀmir took the two sons of the Kanārī and gave them to Nuᶜmān b. Afgham Naṣrī," who freed them, the implicit assumption here being that these two figures of the family, at least, converted and were manumitted. Nöldeke 1979, pp. 2156–2157, de Goeje, 2886.

perplexed: "Have you not said that among all of the Persians there is none such as I," he asked. The Kanārang clarified: This indeed was the case, but it applied to all other noble dynasts besides "Farrukhzād, whose status was higher and whose lineage more ancient than mine."[1597] On the eve of the Arab conquests, the Kanārang and Farrukhzād were in fact coordinating their policies. When Farrukhzād mutinied and left Yazdgird III to his follies with Māhūy and the Turks in the east, he headed back west. His route to Rayy naturally took him through Khurāsān and through the center of the Kanārangīyān's abode in Ṭūs.

It is quite probable even that the two agnatic dynasties had gentilitial affiliation.[1598] For a number of centuries, the Kanārangīyān had maintained a lofty position in Khurāsān, after all. The Ispahbudhān traced their heritage to this same region, and for a long period, as the *spāhbeds* of the *kūst-i khwarāsān*, they were the Kanārangīyāns' overlords. And more often than not, their policies against or on behalf of the Sasanian kings, coincided. Like the Ispahbudhān, the Kanārangīyān had sued for peace, because the Arabs assured them that they only meant to go beyond their territories, to those region wherein resided different peoples: "they [i.e., the Arabs] ... were not coveting the crowns (*deyhīms*) of Parthian kings." Their intent was what they had promised Rustam: to go to the lands beyond Iran, where they could find the sources of the trade.

The Kārinid insurrection

The peace agreements of the Ispahbudhān and the Kanārangīyān with the Arab armies did not sit well with the Kārins. Not only did the Kārins make a staunch stand against the encroaching Arabs—a defensive posture that called for the collaboration of the Kanārangīyān with the Arabs—but there is ample evidence that the dynastic struggle between the two Parthian families continued long after the Arab conquest of their territories. There is no doubt either that the defeat of the Kārins in the course of the conquest of Khurāsān, did not lead to their acquiescence to the nominal lordship of the Arabs over their territories. For as Khalīfat b. Khayyāṭ informs us, shortly after the conquest of Ṭūs and Nīshāpūr by the Arab armies, the Kārins revolted sometime in 33 AH/654 CE.[1599] It is said—perhaps with some exaggeration—that a force of 40,000 gathered around them. Significantly, the Kārins led this revolt in Bādghīs and Herāt. We recall the tradition contained in the *Tārīkh-i Ṭabaristān* that Khusrow I had given parts of Zābulistān to Zarmihr, the eldest of the nine sons of the Kārinid Sukhrā.[1600] The connection of the Kārins to Zābulistān is also maintained in other traditions, except that the son is called Dādburzīn and the king Bahrām

1597 Isfazārī, Muʿīn al-Dīn, *Rowḍāt al-Jannāt fī Owṣāf Madīnat al-Harāt*, Tehran, 1959, edited by Seyyed Muhammad Kazim Imam (Isfazārī 1959), pp. 248–249.

1598 This we cannot establish in reference to concrete information.

1599 Khayyāṭ 1977, p. 167.

1600 Ibn Isfandīyār 1941, p. 151. See §2.5.6.

V Gūr.[1601] While the precise details of the Kārins' association with Zābulistān subsequent to Khusrow I's reforms must be subjected to further investigation, there is no doubt that shortly after the Arab conquest of Khurāsān, a Kārinid revolt did in fact transpire in the east. The Kārins' rebellion was put down, and the Parthian dynasts were defeated by the Arab forces led by ʿAbdallāh b. Khāzim Sulāmī. Kārin himself was ostensibly killed.[1602] This, however, is not the last we will hear of the Kārins, nor of their rivalry with the Ispahbudhān.[1603] One thing is certain: the Arab conquest of Khurāsān further weakened the Parthian Kārin family.

3.4.8 The conquest of Azarbāyjān

To conclude our chapter on the Arab conquests, we must briefly discuss the events transpiring in Azarbāyjān. Before we proceed, we must recall that Azarbāyjān had also come under the control of the Ispahbudhān: both Farrukh Hormozd and Rustam, for example, are called the governors of the region in our sources. When Bukayr b. ʿAbdallāh set out toward Azarbāyjān, therefore, one of the first kings (*mulūk*) of the region to come forward to him was the Ispahbudhān Isfandīyār, who had participated in the battle of Wāj Rūdh and, after being defeated, had fled.[1604] When Isfandīyār fell captive to Bukayr, he asked the latter: "which would you rather have, to conquer the region through war or through peace?" He then suggested that if Bukayr intended to conquer the territory through peace, his only option would be keeping him, Isfandīyār, alive, for "if you [were to] kill me *all of Azarbāyjān [will] rise in avenging my blood, and will wage war against you.*"[1605] He further pointed out that if Bukayr intended to "make no peace treaty involving the people of Azerbaijan, nor join [them], they ... *will disperse into the surrounding Caucasus mountains and those of Asia Minor ... Those who can fortify themselves [there] will [then] do so for some time.*"[1606] Having considered the situation, Bukayr subsequently followed Isfandīyār's advice and made peace with the latter for all those regions in Azarbāyjān over which he had control. Ṭabarī calls Isfandīyār the son of al-Farrukhzār, that is to say, Farrukhzād.[1607] This, too, explains his presence at the battle of Wāj Rūdh alongside Zīnabī Abū 'l-Farrukhān, that is to say, his father.[1608]

[1601]Ferdowsī 1971, vol. VII, p. 387, Ferdowsī 1935, p. 2196. This, probably, is yet another instance of the use of the Ctesian method in Ferdowsī's sources, in this case, probably through Kārinid patronage.

[1602]Khayyāṭ 1977, p. 167.

[1603]See §4.2.

[1604]See page 248ff.

[1605]Balʿamī 1959, p. 335.

[1606]Ṭabarī 1994, p. 32, de Goeje, 2660.

[1607]Sayf calls him the brother of Rustam, in all probability another confusion replete in the sources. For, as we have seen, the two most important sons of Farrukh Hormozd of whom we are aware were Rustam and Farrukhzād. Whether Isfandīyār was a son of Farrukhzād or his brother, however, does not make any difference to the germ of our discussion, for he was in any case an Ispahbudhān. Ṭabarī 1994, p. 21, n. 115.

[1608]See page 248ff.

According to our sources, Farrukhzād had another son, called Bahrām b. Farrukhzād.[1609] In the course of the conquest of Azarbāyjān, however, this Bahrām chose not to submit to the Arab forces. Isfandīyār remarked to Bukayr, therefore, that for the conquest of Azarbāyjān to be complete, "all that ... remained ... was this one war."[1610] This kind of intra-familial Parthian rivalry, we recall, was not uncommon in Sasanian history. Bahrām then engaged the army of ʿUtbah b. Farqad, but was defeated and was forced to flee. At the flight of his brother Bahrām, Isfandīyār then exclaimed to Bukayr that "peace ... [was now] complete and war ha[d] been brought to an end."[1611] As Ṭabarī notes, however, "peace was only complete[d] after ʿUtbah b. Farqad's defeat of Bahrām."[1612] In the peace treaty that was subsequently drawn after the conquest of Azarbāyjān, there was no mention of a ruler of Azarbāyjān. It was addressed to "the people of Azerbaijan, mountains, and plains, borders and frontiers, all people of *whatever religion*."[1613] Once again, the date given for this document, 18 AH/639–640 CE,[1614] is improbable in view of the progress of the conquest elsewhere on the plateau.

Shahrvarāz, the ruler of Darband

Having conquered all of Azarbāyjān, the Arab army then proceeded to the frontier regions of Darband, where for more than a century the Sasanians and the Byzantines had, on and off, cooperated against their mutual enemy the Khazars.[1615] In Bāb al-Abwāb (Darband), we are told, there was a king (*malik*) called Shahrīr or, in Balʿamī's narrative, Shahrīrāz. Ṭabarī calls him Shahrvarāz and confirms that he was "a Persian who was in control of this frontier area [i.e., Darband] and whose origins were from the family of Shahrbarāz, the ruler who had routed the Israelites and driven them out of al-Shām." Shahrvarāz (Shahrīrāz), therefore, was a member of the Mihrān family. The treaty that Shahrvarāz drew up with the Arabs, according to Balʿamī, was one that would thenceforth form the *sunna* (precedent) for the two frontier regions, Caucasia and Transoxiana. In their treaty with Shahrvarāz, the Arabs promised that they would have no armies stationed in the territories under his control and even pledged not to impose any *jizya* or *kharāj*.[1616] In exchange Shahrvarāz promised

[1609]Smith states that he is an "unidentified Azerbaijani ruler." Ṭabarī 1994, p. 32, n. 171.

[1610]In Ṭabarī's narrative the name of Isfandīyār is first given as Jarmīdhih b. al-Farrukhzādh. Ṭabarī 1994, p. 31, de Goeje, 2660.

[1611]Ṭabarī 1994, p. 33, de Goeje, 2661.

[1612]Ṭabarī 1994, p. 33, de Goeje, 2662.

[1613]Ṭabarī 1994, p. 33, de Goeje, 2662. My emphasis. The document also guaranteed that those recruited for military service by the Arabs were "in any one year ... exempt [from paying] the tribute of that year (*wa-man ḥushira min-hum fī sanatin*)." Smith notes that this might "also be rendered as 'those who suffer distress'; that is, drought, crop failure, etc." Ṭabarī 1994, p. 33, n. 172.

[1614]Ṭabarī 1994, p. 34, de Goeje, 2662.

[1615]It must be noted that, the Khazars seem to have been also used as mercenaries by both sides. For a brief history of this region, see footnote 1725 below.

[1616]Balʿamī 1959, p. 337.

to keep two enemies away from the Arabs: the Khazars and the Rūs. For, as he argued for Surāqah b. ʿAbdalraḥmān, these two were "the enemies of the whole world, especially the Arabs."[1617]

Ṭabarī gives us further insight about the peace arrangements between Shahrvarāz and the Arabs. Seeking safe conduct from the Arabs, Shahrvarāz informed them that he was "facing a rabid enemy and different communities who [we]re not of noble descent." He then advised the Arabs that it was not "fitting for noble and intelligent people to assist such people or to ask their help against those of noble descent and origins ... [and that] noblemen [had to stick] close to noblemen, wherever they are ... [and that his] inclinations [we]re the same [as theirs]."[1618] He further explained to them that he was "not a Caucasian nor an Armenian, ... [but the Arabs had] *conquered [his] ... land ... [and his] community*." Shahrvarāz then negotiated with the Arabs: "Our tribute to you will be the military assistance we render you and our carrying out whatever you desire." He, in turn, asked them that they should not "humiliate [them] ... with tribute." Ṭabarī then explains that as a result of the precedence set by the Arab treaty with Shahrvarāz and his followers, "it became a practice for those polytheists who made war on the enemy ... to pay no tribute other than to be ready to fight and were thus exempt from tribute ... of that particular year."[1619] The peace document that was subsequently drawn was addressed, significantly, to Shahrvarāz, "*the inhabitants of Armenia, and the Armenians [in Darband], ... [and also to] those* coming from distant parts *and those who are local and those around them who have joined them*."[1620] Ṭabarī then proceeds to enumerate in detail the tremendous wealth, in precious stones, of the region around Darband through the story of the ruby.[1621]

Significantly, in 653 CE, that is, shortly after Farrukhzād's complicitry with the Arabs, a section of the Armenian nobility who had severed their allegiance from the Byzantines as well as from Farrukhzād, also "submitted to the king of Ishmael. T'ēodoros ... with all the Armenian princes made a pact with death."[1622] And thus, at the expense of the Sasanians, one after another, the Parthian dynastic families of the *kūst-i khwarāsān* and *kūst-i ādurbādagān* made peace with the conquering Arab armies. The Kanārangīyān, the Ispahbudhān,

[1617] Balʿamī 1959, p. 336.

[1618] Ṭabarī 1994, p. 35, de Goeje, 2664.

[1619] Ṭabarī 1994, p. 35, de Goeje, 2664. Smith notes that the relevant passage would mean that this would be the case "whether they actually fight or not ... If they stand ready to fight, they are exempt." Ṭabarī 1994, p. 35, n. 178.

[1620] Ṭabarī 1994, p. 36, de Goeje, 2665.

[1621] Ṭabarī 1994, pp. 40–42, de Goeje, 2669–2671. Balʿamī 1959, pp. 339–340.

[1622] The peace agreements made between the Arabs and the Armenians who had submitted to them are also instructive. According to these the "prince of Ishmael ... [had told them:] I shall not take tribute from you for a three year period. Then you will pay [tribute] with an oath, as much as you may wish. You will keep in your country 15,000 cavalry, and provide sustenance from your country; and I shall reckon it in the royal tax. I shall not request the cavalry for Syria; but wherever else I command they shall be ready for duty. I shall not send amirs to [your] fortresses, nor an Arab army, neither many, nor even down to a single cavalryman." Sebeos 1999, pp. 135–136.

a son of Farrukhzād in Azarbāyjān, and finally some of the Armenian princes, each made a pact with the enemy. Their motive: retaining *de facto* control over their territories. The Mihrāns and the Kārins were on the losing end of these deals made by their Parthian brethren. The saga of the Parthian dynastic families of the *kūst-i khwarāsān* and *kūst-i ādurbādagān* will not be complete, however, until we examine their continued presence in Ṭabaristān in the subsequent centuries. To this, then, we must turn our attention in the next chapter.[1623]

3.5 Epilogue: repercussions for early Islamic history

Our investigation in this chapter of the early Arab conquest of Iran has been methodologically heretical, to say the least. In order to undertake it, we have totally disregarded its *hijra* dating. We had a perfectly justifiably reason for doing so: the *futūḥ* and "the history of Iran at the time of the first Islamic conquests" were *primary themes* of early Islamic tradition,[1624] whereas the *hijra*, annalistic, and caliphal chronological schemes of the early Arabic historical tradition were *secondary themes*.[1625] These *hijra*, annalistic, and caliphal motifs for structuring the narratives of early Islamic history were superimposed *post facto* onto the accounts of the *futūḥ* narrative, hence the "sharp and irresolvable contradictions [which] prevail on not only the dating, but ... [also] the order, of even the most central events in the *history of the expansion of Islam*."[1626]

Uncritically accepting these secondary themes through which the *futūḥ* narratives have been structured, has thus far seriously obstructed scholarly efforts at reaching a satisfactory chronology for the early Arab conquest of the Middle East.[1627] When faced with Sayf's improbable chronology, scholarship regularly accused him of appalling anachronisms, but never attempted to solve the quandary posed by these anachronisms.[1628] Neither was there success in establishing a logical chronological relationship between the conquest of Iraq and Syria.[1629] The adoption of the conventional chronology, even after exhausting

[1623] Lack of space and time has forced us to defer a more detailed study of Azarbāyjān and Khurāsān to a future work.

[1624] Noth 1994, p. 39.

[1625] See footnote 903.

[1626] Noth 1994, p. 41. Hence also the conclusions reached by one of the foremost authorities on the topic who claimed that it "is virtually impossible to accept one sequential or chronological arrangement and to reject another except on grounds that are essentially arbitrary." Donner 1981, p. 128.

[1627] Our point of reference here is primarily the chronology of the *futūḥ* narratives, for as we know many other aspects of early Islamic history have come under serious critical scrutiny.

[1628] See Ṭabarī 1993, p. 11, nn. 73 and 74; p. 15, n. 97, among others.

[1629] The problematic episode of Khālid b. Walīd's desert march is only the most flagrant of these problems. Donner 1981, pp. 119–129, especially p. 120 and p. 311, n. 157; Crone 1991a. Sayf has also been accused of having pushed the conquest of Syria two years earlier to the year 13 of *hijra* (634). In fact, it might be that our newly proposed chronology of the conquest of Iraq will finally make sense of the utter confusion regarding the conquest of Syria.

all other *foreign* traditions at our disposal, therefore, had led to a stalemate in the field.[1630]

The failure in disentangling the puzzles surrounding the Arab conquest of Iran from the disjointed information provided by the *futūḥ* and other sources, however, was hitherto precipitated by the obdurate refusal to integrate the Sasanian dimension of this history into the picture. As our investigations in this chapter demonstrate, the information provided by Sayf on the conditions prevailing in Iran during this period are, in fact, *so detailed* that it is incredible that scholarship has dismissed them for as long as it did—all the more remarkable, given the paucity of our information for this crucial period of history. Here we hope to have finally proven that "a great many of the Persian traditions have [such] thoroughly individual traits ... [that they] cannot be explained away as constructions out of Islamic *futūḥ*."[1631] We also hope to have shown that the majority of traditions concerning the early Arab conquest of Iraq, especially as they are found in the rich accounts of Sayf b. ʿUmar, were probably initially dated relative to the events that were transpiring *in Iran* during the period 628–632 CE.

Proceeding from a heretical methodology, however, has led us not only to equally heretical conclusions, but also to potentially startling implications. As the reader will have noticed, our reconstruction of the chronology of the early conquest of Iraq to the period 628–632 CE, based predominantly on Sasanian chronological indicators and numismatic evidence,[1632] will pose an altogether different set of even more serious chronological quandaries. If this reconstruction is valid, it will in fact have revolutionary implications for our understanding of early Islamic history. Once we accept the remarkable synchrony of the accounts of the early conquest of Iraq with the events that transpired in Iran during the period of 628–632,[1633] our conventional chronological reckoning of dating the Arab conquests to the caliphate of Abū Bakr (12–13 AH/633–634 CE) has to be revised. Once we accept this revision, however, we are confronted with a new quandary: If the early conquest of Iraq did, in fact, take place in the years 7–11 AH/628–632 CE, how will this affect our conventional understanding of early Islamic history? What of the death of the Prophet in 11 AH/632 CE? If the Prophet was alive during the the Arab conquest of Iraq, what of his whereabouts? What was his role in this crucial juncture of history? What of the wars of apostacy (*ridda*), which are presumed to have taken place *after* the death of the Prophet, but *before* any major conquest? If Muhammad was alive, what was his relationship to Abū Bakr and ʿUmar?

[1630] As Noth put it: "Such keen-witted sleuths as de Goeje, Wellhausen, Mednikov, and Caetani were thus unable to resolve this confusion completely, especially since *the non-Arabic sources (Greek, Syriac, Armenian, Coptic)* can provide further help *only at a few points*, and are in any case *demonstrably dependent upon the emergent Arab–Islamic historical tradition for some of their information.*" Noth 1994, p. 42.

[1631] Noth 1994, p. 39.

[1632] See our methodological procedures elaborated in §3.1.2.

[1633] See Table 6.1 on page 468.

It is the nature of scholarship that answering one set of questions often raises new, and perhaps even harder, ones. In our case, these new questions about early Islamic history are of such fundamental importance that satisfactorily answering these will require substantial further research, a feat beyond the scope of present study.[1634] What we shall confine ourselves to in this epilogue, therefore, is simply to suggest one possible answer to these new complex sets of queries, in the hope that it will pave the way for further research.

We will proceed from the chronology of the early conquest of Iraq as established in this chapter.[1635] We have established a new *terminus ante quem* for the early Arab conquest of Iraq, which started with the battle of Ubullah (traditionally dated to 12 AH): this battle took place sometime around Shīrūyih Qubād's death and Ardashīr III's ascension in September 628 CE.[1636] The early conquest of Iraq, therefore, started sometime in the year 7 AH. We have also established that the the battle of Bridge, dated by Sayf to 13 AH, took place at the end of Būrāndukht's second regency, just before Yazdgird III's promotion to kingship in June 632 CE, when factionalism between the Pahlav and the Pārsig prevented the Iranians from following up on their victories.[1637] In the *hijra* calendar, this corresponds to the year 11 AH. Based on these two chronological indicators, the early Arab conquest of Iraq *spread over a period of almost four years*, from circa September 628 to June 632 CE. The *futūḥ* narratives *telescope* these events into the two years 12–13 AH/633–634 CE., during the caliphate of Abū Bakr. This is the most basic observation that we can make on the basis of our analysis. This very basic observation, however, will have potentially revolutionary implications for early Islamic history.[1638]

Abū Bakr's caliphate

At a minimum, the implication of this is that Abū Bakr could not have been the caliph for part of these four years in which the early conquests of Iraq took place.[1639] The contention that Abū Bakr was not functioning as caliph, that is, as the *successor to Muḥammad* during part of this period, however, in turn

[1634] Primarily due to time-pressure, the author was forced to put a stop to her enquiry.

[1635] See §3.3.2, and Table 6.1.

[1636] See page 190ff.

[1637] See §3.3.5, especially 218ff.

[1638] Simply manipulating the date of the *hijra* will not resolve this blatant chronological problem, for four years can never be squeezed into the span of two years, be they lunar or solar!

[1639] Of course, conventional Islamic historiography puts his entire caliphate right after this period. However, we might have to reckon with Ḥamza Iṣfahānī's contention that Būrāndukht's regency "took place *toward the end of the caliphate of Abū Bakr ... [when] three months [remained from the caliphate of] Abū Bakr.*" Ḥamza Iṣfahānī 1961, p. 97, Ḥamza Iṣfahānī 1988, p. 115. How helpful this piece of information is remains to be seen, for it is not clear to which part of Būrāndukht's regency Ḥamza Iṣfahānī is referring. Based on numismatic evidence and our own reconstruction of her reign (see §3.3.4, especially page 208ff), the duration of her combined regencies is 630–632 CE. An additional problem raised by Ḥamza Iṣfahānī's remark is that the Prophet would have already been dead for two years, because the office of caliph was installed only after his death, conventionally dated to 11 AH/632 CE.

raises the question of whether or not the Prophet was already dead when the early conquest of Iraq began.[1640] If the Prophet was indeed alive during at least part of the early conquest of Iraq, however, as the conventional date of 632 for his death would suggest, then what explains his absence from all of the *futūḥ* narratives? As the majority of the *topoi* in early Islamic narratives were *Islamic topoi*, which were added to the tradition *post facto*,[1641] as indeed was also the case with the secondary theme of *hijra*, annalistic, and caliphal arrangement of the tradition, are we then to suppose that the early or later narrators or redactors of the tradition systematically deleted his name from the accounts of the *futūḥ* narratives?[1642] Or, alternatively, was he not significant enough to be included in these? The precise role of Abū Bakr in these wars, the duration of his caliphate, and his relationship to the Prophet would then remain thorny questions for future enquiry.[1643]

The nature of ridda

If the Prophet was alive during the early conquest of Iraq, moreover, how are we to perceive the nature of the *ridda*[1644] as wars of apostasy. Since the early conquest of Iraq occurred in the period 628–632 CE while the Prophet was presumably alive, and for at least two years of which Abū Bakr was not caliph, then the *ridda* wars will acquire a very different meaning indeed. For, in this case, these wars would have taken place, not as the tradition would have us believe, *after the death of the Prophet*, as wars of *apostasy*, but during the lifetime of the Prophet. This would probably mean in turn that, contrary to what the tradition would have us believe, *ridda* had very little Islamic purport, a view articulated by Ferdowsī in his epic. Were the *ridda* a series of wars which were *Islamicized* postfacto, when the early traditionalist superimposed a *hijra* and a *caliphal* dating on these? In this scenario, the *ridda* might still retain their significance as primary theme, but their nature as wars of apostasy would no longer be valid. This, then, would give an added and crucial significance to Lecker's contention that "in *many cases* the *ridda* is a misnomer ... [for] numerous tribes and communities had had no contact whatsoever with the *Muslim state* [to begin with] or had no formal agreements with it ... [other tribes] were [simply]

[1640]Here we might have to reckon with Theophanes' contention that Muḥammad died in the year 629/630 CE. Theophanes 1997, pp. 463–464.

[1641]Noth 1968.

[1642]I am hesitant to accuse them of deliberate forgery, for this in turn brings up the issue of their intent.

[1643]Here, for example, we will have to reckon with Dīnawarī's contention that the deposition of Khusrow II Parvīz and the accession of Shīrūyih Qubād to the throne took place in the year 9 AH (instead of 7 AH/628 CE), and the Prophet died in the same year that Shīrūyih Qubād ascended the throne and Abū Bakr became caliph. Dīnawarī 1960, p. 107, Dīnawarī 1967, p. 116 and p. 120, respectively. This chronology leaves the Prophet alive during the years 7–9 AH, the first two years of the conquest as we have reconstructed them. Dīnawarī's subsequent assertion that Shahrvarāz's usurpation of power (Muharram 9 AH/April 630 CE) took place in the year 12 AH, then clearly involves *hijra* acrobatics. Dīnawarī 1960, p. 111, Dīnawarī 1967, p. 121.

[1644]See footnote 900.

following chieftains who posed as prophets," while still other tribes, previously under the domination of Medina, merely refused to pay the taxation, "while stating their readiness to continue *practicing Islam*."[1645] So one possible scenario that we shall put on the table in light of our analysis is that Muḥammad was alive during the early conquest of Iraq; Abū Bakr was not yet caliph, but simply a general who was leading the Arab armies; and the intention of the Arabs in launching their conquest was mostly not some *ghāzī* predisposition through which they sought to spread their creed, but simply the recognition that with the Sasanians and the Byzantines exhausted through three decades of warfare, with the Pārsīg–Pahlav factional strife debilitating the Sasanians, and with the confusing movement and dislocation of troops all over the region, the time was ripe to pursue their goal of gaining access to trade entrepôts and the riches afforded by these.[1646]

Many more unsettling questions about early Islamic history might proceed from our analysis. In fact, we may have thoroughly misplaced our emphasis by articulating the few that we did. We also may have opened, inadvertently, Pandora's box by our analysis. One observation we can make with comfortable certainty: by the time our thesis is either accepted or rejected through future analysis, the field will have come out of its stasis and, hopefully, be willing, once again, to tackle the chronology of the early Arab conquest of Iran and the Middle East.

[1645]Lecker, M., 'Ridda', in P. Bearman, Th. Bianquis, C.E. Bosworth, E. van Donzel, and W.P. Heinrichs (eds.), *Encyclopaedia of Islam*, Leiden, 2007 (Lecker 2007).
[1646]See our discussion on page 226ff.

CHAPTER 4

Dynastic polities of Ṭabaristān

The general trajectory of events in Ṭabaristān can be integrated into the course of Sasanian history from the reigns of Pīrūz (459–484) and Qubād (488–531) onward. We must follow these to the extent that we can reconstruct them, for they set the stage for events that transpire in the region from the onset of the Arab conquest of Iran—when they overshadow the narrative of the flight of the last Sasanian king, Yazdgird III, to the east—and are pertinent to the later rebellions of Sunbād[1647] (137 AH/755 CE) and Māzīyār (224 AH/839 CE) against the ʿAbbāsid caliphate. Any examination of the history of Ṭabaristān must begin with the region's rich local historiographical tradition, from which we have a number of extant local histories, including, most importantly, the *Tārīkh-i Ṭabaristān* of Ibn Isfandīyār.[1648] While these sources have substantial and peculiar problems of chronology, are late sources, and clearly bear the marks of editorial reworking at the hands of powerful families, including the Parthian dynastic families, they are crucial in that they give us the broad outlines of the history of the region during the Sasanian period, information that is almost totally absent in universal histories such as that of Ṭabarī. Thus, these sources provide us with a context within which we can investigate the history of the region in the post-conquest centuries, and without which this history remains more or less inexplicable. Significantly, some of the information given to us by the *Tārīkh-i Ṭabaristān* can be corroborated by Greek sources as well as numismatic evidence.[1649] As a thorough source-critical approach to the local histories of Ṭabaristān is ideally needed before we can critically examine the history of Ṭabaristān based on them—a study that is beyond the scope of the present work given the confines of time—it is with extreme caution, and with the aid of a rudimentary source-critical approach, therefore, that we will examine the information contained in these. Even with this handicap, however, it is possible to cull valuable information from these sources, as we shall see.

[1647]For a discussion of his rebellion, see §6.4.

[1648]On these sources, see Melville, Charles, 'The Caspian Provinces: A World Apart, Three Local Histories of Mazandaran', *Iranian Studies* 33, (2000), pp. 45–89 (Melville 2000).

[1649]The contention of those scholars who dismiss these local histories based on their late provenance, therefore, can be put to rest.

4.1 The Āl-i Bāvand

4.1.1 Kayūs

According to the *Tārīkh-i Ṭabaristān*, the kingdom of Ṭabaristān had remained in the hands of the family of Jushnasf until the time of Qubād (488–531). For reasons that Ibn Isfandīyār attributes to the workings of time, however, this family's fortunes declined. Qubād, therefore, sent his oldest son Kayūs to Ṭabaristān. The timing of this episode of Ṭabaristān's history would of course depend on the chronology that we choose to adopt about Qubād's age when he ascended the throne.[1650]

Kayūs' rule in Ṭabaristān is confirmed by other sources. Procopius, for instance, calls him Caoses and follows the events that led Qubād and the nobility to forgo appointing Kayūs as Qubād's successor to the Sasanian throne.[1651] Theophanes, who renders his name *Phthasouarsan*, reflecting Kayūs' title as Padhashkhwārgar Shah, that is, the ruler of Ṭabaristān, mentions him under the years 520/521, and 523/524.[1652] Theophanes' account, therefore, points to the second part of Qubād's reign for Kayūs' assumption of power in Ṭabaristān. The arrival of Kayūs in Ṭabaristān supposedly calmed the turbulent situation in the region. During this period Kayūs, presumably from his base in Ṭabaristān, also aided Qubād in expelling the Turks who had invaded Khurāsān.[1653]

When Qubād died and the Khāqān of the Turks attacked Iran once again, Khusrow I (531–579) asked for Kayūs' aid against him. According to Ibn Isfandīyār, Kayūs defeated the Khāqān and set in his stead one of his relatives by the name of Hūshang. He then attacked Ghazna, put his own representative there, and returned to Ṭabaristān with the *kharāj* (taxes) of Turkistān and India as well as a great amount of booty. According to Ibn Isfandīyār, Kayūs then claimed the throne from Khusrow I Nowshīrvān based on his own seniority.[1654] Khusrow I naturally refused, arguing that, among other things, he had the confirmation of the *mōbads* in coming to the throne.[1655] Kayūs then prepared an

[1650]If we accept the tradition that Qubād ascended the throne already at a mature age, that is, in his thirties, then Kayūs could have been installed in Ṭabaristān during the first part of Qubād's reign, that is sometime in 488–496. The adoption of a young age for Qubād's assumption of the throne, however, would put the installation of Kayūs in Ṭabaristān during the second part of his reign, that is in the period between 498 and 531. Ibn Isfandīyār 1941, p. 147; Marʿashī 1966, p. 89. Ibn Isfandīyār acknowledges that his information on Kayūs is an abridged version of that contained in Āmulī, Mowlānā Owliyā, *Tārīkh-i Rūyān*, vol. 64 of *Intishārāt-i bonyād-i farhang-i Irān*, Tehran, 1969, edited by Manuchihr Sotudih (Āmulī 1969), pp. 37–44. However, the extant version of Āmulī's work does not contain any additional information to that provided by Ibn Isfandīyār.

[1651]Procopius 1914, xi. 3, p. 83; II, ix. 12, p. 341; I, xxi. 20, p. 201; I, xxi, 22, p. 201.

[1652]Theophanes 1997.

[1653]Ibn Isfandīyār 1941, p. 148; Marʿashī 1966, p. 92.

[1654]Ibn Isfandīyār 1941, pp. 147–148; Marʿashī 1966, pp. 91–92.

[1655]Ibn Isfandīyār 1941, p. 149. Marʿashī 1966, p. 91. According to Procopius, when Qubād became seriously ill, fearful that at his death "the Persians would make a serious attempt to disregard some of the things which had been decided upon by him," he consulted with one of his closest dynastic partners, Mebodes. The latter advised him to leave a written testament appointing his successor.

army and set out to Ctesiphon in war against his brother. In the process, he was defeated, however.[1656] Having captured Kayūs, Khusrow I assembled the *mōbads* and suggested Kayūs to ask for penitence, and confess to his sins so that he could order his release.[1657] Kayūs responded that he preferred death to the humiliation of confessing to sins, at which point Khusrow I cursed the fortunes for "forcing him to kill a brother like Kayūs."

It is important to highlight the fact that the narrative of Kayūs in Ibn Isfandīyār's version actually starts with an account of the appearance of Mazdak at the time of Qubād.[1658] Ibn Isfandīyār juxtaposes Kayūs' rebellion next to the Mazdakite proclivity of his father and, in doing so, lends credence to the theory that, if not a Mazdakite, Kayūs probably had a strong dose of Mazdakite sympathy. Theophanes explicitly states that Kayūs (Caoses), the Padhashkhwārgar Shah (Phthasouarsan), was a Manichean, who was used by his father Qubād—by means of a promise that he would be appointed as his successor—to lure the Manicheans into an audience, at which point he proceeded to massacre all of them.[1659] If we accept Kayūs' Mazdakite sympathies, then we must assume that the Mazdakite heresy was tolerated in Ṭabaristān during his rule.[1660]

4.1.2 Bāv

From the end of Kayūs' reign onward, however, Ibn Isfandīyār's rendition of the saga of Kayūs' family, the Āl-i Kayūs, becomes very problematic. According to Ibn Isfandīyār, one of the sons of Kayūs was called Shāpūr. Once Khusrow I had killed Kayūs, he kept this Shāpūr, presumably as a hostage, in Madāʾin (Ctesiphon), where he eventually died during Hormozd IV's (579–590) reign.[1661] None of our other sources, however, so far as I can ascertain, provide us with any further information on a son of Kayūs called Shāpūr. Still according to Ibn Isfandīyār, Shāpūr, in turn, had left a son called Bāv. This Bāv allegedly continued to remain in Ctesiphon. From the very inception of Khusrow II Parvīz's

"The document was written by Mebodes himself." When Kayūs, "confident by reason of the law, tried to lay claim to the office … [, however,] Mebodes stood in his way, asserting that *no one ought to assume the royal power by his own initiative but by vote of the Persian notables.* As all the nobility, Mebodes included, came to be in agreement with Qubād's choice of Khusrow I, the latter was chosen over Kayūs." Procopius 1914, xxi. 17–22, pp. 200–201.

1656 Procopius 1914, xxi. 20–26. Also see Ṭabarī 1999, p. 138, n. 356.

1657 Marʿashī 1966, pp. 91–92; Ibn Isfandīyār 1941, p. 150:

توبه کند و اقرار به گناه تا موبدان بشنوند و فرمایم که بند بردارند.

1658 Ibn Isfandīyār 1941, p. 147–148. Ibn Isfandīyār's depiction of Mazdak's uprising is quite ambivalent. While Mazdak is accused of donning the garb of Iblīs (the devil) and leading Qubād astray, when Qubād, at the instigation of Khusrow I Nowshīrvān, massacred Mazdak and his followers, the author accuses Qubād of committing unspeakable injustices, for which he lost his Divine Glory, *farr*. Ibid., pp. 147–148.

1659 Theophanes 1997, pp. 259–260.

1660 In Chapter 5, we will have more to say about the prevalence of Mazdakite (§5.2.7) and Mithraic (see §5.4.1) currents in the quarter of the north.

1661 Ibn Isfandīyār 1941, p. 150, 152; Marʿashī 1966, p. 92.

reign, however, Bāv's power grew substantially. To begin with, during Khusrow II's reign, when the Sasanian monarch was forced to deal with the extensive rebellion of Bahrām-i Chūbīn,[1662] Bāv was among those who remained loyal to Khusrow II, followed him to Byzantium, and left a legacy in aiding him against Bahrām-i Chūbīn. When Khusrow II assumed kingship, furthermore, presumably in remuneration for the services of Bāv, he gave parts of "Azarbāyjān, Iraq, Iṣṭakhr as well as Ṭabaristān to Bāv."[1663] Presumably on Khusrow II's orders, Bāv then went to Khurāsān and Khwārazm where he conquered an extensive territory.

The figure of Bāv in Ibn Isfandīyār's narrative is quite enigmatic, however. For in none of our other sources do we come across a figure called Bāv (Bawi or Boe) with as extensive a power and as central a role as he is given in Ibn Isfandīyār's narrative during the reign of Khusrow II Parvīz. Moreover, the domains supposedly allotted to Bāv by the king, namely, Azarbāyjān, Iraq and Iṣṭakhr, more or less correspond to the territories under the command of the *ērān-spāhbed* of the west (*kūst-i khwarbarān*) from Khusrow I's time onward. Add to this the fact that Ṭabaristān is also said to have been given to Bāv, and the power of Bāv during Khusrow II's rule becomes tremendous. Yet, no trace of such an important persona is left in any of our other sources for this juncture of Sasanian history. The only *ērān-spāhbeds* of the west of whom we have any information, were Vistāhm of the Ispahbudhān family,[1664] and his father the Asparapet, whose name has been rendered by our sources variously as Khurrazād, and significantly, Boe, Bawi, or Shāpūr.[1665] There is, therefore, something extremely peculiar in Ibn Isfandīyār's rendition of the figure of Bāv, as well as his presumed father Shāpūr.

Thus far the figure of Bāv during the reign of Khusrow II Parvīz bears an uncanny resemblance to a powerful figure of late Sasanian history, namely Vistāhm of the Ispahbudhān family. From his involvement in Khusrow II's flight to Byzantium, to his crucial role in aiding Khusrow II against the Parthian dynast Bahrām-i Chūbīn, and finally to his assumption of a post that was tantamount to the *spāhbedī* of the west and part of the east, Bāv's career mirrors almost exactly that of Vistāhm. The wars of Bāv in Khurāsān, moreover, as well as his control of Ṭabaristān, are also reminiscent of the power that Vistāhm assumed in the east and the north.[1666] We have further the curiosity that the name of Bāv himself, as well as that of his presumed father Shāpūr, are also the two names that have been attributed to Vistāhm's father, Asparapet, *the great Parthian and Pahlav aspet* of the Ispahbudhān family, or possibly his

[1662] See §2.6.3 and §6.1.

[1663] Marʿashī 1966, p. 92; Ibn Isfandīyār 1941, p. 152:

به حرب بهرام چوبین اثرها نمود.

[1664] See §2.7.1 and page 107.

[1665] See page 106.

[1666] See §2.7.1.

grandfather, Procopius' Aspebedes. Even the incidental information that the presumed father of Bāv, Shāpūr, died during the rule of Hormozd IV closely parallels the saga of the Ispahbudhān family, when the king murdered the father of Vistāhm and Vindūyih, the powerful Asparapet.[1667] In the figure of Bāv, and onto his saga as depicted in Ibn Isfandīyār's narrative, therefore, the information about three scions of the Ispahbudhān family, Boe, Shāpūr, and Vistāhm, appears to have been edited and superimposed. In the process, this persona seems then to have taken up the name of the original dynast, Boe, or Bāv.

The conflation of the sagas of Ispahbudhān dynasts in the figure of Bāv, however, does not end here in Ibn Isfandīyār's narrative. For the relationships that Bāv came to establish with the ephemeral kings and queens who followed Khusrow II on the throne, form a curious parallel to the story of Farrukh Hormozd as well as Farrukhzād, two further Parthian dynasts of the Ispahbudhān family. In Ibn Isfandīyār's narrative, during the short rule of Shīrūyih Qubād (628), for example, the king reportedly usurped the properties and fortunes of Bāv in Ctesiphon and seized Bāv himself,[1668] putting him under arrest in Iṣṭakhr. When Azarmīdukht ascended the throne (630–631), however, the elite advised her to recall Bāv from Iṣṭakhr to take control of the army. Bāv, however, refused, arguing that only the weak of nature agree to serve under a woman. Refusing Azarmīdukht's invitation to be the general commander of her army, Bāv retired to a fire-temple for a life of prayers.[1669] Here, we clearly have a replica of the story of Azarmīdukht and Farrukh Hormozd, in which Farrukh Hormozd refused to acknowledge the suzerainty of Azarmīdukht, the candidate of the Pārsīg and the Mihrān factions.[1670]

A hero unveiled, once more

What increases our suspicion about Ibn Isfandīyār's purported genealogy of the Āl-i Kayūs is the saga that the author gives of Bāv's activities in Ṭabaristān, at the end of Yazdgird III's rule and the inception of the Arab conquest. For here, there is little doubt that the figure of Bāv is assuming the activities of, this time, Farrukhzād, the son of Farrukh Hormozd. At the onset of the Arab conquests and after the battle of Qādisiya, the last Sasanian king, "the powerful [sic] Yazdgird III," according to Ibn Isfandīyār, recalled Bāv from Iṣṭakhr, and restored (*radd*) to him all his property. That this could not have been possibly the case, considering Yazdgird III's young age and powerlessness, is clear from Ibn Isfandīyār's subsequent remarks. Yazdgird III was in fact forced to recall Bāv, for "on account of the enmity of the Arabs, [the king] could not leave [Bāv] out of his sight."[1671] This replicates the power of Farrukhzād, and

[1667]See pages 105ff, especially page 106.

[1668]It is not clear from where!

[1669]Ibn Isfandīyār 1941, pp. 152–153; Marʿashī 1966, pp. 92–93.

[1670]See §3.3.3.

[1671]Ibn Isfandīyār 1941, p. 153:

بسبب خصومت عرب از خویشتن دور نتوانست کرد.

Yazdgird III's reliance on this power for his protection from the pursuing Arab armies. In all the halting places of Yazdgird III, Ibn Isfandīyār narrates, the king was forced to be in the company of Bāv.[1672] Here then we are given a potentially very significant, but not quite clear piece of information. In Ṭabaristān, Ibn Isfandīyār informs us, "Yazdgird III recalled Gāvbārih [i.e., the Cow Devotee,[1673] Jīl-i Jīlānshāh] with whom we shall deal shortly,[1674] and took over all the region."[1675] The further saga of Farrukhzād and Yazdgird III is then continued in the presumed relationship of Bāv and the king.

According to Ibn Isfandīyār, when the army of Islam was victorious against Yazdgird III, and the king, in flight, went to Rayy, Bāv accompanied the last Sasanian king. Significantly, from Rayy, Bāv got permission from the king to go through Ṭabaristān in order to pray at the fire-temple that his (putative) ancestor, Kayūs, had built in the region, and to join the king later in Gurgān.[1676] Curiously but expectedly, Bāv's stay in Ṭabaristān was prolonged.[1677] When the duration of Bāv's sojourn was extended, he heard the news of the betrayal of Māhūy-i Sūrī and the murder of Yazdgird III.[1678] In summary, all the actions attributed to Bāv by Ibn Isfandīyār during Yazdgird III's reign more or less replicate those undertaken by Farrukhzād: he accompanied Yazdgird III in his flight from Rayy to the east,[1679] then mutinied against him—one of the reasons of which was Yazdgird III's refusal to go to Ṭabaristān—and parted company from him.[1680]

What is most curious, however, is not only that in the career of Bāv we find conflated those of *five generations of Ispahbudhān dynasts*, namely Boe (Aspebedes?), Shāpūr (Asparapet), Vistāhm, Farrukh Hormozd, and Farrukhzād, which, incidentally, reinforces our argument that they do indeed belong to the same family, but also the remarkable fact that as the towering figure of Farrukhzād mysteriously disappears from the scene somewhere in the quarter of the east, after abandoning Yazdgird III, so, too, does the progenitor of the Āl-i Bāvand mysteriously appear in that same region. Indeed, after hearing of the

[1672] Ibn Isfandīyār 1941, p. 153:

در جمله مواقف با او بایست بود.

[1673] For the importance of this epithet, see page 377.
[1674] See §4.3.3.
[1675] Ibn Isfandīyār 1941, p. 153:

بطبرستان گاوباره فرا خواست، جمله ولایت بگرفت.

[1676] Ibn Isfandīyār 1941, p. 154.
[1677] Ibn Isfandīyār 1941, p. 155:

مدّت مقام و مکث او دراز شد.

[1678] Ibn Isfandīyār 1941, p. 155; Marʿashī 1966, p. 93.
[1679] See page 257ff.
[1680] See §3.4.6.

death of Yazdgird III, according to Ibn Isfandīyār, Bāv "shaved his hair" and took up a monastic life at the fire temple in Kūsān [i.e., Qūchān]. Recall that Sebeos likewise maintains that after his mutiny, Farrukhzād fortified himself someplace. Ibn Isfandīyār then briefly describes the conditions in Khurāsān and Ṭabaristān in the post-Bagratuni period just before the Arab conquest: the Turks had wreaked havoc in most of Ṭabaristān and Khurāsān, and "the armies of Islam, under the command of Imām Ḥasan b. ʿAlī and ʿAbdallāh b. ʿUmar ... and Ḥudhayfah," had come to Āmul.[1681] The population of Ṭabaristān therefore, desperate from hardship and adversity, decided that they must find a great king under whose command they could all gather. None, they reckoned, could take up this position except Bāv.[1682] The people of Ṭabaristān, therefore, invited Bāv to become their king. The latter happily accepted their invitation, provided that they agreed that his rule would be absolute.[1683] When they did, Bāv left his monastic life and "cleared the domains of the enemies."[1684] According to Ibn Isfandīyār, the army that attempted the first unsuccessful conquest of Ṭabaristān in 30 AH/650–651 CE was that of Saʿd b. ʿĀṣ. Ibn Isfandīyār does not specify, however, how Bāv received this army or how he cleared the region of all the enemies. Once Bāv had secured the region, he ruled for 15 years, after which he was killed by a certain Valāsh, a figure who subsequently assumed the control of Ṭabaristān for another eight years (circa 665–674). After Bāv's death, presumably around 665, when Ṭabaristān was again in disarray, his son Suhrāb carved out a small kingdom in Kūlā, where he maintained the family's independence for many centuries.[1685] We note here that the *nisba* of Zīnabī Abū 'l-Farrukhān in Ṭabarī's narrative was also said to be Qūlah, i.e., Kūlā.[1686]

All our evidence suggests that the figure named Bāv in this part of the story is none other than Zīnabī Abū 'l-Farrukhān, who in turn is none other than Farrukhzād, the son of Farrukh Hormozd, the dynast from the Ispahbudhān family.[1687] As Farrukhzād mysteriously disappeared from the scene, so too Bāv in one tradition, the Ṭabaristānī tradition, and Zīnabī Abū 'l-Farrukhān in another tradition, the Islamic *futūḥ* narratives, mysteriously appeared on the scene. The disappearance of one and the appearance of the others, moreover, coincided exactly with one and the same juncture of history, that is to say, the point when Farrukhzād abandoned Yazdgird III and, as Zīnabī Abū 'l-Farrukhān, aided the Arabs in the conquest of Rayy and made peace with the conquering Arab army. All our evidence therefore points to the fact that the ancestry of the family of Bāv, and in fact the very name of this dynast,

[1681]This is in all probability part of some Shīʿite popular histories circulating in the region.
[1682]Ibn Isfandīyār 1941, p. 155; Marʿashī 1966, p. 93.
[1683]Ibn Isfandīyār 1941, p. 155; Marʿashī 1966, p. 93.
[1684]Ibn Isfandīyār 1941, p. 155; Marʿashī 1966, p. 93.
[1685]Ibn Isfandīyār 1941, p. 155. For more on Suhrāb, see page 307 below.
[1686]Ṭabarī 1994, p. 26, de Goeje, 2655. See page 250ff.
[1687]For a discussion of the Ispahbudhān, see §3.3.1; for their family tree, see page 471; for Zīnabī's duplicity in the conquest of Rayy, see page 250ff; for his identity, see page 264ff.

has undergone substantial editorial transformation. Whether on purpose or inadvertently, somewhere along the line, the family of Bāv is taken to be the progeny of the Sasanian Kayūs. In view of the familial connection of the Ispahbudhān with the Sasanians there is even a possibility that through marriage such a connection actually did exist. Perhaps it is not incidental that the prevalent dynastic family name of this family later becomes the Āl-i Bāvand or the Bāvandīds, rather than the Āl-i Kayūs. By Ibn Isfandīyār's account, Bāv himself was around throughout the reigns of Khusrow II (591–628) and Yazdgird III (632–651). Considering all the chivalry that he is supposed to have shown during Khusrow II's rule, if one were to hypothetically assume that he was at least 18 years of age at the inception of the king's rule (whence born around 573), then by the time he was murdered by Valāsh after 15 years of rule in Ṭabaristān (around 665), he was nearly a century old. Such a ripe age is a possibility of course, but all other indications seem to point to the fact that this genealogical tradition was forged. To uncover how Bāv is supposed to have dealt with the Arabs, we must first deal with the fortunes of other dynastic families in Ṭabaristān.

4.2 The Kārins in Ṭabaristān

A second important dynastic power that had come to have a substantial interest in Ṭabaristān, from at least the period of Khusrow I onward, when we can trace this,[1688] was the Kārin dynasty. The connection of this family to Ṭabaristān, moreover, at least from this period onward, is contrary to the claim of some,[1689] far from mythical. Ibn Isfandīyār follows the *X^w adāy-Nāmag* tradition in recounting the fortunes of the Kārins and their dominion over the monarchy through the last decades of the fifth century,[1690] ending in Qubād's ousting of the Kārinid Sukhrā with the aid of the Mihrāns,[1691] and Sukhrā's flight, together with his nine sons, to Ṭabaristān.[1692] If Ibn Isfandīyār's rendition of events is to be trusted, the departure of the Kārin family toward Ṭabaristān must have taken place during Qubād's second regency, that is, 498/9–531, at the time that Kayūs held power over Ṭabaristān.[1693] We recall that according to Ibn Isfandīyār, Khusrow I regretted the treatment that his father had inflicted on the Kārins and was keen on retrieving his sons. The Kārins, hearing about this, came together with their army clad in green to the aid of the Sasanian king in his

[1688] As we have seen the power of the Kārins in the Sasanian realm generally predates this.

[1689] Rekaya, M., 'Ḳārinids', in P. Bearman, Th. Bianquis, C.E. Bosworth, E. van Donzel, and W.P. Heinrichs (eds.), *Encyclopaedia of Islam*, Leiden, 2007 (Rekaya 2007).

[1690] Ibn Isfandīyār 1941, p. 151. For the saga of the Kārins during this period, see §2.4, especially §2.4.2.

[1691] See §2.4.4.

[1692] For the conflicting information in our sources about Sukhrā's final destiny, see footnotes 400 and 582.

[1693] Recall that Theophanes mentions Kayūs as Padhashkhwārgar Shah under the years 520–523 CE; see §4.1.1.

war against the Khāqān.[1694] In compensation for their aid, Khusrow I gave the control of Zābulistān to Zarmihr, the eldest son of the late Sukhrā, and parts of Ṭabaristān to a younger son called Kārin,[1695] who became the *ispahbud* of Ṭabaristān.[1696] For all the problems contained in Ibn Isfandīyār's history, the chronological scheme that he presents here is in fact quite sound. For we recall that Kayūs, who had been appointed Padhashkhwārgar Shah by his father Qubād in Ṭabaristān, was in fact murdered by Khusrow I Nowshīrvān when he came to claim the throne. We are here dealing, therefore, with the period in which Khusrow I initiated his military and administrative reforms of the land. If the ruler of Ṭabaristān, Kayūs, is killed by Khusrow I at the inception of his reign, and if his putative progenies Shāpūr and Bāv actually belong to Ispahbudhān family, it follows that after Kayūs' murder in about 531, no one could take over the rule from him: there was, in other words, a power vacuum in Ṭabaristān. This version of events, needless to say, proceeds from our assumption that the presumed progenies of Kayūs, namely Shāpūr and Bāv, actually belong to a different family.

What is most significant about Ibn Isfandīyār's narrative on the measures taken by Khusrow I in Ṭabaristān, however, is the fact that he partitioned the control of the region such that "he did not give the whole to one person, *but divided it*."[1697] Who then were the other groups among whom Ṭabaristān was divided at the inception of Khusrow I's reign? We should recall at this point one significant fact: As our seals testify, Khusrow I gave the *ērān-spāhbedī* of the quarter of the north (*kūst-i ādurbādagān*) to the Parthian Mihrāns.[1698] Over parts of this region, the Mihrāns had ancestral claims at any rate.[1699] So having destroyed his brother Kayūs and having assigned the Mihrāns as the *spāhbeds* of the quarter of the north,[1700] Khusrow I then gave, according to Ibn Isfandīyār, the Kārins the *spāhbedī* of Ṭabaristān. However, we know of no such post, either prior to or after Khusrow I's reforms. In fact, the very division of the realm into four quarters during Khusrow I's rule, we recall, was an innovation where the former function of *ērān-spāhbed* was divided into four.[1701] At any given point after Khusrow I's reforms, therefore, there were supposed to have been only four *spāhbeds* of the Sasanian domains and none of these was called the *spāhbed of Ṭabaristān*.

As we examined in detail in Chapter 2,[1702] Khusrow I had in fact given the Kārins the *ērān-spāhbedī* of the quarter of the east (*kūst-i khwarāsān*)—a region which had originally been the traditional homeland of the Ispahbudhān family.

[1694]Ibn Isfandīyār 1941, p. 151; Marʿashī 1966, pp. 6–7. See pages 113 and 380.

[1695]These parts included Vand Omīd Kūh, Āmul, Lafūr, and Kūh-i Kārin (Farīm).

[1696]Ibn Isfandīyār 1941, pp. 151–152; Marʿashī 1966, p. 7.

[1697]Ibn Isfandīyār 1941, p. 151.

[1698]See page 103.

[1699]See the discussion in §2.5.3.

[1700]For the boundaries of this quarter, see footnote 693; see also footnote 164.

[1701]See page 95.

[1702]See in particular §2.5.6.

This is remarkably confirmed by sigillographic evidence, where we have the seal of Dād-Burz-Mihr (Dādmihr of the Kārin family), "the Parthian *aspbed*, the *ērān-spāhbed* of the side of the east."[1703] Both the *Nihāyat* and Dīnawarī, we recall, confirm that the Kārins were the *spāhbeds* of Khurāsān from the rule of Khusrow I onward. According to Dīnawarī, in Khurāsān the Kārins were in charge of "war and peace, collecting taxation and the administration." Qūmis and Gurgān were also part of the Kārins' governorship.[1704] According to both Dīnawarī and the *Nihāyat*, moreover, Khusrow I's son, Hormozd IV, continued to maintain the Kārins in this position. This assertion of the *X^w adāy-Nāmag* tradition, is likewise corroborated by the second seal of Dād-Burz-Mihr, which belongs to the reign of Hormozd IV.[1705] In his short term of usurping kingship, even Bahrām-i Chūbīn (590–591) confirmed the Kārins' status as the *spāhbeds* of the east.[1706] So, Ibn Isfandīyār's rendition of events, given in the context of the power of various families over Ṭabaristān, is remarkably valid.

As the *ērān-spāhbeds* of the east, therefore, the Kārins controlled not only Khurāsān, but also parts of Ṭabaristān, through the reign of Khusrow I and Hormozd IV. So once Kayūs was out of the picture, in the wake of Khusrow I's reforms, when the *spāhbedī* of the north was given to the Mihrāns and that of the east to the Kārins, the Sasanian king did in fact, as Ibn Isfandīyār claims, "divide Ṭabaristān in such a way that he did not give the whole to one person, but divided it."[1707] Moreover, another region of the southern Caspian Sea, Gīlān, came under the rule of yet another dynastic family, the Āl-i Jāmāsp, as we shall see shortly.[1708]

As part of the land of the Pahlav, however, Khurāsān had prior to this been the traditional homeland of the Ispahbudhān family. The Kārins' claim to the *spāhbedī* of the quarter of the east, therefore, flew in the face of the more ancient heritage of rule of the Ispahbudhān family in these regions. It is, therefore, no surprise that it is in the course of his narrative on the Āl-i Kayūs—whom we postulated to be the adopted progenitors of the Ispahbudhān family—that Ibn Isfandīyār goes into a significant tangent to detail the saga of the Kārinid Sukhrā and the appointment of the family as the rulers in Ṭabaristān by Khusrow I. In sum, Khurāsān and Ṭabaristān were contested by the Parthian families of the Ispahbudhān and the Kārins, while the central and western parts of the region, that is to say, Rayy and the regions to the west of it, were the traditional homelands of the Mihrāns over which they were given the *ērān-spāhbedī* of the north. Thus far the histories of three Parthian dynastic families are intimately connected with the history of Ṭabaristān.

[1703] Gyselen 2001a, seal 1b, p. 36. See page 114 and the table on page 470.

[1704] Dīnawarī 1960, p. 94, Dīnawarī 1967, p. 102; Nihayat 1996, p. 380.

[1705] Gyselen 2001a, seal 1b, p. 36 and seal A, p. 46. See pages 114 and 470.

[1706] Dīnawarī 1960, p. 94, Dīnawarī 1967, p. 102; Nihayat 1996, p. 380. For Bahrām-i Chūbīn's revolt, see page 126ff.

[1707] Ibn Isfandīyār 1941, p. 151.

[1708] See §4.3.1.

After Khusrow II's assumption of power, however, when he gained his very throne thanks to the machinations of his uncles Vindūyih and Vistāhm, the king gave the *spāhbedī* of Khurāsān back to the Ispahbudhān family and their scion Vistāhm. The formal power of the Kārins as the *spāhbeds* of the quarter of the east, therefore, came to an end. Subsequently, as we have seen,[1709] the Ispahbudhān dynast Vistāhm led a significant rebellion against Khusrow II Parvīz, when a long stretch of territory from Khurāsān to Gīlān, including the territories under the Mihrān family, paid allegiance to the Ispahbudhān rebel. What was the position of the Kārins during the almost decade long secessionist revolt of Vistāhm, however? No definitive answer can be given to this question at the moment. In hindsight, the antagonism between the Kārins and the Ispahbudhān in Khurāsān and parts of Ṭabaristān in subsequent years underlines the significant fact that the Kārins' relationship with the Ispahbudhān must have been an extremely contentious one, perhaps purposely aggravated by the Sasanian king Khusrow II when he discharged the Kārins of their office of *ērān-spāhbed* of the east and promoted the Ispahbudhān in their stead.

The precise fate of the Kārins in Khurāsān and Ṭabaristān after Vistāhm's rebellion and during the turbulent Bagratuni and post-Bagratuni history of the region is not clear either. In 596–602, we recall,[1710] Smbat Bagratuni was given the *marzpanate* of Vrkan, that is Gurgān,[1711] in order to quell Vistāhm's rebellion. In this endeavor he was in fact successful: in the midst of Vistāhm's preparation for a second major expedition against Khusrow II, the rebel was killed "with reasonable confidence" in 600.[1712] Smbat Bagratuni was also sent to Khurāsān on a second expedition from 614 to 616/617.[1713] The Kūshāns had asked for Turkish aid, and a great force of 300,000 had thereafter invaded Khurāsān and parts of Ṭabaristān, reaching as far as Rayy. Tangentially we recall that this havoc in the east was occurring precisely in the midst of the Sasanian–Byzantine wars of Khusrow II, which were ravaging the western Sasanian domains. It was in a second campaign a year after this that Smbat reorganized his army and attacked "the nation of Kushans and the Hephthalite king,"[1714] and, defeating the enemy far into their territory, finally settled in Marv.[1715]

In view of the later events and in view of the dynastic and agnatic nature of the power of various Parthian families over their realm, it seems rather certain that while at this juncture of the Sasanian history of the east and the north *de facto* power might have been taken out of the hands of the Kārins, and while the Ispahbudhān rebellion had been quashed by Smbat Bagratuni, *de jure* power continued to remain in the hands of these families; a situation which, in view

1709 §2.7.1.
1710 See page 136ff.
1711 Sebeos 1999, pp. 43–44.
1712 Sebeos 1999, p. 181. See §2.7.2.
1713 Sebeos 1999, p. 50.
1714 Sebeos 1999, p. 52.
1715 Sebeos 1999, p. 53. See page 138ff.

of the simultaneous claims of the Kārins and the Ispahbudhān to the *spāhbedī* of the east—one presumably recent and one with a long ancestral claim to the region—must have continued to create conflict in the territory. Throughout this period turbulence and havoc must have been as much a part of the landscape of the Sasanian domains in the east, as they were in the west during the destructive Sasanian–Byzantine wars of the first three decades of the seventh century.[1716] While Smbat Bagratuni died around 617 CE, both the continued association of the Bagratunis with the east and the ultimate cooperation of this Armenian Parthian dynastic family with the Ispahbudhān family is borne out by the fact that when the unanimous decision of the factions to depose Khusrow II was reached, and Farrukhzād informed Varaztirots‘, the son of Smbat Bagratuni, of their choice for the Iranian throne, the latter responded that the choice of Shīrūyih Qubād as the king "will be pleasing as well to the Kanārangīyān" in Khurāsān.[1717]

We can therefore construct the general contours of the history of Khurāsān and Ṭabaristān by the end of Khusrow II's reign and the inception of the factional strife that swallows the Sasanian kingdom with the murder of this king, during the period of 628–632. Through the first decades of the seventh century, and in fact from the inception of the rebellion of Bahrām-i Chūbīn onward, the north and the eastern parts of the Sasanian domains were struggling through a havoc in which four Parthian dynastic families, the Mihrāns, the Kārins, the Ispahbudhān, and the Kanārangīyān[1718] were the central players in the field. This continued to be the situation on the eve of the Arab conquests of the region, when, on the trail of the last Sasanian king, Yazdgird III, the Arab armies finally reached Khurāsān and Ṭabaristān in 650–651. This picture, however, would not be complete without the introduction of yet another important family on to the scene of Ṭabaristān and Khurāsān.

4.3 The Āl-i Jāmāsp

4.3.1 Jāmāsp

One of the fascinating episodes in the history of Gīlān and Ṭabaristān in the late antique period is the saga of the Sasanian Jāmāsp, beginning with the death of the Sasanian king Pīrūz in 484. In reconstructing this history Ibn Isfandīyār provides us with a unique narrative undoubtedly drawn from the local historical traditions and lore in circulation in the region. The significance of this history is the fact that it revolves around the person of Jāmāsp, one of the most enigmatic sons of Pīrūz, for whom—except for the short period (497–499) when he assumed the crown—we have next to no information in our classical Arabic

[1716] See §2.7.3.

[1717] Ferdowsī 1971, vol. IX, p. 245, Ferdowsī 1935, p. 2901. However, the relationship of the Bagratuni house with the Ispahbudhān family once again deteriorated. Sebeos 1999, p. 92. For the connection of the Kanārangīyān to the house of Farrukhzād, see page 266ff.

[1718] See page 266ff.

sources. Jāmāsp seems to have vanished from the pages of history, precisely because, he met his fate in Ṭabaristān, the history of which is not incorporated in the accounts of the universal histories. Jāmāsp was put on the throne after Qubād's Mazdakite phase with the complicity of the dynastic families.[1719] He remained on the throne for a short period during Qubād's interregnum, that is from about 496 to 499. Most sources, however, are silent about the events that transpired during his short reign. Neither do we know what happened to Jāmāsp once Qubād came to reclaim his throne.[1720] Significantly, two sources maintain that Qubād had Jāmāsp expelled.[1721]

While most sources are silent about Jāmāsp's fate, however, Ibn Isfandīyār provides a wealth of information about this transient king during one of the most important episodes in Sasanian history, the Mazdakite rebellion,[1722] connecting Jāmāsp directly, and significantly, with the history of Ṭabaristān. Ibn Isfandīyār's narrative on Jāmāsp is introduced under the heading of "on the mention of the descendants of Jāmāsp and the story of Gāvbārih."[1723] According to Ibn Isfandīyār, when Qubād is put back on the throne with the consent of the nobility, Jāmāsp objected and went to Armenia. From Darband, he then attacked the Khazars and the Slavs (Suqlāb), and conquering parts of these territories, settled in Armenia and married there. Jāmāsp's activities during this period fit quite well with the international context of the times. The Sasanians, like the Parthians before them, had a long and involved connection with Albania and the rest of the Caucasus.[1724] The late fifth century was a period when, due to a number of factors, the predominantly peaceful Perso-Byzantine relations of the past century were becoming increasingly hostile, and would remain so for the next two centuries. One of the central factors shaping the Perso-Byzantine relations during this period was the appearance of new forces on the Eurasian steppes. While the emergence of the Chionites (Kidarites) in the northeast of the Sasanian territories from the 350s, and that of the Huns in the Ukraine on the eastern European territories of the Byzantine empire, had led the two empires to realize that they needed to join forces against nomadic enemies threatening them both, the disastrous defeat of Pīrūz at the hands of the Hephthalites and the upheavals that this created in the Sasanian empire led Qubād to break the peaceful relations of the past century by attacking the Byzantine empire,

---

[1719] See §2.4.3.

[1720] Bosworth observes that the "fate of Zāmāsp ... is uncertain. Elias of Nisibis alone states that Kawād had him killed. More probable is the leniency toward his brother attributed to Kawād by the well-informed Agathias, that Zāmāsp renounced the throne of his own accord, preferring a life of safe obscurity, and was pardoned ... Procopius in his *The History of the Wars* confuses Jāmāsb with Fīrūz's successor Balāsh/Blasēs." Ṭabarī 1999, pp. 136–137, n. 349, de Goeje, 887. Thaʿālibī and Ferdowsī confirm that Qubād pardoned Jāmāsp, but have nothing to say about the ultimate fate of the latter. Thaʿālibī 1900, pp. 590–593, Thaʿālibī 1989, pp. 381–382, and 384; Ferdowsī 1971, vol. VIII, pp. 40–41, Ferdowsī 1935, p. 1739.

[1721] Christensen 1944, p. 351.

[1722] See §2.4.5.

[1723] See page 302 below for the meaning of this epithet.

[1724] See page 43.

probably in order to engage the disruptive feudal forces against a joint enemy abroad. The first theater of Qubād's war in 502 was Armenia. By then, the Huns had amassed in northern Albania (Arrān). This was the context in which Jāmāsp went, or was exiled to Armenia, where he could have very likely joined an Armenian faction in the war arena. And indeed he seemed to have engaged the enemy at Darband, the famous Pass of Chor. Qubād in fact is also credited with rebuilding the Caspian Gates at Darband after 508.[1725]

There also was a close connection among Armenia, Gīlān, and Ṭabaristān in the previous centuries. This connection is highlighted in Khorenats'i's account.[1726] The Bagratunids' involvement in Khurāsān and Ṭabaristān in subduing the rebellion of Vistāhm gives further evidence of the close involvement of Armenia in Iranian affairs in general, and in Khurāsān and Ṭabaristān in particular. As we have seen, the Armenians were also closely involved in the Parthian confederacy that was created in the quarters of the north and the east, and the turmoil that engulfed the region in the wake of the Arab conquest. The Sasanians, moreover, like the Parthian dynasts, had strong familial relationships with the ruling groups within Armenia. Considering the intimate connection of Iran and Armenia throughout Sasanian history, Ibn Isfandīyār's assertion that Jāmāsp settled in Armenia, therefore, should be reckoned as trustworthy.

[1725]For a succinct overview of Sasanian relations with the Byzantine Empire in late antiquity and the part played by Armenia therein see Howard-Johnston's analysis in Sebeos 1999, pp. xi–xxv. Yazdgird II (438–457) constructed an impressive wall at the Caspian Gates at Darband along the 3 to 3.5 kilometer pass of Chor on the western shores of the Caspian Sea in order to prevent the penetration of the Transcaucasian Huns into his realm. The "Armenians and Albanians wrecked the walls in the rebellion of 450," leading to the occupation of Darband by the Huns during Pīrūz's (459–484) reign. In 464, the latter seems to have received tribute from the Byzantines in exchange for his upkeep of the wall, and the tribute that he was forced to pay to the Hephthalites. Joshua the Stylite 2000, pp. 9–10, n. 37–39 and pp. 82–83, n. 392. At the death of Yazdgird II in 457, the king of Albania was one Vachē, a nephew of the two sons of Yazdgird II, Hormozd III (457–459) and Pīrūz (459–484). Moses Daskhurants'i maintains that the daughter of Yazdgird II's sister was the mother of Vachē whom he had married. Eḷishē 1982, p. 241. The additional information by Moses Daskhurants'i is cited in Thomson's note 5, ibid. During the monarchic dispute that engulfed Iran after the death of Yazdgird II, Vachē, who, according to Eḷishē, was a Christian who had been forced to convert to Zoroastrianism by Yazdgird II, revolted. Even after the Mihrānid Rahām put his protégé Pīrūz in power (see §2.3), Vachē did not submit. The rebellion of Vachē pre-occupied the Sasanians in the Caucasus until 463/464. Pīrūz then asked Vachē to send back his sister and niece to Iran "for they were originally magi and you made them Christians." Eḷishē 1982, pp. 242–243.

[1726]According to Khorenats'i, for example, after "the death of the last Arshak [Arsaces I (247–211 BCE)], king of Persia, our Artashēs made his homonym, Arshak's son Artashēs, king over the land of Persia. *The inhabitants of the mountain which is called in their own tongue the province of Patizhahar [Padhashkhwārgar, i.e., Ṭabaristān], that is, the mountain of Elmants', did not wish to obey him, nor did those who dwelt by the sea and those beyond them.* Similarly the land of the Caspians for that reason rebelled against our king. Therefore Artashēs sent Smbat [an Armenian general from the second century BCE] against them with the entire Armenian army, and the king himself accompanied them for seven days. So Smbat went and subdued them all; he ravaged the land of the Caspians and brought to Armenia more captives than those from Artaz, including their king Zardmanos." Khorenats'i 1978, p. 195. Emphasis added.

4.3.2 Pīrūz

Now according to Ibn Isfandīyār, Jāmāsp's son Narsī had himself a son by the name of Pīrūz. This Pīrūz expanded the territories under his family's rule and conquered the territory up to and presumably including parts of Gīlān. The control of Pīrūz over Gīlān at this juncture is corroborated by Sebeos. Qubād died in 531. If we reckon a similar date for the death of Jāmāsp, the younger brother of Qubād, and count around 35 years for each generation, then the control of Pīrūz over parts of Gīlān can be dated to the late sixth century. It is apt to briefly recall the political situation in Armenia at the time.

The Byzantines, who had come under serious attack by the Avars and the Slavs, especially in the Balkans, began a policy of actively recruiting the Armenian nobility, partly also to rein in the unruly Armenian feudal nobility residing within the enlarged Armenia now under their control. This policy, presumably using some form of coercion, was pursued for three years, by which time the Armenian nobility seem to have had enough of it. The Persians adopted a different policy, seeking the support of the Armenian nobility with cash incentives. The arrival of a financial administrator with a large sum of money triggered, as we have seen, the Vahewuni incident of 594–595 CE, when a group of Armenian nobles rebelled against both the Byzantines and the Persians.[1727] But the rebellion disintegrated shortly after being launched, partly on account of the cooperation of the two empires in putting it down. The Armenian faction that at the end of the conflict remained in the Persian camp were set up in Iṣfahān by Khusrow II Parvīz, around 595.[1728]

As we have seen, in the midst of Vistāhm's rebellion, these Armenian forces also rebelled against the Persian king and decided to join Vistāhm's camp.[1729] But, according to Sebeos, their route to join Vistāhm took them through Gīlān, where they were intercepted by the army of one Pīrūz: "In the land of Gelam, [i.e., Gīlān] Peroz's army arrived in pursuit, and put some of them to the sword. [Others are said to have] committed suicide lest they be captured, while [still] others barely escaped and took refuge in the secure land of Gelam."[1730] In a note, Thomson points out that "Macler suspects that something is wrong and suggests *Persian* or *victorious*" in lieu of *Pīrūz*. Thomson himself maintains that it "would be simplest to suppose that this Peroz was a general who is not mentioned elsewhere in Sebeos."[1731] There is nothing wrong in this case, however, with Sebeos' narrative. Nor do we need to identify this Pīrūz with an unknown Persian general. For the Pīrūz who intercepted the Armenian nobility who were fleeing into Gīlān, is none other than the Āl-i Jāmāsp Pīrūz, the grandson of the Sasanian Jāmāsp who, according to Ibn Isfandīyār, had by then set up his authority over Gīlān.

[1727] See page 133.

[1728] Sebeos 1999, pp. 31-36, 38-43, 175-181.

[1729] See page 133.

[1730] Sebeos 1999, p. 43.

[1731] Macler, F., *Histoire d'Héraclius*, Paris, 1904 (Macler 1904) apud Sebeos 1999, p. 43, n. 268.

4.3.3 Jīl-i Jīlānshāh

Gāvbārih

In Gīlān, Pīrūz married the daughter of one of the princes of Gīlān. From this union was born a son called Jīlānshāh, who in turn had a son called Jīl-i Jīlānshāh.[1732] According to Ibn Isfandīyār, Jīl-i Jīlānshāh became a great king and most of the Gīl (that is, inhabitants of Gīlān) and the Daylamites paid allegiance to him. If Pīrūz of the Āl-i Jāmāsp was in power in Gīlān at the time of Vistāhm's rebellion,[1733] after the Vahewuni incident of 594–595, then by the same reckoning of 35 years per generation, the rule of Jīl-i Jīlānshāh in Gīlān would fall sometime around 630s–660s CE, that is to say, around the period of the attempted Arab conquest of the northern parts of Iran. And this is precisely what happens in Ibn Isfandīyār's narrative.

At this point, Ibn Isfandīyār's account becomes highly symbolic. Jīl-i Jīlānshāh's astrologers told him that the kingdom of Ṭabaristān will one day be his. So Jīl-i Jīlānshāh appointed a regent in his place in Gīlān, picked up two Gīlī cows and set out on foot to the east, toward Ṭabaristān. In fact, after Jīl-i Jīlānshāh had shown so much courage in calming the turbulent situation in Ṭabaristān, as we shall shortly see, the people, according to Ibn Isfandīyār, gave him the epithet Gāvbārih, the Cow Devotee.[1734] Here then comes the account of conquest at which juncture the histories of the Kārins, the Āl-i Bāvand, or rather, the Ispahbudhān, and the Āl-i Jāmāsp all come together in Ibn Isfandīyār's narrative.

Ādhar Valāsh Kārin

In his movement east, Jīl-i Jīlānshāh came across a figure called Ādhar Valāsh, who was the regent of Ṭabaristān. Who then was this Ādhar Valāsh? Once again, Ibn Isfandīyār's narrative proves quite sound, for this Ādhar Valāsh was almost certainly a progeny of the Parthian *spāhbed* Dād-Burz-Mihr (Dādmihr) from the Kārin family.[1735] According to Ibn Isfandīyār and Marʿashī, shortly before Jīl-i Jīlānshāh's takeover of Ṭabaristān, Yazdgird III had given the control of the region, together with Gurgān, to this Ādhar Valāsh.[1736] We recall that in our narrative of Yazdgird III's flight to the east, at one point we came across the information that while Yazdgird III did not accept the invitation of the overlord of Ṭabaristān and Farrukhzād's advice for taking refuge in Ṭabaristān, he had nonetheless appointed the overlord (*ṣaḥib*) of Ṭabaristān as the *ispahbud*,

[1732] Ibn Isfandīyār 1941, p. 151; Marʿashī 1966, pp. 7–8.

[1733] Incidentally, Vistāhm himself took refuge in Gīlān from where he "journeyed to the regions of the Parthians, to the original land of his own principality." Sebeos 1999, p. 42.

[1734] As we will discuss in Chapter 5, page 373ff., the symbolic fetching of two cows in Jīl-i Jīlānshāh's narrative is quite significant in view of the connection between cows and Mihr worship. We will elaborate on this epithet and its connection with Mihr worship in the next chapter; see pages 373 and 377.

[1735] Justi 1895, p. 430. See page 114.

[1736] Ibn Isfandīyār 1941, p. 154. Marʿashī 1966, pp. 9–10. I would like to thank my former student Ranin Kāzemī for pointing this out to me.

for the latter "*had previously held a humbler rank than this.*"[1737] This overlord of humbler rank, we can now ascertain, was none other than the Kārinid Ādhar Valāsh.

We cannot ascertain whether the Kārins' takeover of Ṭabaristān and Gurgān, prior to Jīl-i Jīlānshāh's conquest of the region, was actually with the tacit consent of Yazdgird III, or whether, as is most likely, the Kārins' resumption of power was due to the confusion that ensued in the region after Vistāhm's rebellion,[1738] Smbat Bagratuni's governorship,[1739] and the tumultuous post-Bagratuni period. For all we know, the Kārins might have helped Smbat Bagratuni in his efforts to bring some order back to the region in the aftermath of Vistāhm's rebellion. When Jīl-i Jīlānshāh threatened to attack Ṭabaristān, Ādhar Valāsh is said to have written a letter to Yazdgird III for help. The king requested to be informed of the identity of the attacker. Upon further research into the background of this new figure in Ṭabaristān, the *mōbads* of the king (*mobadān-i ḥaḍrat*) recognized Jīl-i Jīlānshāh and informed Yazdgird III that he was in fact a progeny of Jāmāsp. Reportedly, Yazdgird III thereupon found it prudent (*ṣalāḥ ān dīdand*) to write to Ādhar Valāsh and to communicate to him that as Jīl-i Jīlānshāh was a Sasanian, Ādhar Valāsh should forthwith give the rule over Ṭabaristān to this progeny of Jāmāsp. Yazdgird III, in other words, presumably ordered Ādhar Valāsh to accept the authority of Jīl-i Jīlānshāh of the Āl-i Jāmāsp over himself and his territory.

At any rate, Jīl-i Jīlānshāh assumed the control of the region at the inception of the Arab conquest. Having assumed authority over Ṭabaristān, the new ruler's title became Gīl-i Gīlān Farshvādhjar Shāh. According to Ibn Isfandīyār, he commenced construction from Gīlān to Gurgān—significantly when the rest of Iran was experiencing the destructive effects of conquest—but maintained his capital in Gīlān. We recall, however, Ibn Isfandīyār's narrative on Bāv and the account of how, when Bāv found the region in turmoil, at the invitation of the people in the region, he assumed control, including that of Ṭabaristān, at this same turbulent period of the region's history.

4.4 The Arab conquest of Ṭabaristān

Here then start the accounts of the Arab conquest and the peace treaty made between Suwayd b. Muqarrin, Zīnabī Abū 'l-Farrukhān and Jīl-i Jīlān, as contained in Ṭabarī. At this late juncture of Sasanian history, we recall, the five dynasts in power in the quarters of the north and the east (the *kūst-i ādurbādagān* and *kūst-i khwarāsān*) were Farrukhzad from the Ispahbudhān family, in Khurāsān; Jīl-i Jīlānshāh, the progeny of the Sasanian cadet branch of the Āl-i Jāmāsp, in Gīlān; the Kārinid Ādhar Valāsh, in Ṭabaristān;[1740] the Kanārangīyān,

[1737] Ṭabarī 1990, p. 82, de Goeje, 2875. See page 259.

[1738] See page 132ff.

[1739] See page 138ff.

[1740] See page 302ff.

in Ṭūs and part of Nīshāpūr;[1741] and finally the Mihrānid Sīyāvakhsh, in Rayy and its environs.[1742] As Yazdgird III had fled to Khurāsān and had decided not to take refuge in Ṭabaristān, where, he was told, the rulers of the region would support him and provide him with a safe haven from his enemies, Farrukhzād abandoned him and together with his army headed west in order to make peace with the Arabs. As we have seen, however, most significantly, Farrukhzād suddenly disappears from the scene somewhere in the quarters of the east and the north, at the very same time when Bāv appears in Ibn Isfandīyār's narrative and Zīnabī Abū 'l-Farrukhān in the *futūḥ* narratives. According to the *futūḥ* literature, Zīnabī Abū 'l-Farrukhān then aided the Arab army of Muqarrin, waged war against Sīyāvakhsh-i Mihrān, toppled the Mihrāns from power, and, making peace with the Arabs, assumed the control of Rayy.[1743] As Jīl-i Jīlānshāh was moving east into the territories of the Ispahbudhān, the Kanārangīyān, and the Kārins, Farrukhzād/Bāv/Abū 'l-Farrukhān was moving west to meet the Arab armies. This is why some of our accounts maintain that Farrukhzād/Bāv/Abū 'l-Farrukhān, the *ispahbud-i ispahbudhān*, was the ruler of Khurāsān but had authority over Ṭabaristān. We should also recall that the Turkish threat in Ṭabaristān did not subside during this period, so that when the Arabs first arrived in the environs of Gurgān—a region which was originally under the control of the Kārins and then the base of Smbat Bagratuni in the east[1744]—it is the Turkic ruler Ṣūl whom they found in control of this frontier region.[1745]

4.4.1 Peace treaty with Farrukhzād and Jīl-i Jīlānshāh

It is appropriate to pause here and consider the nature of the allegiances that are made among the dynastic families vis-à-vis each other, and vis-à-vis the Arab army of conquest. For this information sheds further light on the ways in which—with the Sasanian monarchy out of the way—the rivalry among the Parthian dynasts actually provided the most convenient venue for the success of the Arabs and their gradual movement further east. The pattern that emerges in the process of the Arab conquest and diplomacy on the plateau is that, invariably, the Arabs picked sides. They became fully cognizant of the deeply entrenched rivalries among the dynastic families, and they made full use of this. They surely had a lot to work with: vying for power in parts of Khurāsān, Ṭabaristān, and Azarbāyjān were the Sasanian cadet branch of the Āl-i Jāmāsp, and the Parthian families of the Ispahbudhān, the Mihrān, the Kārin, and the Kanārangīyān. This pattern is clearly reflected in Ṭabarī's conquest narratives. For all the disparagement of Sayf b. ʿUmar's traditions, his is one of the most informative sources for precisely the light that it sheds on the Persian side of things.

[1741] See §3.4.7, especially page 271ff.
[1742] See page 249ff.
[1743] See §3.4.4, especially page 250ff.
[1744] See page 136ff.
[1745] See page 253ff.

After the Arab conquest of the quarters of the north and east in 650–651, and through the peace treaties that the Arabs implemented with the Parthian dynastic families, these latter were left free in the administration of their domains. From west to east, all the major dynastic families continued in power subsequent to the nominal conquest of the region. The one possible exception were the Mihrāns, who were toppled in Rayy with the complicity of Zīnabī Abū 'l-Farrukhān, that is to say, Farrukhzād. Rayy, which must have been a long coveted region for them, came under the control of the Ispahbudhān. To the west of Ṭabaristān, in Gīlān, the Sasanian branch of the Āl-i Jāmāsp remained in power. The Āl-i Jāmāspid Jīl-i Jīlānshāh and the Ispahbudhān Farrukhzād, acting in chorus, signed a peace treaty with the Arabs. In exchange for restraining their "robbers and the people on their borders," Farrukhzād, the *ispahbud* of all *ispahbuds*, the ruler of Khurāsān with authority over Ṭabaristān, under whose rule all the other *spāhbeds* were now gathered, and Jīl-i Jīlān of the Āl-i Jāmāsp remained in power, the Arabs agreeing that they would not "have a right to attack" their territories or invade the domains under their control, "or even to approach [them] without [their] permission."[1746] The Parthian Kanārangīyān family, who in all likelihood were a branch of the Ispahbudhān family, likewise retained control over their traditional domains, the region of Ṭūs.[1747] There they aided the Arabs in subduing the Kārins, and in return received full control over Nīshāpūr.[1748] In short, the Kanārangīyān remained in power in Inner Khurāsān.[1749] As a result, the Kārins' territory in the northeast shrank. Nonetheless, a certain Mardānshāh, a Kārinid bearing the title Maṣmughān,[1750] was left in control of Damāvand, Khuwār, Lāriz, and Shirriz,[1751] being promised by the Arabs that "he will not be attacked, nor ... approached save by [his] permission."[1752] The Kārins also continued to hold power in the eastern parts of the region, ruling now under the authority of Āl-i Jāmāsp,[1753] and then under the Āl-i Bāvand, that is to say, under the Ispahbudhān,[1754] at subsequent junctures of the post-conquest history of the region.

[1746]Ṭabarī 1994, pp. 30–31, de Goeje, 2659; Ibn al-Athīr 1862, vol. 3, p. 25.

[1747]See pages 266ff and 276ff.

[1748]See page 271ff.

[1749]In Pourshariati 1995, in the hope of better understanding the post-conquest history of this vast region, we proposed a new conception of Khurāsān into Inner Khurāsān and Outer Khurāsān (see §6.2.1 below). See also Pourshariati 2004. The Kanārangīyān, however, lost whatever control they had over the frontier city of Nisā, in Outer Khurāsān, which later became a base for Arab settlement. Ibid.

[1750]For the possible meaning of the term (grand *moγ*), see Marquart 1931, pp. 113–114. According to Justi, the Maṣmughān belong to the Kārin family, and they trace their ancestry to the righteous Armāyīl (see footnote 172). Justi 1895, p. 199.

[1751]Ṭabarī 1994, p. 27, de Goeje, 2656; Ibn al-Athīr 1862, vol. 3, p. 24. See page 252 for a discussion of the political context.

[1752]Ṭabarī 1994, p. 27, de Goeje, 2656.

[1753]See for instance page 277ff, and §4.5.1 below.

[1754]See page 307 below, as well as the forthcoming work of the author.

The status of Azarbāyjān at this time is less clear,[1755] but considering the *sunna* established as a result of the early conquest, it probably remained under the sovereignty of a cadet branch of the Ispahbudhān family, after Farrukhzād's sons Isfandīyār and Bahrām made peace with the Arabs.[1756] Meanwhile, Shahrvarāz, a progeny of the Mihrānid general Shahrvarāz, while foreign to the region, ended up collaborating with the Arabs in the frontier regions of the Caucasus.[1757] Considering the direction which the history of Iran took after the 650s—when the nobility had to have been in physical control of their agnatic lands and had to have come to terms with the Arab armies, if they were to continue to rule over their territories—and in view of the fact that the army of the Parthian Shahrvarāz had become landless, so to speak, it is rather likely that at least part of this family and the army under their control ended up settling in the frontier regions of the Caucasus.

In short, with the Parthian Āl-i Bāvand (Ispahbudhān) family, the Sasanian Āl-i Jāmāsp, the Kārin, and the Kanārangīyān remaining in control of a truncated quarter of the east and a substantial part of the quarter of the north, no substantive transformation was effected in these territories. We are now in a position to add an actual schematic picture—sometimes, as in the case of Ṭabaristān and Inner Khurāsān more or less clear, and sometimes, as in the case of Azarbāyjān a very probable conjecture about the sociopolitical scene of these regions. As Balʿamī's account makes amply clear, and in view of the fragmentation of authority, especially in Khurāsān and Ṭabaristān, there was an inflationary trend toward the use of the title *ispahbud* in these regions, as each Parthian dynast, as well as the Āl-i Jāmāsp, the first rather justifiably one might add, came to claim the title. Contrary to Rekaya's claims,[1758] this trend was not without historical basis, for by the 650s, the title had been in circulation for more than a century. The title *ispahbud* bestowed a legitimacy that all were keen to preserve and flaunt, for the consumption of their subjects as well as their rivals. How long, however, did these Parthian dynasts and the Āl-i Jāmāsp continue to rule in these territories in the post-conquest centuries? We shall begin to follow the ebb and flow of the rules of these families in what follows.

Dābūyih

According to Ibn Isfandīyār, both Jīl-i Jīlānshāh and Bāv, that is to say, Farrukhzād, ruled for 15 years before they died. Considering that the Arabs signed a peace treaty with these two dynasts around 650–651, their deaths may have occurred around 665. To determine the exact domains under their control, we continue to follow Ibn Isfandīyār's account. Jīl-i Jīlānshāh left two sons:

[1755] See also §3.4.8.

[1756] Ṭabarī 1994, p. 32, de Goeje, 2661; Ibn al-Athīr 1862, vol. 3, pp. 27–28; Balʿamī 1959, pp. 335–340.

[1757] See page 279ff.

[1758] Rekaya, R.M., 'Māzyār: résistance ou intégration d'une province Iranienne au monde Musulman au milieu du IXe siècle ap. J.C.', *Studia Iranica* 2, (1973), pp. 143–192 (Rekaya 1973).

Dābūyih and Bādūspān. Without doubt, Bādūspān is actually a title and not a name, the Arabic form of *pādhūspān*.[1759] Dābūyih, who is said to have a horrific temper, assumed the throne after his father, but kept his seat of government in Gīlān. Meanwhile, Bādūspān became the king of Rūyān.[1760] The manuscript history of the *Tārīkh-i Ṭabaristān* is not clear,[1761] but in the edited version of the manuscript currently at our disposal, it is after narrating the death of Jīl-i Jīlānshāh and the assumption of power of his sons Dābūyih and Bādūspān, that Ibn Isfandīyār starts his account by saying that "after Bāv, when the population of Ṭabaristān had divided into factions, Dābūyih [also] died."[1762] Since Dābūyih remained in Gīlān, it is very probable that his power did not extend much farther in the eastern parts of the region. Now Bāv, that is Farrukhzād, almost certainly controlled Khurāsān, and nominally at least, parts of Ṭabaristān during this period.[1763] In other words, if we follow Ibn Isfandīyār's narrative closely, we realize that Jīl-i Jīlānshāh and Farrukhzād ruled contemporaneously, the former ruling over Gīlān and the latter ruling over Khurāsān but having authority over Ṭabaristān.

Bāv (Farrukhzād), however, did not die a natural death, but was killed by Valāsh, a member of another age-old rival Parthian family, the Kārins.[1764] As the Kārins also launched a major revolt in south-western Khurāsān and Qūhistān at precisely this time,[1765] we are witnessing here a major civil war in the region between the Kārins and the Ispahbudhān, most probably a reflection of the Kārins' attempt at regaining their lost power in the region. At any rate, after the murder of the Ispahbudhān Farrukhzād by the Kārinid Valāsh, the latter assumed control over the region and ruled for eight years, until roughly 673.

Suhrāb

Of all the possible progenies that one might suspect the Ispahbudhān family, specifically Farrukhzād, to have had in Ṭabaristān and Khurāsān itself, only a small child, a certain Suhrāb, is said to have remained.[1766] This might be explained by the intensity of the inter-Parthian rivalry prior to this period, when

[1759] See footnote 411.

[1760] Ibn Isfandīyār 1941, p. 154.

[1761] Melville 2000.

[1762] Ibn Isfandīyār 1941, p. 156.

[1763] Ibn Isfandīyār 1941, p. 156.

[1764] Ibn Isfandīyār 1941, p. 156; Marʿashī 1966, p. 93. In Justi 1895, p. 346, Valāsh is called a grandson of Ādhar Valāsh. So important had the by then legendary figure of Bāv become that, in a thoroughly different context, Ibn Isfandīyār gives a chronologically impossible and clearly legendary story about the murder of Bāv at the hands of the Āl-i Jāmāspid Farrukhān-i Bozorg—on whom see §4.4.2 below—when, presumably, the latter heard of the treachery of Bāv in building Sārī when in fact he had ordered him to construct a city in a different location. Ibn Isfandīyār 1941, p. 59. Significantly, this tradition highlights the fact that a variant of the local lore of the region attributed the construction of Sārī to the Āl-i Bāvand as opposed to the Āl-i Jāmāsp.

[1765] See page 277.

[1766] Ibn Isfandīyār 1941, p. 156. Rendered Surkhāb in Marʿashī 1966, p. 93.

the Kārins might have been successful in more or less decimating the senior members of this family in the region. The defeat of the Ispahbudhān by the Kārins in the post-civil war period might, however, also be partly explained by the fact that part of the Ispahbudhān family was concentrating their efforts in Azarbāyjān at the time of the conquest of the region, and probably remained there in the post-conquest centuries.[1767] In view of our lack of concrete information to this effect, however, this claim remains purely conjectural. After the murder of Bāv (Farrukhzād) by the Kārinid Valāsh, Suhrāb, who was only a young child, allegedly fled with his aged mother to a village near Sārī, thence to the region of Kūlā. Kūlā, we recall, formed in fact the *nisba* of Zīnabī Abū 'l-Farrukhān (*al-Zīnabī b. Qūlah*).[1768] This then might have been an Ispahbudhān home-base. The people of Kūlā, according to Ibn Isfandīyār, with the population of the mountain of Kārin, then gathered around this small child, and murdered the Kārinid Valāsh, and put the child Suhrāb on the throne of Ṭabaristān. The civil war between the Ispahbudhān and the Kārins, in other words, was by no means over. Now sometime prior to this period, Dābūyih, the son of Jīl-i Jīlānshāh had also died.[1769] It is at this point then, that with a recent civil war wreaking havoc in the eastern parts of Ṭabaristān as well as Khurāsān, and with a child dynast of the Ispahbudhān family on the throne of Ṭabaristān, that according to Ibn Isfandīyār, Dhu 'l-Manāqib Farrukhān-i Bozorg, the son of Dābūyih, entered the scene of Ṭabaristān.

4.4.2 Farrukhān-i Bozorg Dhu 'l-Manāqib

A close reading of Ibn Isfandīyār shows that the conquest of Ṭabaristān by Farrukhān-i Bozorg and the inception of his rule over this region do not date to the early Arab conquest, as hitherto believed,[1770] but probably occurred some two decades later, around 673. For, as Ibn Isfandīyār relates, it was "after Bāv, [when] the people of Ṭabaristān had divided into factions, [and] Dābūyih had [also] died," that Dhu 'l-Manāqib Farrukhān-i Bozorg, came with a great army and conquered Ṭabaristān "up to the borders of Nīshāpūr."[1771] In fact, the first Arab or Persian attempt at breaking the treaty previously established with the rulers of the region, took place precisely during this period when the Arab general Maṣqalah b. Hubayrah al-Shaybānī attacked the region,[1772] probably in 54 AH/674 CE,[1773] precisely at the time when Farrukhān-i Bozorg conquered Ṭabaristān and installed himself as the ruler there on the wake of the civil war between the Ispahbudhān and the Kārins in the region. Maṣqalah, together with

[1767]Recall that two other sons of Farrukhzād, Isfandīyār and Bahrām, ruled in Azarbāyjān after they had made peace with the Arabs; see §3.4.8.

[1768]Ṭabarī 1994, p. 26, de Goeje, 2655. See page 250ff.

[1769]Ibn Isfandīyār 1941, p. 156; Marʿashī 1966, pp. 10–11, 157–158.

[1770]Madelung, Wilferd, 'Dabuyids', in Ehsan Yarshater (ed.), *Encyclopaedia Iranica*, New York, 2007a (Madelung 2007a), p. 542 and the sources cited therein.

[1771]Ibn Isfandīyār 1941, p. 156.

[1772]Ibn Isfandīyār 1941, p. 157; Marʿashī 1966, p. 11.

[1773]Madelung 2007a, p. 542.

4,000 men, struggled for two years against Farrukhān-i Bozorg at which point the Arab army was defeated and massacred and Maṣqalah killed. The defeat of Maṣqalah's army was so disastrous and its destruction so total that "the expression *until Maṣqalah returns from Ṭabaristān,* conveying the impossibility of completing a task, for many years afterwards circulated among the people." According to Ibn Isfandīyār, Maṣqalah's tomb still existed on the road from Kajū to Kandūsān and the commoners (*ʿavvam u 'l-nass*) still "slavishly and benightedly (*bi taqlīd o jahl*) went on pilgrimage to it [thinking] that he was one of the Companions (*ṣaḥāba*) of the Prophet!"[1774]

In the process of conquering Ṭabaristān, Farrukhān-i Bozorg brought all the regional rulers under his control. Significantly, the only dynast whose territory he did not conquer was the "progeny of Bāv, whose respect he maintained and whose abode he did not invade."[1775] Through an anecdotal narrative, Ibn Isfandīyār informs us that the Kārinid Maṣmughān Valāsh, the *marzbān* of Damāvand,[1776] was killed and his territory appended to that of Dhu 'l-Manāqib (Farrukhān-i Bozorg).[1777] With the power of the Kārins temporarily overshadowed, and with the shrunken power of the Ispahbudhān respected, therefore, by the end of the seventh century the Sasanian Āl-i Jāmāsp gained power over most of Ṭabaristān, the two other major Parthian dynastic families coming under their suzerainty in the region and the Kanārangīyān remaining in control over Inner Khurāsān. In a sense, by the end of the seventh century, the macrocosmic Sasanian–Parthian confederacy was recreated, in a microcosmic fashion, in the extensive regions of Gīlān and Ṭabaristān. Essentially, this picture did not change until the early ʿAbbāsid caliphate.

According to Ibn Isfandīyār, the next major encounter of Farrukhān-i Bozorg, whom he calls the *ispahbud* of Ṭabaristān, with the Arabs[1778] took place when the schismatic Kharijite leader Qaṭarī b. al-Fujāʿah, the "rebel (*gardankish*) of the [period of] Ḥajjāj b. Yūsuf ... together with the rest of the leaders of the Khawārij [Kharijites], may God curse them, took refuge with the *ispahbud*."[1779]

[1774]Ibn Isfandīyār 1941, p. 158; Marʿashī 1966, p. 125. For the *topos* of the settlement or death of a Companion of the Prophet in a region, see Pourshariati 1995.

[1775]Ibn Isfandīyār 1941, p. 158.

[1776]We postulate that this is the same Kārinid Valāsh who killed Bāv (see page 307), and that he is related, or even identical to Maṣmughān Mardānshāh, who made peace with the Arabs (see page 252 and footnote 1750).

[1777]Ibn Isfandīyār 1941, p. 158.

[1778]There were other attempts by the Arabs to subdue the region. One such attempt was made by Muḥammad b. Ashʿath, when he was appointed as nominal governor of Ṭabaristān by ʿUbaydallāh b. Yazīd, the governor of Kūfa (60–64 AH/679–684 CE). When Farrukhān-i Bozorg delayed forwarding the tribute of Ṭabaristān, Ibn Ashʿath invaded the region, only to be defeated and lose his son in the process. Madelung 2007a, p. 542. This attempt of Muḥammad b. Ashʿath is not mentioned in the *Tārīkh-i Ṭabaristān*, however.

[1779]Including ʿUmar-i Fannāq(?) and Ṣāliḥ-i Miknāq(?). Ibn Isfandīyār 1941, p. 158. Qaṭarī b. al-Fujāʿah took refuge in Ṭabaristān at a time when a split had occurred among the Khawārij, with Qaṭarī assuming the leadership of a small splinter group, while the opposing, larger camp was led by ʿAbd Rabb al-Kabīr. See Sadighi, Ghulam Husayn, *Junbish-hā-i Dīnī-i Irānī*, Tehran, 1996 (Sadighi

Throughout the winter Farrukhān-i Bozorg supplied the forces of Qaṭarī with provisions, fodder and gifts (*nuzl o ʿalaf o hadāyā o tuḥaf*).[1780] Once "their horses became well fed and they themselves strengthened," however, the Kharijites sent messages to the *ispahbud* urging him: "convert to our religion for otherwise we will take control of your region and commence war against you."[1781] Meanwhile, Ḥajjāj sent Sufyān b. Abraṣ to Ṭabaristān in pursuit of Qaṭarī. When Sufyān reached Rayy, Farrukhān-i Bozorg had already taken his army to Damāvand in waiting. He sent a message to Sufyān proposing to him that he would aid him in defeating Qaṭarī in exchange for not being harassed thenceforth in his region. Sufyān agreed to these conditions. The war between Farrukhān-i Bozorg's and Qaṭarī's forces took place in the environs of Simnān, where the latter was defeated and the leaders of the Kharijites were killed.[1782] Farrukhān-i Bozorg thereupon pardoned the weak and the captive (*ḍuʿafā o asīrān*) from among Qaṭarī's army and settled these in Āmul, "their location (*mowḍiʿ*) being to this day visible and called Qaṭrī Kalāda."[1783] In the late seventh century, in other words, a small group of Kharijites settled in Āmul.

4.4.3 Yazīd b. Muhallab's unsuccessful conquest of 716–718

Meanwhile in the rivalry between Qutaybah[1784] and Yazīd b. Muhallab, Farrukhān-i Bozorg—in Ibn Isfandīyār's narrative now often referred to simply as the *ispahbud*—joined the camp of Qutaybah. So while Qutaybah continued his wars of expansion in Khurāsān and Transoxiana, becoming notorious for his harsh rule,[1785] he continued to respect the suzerainty of Farrukhān-i Bozorg in Ṭabaristān. Qutaybah's friendship with Farrukhān-i Bozorg and his

1996), p. 44.

[1780]Ibn Isfandīyār 1941, p. 158.

[1781]Ibn Isfandīyār 1941, p. 158:

چون اسبان فربه و ایشان تن ابادان شدند پیام دادند که تا به دین ما بگرود و اگر نه ولایت از تو باز گیریم و با تو حرب کنیم.

In the interim, Ḥajjāj b. Yūsuf made further unsuccessful efforts to conquer Ṭabaristān. These, however, are not covered in Ibn Isfandīyār's narrative. Madelung 2007a, p. 542.

[1782]This is apparently reported by Ṭabarī with a different twist. Also see Ibn al-Athīr 1862, vol. 5, pp. 29–36. In Ibn Isfandīyār's narrative, the victory of the *ispahbud* over Qaṭarī is underlined and Ḥajjāj b. Yūsuf is portrayed as having recognized this, rewarding Sufyān b. Abraṣ for his failure by spreading dirt on his head. In Ṭabarī's account, on the other hand, Sufyān remained in Ṭabaristān until 82 AH/701 CE in order to subdue the region, albeit unsuccessfully. Madelung 2007a, p. 542.

[1783]Ibn Isfandīyār 1941, p. 160.

[1784]"Qutaybah b. Muslim al-Bāhilī became the governor of Khurāsān in 85 AH/ 704 CE. He was killed when he tried to rebel at the time of Sulaymān's succession in 95 AH/ 714–715 CE. During his governorship he undertook many campaigns beyond Khurāsān ... [he] laid the foundations on which Islamic rule in Central Asia was built." Ṭabarī, *The Waning of the Umayyad Caliphate: Prelude to Revolution: A.D. 738-745/A.H. 121-127*, vol. XXVI of *The History of Ṭabarī*, Albany, 1989b, translated and annotated by Carole Hillenbrand (Ṭabarī 1989b), p. 34, n. 178 and the referenced therein, de Goeje, II, 1697.

[1785]Ibn Isfandīyār 1941, pp. 161–162. As Sadighi maintains, "none of the Arab governors who had come to Khurāsān prior to this, were as oppressive or heavy handed toward the population or reneged on the pacts [that they had made] as much as Qutaybah." Sadighi 1996, p. 47.

rivalry with Yazīd b. Muhallab are highlighted in Ibn Isfandīyār's narrative: whenever Qutaybah would boast about one of his conquests in Khurāsān and Transoxiana, Yazīd b. Muhallab would retort by reminding him that he had not been able to do the same with Ṭabaristān.[1786] As a result, according to Ibn Isfandīyār, Qutaybah recognized even more clearly "that Yazīd was his enemy and the *ispahbud* his friend."[1787] When Sulaymān b. ʿAbdalmalik (715–717) became caliph and ordered Qutaybah's murder, he also encouraged Yazīd b. Muhallab "to undertake that which he had criticized Qutaybah for not fulfilling" and conquer Ṭabaristān himself.[1788] Around this time then, in 98 AH/716 CE, the famous failed conquest of Ṭabaristān at the hands of Yazīd b. Muhallab took place.

In the two-year engagement of Muhallab's forces with those of the *ispahbud*, both sides suffered tremendous loss.[1789] When Muhallab had taken Gurgān and Tammīsha, according to Ibn Isfandīyār, the *ispahbud* retreated to the mountains, following the movement of Yazīd's army to the west from the comfortable distance of the mountain highlands. Yazīd, therefore, was able to reach Sārī and take over the *ispahbud's* palace. When the population of the region dispersed, the *ispahbud* himself contemplated fleeing to the Daylam in order to ask for aid. According to Ibn Isfandīyār, faced with the conquest of Muhallab's army of his capital Sārī, which he himself had constructed,[1790] the *ispahbud went to his father* in order to apprise him of his decision to go to the Daylam.[1791] Here, therefore, we realize that by the time Yazīd b. Muhallab invaded Ṭabaristān, rule could have passed from one *ispahbud*, Dhu 'l-Manāqib Farrukhān-i Bozorg, to his son Dādmihr, who also bore, naturally, the title of *ispahbud*. Alternatively, rule could simply have been shared between father and son during this period. From 673 to 716, therefore, we may be dealing with two generations of *ispahbuds* of the Āl-i Jāmāsp in control of Ṭabaristān. We shall further deal with this in a short while.[1792] The *ispahbud's* father, however, advised against taking refuge with the Daylam, for he argued to his son that at the moment he was still a great ruler with a strong army, and that this would all change were he to flee to the Daylam in despair. Besides, he argued, there was no guarantee of a positive reception on the part of the Daylam for greed might prompt them to side with the enemy as a result of the *ispahbud's* weakness.[1793] Instead, his father advised the *ispahbud* to ask the aid of the Daylam from a safe distance. The Daylam

[1786]Ibn Isfandīyār 1941, p. 162.

[1787]It is interesting to compare the pro-Muhallab account of Sahmī's narrative in the *Taʾrīkh-i Jurjān wa Kitāb Maʿrifa ʿUlamā ʾAhl Jurjān* with the pro-Qutaybah tenor of that of Ibn Isfandīyār. See Pourshariati 1998.

[1788]Ibn Isfandīyār 1941, p. 162.

[1789]It is important to note that the army accompanying Muhallab also included contingents from Khurāsān and Transoxiana, and was, therefore, not a purely Arab army.

[1790]Ibn Isfandīyār 1941, p. 77.

[1791]Ibn Isfandīyār 1941, p. 162.

[1792]See page 312ff.

[1793]Ibn Isfandīyār 1941, p. 162.

responded favorably, and coming to the aid of the *ispahbud*, they surrounded the Arab army massacring 15,000 of them. On the promise of booty, the Turks on the eastern end of Ṭabaristān under the command of Ṣūl also came to the aid of the *ispahbud* and attacked the Arab population of Gurgān, massacring all of them, including members of Muhallab's family.

At the end of this period, therefore, Yazīd b. Muhallab complained to Ḥayyān al-Nabatī, a companion of his own tribe, that "it has been two years that we have been engaged in this *ghazwa and jihād*, and we cannot conquer the land single-handedly, and our people have lost their patience. *No one accepts conversion.* [Pray] seek a solution so that we can leave this region intact. We can take our vengeance on the population of Gurgān [in the future] and prepare ourselves for this on another occasion."[1794] Hence, although Yazīd b. Muhallab established some settlements in Ṭabaristān and Gurgān during the two years of fighting between his forces and those of the *ispahbud*, he cannot be credited with establishing permanent settlements in Gurgān.[1795] So, while Sahmī claims that Muhallab established *khiṭaṭ* in Gurgān,[1796] Ibn Isfandīyār maintains that by the combined efforts of the *ispahbud* and his allies, at the end of this period, no Arab settlements were left in the region.[1797]

Chronology of Farrukhān-i Bozorg's rule

A close reading of Ibn Isfandīyār can help clarify some chronological confusions. First of all, the rule of Farrukhān-i Bozorg does not commence at the inception of the Arab conquest of the region in 650–651 as hitherto believed, but, as we have seen, only around 673. Moreover, according Ibn Isfandīyār, a certain Farrukhān was the *ispahbud* of Ṭabaristān during the attack on the region by Yazīd b. Muhallab in 98 AH/716–717 CE. However, both a father and his son appear here as *ispahbuds* in the narrative, so that it is not clear whether we are dealing with Farrukhān-i Bozorg, or possibly his son Dādmihr. After Muhallab's defeat, the *ispahbud* Farrukhān "once again reconstructed his realm and continued(?) (*dar keshīd*) to rule for seventeen years," that is to say, until approximately 728 CE. After his death, his son Dādmihr then ruled for another

[1794] Ibn Isfandīyār 1941, p. 163:

دو سال گذشت تا بدین غزو و جهاد مشغولیم٠ یك بدست زمین ما را مسلّم نمیشود، و مردم ما ستوه امده اند، کسی مسلمانی قبول نمیکند٠ طریقی اندیش و چاره ای ساز که به سلامت از این ولایت بیرون شویم و مکافات اهل گرگان بدیشان رسانیم و به نوبت دگر تدارك این کار خود فرمائیم٠

The rest of the story here is somewhat confused. The text clearly states that Yazīd b. Muhallab agreed to pay 300,000 *dirhams* in exchange for being given safe passage by the *ispahbud*, but then it maintains that the *ispahbud* returned the payment(?) (*adā'i māl bikard*). Ibid., p. 164. At any rate, Muhallab was not able to leave the territory with any booty. Ibid., p. 165.

[1795] Note, in this connection, the author's article Pourshariati 1998, where this claim was made.

[1796] Sahmī, Abū 'l-Qāsim Ḥamza, *Ta'rīkh-i Jurjān wa Kitāb Ma'rifa 'Ulamā 'Ahl Jurjān*, Haydarabad, 1967, edited by Muhammad A. Khan (Sahmī 1967), pp. 18–20.

[1797] It is possible, of course, that the truth lies somewhere between these two traditions and that in fact a small colony of Arab settlers did end up settling in Gurgān.

twelve years, until about 740 CE. According to this chronology, Farrukhān-i Bozorg therefore ruled for 55 years,[1798] from circa 673 until 728.

We do in fact have coinage of the *ispahbuds* of Ṭabaristān commencing with the 60th year of Yazdgird III (93 AH/711 CE).[1799] The coins of the years 93–103 AH/711–721 CE carry the name Farrukh, while the coins of the period 103–110 AH/721–728 CE bear the name Farrukhān.[1800] Based on this numismatic evidence J. M. Unvala had suggested that we are probably dealing with two figures here. Madelung, siding with J. Walker, proposes that Unvala might have been mistaken, and that we are in fact dealing with one and the same person here, the 17 years of the totality of the coins corresponding to Ibn Isfandīyār's contention that Farrukhān-i Bozorg ruled for seventeen years after Muhallab.[1801] Indeed, according the chronology we just derived using the *Tārīkh-i Ṭabaristān*, these dates coincide remarkably well with the latter part of the reign of Farrukhān-i Bozorg.

Throughout Dādmihr's twelve year long reign (circa 728–740), no soul coveted his realm according to Ibn Isfandīyār. That the author is referring to the Arabs here is clear from his subsequent remark: Until the end of the Umayyads no-one entered Ṭabaristān,[1802] for "the Muslims were preoccupied with revolts and the transfer of the caliphate."[1803] For this Dādmihr, we also have coinage, corroborating once more our chronology based on Ibn Isfandīyār's account: from the years 112 and 120–122 AH/730 and 738–740 CE.[1804] At his death in 741, Dādmihr's son Khurshīd was only a young child. Before his death therefore, Dādmihr entrusted his son to his brother Farrukhān-i Kūchak, making a contract with him that he should rule as a vice-regent until Khurshīd became of age, at which time he should transfer the rule to the latter. Farrukhān-i Kūchak accepted and ruled as vice-regent for eight years, at which point, after a struggle with his cousins, Khurshīd, the Sun-King, assumed the throne of Ṭabaristān, by Ibn Isfandīyār's reckoning sometime in 749 CE.

[1798]This, of course, is a rather unusually long reign, and so it might be the case that, as some part of Ibn Isfandīyār's narrative seems to suggest, we are actually dealing with two generations during this period.

[1799]Significantly the calendar of Ṭabaristān commences with the death of Yazdgird III, making the year one of the calendar 32 AH/652 CE. For this coinage see, Curiel, Raoul and Gyselen, Rika, *Une collection de monnaies de cuivre Arabo-Sasanides*, Paris, 1984 (Curiel and Gyselen 1984), pp. 49-56, as well as Madelung 2007a, and the sources cited therein.

[1800]Madelung 2007a, p. 543.

[1801]Madelung 2007a, p. 543.

[1802]Marʿashī 1966, p. 12, Ibn Isfandīyār 1941, p. 165.

[1803]Ibn Isfandīyār 1941, p. 170:

پس از دوازده سال پادشاهی داذمهر بن فرّخان به امن و رفاهیت فرمان یافت و کسی بدیشان نپرداخت
از آنکه اهل اسلام به خروج و تبدیل خلافت مشغول بودند.

[1804]Madelung 2007a, p. 543.

4.5 Khurshīd Shāh

The manner in which Khurshīd regained his throne and subsequently ruled attests to the agnatic structure of rule that was the norm in the northern regions of the former Sasanian realm. In the face of his cousins' opposition to the transfer of rule to him, Khurshīd obtained the aid of other members of his extended family, namely the three sons of Jushnas, the son of Sārūyih, the son of Farrukhān-i Bozorg, in other words, the sons of his paternal cousin.[1805] After taking the throne, Khurshīd compensated the three brothers for their services: he gave Vandarand and Fahrān (Bahrām?) respectively the governorship of Āmul and Kuhistān (the highland), while keeping the third brother, Farrukhān, in his own service. A maternal cousin, one Shahrkhwāstān, was given the command of the army.[1806]

Through a long narrative Ibn Isfandīyār then details Khurshīd's construction activities and the wealth of his realm. During Khurshīd's reign, Ṭabaristān was heavily engaged in textile production, including silk, as well as in trade, for the Sun-King is said to have constructed bazaars, gathering therein all the tradesmen of Ṭabaristān, and caravansaries.[1807] In fact, a burgeoning economy was already in place during the reign of Khurshīd's grandfather, Farrukhān-i Bozorg, when among the products of Ṭabaristān there was silk, cotton, and wool textiles, besides the varied agricultural products of this rich and lush region of Iran. The bulk of the trade of Ṭabaristān, however, Ibn Isfandīyār informs us, was with the Bulghār and Saqasayn in Turkistān, most of it, it seems, being maritime trade via the Caspian Sea.[1808] It is rather certain, therefore, that a crucial dimension of Farrukhān-i Bozorg's friendship with Qutaybah was the mutual trade interests of the two parties in Transoxiana and Central Asia. Here then Ibn Isfandīyār provides us with further significant information about the saga of one of the Parthian dynastic families, the ambitious Kārins.

4.5.1 The spāhbed Kārin

One of the *spāhbeds* of Khurshīd's realm, according to Ibn Isfandīyār, was a certain Kārin, who had enormous wealth and "four thousand soldiers, and who always sat on a golden throne and wore silk garments." Kārin's orders "were [also] incumbent upon the population under [the control of] the *ispahbud* [i.e., Khurshīd]." His pretensions, however, grew over time, so much so that he became arrogant and did not pay the required deference to the other grandees

[1805] Ibn Isfandīyār 1941, p. 171. Ibn Isfandīyār calls these mistakenly the maternal cousins of Khurshīd. Madelung 2007a, p. 543.

[1806] Ibn Isfandīyār 1941, p. 172. Fahrān is rendered Qahrān in Marʿashī 1966, p. 12. Madelung 2007a, p. 543. This Shahrkhwāstān was a much elder figure for already at the time of Farrukhān-i Bozorg, we see him, advanced in age, as an extremely powerful and wealthy figure who stood in opposition to the open door trade policies of Farrukhān-i Bozorg. Ibn Isfandīyār 1941, p. 77.

[1807] Ibn Isfandīyār 1941, p. 172.

[1808] The voyage of the ships to the latter location from Ṭabaristān is said to have taken three months and the return one week(!). Ibn Isfandīyār 1941, p. 81.

and elite of the realm. He became overbearing, oppressing people.[1809] "The population," Ibn Isfandīyār recounts, "were *awaiting an excuse for rebellion*."[1810] Here, significantly, during the reign of the Āl-i Jāmāsp Khurshīd, the Sun-King, and immediately after the narrative on the power, wealth, and armed forces of the *spāhbed* Kārin, when people were waiting an excuse for rebellion, begins Ibn Isfandīyār account of Sunbād's rebellion.[1811]

4.5.2 Sunbād's murder

Ibn Isfandīyār narrates, that "as we have previously noted,[1812] the caliph Manṣūr killed Abū Muslim." In Rayy, Sunbād heard of the news of the murder of Abū Muslim, and sending all of his treasury and cattle, together with six million *dirhams* as a personal gift, to Khurshīd, rebelled against Manṣūr.[1813] After Sunbād's defeat at the hands of Jawhar b. Marrār, so many of the followers of the rebel had been killed, according to Ibn Isfandīyār, that until the year 300 AH the remains of those slaughtered were still visible in the region of Rayy. In flight, Sunbād set out toward Ṭabaristān and took refuge with Khurshīd.[1814]

In an anecdotal story, Ibn Isfandīyār highlights the arrogance of Sunbād in dealing with one of the cousins of Khurshīd, and indirectly therefore, with Khurshīd himself. In this narrative, Khurshīd sent a certain Ṭūs, his cousin on his father's side, together with presents and gifts and horses, to the reception of Sunbād, somewhere between Ṭabaristān and Qūmis.[1815] When the two parties met, Ṭūs dismounted from his horse and paid his respects to Sunbād. In insolence, however, Sunbād did not reciprocate the respect, and continued to

---

[1809] Ibn Isfandīyār 1941, p. 173.

[1810] Marʿashī 1966, pp. 12–14, Ibn Isfandīyār 1941, p. 173:

دل خلایق از او سیر و ستوه شد و مردم برای عصیان بهانه طلبیدند.

[1811] For a more detailed account of this important rebellion, see §6.4.

[1812] In a long exposition prior to this, Ibn Isfandīyār describes the caliph Manṣūr's final move against Abū Muslim, the leader of the ʿAbbāsid revolution (for more details see our discussion in §6.2). "I have never read," Ibn Isfandīyār maintains, "a stranger story than that of Abū Muslim, for God almighty had given this peasant such submission (*tamkīn*) that he was able to fulfill such an arduous task which he had undertaken." After he had overcome the Umayyads, Ibn Isfandīyār continues, Abū Muslim ordered his *kātib*, one ʿAbdalḥamīd, who was also his *dabīr*, to write a book narrating his exploits. The latter, who was a master of this art, accomplished the task, adding to it many fantastic elements (*gharāyib*) and including all the shortcomings and internal and external states of affairs (*ʿujr o bujr*). Once finished, the book was so bulky that two men were needed in order to lift it. Abū Muslim, however, was not pleased with the account as ʿAbdalḥamīd had portrayed it, and so with an axe, he destroyed it and ordered the *kātib* to rewrite it. After swearing allegiance to Manṣūr, Ibn Isfandīyār continues, Abū Muslim was given permission to return to Khurāsān. Shortly thereafter, however, Manṣūr regretted this decision and ordered the latter to return. Abū Muslim had already passed Ḥulwān when the messenger of Manṣūr reached him in Rayy. He thus left his treasury, together with his representative (*nāyib*) Sunbād in Rayy, and returned to the caliph. Ibn Isfandīyār 1941, pp. 166–167.

[1813] We will discuss Sunbād's revolt in greater detail in §6.4 below; for an elaboration on the significance of treasure in this context, see §6.4.1.

[1814] Ibn Isfandīyār 1941, p. 174.

[1815] de Goeje, III, 120; Ibn al-Athīr 1862, vol. 5, pp. 481–482.

remain mounted on his horse. Ṭūs reminded Sunbād that he was a cousin of Khurshīd and that Sunbād's behavior was unbecoming and disrespectful. Sunbād responded with even more arrogance, at which point Ṭūs beheaded him for all this arrogance.[1816] The *ispahbud* Khurshīd is portrayed by Ibn Isfandīyār as being agitated and saddened over Ṭūs's behavior and to have cursed the latter. Nevertheless, he conveniently seized the wealth that Sunbād had committed to his safe-keeping, and sent the head of Sunbād to the caliph Manṣūr. Significantly, as we will see later,[1817] here Ibn Isfandīyār reiterates the story of the power and the arrogance of the *spāhbed* Kārin.

4.5.3 Khurshīd's death and the final conquest of Ṭabaristān

Manṣūr subsequently asked for the treasures of Abū Muslim and Sunbād, but Khurshīd denied possessing them. This, however, brought him into direct conflict with the caliphate.[1818] In a series of correspondences with Manṣūr, Khurshīd finally agreed to pay the central administration the yearly *kharāj* (taxes) of Ṭabaristān, as it had been calculated in the period of the *akāsirih*, that is to say, at the end of the Sasanian period. It is not clear what exactly had forced Khurshīd to have a turnabout in his dealings with the caliphate. Whatever it was, it was not deemed enough, for Manṣūr, having seen the *kharāj* of Ṭabaristān, became greedy and concocted a ruse to conquer Ṭabaristān.[1819] He had his son Mahdī, from his residence in Rayy, send a messenger to the *ispahbud* Khurshīd to ask his aid in fighting ʿAbd al-Jabbār ʿAbdalraḥmān, who had rebelled in Khurāsān. In his message, he asked permission for part of his army to pass through Ṭabaristān, under the excuse that, as that year was a year of drought, sustenance of the entire army could not be provided if they were all to proceed from a single road. Once the messenger, whose name is not given, but who is said to have been one of the sons of the *ʿajam*, had reached Khurshīd's court, the zeal of the *ʿajam* (*ḥamiyat-i ʿajamiyat*) forced him to warn Khurshīd of Manṣūr's ruse. Khurshīd, however, was suspicious of the messenger and refused to give him an audience, at which point the messenger proclaimed that Fate had ordained that "all this pomp and bounty, together with the kingdom and edifice," should be shattered.[1820]

Mahdī therefore sent an army under the command of Abū 'l-Khaṣīb ʿUmar b. al-ʿAlāʾ,[1821] from the direction of Zārim and Abū ʿAwn b. ʿAbdalmalik from

[1816] Ibn Isfandīyār 1941, p. 174.

[1817] See §6.4.4.

[1818] Marʿashī 1966, pp. 12–14; Ibn Isfandīyār 1941, pp. 174–175.

[1819] Ibn Isfandīyār 1941, p. 175.

[1820] Ibn Isfandīyār 1941, p. 175.

[1821] This Abū 'l-Khaṣīb "had at one time killed someone in Gurgān and had taken refuge with the *ispahbud* [Khurshīd], and for a long while had accumulated property with his [i.e., Khurshīd's] support in the region, and had come to know the terrain of the territory. But, later, he had joined forces with the army of the caliph." Ibn Isfandīyār 1941, p. 176:

ابوالخصیب عمر بن العلاء را، که وقتی بگرگان یکی را کشته بود و پناه با اصفهبد کرده و مدّتها
بحمایت او در ان ولایت وقوفی یافت و مسالك و مابر دانست و باز به لشکر خلیفه پیوسته و قائد

the direction of Gurgān to the region. Khurshīd, not suspecting the caliph, had withdrawn his forces and relocated the population so as to ensure that they would not be harmed by the Arab army passing through the region. Before he realized it, it was too late. Abū 'l-Khaṣīb conquered Āmul, made it his capital and called the population into submission. On account of the oppression that they ostensibly had experienced under Khurshīd, and in order to maintain their property and possessions, one "group after another ... the population accepted Islam."[1822] For two years and seven months the army of Islam stayed in the region and constructed houses,[1823] until Khurshīd, together with 50,000 men set out against them. The spread of cholera at this point was apparently a major factor in the defeat of the forces of Khurshīd. At the defeat of the Āl-i Jāmāspid Khurshīd, the Muslims were preoccupied with the transfer of booty for a whole week (*haft shabānrūz māl naghl mīkardand*). Including in these were the daughters of Khurshīd with beauty as "that of the moon." One was given to ʿAbbās b. Muḥammad al-Hāshimī and named ʾUmmat al-Raḥmān, and the other was given to the caliph. The sons of Khurshīd were equally renamed from Hormozd, Vandād Hormozd, and Dādmihr, to Abū Hārūn ʿĪsā, Mūsā, and Ibrāhīm respectively. The rest of the *haram* was equally divided between the caliph's sons and relatives. The *ispahbud* Khurshīd, declaring that "after this there is no inclination to life and joy, and death is the very solace and respite itself," allegedly committed suicide by taking poison. Thus ends the history of the house of the Sasanian Āl-i Jāmāsp in Ṭabaristān. According to Ibn Isfandīyār, the "kingship of Jīl-i Jīlānshāh to that of Khurshīd and his death was 119 years."[1824]

"The first governor on behalf of the ʿAbbāsids," Ibn Isfandīyār maintains, was Abū 'l-Khaṣīb, and "*the first construction that the Muslims made was the jāmiʿ mosque of Sārī, in the year 144 of hijra.*" Abū 'l-Khaṣīb remained the governor of the region for two years. After him Abū Khuzaymah was sent, who also ruled for two years and "massacred many of the elite from among the Mazdeans (*vujūh o aʿyān-i gabrakān*), until they sent Abū 'l-ʿAbbās Ṭūsī, who set up armed camps (*masālih*) as follows."[1825] Ibn Isfandīyār then proceeds to list 45 camps, together with the number of, presumably, armed men settled in them.[1826] A

لشکر ابوالخصیب گشته بجلادت مقام یافته، دو هزار سقار داد و ب امل تاختن فرمود.

[1822]Marʿashī 1966, p. 13, Ibn Isfandīyār 1941, p. 176:

فوج فوج و قبیله قبیله می امدند و قبول اسلام کرده و املاك و اسباب خویش مسلّم گردانیده.

[1823]Ibn Isfandīyār 1941, p. 177:

و لشکر اسلام دو سال و هفت ماه بکلّی جمع شده زیر طاق خانها ساختند و بمحاصره ان نشستند.

[1824]Ibn Isfandīyār 1941, p. 177. If we put Khurshīd's death two and a half years after that of Sunbād, sometime in 757–758, then calculating backwards, we get the putative date 638–639 for Jīl-i Jīlānshāh's inception of rule, which tallies quite well with our previous estimate of 630s.
[1825]Ibn Isfandīyār 1941, p. 178.
[1826]Ibn Isfandīyār 1941, pp. 178–181.

total of 29,100 men and (and women and children [?]) are listed here, the smallest armed camp having a population between two and three hundred, the average one 500, and the larger ones, between 1,000 and 1,500. It must be noted that there is no certainty that all of these settlers were of Arab ancestry or even Muslims. While some are specifically maintained to be Arabs, the population of other camps are called respectively Ṭūsīs, Ṭabarīs,[1827] Khurāsānīs, Syrian, Khurāsānīs from Nisā and Abīvard, and men from Sughd, Khwārazm, Nisā and Abīvard.[1828] Other regional armies, the ethnic dimension of which is not specified, included those of Jazira, Damascus and Nīshāpūr, for example.[1829] Two camps belonging to Abū 'l-Khaṣīb ʿUmar b. al-ʿAlāʾ with no other population listed, are also mentioned. In one of these the governor is said to have resided, and "the population (*ʿavvām*) visited it believing him to be a Companion of the Prophet."[1830] This, therefore, constituted the beginning of a systematic colonization of Ṭabaristān by the Muslims.

Our narrative of the history of the Sasanians in the late antique period will not be complete, however, unless we turn our attention to a whole different dimension of this history, namely, the spiritual landscape of the Sasanians and their subjects.[1831] For as we shall see in this second part of our study, the agnatic structure of Sasanian society entailed that the Pārsīg–Pahlav dichotomy also replicated itself in the spiritual realm.[1832] Furthermore, the whole series of revolts that erupted in the Pahlav dominions at the inception of the ʿAbbāsid revolution cannot be properly understood before we have undertaken this analysis.[1833]

[1827]Ibn Isfandīyār 1941, p. 179.

[1828]Ibn Isfandīyār 1941, p. 180.

[1829]Ibn Isfandīyār 1941, p. 179.

[1830]Ibn Isfandīyār 1941, pp. 179 and 180 respectively.

[1831]For while during the past two decades, specialists in the field have made tremendous inroads in their assessment of Sasanian religious history, the non-specialist's perspective on this history continues to be informed by the Christensenian thesis. In what follows we shall attempt not only to give a synopsis of recent research in the field, but also to put forth our own analysis.

[1832]See Chapter 5, especially §5.3.3.

[1833]See Chapter 6.

Part II

Religious Currents

CHAPTER 5

Sasanian religious landscape

5.1 Post-Avestan period

For a long period prior to the advent of the Sasanians, the Iranian religious landscape was characterized by a remarkably heterogeneous medley of beliefs and spiritual inclinations. During what Mary Boyce has termed the post-Avestan period,[1834] spanning from the end of the fourth century BCE to the early third century CE, and corresponding to the Seleucid and Arsacid dynasties,[1835] the authorities did not seek to impose centralized control over religious matters and so conditions were set for the development of regional variations in the spiritual landscape of Iran.[1836] While the Avestan communities seem to have retained only a vague memory of the birthplace of Zoroaster[1837] in some distant place in northeastern Iran, for example, it seems to have been during this post-Avestan period that local traditions concerning the birthplace of the prophet were advanced in the Zoroastrian communities of various regions in Iran. As

[1834]Unless otherwise noted the following discussion is indebted to Boyce, Mary, *Zoroastrianism: Its Antiquity and Constant Vigour*, Costa Mesa, 1992 (Boyce 1992), p. 10.

[1835]For the Seleucids, see footnote 75; for the Arsacids, see §1.1.

[1836]After Alexander's conquest, "when the priests of each province rallied from the carnage and destruction of the conquest, they pursued, it seems, independent courses, maintaining only fraternal links with one another." Boyce 1979, p. 79. The regionalism fostered during the Seleucid and Arsacid periods also affected the development of the regional Aramaic scripts in the courts of various provinces. This development, in turn, led to the formation of distinctive scripts in all of the main provinces. Some of the known versions of these scripts are Parthian, Middle Persian, Median, Sogdian and Khwarezmian. The reign of Narseh (293–302) seems to have been the last period in which the Sasanians used the Parthian language in their official inscriptions. Thereafter they presumably attempted to impose Persian "as the sole official language throughout Iran, and forbade altogether the use of written Parthian." Nevertheless, the fact that "a few short *private* inscriptions in Parthian language and script have been found on rock-faces in southern Khorasan, that is, within the territory of Parthia proper" seems to indicate that this language was still patronized in territories under dynastic Parthian control, even though among the aforementioned inscriptions "it is thought that none is later than the fourth century." Boyce 1979, pp. 80 and 116. See, however, our discussion on page 460.

[1837]For the latest work on the ongoing controversy on the date of Zoroaster, see Kingsley, Peter, 'The Greek Origin of the Sixth-Century Dating of Zoroaster', *Bulletin of the School of Oriental and African Studies* 37, (1990), pp. 245–265 (Kingsley 1990), who, by one reckoning, has put the notion of a sixth-century BCE date for Zoroaster to rest.

with other aspects of Iranian social history, the topographical landscape of Iran facilitated centrifugal tendencies in the Iranian religious landscape. Regional communities came to vie with each other over claims to precedence and sanctity in Zoroastrian history. The Atropateneans, the Sīstānis, the Bactrians, and finally the Medes, each co-opted the long-forgotten legends of the birthplace of Zoroaster into the traditions of their localities.[1838] There was besides these the religious tradition of Persis, which pitted itself sometimes against Atropatene (Azarbāyjān), sometimes against Parthava.[1839] The post-Avestan period also gives testimony to religious practices that had remained outside the Mazdean fold. Chief among these was demon-worship (*dev*-worship), a practice that continued to haunt the coalescing Zoroastrian clergy well into the Sasanian period. The ancient Indo-Iranians believed both in beneficent gods and spirits and a number of hostile supernatural beings and malignant spirits. At some point in their history however, they parted ways, leading to the well-known inversion of the Indo-Iranian gods, the *daēvas*, into the "principal agents of evil ... [whom Zoroaster conceived] as adverse gods" and target of his denunciation.[1840] It was a hallmark of Zoroaster's teaching, or those propagated by his followers, that demons and malignant creatures, as well as their worshippers, "all followers of *Drug*, falsehood, became ever more sharply contrasted with divine beings." Angra Mainyu (Ahriman) became the creator of these demonic creatures.[1841] Despite this, the post-Avestan period continued to breed evil-worship. In the Zoroastrian confession of faith, the *Fravarānē*, the recantation of demons forms one of the central dogmas of the faith.[1842] In the *Videvdād* (*The Law against Demons, Vendidad*), besides Nasu, the Demon of Death, several other demons, including Indra, are listed.[1843] Pahlavi literature, most of which reflects—besides its own milieu of production, that is, the late Sasanian and post-conquest period of Iranian history—ancient practices, is practically obsessed with these. The *Dēnkard*, the encyclopedia of Mazdean knowledge, dating to the ninth or tenth century,[1844] gives detailed evidence of the rites of dev-worshippers, of how they

[1838]Boyce 1992, p. 10.

[1839]Eddy 1961, pp. 79–80.

[1840]According to Yarshater, it is not possible to determine with certainty the phases of this development in terms of time, or to say how much of it was due to Zoroaster's reform. From the Gāthās it appears that some Iranian tribes worshipped *daēvas* or practiced their propitiation. Yarshater, Ehsan, 'Iranian Common Beliefs and World-View', in Ehsan Yarshater (ed.), *Cambridge History of Iran: The Seleucid, Parthian, and Sasanian Periods*, vol. 3(1), pp. 343–359, Cambridge University Press, 1983a (Yarshater 1983a), p. 347.

[1841]Yarshater 1983a, p. 347.

[1842]Yasna 1898, *Yasna*, vol. 31 of *Sacred Books of the East*, Oxford University Press, 1898, translated by L.H. Mills (Yasna 1898), §12.

[1843]See for instance Vendidad 1880, *Vendidad*, vol. 4 of *Sacred Books of the East*, Oxford University Press, 1880, translated by James Darmesteter (Vendidad 1880), §19, 43–47; Yarshater 1983a, p. 347.

[1844]While in its extant form the *Dēnkard* dates to the Islamic period, "it is apparent that the whole work, with the exception of Books III and V, represents the religious knowledge available to an educated Mazdean during the Sasanian era." Containing about one quarter of copious summaries of the Avestan Nasks (books), as well as chapters on Mazdean theology, moral precepts, the legend

"prowled around in great secrecy," kept their abode, "body and clothes in a state of filthiness and stench," and of their "chanting services to the demons."[1845]

The post-Avestan period also saw the establishment of Jewish and Christian communities in Iran. The legacy of tolerance during the Arsacid period seems to have provided a very favorable situation for the Jewish communities, so much so that the rise of the Sasanians occasioned fear and apprehension among the rabbis.[1846] As for the Christian communities in Iran during the Arsacid period, it has been observed that "in view of the time necessary to establish even a fairly small community, Christian communities ... [came to exist in Iran] from the beginning of the 2nd century [and that from this period onward] ... these communities consolidated themselves by some form of organization."[1847] As "tolerance was used as a political principle, or merely because of religious indifference," it has been argued furthermore that "the Parthian period was characterized by peace and quiet for non-Zoroastrian minorities."[1848] All are in agreement that the Arsacids, of whose actual religious beliefs and practices we have scant knowledge,[1849] did little to impose an orthodoxy, whatever the nature of this might have been. And so in the post-Avestan period, the Iranian religious landscape came to be dominated by a bewildering array of religious beliefs and practices. This is a primary dimension of the post-Avestan religious landscape about which there is little disagreement in the scholarly community.[1850]

of Zoroaster, and other doctrinal matters, the *Dēnkard* is one of our most important sources of the Mazdean religion. For the *Dēnkard* see, among others, Menasce, J.P. De, 'Zoroastrian Pahlavi Writings', in Ehsan Yarshater (ed.), *Cambridge History of Iran: The Seleucid, Parthian, and Sasanian Periods*, vol. 3(2), pp. 1166–1196, Cambridge University Press, 1983 (Menasce 1983), pp. 1170–1176.

[1845]Dinkard 1911, *Dēnkard: The Complete Text of the Pahlavi Dinkard*, Bombay, 1911, translated by D.M. Madan (Dinkard 1911), p. 219, 7–22, as quoted in Zaehner, R.C., *Zurvan: A Zoroastrian Dilemma*, New York, 1972 (Zaehner 1972), p. 53.

[1846]Widengren, Geo, 'The Status of the Jews in the Sasanian Empire', *Acta Iranica* I, (1961), pp. 117–162 (Widengren 1961), pp. 124–125.

[1847]Asmussen, J.P., 'Christians in Iran', in Ehsan Yarshater (ed.), *Cambridge History of Iran: The Seleucid, Parthian, and Sasanian Periods*, vol. 3(2), pp. 924–949, Cambridge University Press, 1983 (Asmussen 1983), p. 928.

[1848]Asmussen 1983, p. 928.

[1849]Boyce, Mary, 'Arsacids: IV. Arsacid Religion', in Ehsan Yarshater (ed.), *Encyclopaedia Iranica*, pp. 540–541, New York, 1991b (Boyce 1991b).

[1850]As Kreyenbroek maintains, "regional priesthoods enjoyed a large measure of independence during these [i.e., post-Avestan] periods." Kreyenbroek, Philip G., 'Spiritual Authority in Zoroastrianism', *Jerusalem Studies in Arabic and Islam* 17, (1994), pp. 1–16 (Kreyenbroek 1994). While "the *ideal* of a hierarchically structured priesthood headed by a supreme pontiff was present in early Zoroastrianism, and while the local *ratu* presumably had extensive powers, there can have been no question [during the post-Avestan period] ... of a Church united under an uninterrupted line of generally recognized authoritative pontiffs." Kreyenbroek 1994, pp. 3–5. In the Pahlavi books of the Sasanian period the word *dastwar* (*dastūr*) is used for rendering the Avestan *ratu*. Every believer was expected to have a *dastwar* who guided him or her. The *dastwar* could delegate his authority to a priest under him, but he himself "had to recognize the authority of a superior *dastwar*." Ibid., pp. 7–8. Choosing the right *dastwar* seems to have been of crucial importance for the "*the teachings and judgments of various dastwars could differ materially from one another.*" Ibid., p. 9. Emphasis mine. Three accepted teachings (*chāshtag*) are mentioned in a number of Pahlavi books which the *dastwar* was expected to follow, but strong evidence suggests that "the limits of the *dastwars*'

5.2 Orthodoxy – Heterodoxy

5.2.1 Two pillars: the monarchy and the clergy?

The incredible variety of religious practices that constituted the religious landscape of Iran in the post-Avestan period needs to be kept in mind in any appreciation of the subject during the Sasanian period. Until recently, our efforts in this direction were hampered by the long-established paradigm of church-state collaboration in Sasanian studies, and the concomitant theory that the Zoroastrian church, as the orthodox creed, had entrenched itself in Sasanian society. Both aspects of this theory had their base in the ideology promoted by the Sasanians themselves, an ideology that forcefully articulated itself only late in the Sasanian period but which justified itself in reference to the presumed practices of the first Sasanian monarchs. A detailed articulation of it is contained in the famous late Sasanian document, the *Testament of Ardashīr*, but attributed to the first Sasanian king Ardashīr I: "Know that kingship and religion are twins; one cannot exist without the other, for religion is the foundation of royalty and the king is the defender of religion."[1851] Up until recently, this image of a strong and forceful clerical tradition, which, in unison with the monarchy, and according to the ideology of the two pillars of the state, forced upon the believers a strict doctrinal spirituality, was received wisdom in Sasanian studies.

More recent scholarship, however, has argued that this image reflects more the propagandistic endeavors of the clergy and the monarchy, articulated late in the Sasanian and early in the post-conquest period, than the reality of the religious landscape in Iran during the Sasanian period. It has even been suggested that the notion that "the early Sassanian Church ... was dominated by the supremacy of the King of Kings ... [and that] the first steps for the foundation of a State Church" were taken during the reign of Ardashīr I, was nothing but a conscious reconstruction of Sasanian history in later times. The very idea of royalty and religion as twins has been shown to be a literary theme of "regretted

authority was not always clearly delineated and the existence of the Teachings of equal validity ... gave lower-ranking *dastwars* a considerable degree of independence." Ibid., pp. 10–11. What is of practical importance for us, however, is that as long as this system "was based predominantly on an oral tradition, the practical limitations of such a tradition *made it impossible for the highest authorities to control the teachings of local or regional dastwars, except when these were felt to pose a serious threat to the integrity of the faith or the unity of the Church.*" Ibid., p. 13. Emphasis mine. This situation gave considerable authority to the local and regional *dastwars* over their followers. It is important to note that Kreyenbroek's whole study is meant to argue the case for the influence that such a structure of religious authority, especially the roles of the *dastwar* and their disciples (*hāwisht*), might have had on the Muslim Iranian, especially Shīʿite Iranian attitude toward spiritual authority and the rise of the *ʿulamā*, who are "the Islamic counterparts of the Zoroastrian *dastwars*." Ibid., pp. 14–15.

[1851]The popular story of the life of the founder of the Sasanian dynasty, Ardashīr I, and his rise to power, the *Testament of Ardashīr*, was most probably written at the end of the Sasanian period. See Ardashir 1966, *Testament of Ardašīr*, vol. 254 of *Journal Asiatique*, pp. 46–90, 1966, translated by M. Grignaschi (Ardashir 1966), p. 70 and n. 10, translated and cited in Russell, James R., 'Kartīr and Mānī: A Shamanistic Model of their Conflict', in *Acta Iranica 30: Textes et Mémoires, Volume XVI, Papers in Honor of Professor Ehsan Yarshater*, pp. 180–193, 1990a (Russell 1990a), p. 181; Menasce 1983, pp. 1187–1188.

happy bygone mythical times ... or the aspiration of an eschatological future," developed not during the Sasanian period but in the later Islamic periods.[1852] It has been argued convincingly, moreover, that the theories that seek to glorify "the task of the Sasanian kings in establishing a new Zoroastrian church structure and in creating a theocratic state adhering to the Zoroastrian faith" are but exaggerated views of a much more nuanced religio-political landscape.[1853] The Sasanians did attempt to "gain control of the religious establishment by elevating certain priests to high positions, by using religious language and by making generous endowments for religious purposes, but the fusion of state and religion was probably a mere slogan, flaunted by the kings in one direction and by the priests in another, rather than a reality."[1854]

Propaganda, of course, is precisely that: the effort to reconstruct reality so as to give an image of factuality. There are a number of problems with the late Sasanian *topos* of the two pillars of the state. To begin with, and even granting some credibility to this *topos*, it has been observed that the Sasanian effort at creating the image of a national church, and a political ideology that postulated the monarchy's cooperation with the clergy, does not necessarily mean that the monarchical–clerical relationship was always characterized by harmony and close cooperation. On the contrary, the insistence upon an alliance between the throne and altar that infuses the Sasanian national ideology also gives "proof of the opposite: it states an ideal need, it is the reflection of an ideology and not of a historical reality."[1855] Scholars of Sasanian history are generally unanimous in observing that political expediency and not adherence to any particular religious dogma dictated the Sasanian monarchs' relationship vis-à-vis other faiths through most of their history. This can be observed in the Sasanian kings' relationships toward the Jewish and Christian minorities within their realms.[1856] As far as the state's relationship with the national church was concerned, moreover, a close scrutiny of the sources reveals that it was as often, and perhaps more often, characterized by belligerence than congeniality. As Gnoli has observed, it is "in terms of *forces* not always allied and often opposed, that the question of relations between the Church and the State should be considered."[1857] All this is evident in Shāpūr I's (241–272) initial predilection toward Mānī,[1858] Yazdgird I's (399–420) amicable relations with the Christians,

[1852] Although the theme itself can be found in the ancient Indo-Iranian mythology of the twins, the first king (*Yemo*) and the first priest (*Manu*). Gnoli 1989, pp. 138–139, n. 13.

[1853] Shaked, Shaul, *Dualism in Transformation: Varieties of Religion in Sasanian Iran*, vol. 16 of *Jordan Lectures in Comparative Religion*, London, 1994a (Shaked 1994a), p. 1.

[1854] Shaked 1994a, p. 2.

[1855] Gnoli 1989, p. 165.

[1856] Asmussen 1983, p. 933. See also §5.2.8 below.

[1857] Gnoli 1989, p. 169.

[1858] According to the *Dēnkard*, when Shāpūr I attempted to collect the "writings from the Religion which had been dispersed [presumably by Alexander]", he also gathered treaties on "medicine, astronomy, movement, time, space, substance, creation, becoming, passing away, change in quality, growth (?), and other processes and organs. These he added to (?) the Avesta." Boyce observes that

Qubād's (488–531) initial support of Mazdak, and finally the belligerent relationship of Hormozd IV (579–590) with the Zoroastrian clergy, all of which are only the most acute examples of a volatile relationship.[1859] In assessing church-state relations during the Sasanian period it is also prudent to remember that the history of the Zoroastrian church as a monarchy-independent, hierarchically organized church dates only to the fifth century CE, a factor that brings us to the notion of a monolithic Mazdean orthodoxy.

As Bausani has observed, "recent studies have progressively complicated the religious panorama of pre-Islamic Iran, showing that we are not dealing—as some believed when these studies started in Europe—with one Iranian religion, but with various religions or types of religiosity characteristic of one or another branch of the Iranian family."[1860] Besides the religious practices that fell outside the Mazdean fold during the Sasanian period, therefore, we have to reckon with the fact that as the names of the months and days, as well as on coins, crowns, and reliefs of the Sasanian kings bear witness, "Mazdaism was not restricted to the cult of Mazda and the beneficent immortals [Amahraspands]."[1861] Besides Ahūrā Mazda (Ormozd), one may mention three other important gods worshipped during the Sasanian period: Mihr (Mithra),[1862] Anāhitā,[1863] and Bahrām (Wahrām).[1864] While many Sasanian kings were invested by Ahūrā Mazdā, many others received their investiture from other gods.[1865] To give but one example, a new interpretation of the controversial investiture scene of Shāpūr II at Tāq-i Bustān argues convincingly that not only Ahūrā Mazdā but also Mithra is depicted in the relief bestowing Divine Glory on the king.[1866]

The notion that Sasanian Mazdeism was not a monolithic bloc is corroborated by the fact that it is precisely to non-Mazdean sources that we have to resort in order to get a sense of the complexity of the religious landscape of

the "Avesta to which these foreign writings were added was plainly the Zand, that is the Middle Persian translation with its glosses and commentaries." Boyce 1979, p. 113.

1859 Gnoli 1989, p. 169.

1860 Bausani, Alessandro, *Religion in Iran: From Zoroaster to Baha'ullah*, New York, 2000, translated by J.M. Marchesi (Bausani 2000), p. 10.

1861 Duchesne-Guillemin, J., 'Zoroasterian Religion', in Ehsan Yarshater (ed.), *Cambridge History of Iran: The Seleucid, Parthian, and Sasanian Periods*, vol. 3(2), pp. 866–909, Cambridge University Press, 1983 (Duchesne-Guillemin 1983), p. 902. The terms Mazdeism and Zoroastrianism will be used interchangeably as generic terms for the Iranian religion.

1862 See §5.3.1 below.

1863 Arədvī Sūrā Anāhitā (Ardwīsūr Anāhīd), the Strong and Immaculate, was the goddess of the waters (Ābān). Bier, C., Boyce, Mary, and Chaumont, M.L., 'Anāhīd', in Ehsan Yarshater (ed.), *Encyclopaedia Iranica*, New York, 2007 (Bier et al. 2007).

1864 For Bahrām, the god of Victory, see page 411 below.

1865 Duchesne-Guillemin 1983, pp. 902–903. Also see Soudavar, Abolala, *The Aura of the Kings: Legitimacy and Divine Sanction in Iranian Kingship*, vol. 11 of *Bibliotheca Iranica, Intellectual Traditions Series*, 1980 (Soudavar 1980), pp. 48–66. The author would like to express her deep gratitude to Mr. Soudavar for providing her with a copy of his excellent work, although she does reserve judgment about some of his arguments.

1866 Soudavar 1980, pp. 49–52 and nn. 121–129, as well as fig. 46, p. 158.

Iran during the Sasanian period.[1867] The Christian sources in fact often give us a picture of a Mazdeism more pre-occupied with what has been unfortunately termed nature worship, that of sun, fire, and water, with Mihr and Anāhitā as the foremost deities, than with a moralizing Ahūrā Mazdā as the sole object of worship. The worship of Mihr and Anāhitā in fact is even "documented by official iconography ... which has no counterpart in subsequent Zoroastrian literature." Add to this the worship of Nāna, Ba'al, and Nabu "or the bloody worship of Lady Anahid in Staxr ... [and] compare all this with the picture of the Good Religion that is got, for instance, from the [*Dēnkard*, and] we become aware that there is quite a considerable discrepancy" between later *mōbadic* propaganda and actual practice.[1868]

5.2.2 Kirdīr

From the very beginnings of their reign the Sasanians had to contend with the multifarious religious landscape that they had inherited from the Arsacids. This much comes across clearly from the inscriptions of the Sasanian high priest Kirdīr,[1869] which provide some of the earliest evidence at our disposal on the religious landscape of Sasanian society. Kirdīr, who seems to have functioned as a priest and eventually a high priest from the reign of the first Sasanian monarch, Ardashīr I (224?–241 CE), through the reign of Bahrām II (276–293), was also one of the most prolific Sasanian priests: he left his marks in four great inscriptions—more than most kings—intended for public display,[1870] on rock carvings at Sar Mashhad (KSM), Naqsh-i Rostam (KNRm), Kaʿba-i Zartusht (KKZ), and Naqsh-i Rajab (KKRb). In these, he recorded the "deeds of a powerful career and the multitude of titles he received from a succession of appreciative monarchs."[1871]

Kirdīr's inscriptions are a testimony to the efforts that he presumably undertook to establish orthodoxy not only in Iran but also "in the land of non-Iran reached by the horses and men of the King of Kings."[1872] In Iran, Kirdīr boasts of founding a number of Bahrām (Wahrām) fires,[1873] and of bringing the "many

[1867] Gnoli 1989, pp. 166–167.

[1868] Gnoli 1989, p. 165.

[1869] For Kirdīr and a bibliography of the works on his inscriptions see Gignoux, Philippe, *Les quatres inscriptions du mage Kirdīr: textes et concordances*, vol. 9 of *Studia Iranica*, Fribourg-en-Brisgau, 1991c (Gignoux 1991c); and Malandra, W.W., 'Review of Gignoux's *Les quatres inscriptions du mage Kirdīr*', *Journal of the American Oriental Society* 113, (1993), pp. 288–289, review of Gignoux 1991c (Malandra 1993).

[1870] For the significance of Kirdīr's attempt at prominently displaying his inscriptions at venues intended for public consumption, see page 329 below.

[1871] Russell 1990a, p. 181. The text of the Kaʿba-i Zartusht (KKZ) inscription is the best preserved and was the last to be discovered in 1936. With some variations, the inscriptions seem to consist of identical texts. For an attempt at dating these, see Gignoux 1983; Gignoux 1991c, pp. 45–48, 53–73.

[1872] Duchesne-Guillemin 1983, p. 878.

[1873] Three kinds of fires have been distinguished during the Sasanian period: the *Ātakhsh Warahrān* (Bahrām fires), a general category called *Ātakhsh* without particularization, and a third kind named *ʾtwrlwk*. These are thought to resemble the categories of fires still existing among the Parsis in

who held the doctrines of the demons" over to "the worship of gods." He speaks of destroying images, which are the adversary of the Bahrām fires, and establishing in their stead said fires.[1874] As Boyce points out, however, the Sasanian campaign of active iconoclasm was long drawn out. For "cases involving the removal of statues still occur in the *sixth-century* law book, the *Mādigān-i Hazār Dādestān*."[1875] As for dev-worship, even Boyce admits that it appears "in fact to have persisted in certain remote regions (notably mountainous parts of Sogdia) down to the time of the Islamic conquest." One, therefore, is not entitled, argues Boyce, to infer from the evidence that "the early Sasanians succeeded all at once in sweeping an Aegean stable clean."[1876]

Besides subduing sectarians, Kirdīr also boasts of persecuting members of minority religions such as the "Jews, Buddhists and Brahmans and Aramaic and Greek-speaking Christians and Baptizers and Manicheans."[1877] Kirdīr's words resemble those of another high priest of the early Sasanian period, Tansar (Tosar), whose testimonies have come down to us in a redacted form in a sixth century document known as the *Letter of Tansar*.[1878] It has been cogently argued, however, that the generally held view of the Sasanians as the patrons of a systematizing and orthodox Zoroastrian church, the rigorous Sasanian political and religious propaganda, with its archaizing dimensions, in fact the very workings of this attempt at uniformity—as reflected for example in the testimonies of the high priest Kirdīr and the *Letter of Tansar*—are perhaps more a reflection of the uncertainty of the times and the Sasanian struggle with religio-political issues than a genuine reflection of the actual state of affairs. As Shaked observes, "[t]he violence unleashed from time to time against ... [Manicheism and Christianity] is proof enough of the feeling of insecurity on the part of the majority religion, and probably also of the fascination which these alternative modes of piety offered to many Zoroastrian believers."[1879]

India. The "word *ātaxš* appears ... to be largely interchangeable with its cognate *ādur*." Boyce, Mary, 'On the Sacred Fires of the Zoroastrians', *Bulletin of the School of Oriental and African Studies* 31(1), (1968), pp. 52–68 (Boyce 1968), pp. 58, 52–54, and 59 respectively. Boyce also maintains that "Wikander [Wikander, Stig, *Feuerpriester in Kleinasien und Iran*, Lund, 1946 (Wikander 1946), 104f.], may well be right in his contention that fire names with the element Ādur instead of Ātakhsh belong to an older tradition; but the *MHD* [i.e., the sixth-century law book, the *Mādigān-i Hazār Dādestān*] passages do not bear out his general thesis that there was an attempt in Sasanian times to avoid the use of Ādur and words compounded with it." Boyce 1968, p. 59, n. 48. The three fires of Ādhar Gushnasp, Ādhar Farnbagh, and Burzīn Mihr were all Bahrām fires. For these three fires, see respectively pages 362, 363, and 364 below, as well as Gyselen 2003.

[1874]Duchesne-Guillemin 1983, pp. 878–879.

[1875]The iconoclasm of the Sasanians, as Boyce points out, was only directed against the use of cult statues, "for they themselves continued to represent the *yazatas* of Zoroastrianism, including Ohrmozd, in anthropomorphic fashion." In fact, the iconography of the Arsacid period continued throughout the Sasanian reign. Boyce 1979, p. 107.

[1876]"Iran was too vast a country, and open to too many currents of belief, *for the state religion ever to obliterate all other creeds*." Boyce 1979, p. 115. Emphasis added.

[1877]Boyce 1992, p. 142.

[1878]See §2.5.2 for a more detailed discussion of the *Letter of Tansar*.

[1879]Shaked, Shaul, 'Quests and Visionary Journeys in Sasanian Iran', in Jan Assmann and Guy G.

The literary *topos* of a religious and philosophical quest, which was current during this period, provides an apt reflection of the times. In this literature the central and recurring motif is that of an individual who travels the world and observes the tenets of different faiths in search of wisdom and the ability to ascertain the truth behind the plurality of creeds. The *Dādistān i Mēnog Khrad*,[1880] the *Shkand Gumanīk Vizār*,[1881] the works of Mānī, and finally the autobiographical sketch by Bozorg-Mehr contained in the introduction to the Arabic *Kalīla wa Dimna*,[1882] all exhibit an acute awareness of the plurality of faiths, and the admission that no single faith can be considered to have a monopoly on the ultimate spiritual Truth.[1883] Another phenomenon examined by Shaked is the popular currency of undertaking an internal journey, a journey undertaken to the other world to obtain firm faith.[1884]

Kirdīr's journey to the hereafter

Perhaps the most extraordinary testimony to the uncertainty of the times in spiritual matters is contained in the work of the same figure whose purported endeavors to establish Zoroastrian orthodoxy have gained him infamy in Sasanian studies, namely the high priest Kirdīr. As Shaked observes, the contents of Kirdīr's journey, which appear on monuments placed on highways—and thus present personal reflections that are meant to serve a public aim—cannot be deciphered in detail, due to unfamiliar terminology as well as poor preservation. Nonetheless, they provide a fascinating clue to the doubt and anxiety felt about the hereafter by a figure who had achieved infamy as the persecutor of heterodoxy and minority faiths in the nascent Sasanian empire. In these inscriptions, Kirdīr is depicted undertaking a journey to the hereafter in order to bring back reports concerning Heaven and Hell. He is represented by a figure in his likeness and is accompanied by a woman, "probably representing his own self (an idea that in other texts is known by the term *Dēn*)."[1885] Along the way Kirdīr sees deadly persons in different scenes.[1886] While the details of Kirdīr's journey are not very clear, their intent seems obvious: the "inscriptions [reflect] the doubt and anxiety felt about the hereafter." The high Zoroastrian

Stroumsa (eds.), *Transformations of the Inner Self in Ancient Religions*, pp. 65–86, Leiden, 1999 (Shaked 1999), pp. 66–67.

1880 Menog 1884, *Dādistān i Mēnog Khrad*, vol. 24 of *Sacred Books of the East*, Oxford University Press, 1884, translated by E.H. West (Menog 1884).

1881 Vizar 1882, *Shkand Gumānīk Vizār*, vol. 18 of *Sacred Books of the East*, Oxford University Press, 1882, translated by E.W. West (Vizar 1882).

1882 Ibn al-Muqaffaʿ, ʿAbdullāh, *Kalīla wa Dimna*, Beirut, 1947, edited by P. Louis Cheiko (Ibn al-Muqaffaʿ 1947). For the possible identification of Bozorg-Mehr with the Kārinid Dādmihr, see page 114.

1883 Shaked 1999, p. 67–71. Boyce 1979, p. 136.

1884 See also Bausani 2000, pp. 26–27.

1885 This idea of having a twin is also attested in Manicheism where Mānī is said to have received his revelation from a spirit twin. It is not unique to Manicheism either for "men and gods all [were thought to have] had them." See Russell 1990a.

1886 Shaked 1999, pp. 72–73.

priest of the early Sasanian period "feels the need to achieve a vision of [the hereafter] through piety and good deeds and report what he has seen for the edification of his contemporaries and the following generations."[1887] Through the picture that is presented by Kirdīr, in fact, one can grasp the potential complexity of the religious scene during the Sasanian period, a complexity reflected in a religious panorama in which a variety of Zoroastrian religions are competing with Judaism, Christianity, Manicheism, not to mention Buddhism and various Gnostic sects. The currency of the idea of a spiritual journey during the period under consideration is also evidenced in the accounts on Mānī's experience, where this third century Mazdean heretic is said to have been "not only in contact with the spirit world in an intimate way; [but also] to have travelled there and taken others with him."[1888]

The prevalence of visionary journeys, however, was not confined to the early Sasanian period. The *Ardā Wīrāz Nāma* (*The Book of the Righteous Wīrāz*)[1889] exhibits a similar concern with the ability of select individuals to undertake a journey into the hereafter and view the invisible world, *mēnōg*.[1890] Only select individuals, after preparation—usually in the form of taking a dose of *mang* (hemp mixed with wine)—were able to undertake it. The journey was fraught with danger. After all, one journeyed to the realm of the dead and experienced temporary death as a result.[1891] It is important to note that, as Shaked observes, the "vision of [*mēnōg*] comes up again and again in Pahlavi literature." One striking feature of the Pahlavi and early Islamic literature is that they are in fact "practically obsessed with descriptions of visions of the hereafter. To the classical monument of visionary experience, the *Ardā Wīrāz Nāma*, one could add the opening chapters of the book of the *Spirit of Wisdom* [*Dādistān i Mēnog Khrad*] ... and visions of the Amahraspands [which] are alluded to quite frequently in the Pahlavi books, together with the discussion of the possibility of seeing [*mēnōg*], or the organ which is set aside for this kind of vision, the eye of the soul."[1892]

[1887] Shaked 1999, p. 73.

[1888] See Russell 1990a, p. 184, where he outlines the shamanistic nature of Kirdīr's voyage and argues for such a probability also in Mānī's case.

[1889] Arda Wiraz 1999, *Ardā Wīrāz Nāma*, Tehran, 1999, translated by Mihrdad Bahar (Arda Wiraz 1999).

[1890] Gignoux maintains that this "scene of piety troubled by religious uncertainty seems to be set some time after the fall of the Achaemenid empire; but the final redaction of the text probably refers to the early Islamic period." Gignoux, Philippe, 'Ardā Wīrāz', in Ehsan Yarshater (ed.), *Encyclopaedia Iranica*, pp. 356–357, New York, 1991a (Gignoux 1991a), p. 357.

[1891] For a further discussion of the *Ardā Wīrāz Nāma*, see §6.3.1.

[1892] Shaked 1994a, p. 46. It must be noted, however, that some controversy seems to exist as to whether or not one can consider Kirdīr's vision, as well as those in the *Ardā Wīrāz Nāma*, visionary experiences, a claim which apparently would imply shamanistic tendencies in Iranian religions. Opposition to this view is expressed by W. Malandra, who maintains that "the existence of anything like shamanism for ancient Iranian religions remains, at the very best, a weak hypothesis." Malandra 1993. Kirdīr, it has been maintained, "never really had a vision; instead matters concerning the fate of the departed are *reported* by mediums." See Gignoux 1991c, p. 289, and Skjærvø, O., 'Kirdir's Vision: Translation and Analysis', *Archälogische Mitteilungen aus Iran* 16, (1983), pp. 296–

Māni

> SUDDEN CHANGE IN
> MĀNI'S DOCTRINES

It is not incidental, in the framework of religious developments in this period, or as far as the religious history of Iran is concerned, that the same period during which the Sasanian priest Kirdīr was active, was also the heyday of the heretic Māni. Neither is it incidental that throughout the reign of Shāpūr I (241–272), both Kirdīr and Māni vied for the influence with the king, in one instance both accompanying him on his military expeditions. According to one tradition, Māni was not only present at the coronation of Shāpūr I in 241 CE, but also delivered his first speech on that occasion.[1893] During Shāpūr I's reign, Manicheans were given full liberty to proselytize, with Māni himself spending a "long time in the royal suite."[1894] Māni also made extensive missionary trips to the east.[1895] Colpe attributes Shāpūr I's support for Māni to the "preservation of an Iranian frame of doctrine" in his ideas, and his later persecution to a sudden change in his doctrines.[1896] Those who claim Zurvanism[1897] to have been a heretical Mazdean theology[1898] even consider the age of Shāpūr I to have been dominated by it. There is also anecdotal evidence that Shāpūr I "must obviously have been influenced by sorcerers or devil-worshippers."[1899]

Hormozd I's yearlong rule (272–273) saw Kirdīr's rise to power. His rank catapulted from that of *ērpat* (*herbad*), which "implies no superiority over subordinates," to that of *magupat* (*mōbad*), chief of the magi.[1900] On Hormozd I's coins, therefore, Ahūrā Mazdā takes the place of Mithra and Anāhitā. Kirdīr's control over state affairs had become such that, according to some, he was probably responsible for the accession of Bahrām I (273–276) to the throne instead of the elder brother of Hormozd I, Narseh (293–302). He seems to have enjoyed tremendous power at Bahrām I's court, so much so that the King "delivered Māni into his [i.e., Kirdīr's] hands. Māni died in prison and his religion was persecuted, which, according to one account, *proves both the strength*

---

306 (Skjærvø 1983). For the purposes of the present argument, however, whether or not Kirdīr's experiences were visionary are not as relevant as the reflections that they give of his preoccupation with the hereafter.

[1893] Zaehner 1972, p. 36.

[1894] Zaehner 1972, p. 36.

[1895] When the Manichean evangelizer Mar ʿAmmo was dispatched to the east to preach there, he had a "difficult interview with the local goddess who refused to let him in, saying *she had enough religions to deal with already* ... [So] the missionary prayed before the Sun for two days." Russell 1990a, p. 185.

[1896] Colpe, Carsten, 'Development of Religious Thought', in Ehsan Yarshater (ed.), *Cambridge History of Iran: The Seleucid, Parthian, and Sasanian Periods*, vol. 3(2), Cambridge University Press, 1983 (Colpe 1983). Māni's persecution and death on the orders of Bahrām I (273–276) coincided with the alleged consolidation of the Zoroastrian church by Kirdīr.

[1897] See §5.2.4.

[1898] Zaehner 1972, *passim*.

[1899] Zaehner 1972, pp. 34–36. Other deities also continued to be important during Shāpūr I's reign, like the cult of Anāhitā, over whose temple in Iṣṭakhr the reputed ancestor of the Sasanians, Sāsān, presided as a priest. Shāpūr I, for example, called his daughter and queen Ādur Anāhīd, "Fire ... Anāhīd ... a dvandva name, from the name of two deities." Ṭabarī 1999, p. 4, n. 10.

[1900] Duchesne-Guillemin 1983, p. 880.

of state religion and Kardēr's influence on the king of kings."[1901] It is significant, however, that this religious zealot of the early Sasanian period, who is said to have recklessly striven to "establish Zoroastrianism as a state religion at the expense of his opponent Mānī," while leaving numerous inscriptions "is not mentioned among the outstanding religious personalities such as Tōsar/Tansar (under Ardašīr I),[1902] Āturpāt/Ādurbād-ī Mahrspandān (under Šābuhr II),[1903] or Weh-Šābuhr (under Husraw I) in the late Middle Persian literature; ... even in Manichean literature he is barely alluded to, let alone named, which is strange for someone who apparently had Mānī sentenced to death under Wahrām I in 276 CE"[1904]

During the reign of Bahrām II (276–293), Kirdīr's influence reached its apex. His picture appears on the king's reliefs at Naqsh-i Rajab (KKRb), Sar Mashhad (KSM), Naqsh-i Rostam (KNRm), and possibly at Barm-i Delak, the last being Bahrām II's only investiture relief. A host of honorific titles, judge of the empire (*advēnpat*), master of rites, and finally ruler (*patikhāy*) of the fire of Anāhit-Ardashīr at Stakhr and of Lady Anahit, are bestowed on Kirdīr by the king.[1905] His power, at least of persuasion over the king, is said to have been such that for the first time since the advent of the Sasanians, the "all-important ecclesiastical title [of ruler of Anāhitā's temple] became detached from the royal power." In the inscriptions from the reigns of Bahrām II and Bahrām III (293), therefore, Kirdīr boasts, among other things, that through his efforts, the "affairs of Ohrmozd and the gods prospered; and the Mazdayasnian religion and the Magian hierarchy received great honor ... [that] Ahriman and the demons were struck down(?) and their teaching was expelled from the empire ... [that] Jews, Buddhists, Brahmans, two sorts of Christians [!], Manichees and *Zandiks*[1906] were chastised ... idols were destroyed and the dwellings of the demons undone(?) ... [and that finally] fires were established throughout the realm, and the Magians prospered."[1907]

For all Kirdīr's boastings, however, his claims to having subdued various

[1901] Emphasis mine. Duchesne-Guillemin 1983, p. 881. It has been argued, on the other hand, that even during Bahrām I's reign, Kirdīr had a much more humble position than hitherto presumed. For example, he still "had to follow the customary stages of appeal to get an audience with the king." Huyse, Philip, 'Kerdīr and the First Sasanians', in Nicolas Sims-Williams (ed.), *Societas Iranologica Europaea: Proceedings of the Third European Conference of Iranian Studies*, vol. I, Wiesbaden, 1999b (Huyse 1999b), pp. 117–118, n. 55, and pp. 110–120, and the references cited therein.

[1902] See §2.5.2.

[1903] See §5.2.3.

[1904] Huyse 1999b, pp. 109–110. Huyse also argues that while Shāpūr I's inscriptions were most probably set up sometime between 260 and 262, Kirdīr's inscriptions "were all written during the reign of Wahrām II (276–293), who is named in all four inscriptions." It seems likely, though not provable, therefore, Huyse argues, that all the inscriptions were set up toward the end of Bahrām II's life. All in all, a time gap of some thirty years between the engraving of Shāpūr I's (SKZ) and Kirdīr's inscriptions (KKZ) on the Kaʿba is quite "within the bounds of probability." Ibid., p. 112.

[1905] Duchesne-Guillemin 1983, p. 882.

[1906] See §5.2.5.

[1907] Zaehner 1972, p. 24, nn. 1–2. Also see Duchesne-Guillemin 1983, p. 882.

heresies bear witness in fact to the prevalence of these heresies during the third century. The spiritual panorama that they compose, furthermore, is as multifaceted as that which the Sasanians had inherited from the post-Avestan age. More than three-quarters of a century had passed since the inception of Sasanian power. Yet if the inscriptions of Kirdīr are any reflection of reality—they were, after all, cast in stone—the impression they give is that of a continuing heterogeneous religious landscape.

As we have seen, the only doctrine of faith that is actually reflected in Kirdīr's inscriptions at Sar Mashhad (KSM) and Naqsh-i Rajab (KKRb), is the belief in the hereafter.[1908] It has been aptly observed that "this does not go very far to define Kardēr's position in relation to heresy."[1909] Significantly, since Kirdīr expresses himself "only in Middle-Persian, the language of Persis, not as the kings of the 3rd century, in Parthian, Middle Persian, and Greek," he might have been promoting the religious tradition of Persīs over that of Shīz in Azarbāyjān.[1910] After two decades of presumed monarchical-clerical cooperation, through the reigns of Hormozd I (272–273), Bahrām I (273–276), and Bahrām II (276–293), however, Narseh (293–302) comes to power, and we witness, once again, the emergence of the old gods. During his struggle for power under Bahrām II, Narseh concentrated on reverting to the tradition of the first Sasanians. His investiture relief at Naqsh-i Rostam features once again the goddess Anāhitā. In an inscription that he left at Paikuli (NPi) in Kurdistān, Narseh, who had gained the support of the cities in Mesopotamia for whom Kirdīr's theocracy must not have been a welcome episode, claims to rule "in the name of Ohrmazd, *of all the gods* and of the Lady Anāhitā."[1911] He reclaims, moreover, the title of the chief of the Stakhr temple which had remained within the Sasanian family from Bābak's time until Bahrām II had bestowed it on Kirdīr. Thus all "the temporal and spiritual power was again to be concentrated in the king's hand."[1912] Narseh destroyed the recently acquired influence of the clergy over the monarchy in other ways too. He re-established contact with the Manicheans, giving an audience to their leader, Innaios, in consequence of which the persecution of the creed was suspended during his reign.[1913] According to the *Chronique de Seert*, Christians too fared rather well under Narseh.

His inscriptions, furthermore, "name *Parthian* as well as Persian nobles among his supporters, thus illustrating the drawing together of the two imperial peoples, begun under his father Shabuhr I."[1914] In short, for all the talk about the concerted effort of the clergy to gain control of the monarchy, and the *Letter*

[1908]See page 329.

[1909]Duchesne-Guillemin 1983, p. 883.

[1910]This is the belief of Lukonin and there is a high probability that this was in fact the case. But as Duchesne–Guillemin observes, quite correctly, it still does not allow us to decipher the contents of Kirdīr's orthodoxy. Duchesne-Guillemin 1983, p. 883.

[1911]Duchesne-Guillemin 1983, p. 884. Emphasis added.

[1912]Duchesne-Guillemin 1983, p. 885.

[1913]Duchesne-Guillemin 1983, p. 885.

[1914]Boyce 1979, p. 116.

of Tansar's claims of monarchical–clerical cooperation, for the first century of Sasanian rule, the claim can only be maintained for the period 272–293 CE, that is through the combined reigns of Hormozd I, Bahrām I, and Bahrām II. During the short rule of Hormozd II (302–309), the persecution of the Manicheans recommenced and the Mazdean clergy came back into favor, although the king did not "molest the Christians."[1915] And as Hormozd II was invested by Mihr, one might suspect that the primacy of Ahūrā Mazdā was once again questioned by this Sasanian king.[1916]

5.2.3 Āturpāt

Religious life during the long reign of Shāpūr II (309–379) is dominated by the figure of Aturpāt, son of Mahraspand, with whose help the king is said to have taken further steps to consolidate the Mazdean creed. During his reign, for example, a council, presumably under the leadership of Āturpāt, undertook the task of establishing a definitive text of the Avestā in twenty-one *nasks*. In order to establish their veracity, Āturpāt underwent the ordeal of molten metal[1917] and thereby defeated, yet again, all kinds of sectarians and heretics. But the religious landscape of Shāpūr II's kingdom, through most of the fourth century, remained as heterogeneous as ever. The king reportedly introduced himself to emperor Constantius (337–361) as "partners with the stars, brother of the Sun and Moon." In his *Acts of Pusai*, the martyr Pusai[1918] gives evidence of the Zurvanite tendencies in the belief of the Magi.[1919] The king also rekindled the dynasty's ties with the local cult at Stakhr by founding a fire to Anāhitā.[1920] Some scholars even date the initial appearance of the Mazdakite heresy to this period. Presumably, it was partly in opposition to this heresy that Āturpāt underwent his ordeal of fire, and the first attempts at a definition of an orthodox creed were undertaken.[1921] Shāpūr II's reign marks one of the worst episodes

[1915]For the Christians during the Sasanian period, see §5.2.8 below.

[1916]Duchesne-Guillemin 1983, p. 885.

[1917]For the ordeal by fire, see page 356ff.

[1918]*The Acts of Mar Pusai and his Daughter Martha* contains two of the earliest hagiographies of Christian Persians, composed in the late fourth, early fifth centuries. Pusai was a descendant of Roman captives who were settled in Fārs under Shāpūr II. Living "peacefully as a Christian under Sasanian rule," Pusai married a local woman, "taught her, baptized his children and raised and instructed them in Christianity." Together with his family, and following Shāpūr II's orders, he was later moved to Karka de Lēdān, "the new royal foundation fifteen kilometers north of Susa on the Karkeh river." While achieving great honors in his new city, where he was appointed "head of the royal weavers' guild, Pusai ultimately achieved martyrdom when he refused to betray the religion of his parents when interrogated by the chief *mobad*." Walker, Joel Thomas, *The Legend of Mar Qardagh: Narrative and Christian Heroism in Late Antique Iraq*, University of California Press, 2006 (Walker 2006), pp. 222–224. Also see Wiesehöfer, Josef, *Ancient Persia: from 550 BC to 650 AD*, London, 1996 (Wiesehöfer 1996), pp. 192–193.

[1919]For Zurvanism, see §5.2.4 below.

[1920]Duchesne-Guillemin 1983, p. 886.

[1921]For a discussion of this history, as well as a critical survey of the sources at our disposal for the study of the Mazdakite movement, see Yarshater, Ehsan, 'Mazdak', in Ehsan Yarshater (ed.), *Cambridge History of Iran: The Seleucid, Parthian, and Sasanian Periods*, vol. 3(2), pp. 991–1027,

of persecution of Christians, especially in the northwest. But then his reign also coincided with the Byzantine emperor Constantine's official recognition of Christianity. Sasanian scholars are almost unanimous, therefore, in connecting the two phenomena and in highlighting the purely political motives behind this attack on the Christian population of the empire, whom the Sasanians feared might form a fifth column in their domains. In spite of his horrific persecution of Christians, Syrian hagiographers tell us that Shāpūr II was nevertheless personally interested in Christianity.[1922]

During Ardashir II's reign (379–383), Persian ceased to be the sole language of the reliefs and inscriptions. This development, it has been argued, betrays the fact that the tradition of Persīs was no longer considered the dominant tradition in the self-definition of the monarchy, which now sought to distance itself from the traditions of the Persian clergy. The god Mihr appeared on the investiture relief of the king standing on a lotus. This factor might indicate a further token of independence from the traditions of the Persian clergy.[1923]

The role that Yazdgird I (399–420) played in the religious affairs of the Sasanian polity is forever inscribed in his posthumous epithet of the Sinner, coined, most likely, not only by the clergy, but also by the Pahlav dynasts, as we have seen.[1924] Yazdgird I "had a good reputation with the Christians, ... [was] kind to the Jews" and married a Jewess.[1925] Together with Pīrūz (459–484), he was one of the first Sasanian kings to adopt the title *Kai*, thus connecting the Sasanian dynasty to the mythical Kayānids.[1926] The Kayānids were "extolled in the *yašts* of the Avesta." It has been argued, consequently, that Pīrūz's concoction of a Kayānid ancestry also had a religious significance, and that after him, the importance of this part of the Avestā was emphasized, or even that the Avestā came to be recognized as the sacred text during this period.[1927]

In sum, despite the prevalent paradigm in Sasanian studies of an orthodox creed and the church-state confederacy, the available evidence points to a far more volatile and heterogeneous religious climate. Through the fifth century, neither the monarchy nor the Mazdean clergy were able—even if they were so inclined—to impose a uniform orthodoxy. Nowhere is this borne out more clearly than in the socioreligious turmoil that engulfed the Sasanian realm by the late fifth century and well into the first half of the sixth century:

Cambridge University Press, 1983c (Yarshater 1983c), p. 996. See also §5.2.7 below.

[1922] See also §5.2.8.

[1923] The lotus is said to have been a solar symbol imported from Egypt either directly or via Buddhist Gandhara. Duchesne-Guillemin 1983, pp. 888–889.

[1924] See §2.2.2.

[1925] For this and other religious developments during the fifth century, see Duchesne-Guillemin 1983, p. 890.

[1926] For the Kayānids, see footnote 131; for the Kayānid pseudo-genealogy, see page 385.

[1927] This is the thesis of Wikander 1946, with which Duchesne-Guillemin disagrees. Duchesne-Guillemin 1983, p. 892. Once we have established the appropriate context, we will further discuss Pīrūz's religious policies on page 385ff.

the Mazdakite heresy.[1928] It has been argued, in fact, that when Khusrow I (531–579) continued the persecution started by his father, Qubād (488–531), "the Mazdakite upheaval happened to prepare, in a kind of *argumentum ad absurdum*, the advent of a *strong state and of a definitively established Mazdean Church*."[1929] The evidence in the *Dēnkard*, which is thought to be contemporaneous with Khusrow I's rule, together with that of the Sasanian Law Book *Mādigān-i Hazār Dādestān*, in fact, substantiates this: "His present majesty, King of Kings, Khusrow I, son of Kavād, after he had put down irreligion and heresy with the greatest vindictiveness according to the revelation of the Religion in the matter of all heresy, greatly strengthened the system of the four castes and encouraged precise argumentation, and in a diet [i.e., council] of the provinces he issued the following declaration: The truth of the Mazdayasnian religion has been recognized ... What the chief Magians of Ohrmozd have proclaimed, do we proclaim ... with high intent and in concert with the perspicacious, most noble, most honorable, most good Magian men, we do hereby decree that the Avesta and Zand be studied most zealously and ever afresh." And further that: "One was to eradicate the teachings and practices of heretics from the realm of Iran by defeating them utterly; one, to put into practice the teachings of the word of Religion ... in accordance with the teachings and practices of the disciples of Āturpāt, son of Mahraspand, who came from the province of Makrān; *one, not to neglect in the provinces of Iran hospitality to holy men*, the good care of beneficent fire, and the purification of the good waters; one, to cause religion and learning to prosper by being exceedingly zealous ... to propagate it widely ... and jealously to withhold it from evil heretics; one, *to increase in full measure the service and rites of the gods within the provinces of Iran and to smite, smash, and overthrow the idol-temples and disobedience [i.e., unorthodoxy] that comes from the Adversary and the demons*."[1930] What is remarkable here is that for all the talk of monarchical–clerical cooperation in articulating an orthodoxy in prior centuries, neither the monarchy nor the clergy had been able to eradicate heterodoxies as late as Khusrow I's reign. Other evidence from the *Dēnkard* further erodes the image of Khusrow I as the enforcer of a strict orthodoxy. Khusrow I "was not impervious to Greek and Indian influences," so that, ironically, his reign has been described as both orthodox and liberal.[1931]

[1928]For a further discussion of the Mazdakites, see §5.2.7 below.

[1929]Duchesne-Guillemin 1983, p. 893. Emphasis mine. According to Gardīzī, after the destruction of the Mazdakites, Khusrow I Nowshīrvān told the populace to learn the precepts of religion so that they would become experts in it and when a Mazdakite appears, he could not sell his lies to them. Gardīzī 1984, p. 84:

پس اهل مملکت را بفرمود که: دین اموزید، و کار دین را بپردازید تا اندر شناختن و دانستن دین ماهر گردید تا چون مزدکیی بیرون اید مخرقه خویش بر شما روا نتواند کرد.

[1930]Dadestan 1993, *Mādigān-i Hazār Dādestān*, Rechtskasuistik und Gerichtspraxis zu Beginn des siebenten Jahrhunderts in Iran, Wiesbaden, 1993, translated by M. Macuch (Dadestan 1993); as cited in Duchesne-Guillemin 1983, p. 895. Emphasis added.

[1931]Dadestan 1993 apud Duchesne-Guillemin 1983, pp. 894–895.

What is even more significant, however, is that whatever measures Khusrow I might have undertaken in support of a presumed orthodoxy and in cooperation with the clerical classes, these were reversed under his son, Hormozd IV (579–590), who "did not govern with the support of the noblemen and the Magi."[1932] Hormozd IV married a Christian woman and prayed to the martyr St. Sergius, so that he was suspected of converting to Christianity. He superstitiously wore an amulet against death, and put an inordinate emphasis on astrology. By the time of Khusrow II Parvīz (591–628), as a result, any remnants of an orthodox predisposition on the part of the monarchy, whatever their strength, must have been completely obliterated. The unsettled conditions of Iran after the death of Khusrow II Parvīz, when in the span of about four years about eight different monarchs came to the throne either consecutively, or simultaneously,[1933] undermined any effort at a concerted religious policy on the part of the feeble Sasanian monarchs of the period. In short, as Gnoli argues, "Zoroastrianism never succeeded in imposing a spiritual supremacy that was not almost always challenged and in some periods turned out to be downright feeble."[1934]

All this is not to say that the monarchy did not attempt to control the clergy, or that both were not preoccupied with establishing a definition of orthodoxy and heresy. To the contrary, in theory at least, the Sasanian monarchs gave themselves the prerogative of controlling the religious affairs of their realm as a matter of policy.[1935] We have evidence of attempts at delineating the religious posture of an heretic. The Avestā itself testifies to the existence of various kinds of Zoroastrian heresies. The *Hōm Yasht* (Yasht 20), for example, defines an *aṣ̌əmaōγa* as "he who has the words of this religion in his memory, but does not observe them in actions."[1936] In the *Dēnkard*, an *ahlamōγ ī nask ōšmurd* is defined as a "heretic who acknowledges the Nasks of the Avesta." An *ahlamōγ ī frēftār*, the worst heretic, is defined as one "who distorts a precept as it has been taught by the ancient teachers through interpretation."[1937] Late Middle Persian literature strove to depict the early Sasanians as champions of an orthodox faith. According to the *Dēnkard*, for example, Ardashīr I "through the just authority

[1932]Hormozd IV is also accused of having closed the Jewish academies at Susa and Pumbadita. Labourt, J., *Le Christianisme dans l'empire Perse sous la dynastie Sassanide*, Paris, 1897 (Labourt 1897), p. 200ff, as quoted in Duchesne-Guillemin 1983, p. 896.

[1933]See Chapter 3, especially §3.3.

[1934]Gnoli 1989, p. 172.

[1935]Gnoli 1989, p. 170.

[1936]Hom Yasht 1880, *Hōm Yasht*, vol. 5 of *Sacred Books of the East*, Oxford University Press, 1880, translated by L.H. Mills (Hom Yasht 1880), §31.

[1937]Dinkard 1911, 428.9–10, 567.19–21; Shaki, Mansour, 'The Social Doctrine of Mazdak in Light of Middle Persian Evidence', *Archív Orientální* 46, (1978), pp. 289–306 (Shaki 1978), p. 298. As Molè noted, "l'*ahramōkīh* s'opposait à la *pōryōtkēšīh*; leur opposition est fondée sur une exégèse différente de la tradition. Dans le texte du troisième livre du *Dēnkart* nous voyons un *ahramōk* rejeter les écrits des disciples de Zoroastre, mais reconnaître les Gāthās comme révélation divine: aucune doute n'est permis, cet *ahramōk* est un hérétique zoroastrien ou un zoroastrien hérétique." Molè, M., 'Le problème des sectes Zoroastriennes dans les livres Pehlevis', *Oriens* 13-14, (1961), pp. 1–28 (Molè 1961), pp. 14–15.

of Tōsar [i.e., Tansar] commanded that all the scattered teachings [preserved in the provinces on the Arsacid Vologeses' order] to be brought to court. Tōsar set about his business and he accepted one [of those teachings] and left the rest out of the canon, and he issued this decree: the interpretation of all the teachings from the Mazdayasnian religion is our responsibility; from now on there is no lack of certain knowledge concerning them."[1938] The preoccupation with the interpretation of the sacred text, which Tansar claimed as the prerogative of his class and evidently the monarchy, remained one of the cornerstones of the efforts of both parties in controlling the eruption of heresy.

Neither does the aforementioned account intend to downplay the power of the clergy over their flock, or their desire to control the lives of their constituency.[1939] That in spite of all their efforts, neither the state nor the church was thoroughly successful in either of their agendas, however, is again brought out by the Manichean and Mazdakite heresies—the former of which erupted in the third century and continued to menace the Sasanians throughout their later history, and the latter of which started, by some counts, during this same period, but reached its height during the first half of the sixth century. Hindsight, therefore, bears witness that the hold of neither the church nor the monarchy over the population seems to have been so tenacious as to prevent the development of heresy.

But beyond the observation that both church and state were at times preoccupied with leashing heresy—an observation that is neither here nor there, for it does not elucidate the doctrinal aspects of an orthodox creed, nor its social praxis—there is no consensus on popular religious practice within the Sasanian realm. The problem seems to be endemic to the study of Zoroastrianism during the Sasanian period, and has to do with the nature of the sources at our disposal. The contemporary evidence comes mostly from foreign sources, often hostile, usually witness only to conditions in the western parts of the empire, or among the elite with whom the authors of these sources came into contact. They are rarely concerned with the finer doctrinal issues of the creed. The indigenous information, the Middle Persian sources, on the other hand, are, at best, mostly late Sasanian, but generally composed in the ninth and tenth centuries CE. The evidence of the two types of sources cannot be reconciled. What the Middle Persian sources portray as the orthodox creed would make the evidence of the foreign sources tantamount to heresy. The problem is compounded by the fact that both types of sources give only incidental information about popular forms of religiosity.[1940]

[1938] Dinkard 1911, p. 412, II. 12ff, as quoted in Duchesne-Guillemin 1983, p. 877.

[1939] Ełishē, for example, whose ecclesiastical perspective, whence extreme partiality, needs to be kept in mind, notes that the Sasanians "governed their empire by the religion of the magi and *frequently fought against those who would not submit to the same religion; beginning from the years of king Arshak [423–428], son of Tiran, they waged war up to the sixth year of Artashēs, king of Armenia, the son of Vramshapuh.*" As is clear the point of reference here for Ełishē is the non-Iranian religions of the realm or in the regions under Sasanian suzerainty. Ełishē 1982, p. 60.

[1940] See also our discussion on Arabic sources in this context in §6.2.2 below.

5.2.4 Zurvanism

At best only "two major sectarian movements"[1941] have been acknowledged for the duration of Sasanian history, the Zurvanites and the Mazdakites, relegating to the background "various nameless minor movements [that] have been detected within the Middle Persian literature."[1942] Zurvanism, the origins of which have been traced back to the late Achaemenid and the post-Avestan period, has been defined as a monism that was very much influenced by the Mesopotamian and Greek creation myths. A deep doctrinal gulf, it has been argued, separated the Zurvanists from the orthodox Mazdayasnian creed.[1943] The Zurvanite myth of creation postulated "a single eternal Being, the Mainyu of Time (Avestan Zurvān), who begot both Ahūra Mazdā, and Angra Mainyu, that is both good and evil."[1944] The Middle Persian sources, on the other hand, depict a dualistic system of belief in which Zurvan can barely be perceived.[1945] So how did the Sasanians deal with this presumed heresy? For all the contention that the "lucid and comprehensive doctrines taught by Zoroaster left little scope for heresy and schism," one of the foremost authorities in Zoroastrian studies has argued that the orthodoxy promulgated by the Sasanians throughout their reign was in fact the Zurvanite heresy. Indeed, Boyce continues, "ironically,

[1941]Boyce 1992, p. 142.

[1942]Boyce 1992, p. 142.

[1943]An aspect of the doctrinal gulf that Boyce refers to involved the positions that the orthodox Zoroastrians and the Zurvanites maintained on freewill versus pre-destination. In orthodox Zoroastrian cosmogony, Ahūrā Mazdā effected creation in two stages. In the first stage, all creation was brought about in a spiritual and immaterial state, the *mēnōg* state. In the second stage, these acquire a material or *gītīg* existence. These two stages of creation constitute the Act of Creation, the *Bundahishn*. This first Age of the drama of cosmic history is eventually followed by two other periods. The attack of Ahrīman with his conglomerate of evil forces inaugurates the second Age, the period of Mixture (Middle Persian *Gumezishn*). During this second Age this "world is no longer wholly good, but is a blend of good and evil." In this second Age, man needs to make a conscious choice of joining the holy alliance of Ahūrā Mazdā, the six Amahraspands, the beneficent Yazatas, the lesser two of the Ahūrās, and the Sun and the Moon—who through their functions maintain the *asha*—in order to combat the forces of evil. Free Will on the part of the mankind, therefore, is one of the crucial ingredients of the Age of *Gumezishn*. Through Free Will man implicates himself in the progression of cosmic history, whereby gradually the forces of evil will be overcome, restoring the world to its original perfect state. The third glorious Age, the Frashokereti (Middle Persian Frashegird, meaning probably Healing or Renovation) will thereafter be inaugurated. "Therewith history [as we know it] will cease, for the third [Age], that of Separation [Middle Persian *Wizarishn*] will be ushered in." Boyce 1992, pp. 25–26. As opposed to this presumably orthodox myth of creation and cosmic history, the Zurvanite cosmogony holds that a man's role is predestined. In Zurvanite cosmogony, influenced by the Babylonian conceptions of cyclical history, history is divided into great recurrent cycles of time, within which all events repeated themselves. Zurvān, Time, begets both Ahūrā Mazdā and Angra Mainyu. In a later articulation of this myth, Zurvān alone had "always been, and shall be forever more." According to Boyce, the Zurvanite "preoccupation with fate, and the inexorable decrees of Time, obscured the basic Zoroastrian doctrine of the existence of free-will, and the power of each individual to shape his own destiny through the exercise of choice." Boyce 1979, pp. 68–69.

[1944]Boyce 1992, p. 142.

[1945]Duchesne-Guillemin, J., 'Notes on Zervanism in the Light of Zaehner's *Zurvan*', *Journal of Near Eastern Studies* 15(2), (1956), pp. 108–112 (Duchesne-Guillemin 1956), p. 108.

for a dynasty regularly presented as the first creators and defenders of Zoroastrian orthodoxy ... the Sasanians actually weakened the faith through giving prominence to their own Zurvanite beliefs."[1946] The thesis that the Sasanians were actually Zurvanites, also espoused by Arthur Christensen, later came to be further fine tuned in the seminal work of Zaehner, aptly recognizing the continued frustration of the field in its title, *Zurvan: A Zoroastrian Dilemma*.[1947] Zaehner's work paved the "*royal* highway to the solution of the riddle."[1948] The Zurvanites, considered heretical by Zaehner, moved like a pendulum, affected by the pulsation and relaxation of the Mazdean orthodoxy. While Shāpūr I (241–272) eased the implementation of an orthodox creed, during the career of Kirdīr and Shāpūr II (309–379), orthodoxy reasserted itself to the detriment of the Zurvanite creed. The tolerance of Yazdgird I (399–420) led to the bigotry of his successor Yazdgird II (438–457), and while the Mazdakites and the Zurvanites ran riot under Qubād (488–531), Khusrow I (531–579) tightened the grip of orthodoxy. Too many currents were at play during the rule of Khusrow II (591–628), overwhelming the orthodoxy.[1949] It was in the intermittent periods that Zurvanism had liberty to take the field.

Recently, however, Shaked has questioned whether Zurvanism was a heresy at all, or simply a theological doctrine that adopted one of the numerous creation myths in circulation during the Sasanian period. He argued that the "ideas of Time existing at the basis of the cosmos and even at the roots of the division into good and evil were known and current in Zoroastrianism, with Time sometimes being supplemented by the notion of Space or Place." These ideas, according to Shaked, while theoretically akin to Zurvanism, apparently were never considered heretical by Zoroastrian orthodoxy, for "we find them in Zoroastrian writings without a hint of reservation."[1950] The Zurvanites, argues Shaked, were never considered heretical simply because "the adherents of Zurvān as supreme god were simply Zoroastrians."[1951] Shaked's contribution not only argues for the fluidity of Zoroastrian thought during the Sasanian period but also touches upon notions of heresy versus orthodoxy in Sasanian society. The distinction has to do with the disparity that existed between a learned, theologically oriented Zoroastrianism and the popular versions of the

[1946] Boyce 1979, p. 117.

[1947] Zaehner 1972. This path had already been paved in von Wesendok, O.G., *Das Wesen der Lehrer Zarathustras*, Leipzig, 1927 (von Wesendok 1927). For an overview of the scholarship on Zurvanism see Duchesne-Guillemin 1956, pp. 108–109; Boyce, Mary, 'Some Reflections on Zurvanism', *Bulletin of the School of Oriental and African Studies* 19(2), (1957b), pp. 304–316 (Boyce 1957b); Frye, Richard N., 'Zurvanism Again', *Harvard Theological Review* II(2), (1959), pp. 63–73 (Frye 1959).

[1948] Duchesne-Guillemin 1956, p. 108.

[1949] Frye 1959, p. 63.

[1950] On the other hand, Shaked argues, "the myth of Zurvān, in its straightforward formulation (as opposed to the philosophical ideas about the special position of Time and Space), is never found in Iranian sources." Shaked, Shaul, 'The Myth of Zurvan: Cosmogony and Eschatology', in *Messiah and Christos: Studies in the Jewish Origins of Christianity Presented to David Flusser*, vol. 32 of *Texte und Studien zum Antiken Judentum*, pp. 219–240, Tübingen, 1992 (Shaked 1992), p. 231.

[1951] Shaked 1992, pp. 230–231.

faith, practiced, in one form or another, by the majority of its adherents. But how did this theologically defined articulation of faith—whatever its nature—protect itself vis-à-vis the potential outbursts of heresy? The crux of the matter had to do with limiting access and knowledge of the *Zand*, that is to say, the interpretation of the Avesta.

5.2.5 Zandīks

Except for the most crucial and threatening varieties of heretical movements, such as those of the Manicheans and the Mazdakites, the nature of the many heresies in the Sasanian period is lost to us. That other heresies did exist during this period, however, is amply demonstrated by the obsession of the orthodox Zoroastrian articulations of faith with matters of heresy.[1952] While by the Sasanian period Zoroastrianism addressed itself to all mankind, insisted on its universalistic tendencies, and engaged in an active proselytizing effort in its competition with other, similarly inclined religious movements, one cannot totally deny the existence of a "secret element in the Zoroastrian religion"[1953] of the period. The propagation and, for that matter, procurement of religious knowledge during this period was based on a hierarchy of classes or grades of people—which, incidentally, did not correspond to the strict Sasanian social hierarchy.

The teaching of the *Zand* in particular seems to have been actively restricted by the Zoroastrian hierarchy, for *Zand*, that is to say, "the interpretation of the Holy Scriptures, was considered to be the main tool of heretics."[1954] The main articulation of this is found in Masʿūdī, who maintains that "if anyone came forth in their religion with something that contradicted the revealed message, which is the Avesta, and deviated toward the interpretation, which is the *Zand*, they [the Persians] would say: 'He is a *Zandi*'."[1955] Masʿūdī, in turn, must have been very faithful to the sources at his disposal for the *Dēnkard* states the matter quite explicitly: "This, too, thus: One ought not to speak, do, or arrange the business of *Zand* differently from what the original orthodox [spoke,] did, taught and brought forth. *For heresy comes to the world by one who teaches, speaks or does the business of Zand differently from what the orthodox spoke, did, taught and brought forth.*"[1956] The *Dēnkard* continues to warn of the dangers of heresy and of learning the Avestā and *Zand* from wicked people. Its advice to the flock it sought to control was to beware of following a heretic: "not to hear and not to seek from him the instruction of Avesta and *Zand*."[1957] So closely associated

[1952] See also our discussion of heretics on page 337.

[1953] Shaked, Shaul, 'Esoteric Trends in Zoroastrianism', in *Proceedings of the Israeli Academy of Sciences and Humanities*, vol. 3, pp. 175–221, 1969 (Shaked 1969), quoted in Shaked, Shaul, *From Zoroastrian Iran to Islam: Studies in Religious History and Intercultural Contacts*, Aldershot, 1995 (Shaked 1995), pp. 176–177; Molè 1961, pp. 11, 13–14.

[1954] Shaked 1969, p. 189.

[1955] Masʿūdī 1869, vol. 2, pp. 167–168, Masʿūdī 1968, p. 275, also cited in Shaked 1969, p. 188.

[1956] Shaked 1969, p. 189, n. 38. Emphasis added.

[1957] Shaked 1969, p. 190, n. 40.

had the definition of heresy become with the interpretation of the *Zand*, in fact, that *zandīk* became a synonym for heretic. That in fact knowledge of the scriptures was strictly limited to the learned classes, and the masses were oblivious to their meaning is also stated by Niẓām al-Mulk in his *Siyasat Nāma*: when Mazdak was forced to defend his doctrines during his inquisition, he reasoned that it was Zoroaster who had instructed in this way. He argued, furthermore, that "in the Zand and Avesta it stands such as I say, *but the people do not know its meaning.*"[1958] As Shaki observes, there were very tangible reasons for this elitist monopoly of scripture: The "Avestan language had long before Mazdak become laden with ambiguities and obscurities admitting of sundry interpretations."[1959] Shaked therefore argued that "the notion of a hierarchy of religious truths, which existed in the Pahlavi literature, was associated with the notion of the religious hierarchy of the believers in the religion, and that these two hierarchies had some relationship to the *division of the Zoroastrian community into folk religion, on the one side, and a more sophisticated type of religion, developed by the learned, on the other.*"[1960]

5.2.6 Circle of Justice

It is true that the elite–folk dichotomy in the Zoroastrian community did not have an equivalent class basis in that the kings and feudal nobility, not being trained theologians, were as prone to adopting popular forms of religiosity as the masses and the population at large. It is also true, however, that the actual provenance of heresy was thought to have been among the peasantry and the lower strata of Sasanian society. This is clearly reflected in the full-blown articulation of the Circle of Justice, which formulated a very contingent notion of legitimate rule: if the very foundation of the state and the defense of the realm were dependent on the prosperity of the kingdom, which itself could have been achieved only through equitable taxation and the justice meted out to the peasantry, then any injustices inflicted upon the peasantry, in theory at least, gave cause for rebellion and robbed the monarchy of the very basis of its legitimacy. In the Pishdadi section of the national history,[1961] the bilateral dimension of the Circle of Justice and the role of the king in the replenishment of the kingdom are first articulated. In Thaʿālibī's narrative on the mythical king Manūchihr, for example, this dimension of kingship is clearly articulated in the following terms: "The King has a *right* vis-à-vis his subjects and the subjects have *rights* vis-à-vis the king. The populace are obliged toward the king in that they must follow him, and in that they must not desist in giving him advice, that they should be friends to his friends and enemies to his enemies. The king [on the other hand,] has the obligation of caring for his flock, of having their interests in

[1958] Niẓām al-Mulk, *Siyāsat Nāma*, Tehran, 1941, edited by Abbas Iqbal (Niẓām al-Mulk 1941), p. 238; see also Shaki 1978, p. 299.

[1959] Shaki 1978, p. 299.

[1960] Shaked 1969, p. 200. Emphasis added.

[1961] See footnote 131.

mind, and of not demanding from them that which is beyond their capabilities. And if there should appear heavenly or earthly calamities as a result of which their produce and wealth dwindle, the [king] is [obliged] to forego taxation in proportion to the damage."[1962]

The Sasanians were well aware that their conception of justice was a double-edged sword. This is reflected in no uncertain terms in the *Testament of Ardashīr*: "Know that the decay of dynasties begins by [the king] neglecting the subjects without [setting them to do] known works and recognized labours. If unemployment becomes rampant among people, there is produced from it consideration of [various] matters and thought about fundamentals. When they consider this, they consider it with different natures, and as a result their schools of thought become different. From the differences of their schools there is produced enmity and hatred [of each other] among them, while they are united in disliking the kings."[1963] While the *Testament of Ardashīr* has often been quoted for its articulation of Sasanian theory of government and the maxim that kingship and religion are twin brothers, however, the fact that it also contains a blueprint and a scenario for conditions conducive to sedition and heresy has seldom been highlighted. The above passage clearly articulates that sedition acquires an ideological dimension by coalescing into a school of thought. What causes this sedition and leads to the formation of various schools of thought is the king's neglect of his subjects and the implementation of measures whereby unemployment becomes rampant. Turning the maxim of the Circle of Justice on its head, therefore, and given the king's failure to maintain his contract with his subjects, the masses could rebel. The ideology of the Circle of Justice, then, by definition, gave cause for questioning the very legitimacy of the state if it became dysfunctional, and the Sasanians realized this.[1964]

In the Iranian context, the most acute forms of sedition and rebellion are often articulated in the garb of religious heresy among the lower strata of the population. The *Testament of Ardashīr* points out the social sectors which were most susceptible to heretical tendencies, namely, the oppressed lower classes: "The main thing of which I [i.e., Ardashīr I] fear for your [i.e., guardians of religion's] sakes is that the low people should rush and outdo you in the study of religion, in its interpretation and becoming expert in it ... [As a result] there would emerge secret chieftainships among the low people, the peasants and the rabble that you have harassed, tyrannized, deprived, terrorized and belittled. Know that there can never be in one kingdom both a secret chief in religion

[1962] Balʿamī 1959, pp. 37–38; Thaʿālibī 1989, p. 50, Thaʿālibī 1900, p. 67:

و منها انّ للملك على اهل مملكته حقا و انّ لهم عليه حقا. و حق الملك على رعيته انّ يطيعوه و يناصحوه و يوالوا اولياءه و يعادوا اعداءه و حق الرعيت على ملكها ان يصونهم و يحوطهم و يحسن النظر اليهم و لا يكلفهم ما لايطيقونه و ان اصابتهم جائحة سماويه او ارضيّة بنقض من غلاتهم ان يسقط عنهم من الخراج مقدار النقصان.

[1963] Ardashir 1967, *Ahd-i Ardashīr*, Beirut, 1967, edited by I. Abbas (Ardashir 1967), p. 53; Ardashir 1966, p. 49; quoted in Shaked 1969, pp. 214–215.

[1964] For the Mithraic dimension of the Circle of Justice ideology, see page 354 below.

and a manifest chief in kingship without the chief in religion snatching away that which is in the hands of the chief in kingship."[1965] As Shaked himself has pointed out, "the people among whom this danger [of heresy] is possible are *al-sifla* or lower class people and … *al-ʿubbād wa 'l-nussāk*, the pious and the ascetic."[1966]

5.2.7 Mazdakite heresy

The most fertile ground for the cultivation, propagation, and growth of heresy during the Sasanian period, therefore, was amid the lower strata of the population and the peasantry. And it was in fact among this sector of the Iranian population that one of the most potent revolutionary movements in Iranian history, propagating communistic ideals, appeared: the Mazdakite revolution. Whether or not the Mazdakite movement was able to unleash a revolutionary movement that undermined the very foundations of Sasanian society is open to debate.[1967] What seems incontestable, however, is the perceived heretical dimension of the movement. We reiterate once more that the eruption of the Mazdakite ideology with such force so late in Sasanian history attests to the inability of either the clergy or the monarchy to impose an orthodoxy. The history of the Mazdakite movement has been amply dealt with in other accounts.[1968] What follows, therefore, is a selective analysis.

It is generally acknowledged that while the Mazdakite movement came to the fore under the rule of Qubād (488–531), the origin of its doctrines goes back to an earlier period. There seems to be some disagreement, however, over when this earlier phase of the movement began. The figure most often considered the originator of the movement is one Zarādusht, son of Khurragān. This Zarādusht was a *mōbad* or chief *mōbad* of the town of Fasā in Fārs. But there is controversy over the exact identity of this Zarādusht as well as his date, for a second figure called Bundos, a Manichean who "professed new doctrines in opposition to official Manichaeism", is also said to have appeared prior to Mazdak.[1969] It is unlikely that the controversy over the identities of Bundos and Zarādusht will ever be solved with reference to our extant sources. What seems to be clear, however, is that an initial stage of the movement, under the leadership of a figure whom Ibn al-Nadīm calls Mazdak the Older (*al-qadīm*), occurred before the appearance of Mazdak the Younger (*al-akhir*).[1970] Mazdak, son of Bāmdād, according to one account, "renewed the doctrine of Zardusht

[1965] See footnote 1963.

[1966] Shaked 1969, p. 214.

[1967] See our discussion in §2.4.5.

[1968] For a discussion of this history, as well as a critical survey of the sources at our disposal for the study of the movement see, Yarshater 1983c, pp. 991–995; see also §2.4.5.

[1969] Yarshater 1983c, p. 996.

[1970] Ibn al-Nadīm, Muḥammad b. Isḥāq, *al-Fihrist*, Tehran, 1987, translated by Muhammad Riḍā Tajaddod (Ibn al-Nadīm 1987); Yarshater 1983c, p. 995.

Khuragān and gave it a new impetus, to the extent that the sect came to be known by his name."[1971]

As we have seen, it has been argued that the old-Mazdakite movement might in fact be identical with a heresy that erupted during the reign of Shāpūr II (309–379), in opposition to which Aturpāt son of Mahraspand launched his efforts to outline an orthodoxy.[1972] One account places Zarādusht "sometime in the course of the 5th century, presumably during or soon after the reign of Bahrām V Gūr."[1973] Another school of thought dates him to the third century, thereby making him contemporary with Mānī.[1974] The dispute over the identity of Zarādusht betrays the uncertainty of our sources. It does make, however, the question of the prevalence of heresy during the Sasanian period all the more acute. Whether Zarādusht was a contemporary of Mānī, who propagated a heresy that "existed now openly now secretly until the time of Khusrau,"[1975] or whether he lived in the fifth century, makes a difference insofar as the length of time the Sasanians had to reckon with this disruptive heresy. It is noteworthy that those who view Zarādusht as a contemporary of Mānī, maintain that the Zarādushtis were a "sect tolerated for a couple of centuries as one of the numerous heresies of the Zoroastrians."[1976] Chronological problems also plague the period of Mazdak himself. The generally held view, for example, that Mazdak appeared during the reign of Qubād and was destroyed under Khusrow I (531–579) has been challenged.[1977]

Among all the varieties of heresy that might have existed in the Sasanian realm, Mazdakism came to be considered the arch-definition of a Mazdean heresy. Once again, the particular interpretation of the Avestā on which the Mazdakites staked their claim, together with the social ramifications of this interpretation, was the crux of the matter. This intrepretationist dimension of Mazdakite doctrine has been highlighted by, among others, Masʿūdī in his *al-Tanbīh wa 'l-Ashrāf*, where he maintains that "Mazdak was the interpreter (*al-mutaʾawwil*) of the Book of Zoroaster, the Avesta ... and he is first among those who believed in interpretation (*taʾwīl*) and in inner meanings (*bāṭin*)."[1978] In fact while the Manicheans were the first to earn the epithet *zandīk*, the Mazdakites

[1971] Yarshater 1983c, p. 998.

[1972] Zaehner 1972, p. 12. See also our discussion of Āturpāt in §5.2.3.

[1973] Yarshater 1983c, p. 1018.

[1974] Crone 1991b, p. 24.

[1975] Shaki 1978, p. 301; Crone 1991b, p. 24.

[1976] Shaki 1978, p. 301; Crone 1991b, p. 24.

[1977] Crone also advances the thesis that since contemporary foreign sources fail to mention Mazdak, but instead impute heresy to Qubād, while later Middle Persian and Islamic sources link Mazdak to the reigns of both Qubād and Khusrow I, but maintain the charges of heresy against Qubād, this suggests that Mazdak first appeared under Khusrow I and tried to enforce communal access to women and property by raising a peasant revolt, only to be executed along with his followers by Khusrow I in the 530s. Prior to this, however, Qubād had already tried to "enforce communal access to women in the 490s," only to be deposed by the nobility. The two episodes, Crone argues, have been superimposed on each other. Crone 1991b.

[1978] Yarshater 1983c, p. 997.

"came to be considered the *Zindīqs par excellence*" for, as Bīrūnī maintains, the "Manicheans were called *Zindīqs* only metaphorically (*majāzan*)."[1979]

It is not our purpose to prove the peasant dimension of the Mazdakite heresy, for this has been established beyond doubt by other scholars. The Mazdakites came from "the poor, the base, the weak and the ignoble plebeians (*al-fuqarāʾ, al-sifla, al-ḍuʿafāʾ, al-luʾamāʾ, al-ghawghāʾ*)."[1980] It is instructive for our purposes to note that in the midst of crushing the plebeian revolutionaries, Khusrow I also had to deal with the rebellion of one of his brothers, Kayūs, who, according to some of our sources, had adopted the cause of the revolutionaries and challenged Khusrow I's right to accession.[1981]

The Mazdakite interpretation of the Zoroastrian scripture relied ultimately on the Zoroastrian dualistic scheme of the universe, in which man held a central place. Creation was effected with an end in mind: the replication in the *gītīg* (i.e., this world) of the Ahuraic state as it existed in the *mēnōg* (i.e., spiritual state). As Ahūrā Mazdā and his *mēnōg* creation were the very definition of the *just* order of the world, the Zoroastrian worldview burdened man with instrumentality in the scheme of creation: he was the agent for establishing justice in the *gītīg*. The Mazdean worldview, therefore, like the Mazdakite interpretation of it, was predicated upon this-worldly concerns. Man needs to make a conscious choice.[1982] This involved man, above all, in a creation scheme that derived its meaning from the struggle of the good and the just against evil, the very instrument of injustice. This Mazdean scheme was early on incorporated into the Iranian nationalist ideology by not only making kingship sacramental, but also, by extension, making sedition against kingship heretical and the provenance of evil.

Mention has already been made of the purview of, and potential for, rebellion in the articulation of the Circle of Justice.[1983] The worldview espoused by the Circle of Justice ideology can be summed up as a contract between the peasantry and the monarchy, whereby in order to assure its existence, ultimately through the wealth provided by the peasantry, the monarchy undertook to provide for the sustenance of the latter through equitable taxation. As the *Testament of Ardashīr* attests, the monarchy entered into this contract not so much on account of the sacredness of the monarchical office in disposing of its duties, although this claim was made on its behalf, but for utilitarian reasons: the monarchy needed the wealth produced by the peasantry. It may, therefore, be argued that insofar as the Mazdakite rebellion was launched against the

[1979] Yarshater 1983c, p. 997. Emphasis mine.

[1980] Crone 1991b, p. 23, and n. 42 and the sources cited there.

[1981] Theophanes, *Chronographia*, Leipzig, 1883, edited by C. de Boor (Theophanes 1883), pp. 169ff. Cited in Crone 1991b, p. 23, n. 42 and p. 31, n. 237. Crone's claim that later historiography wanted to discredit Kayūs' claim to power by charging him with heresy, is not convincing for, in numerous other instances of contention for power among members of the Sasanian family, no such charges were voiced. Crone 1991b, p. 33. For Kayūs, see §4.1.1.

[1982] See also our discussion on free-will in Mazdeism in footnote 1943.

[1983] See §5.2.6 and footnote 1963.

established hierarchical structure of Sasanian society, of which the Circle of Justice formed the justification and articulation, the movement must have used the interpretation of Zoroastrian scripture to highlight the dysfunction of the state ideology.

5.2.8 Jewish and Christian communities

A variety of forms of the Mazdean creed, even a presumed orthodoxy, were not the only religious currents found in the Sasanian realm, however. While it is safe to assume that the majority of the Iranians partook in some form of their ethnic religion, Zoroastrianism, it is also an established fact that substantial minority religions continued to coexist in Iran. Substantial Jewish settlements existed in the Mesopotamian provinces of the Sasanians, most notably in Asōristān (former Assyria), called in Aramaic *Bēt Aramāyē*.[1984] Jewish settlements also existed in Armenia, in the province of Adiabene, in Media (Māh), and in Azarbāyjān (Atropatene). Some of these settlements were already in existence in Arsacid times. The most eastern evidence for Jewish settlement seems to have been the satrapy of Parthia.[1985] In the south, in Iṣfahān, we find a strong Jewish settlement dating from the period of Shāpūr II (309–379), who resettled them there from the town of Van. Toward the end of the fourth century the Jewish population of Iṣfahān seems to have increased at the prompting of the Jewish wife of Yazdgird I (399–420). After a second migration, the community grew substantially so that by the end of the Sasanian period, the Jewish population of Iṣfahān became a very important factor in the life of the city.[1986] There continued to be also substantial Christian minorities in the Sasanian realm. To give but one example, as Asmussen observes, the "numerous Iranian names of both laymen and clergy in various fifth century Church documents bear witness to the missionary successes of the Syrian church among the Sasanians' fellow countrymen."[1987]

What is of utmost importance for us, however, is that in their relations with the minority communities of Iran, the Sasanians did not have "any articulated legal principle regulating their position except the religious law as contained in the holy canon, the Avesta."[1988] In spite of the hold exerted on the monarchy intermittently by the clergy, the ultimate authority in declaring cases of heresy rested with the monarch in his position as "chief of the magus state, high priest and supreme judge." But equally significant for our purposes is the fact that

[1984] Widengren 1961, pp. 117–162. According to Widengren, their center was in northern Babylonia, but Jewish settlements could also be found in the south, in the Sasanian vassal kingdom of Mesene. Ibid., p. 117.

[1985] Although a separate tradition testifies to the existence of Jewish communities in Khwārazm. If trusted, this would imply that the Jewish community in Khwārazm could have had contact with Soghdiana, although there seems to be thus far no evidence of Jewish settlement in Soghdiana.

[1986] Widengren 1961, p. 119.

[1987] Asmussen 1983, p. 942.

[1988] Widengren 1961, p. 156.

perhaps with a few exceptions, "the king was not led by any religious but by political and economic considerations as far as we are able to judge."[1989]

The central authorities' relations with the Jewish and Christian communities living in their realm was, therefore, not directed by any systematic policy. The reigns of Shāpūr I (241–272), Shāpūr II (309–379),[1990] Yazdgird I (399–420), Bahrām V Gūr (420–438), Qubād (488–531), and even of the rebel Parthian dynast Bahrām-i Chūbīn (590–591), attest to this. Yazdgird I, for example, is said to have given a belt (*kamar*), a mark of honor, to at least one of the exilarchs with whom he had intimate association. The Jewish community may have aided Bahrām V Gūr when he was temporarily deposed, Jews being most certainly recruited in his army. Bahrām-i Chūbīn was supported by rich Jews of the empire, and Khusrow I had a rather benevolent policy toward the community. In short, from the information that we can garner, we get the general impression that the community fared rather well for a substantial portion of the Sasanian period. There were, of course, periods of persecution, at times very intense. Under Bahrām II, the policies of Kirdīr—in whose inscription Jews are mentioned together with other minorities as being smitten in the empire—might point to one such period of crisis for the community. It is not clear, however, to what extent Kirdīr's declarations reflect the actual implementation, or for that matter, success, of the measures he is supposed to have promoted. As far as the Jewish community is concerned, for example, it has been remarked that "it is unclear just how much of [Kirdīr's] boasting is idle ... [for] Talmudic sources have not produced any unequivocal evidence that contemporary Jews were aware of being persecuted."[1991] If the persecution of the community by Kirdīr is open to question, however, the reign of Yazdgird II (438–457) and his son Pīrūz (459–484), who inaugurated "a policy of radical persecution of the Jews," leave dark marks on the Sasanian treatment of this long-established minority community in Iran.[1992]

The Sasanian relationship with the Christian communities of their domain seems to have been equally unaffected by a systematic policy. As Asmussen observes, periods of persecution notwithstanding, "[t]hroughout the whole Sasanid period, Christianity was tolerated ... [so much so that] without reservations on the part of the state, Christians performed services on an equal footing with their Zoroastrian fellow countrymen."[1993] Eḷishē describes in emotive detail, for example, how in the days of Shāpūr, when Christianity was on the rise in the Sasanian realm, the king took measures to stop its spread. But realizing the futility of his efforts, the king ordered "the magi and chief-magi that no

[1989] Widengren 1961, p. 157.

[1990] Eḷishē 1982, pp. 110–111, n. 1 and p. 112.

[1991] See Brody, Robert, 'Judaism in the Sasanian Empire: A Case Study in Religious Coexistence', in Shaul Shaked and Amnon Netzer (eds.), *Irano-Judaica II: Studies Relating to Jewish Contacts with Persian Culture throughout the Ages*, pp. 52–62, 1990 (Brody 1990), p. 60.

[1992] Widengren 1961, pp. 126–147.

[1993] Asmussen 1983, p. 934.

one should molest them [i.e., the Christians] in any way, but that they should remain undisturbed in their own doctrines without fear, magus and Zandik[1994] and Jew and Christian, *and whatever other many sects there were throughout the Persian Empire*." If Eḷishē's observations refer to Shāpūr II (309–379),[1995] during whose reign, by one account, the "only known general persecution of the Christians in the spirit of orthodox Zoroastrianism"[1996] took place, then Shāpūr II's change of policy according to Eḷishē, after "thirty nine or forty years of [severe] persecution," must also be noted. According to some, Yazdgird II's reign (438–457), however, was also clouded by the persecution of Christian Armenians from 441/2–448/9, which, by one account was precipitated by the advice of his magi.[1997] But Yazdgird II's attitude to Christianity itself, as portrayed by Eḷishē, for example, can be characterized as ambiguous at best. As Thomson observes, while "[i]n the first chapter [Yazdgird II] rages when the Christian faith is expounded; at the beginning of the second chapter he reviews all doctrines with a view to choosing the best; [and] in chapter three he states that Christianity is on a par with the Mazdean religion to be the most sublime of all [!]"[1998] It is indicative that, according to Eḷishē, after he began to pursue a more liberal policy toward the Christians, Yazdgird II asked: "What harm have I done, and what crime have I committed against [any] nation, or people or individual? *Are there not many creeds in the land of Aryans, and is not the cult of each openly [performed]? Who has ever forced or compelled [anyone] to accept*

[1994] See §5.2.5.

[1995] Thomson notes that it is not clear whether Eḷishē is referring to Shāpūr III (383–388) mentioned shortly before this observation, or to Shāpūr II "in whose reign there were severe persecutions." Eḷishē 1982, pp. 110–111, n. 1 and p. 112.

[1996] Asmussen 1983, p. 936.

[1997] The two different Armenian historians who cover Yazdgird II's reign in detail, Eḷishē and Łazar P'arpec'i, however, claim two different causes for this persecution. While Eḷishē attributes it to the "malicious plotting of King Yazdkert, abetted by his evil counselors, who see in the Christians potential enemies of the state," Łazar P'arpec'i saw the cause "in Armenia as a personal quarrel between the prince of Siunik' (Vasak), the *marzpan* (governor) of Armenia, and his son-in-law Varazvałan." For a detailed exposition of this see Thomson's introduction in Eḷishē 1982, pp. 3–9.

[1998] Eḷishē 1982, pp. 28, 67, 69–70, and 134–135. In view of his observations here, it is unclear why Thomson continues to argue that "the only Armenian reports of *explicit tolerance* for Christianity in Iran date from *after the reign of Yazdkert*." And notes that these pertain specifically to the reigns of Qubād (488–531) and Khusrow I (531–579). It must be noted significantly, moreover, that with rather convincing grounds, Akinean suspects that many of the actions attributed to Yazdgird II by Eḷishē, as well as descriptions that he gives of the Armenian revolt of 451, bear a striking resemblance to actions undertaken by Khusrow I and the Armenian revolt of 572. If true and if Eḷishē was actually reporting a later version of events, the remarks that he makes on the religious policies of Yazdgird II should therefore be attributed to Khusrow I. See Eḷishē 1982, pp. 23–29. In this respect one might note, for example, the passage where Eḷishē describes the policies of Yazdgird II, and maintains that "he [Yazdgird II] began to give precedence to the junior over the senior, to the unworthy over the honorable, to the ignorant over the knowledgeable ... All the unworthy he promoted and the worthy he demoted, until he had split father and son from each other." Ibid., p. 70. Some of our accounts, as we have seen on page 111, accuse Khusrow I precisely of this policy. The last word on this issue remains outstanding, nevertheless.

the single religion of magism?"[1999] Our overview of the religious landscape in the Sasanian domains, however, would not be complete without a discussion of another age-old Iranian form of worship, that of Mihr (Mithra).

5.3 Mihr worship

While, for obvious reasons, the Mazdakite uprising has attracted much attention in Sasanian scholarship, it has rarely been recognized that of all the forms of Mazdean worship, one in particular was best suited in being exploited for achieving justice: Mihr worship.[2000] This, perhaps, more than any other dimension of the worship, explains its cross-sectional popularity in Iranian history.

The God Mihr belonged to the pre-Avestan, Indo–Iranian pantheon of gods. As such, its worship has had a long heritage in Iranian history. Investigations into Mihr worship, however, have long been hampered by the nature of the sources at our disposal. Much controversy, therefore, surrounds, among other things, the character of this ancient faith as it presented itself in the period under investigation in this study.[2001] Briefly, and most simply put, the primary question revolves around the degrees to which the pre-Avestan forms of the faith were affected by Zoroastrian reforms, if at all. Various answers have been given to this. There are those who argue, for example, that the popularity of pre-Avestan Mihr worship was such that some aspects of this ancient faith, as we can trace these in one of the most ancient documents of the Zoroastrian faith, the *Mihr Yasht*, and parts of other Yashts,[2002] continued into the Zoroastrian period almost completely unaffected by the teachings of Zoroaster. It is for this reason, they argue, that, well after the appearance of Zoroaster, the god Mihr appears as a primary god in these sources. We should keep in mind, these scholars argue, that, while included in the Avestā, the *Mihr Yasht* remains one of the oldest sections of the Zoroastrian holy book, some of its sections being even older than the Gāthās. Parts of these sources, this school of thought argues, have "a striking pagan cast [which] survived unaltered, and are as incongruous to Zoroaster's message as are parts of the Old Testament to Christianity,"[2003] Included in this group are those who argue that Zoroastrian reform, with all its

[1999] Elishē 1982, pp. 134–135. Emphasis added.

[2000] Mihr shared the guardianship of *asha* (order, righteousness, and justice) with the two other Ahuras in the ancient Iranian religions. By one account, once Zoroaster proclaimed Ahūrā Mazdā the most supreme of the three Ahuras, as the one uncreated God, he worshipped him as the "master of *asha*." Boyce 1992, p. 19.

[2001] There has also been an ongoing controversy over the precise relationship of this ancient Iranian faith to Roman Mithraism. See also our discussion at the beginning of §5.3.2.

[2002] "Although the composition of the Yashts in their extant form is later than Zoroaster, their contents predate him, for they contain myths which the eastern Iranians had inherited from pagan times, as well as legends which reflect pre-Zoroastrian heroic ages." Yarshater 1983b, p. 365. Some scholars postulate the date of the composition of the Yashts to be "as far [back] as the mid-second half of the 2nd millennium BCE, and, in some cases, to when the Aryans began to appear on the great plateau." Gnoli 1989, p. 63.

[2003] For an elaboration of this discussion, see, Boyce 1992, p. 38.

efforts at elevating Ahūrā Mazdā to the position of supreme deity, proved incapable of defeating the "Mithraic type of naturism and the Zoroastrian priests had to give in little by little to popular pressure, recognizing, along with the Zoroastrian angels, the gods of the Mithraic pantheon."[2004]

Another school of thought, spearheaded by the late Mary Boyce, argues that with the Zoroastrian reform of the pre-Avestan pantheon of Iranian gods, while Zoroastrianized by becoming one of the *yazatas*, albeit one of the most important ones, Mithra was nonetheless relegated to a second-tier god in the Zoroastrian theology. In the orthodox Mazdean system of belief, they argue, Mihr never acquired the same elevated position as Ahūrā Mazdā. While much investigation will be required in order to settle this controversy, we shall be arguing in the next two sections that important evidence points to the prevalence of Mihr worship among some of the important Parthian dynastic families under investigation here. Even more significantly, we shall maintain that amongst these Pahlav families the God Mihr was bestowed with such primacy that the nature of Mihr worship espoused by some of the Parthian families of the quarter of the north and the east, *could not have been the same as that practiced by Mazdean orthodox population.* The Pahlav and the Pārsīg, therefore, adhered to different schools of religion, as far as we can establish in the course of this study. Before we present our evidence to this effect, a synopsis of the attributes of the ancient Iranian God, Mihr, is necessary.

5.3.1 Mithra

Throughout its long history, Mihr worship had come to be associated with the three functions of Iranian society: the monarchy, the army, and the peasantry. Above all, however, Mihr (Mithra) was the god of Covenants and Pacts, the quintessential deity who, unlike the remoter Ahūrā Mazdā, got his hands dirty, so to speak, in overseeing the proper implementation of pacts and ensuring a just society.

Mithra, Lord Covenant

The ancient Iranians attributed great power among the intangible things to the formal spoken word. "Two forms of legalized utterance were held to be imbued with their own distinct Mainyus [spirits], whose workings were so vividly apprehended that in time they came to be revered as great gods. One was the *mithra*. This was a pact or covenant entered into by two parties—two persons, or tribes, or peoples. The other was the *varuna* . . . apparently an oath taken by a single person."[2005] In this way a great triad of gods was

[2004] Bausani 2000, p. 29. According to one theory, this process of the Zoroastrianization of the ancient faith took already place before the Mazdean religion moved west to be adopted by the Medes and later the Achaemenids. Christensen 1944, p. 31.

[2005] Boyce 1992, p. 55. For Mithra as contract personified, and for the role of Mithra in Iranian belief in general, see Thieme, P., 'The Concept of Mitra in Aryan Belief', in *Mithraic Studies: Proceedings of the First International Congress of Mithraic Studies*, vol. I, pp. 21–39, Manchester University

conceived: Ahūrā Mazdā (Lord Wisdom), Ahūrā Mitra (Lord Covenant), and Ahūrā Varuna (Lord True-Speech).[2006] A declaration of entering into a *mithra* or a *varuna* was thought to invoke the Mainyu "inherent in the words themselves, and this Mainyu was thought to watch thereafter, unsleeping, over those concerned, ready to punish any who broke the faith."[2007] As far as Mihr as a god of contracts was concerned, there "was only one thing sacred about contracts: their inviolability ... [Mithra's] only concern is that, *fair or foul*, contracts must be kept."[2008] Even with this short introduction, the relevance of Mihr worship to the Circle of Justice should become apparent.[2009]

Mithra, the warrior god

Because Mithra/Mihr oversaw a pact entered into by two clans or tribes, if one party would break the covenant, the aggrieved party would then have recourse to Mithra, who, coming to their aid, undertook to set things right by siding with the aggrieved and punishing the covenant breakers. Mithra therefore eventually came to be conceived not only as the god who oversaw the implementation of pacts, but also as an active, warrior god, who undertook to fight on the side of wronged members of society.

The warrior dimension of Mithra was a peculiarly Indo-Iranian trait of the god. In fact it has been argued that one of the chief differences between the Mitra of the Sanskrit *Rig Veda* and the Mithra of the Avestā, is that in the former the god is viewed as one "who defends and rewards those faithful to their solemn contracts," whereas in the latter "he balances this rewarding function ... against his role as the terrible avenger of those who break their contracts."[2010] The active participation of the god on the side of the aggrieved, in fact, "appears to [have] be[en] the genesis of the concept of him as war god, *fighting always on the side of the just*—a concept abundantly attested for this many-sided divinity in his Avestan Yašt."[2011] The *Mihr Yasht* (Yasht 10) articulates this warrior function of the god in detail: "Mithra, whose long arms seize the liar(?), even if he [the culprit] is in the east of the [eastern frontier] he is caught, even if he is in the west [of the western frontier] he is struck down."[2012] In the *Mihr Yasht*,

Press, 1975 (Thieme 1975).

[2006] Boyce, Mary, 'On Mithra, Lord of Fire', in *Acta Iranica 4: Hommages et Opera Minora, Monumentum H.S. Nyberg*, pp. 69–76, Leiden, 1975 (Boyce 1975), p. 69.

[2007] Boyce 1992, p. 54. Another conception of pre-Avestan Mihr worship maintains that in the pre-Zoroastrian communities there existed two types of religiosity. The center of one was the worship of Mazdā, "an omniscient celestial god ... a more or less exact counterpart of the Indian Varuna, god of the sky." A second type of religiosity "more polytheistic and nature-based, centered on the god Mithra, who was accompanied by other nature deities." Bausani 2000, p. 29.

[2008] Thieme 1975, p. 28, n. 17.

[2009] For further elaboration, see page 354 below.

[2010] Thieme 1975, p. 29.

[2011] Boyce 1992, p. 55. My emphasis.

[2012] Mihr Yasht 1883; Mihr Yasht 1959, *The Avestan Hymn to Mithra*, Cambridge University Press, 1959, introduction, translation, and commentary by Ilya Gershevitch (Mihr Yasht 1959), p. 125, as quoted in Thieme 1975, p. 30.

Mithra appears as a "fighting hero on his chariot ... smiting demons and men that break their contracts."[2013] Mithra therefore eventually came to be the deity in charge of implementing justice. The covenant dimension of Mithra also incorporated his attribute as a judge. In the *Mihr Yasht*, the role of Mithra as a mediator "is of remarkable importance: Mithra is the mediator or the arbiter on the cosmological level between the two spirits of Good and Evil, on the socio-juridical level as head of the institution of the *hanāmand* in many respects similar to the institution of *interdictum* in Roman Law, on the socioreligious level as the god of governing relationships, pacts, contracts, and alliances, and *finally on the eschatological level of the individual soul* ... [when] he presides over the Činvat bridge tribunal, midway between Heaven and Hell, compulsory passage of the soul of the faithful departed."[2014] This central aspect of the god as a judge was later also formulated in the terminology of *mīyānchīgh*.[2015]

Mithra in eschatology

The concept of Mihr as judge was gradually to become so central, in fact, that in certain Iranian versions of the myth of creation, Mihr, together with his cohorts Sorūsh and Rashnu,[2016] became the judges of the cosmic battle between Ahūrā Mazdā and Ahrīman in the Zoroastrian eschatology.[2017] In his position as judge, however, Mihr was not considered to be impartial. For "all known varieties of Zoroastrianism uphold the absolute righteousness of Ohrmozd, and it seems natural, from the mythical point of view, that the just judge who is Mihr should be firmly and unequivocally on the side of justice, that is on that of Ohrmozd."[2018] This eschatological dimension of Mihr's function acquires tremendous significance in the late Sasanian and post-conquest history of Iran. It is also very important in deciphering the nature of Mihr worship prevalent among some of the Parthian families, to be discussed shortly.[2019]

According to Shaked, "the eschatological description which places mediators between the two antagonists *preserves a detail which occurred in an older version of the cosmological myth, in which Mihr, with his associates, did indeed preside, as a judge, over the contract between two powers, and that this trait was generally omitted from later Mazdean accounts as the dualist system of thought hardened and became more rigorous.*"[2020] The attributes of Mihr as Lord Covenant

[2013] Thieme 1975, p. 31.

[2014] Belardi, Walter, 'Mithra, Arbiter and Rex', in Ugo Bianchi (ed.), *Mysteria Mithrae*, pp. 689–700, Leiden, 1979 (Belardi 1979), here pp. 697–698.

[2015] Shaked, Shaul, 'Mihr the Judge', *Jerusalem Studies in Arabic and Islam* 2, (1980), pp. 1–31 (Shaked 1980), here p. 10.

[2016] These *yazatas* are worshipped in respectively Sorush Yasht 1883, *Sorūsh Yasht*, vol. 23 of *Sacred Books of the East*, Oxford University Press, 1883, translated by James Darmesteter (Sorush Yasht 1883); and Rashnu Yasht 1883, *Rashnu Yasht*, vol. 23 of *Sacred Books of the East*, Oxford University Press, 1883, translated by James Darmesteter (Rashnu Yasht 1883).

[2017] Shaked 1980, p. 11.

[2018] Shaked 1980, p. 16.

[2019] See §5.4.

[2020] Shaked 1980, p. 17. Emphasis mine

and judge (*mīyānchīgh*), as well as his warrior dimensions are also central to the ideology of Circle of Justice, especially if we consider yet another function of the God, his association with royalty.

Mithra and farr

Much has been said of the conception of kingship in the Iranian world as being contingent on the king's acquisition of Divine Glory, *farr* (*xwarra*, *Khvarenah*, Av. *x*^{v}*arənah*).[2021] It should also be emphasized, however, that according to an ancient myth it was Mithra who took "charge of the fortune [i.e., *farr*, *Khvarenah*] ... at times when that precious commodity [was] in danger of falling into the wrong hands." Perhaps one of the most significant characteristics of Mithra, therefore, was his association with royalty. Mithra bestowed the *farr* on rulers. This aspect of Mithra is set out in the *Zamyād Yasht* (Yasht 19), which is mainly devoted to the *farr*. It contains the myth of how Yima (Jamshīd), the first man-king, lost his *farr* when he lied. After Yima's death, the *farr* passed into the keeping of Mithra, and then into the sea (*Vourukasha*), which was under the protection of Varuna (Vouruna Apąm Napāt).[2022]

Mithra and the Circle of Justice

For the purposes of our discussion of the Circle of Justice it is significant that the "meaning of this myth ... is that since the king, reigning through [*Khvarenah*], maintains thereby social order, when there is no ruler fit to possess it, it returns to the keeping of one of the Ahuras, whose task is primarily to maintain ... [*asha*] order and rightness, in the world of men."[2023] What is equally significant for our purposes is that "Mithra's concern with proper government, arising from his political chieftainship and preoccupation with the covenant ... turned him *into a maker, as well as undoer, of kings*."[2024] Nowhere is the close connection of the Circle of Justice with Mihr worship better illustrated than

[2021] As Bīrūnī maintains, during the annual festival of Mihrigān in the Sasanian period "it was the custom of ... the kings of Iran of crowning themselves on this day with a crown which worked an image of the sun [Mithra] and of the wheel on which he rotates ...," thus confirming their *farr* with the aid of Mithraic symbols. Garsoian, Nina G., 'The Locus of the Death of Kings: Iranian Armenia – the Inverted Image', in *Armenia between Byzantium and the Sasanians*, London, 1985c (Garsoian 1985c), p. 53; Bīrūnī 1984, pp. 337–340, here p. 370. For *farr*, see also footnote 222.

[2022] Zamyad Yasht 1883, §51; Darmesteter, James, *Le Zend Avesta*, Annales du Musée Guimet, 1892, 3 volumes (Darmesteter 1892) apud Mihr Yasht 1959, p. 59.

[2023] Mithra's role as protector of the *farr* is shared with Apąm Napāt, the Grandson of the Waters. According to an ancient Iranian myth, "during the reign of Yima's successor, the evil Zohāk (Aži Dahāka, [i.e., Ḍaḥḥāk]), Mithra keeps the *x*^{v}*arənah* in trust; in time Farīdūn (Θraētaona, [i.e., Fereydūn]) obtains the *x*^{v}*arənah*, defeats Zohāk, and reigns; after him during Minočihr's [i.e., Manūchihr's] childhood, the *x*^{v}*arənah* passes to Sām Narīmān (Kərəsāspa)." See Mihr Yasht 1959, p. 59, where Gershevitch recapitulates Darmesteter's reconstruction of the myth in Darmesteter 1892, p. 625, n. 52. As we shall see, it is no wonder that in the absence of a ruler fit to possess *farr*, in all the major revolts that erupted in Iran in the early ʿAbbāsid period, those of Ustādsīs, Bihāfarīd and Sunbād, it is Mithra who is invoked. For the revolts of Bihāfarīd and Sunbād, see respectively §6.3 and §6.4 below; for Ustādsīs, see, for instance, Sadighi 1938; and Pourshariati 1995.

[2024] Mihr Yasht 1959, p. 60.

in the *Mihr Yasht*, the Hymn to Mithra: "On whom shall I bestow against his expectation an excellent ... powerful kingdom, beautifully strong thanks to a numerous army? [Once he rules] he appeases through Mithra, by honouring the treaty [read, by implementing justice] even the mind of an antagonized, unreconciled, conqueror."[2025] This aspect of Mithra permeates the saga of the Sasanian king Pīrūz (459–484).[2026]

Mithra's nourishing function

There is another very important dimension to Mithra, however. He is the nourishing god who replenishes the earth through rain and vegetation.[2027] In line with Mithra's pre-Avestan eschatological attributes, it has even been argued that "in bringing rain and vegetation, ... [the god must have] exercised what we may call cosmic functions already in proto-Aryan times."[2028] How can we reconcile the three functions of Mithra, the monarchical, warrior, and nourishing functions? It is well worth following in some detail the reasoning of Thieme. "What do rain and vegetation have to do with contracts? Putting the question in this way almost means answering it. According to an archaic, widespread, possibly worldwide belief, a king's moral behavior is responsible for his people's welfare, in particular for their health and for the fertile climate of their country." Ready examples of this include the misdeed of King Romapāda, which resulted in a severe drought; the disastrous plague on the Greek army before Troy, caused by a misdemeanor of Agamemnon toward Apollo; Oedipus's sins causing a pestilence in his realm.[2029] Now, in the *Mihr Yasht*, "the most essential contract, a contract of a thousand fold sacredness ... is a treaty between countries, concluded, of course, between their kings. A king who breaks his treaty exposes his whole country to the wrath."[2030] Here Thieme gives a truncated version of a part of the *Mihr Yasht*: "He wrecks his whole country, the knave who deceitfully breaks his treaty." And he continues: "The converse of this is that Mitra bestows blessings on the country of the king who is faithful to his treaty. Instead of drought and pestilence, which are the natural consequences of a king's wrongdoing, he lets the rain fall, the plants grow, gives strength to the bodies."[2031] The last part of Thieme's wonderful explication might be questioned, however. Most significantly, it is not certain whether the king's breaking of a treaty with another country is what this section of the *Mihr Yasht* refers to, or if it is the king's obligation toward his subjects that is the point. Even if the former, surely this is significant only self-referentially. It is only because the king is inflicting hardship on his own subjects and creating wars

[2025] Mihr Yasht 1959, pp. 127–128; Mihr Yasht 1883, §109.

[2026] See page 380ff.

[2027] Thieme 1975, p. 31.

[2028] Thieme 1975, p. 31. In the *Mihr Yasht*, he carries the epithet *vouru.gaoyaotu*, [lord] of broad cattle pastures. Mihr Yasht 1883, §35.

[2029] Thieme 1975, pp. 31–32.

[2030] Thieme 1975, p. 32.

[2031] Thieme 1975, pp. 32–33.

by breaking treaties with other countries that a king wrecks *his* whole country and exposes *his* whole country to wrath.[2032] The contract implicit between the king and his subjects is spelled out in the *Mihr Yasht*: "If the head of the house who presides over the house, ... the clan who presides over the clan ..., the tribe who presides over the tribe, or *the head of the country who presides over the country*, are false to him, Mithra enraged and provoked comes forth to smash the house, the clan, the country ... [and] the heads of the countries who preside over the countries and the council of premiers of the countries."[2033] It has been justifiably observed, therefore, that the "first condition for a country to be able to honour its treaties is that its internal affairs should be wellregulated, the authorities obeyed, revolutions averted. In the fulfillment of this condition Mithra understandably takes an active part." It is of course natural for the god who provides bounty through replenishing the earth to oversee the welfare of his flock. This function of Mithra replicates, in a sense, that of the king as articulated in the Circle of Justice. This aspect of Mithra's function has, once again, been aptly summarized by Gershevitch. "The provision of material comfort and of sons must be viewed as part and parcel of Mithra's care for the nation's welfare and prosperity, which creates conditions of internal stability, thus leading to treaty-abiding international relations."[2034] As the very incarnation of a god whose purpose it is to ensure justice, moreover, Mithra has "*an endearing affection for the unjustly oppressed, the loyal pauper*."[2035] This we read in the *Mihr Yasht*: "the pauper who follows the doctrine of Truth but is deprived of his rights, the lamenting voice of the latter [invoking Mithra], even though he raises his voice reverently, reaches up to the (heavenly) lights, makes the round of the earth, pervades the seven climes."[2036] That the king's justice is gauged in terms of his equitable behavior toward his subjects, at least in the Iranian context, is borne out by a wealth of tales from medieval Iranian popular literature, whose worldview is infused with pre-Islamic Iranian beliefs.[2037]

Mithra and the ordeal by fire

Besides being the lord of covenants and justice, Mithra was also known as the Lord of Fire, and gradually developed a link with the sun. The epithet of the Lord of Fire seems to have been established in remote antiquity, while the identification with the sun is thought to have been either an Arsacid or a Sasanian phenomenon. Mithra came to be associated with fire because fire came to be associated with truthfulness, and so the ordeal by fire eventually came to establish

[2032] See also Thieme's discussion on Mithra's epithet *vouru.gaoyaotu* (of broad cattle pastures), which also seems to corroborate our argument here. Thieme 1975, pp. 32–33. Emphasis mine.

[2033] Mihr Yasht 1959, p. 83; Mihr Yasht 1883, §18. Emphasis mine.

[2034] Mihr Yasht 1959, p. 32.

[2035] Mihr Yasht 1959, p. 54. Emphasis added.

[2036] Mihr Yasht 1959, pp. 113–115; Mihr Yasht 1883, §§84–85.

[2037] The motif of a king who, in disguise, goes amid his flock only to realize the wretchedness that his policies have caused and thenceforth resolves to rule with justice, is so prevalent in the didactic and popular Iranian tradition that an enumeration of it is beyond the scope of this study.

the veracity of an oath.[2038] In case of Varuna, "the validity of an oath [*varuna*] was judicially tested on occasion by making the man who had sworn it submit to an ordeal by water."[2039] However, since it was "customary to swear to covenants by Mithra ... in the presence of fire," in order to establish their innocence, and prove that they possess *asha* (Vedic *ṛta*), that is to say, that they are among the *ashavan* (Vedic *ṛtavan*), those "accused of breach of undertakings involving two or more persons," underwent the ordeal of fire, which therefore "was associated particularly with Mitra."[2040] In this ordeal "metal was heated, and then poured on the naked breast of the accused. If he survived, he was innocent."[2041] There are many references to ordeals by fire in Persian literature.[2042] The modern Persian expression for taking an oath, *sōgand khordan*, "literally *to drink sulphur* [the substance having a fiery nature], shows that the practice was ancient and widespread."[2043] It is significant that the rite took place at a *Dār-i Mihr* (the abode of Mihr), and the most central deity in its performance was, besides Mithra, Rashnu the Judge, "a hypostasis of one aspect of Mithra's, and the Ahura's helper, with his unerring scales, at the judgment of each individual soul." The element of fire, therefore, was an essential attribute of Mithra and was used as an ancient rite to establish truthfulness.

Mithra, the Sun

But how did the identification of Mithra with the sun come about? According to Boyce, as fire was already associated with truthfulness, a "climate of thought [emerged] which enabled Zoroaster to see fire as the creation and symbol of Asa [*asha*] personified; and his new doctrines, establishing this as a primary article of faith, must have *discouraged the intimate association of Mithra with fire in general*, and have fostered the tendency to link him rather with its particular manifestation, the sun."[2044] Mithra is not identified with the sun in the *Mihr Yasht*. By the Sasanian period, however, "*it was possible to refer to the sun itself as Mihr*."[2045]

The close connection of Mihr worship to ideologies that sought to rebel against the status quo and, in a sense, turn the Circle of Justice ideology on its head, seems beyond dispute. To what extent Mihr worship was connected with the Mazdakite ideology, and which forms of it, requires further research. What seems to be clear, however, is that Mazdakite followers, *al-fuqarāʾ*, *al-sifla*, *al-ḍuʿafāʾ*, *al-luʾamāʾ*, *al-ghawghāʾ*, bear an uncanny resemblance to the "unjustly

[2038] Boyce 1975, p. 69–73.
[2039] Boyce 1975, p. 69–70.
[2040] Boyce 1975, p. 70.
[2041] Boyce, Mary, *A History of Zoroastrianism I: The Early Periord*, Leiden, 1996 (Boyce 1996), pp. 27–28. We recall Āturpāt's voluntary experience of this ordeal; see §5.2.3.
[2042] See Davis, Dick, *Panthea's Children: Hellenistic Novels and Medieval Persian Romances*, New York, 2002 (Davis 2002).
[2043] Boyce 1975, p. 72. Boyce 1996, pp. 34–36.
[2044] Boyce 1975, p. 75.
[2045] Boyce 1975, p. 75. My emphasis.

oppressed, [and] the loyal pauper" for whom Mithra had such an enduring affection. Insofar as the provenance of the heresy is concerned, therefore, and as the evidence of the Mazdakite heresy has shown, the plebeian dimensions of popular religiosity cannot be ignored, even if kings and dynasts were just as ignorant of the requirements of high religion. As we shall see, Mihr worship had a tremendous potential for lending itself to revolutionary upheavals.

5.3.2 Mihr worship in the Achaemenid and the Arsacid periods

That Mihr worship seems to have been a prevalent if not one of the paramount forms of religiosity during the Achaemenid and the post-Avestan period is corroborated on a number of levels. Mithraic theophoric names form the majority of the names found in the Aramaic inscriptions at Persepolis from the time of the Achaemenid king Darius (549–486 BCE). In fact compound names with Mithra outnumber those referring to Ahūrā Mazdā by at least five to three.[2046] As the Greek sources testify, moreover, the prevalence of Mithraic compound names was not confined to Persīs or Parthava during the Achaemenid period.[2047] The literary sources also provide evidence that the worship of Mithra was an important form of worship in Achaemenid Iran. Herodotus informs us, through a curious error, of the cult of a female deity called Mitra whom the Persians had adopted from the Assyrians and Arabs. Xenophon informs us in both *Anabasis* as well as *Cyropaedia* that "the Persian king swore by Mithra." According to Quintus Curtis, Darius III (380–330 BCE) "called upon the sun and Mithras as well as the eternal fire for victory" at the battle of Gaugamela. And finally both Aelian and Pseudo-Callisthenes note that "the [king?] swore by Mithra."[2048] The implication of all this is that "most, if not all, Iranians swore by Mithra, and not just the king or the army." So prevalent was Mihr worship during the Achaemenid, the Hellenistic, and the Arsacid periods, moreover, that one school of thought has argued that through the migration of the Magi from Babylonia to the eastern Mediterranean and Anatolia, the religion reached the Roman military and, in its by now heavily syncretic form, appeared as Roman Mithraism.[2049]

As we already remarked, the religious history of the Parthians has yet to be written.[2050] Nonetheless, the claim that the Parthians were adherents of

[2046]Frye's conclusion is based on the valid observation that "repeated appearance of various theophoric names ... compounded with the name of the same deity, could be used as an indication of the popularity of that deity in naming children." Frye, Richard N., 'Mithra in Iranian History', in John R. Hinnells (ed.), *Mithraic Studies: Proceedings of the First International Congress of Mithraic Studies*, pp. 62–67, Manchester University Press, 1975b (Frye 1975b).

[2047]Frye 1975b, p. 63.

[2048]Frye 1975b, p. 64.

[2049]This is the bare outline of the erudite arguments in Bizet, Joseph and Cumont, Franz, *Les mages Hellénisés: Zoroastre, Ostanès et Hystaspe d'après la tradition Grecque*, Paris, 1938 (Bizet and Cumont 1938).

[2050]Boyce 1991b.

orthodox Zoroastrianism seems to have little to recommend it.[2051] It is true that the Arsacids have been credited with the first codification of the Avestan holy book. The Parthians also used Zoroastrian holy months in their calendar. Considering the confederate nature of the Arsacid polity, and considering the Arsacids' decentralized laissez-faire attitude toward the religious practices in their domains, it may well have been the case that some Parthian dynasts of the Arsacid period were orthodox Zoroastrians. In what follows, however, some significant new evidence as well as a re-assessment of some of the data already at our disposal will be presented in order to make the case that Mihr worship, in contradistinction to orthodox Mazdeism, was the most widespread current of worship in the traditional Parthian domains: the quarters of the east and north. Part of this evidence pertains to the regions under Parthian dynastic control during the Sasanian period, and therefore will be presented as evidence of continuity of religious traditions from the Arsacid to the Sasanian period. In this context the religious history of pre-Christian Armenia—contemporaneous with the first two centuries of Sasanian history—becomes extremely significant. Mihr worship was one of the most popular forms of religiosity in pre-Christian Arsacid Armenia,[2052] so much so that some scholars claim that the region was the provenance of Roman Mithraism. Shaked has argued that "traces of Mihr worship, which, to judge by the Armenian evidence, must have existed from Parthian times, have disappeared." He furthermore maintains, however, that "such worship dedicated specifically to Mihr in the fire temple [existed] seems ... irrefutable."[2053] While "it is difficult to find in the extant literature convincing Iranian parallels to several elements of the [Roman] Mithraic myth in so far as it can be reconstructed from the monuments [in western territories] ... [this] is no proof that they were not there ... We can only manage to reconstruct a small portion of the variegated religious heritage of ancient Iran."[2054] It is in reference to this aspect of Shaked's analysis that we shall present our evidence in §5.4 below.

Theophoric evidence also testifies to the prevalence of Mihr worship among the Arsacids. The ostraca found in Nisā in the Parthian homeland evince "the same picture as at [that presented for] Perspolis under Darius; theophoric names with Mithra are more in evidence than those of other deities."[2055] Mithraic names remained prevalent through the rest of the Arsacid period. At least four Arsacid kings bore the name Mithradates, *bestowed by Mihr*: Mithradates I (171–138 BCE), Mithradates II (124/3–88 BCE), Mithradates III (57–54 BCE), and Mithradates IV (129–147? CE). A significant iconographic feature of Arsacid

[2051] Although the eagerly awaited posthumous volume of Professor Boyce on the religious history of the Arsacids and the Sasanians is certain to clarify a great deal of this.

[2052] See §5.4.4 below.

[2053] Shaked 1994a, p. 46.

[2054] Shaked 1994a, p. 46.

[2055] Frye 1975b, pp. 65.

coins seems also to betray a Mithraic provenance.[2056]

5.3.3 The Pārsīg–Pahlav religious dichotomy

There was a religious dimension to the Pārsīg–Pahlav rivalry during the Sasanian period, and this had to do with the adherence of some of the Parthian dynastic families to Mihr worship.[2057] It is important to bear in mind that this religious rivalry goes back to the rise of the Arsacid dynasty, when the priestly tradition of Persīs articulated its opposition to the Parthians in religious terms.[2058] As Eddy's fascinating study has shown, for more than half a century Persīs resisted Arsacid domination. During the Seleucid period, already from about 280 BCE onward, we have evidence of local dynasts establishing themselves in Persīs. It is only by 140 BCE that the area comes under Arsacid domination. Still, the Persians continued to attack the Arsacids with the same zeal as they had the Seleucids. And this they did in the strongest religious terms. Potent traces of the Persian opposition to the Arsacids is reflected in the first chapter of the *Videvdād* (or *Vendidad*), which has been dated to the middle of the second century BCE. Described as a catalogue of *Unholiness in non-Persian lands*, this section of the *Videvdād* omits one district, Persīs. The Median and the Greco–Bactrian states, in contrast, are listed among the unholy Ahrimanic entities that have been created in opposition to the Ahuraic regional creations. It is Parthia, however, that holds the lion's share of evil territories. Nisā, the original capital of the Arsacids, and the burial site of their early kings, "was guilty of the sin of unbelief; Margiana [Marv] had indulged in sinful lusts; Hyrkania [Gurgān] was guilty of some unnatural sin for which there was no atonement; Rhaga [Rayy], renamed Parthian Arsakeia, had committed another sin without atonement, the sin of utter unbelief. Chorasmia [Khwārazm] had burned corpses, yet another sin without remedy."[2059] It is significant that while each of these territories is labeled unholy land because of a particular sin, Parthava and

[2056] On the reverse side of a substantial number of Arsacid coins, a seated figure is shown holding a bow in a horizontal position. As the *Mihr Yasht* attests, the bow was the chosen weapon of Mithra, with which he struck the *daevas*. Mihr Yasht 1883, §128. Due to the tremendous marksmanship of the Parthian cavalry, the fame of the Parthian bow was widespread among their enemies, especially in the Roman Empire, and classical sources bear witness to this. But the kings who bear these bows on Arsacid coins are not on horseback and the bow is not held in an offensive position. The beardless man holding a bow on the obverse of the majority of Parthian coins is identified by Sellwood as "Apollo seated left on the omphalos and holding a bow." Sellwood, David, 'Parthian Coins', in Ehsan Yarshater (ed.), *Cambridge History of Iran: The Seleucid, Parthian, and Sasanian Periods*, vol. 3(1), pp. 279–299, Cambridge University Press, 1983 (Sellwood 1983), p. 279. Among the classical writers, however, Mithra as the high god was often represented by Apollo.

[2057] See §5.4.2 and §5.4.3.

[2058] As the cradle of the Achaemenid dynasty, Persīs seems to have already begun the Zoroastrianization of its religious tradition toward the middle of the Achaemenid period. According to Gnoli, this process was of crucial importance in the establishment "of that substantial unity between religious tradition and the national tradition, which was to be characteristic of the whole cultural history of ancient, and, in part, medieval Iran." Gnoli 1989, p. 36.

[2059] Eddy 1961, pp. 79–80.

Rayy, however, are depicted as committing the sin of unbelief.[2060] We know furthermore that the Parthians "did not follow magian religious prescriptions, for they both burned and buried the dead."[2061] But from the perspective of the Pārsīgs, perhaps the greatest heresy that the Arsacids had committed was that of dominating Persīs. Thus, as Eddy observes, "the Persians fought their Parthian master. The king from the East whom they had hoped would extirpate the Makedonians [i.e., Alexander's heirs] turned out unhappily for them to be an Arsakid. The resistance of the Persians against the West had to redirect itself against the Orient."[2062]

The early Sasanians continued to use the analogy that Persīs had made between unholy creatures and Parthians. In the investiture scene of Ardashīr I at Naqsh-i Rostam (ANRm), both the king and Ahūrā Mazdā are depicted mounted on horses. Ahūrā Mazdā "offers a ring of investiture with attached flying ribbons to Ardashir." While the mount of the high God tramples Ahrīman, that of the newly invested Sasanian king Ardashīr I tramples the vanquished Arsacid king Ardavān. As Soudavar explains, the message of the scene "is clear: Parthian rule was Ahrimanic and illegitimate, and when the last of the Parthians was vanquished, so was Ahriman."[2063]

The hostility of the Sasanians to the religious traditions of the Parthian dynasts finds further evidence in the history of the rise of Ardashīr I to power in the early third century. While arguing for the general applicability of the *Letter of Tansar* to the reign of Khusrow I Nowshīrvān, Boyce points out a passage which she claims to be appropriate only to the reign of Ardashīr I "and to his reign alone."[2064] In this passage, Gushnāsp accuses Ardashīr I: "The king of kings has *taken away fire temples, extinguished them and blotted them out.*" Boyce points out the dissonance of this information with the generally held contention that the Sasanians zealously promoted sacred fires. "The fires in question," Tansar explains, "*had been those of vassal-kings of the Arsacids*, who had no ancient entitlement to them." The only period to which this information can be applicable, Boyce explains, is that of the rise of the Sasanians. As we shall see, however, this evidence is equally applicable to the reign of Khusrow I and later. The Parthian dynast Bahrām-i Chūbīn, for instance, threatened to destroy Hormozd IV's fire temples, presumably in retaliation for what Khusrow I had done to the Parthian dynasts previously.[2065] In either case, whether the passage refers to the early Sasanian period or to the period of Khusrow I,

[2060] Eddy 1961, pp. 79–80. Also see Boyce 1992, p. 40.

[2061] Eddy 1961, pp. 79–80. Note that cremation as well as interment are against orthodox Zoroastrian doctrine.

[2062] Eddy 1961, pp. 79–80.

[2063] Soudavar 1980, p. 33.

[2064] Tansar 1968, p. 16. See also our discussion of the *Letter of Tansar* in §2.5.2.

[2065] See §2.6.3 and §6.1. Boyce observes that this "quenching of local dynastic fires must have deeply offended the pride and piety of many Zoroastrians." Boyce 1979, p. 108. Boyce's frame of reference, however, is to the presumed Zurvanite-orthodox dimension of the Sasanian–Parthian rivalry; see our discussion in §5.2.4.

it clearly reflects the Sasanian antagonism toward the religious practices of the Parthian families.

Of the three great sacred fires[2066] of the Sasanians, one, the Burzīn Mihr fire, was in fact a Parthian fire established in their homeland sometime during the reign of the Arsacids.[2067] The particular affection of the Parthians for their fire is reflected in the Parthian romance *Vīs o Rāmin*.[2068] Here it is narrated that one of the kings who had "abdicated ... spent his last days in seclusion at its temple." The very burial site of Vīs and Rāmin, who in this romance appear as a Parthian king and queen, was "a royal sepulcher in the mountains above Adur Burzen-Mihr."[2069]

Ādhar Gushnasp fire

While the Burzīn Mihr fire was a Parthian fire, however, the Ādhar Farnbagh[2070] and Ādhar Gushnasp[2071] fires, in Persis and Media respectively, were Sasanian fires.

These fires are postulated to have been constructed in the late Achaemenid or Arsacid period. Their special significance to the Sasanians and the dynasty's promotion of these fires to primary fires, however, begins only in the mid-Sasanian period, that is, the fourth to mid-fifth century. Significantly, it is believed that the Ādhar Gushnasp and the Ādhar Farnbagh fires were promoted in order to "rival the glory of Adur Burzen-Mihr."[2072] Most of our evidence pertaining to these fires, in fact, belongs to this or later periods of Sasanian

[2066]For a synopsis of the stimuli that led to the creation of temples with images during the Achaemenid period, in reaction to which fire temples were created, see Boyce 1979, pp. 62–63. From this period onward, two categories of fires are known to have existed. "The great fires, the cathedral fires ... were all called, it seems, Atar-Verethragnā, Victorious Fire (the name is known only in its later forms, as Atakhsh i Varahram, Atash Bahram.) These were created from the embers of many ordinary fires, purified and consecrated through prolonged rites. The lesser fires were known simply as Fire of Fires (in later parlance *Atakhsh-i Aduran* or *Atash Aduran*.) These were formed from embers from the hearth fires of representatives of each social class, and their temples were roughly equivalent to the parish churches of Christendom." Boyce 1979, pp. 64–65. See also footnote 1873.

[2067]Boyce, Mary, 'Ādur Burzēn Mihr', in Ehsan Yarshater (ed.), *Encyclopaedia Iranica*, pp. 472–473, New York, 1991a (Boyce 1991a), pp. 472–473.

[2068]For *Vīs o Rāmin*, see Minorsky, V., 'Vīs u Rāmin', *Bulletin of the School of Oriental and African Studies* 11, 12, 16, 25, (1946, 1947, 1956, 1962), pp. 741–763, 20–35, 91–92, 275–286 (Minorsky 1946, 1947, 1956, 1962).

[2069]Boyce 1979, pp. 88 and 90 respectively.

[2070]For the legends associated with this fire see Boyce 1991a, pp. 473–475. For the location of the fire see Jackson, William, 'The Location of the Farnbag Fire, the Most Ancient of Zoroastrian Fires', *Journal of the American Oriental Society* 41, (1921), pp. 81–106 (Jackson 1921).

[2071]Boyce, Mary, 'Gushnasp', in Ehsan Yarshater (ed.), *Encyclopaedia Iranica*, pp. 475–476, New York, 1991e (Boyce 1991e). As Boyce observes the identification of the fire with the warrior caste, "to which the kings themselves belonged," was probably effected during the early Sasanian period. "There is no means of knowing whether it was before or after [the late Parthian period] ... when the Median priests annexed the whole of the early Zoroastrian tradition, from the pagan Kayanian down to the Prophet himself, for their own province, transferring it thus from northeast to northwest Iran." Boyce 1991e, p. 475.

[2072]Boyce 1979, p. 123.

rule. As far as the Ādhar Gushnasp fire is concerned, for example, there "is no mention of it in early Sasanian inscriptions; and excavations suggests that it was not until the late fourth century that it was taken to an unusually beautiful site in Azarbaijan."[2073] The first Sasanian monarch mentioned to have lavished gifts to the fire, to have visited the fire on the festivals of Sadih and Nowrūz, and to have made his Indian bride undergo purification there, is Bahrām V Gūr (420–438).[2074] In fact, it was probably this devout and zealous monarch "who first fully acknowledged the royal link with this fire." Archeological evidence, however, gives still later dates. For the "earliest dateable objects found in its [i.e., Ādhar Gushnasp's] ruins come from the reign of … Peroz (459–484)."[2075]

Ādhar Farnbagh fire

The earliest reliable evidence that we have for the Ādhar Farnbagh fire,[2076] furthermore, belongs to the early fifth century, when Yazdgird I (399–420) is "represented as *taking an oath* by both the Farnbag and Burzen-Mihr" fires. Other evidence for the Ādhar Farnbagh fire pertains to even later periods. Bīrūnī maintains, for example, that it was Pīrūz (459–484), the great grandson of Yazdgird I, who "prayed at the shrine of 'Adar Khara' [i.e., Ādhar Farnbagh] for an end to a devastating drought."[2077] The Sasanian solution to the fact that the Parthian fire of Burzīn Mihr was "too holy … to withhold veneration from it," moreover, was a measure which must further have offended the Parthian dynastic families and their followers. After the establishment of the two new fires, the Sasanians began to claim a tripartite hierarchy of fires. They now claimed that "Adur Farnbag … was the special fire of priests, and Adur Gushnasp … that of the warriors, whereas Adur Burzen-Mihr belonged to the lowliest estate, that of the herdsmen and farmers."[2078]

[2073]Boyce 1979, p. 124.

[2074]It is interesting to note, in view of our observations on page 373, that Bahrām V Gūr prohibited slaughtering cows before the fires, for he considered this sacrilegious. The slaughter of cows, the king argued, leads to the disappearance of *farr* from the realm. Ferdowsī 1971, vol. VII, p. 410, Ferdowsī 1935, p. 1678:

مریزید هم خون گاوان و رز — که ننگی بود گاو کشتن به مرز
ز پیری مگر گاو بیکار گشت — بچشم خداوند خود خوار گشت
نباید دگر کشت گاو رهی — که از مرز بیرون شود فرّهی

[2075]Boyce 1979, p. 124. It is also worth noting that this royal fire continued to be "tended in its hill-top sanctuary down to at least the middle of the tenth century." Boyce 1992, p. 153.

[2076]The Ādhar Farnbagh fire was established in Fārs, and Boyce maintains that "it is probable that this is where the fire was first grounded, at some unknown date, presumably in the late Achaemenid or Parthian period." Boyce, Mary, 'Ādur Farnbāg', in Ehsan Yarshater (ed.), *Encyclopaedia Iranica*, p. 474, New York, 1991d (Boyce 1991d).

[2077]"Farnbag means having a share/prosperity through Farnah (*farr*). Farnah is a dialect form of Avestan Khvarenah (Middle Persian Khwarrah, Persian Khara)." As Boyce observes, the Sasanians put this meaning of the name to much propagandistic use, identifying it "at times fully with divine Khvarenah itself." Boyce 1979, p. 123.

[2078]It should be observed that as a Mithra fire (see below), the Burzīn Mihr fire probably addressed the three-fold attributes of this important *yazata*, the kingly, warrior and nourishing functions.

Burzīn Mihr fire

But as the name of the Burzīn Mihr fire, 'Exalted is Mihr,' indicates, Mihr was the principal deity of this Parthian fire. Why would this be the case if the Parthians were in fact orthodox Zoroastrians?[2079] Boyce explains this by maintaining that Burzīn Mihr "is known as a personal name, and is presumed to be that of the unknown founder of the fire."[2080] She believes, in other words, that this major Parthian fire was originally established as a personal fire, as can be the case in Mazdeism. Yet the fire's theophoric name 'exalted is Mihr' would not make any sense, unless the individual in question was not only a Mihr worshipper, but also a powerful political figure, such as an Arsacid king. What lends credence to the conjecture that the Burzīn Mihr fire was a fire dedicated to Mithra/Mihr is further theophoric evidence surrounding this fire. One of the two suggested locations for this fire is Mount Mihr, "five miles from a village called Mihr on the highway between Šāhrūd and Sabsavār [Sabzivār]" in Khurāsān.[2081] The other proposed site is Mount Rīwand, a spur of the Nīshāpūr mountains, near which is a village called Burzīnān.[2082] Another curiosity surrounding this fire deserves mention. Of the three fires, only the Burzīn Mihr fire's name appears without the prefix *Ādur*, *Ādhar* or *Ātakhsh*. It has been suggested, therefore, that this might have been the habitual manner of referring to the Burzīn Mihr fire. The evidence for this is found in a number of seals. One of these seals bears the inscription *Ādur-dukht frāz ō Burzēn-Mihr* (Ādur-dukht in front of Burzēn-Mihr). While the reading of the second seal is not clear, two newly discovered seals[2083] bear the following clear inscription: "Dād-Burz-Mihr, Parthian aspbed, taking refuge in Burzēn-Mih[r]." Recall that these seals belong to the Parthian Kārin dynasty.[2084] Two other seals bear the inscription "*abestān ō Burz-Mihr*, confidence in Burz-Mihr." Gyselen argues, however, that as it is difficult to consider these graphic errors for the name Burzēn-Mihr, one should wonder "who is this Burz-Mihr to whom one is addressing oneself."[2085] The most obvious answer

It is possible, therefore, that in establishing a three-fold division of the fires, the Sasanians were attempting to undermine the all-encompassing functions of Mithra.

[2079] Another exalted temple, probably established during the Arsacid period, was the fire of Karkoy in Sīstān. According to the description of the temple of this fire by the thirteenth century geographer Qazvīnī, the temple had two domes, "bearing horns like that of a great bull." Boyce 1979, p. 153. If, in fact, this is a Parthian fire, the particular symbolism of the cow's horn on this temple is significant. To my knowledge no other Zoroastrian temple is described in the literature with this particular motif. As there seems to be a direct connection between Mihr worship and cow symbolism, at least in some versions of the faith (see 373ff below), the Karkoy fire might be considered another example of the particular Mithraic dimension of Parthian forms of religiosity.

[2080] Boyce 1991a, pp. 472–473.

[2081] William Jackson believed that in his travels he had identified the location of the Burzīn Mihr fire "with reasonable certainty" to be there. Jackson, A.V. William, *From Constantinople to the Home of Omar Khayyam*, New York, 1975 (Jackson 1975).

[2082] Boyce 1991a, p. 472.

[2083] Gyselen 2001a, seal 1b and seal A, pp. 36 and 46.

[2084] See page 114ff.

[2085] Gyselen 2003, pp. 134–135 and the references cited therein.

to this, however, is the one neglected: that the Burzīn Mihr fire is the object of devotion here.

There is no doubt that, as a general rule, during the Sasanian period there was a distinction between the religious tradition espoused by the Pārsīg and that adhered to by the Pahlav dynasts. We are not in a position to argue for this across the board, for we lack evidence to this effect for some important Parthian dynastic families, notably the Sūrens and the Ispahbudhān. What is more, we cannot argue for the dominance of a particular religious tradition within all sectors of a particular agnatic Parthian dynastic family. The distinction between the religious beliefs of the Pārsīg and that of the Pahlav during the Sasanian period, therefore, should be regarded as a general observation.

One key piece of evidence is an observation made by a fifth-century Armenian historian who "refers to a Zoroastrian priest who was master of *both the Persian and Parthian schools of religious thought*."[2086] There is no indication in our sources that any rapprochement between these two schools occurred in subsequent centuries. In fact, all the evidence at our disposal underlines not only a continuing distinction between these two religious schools, but even an outright hostility. The depiction of Khusrow I Nowshīrvān in the *Kārnāmag-i Anōshīravān* lends credence to this observation. Here, Khusrow I claims that "the *mōbadhān mōbadh* submitted [the case] of several persons whom he named *and who belonged to the nobility*. The *religion of these persons was contrary to that which we inherited from our Prophet and the learned men of our faith*." According to the *Kārnāmag-i Anōshīravān*, the *mōbadhān mōbadh* had warned Khusrow I that these people "were proselytizing in secret for their religion and inviting people to adopt it." Khusrow I then had these people brought to him in order to dispute with them. Presumably finding them adamant in their faith, Khusrow I then ordered "that they should be banished" from his capital, his country and his empire, "and that all those who shared their beliefs should follow them."[2087] There is very little doubt that among the nobles in question were members of the Parthian dynastic families. The clergy (*mōbads*) were key enforcers of Khusrow I's reforms, as attested by numerous seals.[2088] As we shall see,[2089] one of the chief accusations of the rebel Bahrām-i Chūbīn against the Sasanians was that the Mihrāns were dejected by the activities of these *mōbads*, by which he undoubtedly meant their attempts to impose Zoroastrian orthodoxy.

Acknowledging this evidence, Boyce admits the existence of a continued doctrinal difference between the Pārsīg and the Parthians during the Sasanian period, but interprets this as Sasanian adherence to the Zurvanite heresy,[2090] versus Parthian adherence to an orthodox form of Mazdeism. The Sasanian

[2086] Boyce 1979, p. 113.

[2087] Anoshiravan 1966, *Kārnāmag-i Anōshīravān*, vol. 254 of *Journal Asiatique*, pp. 16–45, 1966, translated by M. Grignaschi (Anoshiravan 1966), p. 26, apud Boyce 1979, p. 134.

[2088] Gyselen 2002.

[2089] See §6.1, especially page 403.

[2090] See §5.2.4.

adherence to the Zurvanite theology, Boyce argues, "was very probably the main point of difference between Parthian and Persian theology, *a difference which evidently persisted, despite the efforts of the Sasanian clergy.*"[2091] This, she claims, can be substantiated by the evidence of Manichean missionaries in Parthian territories. Although the Manicheans normally rendered the name of their God as Zurvān, when Mānī sent missionaries to Parthia, where his scriptures were translated into Parthian, they "rendered the name of the Manichean gods by ones acceptable to the Zoroastrians of that region." Instead of calling their God Zurvān they "simply translated the name of Mani's supreme God literally, as Father of Greatness." While evidence of Zurvanism can be found among the Sogdians and in the far northeast, Boyce furthermore maintains that "the Parthians appear to have resisted the heresy."[2092]

Contrary to Boyce's claim, however, this difference cannot be explained by the presumed orthodoxy of the Parthians. In fact, the paramount feature of the Sasanian–Parthian religious rivalry in the quarters of the east and the north was the predilection of some of the Parthian dynastic families for Mihr worship. Boyce admits the strength of Mihr worship in northeastern Iran. It is evident, she concedes, that "Mithra worship was *strong among the Iranian peoples to the north-east of Iran proper* ... where *there seem to have been cults where Mithra was the chief god*." This, however, she argues, cannot be taken to mean "that he was ever worshipped alone."[2093] Yet the evidence at our disposal indicates that Mihr was indeed the paramount popular deity among the Parthians—although his worship did not exclude the worship of other *yazatas*.

Ardashīr I / Ardavān

The Mithraic dimension of Parthian religiosity is highlighted in the narrative of the rise of the Sasanians and their defeat of the Arsacids in the *Kārnāmag-i Ardashīr-i Pāpagān*. As in the *Mihr Yasht*, where the true worshippers of Mithra stand in contrast to those who are not Mihr worshippers (*miθrō-druj*),[2094] so too in the *Kārnāmag-i Ardashīr-i Pāpagān*, standing on the side of Mithra, and abiding by his contract, or being in opposition to him and breaking a treaty, is called respectively *mihrān kardan*, to form a Mithra, and *mihr durūjī*, to be false to Mithra. This terminology is in fact replete in the accounts of Ardashīr I's victory over the Arsacid king Ardavān.[2095]

2091 Boyce 1979, pp. 112–113.

2092 Boyce 1979, p. 112.

2093 Boyce, Mary, 'On Mithra's Part in Zoroastrianism', *Bulletin of the School of Oriental and African Studies* 32 (Boyce 1969), p. 16, n. 32.

2094 Mihr Yasht 1883, §9. See also Frawardin Yasht 1883, *Frawardīn Yasht*, vol. 23 of *Sacred Books of the East*, Oxford University Press, 1883, translated by James Darmesteter (Frawardin Yasht 1883), §47, as cited in Jafarey, A., 'Mithra, Lord of the Lands', in Rowman and Littlefield (eds.), *Mithraic Studies: Proceedings of the First International Congress of Mithraic Studies*, pp. 54–61, Manchester University Press, 1975 (Jafarey 1975), p. 58.

2095 Besides the examples below, see Ardashir 1963, p. 186. The *Kārnāmag-i Ardashīr-i Pāpagān* is so replete with Mithraic imagery that a separate study needs to be devoted to it. An example of

The narrative of the rise of the Sasanians in the *Kārnāmag-i Ardashīr-i Pāpagān* contains folkloric elements; a popular provenance that makes the information contained in it all the more significant. Here, the rebellion of the upstart king Ardashīr I against the Arsacid Ardavān commences when Ardashīr I, together with a slave girl of Ardavān, fled from the Arsacid ruler. Halfway through their flight on horses stolen from Ardavān's stable, when the sun had risen, the two were pursued by a ram, the agent that bestows Royal Glory, *farr* (*xwarra*, *Khavernah*), on behalf of the *yazata* Mithra.[2096] The rising sun, the mounted warriors, and finally the ram are all Mithraic imagery that, in line with the function of Mithra as the "maker, as well as undoer, of kings,"[2097] heralds the transference of the *farr* of the last Arsacid, Ardavān, to the first Sasanian king, Ardashīr I. When the ram finally caught up with Ardashīr I, he was consequently assured of kingship.[2098] Later in the narrative, Ardashīr I married the sister of Ardavān. The two brothers of Ardavān, in flight, accused their sister of betrayal and dubbed her a *mihr durūj*, a breaker of the contract, and one who had been false to Mithra.[2099] In fact, this part of the narrative is replete with the terms *mihr durūj* and *Mihr*.[2100] Ardashīr I's enemy in Fārs, with the significantly theophoric name of Mihrak-i Nūshzādān,[2101] broke his collaboration with Ardashīr I by what the *Kārnāmag-i Ardashīr-i Pāpagān* also terms *mihr durūjī*.[2102]

this is the narrative of the *Haftānbūkht* worm who rules, it is argued, on the coast of the Persian Gulf and has his stronghold in the *dizh-i Kalānān*. In the *Shāhnāma*, he is credited with building the city of Kirmān. This powerful worm—called the auspicious worm (*kirm-i farrokh*) in the *Shāhnāma* and *varjāvand* in the *Kārnāmag-i Ardashīr-i Pāpagān*—who is the enemy of Ardashīr I, feeds on the blood of cows, and can be destroyed only if it drinks zinc, as in the ordeal connected with establishing the veracity of a Mithraic oath (see page 356). The worm throws an arrow that is called the arrow of the cavalry of the victorious (*asubārān-i varjāvand*), and his followers are idol worshippers (*uzdih parastandigān*), who have been led astray from the worship of Ahūrā Mazdā and the Amahraspands. This passage contains a host of Mithraic symbols requiring further study. Ardashir 1963, pp. 188–192. The consensus seems to be that the abode of this worm is the coastal part of Persia. A reinvestigation of this story might be open, however, to the possibility that it takes place in northeastern Iran, perhaps in the *dizh-i Kalāt/Kalānān* in Khurāsān. Ardashīr I and a group of his followers, after all, disguise themselves in Khurāsānī attire in order to dupe the worm and his subjects. For Haftānbūkht, see Shaki, Mansour, 'Haftānbūkht', in Ehsan Yarshater (ed.), *Encyclopaedia Iranica*, New York, 2007b (Shaki 2007b) and Shahbazi, Shapur, 'Haftvād', in Ehsan Yarshater (ed.), *Encyclopaedia Iranica*, pp. 535–537, New York, 1991e (Shahbazi 1991e), pp. 535–537.

2096 Ardashir 1963, pp. 176–180. See page 354 and footnote 2261.

2097 Mihr Yasht 1959, p. 60.

2098 Ardashir 1963, p. 182. When Ardavān enquired about the meaning of this, he was told that the ram symbolizes his *farr*. Ferdowsī 1971, vol. VII, p. 128, Ferdowsī 1935, p. 1935:

چنین داد پاسخ که این فرّ اوست   به شاهی و نیك اختری پرّ اوست

2099 Ardashir 1963, p. 195. For a more detailed account, see page 46.

2100 Ardashir 1963, p. 195 (three times), p. 196 (twice).

2101 The *Shāhnāma* calls him Mihrak-i Nūshzād and describes him as having Kayānid ancestry (*Kai Nizhād*). Ferdowsī 1935, p. 1953. In Ṭabarī, Mihrak is "the king of Abarsās, in the district of Ardashīr Khurrah." Ṭabarī 1999, pp. 10–11, and n. 34, de Goeje, 817.

2102 Ardashir 1963, p. 188.

The *X^w adāy-Nāmag* tradition is likewise infused with Mithraic concepts. The Sun as bestower of kingly power, the idea of contract (*peymān*) between the king and his flock, the Circle of Justice, and the concepts of *dād o Mihr* (Justice and Mihr) are recurrent motifs in the *Shāhnāma*. Let us note a few instances in portions dealing with the rise of the Sasanians and their early history. When Bābak dreamt that Sāsān was carrying the three fires of Adhar Gushnasp, Ādhar Farnbagh, and Burzīn Mihr, the dream interpreters informed him that his dream signified that the kingship of Sāsān would appear through the Sun.[2103] When Bābak sent for Sāsān and asked his pedigree, the latter informed him that if he gave him his protection (*zinhār*), that is, refuge—again a thoroughly Mithraic concept—and took his hand in contract (*cho dastam bigīrī peymān bidast*), then he would divulge his ancestry.[2104] When Shāpūr II appointed his brother Ardashīr II as regent for his minor son, Shāpūr III, he did so on condition that Ardashīr II entered *in justice* into a contract with him (*gar bā man az dād peymān konī*).[2105] Ardashīr II kept to the terms of his contract.[2106]

5.4 Mihr worship in the quarters of the north and east

The predominant form of religiosity during the Sasanian era in the northern and northeastern regions of Iran (*kūst-i ādurbādagān* and *kūst-i khwarāsān*) ruled by the Parthian dynastic families, was not the orthodox Zoroastrianism propagated by the Sasanian *mōbads*, but popular religious customs that betray strong currents of Mihr worship. The precise nature of this Mihr worship and the rituals connected with it, and how it differed from the worship of Mihr in the orthodox Zoroastrian systems of belief, cannot be ascertained with any degree of certainty given the evidence at our disposal at this point. What can be asserted, however, is that the Mihr worship prevalent in these regions of Iran was distinct from that which pertained to the orthodox Zoroastrian creed. As

[2103] Ferdowsī 1971, vol. VII, p. 118, Ferdowsī 1935, p. 1925:

کسی را که دیدی تو زینسان به خواب　　به شاهی برارد سر از افتاب

[2104] Ferdowsī 1971, vol. VII, p. 118, Ferdowsī 1935, p. 1925:

وزان پس بدو گفت کی شهریار　　شبان را به جان گر دهی زنهار
بگویم ز گوهر همه هرچه هست　　چو دستم بگیری پیمان بدست

[2105] Ferdowsī 1935, p. 2065:

که گر با من از داد پیمان کنی　　زبان را ز پیمان گروگان کنی

[2106] Ferdowsī 1971, vol. VII, p. 253, Ferdowsī 1935, p. 2069:

نگشت ان دلاور ز پیمان خویش　　به مردی نگه داشت سامان خویش

It should be noted that the use of the term *peymān* here does not seem to have any correspondence with the philosophical and theological terminology of the *right measure* as discussed in Shaked, Shaul, 'Paymān: An Iranian Idea in Contact with Greek Thought and Islam', in *Transition Periods in Iranian History*, vol. 5 of *Societas Iranologica Europaea*, pp. 217–240, Fribourg-en-Brisgau, 1987 (Shaked 1987).

the territories under the control of the Parthian dynastic families were concentrated in the quarters of the north and the east, furthermore, and in line with the Pārsīg–Pahlav political rivalry, a general north–south dichotomy in religious matters seems to have existed through the Sasanian period.

5.4.1 Mihr worship in Ṭabaristān

In the remainder of this chapter, we explore the Mithraic traditions in the quarters of the north and the east, traditionally controlled by the Parthian dynastic families. The primacy of Mihr worship in these regions is reflected in the Iranian national tradition. The stories of a host of primary figures in the mythic sections of this tradition, figures around whom Mihr symbolism coalesce, are appropriated by the Pahlav regions, most notably Ṭabaristān. It must be pointed out from the outset that the association of the events and figures which will be enumerated below with Ṭabaristān was the result of a later identification of the mythical region of Māzandarān from the national tradition with Ṭabaristān.[2107] It has been claimed that this association might have occurred in the late Sasanian period. Regardless, however, of when this identification occurred, it is very likely that it was instigated by the Parthian dynastic families. The fact that the original location of Māzandarān from the national tradition is obscure[2108] does not undermine the significance of the fact that the motifs, symbols, and primary figures of the national tradition, all of which have strong Mithraic associations, were appropriated by regions ruled by Parthian dynastic families during the Sasanian period.

To begin with, according to a tradition contained in the *Videvdād*, the abode of the *yazata* Mithra was in the Alburz mountains.[2109] In the original Iranian myth of creation, however, Mithra's dwelling was on the Peak of Harā. The identification of the primordial Mount Harā with Damāvand in the Alburz mountains may be viewed as an example of the regional development of Zoroastrianism and the appropriation of significant motifs and episodes of the Mazdean religion by various regions.[2110] Only in Ṭabaristān, however, do we find the identification of the *abode of Mithra* with a local mountain chain. When precisely this identification of the dwelling of Mithra with Damāvand came to be made is not clear. What is clear, however, is that the Mithraic myths co-opted by the northern regions run through a number of other episodes of the mythic sections of the Iranian tradition. In the *Videvdād*, therefore, "Mithra is said to approach across the Alburz mountains in front of the sun!"[2111] From

[2107]Yarshater 1983b, pp. 446–447.

[2108]As Yarshater notes the "original location of the lands that the Iranians called Māzandarān as well as the meaning of the name is somewhat problematic. It was applied originally to a hostile land of different cultic beliefs known to the Iranians in their legendary period. Its use as an appellation for Ṭabaristān is fairly late and probably dates from late Sasanian times." Yarshater 1983b, p. 446.

[2109]Vendidad 1880, §19.28.

[2110]See page 321.

[2111]Humback, H., 'Mithra in the Kuṣāṇa Period', in John R. Hinnells (ed.), *Mithraic Studies: Proceedings of the First International Congress of Mithraic Studies*, vol. I, pp. 135–141, 1975 (Humback

Damāvand, Mithra watched over the world, through 360 windows.[2112] Mount Damāvand, the highest peak in the Alburz mountains, was located in Padhashkhwārgar, later considered part of the quarter of the north.[2113]

Fereydūn

Damāvand was not only identified with Mithra, however. It is also the birthplace of the paramount and primary mythic Pīshdādī king of the national tradition, Fereydūn.[2114] His birth took place toward the end of the millennium during which the evil foreigner Ḍaḥḥāk ruled over Iran.[2115] According to the national tradition, when Ḍaḥḥāk destroyed the Pīshdādī king Jamshīd (Yima), Fereydūn's mother took refuge in the Damāvand mountains, where the boy Fereydūn was born and whence he came out of hiding at the age of sixteen.[2116]

What is significant for our purposes about the association of Fereydūn with Ṭabaristān, however, is that potent Mithraic symbols surround this primary mythic king of Iran. In fact, it might be argued that the figure of Fereydūn represents the God Mihr.[2117] According to the *Tārīkh-i Ṭabaristān*, when Ḍaḥḥāk destroyed Jamshīd, the descendants of this Pīshdādī king were left distant from the shadows of the Sun (*az sāyih-i khūrshīd nufūr o mahjūr shudand*).[2118] The deeds of Fereydūn, the king with *farr* (*xwarra, Khvarenah*), and the slayer of Ḍaḥḥāk, therefore, are appropriately compared to that of the luminous Sun by the *Shāhnāma*.[2119] When Fereydūn prepared to battle Ḍaḥḥāk in Ṭabaristān, he first raised his head to the Sun.[2120] In Ṭabaristān, with the aid of the *yazata*

1975), p. 137.

[2112] Yarshater 1983a, p. 351.

[2113] See page 40 for a delimitation of this region.

[2114] According to the Avestā, Fereydūn was born in Varena, "identified in later sources with Var, a village in the area of Lārījān," near Damāvand Vendidad 1880, §1.17. According to *X^w adāy-Nāmag* tradition contained in Ṭabarī, Fereydūn was born in Damāvand itself. For Fereydūn, see Yarshater 1983b, pp. 427–429; Tafazzoli, Ahmad, 'Fereydūn', in Ehsan Yarshater (ed.), *Encyclopaedia Iranica*, New York, 2007 (Tafazzoli 2007); and the sources cited therein. For the Pīshdādī dynasty in the Iranian national history, see Yarshater 1983b, pp. 420–436, as well as footnote 131.

[2115] According to the *Shāhnāma*, the tyrant Ḍaḥḥāk, who ruled Iran for 1000 years, was of Arab descent. His tyranny was caused by the kiss of Ahrīman (the Force of Evil) on his shoulders. Snakes grew in place of this. In order to feed these, the brains of two young boys had to be fed to the tyrant daily. The tyrant's chefs substituted the brain of a sheep for one of these. Kāveh, the blacksmith, seventeen of whose sons had been fed to Ḍaḥḥāk, ultimately led a rebellion that overthrew Ḍaḥḥāk, and returned the crown to the Iranian king, Fereydūn. Ferdowsī 1935, pp. 69–114.

[2116] Ferdowsī 1935.

[2117] Kayūmarth, the first king of the national tradition and the prototype of man in the religious tradition, has also been identified with Mithra, or a brother of Mithra. See Yarshater 1983b, pp. 372–373, and 416. Unlike Fereydūn and a number of other primary figures of the national tradition, however, his figure is not co-opted by the regional traditions of the north.

[2118] Ibn Isfandīyār 1941, p. 57.

[2119] Ferdowsī 1971, vol. I, p. 57:

جهانجوی با فرّ جمشید بود   بکردار تابنده خورشید بود

[2120] Ferdowsī 1971, vol. I, p. 66:

فریدون به خورشید بر برد سر   به کین پدر تنگ بستش کمر

Sorūsh and using the bull-headed mace,[2121] Fereydūn captured Ḍaḥḥāk.[2122] The victory is celebrated on Mihrigān,[2123] one of the most cherished festivals of the Iranians, which therefore came to be associated with the northern regions of Iran, the land of the Pahlav.

Mihrigān

The festival of Mihrigān, as the name implies, was devoted to the God Mihr. Traditionally an autumn festival, through the Sasanian and the early Islamic period, it was "scarcely less well loved than the Spring festival of Nō Rūz."[2124] In fact Bīrūnī observes that "some people have given the preference to Mihrigān by as much as they prefer autumn to spring."[2125] While Mihrigān continued to be celebrated by orthodox Zoroastrians during the Sasanian period, however, it was a festival that was essentially untouched by Zoroastrianism.[2126] As one of the ancient attributes of Mihr was his eschatological function,[2127] so too was the eschatological dimension of Mihrigān very significant, for according to Bīrūnī, "the Iranians who believe in *ta'wīl* ... also believe Mihrigān to be a sign of resurrection and the end of the world, ... For they argue that on this day that which grows reaches its perfection."[2128] Significantly, the festival "was also a time for rallying the forces of good to oppose the demons of the coming winter and darkness," for Mihr "was one of the great fighting divinities *of Zoroastrianism*, a champion for the kingdom of righteousness."[2129] It was also believed that the pact between Ahūrā Mazdā and Ahrīman "which fixes the period of

---

It is worth noting that the *derafsh-i Kāvīyān*, which the legendary hero Kāveh fashioned out of hide, presumably cow's hide, when he instigated a rebellion on behalf of Fereydūn against Ḍaḥḥāk, was also imbued with Mithraic symbolism. It not only symbolizes the just struggle of Kāveh against the unjust usurper Ḍaḥḥāk, but also becomes the symbol of the *farr* for Iranian kings. The *Shāhnāma* maintains that in the darkness of the night, the *derafsh*, being bejeweled, shone like the very sun. Christensen, who pointed out that this legend is not found in the Avestā or other Mazdean theological books and must, therefore, belong to the Sasanian period, argued that the legend probably reflected the fame of the Kārin family, who considered themselves the descendants of Kāveh. As we will discuss in §5.4.3 below, there is every indication that the Kārins were in fact Mihr worshippers. Wikander even argued that the *derafsh* became the national banner of Iran during the Arsacid period. See Christensen 1944, pp. 502–503 and n. 5; and Motlagh, Djalal Khaleghi, 'Derafsh-e Kāvēān', in Ehsan Yarshater (ed.), *Encyclopaedia Iranica*, New York, 2007b (Motlagh 2007b).

2121 Yarshater 1983b, p. 372. The ox-headed mace is also called the mace of Mithra; see footnote 2155 below.

2122 Ibn Balkhī 1995, p. 114.

2123 Tha'ālibī 1900, pp. 35–36; Bīrūnī 1984, pp. 337–338.

2124 Boyce, Mary, 'Iranian Festivals', in Ehsan Yarshater (ed.), *Cambridge History of Iran: The Seleucid, Parthian, and Sasanian Periods*, vol. 3(2), pp. 792–815, Cambridge University Press, 1983a (Boyce 1983a), p. 801.

2125 Bīrūnī 1984, p. 339; Boyce 1983a, p. 801.

2126 Hinnells, John R., 'Reflections on the Bull-Slaying Scene', *Mithraic Studies* 2, (1975), pp. 290–312 (Hinnells 1975), p. 307.

2127 See page 353.

2128 Bīrūnī 1984, p. 339.

2129 Bīrūnī 1984, p. 338; Boyce 1983a, pp. 801–802. Emphasis added. We should stress that Boyce is only referring here to the position of Mihr in Mazdean doctrine.

their struggle, was made at Mihrigān, since *Mihr is the lord of all covenants.*"[2130] Mihrigān was celebrated by the Sasanian kings and commoners alike. For our purposes, its significance, besides its obvious Mithraic provenance, was that it represented the popular celebration of the defeat of Ḍaḥḥāk by Fereydūn. In the popular imagination, Ḍaḥḥāk's defeat took place in Ṭabaristān. Significantly, the very first fire temple built by Fereydūn was also believed to have been in the city of Ṭūs,[2131] in the vicinity of which, we recall, the Burzīn Mihr fire was located. We should add to our list of locations carrying theophoric Mithraic names,[2132] a village called Mihrijān (the Arabicized version of Mihrigān), in the environs of Nīshāpūr.[2133]

In order to defeat Ḍaḥḥāk, a bull-headed mace was constructed for Fereydūn. This mace too is likened to the high Sun in the *Shāhnāma*.[2134] In his fight against the quintessential symbol of injustice, Ḍaḥḥāk, Fereydūn is naturally the quintessential symbol of justice rising from Ṭabaristān. After his defeat of Ḍaḥḥāk, when on the day of Mihr, Fereydūn crowned himself, "the times became bereft of evil and people began to follow the path of wisdom."[2135] The religion of Fereydūn, the *Shāhnāma* finally maintains, is the *worship of Mihrigān*.[2136] Once he defeated Ḍaḥḥāk in Ṭabaristān, from the Alburz mountains, Fereydūn circled around the globe, and saw what was hidden and manifest. With his benevolence he forbade every manifestation of evil and restored every land that had been ridden with destruction. The regions which were barren, he cultivated, making the world paradise incarnate.[2137] Like Mihr, therefore, Fereydūn had his abode in the Damāvand mountains, from where he rose. Like Mihr, raising his head to the Sun, he restored kingship, here to himself. Like Mihr circling the globe from Damāvand, Fereydūn circled the world, and like

---

[2130] Bīrūnī 1984, p. 338; Boyce 1983a, p. 802. Emphasis added.

[2131] Shahristānī, Abū 'l-Fataḥ Muḥammad, *al-Milal wa 'l-Niḥal*, Tehran, 1971, translated by Afdal al-Din Isfahani and edited by Seyyed Muhammad Riza Jalal Na'ini (Shahristānī 1971), p. 269.

[2132] See, for instance, footnote 2081.

[2133] Iṣṭakhrī, *Kitāb al-Masālik wa 'l-Mamālik*, Leiden, 1927, edited by M.J. de Goeje (Iṣṭakhrī 1927), pp. 205, 223.

[2134] Ferdowsī 1971, vol. I, p. 66:

بپیش جهانجوی بردند گرز فروزان به کردار خورشید برز

[2135] Ferdowsī 1971, vol. I, p. 76:

زمانه بی اندوه گشت از بدی گرفتند هر کس رهه بخردی

[2136] Ferdowsī 1935, vol. I, p. 76:

پرستیدن مهرگان دین اوست تن اسانی و خوردن ائین اوست

[2137] Ferdowsī 1971, , vol. I, p. 81:

واز ان پس فریدون به گرد جهان بگردید و دید اشکار و نهان
هر ان چیز کز راه بیداد دید هر ان بوم و بر کان نه اباد دید
بنیکی ببست از همه دست بد چنانك از ره پادشاهان سزد
بیاراست گیتی بسان بهشت بجای گیا سرو گلبن بکشت

Mihr watching over the world through 360 windows,[2138] Fereydūn saw all to be seen and that which was hidden. Like Mihr, he actively destroyed evil and injustice, and as Mihr he had a nourishing function. Finally, like Mihr, he advocated Mihrigān.[2139]

The cow in Mihr worship

The central role of the cow in the narratives of Fereydūn and Ṭabaristān likewise connects Fereydūn to Mihr.[2140] According to Ibn Isfandīyār, when Fereydūn came of age, he left the Damāvand region as a result of its unsuitability for cultivation and migrated to the environs of Shalāb on account of its pastures and the fact that the population of the region subsisted from the breeding of kine and the profits that accrued from this.[2141] At the age of seven Fereydūn would fix halters to the cow's snout and make a riding beast of it. Each day Fereydūn would ride the cow out hunting and in pursuit of other affairs until he reached the prime of his life (*bi rowq-i shabāb resīd*). While seated on the cow, according to the *Tārīkh-i Ṭabaristān*, "one would think that from the *reflection of the heavenly bodies on earth another sun is rising from Taurus.*"[2142] Here, he takes the form of a constellation crossing the sky, to wit, Thawr or Taurus, the sign of the bull. The imagery of the Sun, Taurus, and the riding figure on it, namely

2138 Yarshater 1983a, p. 351.

2139 Significantly, Ferdowsī comments that Fereydūn was not an angel (Amahraspand). It was on account of his justice and kindness that he found the good fortune. Ferdowsī seems to be replying here to what must have been a prevalent popular interpretation of this myth of Fereydūn, for according to Bīrūnī some people thought that during Mihrigān the angels came to the aid of Fereydūn. Bīrūnī 1984, p. 338:

فریدون فرّخ فرشته نبود ... به داد دهش یافت ان نیکویی.

2140 The nature of the terrain in both Ṭabaristān as well as Gīlān is such that the breeding of kine was one of the central economic activities of the region. So much so that to this day cows are a central part of the landscape in this region. The symbolic connection of the cow with Ṭabaristān, however, continues to be especially significant for, except in the lush Caspian provinces, as Insler argues, "cattle never prospered well in the barrenness of Iran." Gathas 1975, *The Gāthās of Zarathustra*, vol. 8 of *Acta Iranica*, 1975, translated by Stanley Insler (Gathas 1975), quoted in Harper, Prudence O., 'The Ox-Headed Mace in Pre-Islamic Iran', in *Papers in Honour of Professor Mary Boyce*, vol. 24 of *Acta Iranica*, pp. 248–265, Leiden, 1985 (Harper 1985), p. 248, n. 9.

2141 Ibn Isfandīyār 1941, p. 57:

که در ان صقع چراخورها باشد و مقیمان او را تعیّش از منافع نتاج و باج گاوان بود.

As Tafazzoli maintains the connection of Fereydūn with cattle in general is noteworthy. The totemic ancestors of the hero are mentioned with the suffix *gāw*, cow. In "Islamic and Middle Persian sources Frēdōn is made a descendant of Jamshēd by ten generations, the names of which are suffixed by the word *gāv*, cow." Tafazzoli 2007; Yarshater 1983b, p. 429. Like the *Tārīkh-i Ṭabaristān*, the association of Fereydūn with the cow is replete in the *Shāhnāma*: he is said to be raised, for example, by a cow. Ferdowsī 1971, vol. I, pp. 57–58, 60–61, 66, 70. For other imagery of the bovine associated with Fereydūn, see Tafazzoli 2007.

2142 Ibn Isfandīyār 1941, p. 57:

چون طفل از حدّ رضاع بفطام رسید، و هفت عام برو گذشت، خطام در بینی گاوان میکرد و مرکب خود میساخت، چنان بود که گویی از عکس افلاك بر روی خاك افتابی دیگر از ثور طلوع میکند.

Fereydūn, the king who is endowed with Divine Glory, replicates in minute detail the Mithraic tauroctony,[2143] except that, unlike Mithras, the young man atop the cow is not depicted as killing the animal.[2144] In this manner and in the prime of his life Fereydūn improved the affairs of his people and managed to gather the inhabitants of the region, including, significantly, those of the Kārin Mountain (Kūh-i Kārin). At this point, according to Ibn Isfandīyār, Fereydūn's followers built him an ox-headed mace (*gorz*) with which he captured Ḍaḥḥāk.[2145] So central was the role of Fereydūn in the popular memory of Ṭabaristān that Ibn Isfandīyār, writing in the thirteenth century, maintains that the remnants of his constructions in his capital Tammīsha (*nishast-i jāy-i khud*) are still in existence.[2146] From the narrative of Fereydūn in the national tradition to the history of Ṭabaristān during the Sasanian period to the accounts of the revolts in the region in the post-conquest period, the cow motif appears with a frequency unparalleled in the narratives of any other region of the Iranian plateau. Mihr worship and cow symbolism were also embraced by the Āl-i Jāmāsp family, the family of Gāvbārih, the Cow-Devotee, who ruled in Ṭabaristān from the sixth through the mid-eighth century.[2147] Finally, it is worth noting that according to Yāqūt, the inhabitants of Ṭūs were called "the cows," Yāqūt expressing disdain about its meaning.[2148]

The cow had always been considered sacred in orthodox Zoroastrianism.[2149] Before the relatively late domestication of the camel and the horse among the Indo-Iranians, the cow was considered the most valuable domesticated animal. From early on, therefore, a cow or a bull (*gāv*) became "traditionally the best offering men could make to the gods." The primordial bull also plays a central role in Zoroastrian cosmogony. In the Zoroastrian myth of creation, it is from the sacrificial slaughter of the cow that all animal life spreads across the *gītig* (material world). Nonetheless, it has been argued that the soteriological dimensions of the sacrifice of the bull was pre-Zoroastrian and in all probability Mithraic. The cow holds a significant place in Mithraic/Mihr religious

[2143]See footnote 2150.

[2144]Ulansey, David, *The Origins of the Mithraic Mysteries: Cosmology and Salvation in the Ancient World*, Oxford University Press, 1989 (Ulansey 1989). In *Āthār al-Bāqiya*, Bīrūnī gives a similar depiction of this mythic episode. When night came, a cow made up of light, with horns of gold, and feet of silver appeared, carrying the wheel of the moon, the whole scene appearing and disappearing at intervals. Bīrūnī gives this under his discussion of the celebration on the day of Mihr of the month of Day, and maintains that Iranians celebrate this festival because on this day Iran freed itself from the rule of Turkistān, and retrieved the cows which the Turkistānis had stolen from them. Bīrūnī 1984, pp. 345–346.

[2145]In the *Āthār al-Bāqiya*, Fereydūn swore on the "blood of the cow that was in [his] ancestor's house" to kill Ḍaḥḥāk. Bīrūnī 1984, p. 339.

[2146]Ibn Isfandīyār 1941, p. 58. For the significance of aspects of Iranian national history in the popular memory of various regions in Iran, as contained in the local historiographical tradition, see Pourshariati 2000.

[2147]See §4.3, especially page 302.

[2148]Yaqūt al-Hamawī 1866, vol. 3, pp. 561–562.

[2149]Boyce, Mary, 'Cattle: II. In Zoroastrianism', in Ehsan Yarshater (ed.), *Encyclopaedia Iranica*, pp. 80–84, New York, 1991c (Boyce 1991c).

rituals, customs, and doctrine. In the Roman Mithraic tauroctony,[2150] the sacrifice of the bull by Mithras is of a central and crucial significance.[2151] Under the Achaemenids, the focal point of the autumnal festival of Mihrigān was the "sacrifice of a bull, or its substitute, to Mithra."[2152] The sacrosanct function of the cow in the Zoroastrian creed, therefore, seems to have a Mithraic heritage. At the initiation ceremony of a Mazdean priest, for example, the *mōbad* is given the famous bull-headed mace, the *gorz*. These *gorzes* are "carried at major ceremonies and decorate the wall of Zoroastrian temples."[2153] A Zoroastrian priest carries the mace "as a symbol of the moral fight which he is taking up against evil."[2154] The *gorz*, like Mihrigān, however, does not have a Zoroastrian origin, and even in the orthodox Zoroastrian creed it is acknowledged as the mace of Mithra.[2155] As Hinnells points out, the designation of "the whole fire temple . . . as *dar-i Mihr*, the gateway or court of Mithra," as well as the ritual dimensions of the cow motif, could "have developed only if Mithra was *traditionally a god of outstanding ritual significance*."[2156]

Manūchihr

Further evidence for the prevalence of Mihr worship in the northern regions is found in the story of the Pīshdādī king Manūchihr,[2157] which begins a new chapter of the Iranian national history. As Yarshater observes, with the advent of Manūchihr, "the world is no longer ruled by a single king." The ferocious feud between the Iranians and the Tūrānians[2158] starts during the reign of this king, where he is the first to have to reckon with a powerful enemy king. A derivative of this king's name, Manush,[2159] is directly connected with the north, for the *Bundahishn* identifies Manush as a mountain belonging to the Alburz

[2150]In Roman Mithraism, in the Mithraea (Mithraic temples) scattered around the Mediterranean world, the central scene of the murals depicts the God Mithras killing a sacred bull.

[2151]Hinnells 1975, p. 308.

[2152]Hinnells 1975, p. 307. This practice continued into the Sasanian period: In gratitude for victory over his enemies, for example, the Sasanian king Yazdgird II (459–484) "increased the sacrifices of fire with white bulls and hairy goats, . . . [and] assiduously multiplied his impure cult." Eḷishē 1982, p. 66.

[2153]Hinnells 1975, p. 308.

[2154]Boyce 1983a, p. 802.

[2155]Besides Ibn Isfandīyār's narrative, the bull-headed mace (*gorz-i gāvsar*) of Fereydūn is also mentioned in the *Shāhnāma*; Ibn Balkhī's *Fārsnāma*, Ṭabarī's *Annals*, and Thaʿālibī's *Ghurar*. Tafazzoli 2007, p. 429 and the references cited there in. For the *gorz*, see Doostkhah, Jalil, 'Gorz', in Ehsan Yarshater (ed.), *Encyclopaedia Iranica*, New York, 1991 (Doostkhah 1991). The ox-headed mace was also the weapon of Rustam, Gēv, Isfandīyār, and Gushtāsp. Harper 1985, p. 248.

[2156]Hinnells 1975, p. 308.

[2157]Manūchihr, whose name (Middle Persian Manushchihr) means from the race of Manu, and is regarded in India as "the first man and father of the human race," is only mentioned in the Avestā once, and then only in the Yashts. Frawardin Yasht 1883, §131; Yarshater 1983b, pp. 432–433.

[2158]For the Tūrānians, Iran's arch-enemies in the national tradition, later identified with the Turks, see Yarshater 1983b, pp. 408–409.

[2159]Zamyad Yasht 1883, §1.

chain, where Manūchihr was born.[2160] In his wars against the Tūrānian Afrāsīyāb, Manūchihr habitually took refuge in Ṭabaristān.[2161] Manūchihr, who was one of the first mythic kings to acquire a reputation for justice and equity (*ʿadl o nīkūyī*),[2162] declared in the *Shāhnāma* that he was both "wrath and warfare as well as justice and Mihr," virtually identifying himself, in other words, with the god. He ordered the people of Iran to engage in agriculture as well as cattle breeding.[2163]

Another important Mithraic aspect of Manūchihr's figure is the popular etymology of his name. According to the *Bundahishn*,[2164] the king acquired his name when the rays of the sun fell on his face at the time of his birth. Manūchihr also inherited the *farr* (*xwarra*) of Fereydūn. Like Fereydūn, Manūchihr acquired this *farr* from the sun Mihr. According to Ibn Balkhī, the father of Manūchihr was called Mīshkhuryār, which Ibn Balkhī translates as the "constant companion of the rays of the sun (*hamīshih āftābyār*)."[2165] Manūchihr's chief achievement, however, was his role as the avenger of the murder of the favorite son of Fereydūn, Iraj, who was killed by his brothers.[2166] As we shall see, the Mithraic motif of revenge for a wrongful murder also appears in the revolts of Bahrām-i Chūbīn in the late sixth century, and of Sunbād in the early ʿAbbāsid period, testifying to the continuity of the Mithraic tradition in the region.[2167]

The collaboration of Manūchihr's *spāhbeds*, Kārin and Ārash, the presumed progenitors of respectively the Kārins and the Mihrāns, with the king of Ṭabaristān is also detailed in the *Tārīkh-i Ṭabaristān*.[2168] The legendary hero Ārash appeared from Ṭabaristān during Manūchihr's war with Tūrān. In order to determine the boundaries between Iran and Tūrān, Ārash, "the best bowman of Iran ... [and] helped by divine guidance," shot an arrow that landed somewhere in the east.[2169] Ārash's arrow left his bow at sunrise, and landed at its destination at sunset, thus mimicking the movement of Mihr's sun chariot.[2170] The bow shot of Ārash established a contract between the two peoples, which, significantly, Afrāsīyāb broke by attacking Iran.[2171] It was to Ārash of Rayy that

[2160] According to Balʿamī some traditions maintain that the birthplace of Manūchihr was Rayy. Balʿamī 1959, p. 33. After his defeat at the hands of Afrāsīyāb, Balʿamī maintains, Manūchihr was held captive in the city of Āmul in Ṭabaristān. Ibid., p. 34.

[2161] Ibn Balkhī 1995, p. 119.

[2162] Thaʿālibī 1900, p. 68, Thaʿālibī 1989, p. 50.

[2163] Thaʿālibī 1989, p. 50, Thaʿālibī 1900, p. 68:

و اوّل من جعل لكل قرية دهقانا و إتخذ اهلها حولا و البسهم لباس المذلة و رالزمهم اذناب البقر.

[2164] Bundahishn 1990, p. 150.

[2165] Ibn Balkhī 1995, p. 67.

[2166] Yarshater 1983b, p. 434.

[2167] See respectively pages 413 and 443 below.

[2168] Ibn Isfandīyār 1941, pp. 60–62.

[2169] Bīrūnī maintains that the bow was shot from the Rūyān mountain in Ṭabaristān. Bīrūnī 1984, pp. 334–335.

[2170] Thaʿālibī 1900, pp. 133–134, Thaʿālibī 1989, pp. 90–91.

[2171] Thaʿālibī 1989, pp. 91, 95, 96. It is important to note that the story of Ārash is not found in

the Parthian Mihrānid dynast Bahrām-i Chūbīn traced his genealogy. Like Fereydūn, all the attributes of Manūchihr, his court in Ṭabaristān, his justice and wrath, his nourishing function, his association with the sun, as well as those of the Ṭabaristānī hero appearing during his reign, Ārash, with his bow that followed the movement of the sun, all these attributes replicate those of the God Mihr.

Exactly when the primary mythic figures of the Pīshdādī section of the national tradition, such as Fereydūn, Manūchihr, and Ārash, acquired such heavily laden Mihr symbolism cannot be ascertained. That an intimate relationship between these figures and the north was established under the patronage of the Parthian dynasts ruling these domains, however, warrants serious consideration. But Mihr symbols are not confined to the mythic history of Ṭabaristān; they are also found in it historical narratives in other crucial ways. The history of the house of Āl-i Jāmāsp, a cadet branch of the Sasanians,[2172] also contains potent symbols of Mihr worship, above all the symbols of the cow and the sun. Before we proceed, we must recall that Jāmāsp (497–499), the brother of Qubād, was not only accused of having Mazdakite proclivity, but also carries the epithet *mihtar-parast* in the *Shāhnāma*. As we shall see in the revolts chapter,[2173] Ferdowsī's rendition of Jāmāsp as a *mihtar-parast* is only the poetic license used by the author for rendering the term *Mihr parast*, a worshipper of Mihr. Therefore, once again, one must entertain the connection of Mihr worship with the Mazdakite doctrine.

Three generations after Jāmāsp, we recall, in the reign of Jīl-i Jīlānshāh, parts of Ṭabaristān were finally conquered by the Āl-i Jāmāsp, a family who had hitherto had their base in Gīlān.[2174] It is appropriate to briefly recall Ibn Isfandīyār's account, which is replete with Mihr symbolism. The astrologers predicted greatness for Pīrūz,[2175] the son of Jāmāsp, and informed him that his grandson will be a great king. Pīrūz's grandson, hearing the same prophecy, left deputies in Gīlān, picked up two cows and went on foot to Ṭabaristān,[2176] which was still reeling from the Arab incursions at the tumultuous end of Yazdgird III's rule. According to Ibn Isfandīyār, his courage earned Jīl-i Jīlānshāh the epithet Gāvbārih, the Cow Devotee. According to ʿAmīd, *bārih* actually means friend (*dūst*). This Mihr symbolism connected with Jāmāsp and his progeny is augmented by Mithraic theophoric names of this dynasty. Among the descendants of Jīl-i Jīlānshāh, we find Dādhmihr (bestowed by Mihr) and Khurshīd

the *Shāhnāma* of Ferdowsī. Thaʿālibī 1989, p. 90, n. 1, Thaʿālibī 1900, pp. 134–135, 139, 140, where the following phrases are specifically used:

ترك الوفـء بعهده، نقض العهد، ناقضا للعهد

2172 See §4.3.

2173 See page 398.

2174 See §4.3.3.

2175 See §4.3.2.

2176 Ibn Isfandīyār 1941, pp. 153–154.

(the Sun).[2177] Except in the Parthian epic-romance of *Samak*, where the main king of Iran is called the Sun-King (Khurshīd Shāh)—a figure who acquires his name in precisely the same manner as the Pīshdādī king Manūchihr, that is, when the rays of the sun touch his nose—to my knowledge, no other historical dynast bears such a theophoric name in the annals of Iranian history of classical antiquity. Khurshīd, moreover, collaborated with the Iranian rebel Sunbād, who revolted against the ʿAbbāsids,[2178] and who encouraged his numerous followers to pray to the Sun and make it their *qibla*.[2179]

5.4.2 Mihr worship among the Mihrān

As we have seen, the Parthian families pitted the fire of Burzīn Mihr against the Sasanians,[2180] took refuge in the said fire as a matter of habit, and continued to use Mithraic theophoric names. Among these Parthian dynasts rose the families of the Mihrāns and the Kārins, whose historical and anecdotal narratives are replete with Mihr worship. The earliest evidence we have for the prevalence of Mihr worship in the quarters of the north and the east during the Sasanian era is provided by the rebellion of the Mihrānid Bahrām-i Chūbīn. As the theophoric name of this dynastic family suggests, Mihr worship was, in all probability, the predominant form of religion among this family and the populations under their control. Incorporated within Bahrām-i Chūbīn's sociopolitical and ideological antagonism toward the Sasanians, was, therefore, as we shall see, a religious rivalry.[2181] Both Bahrām-i Chūbīn and his grandfather, whom Sebeos calls Gołon Mihrān, are given the epithet *Mihrewandak*, Slave of Mihr.[2182] This epithet is reiterated by Ferdowsī, although in a more poetic rendering.[2183] The focal point of the rebel's worship was not the royal fires Ādhar Farnbagh or Ādhar Gushnasp, but the Burzīn Mihr fire, to which Bahrām-i Chūbīn compares himself in the poetic rendering of Ferdowsī. An avowed goal of the Mihrānid rebel was the destruction of the *mōbad*-controlled fire temples of the Sasanians. The Sasanians' destruction of fire temples, as evidenced in the *Letter of Tansar* and *Kārnāmag-i Ardashīr-i Pāpagān*, should therefore be viewed in the context of the continuing Pārsīg–Pahlav religious rivalry. The concomitant Mihrānid agenda of obliterating the celebrations of *Sadih* and *Nowrūz* is surely significant in this connection as well, although the precise meaning of this remains unclear.[2184]

2177 On whom see §4.5; for his coinage, see Justi 1895, p. 430.

2178 See §6.4.

2179 See §6.4.2.

2180 See page 364.

2181 For an in depth discussion of this aspect of Bahrām-i Chūbīn's rebellion, see §6.1.

2182 See pages 103 and 399.

2183 For further discussion, see §6.1, especially page 399.

2184 See footnote 2319. Although it is known that the feast of "Sada was celebrated by the king and commoner alike" during the Sasanian period, the celebration of this festival was specifically associated with the first Sasanian king, Ardashīr I. It is very probable, therefore, that Bahrām-i Chūbīn was here referring to a Zoroastrian feast that was directly associated with the Sasanian

Bahrām-i Chūbīn's rebellion was also attended by strong millennial motifs.[2185] While in the legitimist Sasanian apocalyptic rendition of the rebellion, Bahrām-i Chūbīn is depicted as an illegitimate low-born rebel, in an alternative rendition, most probably articulated by the Mihrāns, Bahrām-i Chūbīn's rebellion is sanctioned by Mihr himself, the very agent of eschatology. Bahrām-i Chūbīn moreover sustains the connection of Mihr worship to Ṭabaristān, claiming descent from the heroic archer Ārash, and from Milād (Mithradates, bestowed by Mithra).

5.4.3 Mihr worship among the Kārin

The Mihrāns, however, were not the only Parthian dynasts of the north that espoused Mihr worship. A strong Mithraic current is also evident among the Kārins, whose home territories had come to be in the quarter of the east, in Ṭabaristān and parts of Inner Khurāsān,[2186] near the Burzīn Mihr fire. Our first evidence to this effect is again theophoric. Of the six known progenies of the towering Kārinid Sukhrā, three bear Mithraic names: Zarmihr (537–558), Dādmihr (558–575), and Mihr (600–620).[2187] Sigillographic evidence further corroborates the Kārin's Mithraic propensities: the seals of Dādmihr, the Kārinid *ērān-spāhbed* of Khurāsān with a clearly Mithraic theophoric name, underline, we recall, that he took refuge into the Burzīn Mihr fire, the regional Parthian fire of Khurāsān.[2188] Apart from theophoric and sigillographic evidence, the most poignant and explicit affirmation of the Kārins' Mihr worship, however, comes through the course of an extremely significant narrative pertaining to the reigns of Pīrūz and Khusrow I. In it, the Kārins are depicted as heroes in whom all the attributes of the *yazata* Mihr coalesce.

Although Pīrūz (459–484) owed his throne to the Mihrānid Rahām,[2189] it was during the reign of this same Sasanian king, we recall, that the Kārins began their spiraling rise to power: they essentially ruled the empire during the reigns of Pīrūz, Bilāsh (484–488), and the young Qubād (488-531).[2190] In reaction to the overpowering and suffocating hold of Sukhrā and the other Kārins on him, where the very taxation of the realm came to Sukhrā's treasury, Qubād was finally able to rid himself of the tremendous hold of the Kārins with the aid of the Mihrānid Shāpūr of Rayy (Shāpūr Rāzī).[2191] According to Ibn Isfandīyār, it was in the aftermath of this and the Mazdakite uprising that Qubād sent the Kārins into exile, the fortunes of the family being resuscitated, once again, by Khusrow I Nowshīrvān, when he gave the *spāhbedī* of the east to the Kārins.[2192]

monarchy. Bīrūnī 1984, p. 350. Boyce 1983a, p. 801.

2185 Czegledy 1958, p. 21. See §6.1.2 for a further examination of this.

2186 For the definition of Inner Khurāsān, see §6.2.1.

2187 Justi 1895, p. 430.

2188 Gyselen 2001a, seals 1b and A, pp. 36 and 46. See page 114.

2189 See §2.3 for a detailed account of this.

2190 See §2.4.2.

2191 See §2.4.4.

2192 See page 114, where we substantiated this claim through sigillographic evidence.

The green-clad army

Now the narrative under examination here deals with the wars of Pīrūz and Khusrow I Nowshīrvān in the east and the role that the Kārins played in these. We can begin by the rendition of this narrative in the work of Ibn Isfandīyār, the Ṭabaristānī author whose work contains—in disjointed form—the saga of his compatriots, the Kārins, from the reign of Pīrūz onward, including the rebellion of the Kārinid Māzīyār during the early ʿAbbāsid period. According to the *Tārīkh-i Ṭabaristān*, in one of Khusrow I's battles against the Turkish Khāqān, unexpectedly, an army of about two to three thousand emerged—it is not clear whence—*all clad in green attire*, so much so that "all except their eyes and [that of?] their horses was covered in green." Donning green and hurling green flags, they aided Khusrow I to victory, setting out to leave the battle arena in the same mysterious way in which they had appeared. None could ascertain their provenance. They disregarded Khusrow I's numerous appeals as to their identity, until he finally dismounted his horse and implored them to God and the fires, when they finally halted to converse with the king and revealed themselves to be Kārins. At this point Ibn Isfandīyār informs us that there is a background to this episode and narrates the story of Pīrūz's disastrous defeat at the hand of the Hephthalites.

As we shall see shortly, in almost all the Arabic, Persian, and Armenian sources, Pīrūz's defeat at the hands of the Hephthalites is explicitly connected to his oath breaking and injustice, and he is represented as a king who epitomizes folly. In all these narratives, moreover, the king's folly, his oath breaking, and the disastrous consequences of these were all amended and set straight by the activities of the Kārins.[2193] Now, as a god who represents the three functions of royalty, warrior caste, and peasantry, Mihr also carries the three colors of white, red, and green, representing each function respectively.[2194] The nourishing function of Mihr seems to have been so important, however, that in all the narratives and rebellions that we shall examine, it was the color green that held paramountcy. Thus, in this narrative of Pīrūz, the color green assumes a primary function. While Pīrūz exemplified *mihr durujī*, to be false to Mithra, therefore, the Kārins donned with the green of Mihr, functioned as their *yazata*, Mihr, toward kingship: they restored and safeguarded the king's crown.

Pīrūz's injustice

It is apt to analyze this episode in more detail. As noted earlier, Mihr cosmogony posits a direct connection between the justice of the king and the replenishment of his kingdom. In the Circle of Justice ideology, unjust kings brought natural calamities upon their subjects.[2195] In Thaʿālibī's narrative this

[2193]See among others, Balʿamī 1959, pp. 128–140; Ibn al-Athīr 1862, vol. 1, pp. 407–410; Ferdowsī 1971, vol. VIII, pp. 9–17.

[2194]Widengren, Geo, 'Bābakīyah and the Mithraic Mysteries', in Ugo Bianchi (ed.), *Mysteria Mithrae*, pp. 675–695, Leiden, 1979 (Widengren 1979).

[2195]See §5.2.6.

connection is explicit. Pīrūz's reign had started unjustly because he had waged an unjust war against his brother Hormozd III (457–459). The brothers' war, in which Hormozd III and three of his family members were killed, wreaked havoc in the land and led to tremendous bloodletting. When Pīrūz ascended the throne, the rain stopped. As a result, rivers dried up and a drought devastated the land. Ṭabarī replicates this narrative: Pīrūz "was a man of limited capability, generally unsuccessful in his undertakings, who *brought down evil and misfortune on his subjects, and the greater part of his sayings and the actions he undertook brought down injury and calamity upon both himself and the people of his realm.*" For seven years continuously during his reign the land was stricken by famine. "Streams, *qanāts*, and springs dried up, trees and reed beds became desiccated ... Dearth, hunger, hardship, and various calamities became general for the people of his realm."[2196]

Presumably realizing his error, Pīrūz began to act with justice. He suspended land and capitation taxation, abolished corvées, forbade hoarding of grain and other foodstuffs, and ordered the rich to share their wealth with the poor. "In this way [Pīrūz] ordered the affairs of his subjects during that period of dearth and hunger so that no one perished of starvation except for one man [!] ... [So Pīrūz] implored his Lord to bestow his mercy on him and his subjects and to send down His rain ... So God aided him by causing it to rain ... Pīrūz's land once more had a profusion of water ... and the trees were restored to a flourishing state."[2197] Pīrūz then commenced his construction activities. Of the three cities that he built, one was in the vicinity of Rayy, called Rām Pīrūz, another between Gurgān and Bāb-i Ṣūl, called Rowshan Pīrūz, and the third in Azarbāyjān, called Shahrām Pīrūz.[2198] It is worth noting that two of these three cities are in the hereditary territory of the Kārin, the Mihrān, and the Ispahbudhān families, the Pahlav regions infused with currents of Mihr worship.

The connection between the justice of the king and the prosperity of the land is of course not peculiar to Iranian notions of kingship. When, however, this connection is accompanied by notions of oath-breaking, as is the case in almost all of the narratives of Pīrūz, it clearly assumes Mithraic characteristics. Once Pīrūz's land was prosperous again, however, he stumbled, once more, by attacking the king of the Hephthalites, Akhshunwār. When the war proved inconclusive, Pīrūz sued for peace. In exchange, Akhshunwār made Pīrūz swear "*with an oath and agreement sworn before God*, that he would never in the future mount raids against him." Pīrūz agreed. Once back in Iran, however, he decided to renew hostilities. He broke his oath against the wishes of "*his viziers and close advisors*, who argued that commencing war *would involve breaking the agreement.*" Having marched out, Pīrūz was confronted with Akhshunwār, who

[2196]Ṭabarī 1999, pp. 111–112, de Goeje, 873.

[2197]Ṭabarī 1999, p. 112, de Goeje, 874. Thaʿālibī 1900, pp. 574–577, Thaʿālibī 1989, pp. 370–371.

[2198]Thaʿālibī 1900, p. 578, Thaʿālibī 1989, p. 371; Ibn Balkhī 1995, pp. 218–219. See also Bosworth's notes in Ṭabarī 1999, p. 113, n. 290, de Goeje, 874.

"publicly adduced before Fayrūz [i.e., Pīrūz] the document with the agreement he had written ... and *warned him about his oath* and his undertaking." Pīrūz's army and his followers "*were, however, in a weakened and defeatist state because of the agreement that had existed between them and the Hephthalites.*" Akhshunwār then proclaimed: "O God, act according to what is in this document."[2199] The theme of Pīrūz's oath-breaking is reiterated in almost all our narratives, including that of Łazar P'arpec'i. The Hephthalite king "sent word to Peroz: 'You have a sworn covenant with me, written and sealed, [not to attack me] if I do not wage war against you ... So remember the covenant ... Return in peace and perish not ...' *When the Aryans heard the arguments of the Hephthalites*, they said to Peroz: 'He is right, and *we are waging an unjust war*'." Łazar P'arpec'i also stresses the episode's association with Ṭabaristān. When Pīrūz and all his sons and people perished as a result of his unjust war, a "few men escaped from the slaughter; reaching Vrkan [i.e., Gurgān, the abode of the Kārins], they told everyone of these grievous events, which caused all the nobles and the rest of the populace in Vrkan to flee to Asorestan."[2200] As a result of Pīrūz's oath-breaking, "the Persian army suffered a defeat the like of which they had never before experienced."[2201]

The theme of oath-taking and oath-breaking also looms large in the *Shāhnāma*'s rendition of Pīrūz's reign.[2202] According to Ferdowsī, when Hormozd III (457–459) ascended the throne, Pīrūz grew jealous and with a number of the elite (*mahān*) approached the Hephthalites. The king of the Hephthalites, Chaghānī, gave him in contract an army (*bih peymān sipāram sipāhī tow rā*), and reminded him that Yazdgird II (438–457) had already given him the control over the regions of Tirmidh and Siyahgird.[2203] With the aid of the Hephthalites, Pīrūz then gained the throne.[2204] Ferdowsī, too, recounts the drought that engulfed Iran, the measures taken by Pīrūz to deal with the calamity, the restoration of the land, and his building activity, followed by his attack on the

[2199]Bosworth notes: "That is, bring upon Fīrūz the stipulated curse for his breaking the agreement he had made with Akhshunwār." Ṭabarī 1999, pp. 113–116, and n. 294, de Goeje, 874–877.

[2200]Parpeci 1991, p. 215.

[2201]The narrative of Pīrūz's war against the Hephthalites, his oath to the enemy, the breaking of this oath, and its consequences are even contained in Procopius, pointing to an original Persian source as the provenance of this and other parts of Procopius' work dealing with Iran. Procopius 1914, I. iii.1–v.1. Pīrūz's oath-breaking is also detailed in Joshua the Stylite 2000, pp. 10–11. The successive wars of Pīrūz against the Huns in the east and Transoxiana hit his domains very hard. He was forced to underwrite these wars by, among other means, demanding a tribute from the Byzantines. According to Joshua the Stylite, in the midst of his wars against the Hephthalites, the king also imposed a poll-tax upon his entire domain. When Bilāsh (484–488) came to power, he "found the Persian treasury empty and the land ravaged by the Huns." Joshua the Stylite 2000, p. 16.

[2202]Ferdowsī 1971, vol. VIII, pp. 8–9:

چو پیمان ازادگان بشکنی   نشان بزرگی به خاك افگنی
مرا با تو پیمان بباید شکست   به ناچار بردن به شمشیر دست

[2203]Ferdowsī 1971, vol. VIII, p. 8, Ferdowsī 1935, p. 2265.

[2204]Ferdowsī 1971, vol. VIII, p. 8, Ferdowsī 1935, p. 2266.

Hephthalites.[2205] While at war, his youngest son, Bilāsh, occupied the throne, but affairs were in the hands of his Kārinid minister Sukhrā.[2206] When the army reached Central Asia, to the agreed upon Oxus border according, this time, to a pact of Bahrām V Gūr (420–438) with Khoshnavāz, Pīrūz decided not to abide by the agreement.[2207]

The issue of contract breaking (*peymān shikanī*) looms large in Ferdowsī's subsequent rendition of events. When the son of the Khāqān heard that Pīrūz had crossed the Oxus with his army, he wrote a letter to the Sasanian king and threatened Pīrūz that if he reneged on his kingly oath, he would not be considered of royal lineage, and further that if Pīrūz broke the oath, he, too, would be forced to break his contract and resort to war. The terminology used in almost the entire narrative is *peymān shikanī* or at times *ʿahd shikanī*.[2208] Significantly, it is to the Kārinid Sukhrā's messenger that the Khāqān communicated his accusation of Pīrūz's breach of contract.[2209] It is noteworthy that both Nöldeke and Bosworth recognized the centrality of oath and oath-breaking in the narrative of Pīrūz's wars in the east, but attributed it to Pīrūz's defeats in these wars.[2210]

The fact that contracts are made under the protection of Mihr, by now readily associated with the Sun, is explicitly stated by Ferdowsī: The Khāqān asked his messenger to tell Pīrūz that he would bring the contract of his ancestor atop a lance, as if it were the sun.[2211] Significantly, on account of

2205 Ferdowsī 1971, vol. VIII, pp. 9–17, Ferdowsī 1935, p. 2269.

2206 Ferdowsī 1971, vol. VIII, pp. 17–29.

2207 Thaʿālibī 1900, pp. 578–579, Thaʿālibī 1989, pp. 372–373; Ferdowsī 1971, vol. VIII, p. 12, Ferdowsī 1935, p. 2270:

نشانی که بهرام یل کرده بود   ز پستی بلندی بر اوارده بود
نوشته یکی عهد شاهنشهان   که از ترك و ایرانیان در جهان
کسی این نشان هیچ برنگذرد   نه از رود بیرون به پی نسپرد ...
چو پیروز شیر اوژن انجا رسید   نشان کرده شاه ایران بدید
چنین گفت یکسر به گردنکشان   که بر پیش ترکان بر این همنشان
مناره برارم به شمشیر و گنج   ز هیتال تا کس نباشد به رنج

2208 Ferdowsī 1935, pp. 2270–2271, Ferdowsī 1971, vol. VIII, pp. 12–13:

چو بشنید فرزند خاقان که شاه   ز جیهون گذر کرد خود با سپاه
همی بشکندعهد بهرام گور   برین بوم و بر تازه شد جنگ و شور ...
یکی نامه بنوشت به افرین   ز دادار بر شهریار زمین
چنین گفت کز عهد شاهان داد   بگردی نخوانمت خسرو نژاد
نه این بود عهد نیاکان تو   گزیده جهاندار و پاکان تو
چو پیمان ازادگان بشکنی   نشان بزرگان به خاك افگنی
مرا با تو پیمان بباید شکست   بناچار بردن بشمشیر دست

2209 Ferdowsī 1971, vol. VIII, p. 21, Ferdowsī 1935, p. 2280.

2210 Bosworth maintains, for example, that the "narrative emphasizes Fīrūz's responsibility, as the breaker of his oath, for the ensuing catastrophe"; but as Nöldeke skeptically observes, "if Fīrūz had been victorious, all mention of his oath-breaking would have been tossed aside!" Ṭabarī 1999, p. 115, n. 292.

2211 Ferdowsī 1971, vol. VIII, p. 14:

بگویش که عهد نیای تو را   بلند اختر و رهنمای تو را
همی بر سر نیزه پیش سپاه   بیارم چو خورشید تابان به راه

Pīrūz's contract-breaking, the Khāqān now accused him of irreligiosity.[2212] The Khāqān beseeched God, who is here rendered as the Righteous Judge (*dāvar-i dādpāk*), in supplication against the unrighteous Pīrūz (*Pīrūz-i bīdādgar*), who sought grandeur through the use of the sword.[2213] And thus the Khāqān set out against Pīrūz. Naturally, Pīrūz suffered a humiliating defeat, losing his life as well as that of the major grandees of the empire in the process. In Procopius' account, when the escape routes of the king were closed, the magi advised the king that he should make sure to meet the Hephthalite leader at "dawn, and then, turning toward the rising sun, make his obeisance. In this way, they explained, he would be able to escape the future ignominy of his deed."[2214] As Trombely and Watt observe, "in reality, Pīrūz was making obeisance to the rising sun (that is, the visible shape of the god Mithra)."[2215] The paradigm for this narrative, without doubt, is "the popular variant of the Iranian myth of creation [where] ... the sun, i.e., Mihr, ... is the arbiter between the two adversaries,"[2216] here co-opted by the Sasanian king Pīrūz.

Another common element in all of the narratives concerning Pīrūz's reign is the central role played by the Kārinid Sukhrā, avenging the king's defeat precipitated by his oath-breaking.[2217] There is little doubt, therefore, that the narrative of Pīrūz's humiliating defeat and all the Mithraic motifs contained in it have to be considered in conjunction with the rise of the Kārins to power and the extremely positive representation of this Parthian dynastic family in most of our narratives. The heroic accounts of the Kārins' role in leashing and highlighting the king's folly and restoring his kingship were inserted in Pīrūz's narratives by the Parthian Kārinid dynastic family. In all probability, likewise, the theme of making and breaking contracts looms large in Pīrūz's narrative because the Parthian Kārins were, like the Mihrāns, Mihr devotees, who inserted their beliefs into these sections of the *X^w adāy-Nāmag* tradition. In fact, in all other substantive narratives in which the Kārins appear, aspects of Mihr worship appear alongside them. This comes across very clearly in the *Tārīkh-i Ṭabaristān*.

As the Kārins' fortunes continued to rise throughout the rule of Bilāsh and the first part of Qubād's reign,[2218] it is, in all probability, primarily on account of this family's power over his kingdom that Qubād started his Mazdakite phase and commenced the reforms that are said to have continued during his son Khusrow I's reign.[2219] According to Ibn Isfandīyār, Qubād substantially reduced the power of the Kārins over his realm by banishing them to

[2212] Ferdowsī 1971, vol. VIII, pp. 14, 21, Ferdowsī 1935, p. 2272.
[2213] Ferdowsī 1935, p. 2273, rendered as *dād o pāk* in Ferdowsī 1971, vol. VIII, p. 15.
[2214] Procopius 1914, I. iii. 1–22.
[2215] Joshua the Stylite 2000, pp. 11–12, n. 44.
[2216] Shaked 1980, p. 18.
[2217] Ṭabarī 1999, p. 117, de Goeje, 877.
[2218] See §2.4.
[2219] See §2.4.5.

Ṭabaristān and Zābulistān. Ibn Isfandīyār's explanatory notes on the Kārin end here, and the narrative of the green-clad army coming to the aid of Khusrow I commences.[2220] When Qubād killed Sukhrā, Ibn Isfandīyār explains, his sons fled from Ṭabaristān to Badakhshān. Hearing of Qubād's death and Khusrow I's regret at his father's treatment of them, the Kārins then came with their green-clad army to Khusrow I's aid against the Khāqān.[2221] In sum, the Kārins wore the color green and assumed their chief deity's role in bestowing and restoring kingship, because they were replicating in Pīrūz's narrative the function of their chief God, Mihr.

Kayānid pseudo-genealogy of the Sasanians.

Under Pīrūz, the Sasanians also challenged the Parthians' territorial and religious legitimacy by concocting their own pseudo-genealogy to rival the pseudo-genealogy of the Arsacids.[2222] The Sasanians now traced their descent, through the Achaemenids, to the Kayānids, and above all to Kai Vīshtāspā. As the father of the last Achaemenid ruler, Darius III (380–330 BCE), was called Vīshtāspā, they identified him with his namesake, the patron of Zoroaster.[2223] With one stroke, therefore, under Pīrūz the Sasanians seem to have effected two feats. On the one hand this was political propaganda par excellence, "since a claim to Kayanian blood gave these kings of the south-west an ancient title to rule also over the north-east."[2224] Insofar as the Sasanians tied their genealogy to the patron of the Mazdean faith, Vīshtāspā, moreover, it gave them religious legitimacy.

There is little doubt, therefore, that the Sasanian concoction of this genealogy was "proclaimed and exploited from the time of Peroz, the son of Yazdgird II (459–484)."[2225] Significantly, it was Pīrūz, as well, who first adopted the title of *Kai*, reviving the ancient title of *Kāvi*, on some of his coins. Naming one of his sons Kavād or Qubād, after the first Kayānid king, Kai Kavād, and another Jāmāsp, after Vīshtāspā's wise counselor, Jāmāsp, was another move in this direction.[2226] Thereafter the use of Kayānid titles among the Sasanians became common. We recall that around this same time, the Sasanians began to

---

[2220]See page 380.

[2221]Ibn Isfandīyār 1941, p. 151.

[2222]Boyce 1979, p. 127.

[2223]In the *X^w adāy-Nāmag* tradition, the Achaemenids, who are represented by only two monarchs and come after the Pīshdādī dynasty, are "treated as part virtually of the Kayanian dynasty." The Kayanids thus meet their end appropriately with Alexander's conquest. Iran then reverts to the period of petty local rulers (*molūk al-tawāʾif*), whose history, that of the Parthians, is basically deleted from the *X^w adāy-Nāmag* tradition. The last Arsacid ruler, Ardavān, then appoints the ancestor of the Sasanians, one Bābak, as the governor of Iṣṭakhr. Bābak, enlightened by dreams, gives his daughter to Sāsān, the last of many bearing this name. The ancestor of this Sāsān, according to the *X^w adāy-Nāmag* tradition, was Dārā (Darius III), the last Achaemenid king. Boyce 1979, pp. 126–127. Yarshater 1983b, pp. 377, 472.

[2224]Boyce 1979, p. 127.

[2225]Boyce 1979, p. 127.

[2226]Boyce 1979, pp. 127–128.

promote the Ādhar Gushnasp and Ādhar Farnbagh fires in rivalry against the Burzīn Mihr fire.[2227]

What led Pīrūz to engage in this politico-religious struggle for legitimacy with the Parthians? Boyce claims that Pīrūz's exploitation of this genealogical tradition and its attendant religious connotations was probably prompted by the Hephthalite threat in the northeastern parts of his realm, "thus making the Sasanians *keenly aware of their need to foster loyalty among their own subjects.*"[2228] But the subjects of the Sasanians in the northeast were Parthians, in whose historical tradition Pīrūz is portrayed in a decidedly negative light.[2229] It might be proposed, therefore, that the Sasanians' propagandistic use of the eastern Kayānid right to power and their promotion of the Ādhar Farnbagh and Ādhar Gushnasp fires against the Pahlav Burzīn Mihr fire reflected the suffocating hold that the Parthian dynastic powers were exerting on Sasanian domains at this juncture of Sasanian history. In the context of this struggle and in an attempt to co-opt the Parthian dynastic families' claim to legitimacy in their ancestral domains, Pīrūz constructed the cities Rām Pīrūz near Rayy, and Rowshan Pīrūz between Gurgān and Bāb-i Ṣūl in these very Pahlav territories.

5.4.4 Mihr worship in Armenia

In the political history chapter we discussed the intimate sociopolitical connections of Iran to Armenia during the Arsacid and Sasanian periods.[2230] The Arsacid descent of the Armenian kings formed a constant and lively reminder for the Sasanians of the sociopolitical presence of the Parthians throughout their rule. In this context, we highlighted the continued intimate association of the Parthian dynastic families of the Sasanian period with Armenia and briefly traced some of the better-known aspects of this relationship, especially that of the Mihrāns. What we must underline in this section, however, and what is of even further crucial importance in the history of Irano–Armenian relations, is that throughout Armenian history, and especially prior to the conversion of the Armenians to Christianity—a process that like all the processes of conversion was drawn-out and complex[2231]—"Iran ... was to be the dominant influence in

[2227] See page 362.

[2228] Boyce 1979, p. 127. Emphasis mine.

[2229] Recall the Kārinid version discussed on page 380ff.

[2230] See page 43. For a synopsis of Armenia's political history, see footnotes 82 and 192.

[2231] As late as the end of the fifth century, we can still see traces of pagan customs in the works of Christian authors. In his accounts of the year 497/8 CE, for example, Joshua the Stylite informs us that during the wicked pagan festival celebrated by the population, pagan myths were chanted, pagan costumes were worn and pagan incense offerings were made. Joshua the Stylite 2000, pp. 32 and 28 respectively. As late as the fourth century, furthermore, shrines to Mihr still existed in Armenia. Clauss, Manfred, *The Roman Cult of Mithras: The God and his Mysteries*, Edinburgh University Press, 2000, translated by R. Gordon (Clauss 2000), p. 4. A primary impetus for the foundation of Armenian historiography, as is readily admitted by scholars of Armenian history, was the Christian church. The general Christian character of Armenian literature is acknowledged. In fact it is known that the "prime concern of the inventor of the Armenian alphabet, Mashtots', was the translation of texts useful for the church." Khorenatsʿi 1978, pp. 32, and 20 respectively. Nevertheless it is

Armenian spiritual matters."[2232]

The Armenians probably became Zoroastrian during the Achaemenid period. For almost a millennium prior to the official Armenian adoption of Christianity in the fourth century CE, therefore, the Armenian religious landscape was informed by Mazdean forms of worship, although strong regional traditions also affected it. It would be logical to presume, therefore, that this spiritual tradition would substantially influence later Armenian religious practice. In fact, so potent a mark Iranian religion had left on the Armenian landscape that, as James Russell observes, "numerous survivals of Armenian Zoroastrianism remain to this day."[2233]

As in post-Avestan and Sasanian Iran, so also in pre-Christian Armenia, no centralized orthodox Zoroastrian church existed. Aramazd (Ohrmozd, Ahūrā Mazdā), sometimes called the *manly god*, was the principal deity, and the father of all gods. Anahit was his progeny, Mihr his son, and Nanē—a female god of Uruk origin—his daughter.[2234] Mimicking the dynastic structure of the Armenian polity, it seems "that the royal family presided over the cult of the supreme God, while local dynasts, the *naxarars*, attended to lesser *yazatas*." Anahit, the Lady, who bears another epithet whose meaning remains unclear (*the golden mother*), had her own separate temple.[2235] Tir, the scribe of Aramazd, and the name of the fourth month in the Armenian calendar,[2236] and *Sandaramet*[2237] were other noteworthy Zoroastrian *yazatas* replicated in Armenia.

Of all the Iranian religious currents prevalent in pre-Christian Armenia, however, Mihr worship was particularly strong.[2238] In fact, so prevalent was Mihr worship in Armenia, we recall, that it has been claimed that this religious

also acknowledged that the "conversion of king Trdat (Tiridates) to Christianity in the early fourth century and the work of Saint Gregory did not bring about an immediate and total rejection of pre-Christian Armenian traditions. Thus, *early Armenian historiography presents us with a fascinating picture of the interplay of cultures pagan and Christian, Iranian and Hellenistic. But the Armenian historians themselves, being Christian, impose upon that complicated amalgam interpretations based upon their own beliefs and ideals, using imagery drawn from the Judeo-Christian world.*" Elishē 1982, p. 1. Emphasis mine. As a result, Garsoian maintains, "any Iranian element lurking beneath the surface of early Christian Armenian civilization can all too easily be overlooked, swamped by Armenian hostility and the highly articulate and well-documented classical tradition which was an indubitable component of the contemporary scene." Garsoian 1985c in Garsoian 1985b, p. 29.

2232 Unless otherwise noted, the following discussion follows Russell 1991, p. 439.

2233 Russell 1991, p. 438.

2234 The "name [Aramazd] is a loan from Parthian, cf. Greek Aramasdēs." The temple of Aramazd "held an image, probably resembling the image of the manly Zeus, destroyed by St. Acindynus." As Russell explains, the Armenians made statues of their gods. These were mostly imported from the west and placed in shrines. The function of Aramazd as a thunder god was probably influenced by a non-Zoroastrian weather god. Russell 1991, p. 439.

2235 As Russell explains, the cult of Anahit might have absorbed symbols of the Mesopotamian goddess Ishtar. Russell 1991, p. 440.

2236 Russell 1991, p. 441.

2237 Derived from a southwest Iranian word, *Spandaramet*, the earth personified. Russell 1991, p. 442.

2238 The following discussion is likewise indebted to James Russell's interesting article Russell 1990b, p. 183.

tradition influenced the development of Roman Mithraism. The very name for a pre-Christian Armenian temple, *mehean*, "from a Middle Iranian derivative of Old Iranian **mā'thryāna* or *mithradāna*,"[2239] testifies to the spread and importance of the cult of Mithra in Armenia. As we have seen, and as Russell also notes, during the Islamic period any Zoroastrian temple was called a *dār-i Mihr* and Armenia was no exception to this general practice. Likewise, any pagan priest was called a Mithraist.[2240] The Armenian king Tiridates I (56–59 and 62–72 CE) invoked Mihr, the god of contracts, in his treaty with the Roman emperor Nero (54–68 CE),[2241] and in an inscription, he referred to himself as the Sun, the very symbol of Mithra.[2242] The high frequency of theophoric names composed with *mihr*, *mrh*, or *meh* among the Armenian Arsacid kings and dynasts in the classical period and late antiquity,[2243] further underlines the significance of Mithra in the Armenian spiritual landscape.[2244] To this day, Mihr remains the seventh month, as well as the eighth day of any month in the Armenian calendar. And in Armenian Christianity, the twenty-first day of Mehekan, Greater Mihrigān in the Zoroastrian calendar, is devoted—appropriate to Mihr's warrior function—to St. George the Soldier.[2245] As late as the nineteenth century, when water seeped from a certain rock, Armenians believed it to be the "urine of Mithra's steed."[2246]

Mithraic elements in hunting and banquet scenes

As Russell notes, the many terracotta figurines that have been found in Parthia and Armenia "of an archer in an Iranian dress on horseback are very likely votive images of Mithra, who is shown hunting on horseback on many Mithraic monuments."[2247] As Garsoian has brilliantly shown, the motifs of the hunting scene, as well as the banquet, so widespread in Parthian Armenian and Sasanian art, have Mithraic provenance. In the Armenian context, as in the Iranian setting, the man on the horse has heroic and supernatural overtones.[2248] Like

[2239]Russell 1991, p. 440. A cave-like temple of Mithra in a village in Armenia has been identified. The temple had already been mentioned by Agat'angelos as a temple of Mithra, *mrhakan mehean*, at Bagayarich (town of god), now Pekeriç. A second cave continues to be associated with Mihr in living Armenian epic. The epic describes a lion Mher (Mithra) and a little Mher, the latter of whom is "guided by a raven ... to a cave at Van, where he waits on horseback, the wheel of destiny (*charkh-e falak*) in his hand, for the end of days when justice will return to earth." Russell 1990b, p. 184.

[2240]Russell 1990b, p. 183.

[2241]Schippmann 1980, p. 56.

[2242]Russell 1991, p. 440.

[2243]As Garsoian observes, the "name Mithra/Mihr is a common component of the onomasticon of Armenia and its neighbors: Mihrdat/Mithradates, Mihran, Mihr-šapuh, Mer Šapuh," etc. Garsoian 1985c, p. 56, n. 90.

[2244]Russell 1990b, pp. 185, 190, 191, 192.

[2245]Russell 1991, p. 440.

[2246]Russell 1991, p. 440.

[2247]Russell 1990b, p. 184.

[2248]The persistent survival of the ideal of the hunter among Iranians is exemplified by a poem which opens with the stanza "La Roi declara ... Qu'ils celèbrent les louangées du Chasseur, maître

its Iranian analogues, "the horse of the evildoers stumbles at the critical moment" in Armenian epic literature.[2249] We recall the horse that kicked Yazdgird I the Sinner to death in Parthava. The imagery of the hunt in Armenian literature and art, therefore, replicates that of the Parthians and the Sasanians, all incorporating potent Mithraic symbolism. Thus "the twin frescoes from the Mithraeum at [Arsacid] Dura Europos[2250] [which depict] the galloping of the god Mithra drawing his bow at a fleeing herd of bucks, onagers, wild boars, and lions, depict *in an identical prefiguration* ... the gesture of the Sasanian royal representation, and thereby identifying their prototype." Just as on a Parthian seal from Nisā we find a rider "crowned with a diadem spearing a wild beast and surmounted by a crescent moon," so on a Sasanian hunter intaglio we find the rider accompanied by the sun and the moon.[2251]

The banquet (*bazm*), a central social function in both the Iranian and Armenian context, and well-represented in Armenian and Iranian literature, also betrays a Mithraic provenance. The banquet, as Garsoian observes, "became one of the settings of the apotheosis at which the gates of eternity opened to reveal the banquet of immortality. The banquet scene ... concludes the series of Mithra's terrestrial exploits preceding his ascension on the chariot of the sun." It is crucial to note that, as Garsoian observes, "in the heavenly vision of ... [the infamous] Sasanian high-priest Kartēr [Kirdīr] described in his inscription at Sar Mashhad [KSM] the central image[2252] is of a golden throne dominating a banquet."[2253]

In the early third century the cult of the *yazata* Vahagn—probably from Parthian Vārhragn, Persian Bahrām—to whom, appropriately, the epithet *brave*

du pact." Mokri, M., *Le Chasseur de Dieu et le mythe du Roi-Aigle*, Wiesbaden, 1967 (Mokri 1967). Cited in Garsoian 1985c, pp. 47–48, n. 74.

2249 Garsoian 1985c, pp. 47–48.

2250 Initially excavated in 1920–22 under the direction of Franz Cumont, Dura Europos, "on the right bank of the Euphrates between Antioch and Seleucia on the Tigris, [was] founded in 303 BCE by Nicanor, a general of Seleucus I ... [It was] brought into the Iranian cultural sphere after the Parthian conquest in about 113 BCE. This domination lasted three centuries." Originally only a fortress it was "constituted as a city only in the late Hellenistic period and had been only sparsely populated throughout the Greek period. It was under the Parthians, however, that the city assumed its essential aspect." Leriche, Pierre and Mackenzie, D.N., 'Duraeuropos', in Ehsan Yarshater (ed.), *Encyclopaedia Iranica*, New York, 2007 (Leriche and Mackenzie 2007).

2251 Garsoian 1985c, p. 54.

2252 "Nous voyons un *cavalier, un prince, éclatant, et il est assis sur un cheval précieux*, et il a une bannière (?) [dans la main?] ... [Et là] un homme [apparait?] ... *et placé sur un trône en or*." Gignoux 1991c, pp. 95–96.

2253 Garsoian 1985c, p. 62, quoting Cumont, Franz, 'The Dura Mithraeum', in John R. Hinnells (ed.), *Mithraic Studies: Proceedings of the First International Congress of Mithraic Studies*, pp. 151–214, Manchester University Press, 1975, edited and translated by E.D. Francis (Cumont 1975), p. 117. According to Garsoian, "Gignoux notes the eschatological interest of this passage and presumes that this banquet was prepared for the righteous ... He takes the sitter in the golden throne to be Rašn [Rashnu] or Vahman ... [the aides to Mithra.]" Garsoian, Nina G., 'L'inscription de *Kartīr Sār Mašhad*', in *Armenia between Byzantium and the Sasanians*, London, 1985d (Garsoian 1985d), pp. 402, 404, 409, n. 11, 37, 39, 47; see also Garsoian 1985c, p. 62, and n. 103. Subsequently Gignoux changed his perspective as to whether the banquet was prepared for the righteous. Gignoux 1991c.

is given and whose name is used for the 27th day of the Armenian month, became particularly strong in Armenia. In the process Vahagn became second only to Aramazd, and, like Mithra, identified with the Sun.[2254] In his narrative on the Christianization of Armenia, Agat'angelos "devotes far more detail to the destruction of Vahagn's temple at Aštišat in Tarōn than to any of the other pagan shrines," the compiler stressing "that St. Gregory was especially desirous of destroying this temple because it was outstanding for its wealth, and because ignorant men still made profane sacrifices at these surviving altars." The first Armenian church was erected on the site of the former temple.[2255] As has recently been suggested with "considerable persuasiveness by James Russell . . . [however] at the beginning of the Sasanian period Vahagn was taking the place of the sun god," Mithra. Thenceforth Vahagn assumes Mithra's place in the "dominant Zoroastrian official trinity of Armenia: [the trinity becoming that of] Ahūrā Mazdā, Anāhit, Vahagn."[2256] We should not lose sight, moreover, of the close correspondence of Mithra and Vahagn. For as Gershevitch and others have shown, in the Mazdean tradition Verethragnā (Avestan Vərəθraɣna)/Bahrām/Vahagn "is the constant companion of [Mithra], thus making the confusion understandable" in the Armenian context.[2257] The white horse in particular is the symbol of Bahrām since the "third incarnation of the god is specified to be as a white horse."[2258]

Divine Glory (*farr*), a necessary prerequisite of kingship, contingent on the king's fulfillment of his contract and the maintenance of the Circle of Justice underwritten by Mihr and represented by a host of Mithraic symbols,[2259] was as integral a part of the discourse of political legitimacy in Armenia as in Iran.[2260]

2254 Russell 1991, p. 441.

2255 Garsoian 1985a, in Garsoian 1985b, pp. 158, 180, n. 74.

2256 Garsoian 1985a, pp. 158 and 180, n. 74 citing Russell, James R., 'Zoroastrian Problems in Armenia: Mihr and Vahagan', in T. Samuelian (ed.), *Classical Armenian Culture*, vol. 4 of *University of Pennsylvania Armenian Texts and Studies*, pp. 1–7, Dudley, 1982 (Russell 1982).

2257 Mihr Yasht 1959, p. 107; Mihr Yasht 1883, §§70–71. See also Bahman Yasht 1880, *Bahman Yasht*, vol. 5 of *Sacred Books of the East*, Oxford University Press, 1880, translated by E.W. West (Bahman Yasht 1880), pp. 243–244, cited in Garsoian 1985c, p. 52, n. 85. In the *Mihr Yasht* we find: "he [Mithra] who is strong and victorious [Verethragnā], [Mihr Yasht 1883, §16] . . . the supernatural god who flies over climes bestowing good fortune [*farr*] . . . bestowing power; victoriousness . . . he increases, [Mihr Yasht 1883, §§67, 127] . . . flying behind [him, Mithra] comes the strong likeness of Ahūrā Mazdā's creature, in the shape of a wild aggressive male boar [Verethragnā] . . . in front of him [Mithra] flies the blazing Fire which (is) the strong Kavyan Fortune [Mihr Yasht 1883, §141]." Garsoian 1985c, pp. 55–56, n. 90. Recall that boar (*gorāz*, *borāz*, or *varāz*) is also the suffix of the name of our towering Mihrānid dynast, Shahrvarāz; see page 146.

2258 Bahman Yasht 1880, §9, cited in Garsoian 1985c, p. 53, n. 87. See also page 411 below.

2259 See our discussion on page 354.

2260 Among the central themes of Ełishē's history, Thomson notes the theme of "the covenant (*ukht*) and the secession (*erkparakut'iwn*) of those who abandoned the covenant. For Ełishē, the covenant is a covenant of the church; he [i.e., Ełishē] emphasizes not merely that the pact to which Armenians swore allegiance was one of *loyalty to God and country*, but that in that pact the church played the leading role." Observing that the concept "of holy covenant as the body of the faithful does not occur in the New Testament," Thomson argues that it nevertheless has a "definite precursor in the Judaism of the second century BCE," for which he gives evidence from 1 Macc. 1:15–16,

As Garsoian observes, "the supernatural aura of both rulers [Armenian and Sasanian] was ... identical. The central Iranian concept of the royal glory, the *kavyan xwarrah* [Armenian *P'ark'*], which identifies, accompanies, and protects the legitimate ruler, but escapes from the usurper, and abandons an evil king, is present in Armenian sources even in a Christian context."[2261] In short, the affinities of the pre-Christian Armenian religious tradition with the Iranian spiritual tradition were so strong, direct, and thorough, having outlived the gradual social Christianization of Armenia, that it has been claimed that the "Armenian religious vocabulary is almost entirely Iranian and covers most Zoroastrian ideas, religious institutions and instruments."[2262]

Obviously, then, the Sasanian connection with Armenia had not only a political dimension, but also a strong cultural and religious one. Through a good part of their history, therefore, the Sasanians were forced to deal not only with an Armenia which was Arsacid and hence a constant reminder of the continued forceful presence of Parthians in their own sociopolitical structure, but also with an Armenia in which currents of Mihr worship were strong. The Mihrāns of the Sasanian domains who had established sociopolitical ties with pre-Christian and Christian Armenia and Albania (Arrān), along with other Iranian Parthian houses, such as the Sūren, whose presence in the pages of Armenian history is replete,[2263] were dealing with Parthian *naxarars* among whom Mihr or Bahrām worship predominated. It was to the Parthian dynast Mihrān, for example, that Vahan Mamikonean argued his case for his loyal behavior toward the Sasanian king Pīrūz,[2264] and it was this same Mihrān who urged the Armenian rebels to convert, or possibly reconvert, and "take refuge in fire and worship the sun."[2265] The Armenian rebels finally resorted to him for rendering

and Daniel 11:18–30. The similarity of the concepts of *ukht* and *erkparakutiwn* with the Mithraic concepts of forming a contract, *mihrān kardan*, literally to form a Mithra, and *mihr durūjī*, to be false to Mithra, is nevertheless striking. Elishē 1982, pp. 9–11.

[2261]Garsoian 1985c, p. 42 and n. 53. "The most common representation of the *xwarrah* ... is that of a ram adorned with flying ribbons." Ibid., p. 44, n. 58, citing Bivar, A.D.H., *Catalogue of the Western Asiatic Seals in the British Museum, Stamp Seals II, the Sasanian Dynasty*, London, 1969 (Bivar 1969), pl. 16. Also see now the excellent work Soudavar 1980, pp. 13–39, where the Mithraic provenance of the ram adorned with flying ribbons, and the flying ribbons (*dastār*) themselves, is convincingly argued. Even the Armenian Holy Cross is depicted "with a pair of stylized wings underneath ... and [is] refer[ed] to as *P'ark' Khāch'* (Glorious Cross)." Soudavar, citing personal correspondence with Russell, ibid., p. 21 and p. 151, figure 24. Soudavar's work is accompanied by fascinating plates which substantiate most of our arguments.

[2262]Russell 1991, p. 443. For a recapitulation of the Iranian dimensions of Armenian sociopolitical and cultural life, see also Garsoian, Nina G., *Des Parthes au Caliphate: quatre lessons sur la formation de l'identité Arménienne*, vol. 10 of *Travaux et mémoires du centre de récherche d'histoire et civilization de Byzance*, Paris, 1997 (Garsoian 1997), especially 'Les elements Iraniens dans l'Armenie paleochretienne,' pp. 9–37.

[2263]As mentioned, we have merely been able to touch upon the intimate relations between Armenia and Iran in this study; see our discussion on page 43.

[2264]Parpeci 1991, pp. 193–196. See page 73.

[2265]Parpeci 1991, pp. 199 and 196.

mediation (*mijnord*).[2266] The chronicler Łazar P'arpec'i must have been thoroughly familiar with the Mithraic beliefs of the Parthian Mihrāns but not necessarily with the beliefs of the Sasanian Pīrūz. When the Mihrānid Bahrām-i Chūbīn solicited the aid of the Armenian dynasts,[2267] therefore, a common recent religious culture probably further strengthened his claim of affinity with them, a dimension of the rebellion that could very well have been deleted from the pages of heavily Christianized Armenian historiography.

The tension and antagonism existing between the Sasanians and the Parthians in religious matters[2268] must have also exacerbated the religious dimension of the Sasanian relationship with pre-Christian Armenia. Mithraism seems to have been so entrenched in Armenia and neighboring Azarbāyjān that it probably even undergirded the cataclysmic rebellion of Bābak Khurramdīn against the ʿAbbāsids in the early ninth century in Azarbāyjān.[2269]

5.5 Conclusion

While underlining their confidence for the continued prevalence of Mihr worship in Iran, scholars have long bemoaned the dearth of evidence to this effect.[2270] Giving a synopsis of the variegated panorama of religious life in Sasanian Iran, however, we have attempted to single out the prevalence of Mihr worship among the Parthian dynasts, especially the Kārins and the Mihrāns, ruling in the quarters of the north and the east (*kūst-i ādurbādagān* and *kūst-i khwarāsān*) of the Sasanian domain. The political rivalry between the Sasanians and the Parthians was exacerbated by religious disparity, if not outright conflict. Like the Pārsīg–Pahlav sociopolitical rivalry, this dichotomy had a geographical dimension. The quarters of the east and the north, regions which continued to be ruled by Parthian dynastic families even after the demise of the Sasanians,[2271] were particularly affected by strong currents of Mihr worship.

Insofar as the Sasanian kings, not being trained theologians, might have adhered to various forms of popular worship, we might argue that Mihr worship was as prevalent among the Sasanian kings as it was among the Parthian dynastic families. If, on the other hand, the orthodoxy that a number of Sasanian kings upheld was in fact the Zurvanite heresy, then clearly the Parthian dynasts of the quarters of the north and east did not partake in it. Enough evidence has hopefully been presented to testify to the prevalence of Mihr worship among the Kārins and the Mihrāns. While little evidence seems to survive for the primacy of Mihr worship among the Ispahbudhān family, we argued that their

2266 Parpeci 1991, p. 193 and n. 1.

2267 See page 128.

2268 We shall provide further evidence of this when discussing Bahrām-i Chūbīn's rebellion in §6.1 below.

2269 Bābak Khurramdīn's rebellion was in all probability a Mithraic socioreligious movement against the caliphate; see footnote 2597. We shall be dealing with this in a later work.

2270 Shaked 1994a, p. 46.

2271 See Chapters 4 and 6.

traditional homeland was Parthava, the regions under the control of the Prince of the Medes, that is to say, Khurāsān and Azarbāyjān.[2272] Considering the strong Mithraic currents present in these regions, it is plausible therefore that this agnatic Parthian dynastic family may also have partaken in the religious dimensions of agnatic worship prevalent in the regions under their control.[2273] What is more, the type of Mihr worship practiced by these Parthian families seems to be substantially different from the devotion of Mihr that was incorporated in the orthodox Zoroastrian creed. As Shaked has argued, "Mihr was ... identified with the Sun, and the worship of the sun could be understood as the worship of Mihr." In orthodox Zoroastrianism, however, "Mihr's position ... is not so central that he would deserve to be placed at the top of the Pantheon." In the orthodox conceptualization of the divine, other gods were clearly "lesser divinities, subordinate to the Creator [Ahūrā Mazdā]."[2274] While Shaked observes that "Ohrmazd himself was also identified with the sun in various Iranian areas, especially in the eastern Iranian provinces, as may be deduced from linguistic evidence," the absence of any reference to Ahūrā Mazdā in any of the rebellions in the quarters of the north and the east investigated in Chapter 6, and the central position of the Sun in all of these, is so conspicuous that we must conclude that these revolts had nothing to do with orthodox Zoroastrianism.[2275] To what extent we can consider Mihr worship in the Pahlav domains as sectarian, strictly speaking, requires a great deal of further investigation. There is one last observation of Shaked that seems especially pertinent to the religious landscape of the regions under study here. As Shaked has argued, the "pluralism of faith that may have prevailed in the Sasanian period ... is to all appearances *not one that entailed necessarily a pluralism of sects.*" There is no reason to assume, in other words, "that every shade of faith had, so to speak, its own church."[2276]

In all the varieties of Iranian religious belief, including Mihr worship, religious identity was closely bound to ethnic identity. In the greater scheme of things, a Mazdean, no matter what his/her popular cosmogonical belief, or who his/her chief *yazata*, was an Iranian, who identified him/herself, if forced, in contradistinction to a non-Mazdean, who was an *anēr*. The coalescence of

[2272]See page 188ff.

[2273]See §1.2 for the concept of agnatic group.

[2274]Boyce 1979, p. 56.

[2275]The evidence that we have gathered calls into question, or should at least be considered side-by-side, Shaked's subsequent claim, viz., that the "religious reality of the Sasanian period was such that Mihr, identified with the sun, was indeed *a central god in the western regions of the empire.*" Shaked 1994a, p. 92. Emphasis added.

[2276]Shaked, Shaul, 'Some Islamic Reports Concerning Zoroastrianism', *Jerusalem Studies in Arabic and Islam* 17, (1994b), pp. 43–84 (Shaked 1994b), p. 46. "It seems clear from what we know of the period from other sources, namely, that there were widespread deviations from the norms of the written religion, and that, as far as we can tell, many of these deviations simply did not exist as separate church structures." Shaked 1994b, p. 46. Significantly, two exceptions seem to be the Sīsāniya sect (the followers of Bihāfarīd, see §6.3, especially page 436) and the followers of Bābak Khurramdīn. Ibid., p. 46–47.

the linguistic, religious, and ethnic dimensions of identity in Sasanian Iran in fact harked back to the Achaemenid period, when the term *airya* was used to connect language, descent, and religious affiliation in Darius I's inscriptions at Bīsetūn (Behistun).[2277] As Gnoli argues, the Avestan tradition "was an Aryan tradition par excellence." Significantly in fact, as Gnoli observes,[2278] while the ethnicon *airya* never appears in the Gāthās, it does appear in the Younger Avestā, in particular in the *Yashts*, and more specifically in the great *Yashts*, namely those dedicated to Anāhitā (Yasht 5),[2279] Tishtrya (Yasht 8),[2280] Mithra (Yasht 10),[2281] and the Fravashis (Yasht 13).[2282] With the assimilation of the "different religious trends that are echoed in the *Yashts*, an assimilation which led to the formation of the Younger Avestā, the tradition we might define as *airya*, began to be an organic part of Zoroastrianism." It was then, Gnoli argues, that "the foundations [were] laid of that *substantial unity between religious tradition and national tradition*, which was to be characteristic of the whole cultural history of ancient and, in part, medieval Iran."[2283] On some very crucial level, the national dimensions of identity as articulated in the *X^w adāy-Nāmag* tradition created a meta-history. The irony of it all was that with the conquest of the plateau by the Arabs, as Crone observes, the Iranians came into contact with a people for whom religious and national identity were equally compounded. Whoever the God of the Arabs was, he spoke Arabic.

While the kingdom of the Sasanians ceased to exist in the Islamic period, the Pārsīg–Pahlav genealogical heritage of the ruling dynasties continued to inform the heritage of those who claimed descent from it, witnessed by the genealogical claims circulating in the tenth centuries among the Samanids, the Buyids, and most importantly, the patrons of the *Shāhnāma*, the family of ʿAbdalrazzāq.[2284] Throughout the Sasanian period, therefore, except for periodic upsurges of centralization, the center–periphery discord, and the localized dimensions of identity, as articulated in an agnatic family structure, remained a paramount feature of Iranian society.[2285] And as the surge of the *ghulāt*[2286] in the medieval period attests, the tension between orthodox and heretic tendencies continued to inform Iranian history. But as attested by the

2277 Gnoli 1989, p. 13.

2278 Gnoli 1989, p. 35.

2279 Aban Yasht 1883, *Ābān Yasht*, vol. 23 of *Sacred Books of the East*, Oxford University Press, 1883, translated by James Darmesteter (Aban Yasht 1883), §§42, 49, 58, 69, and 117.

2280 Tishtar Yasht 1883, *Tishtar Yasht*, vol. 23 of *Sacred Books of the East*, Oxford University Press, 1883, translated by James Darmesteter (Tishtar Yasht 1883), §§36, 56, 58, and 61.

2281 Mihr Yasht 1883, §§4 and 13.

2282 Frawardin Yasht 1883, §§10, 43, 44, 87, and 143.

2283 Gnoli 1989, pp. 35–36.

2284 For ʿAbdalrazzāq, see page 463 below, as well as Pourshariati 1995.

2285 In this sense the history of Iran is no exception to that of any other region in the pre-modern world. One need not put forth an unwarranted claim to continuity to recognize this.

2286 The *ghulāt*, literally the *exaggerators*, were various Shiʿite sects in Iran during the late antique to early modern period. See Babayan, Kathryn, *Mystics, Monarchs and Messiahs: Cultural Landscapes of Early Modern Iran*, Harvard University Press, 2002 (Babayan 2002).

proliferation of the *Shāhnāma* tradition and the strength of its popular dissemination, and as reflected in the prolific popular literature of Iran,[2287] the ethnic and national dimensions of identity have, throughout Iranian history, superseded these centrifugal tendencies.

[2287]The author's research into this will be forthcoming. The concepts of the *ʿajam* versus the Arab or the Turk infuse Iranian popular literature throughout the Qajar period. Their strong currents, in different terminologies, in the modern period of not only Iranian, but also Turkic and Arab modern histories is recognized by all.

CHAPTER 6

Revolts of late antiquity in Khurāsān and Ṭabaristān

In the previous chapter we argued that the histories of the quarter of the east (*kūst-i khwarāsān*) and the quarter of the north (*kūst-i ādurbādagān*) during the Sasanian period, being for the most part controlled by Parthian dynastic families, testify to the existence of popular religious practices prevalent in these regions. Moreover, the predominant popular form of this spirituality in Khurāsān, Ṭabaristān, Gurgān, and the Caspian provinces, as well as in Azarbāyjān,[2288] was Mihr worship. Given also the prevalence of Mihr in pre-Christian Armenia,[2289] it can therefore be said that in an extensive stretch of territory from the northwest to the northeast of Iran, the most popular form of religious practice during the Sasanian period was Mihr worship. The evidence for this in our sources is, as we have seen and will hopefully continue to establish, overwhelming. Moreover, our evidence will underline the substantial and direct continuity of religious practices prevalent in these regions of Iran from the late Sāsānian period through at least the first century and a half of post-conquest Iranian history. In order to establish this we first take up an investigation of the religious dimensions of a revolt whose political ramifications were already examined in Chapter 2: the revolt of Bahrām-i Chūbīn (590–591). We have deferred a detailed study of its religious aspects to this chapter in order to highlight the shared religious landscape of this revolt with those that transpired in the quarters of the east and north of the former Sasanian domains after the eruption of the ʿAbbāsid revolution (747). After our analysis of Bahrām-i Chūbīn's rebellion, we will have to briefly discuss the ʿAbbāsid revolution, before we pick up, once again, our narrative.

6.1 Bahrām-i Chūbīn

The rebellion of the Mihrānid Bahrām-i Chūbīn against Hormozd IV and Khusrow II in 590 was an unprecedented revolt in the history of the Sasanians, for it marked the first significant breakdown of the Sasanian–Parthian confederacy,

[2288] For lack of space and time, we cannot present all our evidence for the latter region here.
[2289] See §5.4.4.

when a Parthian dynast rebelled against the very legitimacy of the kingship of the Sasanians.[2290] As a rebellion against the Sasanians, and in line with the religio-political ideology maintained by the dynasty and promulgated through their ideological machinery,[2291] the revolt of Bahrām-i Chūbīn was naturally considered as the ultimate act of sacrilege. In the religio-political dogma promoted by the Sasanians and the orthodox religious establishment with which it sought at times to form a partnership, any rebellion against the state involved, by definition, apostasy. As it has been so cogently argued by Gnoli,[2292] this definition of apostasy had a long heritage in the religio-political discourse of the Mazdean religion and the Iranian notion of kingship, and was not an invention of the Sasanians. Insofar as there was no clear definition of orthodoxy in the post-Avestan, pre-Sasanian history of Iran, however, the purview of apostasy could not have been very clearly defined prior to the rise of the dynasty. Besides its implicit heretical purport, however, the rebellion of Bahrām-i Chūbīn embodied even more explicit and directly potent signs of heresy. For, as we shall argue in this section, a key feature of the Parthian dynast's rebellion was its promulgation of and adherence to Mithraic currents of religiosity. What is our evidence for this?

6.1.1 Mithraic purview of Bahrām-i Chūbīn's rebellion

A perusal of Ferdowsī's account of Bahrām-i Chūbīn, narrated from the legitimist perspective of the Sasanians as articulated through the *X^w adāy-Nāmag* tradition, gives us a very significant piece of information about this Mihrānid Parthian dynast. While recounting the saga of Bahrām-i Chūbīn, on a number of occasions, Ferdowsī refers to the Parthian dynast as *Bahrām-i Mihtar-parast*.[2293] The only other figure that carries this epithet in the Sasanian sections of Ferdowsī's work is the Sasanian king Jāmāsp,[2294] the progenitor of the Āl-i Jāmāsp dynasty in Gīlān and eventually Ṭabaristān, and the ancestor of Jīl-i Jīlānshāh Gāvbārih, the Cow Devotee. We recall that it was this Jīl-i Jīlānshāh, the Cow Devotee, who, together with the family of Farrukhzād, *aka* Zīnabī, made a pact with the Arab armies.[2295] There is very little doubt that Ferdowsī's epithet of *Mihtar-parast*, applied to Jāmāsp and Bahrām-i Chūbīn, is the author's poetic rendering for *Mihr-parast*, that is to say, a *devotee of Mihr*, and thus signals the Mithraic dimension of the religiosity of these two important dynastic figures in Sasanian history. The literal meaning of this term, "one who is devoted to one's master", makes little sense in this context since both figures in fact rebelled against their overlords. One can only deduce, therefore,

[2290]See §2.6.3.
[2291]See for instance our discussion in §5.2.1.
[2292]Gnoli 1989, *passim*.
[2293]Ferdowsī 1935, pp. 2587–2588.
[2294]Ferdowsī 1935, p. 2298. In assessing the significance of this epithet of Jāmāsp we should also recall that the Sasanian Jāmāsp partook in all probability in the Mazdakite creed; see §4.3.1.
[2295]See §4.4.1.

that using poetic license to suit the rhyme and rhythm of his opus, the poet is simply substituting *mihtar-parast* for the intended *Mihr-parast* (Mihr devotee), giving us the actual religious affiliations of Bahrām-i Chūbīn. Had this been our only evidence of Bahrām-i Chūbīn's Mihr worship, we would not be offering a strong case for it. Ferdowsī's rendition of Bahrām-i Chūbīn as a Mihr worshipper, however, is corroborated by Sebeos, who on two separate occasions refers to the rebel as *Vahram Merhewandak*, where *Merhewandak* or *Mihrewandak* is a literal translation of the *servant of Mithra*.[2296]

Many Mithraic motifs have been infused in Bahrām-i Chūbīn's narrative. Before we get to the crux of the Mithraic framework of Bahrām-i Chūbīn's story, however, it is best to highlight some of the more nuanced reflections of it. According to the *Shāhnāma*, before embarking upon his wars in the east against Sāvih Shāh, who had attacked the Iranian realm during Hormozd IV's reign, and against whom he was called in, Bahrām-i Chūbīn prayed to God.[2297] But from the description that follows it becomes apparent that the god to whom he prayed was not Ahūrā Mazdā, but Mithra, the warrior-god of Justice. In his prayer, Bahrām-i Chūbīn entreated his god, whom he addressed as the Judge of Equity (*dāvar-i dād o pāk*), to make a judgment call: if he reckoned this war to be unjust (*gar īn jang bīdād bīnī hamī*), then he should protect Bahrām-i Chūbīn's enemy Sāvih Shāh. If, on the other hand, he deemed Bahrām-i Chūbīn to be fighting on his side (*vagar man zi bahr-ī tow kūsham hamī*), that is to say, on the side of justice, then the divinity should aid him. Bahrām-i Chūbīn subsequently asked the Judge to confer bliss on him and his army by replenishing the earth after the battle.[2298] Now, like the literary narratives of Pīrūz's war,[2299] all the Mithraic motifs are gathered here in Ferdowsī's narrative. The god in question is a Judge who, based on his decisions as to on whose side Justice resides, will

[2296]For Sebeos' narrative on Bahrām-i Chūbīn's rebellion, see Sebeos 1999, pp. 14–23, especially n. 104, and pp. 168, 169, n. 8. It must be noted that in the accounts of Sebeos, when asking the aid of Mušeł Mamikonean, the Armenian *sparapet*, against Khusrow II, and promising him remuneration, Bahrām-i Chūbīn prayed to Ahūrā Mazdā and other gods besides Mihr: "If I shall be victorious, I swear by the great god Aramazd, by the lord Sun and the Moon, by fire and water, by Mihr and all the gods." This is evidently an indication that the Mihr worship of Bahrām-i Chūbīn did not necessarily exclude his worship of Ahūrā Mazdā, but only points to the primacy of Mihr in the rebel's religious beliefs.

[2297]The *X^w adāy-Nāmag* and the Arabic traditions ignore Bahrām-i Chūbīn's campaigns in the west (see page 125) on behalf of Hormozd IV, the failure of which, according to western sources, was the actual cause of Hormozd IV's disenchantment with Bahrām-i Chūbīn. Instead, for reasons that will become apparent shortly, the emphasis is put on Bahrām-i Chūbīn's campaigns in the east and his tremendous success in that region.

[2298]Ferdowsī 1971, vol. VIII, p. 364, Ferdowsī 1935, p. 2613:

بغلتید در پیش یزدان بخاک　　همی گفت کی داور داد و پاک
گر این جنگ بیداد بینی همی　　ز من ساوه را برگزینی همی
دلم را برزم اندر ارام ده　　بایرانیان بر ورا کام ده
وگر من ز بهر تو کوشم همی　　به رزم اندرون سر فروشم همی
مرا و سپاه مرا شاد کن　　وزین جنگ ما گیتی اباد کن

[2299]See our discussion on page 380ff.

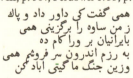

undertake to help the aggrieved party, and subsequently undertakes to replenish the realm that has been destroyed through the acts of the aggressor. Here we have an amalgam of all the Mithraic motifs come together. The warrior dimension of Mihr has already been discussed in detail.[2300] We have also highlighted the intimate connection of Mihr worship, in its Iranian context, with the notions of a just versus an unjust war, as well as the connection of war to notions of just kingship, the Circle of Justice,[2301] and welfare of the realm and the populace. It seems very probable therefore that the god to whom Bahrām-i *Mihrewandak* prays is none other than the warrior god of Justice, the God of Contracts, that is, Mithra.[2302]

Bahrām-i Chūbīn subsequently successfully defended the realm against the aggression of Sāvih Shāh, and his son, Parmūdih. After his defeat, however, Parmūdih asked Bahrām-i Chūbīn for refuge (*zinhār*). Now, "taking refuge (*zinhār*) [into Mithra]" likewise betrays a clear Mithraic terminology, reminiscent of the personal seal of Dād-Burz-Mihr (Dādmihr), the Parthian *spāhbed* of the east of Hormozd IV, who takes refuge (*panāh*) in the Burzīn Mihr fire.[2303] It is in Mithra that an aggrieved party takes refuge seeking his protection, as well as aid against an aggressor and breaker of pacts. Later in the narrative, Bahrām-i Chūbīn openly accused Khusrow II Parvīz of not abiding by the god's contract (*peymān*). Considering the oath-breaking of Khusrow II, moreover, Bahrām-i Chūbīn proclaimed that as it was his camp only that had *justice, Mihr, armour, and hand*, he was certain to be victorious.[2304] The notion of *dast*, hand, as in the hand that will be lent by Mithra to aid the aggrieved and bestow victory, is also patently Mithraic.[2305] In the *Mihr Yasht*, the supplicants have outstretched hands when entreating for the aid of Mithra.[2306] All these Mithraic motifs coalesce in the ways in which Bahrām-i Chūbīn described himself and the enemy. Initially against Sāvih Shāh,[2307] and later against Khusrow II, the Justice of Bahrām-i Chūbīn's cause was always assessed self-referentially.[2308]

2300 See page 352.

2301 See page 354.

2302 See page 351.

2303 Gyselen 2001a, p. 46, seal A. Ferdowsī 1935, pp. 2631–2633.

2304 See footnote 2308.

2305 For a brilliant exposition of this see Soudavar 1980, pp. 13–16. As Soudavar explains, in the rock relief of Shāpūr I in Bīshāpūr where the king's successive victories over Gordian III (238–244), Philip the Arab (244–249) and Valerian (253–260) are depicted, an angel is seen offering a flying ribbon (*dastār*), a purveyor of victory, to "Shāpūr who is depicted with one already floating behind his head." Shāpūr I, moreover, is depicted as "squeezing the wrist of the captive Roman emperor (captivity and submission are termed *dastgir* in Middle and New Persian.)" Ibid., pp. 13–14, nn. 33 and 38, and fig. 2, p. 149.

2306 Mihr Yasht 1959, p. 113; Mihr Yasht 1883, §83.

2307 Ironically, after his rebellion, the Khāqān of the Turks was also on Bahrām-i Chūbīn's side.

2308 Ferdowsī 1971, vol. IX, p. 32, Ferdowsī 1935, p. 2697:

تو پیمان یزدان نداری نگاه   همی ناسزا جویی این پیشگاه ...
بدین کار خاقان مرا یاورست   هم ان کندر ایران و چین لشکراست
که با داد و مهریم و با تیغ و دست   ز دشمن نیاید به ما بر شکست

Ṭabarī's narrative suggests that supernatural forces were at work in the final episode of Bahrām-i Chūbīn's struggle against Khusrow II Parvīz, but fails to identify their agency: When Khusrow II Parvīz "got trapped in a defile," according to Ṭabarī, Bahrām-i Chūbīn pursued him, "but when Bahrām-i Chūbīn was sure that he had Abarwīz in his power something that could not be comprehended [i.e., some supernatural power] took the latter up to the top of the mountain."[2309] In Ferdowsī's narrative, however, this supernatural force is identified as the angel Sorūsh, the right hand aide to the god Mihr. The god Sraoša (Sorūsh), the hypostasis and genius of Discipline, is "in this capacity ... a natural ally of Mithra the guardian of Contract, and of Rašnu the judge ... [This] divine triad remains throughout the development of Zoroastrianism in *charge of prosecuting the wicked* ... [Sraoša's] specific function within the triad ... *must have been that of a punisher*."[2310] While Khusrow II is saved by the angel Sorūsh, however, there is no guarantee that, as a breaker of Contract, he is saved from his wrath.

According to Ferdowsī, when Bahrām-i Chūbīn finally opted to mint coins in the name of Khusrow II Parvīz, he chose a messenger, whom the author compares to Sorūsh.[2311] So although initially Sorūsh supported Bahrām-i Chūbīn, he then apparently switched sides, for it was this same god who ensured Khusrow II Parvīz's victory in his last desperate attempt against the rebel. Khusrow II, having found himself in a cul-de-sac, entreated God, asking him to come to his aid in his hour of weakness. Suddenly and miraculously, Sorūsh appeared from the mountains, riding a horse and wearing a green garb. He grabbed the hand of Khusrow II (*cho nazdīk shod dast-i Khusrow girift*) and carried the king to the heavens, to safety. In tears, Khusrow II then implored the angel to disclose his identity, at which point the latter identified himself as Sorūsh and prognosticated for Khusrow II that he would soon assume the throne and warned him that thenceforth he should act piously.[2312]

Mihr, of course, could be read here as friendship, which given the context, would be rather absurd!

[2309]Ṭabarī 1999, pp. 313–314, de Goeje, 1000.

[2310]Mihr Yasht 1959, p. 193. Emphasis added.

[2311]Ferdowsī 1971, vol. VIII, p. 419:

فرستاده ای جست با رای و هوش   دلاور بسان خجسته سروش

[2312]Ferdowsī 1971, vol. IX, p. 121:

بیزدان چنین گفت کی کردگار   توبی برتر از گردش روزگار
بدین جای بیچارگی دستگیر   تو باشی ننالم به کیوان و تیر
همانگه چو از کوه بر شدخروش   پدید امد از راه فرّخ سروش
همه جامه اش سبز و خنگی بزیر   ز دیدار او گشت خسرو دلیر
چو نزدیك شد دست خسرو گرفت   ز یزدان پاك این نباشد شگفت
چو از پیش بد خواه برداشتش   به اسانی اورد و بگذاشتش
بدو گفت خسرو که نام تو چیست   همی گفت چندی و چندی گریست
فرشته بدو گفت نام سروش   چو ایمن شدی دور باش از خروش
کزین پس شوی در جهان پادشاه   نباید که باشی جز از پارسا

Once again, as in the narrative of the Kārins' aid to Khusrow I Nowshīrvān in his wars in the east,[2313] a green-clad rider, the symbolic representation of Mithra, who in this case happened to be actually his right hand aide, the angel Sorūsh, mysteriously appeared to aid a Sasanian king back to the throne. The fact that Sorūsh here came to the aid of Khusrow II Parvīz rather than Bahrām-i Chūbīn, however, most probably represents a classic case of co-option of the divinity of one enemy's camp into one's own.[2314] In fact the one monarch who is certain to have tampered with the *X^w adāy-Nāmag* tradition when the account did not please him is Khusrow II Parvīz.[2315]

There is little doubt that the rebellion of the Mihrānid Bahrām-i Chūbīn was attended by strong currents of Mihr worship. That the Parthian version of Mihr worship was in fact hostile to the religion advocated by the Sasanian kings of Persīs is also confirmed by Ferdowsī's narrative: the Mihr worship of Bahrām-i *Mihrewandak* was distinct from that of the Sasanian king Khusrow II Parvīz. The clearest reflection of this is Bahrām-i Chūbīn's agenda of destroying the fire temples (*konad bā zamīn rāst ātashkadih*) of the Sasanian realm.[2316] The Pahlav rebel not only promised to renew justice and the traditions of the Arsacid Mithradates (Milād) in the world,[2317] but also claimed to be the very apotheosis of the fiery fire of Burzīn Mihr.[2318] He also promised, as we have seen, to destroy the festivals of *Nowrūz* and *Sadih*.[2319]

I owe this reference to Dr. Asef Kholdani.

[2313]See pages 113 and 380.

[2314]This, it has been argued, for example, was one of the reasons why the Romans adopted the god of their enemy, the Parthians, when they started to worship Mithras on such an extensive and grand scale. Speidel, Michael P., 'Parthia and the Mithraism of the Roman Army', *Études Mithraiques* IV, (1978), pp. 470–485 (Speidel 1978), pp. 470–485.

[2315]The intervention of censoring Sasanian monarchs seems to have been the most acute precisely in the rendition of those periods of their history when their legitimacy was questioned. And this was certainly the case with Khusrow II Parvīz. By adopting the angelology of the enemy, Khusrow II also usurped the legitimacy that the angel is supposed to bestow on the rebel, Bahrām-i Chūbīn. In Bayhaqī, Ibrāhīm b. Muḥammad, *Al-Maḥāsin wa 'l-Masāwī*, Giessen, 1902, edited by F. Schwally (Bayhaqī 1902), we are informed that at the end of Khusrow II Parvīz's wars with Bahrām-i Chūbīn, the monarch "ordered his secretary to write down an account of those wars and relate events in full, from the beginning to the end. The secretary complied, and when they read off the narrative to Xusrau [Khusrow II], its preface did not please him. Thereupon a young secretary wrote an eloquent and rhetorical prologue to the work and presented it to the king. Xusrau ... was delighted with it and ordered the promotion of the young scribe to a higher grade." Bayhaqī 1902, p. 481, quoted in Shahbazi 1990, p. 210. For an example in the case of Bahrām-i Chūbīn's story, see Jāḥiz's comment on page 34.

[2316]The catch of the narrative is that this the rebel claims on behalf of Sāvih Shāh.

[2317]Ferdowsī 1971, vol. IX, p. 32, Ferdowsī 1935, p. 2697:

برافرازم اندر جهان داد را　　کنم تازه آیین میلاد را

[2318]Ferdowsī 1971, vol. IX, p. 32, Ferdowsī 1935, p. 2697:

نبیره جهانجوی گرگین منم　　همان اتش تیز برزین منم

[2319]Yarshater 1983b, p. 458; Ferdowsī 1971, vol. IX, p. 32, Ferdowsī 1935, p. 2697:

Khusrow II Parvīz in fact accused Bahrām-i Chūbīn of irreligion and this, not only in the context of the official Sasanian ideology, where rebellion was tantamount to heresy, but also on account of Bahrām-i Chūbīn's clear apostasy. "Zoroaster has said in the *Zand*," Khusrow II declared to Bahrām-i Chūbīn, "that he who *apostatizes* from the pure religion (*bar gardad az dīn-i pāk*) has no fear and fright of God."[2320] Lest this be construed as apostasy against the state, the literal irreligion and apostasy of Bahrām-i Chūbīn and his followers is further reiterated by Khusrow II Parvīz in Ferdowsī's narrative. At the beginning of his war against Bahrām-i Chūbīn, Khusrow II prayed to the sun, whom he also calls the *Just and Illuminated* (*rowshan-i dādgar*), vowing that if he wins the war, "from the supporters of Bahrām-i Chūbīn, whomever is taken into captivity, he will force them to become the worshippers of the glorious fire (*parastandih farrukh ātash konam*), thereby placating the hearts of the *mōbads* and *herbads*" (*dil-i mowbad o hīrbad khosh konam*) of his domains.[2321] When Bahrām-i Chūbīn became confronted with the possibility of a numerous army gathering around Khusrow II, and recognized that the war, having divided families, had pitted members of his camp against their relatives in Khusrow II's camp, he instructed his army to lure to their side all of their relatives who were of the same inclination and faith (*kih bāshand yik dil bih goftār o kīsh*).[2322] For if they gave their souls to his cause, in contract (*bih peymān*), then in Khusrow II's camp there would remain only the armies of Barda'a and Ardabīl and a few contingents from Armenia.[2323]

The antipathy of Bahrām-i Chūbīn's followers toward the *mōbadic* structure of Khusrow II's regime is reiterated again and again in Ferdowsī's narrative.

به ایران بران رای بد ساوه شاه — که نه تخت ماند نه مهر و کلاه
کند با زمین راست اتشکده — نه نوروز ماند نه جشن سده

[2320]Ferdowsī 1971, vol. IX, p. 34, Ferdowsī 1935, p. 2699:

نشاید کزین کم کنیم ار فزون — که زردشت گوید به زند اندرون
که هر کس که برگردد از دین پاك — ز یزدان ندارد بدل ترس و باك ...
چو بر شاه گیتی شود بد گمان — ببایدش کشتن هم اندر زمان

[2321]Ferdowsī 1971, vol. IX, p. 25, Ferdowsī 1935, p. 2691:

بنالید و سر سوی خورشید کرد — ز یزدان و دلش پر ز امید کرد
چنین گفت کی روشن دادگر — درخت امید از تو اید به بر ...
ز بهرامیان هر که گردد اسیر — بپیش من ارد کسش دستگیر
پرستنده فرّخ اتش کنم — دل موبد و هیربد خوش کنم

[2322]Ferdowsī 1971, vol. IX, p. 42:

فرستید هر کس که دارید خویش — که باشند یك دل به گفتار و کیش

[2323]Ferdowsī 1971, vol. IX, p. 42, Ferdowsī 1935, p. 2708:

سپهبد بپرسید از ان سرکشان — که امد ز خویشان شما را نشان
فرستید هر کس که دارید خویش — که باشند یك دل به گفتار و کیش
گر ایشان بیایند و فرمان کنند — بپیمان روانها گروگان کنند
سپه ماند از بردع و اردبیل — وز ارمینیه سست پی یك دو خیل

When Hormozd IV sent a woman's attire to Bahrām-i Chūbīn as a recompense for his supposed disloyalty, the elite in Bahrām-i Chūbīn's court reminded him of the wise man from Rayy who, at the rise to power of Ardashīr I, had claimed: "I loathe the *mōbad* and the throne of the king (*bīzāram az mowbad o takht-i shāh*) when he does not pay heed to my protection."[2324] In one of his diatribes against Khusrow II Parvīz, while considering Ahūrā Mazdā as deserving of praise, Bahrām-i Chūbīn nevertheless referred to him as *your god* (*Ūrmazd-i shomā*).[2325] According to Simocatta, furthermore, once Khusrow II Parvīz decided to flee his homeland, he "entrusted the reigns of his flight to the supreme God; after looking up to heaven, and turning his thoughts to the Creator, *disregarding the false gods and placing none of his hope in Mithras . . . and by changing faith he also changed fortune toward the better.*"[2326] From Bahrām-i Chūbīn's epithet *Mihrewandak, slave of Mithra,* to his claim that he was the very reincarnation of the Burzīn Mihr fire and that Justice, Mihr, armour and hand—that is to say, Mihr with all his attributes—were on his side, to his platform of destroying the *mōbadic* fires, and his declaration that Khusrow II had broken the contract and Ahūrā Mazdā was *his* (Khusrow II's) god, and finally to the rebel's open declaration that his camp detested the *mōbads*, to Khusrow II's avowed intention of forcibly converting the captive followers of Bahrām-i Chūbīn, there is every indication, therefore, that in the warfare of the Parthian Mihrāns against the Sasanians we are witnessing a continuation of the Pārsīg–Pahlav religious antagonism.

6.1.2 Bahrām-i Chūbīn and the apocalypse

Further evidence for the Mithraic purview of Bahrām-i Chūbīn's rebellion is its messianic character. Indeed, so powerful the image of Bahrām-i Chūbīn as the saviour of Persia seems to have become that it left its mark on the Sasanian apocalyptic literature, where "he assumed the proportions of the Messiah promised in the sacred books."[2327] This messianic dimension of Bahrām-i Chūbīn's rebellion is significant for our purposes, not only on account of its clear Mithraic provenance, but also because the motifs associated with it are replicated in another rebellion that takes place in the same regions, Ṭabaristān and

[2324]Ferdowsī 1935, p. 2646:

نگر تا چه گفت ان خردمند پیر — به ری چون دلش تنگ شد ز اردشیر
که بیزارم از موبد و تخت شاه — چو نیك و بد من ندارد نگاه

With the variant Ferdowsī 1971, vol. VIII, p. 399:

که بیزارم از تخت وز تاج شاه — چو نیك و بد من ندارد نگاه

[2325]"When they bring this message to you, may *your* Ohrmozd be blessed." Ferdowsī 1935, p. 2770.

چو این نامه ارند نزد شما — که فرخنده باد اورمزد شما

[2326]Simocatta 1986, iv.10.I, p. 116. Emphasis mine.
[2327]Czegledy 1958, p. 21.

Khurāsān, more than two centuries posterior to it, namely the revolt of the *ispahbud pīrūz*, the victorious spāhbed, Sunbād.[2328] The superimposition of these motifs on Sunbād's rebellion undoubtedly betray, as we will see, the continued prevalence of Mithraic currents in these regions in the mid-eighth century.

To establish the apocalyptic dimension of Bahrām-i Chūbīn's rebellion, we will make extensive use of Czegledy's excellent article 'Bahrām Chubin and the Persian Apocalyptic Literature'. There is, however, one crucial issue that is lost sight of in Czegledy's fascinating analysis, namely that whenever these apocalyptic accounts take a legitimist tone from the Mihrānid perspective, they are framed by thoroughly Mithraic motifs. This should come as no surprise since Mihr is not only the *yazata* in charge of fulfilling millennial expectations at the apocalypse,[2329] but also the actual historical provenance of Bahrām-i Chūbīn's rebellion is from within a region infused with Mithraic religiosity. As a dynastic leader, the Mihrānid Bahrām-i Chūbīn belonged to the quarter of the north,[2330] and gathered his support from this region as well as from the quarter of the east, in both of which regions one of the most current forms of religiosity was Mihr worship.[2331]

So let us follow in some detail Czegledy's argument, amending it where necessary with our argument as to the Mithraic dimension of the messianic motifs in Bahrām-i Chūbīn's rebellion. According to Czegledy, there are a number of motifs, all historical, with which Bahrām-i Chūbīn's narrative always appears in the apocalyptic sources such as the *Zand i Vahuman Yasn*, *Jamasp Namak* and *Bundahishn*.[2332] These include Bahrām-i Chūbīn's campaigns against the Western and Eastern Turks, through which Balkh, among other major cities, was conquered,[2333] and the tremendous booty that Bahrām-i Chūbīn obtained on these campaigns.[2334] Moreover, even if the narrative is sympathetic to Bahrām-i Chūbīn, as is the case in the romance of Bahrām-i Chūbīn, he is always depicted from the point of view of the legitimist claims of the Sasanians to kingship. In his examination of these accounts, Czegledy further highlights the importance of the *Ctesian method*[2335] in the Iranian historical tradition and shows how it applies in particular to the apocalyptic traditions surrounding Bahrām-i Chūbīn. In the Iranian epic romances, he argues, "many of the ancient heroes of the religion are vested with traits of historic personalities who lived in the ages of the Achaemenids, Arsacidan and Sasanians." Among these ancient Iranian heroes whose myths underwent such an anachronistic adaptation, the most

[2328] See §6.4.

[2329] For the eschatological dimension of Mihr, see page 353.

[2330] We recall, for example, that the *ērān-spāhbed* Gōrgōn of the *kūst-i ādurbādagān* was Bahrām-i Chūbīn's grandfather; see page 103.

[2331] See §5.4.

[2332] On these apocalyptic sources, see Daryaee, Touraj, 'Apocalypse Now: Zoroastrian Reflection on the Early Islamic Centuries', *Medieval Encounters* 4, (1998), pp. 188–202 (Daryaee 1998).

[2333] Czegledy 1958, p. 24.

[2334] Czegledy 1958, pp. 24–25.

[2335] See footnote 609.

important was Spandīyādh, "the hero of Zoroaster's Millennium who, at the time of Vištāsp [Kai Vīshtāspā], thrice vanquished and finally killed Arjāsp, the prince of Tūrān," the archenemy of Iran in the Iranian national epic.[2336] According to Czegledy, one of these anachronistic adaptations in Spandīyādh's story took place under the influence of Bahrām-i Chūbīn's history. Mimicking the historical episodes of Bahrām-i Chūbīn's wars in Transoxiana, Spandīyādh's military campaign was extended beyond the city of Balkh, a feat that was never actually undertaken by him in the Old Iranian epic. In these later versions, however, Spandīyādh crossed the Oxus and progressed as far as the Copper Fortress, the Tūrānian capital, where he killed Arjāsp, the Tūrānian king. We have therefore three new motifs in Spandīyādh's story in the later versions of his epic: 1) his crossing of the Oxus; 2) the mention of the Copper City and; 3) his murder of the Tūrānian prince, all of which follow Bahrām-i Chūbīn's story.[2337] Now, from Tibetan texts of Tun-Huang origin we know that around 750 the Copper City was the name of the capital of the Central Asian Uyghurs. *Madīnatu aṣ-ṣufriya* and, "in part also the Persian *Dizh-i Rōyīn* ... are [therefore] translations of the Turkish *Baqir Baliy* mentioned in the Tibetan text."[2338] In the Persian traditions, the Copper City, *Rūyīn Dizh*, is located either, significantly, in the vicinity of Rām Pīrūz, the city established by the Sasanian king Pīrūz near Rayy,[2339] or in the city of Paykand, about thirty kilometers from Bukhārā.[2340] But it is not only in the *X^w adāy-Nāmag* tradition that we witness a superimposition of Bahrām-i Chūbīn's apocalyptic stories.

According to Czegledy, the figure of Bahrām-i Chūbīn, together with all the motifs of his narrative, were also anachronistically inserted in the most important apocalyptic literature of the Sasanian period. When describing the events of the Fourth Millennium, the *Jāmasp Nāmak* "vividly portrays the emergence of a false pretender. This insignificant and dark (*khvartak ut apa'tāk*) person arrives, with a great army, from Khorasan and, after seizing power, he disappears (*apa'tāk bavet*), in the middle of his reign (*miyān ī pātakhshāhīh*), whereupon the realm is overtaken by foreigners. Then comes the *victorious king* (*Aparvēz Khvatāy*), who conquers large territories, as well as many cities from the Romans. The fortunes of Iran are thenceforth in decline, with misery and great distress, when it is best not to be born to witness the great disasters that engulfs the kingdom at the end of Zoroaster's Millennium."[2341] Czegledy brilliantly points out the parallels of the *Jāmāsp Namak*'s false pretender and the context in which he appears with the figure of Bahrām-i Chūbīn and the history of the Sasanians in the late sixth century. Bahrām-i Chūbīn, too, appeared from Khurāsān as a false pretender. In line with the legitimist dimensions of the *X^w adāy-Nāmag*, he,

[2336] Czegledy 1958, p. 28. For the Tūrānians, see Yarshater 1983b, pp. 408–409.
[2337] Czegledy 1958, p. 29.
[2338] Czegledy 1958, p. 31.
[2339] See page 380ff.
[2340] Czegledy 1958, p. 31.
[2341] Czegledy 1958, p. 33.

too, is depicted as a low-born man, who seized power through violence. And "above all, it was Bahrām-i Chūbīn who disappeared in the midst of his reign. The subsequent rule by foreigners is an obvious reference to the fact that the reign of Khusrov II was reestablished by the Byzantine army."[2342] The story of the victorious king (*Aparvēz Khvatāy*), who took away large territories and many cities from the Romans, refers then to Khusrow II Parvīz's reign, whereas the subsequent decline, when "misery engulfed the land", is a clear reference to the Arab invasion of Iran.[2343] What is even more significant for our purposes, however, is Czegledy's assertion that next, "the text describes the eschatological battle of Mihr and Ēšm [Kheshm]." This, Czegledy believes, is actually portraying "the war of the Mohammedan conquerors against Zoroastrianism."[2344]

Now, in the introductory passages of the *Jāmāsp Nāmak*, when the final collapse of Ērānshahr at the end of the millennium at the hands of the Tāzīyān (i.e., the Arabs) is given in a synopsis, the cause of the calamity is ascribed to the people's oath-breaking (*mihr durujī or peymān shekanī*). People exhibited hatred (*kīn*), envy (*rashk*) and falsehood (*durugh*) against each other.[2345] It is to be remarked, incidentally, that according to our analysis of the Arab conquest and the Pārsīg–Pahlav factional strife, this is precisely what happened. It is significant in this context therefore, that the Mithraic concept of oath-breaking (*mihr durujī, peymān shekanī*) is used here. At any rate, after a detailed description of the wretchedness to which people succumbed at the onset of the Tāzīyān conquest,[2346] the text begins to give a somewhat more detailed chronological narrative of the prior conditions that had led to the final calamity.[2347] It is to this latter section that Czegledy's perceptive identification of Bahrām-i Chūbīn's narrative refers. Here indeed almost all of the historical episodes of Bahrām-i Chūbīn's rebellion, Khusrow II's assumption of the throne with the aid of the Byzantines, his subsequent war against and victories over the latter,[2348] the havoc under his sons and finally the onslaught of the Turks, the Byzantines and the Arabs against the Iranians are one by one briefly depicted.

A Mithraic end-of-time scenario, or as Czegledy puts it, the "*eschatological battle* of Mihr and Ēšm [Kheshm]" is therefore offered. There then comes a passage that Czegledy considers to be interpolated, where the theme of Bahrām-i Chūbīn is repeated through a description of a false pretender. This time the false pretender, together with a large army, arrived, significantly, from the direction of the *kūst-i nēmrōz*, had pretensions to leadership (*khudāvandī*), and through a lot of bloodshed conquered cities and was victorious. At the end, however,

[2342]Czegledy 1958, p. 34.
[2343]Czegledy 1958, pp. 32–34.
[2344]Czegledy 1958, p. 33.
[2345]Jamasp 1941, *Yādgār-i Jāmāsp*, Sokhan, 1941, translated by Sadegh Hedayat (Jamasp 1941), p. 116.
[2346]Jamasp 1941, pp. 116–118.
[2347]Jamasp 1941, p. 118.
[2348]His ultimate defeat is, of course, skipped over.

this rebel fled from the hands of his enemies to Zābulistān and recuperated. In the process, the population of Ērānshahr descended from the heights to utter hopelessness and sought refuge for their own lives.[2349] The end of this false pretender is not described.[2350] In analyzing this section, however, Czegledy maintains that this passage "is obviously closely related to the previous narrative [of Bahrām-i Chūbīn]." It is once again a false pretender that brings misery on Iran. While the end of this figure is not narrated, moreover, Czegledy believes that the whole "passage seems to be an incomplete doublet of the former narrative," the difference being that while in the former Bahrām-i Chūbīn accurately comes from Khurāsān, in this one he comes from the south.[2351] One must not be put off, Czegledy argues, by the fact that in this version our figure appears from Nīmrūz, for we do have certain traditions according to which Bahrām-i Chūbīn comes from Fārs. As far as the mention of Zābulistān is concerned, we do know that, as Nöldeke confirmed, Bahrām-i Chūbīn's "army actually rallied from Hephthalite territory."[2352] The nature of apocalyptic literature—where layers of tradition are superimposed on each other—is such that Czegledy's arguments about this passage might very well be accurate. There is, however, a variant reading of this passage that might actually make more sense. This passage might more appropriately be seen as depicting the revolt of Ustādsīs (circa 767 CE) rather than being a doublet of Bahrām-i Chūbīn's narrative, for all the elements of Ustādsīs' rebellion are incorporated here. Unfortunately, lack of space prevents us from elaborating this point further here.[2353]

The motif of treasure

After the interpolated passage, there is a second narrative in the *Jāmāsp Nāmak* that portrays Bahrām-i Chūbīn in apocalyptic terms. In this passage, a man saw the god (*īzad*) Mihr on the seacoast of Padhashkhwārgar (Ṭabaristān), who told him many secrets. Mihr then sent this man with a message to the king of Padhashkhwārgar. "Why are you maintaining this blind and deaf (*kar o kūr*) kingship," Mihr asked. "You, yourself must assume kingship as your ancestors had," Mihr exhorted the king of Padhashkhwārgar.[2354] "How am I to assume kingship when *I own not an army* or commanders, *nor a treasury* as my ancestors did", the king retorted. At this the envoy showed the king of Padhashkhwārgar the treasures of Afrāsīyāb. Once the king obtained these treasures, he set out with an army from Zābulistān against the enemy. When the Turks, the Arabs and the Romans (Byzantines) learned of the take-over of the treasure of

[2349] Jamasp 1941, p. 119:

از ان فراز به نا امیدی گران رسند.

[2350] Jamasp 1941, p. 119. Czegledy 1958, p. 31.
[2351] Czegledy 1958, p. 31.
[2352] Czegledy 1958, p. 34.
[2353] For the background of Ustādsīs's rebellion, see Pourshariati 1995.
[2354] Jamasp 1941, p. 119. Czegledy 1958, p. 37.

Afrāsīyāb by the king of Padhashkhwārgar, they conspired to capture him and obtain his treasures. The king of Padhashkhwārgar then engaged his enemies in the middle of Ērānshahr, in a region called the White Forest.[2355] With the "power of the gods (Yazdān), the *farra* [Divine Glory] of the Kayānids, and that of the religion of the Mazdeans, with the *farra* of the Padhashkhwārgar and [with the aid of] Mihr, Sorūsh, Rashnu, Ābān, Ādharān and Ātashān," the king of Padhashkhwārgar defeated his enemies.[2356] Then, at Ahūrā Mazdā's order, Sorūsh, along with Pashūtan, came from the fortress of the Kayānids, Kang Dizh. Together with 150 of his companions, wearing black and white clothes, Pashūtan then went to Pārs, to the abode of Ātash (the god of fire) and Ābān (the god of water), reciting the *Yashts* and performing other rituals, thus ending the Age of the Wolf and starting that of the Lamb, when the Zoroastrian religion was established.[2357]

Czegledy aptly recognizes that this section of the *Jāmāsp Nāmak* "*even to a greater degree than the foregoing passages*, betrays that it was composed under the impression of Bahrām Čobīn's historical part."[2358] Padhashkhwārgar is a clear reference to the ancestral territories of the Mihrāns, that is, the regions of Rayy and Ṭabaristān, and the king of Padhashkhwārgar refers to the dynastic leader of these regions in the period under consideration, Bahrām-i Chūbīn. What is even more significant, Czegledy reminds us, is that the envoy urges the king of Padhashkhwārgar to recall his own kingly heritage when contemplating rebellion. It is clear, Czegledy argues, that the dynasty to which the king of Padhashkhwārgar belonged was different from that of the blind and deaf king, in whose person we find an unmistakable reference to Hormozd IV, who was, in fact, blinded by his uncles, the Ispahbudhān Vindūyih and Vistāhm.[2359] Incidentally, we should keep in mind that in the Mithraic conception of kingship, an illegitimate king is also depicted as being blind and deaf: Mithra induces fear "in men who are false to the contract" by carrying "off ... the light of their eyes, the hearing of their ears."[2360] It is Mithra who switches off the "eyesight, [and] deafens the ... ears" of the enemy.[2361] By contrast, it is Mithra who has "a thousand perceptions, [and] ten thousand eyes for seeing all around."[2362] We recall that these were also precisely Fereydūn's attributes, when from the Alburz mountains, he circled the globe and saw all there was to be seen.[2363]

[2355]As Czegledy remarks the "White Forest is an archaism ... [It is in] a more pedantic than apocalyptic style that the compilers [of the *Zand i Vahuman Yasn*] enumerate all the great battles which, according to the Iranian romances, were fought in the White Forest." Czegledy 1958, p. 38. Emphasis added.

[2356]Jamasp 1941, p. 120.

[2357]Jamasp 1941, p. 120.

[2358]Czegledy 1958, p. 37. Emphasis mine.

[2359]See page 127.

[2360]Mihr Yasht 1959, p. 85. Mihr Yasht 1883, §23.

[2361]Mihr Yasht 1959, p. 97. Mihr Yasht 1883, §48.

[2362]Mihr Yasht 1959, pp. 77, 113, 117 and 145 respectively. Mihr Yasht 1883, §§7, 82, 91, 141.

[2363]See page 372.

According to Czegledy, the role of the envoy sent by Mihr to the king of Padhashkhwārgar is replicated in the *Xʷadāy-Nāmag* tradition of the *Shāhnāma* by Bahrām-i Chūbīn's companions. Like the envoy of Mihr, Bahrām-i Chūbīn's companions argued that the Mihrānid himself was entitled to kingship based on his Arsacid lineage.[2364] The reference to Padhashkhwārgar Shāh's initial poverty of means and his subsequent wealth through obtaining the treasury of Afrāsīyāb, Czegledy argues, is a clear reference to "the *vast booty* which Bahrām-i Chūbīn acquired after the defeat of the Hephthalites and Turks and the killing of the Turkish Khaqan."[2365] In short all the motifs of the historical episode of Bahrām-i Chūbīn's rebellion can be found in this apocalyptic narrative. There is, however, one very telling curiosity and difference in this version of Bahrām-i Chūbīn's narrative with the one that preceded it, and Czegledy himself acknowledges this. In this version of the apocalyptic narrative, the king of Padhashkhwārgar actually fulfilled the messianic expectation and reestablished order, legitimate kingship, and the good religion. In Bahrām-i Chūbīn's story there was no such blessed ending: his rebellion ended in terrible defeat. The legitimist tenor of all the Bahrām-i Chūbīn narratives, wherein a base-born rebel severely disrupts the natural order of things, is conspicuously absent in this narrative. "At first sight it appears," Czegledy perceptively realizes, "that the author of this vaticination *does not regard Bahrām-i Chūbīn as a false pretender* ... [and] even looks down upon the reigning king as a deaf and blind king." The narrative has a positive ending, Czegledy believes, because "at this point, all allusions to the history of Bahrām Čobīn come to an end ... So, at this point, we deal with a genuine forecast of the future ... a *victorious* Prince of the Last Days, the king of Patašxvārgar, *alias* Bahrām Čobīn, is heir to the legitimate reign of the Kayanians."[2366]

What Czegledy fails to perceive here, however, is the thoroughly Mithraic provenance of this second, positive depiction of Bahrām-i Chūbīn in the *Jāmāsp Nāmak*. Considering all that has been said about the Mithraic predilections of the Parthian Mihrān dynasty,[2367] and considering the primary eschatological responsibilities of Mihr,[2368] therefore, it is no surprise that in this second narrative—where he is not portrayed as a base-born rebel and the potential destroyer of the legitimate Sasanian kingship, but as an equally legitimate dynast of Kayānid ancestry—it was the god Mihr who shored up the king of Padhashkhwārgar (Ṭabaristān) against the *Aparvēz Khvatāy* (Khusrow II Parvīz). It was Mihr who provided him with Afrāsīyāb's treasury,[2369] and it was Mihr who, true to his function as a warrior god, supplied him with a powerful army.

[2364] Czegledy 1958, p. 37.
[2365] Czegledy 1958, p. 38. Emphasis added.
[2366] Czegledy 1958, p. 38. Emphasis added.
[2367] See §5.4.2.
[2368] See page 353.
[2369] This too, as the *Mihr Yasht* informs us, is a function of Mithra: he "bestows riches and fortune ... and much comfort." Mihr Yasht 1959, p. 127; Mihr Yasht 1883, §108.

In fact, in all versions of the apocalypse in the *Jāmāsp Nāmak*, the Last Days' onslaught starts not with the attack of Ahrīman against Ahūrā Mazdā, but with that of Mihr against Kheshm.[2370] Here, in fact, the *Jāmāsp Nāmak* replicates the narrative found in the *Mihr Yasht*. As a mediator god, or Arbiter, the cosmological role of Mihr is quite significant in the *Mihr Yasht*,[2371] where he bestows legitimate kingship and an army to the king against his enemy: "On whom shall I bestow *against his expectation* [as is the case with Bahrām-i Chūbīn in the positive Mithraic depiction of him] an excellent ... powerful kingdom, beautifully strong *thanks to a numerous army*. Once he rules he appeases through Mithra, by honouring the treaty."[2372]

The Mithraic, messianic dimension of Bahrām-i Chūbīn's second narrative is nowhere better exemplified than in the very name of the hero as it appears in other apocalyptic literature. For while the *Jāmāsp Nāmak* does not mention the name of our hero, the *Zand i Vahuman Yasn* and *Bundahishn* identify him both by his appropriate title Kai Bahrām.[2373] As Czegledy remarks it "is in this name that the motifs of Bahrām's history and the ancient apocalyptic elements are perfectly fused."[2374] What is significant for our purposes is that the name "Wahrām, Vərəṭragna, in the ancient apocalyptic nomenclature, is the customary and well-known expression of the hope that the eschatological victory will be achieved for Ērān by the *Genius of Victory* himself, Wahrām."[2375] In Zoroastrianism, especially in its Mithraic articulations, *Verethragnā* (Wahrām, Bahrām, Pīruz) is the quintessential apotheosis of the god of victory. In the *Mihr Yasht*, specifically, it is *Verethragna* (Bahrām) who flies in front of Mithra.[2376] Most of the divinities that help Kai Bahrām, the Padhashkhwārgar Shāh in the *Jāmāsp Nāmak*, namely, the Divine Fortune (*farr*) of the Kayānids and of the Mazdean religion, Sorūsh, Rashnu, and the gods Ābān, Ādharān and Ātashān, furthermore, are precisely those that accompany Mithra in the *Mihr Yasht*.[2377] Even in the *Bundahishn*, where the positive depiction of Kai Bahrām

[2370]Jamasp 1941, pp. 119–120. For a synopsis of the specific characteristics of the literature of the apocalypse as a genre, see Collins, John, 'Genre, Ideology and Social Movements in Jewish Apocalypticism', in John J. Collins and James H. Charlesworth (eds.), *Mysteries and Revelations: Apocalyptic Studies since the Uppsala Colloquium*, pp. 11–33, Sheffield Academic Press, 1991 (Collins 1991). The legitimist aspect of the genre of apocalypse is particularly pertinent to the present study, of course. As Collins explains, "the genre of apocalypse can be said to have a function, for example, to legitimate the transcendent authorization of the message." Ibid., p. 19. For another important example of the Persian apocalyptic tradition, see Hulgårt, Anders, 'Bahman Yahsht: A Persian Apocalypse', in John J. Collins and James H. Charlesworth (eds.), *Mysteries and Revelations: Apocalyptic Studies since the Uppsala Colloquium*, pp. 114–134, Sheffield Academic Press, 1991 (Hulgårt 1991).

[2371]As Gershevitch maintains, Mithra "came eventually to be thought of as *divine judge par excellence*." Mihr Yasht 1959, pp. 34–35, 53. Belardi 1979, pp. 697–698. Emphasis mine.

[2372]Mihr Yasht 1959, p. 127. Mihr Yasht 1883, §109. Emphasis mine.

[2373]Czegledy 1958, p. 39.

[2374]Czegledy 1958, p. 39.

[2375]Czegledy 1958, p. 39.

[2376]See footnote 2257.

[2377]Among Mihr's companions are listed the Mazdayasnian Religion, Sraoša (Sorūsh), Rašnu

is incorporated, upon closer scrutiny, the ambivalent position of Kai Bahrām toward the Mazdean religion is traceable.[2378]

Czegledy argues that two factors marred the "joy after the great victory [?] of eschatological proportions." One was the actual military defeat of Bahrām-i Chūbīn and the other is the evidence that is provided in Simocatta's writing. For according to the latter, after Khusrow II's flight to the Byzantines, Bahrām-i Chūbīn "*got angry with the clergy* (the *mōbads*), who thought differently."[2379] Czegledy never makes it clear, however, why Bahrām-i Chūbīn should have gotten angry with the clergy. We have said enough thus far to explicate Bahrām-i Chūbīn's presumed anger against them: the Mihrāns rejected the *mōbadic* arm of the *étatiste* endeavors of the Sasanians, because, in addition to their other issues with the Pārsīg, they had a different doctrinal interpretation of faith. It is only in the context of the Mithraic provenance of Bahrām-i Chūbīn's rebellion, therefore, that we can understand why his followers "*continued to expect his return [even] after his final disappearance ... and ... death* ... It was at this time, that Bahrām-i Chūbīn ... *became a messianic figure*, not unlike Ushētar, Ushētar-māh or Sōshyant."[2380]

(Rashnu), the Kavyan Fortune (farr), the Fire Fortune (Īzad-i Ādhar), and the most important of all, Apaṃ Napāt, the grandson of the waters (Ābān). Mihr Yasht 1959, p. 59.

[2378]In the *Bundahishn*, the *farr* of Kai Bahrām came from the seed of the gods (*bidū farra az dūdih-i baghān ast*). Bundahishn 1990, p. 142. Is this a reference to the fact that it is Mihr who bestows Kingly Glory? But then, when Kai Bahrām assumed kingship, he established the religion of Zoroaster (*dīn-i zardusht rā barpā dārad*). It is to be noted that in the primary text of the *Bundahishn* based on which Bahar has edited his text, the phrase *dīn-i zardusht rā barpā dārad* is broken precisely where the word *barpā* comes in. In other words *barpā* comes at the beginning of the next folio. The point is that, if not an editorial change, the word *barpā* can easily have been inserted as a result of a scribal error, or intentionally, instead of *bar*. In this latter case the phrase would read *dīn-i zardusht rā bar dārad* (destroyed Zoroaster's creed). With a slight change, therefore, the meaning of the text would change drastically. Here Kai Bahrām, true to his Mithraic beliefs, and in opposition to the religion established by the *mōbads*, came to destroy the religion of Zoroaster, in which case the rest of the passage would make sense. Thereafter, "none could be found [that adhered to] any [other] creed (*kas bih hīch giravishī peydā natavan kard*)." Then, however, Pashūtan came from Kang Dizh, together with 150 pious (*parhīzgār*) men and destroyed the temple (*butkadih*) that was "the abode of their *secrets* and established the fire of Bahrām in its place." And he rectified the religion and re-established it. If no emendation were to be made, however, the passage as it stands would make little sense: If Kai Bahrām had already established the religion of Zoroaster so that "none can be found [that adhere to] any [other] creed," then why was it necessary for Pashūtan to come once again? Moreover, what temple did Pashūtan destroy which was the abode of their secrets, and why was he obliged to establish in its place the fire of Bahrām, once again?

[2379]Czegledy 1958, p. 39. Emphasis added

[2380]Czegledy 1958, p. 39. There is no doubt that Bahrām-i Chūbīn considered himself the Sōshyant or messiah. The "Soashyant is thought of as being accompanied, like kings and heroes, by Khvarenah [Divine Grace], and it is in *Yasht* 19 [*Zamyād Yasht*] that the extant Avesta has most to tell of him. Khvarenah, ... will accompany the victorious Soashyant ... so that he may restore existence ... he will drive the Drug [Falsehood] out from the world of Asha [Righteousness]." The *farr* (Khvarenah), therefore, is here bestowed upon Bahrām-i Chūbīn by the *yazata* to whose safekeeping it has been given in the absence of a ruler fit to rule, namely the *yazata* Mihr. Zamyad Yasht 1883, §§89, 92, 93; Boyce 1979, p. 42, also pp. 74–75.

The motif of revenge

There is one final element of the millennial dimension of Bahrām-i Chūbīn's rebellion that is significant for our purposes: the motif of revenge. Recall that in the midst of his rebellion, when the Ispahbudhān brothers had first blinded Hormozd IV and then had him killed,[2381] Bahrām-i Chūbīn justified the continuation of his revolt on the basis of revenge for the murdered king.[2382] This comes from a source, namely Dīnawarī, who clearly had access to the positive, popular renditions of Bahrām-i Chūbīn's rebellion as articulated in the epic romance *Bahrām-i Chūbīn Nāma*.[2383] The motif of revenge in Bahrām-i Chūbīn's narrative connects it to the legends of Manūchihr and Afrāsīyāb. In order to explicate this, we might begin with Tord Olsson's analysis of the genre of apocalypse. According to Olsson, a key criterion of *apocalypticism* is its phenomenological parallel in other cultures.[2384] An apocalyptic movement entails "a certain method of interpreting reality *with reference to a cultural heritage* ... [Thus,] the revitalization of mythic material and its *reinterpretation* with *reference to the contemporaneous situation* is a recurrent feature in these movements."[2385] On a more universal level, Olsson argues, apocalyptic activity bespeaks of the belief "in the possibility of the communication between man and the supramundane world, i.e., that *divine secrets or plans relative to the mundane world in the present, past or future, can be revealed to human recipients* ... [Moreover,] these revelatory worldviews are *regularly actualized in situations of conflict or crisis, real or imagined*, or in the *context of the fear of such situations*, ... [when] the social organization, including access to central power, has been affected by a decrease in intra-system communication so that *the cultural integrity of a certain group is jeopardized*."[2386] The apocalyptic activity within such a group then forces the group to "codify or restore their cultural identities or traditional value systems *in opposition to rival communities or groups through revelatory systems of ideas*."[2387] In the Iranian apocalyptic literature, including the *Jāmāsp Nāmak*, the "*legendary motifs* are thus actualized, and reinterpreted, *often in political terms* with reference to the contemporaneous situation or confused with the accounts of recent conflicts with the Arabs and other peoples ... the apocalypses and legends thus deal with the fundamentals of Iranian civilization, culture and religion."[2388] Olsson observes subsequently that in the

[2381] See page 127.

[2382] Dīnawarī 1967, p. 97.

[2383] Christensen, Arthur, *Les gestes des rois dans les traditions de l'Iran antique*, Paris, 1936 (Christensen 1936), p. 59; Shahbazi 2007a.

[2384] Olsson, Tord, 'The Apocalyptic Activity: The Case of *Jāmāsp Nāmag*', in David Hellholm and J.C.B. Mohr (eds.), *Apocalypticism in the Mediterranean World and the Near East*, pp. 21–59, Tübingen, 1983 (Olsson 1983), p. 28.

[2385] Olsson 1983, p. 29. Emphasis added.

[2386] Olsson 1983, pp. 30–31. Emphasis added.

[2387] Olsson 1983, p. 31. Emphasis mine.

[2388] Olsson 1983, pp. 31–32. Emphasis mine.

Jāmāsp Nāmak, Bahrām-i Chūbīn's legend incorporates the "traits of the old legend about the conflict between *Manūščihr* and *Frāsyāp [Afrāsīyāb]*."[2389]

In the Iranian national epic, the ferocious feud between the Iranians and the Tūrānians, we recall, began with the reign of the mythic king, Manūchihr, who was the first to have to reckon with a powerful enemy king.[2390] We also recall Manūchihr's connection with Ṭabaristān,[2391] where he was born on Mount Manush in the Alburz, and where he took refuge during his struggle with the Tūrānian Afrāsīyāb.[2392] By far, however, the chief achievement of Manūchihr in the Iranian national tradition was his role as the avenger of the death of the favorite son of Fereydūn, Iraj, who was murdered by his brothers.[2393] In our subsequent discussion of the religious revolts that transpire in the quarters of the east and the north from the mid-eighth century onward, therefore, besides the currents of Mithraism prevalent in these region, and besides all the motifs, similarly Mithraic, that are imbued within the apocalyptic accounts of Bahrām-i Chūbīn's rebellion, we have to keep in mind the relevance of the old legend of Manūchihr and Afrāsīyāb, and especially the crucial theme of revenge therein.

Before we get to these, however, we must briefly discuss an episode of early Islamic history, the cultural and geographical provenance of which fall outside the purview of this study, namely the ʿAbbāsid revolution. It is precisely in order to underline the extraneous characteristic of this revolution to the concerns of this study, that we must do this.[2394]

6.2 The ʿAbbāsid revolution

In 129 AH/746–747 CE, an obscure figure, carrying the enigmatic name of *father of the Muslims*, Abū Muslim al-Khurāsānī (or al-Marwazī or al-Iṣfahānī), is said to have received instructions from an Imām, Ibrāhīm b. Muḥammad, to launch a call (*daʿwā*) on behalf of an acceptable member of the family of the Prophet (*al-riḍa min al-i Muḥammad*) in the far-eastern corners of the former Sasanian domains and on the edges of the land of the Pahlav.[2395] Donning black garments and raising a black standard in the village of Sefīdanj in Marv, Abū Muslim instructed his followers to do the same and, lighting a fire, signaled the inauguration of a revolution, not just any revolution, but, as the motto of the rebellion indicated, an Islamic revolution. About twelve centuries later, in the

2389 Olsson 1983, p. 39.

2390 As Yarshater notes, there seems to be a certain primacy about Manūchihr. Yarshater 1983b, p. 435.

2391 See page 375ff.

2392 Ibn Balkhī 1995, p. 119.

2393 Yarshater 1983b, p. 434.

2394 A full analysis of the relevance of ʿAbbāsid revolution to the issues discussed in this study must be postponed to the author's forthcoming work. Here we shall only provide a short synopsis.

2395 Crone, Patricia, 'On the Meaning of the ʿAbbāsid Call to al-Riḍā', in C.E. Bosworth (ed.), *The Islamic World from Classical to Modern Times*, pp. 95–111, Princeton, 1989 (Crone 1989). For a synopsis of Abū Muslim's story by Ibn Isfandīyār, see footnote 1812.

heat of the nineteenth century racialist theories smothering the west, and with romanticized obsessions about revolutions percolating in the minds of European orientalists,[2396] gazes were turned to this fascinating episode of the history of the Orient, the ʿAbbāsid revolution. A long history of erudite scholarship was then precipitated, addressing an equally long list of crucial questions, some of which remain unsettled to this day: who was this obscure figure who galvanized the East into launching a revolution? Whence his ethnic origins? Was he an Arab or an Iranian moving the oppressed Iranian *mawālī*[2397] against the yoke of their oppressors? Was this an Arab, Iranian, ʿAbbāsid or Shīʿite revolution? Above all, however, one question was raised: why did the revolution take place in the far eastern corners of Iran, in Khurāsān, of all places? And so, in spite of solitary voices later raised in objection,[2398] the gaze of scholarship was fixated on this northeastern corner of Iran, the frontier region of Khurāsān, where the enigmatic Abū Muslim had launched a revolt almost a millennium and a half earlier.

An overview of the state of the field of this research is in fact quite pertinent to our concerns, and should have ideally appeared here.[2399] But the evidence that we would have to bring in order to fill what we perceive to be one of the most crucial lacunae in the field, is too multifaceted, and so considerations of space preclude their inclusion here.[2400] In order to contextualize our perspective on the ʿAbbāsid revolution in reference to the thesis presented in this study, however, a few words need to be said.

Partly as result of its scholarly heritage, contemporary scholarship on the ʿAbbāsid revolution continues to remain contentious. Precisely because of this, while numerous monographs have attempted to elucidate the socioeconomic, religious, and political dimensions of the revolution, one of the most crucial issues concerning this presumed watershed of early Islamic history has been neglected, namely an investigation into the natural environment in which it unfolded. Except for brief and often artificial asides that have sought to explain the suitability of Khurāsān as a frontier society for Arab mass migration—the latter being a *conditio sine qua non* for the revolution—no systematic study of the relationship between the natural environment of the region and its social

[2396]Scholars such as Van Vloten and Wellhausen, to whom, needless to say, we owe a serious debt for the corpus of scholarship they produced on this and a host of other aspects of the history of the region.

[2397]Crone, Patricia, 'Mawlā', in P. Bearman, Th. Bianquis, C.E. Bosworth, E. van Donzel, and W.P. Heinrichs (eds.), *Encyclopaedia of Islam*, pp. 874–882, Leiden, 2007 (Crone 2007).

[2398]Lassner, Jacob, *The Shaping of ʿAbbāsid Rule*, Princeton University Press, Princeton, 1980 (Lassner 1980).

[2399]The literature on the topic is vast. For an in-depth analysis of the state of the field until a decade ago, see Humphreys 1991, p. 104; Pourshariati 1995. For an update, see Daniel, Elton, 'Arabs, Persians, and the Advent of the Abbasids Reconsidered', *Journal of the American Oriental Society* 117, (1997), pp. 542–548 (Daniel 1997), p. 542.

[2400]These will be hopefully brought together in a sequel to the present work in the near future. For the time being, the reader is referred to Pourshariati 1995, Ch. II and III, as well as Pourshariati 1998, pp. 41–81.

environment has ever been attempted. Examining the scholarship on the topic, one might very well presume that the ʿAbbāsid *daʿwā* exploded on a blank terrain and the ʿAbbāsid *duʿāt* acted on an expansive but *empty* stage. Khurāsān as a geographical entity remains a more or less abstract territorial domain in this scholarship. This abstract conceptualization of the land as a frontier society has also precluded any systematic investigation into the diverse socioeconomic infrastructure of the various parts of this extensive territory and the suitability of each of these to an influx of a substantial population. The notion of a mass migration of the Arab population into the region, embedded within which is the question of the numbers of these Arab migrants, has likewise either been accepted *a priori*, based on nineteenth century research, or has simply been taken for granted.[2401] The question of the pattern of Arab settlement in the region, a question that has hitherto formed the premise of all subsequent studies of the ʿAbbāsid revolution, and a viable indicator for potentially re-assessing the popularity of the revolution, has likewise attracted very little attention.[2402] Above all, with one notable exception,[2403] no systematic study of one of the most crucial issues of early Islamic history in general, and the ʿAbbāsid revolution in particular, namely the issue of *conversion*, has ever been undertaken in the field.[2404] Whether one agrees with Bulliet's thesis or his methodology, his conclusions on conversion remain the only plausible working hypothesis to date and as such must be reckoned with: not until the period between the 790s and the 860s did a substantial population of Iranians convert.[2405] All the outstanding questions related above are closely interconnected and require a brief reconsideration of the topographical and geographical characteristics of

[2401]The question of the numerical strength of this foreign population is of course crucial to any investigation of the topic. In the past decade two dissertations, by Agha and by the author, independently came to the conclusion that the Wellhausanian assessment of the numerical strength of this migration into the region has been exaggerated. Having argued this, the two authors, however, reached different conclusions about the nature of the ʿAbbāsid revolution. See Agha, Saleh Said, *The Agents and Forces that Toppled the Umayyad Caliphate*, Ph.D. thesis, University of Toronto, 1993 (Agha 1993), subsequently published as Agha, Saleh Said, *The Revolution which Toppled the Umayyads: Neither Arab nor ʿAbbāsid*, Leiden, 2003 (Agha 2003); and Pourshariati 1995.

[2402]See Pourshariati 1998, pp. 41–81.

[2403]Bulliet 1979.

[2404]The title of Dennett, Daniel C., *Conversion and the Poll Tax in Early Islam*, Harvard University Press, 1950 (Dennett 1950), is a misnomer, for in this book, an examination of the issue of conversion is not undertaken but simply asserted as a matter of fact. This is also the case with the latest work on the topic, Agha 2003. For an overview of the state of the field on the issue of conversion, see Humphreys 1991, pp. 273–283, where he maintains that in spite of the fact that "conversion to Islam was … a massive process … *it remains one of the most poorly examined fields in Islamic studies.*" Ibid., p. 274. Emphasis mine.

[2405]Bulliet 1979. A caveat to Bulliet's methodology must be mentioned, nonetheless: while conversion entailed a rural–urban migration according to Bulliet, and hence also affected the rural population, his evidence has, per force, been culled from urban literary products and therefore explicates more the urban transformations than the rural conditions. For the majority of the agrarian population of Iran, therefore, we have yet to devise a methodology that addresses the issue of their conversion. See also footnote 2432.

Khurāsān as a frontier region, relegating a more in-depth study of the topic to the future.

6.2.1 Inner–Outer Khurāsān

The Khurāsān that we readily define as a frontier region suitable for mass migration of the Arabs in the wake of the conquests was a vast region. Not all of the varied regions subsumed within this extensive territory had the potential to absorb a serious influx of a foreign population. The relationship between the natural environment of a region to its human population, furthermore, is one of the basic criteria that affect, over time, its evolving social relations. A detailed investigation of the geographical and topographical characteristics of the extensive Khurāsānid territory, therefore, ought to form the very first direction of our research, lest, as Morony puts it, we commit blunders in our subsequent assessment of the history of the region.[2406]

Once such an investigation is undertaken, it becomes apparent that one of the most fruitful ways of conceptualizing the geographical, topographical, and hence social-structural characteristics of Khurāsān in the late antique period, is to follow its natural demarcations and conceive of the land as two distinct territories: Inner and Outer Khurāsān.[2407] An extensive series of impassible mountains, the Greater and Lesser Bālkhān, Kürendagh, Kopet Dāgh, and Bīnālūd, running in a diagonal axis from northwest to southeast, divide Greater Khurāsān naturally into two regions: Inner Khurāsān to the west of this barrier, and Outer Khurāsān to its east. The extensive Khwārazm desert, lying immediately to the north and east of these mountains, provides yet another major divide between these region. As nineteen century travelers have reiterated again and again,[2408] the paucity of passes and corridors through this barrier effectively hampers communication between the two regions. When we habitually promote the conception of Khurāsān as a frontier society, and when we readily argue that by virtue of this, the region was ideal for the purposes of Arab migration and settlement, it behooves us to specify to which part of this extensive region we are referring: the truly frontier cities of Marv, Sarakhs, Nisā, and Abīvard in Outer Khurāsān, or do we have Nīshāpūr, Ṭūs, Qūmis, Bākharz, and Khwāf in Inner Khurāsān in mind? As mentioned, a detailed investigation of this crucial and contextual dimension of the ʿAbbāsid revolution and the natural environment in which it unfurled will be undertaken in a later study.

For now it should be noted that the proposal for viewing Khurāsān in the post-conquest century as having an inward and an outward orientation is not meant as a pedantic exercise in providing alternative terminologies. This

[2406]"Historical events must be understood in their proper physical setting lest one commits blunders in understanding the course of those events." Morony 1984, p. 589.

[2407]I owe this terminology to my former advisor, Richard Bulliet.

[2408]See, among others, Curzon, George N., *Persia and the Persian Question*, London, 1892 (Curzon 1892), pp. 142–143.

geographical delimitation offers a more accurate way of investigating the sociopolitical and cultural inclinations and developments of the two regions during the post-conquest period. The socioeconomic and political forces operating in Outer Khurāsān as well as Central Asia were quite distinct from those affecting the Iranian plateau. As we will be arguing elsewhere, the socioeconomic forces, structures and conditions, and the ideological dynamics that precipitated and sustained the ʿAbbāsid revolution were alien to the Iranian plateau, including the Inner Khurāsān regions.[2409] A close reassessment of the conclusions reached by scholarship based on this new geographical conceptualization of Khurāsān underlines a crucial fact: the geographical spread of the ʿAbbāsid revolution was not in the vast expanse of the Khurāsānid territory, as has been thus far cavalierly maintained, but specifically in *Outer Khurāsān and Transoxiana.* It is perhaps no exaggeration to maintain that the frontier cities of Nisā, Abīvard, Sarakhs, and Marv set aside, the ʿAbbāsid revolution was more of a Central Asian phenomenon than a strictly speaking Khurāsānid one, precisely because the popular base of the revolution followed the pattern of Arab settlement within these regions. The natural environment and the socioeconomic infrastructure operative in Central Asia during the late antique period, can be more readily compared to the western regions of Iran and Mesopotamia than to the Pahlav lands investigated in this study, as Richard Frye already pointed out. While he aptly makes a distinction between what he terms western and eastern Iranian lands, however, he continues to conceptualize a Khurāsān that was undifferentiated in its geographical and topographical environment.[2410] What is missing in Frye's appropriate distinction between eastern and western Iran, is a further fine-tuning of his conceptualization of the eastern Iranian lands: All of Khurāsān, together with Central Asia, is included in his definition of the east. A distinction, however, ought to be made. For the series of mountains that divide Khurāsān into Inner Khurāsān and Outer Khurāsān, also make a division in the infrastructural, social, and economic forces within these regions. As Frye himself underlines, the infrastructure of Central Asia, like western Iran, was marked by a relatively much higher degree of urbanization than the quarters of the east and the north. "It should be noted," Frye remarks, "that whereas in Sasanian Iran the landed aristocracy, the priests, scribes and common folk comprised the four traditional classes or casts, in Transoxiana *the society seems*

[2409]See Pourshariati 1998, pp. 43–44.

[2410]Frye is also the first to point out that the local histories of Iran provide evidence of the Arab–Iranian relationship at the time of the Arab conquest of their territories: "I have reported on one of these ... and have heard of others." These documents, he further maintains, give us evidence that "the Arab conquests loomed very large in the minds of the the people, *at least in later times when the histories were written.*" He even acknowledges that "most *small towns and villages* in Iran and Central Asia were relatively untouched by Islam in the Umayyad period, and their populations were *converted only several centuries or more after the Arab conquests.*" Frye 1975a, p. 94. Emphasis added. The author subsequently published her Pourshariati 1998, and had she undertaken a rereading of the relevant parts of Frye, she would have acknowledged that Frye had already pointed the way.

to have been divided between the landed aristocracy ... the merchants ... and the ordinary folk."[2411] While these social divisions might have been more an idealized depiction, they nevertheless do underline a significant distinction between the Pahlav domains on the one hand, and the Central Asian and Outer Khurāsānid society on the other. Frye's remarks are germane to any investigation of the numerical strength, pattern, and consequence of the Arab settlement in the east, and, therefore, ought to direct the focus of our gaze in deciphering the milieu of the ʿAbbāsid revolution. For as he underlines, a crucial dimension of the economic infrastructure of Central Asia was "the *more important position of the merchant in Central Asia ... as compared with Iran* correspond[ing] to the more significant role which he played in the society of small Central Asian states, *a society which was based on trade.*"[2412] Compared to the predominantly agricultural[2413] economic infrastructure normative for the Pahlav territories, we seriously question whether a similar *agnatic* social structure and the multifarious checks and balances ensuring its cohesion, operated in the urban centers of Outer Khurāsān and Central Asia.

The comparatively much more diverse linguistic and religious landscape operative in the Outer Khurāsānid and Central Asian societies needs to be taken into account as well. As Frye warns us, for example, when examining the linguistic landscape of this part of the east, "one must be careful in interpreting the word Persian in the sources, because it could be used for Sogdian, Khwarzamian, or another Iranian language."[2414] Likewise, the religious landscape of Transoxiana was, comparatively, much more diverse. Buddhism, Manicheism, Nestorian Christianity and local Zoroastrianism, not to mention small colonies of Jews and Hindus, were all part of the picture in Central Asia.[2415] As far as the Iranian religions of Central Asia and Outer Khurāsān are concerned, furthermore, we do not know to what extent a conservative agnatic social structure sustained the religious life of these communities.

As we have argued in a previous study,[2416] on some fundamental level, the conditions that precipitated the eruption of the ʿAbbāsid revolution—whatever the nature of this latter—had very little to do with the regions under investigation in the present study, the land of the Pahlav, the former quarters of the north and the east of the Sasanian domain, of which Inner Khurāsān was an

2411 Frye 1975a, p. 94. Emphasis added.

2412 "The enormous number of wall paintings in Panjikant ... indicates that no town based solely on the surrounding agriculture could have afforded such expensive decorations in so many houses, or would have been interested in such luxuries." Frye 1975a, p. 99. Emphasis added.

2413 We do acknowledge, needless to say, that even the trade economy of Central Asia was ultimately agriculturally sustained.

2414 In contrast, he maintains, when "it is recorded ... that Arabs or non-Arab Muslims spoke Persian, one should accept this as it stands. For Persian or Dari, the Persian spoken at the Sasanian court by the bureaucracy, undoubtedly continued to be a *lingua franca* in the eastern part of the Iranian world, and with the Arab conquest *in Central Asia*, this tongue, Dari, became even more widespread in the east at the expense of local tongues such as Sogdian." Frye 1975a, p. 99.

2415 Frye 1975a, p. 100.

2416 Pourshariati 1998.

integral part. For, except for numerically very small communities of Arabs in these lands, the Arabo-Islamic presence in these regions was practically nonexistent, at least late into the Umayyad period. As Ṭabarī maintained and as the consensus of the scholarship reflects, therefore, not much had changed with the conquest of the regions in the period 640–650 and this remained the case throughout the Umayyad period. The concerns and the platforms of the ʿAbbāsid revolution were alien to the ruling and ruled population of these predominantly Pahlav regions.[2417] Contemporaneous with the ʿAbbāsid revolution, and for close to a century subsequent to it, however, substantial upheavals did in fact take place in the Pahlav regions. There are grounds, therefore, for us to relegate a more detailed investigation of the ʿAbbāsid revolution to a future study. For as we shall presently see, the concerns of the latter had very little to do with the issues that were simmering in the Pahlav lands and the revolutions that were launched there.

6.2.2 Post-conquest Iran and contemporary scholarship

Ever since the nineteenth century, scholarly obsession with the ʿAbbāsid revolution has pre-empted any serious investigation into the socioreligious history of the rest of Iran in the post-conquest period. A number of significant studies in this direction set aside for the moment, the information that one has culled for the post-conquest history of Iran about the social and cultural forces operating in the region has been confined, for the most part, to the political history of various provinces of Iran under the Umayyads. To a large extent this state of research reflects the Arabist predisposition of the field. The nature of the sources at our disposal, however, has also seriously exacerbated the situation. The interruption of the *X^w^adāy-Nāmag* tradition at the end of the Sasanian history, juxtaposed next to the *futūḥ* narratives—all contained within the Islamic historiographical tradition—has created a false dichotomy. This artificial creation of the conquests as a watershed in Iranian history, precipitated by the discontinuity in our sources, has undermined our appreciation of the tremendous degree of social continuity characterizing the post-conquest period of Iran. In its final form, produced three centuries after the events, Islamic historiography was above all a self-conscious attempt at the creation of an Islamic religio-political community. An awareness of the emergence of the ethniconic community of the Arabs, and the centrality of this community in the formation of the Islamic polity, were among the primary stimuli for the rise of this historiography.[2418] This Arabo-Islamic bias of the sources has provided a convenient pretext in

[2417]The case of Gurgān, and the presumed support there for the ʿAbbāsids can also be explained. We intend to deal with this in our forthcoming work.

[2418]While much has been written about the influence of the Judeo-Christian tradition in contradistinction to which the Arabo-Islamic identity was gradually forming, little attention has been paid to the fact that one of the most readily available models of an ethnic community infused with a religious identity was the Iranian model. Among the few scholarly works noting this is Cook and Crone 1977.

modern scholarship for neglecting the socioreligious history of Iran in the immediate post-conquest centuries. All are well aware that on the Iranian plateau alone a number of highly significant revolts erupted simultaneous with, and shortly after, the ʿAbbāsid revolution. Yet, for all the preoccupation with the ʿAbbāsid revolution, and the numerous monographs dealing with this episode of late antique history of Iran, except for a few significant works with which we shall be dealing shortly, modern scholarship has mostly neglected these revolts. The Arabo-Islamist bias of the field in this regard is clear and one need not make apologies for underlining it.[2419]

One of the pioneering attempts at highlighting the artificial and abrupt change of focus in our sources, resulting in a skewed image of the post-conquest history of Iran, was made by Gholam Hossein Sadighi. In his classic account of Iranian religious movements of the second and third Islamic centuries,[2420] Sadighi underlines the partiality of the sources at our disposal. As we have no sources written in Persian in the first three centuries of the Muslim era, we are forced to rely primarily on classical Arabic sources. These sources, however, Sadighi continues, leave many questions pertaining to the Iranian religious scene in the post-conquest period unanswered. The lives of the prophets and leaders of these religious movements remain little known, as do the intellectual, religious, moral, economic, and administrative inclinations and practices of the Iranian population during this period. The "natural antipathy of some of these [classical] authors for the enemies of Islam complicates the task of those" seeking answers.[2421]

This situation is exacerbated by the fact that the Middle Persian (Pahlavi) sources that might have shed more light on the socioreligious history of Iran during the late Sasanian and post-conquest centuries, were composed during the ninth and tenth centuries—that is to say, around the same period in which the Islamic historical corpus was developed[2422]—under the patronage of a by then solidified Mazdean orthodoxy. As Shaked explains, these Middle Persian sources "present a one-sided view of the situation in the Sāsānian and early Islamic period. *They reflect the attitude of an orthodoxy that may have crystallized toward the end of the Sasanian period ... an orthodoxy that must have rejected*

[2419] As the late Mary Boyce has maintained, western scholarship has emphasized the supposed aridity of Zoroastrianism during the seventh century, giving the impression that "this ancient faith had become too mummified by ritual and formality that it needed only the thrust of a conquering sword to crumble into nothingness." Such impressions, Boyce continues, "owe much ... to the misconceptions engendered by the ultimate victory of Islam; and similar analyses of medieval Christianity would undoubtedly have been offered if Saracens and Turks had succeeded in subduing Europe." Boyce 1979, p. 143.

[2420] Sadighi 1938.

[2421] Sadighi 1938, pp. 111–112.

[2422] The fact that the composition of the Middle Persian sources dealing with the history of the Mazdean community, as well as the prolific *Shāhnāma* production, were contemporaneous with the Islamic historical writing, is extremely significant and bespeaks the simultaneous preoccupation of both communities with archaizing efforts toward self-definition.

modes of belief that were unacceptable to it."[2423] Taking issue with the school of thought represented by Sadighi, moreover, Shaked argues that compared to the Middle Persian sources, the value of Islamic sources, composed mainly by authors of "Iranian origin, generally not farther removed from their Zoroastrian ancestry than one to four generations ... [and living amidst] a lively and vigorous Zoroastrian community," have been underrated. It is true, Shaked argues, that these sources betray the Muslim's attitude toward non-Muslims. But precisely because they were not "bound by loyalty to an orthodoxy, they felt free to report views, beliefs, and practices without checking them against the standards of acceptability of a religious establishment."[2424] The variegated information they contain, moreover, is not only "the most important aspect of their contribution to the subject ...," but also a testimony to the diverse religious scene during this period.

Sadighi's work remains to date one of the most elaborate attempts in drawing the contours of the religious history of Iran in the post-conquest centuries. Half a century after his work, however, the void was still felt. Amoretti observes, for example, that "[t]he religious evolution of Iran during the centuries from the Arab conquest to the rise of the Saljuqs was determined by a number of factors which, so far, have not been adequately isolated and analyzed."[2425] Since then, while a number of significant studies have been made,[2426] the issues raised by the revolts that erupted in the wake of the ʿAbbāsid take-over of the caliphate, have not been revisited.[2427] Sadighi highlights the crux of the problem when investigating the Iranian revolts of the second and third century *hijra*. Muslim authors, he argues, provide uneven treatment of the Iranian religio-cultural tradition. As a result, scholars have been led to believe that the Iranians were so troubled at having lost their independence to the Arab conquerers that they no longer had the quietude to occupy themselves with matters of faith.[2428] One can in fact trace a high degree of continuity, Sadighi objects, between the religio-cultural traditions of the Sasanians and those prevalent in Iran during the late Umayyad and early ʿAbbāsid periods. As late as the mid-eighth century—the period under investigation in this chapter—a substantial number of Iranians had yet to abandon their national cult, for traces of Iranian religions and the persistence of their ceremonies and practices can be found everywhere.[2429]

A corollary to these misconceptions about the continuity of Iranian religious traditions is an overestimation of the doctrinal and institutional solidity of Islam and the effect of this on conquered populations. Just as there has been

[2423] Shaked 1994b, p. 43. Emphasis added.
[2424] Shaked 1994b, p. 43.
[2425] Amoretti, B.S., 'Sects and Heresies', in Ehsan Yarshater (ed.), *Cambridge History of Iran: The Seleucid, Parthian, and Sasanian Periods*, vol. 3, p. 481, Cambridge University Press, 1983 (Amoretti 1983).
[2426] To name a few: Bausani 2000; Madelung 1985; Madelung 1988; Madelung 1992; Shaked 1995.
[2427] The few exceptions will be noted as we proceed.
[2428] Sadighi 1938, p. 111.
[2429] Sadighi 1938, p. 111.

a tendency to underestimate the continuity of Iranian religio-cultural traditions in the post-conquest period, so too there has been a corresponding inclination to overestimate the effect of Arab rule and the advent of Islam on the newly conquered territories. One need not adhere to the Wansbroughanian thesis,[2430] or the schools of thought following him, in order to make this claim, although the implications of this thesis for the post-conquest history of Iran and especially the process of conversion are tremendous.[2431] The fallacies of presuming an ideologically cohesive religion appearing as Islam during this period has also been pointed out by Bulliet: "When in the second half of the seventh century CE the Arabs conquered the Persian empire ... they did not bring with them the religion that is described in general books on Islam. They brought with them something far more primitive and undeveloped, a mere germ of later developments ... [T]he society of ... [the] conquered lands was certainly not an Islamic one to begin with ... [The] Muslims in these lands ... at first represented one small element, albeit the ruling element, within a territory that was dominated numerically by adherents of other religions."[2432] Bulliet observes furthermore that "[a]s long as the Muslim population remained a minority or constituted only a bare majority of the entire population of a region, the society of that region as a whole was not an Islamic society, nor the culture of that region an Islamic culture."[2433]

The present work is not a study in change, but an investigation into the continuity of Iranian sociopolitical and religious tradition. It is therefore only indirectly concerned with the issue of conversion. In order to investigate the socioreligious currents that informed the revolts galvanizing Iran from the middle

[2430] Wansbrough, John, *Quranic Studies: Sources and Methods of Scriptural Interpretation*, Oxford University Press, 1977 (Wansbrough 1977).

[2431] As has been observed previously, the conclusions reached by the revisionist school of thought about the Islamic narrative of origin, and by extension its historiographical corpus, are by no means monolithic.

[2432] Bulliet 1979, pp. 1–2. In this context, it has been argued that the many rites and obligations which bound the Zoroastrians to their own priests from cradle to grave, might have found in the "new religion which had yet to create its own hard shell of scholastic dogmatism, and so laid few restraints on independent thought," a respite from the ancestral religion. It might equally be true that "women, too, though in the long run *losers under Islam*, experienced an immediate benefit on conversion through freedom from those laws of purity which pressed so heavily on them in their daily lives." Boyce 1979, p. 149. Yet, as Boyce herself argues, the Iranian masses were little concerned with scholastic matters and "their religious lives, though devout and instructed up to a point, were lived more simply." As far as the actual role and power of women from various strata of the Sasanian society are concerned, furthermore, we know very little of how their lives were led. Moreover, an overriding consideration in any examination of the issue of conversion should be an acute awareness of the ethnic dimension of any variety of Iranian religion. As Boyce underlines, the ancient notion that conversion to a non-Iranian religion, in this case Islam, meant in reality becoming a non-Iranian (*anēr*), a damning indictment, formed a potent hindrance to conversion. Ibid., p. 151. The narrative of the history of three generations of the families of a convert, Dīnār, the issues confronting early converts and the problems they faced in the community from which they apostatized are successfully followed in Bulliet, Richard W., *Islam: The View from the Edge*, Columbia University Press, 1995 (Bulliet 1995), pp. 44–66.

[2433] Bulliet 1979, p. 2.

of the eighth century to the end of the first quarter of the ninth, therefore, we shall start with an observation that is particularly pertinent to our concerns. In his study on Iranian sects and heresies, Amoretti observes that "by concentrating on one area or province, one can attain a more realistic, although possibly still universal vision, which is important for a number of interrelations between the various areas or provinces, and above all take into account whatever each area more or less consciously chose to preserve, in a national sense as one might say today, out of the supranational whole of aims and interests which the caliphate's Islamic ideology expressed in different occasions and forms, within the territorial boundaries of the caliphate."[2434] Amoretti's point of reference was the Iranian plateau as a whole. Our prism in what follows will be the religio-political revolts that transpired from the mid-eighth to the first quarter of the ninth century in the quarters of the north and the east, that is, the regions that remained under Parthian control at least during the first post-conquest century. Having limited our study to these regions, therefore, we shall also confine our conclusions as being pertinent to these same regions.

One can argue that the seminal work of Sadighi has already addressed the topic under investigation. There are two serious shortcomings in Sadighi's work, however, that the present work hopes to address. Firstly, as Widengren perceptively observes, "this meritorious work has not succeeded in *establishing a historical connection between Sasanian and post-Sasanian times* and must be supplemented in this regard."[2435] Viewing the religious revolts that transpired in the quarters of the east and the north up to the middle of the eight century in the context of the history of these regions during the Sasanian period, as discussed amply in the previous chapters, will therefore provide a far clearer picture of precisely how the histories of these regions continued in the post-conquest period. Secondly, while highlighting the heterodox dimension of some of the revolts which he investigated, Sadighi did not properly contextualize the provenance of these revolts, partly because he did not address the Sasanian religious landscape in his work. What then can we add to the picture drawn by Sadighi?

The histories of the quarters of the north and the east connect, in a very direct manner, from the late fifth century to the mid-seventh, when agreements between the Arabs and Farrukhzād, the son of the Prince of the Medes, also known as Zīnabī Abū 'l-Farrukhān[2436] or Bāv,[2437] and his allies Jīl-i Jīlānshāh and the various *spāhbeds*, were effected. The families around whom the accounts of the conquest revolved were not only families having a long heritage in these territories, but also families who continued to the rule in these regions after the conquest: the Parthian Ispahbudhān, Kārins, Mihrāns, and Kanārangīyān, as well as the Sasanian Āl-i Jāmāsp. For almost a century after the conquest, with

[2434] Amoretti 1983, p. 481.

[2435] Widengren 1979, p. 677, n. 7. Emphasis mine.

[2436] See §3.4.6, especially page 264.

[2437] See §4.1.2, especially page 291.

the exception of the Mihrāns, not much had changed in the quarter of the north. In the truncated quarter of the east, what we termed Inner Khurāsān, likewise, very little changed prior to the actual eruption of the ʿAbbāsid revolution.

Contemporary with the ʿAbbāsid revolution and for almost a century afterwards, however, a significant number of popular revolts in Iran and Central Asia shook the nascent ʿAbbāsid regime, forcing it to expend substantial manpower, resources and money to quell these. While these revolts might have shared a number of characteristics, the examination of all under the same rubric is unwarranted. Madelung's contention, moreover, that all of these revolts "*overtly* mixed Persian *and* Islamic religious beliefs and motives,"[2438] under the the generic name of Khurramiya, needs to be reassessed, for this assessment clearly contradicts his assertion that these were anti-Arab and anti-Muslim activities which "reached [their] climax in the great rebellion [of Bābak]".[2439] The Shīʿite heresiographies and other classical Islamic texts that identify the Khurramiya "with the Muslimiya, who considered Abū Muslim as their Imām, prophet or an incarnation of the divine spirit,"[2440] need to be approached with caution and with the understanding that these were in fact later texts that superimposed the conditions of their times onto the presumed origins of these revolts. As Madelung himself observes, the "reports of the Muslim sources about the doctrine and practices of the Khurramiya are mostly summary and biased."[2441] Against Agha's contention, moreover, that "preceding and succeeding Abū Muslim and his followers, the almost uninterrupted string of Iranian rebels, apostates-heretics and heresies [such as Rizām b. Sābiq, Ibn Isḥāq al-Turk, Barāz, and al-Muqannaʿ] came straight from the ranks of Abū Muslim,"[2442] we must note that all but two of these revolts originated in Central Asia. The two exceptions mentioned by Agha are Khidash and Sunbād.[2443] As for Khidash, the one thing that we are certain about is that we are not certain about anything, except that, according to both Ṭabarī and Balādhurī, he began straying away from the Hāshimiya political propaganda espoused by the Abū Muslimites, and according to Balādhurī, he began teaching the doctrines of the Khurramiya.[2444] The sources even suggest that Khidash was preaching some version of Khurramiya doctrine, and it was probably precisely because of this that he was shunned by the ʿAbbāsid Imām.[2445] Accounts of Sunbād's rebellion,

[2438] Madelung, Wilferd, 'Mazdakism and the Khurramiyya', in Ehsan Yarshater (ed.), *Religious Trends in Early Islamic Iran*, Albany, 1998 (Madelung 1998), pp. 1–2.

[2439] Madelung, Wilferd, 'Khurramiyya', in Ehsan Yarshater (ed.), *Encyclopaedia Iranica*, Albany, 2007b (Madelung 2007b).

[2440] Madelung 2007b.

[2441] Madelung 2007b. Madelung notes that this does not apply to the works of the tenth century geographer Maqdisī, which are "based on his personal acquaintance with members of the sect and his reading of some of their books." Maqdisī, however, was also a tenth-century author.

[2442] Agha 2003, p. 215.

[2443] For Sunbād's revolt, see §6.4 below.

[2444] Sharon, M., *Black Banners from the East: the Establishment of the ʿAbbāsid State – Incubation of a Revolt*, Leiden, 1983 (Sharon 1983), p. 167.

[2445] Crone, Patricia, 'Review of Sharon's *Black Banners*', *Bulletin of the School of Oriental and*

on the other hand, follow the thematic motifs of Bahrām-i Chūbīn's rebellion to such an extent, that we will argue that the theme of revenge for Abū Muslim was a later topos incorporated into the narrative of his rebellion. Therefore, generalizations that do not take the regional variations of these revolts into account are unwarranted. Considering this, we shall confine our investigation to two major revolts that transpired in the quarters of the east and north of the former Sasanian domains, namely those of Bihāfarīd Māhfarvardīn in 129–131 AH/747–749 CE,[2446] and of Sunbād, the *ispahbud pīrūz*, in 137 AH/755 CE.[2447]

Our sources, inadequate and biased as they may be, nonetheless portray both revolts as extremely popular uprisings. A simple onomastic glimpse at the name of their leaders underlines their Iranian ethnicon and religion.[2448] Both revolts, moreover, appear to be driven not by an orthodox, elitist Mazdean ideology, but by strong currents of popular Mithraic religiosity. As such, they provide evidence of continuity of the religious currents prevalent in these regions during the Sasanian period. Finally, whether or not they sought to end Arab rule, both revolts had strong political implications for the consolidating ʿAbbāsid regime. We shall begin by addressing the revolt launched by Bihāfarīd Māhfarvardīn, when the ʿAbbāsid proselyte Abū Muslim was in the process of taking over the city of Marv, the *umma 'l-qurā*ʾ of the east, at the edge of the quarter of the east, the territory designated in this study as Outer Khurāsān.

6.3 Bihāfarīd

When the young Abū Muslim declared his call for *al-riḍā min āl-i Muḥammad*, he was well aware of the stiff competition confronting him. Besides the octogenarian Umayyad governor of Khurāsān, Naṣr b. Sayyār, who still maintained *de jure* rule of the province, he also had to reckon with Judayʿ b. ʿAlī al-Kirmānī and al-Ḥārith b. Surayj. The struggle that unfolded among these men on the eve of the ʿAbbāsid revolution, whether sustained by a predominantly Arab or Iranian constituency, originated in the vast regions of Outer Khurāsān and Transoxiana, beyond the Iranian plateau.[2449] With the conquest of Marv[2450] and the flight of Naṣr b. Sayyār to Nīshāpūr, Abū Muslim thought his mission

African Studies 50, (1987), pp. 134–136, review of Sharon 1983 (Crone 1987), p. 136; Madelung, Wilferd, 'Review of Sharon's *Black Banners*', *Journal of Near Eastern Studies* 48, (1989), pp. 70–72, review of Sharon 1983 (Madelung 1989).

[2446] See §6.3.

[2447] See §6.4.

[2448] Given the fact that conversion usually presumes a name change.

[2449] This is an important issue that will be addressed in detail in the author's sequel to this work. For now, the reader is referred to Pourshariati 1995 and Pourshariati 1998. Also see Ibn al-Athīr 1862, pp. 302–305.

[2450] Ṭabarī, *The ʿAbbāsid Revolution: A.D. 743–750/A.H. 126–132*, vol. XXVII of *The History of Ṭabarī*, Albany, 1985, translated and annotated by John Alden Williams (Ṭabarī 1985), p. 81, de Goeje, II, 1929. When al-Ḥārith had conquered Balkh, Jūzjānān and Marv al-Rūd, he informed his companions that his next destination was Marv since "Marv is the main part of Khurāsān, having the largest [number of] cavalrymen." Ibn al-Athīr 1862, p. 183.

accomplished. Little did he know that another adversary, this time with a completely different ideological platform, was incubating a revolt in an unexpected corner of the vast Khurāsānī territory: the region of Nīshāpūr. Of this he was informed by a curious assembly: the Zoroastrian high clergy of Nīshāpūr. The new rebel carried the symbolically significant name Bihāfarīd Māhfarvardīn,[2451] not one of the typically Arab names which the ʿAbbāsid leader had encountered among the supporters of his previous adversaries. His domain was the region of Nīshāpūr, in Inner Khurāsān, unfamiliar to Abū Muslim and his colleagues. His audience, therefore, was not the predominantly Arab, Arabicized Persian, or Iranianized Arab, with which the ʿAbbāsid had been dealing. The man, in other words, was somewhat of an oddity in Abū Muslim's familiar setting. There is very little indication in the sources that there previously existed a relationship between Abū Muslim and Bihāfarīd Māhfarvardīn.[2452] The eruption of his rebellion and the threats inherent in it to both Islam and Mazdeism were relayed to Abū Muslim by Bihāfarīd's staunchest enemies, the *herbads* and the *mōbads*, the Mazdean clergy.

Bīrūnī provides one of the most complete accounts of Bihāfarīd's revolt.[2453] A native, most probably, of Zūzan, in the northern reaches of the Qūhistān region to the south of the extensive region of Nīshāpūr, Bihāfarīd launched his rebellion in Sīrāwand, one of the districts of Nīshāpūr in Khwāf. Of the personal history of the rebel we know very little. According to Bīrūnī, prior to launching his rebellion, Bihāfarīd had spent seven years in China, from where, among other Chinese curiosities, he had brought back a "*green* shirt, which, when folded up, could be held in the grasp of a man's hand, so thin and flexible it was." Upon returning to his native region, Bihāfarīd launched his rebellion. Bīrūnī's account of Bihāfarīd's rebellion clearly draws on popular stories in circulation and therefore provides a unique window on its popular perception. As we shall see, the details of the preparation for his revolt are significant. Bihāfarīd is said to have gone up to a roof one day at night. Upon his descent from the structure, significantly, in the early morning hours, the first man to notice the rebel was a peasant ploughing his field. It was to this peasant that the rebel, donned in the symbolically significant green silk shirt, proclaimed the first item of his doctrine: that he had ascended to the heavens, where he had seen Heaven and Hell, and, inspired by God, who had clothed him in green, he had

[2451] An extensive bibliography of primary sources on Bihāfarīd can be found in Yusofi, Gholam Husayn, 'Behāfarīd', in Ehsan Yarshater (ed.), *Encyclopaedia Iranica*, New York, 2007 (Yusofi 2007), which also provides an excellent synopsis of Bihāfarīd's rebellion. The discussion that follows will only concentrate on those aspects of his revolt which have hitherto gone unnoticed by scholarship. While we have consulted all of the primary and secondary literary sources on the rebel, we shall nonetheless refrain from citing them all. For these, the reader can consult Yusofi 2007; Sadighi 1938; Pourshariati 1995.

[2452] Yusofi 2007.

[2453] Bīrūnī 1984, p. 314. Also see Browne, E.G., *A Literary History of Persia: From the Earliest Times until Ferdowsi*, Bethesda, reprint edn., 1997 (Browne 1997), p. 308; Gardīzī, Abū Saʿīd ʿAbd al-Ḥayy, *Zayn al-Akhbār*, 1968, edited by 'Abd al-Habibi (Gardīzī 1968), p. 120.

descended to earth in order to proclaim his message. The peasant, believing Bihāfarīd, narrated to the people who had gathered around the rebel, how, in fact, he had beheld him descending from the heavens. According to Bīrūnī, Bihāfarīd's doctrines, and his mission as a Prophet, were subsequently believed and led to the conversion of many in the surrounding regions. Our sources, albeit hostile, nevertheless highlight the numerical strength of his supporters. Bihāfarīd, however, "differed from the Magians in most rites," but believed in Zoroaster and claimed for his followers all the institutes of Zoroaster. In the annals of the religious movements in late antique Irān, the Prophet Bihāfarīd Māhfarvardīn established one hitherto unprecedented and crucial innovation: he offered his adherents a new holy book composed, significantly, in Persian. As has been observed, moreover, his message was monotheistic, one of the seven prayers which he instituted being in praise of the one God. It seems clear that Bihāfarīd's doctrines were directed against the orthodox, learned Mazdean creed, for according to Bīrūnī, his followers "strongly oppose[d] the *Zamzamīs amongst the Magians*."[2454]

Although Bihāfarīd can be called a Zoroastrian heretic, in that he seems to have indulged in *Zand* or reinterpretation of the faith, he is also one of the few figures in the history of the faith who radically departed from it. In this sense, he can be compared more readily to Mānī than to Mazdak. Bihāfarīd claimed Prophethood and buttressed this claim with reference to a new holy book that he presented to his followers. He was not there to simply reinterpret the faith, but to substantively change it. His emphasis on worldly concerns, on the other hand, puts him more on a par with Mazdak.

Furthermore, Bihāfarīd appears to have come from a learned background. He must be considered, therefore, a man of knowledge,[2455] at least religious knowledge, for while we know very little of the contents of his holy book, the fact that he produced one indicates a learned background.[2456] Only an extremely restricted group of people in Sasanian society could boast of such skills. Considering all this, it becomes rather evident that, in league with other infamous *zandīks* of the faith, he did not come from the plebeian classes. There are other indicators that point to the potential wealth of our self-proclaimed Prophet. As we have seen, several sources maintain that he traveled to China and Transoxiana, some even claim for trade, and give the duration of his stay in these regions from anywhere between one and seven years. We must remember that China in the regional terminology used at the period referred not to China proper but to the area of the Western Turks.[2457]

[2454]Browne 1997, p. 309. Bīrūnī 1984, pp. 193–194. *Zamzama* or "ritual droning during meals" (Yusofi 2007) was a practice indulged by orthodox Zoroastrians, so much so that Masʿūdī calls the Avestā the *Kitāb al-zamzama*. Sadighi 1938, p. 160.

[2455]Sadighi 1996, p. 152.

[2456]It is of course feasible that he was not necessarily a man of learning himself, but one with access to the services of the learned, a patron of the clerical classes, so to speak. Even so, he must have been personally engaged in the religious discourse current in his society.

[2457]Czegledy 1958, p. 42, n. 85.

In line with Sadighi, we also note that the social dimension of Bihāfarīd's doctrine seems to have been greater than its purely doctrinal aspect.[2458] Some of his most radical departures from the orthodox faith espoused by the established clerics were aimed at ameliorating the lot of the middle classes of the society and undermining that of the nobility and the elite. The most important of these was the ban on close-kin marriage (*khwēdōdah*),[2459] a long-established institution, sanctified hitherto even by the most radical revolutionaries in Sasanian society, the Mazdakites.[2460] Close-kin marriage aimed to ensure the prerogatives of the nobility by keeping wealth, and therefore status, within the higher echelons of Sasanian society. Bihāfarīd's insistence on the interdiction of this institution, therefore, highlights the strong hold that class divisions still had on the community in which he preached and explains why his support base was plebeian and probably mercantile. Regarding marriage customs, he set the uppermost limit of *mahr* (dowry) at 400 *dirhams*. This was still a substantial sum that could only have been afforded by the middle-income sector of his society. Bihāfarīd also introduced some kind of taxation reform, for he propagated the collection of oneseventh of all property and income (*haft yek-i amvāl va kasb-i aʿamāl*) as taxes for the repair of roads and bridges, the construction of caravansaries, care for those with incurable diseases, relief of the poor, and other charitable causes.[2461] His preoccupation with building roads, bridges, and caravansaries, as well as other social aspects of his creed seem to have addressed the concerns of a mercantile, middle class, rather than the lowest or the highest echelons of society. In this, our rebel might have shared similar concerns with the ʿAbbāsid revolutionaries. While the mercantile dimension of his social doctrines is the most blatant, he also seemed, as his charitable and relief efforts indicate, to have been concerned with the lot of the less fortunate, of whom there must have been many during this period.

One of the most interesting religious dimensions of Bihāfarīd's claim to prophethood, however, was his avowed journey into the hereafter during his occultation. It was during this journey that he claimed to have seen Heaven and Hell, and to have received a green cloth from the Divine, before returning to the *gītīg*. The eschatological dimension of Bihāfarīd's doctrine, in fact, is one of the best documented aspects of his faith in our sources and seems to have formed one of the central cores of his dogma.[2462] According to Bīrūnī, he instituted seven prayers for his followers. Four of these were concerned with matters of death and the hereafter: one for death, one for the day of reckoning (*baʿth o ḥisāb*), one for the populations of Heaven and Hell, and one in praise of the

[2458]Sadighi 1938.
[2459]Bīrūnī 1984, pp. 299–300.
[2460]Shaki 1978, pp. 303–305.
[2461]Bīrūnī 1984, p. 315.
[2462]Contra Sadighi 1938, p. 158.

inhabitants of Heaven.[2463] The Prophet's epithet, Māhfarvardīn, also reflects this eschatological concern, for according to Zoroastrian belief it is in the five days of Farvardigān that the souls of the dead return to their abodes. During this period, the relatives of the deceased cleanse their homes and lay out clean spreads on which they put appetizing foods, which they then consume, hoping that the souls of the dead would thereby gain vigor. As eschatology formed one of the basic concerns of the Zoroastrian faith throughout the Sasanian period, Bihāfarīd's doctrine reflected a potent mark of continuity in Iranian expression of spirituality. We should recall at this point, however, that it was the God Mihr who was the quintessential deity for eschatological concerns.[2464]

Among the accounts of Bihāfarīd's journey to the hereafter is Tha'ālibī's *Ghurar*, who adds the following interesting narrative.[2465] In preparation for the proclamation of his Prophethood, Bihāfarīd concocted an elaborate scheme in which he would feign his own death for a period of time, after which he would reappear and claim that he had ascended to the Heavens and had received his prophetic mission from the divine. To this end, in order to sustain himself during his occultation, he prepared imperishable edible provisions which he placed within two pillow-like sacks, hid two garments in a piece of cloth, and then gave orders to construct "a very large dome, from among the best and widest domes … with openings allowed for rain on all sides." After these preparations, he feigned an incurable fatal disease and his subsequent death. Meanwhile, he had asked his wife that, upon his death, she should place him under the dome together with the sacks he had previously prepared. He then willed her to come every week to his shrine and wash her face at the openings in the dome. In this way, our hostile source informs us, the Prophet ensured his provisions, for, lying under the dome, each day, he would consume from the edibles he had prepared and would drink from the seeping rain or from the water with which his wife washed her face, until a year had passed. Sadighi takes issue with Tha'ālibī's narrative, arguing against the logic of this narrative and the fact that Bihāfarīd's presumed instructions for his burial under a covered dome do not tally with Zoroastrian burial customs. But the point is precisely which burial customs, for, as we know, "the officially sanctioned Zoroastrian mode for the disposal of the dead was not scrupulously followed in the Sasanid period."[2466] At any rate the description that Tha'ālibī gives of Bihāfarīd's burial place resembles less a tomb than a shrine, for the construction was to be in the shape of a dome. In fact, the later Bihāfarīdiya expressly argued against the burial practices of the Muslims, for they maintained that the earth was

[2463] As for the remaining three, one had to do with the Unity of God, one with the creation of the skies and earth, and one with the creation of animals and their nourishment.

[2464] See page 353.

[2465] Tha'ālibī 1900, pp. 258–290, Tha'ālibī 1989, pp. 169–170.

[2466] Shaked 1994a, p. 41. He further observes that "[even] the ancient Iranians may well have had several different modes for the disposal of the body, one of which was eventually adopted as the official Zoroastrian practice, while the others continued in use without religious sanction." Ibid., n. 41.

an angel which would be polluted through the burying of a corpse. This last consideration also echoes the Zoroastrian conception of the earth as one of the Amahraspands.[2467] As for the meaning of this narrative, we shall get to it shortly. In any event, when one year had passed, Bihāfarīd awaited that period when the populace would gather to pay their respects at his shrine.[2468] Thaʿālibī's narrative then reaches its climax: in the midst of the commemorations of his death, Bihāfarīd "got up, donned the green shirt and the green cloak, and when people saw him, announced: 'O, people, I am Bihāfarīd, the messenger of God to you'."[2469]

6.3.1 Interlude: *Ardā Wīrāz Nāma*

The most interesting aspect of this narrative, as well as Bihāfarīd's institution of prayers to the dead and to the population of Heaven and Hell is its uncanny resemblance to the narrative of the *Ardā Wīrāz Nāma*, a Zoroastrian work obsessed with the description of the Day of Judgment and Heaven and Hell, painting in colorful detail the rewards and gruesome punishments of its respective occupants.[2470] The *Ardā Wīrāz Nāma* commences with a description of the destructions wrought on Iran after the conquest of Alexander, when kingship, religion, and people succumbed to utter chaos, "doubting the matter of God (*amr-i yazdān*), with many religions and practices."[2471] In order to quell these and achieve certainty about the afterlife for the edification of the disbelievers, the *mōbads* then decided to choose a righteous man and prepare him for a journey to the hereafter. Ardā Wīrāz (or Ardā Virāf) was chosen for the purpose. The *mōbads* then "chose an agreeable place in the *house of mīnū*[2472] measuring 30 *gaz* (*dar khāna-i mīnū jā-ī khūb bih andāza-i sī gām guzīdand*)." There, Ardā Wīrāz washed his body, "donned a new attire, and on a befitting bedstead ... set up a clean and new bed ... He [then] ... prayed ... ate ... and was given wine and *mang*."[2473] While in a semi-dead state, his seven sisters prayed for him for seven days, not leaving his bedside. During this period, the soul

[2467] Spandarmad (Avestan *Spenta Ārmaiti*), Holy Devotion, is the *Amahraspand* presiding over the earth.

[2468] According to Mary Boyce, and based on contemporary practice, the Zoroastrians do not make a sanctuary of a grave. Boyce, Mary, 'Bībī Shahrbānū and the Lady of Pārs', *Bulletin of the School of Oriental and African Studies* 30, (1967), pp. 30–44 (Boyce 1967), p. 30. However, as we have maintained earlier, a uniform burial practice and, by extension, commemoration of the dead cannot be established for the period under consideration. Incidentally, this tradition must have been either incorporated in Bihāfarīd's story at a later date, when the faith of the Prophet was well established and he had gathered enough followers who would undertake a pilgrimage to his shrine. Alternatively, and only if we give any historical credibility to this account, it betrays the status of the historical figure of Bihāfarīd, for only a man of considerable wealth and social standing in the rebel's society could be expected to have his burial site turn into what seems to have been a pilgrimage center.

[2469] Thaʿālibī 1900.

[2470] Compare also with Kirdīr's journey to the hereafter on page 329.

[2471] Arda Wiraz 1999.

[2472] Bahar gives the equivalent of this as the *house of the mīnavī Ātash*, that is, presumably, the fire temple.

[2473] Arda Wiraz 1999, p. 302.

(*ruwān*) of Ardā Wīrāz was taken to the Chinvat Bridge on mount Chagād-i Dāitī (Harā/Alburz). There, Sorūsh, together with Īzad-i Ādhar, awaited him and subsequently guided him on his journey through Heaven, Purgatory, and Hell, and answered all his questions. Upon his return from the realm of the dead after seven days, Ardā Wīrāz's sisters greeted him: "Welcome, O Ardā Wīrāz, our Mazdayasnian Prophet. You have come from the realm of the dead to this abode of the living."[2474]

All the motifs of Ardā Wīrāz's journey into the hereafter—the preparation of a special place for the temporarily deceased to be laid for the duration of his absence, the preparation of nourishment, in Ardā Wīrāz's case before and after his journey, a woman, or women, who keep(s) guard during his absence, the feigning of death, in Ardā Wīrāz's case by taking *mang*, and finally the reappearance of the deceased as a prophet from the hereafter—are also present in the sources narrating Bihāfarīd's presumed occultation and return from the dead. Also significant is the indication that the appearance of Bihāfarīd gives of the turbulent spiritual and social conditions that must have existed during his lifetime, conditions which in their reflection of the spiritual and social anxiety of the age also explain the millennial hope of the appearance of a new Prophet. The uncanny similarity of the two narratives becomes even more interesting, however, when we consider what must be their Mithraic purview.

6.3.2 Mithraic purview of Bihāfarīd's rebellion

In the case of the *Ardā Wīrāz Nāma*, when the soul of Ardā Wīrāz is taken across the *Chinvat Bridge*, it is not only Mihr, but all his associates, including the angels Sorūsh, Rashnu, and Verethragnā Īzad-i Ādhar, that lead the way for Ardā Wīrāz and answer his queries. Here the *Ardā Wīrāz Nāma* itself is perhaps betraying its original Mithraic provenance: Mihr is performing his eschatological function on the individual level where "he presides over the Činvat bridge tribunal, midway between Heaven and Hell, [overseeing] the compulsory passage of the soul of the faithful departed."[2475] Insofar as the eschatological function of Mihr is presumed to date back to remote antiquity,[2476] therefore, we must also date the germs of Ardā Wīrāz's narrative to this same period. Now, while in none of the traditions of Bihāfarīd the name of the divinity that directs Bihāfarīd's entrance into Heaven is provided, his narrative is replete with other symbols of Mihr worship. To begin with, the color of the garment bestowed on Bihāfarīd by the unnamed divinity is the quintessential color of Mithra, green. Invariably, moreover, like the God Mihr, descending from the Harā/Alburz mountain, Bihāfarīd descends either from atop a mountain or a dome. Like Mihr, who appears "*earlier* than the sun, ... [and] travels *in front* of the sun," so, too, Bihāfarīd appears precisely at daybreak. Finally, as with the nourishing

[2474] Arda Wiraz 1999, p. 303.
[2475] Belardi 1979, pp. 697–698.
[2476] See page 353.

function of Mihr, the god of agriculturalists, so, too, in both Bīrūnī's and Majd-i Khwāfī's narrative, Bihāfarīd first appears to a peasant.

While there is no detailed description of Bihāfarīd witnessing the hereafter, moreover, a substantial part of the Prophet's doctrine, not to mention his name, is concerned with the hereafter and death. The eschatological, Mithraic purview of Bihāfarīd's doctrine, therefore, has a lot to recommend itself. Besides its affinities with the *Ardā Wīrāz Nāma* and the eschatological dimensions of his dogma, however, and above and beyond all the other evidence that we have pointed out, there is one other aspect of Bihāfarīd's doctrine which clearly betrays a Mithraic purview: his installment of the Sun as the *qibla*.[2477] The priority of the sun as the paramount symbol of worship in Bihāfarīd's doctrine distinguishes it clearly as a Mithraic creed. For as we have noted, in the Mazdean faith, the sun, while deserving of worship and prayer, was never so central as to be placed, as is the case here, at the top of the pantheon.[2478] So incongruous, in fact, was Bihāfarīd's insistence on sun-worship with what we know to be the monotheistic dimensions of his creed, that it left the late Sadighi perplexed. In view of the monotheistic dimensions of the faith, Sadighi argues, it is not clear why the Prophet attached so much importance to the sun, and neither do we understand the relationship of this astral symbol to God in Bihāfarīd's doctrines.[2479] Sun worship did have a place in the Mazdean faith, being performed three times during the day by the believers. In the case of Bihāfarīd, however, as Sadighi observes, *the only prayers* incumbent upon the believers were those with the Sun as their *qibla*. Bihāfarīd also composed a holy book in Persian for his followers. This does not imply, given the primarily oral tradition in Sasanian Iran, that Bihāfarīd's audience was therefore an educated, that is literate, audience. It does imply, however, as Amoretti observes, that the "Persian language was obviously chosen because, unlike the protagonists of Abū Muslim's revolution, the followers of Bihāfarīd were only local people."[2480]

Predisposed to overestimating the development and spread of Islamic dogma during these early decades, some scholars have observed that aspects of Bihāfarīd's doctrines testify to their synthesis with Islamic injunctions.[2481] Among these they cite his prohibition against close-kin marriage, drinking wine, and

[2477] For the identification of Mithra with the sun, see page 357ff.

[2478] Shaked 1994a, p. 92.

[2479] Sadighi 1938, p. 124.

[2480] Amoretti 1983, p.490. According to Sadighi, it is not clear whether Bihāfarīd's book was written in Pahlavi or Arabic characters. Sadighi 1938, pp. 122–123. The answer to this seems fairly obvious. If, as Sadighi himself admits, the Muslims were oblivious to the proselytizing of the new Prophet as well as to his person, his holy book could not have been written in Arabic characters. After all, to which audience would the book have addressed itself, had it been composed in Arabic characters? In fact, the question of the book's script is a non-issue, for in whichever character, the readership of the book would have been very limited. The language, nonetheless, remained Persian. It might be postulated, nevertheless, that some of the supporters of Bihāfarīd belonged to the more literate sector of society, hence the actual composition of a book for the edification of these.

[2481] Sadighi 1938, p. 127; Daniel, Elton L., *The Political and Social History of Khurasan under Abbasid Rule: 747–820*, Bibliotheca Islamica, 1979 (Daniel 1979), p. 91.

consumption of animals not properly slaughtered. For none of these, however, can we establish with any certainty an Islamic influence. Bihāfarīd's presumed injunction against drinking wine, for example, requires further research. It is not clear whether the ban was against drinking wine or against getting too intoxicated (*sukr*) by it.[2482] If the former was the point of the commandment, then we should observe that to the east of Iran, in a region with which Bihāfarīd had intimate connections,[2483] Shahristānī cites at least two sects among the religions of India, namely the Bihādūniya and the Bāsūya, the adherents of which were prohibited from drinking wine as well. If indeed even modest drinking was prohibited, then Bihāfarīd clearly went against both Mazdean and Mithraic practices. For, in Zoroastrianism, in general, and in Mihr worship, in particular, wine holds a sanctified place.[2484] Drinking wine in moderation is even considered a meritorious act in Zoroastrianism.[2485] In Mihr worship it even holds a central place.[2486] If Bihāfarīd forbade drinking wine, therefore, in this he was dissenting from Mihr worship. As far as the injunction against eating meat is concerned, moreover, we should observe that in the Mazdakite doctrine there was a similar injunction.[2487] The Bāsūya mentioned by Shahristānī, moreover, were also encouraged to desist from lying, to praise fire, and not to eat the flesh of animals not slaughtered for fire. The point is that prohibitions such as eating flesh or drinking wine were prevalent enough in the immediate milieu of Bihāfarīd and need not be explained in Islamic terms. In short, while some of the injunctions of Bihāfarīd might reflect later Islamic dietary practices, to attribute these solely to the latter can be hurried and rash.

As far as the Muslim antagonism toward *khwēdōdah* was concerned, furthermore, we should note that Christian observers had long reprimanded the Zoroastrians for what had seemed to them an abhorrent practice. Never had this affected any anxiety among the Iranians prior to this. There is little reason to suspect, therefore, that Muslim attitude against this practice had inspired Bihāfarīd's ban. For, while, unlike the Christians, the Muslims were in power and their polemics against Iranian practices could have had potentially more force, it is patently clear that Bihāfarīd was oblivious to their concerns. We should not lose sight of the fact that one element of Bihāfarīd's creed would have been the most loathsome to any devout Muslim: his self-proclaimed Prophethood. There could have been no reconciliation between this and Islam, as one of the most basic tenets of the faith—if one follows the Islamic narratives of its own origins—was its belief in the Prophet Muḥammad as the Seal of the Prophets.

[2482] Sadighi 1938, p. 161.

[2483] Among other regions, Bihāfarīd's followers continued to live in Bādghīs.

[2484] Bundahishn 1990, p. 78.

[2485] Widengren 1979, p. 679.

[2486] The evidence for this is substantial; we shall deal with this in a forthcoming project on the connection between Mithraism and the doctrines of the *ʿayyārs*.

[2487] Shaki 1978, p. 305, n. 149, where among others he gives reference to Mīrkhwānd, *Rowḍāt al-Ṣafā*, Tehran, 1960 (Mīrkhwānd 1960), where it is maintained that Mazdak "forbade the people to kill animals and eat their meat and fat."

The observations about Muslim influence on Bihāfarīd's creed also rely on the presumed association of the rebel with the ʿAbbāsids. These stem from a unique tradition in the *Fihrist* of Ibn al-Nadīm, where a connection is established between Abū Muslim and Bihāfarīd.[2488] According to this tradition, when Bihāfarīd's movement had gained momentum, presumably enough to cause anxiety for the movement that was broiling in Outer Khurāsān and Transoxiana, Abū Muslim sent envoys to the self-proclaimed Prophet, inviting him to become a Muslim. This, reportedly, they achieved. Shortly thereafter, as Bihāfarīd had continued to *indulge in prognostication*, however, Abū Muslim turned against the Iranian rebel, and, dispatching ʿAbdallāh b. Saʿīd with an army to Zūzan, had Bihāfarīd captured in Bādghīs and brought to Nīshāpūr. In Nīshāpūr, Abū Muslim ordered the murder of the self-proclaimed Prophet, and had him hung in the *jāmiʿ* mosque, which, incidentally, Abū Muslim himself had only recently constructed when he had made the city his capital. Shortly prior to this, as we shall see, another important ʿAbbāsid general, Ḥumayd b. Qaḥṭabah, had effected another crucial anti-Parthian policy: he had dethroned the Kanārangīyān, undermining their power in Inner Khurāsān after more than half a millennium of rule.[2489] All the evidence, therefore, suggests that Abū Muslim's policies in Iran proper were staunchly anti-Iranian. In view of the ultimate treatment of Bihāfarīd himself at the hands of the Muslims, any ostensible connection between the ʿAbbāsids and the rebel must be considered shortlived at best. Yet, the tradition handed down by Ibn al-Nadīm would have us believe that a man who had only recently launched his own claim to Prophethood, and who had gained a substantial following in the process, suddenly and unexpectedly, had forgone all this only to join the ranks of those who propagated the rule of *al-riḍā min āl-i Muḥammad*. In fact, other traditions put presumed Bihāfarīd's conversion *after his capture* at the hands of the agents of Abū Muslim.

Unlike Abū Muslim and other contenders for power at the time of the ʿAbbāsid revolution, whose sphere of activity was predominantly Outer Khurāsān and Transoxiana, the genesis, progress, and final demise of the rebellion of Bihāfarīd all took place in Inner Khurāsān. There is no indication that Bihāfarīd had any support whatsoever in the regions where Abū Muslim sent his *duʿāt* and found his followers.[2490] As all our sources underline, Bihāfarīd's ultimate goal was the takeover of Nīshāpūr and its dependencies, not that of Marv or the frontier cities of Outer Khurāsān.[2491]

One of the sensitive issues for medieval Islamic authors writing about heterodox revolts was the extent of their popularity. It is a function of the relative objectivity of the Islamic sources, however, as well as the overwhelming

[2488] Ibn al-Nadīm 1987, p. 614.

[2489] See footnote 2562.

[2490] See Pourshariati 1998. Later on, however, some of his followers are mentioned in the vicinity of Marv. Sadighi 1938, p. 165.

[2491] Gardīzī 1968, p. 120; Bīrūnī 1984, pp. 210–211.

popularity of these revolts, that almost all of our sources underline the tremendous support that the movement of Bihāfarīd garnered.[2492] The popularity of the revolt was such in fact, that it led Sadighi to conclude that had the ʿAbbāsid revolution not been led by the energetic Abū Muslim and had Bihāfarīd had more time at his disposal, the post-conquest history of Iran might have taken a different turn from that which ultimately transpired.[2493] But Abū Muslim did suppress Bihāfarīd and murdered him, together with his followers. And, in the final analysis, this rather than any conjectural hypothesis about the presumed affinities between the two movements, must direct our assessment of the nature of their mutual relationship.

Bihāfarīd's movement, however, did not die: in subsequent centuries, it coalesced into a sect. Shahristānī mentions them and observes that the Sīsāniya or Bihāfarīdiya, the followers of Bihāfarīd, had been encouraged by their Prophet to keep their hair hank, and "occupy monasteries [where they] vie[d] with each other in bestowing generously."[2494] According to Shahristānī, they remained "the deadliest enemies of the Zamzamī Majūs."[2495] All of this has led Shaked to argue that whereas all the other varieties of Iranian religions during the Sasanian and early Islamic period "simply did not exist as separate church structures," the sect of the Sīsāniya seems to have been an exception to this rule. They came to have "a full code of religious behavior, as well as a full corpus of doctrine, and something like a separate church, an organization of believers ... [all of which are] the necessary ingredients for the definition of a sect ... [but which] are not frequently encountered in other groups."[2496] In view of our postulate that the Mithraic provenance of the Bihāfarīdiya is valid, it is extremely interesting to note that the one other exception to this rule was yet another Mithraic group, namely the followers of Bābak Khurramdīn, who also seem to have had a rather strict organization.[2497] So abhorrent did the later Bihāfarīdiya and their doctrines remain in Muslim eyes, in fact, that they were singled out as one of the only sects from whom collecting *jizya* was forbidden.

From the paramountcy of sun-worship in Bihāfarīd's doctrine, to its evident eschatological concerns, to the motifs in his narrative that closely follow the functions of Mihr, very little doubt ought to remain about the Mithraic provenance of his movement. In the present state of our knowledge, unfortunately, we cannot ascertain Bihāfarīd's agnatic heritage. As almost all other rebellions

[2492]Ibn al-Nadīm 1987, p. 614; Gardīzī 1968, p. 120; Bīrūnī 1984, p. 210. Other sources give specific numbers. The author of *Ṣuwar al-Aqālīm*, for example, gives the figure 30,000 for the number of adherents. Sadighi 1938, p. 120.

[2493]Sadighi 1938, p. 121.

[2494]As quoted in Shaked 1994b, p. 63. It should be noted that the competition of the Sīsāniya in making charitable donations should caution us against considering the exorbitant demands of the Zoroastrian *mōbads* as a cause for apostasy from the faith.

[2495]As quoted in Shaked 1994b, p. 63.

[2496]Shaked 1994b, pp. 46–47.

[2497]Shaked 1994b, pp. 46–47, who does not, however, recognize the Mithraic purview of either movement.

within the Pahlav domains in the post-conquest period were led by dynastic figures of substantial wealth and power,[2498] and considering the information we have on Bihāfarīd's status, a plebeian background for the self-proclaimed Iranian Prophet is out of the question. Bihāfarīd's rebellion does point to the rise of mercantile interests within the region and a possible antipathy against the interests of the landed gentry. Beyond this, we cannot comment further on the rebel's personal background.

6.4 Sunbād the Sun Worshipper

Less than five years after Abū Muslim al-Marwazī launched the ʿAbbāsid revolution from Outer Khurasan, Transoxiana, and Soghdiana, and effected the transition of the caliphate from the Umayyads to the ʿAbbāsids, the second ʿAbbāsid caliph, Abū Manṣūr al-Dawāniqī (136–158/754–775), had him killed in 755. About two months later a tumultuous popular revolution engulfed the quarters of the north and the east, the domains of the Parthian dynastic families who had remained in power after the Arab conquest of the region, throughout the Umayyad period.[2499] The revolt was led by a figure called Sunbad the Magian,[2500] ostensibly under the banner of revenge for the murder of the ʿAbbāsid leader Abū Muslim. What is striking in the accounts of Sunbād's rebellion, however, is how thoroughly they replicate the *topoi* of the narrative accounts of the rebellion of the Parthian dynast Bahrām-i Chūbīn, a revolt which had transpired in these same regions a century and a half earlier.[2501]

Before we give our evidence for this, it is necessary to give the main themes of the accounts of this enigmatic rebel of the *kūst-i ādurbādagān* and *kūst-i khwarāsān* against the nascent ʿAbbāsid regime. To this end, we shall start with Balʿamī's account, for it contains most of the primary themes of Sunbād's narrative.[2502] Balʿamī informs us that Sunbād was a very wealthy Magian (*ū rā khwāstah-i bisyār būd*) from one of the villages of Nīshāpūr. When the news of the

[2498]For the dynastic background of Sunbād, see §6.4.4; for those of Ustādsīs, Bābak Khurramdīn, and Māzīyār, see the forthcoming work of the author.

[2499]Revisionist historiography on the ʿAbbāsid revolution has in fact been curiously dismissive or simply incongruent in its treatment of the Iranian revolts that erupted subsequent to the ʿAbbāsid revolution. See, for example, Omar, Farouq, *The ʿAbbāsid Caliphate: 132/750-170/786*, Baghdad, 1969 (Omar 1969), pp. 138 and 195; Shaban, M.A., *Islamic History: A New Interpretation*, vol. II, Cambridge University Press, 1971 (Shaban 1971), p. 14. While calling Sunbād's rebellion a minor affair and foregoing a discussion of it, Shaban acknowledges, for example, that the rebellion was potentially dangerous because it threatened to cut off the vital northern route between Khurāsān and the west. As we have argued elsewhere, however, there is every indication that the Khurāsān highway was not functioning during the Umayyad period. Pourshariati 1995, pp. 141–143.

[2500]For Sunbād's rebellion see, among others, Ibn Ṭaqṭaqa, Muḥammad b. ʿAlī b. Ṭabāṭabā, *Taʾrīkh-i Fakhrī*, 1988, translated by Muhammad Vahid Golpaygani (Ibn Ṭaqṭaqa 1988), pp. 232–233. A complete bibliography of sources pertaining to this revolt has been provided by Sadighi 1938, pp. 168–170, and others, including Daniel 1979; Pourshariati 1995. In the present study, only a selection of these will be offered.

[2501]Czegledy had observed this without ever providing an explanation.

[2502]Balʿamī 1959, pp. 1093–1094.

murder of Abū Muslim reached him, Sunbād allegedly became heavy-hearted and subsequently proclaimed that as he was indebted to Abū Muslim, it was only just that he should spend his own wealth in avenging the latter's death. If he were to exhaust his wealth, Sunbād proclaimed, he would be ready to give his life. Remaining true to his promise, Sunbād then distributed his riches and gathered a substantial army and set out, reportedly to avenge Abū Muslim's death. Now, Abū Muslim, according to Balʿamī, had many followers (*shīʿa*) in Khurāsān. So two months after Abū Muslim's murder an army of 60,000 people gathered around the Magian Sunbād and set out from Nīshāpūr toward Iraq. On their way they halted in Rayy, the former Mihrānid capital of the quarter of the north, now under the jurisdiction of the Āl-i Jāmāsp.[2503] Here, one of Sunbād's first acts was to kill Abū ʿUbaydah Ḥanafī, the governor of Rayy from before Manṣūr's time, appointed to the region by the ʿAbbāsid revolutionaries themselves.[2504] In Rayy the number of Sunbād's followers increased substantially, reaching the incredible number of 100,000, likewise eager to avenge the murder of Abū Muslim.[2505] When the shrewd ʿAbbāsid caliph Manṣūr was informed of Sunbād's rebellion, he sent Jawhar b. Marrār al-ʿIjlī to quell the uprising.[2506] In a speech before the battle, Jawhar made the stakes involved quite clear for the mostly Arab forces that had gathered around him: Sunbād's followers were bent on "*exterminat[ing] your religion* and expel[ling] you from your worldly possessions."[2507] Jawhar's forces, we are told, included a comparatively meagre 10,000 men. Somewhere between Hamadān in Media and Rayy, the two forces finally engaged each other, and in spite of the presumed numerical superiority of Sunbād's army, he was defeated by Jawhar. In flight, Sunbād returned back to Rayy *whence he set out for Gurgān*. In Gurgān he was intercepted by the *ispahbud* of the region, rendered by Balʿamī as Hormoz b. al-Farjān (Farrukhān), who forthwith killed Sunbād, presumably *on the order of the ʿAbbāsid caliph, Manṣūr*.[2508]

Balʿamī provides further details: When Sunbād had reached Rayy with his army, he found Abū Muslim's *treasury* there.[2509] Taking over Abū Muslim's treasures, Sunbād now allegedly proclaimed that as he was the one who had

[2503] Nöldeke 1879, pp. 1093–1094. See also §4.5.

[2504] Niẓām al-Mulk 1941, p. 260.

[2505] Niẓām al-Mulk 1941, pp. 260–261.

[2506] Kennedy perceptively points out that Manṣūr sent against the rising rebel "not the Khurasaniya, who might have felt some sympathy for his cause, but the people who had most to lose from his success, i.e., the Arabs of western Iran, led by Jawhar b. Marrar al-ʿIjlī. The ʿIjlīs were the most powerful Arab tribe in the area of Jibal and they followed Jawhar, along with the troops of Fars, Khuzistan and the lightly armed troops of Isfahan and Qum." Kennedy, Hugh, *The Early Abbasid Caliphate*, Totowa, reprint edn., 1981 (Kennedy 1981), p. 64.

[2507] Kennedy 1981, p. 64.

[2508] Nöldeke 1879, p. 419, n. 2365, Nöldeke 1979, pp. 1093–1094. This Farrukhān is probably the cousin of Khurshīd, see page 314. In Ibn Isfandiyār's narrative the name of this cousin is rendered Ṭūs; see §4.5.2.

[2509] Balʿamī 1959, pp. 1093–1094. For Abū Muslim's treasury, see footnote 1812 and page 444ff below.

risen in order to avenge the blood of the revolutionary leader, he was also the most entitled to his wealth. The already wealthy Sunbād, therefore, presumably also usurped Abū Muslim's treasury in Rayy. Sunbād, the alleged avenger of Abū Muslim, then proceeded to disclose one of the most important components of his platform: to end Arab rule over Iran, and implicitly, by extension to restore Iranian hegemony. In the *Siyāsat Nāma*, Niẓām al-Mulk adds further significant information not found in Balʿamī's narrative. Whenever in privacy with the Magians, Sunbād would declare that "the rule of the Arabs had reached its end ... [for he had seen this] prophesied in one of the books of Banī Sāsān." Sunbād's anti-Arab, anti-Muslim stand is underlined in Niẓām al-Mulk's narrative. The rebel declared that he would not cease until he had destroyed the Kaʿba. The Kaʿba, he argued, had been installed as the *qibla* in lieu of the true direction of prayer, namely the Sun. As it had been in former times, Sunbād therefore pledged, he would restore the *sun* as the *qibla*.[2510]

Niẓām al-Mulk's account contains other, perplexing information, however. Shortly after maintaining that Abū Muslim was in fact dead and that he had risen in his revenge, Sunbād is said to have proclaimed to the "people of Iraq and Khurāsān that Abū Muslim was [in fact] *not dead*."[2511] According to Niẓām al-Mulk, Sunbād now argued that when Manṣūr attempted to murder Abū Muslim, the latter murmured the name of God almighty (*nām-i mahīn-i khudā-y-i taʿālā bikhānd*), forthwith turned into a white dove, and flew off to the east. There, in the *Copper Fortress*, Abū Muslim sat in the company of the Mahdī and Mazdak. "The first to appear will be Abū Muslim! Mazdak will be his *vizier*! And I myself, will receive the epistle of Abū Muslim," Sunbād then proclaimed.[2512] This, then, was how Sunbād viewed Abū Muslim and his own relation with the ʿAbbāsid rebel, according to Niẓām al-Mulk's curious narrative.

Niẓām al-Mulk's millennial depiction of Sunbād's rebellion is itself partly a testimony to its posthumous articulation. It contains both the hindsight of the rebel's defeat and his hope for enacting the millennial aspirations of his followers. So total was Sunbād's defeat, in fact, and so many of Sunbād's followers were massacred in the war against Jawhar, that, according to one tradition, until the year 300 AH, their corpses were still extant.[2513] After defeating Sunbād, Jawhar usurped all of Sunbād's wealth as well as Abū Muslim's treasury.[2514] Subsequently, fearing that Manṣūr would seize this wealth, Jawhar

2510 Niẓām al-Mulk 1941, pp. 260–261. Ibn Ṭaqṭaqa 1988, pp. 232–233. For Sunbād's intention of destroying the Kaʿba, also see Ibn al-Athīr 1862, p. 481. Sadighi subsequently concludes that Sunbād "a voulu, comme Bihâfarîd, rétablir l'ancienne coutume [des Iraniennes]." Sadighi 1938, p. 143.

2511 Sadighi 1938, p. 140.

2512 Niẓām al-Mulk 1941, pp. 260–261.

2513 Ibn Isfandīyār 1941, p. 174.

2514 Yaʿqūbi 1969, vol. 2, pp. 441–442; Masʿūdī 1869, vol. 6, pp. 188–189, Masʿūdī 1968, pp. 297–298; Maqdisī, Muṭahhar b. Ṭāhir, *Kitāb al-Badʿ wa ʾl-Taʾrīkh*, Paris, 1919, edited by C. Huart (Maqdisī 1919), vol. 5, p. 82; Niẓām al-Mulk 1941, pp. 260–261.

himself mutinied and rebelled against the ʿAbbāsid caliph.[2515] The motif of treasury, therefore, continues to loom large in Sunbād's narrative.

There is another significant tradition, however, contained in the *Tārīkh-i Ṭabaristān* and other sources about the ultimate fate of Sunbād and that of his treasury, which provides an extremely crucial context for understanding Sunbād's rebellion and the provenance of his narrative.[2516] Ibn Isfandīyār, the author of the *Tārīkh-i Ṭabaristān*, was a native of the region. Having access to local traditions circulating in his homeland around the fate of this regional hero, his account must be deemed more trustworthy than others. According to this author, when the news of Abū Muslim's murder reached Sunbād in Rayy, Sunbād allied himself with the Āl-i Jāmāsp *ispahbud* of Ṭabaristān, Khurshīd, the Sun-King.[2517] According to Ibn Isfandīyār, we recall, before proceeding to war against Jawhar, Sunbād had already sent "all of his *treasury* and beasts of burden in safe-keeping to Khurshīd. Together with these he had sent six million *dirhams* as gifts."[2518] While Sunbād's army was defeated by the forces of Jawhar b. Marrār,[2519] Sunbād himself survived and took refuge with the king of Padhashkhwārgar. Unlike Balʿamī, who calls him the *ispahbud* Farrukhān, Ibn Isfandīyār and most other sources correctly identify this figure as the *ispahbud* Khurshīd, the Āl-i Jāmāsp progeny of Gāvbārih (the cow devotee). We recall, however, that Sunbād was, in fact, killed on his way to Khurshīd by the latter's cousin, Ṭūs.[2520] While Ibn Isfandīyār maintains Ṭūs to be a cousin of Khurshīd, Ibn al-Athīr claims him to have been a governor (*ʿāmil*) on behalf of Khurshīd.[2521] As Sadighi observes the two affiliations were not necessarily mutually exclusive: Ṭūs could have been both a cousin as well as a governor of Khurshīd, since an agnatic structure of power dominated not only the polity of the Parthian dynasts—presumably subservient to the rule of the Āl-i Jāmāsp at this point—but also the Sasanian family of the Āl-i Jāmāsp. While agitated and saddened over Sunbād's murder at the hand of Ṭūs,[2522] according to Ibn Isfandīyār, Khurshīd, nevertheless, conveniently seized the wealth that Sunbād had committed to his safe-keeping, and with one of his representatives, called, significantly, *Pīrūz* (*Verethragnā*, the victorious), he sent the already severed head of Sunbād, together with presents, to the ʿAbbāsid caliph Manṣūr. The latter, not content with what he had received, demanded the treasuries of Abū Muslim usurped by his avenger Sunbād. Once more, therefore, the motif of

2515 Balʿamī, *Tārīkh-nama-i Ṭabarī*, Tehran, 1987, edited by Muhammad Rowshan (Balʿamī 1987), pp. 1093–1094.

2516 Ibn Isfandīyār 1941, pp. 174–175.

2517 Also in Nöldeke 1879; and, without naming Khurshīd, but mentioning Ṭūs, Ibn al-Athīr 1862, vol. 5, pp. 481–482. For Khurshīd, see §4.5.

2518 Ibn Isfandīyār 1941, p. 174.

2519 Ibn Isfandīyār 1941, p. 174.

2520 See §4.5.2.

2521 Ibn al-Athīr 1862, vol. 5, pp. 481–482.

2522 As Sadighi aptly observes, however, Ṭūs as a figure under the authority of Khurshīd, could not have undertaken such an action without the latter's approval. Sadighi 1996, p. 182, n. 3.

treasury appears in the narrative. Khurshīd refused to oblige, and here starts the saga of the destruction of the Āl-i Jāmāsp at the hands of the ʿAbbāsid caliph.[2523] Manṣūr sent Abū ʾl-Khaṣīb ʿUmar b. al-ʿAlāʾ against Khurshīd. It is at this point, we recall,[2524] that, after the final defeat of Khurshīd, the army of Islam settled in the territory for a period of two years and seven months, taking "up residence under the roofs of houses" in the former lands of Khurshīd Shāh.[2525]

6.4.1 Sunbād and Bahrām-i Chūbīn: recurrent narrative motifs

This, then, is the germ of the narrative of the Magian Sunbād Nīshāpūrī: a hero who emerged emerged from the east, with a substantial army and wealth at his disposal. He then came to Ṭabaristān where he entered into an alliance with the Padhashkhwārgar Shāh, the Sun-King, Khurshīd. In the former capital of the Mihrāns, Rayy, however, not only did his army increase, but, even more importantly, he presumably also obtained the treasury of Abū Muslim. Somewhere in the process he claimed to have been an avenger bent on retaliating against the unjust murder of another eastern hero. While his rebellion ultimately ended in defeat, the millennial hope of his cause remained active. For the spirit of his *cause célèbre* had already flown east, to the Copper Fortress.[2526]

This, we realize, is a familiar narrative, one which, once again, superimposes historic events onto a paradigmatic mythic narrative, most likely of popular provenance. It is also thoroughly Mithraic. In what follows, it will be argued that while some aspects of the historicity of the relationship between Sunbād and Abū Muslim are probably valid, the ideological and political platforms of the two rebellions were so distinctly at odds that the primary motif of revenge for the murder of Abū Muslim in Sunbād's narrative, as well as a number of other motifs, are nothing but Mithraic *topoi* borrowed from the rebellion of Bahrām-i Chūbīn, and ultimately from the myth of Manūchihr and Afrāsīyāb. These *topoi* were superimposed onto Sunbād's narrative precisely because, like Bahrām-i Chūbīn, Sunbād's revolt erupted in the quarters of the north and the east, where Mihr worship was the dominant form of religiosity. Once we recognize that the rebellion of Bahrām-i Chūbīn provided the paradigm for the narrative structure of Sunbād's rebellion, some of the details of Sunbād's account, especially the problematic relationship of Sunbād with Abū Muslim, become suspect. They forewarn us about imputing to Sunbād's historic rebellion cultural currents and influences, especially Islamic ones, that were most probably alien to the cultural milieu of Sunbād.

To further identify these motifs, therefore, we shall begin with the regional issue: Sunbād's rebellion engulfed both the quarters of the north and the quarters of the east. One tradition even claims that Sunbād's rebellion actually started in Azarbāyjān and then spread to Rayy and Ṭabaristān. Agapius of

[2523] Ibn Isfandīyār 1941, p. 175. See §4.5.3.
[2524] See page 316.
[2525] Ibn Isfandīyār 1941, p. 175.
[2526] For the Copper Fortress (*Rūyīn Dizh*), see page 406 above.

Manjib maintains that Sunbād, who was one of the commanders of Abū Muslim's army, received the news of the latter's death while in Azarbāyjān, from where he went to Rayy in order to gain the support of the Magians and the Daylamites.[2527] All other sources, however, connect Sunbād's rebellion systematically and intimately to the regions of Nīshāpūr, Rayy, Qūmis, and Gurgān, the same regions, in other words, in which the rebellions of the Parthian dynasts Bahrām-i Chūbīn and Vistāhm had taken place some century and a half prior to this.

The geographical motifs of Sunbād's rebellion, however, go beyond this. Sunbād, like Bahrām-i Chūbīn, emerged from the east. Almost all of our sources maintain that the original homeland of the Magian Sunbād was the region of Nīshāpūr in Inner Khurāsān. Where exactly in the extensive region of Nīshāpūr the rebel came from is not clear. Most sources agree that he was from one of the villages (*qurā*) of Nīshāpūr.[2528] A second geographical motif, however, connects Sunbād's rebellion to even further east. For the putative connection of Sunbād with the unjustly murdered Abū Muslim, a hero who rose in Outer Khurāsān, to the east of Sunbād's native territory, reinforces the eastern provenance of Sunbād's rebellion. Add to this the transmigration of the soul of Abū Muslim to the *Rūyīn Dizh* (Copper Fortress), and we realize that the geographical framework of Sunbād's rebellion replicates that of Bahrām-i Chūbīn. Like Bahrām-i Chūbīn's rebellion, however, the revolt of Sunbād was also intimately connected with Rayy. Almost all of the sources at our disposal highlight the fact that, while a native of Nīshāpūr, it was from Rayy that Sunbād launched his rebellion against the caliph.[2529] In Rayy, furthermore, his army was substantially augmented when the population of the quarters of the north and the east joined his ranks.[2530] It was in Rayy, moreover, that Sunbād, like Bahrām-i Chūbīn, came into the possession of a treasury.

6.4.2 Mithraic purview of Sunbād's rebellion

While obscurity shrouds the relationship of Sunbād with Abū Muslim and his army of the east,[2531] and while the *Rūyīn Dizh* is clearly a legendary motif, however, the actual historical relationship of Sunbād with Ṭabaristān and Rayy is thoroughly historic. It was with the king of Padhashkhwārgar that Sunbād formed a collaboration. To this historic association, however, has been added a legendary myth. As in the Mithraic rendition of Bahrām-i Chūbīn's narrative where the hero acquired a treasury from the God Mihr, so too in Sunbād's narrative, it was in Rayy that the hero obtained a treasury. However, while in

[2527] Agapius of Manjib 1911, p. 538.

[2528] See Balʿamī 1987, p. 1093. Also see Niẓām al-Mulk 1941, pp. 260–261; Ibn Ṭaqṭaqa 1988, pp. 232–233; Yaʿqūbi 1969, vol. 1, p. 442.

[2529] Ibn Isfandīyār 1941, pp. 174–175; Āmulī 1969, pp. 57–59; Khayyāṭ 1977, pp. 416–417; Balʿamī 1987, pp. 1093–1094; Niẓām al-Mulk 1941, pp. 260–261; Ibn Ṭaqṭaqa 1988, pp. 232–233.

[2530] Masʿūdī 1869, vol. 6, pp. 188–189, Masʿūdī 1968, pp. 297–298.

[2531] See below.

the former narrative it was Mihr who bestowed a treasury on the king of Padhashkhwārgar, Kai Bahrām,[2532] in Sunbād's narrative this Mithraic paradigm is inverted and it was Sunbād who gave his treasury in safe-keeping to the king of Padhashkhwārgar, Khurshīd. There remains, however, an amazing historic dimension to this aspect of Sunbād's saga, as well, for the Āl-i Jāmāsp king with whom Sunbād collaborated was in fact called Khurshīd, his very name reflecting the theophoric dimension of his spirituality, for he was the Sun-King. While there is historic certainty about the correspondence of Sunbād with Khurshīd, however, a second motif appearing in Sunbād's narrative is actually quite problematic.

The motif of revenge

This second motif is the purported connection of Sunbād with the figure of Abū Muslim. In this connection the theme of revenge is invariably highlighted in all of our sources. Sunbād supposedly launched his revolt to avenge the death of the leader of the ʿAbbāsid revolution, Abū Muslim. This theme of revenge has also been emphasized by all the secondary literature on the topic. Revenge for the murder of the ʿAbbāsid leader has been considered as one of the primary stimuli for Sunbād's rebellion. One of the explicit conclusions that has followed as a result of this emphasis on vengeance has been the claim that a great many of Sunbād's supporters were remnants of Abū Muslim's army. As most have recognized, however, the connection of Abū Muslim to Sunbād is in fact one of the most problematic aspects of Sunbād's background. Sadighi even expresses despair that the nature of this relationship will perhaps never become clear.[2533] As we have seen, Sadighi underlines the incongruity of Niẓām al-Mulk's narrative. Did Sunbād claim to avenge the murder of Abū Muslim, or did he maintain that the latter was actually alive, and he was only his apostle?[2534] Likewise, while acknowledging that Sunbād was "closely connected with Abu Muslim, whose death was the immediate cause of the outbreak" of his rebellion, Kennedy also expresses despair about Sunbād's postulated association with the ʿAbbāsid revolutionary: As Sunbād "sought to revive the old Persian religion and drive the Arabs out of the country, an aim summed up in his declared intention of sacking the Kaʿba, ... [and as there] is no evidence that Abu Muslim had any intention of ending Arab rule or restoring Zoroastrianism, ... [the most] curious feature of this rebellion ... is the connection of Sunbād with Abū Muslim."[2535]

[2532]See page 411.

[2533]Sadighi 1938.

[2534]Together with other scholars, Sadighi therefore concludes that the "exposition of Niẓām al-Mulk reflects the different doctrines which existed" when Niẓām al-Mulk was writing, doctrines which were prevalent among the sects that had been formed in the centuries following Sunbād's rebellion. Niẓām al-Mulk's rendition of events probably reflects "the state of these doctrines as they evolved, ... [the author having confused] the essential ideas of the leader with the diverse [beliefs] of his followers." Sadighi 1938, p. 140.

[2535]Kennedy 1981, p. 64.

The theme of revenge is also a central part of another narrative discussed in this study, namely that of Bahrām-i Chūbīn.[2536] While initially launching his rebellion against Hormozd IV, we recall, after the subsequent blinding and deposition of the king at the hands of the Ispahbudhān brothers, Bahrām-i Chūbīn went on to sustain his rebellion on the platform of avenging Hormozd IV against the usurper Khusrow II Parvīz.[2537] It is in the theme of the "old legend about the conflict between [Manūchihr] and [Afrāsīyāb],"[2538] superimposed on Bahrām-i Chūbīn's narrative, that Sunbād's rebellion mimics that of the Parthian Mihrānid dynast Bahrām-i Chūbīn. The chief achievement of Manūchihr, as we have mentioned before, was avenging the death of Iraj, who was murdered by his brothers.[2539] This theme, together with all the narratives that replicate it, is thoroughly Mithraic. It is Mithra who "balances [his] rewarding function ... against his role as the terrible avenger of those who break their contracts."[2540] This theme is also incorporated in the narrative of the Kārinid Sukhrā's war against the Hephthalites on behalf of Pīrūz.[2541] There is little doubt, therefore, that Mithraic religio-cultural currents informed Sunbād's rebellion against the ʿAbbāsid caliph, as they did in the revolt of Bahrām-i Chūbīn.

The motif of treasure

What lends credence to the superimposition of Bahrām-i Chūbīn's narrative onto that of Sunbād is a third motif, the motif of *treasury*. In Sunbād's narrative, a systematically highlighted theme is the rebel's supposed acquisition of Abū Muslim's treasury. While the theme of the personal wealth of Sunbād is reiterated in a number of our sources, it is the motif of the *treasury of Abū Muslim* falling into the hands of Sunbād that is highlighted in almost all of our narratives. Significantly, by most accounts, this occurs in Rayy. This incongruous juxtaposition of the motifs of wealth and treasury is nowhere better highlighted than in Balʿamī's narrative. On the one hand, Sunbād is said to have been an independently wealthy acquaintance of Abū Muslim. In this part of the narrative, the affluent Sunbād was so heart-broken by the news of Abū Muslim's death that he vowed to avenge him with an army that he subsequently recruited using his own personal wealth.[2542] In a later section of this same narrative, however, Balʿamī gives a completely different provenance for the wealth of Sunbād: when Sunbād reached Rayy with his army, he found Abū Muslim's treasury there. He then took possession of this treasury arguing that as the avenger of Abū Muslim's blood, he was the most entitled to this treasury.[2543]

[2536]See page 413.
[2537]See page 127ff.
[2538]Olsson 1983, p. 39.
[2539]Yarshater 1983b, p. 434. See also page 375ff.
[2540]Thieme 1975, p. 29.
[2541]Ṭabarī 1999, pp. 116–117, de Goeje, 877. See our discussion on page 380ff.
[2542]This section of the narrative then takes the saga of Sunbād to his death at the hands of the *ispahbud* of Gurgān, Hormoz b. al-Farrukhān (rendered in the text as Farrujān).
[2543]Balʿamī 1987, pp. 1093–1094.

Most of the evidence at our disposal, however, indicates that the theme of Abū Muslim's treasury is in fact a mere *topos*. Indeed, it is never explained clearly why Abū Muslim, going on a temporary visit to Manṣūr, would have carried his treasury with him, and why, of all possible locations, he would have left these in Rayy.[2544] In fact, as Sadighi observes, the account of Abū Muslim's presumed activities in Rayy remain extremely nebulous.[2545] The respective capitals of Abū Muslim in Khurāsān were Marv and Nīshāpūr.[2546] Suspecting the motives of Manṣūr, in a trip wrought with uncertainties of potential war with the caliph, and in anticipation of distributing wealth to his army, Abū Muslim could very well have taken his treasury along with him, but the whole narrative of this episode is so confused in the accounts of our sources that none of this clear. The motif of the treasury and the choice of Rayy, on the other hand, have such an uncanny resemblance with the motifs of Bahrām-i Chūbīn's rebellion and his acquisition of wealth as the king of Padhashkhwārgar,[2547] that it makes the reappearance of this theme in Sunbād's rebellion extremely suspect, to say the least.

6.4.3 Sunbād and the apocalypse

Prominent in the accounts of Sunbād's rebellion is its apocalyptic dimension, whereby the destruction of the agents of *Kheshm*, the Arabs, and their temple, the Kaʿba, and the restoration of the kingdom of Iran, along with the sun as the *qibla* are promised. In its millennial features, Sunbād's movement bears testimony to the continuation of the millennial aspirations as evinced in the rebellion of the Parthian Mihrānid dynast Bahrām-i Chūbīn at the end of the sixth century. As we have seen, Bahram-i Chubin's rebellion later became part and parcel of the apocalyptic literature. Sunbād seems to have had access to this same textual tradition. We recall that according to Niẓām al-Mulk, Sunbād would secretly prognosticate: "the rule of the Arabs has reached its end for I have seen it [foretold] in one of the *books of Banu Sāsān*."[2548] As Sadighi observes, millennial expectations of ending Arab rule preoccupied the Iranian popular imagination in the wake of the Arab conquest and held currency for many centuries thereafter.[2549] Contrary to Rekaya's claims, and those following his school of thought, these millennial expectations prevailed, at least among

[2544]See note 1812.

[2545]Sadighi 1938, p. 137. While the details of Sunbād's association with Rayy, and his activities there are not clear, however, in the connection that Sunbād established with the *ispahbud* of Ṭabaristān, Khurshīd, the rebel's intimate connection with Rayy is beyond any doubt.

[2546]For Abū Muslim's activities, especially his construction activity when he established Nīshāpūr as the capital of Inner Khurāsān, see Pourshariati 1998.

[2547]See pages 408 and 410.

[2548]Niẓām al-Mulk 1941, pp. 260–261. Incidentally, we recall that one of the accusations hurled by Abū Muslim against Bihāfarīd was a similar tendency toward prognostication; see page 435.

[2549]Sadighi 1938, pp. 140–141. Millennial expectations were current during the antique and late antique period throughout the Mediterranean world, Mesopotamia, and Iran, so there is nothing unusual about this phenomenon in the Iranian case. Eddy 1961. What was peculiar to this juncture of Iranian history was that the Arabs, as opposed to, say, Alexander, became the point of reference.

some sectors of the population, for a long period even subsequent to Sunbād's revolt. Bīrūnī, in fact, bears testimony to the prevalence of these expectations during the Buyid period (934–1055): the Buyid assumption of power had apparently also engendered the millennial hope that through them Arab rule would soon be terminated and kingship would be restored to the Iranians.[2550] As Blochet justifiably observes, therefore, when Sunbād declared that he had seen the prognostication of the end of Arab rule "in one of the books of the Banū Sāsān," he was probably sincere: the *Bundahishn*, for instance, maintains that sometime after the "Arabs ... [have] spread their own law and their cursed religion in Iran ... their tyranny will cease, and they will be overthrown."[2551] The apocalypse of the Arab conquest and the millennial expectation of the termination of Arab rule is contained not only in the *Bundahishn*, but also in all other Iranian apocalyptic literature, such as the *Jāmāsp Nāmak* and the *Zand i Vahuman Yasn*. The continuity of the millennial tradition from the revolt of Bahrām-i Chūbīn to that of Sunbād, therefore, is not open to question. Whereas Bahrām-i Chūbīn, in support of an illegitimate or legitimate cause, depending on the apocalyptic tradition one considers, wages a war against the Sasanians, however, Sunbād, from the perspective of his followers, wages an unquestionably *just war* against the Arabs.

Perhaps the most significant current infusing the narrative of Sunbād, like its paradigmatic model, the rebellion of Bahrām-i Chūbīn, is that of Mihr worship. This was to be expected. For the territorial environment of Sunbād's rebellion, like that of Bahrām-i Chūbīn, was one in which Mihr worship was the most predominant form of spirituality. All the symbols, or motifs that betray this symbolism, can be found in the narratives of Sunbād's rebellion: Like Bahrām-i Chūbīn, Sunbād came to acquire an army and a treasury in the capital of the Padhashkhwārgar Shāh. As with Bahrām-i Chūbīn, Sunbād emerged from the east. As Manūchihr and Kai Bahrām, Sunbād rose against an egregious injustice and led a rebellion. Finally, as with the former, Sunbād's protagonist, Abū Muslim, and presumably the rebel himself, found their fate, once again, in the east, in the Rūyīn Dizh. It should be remarked, incidentally, that insofar as both Bahrām-i Chūbīn and Sunbād emerged from the east and returned to this same

[2550]Bīrūnī 1984, p. 303. Having observed the currency of these sentiments, however, Bīrūnī expressed his reservations about these and declared that the choice of the Buyids as the agency for restoring Iranian kingship seemed unwarranted. For, among the governments that had appeared thus far, the astrological configurations signaling the fulfillment of millennial expectations fell more clearly during the period of the ʿAbbāsid *dawla*, who "were a Khurāsānid and eastern government." Bīrūnī subsequently added, however, that "both the ʿAbbāsids, as well as the Buyids, were far from [successful in] reviving Persian kingship and government." Bīrūnī 1984, p. 303. The constant postponement of millennial expectations in the face of actual historical realities is, of course, a chief characteristic of the apocalyptic genre.

[2551]We have used Blochet's French translation here. The relevant chapter is entitled "On the calamities that have befallen the Persian through different ages." Here the restoration of Iran is promised in reference to the Avestā. Blochet, E., *Le messianisme dans l'hétérodoxie Musulmane*, Paris, 1903 (Blochet 1903), pp. 45–46. Blochet concludes, therefore, that "it is possible that this passage of the *Siyāsat Nāma* is an exact reproduction of the proclamation of Sunbād." Ibid., p. 45.

region, they were replicating the movements of the God Mihr, who, riding on his chariot, begins his westward journey in front of the sun only to return to the east, to its point of origin, to recommence the day. Like Bahrām-i Chūbīn-i *Mihrewandak*, who, as a Mihr devotee, wanted to restore the Burzīn Mihr fire, so too Sunbād aspired to destroy the Kaʿba and restore the Sun as the true *qibla*. This, they aimed in historical reality and not simply in mythical fiction. While the movement of the Mihrānid Bahrām-i Chūbīn gained momentum through the support it received from the *kūst-i ādurbādagān* and *kūst-i khwarāsān*, so too did Sunbād work in close collaboration with the Sun-King Khurshīd of the Āl-i Jāmāsp, a dynasty known as the Gāvbārih or Cow Devotees.[2552] Not coincidentally, as we have seen, all the Parthian dynasts had placed themselves under the rule of this same Khurshīd (734–759).[2553] Finally, as Bahrām-i Chūbīn carried a name literally signifying victory (*Bahrām*),[2554] this same epithet was carried by Sunbād, the *pīrūz spāhbed*, literally, the victorious *spāhbed*. In analogy with the epithet of Manūchihr's father, Mīshkhuryār, that is to say, one whose constant companion is the sun,[2555] moreover, it has been conjectured that the etymology of the very name of the rebel, Sunbād, derives from *zunbad*, meaning *guardian of the sun*. The Mithraic purview of Sunbād's rebellion, therefore, must be deemed certain.

6.4.4 Gentilitial background of Sunbād

While the motifs of Abū Muslim's treasury and revenge loom large in Sunbād's narrative, the independent wealth of this historical figure is also highlighted in some of our accounts. Some sources underline the high administrative and/or military function of Sunbād in Nīshāpūr prior to his revolt. Niẓām al-Mulk, for example, calls him a chief (*raʾīs*) of Nīshāpūr and claims that he was an old acquaintance of Abū Muslim (*bar Abū Muslim ḥaqq-i ṣuḥbat-i qadīm dāsht*), whom the latter had appointed commander of the army (*sipahsālār*).[2556] Now the title *sipahsālār* is the equivalent of the title of *spāhbed*. The anonymous *Kitāb al-ʿUyūn wa 'l-Ḥadāʾiq fī 'l-Akhbār al-Ḥaqāʾiq* reiterates Sunbād's acquisition of the title *spāhbed*, maintaining that after Sunbād launched his revolt and conquered Nīshāpūr, Qūmis and Rayy, he came to be called, as we have seen, *fīrūz iṣbahbudh* (*victorious spāhbed*).[2557] If our information is to be trusted in this case, then Sunbād was presumably the *spāhbed* of the east, or part of the east. We can therefore surmise that Sunbād was of a high enough status in the region to warrant him the his acquisition of the title and position of *spāhbed*. As we have seen, ever since its institution by Khusrow I Nowshīrvān, the office

[2552] See page 377.
[2553] See §4.5.
[2554] See page 411.
[2555] Ibn Balkhī 1995, p. 67.
[2556] Niẓām al-Mulk 1941, pp. 260–261.
[2557] Uyun 1869, *Kitāb al-ʿUyūn wa 'l-Ḥadāʾiq fī 'l-Akhbār al-Ḥaqāʾiq*, Leiden, 1869, translated by M.J. de Goeje (Uyun 1869), p. 224.

of *spāhbed* in the quarters of the north and the east of the Sasanian empire was almost always held by Parthian dynastic families. After the Arab conquest of Iran, moreover, the dynamic between the conquering and conquered populations of these regions was such that creating status in the post-conquest period, where no such status existed during the Sasanian period, was basically out of the question. Considering the dearth of Arab juridical, executive, and material presence in these regions, and in the absence of any indication whatsoever of an upheaval in the sociopolitical structure of these regions,[2558] the agnatic nature of the political, social, and religious affiliations of the Parthian dynasts must be considered a constant in the post-conquest period. Except for the disappearance of the Sasanians from the center, whose presence was, nevertheless, continued in the Āl-i Jāmāsp family in the north, and except for the age old re-shuffling of power among the Parthian dynastic families, very little had changed in the wake of the Arab conquest of the quarters of the east and north. Sunbād's social standing, therefore, suggests that he must have come from an agnatic Parthian family, probably, as we shall argue, the Kārins.

There are two traditions concerning the activities of Abū Muslim in Nīshāpūr, before he launched the ʿAbbāsid revolution, within which one might attempt to contextualize the possible acquaintance of Sunbād with Abū Muslim, however transitory this relation. The earlier tradition is given in an anecdotal garb by Nīshāpūrī in the *Taʾrīkh-i Nīsābūr* and is representative of the mostly hostile traditions regarding the ʿAbbāsid revolution and Abū Muslim in Inner Khurāsān. In this narrative Nīshāpūrī informs us that when Abū Muslim came to Nīshāpūr and declared his imminent intention of conquering all of Khurāsān, "some half-witted juveniles cut the tail of his ass." When Abū Muslim saw this, he asked: "What is the name of this quarter?" They said: "The quarter of Būyābād [literally the smelly quarter]." In anger, Abū Muslim retorted that he would soon turn this quarter into the quarter of Gandābād (literally the foul quarter). After he became the governor of Khurāsān, Abū Muslim, true to his word, destroyed the quarter of Būyābād, which "was never reconstructed again."[2559] Typical for the traditions in which the ʿAbbāsids did not find any support in Inner Khurāsān, this tradition of Nīshāpūrī highlights the antagonism of at least part of the population of Nīshāpūr against Abū Muslim.

This narrative resonates with that of the Arab conquest of the Parthian territories of Inner Khurāsān, especially the conquest of Ṭūs and Nīshāpūr in the 650s.[2560] There too, we recall, while the Parthian Kanārangīyān family, in collaboration with the Ispahbudhān family of Farrukhzād, made peace with the Arab armies in exchange for remaining the *de facto* rulers of the territories, a faction of the Nīshāpūrī population opposed both the Arab armies as well as the Kanārangīyān family. This faction, we recall, was led by the Kārins.[2561] The

[2558]The Mihrānid downfall being the exception; see §3.4.4.
[2559]Nīshāpūrī 1965, folio 59. For the story of Būyābād, also see Ibn al-Athīr 1862, vol. 5, p. 258.
[2560]See §3.4.7.
[2561]See our discussion on page 271ff.

narrative of Abū Muslim's hostile reception in Nīshāpūr, therefore, reflects a tradition that betrays opposition to the ᶜAbbāsids and Abū Muslim in parts of the city. The question then becomes the provenance of this narrative. In order to contextualize this we have access to a second narrative contained in the *Shāhnāma-i Abū Manṣūri*. Here we are informed that, after the Arab conquest, the region of Ṭūs and parts of Nīshāpūr remained under the control of the Kanārangīyān family until the takeover of the region by Ḥumayd b. Qaḥṭabah b. Ṭāᵓī, one of the foremost generals of the ᶜAbbāsid army.[2562] As we have discussed in detail elsewhere,[2563] the narratives at our disposal here betray not only the sociopolitical structure of rule in Inner Khurāsān, in Ṭūs and Nīshāpūr specifically, on the eve of the ᶜAbbāsid revolution, but also the intense ᶜAbbāsid struggle against the Umayyads in Inner Khurāsān.[2564] The ᶜAbbāsids had to reckon with the power of the Kanārangīyān family, a Parthian dynastic family who perceptively realized that, after a rule of more than half a millennium, the end of the nominal control of the Umayyads over their territories meant also the demise of their own *de facto* power in these territories. The antagonism of the Ṭūsīs toward the ᶜAbbāsids is even highlighted in the later popular traditions contained in the epic-historic narratives of the *Abū Muslim Nāma*—hence the historicity of the germ of these traditions contained in the epic—where we are informed that the one ᶜAbbāsid *dāᶜī* (missionary) assigned to Ṭūs was unsuccessful in winning the population of the region to the cause of the ᶜAbbāsids.[2565] From the Arab conquest of Inner Khurāsān to the end of the Umayyad rule, besides their control over Ṭūs, the Kanārangīyān had undisputed control only over parts of Nīshāpūr, the Kārins being their hostile adversaries.[2566] We must also recollect the episodic insurgencies led by the Kārins against both the Arab conquerors and the other dynastic powers in some parts of Khurāsān and Nīshāpūr, underlining their continued aspirations, which, however, remained predominantly unfulfilled.[2567] And thus we come to a second tradition concerning Abū Muslim and the positive reception that he receives in parts of Nīshāpūr at the inception of the ᶜAbbāsid revolution. This tradition, we shall argue, is most probably of Kārinid provenance.

This other tradition stands in stark contrast to the one discussed above and actually reflects a very positive historical memory about Abū Muslim's association with Nīshāpūr. No half-witted juvenile cuts the tail of his beast here! This tradition is contained in a later source, Mīrkhwānd, who wrote in the ninth century *hijra* (14–15th century CE). According to this tradition, Sunbād, who was one of the wealthy (*fī 'l-jumlih miknatī dāsht*) fire worshippers of Nīshāpūr, saw Abū Muslim when the latter, coming from the Imām, was heading for

[2562]Qazvini 1984, p. 90. For Ḥumayd b. Qaḥṭabah, see Crone 1980, pp. 188–189.
[2563]Pourshariati 2004.
[2564]Pourshariati 1995, Chapter 1.
[2565]Ṭarsūsī, Abū Ṭāhir ᶜAlī b. Ḥusayn, *Abū Muslim Nāma*, Tehran, nd (Ṭarsūsī nd), p. 635.
[2566]Qazvini 1984, p. 89. Minorsky 1964, p. 273. See our discussion on page 271ff.
[2567]See for instance, page 277ff and §4.5.1.

Marv. Sunbād, according to Mīrkhwānd, saw the signs of statesmanship and prosperity (*āthar-i dowlat va iqbāl*) in Abū Muslim's appearance, took him to his own abode and asked him about his future undertakings.[2568] Initially reluctant, Abū Muslim finally revealed his secrets to the wealthy *magian* of the city. This, then, is the way in which Sunbād is said to have become acquainted with the ʿAbbāsid revolutionary leader Abū Muslim al-Marwazī.

Unlike our previous narrative, moreover, this account betrays a separate provenance. Here we are not dealing with a negative reception of the ʿAbbāsid leader, but one in which a harmonious, positive collaboration is depicted. The provenance of this second narrative, in other words, must be sought alongside those traditions which, like Niẓām al-Mulk's, claim, for example, that Abū Muslim appointed Sunbād as the *spāhbed* of his army, presumably in Inner Khurāsān. By now it must be clear how we view what must have transpired and hence what the provenance of the respective narratives is. While, as our second narrative betrays, there was most probably a historic dimension to Sunbād's collaboration with the ʿAbbāsids, this must be contextualized in the confines of the inter-Parthian dynastic rivalries that continued to engulf the quarters of the north and the east throughout the Umayyad period, and not in a presumed conversion of Sunbād and his followers to the cause of the ʿAbbāsid revolutionaries. While the Kanārangīyān had lost power in Inner Khurāsān with the advent of the ʿAbbāsids to power, another dynastic group must have gained by the victorious launching of the ʿAbbāsid revolution.

As the Kanārangīyān had, in fact, only recently lost power at the hands of the ʿAbbāsid army and their foremost general Ḥumayd b. Qaḥṭabah, Sunbād's dynastic background cannot be sought in the ranks of this deposed dynastic family: Why collaborate, however nominally, with an emerging power that had destroyed one's family fortune just recently? While Sunbād collaborated with the Āl-i Jāmāspid Khurshīd, we should recall that he was actually murdered by another member of this same family.[2569] The tenor of the whole story of his

[2568]Sunbād then prognosticated that his instincts had told him (*marā az ṭarīq-i firāsat chinān bih khāṭir mīresad*) that Abū Muslim would one day overturn the land and "would kill many from among the elite of the Arabs and the *great Iranians* (*ashrāf-i arab va akābir-i ʿajam*)" Mīrkhwānd 1960, pp. 404–405. Zarrinkub cites this story of Mīrkhwānd as a later narration, adopted from popular myths, about the manner of the acquaintance of Sunbād and Abū Muslim. This narrative, he suggests, is taken out from later *Abū Muslim Nāmas* written subsequent to Abū Muslim's death: "the interesting point is that this story does not exist in earlier sources and it seems as if later sources [adopted it from] the myths and stories of the Persian *Abū Muslim Nāma*." Zarrinkub, Abd al-Husayn, *Dow Qarn Sokūt*, 1989, reprinted in German (Zarrinkub 1989). As we are attempting to show, here, however, the late Zarrinkub's distrust of the germ of this tradition was not valid. This story is also given in the later *Taʾrīkh Alfī*. According to this source, Sunbād was a citizen of Nīshāpūr. At the time of the disturbances in Khurāsān, he incited the people of Nīshāpūr to revolt and encouraged them to kill the noble Arabs and the aristocratic Iranians. According to Daniel, Sunbād's "speeches attracted the attention of Abū Muslim, who was very pleased by them and who decided to cultivate Sunbād's friendship. Sunbād and his brother wore black, provided the Abbasid rebels with supplies, and received assistance in fighting the Arabs." Daniel 1979, p. 126.

[2569]See §4.5.2.

murder, moreover, strongly suggests that he could not have been a member of this dynastic family either.

Considering the thematic context of Ibn Isfandīyār's narrative—where the story of Sunbād and his rebellion against Manṣūr is narrated immediately after the story of the rise of the Kārins to power, and where the theme of their arrogance against the Āl-i Jāmāsp, under whose theoretical suzerainty they fell, is highlighted[2570]—and considering the history of the dynastic rivalries within the region during the previous centuries, it is very probable, therefore, that from the two remaining Parthian dynastic families, the Ispahbudhān and the Kārin, Sunbād actually belonged to the Kārin family. There is no reason to assume that the rivalry between the Kanārangīyān and the Kārins in Inner Khurāsān had subsided during the century that had elapsed. In fact, as we have seen,[2571] once before, with the murder of Farrukhzād and their revolt in Inner Khurāsān, the Kārins had already attempted to regain their lost power. While at the beginning of the conquest the power of the Kārins had declined at the expense of the Kanārangīyān in the region, moreover, there is every possibility that the ʿAbbāsids also availed themselves of the dynastic rivalries within the region, and having toppled the Kanārangīyān, once again brought the Kārins back to power. The Kārins' tumultuous relationship with the Āl-i Jāmāsp, moreover, fits very well with the uneasy relationship between Sunbād and the Āl-i Jāmāsp Khurshīd.[2572] This uneasy relationship of the Kārins, now with the Āl-i Jāmāsp, and then with the Āl-i Bāvand,[2573] continued to mark the dynamics between these dynastic powers in the region. There is every indication, therefore, that of all the possible candidates for the agnatic background of Sunbād, the Kārins are the most likely contenders. This background, however, seems to have become obscured as a result of the strength of a more powerful legend that in later centuries was superimposed on the figure of Sunbād: his problematic connection to Abū Muslim.

6.5 Conclusion

The revolts erupting in the Parthian homelands at the inception of the rise of the ʿAbbāsids to power testify not only to the continued currency of Mihr worship, but the persistent aspirations of the Parthians in the northern territories of Iran. Our evidence for the forceful prevalence of Mihr worship, as we have hoped to have shown, is in fact overwhelming. Leaving the late Sadighi at a loss, it is rather evident that Bihāfarīd's revolt was actually a Mithraic revolt. The accounts at our disposal clearly betray the Mithraic motifs of his rebellion, the narratives of the rebel ascribing to Bihāfarīd the role of Mihr himself.

[2570] See §4.5.1.
[2571] See page 307.
[2572] For the Kārins in Ṭabaristān, see §4.2 and §4.5.1.
[2573] Unfortunately, considerations of time and space have not allowed us to follow this latter relationship in more detail.

Considering the currency of millennial beliefs in Bihāfarīd's milieu, moreover, as well his clear prophetic and messianic mission, we can probably also confidently maintain that included in the platform of the rebel was a prognostication for the end of Arab rule. That Mazdean millennial calculations did not tally with the timing of Bihāfarīd's rebellion, as the late Sadighi argued, does not detract from these claims. For as we know, and as reflected in the *Bundahishn* itself, there were many different millennial calculations current among the Iranian populations at this period. Sunbād's historic saga, as well as the *topoi* of his narrative, leave no doubt that his too was a Mithraic rebellion. In fact, it is in Sunbād's narrative that we most clearly see the incredible continuity of Mithraic beliefs in Pahlav regions from the rebellion of Bahrām-i Chūbīn onward.

While the personal background of Bihāfarīd is shrouded in obscurity, moreover, and while in fact a Parthian dynastic background might be a less likely conjecture for this Mihr worshipping rebel, there is every possibility that in the rebellion of Sunbād, the *ispahbud pīrūz*, we are in fact witnessing a Parthian rebellion, probably of the Kārin dynastic family. While this claim can only be postulated, given the information at our disposal, however, it gains tremendous force when considered in conjunction with the later rebellion of the Parthian Kārinid Māzīyār, and his close association with the Azarbāyjānī rebel, Bābak-i Khurramdīn who, incidentally, also launched a Mithraic rebellion. While we must postpone an investigation into these latter rebellions for a sequel to this study, therefore, considering what has already been said of the history of the Pahlav dynasts in the late antique period, and with historical hindsight, we can confidently claim that Parthian political and cultural presence in the northern regions of Iran continued for an inordinate amount of time after the demise of the house of Sāsān. The currency of Parthian agnatic genealogies in the tenth century gives us an incredible vista into the contribution of the Pahlav to Iranian history and culture throughout the late antique, early medieval period.

Conclusion

Further investigation into the currents of Near Eastern studies during the past half century is sure to expose its scholarly predisposition. It is not clear why, exactly, systematic studies of late antique history of Iran were put on the shelf after Christensen's authoritative studies. Not to be misconstrued, there have been many individual scholars who have made significant contributions to the field. Unfortunately, however, as any impartial and cursory inquiry will reveal, their efforts have been against the current and therefore not successful in changing trends in late antique studies of the Middle East.[2574] There has been a systematic neglect of this and the subsequent late antique, early medieval period of Iranian history, and no matter how we justify it, there is no denying it. This trend can be partially explained by the long history of hegemony exerted by classical studies, which have been part and parcel of the birth of modern historiography. Delving into this, however, is to point to the obvious.[2575] There is then the Arabist and Islamist predisposition of the field. Disregarding the explicable nineteenth and early twentieth century history of this current in the field[2576]—coming as it does in the wake of the direct colonial and imperial history of Europe in the Arab Middle East—we still need to reckon with the void left in late antique studies of Iran during the past half century. The discourse of nationalist Iranian scholars of the past two generations, some of whom tenaciously, and at times belligerently, underlined the Iranian contribution to the early medieval history of the Middle East, has also been partly responsible for the subsequent scholarly disregard of the history of Iran during this period. It created a defensive backlash in the field in which any subsequent scholarly effort towards highlighting the Iranian dimension of late antique history of the Middle East became more or less suspect. In this climate, one can scarcely discuss any dimension of Iranian history in a positive light without being accused by some of Iranian cultural chauvinism. This trend is unfortunate and must be remedied. Sound scholarship must not be censored and suffocated, irrespective of

[2574] The momentous *Encyclopaedia Iranica* project has provided a much needed respite in the midst of all this.

[2575] As all are aware, the heritage of modern Europe has been sought in classical antiquity.

[2576] See, for instance, Russell, James R., 'Review of Yamauchi's *Persia and the Bible*', *Jewish Quarterly* 83, (1992), pp. 256–261 (Russell 1992), pp. 256–258.

the implications of its finding. There was then the Iranian revolution of 1978–79, which prompted the creation of an army of modernists and Islamicists in Iranian studies. Valuable as this scholarly surge has been, it has served to further undermine late antique and medieval history of Iran in recent scholarship.

The picture drawn by Christensen of the Sasanian empire left numerous crucial questions unanswered. Above all there remained one critical, perplexing, question: in the span of two decades and in spite of its tremendous power, why did one of the two most powerful empires of late antiquity succumb so rapidly and disastrously into obliteration? The social, ideological, and political trends briefly enumerated above conspired to detract scholarly attention from this crucial question of late antique history of Iran. Arabist and Islamicist concerns have absorbed the lion's share of academic attention. It was fortunate that the ʿAbbāsid revolution redirected scholarly attention to northeastern Iran. Even here, however, it was not the details of Iranian sociopolitical history in the post-conquest century that became the focus of scholarship.[2577] In numerous scholarly works on the topic, brief introductory chapters dealt away with the history of Iran during the Sasanian and Umayyad periods, only to focus their attention on the northeastern territories of Iran in order to dissect the enigma of Abū Muslim and his followers. Crucial questions such as conversion and the course of Iranian history during the Umayyad period were either accepted *a priori*, with very little investigation, as remains the case with the question of conversion, or were not dealt with altogether. The later medieval history of Iran has not fared any better in recent decades.[2578] The dearth of scholarship on these crucial periods of Iranian history to this day remains truly astounding. Foremost among the intended aims of the present work, therefore, has been a plea to the students and scholars of the field to reconsider the lackadaisical manner in which scholarship has treated the late antique and early medieval history of Iran. As we have hoped to have shown in the course of the present study, Iranian history in the period under investigation provides a treasure trove of venues for research, not least of which might have revolutionary implications for the paradigmatic narrative of the origins of Islamic history itself.

After Christensen, scholarship became unduly obsessed with his paradigm of a centralized Sasanian state. There was perhaps an unrecognized ideological locomotive at work here as well. It might be justifiably postulated that the romanticized myth of the *nation*, summoned by the nineteenth and twentieth century conceptions of modern European nation-states, also affected Christensen's implicit ideological assumptions in his study of the Sasanian empire. These theories conceived of centralized modern European states as the epitome of

[2577] See our discussion in §6.2.2.

[2578] To this day substantive accounts of the histories of the Ṭāhirids and the Samanids are nowhere to be found in western languages. Bosworth's monographs on Sīstān and Mottahedeh's work on the Buyids have not been supplemented by further studies. And, after the pioneering efforts of Minorsky on the Caucasus and Azarbāyjān, not a single work on this region's history in late antiquity has appeared.

rationally constructed political organizations that engendered, besides *national identity*, all other benevolent aspects and directions of human sociopolitical organization.[2579] In this conception, one might argue, a decentralized state was considered an inferior state, not capable of rationally mustering all its forces for ameliorating the conditions of its realm. The intimate connection of decentralization with various forms of *feudal* or *semi-feudal*, hence pre-modern, economic and political structures, further underlined the presumed shortcomings of decentralized states. So paradigmatic has this equation of centralization with a more advanced form of political organization become that its marks can be felt on the scholarship on other periods of Iranian and early Islamic history as well. Even the recent revival in Parthian studies, for example, has not remained immune to it: the question of whether or not, and at which point, and to what extent, we can consider the Parthians as being more centralized, and thus implicitly more modern, and in better control of the diverse polities within their realm, has continued to form a bone of contention in the field.[2580]

In the case of the Sasanian state, however, there is surely no reason to continue to presume the equation of centralization with the proper functioning of their government. In order to make our case for the *dynastic* and decentralized nature of the Sasanian state, and while detailing its systematic confederacy with the Parthians, we were obliged to underline those dimensions of this system which made it prone to dysfunction. All with some familiarity with Iran's late antique history will recognize, however, that this is only one side of the picture. For the reverse side of the argument has always been implicit in the picture that we have tried to present in this study, namely that it was precisely because of their decentralized form of government and their confederacy with the Parthians, that the Sasanians became as powerful as they did during the late antique period. The Sasanians could not have functioned, and would not have been able to maintain power for as long as they did, had it not been for their active alliance with the Pahlav dynasties. For the most part, therefore, and in spite of the tensions inherent in it, the decentralized Sasanian political structure was remarkably efficient. It was in fact to the credit of the Sasanians that they acknowledged the sociopolitical and regional centrifugal tendencies embedded in their realm, and set up a system that gave due credit to the realities of Iran in the late antique centuries. In a sense, one might argue that, as with other aspects of their rule, the Sasanians in fact followed the Parthian heritage here as well, and not just during the third century. Just as various Parthian families had agreed to the kingship of the Arsacids, their later history notwithstanding, so

[2579] Elwell Sutton's obituary of Christensen provides interesting clues about the scholar's political orientation. See Sutton, L.P. Elwell, 'Arthur Emanuel Christensen', *Bulletin of the British Society for Middle Eastern Studies* 10, (1983), pp. 59–68 (Sutton 1983). Needless to say, none of this is meant to downplay, by any means, the tremendous debt that Iranian studies owes to the works of this towering Danish scholar.

[2580] This perspective has also affected various theories advanced about the emergence of an Islamic state after the death of the Prophet.

too they came to agree to the kingship of the Sasanians through most of Sasanian history. Had it not been for the irrational attempts of Qubād and Khusrow I at reforming this system with the aim of augmenting monarchical power and establishing an *étatiste* state, the Sasanians would have, in all probability, never experienced the series of Parthian rebellions that shook their realm in the late sixth century. Khusrow II, who owed his very power to the agreement of the Parthians, especially the Ispahbudhān family, was able to recreate the imperial Achaemenid boundaries with the help, predominantly,[2581] of the armies that the Parthian dynasts continued to bring to bear in his campaigns against the Byzantines. The fate of the Sasanians in the "greatest war of antiquity" is in fact a telling testimony to the consequences of Parthian withdrawal of their confederacy from the Sasanians: the sudden and utter defeat of the Sasanian military endeavors against their recently defeated foes, the Byzantines. The fate of Khusrow II might have been very different had he paid heed to the desire of the Parthian dynasts for peace after three decades of internecine warfare. His blind pursuit of imperialistic aims against the Byzantines, however, led the Parthian dynasts to the bosom of the enemy, with the result that important Parthian families made their peace with the shrewd Heraclius.

The Sasanian dynasty, according to James Russell, "has often been presented as consistently intolerant in matters of religion, partly for ease of contrast with its predecessors and probably also *to make the Islamic conquest of Iran somehow justifiable.*"[2582] Indeed, the scholarship that has leapt from the Arab conquest and its rapid success to the ʿAbbāsid revolution and its central premise of conversion to an egalitarian Islam, needed as its foundation the *topos* of a religiously intolerant, doctrinally static, Zoroastrian church, in order to explain the conquest and set the stage for the ʿAbbāsids. Not integrating the results of the last two decades of scholarship on Sasanian religious history, and in view of the dearth of actual scholarship on conversion, this theme of Islamic redemption of the Iranian masses, in other words, needed the image of a suffocating Zoroastrian church in order to uphold it. It needed, furthermore, to uncritically accept the Sasanian ideological *topos* of religion and state as the "twin pillars of government." If the Iranian masses were not suffocating under the yoke of an oppressive Zoroastrian church that acted in concert with the Sasanian state, after all, how could one possibly argue for the speedy and mass conversion of Iranians from their centuries-old ancestral beliefs to a barely formed religious doctrine? If the Iranians freely exercised their spiritual beliefs in a religious landscape that was not doctrinally and structurally hegemonic, centralized, and uniform, why convert? Conveniently set aside was the hallmark of spiritual identity among Iranians: in every variety of Iranian religion, ethnicity was closely

[2581]Zeev Rubin's theory on the barbarization of the standing Sasanian army has to be reckoned with here. Rubin 1995, p. 285.
[2582]Russell 1990a, p. 181. Emphasis added.

intertwined with ancestral beliefs.[2583] Conveniently forgotten, as well, was the agnatic dimension of the Iranian religious experience, where religious practices, rituals, and narratives also had a regional dimension. Perhaps herein lies one of the causes behind the emergence and growth of the Shuʿūbiya movement, once a substantial group of Iranians and the elite sectors of their society had in fact converted. The Shuʿūbiya assuaged their guilt of conversion to a non-ethnic religion by insisting on the disassociation of the former links between ethnicity and religion—taunted this time, ironically, by the Arabs—even while they continued to promote their identity in ethnic terms.[2584]

During the past two decades, the numerous blindspots of this Sasanian *topos* of monarchical–clerical cooperation has been, again and again, explicated. It is time to come up to speed with the results of this research. The religious panorama of the Sasanian realm was far more complex, layered, and multi-faceted than it has been hitherto admitted by the scholars of early Islamic history. Perhaps one of the most important dimensions of this rich religious landscape, moreover, was the prevalence of Mihr worship among a number of powerful Parthian dynastic families and the populace living in their realms, in the quarters of the east *(kūst-i khwarāsān)* and north *(kūst-i ādurbādagan)* of the Sasanian domains.[2585] To this we must add the rich pre-Christian religious traditions of Armenia, themselves strongly influenced by Iranian Mazdean systems of belief, but especially, by Mithraic traditions.[2586] Taking into account the naturally slow process of conversion in Armenia as elsewhere, this meant that during the late antique period, Mihr worship was one of the most significant forms of religiosity in a territory that stretched from Khurāsān, to Ṭabaristān and Gīlān, and further to the west into Azarbāyjān and Armenia. The Pārsīg–Pahlav dichotomy in Iran, therefore, translated itself also into the realm of spirituality in the late antique period.

Apart from its highly ethical and moralistic dimensions, the Mithraic ideology also had the potential for being an ideology of subversion and dissent. Mihr worship was not, as it has been often characterized, *nature* worship. As the God of *contracts* and as the quintessential instrument for implementing *justice*, Mihr equipped its adherents with a powerful weapon in times of hardship, crisis, and uncertainty. It was perhaps the backbone of the Iranian *Circle of Justice* theory of government.[2587] As such, it formed one of the most forceful ideological and social mechanisms with the aid of which one could rebel against oppressive governments. And thus, in rebellion after rebellion in the Pahlav lands, we find not some abstract precepts of a monolithic Mazdean religious ideology at work, but

[2583] Among Islamicists, and besides Minorsky, Crone was one of the few who paid attention to this aspect of Iranian identity.

[2584] Pourshariati 2000. We are well aware that among the anti-Shuʿūbiya, there were those of Iranian ancestry. This, however, is a moot point, that we hope to address in a future study.

[2585] See §5.4.

[2586] See §5.4.4.

[2587] See §5.2.6.

the very specific tenets and symbolism of Mihr worship. In a crucial juncture of Iranian history and, in the face of Parthian pretension and political power in the Pahlav regions, the Sasanian king Pīrūz attempted to launch his own religio-political platform. He promoted the powers of the Ādhar Gushnasp and Ādhar Farnbagh fires, and emphasized Sasanian legitimacy by connecting the ancestry of the dynasty to the Kayānids.[2588] In response, the Kārins redacted the very segments of Pīrūz's reign in the *X^w adāy-Nāmag* history: they infused the narratives of his reign with Kārinid grandeur and wrapped the story of Pīrūz in the Mithraic symbolism of their creed.[2589] Like Mihr, they became the instruments for restoring *farr* to the king. In line with the Circle of Justice ideology, they accused him of being an unjust king. Adopting the green color of Mihr, they indicted him with the Mithraic charge of reneging the *contract* and unleashing hardship. The Parthian Kārins were, undoubtedly, Mihr worshippers.[2590] They highlighted this in their seals when they took refuge in the Burzīn Mihr fire. They used theophoric names that paid tribute to the God they worshipped. What is perhaps most significant for our purposes is that in reality, and not as it has been claimed, in fiction, the Kārin dynasty and its cultural traditions continued to exist well into the post-conquest history of Khurāsān and Ṭabaristān, until at least the ninth century. As we have argued for Sunbād,[2591] and as we hope to show in a sequel to this work for Māzīyār, these rebellions formed a direct continuity with the history of the Kārins in these territories.

The populist Bahrām-i Chūbīn, the *Mihrewandak* and *Mihtar-parast* rebel, was also a Mihr worshipper and articulated this in no uncertain terms in his ideological warfare against Hormozd IV and Khusrow II Parvīz.[2592] The Mihrānid rebel not only flaunted his Parthian genealogy and legitimacy, but also gave voice to the resentment of the populace against the Sasanian appointed *mōbads* in the Pahlav domains. His historic narratives are infused with mythic narratives of Mihr worship. The rebel himself forcefully articulated the superiority of his religion; the family, after all, carried the name of their God as their dynastic name. Galvanizing the Pahlav domains with the Mithraic ideology of dissent, his rebellion was on the verge of collapsing Sasanian power had another towering Parthian dynastic family, the Ispahbudhān, not come to the aid of the feeble Khusrow II Parvīz, enlisting the support of the former foes, the Byzantines, in the process.[2593]

The Parthian dynastic families and their followers were not the only agnatic groups who worshipped Mihr in the northern territories. The Sasanian branch of the Āl-i Jāmāsp in Ṭabaristān also followed the Mithraic creed.[2594] They used

[2588] See page 385.
[2589] See page 380ff.
[2590] See §5.4.3.
[2591] See §6.4.4.
[2592] See §6.1, in particular, page 398.
[2593] See page 128ff.
[2594] See §5.4.1, in particular, page 373ff.

symbolic names such as Khurshīd and Gāvbārih to render their Mihr spirituality. Popular stories depicting their ancestor atop a Mithraic ox, circulated in their territories. The rebel who was their cohort against the newly established ʿAbbāsid caliphate, Sunbād, the *victorious* (*Verethragnā*) *ispahbud*, was working within the same spiritual universe. Sunbād's narrative was, in fact, a Mithraic narrative, following in its accounts the apocalyptic tales of Bahrām-i Chūbīn and the Padhashkhwārgar Shāh Kai Bahrām.[2595] Sunbād's alleged desire for revenge of Abū Muslim's murder was nothing more than a Mithraic *topos* inserted into the saga of this Mithraic hero. Niẓām al-Mulk's post facto rendition of the picture notwithstanding, there was, therefore, very little connection between Sunbād and Abū Muslim, and in all probability, next to no synthesis of Islamic and Mazdean propaganda in the doctrines that Sunbād promoted. Destroying the Kaʿba, yes. But the promotion of *al-riḍā min āl-i Muḥammad*, unlikely! It is, in fact, a reflection of the subtleties with which ancient practices persevere and take on a new color, that Abū Muslim (the father of the Muslims) found his way into the mythic narratives of Mihr worshippers. Mihr worship also provided the spiritual context of the green-clad Prophet Bihāfarīd.[2596] His followers knelt before the sun as their *qibla*. Like Mihr and his right hand aid, Sorūsh, Bihāfarīd appeared at dawn from atop a mountain or a higher structure. And reflecting the nourishing functions of Mihr, preached to the peasants, albeit his message, contained in a holy book in Persian, and thus totally anathema to a Muslim audience, addressed mercantile interests.

As we shall try to establish in a sequel to this study, there is very little doubt as well that the rebellion of Bābak Khurramdīn was a Mithraic rebellion, the rebel being probably of Parthian ancestry himself. Widengren had long ago already identified the Mithraic rituals of the Bābakiya,[2597] a fascinating study which was again conveniently ignored by subsequent meagre scholarship on the rebel. Further symbolic reflections of Bābak's Mihr worship infuse other accounts of his rebellion. From Khurāsān to Azarbāyjān and Armenia, therefore, in an extensive territory, the God Mihr was exalted above other deities in late antique Iranian history. These regions also remained immune from incursions of an alien culture well into subsequent centuries. Herein lies therefore testimony to the continuity and pervasiveness of Mihr worship in Parthian domains through successive centuries, a testimony which ought to be reckoned with when we search for the provenance of Mihr worship in Roman Mithraism.

While it is true that in their official patronage of the *X^w^adāy-Nāmag* tradition the Sasanians virtually deleted the history of the Arsacid dynasty from their accounts, cutting it to half of its actual duration, and manipulating it so as to make their own assumption of power coincide with millennial expectations, it is also true that their efforts in deleting the sagas of the Parthian dynastic families from the accounts of the *Book of Kings* was woefully ineffective. For the

[2595] See §6.4.1.
[2596] See §6.3.2.
[2597] Widengren 1979, *passim*.

X^wadāy-Nāmag tradition gives ample testimony to the editorial manipulation and re-writing of Sasanian history by various Pahlav families. It is on account of this Parthian rewriting of the *X^wadāy-Nāmag* tradition that as soon as the Sasanian section of the *Shāhnāma* gains substance, significantly, with the reign of Pīrūz (459–484), at almost every turn of event, and side-by-side of almost every single Sasanian king, we find as well the saga of the particular Parthian dynastic family that held control over the king. It is in this sense therefore that the *Shāhnāma* becomes a book of kings as much as a book of rebels, an "epic of sedition."[2598] What is crucial to note is that this Parthian historiographical tradition was inserted into both the historical (Sasanian) and some of the mythical (Kayānid) sections of the *Shāhnāma*, predominantly during the Sasanian period. This, then, must also partly explain the various recensions of the *X^wadāy-Nāmag* tradition and the divergences contained therein, observed by the Shuʿūbiya writer Ḥamza Iṣfahānī.[2599] Above and beyond the great intrinsic value of the *Shāhnāma* as a source for reconstructing Sasanian history, therefore, herein also lies the tremendous importance of the Sasanian sections of the opus: the *Shāhnāma* and the *X^wadāy-Nāmag* traditions allow us to follow the fascinating saga of the Pahlav dynasties in the Sasanian domains.

This Parthian role in the transmission of their history, intertwined in the Sasanian accounts of the *Shāhnāma* is explained by their real power within the Pahlav territories, and even in the center of the empire. There is every reason to assume that in their regional capitals such as Rayy, Gurgān, Qūmis, or Ṭūs, the various Parthian dynasts of the Mihrāns, the Kārins, the Ispahbudhān, and the Kanārangīyān, held their own courts and their own mechanisms for retaining their histories and sagas for future generations. It is on account of the Pahlavs' tremendous wealth, allowing the preservation of their chivalrous exploits, that the traditionalists of the conquest underlined, for example, the riches that the Arab conquerors obtained from the capital of the Mihrāns in Rayy, and compared these to the booty collected from the Sasanian capital, Ctesiphon (al-Madāʾin).[2600]

Whether the Parthians cultivated their traditions in a written or through an oral tradition, we can as yet not ascertain with any degree of certainty.[2601] Whatever the case, there is no doubt that, as the *Shāhnāma* bears witness, the Pahlav dynasts continued to *speak the Parthian language* until the end of the Sasanian period and probably for centuries thereafter. When the feeble Shīrūyih Qubād sent messengers to his father, Khusrow II Parvīz, Jālīnūs informed

[2598] Davis 1992, *passim*.

[2599] A comparative analysis of these divergent traditions contained within the *X^wadāy-Nāmag* recensions that have come down to us, is sure to yield important results.

[2600] See §3.4.4, in particular, page 251.

[2601] The fact that our latest written evidence for the Parthian script pertains only to the fourth century is no indication of the non-existence of a later written tradition. Unfortunately, modern archeological investigations of the Pahlav domains are next to nonexistent. There is no telling what future investigations on this neglected and crucial aspect of the pre- and post-conquest history of the Pahlav domains will bring to the fore, were they to be undertaken.

them that he needed to be made privy to the message, "whether it was delivered in the Persian or the Parthian language."[2602] The political and religious Pārsīg-Pahlav dichotomy, therefore, also permeated into the linguistic realm. As the evidence of the Mihrāns in the *Bahrām-i Chūbīn Nāma*[2603] and the *Book of Shahrvarāz and Khusrow*,[2604] the Kārins in the *Ayādgār-i Wuzurgmihr-i Bōkhtagān*,[2605] and the Ispahbudhān in the *Bāvand Nāma*, in which account, presumably, the imploded saga of Bāv (Farrukhzād) of the Ispahbudhān family was spelled out in more detail,[2606] bear witness, the Pahlav systematically preserved their traditions throughout the Sasanian and well into the post-conquest centuries. Add to this the potential that the Sīstānī cycle of the *Shāhnāma* was promoted by the Sūrens,[2607] and the Parthian influence becomes pervasive.

Among the various recensions of the *X*^{w}*adāy-Nāmag* tradition, the *Shāhnāma* of Ferdowsī remains the most fateful in its retention of historical information on the Pahlav during the Sasanian period. And it is to the credit of the collectors of the prose *Shāhnāma*, as well as Ferdowsī, that some of this information cannot be found elsewhere. It is on account of this that the Pahlav identities of some of the presumably legendary figures populating the *Shāhnāma* can now be established in reference to the recently discovered seals of Gyselen. For when the seals of the *spāhbeds* Sēd-hōsh and Gōrgōn from the Kārin family, and Chihr Burzīn from the Mihrān family were discovered, searching through the secondary sources (the so-called universal histories) left Gyselen stranded in identifying them. Little was it known that Shēdōsh (Sēd-hōsh), Gorgēn, and Sīmāh-i Burzīn—the latter's name, after a simple synonymic substitution becoming Chihr Burzīn—were all along roaming the *Shāhnāma* of Ferdowsī. The information in the *Shāhnāma* proves to be quite exhaustive, moreover: every Parthian *spāhbed* from the seals[2608] also appears in Ferdowsī's opus as a

[2602]Ferdowsī 1971, vol. IX, p. 258, Ferdowsī 1935, p. 258:

و لیکن مرا شاه ایران قباد   بسی اندرین پند و اندرز داد
که همداستانی مکن روز و شب   که کس پیش خسرو گشاید دو لب
مگر انکه گفتار او بشنوی   اگر پارسی گوید ار پهلوی

[2603]Mas'ūdī maintains that the "genealogy [of Bahrām-i Chūbīn] was contained in a separate book." Mas'ūdī 1869, vol. 2, pp. 223–224, Mas'ūdī 1968, p. 270. The book was translated into Arabic by Jabalah b. Sālim. Christensen 1936, p. 59.

[2604]Of this book, according to Christensen, "we know nothing but its name ... It would be tempting, however, to see in this book the remote origins of an Arab romance, which existed independently before being incorporated into the collection of *A Thousand and One Nights*, that is the romance of 'Umar b. Nu'mān and his sons." Christensen 1936, p. 61.

[2605]Bozorgmehr 1971.

[2606]Ibn Isfandīyār 1941, p. 4. Ibn Isfandīyār, it should be mentioned, has not a few unkind words to say about this source.

[2607]I am told that to this day, in Sīstān, the Sūrens are jealously guarding their traditions, refusing, unfortunately, academe any access to what seems to be a rich ancestral archive. An entry in *Wikipedia* on the Sūrens is being currently maintained by members of this family. And, if I am not mistaken, one of the towering figures of Iranian art history, Dr. Souren Melikian-Chirvani, traces his genealogy to this very important Parthian family.

[2608]The one possible exception, in fact, is the seal of the *Pārsīg spāhbed*, Wēh-Shābuhr, whom

powerful general, either in the post-reform Sasanian narratives of the *Shāhnāma*, or through the Ctesian method, in its Kayānid sections.[2609]

In their redaction of the *X^w adāy-Nāmag*, the Parthian families, like the Sasanians, were bound to embellish some of the exploits of their family members. We can also deduce that they deleted some of their lesser deeds from the pages of the *X^w adāy-Nāmag* history. They attempted to camouflage their central involvement in those crucial junctures of Sasanian history that subsequently became a source of embarrassment for the family. It is on account of this that the rebellion of Vistāhm cannot be found in some of the extant *X^w adāy-Nāmag* traditions. Through this mechanism, the complicity of Farrukh Hormozd with the Byzantines against Khusrow II is buried or even lost in some of the accounts at our disposal, unless we consult the *Shāhnāma* of Ferdowsī. Through these editorial manipulations of the Ispahbudhān family, Rustam achieves immortality, becoming the penultimate hero of the *Shāhnāma* of Ferdowsī and the subsequent nationalist psyche. His systematic procrastination in the war against the enemy, his very reluctance to lead his army, and his obstinate pursuit of peace, all of this is eclipsed by his heroic aura in the *Shāhnāma* of Ferdowsī.[2610] Farrukhzād's rebellion against Yazdgird III is even deleted from the pages of Sebeos' narrative and is downplayed in the *Shāhnāma*. Incredibly, this towering Pahlav figure subsequently disappears from the pages of all *X^w adāy-Nāmag* narratives. It is a testimony to the primary importance of the theme of Iran in the *futūḥ* narratives that we have the fortune of following, albeit painstakingly, the saga of this Pahlav dynast when he reappears under his bastardized, Arabicized, name Zīnabī in the accounts of the conquest. And so, only by juxtaposing the *X^w adāy-Nāmag* and the *futūḥ* traditions, we are apprised of Farrukhzād's defection from the Sasanian king and his collaboration with the Arab armies. It is one of the ironies of history that, through this process of redaction, the Ispahbudhān inadvertently also erased most traces of their family's great accomplishments, such as the very name of their progenitor, the great Asparapet, or their creation of an autonomous Ṭabaristān after the Arab conquest by Bāv

---

we did not attempt to locate in the sources. Nonetheless, following Gyselen, we may postulate a Sūrenid descent for this *ērān-spāhbed* of the *kūst-i nēmrōz*; see footnote 840.

[2609] Revisiting the *Shāhnāma* as a historical source, therefore, might lead its ardent student to even predict the find of other seals pertaining to powerful generals of late Sasanian period. One such conjectural seal could belong to an *ērān-spāhbed* of the *kūst-i ādurbādagān* by the name of Farrukh Hormozd (see footnote 806).

[2610] It is one of those happenstances of history that in this Rustam seems to be replicating the great deeds of his namesake, the legendary Kayānid hero, Rustam, of the national epic, both attempting to uphold Iranian kingship in spite of its folly. Ironically, by one account, the Rustam cycle in the *Shāhnāma* is itself inspired by the deeds of another Parthian general, this time from another family, in another epoch, and with a different fate: Orodes II's (57–38 BCE) general, Surena, whose actual name was Rustaham Sūren. Sūren's defeat of the Roman general and *triumvir*, Marcus Licinius Crassus, at the battle of Carrhae in 53 BCE, effectively established the Euphrates as the border between the Roman and Parthian empires in subsequent centuries. Shahbazi, Shapur, 'Carrhae', in Ehsan Yarshater (ed.), *Encyclopaedia Iranica*, New York, 2007b (Shahbazi 2007b).

(another alias of Farrukhzād).[2611]

The Parthians played a crucial role in the demise of the Sasanians through their agreement with the Arabs, although some among them, such as the Mihrāns or the Kārins, put up fierce resistance. In a sense, from the Arsacid through the Umayyad period, the dynamics among the Pahlav dynastic families, and between each of these and the central authorities, had not changed. The crucial dimension of the cooperation of the Pahlav who came to terms with the Arabs—as it was worked into the treatises they made with the conquerors—was the understanding that they would continue to control their realm after the collapse of the Sasanian empire. The demise of the Sasanians, therefore, did not mean the demise of the Parthians. As we shall hope to show in a sequel to this study, it is in this sense that, through their very presence in the post-conquest centuries, the Parthian families promoted the continuity of the Iranian national tradition. The very mechanism through which Maᶜmarī compiled the prose *Shāhnāma* in the tenth century, bears witness to the direct part played by the Parthians in creating one of the very first and most important prototypes of the *Book of Kings*, the prose *Shāhnāma* of Abū Manṣūr ᶜAbdalrazzāq (*Shāhnāma-i Abū Manṣūrī*). It was, after all, the very progeny of the Kanārangīyān, the families of ᶜAbdalrazzāq[2612] and Maᶜmarī, who gathered the "*dihqānān*, the wise (*farzānigān*) and sagacious (*jahāndīdigān*) men" of the very heartlands of the Pahlav regions, Ṭūs and Nīshāpūr, in order to compose the prose *Shāhnāma*.[2613]

Parthian genealogical traditions were very much in vogue during the tenth century in the northern and eastern parts of Iran. Leaving aside the genealogical claims of various smaller dynasties that assumed power in Gīlān, Ṭabaristān, and Azarbāyjān during this period, not only did the various patrons of the *Shāhnāma*, Maᶜmarī and Abū Manṣūr ᶜAbdalrazzāq, claim Parthian heritage by tracing their ancestry to the Kanārangīyān, but so did the very dynasty under whose patronage an alleged revival of the Iranian tradition took place, namely, the Samanids, who claimed their descent from none other than the Parthian Mihrāns and the emblematic figure of this family, the rebel Bahrām-i Chūbīn. This they did at a time when the Buyids were claiming Sasanian genealogy and reviving the title of *Shāhānshāh*, King of Kings. In fact, Bīrūnī gives ample evidence of the popularity, as he puts it, of forged genealogical traditions during this period. Forged or not, and even if Bīrūnī's partiality in promoting the ancestral claims of the Buyids were to be denied, there is no doubt that four centuries after the fact, Pārsīg–Pahlav genealogical warfare was still in full sway

[2611] Bāv's story does not belong to the *Shāhnāma* by design, but is found in the *Tārīkh-i Ṭabaristān*, suggesting that the *Xʷadāy-Nāmag* tradition extended beyond Ferdowsī's artificial confines to pre-conquest Iran. The redactional efforts even led in this case to a pseudo-genealogy to the Sasanian Kayūs.

[2612] Bīrūnī's doubts as to the veracity of the genealogy that this family claimed must be dismissed on account of the political rivalries among the Buyids and the Samanids in the tenth century and the role of the ᶜAbdalrazzāq family in this complex situation.

[2613] From Herāt and Sīstān, they probably also gathered the wonderfully diverse Sīstānī cycle of the *Shāhnāma*, a substantial part of which is extant outside the *Shāhnāma*. Qazvini 1984, pp. 34–35.

among the Iranians.[2614] In a sense then, one can perhaps argue that there was no such thing as a *revival* of ancient Iranian traditions during the tenth century, for these had never become extinct to require resurrection in the first place. The interlude of the mid-eighth to the tenth centuries, however, has to be further investigated in order to substantiate this last claim.

The defeat of the Iranians by the Arabs in the course of the conquest has left a scar on the national Iranian historical memory. This was articulated in no uncertain terms by Ferdowsī more than a millennium ago, and has been part and parcel of the Iranian nationalist discourse to this day. For Ferdowsī as well as for some of the scholars who address this juncture of Iranian history, the Arab conquest of Iran marks a watershed. This is a juncture wherein the *pre-Islamic* history of Iran is presumed to have ceased, and the history of *Islamic* Iran to have commenced. This perspective is no longer tenable considering the results of the present study. If substantial Pahlav domains continued to be ruled *de facto* by Parthian dynasts even after the Arab conquests in the seventh century, then the process of the conquest needs to be reassessed and the dichotomous rendition of this juncture of Iranian history as pre- versus post-Islamic history should be deemed a false dichotomy. The Arab conquests were not the watershed that one has made of them.[2615] Shifting paradigms, however, is no easy matter. It might serve us well, therefore, to trust those isolated traditions that do not have the *postfacto* imprint of Islamic narratives of conquests, and portray the conquests as what conquests have always been in the histories of peoples: access to resources, in this case Arab access to the entrepôts of trade. Once we recognize this, it might be easier to fathom why the Arabs did not migrate *en masse* to the Iranian plateau and settle in its various territories, and why the Pahlav agreed to the arrangements that we have delineated. The Arab conquest was not a nineteenth-century British colonial endeavor, but an altogether different matter. If we recognize this, moreover, we can more easily understand why the comparatively meagre Arab settlement and colonization that did in fact take place, was not in the length and breadth of the Iranian lands, but mainly in Outer Khurāsān, *Transoxiana*, and the lands beyond these, just as the Arabs had guaranteed the Parthian dynast Rustam.[2616] This is perhaps the true meaning of those traditions that maintain that the Arab intentions were honorable.[2617]

Another, more crucial, leap of faith, however, has been argued in this investigation, a leap that, nevertheless, and in view of the new evidence presented here, must be taken seriously. The early conquest of Iraq did not begin at the inception of the reign of the last Sasanian king, Yazdgird III, in 632, as it is currently believed, but in 628, at a time that was most opportune for it:

[2614]There is no doubt that Iranian genealogists vied with Arab genealogist during this period. Ibn Balkhī calls the former the Persian genealogists (*nassāb-i Pārsīyān*). Ibn Balkhī 1995, p. 11.

[2615]Insofar as the colonial dimension of the Arab conquest has been highlighted, we should probably also reckon that our scholarly heritage has a nineteenth-century colonial and imperial context.

[2616]For the issue of Arab settlement, see also Pourshariati 1998.

[2617]Ṭabarī 1992, p. 68, de Goeje, 2272.

immediately after the devastating Sasanian–Byzantine wars of 30 years, at the end of Shīrūyih Qubad's reign, when, too little too late, the powers of late antiquity realized in fact that "from the Arab regions strong winds were blowing." The interregnum period of 628–632 was a time of utter confusion. As troops had been dispersed in the wake of the Byzantine–Sasanian war, resulting in the formation of three distinct armies of the Sasanian empire, and as the Pārsīg–Pahlav rivalry had intensified, the perfect power vacuum had been created in Syria, in Iraq, as well as on the Iranian plateau. The Arabs naturally took advantage of this chaotic situation. After we delete what we know to be the postfacto *hijra*, *annalist*, and *caliphal* chronological constructions of the *futūḥ* literature, Sayf's traditions of the early conquest of Iraq synchronize perfectly well with the one chronological given that scholarship had hitherto systematically refused to reckon with: the Sasanian chronological indicators of the reigns of the ephemeral kings and queens of the period 628–632 CE. After all, as Balʿamī informs us, Muḥammad's flight from Mecca to Medina (the *hijra*) did not become the calendar landmark of choice for *all* the various groups within the nascent Muslim community, even in later decades. For a group of Balʿamī's Shīʿite contemporaries, as the author underlines, insisted that the death of Ḥusayn was a more decisive moment in the history of the early Muslim community than the *hijra* of the Prophet.[2618] If the Shīʿites were too biased to lend credibility to this assessment, what ought we do with a tradition describing a group of Balʿamī's contemporaries who claimed Muʿāwiya's assumption of the caliphate to be a more appropriate calendar marker for the Muslims than the *hijra* of Muḥammad from his native city?[2619] While sometime in 16–18 AH/637–639 CE some might have decided to mark Muḥammad's *hijra* as a watershed event in early Islamic history, therefore, up until the tenth century, there was still no consensus on the matter, albeit the dissent was probably voiced by a minority.

How will our chronological reconstruction of the early Arab conquests of Iran affect our reconstruction of early Islamic history, and our appreciation of the Islamic historiographical tradition, especially the *futūḥ* narratives, beyond the strides that scholarship has already made apropos these? If alive, where was the Prophet Muḥammad when the early conquests were taking place? Why does his name not appear in the narratives of the conquest? And what was his relationship to Abū Bakr and ʿUmar? The traditional Islamic narratives of origin cannot quite accommodate the picture that we have presented in this study.

[2618] Balʿamī 1987, p. 87.
[2619] Balʿamī 1987, pp. 87–88.

Tables, figures and map

Key

The following symbols and abbreviations will be used in the tables and the index.

Abbreviations

Khu Khusrow

Hor Hormozd IV

Phl Pahlav faction under the leadership of the Ispahbudhān, including the army of Azarbāyjān.

Prs Pārsīg faction under the leadership of Fīrūzān, including the Nīmrūzī faction and the *army of Persia and the East*.

Shr Shahrvarāz's conquest army from the Byzantine wars.

Arm Armenians

Trk Turks

Dlm Daylam

Marks

* conjectural

↫ collaborator or defector

† died

~~xxx~~ contradictory or inconsistent

⇌ identification

Battle or Raid	King and Faction	CE Date (revised)	Commanders and Generals	
			Iranian	Arab
Ubullah	Ardashīr III (*Prs*, *Phl*)	628	Hormozd^{Prs}, Qubād^{Phl}, Anūshjān^{Phl}, Āzādbih, Jābān	Khālid
Dhāt al-Salāsil	Ardashīr III (*Prs*, *Phl*)	*629	Hormozd$^{\dagger Prs}$, Qubād^{Phl}, Anūshjān^{Phl}	Khālid
Madhār	Ardashīr III (*Prs*, *Phl*)	629–30	Qārīn$^{\dagger Phl}$, Anūshjān$^{\dagger Phl}$, Qubād$^{\dagger Phl}$	Khālid
Walajah	Ardashīr III (*Prs*, *Phl*)	629–30	Bahman Jādhūyih^{Prs}, Andarzghar	Khālid
Ullays	Ardashīr III (*Phl*)	630	Jābān	Khālid
Maqr	Shahrvarāz (*Prs*, *Shr*)	630	Fīrūzān^{Prs}, Jābān, Āzādbih	Khālid
Veh Ardashīr	Shahrvarāz (*Prs*, *Shr*)	630	Bahman Jādhūyih^{Prs}, Āzādbih	Khālid
Anbār	*Shahrvarāz (*Prs*, *Shr*)	*630	Bahman Jādhūyih^{Prs}, Shīrzād	Khālid
ʿAyn Tamr	Shahrvarāz (*Prs*, *Shr*)	630	Mihrān Bahrām-i Chūbīn^{Shr}	Khālid
Dūmat al-Jandal	*Shahrvarāz (*Shr*, **Prs*)	*630	Rūzbih, Zarmihr	Khālid
Ḥuṣayd	*Shahrvarāz (*Shr*, **Prs*)	*630	Zarmihr†, Rūzbih†, Mahbūdhān	Khālid
Firāḍ	Shahrvarāz (*Shr*)	630	Hormozd Jādhūyih^{*Shr}	Muthan
Namāriq	Būrāndukht (*Phl*)	631	Rustam^{Phl}, Narsī^{Phl}, Jābān	Muthan
Kaskar	Būrāndukht (*Phl*)	631	Narsī^{Phl}, Jālīnūs^{Arm}, Tīrūyih^{Phl}, Vindūyih^{Phl}	Abū ʿUbayd
Buwayb	Būrāndukht (*Phl*, *Prs*)	*631	Fīrūzān^{Prs}, Shahrvarāz$^{\dagger Shr}$, Bahman Jādhūyih^{Prs}, Mihrān-i Hamadānī$^{\dagger Phl}$, Rustam^{Phl}, Āzādbih	Muthan
Bridge	Būrāndukht (*Phl*, *Prs*)	632	Bahman Jādhūyih^{Prs}, Jālīnūs^{Arm}	Abū ʿUbayd†

Table 6.1: **Conquest of Iraq:** tentative chronology of the battles during the interregnum (628–632), erroneously dated in the *futūḥ* to 12–13 AH/633–634 CE.

Battles and Conquests	Yazdgird's Location	CE Date	Commanders and Generals	
			Iranian	Arab
Qādisiya	*Ctesiphon*	635	Rustam$^{\dagger Phl}$, Kanārang^{Phl}, Vindūyih^{Phl}, Tīrūyih^{Phl}, Mušeł$^{\dagger Arm}$, Grigor$^{\dagger Arm}$, Mihrān-i Bahrām-i Rāzī^{Phl}, Shahrīyār$^{\dagger Phl}$, Fīrūzān^{Prs}, Hurmuzān^{*Prs}	Sa'd b. Abī Waqqāṣ
Ahvāz	*Ḥulwān*	636	Hurmuzān^{*Prs}	ʿUtbah
Jalūlāʾ	*Ḥulwān*	*637	Mihrān-i Bahrām-i Rāzī$^{\dagger Phl}$, Farrukhzād^{Phl}, Fīrūzān^{Prs}, Varaztirots'^{Arm}	Hāshim b. ʿUtbah
Rām Hurmurz	*Iṣfahān*	637	Hurmuzān^{*Prs}, Sīyāh$^{↫}$	Abū Mūsā ʾAshʿarī
Tustar	*Iṣṭakhr*	637	Hurmuzān$^{*Prs ↫}$	Nuʿmān
Nihāvand	*Kirmān*	642	Varaztirots'^{Arm}, Bahman Jādhūyih^{Prs}, Fīrūzān$^{\dagger Prs}$,	Nuʿmān
Hamadān	*Kirmān*	642	Qārīn^{Phl}, Dīnār$^{↫}$	Nuʿmān
Iṣfahān	*Kirmān*	642	Shahrvarāz Jādhūyih$^{\dagger Phl}$, Fādhūsfān, Bahman Jādhūyih$^{\dagger Prs}$	Nuʿmān
Wāj Rūdh	**Sīstān*	642–43	Mūtā^{Dlm}, Isfandīyār^{Phl}, Varaztirots'$^{\dagger Arm}$, Farrukhzād^{Phl}	Nuʿaym
Fārs	**Sīstān*	*644		Aḥnaf
Rayy	*Marv*	651	Sīyāvakhsh^{Phl}, Farrukhzād$^{Phl ↫}$	Nuʿaym
Damāvand	*Marv*	*651	Mardānshāh^{Phl}	Nuʿaym
Qūmis		~~643~~		Suwayd
Gurgān	*Marv*	~~639~~, *651	Ṣūl^{Trk}	Suwayd
Ṭabaristān	*Marv*	~~643~~, 651	Ṣūl^{Trk}, Farrukhzād$^{Phl ↫}$, Jīl-i Jīlānshāh^{Prs}	Suwayd
Khurāsān	*Marv*†	652	Kanārang$^{Phl ↫}$, Māhūy^{*Phl}	
Nīshāpūr		*652	Kanārang$^{Phl ↫}$, Aswār^{Phl}, Burzīn Shāh^{Phl}	ʿAbdallāh b. ʿĀmir
Azarbāyjān		~~643~~, >651	Isfandīyār$^{Phl ↫}$, Bahrām^{Phl}	Bukayr
Darband			Shahrvarāz^{Shr}	Surāqah
Armenia		653	T'ēodoros$^{Arm ↫}$	
Bādghīs		654	Kārin$^{\dagger Phl}$	Sulāmī

Table 6.2: **Conquest of Iran**: tentative reconstruction, including Yazdgird III's location during his flight.

Seal	King	Kūst	Name	Family
1a	**Khu I**	**East**	**Chihr-Burzēn** (Sīmāh-i Burzīn)	Kārin (*Phl*)
1b	**Hor**	**East**	**Dād-Burz-Mihr** (Dādmihr)	Kārin (***Phl***)
A				
2a	**Khu I**	**South**	**Wahrām Ādurmāh** (Bahrām-i Māh Ādhar)	
2b	**Hor**			
2c	**Khu**	**South**	**Wēh-Shābuhr**	(***Prs***)
B				
2d/1	**Khu II**	**South**	**Pīrag-i Shahrwarāz** (Shahrvarāz)	Mihrān (*Phl*)
2d/2				**Mihrān** (*Phl*)
3a	**Khu II**	*East	**Wistakhm** (Vistāhm)	Ispahbudhān (*Phl*)
3b	**Hor**	**West**		
4a	**Khu I**	**North**	**Gōr-gōn** (Gołon)	**Mihrān** (*Phl*)
4b	**Khu I**	**North**	**Sēd-hōsh**	**Mihrān** (*Phl*)

Table 6.3: **Seals:** the recently discovered seals of eight *spāhbeds*. Information attested on the seals is in boldface.

Figure 6.1: Seal 3b of the *ērān-spāhbed* Vistāhm.

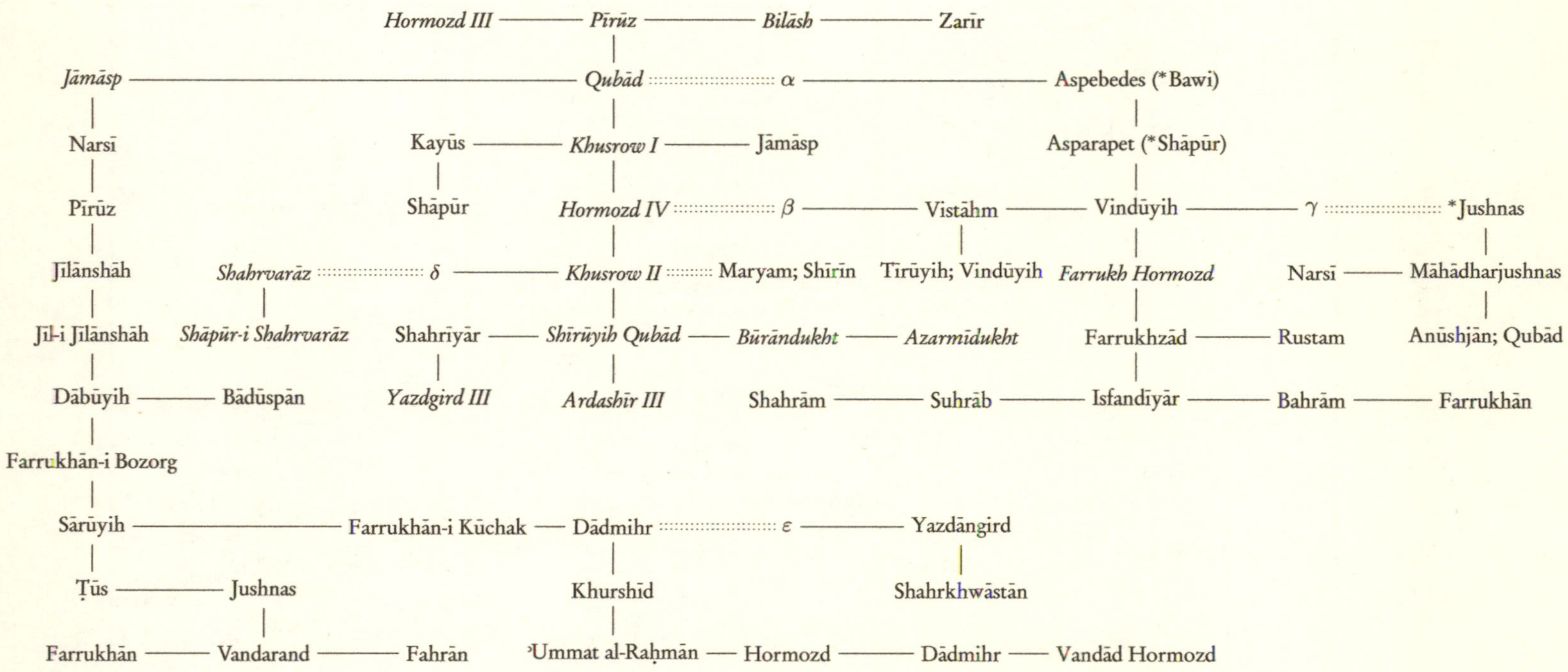

Table 6.4: **Genealogical tree**: the Sasanians (middle), Āl-i Jāmāsp (left), and the Ispahbudhān (right) from the time of Hormozd III. Monarchs are in italics; a double dotted line indicates a marital relationship; a Greek letter denotes a wife whose name is unknown.

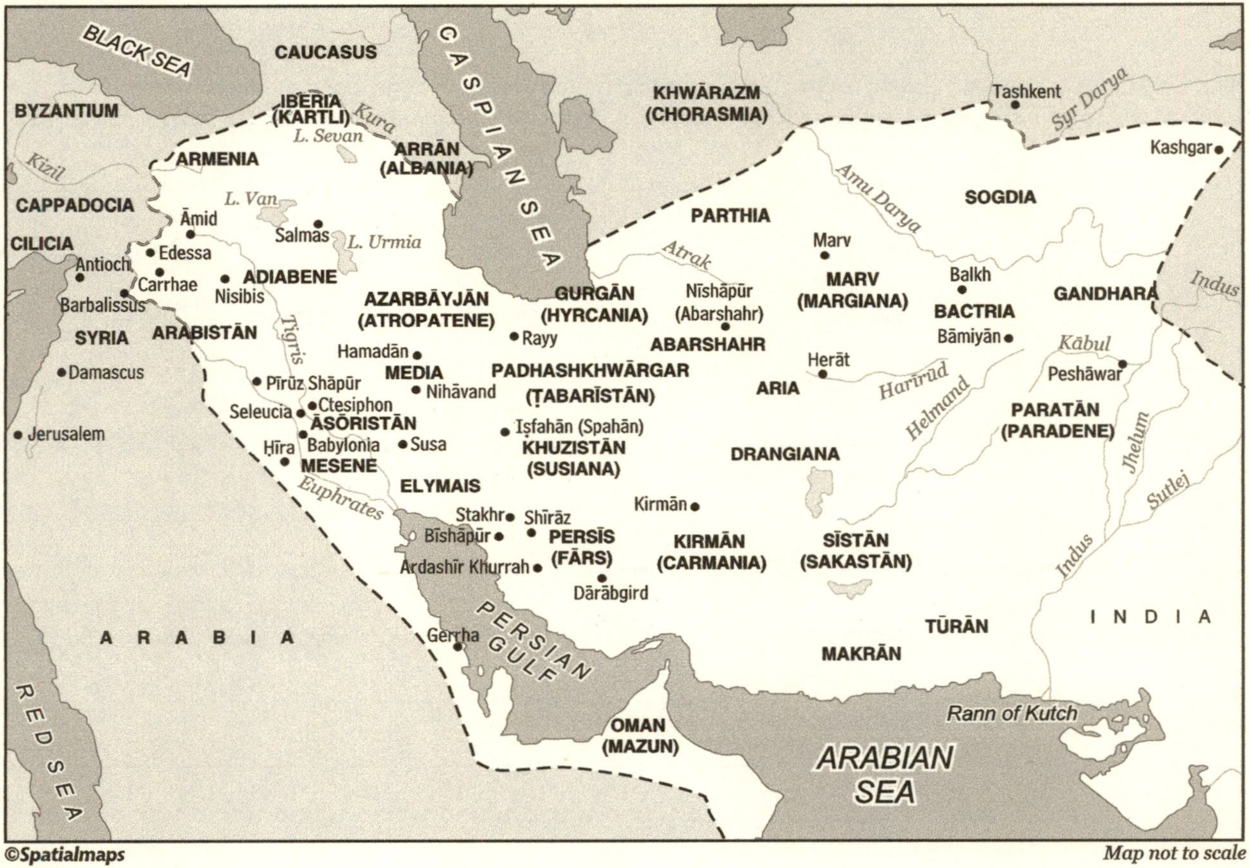

Figure 6.2: **Map of the Sasanian empire**: fourth century CE

Bibliography

For our citation conventions, see p. xii. The numbers between brackets after a reference refer to the pages on which the source is cited.

Aban Yasht 1883, *Ābān Yasht*, vol. 23 of *Sacred Books of the East*, Oxford University Press, 1883, translated by James Darmesteter. [394]

Abbas, I., 'Barmakids', in Ehsan Yarshater (ed.), *Encyclopaedia Iranica*, pp. 806–809, New York, 1991. [175]

Agapius of Manjib, *Kitāb al-ʿUnvān*, vol. 8 of *Patrologia Orientalis*, 1911, edited and translated by A. Vasiliev. [146, 442]

Agha, Saleh Said, *The Agents and Forces that Toppled the Umayyad Caliphate*, Ph.D. thesis, University of Toronto, 1993. [416]

Agha, Saleh Said, *The Revolution which Toppled the Umayyads: Neither Arab nor ʿAbbāsid*, Leiden, 2003. [416, 425]

Altheim, Franz and Stiehl, Ruth, *Ein asiatischer Staat: Feudalismus unter den Sasaniden und ihren Nachbarn*, Wiesbaden, 1954. [41]

Amoretti, B.S., 'Sects and Heresies', in Ehsan Yarshater (ed.), *Cambridge History of Iran: The Seleucid, Parthian, and Sasanian Periods*, vol. 3, p. 481, Cambridge University Press, 1983. [422, 424, 433]

Āmulī, Mowlānā Owliyā, *Tārīkh-i Rūyān*, vol. 64 of *Intishārāt-i bonyād-i farhang-i Irān*, Tehran, 1969, edited by Manuchihr Sotudih. [288, 442]

Anoshiravan 1966, *Kārnāmag-i Anōshīravān*, vol. 254 of *Journal Asiatique*, pp. 16–45, 1966, translated by M. Grignaschi. [365]

Arda Wiraz 1999, *Ardā Wīrāz Nāma*, Tehran, 1999, translated by Mihrdad Bahar. [330, 431, 432]

Ardashir 1963, *Kārnāmag-i Ardashīr-i Pāpagān*, Tehran, 1963, translated by Sadegh Hedayat. [46, 47, 366, 367]

Ardashir 1966, *Testament of Ardašīr*, vol. 254 of *Journal Asiatique*, pp. 46–90, 1966, translated by M. Grignaschi. [324, 343]

Ardashir 1967, *Ahd-i Ardashīr*, Beirut, 1967, edited by I. Abbas. [343]

Asmussen, J.P., 'Christians in Iran', in Ehsan Yarshater (ed.), *Cambridge History of Iran: The Seleucid, Parthian, and Sasanian Periods*, vol. 3(2), pp. 924–949, Cambridge University Press, 1983. [323, 325, 347, 348, 349]

Babayan, Kathryn, *Mystics, Monarchs and Messiahs: Cultural Landscapes of Early Modern Iran*, Harvard University Press, 2002. [394]

Bahman Yasht 1880, *Bahman Yasht*, vol. 5 of *Sacred Books of the East*, Oxford University Press, 1880, translated by E.W. West. [390]

Balādhurī, Aḥmad b. Yaḥyā, *Futūḥ al-Buldān*, Leiden, 1968, edited by M.J. de Goeje. [192, 196, 198, 217, 227, 264, 271, 272]

Balʿamī, *Tarjumih-i Tārīkh-i Ṭabarī*, Tehran, 1959, edited by M.J. Mashkur. [13, 89, 90, 158, 175, 179, 182, 183, 186, 188, 197, 198, 206, 210, 212, 213, 217, 218, 225, 234, 241, 243, 244, 247, 248, 249, 250, 251, 254, 255, 278, 279, 280, 306, 343, 376, 380, 437, 438]

Balʿamī, *Tārīkh-nama-i Ṭabarī*, Tehran, 1987, edited by Muhammad Rowshan. [440, 442, 444, 465]

Bausani, Alessandro, *Religion in Iran: From Zoroaster to Baha'ullah*, New York, 2000, translated by J.M. Marchesi. [326, 329, 351, 352, 422]

Bayhaqī, Ibrāhīm b. Muḥammad, *Al-Maḥāsin wa 'l-Masāwī*, Giessen, 1902, edited by F. Schwally. [402]

Bayhaqī, Ibrāhīm b. Muḥammad, *Taʾrīkh-i Bayhaq*, Tehran, 1938, edited by Ahmad Bahmanyar. [246]

Beeston, A.F.L. and Shahîd, Irfan, 'Ḥīra', in P. Bearman, Th. Bianquis, C.E. Bosworth, E. van Donzel, and W.P. Heinrichs (eds.), *Encyclopaedia of Islam*, Leiden, 2007. [69]

Belardi, Walter, 'Mithra, Arbiter and Rex', in Ugo Bianchi (ed.), *Mysteria Mithrae*, pp. 689–700, Leiden, 1979. [353, 411, 432]

Bickerman, E., 'The Seleucid Period', in Ehsan Yarshater (ed.), *Cambridge History of Iran: The Seleucid, Parthian, and Sasanian Periods*, vol. 3(1), Cambridge University Press, 1983. [19]

Bier, C., Boyce, Mary, and Chaumont, M.L., 'Anāhīd', in Ehsan Yarshater (ed.), *Encyclopaedia Iranica*, New York, 2007. [326]

Bīrūnī, Muḥammad b. Aḥmad, *The Chronology of Ancient Nations*, London, 1879, translation by C.E. Sachau. [14]

Bīrūnī, Muḥammad b. Aḥmad, *Āthār al-Bāqiya*, Tehran, 1984, translated by Akbar Danasirisht. [13, 49, 354, 371, 372, 373, 374, 376, 379, 427, 428, 429, 435, 436, 446]

Bivar, A.D.H., *Catalogue of the Western Asiatic Seals in the British Museum, Stamp Seals II, the Sasanian Dynasty*, London, 1969. [391]

Bivar, A.D.H., 'The Political History of Iran under the Arsacids', in Ehsan Yarshater (ed.), *Cambridge History of Iran: The Seleucid, Parthian, and Sasanian Periods*, vol. 3(1), Cambridge University Press, 1983. [22, 36]

Bivar, A.D.H., 'Gorgān', in Ehsan Yarshater (ed.), *Encyclopaedia Iranica*, New York, 2007a. [20]

Bivar, A.D.H., 'Hayāṭila', in P. Bearman, Th. Bianquis, C.E. Bosworth, E. van Donzel, and W.P. Heinrichs (eds.), *Encyclopaedia of Islam*, Leiden, 2007b. [74]

Bizet, Joseph and Cumont, Franz, *Les mages Hellénisés: Zoroastre, Ostanès et Hystaspe d'après la tradition Grecque*, Paris, 1938. [358]

Blochet, E., *Le messianisme dans l'hétérodoxie Musulmane*, Paris, 1903. [446]

de Blois, F. and Vogelsang, W., 'Dahae', in Ehsan Yarshater (ed.), *Encyclopaedia Iranica*, pp. 581–582, New York, 1991. [19]

Bosworth, C.E., 'Atrak', in Ehsan Yarshater (ed.), *Encyclopaedia Iranica*, New York, 2007a. [19]

Bosworth, C.E., 'Kūmis', in P. Bearman, Th. Bianquis, C.E. Bosworth, E. van Donzel, and W.P. Heinrichs (eds.), *Encyclopaedia of Islam*, Leiden, 2007b. [112]

Bosworth, C.E., 'Zābul, Zābulistān', in P. Bearman, Th. Bianquis, C.E. Bosworth, E. van Donzel, and W.P. Heinrichs (eds.), *Encyclopaedia of Islam*, Leiden, 2007c. [113]

Boyce, Mary, 'The Parthian Gōsān and Iranian Minstrel Tradition', *Journal of the Royal Asiatic Society* 1, (1957a), pp. 10–45. [10, 22]

Boyce, Mary, 'Some Reflections on Zurvanism', *Bulletin of the School of Oriental and African Studies* 19(2), (1957b), pp. 304–316. [340]

Boyce, Mary, 'Bībī Shahrbānū and the Lady of Pārs', *Bulletin of the School of Oriental and African Studies* 30, (1967), pp. 30–44. [431]

Boyce, Mary, 'On the Sacred Fires of the Zoroastrians', *Bulletin of the School of Oriental and African Studies* 31(1), (1968), pp. 52–68. [328]

Boyce, Mary, 'On Mithra's Part in Zoroastrianism', *Bulletin of the School of Oriental and African Studies* 32. [366]

Boyce, Mary, 'On Mithra, Lord of Fire', in *Acta Iranica 4: Hommages et Opera Minora, Monumentum H.S. Nyberg*, pp. 69–76, Leiden, 1975. [352, 357]

Boyce, Mary, *Zoroastrians: Their Religious Beliefs and Practices*, London, 1979. [96, 321, 326, 328, 329, 333, 339, 340, 361, 362, 363, 364, 365, 366, 385, 386, 393, 412, 421, 423]

Boyce, Mary, 'Iranian Festivals', in Ehsan Yarshater (ed.), *Cambridge History of Iran: The Seleucid, Parthian, and Sasanian Periods*, vol. 3(2), pp. 792–815, Cambridge University Press, 1983a. [371, 372, 375, 379]

Boyce, Mary, 'Parthian Writings and Literature', in Ehsan Yarshater (ed.), *Cambridge History of Iran: The Seleucid, Parthian, and Sasanian Periods*, vol. 3(2), pp. 1151–1166, Cambridge University Press, 1983b. [48]

Boyce, Mary, 'Ādur Burzēn Mihr', in Ehsan Yarshater (ed.), *Encyclopaedia Iranica*, pp. 472–473, New York, 1991a. [362, 364]

Boyce, Mary, 'Arsacids: IV. Arsacid Religion', in Ehsan Yarshater (ed.), *Encyclopaedia Iranica*, pp. 540–541, New York, 1991b. [323, 358]

Boyce, Mary, 'Cattle: II. In Zoroastrianism', in Ehsan Yarshater (ed.), *Encyclopaedia Iranica*, pp. 80–84, New York, 1991c. [374]

Boyce, Mary, 'Ādur Farnbāg', in Ehsan Yarshater (ed.), *Encyclopaedia Iranica*, p. 474, New York, 1991d. [363]

Boyce, Mary, 'Gushnasp', in Ehsan Yarshater (ed.), *Encyclopaedia Iranica*, pp. 475–476, New York, 1991e. [362]

Boyce, Mary, *Zoroastrianism: Its Antiquity and Constant Vigour*, Costa Mesa, 1992. [321, 322, 328, 339, 350, 351, 352, 361, 363]

Boyce, Mary, *A History of Zoroastrianism I: The Early Periord*, Leiden, 1996. [357]

Bozorgmehr 1971, *Andarz-nāma-i Bozorgmehr-i Ḥakīm*, Isfahan, 1971, translated by F. Abadani. [126, 461]

Brody, Robert, 'Judaism in the Sasanian Empire: A Case Study in Religious Coexistence', in Shaul Shaked and Amnon Netzer (eds.), *Irano-Judaica II: Studies Relating to Jewish Contacts with Persian Culture throughout the Ages*, pp. 52–62, 1990. [348]

Browne, E.G., *A Literary History of Persia: From the Earliest Times until Ferdowsi*, Bethesda, reprint edn., 1997. [427, 428]

Brunner, Christopher, 'Geographical and Administrative Divisions: Settlements and Economy', in Ehsan Yarshater (ed.), *Cambridge History of Iran: The Seleucid, Parthian, and Sasanian Periods*, vol. 3(2), pp. 747–778, Cambridge University Press, 1983. [22, 39]

Bulliet, Richard W., *Conversion to Islam in the Medieval Period: An Essay in Quantitative History*, Harvard University Press, 1979. [18, 416, 423]

Bulliet, Richard W., *Islam: The View from the Edge*, Columbia University Press, 1995. [423]

Bundahishn 1990, *Bundahish*, Tehran, 1990, translated by Mihrdad Bahar. [264, 376, 412, 434]

Buzandaran 1989, *The Epic Histories: Buzandaran Patmut'iwnk'*, Harvard University Press, 1989, translation and commentary by Nina Garsoian. [64, 72, 128, 131, 136, 154]

Cameron, Averil and Conrad, Lawrence I. (eds.), *The Byzantine and Early Islamic Near East, III: States, Resources and Armies*, Princeton, 1995, papers of the Third Workshop on Late Antiquity and Early Islam. [7]

Chaumont, M.L., 'Armenia and Iran: The pre-Islamic Period', in Ehsan Yarshater (ed.), *Encyclopaedia Iranica*, pp. 417–438, New York, 1991. [12, 43, 68, 71, 131, 153, 154]

Choksy, Jamsheed K., *Conflict and Cooperation: Zoroastrian Subalterns and Muslim Elites in Medieval Iranian Society*, Columbia University Press, 1997. [18]

Christensen, Arthur, *Vazʿ-i Milat va Dowlat va Darbār dar Dowrih-i Shāhanshāhī-i Sāsāniyān*, Tehran, 1935, translated and annotated by Mujtaba Minovi. [48]

Christensen, Arthur, *Les gestes des rois dans les traditions de l'Iran antique*, Paris, 1936. [413, 461]

Christensen, Arthur, *L'Iran sous les Sassanides*, Copenhagen, 1944. [2, 7, 27, 40, 47, 48, 49, 51, 52, 55, 56, 57, 58, 59, 60, 68, 73, 77, 83, 84, 85, 95, 106, 110, 156, 161, 205, 269, 274, 299, 351, 371]

Christensen, Arthur, *The Kayanians*, Bombay, 1993a, translated by F. N. Tumboowalla. [36, 37]

Christensen, Peter, *The Decline of Iranshahr: Irrigation and Environments in the History of the Middle East 500 B.C. to 1500 A.D.*, Copenhagen, 1993b. [17, 40]

Clauss, Manfred, *The Roman Cult of Mithras: The God and his Mysteries*, Edinburgh University Press, 2000, translated by R. Gordon. [386]

Cobb, Paul M. and Kaegi, Walter E., 'Heraclius, Shahrbarāz and Ṭabarī', in Hugh Kennedy (ed.), *Al-Ṭabarī: A Medieval Muslim Historian and His Work*, pp. 121–143, Princeton, 2002. [141, 142, 144, 146, 152]

Colledge, Malcolm A.R., *The Parthians*, New York, 1967. [21]

Colledge, Malcolm A.R., *The Parthian Period*, Leiden, 1986. [21]

Collins, John, 'Genre, Ideology and Social Movements in Jewish Apocalypticism', in John J. Collins and James H. Charlesworth (eds.), *Mysteries and Revelations: Apocalyptic Studies since the Uppsala Colloquium*, pp. 11–33, Sheffield Academic Press, 1991. [411]

Colpe, Carsten, 'Development of Religious Thought', in Ehsan Yarshater (ed.), *Cambridge History of Iran: The Seleucid, Parthian, and Sasanian Periods*, vol. 3(2), Cambridge University Press, 1983. [331]

Cook, Michael and Crone, Patricia, *Hagarism: The Making of the Islamic World*, Cambridge University Press, 1977. [167, 420]

Crone, Patricia, *Slaves on Horses: The Evolution of Islamic Polity*, Cambridge University Press, 1980. [15, 164, 165, 167, 239, 240, 449]

Crone, Patricia, *God's Caliph: Religious Authority in the First Centuries of Islam*, Cambridge University Press, 1986. [35]

Crone, Patricia, 'Review of Sharon's *Black Banners*', *Bulletin of the School of Oriental and African Studies* 50, (1987), pp. 134–136, review of Sharon 1983. [426]

Crone, Patricia, 'On the Meaning of the ʿAbbāsid Call to al-Riḍā', in C.E. Bosworth (ed.), *The Islamic World from Classical to Modern Times*, pp. 95–111, Princeton, 1989. [414]

Crone, Patricia, 'Khālid b. Walīd', in Ehsan Yarshater (ed.), *Encyclopaedia Iranica*, p. 928a, New York, 1991a. [168, 281]

Crone, Patricia, 'Kavād's Heresy and Mazdak's Revolt', *Iran: Journal of Persian Studies* XXIX, (1991b), pp. 21–42. [93, 345, 346]

Crone, Patricia, 'Mawlā', in P. Bearman, Th. Bianquis, C.E. Bosworth, E. van Donzel, and W.P. Heinrichs (eds.), *Encyclopaedia of Islam*, pp. 874–882, Leiden, 2007. [415]

Cumont, Franz, 'The Dura Mithraeum', in John R. Hinnells (ed.), *Mithraic Studies: Proceedings of the First International Congress of Mithraic Studies*, pp. 151–214, Manchester University Press, 1975, edited and translated by E.D. Francis. [389]

Curiel, Raoul and Gyselen, Rika, *Une collection de monnaies de cuivre Arabo-Sasanides*, Paris, 1984. [313]

Curtis, Vesta Sarkhosh, Hillenbrand, Robert, and Rogers, J.M., *The Art and Archaeology of Ancient Persia: New Light on the Parthian and Sasanian Empires*, British Institute of Persian Studies, London, 1998. [24]

Curtis, Vesta Sarkhosh and Malek, H.M., 'History of the Sasanian Queen Boran (AD 629–631)', *Numismatic Chronicle* 158, (1998), pp. 113–129. [208, 209, 217]

Curzon, George N., *Persia and the Persian Question*, London, 1892. [417]

Czegledy, K., 'Bahrām Chubīn and the Persian Apocalyptic Literature', *Acta Orientalia Hungarica* 8, (1958), pp. 21–43. [124, 125, 126, 379, 404, 405, 406, 407, 408, 409, 410, 411, 412, 428]

Dadestan 1993, *Mādigān-i Hazār Dādestān*, Rechtskasuistik und Gerichtspraxis zu Beginn des siebenten Jahrhunderts in Iran, Wiesbaden, 1993, translated by M. Macuch. [336]

Dandamayev, M. and Medvedskaya, I., 'Media', in Ehsan Yarshater (ed.), *Encyclopaedia Iranica*, New York, 2007. [6]

Daniel, Elton, 'Arabs, Persians, and the Advent of the Abbasids Reconsidered', *Journal of the American Oriental Society* 117, (1997), pp. 542–548. [415]

Daniel, Elton L., *The Political and Social History of Khurasan under Abbasid Rule: 747–820*, Bibliotheca Islamica, 1979. [433, 437, 450]

Daniel, Elton L., 'Manuscripts and Editions of Bal'ami's *Tarjamah-yi Tarikh-i Tabari*', *Journal of the American Oriental Society* pp. 282–321. [89]

Darmesteter, James, *Le Zend Avesta*, Annales du Musée Guimet, 1892, 3 volumes. [354]

Daryaee, Touraj, *Soghoot-i Sāsānīyān (The Fall of the Sasanians)*, Tehran, 1994. [223]

Daryaee, Touraj, 'National History or Kayanid History?: The Nature of Sasanid Zoroastrian Historiography', *Iranian Studies* 28, (1995), pp. 129–141. [33, 45]

Daryaee, Touraj, 'Apocalypse Now: Zoroastrian Reflection on the Early Islamic Centuries', *Medieval Encounters* 4, (1998), pp. 188–202. [405]

Daryaee, Touraj, 'The Coinage of Queen Bōrān and its Significance for Late Sasanian Imperial Ideology', *Bulletin of the Asia Institute* 13, (1999), pp. 1–6. [208]

Daryaee, Touraj, 'The Judge and Protector of the Needy during the Sasanian Period', in A.A. Sadeghi (ed.), *Tafazzol Memorial*, pp. 179–187, Tehran, 2001. [197]

Daryaee, Touraj, 'The Changing 'Image of the World': Geography and Imperial Propaganda in Ancient Persia', *Electrum: Studies in Ancient History* 6, (2002), pp. 99–109. [40]

Daryaee, Touraj, 'The Effect of the Arab Muslim Conquest on the Administrative Division of Sasanian Persis/Fars', *Iran: Journal of the British Institute of Persian Studies* 41, (2003), pp. 1–12. [223]

Davis, Dick, *Epic and Sedition: The Case of Ferdowsi's Shāhnāmeh*, University of Arkansas Press, 1992. [36, 460]

Davis, Dick, *Panthea's Children: Hellenistic Novels and Medieval Persian Romances*, New York, 2002. [357]

Debevoise, Neilson C., 'Parthian Problems', *The American Journal of Semitic Languages and Literature* 47, (1931), pp. 73–82. [21]

Debevoise, Neilson C., *A Political History of Parthia*, Chicago University Press, 1938. [21]

Dennett, Daniel C., *Conversion and the Poll Tax in Early Islam*, Harvard University Press, 1950. [416]

Dihkhuda, *Lughat Nāma*, Tehran University Publications, 1998, edited by Muhammad Mo'in and Ja'far Shahidi. [229, 266]

Dīnawarī, Abū Ḥanīfa Aḥmad, *Akhbār al-Ṭiwāl*, Cairo, 1960, edited by Abd al-Mun'im 'Amir Jamal al-Din al-Shayyal. [13, 67, 70, 77, 78, 80, 81, 107, 109, 111, 112, 113, 118, 119, 125, 127, 130, 134, 135, 178, 223, 227, 284, 296]

Dīnawarī, Abū Ḥanīfa Aḥmad, *Akhbār al-Ṭiwāl*, Tehran, 1967, translated by Sadiq Nash'at. [46, 58, 67, 70, 77, 78, 80, 81, 107, 109, 111, 112, 113, 118, 119, 125, 127, 130, 134, 135, 178, 223, 227, 236, 284, 296, 413]

Dinkard 1911, *Dēnkard: The Complete Text of the Pahlavi Dinkard*, Bombay, 1911, translated by D.M. Madan. [323, 337, 338]

Donner, Fred M., *The Early Islamic Conquests*, Princeton University Press, 1981. [7, 69, 80, 164, 165, 166, 168, 190, 193, 211, 213, 218, 281]

Donner, Fred M., 'Centralized Authority and Military Autonomy in the Early Islamic Conquest', in Averil Cameron and Lawrence I. Conrad (eds.), *The Byzantine and Early Islamic Near East, III: States, Resources and Armies*, pp. 337–361, Princeton, 1995. [164]

Donner, Fred M., *Narratives of Islamic Origin: The Beginnings of Islamic Historical Writing*, vol. 14 of *Studies in Late Antiquity and Early Islam*, Princeton, 1998. [162]

Donner, Fred M., 'Baṣra', in Ehsan Yarshater (ed.), *Encyclopaedia Iranica*, New York, 2007a. [237]

Donner, Fred M., 'Sayf b. ʿUmar', in P. Bearman, Th. Bianquis, C.E. Bosworth, E. van Donzel, and W.P. Heinrichs (eds.), *Encyclopaedia of Islam*, Leiden, 2007b. [165]

Doostkhah, Jalil, 'Gorz', in Ehsan Yarshater (ed.), *Encyclopaedia Iranica*, New York, 1991. [375]

Duchesne-Guillemin, J., 'Notes on Zervanism in the Light of Zaehner's *Zurvan*', *Journal of Near Eastern Studies* 15(2), (1956), pp. 108–112. [339, 340]

Duchesne-Guillemin, J., 'Zoroasterian Religion', in Ehsan Yarshater (ed.), *Cambridge History of Iran: The Seleucid, Parthian, and Sasanian Periods*, vol. 3(2), pp. 866–909, Cambridge University Press, 1983. [326, 327, 328, 331, 332, 333, 334, 335, 336, 337, 338]

Dunlop, D.M., 'Barḏaʿa', in P. Bearman, Th. Bianquis, C.E. Bosworth, E. van Donzel, and W.P. Heinrichs (eds.), *Encyclopaedia of Islam*, Leiden, 2007. [116]

Eddy, Samuel K., *The King is Dead: Studies in the Near Eastern Resistance to Hellenism 334–31 B.C.*, University of Nebraska Press, 1961. [34, 35, 322, 360, 361, 445]

Ẹlishē, *History of Vardan and the Armenian War*, Harvard University Press, 1982, translated and commentary by R. Thomson. [12, 43, 44, 64, 65, 70, 71, 300, 338, 348, 349, 350, 375, 387, 391]

Ferdowsī, *Shāhnāma*, Tehran, 1935, edited by S. Nafisi. [68, 69, 70, 77, 78, 79, 80, 81, 102, 104, 108, 113, 119, 120, 121, 122, 123, 124, 125, 126, 128, 130, 132, 147, 148, 153, 154, 155, 156, 174, 175, 180, 228, 229, 230, 236, 261, 266, 267, 269, 278, 298, 299, 363, 367, 368, 370, 372, 382, 383, 384, 398, 399, 400, 402, 403, 404, 461]

Ferdowsī, *Shāhnāma*, Moscow, 1971. [46, 47, 57, 59, 66, 67, 69, 70, 77, 78, 79, 80, 81, 102, 103, 104, 107, 108, 114, 118, 119, 120, 121, 123, 124, 125, 126, 128, 130, 132, 147, 148, 153, 154, 155, 156, 174, 175, 179, 180, 228, 229, 230, 261, 262, 266, 267, 269, 270, 278, 298, 299, 363, 367, 368, 370, 372, 373, 380, 382, 383, 384, 399, 400, 401, 402, 403, 404, 461]

Frawardin Yasht 1883, *Frawardīn Yasht*, vol. 23 of *Sacred Books of the East*, Oxford University Press, 1883, translated by James Darmesteter. [366, 375, 394]

Frye, Richard N., 'Zurvanism Again', *Harvard Theological Review* II(2), (1959), pp. 63–73. [340]

Frye, Richard N., *The Golden Age of Persia: The Arabs in the East*, London, 1975a. [48, 418, 419]

Frye, Richard N., 'Mithra in Iranian History', in John R. Hinnells (ed.), *Mithraic Studies: Proceedings of the First International Congress of Mithraic Studies*, pp. 62–67, Manchester University Press, 1975b. [358, 359]

Frye, Richard N., 'The Political History of Iran Under the Sasanians', in Ehsan Yarshater (ed.), *Cambridge History of Iran: The Seleucid, Parthian, and Sasanian Periods*, vol. 3(1), pp. 119–120, Cambridge University Press, 1983. [50, 52, 56, 57, 74, 161]

Frye, Richard N., 'Feudalism in Iran', *Jerulasem Studies in Arabic Islam* 9, (1987), pp. 13–18. [37]

Frye, Richard N., 'Andragoras', in Ehsan Yarshater (ed.), *Encyclopaedia Iranica*, p. 26, New York, 1991. [20]

Fück, J.W., 'Iyād', in P. Bearman, Th. Bianquis, C.E. Bosworth, E. van Donzel, and W.P. Heinrichs (eds.), *Encyclopaedia of Islam*, Leiden, 2007. [170]

Gardīzī, Abū Saʿīd ʿAbd al-Ḥayy, *Zayn al-Akhbār*, 1968, edited by 'Abd al-Habibi. [427, 435, 436]

Gardīzī, Abū Saʿīd ʿAbd al-Ḥayy, *Taʾrīkh-i Gardīzī*, Tehran, 1984, edited by 'Abd al-Hayy Habibi. [187, 336]

Garsoian, Nina G., 'The Iranian Substratum of Agatʿangelos Cycle', in *Armenia between Byzantium and the Sasanians*, pp. 151–189, London, 1985a, reprinted from Nina G. Garsoian, *East of Byzantium: Syria and Armenia in the Formative Period*, Washington, 1982. [147, 390]

Garsoian, Nina G., *Armenia between Byzantium and the Sasanians*, London, 1985b. [12, 13, 45, 387, 390]

Garsoian, Nina G., 'The Locus of the Death of Kings: Iranian Armenia – the Inverted Image', in *Armenia between Byzantium and the Sasanians*, London, 1985c. [354, 387, 388, 389, 390, 391]

Garsoian, Nina G., 'L'inscription de *Kartīr Sār Mašhad*', in *Armenia between Byzantium and the Sasanians*, London, 1985d. [389]

Garsoian, Nina G., 'Prolegomena to a Study of the Iranian Aspect of Arsacid Armenia', in *Armenia between Byzantium and the Sasanians*, pp. 1–46, London, 1985e. [21, 43, 45]

Garsoian, Nina G., *Des Parthes au Caliphate: quatre lessons sur la formation de l'identité Arménienne*, vol. 10 of *Travaux et mémoires du centre de récherche d'histoire et civilization de Byzance*, Paris, 1997. [391]

Gathas 1975, *The Gāthās of Zarathustra*, vol. 8 of *Acta Iranica*, 1975, translated by Stanley Insler. [373]

Gaube, H., 'Mazdak: Historical Reality or Invention?', *Studia Iranica* 11, (1982), pp. 111–122. [82]

Ghirshman, Roman, *Persian Art, Parthian and Sassanian Dynasties 249 B.C.–651 A.D.*, New York, 1962, translated by Stuart Gilbert and James Emmons. [21]

Gignoux, Philippe, 'Problèmes de distinction et de priorité des sources', in J. Harmatta (ed.), *Prolegomena to the Sources on the History of Pre-Islamic Central Asia*, pp. 137–141, Budapest, 1979. [11]

Gignoux, Philippe, 'Middle Persian Inscriptions', in Ehsan Yarshater (ed.), *Cambridge History of Iran: The Seleucid, Parthian, and Sasanian Periods*, vol. 3(2), pp. 1205–1216, Cambridge University Press, 1983. [38, 327]

Gignoux, Philippe, 'Les quatres régions administratives de l'Iran Sassanide et la symbolique des nombres trois et quatre', *Annali dell'Istituto Universitario Orientale* 44, (1984), pp. 555–572. [95]

Gignoux, Philippe, 'Ardā Wīrāz', in Ehsan Yarshater (ed.), *Encyclopaedia Iranica*, pp. 356–357, New York, 1991a. [330]

Gignoux, Philippe, 'A propos de quelque inscriptions et bulles Sassanides', in *Histoires et Cultes de l'Asie Centrale préislamique: Sources écrites et documents archéologique*, pp. 65–69, 1991b. [95]

Gignoux, Philippe, *Les quatres inscriptions du mage Kirdīr: textes et concordances*, vol. 9 of *Studia Iranica*, Fribourg-en-Brisgau, 1991c. [327, 330, 389, 487]

Gignoux, Philippe, 'Āzarmīgduxt', in Ehsan Yarshater (ed.), *Encyclopaedia Iranica*, New York, 2007a. [206]

Gignoux, Philippe, 'Dastgerd', in Ehsan Yarshater (ed.), *Encyclopaedia Iranica*, New York, 2007b. [38]

Gnoli, Gherardo, 'Farr(ah)', in Ehsan Yarshater (ed.), *Encyclopaedia Iranica*, New York, 2007. [48]

Gnoli, Gherarldo, 'The Quadripartition of the Sassanian Empire', *East and West* 35, (1985), pp. 265–270. [95]

Gnoli, Gherarldo, *The Idea of Iran*, Rome, 1989. [33, 34, 88, 325, 326, 327, 337, 350, 360, 394, 398]

Göbl, Robert, *Sasanian Numismatics*, New York, 1971. [205, 223]

Göbl, Robert, 'Sasanian Coins', in Ehsan Yarshater (ed.), *Cambridge History of Iran: The Seleucid, Parthian, and Sasanian Periods*, vol. 3(1), pp. 322–343, Cambridge University Press, 1983. [137]

Goldziher, 'Islam et Parsism', in *Religion of the Iranian Peoples*, Bombay, 1912, translated by Nariman. [35]

Gutas, Dimitri, *Greek Thought, Arabic Culture: The Graeco-Arabic Translation Movement in Baghdad and Early Abbasid Society (2nd–4th/8th–10th Centuries)*, London, 1998. [35]

Gyselen, Rika, *La géographie administrative de l'empire Sassanide: Les témoignages sigillographiques*, vol. I of *Res Orientales*, Paris, 1989. [36, 40, 115, 184, 197]

Gyselen, Rika, 'La notion Sassanide du Kust î Âdurbâdagân: les premières attestations sigillographiques', *Bulletin de la Société Française de Numismatique* 55, (2000), pp. 213–220. [98]

Gyselen, Rika, *The Four Generals of the Sasanian Empire: Some Sigillographic Evidence*, vol. 14 of *Conferenze*, Rome, 2001a. [11, 39, 60, 63, 95, 98, 100, 101, 103, 104, 105, 108, 109, 110, 115, 116, 117, 120, 121, 124, 125, 142, 156, 216, 296, 364, 379, 400]

Gyselen, Rika, 'Lorsque l'archéologie rencontre la tradition littéraire: les titres des chefs d'armée de l'Iran Sassanide', *Comptes Rendus de l'Académie des Inscriptions et Belles Lettres* Jan, (2001b), pp. 447–459. [98]

Gyselen, Rika, 'Nouveaux matériaux', *Studia Iranica* 24, (2002), pp. 61–69. [12, 85, 90, 98, 126, 186, 365]

Gyselen, Rika, 'Les grands feux de l'empire Sassanide: quelques témoignages sigillographiques', in *Religious themes and texts of pre-Islamic Iran and Central Asia: Studies in honour of Professor Gherardo Gnoli*, Wiesbaden, 2003. [99, 328, 364]

Hamadānī, Ibn al-Faqīh, *al-Buldān*, Leiden, 1885, edited by M.J. de Goeje. [271, 272]

Ḥamdallāh Mustawfī, *Nuzhat al-Qulūb*, Leiden, 1919. [67]

Ḥamza Iṣfahānī, *Taʾrīkh Sinnī Mulūk al-Arḍ wa ʾl-Anbiyāʾ*, Beirut, 1961, edited by Yusuf Ya'qub Maskuni. [170, 192, 246, 262, 283, 483]

Ḥamza Iṣfahānī, *Taʾrīkh Sinnī Mulūk al-Arḍ wa ʾl-Anbiyāʾ*, Tehran, 1988, translation of Ḥamza Iṣfahānī 1961 by Ja'far Shi'ar. [170, 187, 192, 246, 262, 265, 283]

Harper, Prudence O., 'The Ox-Headed Mace in Pre-Islamic Iran', in *Papers in Honour of Professor Mary Boyce*, vol. 24 of *Acta Iranica*, pp. 248–265, Leiden, 1985. [373, 375]

Hinds, Martin, 'The First Arab Conquests in Fārs', in *Studies in Early Islamic History*, pp. 199–232, Princeton, 1996. [236, 237]

Hinnells, John R., 'Reflections on the Bull-Slaying Scene', *Mithraic Studies* 2, (1975), pp. 290–312. [371, 375]

Hoffmann, G., *Auszüge aus syrischen Akten persischer Märtyrer*, vol. 7 of *Abhandlungen für die Kunde des Morgenlandes*, Leipzig, 1980. [49]

Hom Yasht 1880, *Hōm Yasht*, vol. 5 of *Sacred Books of the East*, Oxford University Press, 1880, translated by L.H. Mills. [337]

Howard-Johnston, James, 'The Two Great Powers in Late Antiquity: A Comparison', in Averil Cameron and Lawrence I. Conrad (eds.), *The Byzantine and Early Islamic Near East, III: States, Resources and Armies*, pp. 157–227, 1995. [84]

Hulgårt, Anders, 'Bahman Yahsht: A Persian Apocalypse', in John J. Collins and James H. Charlesworth (eds.), *Mysteries and Revelations: Apocalyptic Studies since the Uppsala Colloquium*, pp. 114–134, Sheffield Academic Press, 1991. [411]

Humback, H., 'Mithra in the Kuṣāṇa Period', in John R. Hinnells (ed.), *Mithraic Studies: Proceedings of the First International Congress of Mithraic Studies*, vol. I, pp. 135–141, 1975. [369]

Humphreys, R. Stephen, *Islamic History: A Framework for Inquiry*, vol. 9, Minneapolis, 1991. [162, 415, 416]

Huyse, Philip, 'Die dreisprachige Inschrift Shâbuhrs I an der Ka'ba-i Zardusht', in *Pahlavi Inscriptions*, vol. 3 of *Corpus Inscriptionum Iranicarum*, 1999a. [38]

Huyse, Philip, 'Kerdīr and the First Sasanians', in Nicolas Sims-Williams (ed.), *Societas Iranologica Europaea: Proceedings of the Third European Conference of Iranian Studies*, vol. I, Wiesbaden, 1999b. [332]

Huyse, Philip, 'Sprachkontakte und Entlehnungen zwischen dem Griechisch / Lateinischen und dem Mitteliranischen', in A. Luther, U. Hartmann, and M. Schuol (eds.), *Grenzüberschreitungen: Formen des Kontakts und Wege des Kulturtransfers zwischen Orient und Okzident im Altertum*, vol. 3 of *Oriens et Occidens*, pp. 197–234, Stuttgart, 2002. [105, 106]

Ibn al-Athīr, ʿIzz al-Dīn, *Al-Kāmil fi 'l-Taʾrīkh*, Beirut, 1862, edited by C.J. Tornberg. [163, 179, 188, 191, 198, 201, 202, 203, 206, 212, 214, 217, 218, 219, 231, 305, 306, 310, 315, 380, 426, 439, 440, 448]

Ibn al-Nadīm, Muḥammad b. Isḥāq, *al-Fihrist*, Tehran, 1987, translated by Muhammad Riḍā Tajaddod. [344, 435, 436]

Ibn Balkhī, *Fārsnāma*, Shiraz, 1995, edited by Mansur Rastgar Fasai. [13, 58, 59, 66, 67, 68, 70, 118, 142, 148, 179, 180, 183, 185, 186, 264, 267, 371, 376, 381, 414, 447, 464]

Ibn Hishām, b. Muḥammad, *Sīrah*, Cairo, 1956. [193]

Ibn Isfandīyār, Muḥammad b. Ḥasan, *Tārīkh-i Ṭabaristān*, Tehran, 1941, edited by 'Abbas Iqbal. [72, 73, 86, 87, 88, 91, 113, 114, 277, 288, 289, 290, 291, 292, 293, 294, 295, 296, 302, 307, 308, 309, 310, 311, 312, 313, 314, 315, 316, 317, 318, 370, 373, 374, 376, 377, 385, 439, 440, 441, 442, 461]

Ibn Saʿd, *Ṭabaqāt al-Kabīr*, Leiden, 1940, edited by E. Sachau. [193]

Ibn Ṭaqṭaqa, Muḥammad b. ʿAlī b. Ṭabāṭabā, *Taʾrīkh-i Fakhrī*, 1988, translated by Muhammad Vahid Golpaygani. [437, 439, 442]

Isfazārī, Muʿīn al-Dīn, *Rowḍāt al-Jannāt fī Owṣāf Madīnat al-Harāt*, Tehran, 1959, edited by Seyyed Muhammad Kazim Imam. [277]

Iṣṭakhrī, *Kitāb al-Masālik wa 'l-Mamālik*, Leiden, 1927, edited by M.J. de Goeje. [372]

Jackson, A.V. William, *From Constantinople to the Home of Omar Khayyam*, New York, 1975. [364]

Jackson, William, 'The Location of the Farnbag Fire, the Most Ancient of Zoroastrian Fires', *Journal of the American Oriental Society* 41, (1921), pp. 81–106. [362]

Jafarey, A., 'Mithra, Lord of the Lands', in Rowman and Littlefield (eds.), *Mithraic Studies: Proceedings of the First International Congress of Mithraic Studies*, pp. 54–61, Manchester University Press, 1975. [366]

Jamasp 1941, *Yādgār-i Jāmāsp*, Sokhan, 1941, translated by Sadegh Hedayat. [407, 408, 409, 411]

Joshua the Stylite, *The Chronicle of Pseudo-Joshua the Stylite*, Liverpool University Press, 2000, translated with notes and introduction by Frank R. Trombley and John W. Watt. [64, 76, 103, 107, 111, 269, 300, 382, 384, 386]

Justi, Ferdinand, *Iranisches Namenbuch*, Marburg, 1895. [102, 106, 114, 117, 119, 120, 143, 146, 157, 163, 179, 184, 187, 197, 198, 205, 206, 251, 302, 305, 307, 378, 379]

Kaegi, Walter, *Byzantium and the Early Islamic Conquests*, Cambridge University Press, 1992. [6, 165, 172, 176, 201, 202]

Keall, E.J., 'Political, Economic, and Social Factors on the Parthian Landscape of Mesapotamia and Western Iran', *Bibliotheca Mesopotamica* 7. [22]

Kellens, J., 'Avesta', in Ehsan Yarshater (ed.), *Encyclopaedia Iranica*, pp. 35–44, New York, 1991. [47]

Kennedy, Hugh, *The Early Abbasid Caliphate*, Totowa, reprint edn., 1981. [438, 443]

Kennedy, Hugh, *The Armies of the Caliphs: Military and Society in the Early Islamic State*, London, 2001. [239]

Khayyāṭ, Khalīfat b., *Taʾrīkh*, Beirut, 1977. [192, 193, 202, 203, 271, 277, 278, 442]

Khorenatsʿi, Moses, *Moses Khorenatsʿi: History of the Armenians*, Harvard University Press, 1978, translated by Robert W. Thomson. [26, 27, 42, 43, 44, 60, 68, 110, 300, 386]

Khurshudian, Eduard, *Die Partischen und Sasanidischen Verwaltungsinstitutionen nach den literarischen und epigraphischen Quellen*, Yerevan, 1998. [49, 61, 62, 83, 115, 120, 126, 186, 195, 267, 268]

Khuzistan 1903, *Chronicon*, Chronica Minora, Paris, 1903, translated by I. Guidi. [236]

Kingsley, Peter, 'The Greek Origin of the Sixth-Century Dating of Zoroaster', *Bulletin of the School of Oriental and African Studies* 37, (1990), pp. 245–265. [321]

Kreyenbroek, Philip G., 'The Zoroastrian Priesthood after the Fall of the Sasanian Empire', in *Transition Periods in Iranian History*, Societas Iranologica Europaea, pp. 151–166, Fribourg-en-Brisgau, 1987. [61]

Kreyenbroek, Philip G., 'Spiritual Authority in Zoroastrianism', *Jerusalem Studies in Arabic and Islam* 17, (1994), pp. 1–16. [323]

Kufi, Abū Muḥammad Aḥmad b. Aʿtham, *Futūḥ*, Tehran, 1921, translation of Kufi 1986 by A.M. Mustowfi al-Hirawi. [271, 274]

Kufi, Abū Muḥammad Aḥmad b. Aʿtham, *al-Futūḥ*, Beirut, 1986. [271, 274, 486]

Labourt, J., *Le Christianisme dans l'empire Perse sous la dynastie Sassanide*, Paris, 1897. [337]

Landua-Tasseron, Ella, 'Sayf b. ʿUmar in Medieval and Modern Scholarship', *Der Islam* 67, (1990), pp. 1–26. [165]

Landua-Tasseron, Ella, 'Features of the pre-Conquest Muslim Armies in the Time of Muḥammad', in *The Byzantine and Early Islamic Near East III: States, Resources and Armies*, pp. 299–337, Princeton, 1995. [163]

Lang, David M., 'Iran, Armenia, and Georgia', in Ehsan Yarshater (ed.), *Cambridge History of Iran: The Seleucid, Parthian, and Sasanian Periods*, vol. 3(1), pp. 505–537, Cambridge University Press, 1983. [13, 43, 44, 73]

Lassner, Jacob, *The Shaping of ʿAbbāsid Rule*, Princeton University Press, Princeton, 1980. [415]

Lecker, M., 'Ridda', in P. Bearman, Th. Bianquis, C.E. Bosworth, E. van Donzel, and W.P. Heinrichs (eds.), *Encyclopaedia of Islam*, Leiden, 2007. [285]

Leder, Stefen, 'The Literary Use of the Khabar', in Averil Cameron and Lawrence I. Conrad (eds.), *The Byzantine and Early Islamic Near East, I: Problems in Literary Source Material*, pp. 277–317, Princeton, 1992. [164, 171]

Lee, A.D., *Information and Frontiers: Roman Foreign Relations in Late Antiquity*, Cambridge University Press, 1993. [41]

Leriche, Pierre and Mackenzie, D.N., 'Duraeuropos', in Ehsan Yarshater (ed.), *Encyclopaedia Iranica*, New York, 2007. [389]

Lockhart, L., 'al-Ahwāz', in P. Bearman, Th. Bianquis, C.E. Bosworth, E. van Donzel, and W.P. Heinrichs (eds.), *Encyclopaedia of Islam*, Leiden, 2007. [236]

Lozinski, Philip, *The Original Homeland of the Parthians*, 's-Gravenhage, 1959. [21]

Lukonin, V.G., *Kultura Sasandskogo Irana*, Moscow, 1969. [38, 487]

Lukonin, V.G., 'Political, Social and Administrative Institutions: Taxes and Trade', in Ehsan Yarshater (ed.), *Cambridge History of Iran: The Seleucid, Parthian, and Sasanian Periods*, vol. 3(2), pp. 119–120, Cambridge University Press, 1983. [23, 37, 41, 48, 49, 50, 106]

Lukonin, V.G., *Tamaddun-i Īrān-i Sāsānī: Īrān dar Sadih-hā-i Sivvum tā Panjum-i Milādī*, Tehran, 1986, translation of Lukonin 1969 by Inayat Allah Riza. [38, 42, 45, 50]

MacKenzie, D.N., *A Concise Pahlavi Dictionary*, Oxford University Press, 1971. [28, 197]

Macler, F., *Histoire d'Héraclius*, Paris, 1904. [301]

Madelung, Wilferd, *Religious Schools and Sects in Medieval Islam*, London, 1985. [18, 422]

Madelung, Wilferd, *Religious Trends in Early Islamic Iran*, Albany, 1988. [17, 422]

Madelung, Wilferd, 'Review of Sharon's *Black Banners*', *Journal of Near Eastern Studies* 48, (1989), pp. 70–72, review of Sharon 1983. [426]

Madelung, Wilferd, *Religious and Ethnic Movements in Medieval Islam*, Brookfield, 1992. [17, 422]

Madelung, Wilferd, 'Mazdakism and the Khurramiyya', in Ehsan Yarshater (ed.), *Religious Trends in Early Islamic Iran*, Albany, 1998. [425]

Madelung, Wilferd, 'Dabuyids', in Ehsan Yarshater (ed.), *Encyclopaedia Iranica*, New York, 2007a. [308, 309, 310, 313, 314]

Madelung, Wilferd, 'Khurramiyya', in Ehsan Yarshater (ed.), *Encyclopaedia Iranica*, Albany, 2007b. [425]

Malandra, W.W., 'Review of Gignoux's *Les quatres inscriptions du mage Kirdīr*', *Journal of the American Oriental Society* 113, (1993), pp. 288–289, review of Gignoux 1991c. [327, 330]

Maqdisī, Muṭahhar b. Ṭāhir, *Kitāb al-Badʿ wa 'l-Taʾrīkh*, Paris, 1919, edited by C. Huart. [439]

Maqdisī, Shams al-Dīn, *Aḥsan al-Taqāsīm fī Maʿrifat al-ʾAqālīm*, Leiden, 1877, edited by M.J. de Goeje. [274]

Marʿashī, Mīr Seyyed Ẓahīr al-Dīn, *Tārīkh-i Ṭabaristān o Rūyān o Māzandarān*, 1966, edited by M. Tasbih with an introduction by Muhammad Javad Mashkur. [113, 114, 288, 289, 290, 291, 292, 293, 295, 302, 307, 308, 309, 313, 314, 315, 316, 317]

Marquart, J., *A Catalogue of the Provincial Capitals of Erānshahr*, Rome, 1931, edited by G. Messina. [39, 40, 73, 139, 244, 305]

Masʿūdī, ʿAlī b. Ḥusayn, *Murūj al-Dhahab wa Maʿādin al-Jawhar*, Paris, 1869, edited by Barbier de Meynard. [14, 125, 132, 341, 439, 442, 461, 487]

Masʿūdī, ʿAlī b. Ḥusayn, *al-Tanbīh wa 'l-Ashrāf*, Beirut, 1965, edited by V.R. Baron Rosen. [36, 186]

Masʿūdī, ʿAlī b. Ḥusayn, *Murūj al-Dhahab*, Tehran, 1968, translation of Masʿūdī 1869 by Abolqasim Payandih. [125, 132, 341, 439, 442, 461]

Melville, Charles, 'The Caspian Provinces: A World Apart, Three Local Histories of Mazandaran', *Iranian Studies* 33, (2000), pp. 45–89. [287, 307]

Menasce, J.P. De, 'Zoroastrian Pahlavi Writings', in Ehsan Yarshater (ed.), *Cambridge History of Iran: The Seleucid, Parthian, and Sasanian Periods*, vol. 3(2), pp. 1166–1196, Cambridge University Press, 1983. [323, 324]

Menog 1884, *Dādistān i Mēnog Khrad*, vol. 24 of *Sacred Books of the East*, Oxford University Press, 1884, translated by E.H. West. [329]

Michael the Syrian, *Chronique de Michel le Syrien*, Paris, 1899, edited and translated by J.-B. Chabot. [146]

Mihr Yasht 1883, *Mihr Yasht*, vol. 23 of *Sacred Books of the East*, Oxford University Press, 1883, translated by James Darmesteter. [147, 352, 355, 356, 360, 366, 390, 394, 400, 409, 410, 411]

Mihr Yasht 1959, *The Avestan Hymn to Mithra*, Cambridge University Press, 1959, introduction, translation, and commentary by Ilya Gershevitch. [352, 354, 355, 356, 367, 390, 400, 401, 409, 410, 411, 412]

Minorsky, V., 'Roman and Byzantine Campaigns in Atropatene', *Bulletin of the School of Oriental and African Studies* 11, (1944), pp. 243–265. [149, 152]

Minorsky, V., 'Vīs u Rāmin', *Bulletin of the School of Oriental and African Studies* 11, 12, 16, 25, (1946, 1947, 1956, 1962), pp. 741–763, 20–35, 91–92, 275–286. [362]

Minorsky, V., 'Caucasia IV', *Bulletin of the School of Oriental and African Studies* 15, (1953), pp. 504–529. [73]

Minorsky, V., 'The Older Preface to the *Shāhnāma*', in *Studi orientalistici in onore de Giorgio Levi Della Vida*, pp. 260–273, Rome, 1964. [272, 449]

Mīrkhwānd, *Rowḍāt al-Ṣafā*, Tehran, 1960. [434, 450]

Mittwoch, E., 'Ayyām al-ʿArab', in Ehsan Yarshater (ed.), *Encyclopaedia Iranica*, New York, 2007. [233]

Mokri, M., *Le Chasseur de Dieu et le mythe du Roi-Aigle*, Wiesbaden, 1967. [389]

Molè, M., 'Le problème des sectes Zoroastriennes dans les livres Pehlevis', *Oriens* 13-14, (1961), pp. 1–28. [337, 341]

Monchi-Zadeh, Davoud, *Topographisch-Historische Studien zum Iranischen Nationalepos*, Wiesbaden, 1975. [66, 67]

Morony, Michael G., *Iraq After the Muslim Conquest*, Princeton University Press, 1984. [166, 168, 193, 212, 417]

Morony, Michael G., 'Arab: II. Arab Conquest of Iran', in Ehsan Yarshater (ed.), *Encyclopaedia Iranica*, pp. 203–210, New York, 1991. [166, 168, 218, 257]

Moshiri, M.I., *Étude[s] de numismatique Iranienne sous les Sassanides*, vol. I, Tehran, 1972. [206]

Moshiri, M.I., *Étude[s] de numismatique Iranienne sous les Sassanides*, vol. II, Tehran, 1997. [206]

Motlagh, Djalal Khaleghi, 'Yikī Mihtarī Būd Gardan-farāz', *Majallih-i Dānishkadih-i Adabīyāt o ʿUlūm-i Insāni-i Dānishgāh-i Ferdowsī* 13, (1977), pp. 197–215. [14]

Motlagh, Djalal Khaleghi, 'Badīhih Sarāyī-i Shafāhī va *Shāhnāma*', in *Jostārhāy-i Shāhnāma-shināsī*, pp. 153–167, Tehran, 2002. [15]

Motlagh, Djalal Khaleghi, 'Bozorgmehr-i Bokhtagān', in Ehsan Yarshater (ed.), *Encyclopaedia Iranica*, New York, 2007a. [114]

Motlagh, Djalal Khaleghi, 'Derafsh-e Kāvēān', in Ehsan Yarshater (ed.), *Encyclopaedia Iranica*, New York, 2007b. [371]

Ibn al-Muqaffaʿ, ʿAbdullāh, *Kalīla wa Dimna*, Beirut, 1947, edited by P. Louis Cheiko. [329]

Narten, J., 'Bahman', in Ehsan Yarshater (ed.), *Encyclopaedia Iranica*, New York, 2007. [198]

Neusner, J., 'Parthian Political Ideology', *Iranica Antiqua* 3, (1963), pp. 40–59. [21, 24, 25, 26]

Nīzāmī, Ganjavī, *Khusrow o Shīrīn*, London, 1844, edited N. Bland. [174]

Nihayat 1996, *Nihāyat al-ʾIrab fī Akhbār al-Furis wa 'l-ʿArab*, vol. 162, Tehran, 1996, translated by M.T. Danish-Pazhuh. [45, 46, 107, 112, 113, 127, 129, 132, 134, 135, 136, 175, 296]

Nīshāpūrī, Abū ʿAbdallāh Ḥākim, *The Histories of Nishapur*, the Hague, 1965, edited by Richard Frye. [271, 272, 273, 274, 448]

Niẓām al-Mulk, *Siyāsat Nāma*, Tehran, 1941, edited by Abbas Iqbal. [342, 438, 439, 442, 445, 447]

Nöldeke, Theodore, *Geschichte der Perser und Araber zur Zeit der Sasaniden*, Leiden, 1879. [7, 14, 45, 60, 61, 62, 68, 69, 76, 141, 143, 144, 153, 161, 175, 178, 182, 187, 209, 222, 223, 229, 438, 440, 489]

Nöldeke, Theodore, 'Das iranische Nationalepos', *Grundriss der iranischen Philologie* II, (1896), pp. 130–211. [76]

Nöldeke, Theodore, *The Iranian National Epic*, Philadelphia, 1979, translated by L. Bogdanov. [33, 34, 37]

Nöldeke, Theodore, *Tārīkh-i Īrāniyān va ʿArab-hā dar zamān-i Sāsāniyān*, Tehran, 1979, translation of Nöldeke 1879 by Abbas Zaryab. [45, 49, 60, 61, 62, 67, 68, 69, 71, 76, 141, 143, 144, 146, 153, 161, 175, 178, 182, 187, 209, 222, 223, 229, 271, 276, 438]

Noth, Albrecht, 'Iṣfahān-Nihāwand. Eine quellenkritische Studie zur frühislamischen Historiographie', *Zeitschrift der Deutschen Morgenländischen Gesellschaft* 118, (1968), pp. 274–296. [227, 241, 247, 284]

Noth, Albrecht, *The Early Arabic Historical Tradition: A Source Critical Study*, Princeton, 1994, second edition in collaboration with Lawrence I. Conrad, translated by Michael Bonner. [15, 162, 163, 165, 166, 167, 168, 169, 171, 281, 282]

Olsson, Tord, 'The Apocalyptic Activity: The Case of *Jāmāsp Nāmag*', in David Hellholm and J.C.B. Mohr (eds.), *Apocalypticism in the Mediterranean World and the Near East*, pp. 21–59, Tübingen, 1983. [413, 414, 444]

Omar, Farouq, *The ʿAbbāsid Caliphate: 132/750-170/786*, Baghdad, 1969. [437]

Omidsalar, Mahmoud, 'Unburdening Ferdowsi', *Journal of the American Oriental Society* 116, (1996), pp. 235–242. [15]

Omidsalar, Mahmoud, 'The Text of Ferdowsi's Shâhnâma and the Burden of the Past', *Journal of the American Oriental Society* 118, (1998), pp. 63–68, review of Olga M. Davidson's *Poet and Hero in the Persian Book of Kings*. [15]

Omidsalar, Mahmoud, 'Could al-Thaʿālibī Have Used the *Shāhnāma* as a Source?', in *Jostārhāy-i Shāhnāma-shināsī*, pp. 113–126, Tehran, 2002. [15]

Parpeci 1991, *History of Łazar P'arpec'i*, vol. 4 of *Columbia University Program in Armenian Studies*, Atlanta, 1991, edited by R.W. Thomson. [43, 60, 71, 72, 73, 74, 75, 77, 382, 391, 392]

Patkanian, M.K., 'D'une histoire de la dynastie des Sassanides', *Journal Asiatique* pp. 101–238, translated by M. Evariste Prud'homme. [49, 106]

Perikhanian, A., 'Iranian Society and Law', in Ehsan Yarshater (ed.), *Cambridge History of Iran: The Seleucid, Parthian, and Sasanian Periods*, vol. 3(2), pp. 627–681, Cambridge University Press, 1983. [27, 28, 29, 64, 94, 106]

Pigulevskaja, Nina, *Les villes de l'état Iranien aux époques Parthe et Sassanide*, Paris, 1963. [38, 40]

Pourshariati, Parvaneh, *Iranian Tradition in Ṭūs and the Arab Presence in Khurāsān*, Ph.D. thesis, Columbia University, 1995. [14, 266, 270, 305, 309, 354, 394, 408, 415, 416, 426, 427, 437, 449]

Pourshariati, Parvaneh, 'Local Histories of Khurāsān and the Pattern of Arab Settlement', *Studia Iranica* 27, (1998), pp. 41–81. [252, 311, 312, 415, 416, 418, 419, 426, 435, 445, 464]

Pourshariati, Parvaneh, 'Local Historiography in Early Medieval Iran and the Taʾrīkh-i Bayhaq', *Journal of Iranian Studies* 33, (2000), pp. 133–164. [246, 374, 457]

Pourshariati, Parvaneh, 'Khurāsān and the Crisis of Legitimacy: A Comparative Historiographical Approach', in Neguin Yavari, Lawrence G. Potter, and Jean-Marc Ran Oppenheim (eds.), *Views From the Edge: Essays in Honor of Richard W. Bulliet*, pp. 208–229, Columbia University Press, 2004. [67, 305, 449]

Pourshariati, Parvaneh, 'Recently Discovered Seals of Wistaxm, Uncle of Khusrow II?', *Studia Iranica* 35, (2006), pp. 163–180. [105, 108]

Procopius, *The History of the Wars*, London, 1914, translated by H.B. Dewing. [45, 72, 102, 103, 106, 107, 111, 267, 268, 269, 288, 289, 382, 384]

Qazvini, Muhammad, '*Muqaddamih-i Qadīm-i Shāhnāma*', in Abbas Iqbal and Ustad Purdavud (eds.), *Bīst Maqalih-i Qazvīnī*, 1984. [35, 272, 449, 463]

Rashnu Yasht 1883, *Rashnu Yasht*, vol. 23 of *Sacred Books of the East*, Oxford University Press, 1883, translated by James Darmesteter. [353]

Rawlison, George, *The Sixth Oriental Monarchy, or The Geography, History, and Antiquities of Parthia, Collected and Illustrated from Ancient and Modern Sources*, New York, 1837. [21]

Rekaya, M., 'Ḳārinids', in P. Bearman, Th. Bianquis, C.E. Bosworth, E. van Donzel, and W.P. Heinrichs (eds.), *Encyclopaedia of Islam*, Leiden, 2007. [294]

Rekaya, R.M., 'Māzyār: résistance ou intégration d'une province Iranienne au monde Musulman au milieu du IXe siècle ap. J.C.', *Studia Iranica* 2, (1973), pp. 143–192. [306]

Robinson, Chase, 'The Conquest of Khuzistān: a Historiographical Reassessment', *Bulletin of the School of Oriental and African Studies* 68, (2004), pp. 14–39. [165, 236, 237, 238, 240]

Robinson, Chase F., *Islamic Historiography: Themes in Islamic History*, Cambridge University Press, 2003. [162, 271]

Rubin, Zeev, 'The Reforms of Khusrow Anūshirwān', in Averil Cameron and Lawrence I. Conrad (eds.), *The Byzantine and Early Islamic Near East, III: States, Resources and Armies*, pp. 227–297, Princeton, 1995. [46, 82, 83, 84, 85, 91, 92, 93, 95, 456]

Rubin, Zeev, 'The Financial Affairs of the Sasanian Empire under Khusrow II Parvez', 2006, MESA talk. [84]

Russell, James R., 'Zoroastrian Problems in Armenia: Mihr and Vahagan', in T. Samuelian (ed.), *Classical Armenian Culture*, vol. 4 of *University of Pennsylvania Armenian Texts and Studies*, pp. 1–7, Dudley, 1982. [390]

Russell, James R., 'Kartīr and Mānī: A Shamanistic Model of their Conflict', in *Acta Iranica 30: Textes et Mémoires, Volume XVI, Papers in Honor of Professor Ehsan Yarshater*, pp. 180–193, 1990a. [324, 327, 329, 330, 331, 456]

Russell, James R., 'On the Armeno-Iranian Roots of Mithraism', in John R. Hinnells (ed.), *Studies in Mithraism*, pp. 553–565, Rome, 1990b. [13, 387, 388]

Russell, James R., 'Armenia and Iran: III Armenian Religion', in Ehsan Yarshater (ed.), *Encyclopaedia Iranica*, pp. 438–444, New York, 1991. [13, 45, 387, 388, 390, 391]

Russell, James R., 'Review of Yamauchi's *Persia and the Bible*', *Jewish Quarterly* 83, (1992), pp. 256–261. [453]

Russell, James R. (ed.), *Armenian and Iranian Studies*, vol. 9 of *Harvard Armenian Texts and Studies*, Cambridge, Mass., 2004. [45]

Sadighi, Ghulam Husayn, *Les mouvements réligieux Iraniens au IIe et au IIIe siècle de l'hégire*, Paris, 1938. [35, 354, 421, 422, 427, 428, 429, 433, 434, 435, 436, 437, 439, 443, 445]

Sadighi, Ghulam Husayn, *Junbish-hā-i Dīnī-i Irānī*, Tehran, 1996. [309, 310, 428, 440]

Safa, D., *Ḥamāsih Sarāyī dar Irān*, Tehran, 1945. [35]

Sahmī, Abū 'l-Qāsim Ḥamza, *Taʾrīkh-i Jurjān wa Kitāb Maʿrifa ʿUlamā ʾAhl Jurjān*, Haydarabad, 1967, edited by Muhammad A. Khan. [312]

Schippmann, Klaus, *Grundzüge der parthischen Geschichte*, Darmstadt, 1980. [21, 22, 23, 24, 25, 388, 492]

Schippmann, Klaus, *Mabānī-i Tārīkh-i Pārtīyān*, Tehran, 2005, translation of Schippmann 1980 by Houshang Sadighi. [21, 23, 24, 25]

Schwartz, Paul, *Iran im Mittelalter nach den arabischen Geographen*, Leipzig, 1896. [215]

Sears, Stuart D., 'The Sasanian Style Drachms of Sistan', *Yarmouk Numismatics* 11, (1999), pp. 18–28. [221]

Sebeos, *The Armenian History Attributed to Sebeos*, Liverpool University Press, 1999, translated with notes by Robert Thomson, Historical Commentary by James Howard-Johnston with assistance from Tim Greenwood. [1, 3, 14, 102, 103, 105, 106, 108, 115, 122, 124, 127, 128, 129, 131, 132, 133, 134, 136, 137, 138, 139, 140, 141, 147, 148, 149, 150, 151, 152, 153, 154, 157, 161, 173, 174, 176, 177, 178, 179, 184, 185, 187, 188, 201, 204, 205, 232, 233, 235, 244, 245, 262, 280, 297, 298, 300, 301, 302, 399]

Seert 1918, *Chronique de Seert*, vol. 13 of *Patrologia Orientalis*, 1918, translated by R. Griveau and A. Scher. [146, 218]

Sellwood, David, 'Parthian Coins', in Ehsan Yarshater (ed.), *Cambridge History of Iran: The Seleucid, Parthian, and Sasanian Periods*, vol. 3(1), pp. 279–299, Cambridge University Press, 1983. [360]

Sellwood, David, 'Amida', in Ehsan Yarshater (ed.), *Encyclopaedia Iranica*, p. 938, New York, 1991. [64]

Shaban, M.A., *Islamic History: A New Interpretation*, vol. II, Cambridge University Press, 1971. [437]

Shahbazi, Shapur, 'On the Xwadāy-Nāmag', *Acta Iranica: Papers in Honor of Professor Ehsan Yarshater* VXI, (1990), pp. 218–223. [2, 33, 34, 116, 117, 402]

Shahbazi, Shapur, 'Army: I. pre-Islamic', in Ehsan Yarshater (ed.), *Encyclopaedia Iranica*, pp. 489–499, New York, 1991a. [163]

Shahbazi, Shapur, 'Bestām o Bendōy', in Ehsan Yarshater (ed.), *Encyclopaedia Iranica*, pp. 181–182, New York, 1991b. [106, 107, 132, 154]

Shahbazi, Shapur, 'Capital Cities', in Ehsan Yarshater (ed.), *Encyclopaedia Iranica*, pp. 768–770, New York, 1991c. [40]

Shahbazi, Shapur, *Ferdowsī: A Critical Bibliography*, Center for Middle Eastern Studies, Harvard University Press, 1991d. [14]

Shahbazi, Shapur, 'Haftvād', in Ehsan Yarshater (ed.), *Encyclopaedia Iranica*, pp. 535–537, New York, 1991e. [367]

Shahbazi, Shapur, 'Bahrām VI Čōbīn', in Ehsan Yarshater (ed.), *Encyclopaedia Iranica*, New York, 2007a. [123, 124, 125, 126, 127, 129, 413]

Shahbazi, Shapur, 'Carrhae', in Ehsan Yarshater (ed.), *Encyclopaedia Iranica*, New York, 2007b. [462]

Shahbazi, Shapur, Schipmman, K., Alram, M., Boyce, Mary, and Toumanoff, C., 'Arsacids', in Ehsan Yarshater (ed.), *Encyclopaedia Iranica*, pp. 525–546, New York, 1991. [19, 20, 126]

Shahîd, Irfan, *Byzantium and the Arabs in the Sixth Century, Volume 1, Part 1: Political and Military History*, Dumbarton Oaks Research Library and Collection, Washington, 1995. [7]

Shahrestan 2002, *Šahrestānīha-ī Ērānšahr: A Middle Persian Text on Late Antique Geography, Epic and History*, Costa Mesa, 2002, translated by Touraj Daryaee. [39, 40]

Shahristānī, Abū 'l-Fataḥ Muḥammad, *al-Milal wa 'l-Niḥal*, Tehran, 1971, translated by Afdal al-Din Isfahani and edited by Seyyed Muhammad Riza Jalal Na'ini. [372]

Shaked, Shaul, 'Esoteric Trends in Zoroastrianism', in *Proceedings of the Israeli Academy of Sciences and Humanities*, vol. 3, pp. 175–221, 1969. [341, 342, 343, 344]

Shaked, Shaul, 'Some Legal and Administrative Terms of the Sasanian Period', in *Momentum H. S. Nyberg*, vol. 5, pp. 213–225, 1975. [126]

Shaked, Shaul, 'Mihr the Judge', *Jerusalem Studies in Arabic and Islam* 2, (1980), pp. 1–31. [353, 384]

Shaked, Shaul, 'Paymān: An Iranian Idea in Contact with Greek Thought and Islam', in *Transition Periods in Iranian History*, vol. 5 of *Societas Iranologica Europaea*, pp. 217–240, Fribourg-en-Brisgau, 1987. [368]

Shaked, Shaul, 'The Myth of Zurvan: Cosmogony and Eschatology', in *Messiah and Christos: Studies in the Jewish Origins of Christianity Presented to David Flusser*, vol. 32 of *Texte und Studien zum Antiken Judentum*, pp. 219–240, Tübingen, 1992. [340]

Shaked, Shaul, *Dualism in Transformation: Varieties of Religion in Sasanian Iran*, vol. 16 of *Jordan Lectures in Comparative Religion*, London, 1994a. [325, 330, 359, 392, 393, 430, 433]

Shaked, Shaul, 'Some Islamic Reports Concerning Zoroastrianism', *Jerusalem Studies in Arabic and Islam* 17, (1994b), pp. 43–84. [393, 422, 436]

Shaked, Shaul, *From Zoroastrian Iran to Islam: Studies in Religious History and Intercultural Contacts*, Aldershot, 1995. [341, 422]

Shaked, Shaul, 'Quests and Visionary Journeys in Sasanian Iran', in Jan Assmann and Guy G. Stroumsa (eds.), *Transformations of the Inner Self in Ancient Religions*, pp. 65–86, Leiden, 1999. [329, 330]

Shaki, Mansour, 'The Social Doctrine of Mazdak in Light of Middle Persian Evidence', *Archív Orientální* 46, (1978), pp. 289–306. [337, 342, 345, 429, 434]

Shaki, Mansour, 'The Cosmogonical and Cosmological Teachings of Mazdak', in *Papers in Honour of Professor Mary Boyce*, vol. 24 of *Acta Iranica*, pp. 527–543, Leiden, 1985. [82]

Shaki, Mansour, 'Dād', in Ehsan Yarshater (ed.), *Encyclopaedia Iranica*, pp. 544–545, New York, 1991. [107]

Shaki, Mansour, 'Gayōmart', in Ehsan Yarshater (ed.), *Encyclopaedia Iranica*, New York, 2007a. [9]

Shaki, Mansour, 'Haftānbūkht', in Ehsan Yarshater (ed.), *Encyclopaedia Iranica*, New York, 2007b. [367]

Sharon, M., *Black Banners from the East: the Establishment of the ʿAbbāsid State – Incubation of a Revolt*, Leiden, 1983. [425, 426, 478, 487]

Simocatta, *The History of Theophylact Simocatta*, Oxford, 1986, English translation with introduction and notes by Michael and Mary Whitby. [29, 30, 92, 93, 106, 125, 126, 404]

Skjærvø, O., 'Kirdir's Vision: Translation and Analysis', *Archälogische Mitteilungen aus Iran* 16, (1983), pp. 296–306. [331]

Sorush Yasht 1883, *Sorūsh Yasht*, vol. 23 of *Sacred Books of the East*, Oxford University Press, 1883, translated by James Darmesteter. [353]

Soudavar, Abolala, *The Aura of the Kings: Legitimacy and Divine Sanction in Iranian Kingship*, vol. 11 of *Bibliotheca Iranica, Intellectual Traditions Series*, 1980. [326, 361, 391, 400]

Speidel, Michael P., 'Parthia and the Mithraism of the Roman Army', *Études Mithraiques* IV, (1978), pp. 470–485. [402]

Sutton, L.P. Elwell, 'Arthur Emanuel Christensen', *Bulletin of the British Society for Middle Eastern Studies* 10, (1983), pp. 59–68. [455]

Ṭabarī, *The ʿAbbāsid Revolution: A.D. 743–750/A.H. 126–132*, vol. XXVII of *The History of Ṭabarī*, Albany, 1985, translated and annotated by John Alden Williams. [426]

Ṭabarī, *The Conquest of Iraq, Southwestern Persia, and Egypt*, vol. XIII of *The History of Ṭabarī*, Albany, 1989a, translated and annotated by Gautier H.A. Juynboll. [198, 215, 216, 234, 235, 236, 237, 238, 239, 240, 241, 242, 243, 244, 245]

Ṭabarī, *The Waning of the Umayyad Caliphate: Prelude to Revolution: A.D. 738-745/A.H. 121-127*, vol. XXVI of *The History of Ṭabarī*, Albany, 1989b, translated and annotated by Carole Hillenbrand. [310]

Ṭabarī, *The Crisis of the Early Caliphate*, vol. 15 of *The History of Ṭabarī*, NY, 1990, translated and annotated by R. Stephen Humphreys. [246, 259, 260, 303]

Ṭabarī, *The Battle of al-Qādisiyyah and the Conquest of Syria and Palestine*, vol. XII of *The History of Ṭabarī*, Albany, 1992, translated and annotated by Yohanan Friedmann. [187, 224, 225, 226, 227, 228, 230, 231, 232, 233, 269, 464]

Ṭabarī, *The Challenge to the Empires*, vol. XI of *The History of Ṭabarī*, Albany, 1993, translated and annotated by Khalid Yahya Blankinship. [16, 164, 165, 168, 169, 170, 190, 191, 192, 193, 194, 195, 196, 197, 198, 199, 200, 201, 202, 203, 204, 206, 207, 208, 209, 210, 211, 212, 213, 214, 215, 217, 218, 219, 220, 234, 281]

Ṭabarī, *The Conquest of Iran*, vol. XIV of *The History of Ṭabarī*, Albany, 1994, translated and annotated by G. Rex Smith. [223, 247, 248, 249, 250, 251, 252, 253, 254, 255, 256, 258, 259, 263, 264, 265, 278, 279, 280, 293, 305, 306, 308]

Ṭabarī, *The Sāsānids, the Byzantines, the Lakhmids, and Yemen*, vol. V of *The History of Ṭabarī*, Albany, 1999, translated and annotated by C.E. Bosworth. [xii, 45, 56, 57, 58, 60, 61, 62, 66, 67, 68, 69, 70, 71, 76, 77, 78, 80, 81, 118, 119, 123, 125, 129, 143, 145, 146, 151, 153, 155, 156, 157, 158, 161, 172, 175, 178, 179, 180, 182, 183, 184, 185, 192, 205, 210, 223, 229, 289, 299, 331, 367, 381, 382, 383, 384, 401, 444]

Ṭabarī, Muḥammad b. Jarīr, *Taʾrīkh al-Rusul wa ʾl-Mulūk (Annales)*, Leiden, 1879–1901, edited by M.J. de Goeje. [xii, 13, 45, 56, 57, 58, 60, 61, 62, 66, 67, 68, 69, 70, 71, 76, 77, 78, 80, 81, 118, 123, 125, 143, 145, 146, 151, 153, 155, 156, 157, 158, 161, 168, 169, 172, 175, 179, 180, 182, 183, 185, 190, 191, 192, 193, 194, 195, 196, 197, 198, 199, 200, 201, 202, 203, 204, 205, 206, 207, 208, 209, 210, 211, 212, 213, 214, 215, 216, 217, 218, 219, 220, 223, 224, 225, 226, 227, 228, 229, 231, 232, 233, 234, 235, 236, 237, 238, 239, 240, 241, 242, 243, 244, 245, 246, 247, 248, 249, 250, 251, 252, 253, 254, 255, 256, 258, 259, 260, 263, 264, 265, 269, 271, 276, 278, 279, 280, 293, 299, 303, 305, 306, 308, 310, 315, 367, 381, 382, 384, 401, 426, 444, 464]

Tafazzoli, Ahmad, *Sasanian Society*, Winona Lake, 2000. [39, 47, 50, 61, 89, 163]

Tafazzoli, Ahmad, 'Fereydūn', in Ehsan Yarshater (ed.), *Encyclopaedia Iranica*, New York, 2007. [370, 373, 375]

Tansar 1968, *Letter of Tansar*, vol. XXXVIII of *Istituto Italiano Per Il Medio Ed Estremo Oriente*, Rome, 1968, translated by Mary Boyce. [86, 87, 88, 91, 361]

Ṭarsūsī, Abū Ṭāhir ʿAlī b. Ḥusayn, *Abū Muslim Nāma*, Tehran, nd. [449]

Tha‘ālibī, Abū Manṣūr, *Ghurar Akhbār Mulūk al-Furs wa Sīyarihim*, Paris, 1900, edited by H. Zotenberg. [13, 45, 58, 59, 60, 66, 69, 70, 77, 113, 114, 120, 121, 122, 124, 130, 154, 155, 159, 174, 178, 179, 183, 211, 259, 262, 270, 299, 343, 371, 376, 377, 381, 383, 430, 431, 496]

Tha‘ālibī, Abū Manṣūr, *Tārīkh-i Tha‘ālibī*, 1989, translation of Tha‘ālibī 1900 by Muhammad Fada'ili. [58, 66, 69, 70, 77, 113, 114, 120, 121, 122, 124, 130, 154, 155, 159, 174, 178, 179, 183, 211, 262, 299, 343, 376, 377, 381, 383, 430]

Theophanes, *Chronographia*, Leipzig, 1883, edited by C. de Boor. [346]

Theophanes, *The Chronicle of Theophanes Confessor: Byzantyine and Near Eastern History AD 284–813*, Oxford, 1997, translated with introduction and commentary by Cyril Mango and Roger Scott. [149, 284, 288, 289]

Thieme, P., 'The Concept of Mitra in Aryan Belief', in *Mithraic Studies: Proceedings of the First International Congress of Mithraic Studies*, vol. I, pp. 21–39, Manchester University Press, 1975. [352, 353, 355, 356, 444]

Tishtar Yasht 1883, *Tishtar Yasht*, vol. 23 of *Sacred Books of the East*, Oxford University Press, 1883, translated by James Darmesteter. [394]

Toumanoff, C., *Studies in Christian Caucasian History*, Georgetown University Press, 1963. [3, 45, 53, 54, 55, 97]

Tyler-Smith, Susan, 'Coinage in the Name of Yazdgerd III (AD 632–651) and the Arab Conquest of Iran', *Numismatic Chronicle* 160, (2000), pp. 135–170. [221, 222]

Ulansey, David, *The Origins of the Mithraic Mysteries: Cosmology and Salvation in the Ancient World*, Oxford University Press, 1989. [374]

Uyun 1869, *Kitāb al-‘Uyūn wa 'l-Ḥadā’iq fi 'l-Akhbār al-Ḥaqā’iq*, Leiden, 1869, translated by M.J. de Goeje. [447]

Vahuman 1883, *Zand-i Vahuman Yasn*, Tehran, 1963, translated by Sadegh Hedayat. [264]

Vendidad 1880, *Vendidad*, vol. 4 of *Sacred Books of the East*, Oxford University Press, 1880, translated by James Darmesteter. [322, 369, 370]

Vizar 1882, *Shkand Gumānīk Vizār*, vol. 18 of *Sacred Books of the East*, Oxford University Press, 1882, translated by E.W. West. [329]

Walker, Joel Thomas, *The Legend of Mar Qardagh: Narrative and Christian Heroism in Late Antique Iraq*, University of California Press, 2006. [334]

Wansbrough, John, *Quranic Studies: Sources and Methods of Scriptural Interpretation*, Oxford University Press, 1977. [423]

Wāqidī, Muḥammad b. ‘Umar, *Kitāb al-Maghāzī*, London, 1966, edited by M. Jones. [193]

Weiskopf, Michael, 'Dara', in Ehsan Yarshater (ed.), *Encyclopaedia Iranica*, pp. 671–672, New York, 1991. [102]

Wenke, Robert J., 'Elymeans, Parthians, and the Evolution of Empires in Southwestern Iran', *Journal of the American Oriental Society* 101, (1981), pp. 303–315. [22]

von Wesendok, O.G., *Das Wesen der Lehrer Zarathustras*, Leipzig, 1927. [340]

Widengren, Geo, 'The Status of the Jews in the Sasanian Empire', *Acta Iranica* I, (1961), pp. 117–162. [323, 347, 348]

Widengren, Geo, *Der Feudalismus im alten Iran*, Cologne, 1969. [37]

Widengren, Geo, 'Bābakīyah and the Mithraic Mysteries', in Ugo Bianchi (ed.), *Mysteria Mithrae*, pp. 675–695, Leiden, 1979. [380, 424, 434, 459]

Widengren, Geo, 'Sources of Parthian and Sasanian History', in Ehsan Yarshater (ed.), *Cambridge History of Iran: The Seleucid, Parthian, and Sasanian Periods*, vol. 3(2), pp. 1261–1284, Cambridge University Press, 1983. [23]

Wiesehöfer, Josef, *Ancient Persia: from 550 BC to 650 AD*, London, 1996. [334]

Wiesehöfer, Josef, *Das Partherreich und seine Zeugnisse: The Arsacid Empire: Sources and Documentation*, Stuttgart, 1998. [21]

Wikander, Stig, *Feuerpriester in Kleinasien und Iran*, Lund, 1946. [328, 335]

Wissemann, Michael, *Die Parther in der augusteischen Dichtung*, Frankfurt, 1982. [22]

Wolski, Józef, *L'empire des Arsacides*, Leuven, 1993. [22]

Yaʿqūbi, Aḥmad b. Abī Yaʿqūb, *Kitâb al-Boldân*, Leiden, 1967, edited by M.J. de Goeje. [272, 497]

Yaʿqūbi, Aḥmad b. Abī Yaʿqūb, *Ibn Wādhih qui Dicitur al-Yaʿqūbī, Historiae*, Leiden, 1969, edited by M.T. Houtsma. [13, 179, 185, 205, 211, 225, 274, 439, 442, 497]

Yaʿqūbi, Aḥmad b. Abī Yaʿqūb, *al-Buldān*, Tehran, 1977, translation of Yaʿqūbi 1967 by M.I. Ayati. [272]

Yaʿqūbi, Aḥmad b. Abī Yaʿqūb, *Taʾrīkh*, Shirkat-i intishārāt-i ʿIlmī va Farhangī, 1983, translation of Yaʿqūbi 1969. [179, 185, 205, 211, 219, 225, 244, 274]

Yaqūt al-Hamawī, *Kitab Muʿjam al-Buldān*, Leipzig, 1866, edited by F. Wüstenfeld as *Jacut's Geographisches Wörterbuch*. [197, 266, 374]

Yarshater, Ehsan, 'Were the Sasanians Heirs to the Achaemenids?', in *La Persia Nel Medioevo*, pp. 517–531, Rome, 1971. [33, 45]

Yarshater, Ehsan, 'Iranian Common Beliefs and World-View', in Ehsan Yarshater (ed.), *Cambridge History of Iran: The Seleucid, Parthian, and Sasanian Periods*, vol. 3(1), pp. 343–359, Cambridge University Press, 1983a. [322, 370, 373]

Yarshater, Ehsan, 'Iranian National History', in Ehsan Yarshater (ed.), *Cambridge History of Iran: The Seleucid, Parthian, and Sasanian Periods*, vol. 3(1), pp. 359–477, Cambridge University Press, 1983b. [9, 13, 14, 33, 35, 36, 39, 45, 46, 47, 265, 350, 369, 370, 371, 373, 375, 376, 385, 402, 406, 414, 444]

Yarshater, Ehsan, 'Mazdak', in Ehsan Yarshater (ed.), *Cambridge History of Iran: The Seleucid, Parthian, and Sasanian Periods*, vol. 3(2), pp. 991–1027, Cambridge University Press, 1983c. [335, 344, 345, 346]

Yasna 1898, *Yasna*, vol. 31 of *Sacred Books of the East*, Oxford University Press, 1898, translated by L.H. Mills. [322]

Yusofi, Gholam Husayn, 'Behāfarīd', in Ehsan Yarshater (ed.), *Encyclopaedia Iranica*, New York, 2007. [427, 428]

Zaehner, R.C., *Zurvan: A Zoroastrian Dilemma*, New York, 1972. [323, 331, 332, 340, 345]

Zakeri, Mohsen, *Sasanid Soldiers in Early Muslim Society: the Origins of ʿAyyārān and Futuwwa*, Wiesbaden, 1995. [29, 274]

Zamyad Yasht 1883, *Zamyād Yasht*, vol. 23 of *Sacred Books of the East*, Oxford University Press, 1883, translated by James Darmesteter. [47, 354, 375, 412]

Zarrinkub, Abd al-Husayn, 'Arab Conquest of Iran and its Aftermath', in Ehsan Yarshater (ed.), *Cambridge History of Iran: The Seleucid, Parthian, and Sasanian Periods*, vol. 4, pp. 1–57, Cambridge University Press, 1975. [168, 187, 248]

Zarrinkub, Abd al-Husayn, *Dow Qarn Sokūt*, 1989, reprinted in German. [450]

Zuhrī, b. ʿAbd al-Ḥakam, *Kitāb Futūḥ Miṣr wa Akhbāriha*, New Haven, 1922, edited by C. Torrey. [144]

Glossary

A

Ahrīman Avestan *Aŋra Mainiiu*: the evil spirit opposing Ahūrā Mazdā (*q.v.*).

ahūra Vedic *asura* (evil god), but in Zoroastrianism one of the three great Lords: Ahūrā Mazdā (*q.v.*), Mithra (*q.v.*), or *Vouruna/Apąm Napaṭ (Varuna; grandson of the waters).

Ahūrā Mazdā Middle Persian *Ohrmazd*, New Persian *Hormozd*, Armenian *Aramazd*, Greek *Aramasdes*, but sometimes also Ζευς (Zeus): Lord Wisdom, the benevolent supreme deity of Zoroastrianism, who opposes and ultimately defeats the evil spirit Ahrīman (*q.v.*).

ʿajam From Arabic *ʿajama* (to mumble); similar in use as Greek *βαρβαρος* (indistinct speech): non-Arabs (from *ʿaraba*, to speak clearly), but in particular, Persians.

Amahraspands Avestan *Aməša Spəṇta* (Bounteous Immortals), the six archangels or emanations of Ahūrā Mazdā: *Vohu Manō* (*Bahman*, Good Thought), *Aša Vahišta* (*Ardwahisht*, *Ordibehesht*, Highest Asha), *Xšaθra Vairiia* (*Shahrewar*, Desirable Dominion), *Spəṇta Ārmaiti* (*Spandarmad*, Holy Devotion), *Hauruuatāṭ* (*Hordād*, Health), and *Amərətāṭ* (*Amurdād*, erroneously also *Mordād*, Immortality). Their names still survive as the eleventh, second, sixth, twelfth, third, and fifth months respectively, in both the Iranian and Zoroastrian calendars, as well as the names of, respectively, the second to the seventh day of each month in the Zoroastrian calendar.

Amesha Spentas See *Amahraspands*.

Anāhitā Avestan *Arəduuī Sūrā Anāhitā* (the Strong and Immaculate), Armenian *Anahit*: goddess of pure waters (*Ābān*) and fertility. The Sasanian kings were often the high-priests of her cult center at Stakhr in Fārs.

anēr Non-Iranian, specifically a non-Zoroastrian.

argbed See *hargbed*.

asha Avestan *aša*, Sanskrit *ṛta*, Middle Persian *arda/ahlaw*: order, righteousness, justice, the moral opposite of *drug* (*q.v.*).

aspbed Middle Persian *aspa-pati*, Armenian *aspet, aspipīdes*: general of the cavalry.

Avestā From Old Persian *upastāwaka* (Praise of God), Middle Persian *abestāg*: collection of Zoroastrian sacred texts, consisting of the *Gāthās* (*q.v.*), the

Yashts (*q.v.*), and other liturgical material; whence Avestan, the old Iranian language of these texts closely related to Old Vedic (Sanskrit), normally divided into Gathic (Old) and Younger Avestan.

ʿayyār Member of secret brother/sisterhoods in Iran during the late antique and medieval periods, often expressing themselves with a Mithraic ideology against the status quo.

azādhān Literally, *the free people*: lower nobility.

B

barīd From Latin *veredus* (post-horse): postal and intelligence service of the Sasanians.

barsom Avestan *barəsman*: sacred twigs in Zoroastrian rituals, bound together in a bundle (the number of twigs in a bundle depends on the particular ceremony). Originally twigs of the *hōm* (*q.v.*) plant were used, but later substituted by those of the pomegranate.

bulla Clay imprint of a seal.

C

caesaropapism From Latin *Caesar* (emperor) and *Papa* (pope): Byzantine model of government in which the emperor was also the head of the Church.

Chinvat Bridge Avestan *cinuuatō pərətu* (bridge of the collector), Middle Persian *chinwad puhl*: narrow bridge on the top of Mount Harā/Alburz (Chagād-i Dāitī) leading to the afterworld, which the soul of the departed, under the guidance of Sorūsh (*q.v.*), has to cross three days after his death, accompanied by his *dēn* (in the form of a fair maiden), after being judged to be righteous by a tribunal presided by Mithra (*q.v.*), the *mīyānchīgh*.

Ctesian method Named after the Greek historian Ctesias, who embellished his stories with mythical material: a method of historical writing in which contemporary histories are anachronistically superimposed onto mythical times.

D

darīgbed Palace superintendent, akin to a Byzantine *cura palatii*.

dastār Flying ribbons symbolizing *farr* (*q.v.*), often in conjunction with a ram.

dastgird Avestan *dasta-kərəta* (handiwork): royal or seigniorial estate.

dastwar Avestan *dasta-bara*, New Persian *dastūr*: religious teacher, spiritual authority; similar to Avestan *ratu*.

daʿwā Religious call.

dayeakordi Armenian *daye'kutʿiwn* from Middle Persian *dāyag* (wet nurse): Armenian form of child rearing through a foster *naxarar* (*q.v.*) family, whence guardianship.

dehkān Middle Persian *dahigān, dehgān*, Syriac *dhgn'*, Arabic *dihqān*: military landlord, presumably after Khusrow I's reforms. Possibly the same as a *shahrīg* (*q.v.*).

dēv Avestan *daēuua*, from Vedic *daiva* (younger god), which acquired in Zoroastrianism the meaning of its moral opposite: evil spirit, demon.

dīwān Army register; treasury for levying land taxes.

driyōšān ǰādaggōw ud dādvar Literally, *protector of the poor and judge*: judiciary office, possibly in replacement of the office of *mōbad* (*q.v.*). See also *jādhū-yih*.

drug Avestan *druj*: falsehood, lie, whence, on a cosmological scale, the evil creation of Ahrīman (*q.v.*).

dvandva From Sanskrit *dva* (two): in onomastics, a compound name formed from the names of two separate deities; e.g., Mihr Hormozd.

E

ērān-dibhērbadh Head of the scribal caste.

ērān-spāhbed Head of the army. Also *spāhbed* (*q.v.*).

ethnicon Ethnic (self-)identification.

exilarch Hereditary leader of the Jews after the Babylonian exile.

F

farr Avestan *x*ʷ*arənah*, Middle Persian *xwarra*, *khvarenah*, Armenian *P'ark'*: the Divine Fortune, associated with legitimate kingship; bestowed by Mithra (*q.v.*).

frashegird Avestan *frašō-kərəti* (making juicy, wonderful): judgment day, the time of healing, renovation.

G

Gāthā Avestan *gāθā*, Middle Persian *gāh*: a sacred hymn from the *Avestā* (*q.v.*), attributed to Zoroaster himself.

ghulāt Literally, *exaggerators*: the name given to various extremist Shīʿite sects in Iran.

gītīg From Avestan *gaēθā* (living beings): material existence.

gumezishn Literally *mixture*: the present, material world, when Ahrīman's (*q.v.*) *drug* (*q.v.*) is mixed with Ahūrā Mazdā's (*q.v.*) *asha* (*q.v.*).

H

ḥadīth Literally *tradition*: an account of the words and deeds of the Prophet Muḥammad, second in authority to the Qurʾān (*q.v.*).

hargbed From Middle Persian *harag* (tax, see *kharāj*) and *pati* (head): chief of finances. Because of the military nature of the office, an alternative proposition is *argbed* (fortress commander).

hazāraft See *hazārbed*.

hazārbed Also *hazāraft*, or erroneously *hazārbandak* (Owner of Thousand Slaves), from Old Persian *hazāra-pati* (chiliarch): Chief of the Thousands, grand intendant, whence also prime minister, *wuzurg framādār* (*q.v.*).

herbad Avestan *aeθra-paiti*, Middle Persian *ērpat*: Zoroastrian priest.

hōm Avestan *haoma*, Vedic *soma*: unidentified plant with psycho-pharmacological properties, used in Zoroastrian rituals, where it is now substituted with harmel (*esfand*) or ephedra; the deity associated with this plant and worshipped in the *Hōm Yasht* (*q.v.*).

Hormozd See Ahūrā Mazdā.

I

ibāha 'l-nisā Literally *permission of women*: Arabic term for the Mazdakite tenet of the "communal sharing of women."

Iblīs From Greek διαβολος (devil, from Middle Persian *dēv*, *q.v.*): the Islamic nomenclature for the devil.

Imām Religious supreme leader.

ispahbud Arabic *isfahbud* or *iṣbahbadh*: New Persian form of *spāhbed* (*q.v.*) or *ērān-spāhbed* (*q.v.*), in the later period, also meaning ruler of a region.

J

jādhūyih Middle Persian *ǰādaggōw*: advocate, spokesman, in particular vis-à-vis the king (see footnote 1092). See also *driyōšān ǰādaggōw ud dādvar*.

jizya Poll (head) tax.

K

Kaʿba Cube shaped shrine in Mecca, believed to be the house of God (Allah) by the Muslims. It constitutes the *qibla* (*q.v.*) for the daily prayers and is the focus of the annual pilgrimage (*ḥajj*).

kārdār Tax collector; akin to Arabic *ʿāmil*.

karīz See *qanāt*.

kharāj From Greek χορηγια (literally organizer of a choir, whence provision, revenue) or Aramaic *ḥarāg*, Middle Persian *harag* (tax): land tax, but sometimes used in the generic sense of tax.

Kheshm Avestan *aēšma-daēuua*, Middle Persian *xēšm* or *ēšm*, Hebrew *Ashmedai*, Greek ασμοδαις: anger, whence in Zoroastrianism the demon Wrath, the chief demon of Ahrīman (*q.v.*). In the apocalypse, the opponent of Mithra.

Khudāynāmag See *X^{w}adāy-Nāmag*.

khvarenah See *farr*.

khwēdōdah Avestan *x^{w}aētuuadaθa*: close-kin (consanguineous) marriage, a practice that was prevalent among Zoroastrian noble families.

Koran See Qurʾān.

kunya In Arabic naming practice, referring to the patronymic construction *Abū* (father of), or its female equivalent *Umm* (mother of); sometimes used instead of the proper name (*ism*).

kūst One of the four quarters (or sides) in which Khusrow I divided the empire, each assigned to an *ērān-spāhbed* (*q.v.*).

kūst-i ādurbādagān The quarter of the north, comprising Azarbāyjān, parts of Gīlān, Ṭabaristān, and northern regions.

kūst-i khwarāsān The quarter of the east, comprising Gurgān, Khurāsān, and eastern regions.

kūst-i khwarbarān The quarter of the west, comprising Sawād, Iraq, and western regions.

kūst-i nēmrōz The quarter of the south, comprising Fārs, Kirmān, and Sīstān.

M

mahistān Avestan *mazišta*, Middle Persian *mahist* (greatest): council of high nobility, senate.

mainyu Avestan *mainiiu*: spirit. See also *menog*.

mang A mixture of hemp and wine, with intoxicating properties. Alternatively, henbane, or a substitute for *hōm* (*q.v.*).

marzbān Old Iranian *marza-panā*, Armenian *marzpan*: margrave, warden of the marches (borders); by extension a military commander, similar sometimes to a *spāhbed* (*q.v.*).

mawlā (pl. *mawālī*). Literally *client*: in the early Islamic period referring to a non-Arab (Iranian) convert.

maẓālim Literally, *not in the right place*: direct dispensation of justice by the ruler.

mēnōg From *mainyu* (*q.v.*): spiritual state.

Mihr See Mithra.

Mihrigān Autumnal festival in celebration of Mithra (*q.v.*), commemorated on the day of Mihr of the month of Mihr, that is to say, 195 days after *Nowrūz* (*q.v.*).

mithraeum Cave-like, often subterranean, temple devoted to the Roman god Mithras (*q.v.*).

Mithra Avestan *Miθra*, Persian *Mihr*: literally *contract*, whence the Indo-Iranian deity of the contract. In Zoroastrianism, one of the three *ahuras* (*q.v.*), whose worship extended greatly beyond orthodox praxis and who became identified with the sun.

Mithras Roman deity, most probably derived from Iranian Mithra (*q.v.*). His cult in the Roman Empire is referred to as *Roman Mithraism*, an extremely popular religious current, which flourished especially during the first three centuries CE, when it rivaled nascent Christianity. See also *tauroctony*.

mōbad Middle Persian *magu-pati*, Parthian *magupat* (chief *moγ*, *q.v.*): Zoroastrian priest holding also an administrative or supervisory office.

mōbadhān mōbadh The mōbad (*q.v.*) of all mōbads, head of the priestly caste.

moɣ Avestan *mōɣu*, Old Persian *maguš*, Middle Persian *magu*, *mgw*, Greek μαγος, Arabic *majūs*: mog, mage, Magian, member of the sacerdotal caste. Originally they may have been a Median tribe of priests. The three wise men from the East adoring the infant Christ (at the Epiphany) were *moɣs* (one of these Magi, Gaspar, is claimed to be the Sūrenid *ērān-spāh-bed* (*q.v.*) Gondofarr, son of general Rustaham Surena). See also *mōbad*.

N

nask Prayer, but by extension one of the twenty parts in which the *Avestā* (*q.v.*) is divided.

naxarar Parthian *naxvadar*: Armenian high nobility.

nisba *Noun of relation*: in Arab nomenclature, the tribe or region to which one belongs; whence, in modern usage, family name.

Nowrūz Literally *new day*: the festival of the Zoroastrian as well as the secular Iranian new year. In modern times, after the calendar reforms and except for certain Parsi calendars, it always falls on the vernal (spring) equinox. During the Sasanian period, due to calendar shifts, the festival fell later in the year.

O

Ohrmazd See Ahūrā Mazdā.

ōstāndār Ruler of an *ōstān* (region, territory), whence governor. The difference with *shahrab* (*q.v.*) is not always clear.

ostracon From Greek οστρακον (shell): piece of pottery with an inscription.

P

pādhūspān Avestan *patikauša-pāna*, Middle Persian *pāygōspān*: protector of the realm, whence governor.

Pahlav Ethnic group, originally called Parni or Dahae. Their name is derived from the Achaemenid term for the region, Parthava, to which they migrated. By extension, Pahlav or Parthian is also used to refer to the Arsacid dynasty, and related dynastic families from this region. The derivation *Pahlavi* refers to a particular script (derived from the Aramaic script), and by extension to the Middle Iranian language written in this script.

Pārsīg From or belonging to the region of *Fārs*, whence Persian. By extension, the faction associating itself with the Sasanians.

Parthian See *Pahlav*.

polis Greek πολις (city): a Hellenistic city-state, often self-sufficient and semi-independent.

Q

qanāt From Akkadian *ḳanū* (reed), Latin *canalis* (canal): underground irrigation canal borrowing into the aquifer inside a mountain slope, thus producing fresh water. Also called *karīz*.

qibla Prayer direction, in the Muslim creed, towards the *Kaʿba* (*q.v.*) in Mecca.

quadripartition The division of the empire by Khusrow I into four quarters or *kūsts* (*q.v.*), each assigned to an *ērān-spāhbed* (*q.v.*).

Qurʾān Muslim holy scripture, believed to be the words of God as revealed to the Prophet Muḥammad.

R

Rashnu Avestan *rašnu*, Middle Persian *rashn*: the *yazata* (*q.v.*) of Justice, whence his close association with Mithra (*q.v.*), worshipped in the *Rashnu Yasht* (*q.v.*).

rathāshtārān sālār From Avestan *raθaēštar* (he who stands on a chariot, warrior): supreme commander of the army. Also *ērān-spāhbed* (*q.v.*).

ridda wars Literally, *wars of apostasy*: a series of battles against Arab tribes that had presumably left the *ʿumma* (*q.v.*) shortly after Muḥammad's death.

Rig Veda Sanskrit *Ṛg Veda*: oldest Hindu scripture, exhibiting strong linguistic and cultural affinities with the *Avestā* (*q.v.*).

S

Sadih From Persian *sad* (hundred): Zoroastrian festival of light, celebrated 50 days (= 100 days and nights) before Nowrūz (*q.v.*).

sanad (plural, *isnād*). Chain of authorities in the transmission of a tradition or *ḥadīth* (*q.v.*).

satrapy Avestan *xšaθra*, Middle Persian *shahr*: realm, whence province, the head of which was a *shahrab* (*q.v.*).

shāhānshāh King of Kings, official title of the Iranian monarch.

shahrab Satrap, governor of a satrapy (*q.v.*) or a royal estate; in the later period, ruler of a *shahr* (province).

shahrdārān Literally, *holder of a shahr* (province or region): in Shāpūr I's inscription ŠKZ, it refers to royal nobility, but in late Sasanian times it could also refer to other high nobility. Sometimes confused with *shahrab* (*q.v.*).

shahrīg Arabic *shahrīj*: a member of the *dehkān* (*q.v.*) class. Sometimes confused with *shahrab* (*q.v.*).

Sorūsh Avestan *sraoša*, Middle Persian *srosh*: the *yazata* (*q.v.*) of Obedience, right hand of Mithra (*q.v.*), worshipped in the *Sorūsh Yasht* (*q.v.*).

Sōshyant Avestan *saošiiant* (he who brings benefit): the redeemer or savior, a Zoroastrian messianic figure, to be born to a virgin from the seed of Zoroaster. To redeem mankind and restore *asha* (*q.v.*) at the time of the *frashegird* (*q.v.*), the third and final Sōshyant, acting as a priest, performs the slaughter of the sacred bull, whose sacrificial fat mixed with *hōm* (*q.v.*) yields the elixir of immortality.

spāhbed Middle Persian *spāda-pati*, Persian *ispahbud* (*q.v.*), Armenian *(a)sparapet*: chief of an army, general. Before Khusrow I's reforms, *spāhbed* also designated the supreme commander, a hereditary post that became the gentilitial name of the Ispahbudhān family; after the reforms, a general in charge of one of the four *kūsts* (*q.v.*). Also *ērān-spāhbed* (*q.v.*).

sparapet Hereditary title of the house of Mamikonean, derived from Parthian *sp'dpty*, Middle Persian *spāhbed* (*q.v.*).

sunna Literally, *way of acting*: precedent, custom.

T

tanutēr Middle Persian *tukhār*: a leading member of an Armenian noble family, *naxarar* (*q.v.*).

tauroctony Scene of Mithras (*q.v.*) ritually slaying a bull. In the depiction, which forms the central mystic dogma of Roman Mithraism and is found in any mithraeum (*q.v.*), Mithras, wearing a Phrygian cap and pants, slays the bull from above while looking away.

topos From Greek *τοπος* (place), whence commonplace: a literary theme or meme.

U

ʾumma The Islamic community.

V

vāspuhrān High ranking elite, princes.

vāstryōshān sālār Middle Persian *wastrā-i ūshān sālār*, from Avestan *vāstriiō-fšuiiaṇt* (farmer): chief of the agriculturalists.

W

wastrā-i ūshān sālār See *vāstryōshān sālār*.

wizarishn From Middle Persian *wizārdan* (to separate): time of separation, redemption, whence the end of the material world, after the Sōshyant (*q.v.*) has defeated the evil forces of Ahrīman (*q.v.*) and his *drug* (*q.v.*) at *frashegird* (*q.v.*).

wuzurgān Grandees.

wuzurg framādār Supreme leader, prime minister. See also *hazārbed*.

X

X^{w}adāy-Nāmag New Persian *Khudāynāmag*: the *Book of the Lords*, that is, *Kings*, whence *Shāhnāma*.

xwarra See *farr*.

Y

Yasht Any of the Avestan hymns to Ahūrā Mazdā, the archangels (*Amahraspands*, *q.v.*), and other *yazatas* (*q.v.*). Some, like the *Mihr Yasht* (see Mithra) and the *Hōm Yasht* (see *hōm*), predate Zoroaster.

yazata Literally, a *being worthy of worship*: any of the lesser deities in the Zoroastrian pantheon, angel.

Z

zandīk Arabic *zindīq*: literally *reader of the Zand* (*q.v.*), but used in the sense of heretic, especially applied to Mazdakites.

Zand Middle Persian translation of the *Avestā* (*q.v.*), together with glosses and commentaries.

Zurvān Avestan *zruuan* (time): the father of the divine twin brothers Ahūrā Mazdā (*q.v.*) and Ahrīman (*q.v.*) according to the Zurvanite branch of Zoroastrianism.

Index

Persian and Armenian figures are listed under their gentilitial name (in boldface), when known (conjectural associations are marked *; see p. 467).

A

abākhtar (north), *listed under* kūst
Ābān
 ~ Jādhūyih, *listed under* Jādhūyih
 deity, *see* Apam Napāt
Abarshahr, *see also* Nīshāpūr, 50, 65, 71, 139, 273, 276
ʿAbbās b. ʿAbdalmuṭṭalib, 227
ʿAbbāsid
 ~ caliphs, *listed under* Caliph
 ~ historiography, 35, 437, 454
 ~ revolution, 315, 397, 414–422, 425, 426, 429, 435–438, 443, 448–450
ʿAbbāsids, 5, 6, 35, 39, 62, 275, 287, 309, 315, 317, 318, 354, 376, 378, 380, 392, 397, 414–422, 425–427, 429, 435–441, 443, 444, 446, 448–451, 454, 456, 459
ʿAbd al-Jabbār b. ʿAbdalraḥmān, 316
ʿAbd Rabb al-Kabīr, 309
ʿAbdalḥamīd, 315
ʿAbdallāh b. ʿAbdallāh b. ʿItbān, 248
ʿAbdallāh b. ʿĀmir, 257, 271–274, 276, 469
ʿAbdallāh b. Khāzim Sulāmī, 278, 469
ʿAbdallāh b. Saʿīd, 435
Abīvard, 318, 417, 418
Abruwān, 61
Abū ʿĀwn b. ʿAbdalmalik, 316
Abū Bakr, *listed under* Caliph
Abū Jaʿfar Zarātusht, 62
Abū ʾl-ʿAbbās Ṭūsī, 317
Abū ʾl-Khaṣīb ʿUmar b. al-ʿAlāʾ, 316–318, 441
Abū Khuzaymah, 317
Abū Manṣūr ʿAbdalrazzāq, 14, 394, 463
 † in 962 CE, 14
 the prose *Shāhnāma* of ~, 14, 271, 463
Abū Mūsā al-ʾAshʿarī, 237, 239, 245, 248, 257, 469
Abū Muslim, 315, 316, 414, 415, 425–427, 433, 435–451, 454, 459
 ~'s call for al-riḍā min āl-i Muḥammad, 414, 426, 435, 459
 † in 755 CE, 315, 437–444, 450
Abū Silt, *listed under* **Kanārangīyān**
Abū ʿUbayd, 207, 210, 211, 213, 468
Abū ʿUbaydah Ḥanafī, 438
 † in 755 CE, 438
Achaemenid
 Darius I, (*ruled 549–486* BCE), 358, 359, 394
 Darius III, (*ruled 380–330* BCE), 19, 29, 358, 385
 Vīshtāspā, father of Darius III, 29, 385
Achaemenids, 1, 20, 22, 23, 26, 34, 36, 37, 45, 110, 140, 351, 358, 359, 375, 385, 387, 405, 456
Ādargulbād (Adergoudounbades), *listed under* **Kanārangīyān**
Ādhar
 deity, *see* Īzad-i Ādhar
 ~ Farnbagh, *listed under* fire

~ Gushnasp, *listed under* fire
~ Narseh, *listed under* **Sāsānid**
~ Valāsh, *listed under* **Kārin**
Adiabene, 50, 347
ādur, *see* Īzad-i Ādhar
Ādur Anāhīd, *listed under* **Sāsānid**
ādurbādagān
north, *listed under* kūst
province, *see* Azarbāyjān
Aelian (historian), 358
Afrāsīyāb, 116, 376, 408–410, 413, 414, 441, 444
Agathias (historian), 299
agnatic, 27–29, 56, 94, 97, 115, 173, 188, 201, 229, 252, 268, 269, 297, 306, 314, 365, 393, 394, 419, 440, 448, 451
ahl al-buyūtāt, 58, 59, 88, 90, 93
•, *variants:* bozorgān; vuzurgān; al-ʿuẓamāʾ
ahlamōγ
~ ī frēftār, 337
~ ī nask ōšmurd, 337
Aḥnaf, 240, 257, 258, 469
Aḥrāʾ, 62
ahramōk, *see* ahlamōγ
Ahrīman, 114, 322, 332, 339, 353, 360, 361, 370, 371, 411, 499, 501, 502, 506, 507
Ahura (Lord), *listed under* Ahūrā Mazdā, Varuna, or Mithra
Ahūrā Mazdā, 326, 327, 331, 334, 339, 346, 350–353, 358, 361, 367, 371, 387, 390, 393, 399, 404, 409, 411, 499, 501, 502, 504, 506, 507
Ahvāz, 194, 227, 236–238, 240, 469, 513
•, *see also* Battle of ~
airya, 394
ʿajam, 158, 192, 217, 218, 250, 251, 255, 316, 395, 499
Akhshunwār, 381, 382
al-ʿAlāʾ b. Ḥaḍramī, 237, 238
Albania, *see* Arrān
Alburz, 137, 369, 370, 372, 375, 409, 414
~ as Harā, 369, 432
Damāvand in ~, 250
Mount Manush in ~, 414
Alexander the Great, 19, 34, 39, 125, 321, 385, 445
† in 323 BCE, 19, 33
demonization of ~, 34, 325, 431
Alexandria, 142, 143
Āl-i Bāvand
Bāv, 107, 289–295, 309, 471
•, *conflation of several members of the* **Ispahbudhān**
† around 665 CE, 293, 294, 306–308, 451
as Farrukh Hormozd, 291
as Farrukhzād, 291–294, 303, 304, 306–309, 424, 461–463
as Vistāhm, 290, 291
Suhrāb, *listed under* **Ispahbudhān**
Āl-i Bāvands, 107, 288, 292, 294, 302, 305–307, 309, 451
Āl-i Jāmāsp
Bādūspān, son of Jīl-i Jīlānshāh, 307, 471
Dābūyih, 306–308, 471
† around 673 CE, 307, 308
Dādmihr (Ibrāhīm), son of Khurshīd, 317, 471
Dādmihr, 311–313, 471
† around 740 CE, 312
Fahrān, 314, 471
Farrukhān, paternal cousin of Khurshīd Shāh, 314, 438, 471
Farrukhān-i Bozorg (Dhu 'l-Manāqib), 307–314, 471
† around 728 CE, 312
Farrukhān-i Kūchak, 313, 471
Hormozd (Abū Hārūn ʿĪsā), son of Khurshīd, 317, 471
Jāmāsp, (*ruled 497–499*), 75, 114, 298–301, 303, 377, 385, 398, 471
† circa 530–540 CE, 301
Jīl-i Jīlānshāh, 255–257, 265, 292, 299, 302–308, 317, 374, 377, 398, 424, 440, 447, 459, 469, 471
† around 665 CE, 306, 307
Jīlānshāh, 302, 471
Jushnas, 314, 471

Khurshīd Shāh, 313–317, 377, 378, 438, 440, 441, 443, 445, 447, 450, 451, 459, 471
† around 757 CE, 317
Narsī, 301, 471
† circa 570–580 CE, 301
Pīrūz, 136, 137, 301, 302, 377, 471
Sārūyih, 314, 471
Ṭūs, 315, 316, 438, 440, 471
ʾUmmat al-Raḥmān, daughter of Khurshīd, 317, 471
Vandād Hormozd (Mūsā), son of Khurshīd, 317, 471
Vandarand, 314, 471
Āl-i Jāmāsps, 137, 296, 298, 301–307, 309, 311, 315, 317, 374, 377, 398, 424, 438, 440, 441, 443, 447, 448, 450, 451, 458, 471
Āl-i Kayūs, *presumed dynasty of Kayūs* **Sāsānid**, *confused with the* **Āl-i Bāvand**
Amahraspands, 49, 198, 326, 330, 339, 367, 373, 431, 499
Amazaspes III Parnabazid, *see also* Arsacids, Georgian, 44
Amesha Spentas, *see* Amahraspands
Āmid, 64, 103, 111, 177, 269
Amida, *see* Āmid
ʿAmr b. al-ʿĀṣ, 192, 193
Āmul, 40, 73, 90, 114, 135, 136, 209, 261, 293, 295, 310, 314, 317, 376
., *see also* mint of ~
Anāhitā, 326, 327, 331–334, 387, 390, 394, 499
Anak, *listed under* ***Sūren**
Anatolia, 141, 358
Anbār, 200, 201, 203, 227, 468, 513
., *see also* Battle of ~
Andarzghar, 195, 468
Andīgān kings, 50
Andragoras, 20
anēr, 393, 423, 499
Angł, 103
Angra Mainyu, *see* Ahrīman
Antioch, 19, 177, 389
Antiochus II, 20
Anūshjān, 191–194, 468, 471
† around 630 CE, 194
Apam Napāt, 354, 412
Aparhatsik', *see* Abarshahr
apocalypticism, 404–406, 408–411, 413, 446, 459
Aprenak, 50
Arabs, *passim*
Aramazd, *see* Ahūrā Mazdā
Ārash, 376, 377, 379
Araxes, 133
Ardā Wīrāz, 330, 431–433
Ardabīl, 116, 117, 130, 403
Ardashīr, *listed under* **Sāsānid**
Ardashīr Khurrah, 38, 61, 76, 147, 367
., *see also* mint of ~
Ardavān, *listed under* **Arsacid**
ʿArfajah b. Harthamah, 237
argbed, 61, 499
ʿāriḍ, 88
aristocracy, *see* ahl al-buyūtāt
Arjāsp, king of Tūrān, 406
Armāyīl, 40, 305
Armenia, *passim*
army
~ of Persia and the East, 150, 155, 156, 159, 173, 181, 196
~ of Gurgān, 254
~ of Khuzistān, 117
~ of Nīmrūz, 128, 155, 156, 173, 177, 184, 198, 199, 245
~ of Sīstān, *see* army of Persia and the East, or of Nīmrūz
~ of Shahrvarāz, 147, 149, 150, 152, 156, 159, 173, 177, 196, 198, 199, 306
~ of Zābulistān, 117
Ispahbudhāni ~ of Azarbāyjān, 150, 152, 159, 173, 177, 184, 199, 204, 244, 248
Arrajān, *see* Veh-az-Amid-Kavād
Arrān (Albania), 73, 116, 299, 300, 391
Arrianus (historian), 26
Arsaces, *listed under* **Arsacid**
Arsacid
Ardavān, (*ruled 216–224*), 9, 42, 45–47, 122, 125, 224, 361, 366, 367, 385

† in 224 CE, 9, 42
Arsaces I, (*ruled 247–211* BCE), 19, 24, 25, 300
Kārin, son of Phraat IV, 26
Koshm, daughter of Phraat IV, 26, 110
Mithradates I, (*ruled 171–138* BCE), 20, 25, 359, 379, 402
Mithradates II, (*ruled 123–88* BCE), 25, 359
Mithradates III, (*ruled 57–54* BCE), 359
Mithradates IV, (*ruled 129–147?*), 359
Orodes II, (*ruled 57–38* BCE), 462
Phraat IV, (*ruled 38–2* BCE), 26, 110
Phraat V, (*ruled 2* BCE–*4* CE), 26
Sūren, son of Phraat IV, 26
Tiridates, brother of Vologeses, king of Armenia, 21
Vologeses, (*ruled 51–78*), 21, 338
Arsacids, 2, 6, 7, 9, 10, 12, 13, 19–27, 33, 35–37, 39, 42–49, 53, 57, 64, 86, 87, 96, 110, 112, 125, 126, 128, 129, 139, 182, 321, 323, 327, 328, 338, 347, 356, 358–362, 364, 366, 367, 371, 385, 386, 389, 402, 405, 410, 455, 459, 463, 504
Armenian ~, 12, 13, 20, 42–45, 57, 72, 300, 359, 386, 388, 391
Georgian ~, 44
religious policy of ~, 24, 323, 359, 360
Arsakeia, *see* Rayy
Arshak, *listed under* **Arshakuni**
Arshakuni
Arshak II, 338
Arshak III, 57
Artashēs, 43, 300, 338
Khosrov III, 43
† in 614 CE, 43
Khusrov I, 42
Tiran, 338
Tiridates I, 43, 388
Tiridates III, 44, 387
Vřamshapuh, 43, 338
† in 614 CE, 43
Artaz, 300
artēshtārān, 47
Asaak, 19
Asāwira, 239–241, 274
Asfādjushnas, 156–158
asha (Av. aša), 339, 350, 354, 357, 412, 499
aṣ̌əmaoγa, *see* ahlamōγ
Ashkanīyān, *see* Arsacids
Ashtāt, *listed under* **Mihrān**
Āsōristān, 150, 347, 382
Asparapet, *listed under* **Ispahbudhān**
aspbed, 98, 100, 101, 105, 115, 117, 216, 296, 364, 499
Aspebedes, *listed under* **Ispahbudhān**
asravān, 47
Assyria, *see* Āsōristān
Aštat, *see* Ashtāt **Mihrān**
Aštišat, 390
Aswār, *listed under* **Kārin**
ātakhsh, *see* Īzad-i Ādhar
āϑravan, *see* āsravān
Atrak, river, 19
Āturpāt, 332, 334, 336, 345, 357
Augusta Antonina, *see* Constantinople
Avars, 301
Avestā, 47, 124, 198, 325, 334–337, 341, 342, 345, 347, 350, 352, 370, 371, 375, 394, 412, 428, 446, 499, 501, 504, 505, 507
Younger ~, 47, 394, 500
ʿAyn Tamr, *see* Battle of ~
ʿayyārs, 87, 434, 500
Āzādbih, governor of Ḥīra, 190, 198, 199, 219, 468
son of ~, 199, 219
azādhān, 29, 48, 500
Azarbāyjān, xi, 6, 8, 39, 73, 103, 116, 117, 125, 127–130, 132, 149–153, 159, 173, 176–178, 184–186, 188, 189, 199, 204, 222, 229, 235, 241, 244, 245, 248, 249, 259, 262, 263, 275, 278, 279, 281, 290, 304, 306, 308, 322, 333, 347, 381, 392, 393, 397, 441, 442, 452, 454, 457, 459, 463, 467, 469, 503

., *variants:* Atr(a)patakan; Atropatene; Ādūrbādagān
Azarmīdukht, *listed under* **Sāsānid**

B

Ba'al, 327
al-Bāb, *see* Darband
Bābak Khurramdīn, 6, 73, 392, 393, 425, 436, 437, 452, 459
Bābak
  ., *listed under* **Sāsānid**
Bābak-i Behruwān, 89
Bābakiya, 459
Babaman Zādigān, ⇌ Shāhīn
Bāb-i Ṣūl, 381, 386
Babylonia, 80, 347, 358
Bactria, *see* Balkh
Badakhshān, 385
Bādghīs, 277, 434, 435, 469
Bādūspān, *listed under* **Āl-i Jāmāsp**
Bagayarich, 388
Baghdād, 203, 219
Bagratuni
  Smbat, 136–140, 142, 151, 153, 154, 173, 174, 275, 297, 298, 303, 304
    ., *variants:* Khusrov-Shum; Khusrow Shenūm
    † in 617 CE, 138, 298
    as governor of Gurgān, 136–139, 297
    as governor of Khurāsān, 138–140, 142, 297, 300, 303
  Varaztirotsʿ, 153, 154, 173, 174, 235, 242, 243, 248, 249, 269, 298, 469
    ., *variants:* Khusrov-Shum; Khusrow Shenūm
    † around 643 CE, 249
Bagrewand, 103
Bahman, 499
Bahman, son of Isfandīyār, 135, 143
Bahrām
  < Av. Vərəθraγna, 362, 389, 390, 411, 432, 440, 459
  > Arm. Vahagn, 389
  ., *variants:* Verethragnā; Vahrām; Vahagn (Arm.); Vərəθraγna (Av.)
  ~ fire, *see* fire
  ~-i Ādargulbād, *listed under* **Kanārangīyān**
  ~-i Āturmāh, *see* below under Māh Ādhar
  ~-i Chūbīn, *listed under* **Mihrān**
  ~-i Māh Ādhar, 101, 119–124
    ., *variants:* Bahrām-i Ādhar Mahān; Bahrām-i Āturmāh; Wahrām-i Ādurmāh (*on seals*)
    † around 580–585 CE, 122
  ~ I, II, III, IV, V (Gūr), *listed under* **Sāsānid**
  ~ VI, ⇌ Bahrām-i Chūbīn **Mihrān**
  deity, 326, 327, 411
  Kai ~, *listed under* Kai
  son of Farrukhzād, *listed under* **Ispahbudhān**
Bahrāmīyān
  Bahrām ~, 68
  Pīrūz ~, 68
  *Mihrāns, 68
Bahrayn, 227
Bahurasīr, *see* Veh Ardashīr
bāj, *see* taxes
Balāsh, *see* Bilāsh under **Sāsānid**
Balkan, 301
Balkh, 20, 73, 74, 76, 126, 139, 175, 266, 322, 405, 406, 426
  Greco–Bactrian states, 360
Bāmdād, *listed under* Mazdak
Barāz, 260, 425
Bardaʿa, 116, 117, 130, 403
barīd, 145, 500
Barmakids, 175
Barshawādgān, 40
Bārusmā, 203
Baṣrah, 36, 190, 192, 227, 236–238, 243, 257, 272
Bāsūya, 434
battle
  ~ of Ahvāz, 236, 469
  ~ of Anbār, 200, 201, 468
  ~ of ʿAyn Tamr, 168, 201, 206, 468
  ~ of Bridge, 168, 198, 213–220, 283, 468
    ., *variants:* Battle of al-Qarqus; al-Quss

~ of Buwayb, 218, 219, 468
~ of Carrhae, 462
~ of Dhāt al-Salāsil, 192–194, 468
~ of Dūmat al-Jandal, 201, 468
~ of Firāḍ, 168, 201, 468
~ of Gaugamela, 358
~ of Ḥuṣayd, 201, 468
~ of Iṣfahān, 197, 213, 241, 247, 253, 469
~ of Jalūlāʾ, 222, 234–237, 242, 244, 245, 257, 469
~ of Kaskar, 201, 211, 212, 216, 468
~ of Madhār, 168, 193, 194, 218, 468
~ of Maqr, 198, 211, 468
~ of Mutʿah, 201
~ of Namāriq, 168, 207, 211–213, 468
~ of Nihāvand, 35, 175, 198, 215, 216, 222, 234, 241–244, 246–248, 252, 275, 469
~ of Qādisiya, 11, 35, 157, 186, 197, 216, 220, 222, 224, 226, 228, 230–236, 242, 244, 257, 269, 291, 469
~ of Rām Hurmurz, 469
~ of Ṭāwūs, 238
~ of Tustar, 469
~ of Ubullah, 190–193, 198, 227, 237, 283, 468
~ of Ullays, 195, 196, 198, 203, 211, 468
~ of Veh Ardashīr, 199, 468
~ of Wāj Rūdh, 248, 249, 278, 469
~ of Walajah, 168, 195, 468
~ of Yarmūk, 202
Kai Khusrow's ~ at Fārāb, 116
Bāvandids, *see* Āl-i Bāvands
Bawi, *listed under* **Ispahbudhān**
Bayhaq, 246
bazm (banquet), 389
Bēt Aramāyē, *see* Āsōristān
Bet-Darāyē, 48
Bēzhan, *listed under* **Kārin**
Bihādūniya, 434
Bihāfarīd, 6, 354, 393, 426–437, 439, 445, 451, 452, 459
† in 749 CE, 436
followers of ~, 393, 436
Bihāfarīdiya, *see* Bihāfarīd, followers
Bilāsh, *listed under* **Sāsānid**
Bīnālūd, 417
Bīsetūn, 394
Bisṭām, 112, 213, 253, 261
Bithynia, 1
Boe, *listed under* **Ispahbudhān**
Bolberd, 74
fortress of ~, 71
gold mines of ~, 71
Bolum, *see* Bolberd
Bozorg-Mehr, ⇌ *Dādmihr **Kārin**, 114, 126, 329
Brahmans, 328, 332, 419
bridge, *see* Battle of ~
Buddhists, 175, 328, 330, 332, 335, 419
Bukayr b. ʿAbdallāh, 278, 279, 469
Bukhārā, 126, 406
Bulghār, 314
bull, *listed under* Fereydūn, Mihr worship, tauroctony, Taurus
bulla, *see* seals
Bundahishn, 339, 375, 376, 405, 411, 412, 446, 452
Bundos the Manichean, 344
Bunyān, 237
Būrāndukht, *listed under* **Sāsānid**
Burāzih, *see* Gurāzih **Sūren**
Burs, 203
Burzīn Mihr, *see* fire of ~
Burzīn Shāh, *listed under* **Mihrān**
Burzīnān, 364
Būst, *see* Bisṭām
Buwayb, *see* Battle of ~
Buyids, 394, 446, 454, 463
Byzantines, *passim*
Byzantium
city, *see* Constantinople
empire, *passim*

C

Cabades, ⇌ Qubād under **Sāsānid**
Caesaria
~ in Cappadocia, 141
~ in Palestine, 177
caesaropapism, 9, 500

Caliph
  ~ Abū Bakr, (*ruled 632–634*), 4, 167, 168, 170, 178, 190, 191, 207, 257, 282–285, 465
    † in 634, 207, 257
  ~ Hārūn al-Rashīd, (*ruled 786–809*), 165
  ~ Mahdī, (*ruled 775–785*), 316, 439
  ~ Manṣūr, (*ruled 754–775*), 315, 316, 437–441, 445, 449, 451
  ~ Muʿāwiya, (*ruled 661–680*), 465
  ~ Muʿtaṣim, (*ruled 833–842*), 62
  ~ Sulaymān b. ʿAbdalmalik, (*ruled 715–717*), 310, 311
  ~ ʿUmar, (*ruled 634–644*), 4, 167, 168, 170, 193, 207, 211, 220, 227, 233, 234, 237–242, 247, 249, 255, 259, 271, 282, 465
  ~ ʿUthmān, (*ruled 644–656*), 257, 259, 271
Caoses, ⇌ Kayūs under **Sāsānid**
Carmenia, 50
Carrhae, *see* Battle of ~
Caspian
  ~ Sea, 19, 20, 36, 72, 92, 112, 231, 296, 300, 314
  ~ gates, 300
Caucasia, 24, 45, 53, 55, 73, 76, 116, 117, 125, 140, 231, 278, 279, 299, 300, 306, 454
Central Asia, 24, 310, 314, 406, 418, 419, 425
Chagād-i Dāitī, *see* Chinvat Bridge
Chaghānī, 382
Chalcedon, 1, 141
Chihr-Burzēn, ⇌ Sīmāh-i Burzīn **Kārin**
Chinvat Bridge, 353, 432, 500
Chionites, *see* Kidarites
Chishmih-i Sū, 66
Chor (pass), 300
Chorasmia, *see* Khwārazm
Chosroids, *see* Arsacids, Georgian
Christians, 13, 323, 325, 327, 328, 330, 332–335, 337, 347–349, 362, 386, 387, 419
  Armenian ~, 12, 44, 349, 386–388, 390–392
Cilicia, 177
Circle of Justice, 59, 93, 342, 343, 346, 347, 352, 354, 356, 357, 368, 380, 390, 400, 457, 458
city
  kingly ~, 38, 39, 500
  polis, 38, 504
coins
  ~ of Arsaces I, 25
  ~ of Azarmīdukht, 208
  ~ of Būrāndukht, 208–209, 217–218
  ~ of Bahrām-i Chūbīn, 132
  ~ of Farrukh Hormozd, 205
  ~ of Hormozd I, 331
  ~ of Kai Pīrūz, 385
  ~ of Khurshīd Shāh, 378
  ~ of Khusrow Parvīz, 137
  ~ of Vistāhm (Pīrūz), 133
  ~ of Yazdgird III, 221–223, 246
  Arsacid ~, 360
confederacy
  church-state ~, 35, 324–326, 333–336, 457
  Sasanian-Parthian ~, 2–5, 12, 13, 15, 17, 29, 33, 37, 42, 45, 53, 56, 59, 62, 83, 97, 101, 110, 122, 127, 133, 135, 140, 159, 172, 173, 182, 211, 249, 309, 397, 455, 456
Constantine, *see* Emperor Constantine or Constans
Constantinople, *see also* Byzantium, 1, 30, 141, 143
Constantius, *see* Emperor Constantius
Copper Fortress, *see* Rūyīn Dizh
cow, *listed under* Fereydūn, Mihr worship, tauroctony
Crassus, 462
Ctesian method, 9, 14, 113, 116–118, 278, 405, 462, 500
Ctesiphon, 35, 41, 68, 77–79, 81, 84, 127, 178, 180, 184, 195, 196, 198–200, 210, 215, 218, 219, 231, 234, 244, 245, 251, 289, 460
cura palatii, 126, 500

D

Dābūyids, progeny of Dābūyih, *listed under* **Āl-i Jāmāsp**
Dābūyih, *listed under* **Āl-i Jāmāsp**
Dād-Burz-Mihr, *see* Dādmihr **Kārin**
Dādmihr
 ~ Kārin, *listed under* **Kārin**
 son of Farrukhān-i Bozorg, *listed under* **Āl-i Jāmāsp**
 son of Khurshīd, *listed under* **Āl-i Jāmāsp**
Dahae, 19, 20, 23, 25, 504
Ḍaḥḥāk, 40, 354, 370–372, 374
dāʿī, 416, 435, 449
Damascus, 141, 207, 318
Damāvand, 40, 47, 90, 253, 305, 309, 310, 369, 370, 372, 373, 469
 •, *see also* Alburz
Dāmghān, 251
Dara, 102, 125, 141
Darband, 215, 216, 231, 242, 279, 280, 299, 300
dār-i Mihr, 357, 375, 388
 •, *see also* mithraeum, mithradāna
darīgbed, 126, 186, 500
Dasht-i Bārīn, 61
Daskhurantsʿi (historian), 300
Dastabā, 243
dastār, 391, 400, 500
dastgird, *see* city, kingly
Dastimaysān, 236
dastwar, 323, 324, 500
Datoyean, 139
daʿwā, 414, 416, 500
dayeakordi, 71, 74, 268, 500
Daylam, 40, 47, 72, 248, 302, 311, 442
dehkān, 85, 92, 211, 250, 260, 463, 500, 505
Dēnkard, 88, 322, 323, 325, 327, 336, 337, 341, 480
derafsh-i Kāvīyān, 117, 217, 371
dev-worship, 322, 328, 331
Dhāt al-Salāsil, *see* Battle of ~
Dhū Qār, 220
Dhu ʾl-Ḥājib, epithet of Bahman Jādhūyih, 196, 198, 202, 213, 217, 241, 247, 248, 253
 † around 642 CE, 213, 248
Dhu ʾl-Manāqib, ⇌ Farrukhān-i Bozorg under **Āl-i Jāmāsp**
dibhērān, 47
Dihistān, 19, 22, 23, 49, 116, 254
 ~ culture, 23
dihqān, *see* dehkān
Dīnār, 243, 244, 252, 275, 469
Dīnawar, 36
Dionysius (historian), 177
dīwān, 227, 501
Dīyārbakr, *see* Āmid
dizh
 ~-i Kalānān, 367
 Rūyīn ~, 126, 266, 406, 439, 441, 442, 446
 Kang ~, 409, 412
driyōšān ǰādaggōw ud dādvar, *see* jādhūyih
drug, 322, 412
Dūmat al-Jandal, *see* Battle of ~
Dumbāvand, *see* Damāvand
Dura Europos, *see also* mithraeum, at Dura Europos, 22, 389
dvandva, 331, 501
Dvin, 149
dynasticism, 2, 20, 35, 53–56
 •, *see also* feudalism; étatism

E

Edessa, 177
Egypt, 20, 141–143, 335
Elias of Nisibis (historian), 299
Eḷmantsʿ, 300
Emperor
 ~ Constans II, (*ruled 641–668*), 176
 ~ Constantine, (*ruled 306–337*), 335
 ~ Constantius, (*ruled 337–361*), 334
 ~ Gordian III, (*ruled 238–244*), 400
 ~ Heraclius, (*ruled 610–641*), 1, 3, 30, 141, 142, 144, 145, 147–149, 151, 152, 174, 176, 177, 196, 201, 202, 456
 ~ Julian, (*ruled 361–363*), 57
  † in 363 CE, 57
 ~ Justinian, (*ruled 527–565*), 102, 110

~ Maurice, (*ruled 582–602*), 30, 127, 143, 154
† in 602 CE, 143
~ Nero, (*ruled 54–68*), 43, 388
~ Philip the Arab, (*ruled 244–249*), 400
~ Phocas, (*ruled 602–610*), 143
~ Tiberius II, (*ruled 574, 578–582*), 93
~ Valerian, (*ruled 253–260*), 400
ērān, 411
ērān-dibhērbadh, 47, 501
ērān-spāhbed, 47, 94, 99, 100, 104, 105, 115–117, 153, 156, 173, 181, 205, 216, 250, 290, 295–297, 379, 405, 462, 470, 501–505
Ērānshahr, 33, 39, 40, 407–409
Ēšm, *see* Kheshm
étatism, 2, 9–11, 26, 55, 56, 412, 456
., *see also* feudalism; dynasticism
Euphrates, 177, 198, 389, 462
exaggerators, *see* ghulāt

F

Fahrān, *listed under* **Āl-i Jāmāsp**
Farghānah, 258
Farhād-i Mihr Burzīn, 68
Farīburz, *listed under* **Mihrān**
Farīm, *see* Kūh-i Kārin
Farnbagh, *see* fire of Ādhar ~
farr, 48, 57, 66, 289, 326, 354, 363, 367, 370, 371, 376, 390, 391, 409, 411, 412, 458, 501, 506
., *variants:* farn; farrah; xwarra; khvarenah; pʻarkʻ(Arm.); Kavyan Fortune; x^varənah (Av.)
ram as symbol of ~, 48, 367, 391, 500
Farrukh Hormozd, *listed under* **Ispahbudhān**
Farrukhān
., ⇌ Farrukh Hormozd **Ispahbudhān**
~-i Bozorg, *listed under* **Āl-i Jāmāsp**
~-i Farrukhzād, *listed under* **Ispahbudhān**
~-i Kūchak, *listed under* **Āl-i Jāmāsp**
cousin of Khurshīd, *listed under* **Āl-i Jāmāsp**
Farrukhzād, *listed under* **Ispahbudhān**
Farrukhzād Ādharmagān, 146
Fārs, 22, 36, 38, 39, 48, 61, 63, 64, 76, 125, 148, 175, 190, 194, 205, 209, 214–217, 221–223, 227, 236–238, 241, 242, 246, 257, 262, 273, 274, 334, 363, 367, 408, 438, 469, 483, 499, 503, 504
Farvardigān, 430
Fasā, 344
Faustus of Byzantium (historian), 156
Fereydūn, 77, 354, 370–377, 409, 414
~ and cow worship, 373
feudalism, 24–26, 37, 41, 49, 52–57, 66
., *see also* dynasticism; étatism
Fiḥl, 207
Firāḍ, *see* Battle of ~
Fīrak Mihrān, *see* Shahrvarāz **Mihrān**
fire
~ of Ādhar Farnbagh, 328, 362, 363, 368, 378, 386, 458
~ of Ādhar Gushnasp, 153, 328, 362, 363, 368, 378, 386, 458
~ of Anāhit-Ardashīr, 332
~ of Bahrām, 327, 362, 412
~ of Burzīn Mihr, 68, 115, 328, 362–365, 368, 372, 378, 379, 386, 400, 402, 404, 447, 458
~ of Farāz-marā-āwar-khudāyā, 61
~ of Kārdādhān, 61
~ of Mājusnasān, 61
~ of Mihr Narsīyān, 61
~ of Zurvāndādhān, 61
~ temple in Karkoy, 364
as a deity, *see* Īzad-i Ādhar
ordeal by ~, 334, 356–357, 367
Firrīm, *see* Kūh-i Kārin
Fīrūzān, 174, 175, 177–181, 183, 196–198, 211, 213–216, 218–220, 223, 231–235, 241–243, 247, 257, 467–469
., *variants:* Khusrow Fīrūz; Pīrūz Khusrow; *Nēw Khusrow; al-Bayrūzān; Bundār
† in 642 CE, 175, 198, 242, 243

frashegird (Healing), 339, 501
Fus Farrukh, *see* Farrukh Hormozd **Ispahbudhān**
futūḥ, 2, 4, 13, 15, 16, 162, 164–166, 168, 170–173, 178, 189, 190, 227, 233, 235, 249, 270, 271, 273, 281–284, 293, 304, 420, 462, 465, 468

G

Gandhara, 335
Gandzak, 149, 152, 153, 176
Gāthās, 322, 350, 394, 499, 501
Gaugamela, *see* Battle of ~
Gāvbārih, Jīl-i Jīlānshāh the Cow Devotee, 292, 299, 302, 374, 377, 398, 440, 447, 459
., *see also* Jīl-i Jīlānshāh **Āl-i Jāmāsp**
Gāwān, *see* Jābān
Gay, *see* Iṣfahān
Gelam, Gelk, *see* Gīlān
Georgia, 43, 44, 48, 73, 74, 102
Gēv, 375
., *see also* under **Kārin**
Ghassanids, 203
ghāzī, 285
Ghazna, 288
ghulāt, 394, 501
Gīlān, 5, 40, 65, 68, 108, 114, 129, 130, 136, 137, 255, 263, 296–298, 300–303, 305, 307, 309, 373, 377, 398, 457, 463, 503
gītīg, 339, 346, 374, 429, 501
Gnostics, 330
gōhar, *see* agnatic
Gołon, *see* Gōrgōn **Mihrān**
Gorāz, *see* Shahrvarāz **Mihrān**
Gordian, *see* Emperor Gordian
Gorgēn Mīlād, 103, 117
., *see also* Gōrgōn **Mihrān**
Gōr-gōn, *see* Gōrgōn **Mihrān**
gorz, *see* ox-headed mace
gōsān, 10
Gostaham, ⇌ Vistāhm
Gousanastades, *see* Gushnāspdād **Kanārangīyān**
Greco-Bactrian states, *see* Balkh
Guaramids, *see* Arsacids, Georgian
Gūdarz, *listed under* **Kārin**
gumezishn (Mixture), 339, 501
Gurdūyih, 163
Gurgān, 20, 23, 36, 49, 67, 90, 112, 136, 137, 139, 209, 248, 250, 253–257, 261, 274, 292, 296, 297, 302–304, 311, 312, 316, 317, 360, 381, 382, 386, 397, 420, 438, 442, 444, 460, 469, 503
., *see also* mint of ~
Gurgēn Mīlād, *see* Gōrgōn **Mihrān**
Gushnasp, *see* fire of Ādhar ~
Gushnāsp, ruler of Ṭabaristān, 86–88, 91, 361
., *see also* Letter of Tansar
Gushnāspdād, *listed under* **Kanārangīyān**
Gushtāsp, 375

H

ḥadīth, 165, 501, 505
Haftānbūkht, 367
Hajar, 226
Ḥajjāj b. Yūsuf, 309, 310
Hamadān, 90, 152, 243, 248, 249, 438, 469
hanāmand, 353
hargbed, 61, 501
al-Ḥārith b. Surayj, 426
Ḥarrān, *see* battle, Carrhae
Hārūn al-Rashīd, *listed under* Caliph
Hāshim b. ʿUtbah, 235, 469
al-Hāshimī, ʿAbbās b. Muḥammad, 317
Hāshimiya, 425
hazārbed, 60, 62, 63, 73, 100, 104, 501, 506
Hecatompylos, *see* Qūmis
Hellenistic, 23, 38, 48, 358, 387
Hephthalites, 75, 76, 114, 116, 126, 139, 267, 297, 299, 300, 380–382, 384, 386, 408, 410, 444
Heraclius, *see* Emperor Heraclius
Herāt, 65, 71, 139, 209, 266, 277, 463
., *see also* mint of ~
herbad, 61, 85, 86, 243, 331, 403, 427, 502
Herodotus, 358

hijra, 1, 15, 167–171, 190–195, 199, 200, 202, 214, 220, 235, 248, 253, 281, 283, 284, 317, 422, 449, 465
Ḥīra, 69, 109, 170, 178, 190, 192, 198, 199, 202, 207, 211, 219, 227
Hishām b. Muḥammad, 172
Hormozd
~ I, II, III, IV, *listed under* **Sāsānid**
~ V, ⇌ Farrukh Hormozd **Ispahbudhān**
general, 191–196, 468
† around 629 CE, 193, 194, 196
son of Khurshīd, *listed under* **Āl-i Jāmāsp**
son of Yazdgird II, *listed under* **Sāsānid**
Hormozd-Ardashīr, *see* Ahvāz
Hrev, *see* Herāt
Ḥudhayfah, 243, 248, 293
hūiti, *see* hutukhshān
Ḥulwān, 215, 216, 235, 242, 245, 315, 469
Ḥumayd b. Qaḥṭabah, 435, 449, 450
Huns, 65, 72–74, 299, 300, 382
•, *see also* Hephthalites, Kidarites
Hurmuzān, xii, 232, 233, 236–238, 240–242, 245, 247, 257, 469
Hurmuzjird, 203
Ḥusayn, 465
† in 680 CE, 465
Hūshang, *listed under* **Sāsānid**
Ḥuṣayd, *see* Battle of ~
hutukhshān, 47
Hydaspes, *see* Vīshtāspā **Achaemenid**
Hyrcania, *see* Gurgān

I

ibāha 'l-nisā, 82, 93, 502
Iberia, 44, 50, 103
Iblīs, 289, 502
Ibn al-Kalbī, 259
Ibn Ashʿath Muḥammad, 309
Ibn Isḥāq al-Turk, 425
Ibn Isḥāq, 14, 172
ʾIkramah, 145, 172
Imām, 293, 414, 425, 502
Indra (dev), 322
Innaios, 333
inscriptions
•, *see also* Kirdīr
~ at Barm-i Delak, 332
~ at Naqsh-i Rajab, 50
~ at Naqsh-i Rostam, 333
~ at Persepolis, 358
~ of Tiridates I, 388
~ of Tāq-i Bustān, 326
Ardashīr I's ~ at Naqsh-i Rostam (ANRm), 361
Kirdīr's ~ at Naqsh-i Rajab (KKRb), 327, 332, 333
Kirdīr's ~ at Naqsh-i Rostam (KNRm), 327, 332
Kirdīr's ~ at Kaʿba-i Zartusht (KKZ), 327, 332
Kirdīr's ~ at Sar Mashhad (KSM), 327, 332, 333, 389
Shāpūr I's ~ at Ḥājī Ābād (ŠH), 48
Shāpūr I's ~ at Kaʿba-i Zartusht (ŠKZ), 38, 49, 50, 64, 505
Shāpur I's ~ at Bīshāpūr, 400
Darius' ~ at Bīsetūn (Beh), 394
Narseh's ~ at Paikuli (NPi), 321, 333
Iraj, 414, 444
Iraq, *passim*, 4, 15, 503
•, *see also* Mesopotamia
iṣbahbadh al-bilād, *see* ērān-spāhbed
Isdigousnas, *see* Īzadgushasp **Mihrān**
Iṣfahān, 49, 133, 136, 139, 197, 213, 238, 241, 242, 244–248, 253, 258, 259, 265, 301, 347, 438, 469, 514
•, *see also* Battle of ~
Isfandīyār, *listed under* **Ispahbudhān**
Isfandīyārs, 49, 60, 135, 143, 375, 406
Ishmaelites, ⇌ Arabs
Ishtar, 387
isnād, 145, 162, 193, 218, 505
ispahbud, xi, 114, 180, 185, 254–256, 265, 295, 302, 304–306, 309–314, 316, 317, 405, 426, 438, 440, 444, 445, 452, 459, 502, 505
•, *see also* spāhbed
Ispahbudhān, 3, 8, 27, 42, 49, 63, 83, 96, 99, 101, 104, 106–108, 110–112, 115, 118, 122, 127–133,

136, 137, 143, 146, 148, 151, 153–156, 159, 163, 164, 173, 176, 177, 181, 182, 186–189, 197, 204–208, 212, 228, 231, 244, 248–250, 257, 259, 260, 262–264, 268, 269, 274–278, 280, 290–298, 302–309, 365, 381, 392, 409, 413, 424, 444, 448, 451, 456, 458, 460–462, 467, 470, 471, 505

Ispahbudhān

Asparapet, maternal uncle of Khusrow II, 105–108, 111, 112, 117, 122, 127, 132, 188, 290–292, 462, 471

., *variants:* Parthian and Pahlaw aspet; sparapet; Aspebedes (*by Simocatta*)

† in 586 CE, 106, 108, 112, 122, 127, 131, 291

named Khurbundād(ūyih); Kharrād, 107, 290

named Shāpūr, 106, 107, 290–292, 295, 471

Aspebedes, maternal uncle of Khusrow I, 106, 107, 111, 212, 268, 291, 292, 471

† around 532 CE, 111, 268

Bahrām, 279, 306, 308, 469, 471

Bawi, 107, 290, 471

., *variants:* Bāv; Boe

Boe, 107, 290–292

Farrukh Hormozd, (*ruled 631*), 143–147, 150–153, 155, 156, 159, 169, 173, 174, 176–179, 184–190, 200, 204–208, 210, 224, 228, 235, 244, 248, 257, 262–264, 275, 276, 278, 291–293, 393, 424, 438, 440, 462, 471

., *variants:* Farrukhān; Khurrukhān; Farruhān; Fus Farrukh; Zādhān Farrukh-i Shahrdārān; Pusfarrukh; Saqrūkh; Khoṙokh Ormizd; Hormozd V

., *sometimes confused with his son Farrukhzād*

., *appears as Bāv in Tārīkh-i Ṭabaristān; see under* **Āl-i Bāvand**

† in 631 CE, 185–187, 206, 207, 210

Farrukhān-i Farrukhzād, 251, 471

Farrukhzād, 126, 150, 151, 153–156, 158, 159, 173, 175, 176, 183, 184, 186–189, 204, 208, 210, 222, 228–232, 234, 235, 241–246, 248, 250–257, 259–266, 269, 270, 272, 275–281, 291–294, 298, 302–309, 398, 424, 448, 451, 461–463, 469, 471

., *variants:* al-Zīnabī Abū 'l-Farrukhān; Vabī Farrukhān; Khurrazād-Mihr; Khoṙokhazat

., *sometimes called Farrukhān and confused with his father Farrukh Hormozd*

., *appears as Bāv in Tārīkh-i Ṭabaristān; see under* **Āl-i Bāvand**

† around 665 CE, 293, 294, 306–308, 451

Isfandīyār, 248, 249, 278, 279, 306, 308, 469, 471

., *variants:* Jarmīdhih b. al-Farrukhzād; Isfandīyādh b. al-Farrukhzār

Rustam, 148–153, 156, 157, 163, 173, 176, 185–189, 197, 206–220, 222–232, 234, 235, 244, 246, 248, 257, 259, 263, 269, 275–278, 462, 464, 468, 469, 471

† in 635 CE, 216, 228, 233–235, 244

Shahrām, 251, 471

Suhrāb, 293, 307, 308, 471

Tīrūyih, son of Vistāhm, 163, 189, 212, 232, 468, 469, 471

Vindūyih, 106–108, 112, 117, 122, 127, 128, 131, 132, 134, 153, 155, 158, 163, 187–189, 204, 212, 231, 268, 291, 297, 409, 471

., *variants:* Vndoy; Bindūya; Binduwān; Bindū; Bindoes

† around 594 CE, 112, 132, 138, 155, 163, 189

Vindūyih, son of Vistāhm, 134, 163, 189, 212, 232, 468, 469, 471
Vistāhm, 8, 52, 63, 68, 80, 96, 106–108, 110, 112, 117, 118, 122, 127, 128, 131–138, 143, 151, 154, 155, 158, 163, 181, 182, 187–189, 212, 213, 232, 250, 268, 270, 275, 290–292, 297, 300–303, 409, 442, 462, 470, 471
., *variants:* Bisṭām; Wistakhm (*on seals*); Gostaham; Vstam; Bestam
., *appears sometimes as Bāv in Tārīkh-i Ṭabaristān; see under* **Āl-i Bāvand**
∼ in Dīnawarī, 109, 110
† in 600 CE, 112, 137, 138, 155, 189, 297
Iṣṭakhr, *see* Stakhr
Istanbul, *see* Constantinople
Iyād, 169, 201, 202
Īzadgushasp, *listed under* **Mihrān**
Īzad Gushnasp, *listed under* **Mihrān**
Īzad-i Ādhar, 327, 409, 411, 412, 432

J

Jabalah b. Sālim, 461
Jābān, 190, 195, 196, 199, 211–213, 468
jādaggōw, *see* jādhūyih
jādhūyih, 107, 115, 195, 197, 258, 265, 501, 502
Ābān ∼, ⇌ *Farrukhzād **Ispahbudhān**, 197, 258, 264, 265
Bahman ∼, *variants:* Dhu 'l-Ḥājib; *Mardānshāh, 195–202, 212, 213, 217–219, 241, 242, 247, 248, 253, 468, 469
† around 642 CE, 213, 248
Hormozd ∼, 197, 202, 203, 468
Rustam ∼, ⇌ *Rustam **Ispahbudhān**, 197
Shahrvarāz ∼, *listed under* **Mihrān**
Jāḥiz, 34, 402
Jālīnūs, 157, 158, 213, 216, 217, 225, 226, 232, 460, 468
Jalūlā', *see* Battle of ∼
Jāmāsp
brother of Qubād, *listed under* **Āl-i Jāmāsp**
brother of Khusrow I, *listed under* **Sāsānid**
counselor of Vīshtāspā, 385
Jāmāsp Nāmak, 405–411, 413, 414, 446
Jamshīd, 354, 370, 373
Javitean Khusrow, ⇌ Varaztirots' **Bagratuni**
Jawhar b. Marrār al-ʿIjlī, 315, 438–440
Jazira, 318
Jerusalem, 139, 141–143, 176, 177
Jews, 323, 325, 328, 330, 332, 335, 337, 347–349, 419
Jibāl, 194, 215, 235, 238, 242, 438
jihād, 312
Jīlānshāh, *listed under* **Āl-i Jāmāsp**
Jīl-i Jīlānshāh, *listed under* **Āl-i Jāmāsp**
Jirih, 61
jīzya, *see* taxes
Johannes of Ephesus (historian), 120
Julian, *see* Emperor Julian
Jundaysābūr, 237
Jushnas, *listed under* **Āl-i Jāmāsp**
Jushnasf, 288
Jushnasmāh, *see* Māhādharjushnas
Justinian, *see* Emperor Justinian
Justinus (historian), 25
Jūzjānān, 259, 426

K

Kaʿba, 439, 443, 445, 447, 459, 502, 505
Kaʿba-i Zartusht, *see* inscriptions
Kābul, 86
Kābulshāh, 46
Kadiköy, *see* Chalcedon
Kai
∼ Khusrow, 39, 116–118
∼ Bahrām, 411, 412, 443, 446, 459
∼ Kavād, 39, 385
∼ Vīshtāspā, 385, 406
Kajū, 309
Kalāt, 266
Kāmindār, daughter of Narsī, 192
Kamsarakan, 74
Kārinid descent of ∼, 42
kanārang, 154, 261, 265–267, 269, 271, 272
Kanārangīyān, 3, 42, 49, 67, 68, 111, 154, 155, 173, 177, 233, 265–272,

274–277, 280, 298, 303–306, 309, 424, 435, 448–451, 460, 463

Kanārangīyān

Ādhargulbād, 111, 267–269

† around 540 CE, 269

Abū Silt Kanārī, 276

Bahrām, 268, 269

Gushnāspdād, 267, 268

† around 488 CE, 268

Kanārang-i Ṭūs, 232, 263, 265, 266, 269–273, 275–277, 469

., *variants:* Kanāra; Kanāz

Kanāra, 154, 232

Salim, 276

Shahrīyār, 232, 233, 269, 469

† in 635 CE, 233, 269

Kandūsān, 309

kārdār, 61, 90

Kardārīgan, 92, 146

Kardarigas, ⇌ Farrukh Hormozd **Ispahbudhān**, 149

Karēn, *see* Kārins

Kārin

spāhbed of Khurshīd, *listed under* **Kārin**

son of Sukhrā, *listed under* **Kārin**

son of Phraat IV, *listed under* **Arsacid**

Kārin

Ādhar Valāsh, 302, 303, 307

Aswār, 273, 274, 276, 469

Bīzhan, 117

Burzīn Shāh, 273, 274, 276, 469

Dādburzīn, 113, 277

., *perhaps a Ctesian reflection of Dādmihr below*

Dādmihr, 68, 114, 115, 121, 122, 126, 296, 302, 329, 379, 400

., *variants:* Dādburzīnmihr; Burzmihr; Dād-Burz-Mihr (*on seals*); *Bozorg-Mehr; *Dādburzīn

† in 575 CE, 379

Gēv, 117

Gūdarz, 116, 117

Kārin, rebel against the Arabs, 277, 278, 469

† around 654 CE, 278

Kārin, son of Sukhrā, 113, 295

Kārin, spāhbed of Khurshīd, 314–316

Mardānshāh Maṣmughān, 253, 305, 309, 469

Mihr, son of Sukhrā, 379

† in 620 CE, 379

Perozamat, 42

., *see also* Kamsarakan

Qārin, general, 193–196, 243, 468, 469

† around 630 CE, 194–196

Rahām, 117

Sīmāh-i Burzīn, 119–122, 461

., *variants:* Chihr-Burzēn (*on seals*)

† around 580–585 CE, 122

Sukhrā, 73, 75–81, 101, 104, 113, 114, 117, 120, 151, 274, 277, 294–296, 379, 383–385, 444

† around 495 CE, 81, 385

*Sunbād, 6, 275, 287, 315–317, 354, 376, 378, 405, 425, 426, 437–452, 458, 459

† in 755, 315–316, 438, 440, 444

Valāsh, 293, 294, 307–309

† around 674 CE, 308, 309

Zarmihr, 73–75, 77

Zarmihr, son of Sukhrā, 73, 81, 113, 114, 151, 209, 277, 295, 379

† in 558 CE, 379

Karin (city), 71

Kārins, 3, 6, 26, 42, 49, 50, 68, 73–81, 83, 96, 99, 101, 104, 112–118, 120–122, 129, 130, 135, 151, 193, 209, 243, 244, 252, 253, 260, 274–278, 281, 294–298, 302–309, 314, 329, 364, 371, 374, 376, 378–386, 392, 402, 424, 444, 448, 449, 451, 452, 458, 460, 461, 463, 469, 470

karīz, *see* qanāt

Karka de Lēdān, 334

Karkeh (river), 334

Karkoy, *listed under* fire

Kārnāmag-i Ardashīr-i Pāpagān, 46, 366, 367, 378
Kartli, *see* Iberia
Kaskar, 212
., *see also* Battle of ~
Katishk', 65
Kavād, *listed under* Kai; for Qubād, see under **Sāsānid**
Kāveh, 370, 371
Kayānids, 33, 39, 77, 86, 103, 104, 126, 264, 335, 362, 367, 385, 386, 409–411, 458, 460, 462
., *see also* Kai
Sāsānid pseudo-genealogy to ~, 33, 77, 335, 385–386
Kayūmarth, 9, 36, 370
Kayūs, *listed under* **Sāsānid**
Keresaspā, *see* Sām Narīmān
Khālid b. Walīd, 4, 166, 168, 170, 190–193, 199, 200, 202, 281, 478
Khalīfat b. Khayyāṭ, 190, 203, 277
Khāqān, 78, 103, 104, 113, 124, 126, 129, 209, 261, 288, 295, 380, 383–385, 400
kharāj, *see* taxes
Kharijites, 309, 310
Kharrād-i Mihr Pīrūz, 68
Khashm, *see* Kheshm
Khazars, 123, 231, 279, 280, 299
Khekewand, 137
Kheshm, xii, 407, 411, 445, 502
Khidash, 425
Khodā Nāmah, *see* X^{w}adāy-Nāmag
Khoṙeam, ⇌ Shahrvarāz **Mihrān**
Khoṙokh Ormizd, *see* Farrukh Hormozd **Ispahbudhān**
Khoshnavāz, 383
Khrokht, 139
Khudāynāmag, *see* X^{w}adāy-Nāmag
Khuramdīn, *see* Mazdakites
Khurāsān, 5, 8, 19, 20, 22, 39, 68, 74, 108, 111–115, 129–131, 134, 136–139, 153, 183, 185–187, 189, 195, 209, 210, 215, 216, 232, 242–244, 246, 249, 252–259, 261–267, 270–278, 281, 288, 290, 293, 296–298, 300, 303–308, 310, 311, 315, 316, 318, 321, 364, 367, 379, 393, 397, 405, 406, 408, 414–418, 426, 427, 437–439, 445, 446, 448–450, 457–459, 469, 503
~ highway, 437
Inner ~, 266, 305, 306, 309, 379, 417–419, 425, 427, 435, 442, 445, 448–451
Outer ~, 155, 266, 305, 417–419, 426, 435, 437, 442, 464
Khuraybah, 192
Khurbundād, *see* Bawi **Ispahbudhān**
Khurramiya, 425
Khurshīd Shāh, *listed under* **Āl-i Jāmāsp**
Khushnavāz, 77
Khusrov, *listed under* **Arshakuni**
Khusrov-Shum, ⇌ Smbat or Varaztirots' **Bagratuni**
Khusrow
., *variants:* Xusrau; Kisrā; Chosroes
~ I (Nowshīrvān), II (Parvīz), *listed under* **Sāsānid**
~ Shenūm, 140, 174, 235, 242, 243, 248, 249
., ⇌ Smbat or Varaztirots' **Bagratuni**
Khizravān ~, 130
Kai ~, *listed under* Kai
son of Yazdgird I, *listed under* **Sāsānid**
Khuṭrāniya, 80
Khuzistān, 36, 117, 165, 217, 221–223, 235–238, 242, 257, 262, 438, 491
khwarāsān (east), *listed under* kūst
Khwārazm, 39, 86, 290, 318, 321, 347, 360, 417, 419
khwarbarān (west), *listed under* kūst
Khwarezmia, *see* Khwārazm
khwēdōdah, 429, 433, 434, 502
Kidarites, 76, 299
., *see also* Hephthalites, Huns
Kirdīr, 327–333, 340, 348, 389, 431
., *see also* under inscriptions
Kirmān, 39, 50, 209, 217, 222, 223, 246, 257, 265, 367, 469, 503
., *see also* mint of ~

al-Kirmānī, Juday' b. 'Alī, 426
Komsh, *see* Qūmis
Kopet Dāgh, 23, 417
~ culture, 23
Koran, *see* Qur'ān
Koshm, *listed under* **Arsacid**
Kotit, lord of Amatunik', 133
Kūfa, 36, 165, 192, 218, 243, 272, 309
Kūh-i Kārin, 114, 295, 308, 374
Kūlā, 252, 293, 308
Kurdistān, 237, 238, 333
Kürendagh, 417
Kūshān, 136, 137, 139, 297
kūst, 39, 49, 95, 157, 503
~-i ādurbādagān, xi, 4, 6, 17, 39, 42, 84, 95–97, 100–104, 116, 117, 125, 127, 129, 130, 133, 136, 151, 165, 172, 215, 216, 222, 249, 250, 252, 263, 280, 281, 289, 295, 303, 359, 366, 368–370, 378, 392, 393, 397, 405, 414, 418, 419, 424–426, 437, 438, 441, 442, 447, 448, 450, 457, 462, 503
~-i khwarāsān, 4, 6, 17, 39, 42, 96, 97, 99, 115, 120, 122, 127, 130, 133, 136, 151, 165, 172, 188, 215, 216, 222, 249, 250, 262, 263, 274, 275, 277, 280, 281, 292, 295, 303, 359, 366, 368, 369, 378, 379, 392, 393, 397, 405, 414, 418, 419, 424–426, 437, 441, 442, 447, 448, 450, 457, 503
~-i khwarbarān, 40, 100, 106, 108, 115, 117, 131, 188, 215, 216, 221, 290, 503
~-i nēmrōz, 39, 64, 95, 100, 120, 121, 150, 153, 156, 157, 173, 181, 215–217, 221, 407, 462, 503

L

Lafūr, 114, 295
Lakhmids, 69
Lārījān, 370
Lazistān, 102, 103
letter (as topos)
~ of Tansar, 40, 85–92, 328, 334, 361, 378
Ādhar Valāsh's ~ to Yazdgird III, 303
Bahrām-i Chūbīn's ~ to Mušeł Mamikonean, 128, 129
Farrukzād's ~ to the Arabs, 256
Kanārang's ~s to the Arabs, 271–273
Khālid's ~ to general Hormozd, 191, 193
Khālid's ~ to the kings of Persia, 199, 200
Khāqān's ~ to Pīrūz, 383
Khusrow I's ~ to his pādhūspān, 83
Khusrow II's ~ to Farrukhān, 144, 145, 149, 152
Khusrow II's ~ to Shahrvarāz, 144, 145, 147, 152
Māhūy's ~ to Yazdgird III, 260
Persian nobility's ~ to Shāpūr Mihrān, 75
Qubād's ~ to Sukhrā, 79
Rustam's ~ to Farrukhzād, 156, 228–230
Shahrvarāz's ~ to Muthannā, 203
Shīrūyih Qubād's ~ to Heraclius, 176
Shīrūyih Qubād's ~ to Khusrow II, 154
Vistāhm's ~s to Khusrow II, 135
Yazdgird III's ~ to Farrukhzād, 262
Yazdgird III's ~ to Māhūy, 265
Yazdgird III's ~ to the Kanārang, 265, 266

M

mace, *see* ox-headed mace
al-Madā'in, *see* Ctesiphon
Madhār, *see* Battle of ~
Māh Afrīdhan, 240
Māh Dīnār, *see* Nihāvand
Māh Isfand, 158
Māhādharjushnas, 179–182, 192–194, 211, 212, 471
., *variants:* Mih Ādhar Jushnas; Jushnasmāh; Mihr Ḥasīs
† in 630 CE, 181, 182, 212
Māhawayh, *see* Māhūy
Mahbūdhān, 201, 468

Mahdī, *listed under* Caliph
Māhfarvardīn, 426–428, 430
mahistān, 25, 503
Mahoe, *see* Māhūy
mahr, *see* marriage, dowry
Mahraspand, 334, 336, 345
Māhūy, 259-263, 265, 266, 277, 292, 469
Māhyāy, 183
Makrān, 336
Mamak, *listed under* **Mamikonean**
Mamikonean
  Dawit', 157, 232
  Mamak, 133
  Mušeł, 127, 128, 154, 399
  Mušeł, son of Dawit', 157, 232, 233, 469
    † in 635 CE, 157, 233
  Vahan, 71–75, 391
Mamikoneans, 128, 129
Manādhir, 237
mang, 330, 431, 432, 503
Mānī, 325, 329–332, 345, 366, 428
  † around 276 CE, 331, 332
Manicheans, 289, 328–334, 338, 341, 344, 345, 366, 419
Manṣūr, *listed under* Caliph
Manu, 325
Manūchihr, 77, 342, 354, 375–378, 413, 414, 441, 444, 446, 447
Maqr, *see* Battle of ~
Mar ʿAmmo, 331
Mardānshāh
  pādhūspān of Nīmrūz, *listed under* ***Sūren**
  general, 212, 213
    † in 631 CE, 212, 213
  ~ Maṣmughān, *listed under* **Kārin**
  Pārsīg leader, probably Bahman Jādhūyih, 196–198, 202, 217, 219, 241, 247, 248, 253
    † around 642 CE, 213, 248
Margiana, *see* Marv
Marj al-Rāhiṭ, 203
Marmara, sea of, 141
marriage
  close-kin ~, *see* khwēdōdah
  dowry (mahr), 429
Marv, 50, 139, 238, 246, 257, 259-261, 265, 272, 297, 360, 414, 417, 418, 426, 435, 445, 450
Marv al-Rūd, 39, 259, 426
Marwanids, 239
Maryam, queen, 174, 236
marzbān, 43, 48, 70, 77, 103, 120, 125, 130, 136, 138, 153, 174, 190, 198, 231, 251, 259, 261, 263, 265, 271, 274, 309, 503
Mashtots', 44, 386
Maṣqalah b. Hubayrah al-Shaybānī, 308, 309
  † around 676 CE, 309
Maurice, *see* Emperor Maurice
Maysān, 236
maẓālim, 58, 503
Māzandarān, 72, 230, 369
  ., *see also* Ṭabaristān
Mazdak, 40, 114, 289, 326, 342, 344, 345, 428, 434, 439
  Zarādusht ~ the Older, 344, 345
Mazdakites, 81, 82, 86, 87, 93, 97, 289, 334, 336, 338-341, 344-346, 357, 377, 398, 429, 434, 507
  rebellion of the ~, 76, 78, 82, 83, 85-88, 93, 94, 99, 101, 116, 344, 346, 350, 379, 384
Māzīyār, 6, 287, 380, 437, 452, 458
Mebodes, 288
Mecca, 1, 167, 465
Media, 6, 20, 36, 40, 97, 130, 149, 152, 241, 321, 322, 347, 351, 360, 362, 438
Medina, 1, 167, 210, 465
mehean, *see* mithradāna, dār-i Mihr
Mehekan, *see* Mihragān
mēnōg, 330, 339, 346, 503
mercantile economy, *see* trade
Mermeroes, *listed under* **Mihrān**
  iṣbahbadh al-bilād, ⇌ Shāpūr Rāzī **Mihrān**
Mesene, 347
Mesopotamia, 19, 37–39, 41, 50, 52, 140, 141, 166, 333, 347, 418
  ., *see also* Iraq

religion of ~, 339, 387
Mher, *see* Mihr
Mihr (mountain), 364
Mihr (village), 364
mihr durujī, 366, 367, 380, 391, 400, 407
., *see also* Mithra
Mihr Ḥasīs, ⇌ Māhādharjushnas
Mihr Hormozd, *listed under* ***Sūren**
Mihr Narseh, *listed under* **Sūren**
Mihr worship, 5, 6, 13, 17, 87, 327, 350–354, 357–360, 366, 368, 369, 371, 373, 377–379, 381, 384, 392, 393, 397, 399, 400, 402, 405, 433, 434, 441, 446, 451, 457–459
~ and Roman Mithraism, *see* Roman Mithraism
~ and banquet scene, 389
~ and hunting scene, 388
~ and the Circle of Justice, *see* Circle of Justice
~ in Armenia, 13, 359, 386–392, 397
~ in Ferdowsī, 377, 399
Pīshdādīs and ~, 377
the cow in ~, 364, 374, 375, 398, 447
Mihr, son of Sukhrā, *listed under* **Kārin**
Mihrak-i Nūshzādān, 46, 367
Mihrān
~ al-Hamadānī, *listed under* **Mihrān**
~-i Bahrām-i Rāzī, *listed under* **Mihrān**
general of Pīrūz, *listed under* **Mihrān**
sister of Khusrow II, *listed under* **Sāsānid**
son of Bahrām-i Chūbīn, *listed under* **Mihrān**
Mihrān
Ashtād (dibīr), 50
Ashtāt, 71–73, 75
Bahrām Gushnāsp, 125
Bahrām-i Chūbīn, (*ruled 590–591*), 6, 8, 29, 34, 52, 68, 80, 81, 95, 96, 103, 104, 109, 110, 112, 113, 118, 119, 121–135, 138, 154, 156, 157, 181, 182, 188, 201, 206, 249, 250, 264, 274, 290, 296, 298, 348, 361, 365, 376–379, 392, 397–414, 426, 437, 441, 442, 444–447, 452, 458, 459, 461, 463, 468
† in 591 CE, 96, 129, 412
Farīburz, 102, 117
Gōrgōn, 101–104, 107, 117, 125, 378, 405, 461, 470
., *variants:* Gurgēn Mīlād; Gōrgēn; Gōr-gōn (*on seals*); Glon; Gołon Mihrewandak
Gorduyih, 81
Īzad Gushnasp, 71–75
Īzadgushasp, 102, 117, 119–122
† around 580–585 CE, 119
supporter of Bahrām-i Chūbīn, 119
Mihrān, general of Pīrūz, 73–75, 391
Mihrān-i Bahrām-i Chūbīn, 201, 206
Mihrān-i Bahrām-i Rāzī, 232, 235, 245, 469
† around 637 CE, 235
Mihrān-i Hamadānī, 219, 227, 468
† around 631 CE, 219
Mihrānsitād, 103, 104, 117, 124
† around 592 CE, 124
Mihrbundādh, 219
Mihrfīrūz, 72, 73
Mirranes, 102
Nastūh, 104, 117, 124
Pīrān Gushnasp, 48
Rahām, 68, 71, 300, 379
Sēd-hōsh, 101, 102, 104, 116, 117, 461
., *variants:* Shēdōsh
Sīyāvakhsh-i Mihrān-i Chūbīn, 206, 249–252, 263, 265, 304, 469
., ⇌ *Sīyāvakhsh-i Rāzī
Sīyāvakhsh-i Rāzī, 206, 210, 250
., ⇌ *Sīyāvakhsh-i Mihrān-i Chūbīn
† in 631 CE, 206, 210
Shāpūr Rāzī, 79–81, 101, 103, 104, 111, 268, 269, 379
Shāpūr, 74, 75

Shāpūr-i Shahrvarāz, (*ruled* *631), 202, 204, 205, 207, 210, 471
† in 631 CE, 210
Shahrēn, 48
Shahrīrāz, 279
*Shahrvarāz Jādhūyih, 197, 247, 469
† in 642 CE, 247
Shahrvarāz, (*ruled 630*), 101, 102, 110, 137, 141–153, 155–157, 159, 169, 173, 174, 176–185, 192, 196–205, 207, 209–212, 219, 247, 284, 306, 390, 461, 467, 468, 470, 471
., *variants:* Gorāz; Pīrag-i Shahrwarāz (*on seals*); Khořeam
† in 630 CE, 182–184, 203, 207, 209
Shahrvarāz, commander of the cavalry, 219, 468
† around 631 CE, 219
Shahrvarāz, ruler of al-Bāb, 231, 254, 279, 280, 306, 469
Mihrāns, xi, 3, 6, 8, 42, 44, 48–51, 57, 68, 70–76, 78, 80, 81, 83, 95, 96, 99–104, 107, 110, 112, 113, 115–120, 122, 124, 125, 127, 129–131, 135, 137, 142, 149–151, 153, 157, 159, 173, 177, 180–183, 189, 196, 197, 201, 202, 204–206, 210, 211, 219, 231, 232, 247, 249–254, 263–265, 268, 269, 275, 279, 281, 291, 294–298, 300, 304–306, 365, 376–379, 381, 384, 386, 390–392, 397, 398, 402, 404, 405, 409, 410, 412, 424, 425, 438, 441, 444, 445, 447, 448, 458, 460, 461, 463, 468, 470, 527
Mihrānsitād, *listed under* **Mihrān**
Mihrbundādh, *listed under* **Mihrān**
Mihrdād, *see* Mithradates
Mihrewandak, 103, 378, 399, 400, 402, 404, 447, 458
Bahrām-i Chūbīn ~, *see* Bahrām-i Chūbīn **Mihrān**
Gołon ~, *see* Gōrgōn **Mihrān**
Mihrigān, 354, 371–373, 375, 388, 503
Mihrijān, *see* Mihrigān
Mihrijān (village), 372
Mihrijān Qadhaq, 236, 237, 240
miǰnord, 74, 392
Milād, ⇌ Mithradates I **Arsacid**
mint
~ WYHC, 209, 222
~ of Āmul, 209
~ of Ardashīr Khurrah, 217
~ of Gurgān, 209
~ of Herāt, 209
~ of Hormozd Ardashīr, 217
~ of Kirmān, 209, 217, 222, 223
~ of Nīshāpūr, 209
~ of Nihāvand, 205
~ of Qum, 209
~ of Rayy, 209
~ of Sīstān, 217, 221, 222
~ of Stakhr, 205, 217
~ of Visp-shad-Husrav, 209, 222
Mirian III Chosroid, *see also* Arsacids, Georgian, 44
Mihrānid descent of ~, 44
Mīrūy, 230
Mīshkhuryār, father of Manūchihr, 376, 447
Mithra, 68, 147, 326, 327, 331, 335, 351–354, 356–360, 364, 366, 367, 369–372, 375, 377, 386–390, 393, 398, 399, 401, 402, 404, 408–412, 432, 442, 499, 502, 503, 505, 506
., *see also* Mihr worship; miǰnord
., *variants:* Mitra; Mihr; Mher
~ as Apollo, 360
~ as judge, 351–357, 366, 368, 373, 383, 391, 400, 404, 500, 505
~ as the sun, 327, 354, 357, 372, 376, 378, 383, 384, 388–390, 393, 432
~ic mysteries, *see* Roman Mithraism
eschatological role of ~, 353, 371, 379, 405, 407, 411, 432
mace of ~, *see* ox-headed mace
three functions of ~, 334, 352–356, 364, 367, 371, 373, 376, 380, 388, 400, 411, 433
mithradāna, 388
., *see also* mithraeum

Mithradates, *listed under* **Arsacid**
mithraeum, 375, 388, 503, 506
  ., *see also* mithradāna, dār-i Mihr
  ~ at Dura Europos, 389
Mithras, 374, 375, 402, 503, 506
  ., *see also* Roman Mithraism
mīyānchīgh, *see* Mithra, as judge
mōbad, 33, 46, 61, 62, 66, 68, 90, 91, 114, 120, 288, 289, 303, 327, 331, 344, 365, 368, 375, 378, 403, 404, 412, 427, 431, 436, 458, 501, 503, 504
  mōbadhān ~, 46, 47, 61, 90, 91, 344, 365, 503
Muʿāwiya, *listed under* Caliph
mufattish, 88, 89
Mughīrah b. Shuʿbah, 228, 247
Muḥammad (Prophet), 4, 6, 162, 167, 193, 226, 255, 271, 282–285, 434, 465, 501, 505
  † in 632 CE, 4, 162, 166, 168, 170, 191, 282–284
  as Seal of the Prophets, 434
Mundhir, king of Ḥīra, 69
al-Muqannaʿ, 425
Muqarrin, *listed under* Nuʿaym; Nuʿmān; Suwayd
Murghāb, 23
  ~ culture, 23
Musaylimah, 190, 191
Mushel, *listed under* **Mamikonean**
Muslimiya, 425
Mutʿah, *see* Battle of ~
Mūtā (Daylam), 248, 469
Muʿtaṣim, *listed under* Caliph
Muthannā b. Ḥāritha, 166, 178, 192, 202, 203, 207, 210, 211, 218–220, 227, 468
Mystacon, Magister Militum per Armeniam, 128

N

Nabateans, 36
Nabu, 327
nāf, *see* agnatic
Nahr al-Marʾāt, 192
Nahr Tīrā, 237
Nakhārjān, *see* naxarar
Namāriq, *see* Battle of ~
Namazga VI culture, 23
Nāmdār Jushnas, 180, 181, 196
Namir, 169, 201, 202
Nāna, 327
Nanē, 387
Narisanka, ⇌ Andragoras
Narseh, *listed under* **Sāsānid**
Narsī
  brother of Māhādharjushnas, 192, 211–213, 468, 471
  son of Jāmāsp, *listed under* **Āl-i Jāmāsp**
Naṣr b. Sayyār, 426
Nuʿmān b. Afgham Naṣrī, 276
Nastūh, *listed under* **Mihrān**
Nasu (dev), 322
naxarar, 43, 136, 153, 154, 243, 387, 391, 504
  ., *variants:* naxvadar; Nakhārjān; Tukhār
naxvadar, *see* naxarar
nēmrōz (south), *listed under* kūst
Nero, *see* Emperor Nero
Nestorians, 419
Nēw-Shābuhr, *see* Nīshāpūr
Nēw Khusrow, *see* Fīrūzān
Nicanor, 389
Nihāvand, 244
  ., *see also* Battle of ~
  ., *see also* mint of ~
  Kārīnid domains of ~, 49, 115, 243
Nikbī ben Massoud (historian), 187
nīmrūz (south), *listed under* kūst
Nisā, 22, 266, 276, 305, 318, 359, 389, 417, 418
Nīshāpūr, xi, 39, 65, 70, 71, 113, 139, 209, 270–274, 276, 277, 304, 305, 308, 318, 364, 372, 417, 426, 427, 435, 437, 438, 441, 442, 445, 447–450, 463, 469
  ., *see also* mint of ~
Nīzak Tarkhān, 260
Nowbahār, 175
Nowrūz, 363, 371, 378, 402, 503–505
Nuʿaym b. Muqarrin, 248, 250–253, 304, 469

Nubia, 143
Nu'mān b. Muqarrin, 241, 469

O

oath breaking, *see* mihr durujī
Oman, 227
Ormi, *see* Urumiya
Ormozd, *see* Ahūrā Mazdā
Orodes, *listed under* **Arsacid**
Osrhoene, 177
ōstāndār, 247, 504
ox-headed mace, 371, 372, 374, 375
  ., *variants:* gorz-i gāvsar; gurz; mace of Mithra
Oxus, 126, 139, 229, 240, 276, 383, 406

P

Padhashkhwārgar, 40, 47, 288, 289, 294, 295, 300, 370, 408–411, 440–443, 445, 446, 459
  ., *see also* Ṭabaristān
padhghuspān, *see* pādhūspān
pādhūspān, 83, 143, 157, 158, 181, 197, 247, 248, 274, 307, 504
Pahlav, *see* Parthians
Panjikant, 419
Parmūdih, 400
Parnabazids, *see* Arsacids, Georgian
Parni, 19, 20, 23, 25, 504
Pārsīg, *passim*
Parsis, 327, 504
Partav (in Arrān), *see* Barda'a
Parthava, 20, 42, 504
Parthian and Pahlaw aspet, *see* Asparapet **Ispahbudhān**
Parthians, *passim*
Pashūtan, 409, 412
Patizhahar, *see* Padhashkhwārgar
Paykand, 406
Pekeriç, *see* Bagayarich
Pērōzāpāt, *see* Barda'a
Persepolis, 359
Persīs, 22, 27, 36, 49, 53, 56, 67, 98, 120, 123, 125, 130, 156, 215, 322, 333, 335, 358, 360–362, 402
Petra, 103
peymān (contract), *see* Mithra
Phabrizius, *see* Farīburz **Mihrān**
Philip, *see* Emperor Philip
Phocas, *see* Emperor Phocas
Phraat, *listed under* **Arsacid**
Phraataces, ⇌ Phraat V **Arsacid**
Phthasouarsan, ⇌ Kayūs under **Sāsānid**
Pīrag-i Shahrwarāz, *see* Shahrvarāz **Mihrān**
Pīrūz
  ., *listed under* **Sāsānid**
  ∼ Khusrow, *see also* Fīrūzān
  ∼ Khusrow, general
  † around 631 CE, 175
  brother of Khusrow I, *listed under* **Sāsānid**
  grandson of Jāmāsp, *listed under* **Āl-i Jāmāsp**
Pīshdādī, 33, 342, 370, 375, 377, 378, 385
Pliny (historian), 37
Plutarch (historian), 64
pōryōtkēshīh, 337
Prince of the Medes, ⇌ Farrukh Hormozd **Ispahbudhān**
Pseudo-Callisthenes (historian), 358
Pumbadita, 337
Pūrān, *see* Būrāndukht **Sāsānid**
Pusai, 334
Pūshang, 39

Q

Qādisiya, *see* Battle of ∼
Qajars, 395
qanāt, 274, 502, 504
Qa'qā b. 'Amr, 231, 233–235, 248
Qārin, *listed under* **Kārin**
Qārin Kūh, *see* Kūh-i Kārin
Qaṭarī b. al-Fujā'ah, 309, 310
  † circa 685–695 CE, 310
Qazvīn, 251
Qazvīnī, 364
qibla, 378, 433, 439, 445, 447, 459, 505
Qihā, 251
quadripartition, *see* reforms of Khusrow I **Sāsānid**
quarter, *see* kūst
Qubād
  ., *listed under* **Sāsānid**

~ II, ⇌ Shīrūyih Qubād
son of Jāmāsp, *listed under* **Sāsānid**
son of Māhādharjushnas, 191–194, 468, 471
† around 630 CE, 194
Qūchān, 19, 293
Qūhistān, 113, 246, 307, 427
Quintus Curtis (historian), 358
Qūlah, *see* Kūlā
Qum, 252, 438
Qūmis, 39, 90, 112, 137, 139, 250, 251, 253, 255, 296, 315, 417, 442, 447, 460, 469
Qur'ān, 501, 502, 505
Qutaybah b. Muslim al-Bāhilī, 223, 310, 311, 314
† around 714 CE, 310, 311
Ibn Qutaybah, 178

R

Rādih Kūh, 266
Rādihkān, 266
Rahām, *listed under* **Kārin**; **Mihrān**
ra'īs, 88, 447
Rām Pīrūz, 381, 386, 406
Rām Hurmurz, 236, 237, 469, 514
., *see also* Battle of ~
Rashnu, 353, 357, 389, 401, 409, 411, 412, 432, 505
raϑaēštar, *see* artēshtārān
rathāshtārān sālār, 61, 63, 505
ratu, *see* dastwar
Rayy, 47, 49, 50, 68, 80, 90, 112, 124, 125, 127, 130, 133–135, 139, 189, 206, 209, 222, 236, 244, 246, 248–253, 256, 258, 259, 261, 263–265, 275, 277, 292, 293, 296, 297, 304, 305, 310, 315, 316, 360, 361, 376, 379, 381, 386, 404, 406, 409, 438–442, 444, 445, 447, 460, 469
., *see also* mint of ~
., *variants:* Razz; Ṙeyy; Rhaga
~ and the Mihrāns, 68, 80, 124, 125, 127, 189, 206, 249, 264, 265, 296, 304, 305, 376, 409, 438, 441, 460
Rev, Iberian king, *see also* Arsacids, Georgian, 44
Rewan, 71
Rhaga, *see* Rayy
Rib'ī b. 'Āmir, 227
ridda wars, 4, 162, 166, 190, 193, 237, 282, 284, 505
Rig Veda, 352
Rīwand, 364
Rizām b. Sābiq, 425
Roman Mithraism, 6, 24, 350, 358, 359, 374, 375, 388, 389, 402, 459, 503, 506
Romapāda, 355
Rome, *see also* Byzantium, 20–22, 24
Rostam, Ṙostom, *see* Rustam
Rowshan Pīrūz, 381, 386
Rōyān, *see* Rūyān
Rūdbār, 229, 230
., *see also* Oxus
Rumiyūzān, 143
., ⇌ Shahrvarāz **Mihrān**
Rūs, 280
Rustaham, *listed under* **Sūren**
Rustam, *listed under* **Ispahbudhān**
~ Jādhūyih, *listed under* jādhūyih
mythical ~, 76, 118, 375, 462
Rūyān, 40, 135, 136, 307, 376
Rūzbih, 201, 468
† around 630 CE, 201

S

Sābāṭ, 219, 231
Sabzivār, 364
Sa'd b. 'Āṣ, 272, 293
Sadih, 363, 378, 402, 505
Sahak I the Great, 43, 60
Sūrenid descent of ~, 60
Saint Acindynus, 387
Saint George the Soldier, 388
Saint Gregory the Illuminator, 44, 387, 390
Sūrenid descent of ~, 44, 131
Saint Sergius, 337
Ṣāliḥ-i Miknāq, 309
Salim, *listed under* **Kanārangīyān**
Saljuqs, 422
Sām Narīmān, 354
Samak, 378
Samak-i 'Ayyār, 22

Samanids, 394, 454, 463
sanad, *see* isnād
Sandaramet, *see* Spandarmad, 387
Saoshyant, *see* Sōshyant
Šapuh Mihrān, *see* Shāpūr **Mihrān**
Saqasayn, 314
Sarakhs, 260, 417, 418
Sārī, 261, 307, 308, 311, 317
Sārūyih, *listed under* **Āl-i Jāmāsp**
Sasanian
 ∼ historiography, 34–36
 ∼ propaganda, 9, 10, 22, 33–35, 459
 ∼ kings, *listed under* **Sāsānid**
Sāsānid
 Ādhar Narseh, son of Hormozd II, 56
 † in 309 CE, 56
 Ādur Anāhīd, daughter of Shāpūr I, 331
 Ardashīr I, (*ruled 224–241*), 8, 38, 42, 45–47, 49–51, 56, 64, 83, 85–87, 224, 324, 327, 337, 343, 361, 366, 367, 378, 404
 Ardashīr II, (*ruled 379–383*), 42, 57, 58, 335, 368
 † in 383 CE, 57
 Ardashīr III, (*ruled 628–630*), 150, 151, 169, 173, 176, 178–181, 183, 188, 189, 191–196, 198–200, 209, 211, 212, 283, 468, 471
 ., *variants:* Ardashīr b. Shīrā; Ardashīr Shīrūyih
 † in 630 CE, 169, 181, 183, 188, 196, 198, 199, 209
 Azarmīdukht, (*ruled 630–631*), 169, 183, 185–187, 189, 190, 203–211, 217, 291, 471
 † in 631 CE, 185–187, 207–210, 217
 Bābak, 333, 368, 385
 Būrāndukht, (*ruled 630–632*), 11, 151, 169, 170, 175, 178, 183–187, 189, 190, 198–200, 203–205, 207–214, 217, 218, 220, 222, 242, 283, 468, 471
 ., *variants:* Bor; Turān Dukht; Dukht-i Zabān; Pūrān
 † in 632 CE, 185, 218, 220
 Bahrām I, (*ruled 273–276*), 331–334
 † in 276 CE, 331
 Bahrām II, (*ruled 276–293*), 21, 327, 332–334, 348
 † in 293 CE, 327
 Bahrām III, (*ruled 293*), 332
 † in 293 CE, 332
 Bahrām IV, (*ruled 388–399*), 58
 † in 399 CE, 58
 Bahrām V Gūr, (*ruled 420–438*), 34, 43, 59–62, 64, 67–70, 109, 113, 278, 345, 348, 363, 383
 Bilāsh, (*ruled 484–488*), 75–78, 267, 379, 382–384, 471
 Hūshang, 288
 Hormozd Ardashīr, 21
 Hormozd I, (*ruled 272–273*), 46, 47, 331, 333, 334
 Hormozd II, (*ruled 302–309*), 56, 334
 † in 309 CE, 56
 Hormozd III, (*ruled 457–459*), 71, 300, 381, 382, 471
 † in 459 CE, 71, 381
 Hormozd IV, (*ruled 579–590*), 63, 91, 92, 94–97, 99–102, 104–106, 108, 111–113, 118–124, 126, 127, 129, 131, 132, 155, 182, 192, 250, 274, 289, 296, 326, 337, 361, 397, 399, 400, 404, 444, 458, 467, 471
 ∼'s killing of the nobles, 63, 106, 108, 112, 114, 118–123, 127, 131, 291
 † in 590 CE, 96, 123, 127, 132, 155, 409, 413, 444
 Byzantine wars of ∼, 123, 146
 Hormozd, son of Yazdgird II, 70
 Jāmāsp, brother of Khusrow I, 110, 111, 268, 471
 † around 532 CE, 111
 Jāmāsp, brother of Qubād, (*ruled 497–499*)
 ., *listed under* **Āl-i Jāmāsp**
 Kayūs, 110, 288, 289, 291, 292, 294–296, 346, 463, 471

., *variants:* Caoses; Kaus; Phthasouarsan
† around 531 CE, 289, 295
Khusrow I Nowshīrvān, (*ruled 531–579*), xi, 7, 8, 34, 35, 39, 40, 44, 49, 52, 63, 64, 82–84, 86–97, 99–105, 107–122, 124–126, 128, 129, 131, 161, 192, 209, 216, 231, 243, 250, 252, 268, 269, 274, 277, 288–290, 294–296, 336, 345, 346, 349, 361, 365, 379, 380, 385, 402, 447, 456, 471, 505
~'s war against the Turks, 380
absolutist power of ~, 52, 58, 84, 85, 91, 97, 99, 101
armies of ~, 92, 101, 102, 117
reforms of ~, 8, 11, 69, 78, 80, 83, 85, 86, 88, 89, 91–99, 101, 104, 107, 110, 115, 117, 118, 121, 123, 128, 182, 188, 278, 295, 296, 384, 500, 503, 505
religious policies of ~, 336, 337, 340, 345, 348, 349, 361, 365
Khusrow II Parvīz, (*ruled 591–628*), 3, 8, 34, 39, 40, 59, 63, 68, 94–97, 99–102, 104, 106, 108–110, 112, 122, 125, 127–138, 140–150, 152–159, 173–177, 179, 181, 184, 186, 187, 189, 193, 197, 200, 205, 212, 213, 229, 239, 250, 274, 275, 284, 289–291, 294, 297, 301, 337, 340, 397, 400–404, 407, 410, 412, 444, 456, 458, 460, 462, 471
~'s war against the Turks, 139
† in 628 CE, 4, 8, 150, 155, 156, 158, 172–174, 262, 298, 337
armies of ~, 136, 142, 148, 154
Byzantine wars of ~, 1, 110, 140–145, 147, 153, 297
deposition of ~, 140, 142, 147, 148, 151–159, 161, 171, 173, 175, 177, 180, 181, 189, 213, 232, 269, 298, 399
Khusrow III, 155
Khusrow, prince, 67, 69, 109
Mihrān, sister of Khusrow II, wife of Shahrvarāz, 205, 471
Narseh, (*ruled 293–302*), 63, 321, 331, 333
Pīrūz, (*ruled 459–484*), 34, 65, 70–77, 86, 92, 287, 298, 300, 335, 348, 355, 363, 379–386, 391, 392, 399, 406, 458, 460
., *variants:* Peroz; Fīrūz
† in 484 CE, 75–77, 298
Hephthalite wars of ~, 74–77, 299, 380–384
Qubād, (*ruled 488–497, 499–531*), 39, 40, 52, 58, 64, 73, 75–83, 87, 92, 96, 101, 103, 104, 106, 107, 110, 111, 113, 114, 135, 212, 267–269, 287–289, 294, 295, 299–301, 326, 336, 340, 344, 345, 348, 349, 377, 379, 384, 385, 456, 471
., *variants:* Cabades; Kavad; Kouades
† in 531 CE, 113, 288, 301, 385
Qubād, son of Jāmāsp, 111, 268
Sāsān, 5, 8, 42, 125, 127, 130, 157, 173, 182, 249, 331, 368, 385, 439, 445, 446, 452
Shāpūr I, (*ruled 241–272*), 8, 21, 38, 46–48, 50, 56, 83, 325, 331, 332, 340, 348, 400, 505
Shāpūr II, (*ruled 309–379*), 52, 56–58, 83, 92, 128, 326, 334, 335, 340, 345, 347–349, 368
† in 379 CE, 58
Shāpūr III, (*ruled 383–388*), 57, 58, 349, 368
Shāpūr, son of Kayūs, 289, 471
† circa 579–590 CE, 289
Shāpūr, son of Yazdgird I, 43, 68
† in 420 CE, 43, 68
Shīrūyih Qubād, (*ruled 628*), 148, 153, 154, 156–158, 169, 173–179, 189–193, 200, 209, 236, 269, 283, 284, 291, 298, 460, 465, 471
., *variants:* Shīrā b. Kisrā; Qubād II
† in 628 CE, 177, 178, 191, 209
Shahrīyār, brother of Shīrūyih Qubād, 471

† in 628 CE, 175
Yazdgird I, (*ruled 399–420*), 58–62, 64–69, 109, 110, 266, 325, 335, 340, 347, 348, 363
~ the Sinner, 59, 66, 67, 267, 335
† in 420 CE, 43, 66, 68, 69, 109, 267, 389
Yazdgird II, (*ruled 438–457*), 34, 59–62, 64, 70, 71, 300, 340, 348, 349, 375, 382, 385
† in 457 CE, 71, 300
Yazdgird III, (*ruled 632–651*), 4, 9, 36, 161, 169–172, 185, 191, 207–209, 215, 219–225, 229, 231, 235, 236, 238–240, 242, 244–246, 250, 257–266, 269–271, 276, 277, 283, 291–294, 302, 303, 313, 377, 462, 464, 469, 471
† in 651 CE, 2, 220, 257, 259, 263, 272, 292, 293
flight of ~, 236, 241, 244–246, 253, 257–260, 262, 263, 265, 270, 287, 292, 298, 302, 304
Zarīr, brother of Bilāsh, 76
Sāvih Shāh, 399, 400, 402
Sawād, 108, 109, 131, 178, 194, 195, 199, 203, 207, 211, 214, 216, 220, 224, 225, 227, 231, 232, 503
., *see also* kūst-i khwarāsān
spāhbed of ~, 108, 109, 131
Sayf b. ʿUmar, 15, 16, 162, 165–172, 189–216, 218–220, 224, 225, 227–230, 232–234, 236, 238, 240–242, 247–249, 251, 254, 258, 263, 278, 281–283, 304, 465
† around 796 CE, 165
seals
~ of Chihr-Burzēn, 99, 121, 122, 461, 470
, ⇌ Sīmāh-i Burzīn **Kārin**
~ of Dād-Burz-Mihr, 99, 100, 115, 120, 121, 216, 296, 302, 364, 379, 400, 470
, ⇌ Dādmihr **Kārin**
~ of Gōr-gōn, 99–104, 107, 117, 461, 470
, ⇌ Gōrgōn **Mihrān**
~ of Pīrag-i Shahrwarāz, 99–102, 110, 142, 150, 152, 153, 182, 470
, ⇌ Shahrvarāz **Mihrān**
~ of Sēd-hōsh, 99–102, 104, 107, 116, 117, 461, 470
, ⇌ Sēd-hōsh **Mihrān**
~ of Wēh-Shābuhr, 99–101, 156, 216, 461, 470
~ of Wahrām Ādurmāh, 99, 101, 120–122, 124, 470
, ⇌ Bahrām-i Māh Ādhar
~ of Wistakhm, 63, 99, 104, 107–110, 470
, ⇌ Vīstāhm **Ispahbudhān**
Sēd-hōsh, *listed under* **Mihrān**
Sefīdanj, 414
Seleucia, 20, 389
Seleucids, 19, 20, 37, 321, 360, 361
Seleucus, 19, 389
Shāhanshāh, 48, 56, 182, 463, 505
Shāhīn, 141, 143, 146, 151
shahrab, 38, 49, 238, 505
Shahrām, *listed under* **Ispahbudhān**
Shahrām Pīrūz, 381
Shahrapan Bandakan, 139
shahrdārān, 48, 55, 505
shahrīg, 238, 274, 505
Shahrīrāz, *listed under* **Mihrān**
Shahrīyār, *listed under* **Kanārangīyān**
Shahrkhwāstān, maternal cousin of Khurshīd Shāh, 314, 471
Shāhrūd, 364
Shahrvarāz
., *listed under* **Mihrān**
~ Jādhūyih, *listed under* ***Mihrān**
ruler of al-Bāb, *listed under* **Mihrān**
Shalāb, 373
Shamṭā, 175
Shāpūr
., *listed under* **Mihrān**
~ I, II, III, *listed under* **Sāsānid**
~ Kharrād, ⇌ Asparapet **Ispahbudhān**
son of Yazdgird I, *listed under* **Sāsānid**
Shāpūr Rāzī, *listed under* **Mihrān**
Shēdōsh, *see* Sēd-hōsh **Mihrān**

Shemīrān, 266
., *variants:* Shamīlān
Shīrāz, 79, 81
Shīrīn, wife of Khusrow II, 174, 471
Shīrūyih Qubād, *listed under* **Sāsānid**
Shīrzād, 200, 201, 468
Shīz, 333
Shuʿūbiya, 230, 457, 460
Sibylline Oracles, 34
Sīmāh-i Burzīn, *listed under* **Kārin**
Simnān, 310
Sīrāwand, 427
Sīsāniya, *see* Bihāfarīd, followers
Sīstān, 39, 49, 50, 64, 77, 130, 150, 155–159, 177, 215, 217, 221, 222, 246, 257, 322, 364, 454, 461, 463, 469, 503
., *see also* mint of ~
Siunik', 349
Siwni
Grigor, 157, 232, 233, 469
† in 635 CE, 157, 233
Step'anos, 133
Sīyāh, 238–240, 245, 469
Siyahgird, 382
Sīyāvakhsh
~-i Mihrān-i Chūbīn, *listed under* **Mihrān**
~-i Rāzī, *listed under* **Mihrān**
Slav, 299, 301
slaves, 38, 63, 90
Smbat, *listed under* **Bagratuni**
Smbat (Armenian general), 300
Sogdians, 48, 318, 321, 328, 347, 366, 419, 437
Sorūsh, 353, 371, 401, 402, 409, 411, 432, 459, 500, 505
Sōshyant, 412, 505, 506
Spahān, *see* Iṣfahān
spāhbed, xi, 61, 94, 95, 98–110, 112, 114–117, 120–123, 125, 128, 129, 131, 132, 138, 142, 143, 150, 151, 153, 155–157, 173, 180, 181, 185, 186, 196, 205, 216, 250, 252, 254, 256, 259, 260, 262, 263, 272, 274–277, 290, 295–298, 302, 305, 314–316, 376, 379, 400, 405, 424, 447, 448, 450, 461, 462, 470, 501–506
., *see also* ispahbud
Spandarmad, 49, 387, 499
Spandīyādh, *see* Isfandīyārs
sparapet, *see also* Asparapet **Ispahbudhān**
Mamikonean ~, 105, 128
Sraoša, *see* Sorūsh
Stakhr, 239, 245, 290, 291, 327, 331–334, 385, 469
., *see also* mint of ~
., *variants:* Iṣṭakhr; Staxr
Strabo (historian), 25
stūrīh, *see* marriage, substitute
Sufyān b. Abraṣ, 310
Suhrāb, *listed under* **Āl-i Bāvand**
Sukhrā, *listed under* **Kārin**
Ṣūl, 253–255, 304, 312, 469
Sulaymān b. ʿAbdalmalik, *listed under* Caliph
sun worship, *see* Mithra as the sun
Sunbād, *listed under* ***Kārin**
Sūq al-Ahwāz, 237
Suqlāb, *see* Slav
Surāqah b. ʿAbdalraḥmān, 280
Surāqah b. ʿAmr, 280, 469
Sūren, son of Phraat IV, *listed under* **Arsacid**
Sūren
*Anak, 106, 131
Ardashīr, 50
Gondofarr, 504
Gurāzih, 60
Kārdār, son of Mihr Narseh, 61
Kalbūy, 230
*Māhūy, 259–263, 265, 266, 277, 292, 469
Mājusnas, 61
*Mardānshāh, 157, 158, 181, 197
† in 626 CE, 158, 197
*Mihr Hormozd, 157–159, 173, 501
Mihr Narseh, 60–62, 64–66, 68, 70, 71
Rustaham Surena, 64, 76, 462, 504
Rustam, 117, 118
Zurvāndād, 61

Surena, ⇌ Rustaham **Sūren**
Sūrens, 3, 26, 42–44, 49–51, 57, 59–66, 68, 70, 76, 79, 101, 118, 131, 155–158, 173, 221, 230, 265, 365, 391, 461, 462, 504
Susa, 236–238, 245, 334, 337
Suwayd b. Muqarrin, 178, 192, 253–256, 303, 469
Syria, 4, 20, 40, 141, 143, 144, 168, 172, 199–202, 280, 281, 318

T

Ṭabaristān, 5, 6, 20, 22, 39, 40, 47, 72, 73, 80, 86, 107, 113, 114, 117, 129, 130, 135–137, 165, 230, 244, 246, 248–250, 252–257, 259–261, 263, 265, 274, 275, 281, 287–300, 302–318, 369, 370, 372–374, 376, 377, 379, 380, 382, 385, 397, 398, 404, 408–410, 414, 440–442, 445, 451, 457, 458, 462, 463, 469, 503
., *see also* Māzandarān; Padhashkhwārgar
Ṭabasayn, 246, 257
Taghlib, 169, 201, 202
Ṭāhirids, 272, 454
Ṭahmūrath, 264
Ṭāliqān, 139, 259
Tamīm, 165
Tammīsha, 114, 311, 374
Tansar, 85–87, 328, 332, 338
., *see also* Letter of Tansar
tanutēr, 140, 154, 174, 506
Ṭāq-i Kisrā, 84
Tarōn, 128, 390
Tarsus, 177
tauroctony, 374, 375
Taurus (constellation), 373
Ṭāwūs, *see* Battle of ~
taxes, 41, 61, 69, 90, 112, 114, 146, 175, 229, 237, 253, 280, 342, 343, 346
bāj, 79
kharāj, 90, 254, 273, 279, 288, 316, 501, 502
poll ~, 91, 191, 193, 228, 247, 255, 279, 382, 436, 502
reform, 82, 85, 89, 90, 123, 379, 381
Tāzīyān (Arabs), 407
T'ēodoros
Ṙshtuni, 280, 469
prince of Armenia, 176
Thomas of Marga (historian), 175
Tiberius, *see* Emperor Tiberius
Tigris, 199, 203, 389
Tikrīt, 219
Tīr, 163, 387, 402
Tiridates, *listed under* **Arshakuni; Arsacid**
Tirmidh, 382
Tīrūyih, *listed under* **Ispahbudhān**
Tīsfūn, *see* Ctesiphon
tōkhm, *see* agnatic
Tōsar, *see* Tansar
trade, 5, 88–91, 226, 229, 230, 232, 240, 277, 314, 419, 428, 429, 464
traitor (as topos), 243, 251
Transcaucasia, 149
Transoxiana, 5, 22, 74, 76, 279, 310, 311, 314, 382, 406, 418, 419, 426, 428, 435, 437, 464
Trdat, *see* Tiridates **Arshakuni**
treasury (as topos)
Abū Muslim's ~ acquired by Jawhar, 439
Abū Muslim's ~ acquired by Sunbād, 315, 438, 440–442, 444, 445, 447
Afrāsīyāb's ~ acquired by Padhashkhwārgar Shāh, 408, 410, 443, 445
Khāqān's ~ acquired by Bahrām-i Chūbīn, 410, 442, 445
Mihrān's ~ acquired by Farrukhzād, 251
Pīrūz's ~ acquired by Sukhrā, 79
Smbat Bagratuni's ~ acquired by the Arabs, 243
Sunbād's ~ acquired by Khurshīd, 315, 316, 440, 441, 443
Yazdgird III's ~ acquired by Farrukhzād, 244, 245, 258
Trogus (historian), 25
True Cross, 176
Tukhār, *see* Varaztirots' **Bagratuni**
tukhār, *see* naxarar or tanutēr

Tukharistan, 139
Tu'mas, 176
Tun-Huang, 406
Tūrāns, 33, 77, 375, 376, 406, 414
Turkistān, 288, 314, 374
Turkmenistan, 23
Turks, 92, 139, 270, 400, 405, 407, 408, 410, 421, 428
Ṭūs
  city, 66, 67, 90, 261, 265–267, 269–274, 276, 277, 304, 305, 318, 372, 374, 417, 448, 449, 460, 463
  commander of Kai Khusrow, 117
  ., **Asparapet* **Ispahbudhān**
  cousin of Khurshīd, *listed under* **Āl-i Jāmāsp**
Tustar, 237–240, 245
  ., *see also* Battle of ~

U

ʿUbaydallāh b. Yazīd, 309
Ubullah, *see* Battle of ~; Baṣra
Ukraine, 299
ʿulamā, 324
Ullays, 190
  ., *see also* Battle of ~
ʿUmar, *listed under* Caliph
ʿUmar b. Nuʿmān, 461
ʿUmar-i Fannāq, 309
Umayyads, *see also* Caliph, 5, 35, 313, 315, 418, 420, 422, 426, 437, 449, 450, 454, 463
ʾumma, 1, 166, 505, 506
ʾUmmat al-Raḥmān, *listed under* **Āl-i Jāmāsp**
Urarta, 43
Uruk, 20, 387
Urumiya, 125, 152
Usayyid, 165, 233
Ushētar, 412
Ushētar-māh, 412
Ustādsīs, 354, 408, 437
ʿUtbah b. Farqad, 279
ʿUtbah b. Ghazwān, 168, 190, 193, 227, 237, 469
ʿUthmān, *listed under* Caliph
Uyghurs, 406

V

Vachē, king of Albania, 300
Vahagn, 389, 390
  < Av. Vərəθraγna, 362, 390, 411, 432, 440, 459
  ~ and Mihr, 390
  ~ as Bahrām, *see* Bahrām
Vahan, *listed under* **Mamikonean**
Vahewuni rebellion, 133–134, 301, 302
Vakhtang I Gorgasali, 73
Valakhsh, ⇌ Vologeses **Arsacid**
Valerian, *see* Emperor Valerian
Vand Omīd Kūh, 114, 295
Vandād Hormozd, son of Khurshīd, *listed under* **Āl-i Jāmāsp**
Vandarand, *listed under* **Āl-i Jāmāsp**
Varāz, 50
  Ardashīr ~, 50
Varaztirots' Jāvītān, *listed under* **Bagratuni**
Varena, 370
varjāvand, *see* Haftānbukht
Varrames, *see* Bahrām **Kanārangīyān**
Varuna, *see also* Apam Napāt, 351, 352, 354, 357, 499
  ., *variants:* Vouruna Apąm Napāt
Varazvaḷan, 349
vāspuhrān, 48, 55, 506
vāstryōfšuyant, *see* vāstryōshān
vāstryōshān, 47
vāstryōshān sālār, 47, 61, 63, 506
Veh Ardashīr, 38, 77, 199, 200, 209, 468, 514
  ., *see also* Battle of ~
Veh-az-Amid-Kavād, 209
Vehṙot, *see* Oxus
Vendidad, *see* Videvdād
victory (deity), *see* Bahrām < Av. Vərəθraγna
Videvdād, 322, 360, 369
Vilāsh, *listed under* **Kārin**
Vindūyih, *listed under* **Ispahbudhān**
Vīs o Rāmīn, 22
Vīshtāspā, *listed under* Kai; **Achaemenid**
Vistāhm, *listed under* **Ispahbudhān**
Vohu Manah, *see* Bahman

Vologeses, *listed under* **Arsacid**; for
Bilāsh, see under **Sāsānid**
Vram, *see* Bahrām
Vrkan, *see* Gurgān

W

Wahrām Ādurmāh, *see* seals of ~
Wāj Rūdh, *see* Battle of ~
Walajah, *see* Battle of ~
Wāqidī, 235
Waqqāṣ, Saʿd b. Abī, 185, 226, 231, 234, 237, 469
wastrā-i ūshān sālār, *see* vāstryōshān sālār
wealth (as topos), 227, 238, 251, 280, 314
Wēh-Shābuhr, *see* seals of ~
probably a Sūren, 156
Weh-Shāpūr, 332
White Forest, 409
Wistakhm, *see* Vistāhm **Ispahbudhān**
wizarishn (Redemption), 339, 506
wuzurg framādār, 62, 506
wuzurgān, 48, 506

X

Xenophon (historian), 358
X^{w}adāy-Nāmag, 2, 4, 7, 9–11, 13–16, 22, 23, 34–36, 45, 58, 59, 62, 75, 87, 99, 116, 122, 135, 146, 159, 161, 171, 172, 174, 178, 181, 189, 191, 194, 195, 260, 262, 263, 270, 294, 296, 368, 370, 384, 385, 394, 398, 399, 402, 406, 410, 420, 458–463, 502, 506
Parthian redaction of ~, 159, 262, 264, 462–463

Y

Yamāmah, 190, 193
Yarmūk, *see* Battle of ~
Yasht, 335, 350, 352, 375, 394
Yazdān, *see* Īzad Gushnasp **Mihrān**
Yazdgird I, II, III, *listed under* **Sāsānid**
Yazdīn, 175
Yazdwšnasp, *see* Īzadgushasp **Mihrān**
Yazīd b. Muhallab, 310–313
Yazīd b. Sīyāh al-Uswārī, 240
Yemen, 40, 116, 117
Yemo, 325
Yĕzatvšnasp, *see* Īzad Gushnasp **Mihrān**
Yima, *see* Jamshīd

Z

Zābulistān, 68, 77, 113, 117, 209, 229, 277, 278, 295, 385, 408
Zād Farrukh, 146–152, 155
., ⇌ Farrukh Hormozd or Farrukhzād **Ispahbudhān**
Zāmāsp, *see* Jāmāsp under **Āl-i Jāmāsp**
Zames, *see* Jāmāsp, brother of Khusrow I, under **Sāsānid**
Zamzamī, *see* mōbad
Zand, 124, 326, 336, 341, 342, 403, 428, 507
Zand i Vahuman Yasn, 405, 409, 411, 446
zandīk, 165, 332, 341, 342, 345, 349, 428, 507
Zarādushti, *see* Mazdak
Zarang, 40
Zardmanos, 300
Zārim, 316
Zarmihr, *listed under* **Kārin**
Zarmihr, commander, 201, 468
† around 630 CE, 201
Zayd b. Hārithah, 193
Zīks, 49
al-Zīnabī Abū 'l-Farrukhān, 248, 250–253, 256, 263–265, 278, 293, 303–305, 308, 398, 424, 462
., ⇌ Farrukhzād **Ispahbudhān**
zindik, zindīq, *see* zandīk
zinhār (refuge), *see* Mithra
Zoroaster, 322, 339, 342, 350, 357, 385, 403, 406, 412, 428, 501
regional legends of ~, 321, 322, 369
Zuhrah b. Ḥawiyah, 226, 227
Zurvān, 339, 340, 366, 507
Zurvanism, 331, 334, 339, 340, 365, 366, 392
Zūzan, 427, 435